OFFICIAL WNBA GUIDE AND REGISTER
2006 EDITION

Editors

Erin Farrell

Jay Moore

Contributing editors

Chris Mattia

Sporting News contributors:
Page layout: Chad Painter, David Niehaus
Programmer: Keith Camden

ISBN: 0-89204-852-2

10 9 8 7 6 5 4 3 2 1

CONTENTS

2006 SEASON

Team Information

REVIEW

RECORDS

Regular Season

Playoff Records

Finals Records

OFFICIAL WNBA RULES

WNBA PLAYER PROFILES

NEW YORK OFFICE
Women's National Basketball Association
Olympic Tower, 645 Fifth Avenue
New York, NY 10022
Main Number: 212-688-WNBA (9622)
Main Fax Number: 212-750-WNBA (9622)
www.wnba.com

NEW JERSEY OFFICE
WNBA Enterprises, LLC
450 Harmon Meadow Boulevard
Secaucus, NJ 07094
Main Number: 201-865-7700
Fax Number: 201-974-1143

President ....Donna Orender
Chief of Basketball Operations and Player Relations .... Reneé Brown
Vice President, Business Operations ....Mary Ellen Curran
Vice President, Team Development and Services ....Michael Ginn
Vice President, Business Development...Molly Mullady
Vice President, Marketing Communications...Mike Bass
General Counsel ....Jamin S. Dershowitz
Senior Director, Player Personnel ....Angela Taylor
Senior Director, Basketball Operations ....Wade Morehead
Senior Director, WNBA Programming ....Stephanie Schwartz
Senior Director, Team Business Development.. Kristin Bernert
Director, Marketing Partnerships ....Carolanne McAuliffe
Director, WNBA Communications ....Ron Howard
Director, Security ....Kelley Hardwick
Senior Manager, Basketball Operations ....Thomas Tedesco
Senior Manager, Communications ....Dina Pappas
Manager, Community Relations ....Maggie Glenn
Manager, Marketing Partnerships ....Christie Howard
Manager, Marketing Partnerships...Jessica Rotoli
Editor, Interactive Services, WNBA.com ....Matthew Wurst
Special Coordinator to the Executive Office ....Brad Barnett
Coordinator, Basketball Communications ....Jay Moore
Coordinator, Business Operations ....Anne Wright
Coordinator, Communications ....Christina Nishihara
Coordinator, Marketing Partnerships..Alanna LeGall
Coordinator, Marketing Partnerships ....Hiroshi Okuda
Coordinator, Player Programs ....Bonnie Thurston
Senior Assistant, Marketing Partnerships ....LaShawn Carter
Administrative Assistant to the President ....Kate Galiani
Administrative Assistant to the President..Floretta Gibbs
Administrative Assistant to the President...Courtney Green
Staff Assistant, Player Personnel ....Nikeisha Plummer
Supervisor of Officials ....Dee Kantner
Special Advisor ....Rebecca Lobo
Team Business Development..Paula Hanson, Jerry Murphy

Donna Orender — President

Donna Orender was named President of the Women's National Basketball Association in February 2005. Bringing more than 20 years of sports business experience, she oversees all business and league operations for the league.

Prior to joining the WNBA, Orender spent more than 17 years with the PGA Tour, serving most recently as Senior Vice President of Strategic Development in the Office of the Commissioner. While at the Tour, Orender was responsible for the development and management of strategic direction across all business lines including new media, Internet, advertising and brand management. In addition, she ran the Tour's worldwide television and production businesses for nine years prior to being named senior vice president.

Orender's television production career began at ABC Sports and continued at SportsChannel. Orender also owned her own production company, Primo Donna Productions.

A graduate of Queens College in New York, Orender did graduate studies in social work at Adelphi University. She comes to the WNBA with a significant basketball history and a true passion for the game. She played three seasons in the Women's Professional Basketball League (WBL), where she was an All-Star. She also was an All-American basketball player during her collegiate years.

Orender's community and philanthropic activities include serving on the boards of Beth El—The Beaches Synagogue, the Monique Burr Foundation for Children, Inc., the Jacksonville Film & Television Advisory Council, the University of North Florida College of Arts and Science Advisory Council and Maccabi USA/Sports for Israel. In addition, she served as Co-Chair for the USA Women's Basketball team for the 16th World Maccabiah Games in Israel and participates in the National Minority Golf Foundation Mentor Program.

Among her many accolades, Orender was recently named to the prestigious *Sporting News*' annual "Power 100" list, as well as FoxSports.com's "Top 10 Most Powerful Women in Sports" list. She became the first woman honored by the UJA-Federation of New York's Entertainment, Media & Communications Division for her loyal and longstanding dedication to community in March 2006.

Orender is married to MG Orender, Honorary President of the PGA of America and owner/partner in Hampton Golf, Inc. She has twin boys, Jacob and Zachary (7) and two stepchildren, Morgan and Colleen.

Reneé Brown — Chief of Basketball Operations & Player Relations

Reneé Brown, WNBA Chief of Basketball Operations and Player Relations, oversees all player-scouting and acquisition and the administration of all player-related and on-court operations policies including scheduling, officiating, game conduct and discipline. Brown joined the WNBA in September 1996 as Director of Player Personnel. She was named Senior Vice President in 2004.

During the 1995-96 season, Brown served as an assistant coach to Tara VanDerveer for the gold medal-winning USA Basketball Women's National Team in Colorado Springs, where she helped with game preparation, player conditioning and scouting. Since 2000, she has served on the Executive Committee for USA Basketball as the Vice President for the Senior Women's Programs. In 2004, she presided as the Chair for the Women's Senior National Team Committee and will continue that role through 2008. Brown also will sit on the USA Basketball Board of Directors through 2008.

Brown, a 1978 graduate of the University of Nevada-Las Vegas, also received a master's in education from UNLV in 1981. She was an assistant coach for the women's basketball teams at the University of Kansas, Stanford University and San Jose State University. Her Stanford team won the NCAA tournament in 1990 and earned a trip to the Final Four in 1991.

Mary Ellen Curran — Vice President, Business Operations

Mary Ellen Curran was named Vice President of Business Operations for the WNBA in October 2005. In this role, Curran oversees all league events, brand management and marketing, league administration and merchandising.

Curran came to the NBA in November 2002 as Director of Community Relations. As such, she was responsible for the planning and execution of community based initiatives for both the NBA and WNBA including Read to Achieve, WNBA Be Smart, Be Fit, Be Yourself, Breast Health Awareness and Junior NBA/WNBA. She also helped to develop nonprofit and corporate partnerships to expand NBA/WNBA programs nationwide and to provide additional resources to teams for Community Relations programs.

Before joining the NBA, Curran held the position of Vice President at Carlson Draddy & Associates, a strategic marketing firm. Curran's sports background also includes holding management positions at the NHL, USTA, and USTA New England.

A graduate of College of the Holy Cross in Worcester, Mass., Curran was a member of the women's varsity tennis team.

Michael Ginn — Vice President, Team Development and Services

Michael Ginn is Vice President of Team Development and Services. He works closely with the MTBO group to provide strategic resources for teams on a day-to-day basis in the areas of sponsorship and ticket sales, marketing, business planning and strategy.

He brings more than 20 years of management experience in sales, business development and marketing. Prior to joining the WNBA, Michael was a key member of the team that created Wannado Entertainment and Wannado City, a role-playing theme park. He was responsible for advertising sales and business development. Michael also was instrumental in the success of Turner Broadcasting for more than 13 years, most recently as the SVP of sales and marketing for Latin America. Michael also held positions in Turner's international group and with CNN, in Los Angeles and Chicago.

Ginn is a graduate of Kent State University. He, his wife, Dafne, their daughter Erin and their two dogs, Otis and Max, reside in N.Y.

Molly Mullady — Vice President, Business Development

Molly Mullady serves as Vice President of Business Development for the WNBA. She directs all of the league's sales efforts and is responsible for developing strategic and tactical marketing partnerships that support brand positioning, advertising and promotion.

Mullady joined the WNBA in January 2006 with more than 13 years of sales experience, most recently serving as Director of Corporate Partnerships for the Philadelphia Eagles and Lincoln Financial Field. Her responsibilities included incorporating promotions, television, radio, print, online and in-stadium elements into integrated corporate partnerships. She also was responsible for select online initiatives; special event development and new business generation.

Prior to her position with the Eagles, Mullady served as the Director of New Business Development, Corporate Sales for Palace Sports & Entertainment. Joining the Palace in September 1996, she was involved in sponsorship sales for the NBA Detroit Pistons, WNBA Detroit Shock, IHL Detroit Vipers, Palace of Auburn Hills, Pine Knob Music Theatre and Meadow Brook Music Festival.

Mullady began her career in sports marketing with International Management Group (IMG) in Cleveland. She rose to the position of Director of Sales and Marketing for IMG Latin America based in New York and then in Miami. She sold sponsorships for events such as the ATP Mexican Open Tennis Championships, Argentine Open Golf Championships, International Gymnastics Exhibitions and regional tours by various classical artists.

Mullady graduated with honors from St. Lawrence University in 1991 with a double major in government and Spanish. She is a proud member of the Board of Directors for Special Olympics Pennsylvania.

Jamin S. Dershowitz — General Counsel

As the WNBA's General Counsel, Jamin Dershowitz is responsible for overseeing the legal affairs of the league and for administering the salary cap. He has been with the WNBA since its inception and has been a member of the NBA Legal Department since 1993.

A graduate of Yale Law School in 1988, Dershowitz began his legal career as a law clerk for Judge Joseph Tauro of the United States District Court for the District of Massachusetts. He then worked for the New York Legal Aid Society, representing indigent people accused of crimes. At the NBA, Dershowitz has worked on a variety of legal matters, including salary cap administration, collective bargaining, Internet and new technologies and the NBA's relationship with USA Basketball.

Angela Taylor — Senior Director, Player Personnel

As Senior Director, Player Personnel for the WNBA League Office, Angela Taylor heads the Player Personnel Department and is responsible for all player-related matters and issues. Now in her ninth year with the WNBA, Taylor's responsibilities include collegiate & international player evaluation, player marketing and player programs (including WNBA player orientation, appearances throughout the year and tuition assistance). Taylor also works with various other WNBA departments as it pertains to league business.

Taylor joined the WNBA in June 1997 as Coordinator, Player Personnel and was promoted to Manager in October 1999. She was named Director in October 2004 and Senior Director in October 2005.

Prior to joining the WNBA staff, Taylor was an assistant coach for the women's basketball teams at Stanford University, Texas A&M University and the University of Arizona. A four-year varsity letterwinner at Stanford University, Taylor helped guide the Stanford women's basketball team to two NCAA national championships (1990 & 1992), three Final Fours (1990-92) and one Sweet Sixteen appearance (1993). Additionally, as an assistant coach at Stanford, Taylor's teams went to back-to-back Final Fours in 1996 and 1997. While at Stanford, she had the opportunity to work with 1996 Olympic gold medal-winning head coach Tara VanDerveer.

Taylor graduated from Stanford University in 1993 with a Bachelor of Arts degree in economics and earned her MBA with an emphasis in marketing and management at New York University's Stern School of Business in May 2002.

Wade Morehead — Senior Director, Basketball Operations

Wade Morehead was named WNBA Senior Director, Basketball Operations in May 2005 and is responsible for all on-court operations including scheduling, officiating, game conduct, discipline and compliance.

Morehead, who has 13 years of experience in professional basketball, served the previous four years as Deputy Commissioner of the Continental Basketball Association where he was responsible for all league operations, events and franchise development. A member of the USA Basketball Board of Directors (1999, 2002-05), Morehead served in several capacities for the CBA during his 12 seasons, including public and media relations (assistant director, media relations) and basketball operations (coordinator to senior vice president).

During the 2000-01 season, Morehead served as Vice President, Basketball Operations for the Phoenix-based Harlem Globetrotters. He was responsible for the operations and logistics of three touring teams that played more than 280 games in approximately 100 days. Additional responsibilities included conducting 15 nationwide youth basketball camps and served as account supervisor of apparel, ground transportation, travel and competition partnerships.

Morehead earned a bachelor's degree in communications from the University of Tulsa in 1991, and a master's degree in sports management from the University of Tennessee in 1994.

Raised in Littleton, Colo., Morehead now resides in New Jersey with his wife Amy and two sons.

Stephanie Schwartz — Senior Director, WNBA Programming

After 18 years working with the NBA, Stephanie joined the WNBA as Senior Director, WNBA Programming in January 2006.

Prior to her appointment to the WNBA she served as Senior Director, Ethnic Programming and Marketing, overseeing the NBA and WNBA's Ethnic Initiatives and business development within the ethnic business community.

Previous to that position, she served as Senior Director, International Programming where she oversaw the global operation of NBA and WNBA Television Programming, Production, and Promotion.

She graduated from Columbia University with a bachelor's degree and holds an MBA in International Business from Fordham University.

Kristin Bernert — Senior Director, Team Business Development

Kristin Bernert enters her first season as Senior Director, WNBA Team Business Development. In her role, she serves as a consultant to the teams in all aspects of their business operations.

Before joining the WNBA league office, she served as Vice President of Operations for the Detroit Shock where she was responsible for the coordination of all aspects of Shock business, including ticket sales, marketing, corporate sponsorship, community relations, public relations and event operations.

Prior to joining the Shock, Bernert served in the corporate marketing department for the Cleveland Indians. This was her first entry into the professional sports arena after working at The Ohio State University as Assistant Director of Athletics Marketing and at Bowling Green State University (BGSU) as Assistant Athletics Director for Marketing and Communications.

A native of Stow, Ohio, Bernert received her bachelor's from Siena College in 1996 and her master's from Ohio State in 1998.

Carolanne McAuliffe — Director, Marketing Partnerships

As Director, WNBA Marketing Partnerships, Carolanne McAuliffe is responsible for overseeing the development and execution of the League's existing marketing partner programs as well as playing a key role with the new business development team. Such marketing partner programs include the Be Fit Tour, All-Star Weekend, All-Star Balloting and Read to Achieve. In addition, McAuliffe works closely with WNBA account managers on the day-to-day management of all WNBA partners. She joined as Senior Manager, WNBA Marketing Partnerships in June 2001 and was named Director in October, 2004.

Prior to joining the WNBA, McAuliffe worked for Host Communications, Inc. as Vice President/General Manager of the Women's Sports Division and later as Vice President, Host Sports, Client Development. In both roles, she developed relationships with NCAA Corporate Partners and helped to coordinate partner promotional related activities and on-site activation at NCAA Championships including the Men's and Women's Final Four. Prior to working on the NCAA property, she oversaw the sales and marketing of the Metro Atlantic Athletic Conference, as the Director of MAAC Properties.

McAuliffe graduated from University of Massachusetts, Amherst in 1989 with a bachelor's in Athletic Administration.

Ron Howard — Director, WNBA Communications

As Director, WNBA Communications, Ron Howard is responsible for all sports, marketing, corporate and non-sports communications strategies and programs at large for the league. In this role he also serves as the primary league contact for WNBA team public relations departments. He was named to the position in November of 2005.

Howard joins the WNBA with more than 20 years of professional sports experience in public relations, marketing communications and crisis management. Most recently, he served as Director of Marketing Communications for the Philadelphia Eagles.

During his time with the Eagles, Howard assisted the league office at seven Super Bowls and the Pro Bowl.

A native of New York City, Howard earned a degree in American Studies from Amherst College where he played both football and baseball. He and his wife, Karen, have a son, Reid.

Dee Kantner — Supervisor of Officials

As WNBA Supervisor of Officials, Dee Kantner is responsible for recruiting, training and supervising officials and assisting in rules development for the league. She served as the league's inaugural WNBA Supervisor of Officials in 1997 and 1998. As Director of Referee Development for the WNBA in 2003 and 2004, Kantner assisted on a part-time basis in the recruitment and training of WNBA referees.

Kantner continues to officiate a full schedule of women's collegiate games and previously served as an NBA referee for five seasons. She has officiated ten women's NCAA Final Fours, including five national championship games and was named the Naismith Award winner as the 1997 Official of the Year, as well as the 1996 Atlantic Coast Conference Women's Official of the Year. Kantner has extensive FIBA officiating experience, including the 1994 and 1998 Women's World Championship and the 2000 Olympics, and spent two seasons as a referee in the CBA.

Kantner graduated from the University of Pittsburgh, where she was a four-year member of the women's field hockey team and participated in one season of basketball and track. She currently resides in Charlotte, N.C.

WNBA SCHEDULE

- 2006 Composite Schedule

- 2006 WNBA Key Dates

- 2006 TV Schedule

- 2006 Playoffs Schedule

2006 WNBA Schedule

Date	Road Team	at	Home Team	Eastern Time
Saturday, May 20	Phoenix	at	Sacramento	4 p.m.
Saturday, May 20	Chicago	at	Charlotte	6 p.m.
Saturday, May 20	New York	at	Connecticut	7 p.m.
Saturday, May 20	Detroit	at	Indiana	7 p.m.
Sunday, May 21	San Antonio	at	Houston	6 p.m.
Sunday, May 21	Los Angeles	at	Seattle	9 p.m.
Tuesday, May 23	Los Angeles	at	Charlotte	7 p.m.
Tuesday, May 23	New York	at	Washington	7 p.m.
Tuesday, May 23	Sacramento	at	Chicago	8 p.m.
Tuesday, May 23	Indiana	at	San Antonio	8 p.m.
Tuesday, May 23	Connecticut	at	Minnesota	9 p.m.
Tuesday, May 23	Houston	at	Seattle	11 p.m.
Wednesday, May 24	Minnesota	at	Detroit	7:30 p.m.
Thursday, May 25	Washington	at	Charlotte	7 p.m.
Thursday, May 25	Los Angeles	at	San Antonio	8 p.m.
Thursday, May 25	Seattle	at	Phoenix	10 p.m.
Thursday, May 25	Houston	at	Sacramento	10 p.m.
Friday, May 26	Indiana	at	Chicago	8:30 p.m.
Saturday, May 27	Detroit	at	Connecticut	4 p.m.
Saturday, May 27	Minnesota	at	Washington	5 p.m.
Tuesday, May 30	New York	at	Indiana	7 p.m.
Tuesday, May 30	Los Angeles	at	Chicago	9 p.m.
Wednesday, May 31	Los Angeles	at	Minnesota	8 p.m.
Wednesday, May 31	Indiana	at	Houston	8:30 p.m.
Wednesday, May 31	Seattle	at	Sacramento	10 p.m.
Wednesday, May 31	San Antonio	at	Phoenix	10 p.m.
Thursday, June 1	Connecticut	at	Charlotte	7 p.m.
Thursday, June 1	New York	at	Detroit	7:30 p.m.
Friday, June 2	Indiana	at	Minnesota	8 p.m.
Friday, June 2	Chicago	at	Houston	8:30 p.m.
Friday, June 2	Phoenix	at	Seattle	10 p.m.
Friday, June 2	San Antonio	at	Sacramento	10 p.m.
Saturday, June 3	Los Angeles	at	New York	4 p.m.
Saturday, June 3	Charlotte	at	Connecticut	4 p.m.
Saturday, June 3	Detroit	at	Washington	4 p.m.
Sunday, June 4	Minnesota	at	Houston	6 p.m.
Sunday, June 4	Detroit	at	Chicago	7 p.m.
Sunday, June 4	San Antonio	at	Seattle	9 p.m.
Tuesday, June 6	Houston	at	Washington	7 p.m.
Tuesday, June 6	Sacramento	at	Phoenix	10:30 p.m.
Wednesday, June 7	Connecticut	at	New York	11 a.m.
Wednesday, June 7	Washington	at	Indiana	7 p.m.
Wednesday, June 7	Chicago	at	Seattle	10 p.m.
Wednesday, June 7	Detroit	at	Los Angeles	10:30 p.m.
Friday, June 9	Seattle	at	Connecticut	7 p.m.
Friday, June 9	Indiana	at	Charlotte	7 p.m.
Friday, June 9	Minnesota	at	San Antonio	8 p.m.
Friday, June 9	New York	at	Houston	8:30 p.m.
Friday, June 9	Detroit	at	Phoenix	10 p.m.
Friday, June 9	Chicago	at	Los Angeles	10:30 p.m.
Saturday, June 10	New York	at	San Antonio	8 p.m.
Saturday, June 10	Chicago	at	Sacramento	10 p.m.
Sunday, June 11	Washington	at	Connecticut	4 p.m.
Sunday, June 11	Seattle	at	Indiana	6 p.m.

Sunday, June 11	Houston	at	Minnesota	6 p.m.
Tuesday, June 13	Charlotte	at	Washington	7 p.m.
Tuesday, June 13	Indiana	at	New York	7:30 p.m.
Tuesday, June 13	Phoenix	at	Los Angeles	10:30 p.m.
Wednesday, June 14	Seattle	at	Minnesota	8 p.m.
Wednesday, June 14	Sacramento	at	Houston	8:30 p.m.
Thursday, June 15	Washington	at	Charlotte	7 p.m.
Thursday, June 15	Seattle	at	Chicago	8 p.m.
Friday, June 16	Houston	at	New York	7:30 p.m.
Friday, June 16	Indiana	at	Detroit	7:30 p.m.
Friday, June 16	Minnesota	at	San Antonio	8 p.m.
Friday, June 16	Connecticut	at	Phoenix	10 p.m.
Saturday, June 17	Seattle	at	Sacramento	4 p.m.
Saturday, June 17	New York	at	Washington	6 p.m.
Saturday, June 17	Houston	at	Detroit	7:30 p.m.
Saturday, June 17	San Antonio	at	Chicago	8 p.m.
Saturday, June 17	Connecticut	at	Los Angeles	10:30 p.m.
Sunday, June 18	Phoenix	at	Minnesota	6 p.m.
Sunday, June 18	Charlotte	at	Indiana	6 p.m.
Sunday, June 18	Sacramento	at	Los Angeles	9:30 p.m.
Tuesday, June 20	Connecticut	at	Charlotte	7 p.m.
Wednesday, June 21	Chicago	at	Indiana	7 p.m.
Wednesday, June 21	Washington	at	New York	7:30 p.m.
Wednesday, June 21	Phoenix	at	Seattle	10 p.m.
Wednesday, June 21	San Antonio	at	Sacramento	10 p.m.
Wednesday, June 21	Houston	at	Los Angeles	10:30 p.m.
Thursday, June 22	Detroit	at	Charlotte	11:30 a.m.
Thursday, June 22	Minnesota	at	Connecticut	7 p.m.
Friday, June 23	Connecticut	at	Chicago	8:30 p.m.
Friday, June 23	Charlotte	at	Houston	8:30 p.m.
Friday, June 23	Los Angeles	at	Sacramento	10 p.m.
Friday, June 23	San Antonio	at	Seattle	10 p.m.
Friday, June 23	Indiana	at	Phoenix	10 p.m.
Saturday, June 24	Washington	at	Detroit	12 p.m.
Saturday, June 24	New York	at	Minnesota	8 p.m.
Sunday, June 25	Connecticut	at	Washington	6 p.m.
Sunday, June 25	Charlotte	at	Detroit	5 p.m.
Sunday, June 25	Seattle	at	Houston	6 p.m.
Sunday, June 25	Chicago	at	Phoenix	9 p.m.
Sunday, June 25	Indiana	at	Sacramento	9 p.m.
Sunday, June 25	San Antonio	at	Los Angeles	9:30 p.m.
Tuesday, June 27	Houston	at	Connecticut	7 p.m.
Tuesday, June 27	Indiana	at	Washington	7 p.m.
Tuesday, June 27	Charlotte	at	New York	7:30 p.m.
Tuesday, June 27	Detroit	at	San Antonio	8 p.m.
Tuesday, June 27	Sacramento	at	Seattle	10 p.m.
Wednesday, June 28	Minnesota	at	Phoenix	3:30 p.m.
Wednesday, June 28	Seattle	at	Los Angeles	10:30 p.m.
Thursday, June 29	Washington	at	Houston	1 p.m.
Thursday, June 29	Detroit	at	Indiana	7 p.m.
Thursday, June 29	San Antonio	at	New York	7:30 p.m.
Thursday, June 29	Charlotte	at	Chicago	8 p.m.
Thursday, June 29	Minnesota	at	Sacramento	10 p.m.
Friday, June 30	Detroit	at	Connecticut	7 p.m.
Friday, June 30	Phoenix	at	Los Angeles	10:30 p.m.
Saturday, July 1	Sacramento	at	Charlotte	6 p.m.

Saturday, July 1	Connecticut	at	Indiana	7 p.m.
Saturday, July 1	Chicago	at	San Antonio	8 p.m.
Saturday, July 1	Minnesota	at	Seattle	10 p.m.
Saturday, July 1	Washington	at	Los Angeles	10:30 p.m.
Sunday, July 2	Sacramento	at	Houston	6 p.m.
Sunday, July 2	Washington	at	Phoenix	9 p.m.
Monday, July 3	San Antonio	at	Los Angeles	10:30 p.m.
Wednesday, July 5	Washington	at	Minnesota	8 p.m.
Wednesday, July 5	Houston	at	Los Angeles	10:30 p.m.
Thursday, July 6	Charlotte	at	Connecticut	7 p.m.
Thursday, July 6	Sacramento	at	New York	7:30 p.m.
Thursday, July 6	Phoenix	at	Detroit	7:30 p.m.
Friday, July 7	Sacramento	at	Washington	7 p.m.
Friday, July 7	Houston	at	San Antonio	8 p.m.
Friday, July 7	Detroit	at	Minnesota	8 p.m.
Friday, July 7	New York	at	Chicago	8:30 p.m.
Friday, July 7	Indiana	at	Los Angeles	10:30 p.m.
Saturday, July 8	Phoenix	at	Connecticut	3 p.m.
Saturday, July 8	Charlotte	at	Los Angeles	10:30 p.m.
Sunday, July 9	Phoenix	at	New York	4 p.m.
Sunday, July 9	Chicago	at	Washington	4 p.m.
Sunday, July 9	San Antonio	at	Minnesota	6 p.m.
Sunday, July 9	Detroit	at	Houston	6 p.m.
Sunday, July 9	Charlotte	at	Sacramento	9 p.m.
Sunday, July 9	Indiana	at	Seattle	9 p.m.
Wednesday, July 12	WNBA All-Star Game	at	New York	7:30 p.m.
Friday, July 14	San Antonio	at	Charlotte	7 p.m.
Friday, July 14	Houston	at	Chicago	8:30 p.m.
Friday, July 14	Los Angeles	at	Phoenix	10 p.m.
Friday, July 14	New York	at	Seattle	10 p.m.
Saturday, July 15	Connecticut	at	Sacramento	4 p.m.
Saturday, July 15	Indiana	at	Charlotte	6 p.m.
Sunday, July 16	San Antonio	at	Detroit	5 p.m.
Sunday, July 16	Los Angeles	at	Minnesota	6 p.m.
Sunday, July 16	Houston	at	Indiana	6 p.m.
Sunday, July 16	Washington	at	Chicago	7 p.m.
Sunday, July 16	New York	at	Phoenix	9 p.m.
Sunday, July 16	Connecticut	at	Seattle	9 p.m.
Tuesday, July 18	Phoenix	at	Indiana	1 p.m.
Tuesday, July 18	Sacramento	at	Seattle	3 p.m.
Tuesday, July 18	Houston	at	San Antonio	8 p.m.
Tuesday, July 18	New York	at	Los Angeles	10 p.m.
Wednesday, July 19	Phoenix	at	Washington	11:30 a.m.
Wednesday, July 19	Charlotte	at	Detroit	12 p.m.
Wednesday, July 19	Chicago	at	Minnesota	1 p.m.
Thursday, July 20	Seattle	at	Charlotte	11:30 a.m.
Thursday, July 20	New York	at	Sacramento	2:30 p.m.
Thursday, July 20	Chicago	at	Connecticut	7 p.m.
Thursday, July 20	Minnesota	at	Houston	8:30 p.m.
Friday, July 21	Los Angeles	at	Detroit	7:30 p.m.
Friday, July 21	Washington	at	San Antonio	8 p.m.
Saturday, July 22	Phoenix	at	Charlotte	6 p.m.
Saturday, July 22	Los Angeles	at	Indiana	7 p.m.
Saturday, July 22	Seattle	at	New York	7:30 p.m.
Saturday, July 22	Chicago	at	Detroit	7:30 p.m.
Saturday, July 22	Sacramento	at	Minnesota	8 p.m.

Saturday, July 22	Connecticut	at	San Antonio	8 p.m.
Sunday, July 23	Seattle	at	Washington	6 p.m.
Monday, July 24	Connecticut	at	New York	7:30 p.m.
Tuesday, July 25	Sacramento	at	Indiana	7 p.m.
Tuesday, July 25	Minnesota	at	Charlotte	7 p.m.
Tuesday, July 25	New York	at	Chicago	8 p.m.
Tuesday, July 25	Washington	at	Connecticut	7:30 p.m.
Tuesday, July 25	Los Angeles	at	Houston	8:30 p.m.
Tuesday, July 25	Seattle	at	Phoenix	9:30 p.m.
Wednesday, July 26	Sacramento	at	Detroit	7:30 p.m.
Wednesday, July 26	Los Angeles	at	San Antonio	8 p.m.
Thursday, July 27	Chicago	at	Washington	7 p.m.
Thursday, July 27	Charlotte	at	Minnesota	8 p.m.
Thursday, July 27	Phoenix	at	Houston	8:30 p.m.
Friday, July 28	Sacramento	at	Connecticut	7 p.m.
Friday, July 28	Phoenix	at	San Antonio	8 p.m.
Friday, July 28	Minnesota	at	Chicago	8:30 p.m.
Friday, July 28	Detroit	at	Seattle	10 p.m.
Saturday, July 29	New York	at	Charlotte	6 p.m.
Saturday, July 29	Washington	at	Indiana	7 p.m.
Sunday, July 30	San Antonio	at	Connecticut	4 p.m.
Sunday, July 30	Minnesota	at	New York	4 p.m.
Sunday, July 30	Houston	at	Phoenix	7 p.m.
Sunday, July 30	Indiana	at	Chicago	7 p.m.
Sunday, July 30	Charlotte	at	Washington	7:30 p.m.
Sunday, July 30	Los Angeles	at	Seattle	9 p.m.
Sunday, July 30	Detroit	at	Sacramento	9 p.m.
Tuesday, August 1	Los Angeles	at	Washington	7 p.m.
Tuesday, August 1	New York	at	Connecticut	7 p.m.
Tuesday, August 1	Phoenix	at	Chicago	8 p.m.
Tuesday, August 1	Seattle	at	Minnesota	8 p.m.
Tuesday, August 1	Charlotte	at	San Antonio	8 p.m.
Tuesday, August 1	Indiana	at	Detroit	8 p.m.
Tuesday, August 1	Houston	at	Sacramento	10 p.m.
Thursday, August 3	Los Angeles	at	Connecticut	7 p.m.
Thursday, August 3	Minnesota	at	Indiana	7 p.m.
Thursday, August 3	Detroit	at	New York	7:30 p.m.
Thursday, August 3	Sacramento	at	San Antonio	8 p.m.
Thursday, August 3	Charlotte	at	Phoenix	10 p.m.
Thursday, August 3	Washington	at	Seattle	10 p.m.
Friday, August 4	Houston	at	Minnesota	8 p.m.
Friday, August 4	Detroit	at	Chicago	8:30 p.m.
Saturday, August 5	San Antonio	at	Indiana	7 p.m.
Saturday, August 5	Chicago	at	New York	7:30 p.m.
Saturday, August 5	Los Angeles	at	Phoenix	10 p.m.
Saturday, August 5	Washington	at	Sacramento	10 p.m.
Saturday, August 5	Charlotte	at	Seattle	10 p.m.
Sunday, August 6	Connecticut	at	Houston	6 p.m.
Sunday, August 6	New York	at	Detroit	6 p.m.
Sunday, August 6	San Antonio	at	Minnesota	7 p.m.
Tuesday, August 8	San Antonio	at	Washington	7 p.m.
Tuesday, August 8	Houston	at	Charlotte	7 p.m.
Tuesday, August 8	Seattle	at	Detroit	7:30 p.m.
Tuesday, August 8	Indiana	at	New York	7:30 p.m.
Tuesday, August 8	Connecticut	at	Chicago	8 p.m.
Tuesday, August 8	Minnesota	at	Phoenix	9:30 p.m.

Wednesday, August 9	Sacramento	at	Los Angeles	3:30 p.m.
Wednesday, August 9	Connecticut	at	Indiana	7 p.m.
Thursday, August 10	Chicago	at	Detroit	7:30 p.m.
Thursday, August 10	Seattle	at	San Antonio	8 p.m.
Thursday, August 10	Phoenix	at	Houston	8:30 p.m.
Thursday, August 10	Minnesota	at	Sacramento	10 p.m.
Friday, August 11	Indiana	at	Connecticut	7 p.m.
Friday, August 11	Detroit	at	Washington	7 p.m.
Friday, August 11	Charlotte	at	New York	7:30 p.m.
Saturday, August 12	Seattle	at	Houston	2 p.m.
Saturday, August 12	Chicago	at	Charlotte	6 p.m.
Saturday, August 12	Phoenix	at	San Antonio	8 p.m.
Sunday, August 13	Washington	at	New York	1:30 p.m.
Sunday, August 13	Connecticut	at	Detroit	5 p.m.
Sunday, August 13	Chicago	at	Indiana	6 p.m.
Sunday, August 13	Minnesota	at	Los Angeles	9:30 p.m.
Sunday, August 13	Sacramento	at	Phoenix	10 p.m.

2006 WNBA 10th ANNIVERSARY SEASON

KEY DATES
(Eastern times shown)

April 3	WNBA Predraft Camp — Boston, Mass.
April 5	WNBA Draft — Boston, Mass.
April 20-22	Rookie Orientation — Chicago
April 21-23	WNBA Referee Orientation — Jersey City, N.J.
April 23	Training Camp Begins
April 29	Preseason Games Begin
May 2	Training Camp Roster Cut-Down (18 to 15), 3 p.m.
May 19	Final Roster Cut-Down (15 to 11), 3 p.m.
May 20	Regular Season Begins
June 29	Mid-Season Cut-Down
July 12	WNBA All-Star Game — Madison Square Garden, New York
July 20	Trading Deadline, 8 p.m.
August 13	Regular Season Ends
August 16	Playoff Rosters Due, 3 p.m.
August 17	Playoffs Begin
September 9	Last possible Finals Date

2006 WNBA TELEVISION SCHEDULE

(Eastern starting times shown)

ABC SCHEDULE

Saturday, May 20	Phoenix	at	Sacramento	4 p.m.
Saturday, May 27	Detroit	at	Connecticut	4 p.m.
Saturday, June 3	Los Angeles	at	New York	4 p.m.
Saturday, July 15	Connecticut	at	Sacramento	4 p.m.
Saturday, August 12	Seattle	at	Houston	2 p.m.
Sunday, August 13	Washington	at	New York	1:30 p.m.

ESPN SCHEDULE

July 12, 2006	2006 WNBA All-Star Game	7:30 p.m.

ESPN2 SCHEDULE

Tuesday, May 23	Connecticut	at	Minnesota	9 p.m.
Tuesday, May 23	Houston	at	Seattle	11 p.m.
Tuesday, May 30	New York	at	Indiana	7 p.m.
Tuesday, May 30	Los Angeles	at	Chicago	9 p.m.
Tuesday, June 6	Sacramento	at	Phoenix	10:30 p.m.
Tuesday, June 13	Charlotte	at	Washington	7 p.m.
Tuesday, June 27	Sacramento	at	Seattle	10 p.m.
Saturday, July 8	Phoenix	at	Connecticut	3 p.m.
Tuesday, July 18	Houston	at	San Antonio	8 p.m.
Tuesday, July 18	New York	at	Los Angeles	10 p.m.
Tuesday, July 25	Washington	at	Connecticut	7:30 p.m.
Tuesday, July 25	Seattle	at	Phoenix	9:30 p.m.
Tuesday, August 1	Indiana	at	Detroit	8 p.m.
Tuesday, August 1	Houston	at	Sacramento	10 p.m.
Tuesday, August 8	Minnesota	at	Phoenix	10 p.m.

Playoffs Schedule

FIRST ROUND

Thursday, August 17	One East / One West First Round – Game #1
Friday, August 18	One East / One West First Round – Game #1
Saturday, August 19	One East / One West First Round – Game #2
Sunday, August 20	One East / One West First Round – Game #2
Monday, August 21	One East / One West First Round – Game #3*
Tuesday, August 22	One East / One West First Round – Game #3*

Conference Finals

Thursday, August 24	Game #1 – Eastern Conf. / Western Conf.
Saturday, August 26	Game #2 – Eastern Conf. / Western Conf.
Sunday, August 27	Game #3 – Eastern Conf. / Western Conf.*

Finals

Wednesday, August 30	Game #1
Friday, September 1	Game #2
Sunday, September 3	Game #3
Wednesday, September 6	Game #4*
Saturday, September 9	Game #5*

* - if necessary

TEAM DIRECTORIES

- Team Personnel

- Game Schedules

- 2006 Rosters

- 2005 Results

CHARLOTTE STING
EASTERN CONFERENCE

333 E. Trade St.
Charlotte, NC 28202
Telephone: (704) 688-8600
Fax: (704) 688-8733
Ticket Information: (704) 424-WNBA

www.charlottesting.com
Arena: Charlotte Bobcats Arena
 WNBA capacity (8,506)
Radio: WNMX Mix 106.1
Television: TBD

2006 SEASON
TEAM DIRECTORY

Owner	Robert L. Johnson
President/Chief Operating Officer	Ed Tapscott
General Manager	Trudi Lacey
Head Coach	Tyrone "Muggsy" Bogues
Assistant Coaches	Earl Cureton, Shelley Patterson
Athletic Trainer	TBD
Strength and Conditioning Coach	Jodi Hopkins
Equipment Manager	James McCullough
Video Coordinator	Dwayne Killings
Basketball Operations Manager	Tim Burke
Executive Vice President/General Counsel	Jonathan Fine
Executive Vice President of Administration	Colleen Millsap
Chief Operating Officer Charlotte Bobcats Arena	Barry Silberman
Executive VP of Business Operations/Chief Financial Officer	Peter Smul
Executive Vice President of Media Right and Entertainment	Naomi Travers
Executive Vice President / Chief Marketing Officer	Chris Weiller
Senior Vice President of Finance	Mike Behrman
Senior Vice President of Broadcasting and Game Entertainment	John Guagliano
Senior Vice President of Business Operations	Steve Swetoha
Vice President of Finance / Controller	Sheryl Allen
Vice President of Community Relations	LaRita Barber
Vice President of Marketing	Jason Brannon
Vice President of Public Relations	Scott Leightman
Vice President of Government Relations	Ed Lewis
Vice President of Human Resources	Kay Lowery
Vice President of Special Events	Polly Pearce
Vice President of Corporate Partnerships	Tod Rosensweig
Director of Ticket Sales	Chris Gargani
Director of Creative Services	Bo Hussey
Director of Group Sales	Christie Hussey
Director of Game Operations	John Leach
Director of Public Relations	TBD
Public Relations Coordinator	Malinda Murray
Team Photographer	Kent Smith
Radio Announcers	Sam Smith, Stephanie Ready

Robert L. Johnson

Trudi Lacey

Tyrone Bogues

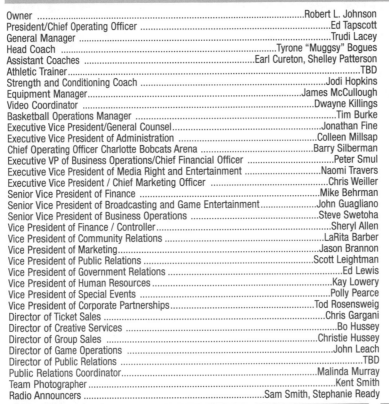

May

S	M	T	W	T	F	S
	1	2	3	4	5	6
7	8	9	10	11	12	13
14	15	16	17	18	19	20 Chi
21	22	23 LA	24	25	26	27
28	29	30	31			

June

S	M	T	W	T	F	S
				1 Con	2	3 Con
4	5	6	7	8 Ind	9	10
11	12	13 Was	14	15 Was	16	17
18 Ind	19	20 Con	21	22 Det	23 Hou	24
25 Det	26	27 NY	28	29 Chi	30	

July

S	M	T	W	T	F	S
						1 Sac
2	3	4	5	6 Con	7	8 LA
9 Sac	10	11 ★12		13	14 SA	15 Ind
16	17	18	19 Det	20 Sea	21	22 Pho
23	24	25 Min	26	27 Min	28	29 NY
30 Was	31					

August

S	M	T	W	T	F	S
		1	2	3 SA	4 Pho	5 Sea
6	7	8 Hou	9	10	11 NY	12 Chi
13	14	15	16	17	18	19
20	21	22	23	24	25	26
27	28	29	30			

▮ = Home ☐ = Away ★ 2006 WNBA All-Star Game at New York

2006 ROSTER

No.	Player	Pos.	Ht./Wt.	Metric	Born	College/Country
10	LaToya Bond	G	5-7/132	1.7/59.9	2/13/84	Missouri
1	Tasha Butts	G	5-11/160	1.8/72.6	3/10/82	Tennessee
25	Monique Currie	G/F	6-0/177	1.83/80.4	2/25/83	Duke
30	Helen Darling	G	5-6/164	1.68/74.5	8/29/78	Penn State
3	Summer Erb	C	6-6/240	1.98/109	7/25/77	North Carolina State
21	Allison Feaster	G	5-11/168	1.8/76.3	2/11/76	Harvard
42	Tye'sha Fluker	C	6-5/209	1.96/94.9	12/27/84	Tennessee
3	Alexis Kendrick	G	5-7/145	1.7/65.8	1/3/84	Georgia
8	Edwige Lawson	G	5-6/130	1.68/59	5/14/79	France
33	Yelana Leuchanka	C	6-5/195	1.96/88.5	4/30/83	West Virginia
57	Caity Matter	G	5-9/167	1.75/75.8	8/22/82	Ohio State
13	Kelly Mazzante	G	6-0/155	1.83/70.4	2/2/82	Penn State
4	Janel McCarville	F/C	6-2/220	1.88/99.9	11/3/82	Minnesota
7	Ezria Parsons	F	6-0/169	1.83/76.7	3/1/83	South Florida
2	Sheri Sam	G/F	6-0/160	1.83/72.6	5/5/74	Vanderbilt
50	Tangela Smith	F/C	6-4/160	1.93/72.6	4/1/77	Iowa
55	Tammy Sutton-Brown	C	6-4/199	1.93/90.3	1/27/78	Rutgers
9	Stacey Thomas	F	5-10/154	1.78/69.9	8/29/78	Michigan
12	Ayana Walker	F	6-3/143	1.91/64.9	9/10/79	Louisiana Tech

Coach—Tyrone "Muggsy" Bogues
Assistant coaches—Earl Cureton, Shelley Patterson
Trainer—TBD

2005 REVIEW

Results

May
21—Washington	*42-60	0-1
22—at Indiana	*58-68	0-2
26—Phoenix	*58-68	0-3
28—Los Angeles	84-75	1-3

June
02—at San Antonio	*62-69	1-4
04—at Minnesota	*67-73	1-5
10—at Detroit	*55-69	1-6
12—Seattle	*60-62	1-7
16—Indiana	*57-60	1-8
23—San Antonio	*49-64	1-9
25—New York	67-61	2-9
28—Washington	*†61-66	2-10
30—at Washington	*50-65	2-11

July
02—at Houston	*65-75	2-12
07—Minnesota	66-58	3-12
12—at Los Angeles	*59-71	3-13
13—at Phoenix	*62-82	3-14
17—Houston	*55-67	3-15
19—Connecticut	*55-64	3-16
22—at Connecticut	*63-73	3-17
23—Indiana	*46-63	3-18
26—at Sacramento	*54-64	3-19
29—at Seattle	*68-79	3-20

August
02—at Washington	*63-65	3-21
04—Sacramento	*58-76	3-22

06—Detroit	‡82-73	4-22
09—at Detroit	*64-71	4-23
12—New York	*‡74-82	4-24
14—at New York	*65-73	4-25
18—at Connecticut	*70-84	4-26
20—at Indiana	*53-62	4-27
23—Detroit	56-49	5-27
25—at New York	78-66	6-27
27—Connecticut	*69-78	6-28

*Loss. †Single overtime. ‡Double overtime.

TEAM LEADERS

Points: Tangela Smith (421).
Field goals: Tangela Smith (169).
Free throws: Tammy Sutton-Brown (96).
Three pointers: Allison Feaster (37).
Rebounds: Tammy Sutton-Brown (179).
Assists: Dawn Staley (121).
Steals: Tangela Smith (51).
Blocked shots: Tammy Sutton-Brown (37).

TEAM-BY-TEAM RESULTS

vs. Connecticut: 0-4
vs. Detroit: 2-2
vs. Houston: 0-2
vs. Indiana: 0-4
vs. Los Angeles: 1-1
vs. Minnesota: 1-1
vs. New York: 2-2
vs. Phoenix: 0-2
vs. Sacramento: 0-2
vs. San Antonio: 0-2
vs. Seattle: 0-2
vs. Washington: 0-4

CHICAGO SKY
EASTERN CONFERENCE

UIC Pavilion
525 South Racine
Chicago, IL 60607
Phone: (312) 828-9550
Ticket Information: (877) 329-9622

www.chicagosky.net
Arena: UIC Pavilion (6,500)
TV: WTTW Channel 11
    WCIU TV

2006 SEASON
TEAM DIRECTORY

Owner	Michael Alter
President/CEO	Margaret Stender
General Manager/Head Coach	Dave Cowens
Director of Game Operations and Finance	Steve Goldsher
Director of Sales	Ian McCoy
Director of Media and Community Relations	Marla Krause
Director of Marketing	Lynne Hairston
ATC/Director of Basketball Operations	Georgia Fischer
Assistant Coach	Steven Key
Video Coordinator	Michael Fischer
Strength and Conditioning Coach	Kathleen Weber
Game Operations Assistant	Eric Olton
Account Executive	Olga Gvozdenovic
Account Executive	Ibrahim Fetuga
Account Executive	Mindy Gilbert
Account Executive	Wendy Ellis
Account Executive	RaShaan Davis
Media Relations/Basketball Operations Assistant	Kristi Faulkner
Marketing Assistant	Michelle Fasulko
Office Manager	Sara Parker

Michael Alter

Margaret Stender

Dave Cowens

May

S	M	T	W	T	F	S
	1	2	3	4	5	6
7	8	9	10	11	12	13
14	15	16	17	18	19	20 Cha
21	22	23 Sac	24	25	26 Ind	27
28	29	30 LA	31			

June

S	M	T	W	T	F	S
				1	2 Hou	3
4 Det	5	6	7 Sea	8	9 LA	10 Sac
11	12	13	14	15 Sea	16	17 SA
18	19	20	21 Ind	22	23 Con	24
25 Pho	26	27	28	29 Cha	30	

July

S	M	T	W	T	F	S
						1 SA
2	3	4	5	6	7 NY	8
9 Was	10	11	★12	13	14 Hou	15
16 Was	17	18	19 Min	20 Con	21	22 Det
23	24	25 NY	26	27 Was	28 Min	29
30 Ind	31					

August

S	M	T	W	T	F	S
		1	2	3 Pho	4 Det	5 NY
6	7	8 Con	9	10 Det	11	12 Cha
13 Ind	14	15	16	17	18	19
20	21	22	23	24	25	26
27	28	29	30			

▓ = Home   ☐ = Away   ★ 2006 WNBA All-Star Game at New York

2006 ROSTER

No.	Player	Pos.	Ht./Wt.	Metric	Born	College/Country
12	Stacey Dales	G/F	6-0/155	1.83/70.4	9/5/79	Oklahoma
4	Candice Dupree	F/C	6-2/162	1.88/73.5	8/16/84	Temple
1	Kerri Gardin	F	6-1/170	1.86/77.2		Virgina Tech
3	Jennifer Harris	G	5-10/147	1.78/66.7		Washborn
23	Deanna Jackson	F	6-2/155	1.88/70.4	12/15/79	Alabama Birmingham
24	Amanda Lassiter	F	6-1/160	1.86/72.6	6/9/79	Missouri
32	Stacey Lovelace	F	6-4/170	1.93/77.2	12/5/74	Purdue
	Julie McBride					
15	Nikki McCray	G	5-11/158	1.8/71.7	12/17/71	Tennessee
2	Chelsea Newton	G	5-11/150	1.8/68.1	2/17/83	Rutgers
50	Bernadette Ngoyisa	C	6-4/195	1.93/88.5	8/26/82	Congo (Zaire)
11	Jia Perkins	G	5-8/155	1.73/70.4	2/23/82	Texas Tech
5	Elaine Powell	G	5-9/147	1.75/66.7	8/9/75	Louisiana State
43	Ashley Robinson	C	6-4/180	1.93/81.7	8/12/82	Tennessee
	Holly Tyler					
21	Brooke Wyckoff	F	6-1/183	1.86/83.1	3/30/80	Florida State
7	Francesca Zara	G	5-10/146	1.78/66.3	12/8/76	Italy

Head coach—Dave Cowens
Assistant coach—Steven Key
Strength and Conditioning coach—Kathleen Weber

CONNECTICUT SUN
EASTERN CONFERENCE

1 Mohegan Sun Blvd.
Uncasville, CT 06382
Tel: (860) 862-4000
Fax: (860) 862-4006, 862-4010
Ticket Information: (877) 786-8499

www.connecticutsun.com
Arena: Mohegan Sun Arena (9,341)
Radio: WXLM 102.3 FM
TV: FOX 61/WB 20

2006 SEASON
TEAM DIRECTORY

Owner	The Mohegan Tribe
Chief Executive Officer/Governor	Mitchell Etess
Chief Operating Officer/Alternate Governor	Jeffrey Hartmann
President/Alternate Governor	Paul Munick
General Manager	Christopher Sienko
Head Coach	Mike Thibault
Assistant Coaches	Scott Hawk, Bernadette Mattox
Head Athletic Trainer	Jen Brodeur
Strength and Conditioning Coach	Lisa Ciaravella
Director of Marketing	Lisa Weistart
Director of Business Operations	Dave Martinelli
Consumer Sales Manager	Todd McDonald
Media Relations Manager	Bill Tavares
Community Relations Manager	Tina James
Game Operations Manager	Bruce Cohn
Consumer Sales Representatives	Michael Reynolds, Annmarie Gengo, Matt Edwards
Basketball Operations Coordinator	Bill Tinnel
Consumer Sales Assistant	Rachel Manke
Media Relations Assistant	Sarah Emmett
Administrative Assistant	Sarah Ford
Video Coordinator	Jon Whitkin
Equipment Manager	Tara Peterson
Team Physicians	Diana Heiman, MD; Patricia Stuart, MD
Director of Box Office Operations	April Paris
Vice President Sponsorship/Sales	Jenna Miller-Wassell
Event Production Supervisor	Frank Pavlich
Radio Play-by-Play	Bob Heussler
TV Play-by-Play	Mike Gorman
TV Color	Rebecca Lobo

Paul Munick

Christopher Sienko

Mike Thibault

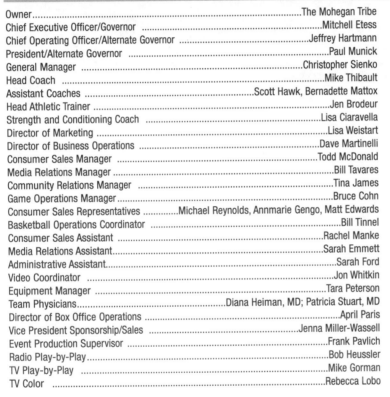

May						
S	M	T	W	T	F	S
	1	2	3	4	5	6
7	8	9	10	11	12	13
14	15	16	17	18	19	20 NY
21	22	23 Min	24	25	26	27 Det
28	29	30	31			

June						
S	M	T	W	T	F	S
				1	2 Cha	3 Cha
4	5	6	7 NY	8	9 Sea	10
11 Was	12	13	14	15	16 Pho	17 LA
18	19	20	21	22 Min	23 Chi	24
25 Was	26	27 Hou	28	29	30 Det	

July						
S	M	T	W	T	F	S
						1 Ind
2	3	4	5	6 Cha	7	8 Pho
9	10	11 ★12	13	14	15 Sac	
16 Sea	17	18	19	20 Chi	21	22 SA
23	24 NY	25 Was	26	27	28 Sac	29
30 SA	31					

August						
S	M	T	W	T	F	S
		1	2 NY	3	4 LA	5
6 Hou	7	8 Chi	9 Ind	10	11 Ind	12
13 Det	14	15	16	17	18	19
20	21	22	23	24	25	26
27	28	29	30			

▨ = Home   ☐ = Away   ★ 2006 WNBA All-Star Game at New York

2006 ROSTER

No.	Player	Pos.	Ht./Wt.	Metric	Born	College/Country
22	Jessica Brungo	F	6-1/165	1.86/74.9	4/16/82	Penn State
10	Jamie Carey	G	5-6/135	1.68/61.3	3/12/81	Texas
23	Monique Coker	F	6-1/180	1.86/81.7	11/28/82	Old Dominion
33	Katie Cronin	G	6-0/155	1.83/70.4	9/8/77	Colorado State
34	Jennifer Derevjanik	G	5-10/140	1.78/63.6	3/29/82	George Mason
32	Katie Douglas	G/F	6-0/165	1.83/74.9	5/7/79	Purdue
12	Margo Dydek	C	7-2/223	2.19/101.2	4/28/74	Poland
15	Asjha Jones	F/C	6-2/196	1.88/89	8/1/80	Connecticut
9	Donna Loffhagen	F	6-2/183	1.88/83.1	4/29/78	New Zealand
24	Megan Mahoney	F	6-0/160	1.83/72.6	2/18/83	Kansas State
11	Taj McWilliams-Franklin	F/C	6-2/184	1.88/83.5	10/20/70	St. Edwards
31	Erin Phillips	G	5-7	1.7	5/19/85	Australia
42	Nykesha Sales	G/F	6-0/184	1.83/83.5	5/10/76	Connecticut
14	Laura Summerton	C	6-2/167	1.88/75.8	12/13/83	Australia
13	Lindsay Whalen	G	5-8/150	1.73/68.1	5/9/82	Minnesota
43	Le'coe Willingham	F	6-0/200	1.83/90.8	2/10/81	Auburn

Head coach—Mike Thibault
Assistant coaches—Scott Hawk, Bernadette Mattox
Trainer—Jen Brodeur

2005 REVIEW

RESULTS

May

21—at Detroit	*67-78	0-1
22—at Washington	69-67	1-1
28—Phoenix	85-68	2-1

June

04—San Antonio	80-69	3-1
07—Seattle	81-69	4-1
10—at Houston	77-57	5-1
11—at San Antonio	78-69	6-1
18—Detroit	73-63	7-1
20—at Los Angeles	90-70	8-1
22—at Seattle	*86-95	8-2
24—at Sacramento	61-50	9-2
25—at Phoenix	77-69	10-2

28—Sacramento	70-66	11-2
30—Minnesota	71-56	12-2

July

07—at New York	*79-89	12-3
13—at Indiana	*53-64	12-4
15—Houston	70-66	13-4
17—at Minnesota	72-53	14-4
19—at Charlotte	64-55	15-4
20—at Detroit	*57-66	15-5
22—Charlotte	73-63	16-5
26—Indiana	68-55	17-5
28—New York	73-70	18-5
30—Detroit	*66-75	18-6

August

02—at New York	72-65	19-6
06—at Indiana	74-65	20-6
09—Los Angeles	64-51	21-6
11—at Washington	80-65	22-6
14—Washington	80-77	23-6
18—Charlotte	84-70	24-6
20—New York	*58-64	24-7
23—Indiana	*63-69	24-8
26—Washington	81-47	25-8
27—at Charlotte	78-69	26-8

*Loss.

TEAM LEADERS

Points: Nykesha Sales (532).
Field goals: Nykesha Sales (201).
Free throws: Lindsay Whalen (125).
Three pointers: Nykesha Sales (49).
Rebounds: Taj McWilliams-Franklin (248).
Assists: Lindsay Whalen (172).
Steals: Nykesha Sales (61).
Blocked shots: Margo Dydek (71).

TEAM-BY-TEAM RESULTS

vs. Charlotte: 4-0
vs. Detroit: 1-3
vs. Houston: 2-0
vs. Indiana: 2-2
vs. Los Angeles: 2-0
vs. Minnesota: 2-0
vs. New York: 2-2
vs. Phoenix: 2-0
vs. Sacramento: 2-0
vs. San Antonio: 2-0
vs. Seattle: 1-1
vs. Washington: 4-0

DETROIT SHOCK
EASTERN CONFERENCE

Four Championship Drive
Auburn Hills, MI 48326-1752
Phone: (248) 377-0100
Fax: (248) 377-3260
Ticket Information: (248) 377-0100

www.detroitshock.com
Arena: The Palace of Auburn Hills
         WNBA capacity (11,268)
Radio: 1310 AM
TV: TBD

2006 SEASON
TEAM DIRECTORY

Managing Partner ....William Davidson
Legal Counsel ....Oscar H. Feldman
President and CEO ....Tom Wilson
Chief Operating Officer ....Alan Ostfield
Head Coach ....Bill Laimbeer
Assistant Coaches ....Rick Mahorn, Cheryl Reeve
Athletic Trainer ....Mike Perkins
Vice President of Brand Management ....Craig Turnbull
Director of Business Operations & Brand Management..........................Alicia Jeffreys
Director of Basketball Operations & Public Relations............................John Maxwell
Media Relations Assistant..Jackie Begin
Director of Strategic Communications..Dave Wieme
Director of Community Relations ....Dennis Sampier
Basketball Operations Manager ....Rachel Sutton
Sales and Marketing Coordinators ....Dan Edelstein, Carley Knox, Jenny Smith
Brand Marketing Coordinator ....Shana Gillis
Brand Management Assistants ....Mike Huff
Web Services Manager...Dena Krischer
Television/Radio Broadcaster...Matt Shepard
Team Physician ....Dr. Ben Paolucci
Team Photographer ....Allen Einstein

Tom Wilson

Bill Laimbeer

May

S	M	T	W	T	F	S
	1	2	3	4	5	6
7	8	9	10	11	12	13
14	15	16	17	18	19	20 Ind
21	22	23	24 Min	25	26	27 Con
28	29 Ind	30	31			

June

S	M	T	W	T	F	S
				1 NY	2	3 Was
4 Chi	5	6	7 LA	8	9 Pho	10
11	12	13	14	15	16 Ind	17 Hou
18	19	20	21	22 Cha	23	24 Was
25 Cha	26	27	28	29	30 Con	

July

S	M	T	W	T	F	S
						1
2	3	4	5	6 Pho	7 Min	8
9 Hou	10	11 ★12	13	14	15	
16 SA	17	18	19 Cha	20	21 LA	22 Chi
23	24	25	26 Sac	27 SA	28 Sea	29
30 Sac	31					

August

S	M	T	W	T	F	S
		1	2	3 Ind	4 NY	5 Chi
6 NY	7	8 Sea	9	10 Chi	11 Was	12
13 Con	14	15	16	17	18	19
20	21	22	23	24	25	26
27	28	29	30			

▢ = Home   ▢ = Away   ★ 2006 WNBA All-Star Game at New York

26

2006 ROSTER

No.	Player	Pos.	Ht./Wt.	Metric	Born	College/Country
21	Jacqueline Batteast	F	6-2/175	1.88/79.5	3/26/83	Notre Dame
45	Kara Braxton	F	6-6/190	1.98/86.3	2/18/83	Georgia
32	Swin Cash	F	6-1/165	1.86/74.9	9/22/79	Connecticut
20	Ryan Coleman	G	5-8/152	1.73/69	7/2/83	Eastern Michigan
35	Cheryl Ford	C	6-3/191	1.91/86.7	6/6/81	Louisiana Tech
11	Kedra Holland-Corn	G	5-7/136	1.7/61.7	11/5/74	Georgia
14	Deanna Nolan	G/F	5-10/160	1.78/72.6	8/25/79	Georgia
23	Plenette Pierson	F/C	6-2/170	1.88/77.2	8/31/81	Texas Tech
00	Ruth Riley	C	6-5/195	1.96/88.5	8/28/79	Notre Dame
30	Katie Smith	G	5-11/180	1.8/81.7	6/4/74	Ohio State
43	Zane Teilane	C	6-7/170	2.01/77.2	9/24/83	Western Illinois

Head coach—Bill Laimbeer
Assistant coaches—Rick Mahorn, Cheryl Reeve
Trainer—Mike Perkins

2005 REVIEW

RESULTS

May

21—Connecticut	78-67	1-0
22—at New York	78-71	2-0
24—San Antonio	74-65	3-0

June

03—New York	†68-66	4-0
08—Seattle	*61-76	4-1
10—Charlotte	69-55	5-1
12—at New York	*69-72	5-2
15—at Indiana	*†79-84	5-3
18—at Connecticut	*63-73	5-4
24—Washington	*55-69	5-5
26—Los Angeles	79-73	6-5

July

01—Sacramento	*63-80	6-6

05—Houston	*66-75	6-7
07—at Washington	76-62	7-7
13—at Minnesota	*61-71	7-8
15—at Indiana	*57-62	7-9
17—Indiana	*58-59	7-10
20—Connecticut	66-57	8-10
23—at Seattle	*71-74	8-11
24—at Sacramento	*51-91	8-12
30—at Connecticut	75-66	9-12
31—Phoenix	66-63	10-12

August

02—at Houston	*61-62	10-13
06—at Charlotte	*‡73-82	10-14
07—New York	72-67	11-14
09—Charlotte	71-64	12-14

11—Minnesota	†72-66	13-14
13—at San Antonio	60-59	14-14
16—at Phoenix	*51-58	14-15
19—at Los Angeles	*67-74	14-16
21—Washington	66-52	15-16
23—at Charlotte	*49-56	15-17
25—Indiana	55-40	16-17
27—at Washington	*67-76	16-18

*Loss. †Single overtime. ‡Double overtime

TEAM LEADERS

Points: Deanna Nolan (524).
Field goals: Deanna Nolan (184).
Free throws: Deanna Nolan (128).
Three pointers: Deanna Nolan (28).
Rebounds: Cheryl Ford (322).
Assists: Deanna Nolan (121).
Steals: Deanna Nolan (55).
Blocked shots: Ruth Riley (46).
Blocked shots: Cheryl Ford (46).

TEAM-BY-TEAM RESULTS

vs. Charlotte: 2-2
vs. Connecticut: 3-1
vs. Houston: 0-2
vs. Indiana: 1-3
vs. Los Angeles: 1-1
vs. Minnesota: 1-1
vs. New York: 3-1
vs. Phoenix: 1-1
vs. Sacramento: 0-2
vs. San Antonio: 2-0
vs. Seattle: 0-2
vs. Washington: 2-2

HOUSTON COMETS
WESTERN CONFERENCE

1510 Polk St.
Houston, TX 77002
Tel: (713) 758-7200
Fax: (713) 758-7339
Ticket Information: (713) 627-WNBA

www.houstoncomets.com
Arena: Toyota Center
WNBA capacity (10,063)
Radio Station: SportsRadio 610
TV Station: FSN Southwest

2006 SEASON
TEAM DIRECTORY

Owner	Leslie L. Alexander
President & Chief Executive Officer	George N. Postolos
Comets President & Chief Executive Officer	Andréa Bouchey Young
Chief Financial Officer	Marcus Jolibois
Senior Vice President, Sales, Marketing & Broadcasting	Thaddeus Brown
Senior Vice President, Business Development	David Carlock
Vice President, Corporate Development	Greg Elliot
Vice President & General Manager of Toyota Center	Doug Hall
Vice President, Marketing	John Dillon
Vice President, Human Resources	Vivian L. Mora
Vice President, Ticket Sales & Services	Mark Norelli
Executive Vice President of Basketball	Carroll Dawson
Head Coach & General Manager	Van Chancellor
Assistant Coaches	Kevin Cook, Karleen Thompson
Director of Player Personnel	Tom Cross
Coordinator of Sports Medicine	Michelle T. Leget
Head Athletic Trainer	Samantha Hicks
Video Coordinator	Harold Liggans
Equipment Manager	Anthony Nila
Basketball Operations Executive Assistant	Sandie Largent
Director of Broadcasting	Joel Blank
Senior Director of Finance	David Jackson
Director of Community Relations	Sarah Joseph
Director of Ticket Operations	Josh Logan
Manager of Comets Ticket Sales & Services	April Sanders
Manager of Marketing Operations & Partnerships	Kyle Simpson
Comets Media Relations Coordinator	Allan Rojas
Comets Account Representatives	Nicole Hernandez, Mandy Love, Jesse Salazar, Toi Tyo
Comets Group Sales Representatives	Jason Betts, Elana Washington
Business & Travel Coordinator	Geraldine Chell
Comets Broadcasters	Radio: Craig Ackerman, TBD
	TV: TBD

Leslie Alexander

Andréa Bouchey Young

Van Chancellor

May

S	M	T	W	T	F	S
	1	2	3	4	5	6
7	8	9	10	11	12	13
14	15	16	17	18	19	20
21 SA	22	23 Sea	24	25 Sac	26	27
28	29	30	31 Ind			

June

S	M	T	W	T	F	S
				1	2 Chi	3
4 Min	5	6 Was	7	8	9 NY	10
11 Min	12	13	14 Sac	15	16 NY	17 Det
18	19	20	21 LA	22	23 Cha	24
25 Sea	26	27 Con	28	29 Was	30	

July

S	M	T	W	T	F	S
						1
2 Sac	3	4	5 LA	6	7 SA	8
9 Det	10	11	★12	13	14 Chi	15
16 Ind	17	18 SA	19	20 Min	21	22
23	24	25 LA	26	27 Pho	28	29
30 Pho	31					

August

S	M	T	W	T	F	S
		1	2	3 Sac	4	5 Min
6 Con	7	8 Cha	9	10 Pho	11	12 Sea
13	14	15	16	17	18	19
20	21	22	23	24	25	26
27	28	29	30			

 = Home   = Away   ★ 2006 WNBA All-Star Game at New York

2006 ROSTER

No.	Player	Pos.	Ht./Wt.	Metric	Born	College/Country
25	Dominique Canty	G/F	5-9/162	1.75/73.5	3/2/77	Alabama
4	Kayte Christensen	F	6-2/171	1.88/77.6	11/16/80	UC Santa Barbara
20	Tamecka Dixon	G	5-9/148	1.75/67.1	12/14/75	Kansas
15	Roneeka Hodges	G	5-11/165	1.8/74.8	7/19/82	Florida State
55	Anastasia Kostaki	G	5-7/137	1.7/62.1	3/26/78	Greece
21	Sancho Lyttle	C	6-4/175	1.93/79.4	9/20/83	Houston
41	Megan Moody	G/F	6-2/167	1.88/75.8	11/3/83	Tulsa
9	Astou Ndiaye-Diatta	F	6-3/182	1.91/82.6	11/5/73	Southern Nazarene
24	Tari Phillips	C	6-2/200	1.88/90.7	3/6/70	Central Florida
52	Liz Shimek	F	6-1/195	1.85/88.5	5/25/84	Michigan State
42	Charlene Smith	G	5-8/153	1.73/69.5	12/22/81	DePaul
2	Michelle Snow	C	6-5/158	1.96/71.7	3/20/80	Tennessee
5	Dawn Staley	G	5-6/134	1.68/60.8	5/4/70	Virginia
44	Tiffany Stansbury	F/C	6-3/183	1.91/83.1	1/16/83	North Carolina State
22	Sheryl Swoopes	F	6-0/145	1.83/65.8	3/25/71	Texas Tech
7	Tina Thompson	F	6-2/178	1.88/80.7	2/10/75	Southern California
8	Mistie Williams	F	6-3/205	1.91/93.1	12/2/83	Duke

Head coach—Van Chancellor
Assistant coaches—Kevin Cook, Karleen Thompson
Trainer—Samantha Hicks

2005 REVIEW

RESULTS

May
21—at San Antonio	78-70	1-0
22—Minnesota	79-65	2-0
27—at Seattle	*69-79	2-1
29—Indiana	‡86-78	3-1

June
04—Phoenix	59-57	4-1
07—Minnesota	*58-62	4-2
10—Connecticut	*57-77	4-3
13—at Sacramento	*68-74	4-4
15—at Los Angeles	*64-83	4-5
18—at San Antonio	75-69	5-5
25—San Antonio	62-44	6-5
28—Seattle	71-67	7-5

July
02—Charlotte	75-65	8-5
05—at Detroit	75-66	9-5
07—at Indiana	65-63	10-5
12—New York	*†65-68	10-6
15—at Connecticut	*66-70	10-7
17—at Charlotte	67-55	11-7
19—Sacramento	58-54	12-7
21—Washington	*65-70	12-8
23—Los Angeles	*59-69	12-9
26—at Washington	83-65	13-9
27—at New York	71-69	14-9
30—San Antonio	*63-68	14-10

August
02—Detroit	62-61	15-10
05—at Phoenix	*75-80	15-11
07—at Sacramento	*45-55	15-12
09—at Seattle	*68-71	15-13
14—Seattle	75-72	16-13
16—at Minnesota	*62-73	16-14
18—Phoenix	77-66	17-14
21—at Los Angeles	*50-55	17-15
25—at Phoenix	80-72	18-15
27—Los Angeles	77-51	19-15

*Loss. †Single overtime.
‡Double overtime

TEAM LEADERS

Points: Sheryl Swoopes (614).
Field goals: Sheryl Swoopes (217).
Free throws: Sheryl Swoopes (153).
Three pointers: Sheryl Swoopes (27).
Rebounds: Michelle Snow (225).
Assists: Sheryl Swoopes (141).
Steals: Sheryl Swoopes (66).
Blocked shots: Michelle Snow (38).

TEAM-BY-TEAM RESULTS

vs. Charlotte: 2-0
vs. Connecticut: 0-2
vs. Detroit: 2-0
vs. Indiana: 2-0
vs. Los Angeles: 1-3
vs. Minnesota: 1-2
vs. New York: 1-1
vs. Phoenix: 3-1
vs. Sacramento: 1-2
vs. San Antonio: 3-1
vs. Seattle: 2-2
vs. Washington: 1-1

INDIANA FEVER
EASTERN CONFERENCE

125 S. Pennsylvania St.
Indianapolis, IN 46204
Tel: (317) 917-2500
Fax: (317) 917-2599
Ticket Information: (317) 917-2500
Single Game Ticket Information: (877) WNBA-TIX

www.feverbasketball.com
Arena: Conseco Fieldhouse
         WNBA capacity (9,823)
Radio Station: WIBC 1070 AM
TV Station: FOX Sports Midwest, WB4

2006 SEASON
TEAM DIRECTORY

Pacers Sports & Entertainment Ownership ....Herb Simon, Melvin Simon
President, Pacers Sports & Entertainment ....Donnie Walsh
Senior VP/Chief Operating Officer & General Manager ....Kelly Krauskopf
Senior VP/Executive Director of Conseco Fieldhouse ....Rick Fuson
Senior VP/Chief Financial Officer ....Kevin Bower
Senior VP/Marketing ....Larry Mago
Senior VP/Basketball Administration ....David Morway
Head Coach ....Brian Winters
Assistant Coaches ....Lin Dunn, Julie Plank
Trainer ....Holly Heitzman-Allison
Strength Coach ....Greg Moore
Operations Coordinator ....Elizabeth Linkous
Video Coordinator ....Vance Catlin
Administrative Assistant...Michelle Cassaday
Team Physician ....David Harsha, M.D.
Team Orthopedist...Scott A. Lintner, M.D.
Director of Business Operations ....Julie Graue
Director of Game Operations/Promotions ....Jeff Scalf
Director of Group Events ....Rob Robinson
Director of Sponsorship Sales ....Mike McClure
Director of Media Relations ....Kevin Messenger
Director of Inside Sales and Fever Ticket Sales ....Ben Milsom
Manager of Community Relations ....Dan Gaines
Game Operations Manager ....Doug Morgan
Promotions Managers ....Karen Atkeson, Dean Heaviland
Sponsorship Service Coordinator ....Ramona Christen
Public Information Assistant...Tim Edwards
Dance Teams Coordinator/Choreographer ....Stacey Austin
Radio/TV Play-by-Play ....Chris Denari, Kevin Lee (radio only)
Radio/TV Analysts ....Debbie Antonelli (TV), Jane Schott (radio)
Public Address Announcer ....Kevin Cole
Team Photographer ....Frank McGrath
Statistics Crew Directors ....Gwynda Eversole, Bill York
Statistics Crew..Bob Bernath, Trudy Bernath, Clara Caito,
                          Marie Kabrich, Beth Masariu, Judy Schneider,
              Janice Verplank, Ed Whitehead, Rick York, Pam Zwickel
Media Room Attendants ....Martha Kalb, Susan Kessler,
                                                         Barbara Meiers,Dana Whitehead

Donnie Walsh

Kelly Krauskopf

Brian Winters

= Home   **= Away**   ★ 2006 WNBA All-Star Game at New York

No.	Player	Pos.	Ht./Wt.	Metric	Born	College/Country
22	La'Tangela Atkinson	G	6-2/169	1.88/76.7	3/22/84	North Carolina
41	Tully Bevilaqua	G	5-7/145	1.7/65.8	7/19/72	Australia
14	Coretta Brown	G	5-9/150	1.75/68.1	10/21/80	North Carolina
24	Tamika Catchings	F	6-1/167	1.86/75.8	7/21/79	Tennessee
30	Anna DeForge	G	5-10/160	1.78/72.6	4/14/76	Nebraska
31	Linda Frohlich	F	6-2/185	1.88/84	6/23/79	Nevada-Las Vegas
32	Ebony Hoffman	C	6-2/215	1.88/97.6	8/27/82	Southern California
0	Olympia Scott	C	6-2/175	1.88/79.5	8/5/76	Stanford
32	Kristen Sharp	G	5-9/149	1.75/67.6	4/18/81	Cincinnati
23	Charlotte Smith	F	6-0/148	1.83/67.2	8/23/73	North Carolina
35	Kasha Terry	C	6-3/185	1.91/84	10/21/83	Gerogia Tech
15	Tan White	G	5-7/154	1.7/69.9	9/27/82	Mississippi State
44	Tamika Whitmore	F	6-2/190	1.88/86.3	6/5/77	Memphis
23	Lenae Williams	G	5-11/155	1.8/70.4	7/14/79	DePaul

Head coach—Brian Winters
Assistant coaches—Lin Dunn, Julie Plank
Trainer—Holly Heitzman-Allison

2005 REVIEW

RESULTS

May

22—Charlotte	68-58	1-0
24—Phoenix	83-76	2-0
26—at New York	67-59	3-0
29—at Houston	*‡78-86	3-1

June

01—Sacramento	61-60	4-1
04—at Seattle	*77-83	4-2
07—at Sacramento	*51-65	4-3
10—New York	62-59	5-3
15—Detroit	†84-79	6-3
16—at Charlotte	60-57	7-3
18—at Washington	*‡78-88	7-4
24—Minnesota	57-55	8-4
28—Los Angeles	*58-61	8-5

July

07—Houston	*63-65	8-6
13—Connecticut	64-53	9-6
15—Detroit	62-57	10-6
17—at Detroit	59-58	11-6
19—at Minnesota	*45-66	11-7
21—San Antonio	66-53	12-7
23—at Charlotte	63-46	13-7
26—at Connecticut	*55-68	13-8
29—Washington	62-58	14-8
31—at New York	*53-67	14-9

August

04—Seattle	78-68	15-9
06—Connecticut	*65-74	15-10
07—at Washington	*60-61	15-11

11—at San Antonio	57-50	16-11
13—at Los Angeles	*59-69	16-12
14—at Phoenix	62-56	17-12
18—Washington	67-57	18-12
20—Charlotte	62-53	19-12
23—at Connecticut	69-63	20-12
25—at Detroit	*40-55	20-13
27—New York	75-50	21-13

*Loss. †Single overtime. ‡Double overtime

TEAM LEADERS

Points: Tamika Catchings (501).
Field goals: Tamika Catchings (157).
Free throws: Tamika Catchings (152).
Three pointers: Tully Bevilaqua (44).
Rebounds: Tamika Catchings (264).
Assists: Tamika Catchings (143).
Steals: Tamika Catchings (90).
Blocked shots: Kelly Schumacher (24).

TEAM-BY-TEAM RESULTS

vs. Charlotte: 4-0
vs. Connecticut: 2-2
vs. Detroit: 3-1
vs. Houston: 0-2
vs. Los Angeles: 0-2
vs. Minnesota: 1-1
vs. New York: 3-1
vs. Phoenix: 2-0
vs. Sacramento: 1-1
vs. San Antonio: 2-0
vs. Seattle: 1-1
vs. Washington: 2-2

LOS ANGELES SPARKS
WESTERN CONFERENCE

2151 E. Grand Ave. #100
El Segundo, CA 90245
Tel: (310) 341-1000
Fax: (310) 341-1029
Ticket Information: (877) 44-SPARKS

www.lasparks.com
Arena: STAPLES Center
         WNBA capacity (13,141)
Radio: Progressive Talk AM 1150
TV: Fox Sports West, FSN Prime Ticket

2006 SEASON
TEAM DIRECTORY

Chairman ....Dr. Jerry Buss
President ....Johnny Buss
Chief Financial Officer ....Joe McCormack
General Counsel..Jim Perzik
General Manager ....Penny Toler
Assistant, General Manager ....Rondre Jackson
Senior Assistant to the President ....Brandi Bratcher
Head Coach ....Joe "Jellybean" Bryant
Assistant Coaches ....TBA
Team Physicians ....Dr. John Moe, Dr. Stephen Lombardo
Head Athletic Trainer ....Marco Nunez
Assistant Trainer ....Tiffany Maston
Team Manager ....Thomas Archie
Assistant Manager..Specelle Williams
Video Coordinator ....Dominic Sermeno
Exec. Dir. Corporate Sponsorship ....Eva Campbell, Ron Rockoff
Exec. Dir. Multimedia Marketing ....Keith Harris
Director, Advertising ....Michael Harris
Public Relations Coordinator..Ashley King
Assistant Public Relations Coordinator ....Jonathan Daillak
Community Relations Coordinator ....Andrea Smith
Director, Corporate Marketing ....Robin McLaughlin
Director, Event Production and Game Operations ....Ian Levitt
Director, Ticket Operations...Veronica Lawlor
Assistant Directors, Ticket Operations ....Jim Bakken, Charles Bingham
Account Executives, Ticket Operations..........................Joe Bucz, Pati Freund, James Brown
Office Coordinator ....Kim Bourgeois

Johnny Buss

Penny Toler

Joe Bryant

May

S	M	T	W	T	F	S
	1	2	3	4	5	6
7	8	9	10	11	12	13
14	15	16	17	18	19	20
21 Sea	22	23 Cha	24	25 SA	26	27
28	29	30 Chi	31 Min			

June

S	M	T	W	T	F	S
				1	2 NY	3
4	5	6	7 Det	8	9 Chi	10
11	12	13 Pho	14	15	16	17 Con
18 Sac	19	20	21 Hou	22	23 Sac	24
25 SA	26 SA	27	28	29	30 Pho	

July

S	M	T	W	T	F	S
						1 Was
2	3 SA	4	5 Hou	6	7 Ind	8 Cha
9	10	11 ★12		13	14 Pho	15
16 Min	17	18 NY	19	20	21 Det	22 Ind
23	24	25 Hou	26	27	28	29
30 Sea	31					

August

S	M	T	W	T	F	S
		1	2 Was	3	4 Con	5 Pho
6	7	8	9 Sac	10	11	12
13 Min	14	15	16	17	18	19
20	21	22	23	24	25	26
27	28	29	30			

■ = Home □ = Away ★ 2006 WNBA All-Star Game at New York

2006 ROSTER

No.	Player	Pos.	Ht./Wt.	Metric	Born	College/Country
25	Jennifer Butler	C	6-3/175	1.91/79.5	4/21/81	Massachusetts
23	Willnett Crockett	F	6-2	1.88	7/5/84	Connecticut
21	Brandi Davis	G	6-0/172	1.83/78.1	1/1/83	Oregon
5	Ha Eun-joo	C	6-8	2.03		South Korea
10	Doneeka Hodges-Lewis	G	5-9/160	1.75/72.6	7/19/82	Louisiana State
1	Chamique Holdsclaw	F	6-2/172	1.88/78.1	8/9/77	Tennessee
2	Temeka Johnson	G	5-3/145	1.6/65.8	9/6/82	Louisiana State
9	Lisa Leslie	C	6-5/170	1.96/77.2	7/7/72	Southern California
4	Mwadi Mabika	G	5-11/165	1.8/74.9	7/27/76	Congo (Zaire)
33	Raffaella Masciadri	G	6-0/169	1.83/76.7	9/30/80	University of Como
3	Shannon Mathews	G	5-6/153	1.68/69.5	6/28/83	Gonzaga
12	Brandi McCain	G	5-3/135	1.6/61.3	9/21/79	Florida
31	Jessica Moore	C	6-3/180	1.91/81.7	7/9/82	Connecticut
15	Tamara Moore	G	5-10/176	1.78/79.9	4/11/80	Wisconsin
14	Emmeline Ndongue	C	6-2	1.88	4/25/83	France
00	Murriel Page	C	6-2/160	1.88/72.6	9/18/75	Florida
34	Tiffany Porter-Talbert	G	5-7	1.7	10/21/84	Western Kentucky
32	Christi Thomas	F	6-3/185	1.91/84	8/14/82	Georgia
	Dalivorka Vilipic	F/C	6-4/207	1.93/94	3/30/75	Yugoslavia
20	Abiola Wabara	F	6-0/174	1.83/79		Baylor
40	Lisa Willis	G	5-11/170	1.8/77.2	6/13/84	UCLA

Head coach—Joe "Jellybean" Bryant
Assistant coaches—TBA
Trainer—Marco Nunez

2005 REVIEW

RESULTS

May

21—at Seattle	68-50	1-0
25—at Minnesota	*65-68	1-1
26—at Washington	84-75	2-1
28—at Charlotte	*75-84	2-2
31—San Antonio	81-70	3-2

June

04—at Sacramento	*53-81	3-3
08—Phoenix	*63-66	3-4
11—Sacramento	81-74	4-4
15—Houston	83-64	5-4
18—Minnesota	69-56	6-4
20—Connecticut	*70-90	6-5

24—Seattle	76-65	7-5
26—at Detroit	*73-79	7-6
28—at Indiana	61-58	8-6

July

02—Phoenix	86-63	9-6
05—New York	*55-67	9-7
12—Charlotte	71-59	10-7
16—Seattle	*70-78	10-8
19—Washington	*68-74	10-9
23—at Houston	69-59	11-9
26—at Phoenix	*60-77	11-10
29—at Sacramento	*59-79	11-11
31—at Seattle	*72-77	11-12

August

05—at San Antonio	66-63	12-12
07—at Minnesota	*72-76	12-13
09—at Connecticut	*51-64	12-14
10—at New York	*69-74	12-15
13—Indiana	69-59	13-15
16—Sacramento	*63-72	13-16
19—Detroit	74-67	14-16
21—Houston	55-50	15-16
23—Minnesota	74-63	16-16
26—at San Antonio	70-67	17-16
27—at Houston	*51-77	17-17

*Loss.

TEAM LEADERS

Points: Chamique Holdsclaw (561).
Field goals: Chamique Holdsclaw (216).
Free throws: Chamique Holdsclaw (126).
Three pointers: Doneeka Hodges (31).
Rebounds: Lisa Leslie (248).
Assists: Chamique Holdsclaw (104).
Steals: Lisa Leslie (67).
Blocked shots: Lisa Leslie (71).

TEAM-BY-TEAM RESULTS

vs. Charlotte: 1-1
vs. Connecticut: 0-2
vs. Detroit: 1-1
vs. Houston: 3-1
vs. Indiana: 2-0
vs. Minnesota: 2-2
vs. New York: 0-2
vs. Phoenix: 1-2
vs. Sacramento: 1-3
vs. San Antonio: 3-0
vs. Seattle: 2-2
vs. Washington: 1-1

33

MINNESOTA LYNX
WESTERN CONFERENCE

Target Center
600 First Avenue North
Minneapolis, MN 55403
Tel: (612) 673-1600
Fax: (612) 673-1699
Ticket Information: (612) 673-8400

www.lynxbasketball.com
Arena: Target Center
         WNBA capacity (11,380)
Radio: BOB 106.1 FM
TV: FSN North

2006 SEASON
TEAM DIRECTORY

Owner	Glen Taylor
President	Chris Wright
Chief Operating Officer	Roger Griffith
Head Coach	Suzie McConnell Serio
Assistant Coaches	Carolyn Jenkins, TBD
Trainer	Alisha Hvistendahl
Operations Manager	Katie Murphy
Public Relations Coordinator	Matt Slieter
Public Relations Manager	Mike Cristaldi
Vice President of Communications	Ted Johnson
Vice President of Marketing	Jason LaFrenz
Director of Ticket Sales	Bryant Pfeiffer
Vice President of Business Development	Conrad Smith
Vice President of Corporate Sales	Ethan Casson
Vice President of Fan/Guest Relations	Jeff Munneke
Community Relations Manager	Katie Mattis
Box Office Manager	Molly Tomczak

Roger Griffith

Suzie McConnell Serio

May

S	M	T	W	T	F	S
	1	2	3	4	5	6
7 Hou	8	9	10	11	12	13
14	15	16	17	18	19	20
21	22	23 Con	24 Det	25	26	27 Was
28	29	30	31 LA			

June

S	M	T	W	T	F	S
				1	2 Ind	3
4 Hou	5	6	7	8	9 SA	10
11 Hou	12	13	14 Sea	15	16 SA	17
18 Pho	19	20	21	22 Con	23	24 NY
25	26	27	28 Pho	29 Sac	30	

July

S	M	T	W	T	F	S
						1 Sea
2	3	4	5 Was	6	7 Det	8
9 SA	10	11	★ 12	13	14	15
16 LA	17	18	19 Chi	20 Hou	21	22 Sac
23	24	25 Cha	26	27 Cha	28 Chi	29
30 NY	31					

August

S	M	T	W	T	F	S
		1	2 Sea	3	4 Ind	5 Hou
6 SA	7	8 Pho	9	10 Sac	11	12
13 LA	14	15	16	17	18	19
20	21	22	23	24	25	26
27	28	29	30			

■ = Home   □ = Away   ★ 2006 WNBA All-Star Game at New York

2006 ROSTER

No.	Player	Pos.	Ht./Wt.	Metric	Born	College/Country
25	Svetlana Abrosimova	F	6-2/169	1.88/76.7	7/9/80	Connecticut
21	Ambrosia Anderson	F	6-0/167	1.83/75.8	3/14/84	BYU
33	Seimone Augustus	G	6-0/179	1.83/81.3	4/30/84	Lousiana State
31	Brittany Davis	F	6-1/187	1.86/84.9	1/7/84	Florida
5	Megan Duffy	G	5-7/135	1.7/61.3	7/13/84	Notre Dame
8	Kristi Harrower	G	5-4/139	1.63/63.1	3/4/75	Australia
55	Vanessa Hayden	C	6-4/240	1.93/109	6/5/82	Florida
23	Amber Jacobs	G	5-8/152	1.73/69	6/29/82	Boston College
13	Chandi Jones	G	5-9/150	1.75/68.1	3/25/82	Houston
1	Tynesha Lewis	G	5-10/152	1.78/69	5/8/79	North Carolina State
44	Kristen Mann	F	6-1/185	1.86/84	8/10/83	Cal-Santa Barbara
11	Nuria Martinez	G	5-9/167	1.75/75.8	2/29/84	Spain
3	Nicole Ohlde	F/C	6-5/180	1.96/81.7	3/13/82	Kansas State
32	Jess Strom	G	5-9/149	1.75/67.6	4/29/83	Penn State
10	Shona Thorburn	G	5-9/149	1.75/67.6	8/7/82	Utah
34	Adrian Williams	F/C	6-4/170	1.93/77.2	2/15/77	Southern California
20	Tamika Williams	F	6-2/195	1.88/88.5	4/12/80	Connecticut

Head coach—Suzie McConnell Serio
Assistant coaches—Carolyn Jenkins, TBD
Trainer—Alisha Hvistendahl

2005 REVIEW

RESULTS

May

22—at Houston	*65-79	0-1
25—Los Angeles	68-65	1-1
29—Sacramento	*66-67	1-2

June

03—at Washington	*71-74	1-3
04—Charlotte	73-67	2-3
07—at Houston	62-58	3-3
11—Washington	78-60	4-3
15—at Seattle	†86-81	5-3
17—at Sacramento	*50-67	5-4
18—at Los Angeles	*56-69	5-5
22—Phoenix	75-59	6-5
24—at Indiana	*55-57	6-6

26—Seattle	73-70	7-6
28—San Antonio	63-53	8-6
30—at Connecticut	*56-71	8-7

July

07—at Charlotte	*58-66	8-8
13—Detroit	71-61	9-8
15—at New York	64-60	10-8
17—Connecticut	*53-72	10-9
19—Indiana	66-45	11-9
24—New York	*47-59	11-10
26—at San Antonio	*71-78	11-11
29—Phoenix	*65-69	11-12
31—at Sacramento	*54-67	11-13

August

03—at Phoenix	*64-70	11-14
07—Los Angeles	76-72	12-14
09—San Antonio	76-72	13-14
11—at Detroit	*†66-72	13-15
12—Seattle	*66-72	13-16
16—Houston	73-62	14-16
18—at Seattle	*60-76	14-17
21—at Phoenix	*69-83	14-18
23—at Los Angeles	*63-74	14-19
27—Sacramento	*52-61	14-20

*Loss. †Single overtime.

TEAM LEADERS

Points: Nicole Ohlde (382).
Field goals: Nicole Ohlde (133).
Free throws: Nicole Ohlde (116).
Three pointers: Katie Smith (35).
Rebounds: Nicole Ohlde (194).
Assists: Kristi Harrower (96).
Steals: Svetlana Abrosimova (48).
Blocked shots: Vanessa Hayden (68).

TEAM-BY-TEAM RESULTS

vs. Charlotte: 1-1
vs. Connecticut: 0-2
vs. Detroit: 1-1
vs. Houston: 2-1
vs. Indiana: 1-1
vs. Los Angeles: 2-2
vs. New York: 1-1
vs. Phoenix: 1-3
vs. Sacramento: 0-4
vs. San Antonio: 2-1
vs. Seattle: 2-2
vs. Washington: 1-1

NEW YORK LIBERTY
EASTERN CONFERENCE

Madison Square Garden
Two Pennsylvania Plaza
New York, NY 10121-0091
Phone: (212) 564-WNBA
www.nyliberty.com

Arena: Madison Square Garden (19,763)
Radio: WWRL (1600 AM)
TV: MSG Network (cable)

2006 SEASON
TEAM DIRECTORY

President and Chief Executive Officer, Cablevision
Systems Corporation; Chairman, Madison Square Garden ....James L. Dolan
Vice Chairman, Cablevision Systems Corporation;
Vice Chairman, Madison Square Garden ....Hank J. Ratner
President and Chief Operating Officer, MSG Sports ....Steve Mills
President, Basketball Operations, Knicks ....Isiah Thomas
President and General Manager, New York Rangers ....Glen Sather
Executive Vice President, Finance...Robert Pollichino
Senior Vice President & General Manager ....Carol Blazejowski
Senior Vice President, Finance & Controller ....John Cudmore
Senior Vice President, Sports Team Operations ....Mark Piazza
Senior Vice President, Legal Affairs, Madison Square Garden ....Marc Schoenfeld
Vice President, MSG Legal & Business Affairs...Rana Dershowitz
Vice President, Marketing and Communications..Amy Scheer
President, MSG Networks ....Michael Bair
President, Facilities ....Tim Hassett
President, MSG Entertainment ....Jay Marciano
Executive Vice President, Advertising Sales ....Mike Chico
Senior Vice President, Sports & Facility Event Sales......................................Joel Fisher
Senior Vice President, Team Sales, Tickets/Suites ....Brian Lafemina
Senior Vice President, Human Resources ....Rusty McCormack
Senior Vice President, Communications ....Barry Watkins
Head Coach ....Pat Coyle
Assistant Coaches ....Marianne Stanley, Nick DiPillo
Manager, Scouting & Video Operations ....Catherine Proto
Head Athletic Trainer/Manager, Basketball Operations ....Lisa White
Equipment Manager ....Rob Mangan
Vice President, Publicity, Sports Teams ....Dan Schoenberg
Vice President, Event Presentation ....Gary Winkler
Manager, Marketing Programs & Promotions ....Melissa Abbe
Manager, Event Presentation ....Michael Chant
Manager, Entertainment Marketing ....Michelle Harris
Manager, Marketing ....Christine Sipples
Coordinator, Communications ....Sarah Jamieson
Team Physician...Dr. Susan Scott
Director, Player Care...Dr. Lisa Callahan
TV Announcers ....Gus Johnson, Bob Wischusen, Doris Burke
Radio Announcers ....Bob Wischusen, Vera Jones

Carol Blazejowski

Pat Coyle

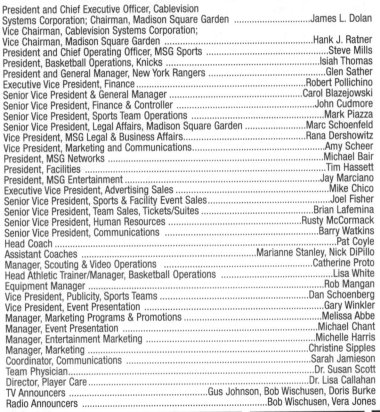

May						
S	M	T	W	T	F	S
	1	2	3	4	5	6
7	8	9	10	11	12	13
14	15	16	17	18	19	20 Con
21	22	23 Was	24	25	26	27
28	29	30 Ind	31			

June						
S	M	T	W	T	F	S
				1 Det	2	3 LA
4	5	6	7	8	9 Hou	10 SA
11	12	13 Ind	14	15	16 Hou	17 Was
18	19	20	21 Was	22	23	24 Min
25	26	27 Cha	28	29 Cha	30	

July						
S	M	T	W	T	F	S
						1
2	3	4	5	6 Sac	7 Chi	8
9 Pho	10	11 ★12	13	14 Sea	15	
16 Pho	17	18 LA	19	20 Sac	21	22 Sea
23	24 Con	25 Chi	26	27	28	29 Cha
30 Min	31					

August						
S	M	T	W	T	F	S
		1 Con	2	3 Det	4	5 Chi
6 Det	7	8 Ind	9	10	11 Cha	12
13 Was	14	15	16	17	18	19
20	21	22	23	24	25	26
27	28	29	30			

▓ = Home   ☐ = Away   ★ 2006 WNBA All-Star Game at New York

2006 ROSTER

No.	Player	Pos.	Ht./Wt.	Metric	Born	College/Country
10	Sherill Baker	G	5-8/125	1.73/56.8	12/3/82	Georgia
22	Ashley Battle	F	6-0/183	1.83/83.1	5/31/82	Connecticut
24	Edwina Brown	G	5-9/163	1.75/74	7/1/78	Texas
6	Kiesha Brown	G	5-9/146	1.75/66.3	1/13/79	Georgia
20	Shameka Christon	G/F	6-1/170	1.86/77.2	2/15/82	Arkansas
54	Barbara Farris	F	6-3/195	1.91/88.5	9/10/76	Tulane
32	Emile Gomis	G	5-9/135	1.75/61.3	10/18/83	France
25	Becky Hammon	G	5-6/136	1.68/61.7	3/11/77	Colorado State
24	Cathrine Kraayeveld	F	6-4/180	1.93/81.7	9/30/81	Oregon
21	Loree Moore	G	5-9/165	1.75/74.9	3/21/83	Tennessee
14	Christelle N'Garsanet	C	6-3/168	1.91/76.3	6/23/83	Missouri
2	Brooke Queenan	F	6-2/185	1.88/84	4/10/84	Boston College
17	Kelly Schumacher	F/C	6-5/183	1.96/83.1	10/14/77	Connecticut
5	Erin Thorn	G	5-10/150	1.78/68.1	5/19/81	Brigham Young
3	Iciss Tillis	F	6-5/165	1.96/74.9	12/6/81	Duke
7	Svetlana Volnaya	G/F	6-1/163	1.86/74	10/13/78	Louisiana State

Head coach—Pat Coyle
Assistant coaches—Marianne Stanley, Nick DiPillo
Trainer—Lisa White

2005 REVIEW

RESULTS

May

| 22—Detroit | *71-78 | 0-1 |
| 26—Indiana | *59-67 | 0-2 |

June

01—at Washington	77-68	1-2
03—at Detroit	*†66-68	1-3
05—Washington	61-58	2-3
10—at Indiana	*59-62	2-4
12—Detroit	72-69	3-4
18—Phoenix	65-54	4-4
21—San Antonio	77-59	5-4
25—at Charlotte	*61-67	5-5
30—Sacramento	*50-61	5-6

July

02—at San Antonio	*57-69	5-7
05—at Los Angeles	67-55	6-7
07—Connecticut	89-79	7-7
12—at Houston	†68-65	8-7
15—Minnesota	*60-64	8-8
19—at Seattle	*78-87	8-9
21—at Phoenix	80-70	9-9
22—at Sacramento	73-63	10-9
24—at Minnesota	59-47	11-9
27—Houston	*69-71	11-10
28—at Connecticut	*70-73	11-11
31—Indiana	67-53	12-11

August

02—Connecticut	*65-72	12-12
06—Seattle	79-67	13-12
07—at Detroit	*67-72	13-13
10—Los Angeles	74-69	14-13
12—at Charlotte	‡82-74	15-13
14—Charlotte	73-65	16-13
16—Washington	72-66	17-13
20—at Connecticut	64-58	18-13
23—at Washington	*†69-82	18-14
25—Charlotte	*66-78	18-15
27—at Indiana	*50-75	18-16

*Loss. †Single overtime. ‡Double overtime.

TEAM LEADERS

Points: Becky Hammon (473).
Field goals: Ann Wauters (151).
Free throws: Becky Hammon (118).
Three pointers: Becky Hammon (65).
Rebounds: Elena Baranova (227).
Assists: Becky Hammon (146).
Steals: Becky Hammon (60).
Blocked shots: Elena Baranova (46).

TEAM-BY-TEAM RESULTS

vs. Charlotte: 2-2
vs. Connecticut: 2-2
vs. Detroit: 1-3
vs. Houston: 1-1
vs. Indiana: 1-3
vs. Los Angeles: 2-0
vs. Minnesota: 1-1
vs. Phoenix: 2-0
vs. Sacramento: 1-1
vs. San Antonio: 1-1
vs. Seattle: 1-1
vs. Washington: 3-1

PHOENIX MERCURY
WESTERN CONFERENCE

201 East Jefferson
Phoenix, AZ 85004
Tel: (602) 514-8333
Fax: (602) 514-8303
Ticket Information: (602) 379-7878

www.phoenixmercury.com
Arena: US Airways Center
WNBA capacity (10,746)
Radio: ESPN Radio 860 AM
TV: Fox Sports Net Arizona

2006 SEASON
TEAM DIRECTORY

Chairman and CEO	Jerry Colangelo
Vice Chairman and Managing Partner	Robert Sarver
President and COO, Phoenix Suns	Rick Welts
President and COO, Phoenix Mercury	Jay Parry
Vice President and General Manager	Seth Sulka
Vice President, Corporate Sales	Lynn Agnello
Director of Marketing	Amber Cox
Head Coach	Paul Westhead
Assistant Coaches	Corey Gaines, Julie Hairgrove
Trainer	TBA
Basketball Communications Manager	Vince Kozar
Corporate Sales Account Manager	Carlissa Henry
Director of Game Operations	Kip Helt
Director of Ticket Sales	Mike Tomon
Season Ticket Manager	Adam Somers

Jay Parry

Seth Sulka

Paul Westhead

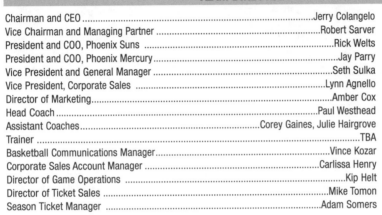

May

S	M	T	W	T	F	S
	1	2	3	4	5	6
7	8	9	10	11	12	13
14	15	16	17	18	19	20 Sac
21	22	23	24	25 Sea	26	27
28	29	30	31 SA			

June

S	M	T	W	T	F	S
				1	2 Sea	3
4	5	6 Sac	7	8	9 Det	10
11	12	13 LA	14	15	16 Con	17
18 Min	19	20	21 Sea	22	23 Ind	24
25 Chi	26	27	28 Min	29	30 LA	

July

S	M	T	W	T	F	S
						1
2 Was	3	4	5	6 Det	7	8 Con
9 NY	10	11 ★12		13	14 LA	15
16 NY	17	18 Ind	19	20	21	22 Cha
23	24	25 Sea	26	27 Hou	28 SA	29
30 Hou	31					

August

S	M	T	W	T	F	S
		1	2 Chi	3	4 Cha	5 LA
6	7	8 Min	9	10 Hou	11	12 SA
13 Sac	14	15	16	17	18	19
20	21	22	23	24	25	26
27	28	29	30			

■ = Home   □ = Away   ★ 2006 WNBA All-Star Game at New York

2006 ROSTER

No.	Player	Pos.	Ht./Wt.	Metric	Born	College/Country
50	Tera Bjorklund	C	6-4/175	1.93/79.5	6/29/82	Colorado
25	Sandora Irvin	F	6-3/185	1.91/84	2/23/82	Texas Christian
35	Tamicha Jackson	G	5-6/120	1.68/54.5	4/22/78	Louisiana Tech
31	Jennifer Lacy	F	6-3	1.91	3/21/83	Pepperdine
8	Kelly Miller	G	5-10/140	1.78/63.6	9/6/78	Georgia
32	Bridget Pettis	G	5-9/150	1.75/68.1	1/1/71	Florida
23	Cappie Pondexter	G	5-9/160	1.75/72.6	1/7/83	Rutgers
52	Kristen Rasmussen	F	6-2/172	1.88/78.1	11/1/78	Michigan State
10	Crystal Smith	G	5-6	1.68	3/12/84	Iowa
12	Belinda Snell	F	5-9/170	1.75/77.2	10/1/81	Australia
54	Mandisa Stevenson	F/C	6-3/166	1.91/75.4	2/4/82	Auburn
43	Ann Strother	F	6-3/162	1.91/73.5	12/11/83	Connecticut
3	Diana Taurasi	G	6-0/172	1.83/78.1	6/11/82	Connecticut
7	Kamila Vodichkova	F/C	6-4/190	1.93/86.3	12/19/72	Czech Republic
33	Angelina Williams	F	6-0/150	1.83/68.1	7/21/83	Illinois
50	Shereka Wright	F	5-10/155	1.78/70.4	9/21/81	Purdue

Head coach—Paul Westhead
Assistant coach—Corey Gaines, Julie Hairgrove
Trainer—TBA

2005 REVIEW

RESULTS

May

21—Sacramento	*72-77	0-1
24—at Indiana	*76-83	0-1
26—at Charlotte	68-58	1-2
28—at Connecticut	*68-85	1-3

June

02—Seattle	*67-78	1-4
04—at Houston	*57-59	1-5
08—at Los Angeles	66-63	2-5
10—at Sacramento	*61-73	2-6
15—San Antonio	76-62	3-6
18—at New York	*54-65	3-7
21—at Washington	*56-77	3-8

22—at Minnesota	*59-75	3-9
25—Connecticut	*69-77	3-10

July

02—at Los Angeles	*63-86	3-11
05—at San Antonio	76-69	4-11
06—Seattle	73-61	5-11
13—Charlotte	82-62	6-11
15—Washington	77-66	7-11
21—New York	*70-80	7-12
23—at San Antonio	66-49	8-12
26—Los Angeles	77-60	9-12
29—at Minnesota	69-65	10-12
31—at Detroit	*63-66	10-13

August

03—Minnesota	70-64	11-13
05—Houston	80-75	12-13
12—Sacramento	76-62	13-13
14—Indiana	*56-62	13-14
16—Detroit	58-51	14-14
18—at Houston	*66-77	14-15
19—San Antonio	91-57	15-15
21—Minnesota	83-69	16-15
23—at Sacramento	*70-76	16-16
25—Houston	*72-80	16-17
27—at Seattle	*74-85	16-18

*Loss.

TEAM LEADERS

Points: Diana Taurasi (527).
Field goals: Diana Taurasi (175).
Free throws: Diana Taurasi (121).
Three pointers: Diana Taurasi (56).
Rebounds: Kamila Vodichkova (196).
Assists: Diana Taurasi (150).
Steals: Anna DeForge (41).
Blocked shots: Maria Stepanova (38).

TEAM-BY-TEAM RESULTS

vs. Charlotte: 2-0
vs. Connecticut: 0-2
vs. Detroit: 1-1
vs. Houston: 1-3
vs. Indiana: 0-2
vs. Los Angeles: 2-1
vs. Minnesota: 3-1
vs. New York: 0-2
vs. Sacramento: 1-3
vs. San Antonio: 4-0
vs. Seattle: 1-2
vs. Washington: 1-1

SACRAMENTO MONARCHS
WESTERN CONFERENCE

ARCO Arena
One Sports Parkway
Sacramento, CA 95834
Tel: (916) 928-0000
Fax: (916) 928-0727
Ticket Information: (916) 419-WNBA

www.sacramentomonarchs.com
Arena: ARCO Arena (17,317)
Radio Station: Sports 1140 AM KHTK
TV Station: KXTV (News10), CSN (Comcast SportsNet Sacramento)

2006 SEASON
TEAM DIRECTORY

John Whisenant

Ownership	Maloof Family
President	John Thomas
Head Coach/General Manager	John Whisenant
Assistant Coaches	Tom Abatemarco, Monique Ambers
Advanced Scout/Video Coordinator	Steve Shuman
Head Athletic Trainer	Jill Jackson
Strength and Conditioning Coach	TBA
Scout	Lady Grooms
Administrative Assistant, Monarchs Basketball Operations	Kristina Anderson
Equipment Manager	Jill Culbertson
Senior Vice President, Business Operations	John Rinehart
Senior Vice President, Arena Services	Mark Stone
Vice President, Arena Programming	Mike Duncan
Vice President, Human Resources	Donna Ruiz
Vice President, Service and Development	Tom Peterson
Vice President, Strategic Alliances	Tom Hunt
Vice President, Strategic Alliances Sales	Eric Mastalir
Vice President, Marketing & Monarchs Business Operations	Danette Leighton
Manager, Marketing & Monarchs Business Operations	Kimberly Knight
Manager, Basketball Operations	Pam Kay
Manager, Media Relations	Rebecca Brutlag
Manager, Team & Fan Relations	Ruthie Bolton
Media Relations & Marketing Assistant	Emily Arno
Radio/Television Play-by-Play	Jim Kozimor
Radio/Television Analyst	Krista Blunk

May

S	M	T	W	T	F	S
	1	2	3	4	5	6
7	8	9	10	11	12	13
14	15	16	17	18	19	20 Pho
21	22	23 Chi	24	25 Hou	26	27
28	29	30	31 Sea			

June

S	M	T	W	T	F	S
				1	2 SA	3
4	5	6 Pho	7	8	9	10 Chi
11	12	13	14 Hou	15	16	17 Sea
18 LA	19	20	21 SA	22	23 SA	24
25 Ind	26	27 Sea	28	29 Min	30	

July

S	M	T	W	T	F	S
						1 Cha
2 Hou	3	4	5	6 NY	7 Was	8
9 Cha	10	11 ★12	13	14	15 Con	
16	17	18 Sea	19	20 NY	21	22 Min
23	24	25 Ind	26 Det	27	28 Con	29
30 Det	31					

August

S	M	T	W	T	F	S
		1	2 Hou	3 SA	4	5 Was
6	7	8	9 LA	10 Min	11	12
13 Pho	14	15	16	17	18	19
20	21	22	23	24	25	26
27	28	29	30			

▓ = Home ☐ = Away ★ 2006 WNBA All-Star Game at New York

2006 ROSTER

No.	Player	Pos.	Ht./Wt.	Metric	Born	College/Country
43	Lamisha Augustine	F	6-1/146	1.86/66.3	2/7/82	San Jose State
32	Rebekkah Brunson	F	6-3/175	1.91/79.5	12/11/81	Georgetown DC
7	Erin Buescher	F/C	6-3/181	1.91/82.2	6/5/79	The Masters College
5	Scholanda Dorrell	G	5-10/155	1.78/70.4	1/9/83	Lousiana State
31	Cisti Greenwalt	C	6-5/183	1.96/83.1	4/4/83	Texas Tech
33	Yolanda Griffith	F/C	6-3/175	1.91/79.5	3/1/70	Florida Atlantic
4	Kristin Haynie	G	5-9/147	1.75/66.7	6/17/83	Michigan State
35	Dionnah Jackson	G	5-9/155	1.75/70.4	8/15/82	Oklahoma
20	Kara Lawson	G	5-10/172	1.78/78.1	2/14/81	Tennessee
9	Hamchetou Maiga-Ba	G/F	6-1/160	1.86/72.6	4/25/78	Old Dominion
12	Anne O'neil	G	5-11/160	1.8/72.6	12/8/81	Iowa State
21	Ticha Penicheiro	G	5-11/149	1.8/67.6	9/18/74	Old Dominion
14	Nicole Powell	G/F	6-2/170	1.88/77.2	6/22/82	Stanford
3	Chameka Scott	G	6-0/155	1.83/70.4	5/9/84	Baylor
8	Kim Smith	F	5-11/155	1.8/70.4	5/7/84	Utah
22	DeMya Walker	F	6-3/168	1.91/76.3	11/28/77	Virginia
51	Brittany Wilkins	C	6-3/185	1.91/84	6/15/83	Iowa State

Head coach—John Whisenant
Assistant coaches—Tom Abatemarco, Monique Ambers
Trainer—Jill Jackson

2005 REVIEW

Results

May

21—at Phoenix	77-72	1-0
27—at San Antonio	71-67	2-0
29—at Minnesota	67-66	3-0

June

01—at Indiana	*60-61	3-1
04—Los Angeles	81-53	4-1
07—Indiana	65-51	5-1
10—Phoenix	73-61	6-1
11—at Los Angeles	*74-81	6-2
13—Houston	74-68	7-2
17—Minnesota	67-50	8-2
24—Connecticut	*50-61	8-3
26—at Washington	62-57	9-3

28—at Connecticut	*66-70	9-4
30—at New York	61-50	10-4

July

01—at Detroit	80-63	11-4
03—at Seattle	*67-74	11-5
14—San Antonio	72-61	12-5
16—Washington	73-59	13-5
19—at Houston	*54-58	13-6
22—New York	*63-73	13-7
24—Detroit	91-51	14-7
26—Charlotte	64-54	15-7
29—Los Angeles	79-59	16-7
31—Minnesota	67-54	17-7

August

02—at San Antonio	67-57	18-7
04—at Charlotte	76-58	19-7
07—Houston	55-45	20-7
12—at Phoenix	*62-76	20-8
16—at Los Angeles	72-63	21-8
18—San Antonio	64-57	22-8
20—Seattle	75-65	23-8
23—Phoenix	76-70	24-8
25—at Seattle	*63-76	24-9
27—at Minnesota	61-52	25-9

*Loss.

TEAM LEADERS

Points: Yolanda Griffith (469).
Field goals: Yolanda Griffith (173).
Free throws: Yolanda Griffith (123).
Three pointers: Nicole Powell (66).
Rebounds: Yolanda Griffith (223).
Assists: Ticha Penicheiro (149).
Steals: Ticha Penicheiro (48).
Blocked shots: Yolanda Griffith (31).

TEAM-BY-TEAM RESULTS

vs. Charlotte: 2-0
vs. Connecticut: 0-2
vs. Detroit: 2-0
vs. Houston: 2-1
vs. Indiana: 1-1
vs. Los Angeles: 3-1
vs. Minnesota: 4-0
vs. New York: 1-1
vs. Phoenix: 3-1
vs. San Antonio: 4-0
vs. Seattle: 1-2
vs. Washington: 2-0

SAN ANTONIO SILVER STARS
WESTERN CONFERENCE

AT&T Center
One SBC Center
San Antonio, TX 78219
Phone: (210) 444-5000 Fax: (210) 444-5003
Ticket Info: (210) 444-5050

www.sasilverstars.com
Arena: AT&T Center
WNBA capacity (9,877)
Radio: KTKR 760 AM
TV: KRRT WB-35

2006 SEASON
TEAM DIRECTORY

Owner...Spurs Sports & Entertainment (SS&E)
Chairman & CEO ....Peter Holt
Executive Vice President/Business Operations, Governor ....Russ Bookbinder
Executive Vice President/Finance and Corporate Development ....Rick Pych
Chief Operating Officer, Alternate Governor ....Clarissa Davis-Wrightsil
Silver Stars Administrative Assistant ....Jessica Peoples
Senior Vice President/Broadcasting..Lawrence Payne
Vice President/Marketing...Bruce Guthrie
Vice President/Ticket Sales and Services..Joe Clark
Vice President/Community Relations...Alison Fox
Vice President/Finance ....Lori Warren
Vice President/Human Resources..Paula Winslow
Vice President/Public Affairs and Corporate Administration ....Leo Gomez
Vice President and GM/AT&T Center ....John Sparks
Head Coach/General Manager ....Dan Hughes
Assistant Coaches ....Brian Agler, Sandy Brondello
Video Coordinator...Michael Wholey
Strength & Conditioning Coach ....Eric Rashid
Athletic Trainer ....Tonya Holley
Equipment Manager ....Will Grove
Team Physicians ....David R. Schmidt, M.D.; Paul Saenz, D.O.;
Timothy S. Palomera, M.D.
Media Services Manager ....Leigh Anne Gullett
Game Operations Manager ....Chris Garcia
Game Operations Coordinator...Brian Ricketts
Ticket Manager...Arthur Serna
Radio/TV Play-by-Play ....Andrew Monaco
TV Analyst ....Fran Harris

Clarissa
Davis-Wrightsil

Dan Hughes

May

S	M	T	W	T	F	S
	1	2	3	4	5	6
7	8	9	10	11	12	13
14	15	16	17	18	19	20
21 Hou	22	23 Ind	24	25 LA	26	27
28	29	30	31 Pho			

June

S	M	T	W	T	F	S
				1	2 Sac	3
4 Sea	5	6	7	8	9 Min	10 NY
11	12	13	14	15	16 Min	17 Chi
18	19	20	21 Sac	22	23 Sea	24
25	26	27 Det	28	29 NY	30	

July

S	M	T	W	T	F	S
						1 Chi
2	3	4	5	6	7 Hou	8
9 Min	10	11 ★12	13	14 Cha	15	
16 Det	17	18 Hou	19	20	21 Was	22 Con
23	24	25	26 LA	27	28 Pho	29
30 Con	31					

August

S	M	T	W	T	F	S
		1 Cha	2	3	4 Sac	5 Ind
6 Min	7	8 Was	9	10 Sea	11	12 Pho
13	14	15	16	17	18	19
20	21	22	23	24	25	26
27	28	29	30			

■ = Home   □ = Away   ★ 2006 WNBA All-Star Game at New York

2006 ROSTER

No.	Player	Pos.	Ht./Wt.	Metric	Born	College/Country
7	Chantelle Anderson	C	6-6/192	1.98/87.2	1/22/81	Vanderbilt
10	Agnieszka Bibrzycka	G	6-2/168	1.88/76.3	10/21/2	Poland
00	Sylvia Crawley	F	6-5/187	1.96/84.9	9/27/72	North Carolina
6	Jae Cross	G	5-8/150	1.73/68.1	1/20/76	Australia
43	Shyra Ely	F	6-2/182	1.88/82.6	8/9/83	Tennessee
44	Katie Feenstra	C	6-8/240	2.03/109	11/17/82	Liberty
3	Marie Ferdinand	G	5-9/153	1.75/69.5	10/13/78	Louisiana State
8	Dalma Ivanyi	G	5-10/135	1.78/61.3	3/18/76	Florida International
14	Shannon Johnson	G	5-7/152	1.7/69	8/18/74	South Carolina
55	Vickie Johnson	G	5-9/150	1.75/68.1	4/15/72	Louisiana Tech
32	LaToya Thomas	F	6-2/165	1.88/74.9	7/6/81	Mississippi State
53	Kendra Wecker	F	5-11/172	1.8/78.1	12/16/82	Kansas State
33	Sophia Young	F	6-1/165	1.86/74.9	12/15/83	Baylor
5	Shanna Zolman	G	5-10/155	1.78/70.4	9/7/83	Tennessee

Head coach—Dan Hughes
Assistant coaches—Brian Agler, Sandy Brondello
Trainer—Tonya Holley

2005 REVIEW

RESULTS

May

21—Houston	*70-78	0-1
24—at Detroit	*65-74	0-2
27—Sacramento	*67-71	0-3
29—at Seattle	*51-79	0-4
31—at Los Angeles	*70-81	0-5

June

02—Charlotte	69-62	1-5
04—at Connecticut	*69-80	1-6
07—Washington	71-62	2-6
11—Connecticut	*69-78	2-7
15—at Phoenix	*62-76	2-8
18—Houston	*69-75	2-9

21—at New York	*59-77	2-10
23—at Charlotte	64-49	3-10
25—at Houston	*44-62	3-11
28—at Minnesota	*53-63	3-12
30—Seattle	81-69	4-12

July

02—New York	69-57	5-12
05—Phoenix	*69-76	5-13
14—at Sacramento	*61-72	5-14
15—at Seattle	*70-92	5-15
21—at Indiana	*53-66	5-16
23—Phoenix	*49-66	5-17
26—Minnesota	78-71	6-17

| 28—at Washington | *58-73 | 6-18 |
| 30—at Houston | 68-63 | 7-18 |

August

02—Sacramento	*57-67	7-19
05—Los Angeles	*63-66	7-20
09—at Minnesota	*72-76	7-21
11—Indiana	*50-57	7-22
13—Detroit	*59-60	7-23
18—at Sacramento	*57-64	7-24
19—at Phoenix	*57-91	7-25
23—Seattle	*51-78	7-26
26—Los Angeles	*67-70	7-27

*Loss.

TEAM LEADERS

Points: Marie Ferdinand (388).
Field goals: Marie Ferdinand (132).
Free throws: Shannon Johnson (113).
Three pointers: Shannon Johnson (28).
Rebounds: Wendy Palmer-Daniel (193).
Assists: Shannon Johnson (158).
Steals: Shannon Johnson (46).
Steals: Marie Ferdinand (46).
Blocked shots: Katie Feenstra (44).

TEAM-BY-TEAM RESULTS

vs. Charlotte: 2-0
vs. Connecticut: 0-2
vs. Detroit: 0-2
vs. Houston: 1-3
vs. Indiana: 0-2
vs. Los Angeles: 0-3
vs. Minnesota: 1-2
vs. New York: 1-1
vs. Phoenix: 0-4
vs. Sacramento: 0-4
vs. Seattle: 1-3
vs. Washington: 1-1

SEATTLE STORM
WESTERN CONFERENCE

351 Elliott Ave. W., Suite 500
Seattle, WA 98119
Tel: (206) 281-5800 Fax: (206) 281-5839
Ticket Information: (206) 217-WNBA
www.storm.wnba.com

Arena: KeyArena at Seattle Center
WNBA capacity (9,686)
Training facility: The Furtado Center
Radio: SportsRadio KJR 950 AM
TV: Fox Sports Net (FSN)

2006 SEASON
TEAM DIRECTORY

Chairman ....Howard Schultz
President and CEO ....Wally Walker
Chief Operating Officer...Karen Bryant
Head Coach & Director of Player Personnel ....Anne Donovan
Assistant Coaches ....Jessie Kenlaw, Heidi VanDerveer
Director of Basketball Operations ....Missy Bequette
Head Athletic Trainer ....Annmarie Henkel
Strength & Conditioning Coach...TBA
Equipment Manager..TBA
Video Coordinator ....Ayana Clinton
Executive Vice President of Sales & Marketing ....Mike Humes
Vice President of Sales & Marketing ....Brian Byrnes
Vice President, Corporate Sponsorship & Entertainment........................John Croley
Senior Director of Public Relations & Community Relations ....Valerie O'Neil
Community Relations Coordinator ....Dallas Pride
Business Development Manager of Client Services ....Arlene Escobar
Public Relations Manager ....Jennifer Carroll
Public Relations Coordinator ....Mark Rosenberg
Sales Development Representatives ....Amy Burdick, Kris Kohlemain,
Susie Young, Kyle Waters
Play-By-Play Announcer (Radio)...David Locke
Color Analyst (Radio) ....Elise Woodward
Play-By-Play Announcer (TV) ....TBA
Color Analyst (TV)..TBA

Karen Bryant

Anne Donovan

May

S	M	T	W	T	F	S
	1	2	3	4	5	6
7	8	9	10	11	12	13
14	15	16	17	18	19	20
21 LA	22	23 Hou	24	25 Pho	26	27
28	29	30	31 Sac			

June

S	M	T	W	T	F	S
				1	2 Pho	3
4 SA	5	6	7 Chi	8	9 Con	10
11 Ind	12	13	14 Min	15 Chi	16	17 Sac
18	19	20	21 Pho	22	23 SA	24
25 Hou	26	27 Sac	28 LA	29	30	

July

S	M	T	W	T	F	S
						1 Min
2	3	4	5	6	7	8
9 Ind	10	11	★12	13	14 NY	15
16 Con	17	18 Sac	19	20 Cha	21	22 NY
23	24	25 Pho	26	27	28 Det	29
30 LA	31					

August

S	M	T	W	T	F	S
	1 Min	2	3 Was	4	5 Cha	6
7 Det	8	9	10 SA	11	12 Hou	13
14	15	16	17	18	19	20
21	22	23	24	25	26	27
28	29	30	31			

▨ = Home   ☐ = Away   ★ 2006 WNBA All-Star Game at New York

2006 ROSTER

No.	Player	Pos.	Ht./Wt.	Metric	Born	College/Country
9	Suzy Batkovic	C	6-4/203	1.93/92.2	12/17/80	Australia
10	Sue Bird	G	5-9/150	1.75/68.1	10/16/80	Connecticut
33	Janell Burse	C	6-5/199	1.96/90.3	5/19/79	Tulane
8	Iziane Castro Marques	G	6-0/140	1.83/63.6	3/13/82	Brazil
4	Simone Edwards	C	6-4/164	1.93/74.5	11/17/73	Iowa
34	Dalila Eshe	F	6-3/170	1.91/77.2	6/2/84	Florida
32	Shaunzinski Gortman	G	5-10/158	1.78/71.7	12/7/79	South Carolina
15	Lauren Jackson	F/C	6-5/187	1.96/84.9	5/11/81	Australia
5	Tiffani Johnson	C	6-4/240	1.93/109	12/27/75	Tennessee
22	Betty Lennox	G	5-8/143	1.73/64.9	12/4/76	Louisiana Tech
3	Wendy Palmer	F	6-2/165	1.88/74.9	8/12/74	Virginia
44	Lindsay Taylor	C	6-8/200	2.03/90.8	5/20/81	UC Santa Barbara
11	Barbara Turner	G/F	6-0/172	1.83/78.1	6/8/84	Connecticut
1	Toccara Williams	G	5-8/138	1.73/62.7	1/11/82	Texas A&M
30	Tanisha Wright	G	5-11/165	1.8/74.9	11/29/83	Penn State

Head coach—Anne Donovan
Assistant coaches—Jessie Kenlaw, Heidi VanDerveer
Trainer—Annmarie Henkel

2005 REVIEW

RESULTS

May
21—Los Angeles	*50-68	0-1
27—Houston	79-69	1-1
29—San Antonio	79-51	2-1

June
02—at Phoenix	78-67	3-1
04—Indiana	83-77	4-1
07—at Connecticut	*69-81	4-2
08—at Detroit	76-61	5-2
10—at Washington	*52-64	5-3
12—at Charlotte	62-60	6-3
15—Minnesota	*†81-86	6-4
22—Connecticut	95-86	7-4

24—at Los Angeles	*65-76	7-5
26—at Minnesota	*70-73	7-6
28—at Houston	*67-71	7-7
30—at San Antonio	*69-81	7-8

July
03—Sacramento	74-67	8-8
06—at Phoenix	*61-73	8-9
13—Washington	*71-78	8-10
15—San Antonio	92-70	9-10
16—at Los Angeles	78-70	10-10
19—New York	87-78	11-10
23—Detroit	74-71	12-10
29—Charlotte	79-68	13-10
31—Los Angeles	77-72	14-10

August
04—at Indiana	*68-78	14-11
06—at New York	*67-79	14-12
09—Houston	71-68	15-12
12—at Minnesota	72-66	16-12
14—at Houston	*72-75	16-13
18—Minnesota	76-60	17-13
20—at Sacramento	*65-75	17-14
23—at San Antonio	78-51	18-14
25—Sacramento	76-63	19-14
27—Phoenix	85-74	20-14

*Loss. †Single overtime.

TEAM LEADERS

Points: Lauren Jackson (597).
Field goals: Lauren Jackson (206).
Free throws: Lauren Jackson (151).
Three pointers: Sue Bird (45).
Rebounds: Lauren Jackson (313).
Assists: Sue Bird (176).
Steals: Lauren Jackson (36).
Blocked shots: Lauren Jackson (67).

TEAM-BY-TEAM RESULTS

vs. Charlotte: 2-0
vs. Connecticut: 1-1
vs. Detroit: 2-0
vs. Houston: 2-2
vs. Indiana: 1-1
vs. Los Angeles: 2-2
vs. Minnesota: 2-2
vs. New York: 1-1
vs. Phoenix: 2-1
vs. Sacramento: 2-1
vs. San Antonio: 3-1
vs. Washington: 0-2

WASHINGTON MYSTICS
EASTERN CONFERENCE

Verizon Center
401 F Street, N.W. Suite 750
Washington, DC 20004
Tel: (202) 266-2200
Fax: (202) 266-2200

Ticket Information: (877) DCHOOP1 (324-6671)
www.washingtonmystics.com
Arena: Verizon Center (20,173)
Radio: Progressive Talk 1260
TV: Comcast SportsNet

2006 SEASON
TEAM DIRECTORY

Owner	Lincoln Holdings LLC
Chairman	Ted Leonsis
President	Sheila Johnson
Chief Operating Officer	Curtis Symonds
Executive Assistant	Sheila Robinson
Senior Vice President, Sponsorship	Rick Moreland
VP, Marketing & Business Development	Neville Waters
Director, Public Relations	Ketsia Colimon
Assistant Director, Public Relations	Nicole Boden
Director, Game Operations	Jacque Coleman
Director, Marketing	Stacey Girard
Senior Account Manager	Tamara Edgerton
Account Executive	Jimmelle Melvin
Customer Service Manager	Bill Holt
Customer Service Coordinator	Eboni Tyler
General Manager	Linda Hargrove
Coordinator	Rebecca Hunt
Head Coach	Richie Adubato
Assistant Coach	Marynell Meadors
Head Trainer	TBA
Strength & Conditioning Coach	Jonathan Jones
Equipment Manager/Video Coordinator	Dave Avery

Ted Leonsis

Sheila Johnson

Richie Adubato

May

S	M	T	W	T	F	S
	1	2	3	4	5	6
7	8	9	10	11	12	13
14	15	16	17	18	19	20
21	22	23 NY	24 Cha	25	26	27 Min
28	29	30	31			

June

S	M	T	W	T	F	S
				1	2	3 Det
4	5	6 Hou	7 Ind	8	9	10
11 Con	12	13 Cha	14	15 Cha	16	17 NY
18	19	20	21 NY	22	23	24 Det
25 Con	26	27 Ind	28	29 Hou	30	

July

S	M	T	W	T	F	S
						1 LA
2 Pho	3	4	5 Min	6	7 Sac	8
9 Chi	10	11 ★12	13	14	15	
16 Chi	17	18	19 Pho	20	21 SA	22
23 Sea	24	25 Con	26 Chi	27	28 Chi	29 Ind
30 Cha	31					

August

S	M	T	W	T	F	S
		1	2 LA	3	4 Sea	5 Sac
6	7	8 SA	9	10	11 Det	12
13 NY	14	15	16	17	18	19
20	21	22	23	24	25	26
27	28	29	30	31		

■ = Home □ = Away ★ 2006 WNBA All-Star Game at New York

2006 ROSTER

No.	Player	Pos.	Ht./Wt.	Metric	Born	College/Country
20	Alana Beard	G/F	5-11/160	1.8/72.6	5/14/82	Duke
19	Nikki Blue	G	5-8	1.73	5/29/84	UCLA
00	Latasha Byears	F	5-11/206	1.8/93.5	8/12/73	DePaul
50	Kaayla Chones	C	6-3/180	1.91/81.7	1/11/81	North Carolina State
2	Tamara James	F	5-10	1.78	6/13/84	Miami
44	Chasity Melvin	F/C	6-3/185	1.91/84	5/3/76	North Carolina State
9	Coco Miller	G	5-9/140	1.75/63.6	9/6/78	Georgia
17	Crystal Robinson	F	5-11/155	1.8/70.4	1/22/74	SE Oklahoma State
43	Nakia Sanford	F/C	6-4/200	1.93/90.8	5/10/76	Kansas
31	Aiysha Smith	F	6-2/173	1.88/78.5	7/18/80	Louisiana State
42	Nikki Teasley	G	6-0/169	1.83/76.7	3/22/79	North Carolina
11	Rita Williams	G	5-6/135	1.68/61.3	1/14/76	Connecticut
	Tiffany Williams					

Head coach—Richie Adubato
Assistant coaches—Marynell Meadors
Trainer—TBA

2005 REVIEW

RESULTS

May

21—at Charlotte	60-42	1-0
22—Connecticut	*67-69	1-1
26—Los Angeles	*75-84	1-2

June

01—New York	*68-77	1-3
03—Minnesota	74-71	2-3
05—at New York	*58-61	2-4
07—at San Antonio	*62-71	2-5
10—Seattle	64-52	3-5
11—at Minnesota	*60-78	3-6
18—Indiana	‡88-78	4-6
21—Phoenix	77-56	5-6
24—at Detroit	69-55	6-6

26—Sacramento	*57-62	6-7
28—at Charlotte	†66-61	7-7
30—Charlotte	65-50	8-7

July

07—Detroit	*62-76	8-8
13—at Seattle	78-71	9-8
15—at Phoenix	*66-77	9-9
16—at Sacramento	*59-73	9-10
19—at Los Angeles	74-68	10-10
21—at Houston	70-65	11-10
26—Houston	*65-83	11-11
28—San Antonio	73-58	12-11
29—at Indiana	*58-62	12-12

August

02—Charlotte	65-63	13-12
07—Indiana	61-60	14-12
11—Connecticut	*65-80	14-13
14—at Connecticut	*77-80	14-14
16—at New York	*66-72	14-15
18—at Indiana	*57-67	14-16
21—at Detroit	*52-66	14-17
23—New York	†82-69	15-17
26—at Connecticut	*47-81	15-18
27—Detroit	76-67	16-18

*Loss. †Single overtime. ‡Double overtime.

TEAM LEADERS

Points: Alana Beard (422).
Field goals: Alana Beard (155).
Free throws: Chasity Melvin (93).
Three pointers: Charlotte Smith-Taylor (42).
Rebounds: Chasity Melvin (199).
Assists: Temeka Johnson (177).
Steals: DeLisha Milton-Jones (57).
Blocked shots: DeLisha Milton-Jones (18).

TEAM-BY-TEAM RESULTS

vs. Charlotte: 4-0
vs. Connecticut: 0-4
vs. Detroit: 2-2
vs. Houston: 1-1
vs. Indiana: 2-2
vs. Los Angeles: 1-1
vs. Minnesota: 1-1
vs. New York: 1-3
vs. Phoenix: 1-1
vs. Sacramento: 0-2
vs. San Antonio: 1-1
vs. Seattle: 2-0

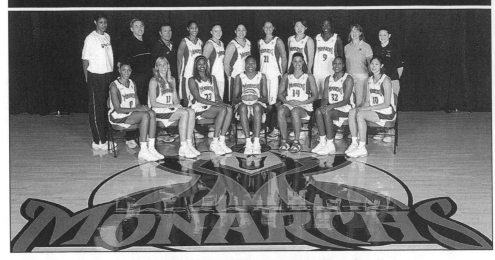

SACRAMENTO MONARCHS, 2005 WNBA Champions

Front Row (l to r) — Olympia Scott, Erin Buescher, DeMya Walker, Yolanda Griffith, Nicole Powell, Rebekkah Brunson, Sui Feifei.
Back Row (l to r) — Assistant Coach Monique Ambers, Head Coach/General Manager John Whisenant, Assistant Coach Tom Abatemarco, Chelsea Newton, Kristin Haynie, Kara Lawson, Ticha Penicheiro, Miao Li Jie, Hamchétou Maïga-Ba, Head Athletic Trainer Jill Jackson, Equipment Manager Jill Culbertson.

FINAL STANDINGS

EASTERN CONFERENCE

TEAM	W	L	PCT	GB	HOME	ROAD	LAST-10	STREAK
Connecticut	26	8	.765	0	14-3	12-5	8-2	Won 2
Indiana	21	13	.618	5	14-3	7-10	6-4	Won 1
New York	18	16	.529	8	10-7	8-9	6-4	Lost 3
Detroit	16	18	.471	10	12-5	4-13	6-4	Lost 1
Washington	16	18	.471	10	10-7	6-11	4-6	Won 1
Charlotte	6	28	.176	20	5-12	1-16	3-7	Lost 1

WESTERN CONFERENCE

TEAM	W	L	PCT	GB	HOME	ROAD	LAST-10	STREAK
Sacramento	25	9	.735	0	15-2	10-7	8-2	Won 1
Seattle	20	14	.588	5	14-3	6-11	6-4	Won 3
Houston	19	15	.559	6	11-6	8-9	5-5	Won 2
Los Angeles	17	17	.500	8	11-6	6-11	5-5	Lost 1
Phoenix	16	18	.471	9	11-6	5-12	5-5	Lost 3
Minnesota	14	20	.412	11	11-6	3-14	3-7	Lost 4
San Antonio	7	27	.206	18	5-12	2-15	1-9	Lost 9

TEAM STANDINGS

OFFENSIVE

TEAM	G	FG	FGA	PCT	FG3	FG3A	PCT	FT	FTA	PCT	OFF	DEF	REB	AST	PF	DQ	STL	TO	BLK	PTS	AVG
Sea.	34	906	2066	.439	142	429	.331	544	688	.791	323	776	1099	520	657	0	201	516	158	2498	73.5
Conn.	34	916	2025	.452	130	373	.349	512	688	.744	322	788	1110	573	624	1	236	452	130	2474	72.8
Phoe.	34	826	1994	.414	178	539	.330	531	693	.766	342	720	1062	549	697	1	243	517	179	2361	69.4
Sac.	34	853	1986	.430	129	360	.358	494	721	.685	369	674	1043	527	684	0	304	500	108	2329	68.5
L.A.	34	873	2042	.428	124	387	.320	456	630	.724	321	683	1004	551	737	0	264	492	136	2326	68.4
N.Y.	34	828	1860	.445	208	605	.344	452	552	.819	242	732	974	498	613	1	214	462	112	2316	68.1
Hou.	34	860	1920	.448	62	205	.302	527	690	.764	276	684	960	467	581	1	246	425	105	2309	67.9
Wash.	34	847	1968	.430	181	510	.355	388	546	.711	266	677	943	517	697	1	260	435	76	2263	66.6
Det.	34	831	2060	.403	76	238	.319	509	774	.658	412	803	1215	474	761	1	241	571	155	2247	66.1
Minn.	34	801	1946	.412	172	492	.350	437	601	.727	310	715	1025	531	624	0	258	536	127	2211	65.0
Ind.	34	784	1958	.400	150	468	.321	452	595	.760	341	671	1012	493	668	1	336	477	95	2170	63.8
S.A.	34	764	1833	.417	110	339	.324	503	652	.771	256	690	946	433	650	0	195	535	90	2141	63.0
Cha.	34	772	1913	.404	104	301	.346	447	624	.716	316	609	925	493	727	1	284	535	113	2095	61.6

DEFENSIVE

TEAM	FG	FGA	PCT	FG3	FG3A	PCT	FT	FTA	PCT	OFF	DEF	REB	AST	PF	DQ	STL	TO	BLK	PTS	AVG	DIFF
Sac.	751	1823	.412	113	376	.301	478	653	.732	273	694	967	463	723	0	235	622	132	2093	61.6	6.9
Ind.	775	1798	.431	123	367	.335	460	642	.717	279	711	990	435	644	2	234	558	113	2133	62.7	1.1
Conn.	835	2100	.398	122	400	.305	452	599	.755	350	728	1078	495	675	2	258	442	79	2244	66.0	6.8
Hou.	848	1944	.436	148	423	.350	419	559	.750	274	687	961	541	685	1	197	481	111	2263	66.6	1.3
N.Y.	859	2012	.427	125	398	.314	442	608	.727	345	685	1030	473	590	1	275	411	86	2285	67.2	0.9
Det.	784	1945	.403	154	456	.338	565	754	.749	273	745	1018	473	744	1	272	520	136	2287	67.3	-1.2
Minn.	862	2019	.427	129	376	.343	435	592	.735	344	711	1055	537	665	0	275	487	144	2288	67.3	-2.3
Wash.	833	1872	.445	150	433	.346	489	648	.755	267	757	1024	545	638	0	205	504	108	2305	67.8	-1.2
Cha.	851	1888	.451	124	339	.366	509	713	.714	355	700	1055	496	654	0	269	534	146	2335	68.7	-7.1
L.A.	818	1955	.418	182	519	.351	527	709	.743	332	709	1041	567	654	0	247	544	115	2345	69.0	-0.6
Phoe.	855	1993	.429	121	332	.364	523	720	.726	319	705	1024	470	672	0	265	483	112	2354	69.2	-0.2
S.A.	898	2059	.436	142	408	.348	463	611	.758	351	704	1055	563	685	1	283	429	148	2401	70.6	-7.6
Sea.	892	2163	.412	133	419	.317	490	646	.759	334	686	1020	568	691	0	267	438	154	2407	70.8	2.7

TEAM COMPARISONS

TEAM	Points Per Game OWN	OPP	Field Goal Percentage OWN	OPP	Turnovers Per Game OWN	OPP	Rebound Percentages OFF	DEF	Below 70 Pts. OWN	OPP	Overtime Games W	L	3 PTS or Less W	L	10 PTS or More W	L
Charlotte	61.6	68.6	.404	.451	15.7	15.7	.311	.632	29	20	1	2	0	3	1	16
Connecticut	72.7	66.0	.452*	.398*	13.2	13.0	.307	.692	11	26	0	0	3	0	15	3
Detroit	66.0	67.2	.403	.403	16.7	15.2	.356*	.746*	22	20	2	2	3	4	5	6
Houston	67.9	66.5	.448	.436	12.5*	14.1	.287	.714	20	21	1	1	5	2	7	6
Indiana	63.8	62.7	.400	.431	14.0	16.4	.324	.706	27	28	1	2	5	3	7	7
Los Angeles	68.4	68.9	.428	.418	14.4	16.0	.312	.673	18	18	0	0	3	2	10	7
Minnesota	65.0	67.2	.412	.427	15.7	14.3	.304	.675	23	19	1	1	2	3	6	10
New York	68.1	67.2	.445	.427	13.5	12.0	.261	.680	20	22	2	2	3	4	9	5
Phoenix	69.4	69.2	.414	.429	15.2	14.2	.327	.693	17	19	0	0	1	2	10	10
Sacramento	68.5	61.5*	.430	.412	14.7	18.2*	.347	.712	19	26	0	0	1	1	16	4
San Antonio	62.9	70.6	.417	.436	15.7	12.	.267	.663	27	15	0	0	0	3	3	15
Seattle	73.4*	70.7	.439	.412	15.1	12.8	.320	.699	11	1	0	1	3	2	10	9
Washington	66.5	67.7	.430	.445	12.7	14.8	.260	.717	23	19	3	0	3	3	8	9

* —League Leader
REBOUND PERCENTAGES
OFF. Percentage of a given team's missed shots which that team rebounds.
DEF. Percentage of opponents' missed shots which a given team rebounds.

SCORING AVERAGE

	G	FG	FT	PTS	AVG
Swoopes, Hou.	33	217	153	614	18.6
Jackson, Sea.	34	206	151	597	17.6
Holdsclaw, L.A.	33	216	126	561	17.0
Taurasi, Pho.	33	175	121	527	16.0
Nolan, Det.	33	184	128	524	15.9
Sales, Ct.	34	201	81	532	15.6
Leslie, L.A.	34	204	102	517	15.2
Catchings, Ind.	34	157	152	501	14.7
Beard, Was.	30	155	80	422	14.1
Hammon, N.Y.	34	145	118	473	13.9
McWilliams-Franklin, Ct.	34	180	107	471	13.9
Griffith, Sac.	34	173	123	469	13.8
Wauters, N.Y.	28	151	79	383	13.7
Smith, Cha.	31	169	83	421	13.6
Taylor, Pho.	29	121	102	382	13.2
DeForge, Pho.	33	142	102	433	13.1
Ferdinand, S.A.	31	132	104	388	12.5
Lennox, Sea.	28	123	76	346	12.4
Bird, Sea.	30	130	59	364	12.1
Whalen, Ct.	34	135	125	411	12.1

REBOUNDS PER GAME

	G	OFF	DEF	TOT	AVG
Ford, Det.	33	113	209	322	9.8
Jackson, Sea.	34	96	217	313	9.2
Catchings, Ind.	34	69	195	264	7.8
Leslie, L.A.	34	70	178	248	7.3
McWilliams-Franklin, Ct.	34	78	170	248	7.3
Vodichkova, Pho.	28	60	136	196	7.0
Baranova, N.Y.	33	39	188	227	6.9
Snow, Hou.	33	68	157	225	6.8
Holdsclaw, L.A.	33	86	137	223	6.8
Wauters, N.Y.	28	47	137	184	6.6
Griffith, Sac.	34	87	136	223	6.6
Dydek, Ct.	31	27	168	195	6.3
Burse, Sea.	34	81	118	199	5.9
Melvin, Was.	34	82	117	199	5.9
Ohlde, Min.	34	63	131	194	5.7
Palmer-Daniel, S.A.	34	53	140	193	5.7
Brunson, Sac.	34	75	112	187	5.5
Williams, Ind.	34	74	112	186	5.5
Sutton-Brown, Cha.	34	64	115	179	5.3
Hayden, Min.	31	48	115	163	5.3

ASSISTS PER GAME

	G	AST	AVG
Bird, Sea	30	176	5.9
Johnson, Was.	34	177	5.2
Whalen, Ct.	34	172	5.1
Johnson, S.A.	34	158	4.6
Taurasi, Pho.	33	150	4.5
Staley, Hou.	33	149	4.5
Penicheiro, Sac.	34	149	4.4
Hammon, N.Y.	34	146	4.3
Swoopes, Hou.	33	141	4.3
Catchings, Ind.	34	143	4.2
Nolan, Det.	33	121	3.7
Taylor, Pho.	29	94	3.2
Holdsclaw, L.A.	33	104	3.2
Canty, Hou.	33	101	3.1
Beard, Was.	30	90	3.0
Douglas, Ct.	32	94	2.9
Harrower, Min.	34	96	2.8
Johnson, N.Y.	34	92	2.7
Darling, Cha.	31	83	2.7
Sam, Cha.	34	91	2.7
Powell, Det.	29	77	2.7

FIELD GOAL PCT

	FG	FGA	PCT
Snow, Hou.	152	276	.551
Wauters, N.Y.	151	279	.541

	FG	FGA	PCT
Walker, Sac.	125	234	.534
Burse, Sea.	127	243	.523
Palmer-Daniel, S.A.	125	242	.517
Sutton-Brown, Cha.	111	218	.509
McWilliams-Franklin, Ct.	180	364	.495
Vodichkova, Pho.	127	257	.494
Melvin, Was.	150	305	.492
Griffith, Sac.	173	357	.485

3-PT FIELD GOAL PCT.

	3FG	3GA	PCT
Koehn, Was.	35	75	.467
Hodges, L.A.	31	69	.449
Lawson, Sac.	36	81	.444
Bird, Sea.	45	103	.437
Feaster, Cha.	37	86	.430
Sales, Ct.	49	116	.422
Jones, Min.	29	69	.420
Smith-Taylor, Was.	42	100	.420
Powell, Sac.	66	159	.415
Lovelace, Min.	26	63	.413

FREE THROW PCT.

	FT	FTA	PCT
Hammon, N.Y.	118	131	.901
Arcain, Hou.	83	94	.883
Lennox, Sea.	76	87	.874
Whitmore, L.A.	92	106	.868
Taylor, Pho.	102	118	.864
Bird, Sea.	59	69	.855
Christon, N.Y.	65	76	.855
DeForge, Pho.	102	120	.850
Swoopes, Hou.	153	180	.850
Miller, Ind.	67	79	.848

STEALS PER GAME

	G	STL	AVG
Catchings, Ind.	34	90	2.65
Swoopes, Hou.	33	66	2.00
Leslie, L.A.	34	67	1.97
Bevilaqua, Ind.	31	60	1.94
Sales, Ct.	34	61	1.79
Hammon, N.Y.	34	60	1.76
Milton-Jones, Was.	33	57	1.73
Nolan, Det.	33	55	1.67
Smith, Cha.	31	51	1.65
Arcain, Hou.	34	55	1.62

BLOCKS PER GAME

	G	BLK	AVG
Dydek, Ct.	31	71	2.29
Hayden, Min.	31	68	2.19
Leslie, L.A.	34	71	2.09
Jackson, Sea.	34	67	1.97
Ford, Det.	33	46	1.39
Riley, Det.	33	46	1.39
Baranova, N.Y.	33	46	1.39
Feenstra, S.A.	34	44	1.29
Burse, Sea.	34	40	1.18
Snow, Hou.	33	38	1.15

MINUTES PER GAME

	G	MIN	AVG
Swoopes, Hou.	33	1225	37.1
Nolan, Det.	33	1213	36.8
Holdsclaw, L.A.	33	1183	35.8
Hammon, N.Y.	34	1180	34.7
Jackson, Sea.	34	1176	34.6
Catchings, Ind.	34	1174	34.5
Smith, Cha.	31	1063	34.3
DeForge, Pho.	33	1131	34.3
Bird, Sea.	30	1020	34.0
Beard, Was.	30	1015	33.8

REVIEW 2005 Regular Season

CHARLOTTE STING

PLAYER	G	GS	MIN	FG	FGA	PCT	3FG	3FGA	PCT	FT	FTA	PCT	OFF	DEF	TOT	AST	PF	DQ	STL	TO	BLK	PTS	AVG
Tangela Smith	31	31	1063	169	405	.417	0	7		0	83	104	.798	45	117	162	41	105	1	51	84	32	421	13.6
Sheri Sam	34	33	1075	146	377	.387	18	56	.321	77	108	.713	53	92	145	91	87	1	44	100	2	387	11.4
T. Sutton-Brown	34	33	887	111	218	.509	0	0		0	96	141	.681	64	115	179	14	138	5	30	69	37	318	9.4
Allison Feaster	21	21	666	61	162	.377	37	86	.430	33	39	.846	9	28	37	51	52	0	14	38	2	192	9.1
A. Goodson (*)	10	0	215	30	71	.423	1	1	1.000	9	15	.600	17	18	35	6	22	1	3	18	1	70	7.0
A. Goodson (!)	33	0	486	59	144	.410	2	3	.667	22	36	.611	33	38	71	21	40	1	11	34	1	142	4.3
Dawn Staley (>)	23	23	684	53	131	.405	17	42	.405	23	30	.767	7	46	53	121	47	0	30	42	0	146	6.3
Jia Perkins	30	11	464	64	151	.424	3	9	.333	19	30	.633	24	20	44	32	45	0	29	32	9	150	5.0
Tynesha Lewis (>)	10	1	166	19	61	.311	1	12	.083	8	16	.500	10	10	20	13	7	0	3	11	3	47	4.7
Teana Miller	31	1	362	44	91	.484	0	0		0	25	36	.694	29	36	65	7	71	0	14	26	18	113	3.6
Helen Darling	31	11	600	27	88	.307	10	32	.313	43	58	.741	5	42	47	83	73	1	41	51	0	107	3.5
Kelly Mazzante	27	2	226	21	72	.292	14	46	.304	8	10	.800	14	17	31	7	9	0	9	7	0	64	2.4
K. Rasmussen (*)	3	0	29	2	4	.500	2	3	.667	0	0		0	2	3	5	2	8	0	1	1	0	6	2.0
K. Rasmussen (!)	27	19	551	49	102	.480	7	18	.389	22	30	.733	28	53	81	24	64	0	14	20	16	127	4.7
Janel McCarville	28	3	311	17	50	.340	0	0		0	16	25	.640	32	44	76	11	39	0	12	22	7	50	1.8
Ayana Walker (*)	9	0	92	4	16	.250	0	0		0	4	8	.500	4	14	18	6	11	0	2	3	2	12	1.3
Ayana Walker (!)	21	11	333	29	68	.426	0	0		0	13	20	.650	20	45	65	19	26	0	8	19	12	71	3.4
Caity Matter	10	0	56	3	13	.231	1	7	.143	2	2	1.000	0	3	3	6	4	0	1	2	0	9	0.9
Jessica Moore (>)	6	0	49	1	3	.333	0	0		0	1	2	.500	1	4	5	2	9	1	0	4	0	3	0.5
TEAM TOTALS	34	-	6945	772	1913	.404	104	301	.346	447	624	.716	316	609	925	493	727	10	284	535	113	2095	61.6
OPPONENTS	34	-	6945	851	1888	.451	124	339	.366	509	713	.714	355	700	1055	496	654	3	269	534	146	2335	68.7

CONNECTICUT SUN

PLAYER	G	GS	MIN	FG	FGA	PCT	3FG	3FGA	PCT	FT	FTA	PCT	OFF	DEF	TOT	AST	PF	DQ	STL	TO	BLK	PTS	AVG
Nykesha Sales	34	34	1074	201	482	.417	49	116	.422	81	108	.750	36	88	124	74	96	0	61	64	10	532	15.6
T. McWilliams-Franklin	34	34	1087	180	364	.495	4	18	.222	107	136	.787	78	170	248	65	80	1	37	59	25	471	13.9
Lindsay Whalen	34	34	1047	135	290	.466	16	46	.348	125	156	.801	29	99	128	172	90	0	42	89	2	411	12.1
Katie Douglas	32	32	998	119	288	.413	31	110	.282	82	106	.774	45	85	130	94	57	0	48	54	4	351	11.0
Asjha Jones	33	4	705	133	275	.484	2	5	.400	33	56	.589	54	67	121	40	70	0	10	51	7	301	9.1
Margo Dydek	31	30	671	87	162	.537	1	2	.500	50	65	.769	27	168	195	38	62	0	8	47	71	225	7.3
Brooke Wyckoff	34	1	596	35	88	.398	22	52	.423	13	20	.650	25	70	95	35	82	0	13	28	9	105	3.1
Le'coe Willingham	18	0	91	7	17	.412	0	0		0	10	20	.500	10	7	17	3	16	0	2	14	0	24	1.3
Jaime Carey	15	0	86	7	19	.368	4	13	.308	0	0		0	2	4	6	7	9	0	2	4	0	18	1.2
Laura Summerton	11	0	43	3	9	.333	0	0		0	4	5	.800	5	5	10	3	11	0	2	4	0	10	0.9
Jennifer Derevjanik	34	1	359	8	22	.364	1	7	.143	7	16	.438	10	20	30	40	47	0	11	26	2	24	0.7
Jessica Brungo	12	0	47	1	9	.111	0	4		0	0	0		0	1	5	6	2	4	0	0	2	0	2	0.2
TEAM TOTALS	34	-	6800	916	2025	.452	130	373	.349	512	688	.744	322	788	1110	573	624	1	236	452	130	2474	72.8
OPPONENTS	34	-	6800	835	2100	.398	122	400	.305	452	599	.755	350	728	1078	495	675	8	258	442	79	2244	66.0

DETROIT SHOCK

PLAYER	G	GS	MIN	FG	FGA	PCT	3FG	3FGA	PCT	FT	FTA	PCT	OFF	DEF	TOT	AST	PF	DQ	STL	TO	BLK	PTS	AVG
Deanna Nolan	33	33	1213	184	462	.398	28	90	.311	128	160	.800	31	125	156	121	64	0	55	100	14	524	15.9
Cheryl Ford	33	33	932	120	279	.430	0	0		0	73	150	.487	113	209	322	26	143	6	33	69	46	313	9.5
Katie Smith (*)	13	9	394	40	107	.374	18	55	.327	26	34	.765	11	17	28	26	27	0	5	17	3	124	9.5
Katie Smith (!)	36	32	1160	140	368	.380	53	159	.333	97	124	.782	23	60	83	87	73	0	30	71	5	430	11.9
P. Pierson (*)	23	0	444	55	126	.437	1	1	1.000	67	96	.698	27	35	62	21	54	0	14	42	6	178	7.7
P. Pierson (!)	35	11	762	91	231	.394	1	2	.500	87	125	.696	46	75	121	34	93	0	24	74	9	270	7.7
Ruth Riley	33	33	855	100	267	.375	3	12	.250	48	60	.800	43	113	156	39	131	4	23	68	46	251	7.6
Kara Braxton	33	2	455	97	210	.462	0	1		0	33	60	.550	42	58	100	14	78	0	18	52	13	227	6.9
Chandi Jones (>)	21	0	329	46	113	.407	18	37	.486	15	20	.789	8	23	31	23	42	0	13	23	2	125	5.9
Swin Cash	21	21	458	48	126	.381	2	10	.200	21	32	.656	42	46	88	43	44	1	12	47	6	119	5.7
Elaine Powell	29	21	671	62	142	.437	0	2		0	39	65	.600	25	55	80	77	62	0	29	51	4	163	5.6
Ayana Walker (>)	12	11	241	25	52	.481	0	0		0	9	12	.750	16	31	47	13	15	0	6	16	10	59	4.9
Sheila Lambert	12	5	152	14	45	.311	1	7	.143	4	5	.800	2	15	17	21	11	0	8	24	1	33	2.8
Barbara Farris	34	1	444	25	73	.342	0	0		0	33	54	.611	31	53	84	19	55	0	8	43	1	83	2.4
Andrea Stinson	18	1	102	8	23	.348	2	10	.200	4	6	.667	6	6	12	13	6	0	3	4	0	22	1.2
Niele Ivey (>)	12	0	102	5	23	.217	3	12	.250	1	1	1.000	5	7	12	10	14	0	6	5	0	14	1.1
Stacey Thomas (>)	17	0	133	2	12	.167	0	1		0	8	20	.400	10	10	20	8	15	0	8	3	3	12	0.7
TEAM TOTALS	34	-	6925	831	2060	.403	76	238	.319	509	774	.658	412	803	1215	474	761	11	241	571	155	2247	66.1
OPPONENTS	34	-	6925	784	1945	.403	154	456	.338	565	754	.749	273	745	1018	473	744	10	272	520	136	2287	67.3

HOUSTON COMETS

PLAYER	G	GS	MIN	FG	FGA	PCT	3FG	3FGA	PCT	FT	FTA	PCT	OFF	DEF	TOT	AST	PF	DQ	STL	TO	BLK	PTS	AVG
													—REBOUNDS—									SCORING	
Sheryl Swoopes	33	33	1225	217	486	.447	27	75	.360	153	180	.850	27	92	119	141	54	0	66	72	26	614	18.6
Michelle Snow	33	33	966	152	276	.551	0	0	0	92	130	.708	68	157	225	40	120	4	20	65	38	396	12.0
Janeth Arcain	34	34	1079	128	304	.421	3	16	.188	83	94	.883	20	73	93	53	85	0	55	56	6	342	10.1
Tina Thompson	15	15	439	62	150	.413	12	40	.300	16	21	.762	17	40	57	22	32	0	12	32	4	152	10.1
Dominique Canty	33	32	997	95	238	.399	0	4	0	80	110	.727	25	83	108	101	75	0	29	67	2	270	8.2
K. Rasmussen (>)	24	19	522	47	98	.480	5	15	.333	22	30	.733	26	50	76	22	56	0	13	19	16	121	5.0
Sancho Lyttle	33	0	460	59	101	.584	0	0	0	22	40	.550	35	90	125	17	45	0	20	23	3	140	4.2
Tari Phillips	32	1	366	40	94	.426	0	0	0	31	48	.646	30	49	79	14	56	0	11	30	8	111	3.5
Dawn Staley (*)	10	3	221	10	28	.357	4	14	.286	9	10	.900	2	15	17	28	23	1	6	12	1	33	3.3
Dawn Staley (!)	33	26	905	63	159	.396	21	56	.375	32	40	.800	9	61	70	149	70	1	36	54	1	179	5.4
A. Goodson (>)	23	0	271	29	73	.397	1	2	.500	13	21	.619	16	20	36	15	18	0	8	16	0	72	3.1
Edwige Lawson (*)	17	0	114	8	24	.333	5	13	.385	4	4	1.000	1	6	7	4	5	0	2	12	1	25	1.5
Edwige Lawson (!)	19	0	126	8	28	.286	5	15	.333	6	6	1.000	1	8	9	4	7	0	2	12	1	27	1.4
Roneeka Hodges	26	0	188	13	47	.277	5	26	.192	2	2	1.000	9	8	17	7	8	0	3	3	0	33	1.3
Kiesha Brown (*)	4	0	18	0	0	0	0	0	0	0	0	0	0	1	1	2	1	0	1	2	0	0	0
Kiesha Brown (!)	6	0	32	1	2	.500	0	1	0	0	0	0	0	1	1	2	1	0	3	4	0	2	0.3
Felicia Ragland	4	0	9	0	1	0	0	0	0	0	0	0	0	0	0	1	3	0	0	0	0	0	0
TEAM TOTALS	34	-	6875	860	1920	.448	62	205	.302	527	690	.764	276	684	960	467	581	5	246	425	105	2309	67.9
OPPONENTS	34	-	6875	848	1944	.436	148	423	.350	419	559	.750	274	687	961	541	685	11	197	481	111	2263	66.6

INDIANA FEVER

PLAYER	G	GS	MIN	FG	FGA	PCT	3FG	3FGA	PCT	FT	FTA	PCT	OFF	DEF	TOT	AST	PF	DQ	STL	TO	BLK	PTS	AVG
													—REBOUNDS—									SCORING	
Tamika Catchings	34	34	1174	157	410	.383	35	123	.285	152	193	.788	69	195	264	143	96	1	90	91	16	501	14.7
Kelly Miller	34	34	1057	122	278	.439	37	114	.325	67	79	.848	26	60	86	81	81	1	40	53	2	348	10.2
Natalie Williams	34	34	804	103	248	.415	0	0	0	45	67	.672	74	112	186	31	105	3	56	12	251	7.4	
Tan White	34	3	693	85	254	.335	25	81	.309	47	58	.810	21	32	53	53	62	1	30	70	7	242	7.1
Tully Bevilaqua	31	31	873	63	162	.389	44	116	.379	24	44	.545	12	51	63	80	69	0	60	51	0	194	6.3
J. Streimikyte	34	20	686	82	178	.461	3	6	.500	19	27	.704	37	64	101	32	75	0	29	36	11	186	5.5
Deanna Jackson	34	0	472	56	139	.403	0	3	0	50	68	.735	37	40	77	23	55	0	17	32	12	162	4.8
Kelly Schumacher	34	14	516	58	138	.420	2	11	.182	17	21	.810	26	42	68	14	59	0	10	33	24	135	4.0
Ebony Hoffman	33	0	497	47	116	.405	1	2	.500	25	30	.833	34	63	97	16	59	0	21	23	10	120	3.6
Yolanda Paige	13	0	78	6	22	.273	1	5	.200	3	4	.750	2	7	9	13	1	0	2	6	0	16	1.2
Coretta Brown	6	0	39	2	5	.400	2	5	.400	0	0	0	0	2	2	3	1	0	1	3	0	6	1.0
J. Benningfield	10	0	52	3	8	.375	0	2	0	3	4	.750	3	3	6	4	5	0	1	4	1	9	0.9
TEAM TOTALS	34	-	6925	784	1958	.400	150	468	.321	452	595	.760	341	671	1012	493	668	6	336	477	95	2170	63.8
OPPONENTS	34	-	6925	775	1798	.431	123	367	.335	460	642	.717	279	711	990	435	644	7	234	558	113	2133	62.7

LOS ANGELES SPARKS

PLAYER	G	GS	MIN	FG	FGA	PCT	3FG	3FGA	PCT	FT	FTA	PCT	OFF	DEF	TOT	AST	PF	DQ	STL	TO	BLK	PTS	AVG
													—REBOUNDS—									SCORING	
C. Holdsclaw	33	33	1183	216	450	.480	3	13	.231	126	160	.788	86	137	223	104	94	2	38	99	16	561	17.0
Lisa Leslie	34	34	1096	204	464	.440	7	34	.206	102	174	.586	70	178	248	87	122	2	67	100	71	517	15.2
Tamika Whitmore	34	34	917	115	265	.434	5	19	.263	92	106	.868	54	89	143	42	110	1	33	57	14	327	9.6
Nikki Teasley	19	19	551	45	135	.333	29	94	.309	22	26	.846	6	47	53	70	38	0	23	47	4	141	7.4
Mwadi Mabika	17	14	367	39	122	.320	11	49	.224	10	20	.500	8	19	27	29	43	0	15	14	0	99	5.8
Doneeka Hodges	32	11	669	65	157	.414	31	69	.449	17	25	.680	8	39	47	77	35	0	18	48	7	178	5.6
Tamecka Dixon	30	23	607	63	154	.409	0	5	0	34	40	.850	24	43	67	77	73	0	24	40	2	160	5.3
Laura Macchi	13	1	148	21	53	.396	9	28	.321	12	17	.706	6	12	18	7	23	0	8	13	1	63	4.8
Christi Thomas	32	0	520	48	96	.500	4	12	.333	22	32	.688	28	76	104	17	102	1	11	25	19	122	3.8
R. Masciadri	33	1	463	44	104	.423	19	46	.413	15	20	.750	20	27	47	23	51	0	15	21	1	122	3.7
Edniesha Curry	13	0	113	7	23	.304	6	16	.375	3	6	.500	4	7	11	12	16	0	7	10	1	23	1.8
M. Nieuwveen (>)	7	0	16	2	3	.667	0	0	0	0	0	0	0	2	2	0	5	0	0	2	0	4	0.6
Jessica Moore (*)	15	0	109	4	8	.500	0	0	0	0	0	0	4	4	8	1	21	0	4	5	0	8	0.5
Jessica Moore (!)	21	0	158	5	11	.455	0	0	0	1	2	.500	5	8	13	3	30	1	4	9	0	11	0.
Gordana Grubin (>)	9	0	41	0	8	0	0	2	0	1	4	.250	1	5	6	5	4	0	1	2	0	1	0.1
TEAM TOTALS	34	-	6800	873	2042	.428	124	387	.320	456	630	.724	321	683	1004	551	737	6	264	492	136	2326	68.4
OPPONENTS	34	-	6800	818	1955	.418	182	519	.351	527	709	.743	332	709	1041	567	654	6	247	544	115	2345	69.0

MINNESOTA LYNX

PLAYER	G	GS	MIN	FG	FGA	PCT	3FG	3FGA	PCT	FT	FTA	PCT	OFF	DEF	TOT	AST	PF	DQ	STL	TO	BLK	PTS	AVG
Katie Smith (>)	23	23	766	100	261	.383	35	104	.337	71	90	.789	12	43	55	61	46	0	25	54	2	306	13.3
Nicole Ohlde	34	34	1038	133	292	.455	0	2	0	116	142	.817	63	131	194	78	92	1	21	84	22	382	11.2
S. Abrosimova (>)	31	31	777	109	276	.395	33	82	.402	53	73	.726	29	78	107	60	86	0	48	80	6	304	9.8
Chandi Jones (*)	10	9	281	29	83	.349	11	32	.344	12	19	.632	10	23	33	30	26	0	13	17	3	81	8.1
Chandi Jones (!)	31	9	610	75	196	.383	29	69	.420	27	38	.711	18	46	64	53	68	0	26	40	5	206	6.6
Vanessa Hayden	31	25	595	103	238	.433	0	0	0	40	72	.556	48	115	163	23	110	2	15	63	68	246	7.9
Stacey Lovelace	34	2	594	70	173	.405	26	63	.413	43	54	.796	35	72	107	31	57	0	24	37	11	209	6.1
Tamika Williams	34	9	758	86	156	.551	0	3	0	25	46	.543	76	95	171	39	52	0	30	41	2	197	5.8
Kristi Harrower	34	34	832	53	151	.351	22	68	.324	28	36	.778	11	71	82	96	37	0	38	54	1	156	4.6
Amber Jacobs	33	0	478	40	104	.385	20	53	.377	21	29	.724	4	15	19	68	34	0	19	46	4	121	3.7
Amanda Lassiter	31	3	388	38	115	.330	24	72	.333	7	11	.636	10	36	46	23	55	0	14	29	4	107	3.5
Kristen Mann	24	0	185	30	60	.500	0	9	0	11	16	.688	11	24	35	11	16	0	8	7	1	71	3.0
Tynesha Lewis (*)	11	0	90	10	27	.370	1	3	.333	7	9	.778	0	5	5	7	7	0	3	11	1	28	2.5
Tynesha Lewis (!)	21	1	256	29	88	.330	2	15	.133	15	25	.600	10	15	25	20	14	0	6	22	4	75	3.6
S. King Borchardt (>)	3	0	17	0	1	0	0	0	0	0	3	4	.750	0	1	1	1	2	0	0	1	3	1.0
Stacey Thomas (*)	1	0	3	0	2	0	0	0	0	0	0	0	1	1	2	0	0	0	0	0	0	0	0.0
Stacey Thomas (!)	18	0	136	2	14	.143	0	1	0	8	20	.400	11	11	22	8	15	0	8	3	3	12	0.7
Nuria Martinez (>)	1	0	2	0	1	0	0	1	0	0	0	0	0	0	0	0	0	0	0	0	0	0	0.0
J. Batteast	8	0	46	0	6	0	0	0	0	0	0	0	0	5	5	3	4	0	0	3	1	0	0.0
TEAM TOTALS	34	-	6850	801	1946	.412	172	492	.350	437	601	.727	310	715	1025	531	624	3	258	536	127	2211	65.0
OPPONENTS	34	-	6850	862	2019	.427	129	376	.343	435	592	.735	344	711	1055	537	665	4	275	487	144	2288	67.3

NEW YORK LIBERTY

PLAYER	G	GS	MIN	FG	FGA	PCT	3FG	3FGA	PCT	FT	FTA	PCT	OFF	DEF	TOT	AST	PF	DQ	STL	TO	BLK	PTS	AVG
Becky Hammon	34	34	1180	145	336	.432	65	178	.365	118	131	.901	20	94	114	146	77	0	60	107	2	473	13.9
Ann Wauters	28	28	879	151	279	.541	2	2	1.000	79	105	.752	47	137	184	41	91	1	18	71	23	383	13.7
Vickie Johnson	34	34	1023	129	272	.474	30	84	.357	65	84	.774	37	81	118	92	56	0	23	44	2	353	10.4
Shameka Christon	34	9	809	111	270	.411	24	89	.270	65	76	.855	25	67	92	41	100	1	33	50	19	311	9.1
Elena Baranova	33	33	953	104	236	.441	33	85	.388	47	55	.855	39	188	227	59	79	1	25	59	46	288	8.7
Crystal Robinson	32	31	969	85	224	.379	34	107	.318	30	38	.789	29	71	100	58	86	1	21	38	5	234	7.3
C. Kraayeveld	17	0	196	23	55	.418	9	24	.375	14	15	.933	13	14	27	5	21	0	4	17	8	69	4.1
La'Keshia Frett	33	1	361	42	88	.477	0	0	0	14	19	.737	15	23	38	18	52	0	12	18	4	98	3.0
Erin Thorn	21	0	203	21	54	.389	10	29	.345	4	4	1.000	4	10	14	13	12	0	4	7	0	56	2.7
Tamara Moore (>)	7	0	48	4	6	.667	1	3	.333	2	2	1.000	0	7	7	6	6	0	0	4	0	11	1.6
DeTrina White	13	0	90	4	11	.364	0	0	0	8	12	.667	9	13	22	0	15	0	4	3	3	16	1.2
Edwige Lawson (>)	2	0	12	0	4	0	0	2	0	2	2	1.000	0	2	2	2	0	0	0	0	0	2	1.0
Loree Moore	24	0	182	9	23	.391	0	2	0	4	9	.444	4	23	27	19	12	0	10	25	0	22	0.9
Amisha Carter	3	0	13	0	1	0	0	0	0	0	0	0	0	2	2	4	0	0	1	0	0	0	0.0
Jennifer Smith	2	0	7	0	1	0	0	0	0	0	0	0	0	0	0	0	0	0	0	0	0	0	0.0
TEAM TOTALS	34	-	6925	828	1860	.445	208	605	0.344	452	552	.819	242	732	974	498	613	4	214	462	112	2316	68.1
OPPONENTS	34	-	6925	859	2012	.427	125	398	0.314	442	608	.727	345	685	1030	473	590	5	275	411	86	2285	67.2

PHOENIX MERCURY

PLAYER	G	GS	MIN	FG	FGA	PCT	3FG	3FGA	PCT	FT	FTA	PCT	OFF	DEF	TOT	AST	PF	DQ	STL	TO	BLK	PTS	AVG
Diana Taurasi	33	33	1089	175	427	.410	56	179	.313	121	151	.801	22	116	138	150	111	2	38	112	28	527	16.0
Penny Taylor	29	29	852	121	261	.464	38	94	.404	102	118	.864	38	82	120	94	86	2	38	77	1	382	13.2
Anna DeForge	33	33	1131	142	364	.390	47	144	.326	102	120	.850	31	83	114	80	66	0	41	81	7	433	13.1
K. Vodichkova	28	25	821	127	257	.494	3	7	.429	48	72	.667	60	136	196	63	86	2	28	58	22	305	10.9
M. Stepanova (>)	15	14	409	68	144	.472	0	0	0	26	40	.650	29	51	80	23	33	0	20	22	38	162	10.8
P. Pierson (>)	12	11	318	36	105	.343	0	1	0	20	29	.690	19	40	59	13	39	2	10	32	13	92	7.7
Shereka Wright	25	5	346	24	59	.407	11	35	.314	35	52	.673	18	32	50	23	13	0	14	28	3	94	3.8
Sandora Irvin	12	0	122	14	44	.318	4	8	.500	12	15	.800	16	18	34	5	20	0	5	2	6	44	3.7
Belinda Snell	20	0	226	19	55	.345	11	37	.297	16	18	.889	19	17	36	18	31	0	7	11	1	65	3.3
Ashley Robinson	34	15	659	42	129	.326	0	1	0	19	38	.500	48	70	118	31	108	3	20	38	34	103	3.0
Gwen Jackson	11	2	121	13	26	.500	2	4	.500	3	6	.500	8	15	23	3	12	0	0	13	3	31	2.8
Angelina Williams	16	0	149	15	50	.300	4	18	.222	6	7	.857	9	14	23	9	17	0	4	11	7	40	2.5
Niele Ivey (*)	14	0	152	8	24	.333	2	10	.200	6	6	1.000	3	7	10	20	17	0	6	6	0	24	1.7
Niele Ivey (!)	26	0	254	13	47	.277	5	22	.227	7	7	1.000	8	14	22	30	31	0	12	11	0	38	1.5
K. Christensen (>)	1	0	108	7	15	.467	0	0	0	4	7	.571	9	13	22	7	25	1	7	10	5	18	1.6
Lisa Harrison	27	2	297	15	34	.441	0	1	0	11	14	.786	13	26	39	10	33	0	5	12	1	41	1.5
TEAM TOTALS	34	-	6800	826	1994	.414	178	539	.330	531	693	.766	342	720	1062	549	697	12	243	517	179	2361	69.4
OPPONENTS	34	-	6800	855	1993	.429	121	332	.364	523	720	.726	319	705	1024	470	672	3	265	483	112	2354	69.2

SACRAMENTO MONARCHS

PLAYER	G	GS	MIN	FG	FGA	PCT	3FG	3FGA	PCT	FT	FTA	PCT	—REBOUNDS—			AST	PF	DQ	STL	TO	BLK	SCORING	
													OFF	DEF	TOT							PTS	AVG
DeMya Walker	22	19	598	125	234	.534	1	1	1.000	60	93	.645	47	70	117	48	66	1	28	78	13	311	14.1
Yolanda Griffith	34	33	962	173	357	.485	0	0	0	123	174	.707	87	136	223	52	98	0	42	68	31	469	13.8
Nicole Powell	34	34	988	120	317	.379	66	159	.415	58	72	.806	32	92	124	62	83	0	39	44	16	364	10.7
Kara Lawson	24	1	508	65	148	.439	36	81	.444	26	31	.839	7	26	33	37	28	0	13	22	3	192	8.0
R. Brunson	34	16	722	105	246	.427	0	0	0	55	92	.598	75	112	187	16	61	0	28	42	15	265	7.8
Ticha Penicheiro	34	33	927	54	172	.314	8	41	.195	79	100	.790	8	89	97	149	64	0	48	67	6	195	5.7
Chelsea Newton	34	34	715	60	149	.403	6	25	.240	22	36	.611	32	34	66	55	102	0	24	37	9	148	4.4
H. Maiga	34	0	408	59	131	.450	0	0	0	11	35	.314	31	36	67	30	69	0	24	42	6	129	3.8
Kristin Haynie	30	0	434	40	117	.342	5	32	.156	19	23	.826	19	43	62	43	41	0	33	35	1	104	3.5
Erin Buescher	23	0	209	28	40	.700	0	0	0	20	34	.588	14	15	29	14	29	0	16	26	5	76	3.3
Miao Li Jie	18	0	135	9	30	.300	6	20	.300	7	7	1.000	0	4	4	13	13	0	5	15	1	31	1.7
O. Scott-Richardson	18	0	170	14	39	.359	0	0	0	10	20	.500	17	16	33	5	27	0	4	22	2	38	2.1
Sui Feifei	5	0	24	1	6	.167	1	1	1.000	4	4	1.000	0	1	1	3	3	0	0	2	0	7	1.4
TEAM TOTALS	34	-	6800	853	1986	.430	129	360	.358	494	721	.685	369	674	1043	527	684	1	304	500	108	2329	68.5
OPPONENTS	34	-	6800	751	1823	.412	113	376	.301	478	653	.732	273	694	967	463	723	0	235	622	132	2093	61.6

SAN ANTONIO SILVER STARS

PLAYER	G	GS	MIN	FG	FGA	PCT	3FG	3FGA	PCT	FT	FTA	PCT	—REBOUNDS—			AST	PF	DQ	STL	TO	BLK	SCORING	
													OFF	DEF	TOT							PTS	AVG
Marie Ferdinand	31	31	999	132	358	.369	20	65	.308	104	134	.776	40	76	116	68	74	0	46	70	5	388	12.5
W. Palmer-Daniel	34	29	882	125	242	.517	24	56	.429	52	70	.806	53	140	193	33	74	0	20	42	7	326	9.6
Shannon Johnson	34	33	1104	88	241	.365	28	90	.311	113	136	.831	17	74	91	158	78	1	46	113	5	317	9.3
LaToya Thomas	21	12	505	69	161	.429	3	7	.429	44	49	.898	18	50	68	22	42	0	7	33	8	185	8.8
Katie Feenstra	34	14	673	104	222	.468	0	0	0	90	128	.703	57	118	175	6	90	0	9	62	44	298	8.8
C. Anderson	34	19	669	83	178	.466	0	0	0	37	46	.804	28	62	90	11	106	5	8	55	15	203	6.0
Shyra Ely	31	11	528	50	132	.379	9	31	.290	30	39	.769	11	51	62	27	42	0	7	33	4	139	4.5
Bernadette Ngoyisa	26	0	251	46	81	.568	0	0	0	19	26	.731	17	44	61	5	45	1	5	25	2	111	4.3
Kendra Wecker	1	0	11	2	6	.333	0	3	.000	0	0	0	0	0	0	2	0	0	1	1	0	4	4.0
Dalma Ivanyi	30	14	577	25	67	.373	20	54	.444	5	8	.625	5	45	50	68	48	0	26	53	0	75	2.5
Nikki McCray	23	5	302	15	62	.242	1	20	.050	7	11	.636	7	13	20	16	26	0	11	18	0	38	1.7
Edna Campbell	28	2	248	21	67	.313	5	19	.263	1	1	1.000	2	12	14	14	20	0	7	15	0	48	1.7
Tai Dillard	10	0	51	4	16	.250	0	3	.000	1	4	.250	1	5	6	3	5	0	2	3	0	9	0.9
TEAM TOTALS	34	-	6800	764	1833	.417	110	339	.324	503	652	.771	256	690	946	433	650	7	195	535	90	2141	63.0
OPPONENTS	34	-	6800	898	2059	.436	142	408	.348	463	611	.758	351	704	1055	563	685	1	283	429	148	2401	70.6

SEATTLE STORM

PLAYER	G	GS	MIN	FG	FGA	PCT	3FG	3FGA	PCT	FT	FTA	PCT	—REBOUNDS—			AST	PF	DQ	STL	TO	BLK	SCORING	
													OFF	DEF	TOT							PTS	AVG
Lauren Jackson	34	34	1176	206	450	.458	34	118	.288	151	181	.834	96	217	313	57	100	2	36	59	67	597	17.6
Betty Lennox	28	26	800	123	314	.392	24	78	.308	76	87	.874	21	103	124	57	82	0	35	75	5	346	12.4
Sue Bird	30	30	1020	130	294	.442	45	103	.437	59	69	.855	21	51	72	176	46	0	29	87	6	364	12.1
Janell Burse	34	34	859	127	243	.523	0	0	0	86	123	.699	81	118	199	23	139	6	19	78	40	340	10.0
I. Castro Marques	33	32	879	93	242	.384	24	72	.333	59	73	.808	23	74	97	49	73	0	18	59	4	269	8.2
Suzy Batkovic	29	0	461	76	174	.437	2	7	.286	45	58	.776	26	68	94	26	85	1	17	32	24	199	6.9
Tanisha Wright	34	8	528	49	106	.462	0	1	.000	24	36	.667	20	37	57	53	60	1	18	40	3	122	3.6
Alicia Thompson	30	1	329	32	81	.395	7	22	.318	12	16	.750	10	35	45	14	17	0	4	18	4	83	2.8
Francesca Zara	34	4	413	34	85	.400	5	22	.227	17	21	.810	11	28	39	51	29	0	16	41	1	90	2.6
Simone Edwards	28	0	201	24	41	.585	0	0	0	7	12	.583	9	22	31	3	13	0	4	4	2	55	2.0
M. Stevenson (>)	4	1	53	3	12	.250	0	1	.000	0	0	0	2	4	6	1	3	0	2	4	0	6	1.5
N. Vodopyanova	17	0	98	8	22	.364	1	5	.200	8	12	.667	3	17	20	10	9	0	3	8	2	25	1.5
Ashley Battle (>)	2	0	8	1	2	.500	0	0	0	0	0	0	0	2	2	0	1	0	0	1	0	2	1.0
TEAM TOTALS	34	-	6825	906	2066	.439	142	429	.331	544	688	.791	323	776	1099	520	657	10	201	516	158	2498	73.5
OPPONENTS	34	-	6825	892	2163	.412	133	419	.317	490	646	.759	334	686	1020	568	691	0	267	438	154	2407	70.8

WASHINGTON MYSTICS

PLAYER	G	GS	MIN	FG	FGA	PCT	3FG	3FGA	PCT	FT	FTA	PCT	OFF	DEF	TOT	AST	PF	DQ	STL	TO	BLK	PTS	AVG
Alana Beard	30	30	1015	155	408	.380	32	101	.317	80	105	.762	25	105	130	90	87	0	45	63	9	422	14.1
D. Milton-Jones	33	30	1069	138	331	.417	39	119	.328	79	99	.798	45	127	172	58	117	4	57	75	18	394	11.9
Chasity Melvin	34	34	1051	150	305	.492	4	16	.250	93	138	.674	82	117	199	25	113	1	31	61	14	397	11.7
Temeka Johnson	34	34	973	125	273	.458	13	43	.302	52	66	.788	13	91	104	177	99	2	44	88	1	315	9.3
C. Smith-Taylor	34	34	1036	87	190	.458	42	100	.420	30	46	.652	34	94	128	71	93	0	22	46	11	246	7.2
Coco Miller..............	34	4	500	68	160	.425	9	24	.375	8	10	.800	24	35	59	44	53	0	26	28	3	153	4.5
Laurie Koehn	30	0	230	37	79	.468	35	75	.467	4	5	.800	4	7	11	10	15	0	2	6	0	113	3.8
Nakia Sanford	27	0	293	29	60	.483	0	0	0	30	62	.484	15	30	45	6	50	0	10	17	11	88	3.3
Murriel Page	34	4	589	47	119	.395	6	22	.273	8	8	1.000	21	62	83	25	56	0	15	23	9	108	3.2
Kaayla Chones	12	0	61	6	14	.429	0	0	0	2	3	.667	2	4	6	1	9	0	1	4	0	14	1.2
Tamicha Jackson	8	0	66	4	26	.154	1	9	.111	0	2	0	1	5	6	10	5	0	5	4	0	9	1.1
Kiesha Brown (>)	2	0	14	1	2	.500	0	1	0	0	0	0	0	0	0	0	0	0	2	2	0	2	1.0
M. Amachree	3	0	3	0	1	0	0	0	0	2	2	1.000	0	0	0	0	0	0	0	0	0	2	0.7
TEAM TOTALS	34	-	6900	847	1968	.430	181	510	.355	388	546	.711	266	677	943	517	697	7	260	435	76	2263	66.6
OPPONENTS............	34	-	6900	833	1872	.445	150	433	.346	489	648	.755	267	757	1024	545	638	0	205	504	108	2305	67.8

(*) Statistics with this team only   (!) Totals with all teams   (>) Did not finish season with team

PLAYOFF RESULTS

FIRST ROUND

Connecticut defeats Detroit, 2-0

| August 31 | Connecticut 73, Detroit 62 |
| September 2 | Connecticut 75, Detroit 67 |

Indiana defeats New York, 2-0

| August 30 | Indiana 63, New York 51 |
| September 1 | Indiana 58, New York 50 |

Sacramento defeats Los Angeles, 2-0

| August 31 | Sacramento 75, Los Angeles 72 |
| September 2 | Sacramento 81, Los Angeles 63 |

Houston defeats Seattle, 2-1

August 30	Seattle 75, Houston 67
September 1	Houston 67, Seattle 64
September 3	Houston 75, Seattle 58

CONFERENCE FINALS

Connecticut defeats Indiana, 2-0

| September 8 | Connecticut 73, Indiana 68 |
| September 10 | Connecticut 77, Indiana 67 (OT) |

Sacramento defeats Houston, 2-0

| September 8 | Sacramento 73, Houston 69 |
| September 10 | Sacramento 74, Houston 65 |

WNBA FINALS

Sacramento defeats Connecticut, 3-1

September 14	Sacramento 69, Connecticut 65
September 15	Connecticut 77, Sacramento 70 (OT)
September 18	Sacramento 66, Connecticut 55
September 20	Sacramento 62, Connecticut 59

TEAM STANDINGS

OFFENSIVE

TEAM	G	FG	FGA	PCT	FG3	FG3A	PCT	FT	FTA	PCT	OFF	DEF	REB	AST	PF	DQ	STL	TO	BLK	PTS	AVG
Sac..........	8	215	487	.441	37	8	.463	103	143	.720	69	184	253	133	151	0	54	103	16	570	71.3
Conn........	8	187	445	.420	41	114	.360	139	192	.724	70	190	260	108	135	0	54	110	41	554	69.3
Hou..........	5	123	271	.454	11	33	.333	86	109	.789	34	106	140	67	85	0	34	70	11	343	68.6
L.A..........	2	48	110	.436	11	30	.367	28	42	.667	14	25	39	35	46	0	17	31	5	135	67.5
Sea..........	3	70	175	.400	11	48	.229	46	52	.885	17	62	79	40	63	0	18	40	7	197	65.7
Det..........	2	48	135	.356	6	18	.333	27	36	.750	27	42	69	24	49	0	13	25	8	129	64.5
Ind.	4	83	236	.352	21	46	.457	69	86	.802	50	75	125	46	87	0	34	36	11	256	64.0
N.Y..........	2	35	94	.372	7	25	.280	24	29	.828	6	39	45	19	45	0	5	25	4	101	50.5

DEFENSIVE

Team	FG	FGA	PCT	FG3	FG3A	PCT	FT	FTA	PCT	OFF	DEF	REB	AST	PF	DQ	STL	TO	BLK	PTS	AVG	DIFF
N.Y	34	103	.330	11	24	.458	42	52	.808	21	44	65	23	34	0	14	15	9	121	60.5	5.7
Ind.	81	194	.418	16	46	.348	73	93	.785	25	85	110	48	79	0	17	50	12	251	62.8	1.2
Sac.	193	459	.420	37	109	.339	102	150	.680	65	160	225	116	146	0	60	123	35	525	65.6	5.7
Conn.	198	524	.378	34	79	.430	101	133	.759	91	166	257	109	168	0	62	89	16	53	66.4	2.9
Hou.	129	300	.430	21	67	.313	65	77	.844	36	105	141	73	107	0	31	69	12	344	68.8	-0.2
Sea.	73	159	.459	5	17	.294	58	70	.829	16	67	83	41	52	0	20	39	4	209	69.7	-4.0
Det........	46	108	.426	12	30	.400	44	59	.746	18	48	66	24	34	0	13	24	10	148	74.0	-9.5
L.A.	55	106	.519	9	22	.409	37	55	.673	15	48	63	38	41	0	12	31	5	156	78.0	-10.5

TEAM COMPARISONS

TEAM	Points Per Game OWN	OPP	Field Goal Percentage OWN	OPP	Turnovers Per Game OWN	OPP	Rebound Percentages OFF	DEF	Below 70 Pts. OWN	OPP	Overtime Games W	L	3 PTS or Less W	L	10 PTS or More W	L
Connecticut..........69.2	66.3	.420	.378	13.7	11.1	.297	.676	3	7	2	0	0	1	2	1
Detroit.................64.5	74.0	.356	.426	12.5	12.0	.360	.700	2	0	0	0	0	0	0	1
Houston 68.6	68.8	.454*	.430	14.0	13.8	.245	.746	4	2	0	1	1	0	1	0
Indiana 64.0	62.7	.352	.418	9.0*	12.5	.370	.750	4	2	0	1	0	0	1	1
Los Angeles 67.5	78.0	.436	.519	15.5	15.5*	.226	.625	1	0	0	0	0	1	0	1
New York 50.5	60.5*	.372	.330*	12.5	7.5	.120	.650	2	2	0	0	0	0	0	1
Sacramento........71.2*	65.6	.441	.420	12.8	15.3	.301	.739	3	6	1	1	2	0	2	0
Seattle 65.6	69.6	.400	.459	13.3	13.0	.202	.795	2	2	0	0	0	1	0	1

* - League Leader

REBOUND PERCENTAGES
OFF. - Percentage of a given team's missed shots which that team rebounds.
DEF. - Percentage of opponents' missed shots which a given team rebounds.

INDIVIDUAL PLAYOFF STATISTICS, TEAM BY TEAM

CONNECTICUT SUN

PLAYER	G	GS	MIN	FG	FGA	PCT	FG3	FG3A	PCT	FT	FTA	PCT	OFF	DEF	TOT	AST	PF	DQ	STL	TO	BLK	PTS	AVG
T. McWilliams-Franklin 8	8	284	48	94	.511	1	3	.333	30	38	.789	22	53	75	13	23	0	9	16	11	127	15.9	
Nykesha Sales 8	8	270	37	101	.366	16	38	.421	25	31	.806	10	22	32	19	20	0	16	16	8	115	14.4	
Katie Douglas 8	8	278	31	67	.463	15	38	.395	19	29	.655	12	25	37	18	17	0	11	8	1	96	12.0	
Lindsay Whalen 7	7	220	19	57	.333	3	15	.200	37	48	.771	6	18	24	23	11	0	6	20	1	78	11.1	
Asjha Jones 8	0	178	29	60	.483	0	2	0	13	23	.565	8	20	28	7	23	0	2	11	4	71	8.9	
Margo Dydek 8	8	146	14	38	.368	1	1	1.000	7	11	.636	8	34	42	4	19	0	3	16	13	36	4.5	
Brooke Wyckoff 8	0	109	5	12	.417	4	10	.400	4	6	.667	3	12	15	3	13	0	1	5	2	18	2.3	
Jaime Carey 6	0	71	2	9	.222	1	6	.167	0	0	0	0	2	2	7	5	0	1	4	0	5	0.8	
J. Derevjanik 8	1	82	2	5	.400	0	1	0	2	4	.500	1	3	4	14	4	0	5	6	0	6	0.8	
Le'coe Willingham ..3	0	10	0	2	0	0	0	0	2	2	.000	0	1	1	0	0	0	0	1	1	2	0.7	
Laura Summerton....2	0	2	0	0	0	0	0	0	0	0	0	0	0	0	0	0	0	0	0	0	0	0	
TEAM TOTALS.........8	-	1650	187	445	.420	41	114	.360	139	192	.724	70	190	260	108	135	0	54	110	41	554	69.3	
OPPONENTS 8	-	1650	198	524	.378	34	79	.430	101	133	.759	91	166	257	109	168	0	62	89	16	531	66.4	

DETROIT SHOCK

PLAYER	G	GS	MIN	FG	FGA	PCT	FG3	FG3A	PCT	FT	FTA	PCT	OFF	DEF	TOT	AST	PF	DQ	STL	TO	BLK	PTS	AVG
Deanna Nolan..........2	2	79	15	37	.405	1	4	.250	6	7	.857	1	7	8	7	4	0	2	6	2	37	18.5	
Katie Smith............2	2	67	7	26	.269	2	10	.200	5	5	1.000	2	4	6	1	5	0	2	2	0	21	10.5	
Cheryl Ford............2	2	49	8	18	.444	0	0	0	3	5	.600	7	7	14	2	11	1	1	3	2	19	9.5	
Ruth Riley..............2	2	54	7	17	.412	3	3	1.000	0	0	0	3	8	11	0	10	1	1	5	2	17	8.5	
Swin Cash 2	2	51	4	13	.308	0	1	0	8	11	.727	5	4	9	7	4	0	3	4	2	16	8.0	
Kara Braxton 2	0	36	5	18	.278	0	0	0	5	6	.833	4	3	7	2	5	0	3	0	0	15	7.5	
Plenette Pierson.....2	0	20	2	5	.400	0	0	0	0	0	0	3	3	6	0	5	0	1	0	0	4	2.0	
Elaine Powell 2	0	32	0	0	0	0	0	0	0	0	0	2	5	7	5	5	0	3	2	0	0	0	
Barbara Farris 2	0	12	0	1	0	0	0	0	0	0	0	0	1	1	0	0	0	0	0	0	0	0	
TEAM TOTALS 2	-	400	48	135	.356	6	18	.333	27	36	.750	27	42	69	24	49	0	13	25	8	129	64.5	
OPPONENTS 2	-	400	46	108	.426	12	30	.400	44	59	.746	18	48	66	24	34	0	13	24	10	148	74.0	

HOUSTON COMETS

PLAYER	G	GS	MIN	FG	FGA	PCT	FG3	FG3A	PCT	FT	FTA	PCT	OFF	DEF	TOT	AST	PF	DQ	STL	TO	BLK	PTS	AVG
Sheryl Swoopes 5	5	189	35	87	.402	5	14	.357	17	21	.810	8	20	28	19	17	0	7	15	2	92	18.4	
Tina Thompson........5	5	168	28	57	.491	3	10	.300	10	14	.714	10	18	28	6	15	0	2	9	6	69	13.8	
Michelle Snow 5	5	152	18	34	.529	0	0	0	16	23	.696	1	26	27	4	15	0	5	16	3	52	10.4	
Janeth Arcain 5	5	138	16	33	.485	0	1	0	12	12	1.000	1	9	10	6	5	0	6	2	0	44	8.8	
Dominique Canty 5	5	162	12	30	.400	0	0	0	16	20	.800	11	11	22	17	12	0	1	14	0	40	8.0	
Dawn Staley 5	0	125	6	13	.462	3	8	.375	6	7	.857	0	4	4	14	9	0	9	7	0	21	4.2	
Tari Phillips............5	0	53	5	12	.417	0	0	0	3	4	.750	1	8	9	1	6	0	1	4	0	13	2.6	
Kiesha Brown 1	0	1	0	0	0	0	0	0	2	2	1.000	0	0	0	0	1	0	0	0	0	2	2.0	
Sancho Lyttle 5	0	34	3	5	.600	0	0	0	4	6	.667	2	10	12	0	5	0	2	0	0	10	2.0	
Edwige Lawson 1	0	1	0	0	0	0	0	0	0	0	0	0	0	0	0	0	0	0	0	0	0	0	

56

PLAYER	G	GS	MIN	FG	FGA	PCT	FG3	FG3A	PCT	FT	FTA	PCT	OFF	DEF	TOT	AST	PF	DQ	STL	TO	BLK	PTS	AVG
Roneeka Hodges, ...2	0	2	0	0	0	0	0	0	0	0	0	0	0	0	0	0	0	0	1	1	0	0	0
TEAM TOTALS.........5	-	1025	123	271	.454	11	33	.333	86	109	.789	34	106	140	67	85	0	34	70	11	343	68.6
OPPONENTS 5	-	1025	129	300	.430	21	67	.313	65	77	.844	36	105	141	73	107	0	31	69	12	344	68.8

INDIANA FEVER

PLAYER	G	GS	MIN	FG	FGA	PCT	FG3	FG3A	PCT	FT	FTA	PCT	OFF	DEF	TOT	AST	PF	DQ	STL	TO	BLK	PTS	AVG
Tamika Catchings....4	4	146	21	59	.356	5	12	.417	22	28	.786	13	24	37	9	13	1	8	11	1	69	17.3
Natalie Williams 4	4	134	17	40	.425	0	1	0	13	16	.813	13	17	30	6	14	0	5	1	2	47	11.8
Kelly Miller 4	4	155	12	39	.308	9	17	.529	7	10	.700	0	7	7	10	13	0	5	5	0	40	10.0
Deanna Jackson.......4	0	84	10	23	.435	1	1	1.000	14	17	.824	4	10	14	2	17	1	2	1	2	35	8.8
Tully Bevilaqua 4	4	152	8	25	.320	6	14	.429	5	7	.714	1	8	9	11	12	0	7	10	1	27	6.8
Kelly Schumacher.....4	0	42	9	19	.474	0	0	0	2	2	1.000	7	1	8	2	6	0	2	0	4	20	5.0
J. Streimikyte 4	4	96	6	23	.261	0	0	0	6	6	1.000	10	8	18	5	11	0	5	6	1	18	4.5
Tan White 4	0	16	0	8	0	0	1	0	0	0	0	2	0	2	1	1	0	0	0	0	0	0
TEAM TOTALS.........4	-	825	83	236	.352	21	46	.457	69	86	.802	50	75	125	46	87	0	34	36	11	256	64.0
OPPONENTS 4	-	825	81	194	.418	16	46	.348	73	93	.785	25	85	110	48	79	0	17	50	12	251	62.8

LOS ANGELES SPARKS

PLAYER	G	GS	MIN	FG	FGA	PCT	FG3	FG3A	PCT	FT	FTA	PCT	OFF	DEF	TOT	AST	PF	DQ	STL	TO	BLK	PTS	AVG
Chamique Holdsclaw ..2	2	78	14	27	.519	1	1	1.000	2	5	.400	3	7	10	2	6	0	4	6	0	31	15.5
R. Masciadri 2	1	47	8	17	.471	4	10	.400	4	4	1.000	2	1	3	4	6	0	1	1	0	24	12.0
Nikki Teasley 2	1	61	7	21	.333	2	11	.182	6	9	.667	2	3	5	14	4	0	3	3	0	22	11.0
Lisa Leslie 2	2	67	5	14	.357	0	0	0	8	13	.615	4	9	13	7	8	0	5	2	3	18	9.0
Tamika Whitmore 2	2	48	6	14	.429	1	1	1.000	5	8	.625	2	1	3	1	7	0	1	7	0	18	9.0
Christi Thomas 2	0	38	3	4	.750	1	1	1.000	1	1	1.000	1	1	2	2	7	0	0	2	2	8	4.0
Laura Macci 2	0	9	2	4	.500	1	1	1.000	2	2	1.000	0	0	0	1	0	0	0	0	0	7	3.5
Mwadi Mabika 1	1	11	1	4	.250	0	2	0	0	0	0	0	0	0	0	0	0	2	0	0	2	2.0
Doneeka Hodges 2	0	13	1	2	.500	1	2	.500	0	0	0	0	1	1	2	0	0	1	2	0	3	1.5
Tamecka Dixon........2	1	12	1	2	.500	0	0	0	0	0	0	0	1	1	2	4	0	1	1	0	2	1.0
Edniesha Curry........2	0	16	0	1	0	0	1	0	0	0	0	0	1	1	1	3	0	1	5	0	0	0
TEAM TOTALS.........2	-	400	48	110	.436	11	30	.367	28	42	.667	14	25	39	35	46	0	17	31	5	135	67.5
OPPONENTS 2	-	400	55	106	.519	9	22	.409	37	55	.673	15	48	63	38	41	0	12	31	5	156	78.0

NEW YORK LIBERTY

PLAYER	G	GS	MIN	FG	FGA	PCT	FG3	FG3A	PCT	FT	FTA	PCT	OFF	DEF	TOT	AST	PF	DQ	STL	TO	BLK	PTS	AVG
Vickie Johnson 2	2	73	10	22	.455	0	3	0	6	8	.750	0	6	6	7	7	0	1	4	0	26	13.0
Becky Hammon 2	2	76	9	20	.450	2	7	.286	3	3	1.000	0	7	7	4	8	1	0	10	0	23	11.5
La'Keshia Frett 2	1	47	5	12	.417	0	0	0	5	6	.833	2	2	4	1	7	0	0	2	0	15	7.5
Shameka Christon ..2	1	47	4	12	.333	2	4	.500	1	2	.500	0	5	5	1	7	0	0	2	1	11	5.5
Elena Baranova 2	2	59	3	10	.300	1	3	.333	2	2	1.000	1	7	8	2	4	0	3	1	2	9	4.5
C. Kraayeveld 2	0	37	1	3	.333	1	1	1.000	5	6	.833	2	5	7	0	6	0	0	2	0	8	4.0
Crystal Robinson 2	2	50	2	13	.154	1	7	.143	2	2	1.000	1	7	8	4	5	0	1	1	1	7	3.5
Erin Thorn...............2	0	10	1	2	.500	0	0	0	0	0	0	0	0	0	1	0	0	0	0	2	1.0
Loree Moore 1	0	1	0	0	0	0	0	0	0	0	0	0	0	0	0	0	0	0	0	0	0	0
TEAM TOTALS.........2	-	400	35	94	.372	7	25	.280	24	29	.828	6	39	45	19	45	0	5	25	4	101	50.5
OPPONENTS 2	-	400	34	103	.330	11	24	.458	42	52	.808	21	44	65	23	34	0	14	15	9	121	60.5

SACRAMENTO MONARCHS

PLAYER	G	GS	MIN	FG	FGA	PCT	FG3	FG3A	PCT	FT	FTA	PCT	OFF	DEF	TOT	AST	PF	DQ	STL	TO	BLK	PTS	AVG
Yolanda Griffith 8	8	246	53	108	.491	0	0	0	32	45	.711	27	39	66	11	20	0	10	10	4	138	17.3
Kara Lawson 8	2	208	29	67	.433	15	29	.517	17	18	.944	2	27	29	18	9	0	8	11	1	90	11.3
Nicole Powell 8	8	257	30	78	.385	20	42	.476	8	10	.800	2	18	20	15	16	0	7	12	1	88	11.0
DeMya Walker 6	0	165	26	52	.500	0	0	0	9	12	.750	7	11	18	21	19	0	3	17	0	61	10.2
R. Brunson 8	8	194	25	56	.446	0	0	0	5	11	.455	13	31	44	10	27	0	5	9	4	55	6.9
Chelsea Newton 8	8	182	18	42	.429	2	4	.500	8	12	.667	4	10	14	8	19	0	2	11	0	46	5.8
Ticha Penicheiro......6	6	162	10	31	.323	0	4	0	12	15	.800	2	22	24	31	9	0	6	14	1	32	5.3
Hamchetou Maiga ..8	0	82	13	26	.500	0	0	0	4	6	.667	5	8	13	4	16	0	5	8	3	30	3.8
Kristin Haynie 8	0	103	7	19	.368	0	0	0	4	6	.667	4	10	14	8	8	0	8	4	0	18	2.3
O. Scott-Richardson..7	0	38	4	8	.500	0	0	0	1	2	.500	2	5	7	5	8	0	0	3	1	9	1.3

57

PLAYER	G	GS	MIN	FG	FGA	PCT	FG3	FG3A	PCT	FT	FTA	PCT	OFF	DEF	TOT	AST	PF	DQ	STL	TO	BLK	PTS	AVG
Erin Buescher..........3	0	13	0	0		0	0	0		3	6	.500	1	3	4	2	0	0	0	1	1	3	1.0
TEAM TOTALS.........8	-	1650	215	487	.441	37	80	.463	103	143	.720	69	184	253	133	151	0	54	103	16	570	71.3	
OPPONENTS 8	-	1650	193	459	.420	37	109	.339	102	150	.680	65	160	225	116	146	0	60	123	35	525	65.6	

SEATTLE STORM

PLAYER	G	GS	MIN	FG	FGA	PCT	FG3	FG3A	PCT	FT	FTA	PCT	OFF	DEF	TOT	AST	PF	DQ	STL	TO	BLK	PTS	AVG
Betty Lennox 3	3	94	15	38	.395	3	12	.250	13	14	.929	1	13	14	8	9	0	3	6	0	46	15.3	
Lauren Jackson 3	3	102	17	39	.436	4	13	.308	5	6	.833	4	20	24	2	11	0	4	8	4	43	14.3	
Janell Burse 3	3	90	11	18	.611	0	0	0	6	6	1.000	8	6	14	3	11	0	3	2	1	28	9.3	
Sue Bird 3	3	103	9	33	.273	2	15	.133	7	8	.875	1	4	5	13	6	0	3	4	0	27	9.0	
I. Castro Marques 3	3	86	6	18	.333	1	6	.167	4	4	1.000	0	3	3	4	12	0	2	8	0	17	4.7	
Suzy Batkovic..........3	0	43	6	12	.500	0	0	0	2	5	.400	2	8	10	0	8	0	0	5	2	14	4.7	
Francesca Zara.......3	0	26	4	6	.667	1	1	1.000	2	2	1.000	0	0	0	2	0	0	0	5	0	11	3.7	
Tanisha Wright 3	0	38	1	5	.200	0	0	0	7	7	1.000	1	4	5	7	6	0	3	2	0	9	3.0	
Alicia Thompson 1	0	10	1	4	.250	0	1	0	0	0	0	0	3	3	0	0	0	0	0	0	2	2.0	
Simone Edwards 2	0	5	0	1	0	0	0	0	0	0	0	0	1	1	1	0	0	0	0	0	0	0	
N. Vodopyanova.......1	0	3	0	1	0	0	0	0	0	0	0	0	0	0	0	0	0	0	0	0	0	0	
TEAM TOTALS.........3	-	600	70	175	.400	11	48	.229	46	52	.885	17	62	79	40	63	0	18	40	7	197	65.7	
OPPONENTS 3	-	600	73	159	.459	5	17	.294	58	70	.829	16	67	83	41	52	0	20	39	4	209	69.7	

INDIVIDUAL FINALS STATISTICS, TEAM BY TEAM

CONNECTICUT SUN

PLAYER	G	GS	MIN	FG	FGA	PCT	FG3	FG3A	PCT	FT	FTA	PCT	OFF	DEF	TOT	AST	PF	DQ	STL	TO	BLK	PTS	AVG
Nykesha Sales 4	4	140	23	63	.365	10	24	.417	13	17	.765	4	7	11	12	9	0	7	10	3	69	17.3	
T. McWilliams-Franklin 4	4	142	24	48	.500	0	1	0	10	15	.667	14	35°	49	6	10	0	3	8	6	58	14.5	
Katie Douglas 4	4	138	19	42	.452	6	19	.316	7	11	.636	5	13	18	9	10	0	7	4	1	51	12.8	
Asjha Jones 4	0	92	12	26	.462	0	1	0	9	15	.600	5	9	14	2	14	0	2	8	3	33	8.3	
Lindsay Whalen 3	3	74	5	19	.263	0	4	0	2	4	.500	2	4	6	9	3	0	3	9	1	12	4.0	
Margo Dydek 4	4	63	5	16	.313	0	0	0	1	1	1.000	3	17	20	3	9	0	2	8	7	11	2.8	
Brooke Wyckoff 4	0	60	4	10	.400	3	8	.375	0	0	0	0	6	6	2	5	0	0	3	2	11	2.8	
J. Derevjanik 4	1	56	2	4	.500	1	0	0	2	4	.500	0	2	2	5	2	0	4	5	0	6	1.5	
Le'coe Willingham ..2	0	9	0	2	0	0	0	0	2	2	1.000	0	1	1	0	0	0	0	1	0	2	1.0	
Jaime Carey 4	0	50	1	7	.143	1	5	.200	0	0	0	0	2	2	7	5	0	1	3	0	3	0.8	
Laura Summerton....1	0	1	0	0	0	0	0	0	0	0	0	0	0	0	0	0	0	0	0	0	0	0	
TEAM TOTALS.........4	-	825	95	237	.401	20	63	.317	46	69	.667	33	96	129	55	67	0	29	61	23	256	64.0	
OPPONENTS 4	-	825	101	256	.395	18	39	.462	47	63	.746	35	93	128	62	66	0	29	43	6	267	66.8	

SACRAMENTO MONARCHS

PLAYER	G	GS	MIN	FG	FGA	PCT	FG	FGA	PCT	FT	FTA	PCT	OFF	DEF	TOT	AST	PF	DQ	STL	TO	BLK	PTS	AVG
Yolanda Griffith 4	4	123	28	57	.491	0	0	0	18	27	.667	17	22	39	5	11	0	5	7	2	74	18.5	
Nicole Powell 4	4	136	18	48	.375	13	25	.520	2	4	.500	1	11	12	5	5	0	4	3	1	51	12.8	
Kara Lawson 4	0	103	12	29	.414	5	10	.500	12	12	1.000	0	9	9	6	3	0	4	2	1	41	10.3	
DeMya Walker 4	0	112	17	38	.447	0	0	0	3	4	.750	2	8	10	14	12	0	3	10	0	37	9.3	
R. Brunson 4	4	89	10	27	.370	0	0	0	3	4	.750	6	14	20	5	14	0	2	4	1	23	5.8	
Chelsea Newton 4	4	75	7	18	.389	0	2	0	3	4	.750	2	6	8	4	10	0	1	4	0	17	4.3	
Ticha Penicheiro 4	4	98	3	18	.167	0	2	0	4	6	.667	1	14	15	16	4	0	2	9	1	10	2.5	
Kristin Haynie 4	0	52	2	10	.200	0	0	0	2	2	1.000	3	5	8	6	3	0	5	1	0	6	1.5	
O. Scott-Richardson..3	0	7	2	4	.500	0	0	0	0	0	0	1	1	2	0	0	0	0	0	0	4	1.3	
Hamchetou Maiga ..4	0	28	2	7	.286	0	0	0	0	0	0	2	2	4	1	4	0	3	2	0	4	1.0	
Erin Buescher 1	0	2	0	0	0	0	0	0	0	0	0	0	1	1	0	0	0	0	0	0	0	0	
TEAM TOTALS.........4	-	825	101	256	.395	18	39	.462	47	63	.746	35	93	128	62	66	0	29	43	6	267	66.8	
OPPONENTS 4	-	825	95	237	.401	20	63	.317	46	69	.667	33	96	129	55	67	0	29	61	23	256	64.0	

FINALS BOX SCORES

GAME 1

at Mohegan Sun Arena, September 14, 2005

OFFICIALS: Tina Napier, Daryl Humphrey, Michael Price   TIME OF GAME: 1:51   ATTENDANCE: 8,157

SCORE BY PERIODS	1	2	FINAL
Monarchs	27	42	69
Sun	31	34	65

VISITOR: Sacramento Monarchs (1-0)

NO	PLAYER	MIN	FG	FGA	3P	3PA	FT	FTA	OR	DR	TOT	A	PF	ST	TO	BS	PTS
14	Nicole Powell, F	32	4	9	2	3	0	0	1	4	5	2	1	1	0	1	10
32	Rebekkah Brunson, F	26	2	10	0	0	1	1	2	4	6	0	2	2	0	0	5
33	Yolanda Griffith, C	28	11	17	0	0	3	5	3	6	9	0	2	0	2	0	25
2	Chelsea Newton, G	20	2	4	0	0	2	2	1	1	2	0	1	0	0	0	6
21	Ticha Penicheiro, G	21	0	1	0	0	2	2	0	1	1	8	1	1	3	0	2
9	Hamchetou Maiga	8	1	3	0	0	0	0	2	0	2	0	0	1	0	0	2
20	Kara Lawson	24	3	9	1	4	2	2	0	0	0	1	0	1	0	0	9
22	DeMya Walker	24	4	10	0	0	0	0	0	1	1	3	2	1	2	0	8
4	Kristin Haynie	15	1	4	0	0	0	0	1	1	2	3	1	1	0	0	2
0	O. Scott-Richardson	2	0	0	0	0	0	0	0	1	1	0	0	0	0	0	0
11	Erin Buescher						DNP		Coach's Decision								
	TOTALS:	200	28	67	3	7	10	12	10	19	29	17	10	8	7	1	69
	PERCENTAGES:		41.8	42.9	83.3												

TM REB: 8 TOT TO: 7 (8 PTS)

HOME: CONNECTICUT SUN (0-1)

NO	PLAYER	MIN	FG	FGA	3P	3PA	FT	FTA	OR	DR	TOT	A	PF	ST	TO	BS	PTS
32	Rebekkah Brunson, F	26	2	10	0	0	1	1	2	4	6	0	2	2	0	0	5
11	T. McWilliams-Franklin, F	31	4	6	0	0	0	0	3	7	10	2	2	1	3	1	8
42	Nykesha Sales, F	33	7	17	4	7	5	5	0	2	2	4	2	1	3	0	23
12	Margo Dydek, C	24	2	6	0	0	1	1	3	4	7	2	2	0	3	4	5
13	Lindsay Whalen, G	25	3	9	0	3	1	2	0	0	0	2	1	1	0	0	7
32	Katie Douglas, G	33	6	10	2	4	0	0	0	5	5	2	1	1	1	0	14
15	Asjha Jones	18	1	2	0	0	0	0	1	2	3	2	3	2	1	2	2
34	Jennifer Derevja	11	1	1	0	0	0	0	0	1	1	0	1	0	1	0	2
21	Brooke Wyckoff	12	1	3	0	2	0	0	0	0	0	1	0	0	1	0	2
43	Le'coe Willingham	7	0	2	0	0	2	2	0	1	1	0	0	0	1	0	2
10	Jamie Carey	6	0	0	0	0	0	0	0	0	0	0	0	0	1	0	0
14	Laura Summerton						DNP - Coach's Decision										
	TOTALS:	200	25	56	6	16	9	10	7	22	29	15	12	6	15	7	65
	PERCENTAGES:		44.6	37.5	90.0												

GAME 2
at Mohegan Sun Arena, September 15, 2005

OFFICIALS: Sue Blauch, Lisa Mattingly, Bryan Enterline   TIME OF GAME: 2:22   ATTENDANCE: 8,444

SCORE BY PERIODS	1	2	OT	FINAL
Monarchs	39	31	0	70
Suns	38	32	7	77

VISITOR: Sacramento Monarchs (1-1)

NO	PLAYER	MIN	FG	FGA	3P	3PA	FT	FTA	OR	DR	TOT	A	PF	ST	TO	BS	PTS
32	Rebekkah Brunson, F	26	2	10	0	0	1	1	2	4	6	0	2	2	0	0	5
14	Nicole Powell, F	39	5	15	4	9	2	4	0	5	5	2	2	2	1	0	16
32	Rebekkah Brunson, F	16	0	3	0	0	0	0	0	3	3	1	4	0	1	0	0
33	Yolanda Griffith, C	37	7	17	0	0	2	4	6	3	9	3	4	1	0	1	16
2	Chelsea Newton, G	23	4	8	0	2	1	2	1	1	2	3	4	0	2	0	9
21	Ticha Penicheiro, G	21	0	2	0	1	0	0	0	2	2	2	0	0	4	0	0
20	Kara Lawson	29	4	7	1	2	2	2	0	4	4	2	1	2	0	1	11
22	DeMya Walker	34	6	10	0	0	2	2	0	6	6	2	4	0	4	0	14
4	Kristin Haynie	15	0	2	0	0	2	2	1	1	2	1	0	2	1	0	2
9	Hamchetou Maiga	5	0	0	0	0	0	0	0	0	0	3	0	1	0	0	0
0	O. Scott-Richardson	4	1	3	0	0	0	0	1	0	1	0	0	0	0	0	2
11	Erin Buescher	2	0	0	0	0	0	0	0	1	1	0	0	0	0	0	0
	TOTALS:	225	27	67	5	14	11	16	9	26	35	16	22	7	14	2	70
	PERCENTAGES:		40.3	35.7	68.8												

HOME: CONNECTICUT SUN (1-1)

NO	PLAYER	MIN	FG	FGA	3P	3PA	FT	FTA	OR	DR	TOT	A	PF	ST	TO	BS	PTS
11	T. McWilliams-Franklin, F	41	8	17	0	1	8	11	4	12	16	2	2	1	1	1	24

NO	PLAYER	MIN	FG	FGA	3P	3PA	FT	FTA	OR	DR	TOT	A	PF	ST	TO	BS	PTS
42	Nykesha Sales, F	37	7	16	3	5	2	2	3	0	3	4	3	3	2	2	19
12	Margo Dydek, C	11	0	3	0	0	0	0	0	6	6	1	0	1	1	0	0
32	Katie Douglas, G	41	7	15	1	5	1	4	1	2	3	3	3	3	1	1	16
34	Jennifer Derevja, G	24	1	2	0	1	1	2	0	0	0	4	0	2	2	0	3
15	Asjha Jones	23	1	5	0	0	1	2	1	4	5	0	4	0	4	0	3
10	Jamie Carey	21	1	3	1	2	0	0	0	0	0	4	2	0	2	0	3
21	Brooke Wyckoff	27	3	5	3	4	0	0	0	2	2	1	0	0	1	0	9
14	Laura Summerton						DNP - Coach's Decision											
13	Lindsay Whalen						DNP - Ankle											
43	Le'coe Willingham						DNP - Coach's Decision											
	TOTALS:	225	28	66	8	18	13	21	9	26	35	19	14	10	14	4	77
	PERCENTAGES:		42.4	44.4	61.9												

GAME 3
at ARCO Arena, September 18, 2005

OFFICIALS: June Courteau, Bob Trammell, Kurt Walker   TIME OF GAME: 2:08   ATTENDANCE: 14,073

SCORE BY PERIODS	1	2	FINAL
Sun	31	24	55
Monarchs	35	31	66

VISITOR: Connecticut Sun (5-2)

NO	PLAYER	MIN	FG	FGA	3P	3PA	FT	FTA	OR	DR	TOT	A	PF	ST	TO	BS	PTS
42	Nykesha Sales, F	36	6	16	2	6	3	6	0	4	4	2	2	2	2	1	17
11	T. McWilliams-Franklin ,F	35	7	11	0	0	2	4	3	10	13	2	3	0	2	3	16
12	Margo Dydek, C	19	3	4	0	0	0	0	0	6	6	0	4	1	2	2	6
32	Katie Douglas, G	31	2	7	1	5	1	1	1	2	3	0	5	0	2	0	6
13	Lindsay Whalen, G	23	1	4	0	1	0	0	0	0	0	2	1	1	5	1	2
15	Asjha Jones	24	2	7	0	1	3	6	1	0	1	0	2	0	1	0	7
34	Jennifer Derevja	12	0	0	0	0	1	2	0	1	1	1	0	1	1	0	1
21	Brooke Wyckoff	9	0	0	0	0	0	0	0	1	1	0	1	0	0	1	0
10	Jamie Carey	11	0	3	0	2	0	0	0	1	1	0	2	0	0	0	0
14	Laura Summerton						DNP - Coach's Decision											
43	Le'coe Willingham						DNP - Coach's Decision											
	TOTALS:	200	21	52	3	15	10	19	5	25	30	7	20	5	15	8	55
	PERCENTAGES:		40.4	20.0	52.6												

HOME: SACRAMENTO MONARCHS (6-1)

NO	PLAYER	MIN	FG	FGA	3P	3PA	FT	FTA	OR	DR	TOT	A	PF	ST	TO	BS	PTS
14	Nicole Powell, F	35	4	14	4	8	0	0	0	1	1	1	0	1	0	0	12
32	Rebekkah Brunson, F	22	3	6	0	0	0	0	2	3	5	3	5	0	0	0	6
33	Yolanda Griffith, C	30	7	12	0	0	5	8	5	6	11	2	2	2	3	1	19
2	Chelsea Newton, G	16	1	3	0	0	0	0	0	1	1	0	4	1	1	0	2
21	Ticha Penicheiro, G	31	1	7	0	1	1	2	1	5	6	3	2	1	1	0	3
20	Kara Lawson	24	4	7	2	2	6	6	0	4	4	0	1	0	1	0	16
22	DeMya Walker	28	3	11	0	0	0	0	1	1	2	4	2	1	0	0	6
4	Kristin Haynie	9	1	1	0	0	0	0	0	2	2	2	1	0	0	0	2
9	Hamchetou Maiga	5	0	3	0	0	0	0	0	0	0	0	1	1	0	0	0
11	Erin Buescher						DNP - Coach's Decision											
0	O. Scott-Richardson						DNP - Coach's Decision											
	TOTALS:	200	24	64	6	11	12	16	9	23	32	15	18	7	6	1	66
	PERCENTAGES:		37.5	54.5	75.0												

GAME 4
at ARCO Arena, September 20, 2005

OFFICIALS: Michael Price, Tina Napier, Bryan Enterline   TIME OF GAME: 2:09   ATTENDANCE:15,002

SCORE BY PERIODS	1	2	FINAL
Sun	31	28	59
Monarchs	25	37	62

VISITOR: Connecticut Sun (5-3)

NO	PLAYER	MIN	FG	FGA	3P	3PA	FT	FTA	OR	DR	TOT	A	PF	ST	TO	BS	PTS
42	Nykesha Sales, F	34	3	14	1	6	3	4	1	1	2	2	2	1	3	0	10
11	T. McWilliams-Franklin ,F	35	5	14	0	0	0	0	4	6	10	0	3	1	2	1	10
12	Margo Dydek, C	9	0	3	0	0	0	0	0	1	1	0	3	0	2	1	0

NO	PLAYER	MIN	FG	FGA	3P	3PA	FT	FTA	OR	DR	TOT	A	PF	ST	TO	BS	PTS
32	Katie Douglas, G	33	4	10	2	5	5	6	3	4	7	4	1	3	0	0	15
13	Lindsay Whalen, G	26	1	6	0	0	1	2	2	4	6	5	1	1	4	0	3
15	Asjha Jones	27	8	12	0	0	5	7	2	3	5	0	5	0	2	1	21
21	Brooke Wyckoff	12	0	2	0	2	0	0	0	3	3	0	4	0	1	1	0
34	Jennifer Derevja	9	0	1	0	0	0	0	0	0	0	0	1	1	1	0	0
10	Jamie Carey	12	0	1	0	1	0	0	0	1	1	3	1	1	0	0	0
43	Le'coe Willingham	2	0	0	0	0	0	0	0	0	0	0	0	0	0	0	0
14	Laura Summerton	1	0	0	0	0	0	0	0	0	0	0	0	0	0	0	0
	TOTALS:	200	21	63	3	14	14	19	12	23	35	14	21	8	15	4	59
	PERCENTAGES:		33.3	21.4	73.7												

HOME: SACRAMENTO MONARCHS (7-1)

NO	PLAYER	MIN	FG	FGA	3P	3PA	FT	FTA	OR	DR	TOT	A	PF	ST	TO	BS	PTS
14	Nicole Powell, F	30	5	10	3	5	0	0	0	1	1	0	2	0	2	0	13
32	Rebekkah Brunson, F	25	5	8	0	0	2	3	2	4	6	1	3	0	3	1	12
33	Yolanda Griffith, C	28	3	11	0	0	8	10	3	7	10	0	3	2	2	0	14
2	Chelsea Newton, G	16	0	3	0	0	0	0	0	3	3	1	1	0	1	0	0
21	Ticha Penicheiro, G	25	2	8	0	0	1	2	0	6	6	3	1	0	1	1	5
22	DeMya Walker	26	4	7	0	0	2	2	1	0	1	5	4	1	4	0	9
20	Kara Lawson	26	1	6	1	2	2	2	0	1	1	3	1	1	1	0	5
4	Kristin Haynie	13	0	3	0	0	0	0	1	1	2	0	1	2	0	0	0
9	Hamchetou Maiga	10	1	1	0	0	0	0	0	2	2	1	0	1	1	0	2
0	O. Scott-Richardson	1	1	1	0	0	0	0	0	0	0	0	0	0	0	0	2
11	Erin Buescher					DNP - Coach's Decision											
	TOTALS:	200	22	58	4	7	14	19	7	25	32	14	16	7	15	2	62
	PERCENTAGES:		37.9	57.1	73.7												

ALL-STAR GAME BOX SCORE

at Mohegan Sun Arena, July 9, 2005

OFFICIALS: Tina Napier, Daryl Humphrey, Bryan Enterline TIME OF GAME: 1:52 ATTENDANCE: 9,168

SCORE BY PERIODS	1	2	FINAL
West	52	70	122
East	43	56	99

VISITOR: All-Star West (1-0)

NO	PLAYER	MIN	FG	FGA	3P	3PA	FT	FTA	OR	DR	TOT	A	PF	ST	TO	BS	PTS
15	Lauren Jackson, F	20	3	10	1	4	2	2	2	2	4	2	1	3	2	0	9
22	Sheryl Swoopes, F	25	6	13	2	3	1	2	1	3	4	2	2	0	1	0	15
33	Yolanda Griffith, C	19	5	10	0	1	2	4	7	7	14	0	0	0	1	1	12
3	Diana Taurasi, G	24	3	8	2	6	2	2	1	1	2	4	0	1	2	0	10
10	Sue Bird, G	19	5	6	3	3	1	2	1	3	4	3	0	1	0	0	14
3	Marie Ferdinand	13	5	8	0	0	0	0	0	0	0	1	1	2	1	0	10
1	Chamique Holdsclaw	16	4	12	0	0	6	6	4	2	6	1	1	0	1	0	14
9	Lisa Leslie	20	2	8	0	1	5	7	1	3	4	1	2	0	1	0	9
30	Katie Smith	20	4	9	4	6	4	4	1	3	4	1	1	1	0	0	16
2	Michelle Snow	14	3	3	0	0	2	2	2	1	3	1	1	0	0	1	8
22	DeMya Walker	10	2	3	0	0	1	2	0	1	1	0	2	1	0	1	5
	TOTALS:	200	42	90	12	24	26	33	20	26	46	16	11	9	9	3	122
	PERCENTAGES:		46.7	50.0	78.8												

HOME: ALL-STAR EAST (0-1)

NO	PLAYER	MIN	FG	FGA	3P	3PA	FT	FTA	OR	DR	TOT	A	PF	ST	TO	BS	PTS
24	Tamika Catchings, F	24	7	11	0	2	4	5	2	4	6	2	3	2	1	0	18
32	Swin Cash, F	17	1	7	0	2	0	0	3	2	5	1	0	0	1	0	2
00	Ruth Riley, C	16	4	5	0	0	2	2	0	1	1	3	0	0	0	0	10
5	Dawn Staley, G	18	1	5	0	3	0	0	1	1	2	4	3	0	2	0	2
25	Becky Hammon, G	21	7	14	4	6	0	0	3	3	6	4	1	0	3	0	18
20	Alana Beard	20	1	9	0	4	0	0	1	4	5	2	0	0	3	1	2
11	Taj McWilliams-Franklin	17	2	5	0	1	4	5	1	1	2	3	2	1	1	0	8
42	Nykesha Sales	20	5	10	1	2	0	0	2	2	4	2	2	1	1	0	11
14	Deanna Nolan	22	7	1	4	8	2	2	2	2	4	1	2	1	3	0	20
35	Cheryl Ford	12	2	3	0	0	0	0	1	4	5	0	3	0	1	0	4
12	Ann Wauters	13	1	4	0	0	2	2	2	1	3	0	0	0	1	1	4
	TOTALS:	200	38	94	9	28	14	16	18	25	43	20	19	5	17	2	99
	PERCENTAGES:		40.4	32.1	87.5												

SEATTLE STORM, 2004 WNBA Champions

Front Row (l to r) — Adia Barnes, Betty Lennox, Tully Bevilaqua, Michelle Greco, Sue Bird, Trina Frierson, Alicia Thompson. Back Row (l to r) — Janell Burse, Assistant Coach Jenny Boucek, Kamila Vodichkova, Simone Edwards, Head Coach Anne Donovan, Lauren Jackson, Sheri Sam, Assistant Coach Jessie Kenlaw

FINAL STANDINGS

EASTERN CONFERENCE

TEAM	W	L	PCT	GB	HOME	ROAD	LAST-10	STREAK
Connecticut	18	16	.529	-	10-7	8-9	6-4	Won 1
New York	18	16	.529	-	11-6	7-10	6-4	Won 3
Detroit	17	17	.500	1	8-9	9-8	6-4	Won 3
Washington	17	17	.500	1	11-6	6-11	7-3	Lost 1
Charlotte	16	18	.471	2	10-7	6-11	4-6	Lost 3
Indiana	15	19	.441	3	10-7	5-12	3-7	Lost 4

WESTERN CONFERENCE

TEAM	W	L	PCT	GB	HOME	ROAD	LAST-10	STREAK
Los Angeles	25	9	.735	-	15-2	10-7	8-2	Won 1
Seattle	20	14	.588	5	13-4	7-10	4-6	Lost 1
Minnesota	18	16	.529	7	11-6	7-10	4-6	Lost 1
Sacramento	18	16	.529	7	10-7	8-9	7-3	Won 3
Phoenix	17	17	.500	8	10-7	7-10	5-5	Won 1
Houston	13	21	.382	12	9-8	4-13	3-7	Lost 3
San Antonio	9	25	.265	16	6-11	3-14	3-7	Won 1

TEAM STANDINGS

OFFENSIVE

TEAM	G	FG	FGA	PCT	FG3	FG3A	PCT	FT	FTA	PCT	OFF	DEF	REB	AST	PF	DQ	STL	TO	BLK	PTS	AVG
L.A.	34	904	2069	.437	157	414	.379	530	722	.734	312	809	1121	626	731	6	262	529	148	2495	73.4
Sea.	34	873	2025	.431	167	439	.380	524	676	.775	350	709	1059	552	665	8	302	499	131	2437	71.7
Det.	34	874	2097	.417	62	209	.297	556	792	.702	397	773	1170	564	648	6	277	513	148	2366	69.6
Conn.	34	876	2051	.427	149	467	.319	434	590	.736	321	724	1045	572	610	1	299	462	96	2335	68.7
Wash.	34	873	2088	.418	105	283	.371	474	661	.717	337	726	1063	467	652	1	255	424	128	2325	68.4
Sac.	34	874	2072	.422	129	365	.353	435	604	.720	389	635	1024	519	641	3	314	485	118	2312	68.0
Phoe.	34	826	1922	.430	192	519	.370	456	598	.763	264	652	916	501	748	13	282	464	137	2300	67.6
N.Y.	34	819	1932	.424	216	617	.350	398	531	.750	263	741	1004	539	587	3	209	506	124	2252	66.2
Ind.	34	791	2011	.393	166	481	.345	450	580	.776	396	705	1101	555	639	12	261	486	134	2198	64.6
S.A.	34	812	1940	.419	79	247	.320	488	628	.777	302	701	1003	493	628	5	272	513	106	2191	64.4
Hou.	34	798	1933	.413	123	358	.344	458	615	.745	311	724	1035	451	555	2	242	484	107	2177	64.0
Minn.	34	767	1900	.404	177	542	.327	454	640	.709	332	724	1056	526	660	3	257	613	139	2165	63.7
Cha.	34	745	1744	.427	166	459	.362	436	590	.739	256	616	872	426	648	4	210	479	134	2092	61.5

DEFENSIVE

Team	FG	FGA	PCT	FG3	FG3A	PCT	FT	FTA	PCT	OFF	DEF	REB	AST	PF	DQ	STL	TO	BLK	PTS	AVG	DIFF
Cha.	800	1932	.414	130	349	.372	438	587	.746	368	628	996	516	595	2	243	437	114	2168	63.8	-2.2
Minn.	804	1972	.408	92	330	.279	490	669	.732	323	713	1036	508	676	10	333	502	133	2190	64.4	-0.7
Hou.	834	2008	.415	152	434	.350	391	531	.736	335	720	1055	539	655	4	258	471	129	2211	65.0	-1.0
Phoe.	784	1845	.425	133	348	.382	534	724	.738	309	711	1020	456	660	0	226	536	137	2235	65.7	+1.9
Sac.	803	1872	.429	161	458	.352	474	631	.751	310	676	986	513	646	5	241	593	117	2241	65.9	+2.1
Ind.	804	1865	.431	121	352	.344	516	695	.742	281	688	969	514	603	1	268	466	162	2245	66.0	-1.4
Sea.	851	1989	.428	139	391	.355	423	592	.715	303	679	982	507	678	4	252	527	137	2264	66.6	+5.1
N.Y.	867	2096	.414	132	416	.317	431	579	.744	371	730	1101	517	589	7	288	430	123	2297	67.6	-1.3
Conn.	858	1996	.430	145	384	.378	443	599	.740	306	757	1063	565	627	4	239	492	113	2304	67.8	+0.9
L.A.	815	2095	.389	174	511	.341	557	761	.732	339	727	1066	532	704	8	288	523	114	2361	69.4	+3.9
S.A.	888	2003	.443	172	469	.367	416	564	.738	324	710	1034	575	624	7	280	492	129	2364	69.5	-5.1
Det.	860	2098	.410	191	533	.358	470	609	.772	325	730	1055	515	728	12	289	496	131	2381	70.0	-0.4
Wash.	864	2013	.429	146	425	.344	510	686	.743	336	770	1106	534	627	3	237	492	111	2384	70.1	-1.7
AVG.'S	833	1983	.420	145	415	.350	469	633	.741	325	711	1036	522	647	5	265	497	127	2280	67.1	—
	10832	25784	—	1888	5400	—	6093	8227	—	4230	9239	13469	6791	8412	67	3442	6457	1650	29645	—	—

TEAM COMPARISONS

TEAM	Points Per Game OWN	OPP	Field Goal Percentage OWN	OPP	Turnovers Per Game OWN	OPP	Rebound Percentages OFF	DEF	TOT	Below 70 Pts. Games OWN	OPP	Overtime Games W	L	3 PTS or Less W	L	10 PTS or More W	L
Charlotte	61.5	63.8*	.427	.414	14.1	12.9	.290	.626	.458	28	25	2	1	4	1	4	11
Connecticut	68.7	67.8	.427	.430	13.6	14.5	.298	.703	.500	17	23	2	2	2	5	7	7
Detroit	69.6	70.0	.417	.410	15.1	14.6	.352	.704	.528	17	17	1	1	1	5	7	7
Houston	64.0	65.0	.413	.415	14.2	13.9	.302	.684	.493	27	22	1	1	1	2	6	6
Indiana	64.6	66.0	.393	.431	14.3	13.7	.365*	.715*	.540*	22	23	0	2	4	2	6	6
Los Angeles	73.4*	69.4	.437*	.389*	15.6	15.4	.300	.705	.502	13	17	4	1	9	0	11	4
Minnesota	63.7	64.4	.404	.408	18.0	14.8	.318	.691	.505	27	25	2	0	6	2	5	9
New York	66.2	67.6	.424	.414	14.9	12.6	.265	.666	.466	23	21	2	2	2	3	4	9
Phoenix	67.6	65.7	.430	.425	13.6	15.8	.271	.678	.475	18	21	0	1	1	5	11	4
Sacramento	68.0	65.9	.422	.429	14.3	17.4*	.365	.672	.519	20	21	0	3	2	3	8	5
San Antonio	64.4	69.5	.419	.443	15.1	14.5	.298	.684	.491	23	18	1	2	0	4	5	14
Seattle	71.7	66.6	.431	.428	14.7	15.5	.340	.701	.520	16	21	1	0	4	6	11	1
Washington	68.4	70.1	.418	.429	12.5*	14.5	.304	.684	.494	20	17	1	1	5	3	7	9
COMPOSITE; 221 games	67.1		.420		14.6		.314	.686		271	271	17		41		92	

* - League Leader

REBOUND PERCENTAGES

OFF. - Percentage of a given team's missed shots which that team rebounds.

DEF. - Percentage of opponents' missed shots which a given team rebounds.

TOT. - Average of offensive and defensive rebound percentages.

SCORING AVERAGE

	G	FG	FT	PTS	AVG
Jackson, Sea.	31	220	142	634	20.5
Thompson, Hou.	26	180	116	520	20.0
Leslie, L.A.	34	223	146	598	17.6
Taurasi, Pho.	34	209	98	578	17.0
Catchings, Ind.	34	180	152	568	16.7
Cash, Det.	32	180	158	526	16.4
Sales, Ct.	34	210	56	517	15.2
Swoopes, Hou.	31	181	77	459	14.8
Griffith, Sac.	34	177	140	494	14.5
Mabika, L.A.	31	159	89	445	14.4
DeForge, Pho.	34	165	88	488	14.4
Thomas, S.A.	31	171	95	440	14.2
Nolan, Det.	34	166	99	464	13.6
Hammon, N.Y.	34	153	97	460	13.5
P. Taylor, Pho.	33	150	93	434	13.2
Beard, Was.	34	159	107	446	13.1
Bird, Sea.	34	151	73	439	12.9
McWilliams-Frank, Ct.	34	168	77	413	12.1
Robinson, N.Y.	28	122	40	339	12.1
Feaster, Cha.	33	132	79	388	11.8

REBOUNDS PER GAME

	G	OFF	DEF	TOT	AVG
Leslie, L.A.	34	60	276	336	9.9
Ford, Det.	31	104	193	297	9.6
Snow, Hou.	31	62	177	239	7.7
Catchings, Ind.	34	79	170	249	7.3
Baranova, N.Y.	34	33	213	246	7.2
Griffith, Sac.	34	122	124	246	7.2
McWilliams-Frank, Ct.	34	83	161	244	7.2
Goodson, S.A.	34	89	146	235	6.9
Williams, Ind.	34	93	142	235	6.9
Jackson, Sea.	31	64	143	207	6.7
Cash, Det.	32	78	130	208	6.5
Sutton-Brown, Cha.	34	63	148	211	6.2
Thompson, Hou.	26	44	113	157	6.0
Williams, Min.	34	82	123	205	6.0
Riley, Det.	34	68	131	199	5.9
Ohlde, Min.	34	83	111	194	5.7
Palmer, Ct.	33	47	135	182	5.5
Lennox, Sea.	32	28	131	159	5.0
Sanford, Was.	31	53	101	154	5.0
2 tied					4.9

ASSISTS PER GAME

	G	AST	AVG
Teasley, L.A.	34	207	6.1
Bird, Sea.	34	184	5.4
Staley, Cha.	34	171	5.0
Penicheiro, Sac.	33	163	4.9
Whalen, Ct.	31	148	4.8
Powell, Det.	30	134	4.5
Hammon, N.Y.	34	150	4.4
Johnson, S.A.	31	136	4.4
Cash, Det.	32	135	4.2
Taurasi, Pho.	34	132	3.9
Johnson, N.Y.	34	124	3.6
Dixon, L.A.	32	112	3.5
Darling, Min.	33	115	3.5
Catchings, Ind.	34	115	3.4
Nolan, Det.	34	112	3.3
DeForge, Pho.	34	107	3.1
Miller, Ind.	34	106	3.1
Swoopes, Hou.	31	91	2.9
Sales, Ct.	34	97	2.9
Beard, Was.	34	91	2.7

FIELD GOAL PCT

	FG	FGA	PCT
Williams, Min.	102	189	.540
Griffith, Sac.	177	341	.519
Leslie, L.A.	223	451	.494
Thomas, S.A.	171	350	.489
P. Taylor, Pho.	150	310	.484
Jackson, Sea.	220	460	.478
McWilliams-Frank, Ct	168	352	.477
Sutton-Brown, Cha.	106	224	.473
Cash, Det.	180	384	.469
Baranova, N.Y.	146	315	.463

3-PT FIELD GOAL PCT.

	3FG	3GA	PCT
Smith-Taylor, Cha.	29	58	.500
Baranova, N.Y.	53	115	.461
Jackson, Sea.	52	115	.452
Bird, Sea.	64	146	.438
Smith, Min.	60	139	.432
P. Taylor, Pho.	41	96	.427
Teasley, L.A.	68	165	.412
Miller, Ind.	46	112	.411
Thompson, Hou.	44	108	.407
Bolton, Sac.	32	79	.405

FREE THROW PCT.

	FT	FTA	PCT
Smith, Min.	98	109	.899
Johnson, N.Y.	62	70	.886
Miller, Ind.	50	57	.877
Feaster, Cha.	79	91	.868
DeForge, Pho.	88	102	.863
P. Taylor, Pho.	93	108	.861
Ferdinand, S.A.	55	64	.859
Bird, Sea.	73	85	.859
Swoopes, Hou.	77	90	.856
Sam, Sea.	65	76	.855

STEALS PER GAME

	G	STL	AVG
Griffith, Sac.	34	75	2.21
Sales, Ct.	34	75	2.21
Beard, Was.	34	69	2.03
Catchings, Ind.	34	67	1.97
Nolan, Det.	34	66	1.94
Penicheiro, Sac.	33	64	1.94
Hammon, N.Y.	34	58	1.71
P. Taylor, Pho.	33	52	1.58
Sam, Sea.	34	53	1.56
Johnson, S.A.	31	48	1.55

BLOCKS PER GAME

	G	BLK	AVG
Leslie, L.A.	34	98	2.88
Sutton-Brown, Cha.	34	71	2.09
Jackson, Sea.	31	62	2.00
Baranova, N.Y.	34	58	1.71
Riley, Det.	34	53	1.56
Dydek, S.A.	34	48	1.41
McWilliams-Frank, Ct.	34	45	1.32
Ohlde, Min.	34	45	1.32
Burse, Sea.	29	36	1.24
Griffith, Sac.	34	41	1.21

MINUTES PER GAME

	G	MIN	AVG
Thompson, Hou.	26	943	36.3
Holdsclaw, Was.	23	801	34.8
Smith, Min.	23	800	34.8
Cash, Det.	32	1105	34.5
Jackson, Sea.	31	1070	34.5
Swoopes, Hou.	31	1070	34.5
DeForge, Pho.	34	1152	33.9
Leslie, L.A.	34	1150	33.8
Catchings, Ind.	34	1149	33.8
Staley, Cha.	34	1143	33.6

CHARLOTTE STING

Player	G	Min	FGM	FGA	Pct	FTM	FTA	Pct	Off	Def	Tot	Ast	PF	Dq	Stl	TO	Blk	Pts	Avg	Hi
Allison Feaster 33		1052	132	332	.398	79	91	.868	22	62	84	60	61	0	27	68	6	388	11.8	23
Tammy Sutton-Brown 34		970	106	224	.473	113	162	.698	63	148	211	15	111	1	31	71	71	325	9.6	22
Dawn Staley 34		1143	106	246	.431	66	87	.759	12	46	58	171	83	0	43	74	2	302	8.9	19
C. Smith-Taylor 34		977	99	206	.481	53	73	.726	50	89	139	40	109	1	18	55	13	280	8.2	18
Tynesha Lewis 34		617	91	210	.433	44	58	.759	23	34	57	44	47	1	27	44	7	246	7.2	19
Andrea Stinson 34		777	79	191	.414	34	44	.773	25	94	119	49	60	1	27	41	7	203	6.0	16
Nicole Powell 31		384	50	121	.413	8	10	.800	10	61	71	16	37	0	15	22	4	132	4.3	14
Teana Miller 9		77	14	27	.519	7	14	.500	9	9	18	0	21	0	2	5	6	35	3.9	10
Kelly Mazzante 34		339	31	92	.337	4	6	.667	9	24	33	9	22	0	7	20	2	79	2.3	15
O. Scott-Richardson ..34		398	27	67	.403	19	32	.594	28	37	65	10	78	0	9	36	13	73	2.1	16
La'Keshia Frett(>) 10		71	6	13	.462	3	6	.500	3	7	10	4	4	0	1	10	2	15	1.5	4
Mery Andrade 12		65	3	7	.429	3	3	1.000	1	3	4	7	12	0	0	3	1	9	0.8	7
Jia Perkins 4		17	0	5	.000	3	4	.750	1	2	3	1	2	0	3	1	0	3	0.8	2
Tera Bjorklund 4		13	1	3	.333	0	0	—	0	0	0	0	1	0	0	1	0	2	0.5	2
Charlotte.....................34		6900	745	1744	.427	436	590	.739	256	616	872	426	648	4	210	479	134	2092	61.5	74
Opponents 34		6900	800	1932	.414	438	587	.746	368	628	996	516	595	2	243	437	114	2168	63.8	87

3-pt. FG: Charlotte 166-459 (.362)
Feaster 45-143 (.315); Staley 24-59 (.407); Smith-Taylor 29-58 (.500); Lewis 20-50 (.400); Stinson 11-37 (.297)
Powell 24-58 (.414); Mazzante 13-52 (.250); Scott-Richardson 0-1 (.000); Andrade 0-1 (.000); Opponents 130-349 (.372)

CONNECTICUT SUN

Player	G	Min	FGM	FGA	Pct	FTM	FTA	Pct	Off	Def	Tot	Ast	PF	Dq	Stl	TO	Blk	Pts	Avg	Hi
Nykesha Sales 34		1096	210	486	.432	56	77	.727	33	102	135	97	98	0	75	76	8	517	15.2	28
T. McWilliams-Franklin34		1133	168	352	.477	77	128	.602	83	161	244	63	96	1	48	73	45	413	12.1	22
Katie Douglas 34		1120	125	321	.389	61	77	.792	33	99	132	90	73	0	50	52	13	364	10.7	25
Wendy Palmer 33		786	108	253	.427	68	85	.800	47	135	182	30	77	0	23	40	5	297	9.0	21
Lindsay Whalen..........31		946	83	183	.454	89	122	.730	21	69	90	148	72	0	30	94	0	275	8.9	21
Asjha Jones 34		699	96	239	.402	41	48	.854	51	67	118	39	82	0	20	53	18	235	6.9	16
Le'coe Willingham.......23		175	24	38	.632	20	26	.769	22	21	43	7	16	0	8	12	2	68	3.0	12
Candace Futrell..........20		144	11	38	.289	13	16	.813	7	12	19	10	20	0	5	7	1	42	2.1	8
Debbie Black 34		347	26	56	.464	3	4	.750	13	23	36	47	35	0	19	15	0	55	1.8	6
Jessica Brungo.........33		314	18	59	.305	4	5	.800	10	27	37	27	21	0	4	12	4	50	1.5	6
Jen Derevjanik 23		140	7	26	.269	2	2	1.000	1	8	9	14	20	0	8	10	0	19	0.8	6
Connecticut 34		6900	876	2051	.427	434	590	.736	321	724	1045	572	610	1	299	462	96	2335	68.7	83
Opponents 34		6900	858	1996	.430	443	599	.740	306	757	1063	565	627	4	239	492	113	2304	67.8	85

3-pt. FG: Connecticut 149-467 (.319)
Sales 41-129 (.318); McWilliams-Franklin 0-12 (.000); Douglas 53-153 (.346); Palmer 13-41 (.317); Whalen 20-57 (.351)
Jones 2-6 (.333); Willingham 0-1 (.000); Futrell 7-17 (.412); Black 0-1 (.000); Brungo 10-38 (.263); Derevjanik 3-12 (.250);
Opponents 145-384 (.378)

DETROIT SHOCK

Player	G	Min	FGM	FGA	Pct	FTM	FTA	Pct	Off	Def	Tot	Ast	PF	Dq	Stl	TO	Blk	Pts	Avg	Hi
Swin Cash 32		1105	180	384	.469	158	219	.721	78	130	208	135	84	0	44	81	29	526	16.4	29
Deanna Nolan...........34		1138	166	435	.382	99	124	.798	29	105	134	112	75	1	66	90	12	464	13.6	29
Ruth Riley 34		1037	153	343	.446	71	87	.816	68	131	199	50	121	2	31	82	53	378	11.1	26
Cheryl Ford 31		912	118	287	.411	93	158	.589	104	193	297	34	118	3	41	54	25	329	10.6	21
Merlakia Jones 33		517	76	205	.371	24	32	.750	23	46	69	21	41	0	19	26	2	180	5.5	16
Barbara Farris............26		422	41	80	.513	36	54	.667	28	33	61	7	46	0	8	26	2	118	4.5	15
Elaine Powell 30		760	52	138	.377	29	50	.580	31	53	84	134	67	0	36	61	8	133	4.4	10
Chandi Jones 31		397	37	103	.359	25	31	.806	8	26	34	45	41	0	18	40	5	107	3.5	14
Iciss Tillis 31		287	35	74	.473	7	12	.583	13	26	39	13	23	0	9	23	8	83	2.7	8
Isabel Sanchez 10		62	6	14	.429	8	11	.727	3	2	5	3	6	0	2	11	0	22	2.2	7
Ayana Walker 18		148	8	28	.286	2	6	.333	10	16	26	6	13	0	1	5	4	18	1.0	4
Jae Cross(>)...............5		15	0	0	---	3	4	.750	0	1	1	1	1	0	0	2	0	3	0.6	2
Stacy Stephens 7		36	2	6	.333	0	2	.000	2	7	9	3	7	0	0	2	0	4	0.6	2
Amisha Carter.............2		13	0	0	---	1	2	.500	0	4	4	0	5	0	2	3	0	1	0.5	1
Stacey Thomas 1		1	0	0	---	0	0	---	0	0	0	0	0	0	0	0	0	0	0.0	0
Detroit.......................34		6850	874	2097	.417	556	792	.702	397	773	1170	564	648	6	277	513	148	2366	69.6	88
Opponents 34		6850	860	2098	.410	470	609	.772	325	730	1055	515	728	12	289	496	131	2381	70.0	97

3-pt. FG: Detroit 62-209 (.297)
Cash 8-23 (.348); Nolan 33-114 (.289); Riley 1-2 (.500); M. Jones 4-15 (.267); C. Jones 8-32 (.250); Tillis 6-18 (.333)
Sanchez 2-5 (.400); Opponents 191-533 (.358)

HOUSTON COMETS

Player	G	Min	FGM	FGA	Pct	FTM	FTA	Pct	Off	Def	Tot	Ast	PF	Dq	Stl	TO	Blk	Pts	Avg	Hi
Tina Thompson 26		943	180	448	.402	116	147	.789	44	113	157	48	68	0	22	70	23	520	20.0	35
Sheryl Swoopes 31		1070	181	429	.422	77	90	.856	38	115	153	91	56	0	47	59	16	459	14.8	33
Michelle Snow 31		893	104	229	.454	68	113	.602	62	177	239	31	89	0	28	71	35	276	8.9	15
Kedra Holland-Corn....27		703	59	159	.371	28	41	.683	19	47	66	53	51	0	40	47	3	177	6.6	21
Sheila Lambert 34		788	75	177	.424	40	51	.784	19	49	68	88	46	0	26	82	4	197	5.8	19
Dominique Canty 32		770	63	150	.420	51	72	.708	40	44	84	64	61	0	32	45	1	177	5.5	12
Tiffani Johnson 33		660	59	118	.500	24	32	.750	30	92	122	27	72	1	9	31	17	142	4.3	12
Felicia Ragland 34		517	44	120	.367	11	13	.846	19	48	67	38	48	0	25	32	3	118	3.5	11
Octavia Blue 13		155	16	42	.381	12	13	.923	12	9	21	5	10	0	1	7	0	44	3.4	13
Lucienne Berthieu......16		134	12	34	.353	13	18	.722	12	15	27	4	28	1	6	9	2	37	2.3	11
P. Johns Kimbrough ..19		157	3	17	.176	16	21	.762	16	13	29	1	21	0	4	8	3	22	1.2	10
LaTonya Johnson 6		36	2	7	.286	0	2	.000	0	1	1	1	3	0	2	2	0	6	1.0	3
Gordana Grubin...........5		24	0	3	.000	2	2	1.000	0	1	1	0	2	0	0	3	0	2	0.4	2
Houston 34		6850	798	1933	.413	458	615	.745	311	724	1035	451	555	2	242	484	107	2177	64.0	97
Opponents 34		6850	834	2008	.415	391	531	.736	335	720	1055	539	655	4	258	471	129	2211	65.0	82

3-pt. FG: Houston 123-358 (.344)
Thompson 44-108 (.407); Swoopes 20-65 (.308); Holland-Corn 31-97 (.320); Lambert 7-27 (.259); Canty 0-2 (.000); Blue 0-4 (.000)
Ragland 19-49 (.388); L. Johnson 2-6 (.333); Opponents 152-434 (.350)

INDIANA FEVER

Player	G	Min	FGM	FGA	Pct	FTM	FTA	Pct	Off	Def	Tot	Ast	PF	Dq	Stl	TO	Blk	Pts	Avg	Hi
Tamika Catchings 34		1149	180	468	.385	152	178	.854	79	170	249	115	90	2	67	77	38	568	16.7	30
Natalie Williams 34		956	133	293	.454	83	119	.697	93	142	235	62	122	3	40	65	23	349	10.3	19
Kelly Miller 34		1096	126	326	.386	50	57	.877	28	80	108	106	81	3	37	74	5	348	10.2	20
Kelly Schumacher.......32		601	92	196	.469	35	45	.778	36	68	104	25	67	0	10	52	31	224	7.0	17
Deanna Jackson.........34		804	92	251	.367	52	73	.712	57	56	113	53	82	3	29	52	6	236	6.9	19
Kristen Rasmussen 33		692	56	135	.415	30	38	.789	41	72	113	47	51	0	21	35	14	152	4.6	12
Stephanie White 22		450	27	72	.375	24	34	.706	8	20	28	52	30	0	24	30	5	91	4.1	12
Coretta Brown............26		398	37	108	.343	10	16	.625	10	24	34	41	31	0	7	31	1	104	4.0	11
Niele Ivey 15		179	11	37	.297	4	6	.667	2	8	10	18	20	0	4	6	3	34	2.3	8
Ebony Hoffman 30		334	26	83	.313	3	4	.750	34	53	87	21	51	1	15	27	5	60	2.0	9
Kate Starbird.............12		117	6	23	.261	5	6	.833	6	3	9	11	7	0	6	9	0	20	1.7	9
Astou Ndiaye-Diatta ..10		74	5	19	.263	2	4	.500	2	9	11	4	7	0	1	8	3	12	1.2	6
Indiana 34		6850	791	2011	.393	450	580	.776	396	705	1101	555	639	12	261	486	134	2198	64.6	85
Opponents 34		6850	804	1865	.431	516	695	.742	281	688	969	514	603	1	268	466	162	2245	66.0	83

3-pt. FG: Indiana 166-481 (.345)
Catchings 56-167 (.335); Williams 0-4 (.000); Miller 46-112 (.411); Schumacher 5-13 (.385); Jackson 0-12 (.000); Ivey 8-24 (.333)
Rasmussen 10-27 (.370); White 13-39 (.333); Brown 20-56 (.357); Hoffman 5-17 (.294); Starbird 3-10 (.300);
Opponents 121-352 (.344)

LOS ANGELES SPARKS

Player	G	Min	FGM	FGA	Pct	FTM	FTA	Pct	Off	Def	Tot	Ast	PF	Dq	Stl	TO	Blk	Pts	Avg	Hi
Lisa Leslie 34		1150	223	451	.494	146	205	.712	60	276	336	88	130	5	50	110	98	598	17.6	31
Mwadi Mabika 31		965	159	383	.415	89	108	.824	39	83	122	75	88	0	36	48	3	445	14.4	26
Nikki Teasley..............34		1105	108	278	.388	52	68	.765	29	87	116	207	89	0	43	103	7	336	9.9	25
DeLisha Milton-Jones 19		604	65	161	.404	45	62	.726	35	55	90	31	63	1	23	48	10	186	9.8	20
Tamecka Dixon 32		913	119	269	.442	68	87	.782	32	78	110	112	86	0	36	71	1	311	9.7	20
Tamika Whitmore 34		595	77	173	.445	49	72	.681	38	68	106	17	73	0	12	34	5	210	6.2	18
Laura Macchi 25		410	52	106	.491	41	55	.745	23	38	61	14	56	0	21	29	6	152	6.1	16
Christi Thomas 31		547	66	143	.462	28	41	.683	43	77	120	23	80	0	18	27	14	165	5.3	14
Doneeka Hodges 24		245	16	52	.308	7	10	.700	3	19	22	16	9	0	10	17	2	43	1.8	9
Raffaella Masciadri ...17		116	10	25	.400	4	10	.400	1	4	5	8	23	0	1	5	0	28	1.6	7
Monique Coker 3		14	1	1	1.000	0	0	---	1	0	1	3	2	0	0	3	1	3	1.0	3
Teresa Weatherspoon 34		292	8	25	.320	0	0	---	6	23	29	32	27	0	12	26	1	17	0.5	4
Mfon Udoka 3		19	0	2	.000	1	4	.250	2	1	3	0	5	0	0	1	0	1	0.3	1
Los Angeles 34		6975	904	2069	.437	530	722	.734	312	809	1121	626	731	6	262	529	148	2495	73.4	96
Opponents 34		6975	815	2095	.389	557	761	.732	339	727	1066	532	704	8	288	523	114	2361	69.4	93

3-pt. FG: Los Angeles 157-414 (.379)
Leslie 6-22 (.273); Mabika 38-94 (.404); Teasley 68-165 (.412); Milton-Jones 11-37 (.297); Dixon 5-11 (.455); Whitmore 7-16 (.438)
Macchi 7-26 (.269); Thomas 5-11 (.455); Hodges 4-17 (.235); Masciadri 4-11 (.364); Coker 1-1 (1.000); Weatherspoon 1-3 (.333);
Opponents 174-511 (.341)

MINNESOTA LYNX

Player	G	Min	FGM	FGA	Pct	FTM	FTA	Pct	Off	Def	Tot	Ast	PF	Dq	Stl	TO	Blk	Pts	Avg	Hi
Katie Smith	23	800	137	318	.431	98	109	.899	17	67	84	52	63	1	23	51	6	432	18.8	34
Nicole Ohlde	34	1018	136	308	.442	125	177	.706	83	111	194	60	103	1	16	74	45	397	11.7	21
Tamika Williams	34	978	102	189	.540	49	87	.563	82	123	205	38	65	0	39	66	5	254	7.5	22
Svetlana Abrosimova	22	462	49	139	.353	28	46	.609	17	57	74	45	42	0	30	43	2	146	6.6	21
Teresa Edwards	34	697	74	200	.370	21	30	.700	29	61	90	79	37	0	47	93	8	194	5.7	18
Vanessa Hayden	29	350	66	159	.415	21	38	.553	23	61	84	7	65	0	7	34	29	153	5.3	18
Helen Darling	33	707	43	130	.331	42	63	.667	11	56	67	115	83	0	30	74	4	140	4.2	14
Amanda Lassiter	33	563	47	135	.348	6	9	.667	15	65	80	37	74	0	21	40	22	127	3.8	15
Stacey Lovelace	34	388	49	122	.402	20	24	.833	25	41	66	20	47	0	18	45	9	121	3.6	12
Amber Jacobs	32	391	31	100	.310	20	22	.909	3	33	36	47	36	0	13	45	0	101	3.2	11
Michele Van Gorp	8	66	9	19	.474	4	8	.500	6	7	13	1	8	0	0	7	1	22	2.8	13
Tasha Butts	30	423	24	80	.300	18	25	.720	21	41	62	25	37	1	13	23	7	76	2.5	13
Gwen Slaughter	3	7	0	1	.000	2	2	1.000	0	1	1	0	0	0	0	0	1	2	0.7	2
Minnesota	34	6850	767	1900	.404	454	640	.709	332	724	1056	526	660	3	257	613	139	2165	63.7	85
Opponents	34	6850	804	1972	.408	490	669	.732	323	713	1036	508	676	10	333	502	133	2190	64.4	88

3-pt. FG: Minnesota 177-542 (.327)
Smith 60-139 (.432); Ohlde 0-2 (.000); Williams 1-4 (.250); Abrosimova 20-53 (.377); Edwards 25-85 (.294); Darling 12-55 (.218)
Lassiter 27-89 (.303); Lovelace 3-17 (.176); Jacobs 19-60 (.317); Van Gorp 0-1 (.000); Butts 10-37 (.270); Opponents 92-330 (.279)

NEW YORK LIBERTY

Player	G	Min	FGM	FGA	Pct	FTM	FTA	Pct	Off	Def	Tot	Ast	PF	Dq	Stl	TO	Blk	Pts	Avg	Hi
Becky Hammon	34	1130	153	354	.432	97	116	.836	17	101	118	150	73	0	58	118	2	460	13.5	28
Crystal Robinson	29	890	122	279	.437	40	43	.930	19	64	83	58	77	2	24	33	8	339	12.1	22
Elena Baranova	34	1048	146	315	.463	49	53	.925	33	213	246	67	88	0	37	80	58	394	11.6	27
Vickie Johnson	34	1119	121	293	.413	62	70	.886	37	84	121	124	75	0	25	71	4	321	9.4	18
Tari Phillips	13	311	33	95	.347	21	46	.457	28	42	70	16	41	1	14	33	10	87	6.7	13
Ann Wauters	13	271	29	66	.439	23	29	.793	10	30	40	21	28	0	4	21	8	82	6.3	15
Shameka Christon	33	560	67	189	.354	33	51	.647	19	49	68	23	71	0	9	32	9	191	5.8	18
Bethany Donaphin	26	479	49	106	.462	33	61	.541	30	41	71	16	60	0	11	21	8	131	5.0	14
La'Keshia Frett(*)	16	276	41	85	.482	20	31	.645	14	26	40	14	25	0	9	14	5	102	6.4	10
La'Keshia Frett(!)	26	347	47	98	.480	23	37	.622	17	33	50	18	29	0	10	24	7	117	4.5	10
DeTrina White	31	420	37	68	.544	8	17	.471	51	67	118	9	37	0	8	36	10	82	2.6	10
Erin Thorn	17	156	12	45	.267	1	2	.500	0	8	8	8	5	0	4	9	1	34	2.0	8
K.B. Sharp	30	240	9	37	.243	11	12	.917	5	16	21	33	7	0	6	20	1	29	1.0	6
New York	34	6900	819	1932	.424	398	531	.750	263	741	1004	539	587	3	209	506	124	2252	66.2	80
Opponents	34	6900	867	2096	.414	431	579	.744	371	730	1101	517	589	7	288	430	123	2297	67.6	88

3-pt. FG: New York 216-617 (.350)
Hammon 57-170 (.335); Robinson 55-144 (.382); Baranova 53-115 (.461); Johnson 17-60 (.283); Wauters 1-3 (.333); Thorn 9-31 (.290); Christon 24-82 (.293); Sharp 0-12 (.000); Opponents 132-416 (.317)

PHOENIX MERCURY

Player	G	Min	FGM	FGA	Pct	FTM	FTA	Pct	Off	Def	Tot	Ast	PF	Dq	Stl	TO	Blk	Pts	Avg	Hi
Diana Taurasi	34	1130	209	503	.416	98	129	.760	28	121	149	132	117	4	43	90	25	578	17.0	29
Anna DeForge	34	1152	165	396	.417	88	102	.863	23	100	123	107	51	0	51	68	8	488	14.4	31
Penny Taylor	33	1076	150	310	.484	93	108	.861	51	109	160	82	108	1	52	81	14	434	13.2	25
Plenette Pierson	31	803	112	253	.443	66	109	.606	46	85	131	26	102	4	26	49	17	290	9.4	24
Adrian Williams(>)	11	145	27	60	.450	11	14	.786	10	11	21	5	16	0	11	15	5	65	5.9	14
Gwen Jackson(*)	14	136	23	45	.511	9	11	.818	11	16	27	4	11	0	3	4	1	56	4.0	12
Gwen Jackson(!)	33	426	46	93	.495	24	32	.750	31	50	81	15	34	0	6	15	4	117	3.5	17
Slobodanka Tuvic	33	691	37	99	.374	17	24	.708	25	98	123	32	115	2	25	41	37	91	2.8	9
Tamara Moore	32	387	27	61	.443	25	29	.862	7	21	28	53	46	0	26	34	9	82	2.6	9
Nikki McCray	27	371	30	67	.448	4	7	.571	10	19	29	13	35	0	7	18	0	69	2.6	10
Shereka Wright	24	243	13	42	.310	25	32	.781	17	10	27	8	19	0	3	15	1	57	2.4	16
Kayte Christensen	32	407	19	49	.388	12	19	.632	27	42	69	23	89	2	21	26	7	50	1.6	5
Jae Cross(*)	13	128	6	18	.333	5	7	.714	5	8	13	12	10	0	5	7	2	20	1.5	7
Jae Cross(!)	18	143	6	18	.333	8	11	.727	5	9	14	13	11	0	5	9	2	23	1.3	7
Ashley Robinson	19	130	7	14	.500	3	7	.429	4	9	13	2	22	0	8	4	10	17	0.9	4
Lindsay Taylor	5	26	1	5	.200	0	0	---	0	3	3	2	7	0	1	1	1	3	0.6	9
Phoenix	34	6825	826	1922	.430	456	598	.763	264	652	916	501	748	13	282	464	137	2300	67.6	87
Opponents	34	6825	784	1845	.425	534	724	.738	309	711	1020	456	660	0	226	536	137	2235	65.7	82

3-pt. FG: Phoenix 192-519 (.370)
Taurasi 62-188 (.330); DeForge 70-181 (.387); P. Taylor 41-96 (.427); Pierson 0-3 (.000); Jackson(*) 1-5 (.200); Tuvic 0-1 (.000)
Jackson(!) 1-6 (.167); Moore 3-10 (.300); McCray 5-11 (.455); Wright 6-13 (.462); Cross(*) 3-7 (.429); Cross(!) 3-7 (.429)
Robinson 0-1 (.000); L. Taylor 1-3 (.333); Opponents 133-348 (.382)

SACRAMENTO MONARCHS

Player	G	Min	FGM	FGA	Pct	FTM	FTA	Pct	Off	Def	Tot	Ast	PF	Dq	Stl	TO	Blk	Pts	Avg	Hi
Yolanda Griffith	34	1031	177	341	.519	140	186	.753	122	124	246	42	99	2	75	59	41	494	14.5	23
Tangela Smith	34	908	165	401	.411	45	56	.804	46	92	138	50	86	0	38	53	25	380	11.2	21
Kara Lawson	34	827	103	245	.420	37	44	.841	12	65	77	68	41	0	21	53	8	294	8.6	21
DeMya Walker	34	884	111	267	.416	62	103	.602	72	71	143	86	109	1	26	86	13	284	8.4	19
Ticha Penicheiro	33	970	63	178	.354	50	70	.714	14	88	102	163	64	0	64	72	2	199	6.0	15
Ruthie Bolton	34	469	57	154	.370	14	19	.737	17	32	49	31	45	0	23	15	0	160	4.7	14
Rebekkah Brunson	34	494	59	140	.421	33	46	.717	42	80	122	19	48	0	23	29	13	151	4.4	12
Tanty Maiga	34	480	62	132	.470	16	29	.552	35	36	71	25	63	0	29	49	6	140	4.1	17
Edna Campbell	22	332	29	76	.382	0	2	.000	3	16	19	16	24	0	5	15	2	74	3.4	15
Chantelle Anderson	30	231	25	64	.391	27	37	.730	14	20	34	5	46	0	3	25	6	77	2.6	10
Lady Grooms	28	235	19	66	.288	11	12	.917	10	8	18	11	14	0	7	2	2	49	1.8	10
Giuliana Mendiola	6	39	4	8	.500	0	0	---	2	3	5	3	2	0	0	3	0	10	1.7	5
Sacramento	34	6900	874	2072	.422	435	604	.720	389	635	1024	519	641	3	314	485	118	2312	68.0	85
Opponents	34	6900	803	1872	.429	474	631	.751	310	676	986	513	646	5	241	593	117	2241	65.9	85

3-pt. FG: Sacramento 129-365 (.353)
Griffith 0-1 (.000); Smith 5-29 (.172); Lawson 51-134 (.381); Walker 0-10 (.000); Penicheiro 23-68 (.338); Bolton 32-79 (.405)
Campbell 16-39 (.410); Mendiola 2-5 (.400); Opponents 161-458 (.352)

SAN ANTONIO SILVER STARS

Player	G	Min	FGM	FGA	Pct	FTM	FTA	Pct	Off	Def	Tot	Ast	PF	Dq	Stl	TO	Blk	Pts	Avg	Hi
LaToya Thomas	31	964	171	350	.489	95	113	.841	48	90	138	42	99	1	25	56	11	440	14.2	26
Marie Ferdinand	17	509	67	162	.414	55	64	.859	18	36	54	29	34	0	32	35	2	199	11.7	26
Adrienne Goodson	34	1068	142	317	.448	84	102	.824	89	146	235	60	77	1	28	67	2	372	10.9	22
Shannon Johnson	31	954	89	234	.380	82	107	.766	14	68	82	136	69	2	48	99	4	287	9.3	25
Agnieszka Bibrzycka	24	465	55	151	.364	23	26	.885	5	23	28	40	38	0	21	32	7	159	6.6	19
Margo Dydek	34	682	90	208	.433	44	58	.759	30	138	168	60	70	0	20	64	48	225	6.6	15
Jessie Hicks	27	371	52	111	.468	23	38	.605	23	34	57	18	57	1	17	34	13	127	4.7	12
Semeka Randall	29	462	53	143	.371	30	48	.625	26	34	60	20	41	0	22	28	4	136	4.7	10
Adrian Williams(*)	12	149	15	45	.333	2	7	.286	6	22	28	8	19	0	8	12	1	32	2.7	10
Adrian Williams(!)	23	294	42	105	.400	13	21	.619	16	33	49	13	35	0	19	27	6	97	4.2	14
Jocelyn Penn	1	3	2	2	1.000	0	0	---	0	1	1	0	0	0	0	0	0	4	4.0	4
Gwen Jackson(>)	19	290	23	48	.479	15	21	.714	20	34	54	11	23	0	3	11	3	61	3.2	17
Nevriye Yilmaz	7	77	6	24	.250	6	6	1.000	3	7	10	2	15	0	3	4	1	19	2.7	8
Toccara Williams	26	417	16	46	.348	22	29	.759	7	32	39	43	36	0	35	31	5	55	2.1	10
Tai Dillard	23	205	16	54	.296	0	1	.000	2	12	14	19	18	0	4	14	1	37	1.6	11
Mandisa Stevenson	29	259	15	45	.333	7	8	.875	11	24	35	5	32	0	6	11	4	38	1.3	9
San Antonio	34	6875	812	1940	.419	488	628	.777	302	701	1003	493	628	5	272	513	106	2191	64.4	82
Opponents	34	6875	888	2003	.443	416	564	.738	324	710	1034	575	624	7	280	492	129	2364	69.5	87

3-pt. FG: San Antonio 79-247 (.320)
Thomas 3-8 (.375); Ferdinand 10-27 (.370); Goodson 4-16 (.250); Johnson 27-76 (.355); Bibrzycka 26-84 (.310); Dydek 1-2 (.500)
Randall 0-5 (.000); Jackson(>) 0-1 (.000); Yilmaz 1-7 (.143); T. Williams 1-2 (.500); Dillard 5-18 (.278); Stevenson 1-1 (1.000);
Opponents 172-469 (.367)

SEATTLE STORM

Player	G	Min	FGM	FGA	Pct	FTM	FTA	Pct	Off	Def	Tot	Ast	PF	Dq	Stl	TO	Blk	Pts	Avg	Hi
Lauren Jackson	31	1070	220	460	.478	142	175	.811	64	143	207	51	93	0	31	67	62	634	20.5	33
Sue Bird	34	1136	151	326	.463	73	85	.859	22	84	106	184	48	0	51	87	5	439	12.9	25
Betty Lennox	32	920	139	330	.421	58	68	.853	28	131	159	79	89	0	34	77	3	358	11.2	23
Sheri Sam	34	1018	117	284	.412	65	76	.855	42	97	139	82	108	1	53	63	6	310	9.1	21
Kamila Vodichkova	34	873	94	241	.390	84	108	.778	65	103	168	55	110	5	32	73	12	273	8.0	18
Janell Burse	29	514	51	119	.429	39	67	.582	51	45	96	19	84	2	23	41	36	141	4.9	12
Tully Bevilaqua	34	358	24	60	.400	20	29	.690	6	20	26	29	48	0	38	26	2	79	2.3	10
Alicia Thompson	23	182	24	54	.444	1	2	.500	8	16	24	9	9	0	6	7	0	52	2.3	9
Michelle Greco	13	73	10	18	.556	9	13	.692	3	7	10	8	6	0	3	8	0	29	2.2	6
Simone Edwards	23	257	20	55	.364	8	19	.421	25	31	56	5	25	0	8	13	3	48	2.1	8
Adia Barnes	34	402	21	69	.304	22	31	.710	33	30	63	31	38	0	23	24	2	67	2.0	7
Trina Frierson	5	22	2	9	.222	3	3	1.000	3	2	5	0	7	0	0	1	0	7	1.4	3
Seattle	34	6825	873	2025	.431	524	676	.775	350	709	1059	552	665	8	302	499	131	2437	71.7	93
Opponents	34	6825	851	1989	.428	423	592	.715	303	679	982	507	678	4	252	527	137	2264	66.6	85

3-pt. FG: Seattle 167-439 (.380)
Jackson 52-115 (.452); Bird 64-146 (.438); Lennox 22-83 (.265); Sam 11-42 (.262); Vodichkova 1-2 (.500); Bevilaqua 11-26 (.423)
Thompson 3-16 (.188); Greco 0-2 (.000); Barnes 3-6 (.500); Frierson 0-1 (.000); Opponents 139-391 (.355)

WASHINGTON MYSTICS

Player	G	Min	FGM	FGA	Pct	FTM	FTA	Pct	Off	Def	Tot	Ast	PF	Dq	Stl	TO	Blk	Pts	Avg	Hi
Chamique Holdsclaw	23	801	162	403	.402	106	132	.803	51	140	191	56	67	0	39	57	18	437	19.0	29
Alana Beard	34	1025	159	380	.418	107	149	.718	28	115	143	91	98	0	69	80	34	446	13.1	27
Chasity Melvin	34	825	104	256	.406	85	111	.766	63	68	131	37	89	0	15	52	18	293	8.6	22
S. Dales-Schuman	31	782	87	228	.382	40	55	.727	17	47	64	78	61	0	20	37	3	254	8.2	17
Murriel Page	33	809	81	175	.463	22	40	.550	40	100	140	36	85	1	25	30	16	184	5.6	13
Nakia Sanford	31	653	63	126	.500	43	75	.573	53	101	154	18	99	0	18	37	16	169	5.5	17
Tamicha Jackson	25	405	57	135	.422	11	16	.688	7	30	37	45	21	0	20	28	1	135	5.4	17
Coco Miller	33	637	72	167	.431	11	14	.786	35	28	63	43	60	0	18	27	3	160	4.8	15
Kiesha Brown	26	371	35	88	.398	21	24	.875	9	41	50	42	21	0	13	33	2	104	4.0	13
Aiysha Smith.............	29	403	42	103	.408	22	34	.647	26	43	69	15	38	0	17	21	12	115	4.0	10
Kaayla Chones	13	115	11	27	.407	6	11	.545	8	9	17	4	13	0	1	11	4	28	2.2	7
Shaunzinski Gortman	.4	24	0	0	---	0	0	---	0	4	4	2	0	0	0	2	1	0	0.0	0
Washington	34	6850	873	2088	.418	474	661	.717	337	726	1063	467	652	1	255	424	128	2325	68.4	84
Opponents	34	6850	864	2013	.429	510	686	.743	336	770	1106	534	627	3	237	492	111	2384	70.1	96

3-pt. FG: Washington 105-283 (.371)

Holdsclaw 7-17 (.412); Beard 21-56 (.375); Dales-Schuman 40-119 (.336); Page 0-3 (.000); Jackson 10-25 (.400); Miller 5-19 (.263) Brown 13-28 (.464); Smith 9-16 (.563); Opponents 146-425 (.344)

(*) Statistics with this team only
(!) Totals with all teams
(>) Continued season with another team

PLAYOFF RESULTS

FIRST ROUND

Connecticut defeats Washington, 2-1

September 25	Washington 67, Connecticut 59
September 27	Connecticut 80, Washington 70
September 29	Connecticut 76, Washington 56

New York defeates Detroit, 2-1

September 24	New York 75, Detroit 62
September 26	Detroit 76, New York 66
September 28	New York 66, Detroit 64

Sacramento defeats Los Angeles, 2-1

September 24	Sacramento 72, Los Angeles 52
September 26	Los Angeles 71, Sacramento 57
September 28	Sacramento 73, Los Angeles 58

Seattle defeats Minnesota, 2-0

| September 25 | Seattle 70, Minnesota 58 |
| September 27 | Seattle 64, Minnesota 54 |

CONFERENCE FINALS

Connecticut defeats New York, 2-0

| October 1 | Connecticut 61, New York 51 |
| October 3 | Connecticut 60, New York 57 |

Seattle defeats Sacramento, 2-1

October 1	Sacramento 74, Seattle 72 (OT)
October 3	Seattle 66, Sacramento 54
October 5	Seattle 82, Sacramento 62

WNBA FINALS

Seattle defeats Connecticut, 2-1

October 8	Connecticut 68, Seattle 64
October 10	Seattle 67, Connecticut 65
October 12	Seattle 74, Connecticut 60

TEAM STANDINGS

OFFENSIVE

TEAM	G	FG	FGA	PCT	FG3	FG3A	PCT	FT	FTA	PCT	OFF	DEF	REB	AST	PF	DQ	STL	TO	BLK	PTS	AVG
Sea..........	8	209	492	.425	42	91	.462	99	126	.786	85	175	260	133	144	0	67	127	31	559	69.9
Det.	3	71	167	.425	5	15	.333	55	78	.705	30	66	96	45	44	0	27	41	13	202	67.3
Conn.......	8	191	470	.406	37	102	.363	110	143	.769	78	173	251	114	128	0	71	105	20	529	66.1
Sac.......	6	148	363	.408	20	72	.278	76	103	.738	61	114	175	89	97	0	66	84	33	392	65.3
Wash.......	3	67	170	.394	7	23	.304	52	66	.788	34	70	104	31	58	0	17	40	15	193	64.3
N.Y..........	5	120	291	.412	38	106	.358	37	50	.740	45	84	129	74	98	1	39	67	20	315	63.0
L.A...........	3	67	170	.394	13	40	.325	34	38	.895	25	68	93	46	66	1	16	52	10	181	60.3
Minn........	2	42	100	.420	9	27	.333	19	30	.633	16	38	54	27	33	0	11	40	8	112	56.0

DEFENSIVE

Team	FG	FGA	PCT	FG3	FG3A	PCT	FT	FTA	PCT	OFF	DEF	REB	AST	PF	DQ	STL	TO	BLK	PTS	AVG	DIFF
Sea.	190	463	.410	32	100	.320	83	120	.692	69	150	219	104	135	0	78	128	38	495	61.9	+8.0
Conn.	186	477	.390	26	82	.317	108	137	.788	86	176	262	92	147	0	58	112	34	506	63.3	+2.9

Team	FG	FGA	PCT	FG3	FG3A	PCT	FT	FTA	PCT	OFF	DEF	REB	AST	PF	DQ	STL	TO	BLK	PTS	AVG	DIFF
N.Y.	116	276	.420	13	39	.333	78	107	.729	54	110	164	74	64	0	44	70	17	323	64.6	-1.6
Sac.	144	340	.424	38	84	.452	75	87	.862	54	128	182	102	123	1	37	105	21	401	66.8	-1.5
Minn.	55	125	.440	7	20	.350	17	25	.680	20	41	61	40	34	0	24	27	10	134	67.0	-11.0
L.A.	74	186	.398	11	41	.268	43	59	.729	35	66	101	48	45	0	30	38	14	202	67.3	-7.0
Det.	78	181	.431	29	74	.392	22	31	.710	29	52	81	50	62	1	20	42	11	207	69.0	-1.7
Wash.	72	175	.411	15	36	.417	56	68	.824	27	65	92	49	58	0	23	34	5	215	71.7	-7.3
Avgs	114	278	.412	21	60	.359	60	79	.760	47	99	145	70	84	0	39	70	19	310	65.3	—
Totals	915	2223	—	171	476	—	482	634	---	374	788	1162	559	668	2	314	556	150	2483	—	—

TEAM COMPARISONS

TEAM	Points Per Game		Field Goal Percentage		Turnovers Per Game		Rebound Percentages			Below 70 Pts.		Overtime Games		3 PTS or Less		10 PTS or More	
	OWN	OPP	OWN	OPP	OWN	OPP	OFF	DEF	TOT	OWN	OPP	W	L	W	L	W	L
Connecticut	66.1	63.3	.406	.390*	13.1*	14.0	.307	.668	.488	6	6	0	0	1	1	3	1
Detroit	67.3	69.0	.425*	.431	13.7	14.0	.366*	.695	.530	2	2	0	0	0	1	1	1
Los Angeles	60.3	67.3	.394	.398	17.3	12.7	.275	.660	.467	2	1	0	0	0	0	1	2
Minnesota	56.0	67.0	.420	.440	20.0	13.5	.281	.655	.468	2	1	0	0	0	0	0	2
New York	63.0	64.6	.412	.420	13.4	14.0	.290	.609	.450	4	4	0	0	1	1	1	2
Sacramento	65.3	66.8	.408	.424	14.0	17.5*	.323	.679	.501	3	3	1	0	1	0	2	3
Seattle	69.9*	61.9*	.425	.410	15.9	16.0	.362	.717	.539*	4	7	0	1	1	1	5	0
Washington	64.3	71.7	.394	.411	13.3	11.3	.343	.722*	.533	2	1	0	0	0	0	0	2
COMPOSITE; 19 games	65.3	65.3	.412	.412	14.6	14.6	.322	.678	—	25	25	1	1	4	4	13	13

* - League Leader

REBOUND PERCENTAGES
OFF. - Percentage of a given team's missed shots which that team rebounds.
DEF. - Percentage of opponents' missed shots which a given team rebounds.
TOT. - Average of offensive and defensive rebound percentages.

INDIVIDUAL PLAYOFF STATISTICS, TEAM BY TEAM

CONNECTICUT SUN

Player	G	Min	FGM	FGA	Pct	FTM	FTA	Pct	Off	Def	Tot	Ast	PF	Dq	Stl	TO	Blk	Pts	Avg	Hi
Nykesha Sales	8	260	44	102	.431	15	22	.682	12	31	43	11	22	0	25	20	6	118	14.8	32
Lindsay Whalen	8	255	30	65	.462	43	53	.811	5	13	18	41	23	0	11	17	3	107	13.4	21
T. McWilliams-Franklin	8	252	35	87	.402	12	18	.667	19	40	59	15	22	0	12	13	6	83	10.4	18
Katie Douglas	8	268	23	66	.348	25	27	.926	9	23	32	22	19	0	10	16	0	82	10.3	18
Asjha Jones	8	171	26	53	.491	7	11	.636	8	13	21	11	10	0	5	18	1	59	7.4	14
Wendy Palmer	8	156	18	49	.367	5	8	.625	10	25	35	1	11	0	3	8	3	44	5.5	16
Le'coe Willingham	8	60	7	18	.389	3	4	.750	8	11	19	1	4	0	3	1	1	17	2.1	5
Debbie Black	8	73	4	14	.286	0	0	—	2	9	11	7	12	0	4	6	0	9	1.1	5
Jessica Brungo	8	101	3	15	.200	0	0	—	5	8	13	5	5	0	1	2	0	8	1.0	6
Candace Futrell	2	3	1	1	1.000	0	0	—	0	0	0	0	0	0	0	0	0	2	1.0	2
Jen Derevjanik	1	1	0	0	—	0	0	—	0	0	0	0	0	0	0	0	0	0	0.0	0
Connecticut	8	1600	191	470	.406	110	143	.769	78	173	251	114	128	0	71	105	20	529	66.1	80
Opponents	8	1600	186	477	.390	108	137	.788	86	176	262	92	147	0	58	112	34	506	63.3	74

3-pt. FG: Connecticut 37-102 (.363)
Sales 15-29 (.517); Whalen 4-11 (.364); McWilliams-Franklin 1-2 (.500); Douglas 11-37 (.297); Palmer 3-12 (.250); Black 1-1 (1.000); Brungo 2-10 (.200); Opponents 26-82 (.317)

DETROIT SHOCK

Player	G	Min	FGM	FGA	Pct	FTM	FTA	Pct	Off	Def	Tot	Ast	PF	Dq	Stl	TO	Blk	Pts	Avg	Hi
Deanna Nolan	3	119	18	45	.400	14	15	.933	3	11	14	7	5	0	5	10	0	54	18.0	20
Cheryl Ford	3	111	17	38	.447	14	22	.636	5	27	32	1	3	0	4	8	7	48	16.0	21
Ruth Riley	3	95	9	21	.429	11	15	.733	7	8	15	9	9	0	2	2	6	29	9.7	13
Merlakia Jones	3	61	11	26	.423	1	1	1.000	3	9	12	2	8	0	4	2	0	23	7.7	13
Elaine Powell	3	97	7	14	.500	9	17	.529	4	2	6	21	7	0	10	8	0	23	7.7	10
Barbara Farris	3	78	6	17	.353	6	8	.750	8	7	15	2	5	0	1	5	0	18	6.0	11
Chandi Jones	2	10	1	4	.250	0	0	---	0	0	0	1	2	0	0	1	0	2	1.0	2
Stacey Thomas	3	7	1	1	1.000	0	0	---	0	1	1	0	1	0	1	0	0	3	1.0	3
Iciss Tillis	3	18	1	1	1.000	0	0	---	0	1	1	1	3	0	0	1	0	2	0.7	2
Ayana Walker	2	4	0	0	---	0	0	---	0	0	0	0	1	0	0	1	0	0	0.0	0
Detroit	3	600	71	167	.425	55	78	.705	30	66	96	45	44	0	27	41	13	202	67.3	76
Opponents	3	600	78	181	.431	22	31	.710	29	52	81	50	62	1	20	42	11	207	69.0	75

3-pt. FG: Detroit 5-15 (.333)
Nolan 4-13 (.308); M. Jones 0-1 (.000); Thomas 1-1 (1.000); Opponents 29-74 (.392)

LOS ANGELES SPARKS

Player	G	Min	FGM	FGA	Pct	FTM	FTA	Pct	Off	Def	Tot	Ast	PF	Dq	Stl	TO	Blk	Pts	Avg	Hi
Mwadi Mabika	3	107	17	46	.370	15	16	.938	3	5	8	10	10	0	7	6	0	56	18.7	22
Lisa Leslie	3	110	14	31	.452	6	8	.750	4	22	26	2	10	0	1	8	8	34	11.3	13
Tamecka Dixon	3	100	12	30	.400	7	8	.875	4	13	17	9	12	1	2	10	0	31	10.3	17
Christi Thomas	3	100	12	22	.545	0	0	—	11	12	23	2	14	0	1	2	1	24	8.0	12
Nikki Teasley	3	88	5	19	.263	4	4	1.000	1	2	3	16	10	0	2	14	1	19	6.3	16
Tamika Whitmore	3	39	4	10	.400	2	2	1.000	0	6	6	1	4	0	0	3	0	10	3.3	6
Laura Macchi	1	15	1	6	.167	0	0	—	1	3	4	1	4	0	1	0	0	2	2.0	2
Doneeka Hodges	3	29	2	5	.400	0	0	—	0	4	4	4	0	0	1	3	0	5	1.7	5
Raffaella Masciadri	1	2	0	0	—	0	0	—	0	0	0	0	0	0	0	0	0	0	0.0	0
Teresa Weatherspoon	2	10	0	1	.000	0	0	—	1	1	2	1	1	0	1	3	0	0	0.0	0
Los Angeles	3	600	67	170	.394	34	38	.895	25	68	93	46	66	1	16	52	10	181	60.3	71
Opponents	3	600	74	186	.398	43	59	.729	35	66	101	48	45	0	30	38	14	202	67.3	73

3-pt. FG: Los Angeles 13-40 (.325)
Mabika 7-20 (.350); Thomas 0-1 (.000); Teasley 5-15 (.333); Whitmore 0-2 (.000); Macchi 0-1 (.000); Hodges 1-1 (1.000); Opponents 11-41 (.268)

MINNESOTA LYNX

Player	G	Min	FGM	FGA	Pct	FTM	FTA	Pct	Off	Def	Tot	Ast	PF	Dq	Stl	TO	Blk	Pts	Avg	Hi
Nicole Ohlde	2	74	11	23	.478	6	10	.600	4	6	10	9	5	0	1	6	0	28	14.0	17
Tamika Williams	2	72	10	16	.625	4	4	1.000	5	12	17	6	4	0	1	1	0	24	12.0	16
Svetlana Abrosimova	2	67	8	23	.348	2	4	.500	3	6	9	3	7	0	1	3	2	20	10.0	14
Amanda Lassiter	2	30	3	7	.429	0	0	---	0	4	4	1	5	0	2	4	3	9	4.5	9
Amber Jacobs	2	36	3	5	.600	1	2	.500	0	1	1	2	0	0	0	4	0	8	4.0	8
Helen Darling	2	44	2	9	.222	1	2	.500	2	1	3	4	0	0	3	11	0	7	3.5	4
Teresa Edwards	2	43	1	6	.167	3	4	.750	1	4	5	2	5	0	3	4	1	6	3.0	4
Stacey Lovelace	2	17	2	4	.500	2	4	.500	1	2	3	1	0	0	1	0	0	6	3.0	6
Vanessa Hayden	2	16	2	7	.286	0	0	---	0	2	2	0	2	0	0	3	1	4	2.0	2
Tasha Butts	1	1	0	0	---	0	0	---	0	0	0	0	1	0	0	2	0	0	0.0	0
Minnesota	2	400	42	100	.420	19	30	.633	16	38	54	27	33	0	11	40	8	112	56.0	58
Opponents	2	400	55	125	.440	17	25	.680	20	41	61	40	34	0	24	27	10	134	67.0	70

3-pt. FG: Minnesota 9-27 (.333)
Williams 0-2 (.000); Abrosimova 2-8 (.250); Lassiter 3-6 (.500); Jacobs 1-2 (.500); Darling 2-3 (.667); Edwards 1-5 (.200) Lovelace 0-1 (.000); Opponents 7-20 (.350)

NEW YORK LIBERTY

Player	G	Min	FGM	FGA	Pct	FTM	FTA	Pct	Off	Def	Tot	Ast	PF	Dq	Stl	TO	Blk	Pts	Avg	Hi
Crystal Robinson	5	175	29	58	.500	4	5	.800	4	12	16	13	16	1	9	8	2	75	15.0	17
Becky Hammon	5	178	20	51	.392	4	5	.400	0	13	13	17	12	0	6	19	0	53	10.6	20
La'Keshia Frett	5	116	20	48	.417	4	4	1.000	5	12	17	6	12	0	4	7	3	44	8.8	20
Elena Baranova	5	154	15	38	.395	8	10	.800	7	27	34	10	18	0	4	12	9	42	8.4	17
Vickie Johnson	5	161	18	39	.359	11	12	.917	11	11	22	16	10	0	5	4	1	41	8.2	19
Shameka Christon	5	63	8	21	.381	6	9	.667	4	5	9	4	13	0	2	3	0	28	5.6	13
Bethany Donaphin	5	96	10	25	.400	2	5	.400	8	3	11	2	9	0	7	5	2	22	4.4	6
Erin Thorn	2	3	1	1	1.000	0	0	---	0	0	0	0	0	0	0	0	0	3	1.5	3
K.B. Sharp	5	20	2	5	.400	0	0	---	0	1	1	5	2	0	0	2	0	5	1.0	5
DeTrina White	5	34	1	5	.200	0	0	---	3	3	6	1	6	0	2	4	0	2	0.4	2
New York	5	1000	120	291	.412	37	50	.740	45	84	129	74	98	1	39	67	20	315	63.0	75
Opponents	5	1000	116	276	.420	78	107	.729	54	110	164	74	64	0	44	70	17	323	64.6	76

3-pt. FG: New York 38-106 (.358)
Robinson 13-33 (.394); Hammon 11-33 (.333); Frett 0-1 (.000); Baranova 4-13 (.308); Johnson 2-10 (.200); Christon 6-14 (.429) Thorn 1-1 (1.000); Sharp 1-1 (1.000); Opponents 13-39 (.333)

SACRAMENTO MONARCHS

Player	G	Min	FGM	FGA	Pct	FTM	FTA	Pct	Off	Def	Tot	Ast	PF	Dq	Stl	TO	Blk	Pts	Avg	Hi
Tangela Smith	6	185	38	86	.442	17	22	.773	11	20	31	8	17	0	9	11	12	95	15.8	24
Yolanda Griffith	6	204	31	63	.492	20	24	.833	20	29	49	8	15	0	12	12	6	82	13.7	17
DeMya Walker	6	173	30	54	.556	11	17	.647	11	9	20	14	12	0	6	18	8	71	11.8	17
Kara Lawson	6	153	20	54	.370	8	9	.889	3	12	15	11	10	0	8	5	1	58	9.7	17
Edna Campbell	6	102	10	25	.400	0	0	---	0	11	11	5	6	0	3	2	0	26	4.3	8
Ticha Penicheiro	6	193	6	27	.222	11	16	.688	4	16	20	32	17	0	15	19	2	25	4.2	8
Rebekkah Brunson	6	80	7	20	.350	5	7	.714	8	9	17	3	6	0	5	3	4	19	3.2	5
Ruthie Bolton	6	53	5	18	.167	3	4	.750	3	4	7	3	7	0	2	3	0	13	2.2	5
Chantelle Anderson	2	11	1	2	.500	1	2	.500	0	2	2	1	1	0	0	1	0	3	1.5	4
Tanty Maiga	6	68	2	13	.154	0	4	.250	3	3	6	4	11	0	7	7	0	5	0.8	2
Lady Grooms	1	3	0	1	.000	0	0	---	0	0	0	0	0	0	0	0	0	0	0.0	0
Sacramento	6	1225	148	363	.408	76	103	.738	61	114	175	89	97	0	66	84	33	392	65.3	74
Opponents	6	1225	144	340	.424	75	87	.862	54	128	182	102	123	1	37	105	21	401	66.8	82

3-pt. FG: Sacramento 20-72 (.278)
Smith 2-9 (.222); Lawson 10-24 (.417); Campbell 6-14 (.429); Penicheiro 2-15 (.133); Bolton 0-9 (.000); Maiga 0-1 (.000) Opponents 38-84 (.452)

SEATTLE STORM

Player	G	Min	FGM	FGA	Pct	FTM	FTA	Pct	Off	Def	Tot	Ast	PF	Dq	Stl	TO	Blk	Pts	Avg	Hi
Lauren Jackson	8	287	53	113	.469	35	39	.897	20	40	60	11	23	0	8	16	9	157	19.6	31
Betty Lennox	8	251	44	97	.454	21	24	.875	4	25	29	21	21	0	8	23	1	117	14.6	27

REVIEW 2004 Playoffs

Player	G	Min	FGM	FGA	Pct	FTM	FTA	Pct	Off	Def	Tot	Ast	PF	Dq	Stl	TO	Blk	Pts	Avg	Hi
Sue Bird	8	233	23	61	.377	16	21	.762	5	21	26	42	13	0	12	16	0	68	8.5	12
Sheri Sam	8	248	25	76	.329	6	9	.667	13	31	44	28	21	0	10	25	0	59	7.4	12
Kamila Vodichkova	8	204	19	47	.404	11	18	.611	13	17	30	6	16	0	7	13	7	49	6.1	14
Alicia Thompson	8	83	15	33	.455	3	3	1.000	6	9	15	6	6	0	2	7	1	39	4.9	10
Janell Burse	8	109	12	27	.444	3	4	.750	10	8	18	1	17	0	9	8	10	27	3.4	6
Tully Bevilaqua	8	111	8	17	.471	3	4	.750	3	13	16	11	12	0	8	9	1	22	2.8	9
Simone Edwards	7	54	6	9	.667	0	0	---	7	7	14	1	5	0	2	1	1	12	1.7	6
Adia Barnes	6	39	3	11	.273	1	4	.250	4	4	8	5	10	0	3	1	1	7	1.2	3
Michelle Greco	4	6	1	1	1.000	0	0	---	0	0	0	0	0	0	1	0	0	2	0.5	2
Seattle	8	1625	209	492	.425	99	126	.786	85	175	260	133	144	0	67	127	31	559	69.9	82
Opponents	8	1625	190	463	.410	83	120	.692	69	150	219	104	135	0	78	128	38	495	61.9	74

3-pt. FG: Seattle 42-91 (.462)
Jackson 16-22 (.727); Lennox 8-18 (.444); Bird 6-20 (.300); Sam 3-12 (.250); Thompson 6-12 (.500); Bevilaqua 3-7 (.429);
Opponents 32-100 (.320)

WASHINGTON MYSTICS

Player	G	Min	FGM	FGA	Pct	FTM	FTA	Pct	Off	Def	Tot	Ast	PF	Dq	Stl	TO	Blk	Pts	Avg	Hi
Alana Beard	3	102	18	41	.439	13	13	1.000	2	13	15	9	8	0	6	10	8	50	16.7	22
Chasity Melvin	3	104	13	31	.419	15	21	.714	7	18	25	6	10	0	1	2	4	41	13.7	17
S. Dales-Schuman	3	87	8	20	.400	10	15	.667	6	9	15	5	8	0	2	8	0	27	9.0	10
Tamicha Jackson	3	42	6	13	.462	2	2	1.000	0	1	1	4	7	0	0	2	0	17	5.7	17
Coco Miller	3	51	7	19	.368	2	2	1.000	3	4	7	2	2	0	5	2	0	16	5.3	8
Aiysha Smith	3	53	5	15	.333	4	5	.800	5	3	8	1	5	0	1	4	0	15	5.0	10
Nakia Sanford	3	62	4	12	.333	5	6	.833	8	11	19	0	12	0	2	7	1	13	4.3	6
Murriel Page	3	90	5	16	.313	1	2	.500	3	11	14	4	5	0	3	1	1	11	3.7	5
Kiesha Brown	2	3	1	1	1.000	0	0	—	0	0	0	0	0	0	0	0	0	3	1.5	3
Kaayla Chones	2	4	0	1	.000	0	0	—	0	0	0	0	1	0	0	0	1	0	0.0	0
Shaunzinski Gortman	1	2	0	1	.000	0	0	—	0	0	0	0	0	0	0	0	0	0	0.0	0
Washington	3	600	67	170	.394	52	66	.788	34	70	104	31	58	0	17	40	15	193	64.3	70
Opponents	3	600	72	175	.411	56	68	.824	27	65	92	49	58	0	23	34	5	215	71.7	80

3-pt. FG: Washington 7-23 (.304)
Beard 1-4 (.250); Dales-Schuman 1-9 (.111); Jackson 3-5 (.600); Smith 1-4 (.250); Brown 1-1 (1.000); Opponents 15-36 (.417)

(*) Statistics with this team only
(!) Totals with all teams
(>) Continued season with another team

REVIEW 2004 Playoffs/Finals

INDIVIDUAL FINALS STATISTICS, TEAM BY TEAM

CONNECTICUT SUN

Player	G	Min	FGM	FGA	Pct	FTM	FTA	Pct	Off	Def	Tot	Ast	PF	Dq	Stl	TO	Blk	Pts	Avg	Hi
Nykesha Sales	3	100	22	41	.537	6	7	.857	6	14	20	2	9	0	10	8	4	57	19.0	32
Katie Douglas	3	102	11	32	.344	11	13	.846	3	10	13	4	6	0	7	6	0	38	12.7	18
Lindsay Whalen	3	97	10	27	.370	9	15	.600	0	5	5	18	9	0	4	6	2	30	10.0	11
T. McWilliams-Franklin	3	98	10	32	.313	2	4	.500	7	12	19	6	8	0	5	5	3	22	7.3	10
Asjha Jones	3	59	9	17	.529	1	4	.250	3	3	6	3	4	0	2	9	0	19	6.3	12
Wendy Palmer	3	53	7	17	.412	1	2	.500	3	7	10	0	5	0	1	3	2	16	5.3	16
Le'coe Willingham	3	26	3	9	.333	1	1	1.000	4	6	10	0	0	0	0	1	0	7	2.3	5
Candace Futrell	1	2	1	1	1.000	0	0	—	0	0	0	0	0	0	0	0	0	2	2.0	2
Debbie Black	3	27	1	5	.200	0	0	—	0	4	4	1	6	0	2	3	0	2	0.7	2
Jessica Brungo	3	36	0	5	.000	0	0	—	1	3	4	2	3	0	1	0	0	0	0.0	0
Connecticut	3	600	74	186	.398	31	46	.674	27	64	91	36	50	0	31	42	11	193	64.3	68
Opponents	3	600	77	197	.391	41	52	.788	36	74	110	37	53	0	22	47	10	205	68.3	74

3-pt. FG: Connecticut 14-42 (.333)
Sales 7-11 (.636); Douglas 5-16 (.313); Whalen 1-6 (.167); Palmer 1-6 (.167); Brungo 0-3 (.000); Opponents 10-27 (.370)

SEATTLE STORM

Player	G	Min	FGM	FGA	Pct	FTM	FTA	Pct	Off	Def	Tot	Ast	PF	Dq	Stl	TO	Blk	Pts	Avg	Hi
Betty Lennox	3	103	25	50	.500	14	16	.875	2	11	13	6	10	0	4	8	0	67	22.3	27
Lauren Jackson	3	111	16	45	.356	9	11	.818	7	17	24	6	6	0	4	6	4	44	14.7	16
Sue Bird	3	94	9	23	.391	11	13	.846	3	11	14	11	7	0	4	10	0	30	10.0	12
Kamila Vodichkova	3	64	8	21	.381	5	9	.556	5	10	15	2	6	0	1	7	2	21	7.0	14
Sheri Sam	3	82	5	19	.263	2	3	.667	5	7	12	7	7	0	4	5	0	12	4.0	5
Alicia Thompson	3	38	4	11	.364	2	0	---	4	4	8	3	3	0	1	4	0	10	3.3	8
Simone Edwards	3	30	4	7	.571	0	0	---	6	6	12	1	3	0	0	2	1	8	2.7	6
Tully Bevilaqua	3	37	3	7	.429	0	0	---	1	3	4	1	7	0	2	3	0	7	2.3	4
Janell Burse	3	33	3	12	.250	0	0	---	2	5	7	0	2	0	2	1	3	6	2.0	4
Adia Barnes	2	7	0	2	.000	0	0	---	1	0	1	0	2	0	0	0	0	0	0.0	0
Michelle Greco	1	1	0	0	---	0	0	---	0	0	0	0	0	0	0	0	0	0	0.0	0

| | | | | | REBOUNDS | | | | | | | | | | | | | SCORING | | | |
Player	G	Min	FGM	FGA	Pct	FTM	FTA	Pct	Off	Def	Tot	Ast	PF	Dq	Stl	TO	Blk	Pts	Avg	Hi
Seattle	3	600	77	197	.391	41	52	.788	36	74	110	37	53	0	22	47	10	205	68.3	74
Opponents	3	600	74	186	.398	31	46	.674	27	64	91	36	50	0	31	42	11	193	64.3	68

3-pt. FG: Seattle 10-27 (.370)
Lennox 3-5 (.600); Jackson 3-5 (.600); Bird 1-8 (.125); Sam 0-2 (.000); Thompson 2-6 (.333); Bevilaqua 1-1 (1.000); Opponents 14-42 (.333)

(*) Statistics with this team only
(!) Totals with all teams
(>) Continued season with another team

FINALS BOX SCORES

GAME 1
At Mohegan Sun Arena, October 8, 2004

OFFICIALS: June Courteau, Lisa Mattingly, Michael Price.   TIME OF GAME: 1:59.   ATTENDANCE: 9,341.

SCORE BY PERIODS	1	2	FINAL
Seattle	29	35	64
Connecticut	33	35	68

VISITORS: Seattle, 4-2. Head Coach: Anne Donovan.

NO	PLAYER	MIN	FG	FGA	3P	3PA	FT	FTA	OR	DR	TOT	A	PF	ST	TO	TEC	PTS
15	Lauren Jackson, F	40	6	19	2	4	2	2	5	1	6	1	1	2	3	0	16
55	Sheri Sam, F	24	2	7	0	1	1	1	2	1	3	2	2	2	2	0	5
7	Kamila Vodichkova, C	21	1	4	0	0	0	0	0	6	6	0	0	1	3	0	2
10	Sue Bird, G	32	4	11	1	4	3	4	3	3	6	4	5	0	6	0	12
22	Betty Lennox, G	38	7	17	3	4	0	0	2	6	8	3	3	1	1	0	17
33	Janell Burse	11	2	5	0	0	0	0	0	2	2	0	2	0	0	0	4
43	Alicia Thompson	16	1	7	0	3	0	0	3	0	3	2	1	0	2	0	2
44	Tully Bevilaqua	10	2	2	0	0	0	0	0	0	0	0	3	0	0	0	4
4	Simone Edwards	8	1	2	0	0	0	0	5	3	8	1	0	0	0	0	2
32	Adia Barnes									DNP							
20	Michelle Greco									DNP							
	TOTALS	200	26	74	6	16	6	7	20	22	42	13	17	6	17	0	64
	PERCENTAGES		35.1	37.5		85.7											

TM REB: 6 TOT TO: 18 (7 PTS)

HOME: Connecticut, 5-1. Head Coach: Mike Thibault.

NO	PLAYER	MIN	FG	FGA	3P	3PA	FT	FTA	OR	DR	TOT	A	PF	ST	TO	TEC	PTS
3	Wendy Palmer, F	30	7	13	1	3	1	2	3	4	7	0	2	1	1	0	16
42	Nykesha Sales, F	32	3	7	0	0	1	2	4	5	9	2	1	4	4	0	7
11	McWilliams-Frank, C	33	5	12	0	0	0	1	1	6	7	3	3	4	0	0	10
13	Lindsay Whalen, G	32	4	9	1	2	2	4	0	3	3	9	2	2	2	0	11
32	Katie Douglas, G	31	6	11	3	6	3	4	0	2	2	2	1	2	4	0	18
43	Le'coe Willingham	4	0	0	0	0	0	0	0	1	1	0	0	0	0	0	0
15	Asjha Jones	13	3	4	0	0	0	1	0	1	1	0	1	0	3	0	6
22	Jessica Brungo	17	0	4	0	2	0	0	1	2	3	2	1	0	0	0	0
24	Debbie Black	8	0	1	0	0	0	0	0	0	0	1	3	2	1	0	0
34	Jen Derevjanik									DNP							
12	Candace Futrell									DNP							
	TOTALS	200	28	61	5	13	7	14	9	24	33	19	14	15	15	0	68
	PERCENTAGES		45.9	38.5		50.0											

TM REB: 8 TOT TO: 15 (17 PTS)
BLOCKED SHOTS: Storm 3: Burse 2; Jackson 1. Sun 6: McWilliams-Franklin 2; Whalen 2; Palmer 1, Sales 1.
TECHNICAL FOULS: Storm 0. Sun 0.

	ILL	PTO	FBP	PIP	2PT
Seattle	0	17	9	26	28
Connecticut	0	7	15	34	11

FLAGRANT FOUL: Storm, 0. Sun, 0.

GAME 2
At Key Arena, October 10, 2004

OFFICIALS: Bob Trammell, Sally Bell, Tina Napier.   TIME OF GAME: 2:10.   ATTENDANCE: 17,072.

SCORE BY PERIODS	1	2	FINAL
Connecticut	30	35	65
Seattle	35	32	67

VISITORS: Connecticut, 5-2. Head Coach: Mike Thibault.

No	Player	MIN	FG	FGA	3P	3PA	FT	FTA	OR	DR	TOT	A	PF	ST	TO	TEC	PTS
3	Wendy Palmer, F	14	0	2	0	1	0	0	0	2	2	0	1	0	2	0	0
42	Nykesha Sales, F	35	14	22	4	6	0	0	0	5	5	0	3	4	2	0	32
11	McWilliams-Franklin, C	32	1	11	0	0	0	0	4	3	7	1	2	0	3	0	2
32	Katie Douglas, G	37	5	10	2	4	2	3	2	3	5	0	1	3	2	0	14
13	Lindsay Whalen, G	30	3	9	0	2	3	4	0	1	1	7	4	1	2	0	9
22	Jessica Brungo	7	0	0	0	0	0	0	0	0	0	0	1	0	0	0	0
15	Asjha Jones	21	0	2	0	0	1	2	1	1	2	2	1	1	3	0	1
24	Debbie Black	12	1	3	0	0	0	0	0	3	3	0	2	0	2	0	2
43	Le'coe Willingham	12	2	5	0	0	1	1	1	3	4	0	0	0	0	0	5
34	Jen Derevjanik									DNP							
12	Candace Futrell									DNP							
	TOTALS	200	26	64	6	13	7	10	8	21	29	10	15	9	16	1	65
	PERCENTAGES	40.6	46.2	70.0													

TM REB: 8 TOT TO: 16 (14 PTS)

HOME: Seattle, 5-2. Head Coach: Anne Donovan.

No	Player	MIN	FG	FGA	3P	3PA	FT	FTA	OR	DR	TOT	A	PF	ST	TO	TEC	PTS
15	Lauren Jackson, F	37	5	15	1	1	4	4	2	9	11	2	1	1	2	0	15
55	Sheri Sam, F	29	1	6	0	0	0	0	1	3	4	3	4	2	2	0	2
7	Kamila Vodichkova, C	22	2	9	0	0	1	2	4	1	5	2	2	0	2	0	5
10	Sue Bird, G	31	2	6	0	3	6	7	0	3	3	1	0	3	2	0	10
22	Betty Lennox, G	31	11	16	0	0	5	5	0	2	2	1	3	1	4	0	27
33	Janell Burse	12	0	4	0	0	0	0	1	2	3	0	0	2	1	0	0
4	Simone Edwards	8	0	0	0	0	0	0	0	0	0	0	2	0	0	0	0
44	Tully Bevilaqua	14	0	2	0	0	0	0	0	1	1	1	2	0	1	0	0
43	Alicia Thompson	13	3	3	2	2	0	0	1	2	3	0	2	1	2	0	8
32	Adia Barnes	3	0	1	0	0	0	0	0	0	0	0	0	0	0	0	0
20	Michelle Greco									DNP							
	TOTALS	200	24	62	3	6	16	18	9	23	32	10	16	10	16	0	67
	PERCENTAGES	38.7	50.0	88.9													

TM REB: 12 TOT TO: 16 (14 PTS)
BLOCKED SHOTS: Sun 4: Sales 2; Palmer 1; McWilliams-Franklin 1. Storm 4: Vodichkova 2; Jackson 1; Burse 1.
TECHNICAL FOULS: Sun 1: Thibault 1. Storm 0.

	ILL	PTO	FBP	PIP	2PT
Connecticut	0	14	8	26	13
Seattle	0	14	16	26	10

FLAGRANT FOUL: Storm, 0. Sun, 0.

GAME 3

At Key Arena, October 12, 2004

OFFICIALS: June Courteau, Lisa Mattingly, Roy Gulbeyan.   TIME OF GAME: 2:07.   ATTENDANCE: 17,072.

SCORE BY PERIODS	1	2	FINAL
Connecticut	36	24	60
Seattle	37	37	74

VISITORS: Connecticut, 5-3. Head Coach: Mike Thibault.

No	Player	MIN	FG	FGA	3P	3PA	FT	FTA	OR	DR	TOT	A	PF	ST	TO	TEC	PTS
3	Wendy Palmer, F	9	0	2	0	2	0	0	0	1	1	0	2	0	0	0	0
42	Nykesha Sales, F	33	5	12	3	5	5	5	2	4	6	0	5	2	2	0	18
11	McWilliams-Franklin, C	33	4	9	0	0	2	3	2	3	5	2	3	1	2	1	10
32	Katie Douglas, G	34	0	11	0	6	6	6	1	5	6	2	4	2	0	0	6
13	Lindsay Whalen, G	35	3	9	0	2	4	7	0	1	1	2	3	1	2	0	10
15	Asjha Jones	25	6	11	0	0	0	1	2	1	3	1	2	1	3	0	12
22	Jessica Brungo	12	0	1	0	1	0	0	0	1	1	0	1	0	1	0	0
43	Le'coe Willingham	10	1	4	0	0	0	0	3	2	5	0	0	0	1	0	2
24	Debbie Black	7	0	1	0	0	0	0	0	1	1	0	1	0	0	0	0
12	Candace Futrell	2	1	1	0	0	0	0	0	0	0	0	0	0	0	0	2
34	Jen Derevjanik									DNP							
	TOTALS	200	20	61	3	16	17	22	10	19	29	7	21	7	11	1	60
	PERCENTAGES	32.8	18.8	77.3													

TM REB: 8 TOT TO: 11 (13 PTS)

HOME: Seattle, 6-2. Head Coach: Anne Donovan.

No	Player	MIN	FG	FGA	3P	3PA	FT	FTA	OR	DR	TOT	A	PF	ST	TO	TEC	PTS
15	Lauren Jackson, F	34	5	11	0	0	3	5	0	7	7	3	4	1	1	1	13
55	Sheri Sam, F	29	2	6	0	1	1	2	2	3	5	2	1	0	1	0	5
7	Kamila Vodichkova, C	21	5	8	0	0	4	7	1	3	4	0	4	0	2	0	14
10	Sue Bird, G	31	3	6	0	1	2	2	0	5	5	6	2	1	2	0	8
22	Betty Lennox, G	34	7	17	0	1	9	11	0	3	3	2	4	2	3	0	23
43	Alicia Thompson	9	0	1	0	1	0	0	0	2	2	1	0	0	0	0	0
33	Janell Burse	10	1	3	0	0	0	0	1	1	2	0	0	0	0	0	2
4	Simone Edwards	14	3	5	0	0	0	0	1	3	4	0	1	0	2	0	6
44	Tully Bevilaqua	13	1	3	1	1	0	0	1	2	3	0	2	2	2	0	3
32	Adia Barnes	4	0	1	0	0	0	0	1	0	1	0	2	0	0	0	0
20	Michelle Greco	1	0	0	0	0	0	0	0	0	0	0	0	0	0	0	0
	TOTALS	200	27	61	1	5	19	27	7	29	36	14	20	6	13	1	74
	PERCENTAGES		44.3		20.0		70.4										

TM REB: 15 TOT TO: 13 (11 PTS)
BLOCKED SHOTS: Sun 1: Sales, 1. Storm 3: Jackson 2; Edwards 1.
TECHNICAL FOULS: Sun 1: McWilliams-Franklin 1. Storm 1: Jackson 1.

	ILL	PTO	FBP	PIP	2PT
Connecticut	0	11	1	32	8
Seattle	0	13	7	36	4

FLAGRANT FOUL: Storm, 0. Sun, 0.

At Radio City Music Hall, August 5, 2004

OFFICIALS: June Courteau, Sally Bell, Nan Sisk. TIME OF GAME: 1:53.

SCORE BY PERIODS	1	2	FINAL
WNBA All-Stars	20	38	58
USAB National	39	35	74

VISITORS: WNBA All-Stars

Player	MIN	FG	FGA	3P	3PA	FT	FTA	OR	DR	TOT	A	PF	ST	TO	BS	PTS
Nikki Teasley, G	17	1	6	0	4	0	0	1	3	4	0	3	1	4	0	2
Anna DeForge, G	16	0	5	0	5	2	2	0	1	1	0	0	1	0	0	2
Cheryl Ford, F	25	5	9	0	0	0	0	1	4	5	2	4	4	2	1	10
Nykesha Sales, F	18	3	9	1	2	0	0	0	3	3	1	1	4	0	0	7
T. McWilliams-Franklin, C	31	2	6	0	0	5	7	0	2	2	0	1	1	2	1	9
Natalie Williams	25	1	4	0	0	3	4	4	2	6	4	3	4	3	2	5
Becky Hammon	16	1	7	0	4	0	0	0	1	1	1	0	2	1	0	2
Allison Feaster	16	0	5	0	2	1	2	0	0	0	0	1	3	0	0	1
Mwadi Mabika	15	5	11	0	2	1	1	1	2	3	2	0	1	0	0	11
Deanna Nolan	12	1	7	0	1	1	2	2	1	3	2	1	2	2	0	3
Lindsay Whalen	9	2	3	0	0	2	2	1	1	2	2	0	0	4	0	6
TOTALS	200	21	72	1	20	15	20	10	20	30	14	14	23	18	4	58
PERCENTAGES		29.2		5.0		75.0										

Team Rebounds: 9   Total TO: 19

HOME: USA Basketball

Player	MIN	FG	FGA	3P	3PA	FT	FTA	OR	DR	TOT	A	PF	ST	TO	BS	PTS
Dawn Staley, G	24	0	4	0	0	0	0	0	0	0	3	2	2	5	0	0
Shannon Johnson, G	20	3	4	2	2	0	0	1	2	3	3	1	0	3	0	8
Tamika Catchings, F	27	4	11	2	4	2	2	5	6	11	1	1	0	3	0	12
Tina Thompson, F	24	5	13	1	6	0	0	2	5	7	2	4	2	5	0	11
Lisa Leslie, C	22	6	12	0	1	3	4	2	10	12	1	2	0	5	1	15
Sue Bird	20	1	4	0	3	0	0	0	1	1	3	1	1	2	0	2
Yolanda Griffith	18	5	14	0	0	1	2	11	4	15	0	1	0	1	0	11
Swin Cash	16	4	7	0	0	1	2	4	2	6	2	3	2	2	0	9
Diana Taurasi	16	0	4	0	3	0	0	0	4	4	2	2	1	2	0	0
Ruth Riley	13	2	7	0	0	2	2	0	3	3	0	3	0	0	0	6
Katie Smith						DNP										
Sheryl Swoopes						DNP										
TOTALS	200	30	80	5	19	9	12	25	37	62	17	20	8	28	1	74
PERCENTAGES		37.5		26.3		75.0										

Team Rebounds: 8   Total TO: 28
TECHNICAL FOULS: None.

	FBP	PIP
WNBA All-Stars	8	22
USA Basketball	6	42

FLAGRANT FOUL: None.

2003 SEASON IN REVIEW

DETROIT SHOCK, 2003 WNBA CHAMPIONS

Front Row (l. to r.) – Sheila Lambert, Assistant Coach Korie Hlede, Assistant Coach Pamela McGee, Head Coach Bill Laimbeer, Assistant Coach Laurie Byrd, Elaine Powell, Kedra Holland-Corn.
Back Row (l. to r.) – Allison Curtin, Swin Cash, Stacey Thomas, Barbara Farris, Ayana Walker, Ruth Riley, Petra Ujhelyi, Cheryl Ford, Astou Ndiaye-Diatta, Deanna Nolan, Team Trainer Laura Ramus.

FINAL STANDINGS

EASTERN CONFERENCE

TEAM	W	L	PCT	GB	HOME	ROAD	LAST-10	STREAK
Detroit	25	9	.735	-	13-4	12-5	7-3	Won 4
Charlotte	18	16	.529	7	13-4	5-12	5-5	Lost 1
Connecticut	18	16	.529	7	10-7	8-9	5-5	Won 3
Cleveland	17	17	.500	8	11-6	6-11	6-4	Won 1
Indiana	16	18	.471	9	11-6	5-12	3-7	Lost 1
New York	16	18	.471	9	11-6	5-12	5-5	Lost 2
Washington	9	25	.265	16	3-14	6-11	4-6	Lost 4

WESTERN CONFERENCE

TEAM	W	L	PCT	GB	HOME	ROAD	LAST-10	STREAK
Los Angeles	24	10	.706	-	11-6	13-4	6-4	Won 5
Houston	20	14	.588	4	14-3	6-11	5-5	Lost 3
Sacramento	19	15	.559	5	12-5	7-10	7-3	Lost 1
Minnesota	18	16	.529	6	11-6	7-10	5-5	Lost 2
Seattle	18	16	.529	6	13-4	5-12	4-6	Won 2
San Antonio	12	22	.353	12	9-8	3-14	4-6	Lost 2
Phoenix	8	26	.235	16	6-11	2-15	3-7	Lost 1

TEAM STANDINGS
OFFENSIVE

TEAM	G	FG	FGA	PCT	FG3	FG3A	PCT	FT	FTA	PCT	OFF	DEF	REB	AST	PF	DQ	STL	TO	BLK	PTS	AVG
Det.	34	902	2004	.450	125	323	.387	624	882	.707	379	851	1230	545	605	3	263	608	158	2553	75.1
L.A.	34	894	2140	.418	174	528	.330	537	678	.792	336	813	1149	587	682	12	242	470	161	2499	73.5
Sea.	34	890	2045	.435	166	500	.332	442	567	.780	342	732	1074	548	644	8	232	465	138	2388	70.2
Conn.	34	864	2102	.411	177	549	.322	479	646	.741	333	762	1095	520	663	5	270	434	111	2384	70.1
Minn.	34	875	1978	.442	180	524	.344	450	624	.721	361	718	1079	580	634	6	242	558	101	2380	70.0
Ind.	34	839	2011	.417	210	600	.350	449	563	.798	334	654	988	539	668	5	299	474	121	2337	68.7
Wash.	34	896	2191	.409	157	505	.311	381	507	.751	382	703	1085	568	676	5	213	462	99	2330	68.5
Sac.	34	862	2107	.409	150	473	.317	425	626	.679	349	718	1067	568	641	7	297	461	122	2299	67.6
Hou.	34	828	1916	.432	115	344	.334	473	600	.788	266	764	1030	465	490	2	231	450	129	2244	66.0
N.Y.	34	825	1923	.429	181	500	.362	412	537	.767	271	686	957	527	587	5	262	470	128	2243	66.0
Clev.	34	815	1975	.413	135	425	.318	464	643	.722	349	720	1069	517	639	4	226	466	86	2229	65.6
Cha.	34	787	1881	.418	187	517	.362	456	590	.773	342	629	971	499	697	3	279	497	115	2217	65.2
S.A.	34	792	2068	.383	93	315	.295	538	736	.731	350	795	1145	428	728	8	187	513	167	2215	65.1
Phoe.	34	801	2095	.382	116	349	.332	379	556	.682	357	643	1000	461	664	8	310	479	111	2097	61.7

DEFENSIVE

Team	FG	FGA	PCT	FG3	FG3A	PCT	FT	FTA	PCT	OFF	DEF	REB	AST	PF	DQ	STL	TO	BLK	PTS	AVG	DIFF
Hou.	824	2030	.406	169	500	.338	325	448	.725	298	708	1006	516	634	2	227	430	122	2142	63.0	+3.0
Cha.	790	1902	.415	138	407	.339	477	667	.715	386	621	1007	491	606	2	264	469	104	2195	64.6	+0.6
Clev.	809	1927	.420	127	355	.358	465	607	.766	300	704	1004	510	659	9	223	467	135	2210	65.0	+0.6
Sac.	816	1991	.410	149	467	.319	435	597	.729	345	751	1096	516	640	9	224	576	141	2216	65.2	+2.4
N.Y.	821	1959	.419	155	467	.332	459	581	.790	326	736	1062	506	614	5	269	480	96	2256	66.4	-0.4
Phoe.	834	1867	.447	136	371	.367	466	626	.744	303	811	1114	509	667	4	275	610	146	2270	66.8	-5.1
Sea.	844	2039	.414	145	437	.332	441	591	.746	352	689	1041	456	570	9	245	459	104	2274	66.9	+3.4
Ind.	837	1908	.439	157	421	.373	490	638	.768	309	677	986	570	631	4	227	512	170	2321	68.3	+0.5
Minn.	878	2067	.425	141	446	.316	473	633	.747	337	652	989	528	666	10	271	471	126	2370	69.7	+0.3
Det.	911	2286	.399	161	541	.298	412	556	.741	390	674	1064	504	774	5	309	497	129	2395	70.4	+4.6
Conn.	864	2104	.411	172	536	.321	509	673	.756	366	812	1178	553	669	8	252	476	88	2409	70.9	-0.7
S.A.	867	2176	.398	149	482	.309	544	745	.730	389	783	1172	530	669	8	275	424	140	2427	71.4	-6.2
L.A.	866	2147	.403	196	540	.363	504	702	.718	316	789	1105	572	654	6	241	468	127	2432	71.5	+2.0
Wash.	909	2033	.447	171	482	.355	509	691	.737	334	781	1115	591	565	0	251	468	119	2498	73.5	-4.9
AVG'S	848	2031	.417	155	461	.336	465	625	.743	339	728	1067	525	644	6	254	486	125	2315	68.1	---
	1187028436		---	2166	6452	---	6509	8755	---	4751101881	4939735	29018		8135536807		174732415				---	---

TEAM COMPARISONS

TEAM	Points Per Game		Field Goal Percentage		Turnovers Per Game		Rebound Percentages			Below 70 Pts.		Overtime Games		3 PTS or Less		10 PTS or More	
	OWN	OPP	OWN	OPP	OWN	OPP	OFF	DEF	TOT	OWN	OPP	W	L	W	L	W	L
Charlotte	65.2	64.6	.418	.415	14.6	13.8	.355	.620	.487	26	24	1	1	4	1	8	7
Cleveland	65.6	65.0	.413	.420	13.7	13.7	.331	.706	.519	21	22	1	0	2	3	8	8
Connecticut	70.1	70.9	.411	.411	12.8*	14.0	.291	.676	.483	16	18	0	2	3	4	7	8
Detroit	75.1*	70.4	.450*	.399	17.9	14.6	.360*	.686	.523*	12	18	4	0	6	2	11	5
Houston	66.0	63.0*	.432	.406	13.2	12.6	.273	.719	.496	24	27	0	1	3	3	9	4
Indiana	68.7	68.3	.417	.439	13.9	15.1	.330	.679	.505	20	19	2	0	1	1	10	7
Los Angeles	73.5	71.5	.418	.403	13.8	13.8	.299	.720*	.509	12	15	2	1	8	2	4	3
Minnesota	70.0	69.7	.442	.425	16.4	13.9	.356	.681	.518	16	15	1	1	3	4	4	5
New York	66.0	66.4	.429	.419	13.8	14.1	.269	.678	.473	22	24	0	2	2	3	6	8
Phoenix	61.7	66.8	.382	.447	14.1	17.9*	.306	.680	.493	28	24	1	2	3	6	3	9
Sacramento	67.6	65.2	.409	.410	13.6	16.9	.317	.675	.496	24	21	1	0	1	6	9	6
San Antonio	65.1	71.4	.383	.398*	15.1	12.5	.309	.671	.490	22	16	1	0	1	2	6	13
Seattle	70.2	65.6	.435	.414	13.7	13.5	.332	.675	.503	15	21	0	2	4	2	11	6
Washington	68.5	73.5	.409	.447	13.6	13.8	.328	.678	.503	18	12	0	2	1	3	2	9
COMPOSITE; 238 games																	
	68.1		.417		14.3		.318	.682		276	276	14		42		98	

* - League Leader
REBOUND PERCENTAGES
OFF. - Percentage of a given team's missed shots which that team rebounds.
DEF. - Percentage of opponents' missed shots which a given team rebounds.
TOT. - Average of offensive and defensive rebound percentages.

SCORING AVERAGE

	G	FG	FT	PTS	AVG
Jackson, Sea.	33	254	151	698	21.2
Holdsclaw, Was.	27	204	140	554	20.5
Catchings, Ind.	34	221	155	671	19.7
Leslie, L.A.	23	165	82	424	18.4
Smith, Min.	34	208	126	620	18.2
Thompson, Hou.	28	176	81	472	16.9
Cash, Det.	33	195	146	548	16.6
Sales, Ct.	34	194	116	548	16.1
Swoopes, Hou.	31	175	110	484	15.6
Ferdinand, S.A.	34	139	176	470	13.8
Griffith, Sac.	34	161	147	469	13.8
Mabika, L.A.	32	158	97	441	13.8
Dixon, L.A.	30	159	83	412	13.7
Williams, Ind.	34	176	105	457	13.4
Johnson, N.Y.	32	158	79	430	13.4
Milton, L.A.	31	139	115	416	13.4
Melvin, Cle.	34	159	123	444	13.1
Smith, Sac.	34	188	41	430	12.6
Miller, Was.	33	172	37	413	12.5
Feaster, Cha.	34	142	66	422	12.4

REBOUNDS PER GAME

	G	OFF	DEF	TOT	AVG
Holdsclaw, Was.	27	72	222	294	10.9
Ford, Det.	32	99	235	334	10.4
Leslie, L.A.	23	76	155	231	10.0
Jackson, Sea.	33	82	225	307	9.3
Phillips, N.Y.	33	99	181	280	8.5
Catchings, Ind.	34	82	190	272	8.0
Snow, Hou.	34	76	187	263	7.7
Williams, Ind.	34	109	146	255	7.5
Williams, Pho.	34	68	184	252	7.4
Dydek, S.A.	34	45	206	251	7.4
Griffith, Sac.	34	92	156	248	7.3
Milton, L.A.	31	59	161	220	7.1
McWilliams-Franklin, Ct.	34	78	149	227	6.7
Melvin, Cle.	34	82	133	215	6.3
Jackson, S.A.	33	86	119	205	6.2
Williams, Min.	34	92	117	209	6.1
Riley, Det.	34	59	142	201	5.9
Sutton-Brown, Cha.	34	73	128	201	5.9
Thompson, Hou.	28	39	126	165	5.9
Cash, Det.	33	65	128	193	5.8

ASSISTS PER GAME

	G	AST	AVG
Penicheiro, Sac.	34	229	6.7
Bird, Sea.	34	221	6.5
Teasley, L.A.	34	214	6.3
S. Johnson, Ct.	34	196	5.8
Staley, Cha.	34	174	5.1
Weatherspoon, N.Y.	34	149	4.4
Edwards, Min.	34	148	4.4
Jackson, Pho.	34	146	4.3
Powell, Det.	33	129	3.9
Swoopes, Hou.	31	121	3.9
Darling, Cle.	34	128	3.8
Cash, Det.	33	119	3.6
Catchings, Ind.	34	114	3.4
Dales-Schuman, Was.	34	114	3.4
Holdsclaw, Was.	27	89	3.3
Burgess, Was.	34	112	3.3
Azzi, S.A.	34	111	3.3
Dixon, L.A.	30	89	3.0
Stinson, Cha.	34	97	2.9
Abrosimova, Min.	30	82	2.7

FIELD GOAL PCT.

	FG	FGA	PCT
Williams, Min.	129	193	.668
Snow, Hou.	126	253	.498
Riley, Det.	115	231	.498
Griffith, Sac.	161	332	.485
Williams, Ind.	176	363	.485
Jackson, Sea.	254	526	.483
Melvin, Cle.	159	333	.477
Vodichkova, Sea.	101	213	.474
Ford, Det.	128	270	.474
Rasmussen, Ind.	94	200	.470

3-PT FIELD GOAL PCT.

	3FG	3GA	PCT
Hammon, N.Y.	23	49	.469
Brondello, Sea.	21	48	.437
Teasley, L.A.	70	165	.424
Miller, Cha.	22	52	.423
Nolan, Det.	48	114	.421
Enis, Cha.	26	62	.419
Campbell, Sac.	46	111	.414
Jackson, Cle.	29	70	.414
DeForge, Pho.	61	148	.412
Holland-Corn, Det.	50	124	.403

FREE THROW PCT.

	FT	FTA	PCT
Hammon, N.Y.	39	41	.951
White, Ind.	45	48	.937
Holdsclaw, Was.	140	155	.903
Swoopes, Hou.	110	124	.887
Bird, Sea.	61	69	.884
Dixon, L.A.	83	94	.883
Smith, Min.	126	143	.881
Teasley, L.A.	98	112	.875
Mabika, L.A.	97	112	.866
Johnson, N.Y.	79	92	.859

STEALS PER GAME

	G	STL	AVG
Swoopes, Hou.	31	77	2.48
Catchings, Ind.	34	72	2.12
Penicheiro, Sac.	34	61	1.79
Ferdinand, S.A.	34	58	1.71
Phillips, N.Y.	33	56	1.70
Griffith, Sac.	34	57	1.68
Williams, Pho.	34	57	1.68
Milton, L.A.	31	49	1.58
Feaster, Cha.	34	52	1.53
Jackson, Pho.	34	52	1.53

BLOCKS PER GAME

	G	BLK	AVG
Dydek, S.A.	34	100	2.94
Leslie, L.A.	23	63	2.74
Jackson, Sea.	33	64	1.94
Snow, Hou.	34	62	1.82
Riley, Det.	34	58	1.71
Sutton-Brown, Cha.	34	50	1.47
Milton, L.A.	31	41	1.32
Baranova, N.Y.	33	43	1.30
Griffith, Sac.	34	39	1.15
Catchings, Ind.	34	35	1.03

MINUTES PER GAME

	G	MIN	AVG
Catchings, Ind.	34	1210	35.6
Holdsclaw, Was.	27	948	35.1
Milton, L.A.	31	1086	35.0
Teasley, L.A.	34	1189	35.0
Swoopes, Hou.	31	1084	35.0
Smith, Min.	34	1185	34.9
Thompson, Hou.	28	974	34.8
Dixon, L.A.	30	1042	34.7
Leslie, L.A.	23	792	34.4
Jackson, Sea.	33	1109	33.6

CHARLOTTE STING

Player	G	Min	FGM	FGA	Pct	FTM	FTA	Pct	Off	Def	Tot	Ast	PF	Dq	Stl	TO	Blk	Pts	Avg	Hi
Allison Feaster 34		1096	142	378	.376	66	78	.846	37	76	113	73	75	0	52	72	9	422	12.4	23
Andrea Stinson 34		1000	147	321	.458	60	79	.759	28	112	140	97	70	0	48	75	5	377	11.1	23
Shalonda Enis...........29		613	82	188	.436	62	77	.805	62	63	125	16	63	0	29	41	2	252	8.7	29
Tammy Sutton-Brown 34		864	98	233	.421	90	131	.687	73	128	201	15	132	2	19	59	50	286	8.4	21
Dawn Staley 34		1086	90	216	.417	61	73	.836	14	44	58	174	76	0	49	78	4	269	7.9	20
Kelly Miller 34		523	68	167	.407	31	40	.775	20	33	53	47	44	0	18	35	2	189	5.6	14
Rushia Brown 34		483	53	116	.457	19	23	.826	34	49	83	16	88	1	29	35	10	125	3.7	14
Charlotte Smith-Tayl ..27		443	31	98	.316	24	36	.667	23	37	60	18	54	0	10	24	2	95	3.5	10
Teana McKiver 31		341	41	78	.526	23	31	.742	37	54	91	6	58	0	14	27	24	105	3.4	15
Tynesha Lewis 23		234	26	62	.419	11	12	.917	11	22	33	20	18	0	10	16	6	70	3.0	13
Marla Brumfield 25		123	6	16	.375	6	6	1.000	1	9	10	14	13	0	1	6	1	18	0.7	6
Erin Buescher 14		44	3	8	.375	3	4	.750	2	2	4	3	6	0	0	2	0	9	0.6	3
Charlotte...................34		6850	787	1881	.418	456	590	.773	342	629	971	499	697	3	279	497	115	2217	65.2	92
Opponents 34		6850	790	1902	.415	477	667	.715	386	621	1007	491	606	2	264	469	104	2195	64.6	83

3-pt. FG: Charlotte 187-517 (.362)
Feaster 72-205 (.351); Stinson 23-75 (.307); Enis 26-62 (.419); Staley 28-72 (.389); Miller 22-52 (.423); Brown 0-2 (.000)
Smith-Taylor 9-32 (.281); McKiver 0-1 (.000); Lewis 7-13 (.538); Brumfield 0-3 (.000); Opponents 138-407 (.339)

CLEVELAND ROCKERS

Player	G	Min	FGM	FGA	Pct	FTM	FTA	Pct	Off	Def	Tot	Ast	PF	Dq	Stl	TO	Blk	Pts	Avg	Hi
Chasity Melvin 34		1061	159	333	.477	123	176	.699	82	133	215	52	108	0	28	67	22	444	13.1	22
Penny Taylor 34		898	143	340	.421	78	95	.821	44	104	148	80	53	0	38	60	10	398	11.7	33
LaToya Thomas.........32		852	137	296	.463	71	90	.789	63	101	164	37	62	1	28	42	13	345	10.8	23
Betty Lennox.............34		560	100	269	.372	26	36	.722	19	70	89	32	77	0	14	58	4	258	7.6	23
Deanna Jackson 34		763	83	198	.419	50	70	.714	37	52	89	51	92	1	20	33	13	245	7.2	30
Merlakia Jones 34		672	66	196	.337	28	39	.718	18	79	97	44	59	0	22	36	3	164	4.8	14
Helen Darling 34		832	44	143	.308	30	41	.732	25	62	87	128	87	2	39	74	6	141	4.1	10
Lucienne Berthieu......22		201	27	52	.519	30	46	.652	20	22	42	6	38	0	10	22	4	84	3.8	15
P. Johns Kimb 30		416	35	63	.556	19	34	.559	31	51	82	19	35	0	12	19	10	89	3.0	13
Jennifer Rizzotti 33		525	20	72	.278	9	16	.563	4	38	42	65	22	0	14	35	0	59	1.8	8
Tracy Henderson 11		45	1	13	.077	0	0	---	6	8	14	3	6	0	1	4	1	2	0.2	2
Cleveland 34		6825	815	1975	.413	464	643	.722	349	720	1069	517	639	4	226	466	86	2229	65.6	89
Opponents 34		6825	809	1927	.420	465	607	.766	300	704	1004	510	659	9	223	467	135	2210	65.0	81

3-pt. FG: Cleveland 135-425 (.318)
Melvin 3-11 (.273); Taylor 34-99 (.343); Thomas 0-6 (.000); Lennox 32-103 (.311); Jackson 29-70 (.414); Jones 4-13 (.308)
Darling 23-71 (.324); Berthieu 0-1 (.000); Rizzotti 10-51 (.196); Opponents 127-355 (.358)

CONNECTICUT SUN

Player	G	Min	FGM	FGA	Pct	FTM	FTA	Pct	Off	Def	Tot	Ast	PF	Dq	Stl	TO	Blk	Pts	Avg	Hi
Nykesha Sales 34		1106	194	468	.415	116	144	.806	27	118	145	92	107	3	46	73	13	548	16.1	31
Shannon Johnson 34		1107	138	319	.433	125	171	.731	39	95	134	196	77	0	44	107	3	420	12.4	31
Katie Douglas 28		843	120	274	.438	49	68	.721	33	73	106	56	38	0	31	28	11	336	12.0	28
McWilliams-Franklin ..34		983	133	301	.442	76	102	.745	78	149	227	49	103	1	43	54	33	354	10.4	28
Adrienne Johnson 34		584	69	195	.354	18	24	.750	23	35	58	18	36	0	17	21	1	173	5.1	15
Wendy Palmer............32		433	58	147	.395	23	28	.821	29	77	106	16	62	0	11	35	3	149	4.7	20
Brooke Wyckoff.........34		755	55	142	.387	26	36	.722	48	98	146	35	109	1	33	39	19	156	4.6	17
Jessie Hicks 27		253	37	80	.463	24	25	.960	23	25	48	6	47	0	11	26	9	98	3.6	12
Rebecca Lobo............25		297	25	88	.284	2	9	.222	9	43	52	5	33	0	6	14	15	59	2.4	12
Courtney Coleman 20		141	11	20	.550	14	30	.467	8	14	22	1	18	0	8	13	2	36	1.8	6
Debbie Black 34		373	24	68	.353	6	9	.667	16	35	51	46	33	0	20	18	2	55	1.6	8
Connecticut 34		6875	864	2102	.411	479	646	.741	333	762	1095	520	663	5	270	434	111	2384	70.1	91
Opponents 34		6875	864	2104	.411	509	673	.756	366	812	1178	553	669	8	252	476	88	2409	70.9	103

3-pt. FG: Connecticut 177-549 (.322)
Sales 44-114 (.386); S. Johnson 19-73 (.260); Douglas 47-123 (.382); McWilliams-Frank 12-43 (.279); A. Johnson 17-49 (.347)
Palmer 10-46 (.217); Wyckoff 20-70 (.286); Lobo 7-28 (.250); Black 1-3 (.333); Opponents 172-536 (.321)

DETROIT SHOCK

Player	G	Min	FGM	FGA	Pct	FTM	FTA	Pct	Off	Def	Tot	Ast	PF	Dq	Stl	TO	Blk	Pts	Avg	Hi
Swin Cash 33		1097	195	430	.453	146	214	.682	65	128	193	119	76	0	43	108	23	548	16.6	26
Deanna Nolan 32		954	136	312	.436	76	96	.792	12	95	107	83	65	0	41	69	14	396	12.4	27
Cheryl Ford 32		956	128	270	.474	88	129	.682	99	235	334	27	109	1	32	79	31	344	10.8	20
Ruth Riley 34		995	115	231	.498	97	127	.764	59	142	201	64	128	2	25	82	58	327	9.6	19
Kedra Holland-Corn...34		694	107	232	.461	48	63	.762	12	45	57	63	26	0	36	59	3	312	9.2	23
Elaine Powell 33		938	105	233	.451	79	106	.745	43	63	106	129	65	0	45	79	9	296	9.0	16

Player	G	Min	FGM	FGA	Pct	FTM	FTA	Pct	REBOUNDS Off	Def	Tot	Ast	PF	Dq	Stl	TO	Blk	SCORING Pts	Avg	Hi
Barbara Farris	34	522	43	99	.434	41	63	.651	29	53	82	23	62	0	10	41	4	127	3.7	14
Sheila Lambert	27	187	24	66	.364	32	41	.780	10	18	28	14	15	0	5	29	0	87	3.2	14
Stacey Thomas(*)	11	82	5	16	.313	4	11	.364	5	11	16	5	10	0	9	6	1	15	1.4	6
Stacey Thomas(!)	30	269	20	62	.323	14	27	.519	15	28	43	15	24	0	20	16	9	61	2.0	9
Astou Ndiaye-Diatta	11	70	10	21	.476	0	2	.000	5	9	14	1	3	0	3	9	1	20	1.8	10
Ayana Walker	34	271	24	70	.343	8	21	.381	34	37	71	10	33	0	10	19	11	56	1.6	14
Tamara Moore(>)	15	66	8	16	.500	5	6	.833	3	6	9	4	5	0	4	6	2	21	1.4	5
Petra Ujhelyi	14	68	2	8	.250	0	3	.000	3	9	12	3	8	0	0	10	1	4	0.3	2
Detroit	34	6900	902	2004	.450	624	882	.707	379	851	1230	545	605	3	263	608	158	2553	75.1	103
Opponents	34	6900	911	2286	.399	412	556	.741	390	674	1064	504	774	5	309	497	129	2395	70.4	92

3-pt. FG: Detroit 125-323 (.387).
Cash 12-40 (.300); Nolan 48-114 (.421); Holland-Corn 50-124 (.403); Powell 7-20 (.350); Lambert 7-16 (.438); Thomas(*) 1-5 (.200)
Thomas(!) 7-27 (.259); Moore(>) 0-4 (.000); Opponents 161-541 (.298)

HOUSTON COMETS

Player	G	Min	FGM	FGA	Pct	FTM	FTA	Pct	REBOUNDS Off	Def	Tot	Ast	PF	Dq	Stl	TO	Blk	SCORING Pts	Avg	Hi
Tina Thompson	28	974	176	426	.413	81	104	.779	39	126	165	47	65	0	18	69	23	472	16.9	30
Cynthia Cooper	4	144	16	38	.421	25	28	.893	2	8	10	22	9	0	4	14	1	64	16.0	22
Sheryl Swoopes	31	1084	175	434	.403	110	124	.887	32	111	143	121	48	0	77	73	26	484	15.6	29
Janeth Arcain	34	1136	151	324	.466	79	94	.840	24	112	136	67	64	0	41	50	1	390	11.5	20
Michelle Snow	34	1025	126	253	.498	62	85	.729	76	187	263	42	120	2	35	68	62	314	9.2	19
Dominique Canty	32	648	55	145	.379	62	93	.667	36	64	100	56	62	0	22	49	1	172	5.4	14
Ukari Figgs	34	952	52	124	.419	19	22	.864	11	70	81	82	33	0	26	59	1	149	4.4	13
Tiffani Johnson	22	359	30	62	.484	17	23	.739	19	44	63	13	33	0	3	20	7	77	3.5	8
Mfon Udoka	25	251	32	64	.500	16	23	.696	22	29	51	4	38	0	4	21	2	80	3.2	12
Kelley Gibson	26	209	14	42	.333	0	0	---	4	12	16	8	14	0	1	9	5	38	1.5	9
Octavia Blue	16	37	1	4	.250	2	4	.500	1	1	2	2	3	0	2	2	0	4	0.3	2
Itoro Umoh-Coleman	3	6	0	0	---	0	0	---	0	0	0	1	1	0	0	1	0	0	0.0	0
Houston	34	6825	828	1916	.432	473	600	.788	266	764	1030	465	490	2	231	450	129	2244	66.0	83
Opponents	34	6825	824	2030	.406	325	448	.725	298	708	1006	516	634	2	227	430	122	2142	63.0	91

3-pt. FG: Houston 115-344 (.334).
Thompson 39-114 (.342); Cooper 7-18 (.389); Swoopes 24-79 (.304); Arcain 9-37 (.243); Snow 0-1 (.000); Canty 0-1 (.000)
Figgs 26-69 (.377); Udoka 0-1 (.000); Gibson 10-24 (.417); Opponents 169-500 (.338)

INDIANA FEVER

Player	G	Min	FGM	FGA	Pct	FTM	FTA	Pct	REBOUNDS Off	Def	Tot	Ast	PF	Dq	Stl	TO	Blk	SCORING Pts	Avg	Hi
Tamika Catchings	34	1210	221	512	.432	155	183	.847	82	190	272	114	122	2	72	102	35	671	19.7	32
Natalie Williams	34	1054	176	363	.485	105	148	.709	109	146	255	46	138	2	43	70	21	457	13.4	24
Stephanie White	28	577	60	173	.347	45	48	.938	14	27	41	58	60	0	34	37	6	194	6.9	16
Kristen Rasmussen	33	814	94	200	.470	31	39	.795	44	71	115	64	65	0	24	48	15	226	6.8	16
Coretta Brown	30	522	61	164	.372	28	33	.848	11	30	41	31	30	0	21	36	4	186	6.2	26
Kelly Schumacher	34	480	81	169	.479	23	27	.852	40	59	99	20	63	0	7	32	24	189	5.6	22
Niele Ivey	27	651	45	116	.388	12	17	.706	5	27	32	71	40	0	29	28	7	135	5.0	14
Nikki McCray	34	734	52	138	.377	20	24	.833	18	33	51	49	67	1	37	44	2	131	3.9	11
Coquese Washington	20	348	19	67	.284	11	13	.846	2	27	29	48	32	0	14	30	2	63	3.2	18
Zuzi Klimesova	1	3	0	1	.000	2	2	1.000	0	0	0	0	1	0	0	0	0	2	2.0	2
Bridget Pettis	31	148	15	52	.288	13	17	.765	5	14	19	8	17	0	4	8	1	49	1.6	9
Leigh Aziz	7	44	4	14	.286	2	4	.500	2	7	9	1	5	0	0	3	4	10	1.4	4
Sonja Henning(*)	23	290	11	42	.262	2	8	.250	2	23	25	29	28	0	14	13	0	24	1.0	6
Sonja Henning(!)	24	295	11	43	.256	2	8	.250	2	23	25	29	28	0	15	13	0	24	1.0	6
Indiana	34	6875	839	2011	.417	449	563	.798	334	654	988	539	668	5	299	474	121	2337	68.7	94
Opponents	34	6875	837	1908	.439	490	638	.768	309	677	986	570	631	4	227	512	170	2321	68.3	91

3-pt. FG: Indiana 210-600 (.350).
Catchings 74-191 (.387); Williams 0-1 (.000); White 29-84 (.345); Rasmussen 7-15 (.467); Brown 36-100 (.360); Ivey 33-84 (.393)
Schumacher 4-9 (.444); McCray 7-32 (.219); Washington 14-48 (.292); Pettis 6-27 (.222); Henning(*) 0-9 (.000)
Henning(!) 0-9 (.000); Opponents 157-421 (.373)

LOS ANGELES SPARKS

Player	G	Min	FGM	FGA	Pct	FTM	FTA	Pct	REBOUNDS Off	Def	Tot	Ast	PF	Dq	Stl	TO	Blk	SCORING Pts	Avg	Hi
Lisa Leslie	23	792	165	373	.442	82	133	.617	76	155	231	46	93	3	31	65	63	424	18.4	31
Mwadi Mabika	32	1042	158	388	.407	97	112	.866	34	107	141	82	105	3	30	74	18	441	13.8	28
Tamecka Dixon	30	1042	159	364	.437	83	94	.883	41	85	126	89	83	0	35	69	10	412	13.7	28
DeLisha Milton-Jones	31	1086	139	328	.424	115	143	.804	59	161	220	64	109	0	49	79	41	416	13.4	23
Nikki Teasley	34	1189	112	288	.389	98	112	.875	30	145	175	214	68	0	39	108	15	392	11.5	23
Latasha Byears	5	72	10	25	.400	8	11	.727	12	9	21	2	12	0	0	2	2	28	5.6	7
Vanessa Nygaard	11	168	16	36	.444	3	4	.750	11	8	19	5	22	1	3	4	0	41	3.7	14
Jennifer Gillom	33	397	40	97	.412	16	21	.762	18	37	55	21	65	1	16	9	3	103	3.1	12
Rhonda Mapp	24	255	30	60	.500	2	4	.500	26	42	68	6	45	0	7	12	6	62	2.6	12
Sophia Witherspoon	23	235	17	53	.321	12	14	.857	6	13	19	4	17	0	7	7	0	56	2.4	10

REVIEW 2003 Regular Season

Player	G	Min	FGM	FGA	Pct	FTM	FTA	Pct	Off	Def	Tot	Ast	PF	Dq	Stl	TO	Blk	Pts	Avg	Hi
Nicky McCrimmon	33	299	28	63	.444	7	8	.875	7	22	29	32	20	0	19	17	1	68	2.1	12
Shaquala Williams	25	229	19	53	.358	10	14	.714	11	21	32	19	25	0	6	7	0	49	2.0	13
Lynn Pride(*)	4	28	0	5	.000	1	4	.250	3	3	6	0	9	1	0	3	0	1	0.3	1
Lynn Pride(!)	17	94	7	19	.368	4	8	.500	11	12	23	1	20	1	3	11	1	18	1.1	6
Chandra Johnson	8	45	1	5	.200	3	4	.750	2	4	6	3	6	0	0	4	1	6	0.8	4
Jenny Mowe	1	21	0	2	.000	0	0	---	0	1	1	0	3	0	1	1	0	0	0.0	0
Los Angeles	34	6900	894	2140	.418	537	678	.792	336	813	1149	587	682	12	242	470	161	2499	73.5	97
Opponents	34	6900	866	2147	.403	504	702	.718	316	789	1105	572	654	6	241	468	127	2432	71.5	92

3-pt. FG: Los Angeles 174-528 (.330).
Leslie 12-37 (.324); Mabika 28-106 (.264); Dixon 11-52 (.212); Milton-Jones 23-61 (.377); Teasley 70-165 (.424); Byears 0-1 (.000)
Nygaard 6-17 (.353); Gillom 7-26 (.269); Mapp 0-1 (.000); Witherspoon 10-29 (.345); McCrimmon 5-12 (.417); Williams 1-16 (.063)
Johnson 1-5 (.200); Opponents 196-540 (.363)

MINNESOTA LYNX

Player	G	Min	FGM	FGA	Pct	FTM	FTA	Pct	Off	Def	Tot	Ast	PF	Dq	Stl	TO	Blk	Pts	Avg	Hi
Katie Smith	34	1185	208	455	.457	126	143	.881	40	98	138	84	112	2	25	67	6	620	18.2	34
Sheri Sam	34	953	138	360	.383	74	105	.705	46	96	142	88	70	0	38	48	6	374	11.0	20
Svetlana Abrosimova	..30	792	112	285	.393	69	98	.704	44	97	141	82	79	0	44	90	11	318	10.6	23
Tamika Williams	34	1121	129	193	.668	45	93	.484	92	117	209	44	78	0	34	58	10	303	8.9	16
Janell Burse	29	438	76	155	.490	54	70	.771	40	68	108	19	81	2	13	42	28	206	7.1	21
Michele Van Gorp	..31	528	70	162	.432	35	52	.673	32	75	107	17	87	2	10	56	20	175	5.6	17
Teresa Edwards	34	854	63	168	.375	31	40	.775	24	81	105	148	60	0	41	92	11	181	5.3	15
Jordan Adams	10	96	13	33	.394	2	2	1.000	10	13	23	4	10	0	2	10	3	33	3.3	13
Kristi Harrower	31	499	32	87	.368	8	13	.615	9	30	39	72	15	0	18	39	3	88	2.8	10
Shaunzinski Gortman	25	200	21	49	.429	3	4	.750	9	23	32	14	25	0	11	20	1	50	2.0	11
Lynn Pride(>)	13	66	7	14	.500	3	4	.750	8	9	17	1	11	0	3	8	1	17	1.3	6
Georgia Schweitzer	...16	118	6	17	.353	0	0	---	7	11	18	7	6	0	3	8	1	15	0.9	5
Minnesota	34	6850	875	1978	.442	450	624	.721	361	718	1079	580	634	6	242	558	101	2380	70.0	85
Opponents	34	6850	878	2067	.425	473	633	.747	337	652	989	528	666	10	271	471	126	2370	69.7	88

3-pt. FG: Minnesota 180-524 (.344).
Smith 78-200 (.390); Sam 24-73 (.329); Abrosimova 25-82 (.305); Williams 0-2 (.000); Burse 0-2 (.000); Van Gorp 0-1 (.000)
Edwards 24-80 (.300); Adams 5-12 (.417); Harrower 16-43 (.372); Gortman 5-20 (.250); Schweitzer 3-9 (.333);
Opponents 141-446 (.316)

NEW YORK LIBERTY

Player	G	Min	FGM	FGA	Pct	FTM	FTA	Pct	Off	Def	Tot	Ast	PF	Dq	Stl	TO	Blk	Pts	Avg	Hi
Becky Hammon	11	257	50	87	.575	39	41	.951	1	20	21	18	13	0	10	27	1	162	14.7	33
Vickie Johnson	32	1042	158	345	.458	79	92	.859	30	65	95	75	65	0	29	55	7	430	13.4	27
Crystal Robinson	33	1078	143	326	.439	47	56	.839	13	57	70	63	94	0	40	43	13	395	12.0	22
Tari Phillips	33	1033	142	358	.397	87	134	.649	99	181	280	56	118	3	56	92	28	372	11.3	20
Elena Baranova	33	850	107	257	.416	31	35	.886	45	136	181	64	69	0	36	62	43	278	8.4	20
Tamika Whitmore	33	823	110	242	.455	50	76	.658	38	84	122	25	100	1	35	57	22	271	8.2	21
Linda Frohlich	26	214	31	72	.431	14	22	.636	11	25	36	15	26	0	6	14	8	83	3.2	12
K.B. Sharp	30	398	28	71	.394	31	39	.795	11	21	32	37	15	0	14	26	0	94	3.1	14
Teresa Weatherspoon	34	824	37	96	.385	24	32	.750	19	78	97	149	60	0	28	62	5	98	2.9	13
Erin Thorn	23	181	13	42	.310	10	10	1.000	3	8	11	16	8	0	4	13	1	44	1.9	12
Lindsey Yamasaki	24	148	6	27	.222	0	0	---	1	11	12	9	19	1	4	5	0	16	0.7	3
Bethany Donaphin	1	2	0	0	---	0	0	---	0	0	0	0	0	0	0	0	0	0	0.0	0
New York	34	6850	825	1923	.429	412	537	.767	271	686	957	527	587	5	262	470	128	2243	66.0	90
Opponents	34	6850	821	1959	.419	459	581	.790	326	736	1062	506	614	5	269	480	96	2256	66.4	90

3-pt. FG: New York 181-500 (.362).
Hammon 23-49 (.469); Johnson 35-96 (.365); Robinson 62-168 (.369); Phillips 1-5 (.200); Baranova 33-91 (.363); Whitmore 1-3
(.333); Frohlich 7-13 (.538); Sharp 7-24 (.292); Weatherspoon 0-4 (.000); Thorn 8-33 (.242); Yamasaki 4-14 (.286);
Opponents 155-467 (.332)

PHOENIX MERCURY

Player	G	Min	FGM	FGA	Pct	FTM	FTA	Pct	Off	Def	Tot	Ast	PF	Dq	Stl	TO	Blk	Pts	Avg	Hi
Anna DeForge	34	1065	147	357	.412	50	69	.725	32	73	105	72	61	0	51	53	12	405	11.9	24
Adrian Williams	34	985	141	351	.402	52	85	.612	68	184	252	31	95	1	57	73	19	334	9.8	20
Tamicha Jackson	34	958	124	361	.343	24	58	.810	24	58	82	146	62	0	52	76	4	300	8.8	20
Slobodanka Tuvic	17	365	45	116	.388	37	46	.804	31	36	67	12	61	2	10	32	15	127	7.5	17
Kayte Christensen	30	659	78	161	.484	50	83	.602	61	65	126	16	104	4	25	39	16	206	6.9	16
Plenette Pierson	33	602	67	177	.379	64	101	.634	37	43	80	22	87	1	19	42	13	198	6.0	26
Lisa Harrison	33	838	74	179	.413	35	51	.686	42	76	118	36	58	0	29	34	6	183	5.5	16
I. Castro Marque	16	178	25	71	.352	11	18	.611	6	6	12	9	11	0	6	10	1	69	4.3	12
Edwina Brown	34	524	41	152	.270	36	44	.818	29	42	71	62	44	0	30	47	7	118	3.5	15
Nevriye Yilmaz	5	34	7	15	.467	0	2	.000	3	0	3	2	7	0	0	4	0	14	2.8	10

Player	G	Min	FGM	FGA	Pct	FTM	FTA	Pct	Off	Def	Tot	Ast	PF	Dq	Stl	TO	Blk	Pts	Avg	Hi
Stacey Thomas(>)	19	187	15	46	.326	10	16	.625	10	17	27	10	14	0	11	10	8	46	2.4	9
Tamara Moore(*)	11	110	11	26	.423	11	13	.846	3	16	19	8	9	0	5	10	4	33	3.0	8
Tamara Moore(!)	26	176	19	42	.452	16	19	.842	6	22	28	12	14	0	9	16	6	54	2.1	8
Sonja Mallory	6	44	4	9	.444	2	2	1.000	4	6	10	0	7	0	1	6	4	10	1.7	4
Felicia Ragland	3	39	1	12	.083	2	2	1.000	0	2	2	2	4	0	2	3	0	5	1.7	5
Edniesha Curry	20	205	13	35	.371	2	3	.667	1	10	11	24	25	0	9	15	0	33	1.7	8
Dalma Ivanyi	4	34	3	8	.375	0	0	---	2	2	4	2	4	0	0	2	1	6	1.5	2
Tracy Reid	2	12	1	3	.333	0	0	---	1	0	1	1	4	0	2	1	0	2	1.0	2
Michaela Pavlickova	8	29	3	7	.429	0	0	---	1	3	4	1	1	0	1	2	0	6	0.8	2
Grace Daley	3	28	1	5	.200	0	0	---	1	1	2	3	2	0	3	1	2	2	0.7	2
Gergana Slavtcheva	2	12	0	2	.000	0	0	---	0	0	0	1	2	0	1	0	0	0	0.0	0
Charmin Smith	4	17	0	2	.000	0	0	---	1	3	4	1	2	0	0	0	0	0	0.0	0
Phoenix	34	6925	801	2095	.382	379	556	.682	357	643	1000	461	664	8	310	479	111	2097	61.7	89
Opponents	34	6925	834	1867	.447	466	626	.744	303	811	1114	509	667	4	275	610	146	2270	66.8	82

3-pt. FG: Phoenix 116-349 (.332).
DeForge 61-148 (.412); Williams 0-1 (.000); Jackson 35-99 (.354); Tuvic 0-4 (.000); Pierson 0-2 (.000); Harrison 0-3 (.000)
Castro Marques 8-27 (.296); Brown 0-3 (.000); Thomas(>) 6-22 (.273); Moore(*) 0-5 (.000); Moore(!) 0-9 (.000); Ragland 1-5 (.200)
Curry 5-22 (.227); Ivanyi 0-2 (.000); Daley 0-2 (.000); Slavtcheva 0-2 (.000); Smith 0-2 (.000); Opponents 136-371 (.367)

SACRAMENTO MONARCHS

Player	G	Min	FGM	FGA	Pct	FTM	FTA	Pct	Off	Def	Tot	Ast	PF	Dq	Stl	TO	Blk	Pts	Avg	Hi
Yolanda Griffith	34	1015	161	332	.485	147	190	.774	92	156	248	46	125	3	57	75	39	469	13.8	27
Tangela Smith	34	986	188	427	.440	41	58	.707	61	126	187	52	103	2	43	56	32	430	12.6	24
DeMya Walker	34	740	111	242	.459	83	143	.580	61	88	149	47	95	0	25	69	23	307	9.0	21
Edna Campbell	34	724	98	244	.402	25	33	.758	17	53	70	43	42	0	21	43	5	267	7.9	15
Kara Lawson	34	769	89	227	.392	31	40	.775	30	77	107	56	45	0	15	42	5	263	7.7	24
Ticha Penicheiro	34	1089	62	205	.302	44	76	.579	29	90	119	229	76	1	61	81	1	183	5.4	16
Ruthie Bolton	33	521	55	175	.314	20	26	.769	15	42	57	35	52	0	33	21	2	149	4.5	13
Lady Grooms	34	470	45	112	.402	21	26	.808	15	31	46	29	27	0	17	21	5	111	3.3	13
Tanty Maiga	22	190	17	52	.327	8	20	.400	13	24	37	14	27	0	18	14	2	42	1.9	6
Chantelle Anderson	26	171	19	44	.432	4	12	.333	7	17	24	5	33	1	5	17	5	42	1.6	8
La'Keshia Frett	24	150	17	47	.362	1	2	.500	9	14	23	12	16	0	2	10	3	36	1.5	7
Sacramento	34	6825	862	2107	.409	425	626	.679	349	718	1067	568	641	7	297	461	122	2299	67.6	89
Opponents	34	6825	816	1991	.410	435	597	.729	345	751	1096	516	640	9	224	576	141	2216	65.2	79

3-pt. FG: Sacramento 150-473 (.317)
Griffith 0-2 (.000); Smith 13-49 (.265); Walker 2-15 (.133); Campbell 46-111 (.414); Lawson 54-135 (.400); Penicheiro 15-60 (.250)
Bolton 19-98 (.194); Grooms 0-1 (.000); Frett 1-2 (.500); Opponents 149-467 (.319)

SAN ANTONIO SILVER STARS

Player	G	Min	FGM	FGA	Pct	FTM	FTA	Pct	Off	Def	Tot	Ast	PF	Dq	Stl	TO	Blk	Pts	Avg	Hi
Marie Ferdinand	34	1116	139	384	.362	176	223	.789	28	99	127	90	87	0	58	85	6	470	13.8	26
Margo Dydek	34	926	156	346	.451	94	130	.723	45	206	251	58	113	1	19	80	100	406	11.9	27
Adrienne Goodson	33	969	141	357	.395	81	102	.794	74	111	185	71	96	2	24	85	6	371	11.2	26
Gwen Jackson	33	975	114	286	.399	56	88	.636	86	119	205	20	85	1	15	46	17	289	8.8	16
Jennifer Azzi	34	1136	85	211	.403	51	65	.785	10	81	91	111	98	2	27	61	9	260	7.6	18
Sylvia Crawley	33	564	50	130	.385	15	22	.682	39	66	105	19	76	1	18	40	19	115	3.5	13
Semeka Randall	33	339	32	90	.356	24	45	.533	25	28	53	23	41	0	11	44	0	88	2.7	14
LaQuanda Quick	26	168	21	79	.266	2	2	1.000	8	25	33	5	21	0	1	10	3	59	2.3	22
Tausha Mills	29	185	20	49	.408	18	31	.581	27	28	55	7	58	1	4	23	2	58	2.0	7
LaTonya Johnson	31	279	18	71	.254	16	22	.727	7	18	25	19	31	0	3	14	1	58	1.9	7
Tai Dillard	24	168	16	65	.246	5	6	.833	1	14	15	15	22	0	7	14	4	41	1.7	9
San Antonio	34	6825	792	2068	.383	538	736	.731	350	795	1145	428	728	8	187	513	167	2215	65.1	88
Opponents	34	6825	867	2176	.398	544	745	.730	389	783	1172	530	669	8	275	424	140	2427	71.4	99

3-pt. FG: San Antonio 93-315 (.295)
Ferdinand 16-52 (.308); Dydek 0-1 (.000); Goodson 8-36 (.222); Jackson 5-30 (.167); Azzi 39-97 (.402); Randall 0-1 (.000)
Quick 15-52 (.288); Johnson 6-23 (.261); Dillard 4-23 (.174); Opponents 149-482 (.309)

SEATTLE STORM

Player	G	Min	FGM	FGA	Pct	FTM	FTA	Pct	Off	Def	Tot	Ast	PF	Dq	Stl	TO	Blk	Pts	Avg	Hi
Lauren Jackson	33	1109	254	526	.483	151	183	.825	82	225	307	62	106	1	38	69	64	698	21.2	34
Sue Bird	34	1136	155	368	.421	61	69	.884	22	91	113	221	47	0	48	110	1	420	12.4	27
Kamila Vodichkova	28	709	101	213	.474	82	101	.812	55	88	143	31	101	4	20	53	21	284	10.1	18
Sandy Brondello	34	975	117	282	.415	25	31	.806	19	37	56	69	58	0	31	37	2	280	8.2	21
Adia Barnes	16	396	32	84	.381	12	21	.571	26	39	65	23	36	1	11	18	7	88	5.5	12
Amanda Lassiter	32	733	60	156	.385	19	30	.633	33	79	112	42	92	2	27	42	26	163	5.1	16
Simone Edwards	34	577	61	134	.455	35	56	.625	54	79	133	16	55	0	10	31	9	157	4.6	16
Alisa Burras	27	270	35	75	.467	19	27	.704	27	34	61	5	58	0	5	25	5	89	3.3	12
Rita Williams	32	381	28	75	.373	11	15	.733	3	19	22	41	34	0	14	27	0	78	2.4	9

Player	G	Min	FGM	FGA	Pct	FTM	FTA	Pct	Off	Def	Tot	Ast	PF	Dq	Stl	TO	Blk	Pts	Avg	Hi
LaTonya Massaline(*)	11	121	13	33	.394	5	5	1.000	7	4	11	5	8	0	4	5	0	33	3.0	9
LaTonya Massaline(!)	24	222	20	63	.317	7	7	1.000	12	9	21	8	12	0	5	10	0	53	2.2	15
Tully Bevilaqua 31		252	17	51	.333	16	21	.762	9	17	26	32	30	0	14	20	1	58	1.9	14
Sun-Min Jung...........17		118	13	32	.406	4	4	1.000	1	9	10	1	13	0	5	5	0	30	1.8	10
Mactabene Amachree ..7		47	3	10	.300	2	4	.500	4	10	14	0	3	0	5	9	2	8	1.1	4
Danielle McCulley 7		26	1	6	.167	0	0	---	0	1	1	0	3	0	0	4	0	2	0.3	2
Seattle 34		6850	890	2045	.435	442	567	.780	342	732	1074	548	644	8	232	465	138	2388	70.2	93
Opponents 34		6850	844	2039	.414	441	591	.746	352	689	1041	456	570	9	245	459	104	2274	66.9	95

3-pt. FG: Seattle 166-500 (.332)

Jackson 39-123 (.317); Bird 49-140 (.350); Vodichkova 0-5 (.000); Brondello 21-48 (.438); Barnes 12-31 (.387); Jung 0-7 (.000)
Lassiter 24-73 (.329); Williams 11-43 (.256); Massaline(*) 2-8 (.250); Massaline(!) 6-20 (.300); Bevilaqua 8-21 (.381)
McCulley 0-1 (.000); Opponents 145-437 (.332)

WASHINGTON MYSTICS

Player	G	Min	FGM	FGA	Pct	FTM	FTA	Pct	Off	Def	Tot	Ast	PF	Dq	Stl	TO	Blk	Pts	Avg	Hi
Chamique Holdsclaw	27	948	204	480	.425	140	155	.903	72	222	294	89	74	0	34	72	15	554	20.5	34
Coco Miller 33		1076	172	382	.450	37	53	.698	55	72	127	86	95	1	39	53	7	413	12.5	23
S. Dales-Schuman 34		998	122	298	.409	39	55	.709	44	57	101	114	97	2	29	72	12	340	10.0	20
Asjha Jones 34		748	121	279	.434	41	55	.745	62	73	135	52	109	1	16	63	25	290	8.5	21
Murriel Page 34		850	83	220	.377	42	56	.750	62	90	152	35	101	0	18	41	24	213	6.3	19
Annie Burgess 34		841	50	134	.373	15	25	.600	24	55	79	112	47	1	27	52	1	131	3.9	15
Aiysha Smith..............31		422	41	120	.342	17	34	.500	21	44	65	10	44	0	11	26	9	104	3.4	10
Helen Luz 20		165	19	53	.358	9	10	.900	2	8	10	21	16	0	6	11	2	59	3.0	9
Nakia Sanford............17		134	20	40	.500	9	20	.450	10	16	26	1	35	0	3	14	2	49	2.9	10
Jocelyn Penn 30		288	31	78	.397	22	33	.667	19	33	52	16	28	0	15	20	1	86	2.9	13
Kiesha Brown 27		269	24	72	.333	2	3	.667	6	26	32	28	23	0	13	22	1	60	2.2	9
Zuzana Zirkova 6		30	2	4	.500	6	6	1.000	0	2	2	1	3	0	0	2	0	11	1.8	5
LaTonya Massaline(>)13		101	7	30	.233	2	2	1.000	5	5	10	3	4	0	1	5	0	20	1.5	15
Sonja Henning(>) 1		5	0	1	.000	0	0	---	0	0	0	0	1	0	0	1	0	0	0.0	0
Washington................34		6875	896	2191	.409	381	507	.751	382	703	1085	568	676	5	213	462	99	2330	68.5	92
Opponents 34		6875	909	2033	.447	509	691	.737	334	781	1115	591	565	0	251	468	119	2498	73.5	97

3-pt. FG: Washington 157-505 (.311)

Holdsclaw 6-35 (.171); Miller 32-89 (.360); Dales-Schuman 57-160 (.356); Jones 7-17 (.412); Page 5-12 (.417); Burgess 16-58
(.276); Smith 5-34 (.147); Luz 12-40 (.300); Penn 2-13 (.154); Brown 10-33 (.303); Zirkova 1-2 (.500); Massaline(>) 4-12 (.333)
Opponents 171-482 (.355)

(*) Statistics with this team only
(!) Totals with all teams
(>) Continued season with another team

PLAYOFF RESULTS

FIRST ROUND

Los Angeles defeats Minnesota, 2-1

August 28	Minnesota 74, Los Angeles 72
August 30	Los Angeles 80, Minnesota 69
September 1	Los Angeles 74, Minnesota 64

Sacramento defeats Houston, 2-1

August 29	Sacramento 65, Houston 59
August 31	Houston 69, Sacramento 48
September 2	Sacramento 70, Houston 68

Detroit defeats Cleveland, 2-1

August 29	Detroit 76, Cleveland 74
August 31	Cleveland 66, Detroit 59
September 2	Detroit 77, Cleveland 63

Connecticut defeats Charlotte, 2-0

August 28	Connecticut 68, Charlotte 66
August 30	Connecticut 68, Charlotte 62

CONFERENCE FINALS

Detroit defeats Connecticut, 2-0

September 5	Detroit 73, Connecticut 63
September 7	Detroit 79, Connecticut 73

Los Angeles defeats Sacramento, 2-1

September 5	Sacramento 77, Los Angeles 69
September 7	Los Angeles 79, Sacramento 54
September 9	Los Angeles 66, Sacramento 63

FINALS

Detroit defeats Los Angeles, 2-1

September 12	Los Angeles 75, Detroit 63
September 14	Detroit 62, Los Angeles 61
September 16	Detroit 83, Los Angeles 78

TEAM STANDINGS
OFFENSIVE

TEAM	G	FG	FGA	PCT	FG3	FG3A	PCT	FT	FTA	PCT	OFF	DEF	REB	AST	PF	DQ	STL	TO	BLK	PTS	AVG
L.A.	9	246	564	.436	40	123	.325	122	154	.792	80	197	277	177	182	2	76	116	48	654	72.7
Det.	8	202	516	.391	41	103	.398	127	160	.794	87	195	282	139	141	0	53	109	38	572	71.5
Minn.	3	69	175	.394	14	44	.318	55	72	.764	25	58	83	53	56	0	29	47	8	207	69.0
Conn.	4	103	221	.466	12	48	.250	54	67	.806	26	83	109	65	75	0	26	38	13	272	68.0
Clev.	3	67	173	.387	10	35	.286	59	77	.766	22	74	96	42	67	0	22	39	12	203	67.7
Hou.	3	71	184	.386	10	37	.270	44	54	.815	33	68	101	39	50	0	22	34	12	196	65.3
Cha.	2	44	112	.393	13	31	.419	27	34	.794	21	31	52	28	40	1	12	22	7	128	64.0
Sac.	6	141	347	.406	21	75	.280	74	96	.771	51	137	188	84	106	0	24	82	19	377	62.8

DEFENSIVE

Team	FG	FGA	PCT	FG3	FG3A	PCT	FT	FTA	PCT	OFF	DEF	REB	AST	PF	DQ	STL	TO	BLK	PTS	AVG	DIFF
Hou.	71	174	.408	11	41	.268	30	40	.750	25	75	100	38	56	0	9	42	11	183	61.0	+4.3
L.A.	213	543	.392	38	114	.333	145	181	.801	83	191	274	151	150	0	63	125	35	609	67.7	+5.0
Cha.	51	103	.495	5	16	.313	29	38	.763	14	40	54	34	36	0	13	18	6	136	68.0	-4.0
Sac.	154	368	.418	24	77	.312	78	102	.765	58	130	188	104	110	0	49	72	29	410	68.3	-5.5
Det.	195	491	.397	35	120	.292	128	157	.815	64	193	257	124	163	1	57	90	35	553	69.1	+2.4
Conn.	98	238	.412	27	57	.474	57	76	.750	48	78	126	64	71	1	24	49	10	280	70.0	-2.0
Clev.	74	195	.379	13	41	.317	51	65	.785	28	77	105	51	66	0	22	44	16	212	70.7	-3.0
Minn.	87	180	.483	8	30	.267	44	55	.800	25	59	84	61	65	1	27	47	15	226	75.3	-6.3
Averages	118	287	.411	20	62	.325	70	89	.787	43	105	149	78	90	0	33	61	20	326	68.7	---
Totals	943	2292	---	161	406	---	562	714	---	345	843	1188	627	717	3	264	487	157	2609	---	---

TEAM COMPARISONS

TEAM	Points Per Game OWN	OPP	Field Goal Percentage OWN	OPP	Turnovers Per Game OWN	OPP	Rebound Percentages OFF	DEF	TOT	Below 70 Pts. OWN	OPP	Overtime Games W	L	3 PTS or Less W	L	10 PTS or More W	L
Charlotte	64.0	68.0	.393	.495	11.0	9.0	.344*	.689	.517	2	2	0	0	0	1	0	0
Cleveland	67.7	70.7	.387	.379*	13.0	14.7	.222	.725	.474	2	1	0	0	1	0	0	1
Connecticut	68.0	70.0	.466*	.412	9.5*	12.3	.250	.634	.442	3	2	0	0	1	0	0	0
Detroit	71.5	69.1	.391	.397	13.6	11.3	.311	.753*	.532*	3	4	0	0	2	0	2	1
Houston	65.3	61.0*	.386	.408	11.3	14.0	.306	.731	.518	3	2	0	0	0	1	1	0
Los Angeles	72.7*	67.7	.436	.392	12.9	13.9	.295	.704	.499	3	6	0	0	1	2	4	0
Minnesota	69.0	75.3	.394	.483	15.7	15.7*	.298	.699	.498	2	0	0	0	1	0	0	2
Sacramento	62.8	68.3	.406	.418	13.7	12.0	.282	.703	.492	4	5	0	0	1	1	0	2
COMPOSITE: 19 games	68.7	---	.411	---	12.8	---	.290	.710	---	22	22	0	---	6	---	7	---

* - League Leader
REBOUND PERCENTAGES
OFF. - Percentage of a given team's missed shots which that team rebounds.
DEF. - Percentage of opponents' missed shots which a given team rebounds.
TOT. - Average of offensive and defensive rebound percentages.

INDIVIDUAL PLAYOFF STATISTICS, TEAM BY TEAM
CHARLOTTE STING

Player	G	Min	FGM	FGA	Pct	FTM	FTA	Pct	REBOUNDS Off	Def	Tot	Ast	PF	Dq	Stl	TO	Blk	SCORING Pts	Avg	Hi
Andrea Stinson	2	64	12	28	.429	9	9	1.000	4	5	9	7	4	0	2	4	0	36	18.0	25
Allison Feaster	2	63	7	20	.350	3	4	.750	2	3	5	1	5	0	2	0	0	21	10.5	12
Dawn Staley	2	58	6	17	.353	2	5	.400	1	4	5	7	6	0	4	4	0	18	9.0	15
Shalonda Enis	2	58	4	10	.400	6	6	1.000	5	7	12	1	9	1	2	6	2	15	7.5	11
Tynesha Lewis	2	29	4	8	.500	5	6	.833	2	1	3	4	2	0	0	0	1	14	7.0	9
Kelly Miller	2	23	4	10	.400	0	0	---	0	1	1	2	2	0	1	0	0	8	4.0	6
Rushia Brown	2	46	3	7	.429	1	2	.500	3	5	8	4	4	0	2	4	0	7	3.5	6
Tammy Sutton-Brown	2	32	2	7	.286	0	0	---	1	5	6	0	5	0	0	2	3	4	2.0	4
Marla Brumfield	2	7	1	2	.500	1	2	.500	0	0	0	1	1	0	1	0	0	3	1.5	3
C. Smith-Taylor	2	7	1	1	1.000	0	0	---	1	0	1	1	0	0	0	0	0	2	1.0	2
Teana McKiver	2	13	0	2	.000	0	0	---	2	0	2	0	2	0	0	0	1	0	0.0	0
Charlotte	2	400	44	112	.393	27	34	.794	21	31	52	28	40	1	12	22	7	128	64.0	66
Opponents	2	400	51	103	.495	29	38	.763	14	40	54	34	36	0	13	18	6	136	68.0	68

3-pt. FG: Charlotte 13-31 (.419)
Stinson 3-7 (.429); Feaster 4-10 (.400); Staley 4-8 (.500); Enis 1-3 (.333); Lewis 1-1 (1.000); Miller 0-2 (.000); Opponents 5-16 (.313)

CONNECTICUT SUN

Player	G	Min	FGM	FGA	Pct	FTM	FTA	Pct	Off	Def	Tot	Ast	PF	Dq	Stl	TO	Blk	Pts	Avg	Hi
McWilliams-Franklin	4	122	24	47	.511	16	17	.941	9	21	30	5	10	0	6	6	2	65	16.3	20
Nykesha Sales	4	131	17	40	.425	13	18	.722	1	12	13	9	12	0	5	7	3	47	11.8	22
Shannon Johnson	4	131	13	29	.448	14	18	.778	3	9	12	19	11	0	7	11	1	45	11.3	16
Katie Douglas	4	126	10	30	.333	6	7	.857	2	8	10	12	9	0	3	1	1	29	7.3	13
Wendy Palmer	4	64	13	22	.591	2	3	.667	1	11	12	3	9	0	0	7	0	29	7.3	13
Rebecca Lobo	2	38	4	10	.400	0	0	---	3	5	8	5	4	0	0	2	4	9	4.5	9
Brooke Wyckoff	4	89	7	16	.438	3	4	.750	3	9	12	5	11	0	2	2	1	18	4.5	9
Adrienne Johnson	3	43	6	9	.667	0	0	---	0	4	4	4	2	0	1	0	0	12	4.0	10
Jessie Hicks	4	27	5	8	.625	0	0	---	3	3	6	1	5	0	0	2	1	10	2.5	4
Debbie Black	4	29	4	10	.400	0	0	---	1	1	2	2	2	0	2	0	0	8	2.0	6
Connecticut	4	800	103	221	.466	54	67	.806	26	83	109	65	75	0	26	38	13	272	68.0	73
Opponents	4	800	98	238	.412	57	76	.750	48	78	126	64	71	1	24	49	10	280	70.0	79

3-pt. FG: Connecticut 12-48 (.250)
McWilliams-Frank 1-5 (.200); Sales 0-6 (.000); S. Johnson 5-10 (.500); Douglas 3-12 (.250); Palmer 1-4 (.250); Lobo 1-4 (.250)
Wyckoff 1-6 (.167); A. Johnson 0-1 (.000); Opponents 27-57 (.474)

CLEVELAND ROCKERS

Player	G	Min	FGM	FGA	Pct	FTM	FTA	Pct	Off	Def	Tot	Ast	PF	Dq	Stl	TO	Blk	Pts	Avg	Hi
Chasity Melvin	3	104	12	31	.387	26	34	.765	3	10	13	5	10	0	2	8	4	50	16.7	21
Penny Taylor	3	99	16	36	.444	10	12	.833	1	12	13	3	10	0	6	6	1	45	15.0	17
LaToya Thomas	3	100	14	32	.438	13	17	.765	6	17	23	4	11	0	1	6	4	41	13.7	17
Betty Lennox	3	45	9	19	.474	1	2	.500	1	6	7	3	7	0	3	4	0	21	7.0	14
Deanna Jackson	3	60	4	20	.200	4	6	.667	2	10	12	2	7	0	2	0	0	12	4.0	6
Jennifer Rizzotti	3	36	4	6	.667	0	0	---	0	2	2	0	2	0	0	1	0	12	4.0	9
Helen Darling	3	83	2	13	.154	4	4	1.000	4	8	12	13	11	0	6	10	0	9	3.0	5
Tracy Henderson	1	3	1	1	1.000	0	0	---	0	1	1	0	1	0	0	0	0	2	2.0	2
Merlakia Jones	3	37	2	5	.400	1	2	.500	3	2	5	0	2	0	0	2	0	5	1.7	3
Lucienne Berthieu	3	13	2	9	.222	0	0	---	2	2	4	1	5	0	1	2	1	4	1.3	4
P. Johns Kimb	3	20	1	1	1.000	0	0	---	0	4	4	3	1	0	1	0	2	2	0.7	2
Cleveland	3	600	67	173	.387	59	77	.766	22	74	96	42	67	0	22	39	12	203	67.7	74
Opponents	3	600	74	195	.379	51	65	.785	28	77	105	51	66	0	22	44	16	212	70.7	77

3-pt. FG: Cleveland 10-35 (.286)
Melvin 0-1 (.000); Taylor 3-10 (.300); Thomas 0-2 (.000); Lennox 2-5 (.400); Jackson 0-2 (.000); Rizzotti 4-6 (.667);
Darling 1-8 (.125); Jones 0-1 (.000); Opponents 13-41 (.317)

DETROIT SHOCK

Player	G	Min	FGM	FGA	Pct	FTM	FTA	Pct	Off	Def	Tot	Ast	PF	Dq	Stl	TO	Blk	Pts	Avg	Hi
Swin Cash	8	289	43	104	.413	42	52	.808	24	27	51	35	21	0	4	28	5	130	16.3	26
Deanna Nolan	8	257	44	96	.458	15	16	.938	4	25	29	21	21	0	10	13	2	124	15.5	26
Ruth Riley	8	258	41	106	.387	21	26	.808	15	34	49	20	26	0	5	13	20	103	12.9	27
Cheryl Ford	8	232	24	74	.324	19	23	.826	25	55	80	4	30	0	11	10	6	67	8.4	17
Kedra Holland-Corn	8	155	21	53	.396	8	10	.800	2	10	12	15	7	0	10	12	0	65	8.1	16
Elaine Powell	8	219	16	46	.348	7	11	.636	6	24	30	38	17	0	7	13	4	41	5.1	9
Barbara Farris	8	133	10	25	.400	11	17	.647	8	12	20	4	14	0	1	10	0	31	3.9	6
Ayana Walker	4	24	1	5	.200	3	3	1.000	3	3	6	0	0	0	4	1	1	5	1.3	3
Sheila Lambert	7	14	2	6	.333	0	0	---	0	2	2	1	3	0	0	4	0	5	0.7	3
Astou Ndiaye-Diatta	2	6	0	0	---	1	2	.500	0	0	0	1	1	0	0	0	0	1	0.5	1
Stacey Thomas	4	13	0	1	.000	0	0	---	3	0	3	3	1	0	1	1	0	0	0.0	0
Detroit	8	1600	202	516	.391	127	160	.794	87	195	282	139	141	0	53	109	38	572	71.5	83
Opponents	8	1600	195	491	.397	128	157	.815	64	193	257	124	163	1	57	90	35	553	69.1	78

3-pt. FG: Detroit 41-103 (.398)
Cash 2-10 (.200); Nolan 21-47 (.447); Holland-Corn 15-32 (.469); Powell 2-10 (.200); Farris 0-1 (.000); Lambert 1-3 (.333);
Opponents 35-120 (.292)

HOUSTON COMETS

Player	G	Min	FGM	FGA	Pct	FTM	FTA	Pct	Off	Def	Tot	Ast	PF	Dq	Stl	TO	Blk	Pts	Avg	Hi
Sheryl Swoopes	3	110	20	46	.435	15	16	.938	2	17	19	13	8	0	4	5	2	56	18.7	27
Tina Thompson	3	106	18	46	.391	6	7	.857	3	11	14	5	9	0	2	6	6	45	15.0	21
Janeth Arcain	3	107	12	31	.387	12	13	.923	6	8	14	3	5	0	8	7	0	37	12.3	13
Michelle Snow	3	89	10	25	.400	5	8	.625	12	17	29	5	10	0	4	5	4	25	8.3	16
Ukari Figgs	3	81	6	15	.400	0	0	---	1	5	6	7	4	0	1	3	0	17	5.7	8
Dominique Canty	3	48	3	9	.333	5	8	.625	7	4	11	5	7	0	1	3	0	11	3.7	6
Kelley Gibson	2	18	2	5	.400	0	0	---	0	1	1	0	1	0	0	0	0	4	2.0	4
Mfon Udoka	1	6	0	0	---	1	2	.500	0	1	1	0	2	0	0	2	0	1	1.0	1
Octavia Blue	1	4	0	1	.000	0	0	---	0	0	0	1	0	0	0	2	0	0	0.0	0
Tiffani Johnson	3	31	0	6	.000	0	0	---	2	4	6	0	4	0	2	1	0	0	0.0	0
Houston	3	600	71	184	.386	44	54	.815	33	68	101	39	50	0	22	34	12	196	65.3	69
Opponents	3	600	71	174	.408	30	40	.750	25	75	100	38	56	0	9	42	11	183	61.0	70

3-pt. FG: Houston 10-37 (.270)
Swoopes 1-10 (.100); Thompson 3-13 (.231); Arcain 1-5 (.200); Figgs 5-7 (.714); Gibson 0-2 (.000); Opponents 11-41 (.268)

LOS ANGELES SPARKS

Player	G	Min	FGM	FGA	Pct	FTM	FTA	Pct	Off	Def	Tot	Ast	PF	Dq	Stl	TO	Blk	Pts	Avg	Hi
Lisa Leslie	9	327	74	137	.540	38	54	.704	22	58	80	23	39	1	12	24	28	187	20.8	26
DeLisha Milton-Jones	9	338	47	106	.443	27	35	.771	20	37	57	25	40	1	17	20	13	131	14.6	20
Mwadi Mabika	9	344	53	121	.438	11	13	.846	10	40	50	21	29	0	14	20	2	129	14.3	29
Tamecka Dixon	9	316	40	94	.426	26	27	.963	8	21	29	29	27	0	14	11	2	110	12.2	18
Nikki Teasley	9	312	22	67	.328	16	20	.800	11	29	40	71	23	0	12	27	0	70	7.8	13
Vanessa Nygaard	5	24	3	5	.600	0	0	---	3	2	5	0	1	0	1	1	1	8	1.6	3
Nicky McCrimmon	7	54	4	18	.222	0	0	---	0	4	4	7	5	0	2	4	0	9	1.3	3
Sophia Witherspoon	5	14	1	5	.200	3	4	.750	0	2	2	0	1	0	1	2	0	5	1.0	5
Lynn Pride	6	36	2	6	.333	1	1	1.000	6	3	9	1	10	0	2	3	1	5	0.8	3
Jennifer Gillom	6	22	0	5	.000	0	0	---	0	1	1	0	5	0	1	0	1	0	0.0	0
Shaquala Williams	4	13	0	0	---	0	0	---	0	0	0	0	2	0	0	0	0	0	0.0	0
Los Angeles	9	1800	246	564	.436	122	154	.792	80	197	277	177	182	2	76	116	48	654	72.7	80
Opponents	9	1800	213	543	.392	145	181	.801	83	191	274	151	150	0	63	125	35	609	67.7	83

3-pt. FG: Los Angeles 40-123 (.325).
Leslie 1-3 (.333); Milton-Jones 10-18 (.556); Mabika 12-34 (.353); Dixon 4-12 (.333); Teasley 10-45 (.222); Nygaard 2-2 (1.000)
McCrimmon 1-6 (.167); Witherspoon 0-3 (.000); Opponents 38-114 (.333)

MINNESOTA LYNX

Player	G	Min	FGM	FGA	Pct	FTM	FTA	Pct	Off	Def	Tot	Ast	PF	Dq	Stl	TO	Blk	Pts	Avg	Hi
Katie Smith	3	120	18	42	.429	11	12	.917	3	10	13	9	11	0	1	8	0	52	17.3	23
Tamika Williams	3	116	17	28	.607	16	24	.667	12	10	22	3	5	0	7	4	1	50	16.7	17
Sheri Sam	3	74	10	28	.357	6	8	.750	5	11	16	8	6	0	6	8	0	26	8.7	11
Svetlana Abrosimova	3	69	6	22	.273	8	8	1.000	1	4	5	4	8	0	4	8	1	23	7.7	10
Teresa Edwards	3	83	6	19	.316	4	4	1.000	1	9	10	19	6	0	5	8	1	20	6.7	8
Janell Burse	3	42	6	18	.333	4	6	.667	2	7	9	2	3	0	4	3	2	16	5.3	6
Kristi Harrower	3	65	4	11	.364	1	2	.500	1	6	7	5	6	0	1	3	0	11	3.7	6
Michele Van Gorp	3	31	2	7	.286	5	8	.625	0	1	1	3	11	0	1	4	3	9	3.0	5
Minnesota	3	600	69	175	.394	55	72	.764	25	58	83	53	56	0	29	47	8	207	69.0	74
Opponents	3	600	87	180	.483	44	55	.800	25	59	84	61	65	1	27	47	15	226	75.3	80

3-pt. FG: Minnesota 14-44 (.318)
Smith 5-14 (.357); Sam 0-4 (.000); Abrosimova 3-7 (.429); Edwards 4-12 (.333); Harrower 2-7 (.286); Opponents 8-30 (.267)

SACRAMENTO MONARCHS

Player	G	Min	FGM	FGA	Pct	FTM	FTA	Pct	Off	Def	Tot	Ast	PF	Dq	Stl	TO	Blk	Pts	Avg	Hi
Yolanda Griffith	6	200	36	67	.537	31	34	.912	19	34	53	7	16	0	7	12	6	103	17.2	27
Tangela Smith	6	176	29	73	.397	14	20	.700	9	37	46	11	17	0	5	11	3	77	12.8	17
DeMya Walker	6	170	24	55	.436	11	20	.550	14	13	27	10	17	0	1	21	3	59	9.8	16
Edna Campbell	6	148	17	36	.472	2	2	1.000	1	3	4	11	11	0	1	8	0	40	6.7	12
Kara Lawson	6	154	9	42	.214	7	8	.875	2	21	23	16	8	0	1	4	2	32	5.3	12
Ticha Penicheiro	6	143	8	24	.333	7	8	.875	1	13	14	18	12	0	6	7	3	25	4.2	16
Ruthie Bolton	6	91	6	28	.214	0	0	---	2	8	10	6	10	0	2	5	0	15	2.5	6
Lady Grooms	6	65	7	12	.583	1	2	.500	2	3	5	3	3	0	1	5	0	15	2.5	6
La'Keshia Frett	1	9	1	2	.500	0	0	---	0	0	0	0	1	0	1	0		2	2.0	2
Chantelle Anderson	5	29	3	5	.600	1	2	.500	0	3	3	0	7	0	0	4	2	7	1.4	3
Tanty Maiga	4	15	1	3	.333	0	0	---	1	2	3	2	4	0	0	5	0	2	0.5	2
Sacramento	6	1200	141	347	.406	74	96	.771	51	137	188	84	106	0	24	82	19	377	62.8	77
Opponents	6	1200	154	368	.418	78	102	.765	58	130	188	104	110	0	49	72	29	410	68.3	79

3-pt. FG: Sacramento 21-75 (.280)
Smith 5-15 (.333); Campbell 4-16 (.250); Lawson 7-23 (.304); Penicheiro 2-8 (.250); Bolton 3-12 (.250); Frett 0-1 (.000)
Opponents 24-77 (.312)

(*) Statistics with this team only (!) Totals with all teams (>) Continued season with another team

INDIVIDUAL FINALS STATISTICS, TEAM BY TEAM

DETROIT SHOCK

Player	G	Min	FGM	FGA	Pct	FTM	FTA	Pct	Off	Def	Tot	Ast	PF	Dq	Stl	TO	Blk	Pts	Avg	Hi
Deanna Nolan	3	92	15	35	.429	10	10	1.000	2	6	8	9	7	0	5	6	1	46	15.3	17
Ruth Riley	3	97	18	43	.419	8	10	.800	5	10	15	9	10	0	0	5	10	44	14.7	27
Swin Cash	3	116	14	41	.341	10	13	.769	8	14	22	16	4	0	0	6	1	38	12.7	16
Cheryl Ford	3	99	10	30	.333	9	10	.900	11	19	30	2	10	0	5	4	5	29	9.7	11
Kedra Holland-Corn	3	56	9	21	.429	4	4	1.000	1	4	5	4	1	0	5	7	0	29	9.7	16
Elaine Powell	3	84	5	15	.333	1	2	.500	3	11	14	9	7	0	4	3	2	11	3.7	7
Barbara Farris	3	42	2	7	.286	4	4	1.000	2	5	7	3	4	0	0	5	2	8	2.7	4
Sheila Lambert	2	8	1	3	.333	0	0	---	0	1	1	0	1	0	0	1	0	3	1.5	3
Stacey Thomas	2	5	0	0	---	0	0	---	0	1	1	0	0	0	0	0	0	0	0.0	0
Ayana Walker	1	1	0	0	---	0	0	---	0	0	0	0	0	0	0	0	0	0	0.0	0
Detroit	3	600	74	195	.379	46	53	.868	32	71	103	52	44	0	19	38	19	208	69.3	83
Opponents	3	600	76	200	.380	44	51	.863	30	76	106	51	57	1	22	31	16	214	71.3	78

3-pt. FG: Detroit 14-36 (.389) Nolan 6-16 (.375); Cash 0-3 (.000); Holland-Corn 7-12 (.583); Powell 0-3 (.000); Lambert 1-2 (.500)
Opponents 18-53 (.340)

LOS ANGELES SPARKS

Player	G	Min	FGM	FGA	Pct	FTM	FTA	Pct	Off	Def	Tot	Ast	PF	Dq	Stl	TO	Blk	Pts	Avg	Hi
DeLisha Milton-Jones ..3		115	18	47	.383	14	16	.875	7	12	19	7	12	0	7	7	5	56	18.7	19
Lisa Leslie 3		119	21	50	.420	12	16	.750	10	28	38	7	13	1	6	9	7	54	18.0	23
Mwadi Mabika 3		118	16	42	.381	7	7	1.000	3	16	19	7	6	0	4	6	1	42	14.0	29
Tamecka Dixon 3		106	13	31	.419	9	9	1.000	2	6	8	6	11	0	2	3	2	37	12.3	15
Nikki Teasley.............3		111	6	22	.273	2	3	.667	4	11	15	24	9	0	3	4	0	19	6.3	10
Vanessa Nygaard 1		4	1	1	1.000	0	0	---	1	1	2	0	0	0	0	0	0	3	3.0	3
Nicky McCrimmon 2		5	1	3	.333	0	0	---	0	0	0	0	1	0	0	0	0	3	1.5	3
Jennifer Gillom 1		1	0	0	---	0	0	---	0	0	0	0	1	0	0	0	0	0	0.0	0
Lynn Pride 3		13	0	1	.000	0	0	---	3	0	3	0	4	0	1	1	0	0	0.0	0
Sophia Witherspoon 2		8	0	3	.000	0	0	---	0	2	2	0	0	0	0	0	0	0	0.0	0
Los Angeles 3		600	76	200	.380	44	51	.863	30	76	106	51	57	1	22	31	16	214	71.3	78
Opponents 3		600	74	195	.379	46	53	.868	32	71	103	52	44	0	19	38	19	208	69.3	83

3-pt. FG: Los Angeles 18-53 (.340).
Milton-Jones 6-9 (.667); Leslie 0-1 (.000); Mabika 3-10 (.300); Dixon 2-7 (.286); Teasley 5-19 (.263); Nygaard 1-1 (1.000); McCrimmon 1-3 (.333); Witherspoon 0-3 (.000); Opponents 14-36 (.389).

(*) Statistics with this team only (!) Totals with all teams (>) Continued season with another team

---

FINALS BOX SCORES

GAME 1

At STAPLES Center, September 12, 2003

OFFICIALS: Lisa Mattingly, Bob Trammell, June Courteau   TIME OF GAME: 1:54   ATTENDANCE: 10,264

SCORE BY PERIODS	1	2	FINAL
Detroit	21	42	63
Los Angeles	42	33	75

VISITORS: Detroit: 4-2. Head Coach: Bill Laimbeer

No Player	MIN	FG	FGA	3P	3PA	FT	FTA	OR	DR	TOT	A	PF	ST	TO	TEC	PTS
32 Swin Cash, F.................40		5	15	0	0	6	6	4	3	7	4	1	0	1	0	16
35 Cheryl Ford, F...............37		3	14	0	0	5	6	7	5	12	0	2	2	2	0	11
00 Ruth Riley, C................32		2	10	0	0	2	2	1	5	6	1	5	0	3	0	6
14 Deanna Nolan, G............36		6	13	1	5	2	2	1	4	5	2	1	1	2	0	15
5 Elaine Powell, G............19		1	5	0	1	0	0	1	4	5	3	1	1	1	0	2
11 Kedra Holland-Corn........17		2	8	2	5	2	2	1	0	1	1	0	3	4	0	8
54 Barbara Farris 12		0	2	0	0	2	2	1	3	4	3	1	0	2	0	2
31 Sheila Lambert................7		1	3	1	2	0	0	0	1	1	0	1	0	0	0	3
44 Ndiaye-Diatta	DNP															
9 Stacey Thomas	DNP															
12 Ayana Walker	DNP															
TOTALS 200		20	70	4	13	19	20	16	25	41	14	12	7	15	0	63
PERCENTAGES.................28.6		30.8	95.0													

TM REB: 9. TOT TO: 15 (24 PTS)

HOME: Los Angeles: 5-2   Head Coach: Michael Cooper

No Player	MIN	FG	FGA	3P	3PA	FT	FTA	OR	DR	TOT	A	PF	ST	TO	TEC	PTS
8 Milton-Jones, F..............39		6	16	2	3	5	6	2	7	9	3	5	2	1	1	19
4 Mwadi Mabika, F 39		4	11	1	5	0	0	1	4	5	4	2	2	3	1	9
9 Lisa Leslie, C 40		10	18	0	0	3	4	2	10	12	3	5	1	4	1	23
42 Nikki Teasley, G.............40		2	11	1	10	1	1	2	5	7	11	4	1	1	0	6
21 Tamecka Dixon, G 34		4	11	2	4	5	5	1	2	3	1	4	1	2	0	15
31 Vanessa Nygaard............4		1	1	1	1	0	0	1	1	2	0	0	0	0	0	3
34 Lynn Pride.....................3		0	1	0	0	0	0	1	0	1	0	1	0	0	0	0
12 Nicky McCrimmon............1		0	0	0	0	0	0	0	0	0	0	0	0	0	0	0
22 Jennifer Gillom	DNP															
20 Shaquala Williams..............	DNP															
13 Sophia Witherspoon	DNP															
TOTALS 200		27	69	7	23	14	16	10	29	39	22	21	7	11	3	75
PERCENTAGES.................39.1		30.4	87.5													

TM REB: 6. TOT TO: 11 (9 PTS)

BLOCKED SHOTS: Shock 7:Cash1,Ford3,Riley3. Sparks 6: Milton-Jones2,Leslie3,Dixon1.
TECHNICAL FOULS: Shock 0. Sparks 3: Milton-Jones1,Mabika 1,Leslie 1.

	ILL	PTO	FBP	PIP	2PT
DET.............0		9	7	20	10
LA...............0		24	3	18	13

FLAGRANT FOUL
None.

GAME 2

At The Palace of Auburn Hills, September 14, 2003

OFFICIALS: Matthew Boland, Sally Bell, Roy Gulbeyan.   TIME OF GAME: 1:54.   ATTENDANCE: 17,846

SCORE BY PERIODS	1	2	FINAL
Los Angeles	22	39	61
Detroit	38	24	62

VISITORS: Los Angeles: 5-3. Head Coach: Michael Cooper

No Player	MIN	FG	FGA	3P	3PA	FT	FTA	OR	DR	TOT	A	PF	ST	TO	TEC	PTS
4 Mwadi Mabika, F	39	1	11	0	2	2	2	0	5	5	1	1	1	1	0	4
8 Milton-Jones, F	36	6	18	2	3	4	4	2	1	3	3	3	3	3	0	18
9 Lisa Leslie, C	40	6	13	0	1	6	8	4	11	15	1	2	3	3	0	8
21 Tamecka Dixon, G	36	4	9	0	0	0	0	0	2	2	1	2	0	1	0	8
42 Nikki Teasley, G	36	3	5	3	5	1	2	1	4	5	6	2	1	1	0	10
34 Lynn Pride	4	0	0	0	0	0	0	1	0	1	0	0	0	1	0	0
12 Nicky McCrimmon	4	1	3	1	3	0	0	0	0	0	0	1	0	0	0	3
13 Sophia Witherspoon	4	0	1	0	1	0	0	0	2	2	0	0	0	1	0	0
22 Jennifer Gillom	1	0	0	0	0	0	0	0	0	0	0	1	0	0	0	0
31 Vanessa Nygaard							DNP									
20 Shaquala Williams							DNP									
TOTALS	200	21	60	6	15	13	16	8	25	33	12	12	8	11	0	61
PERCENTAGES	35.0	40.0	81.3													

TM REB: 8. TOT TO: 11 (9 PTS)

HOME: Detroit: 5-2. Head Coach: Bill Laimbeer

No Player	MIN	FG	FGA	3P	3PA	FT	FTA	OR	DR	TOT	A	PF	ST	TO	TEC	PTS
32 Swin Cash, F	36	4	12	0	2	1	1	1	2	3	3	1	0	2	0	9
35 Cheryl Ford, F	33	4	9	0	0	0	0	2	5	7	2	4	2	1	0	8
00 Ruth Riley, C	31	5	14	0	0	1	2	0	3	3	5	2	0	2	0	11
14 Deanna Nolan, G	30	5	11	2	5	2	2	0	2	2	3	2	3	3	0	14
5 Elaine Powell, G	29	1	4	0	0	0	0	2	6	8	1	3	1	0	0	2
11 Kedra Holland-Corn	22	6	11	4	5	0	0	0	4	4	3	0	1	1	0	16
54 Barbara Farris	14	1	2	0	0	0	0	0	2	2	0	2	0	2	0	2
9 Stacey Thomas	4	0	0	0	0	0	0	0	1	1	0	0	0	0	0	0
12 Ayana Walker	1	0	0	0	0	0	0	0	0	0	0	0	0	0	0	0
31 Sheila Lambert							DNP									
44 Ndiaye-Diatta							DNP									
TOTALS	200	26	63	6	12	4	5	5	25	30	17	14	7	11	0	62
PERCENTAGES	41.3	50.0	80.0													

TM REB: 9. TOT TO: 12 (14 PTS)

BLOCKED SHOTS: Sparks 5: Milton-Jones, Mabika 1, Leslie 2, Dixon. Shock 6: Ford 1, Riley 4, Powell 1.

TECHNICAL FOULS: None

	ILL	PTO	FBP	PIP	2PT
LA	0	14	6	20	7
DET	0	9	6	22	8

FLAGRANT FOUL: None

GAME 3

At The Palace of Auburn Hills, September 16, 2003

OFFICIALS: June Courteau, Lisa Mattingly, Michael Price. TIME OF GAME: 2:02. ATTENDANCE: 22,076

SCORE BY PERIODS	1	2	FINAL
Los Angeles	37	41	78
Detroit	42	41	83

VISITORS: Los Angeles 5-4. Head Coach: Michael Cooper

No Player	MIN	FG	FGA	3P	3PA	FT	FTA	OR	DR	TOT	A	PF	ST	TO	TEC	PTS
8 Milton-Jones, F	40	6	13	2	3	5	6	3	4	7	1	4	2	3	0	19
4 Mwadi Mabika, F	40	11	20	2	3	5	5	2	7	9	2	3	1	2	0	29
9 Lisa Leslie, C	39	5	19	0	0	3	4	4	7	11	3	6	2	2	0	13
21 Tamecka Dixon, G	36	5	11	0	3	4	4	1	2	3	4	5	1	0	0	14
42 Nikki Teasley, G	35	1	6	1	4	0	0	1	2	3	7	3	1	2	0	3
34 Lynn Pride	6	0	0	0	0	0	0	1	0	1	0	3	0	0	0	0
13 Sophia Witherspoon	4	0	2	0	2	0	0	0	0	0	0	0	0	0	0	0
31 Vanessa Nygaard							DNP									
20 Shaquala Williams							DNP									
22 Jennifer Gillom							DNP									
12 Nicky McCrimmon							DNP									
TOTALS	200	28	71	5	15	17	19	12	22	34	17	24	7	9	0	78
PERCENTAGES	39.4	33.3	89.5													

TM REB: 8. TOT TO: 9 (11 PTS)

HOME: Detroit 6-2. Head Coach: Bill Laimbeer

No Player	MIN	FG	FGA	3P	3PA	FT	FTA	OR	DR	TOT	A	PF	ST	TO	TEC	PTS
32 Swin Cash, F	40	5	14	0	1	3	6	3	9	12	9	2	0	3	0	13
35 Cheryl Ford, F	29	3	7	0	0	4	4	2	9	11	0	4	1	1	0	10
00 Ruth Riley, C	34	11	19	0	0	5	6	4	2	6	3	3	0	0	0	27
5 Elaine Powell, G	36	3	6	0	2	1	2	0	1	1	5	3	2	2	0	7
14 Deanna Nolan, G	26	4	11	3	6	6	6	1	0	1	4	4	1	1	0	17
11 Kedra Holland-Corn	17	1	2	1	2	2	2	0	0	0	0	1	1	2	0	5
54 Barbara Farris	16	1	3	0	0	2	2	1	0	1	0	1	0	1	0	4
31 Sheila Lambert	1	0	0	0	0	0	0	0	0	0	0	0	0	1	0	0
9 Stacey Thomas	1	0	0	0	0	0	0	0	0	0	0	0	0	0	0	0
44 Ndiaye-Diatta						DNP										
12 Ayana Walker						DNP										
TOTALS	200	28	62	4	11	23	28	11	21	32	21	18	5	11	0	83
PERCENTAGES	45.2	36.4	82.1													

TM REB: 10. TOT TO: 11 (12 PTS)
BLOCKED SHOTS: Sparks 5: Milton-Jones 2, Leslie 2, Pride 1. Shock 6: Ford 1, Riley 3, Powell 1, Nolan 1.
TECHNICAL FOULS: None.

	ILL	PTO	FBP	PIP	2PT
LA	0	12	9	34	12
DET	0	11	7	32	8

FLAGRANT FOUL: None.

ALL-STAR GAME BOX SCORE

At Madison Square Garden, July 12, 2003

OFFICIALS: Roy Gulbeyan, Guc Blauoh, Lamont Simpson. TIME OF GAME: 2:05 ATTENDANCE: 18,610.

SCORE BY PERIODS	1	2	FINAL
West	38	46	84
East	46	29	75

VISITORS: West

No Player	MIN	FG	FGA	3P	3PA	FT	FTA	OR	DR	TOT	A	PF	ST	TO	TEC	PTS
22 Sheryl Swoopes, F	21	1	4	0	1	2	4	0	4	4	4	1	1	2	0	4
9 Lisa Leslie, F	16	7	10	1	2	2	2	1	2	3	0	2	1	2	0	17
15 Lauren Jackson, C	19	3	7	1	2	2	3	1	3	4	0	0	0	0	0	9
10 Sue Bird, G	21	3	8	1	4	4	5	1	3	4	2	1	0	2	0	11
21 Tamecka Dixon, G	14	0	2	0	0	0	0	1	2	3	1	0	0	2	0	0
33 Yolanda Griffith	25	6	8	0	0	2	3	2	5	7	1	3	2	6	0	14
42 Nikki Teasley	24	2	6	2	5	4	4	0	6	6	6	0	5	0	0	10
33 Adrian Williams	19	4	6	0	0	1	2	1	5	6	0	1	2	1	0	9
3 Marie Ferdinand	19	3	7	0	1	0	0	0	0	0	1	4	2	3	0	6
30 Katie Smith	15	1	4	0	0	0	0	0	0	0	0	1	0	1	0	2
12 Margo Dydek	7	1	3	0	0	0	0	1	1	2	0	0	1	1	0	2
7 Tina Thompson			DNP													
14 Cynthia Cooper			DNP													
TOTALS	200	31	65	5	15	17	23	8	31	39	15	13	14	20	0	84
PERCENTAGES	47.7	33.3	73.9													

TM REB: 6. TOT TO: 20 (21 PTS)

HOME: East

No Player	MIN	FG	FGA	3P	3PA	FT	FTA	OR	DR	TOT	A	PF	ST	TO	TEC	PTS
24 Tamika Catchings, F	30	6	15	4	6	1	2	2	2	4	2	4	2	5	0	17
1 Chamique Holdsclaw, F	15	3	8	0	1	0	0	0	1	1	0	0	1	0	0	6
24 Tari Phillips, C	20	6	12	0	0	1	1	2	5	7	1	4	2	1	0	13
5 Dawn Staley, G	24	1	6	1	4	2	2	0	4	4	7	1	0	4	0	5
11 Weatherspoon, G	16	0	1	0	0	0	2	1	2	3	2	0	3	0	0	0
14 Deanna Nolan	22	5	10	3	7	2	3	2	4	6	1	1	1	0	0	15
12 Natalie Williams	22	3	5	0	0	0	0	7	4	11	1	1	3	1	0	6
32 Swin Cash	19	3	13	0	4	0	0	1	1	2	1	1	2	1	0	6
14 Shannon Johnson	2	0	5	0	1	0	0	0	1	1	2	1	0	1	0	0
42 Nykesha Sales	11	3	6	1	3	0	0	0	1	1	0	1	1	1	0	7
35 Cheryl Ford	9	0	2	0	0	0	0	0	1	1	0	2	0	2	0	0
25 Becky Hammon			DNP													
TOTALS	200	30	83	9	26	6	10	15	26	41	17	16	12	19	0	75
PERCENTAGES	36.1	34.6	60.0													

TM REB: 11. TOT TO: 20 (30 PTS)
BLOCKED SHOTS: West 5: Jackson 3, Griffith 2. East 4: Holdsclaw 1, Phillips 2, Ford 1.
TECHNICAL FOULS: None.

	ILL	PTO	FBP	PIP	2PT
West	0	30	16	50	8
East	0	21	4	28	10

FLAGRANT FOUL: None.

2002 SEASON IN REVIEW

Front Row (l. to r.) - Marlies Askamp, M. Nikki Teasley, DeLisha Milton, President Johnny Buss, Lisa Leslie, Vedrana Grgin-Fonseca, Erika DeSouza. Back Row (l. to r.) - Head Coach Michael Cooper, Assistant Coach Glenn McDonald, General Manager Penny Toler, Assistant Coach Karleen Thompson, Latasha Byears, Nicky McCrimmon, Tamecka Dixon, Mwadi Mabika, Sophia Witherspoon, Team Trainer Sandee Teruya, Team Manager Thomas Archie, Assistant to the General Manager Rondre Jackson, Video Coordinator Ryan Weisenberg.

FINAL STANDINGS

EASTERN CONFERENCE

TEAM	W	L	PCT	GB	HOME	ROAD	LAST-10	STREAK
New York	18	14	.562	-	10-6	8-8	5-5	Lost 2
Charlotte	18	14	.562	-	11-5	7-9	5-5	Won 4
Washington	17	15	.531	1	9-7	8-8	2-8	Lost 1
Indiana	16	16	.500	2	10-6	6-10	7-3	Won 2
Orlando	16	16	.500	2	10-6	6-10	6-4	Won 2
Miami	15	17	.469	3	9-7	6-10	5-5	Won 1
Cleveland	10	22	.312	8	4-12	6-10	2-8	Lost 6
Detroit	9	23	.281	9	7-9	2-14	5-5	Lost 2

WESTERN CONFERENCE

TEAM	W	L	PCT	GB	HOME	ROAD	LAST-10	STREAK
Los Angeles	25	7	.781	-	12-4	13-3	7-3	Won 3
Houston	24	8	.750	1	14-2	10-6	8-2	Won 1
Utah	20	12	.625	5	12-4	8-8	5-5	Won 1
Seattle	17	15	.531	8	10-6	7-9	7-3	Lost 1
Portland	16	16	.500	9	9-7	7-9	3-7	Lost 4
Sacramento	14	18	.437	11	10-6	4-12	8-2	Won 1
Phoenix	11	21	.344	14	10-6	1-15	3-7	Lost 1
Minnesota	10	22	.312	15	7-9	3-13	3-7	Lost 3

TEAM STANDINGS
OFFENSIVE

TEAM	G	FG	FGA	PCT	FG3	FG3A	PCT	FT	FTA	PCT	OFF	DEF	REB	AST	PF	DQ	STL	TO	BLK	PTS	AVG
L.A.	32	891	2002	.445	194	515	.377	476	645	.738	329	814	1143	583	664	18	257	517	161	2452	76.6
Utah	32	843	1911	.441	89	247	.360	643	844	.762	347	721	1068	478	665	7	228	522	178	2418	75.6
Orl.	32	808	1914	.422	145	461	.315	493	646	.763	320	595	915	446	669	6	295	456	113	2254	70.4
Cha.	32	770	1790	.430	211	527	.400	490	663	.739	302	653	955	496	647	9	241	408	105	2241	70.0
Port.	32	829	1951	.425	127	391	.325	410	564	.727	307	641	948	492	623	1	239	493	120	2195	68.6
Sea.	32	794	1948	.408	182	506	.360	418	543	.770	362	633	995	514	623	5	282	477	151	2188	68.4
Sac.	32	780	1945	.401	112	395	.284	494	653	.757	301	648	949	500	675	8	247	456	109	2166	67.7
Wash.	32	806	1910	.422	164	443	.370	359	478	.751	330	708	1038	516	583	3	221	455	94	2135	66.7
Det.	32	766	1919	.399	110	364	.302	472	651	.725	360	719	1079	478	609	1	201	541	132	2114	66.1
Ind.	32	731	1825	.401	180	543	.331	455	580	.784	315	633	948	447	559	6	268	438	100	2097	65.5
Phoe.	32	793	1889	.420	100	328	.305	405	538	.753	292	626	918	427	623	1	267	501	94	2091	65.3
N.Y.	32	772	1740	.444	145	400	.363	400	567	.705	260	610	870	496	638	5	261	458	100	2089	65.3
Hou.	32	755	1778	.425	109	332	.328	453	585	.774	299	702	1001	450	467	1	260	455	126	2072	64.8
Clev.	32	760	1820	.418	121	374	.324	430	553	.778	295	674	969	480	567	8	225	451	83	2071	64.7
Miami	32	774	1856	.417	129	389	.332	369	529	.698	296	573	869	476	643	4	274	435	96	2046	63.9
Minn.	32	727	1775	.410	166	500	.332	383	578	.663	309	650	959	466	617	7	226	529	102	2003	62.6

DEFENSIVE

Team	FG	FGA	PCT	FG3	FG3A	PCT	FT	FTA	PCT	OFF	DEF	REB	AST	PF	DQ	STL	TO	BLK	PTS	AVG	DIFF
Hou.	705	1880	.375	151	489	.309	331	452	.732	309	664	973	446	606	7	262	464	71	1892	59.1	+5.6
N.Y.	691	1733	.399	149	434	.343	484	645	.750	312	649	961	410	597	2	228	478	88	2015	63.0	+2.3
Miami	745	1722	.433	129	382	.338	469	614	.764	278	693	971	446	588	4	222	515	104	2088	65.3	-1.3
Sea.	783	1818	.431	102	342	.298	435	587	.741	307	662	969	488	563	5	254	531	125	2103	65.7	+2.7
Minn.	747	1807	.413	141	389	.362	469	613	.765	302	612	914	495	618	4	273	465	117	2104	65.8	-3.2
Wash.	786	1903	.413	147	446	.330	397	538	.738	309	680	989	442	570	3	237	441	101	2116	66.1	+0.6
Ind.	804	1817	.442	162	464	.349	359	503	.714	288	644	932	507	647	9	226	470	145	2129	66.5	-1.0
Cha.	778	1807	.431	133	372	.358	444	598	.742	295	620	915	489	600	2	208	424	103	2133	66.7	+3.4
Clev.	797	1834	.435	149	441	.338	397	521	.762	278	640	918	530	613	5	242	428	109	2140	66.9	-2.2
Port.	819	1885	.434	126	348	.362	463	647	.716	334	678	1012	486	616	6	272	508	139	2227	69.6	-1.0
L.A.	796	2040	.390	163	521	.313	480	649	.740	314	645	959	508	623	6	275	453	111	2235	69.8	+6.8
Orl.	804	1862	.432	156	422	.370	491	668	.735	362	684	1046	519	637	9	251	541	108	2255	70.5	-0.0
Det.	828	1984	.417	146	447	.327	464	605	.767	314	669	983	465	637	4	277	443	139	2266	70.8	-4.8
Phoe.	850	1870	.455	155	388	.399	436	608	.717	309	692	1001	532	600	6	268	491	127	2291	71.6	-6.3
Sac.	815	1944	.419	149	453	.329	515	681	.756	352	723	1075	493	633	8	233	496	128	2294	71.7	-4.0
Utah	851	2067	.412	126	377	.334	516	688	.750	361	645	1006	489	724	10	260	444	149	2344	73.3	+2.3
Avg	787	1873	.420	143	420	.340	447	601	.743	314	663	977	484	617	6	249	475	117	2165	67.6	—
Totals	12599	29973		2284	6715		7150	9617		5024	10600	15624	7745	9872	90	3988	7592	1864	34632	—	—

TEAM COMPARISONS

TEAM	Points Per Game		Field Goal Percentage		Turnovers Per Game		Rebound Percentages			Below 70 Pts.		Overtime Games		3 PTS or Less		10 PTS or More	
	OWN	OPP	OWN	OPP	OWN	OPP	OFF	DEF	TOT	OWN	OPP	W	L	W	L	W	L
Charlotte	70.0	66.7	.430	.431	12.8*	13.3	.328	.689	.508	14	23	2	0	1	6	11	5
Cleveland	64.7	66.9	.418	.435	14.1	13.4	.316	.708	.512	24	22	0	4	1	2	7	8
Detroit	66.1	70.8	.399	.417	16.9	13.8	.350	.696	.523	22	14	0	2	3	3	4	12
Houston	64.8	59.1*	.425	.375*	14.2	14.5	.310	.694	.502	24	29	1	0	5	1	13	3
Indiana	65.5	66.5	.401	.442	13.7	14.7	.328	.687	.508	21	19	0	1	2	1	6	9
Los Angeles	76.6*	69.8	.445*	.390	16.2	14.2	.338	.722*	.530*	9	17	2	1	0	2	13	2
Miami	63.9	65.3	.417	.433	13.6	16.1	.299	.673	.486	26	21	2	1	1	2	3	7
Minnesota	62.6	65.8	.410	.413	16.5	14.5	.336	.683	.509	24	20	1	2	3	6	3	10
New York	65.3	63.0	.444	.399	14.3	14.9	.286	.662	.474	19	23	0	1	3	3	9	5
Orlando	70.4	70.5	.422	.432	14.3	16.9*	.319	.622	.470	14	17	3	0	4	3	6	5
Phoenix	65.3	71.6	.420	.455	15.7	15.3	.297	.670	.483	18	14	0	0	4	4	2	12
Portland	68.6	69.6	.425	.434	15.4	15.9	.312	.657	.485	15	16	0	2	3	4	7	7
Sacramento	67.7	71.7	.401	.419	14.3	15.5	.294	.648	.471	18	11	2	2	6	3	4	12
Seattle	68.4	65.7	.408	.431	14.9	16.6	.354*	.673	.513	18	19	1	1	2	2	9	5
Utah	75.6	73.3	.441	.412	16.3	13.9	.350	.666	.508	9	12	2	0	3	1	9	5
Washington	66.7	66.1	.422	.413	14.2	13.8	.327	.696	.511	23	21	1	0	3	1	6	5
COMPOSITE; 256 games	67.6		.420		14.8		.322	.678		298	17			44		112	

* - League Leader

REBOUND PERCENTAGES — OFF. - Percentage of a given team's missed shots which that team rebounds. DEF. - Percentage of opponents' missed shots which a given team rebounds. TOT. - Average of offensive and defensive rebound percentages.

SCORING AVERAGE

	G	FG	FT	PTS	AVG
Holdsclaw, Was.	20	149	88	397	19.9
Catchings, Ind.	32	184	150	594	18.6
Swoopes, Hou.	32	221	127	592	18.5
Jackson, Sea.	28	186	68	482	17.2
Leslie, L.A.	31	189	133	523	16.9
Mabika, L.A.	32	188	99	539	16.8
Thompson, Hou.	29	176	93	485	16.7
Smith, Min.	31	162	126	512	16.5
S. Johnson, Orl.	31	157	164	499	16.1
Goodson, Utah	32	189	117	503	15.7
Ferdinand, Utah	32	176	132	489	15.3
Gillom, Pho.	31	166	105	473	15.3
Cash, Det.	32	144	173	474	14.8
Smith, Sac.	32	184	86	469	14.7
Sam, Mia.	32	191	55	463	14.5
Bird, Sea.	32	151	102	461	14.4
Phillips, N.Y.	32	183	85	451	14.1
Sales, Orl.	32	155	84	431	13.5
Dydek, Utah	30	139	114	394	13.1
Taylor, Cle.	30	133	87	391	13.0

REBOUNDS PER GAME

	G	OFF	DEF	TOT	AVG
Holdsclaw, Was.	20	54	178	232	11.6
Leslie, L.A.	31	78	244	322	10.4
Dydek, Utah	30	52	210	262	8.7
Catchings, Ind.	32	92	184	276	8.6
Williams, Utah	31	105	150	255	8.2
Thompson, Hou.	29	67	150	217	7.5
Williams, Min.	31	96	133	229	7.4
Phillips, N.Y.	32	69	154	223	7.0
Cash, Det.	32	77	145	222	6.9
Williams, Pho.	32	64	156	220	6.9
Scott-Richardson, Ind.	31	80	131	211	6.8
Jackson, Sea.	28	66	124	190	6.8
Milton, L.A.	32	65	146	211	6.6
Melvin, Cle.	32	84	110	194	6.1
Sutton-Brown, Cha.	32	76	115	191	6.0
Palmer, Det.-Orl.	32	47	142	189	5.9
Smith, Sac.	32	56	132	188	5.9
Bullett, Was.	32	46	140	186	5.8
Goodson, Utah	32	91	90	181	5.7
Stinson, Cha.	32	37	140	177	5.5

ASSISTS PER GAME

	G	AST	AVG
Penicheiro, Sac.	24	192	8.0
Bird, Sea.	32	191	6.0
Weatherspoon, N.Y.	32	181	5.7
S. Johnson, Orl.	31	163	5.3
Staley, Cha.	32	164	5.1
Azzi, Utah	32	158	4.9
Teasley, L.A.	32	140	4.4
Black, Mia.	32	137	4.3
Dixon, L.A.	30	119	4.0
Catchings, Ind.	32	118	3.7
Burgess, Was.	26	93	3.6
Figgs, Por.	31	104	3.4
Swoopes, Hou.	32	107	3.3
Rizzotti, Cle.	26	85	3.3
Grubin, Pho.	32	104	3.3
Nagy, Sac.	24	73	3.0
Powell, Orl.-Det.	30	90	3.0
Jackson, Por.	32	95	3.0

	G	AST	AVG
Canty, Det.	28	83	3.0
Mabika, L.A.	32	92	2.9

FIELD GOAL PCT.

	FG	FGA	PCT
Burras, Por.	117	186	.629
Williams, Min.	124	221	.561
Wauters, Cle.	120	217	.553
Sutton-Brown, Cha.	129	243	.531
Griffith, Sac.	93	179	.520
Harrison, Pho.	120	242	.496
Phillips, N.Y.	183	373	.491
Milton, L.A.	132	271	.487
Scott-Richardson, Ind.	113	232	.487
Walker, Por.	139	287	.484

3-PT FIELD GOAL PCT.

	3FG	3GA	PCT
Miller, Cha.	24	51	.471
Azzi, Utah	41	92	.446
Washington, Hou.-Ind.	22	52	.423
Johnson, N.Y.	32	76	.421
Milton, L.A.	21	50	.420
Feaster, Cha.	79	189	.418
Witherspoon, L.A.	28	67	.418
Stinson, Cha.	29	70	.414
Bird, Sea.	57	142	.401
2 tied			.400

FREE THROW PCT.

	FT	FTA	PCT
Bird, Sea.	102	112	.911
Figgs, Por.	59	65	.908
Arcain, Hou.	98	111	.883
Douglas, Orl.	58	67	.866
Moore, Mia.-Min.	54	63	.857
Grooms, Sac.	71	83	.855
Taylor, Cle.	87	102	.853
Smith, Sac.	86	101	.851
Wauters, Cle.	74	87	.851
Rasmussen, Mia.	39	46	.848

STEALS PER GAME

	G	STL	AVG
Catchings, Ind.	32	94	2.94
Swoopes, Hou.	32	88	2.75
Penicheiro, Sac.	24	64	2.67
Sam, Mia.	32	69	2.16
Sales, Orl.	32	60	1.88
Black, Mia.	32	59	1.84
Phillips, N.Y.	32	58	1.81
Bird, Sea.	32	55	1.72
Jackson, Por.	32	55	1.72
Bullett, Was.	32	54	1.69

BLOCKS PER GAME

	G	BLK	AVG
Dydek, Utah	30	107	3.57
Leslie, L.A.	31	90	2.90
Jackson, Sea.	28	81	2.89
Riley, Mia.	26	41	1.58
Smith, Sac.	32	46	1.44
Catchings, Ind.	32	43	1.34
Whitmore, N.Y.	32	43	1.34
Bullett, Was.	32	37	1.16
Crawley, Por.	32	37	1.16
Sutton-Brown, Cha.	32	36	1.13

MINUTES PER GAME

Player	G	MIN	AVG	Player	G	MIN	AVG
Smith, Min.	31	1138	36.7	S. Johnson, Orl.	31	1110	35.8
Catchings, Ind.	32	1167	36.5	Penicheiro, Sac.	24	853	35.5
Thompson, Hou.	29	1052	36.3	Bird, Sea.	32	1121	35.0
Swoopes, Hou.	32	1154	36.1	Arcain, Hou.	32	1116	34.9
Azzi, Utah	32	1151	36.0	Goodson, Utah	32	1101	34.4

INDIVIDUAL STATISTICS, TEAM BY TEAM

CHARLOTTE STING

Player	G	Min	FGM	FGA	Pct	FTM	FTA	Pct	Off	Def	Tot	Ast	PF	Dq	Stl	TO	Blk	Pts	Avg	Hi
Andrea Stinson	32	950	159	349	.456	64	93	.688	37	140	177	91	56	0	37	52	9	411	12.8	27
Tammy Sutton-Brown	32	885	129	243	.531	124	174	.713	76	115	191	15	125	3	29	49	36	382	11.9	22
Allison Feaster	32	956	115	292	.394	70	85	.824	37	81	118	61	79	0	39	40	12	379	11.8	24
Dawn Staley	32	1061	84	231	.364	77	101	.762	8	48	56	164	67	0	48	80	0	278	8.7	19
Charlotte Smith-Taylor	32	890	91	222	.410	40	54	.741	39	82	121	53	113	3	21	60	17	256	8.0	14
Kelly Miller	32	554	79	177	.446	29	38	.763	31	37	68	49	39	0	22	27	1	211	6.6	23
Shalonda Enis	4	59	5	18	.278	9	9	1.000	6	3	9	3	4	0	1	1	2	19	4.8	11
Tonya Edwards	29	303	36	99	.364	33	46	.717	11	30	41	24	28	0	16	17	2	112	3.9	14
Erin Buescher	29	392	33	82	.402	25	36	.694	32	59	91	18	61	1	13	27	15	95	3.3	11
Summer Erb	31	342	35	62	.565	18	25	.720	20	51	71	10	70	2	13	35	11	88	2.8	11
Keisha Anderson	7	31	3	12	.250	0	0	—	2	4	6	5	4	0	0	3	0	7	1.0	5
Elena Shakirova	1	5	0	0	—	1	2	.500	1	0	1	0	0	0	1	0	1	1	1.0	1
Sheila Lambert	3	16	1	3	.333	0	0	—	2	1	3	3	1	0	1	2	0	2	0.7	2
Shanda Owens	2	8	0	0	—	0	0	—	0	2	2	0	0	0	0	0	0	0	0.0	0
Charlotte	32	6450	770	1790	.430	490	663	.739	302	653	955	496	647	9	241	408	105	2241	70.0	94
Opponents	32	6450	778	1807	.431	444	598	.742	295	620	915	489	600	2	208	424	103	2133	66.7	87

3-pt. FG: Charlotte 211-527 (.400) Stinson 29-70 (.414); Feaster 79-189 (.418); Staley 33-83 (.398); Smith-Taylor 34-91 (.374); Miller 24-51 (.471); Enis 0-3 (.000) Edwards 7-25 (.280); Buescher 4-11 (.364); Anderson 1-4 (.250); Opponents 133-372 (.358)

CLEVELAND ROCKERS

Player	G	Min	FGM	FGA	Pct	FTM	FTA	Pct	Off	Def	Tot	Ast	PF	Dq	Stl	TO	Blk	Pts	Avg	Hi
Penny Taylor	30	908	133	320	.416	87	102	.853	51	107	158	68	66	0	37	58	11	391	13.0	27
Chasity Melvin	32	1055	153	330	.464	90	131	.687	84	110	194	57	104	2	28	74	18	399	12.5	30
Merlakia Jones	32	1094	157	393	.399	62	79	.785	33	143	176	72	60	0	44	55	4	391	12.2	27
Ann Wauters	28	802	120	217	.553	74	87	.851	45	95	140	39	74	0	16	59	21	314	11.2	20
Jennifer Rizzotti	26	695	54	135	.400	32	40	.800	5	65	70	85	53	3	23	45	3	178	6.8	16
Rushia Brown	28	468	42	105	.400	28	38	.737	29	46	75	27	54	0	21	39	8	112	4.0	11
Deanna Jackson	18	143	19	46	.413	17	24	.708	10	17	27	6	11	0	2	9	1	55	3.1	14
Mery Andrade	32	665	34	111	.306	18	23	.783	17	39	56	67	82	2	29	41	6	91	2.8	11
Brandi McCain	31	392	25	86	.291	12	16	.750	4	22	26	41	29	0	11	34	3	83	2.7	9
Lucienne Berthieu	5	16	3	7	.429	2	4	.500	3	1	4	0	5	0	0	0	0	8	1.6	5
Tracy Henderson	23	173	16	41	.390	3	3	1.000	12	22	34	3	26	1	3	18	7	35	1.5	5
Tricia Bader Binford	18	132	4	26	.154	5	6	.833	1	6	7	15	3	0	6	7	1	14	0.8	5
Paige Sauer	1	7	0	3	.000	0	0	—	1	1	2	0	0	0	1	1	0	0	0.0	0
Cleveland	32	6550	760	1820	.418	430	553	.778	295	674	969	480	567	8	221	451	83	2071	64.7	99
Opponents	32	6550	797	1834	.435	397	521	.762	278	640	918	530	613	5	242	428	109	2140	66.9	103

3-pt. FG: Cleveland 121-374 (.324) Taylor 38-111 (.342); Melvin 3-6 (.500); Jones 15-54 (.278); Wauters 0-1 (.000); Rizzotti 38-99 (.384); Brown 0-1 (.000) Jackson 0-3 (.000); Andrade 5-26 (.192); McCain 21-58 (.362); Berthieu 0-1 (.000); Bader Binford 1-14 (.071); Opponents 149-441 (.338)

DETROIT SHOCK

Player	G	Min	FGM	FGA	Pct	FTM	FTA	Pct	Off	Def	Tot	Ast	PF	Dq	Stl	TO	Blk	Pts	Avg	Hi
Swin Cash	32	1079	144	353	.408	173	227	.762	77	145	222	86	85	0	37	100	31	474	14.8	25
Wendy Palmer(‡)	16	464	65	153	.425	35	53	.660	27	69	96	20	44	0	13	34	2	184	11.5	20
Deanna Nolan	32	804	103	248	.415	29	36	.806	17	70	87	62	74	1	27	61	12	277	8.7	18
Astou Ndiaye-Diatta	32	776	126	270	.467	23	39	.590	44	118	162	39	65	0	17	58	12	275	8.6	15
Elaine Powell(*)	15	397	54	121	.446	34	40	.850	26	37	63	60	19	0	23	41	8	148	9.9	18
Elaine Powell(†)	30	705	89	220	.405	50	66	.758	33	62	95	90	50	0	43	71	12	236	7.9	18
Dominique Canty	28	625	52	154	.338	55	76	.724	24	45	69	83	59	0	21	56	4	160	5.7	17
Ayana Walker	32	548	63	167	.377	34	49	.694	56	62	118	17	56	0	12	29	34	162	5.1	16
Barbara Farris	32	564	49	117	.419	45	61	.738	29	65	94	16	62	0	12	38	9	143	4.5	14
Edwina Brown	28	549	43	131	.328	23	32	.719	29	53	82	58	73	0	25	60	7	115	4.1	12
Kelly Santos	12	169	16	42	.381	12	20	.600	12	20	32	7	20	0	3	14	9	44	3.7	9
Lenae Williams	27	177	30	101	.297	0	5	.000	7	12	19	4	15	0	4	14	0	73	2.7	8

Player	G	Min	FGM	FGA	Pct	FTM	FTA	Pct	Off	Def	Tot	Ast	PF	Dq	Stl	TO	Blk	Pts	Avg	Hi
									REBOUNDS									SCORING		
Stacy Clinesmith	12	105	8	21	.381	5	6	.833	1	4	5	17	6	0	1	6	1	27	2.3	8
Jill Chapman-Daily	19	119	10	27	.370	2	3	.667	11	15	26	0	20	0	3	8	2	22	1.2	4
Begona Garcia	8	64	2	11	.182	2	4	.500	0	4	4	9	8	0	3	11	0	8	1.0	6
O. Zakaluzhnaya(‡)	3	10	1	3	.333	0	0	—	0	0	0	3	0	0	0	1		2	0.7	2
Detroit	32	6450	766	1919	.399	472	651	.725	360	719	1079	478	609	1	201	541	132	2114	66.1	91
Opponents	32	6450	828	1984	.417	464	605	.767	314	669	983	465	637	4	277	443	139	2266	70.8	94

3-pt. FG: Detroit 110-364 (.302) Cash 13-63 (.206); Palmer(‡) 19-60 (.317); Nolan 42-114 (.368); Ndiaye-Diatta 0-2 (.000); Powell(*) 6-22 (.273); Canty 1-5 (.200) Powell(†) 8-33 (.242); Walker 2-9 (.222); Farris 0-1 (.000); Brown 6-12 (.500); Williams 13-54 (.241); Clinesmith 6-15 (.400) Chapman-Daily 0-1 (.000); Garcia 2-6 (.333); Opponents 146-447 (.327).

HOUSTON COMETS

Player	G	Min	FGM	FGA	Pct	FTM	FTA	Pct	Off	Def	Tot	Ast	PF	Dq	Stl	TO	Blk	Pts	Avg	Hi
									REBOUNDS									SCORING		
Sheryl Swoopes	32	1154	221	509	.434	127	154	.825	30	128	158	107	50	0	88	87	23	592	18.5	32
Tina Thompson	29	1052	176	408	.431	93	113	.823	67	150	217	62	76	0	25	92	20	485	16.7	31
Janeth Arcain	32	1116	128	302	.424	98	111	.883	42	84	126	86	49	0	51	71	6	364	11.4	23
Tiffani Johnson	32	815	77	178	.433	47	58	.810	73	100	173	39	67	0	17	38	24	201	6.3	13
Rita Williams(*)	9	85	5	11	.455	7	10	.700	0	6	6	7	11	0	11	10	0	19	2.1	15
Rita Williams(†)	29	569	44	146	.301	32	44	.727	10	33	43	50	45	0	32	39	2	139	4.8	17
Michelle Snow	32	480	45	96	.469	34	57	.596	31	88	119	13	59	0	12	22	26	125	3.9	16
Grace Daley	23	185	16	37	.432	29	47	.617	13	10	23	16	15	0	3	17	1	63	2.7	19
C. Washington(‡)	21	349	17	50	.340	2	2	1.000	7	34	41	31	38	1	13	20	0	44	2.1	6
Kelley Gibson	29	276	21	55	.382	4	6	.667	3	17	20	14	21	0	8	21	7	60	2.1	13
Sonja Henning(*)	23	521	18	52	.346	5	11	.455	10	48	58	51	42	0	23	36	6	44	1.9	8
Sonja Henning(†)	31	728	26	74	.351	7	15	.467	18	66	84	66	57	0	32	43	7	62	2.0	8
Tynesha Lewis	17	145	13	30	.433	5	8	.625	6	12	18	9	18	0	3	34	3	34	2.0	12
Rebecca Lobo	21	132	15	32	.469	1	4	.250	9	14	23	12	10	0	1	11	5	34	1.6	9
Tammy Jackson	5	69	3	8	.375	0	2	.000	7	6	13	1	7	0	3	6	3	6	1.2	2
Amanda Lassiter(‡)	6	46	0	10	.000	1	2	.500	1	5	6	2	4	0	2	2	1	1	0.2	1
Houston	32	6425	755	1778	.425	453	585	.774	299	702	1001	450	467	1	260	455	126	2072	64.8	89
Opponents	32	6425	705	1880	.375	331	452	.732	309	664	973	446	606	7	262	464	71	1892	59.1	75

3-pt. FG: Houston 109-332 (.328) Swoopes 23-80 (.288); Thompson 40-108 (.370); Arcain 10-37 (.270); Johnson 0-2 (.000); Williams(*) 2-6 (.333); Snow 1-2 (.500) Williams(†) 19-73 (.260); Daley 2-8 (.250); Washington(‡) 8-21 (.381); Gibson 14-36 (.389); Henning(*) 3-12 (.250) Henning(†) 3-16 (.188); Lewis 3-8 (.375); Lobo 3-7 (.429); Lassiter(‡) 0-5 (.000); Opponents 151-489 (.309).

INDIANA FEVER

Player	G	Min	FGM	FGA	Pct	FTM	FTA	Pct	Off	Def	Tot	Ast	PF	Dq	Stl	TO	Blk	Pts	Avg	Hi
									REBOUNDS									SCORING		
Tamika Catchings	32	1167	184	439	.419	150	184	.815	92	184	276	118	105	2	94	82	43	594	18.6	32
Nikki McCray	32	1058	132	318	.415	84	103	.816	29	68	97	70	73	2	28	82	3	369	11.5	30
Olympia Scott-Richar	31	975	113	232	.487	66	82	.805	80	131	211	52	127	2	38	69	13	292	9.4	31
Rita Williams(‡)	20	484	39	135	.289	25	34	.735	10	27	37	43	34	0	21	29	2	120	6.0	17
Alicia Thompson	18	314	39	109	.358	12	17	.706	12	30	42	14	20	0	7	18	2	97	5.4	16
Nadine Malcolm	29	599	58	158	.367	28	37	.757	22	39	61	21	42	0	13	34	3	156	5.4	19
C. Washington(*)	11	325	26	70	.371	14	20	.700	7	26	33	48	22	0	23	24	2	80	7.3	14
C. Washington(†)	32	674	43	120	.358	16	22	.727	14	60	74	79	60	1	36	44	2	124	3.9	14
Bridget Pettis	32	375	38	107	.355	28	39	.718	17	22	39	17	22	0	8	24	0	113	3.5	15
Kelly Schumacher	31	352	45	89	.506	18	26	.692	18	41	59	13	49	0	7	21	23	108	3.5	15
Niele Ivey	31	439	25	71	.352	17	21	.810	6	22	28	39	31	0	16	22	3	86	2.8	9
Jackie Moore	18	128	16	38	.421	10	14	.714	9	20	29	3	16	0	5	14	1	42	2.3	13
Monica Maxwell	18	170	14	47	.298	2	2	1.000	12	19	31	7	16	0	7	6	4	35	1.9	6
Zuzi Klimesova	11	39	2	12	.167	1	1	1.000	1	4	5	2	2	0	1	2	1	5	0.5	5
Indiana	32	6425	731	1825	.401	455	580	.784	315	633	948	447	559	6	268	438	100	2097	65.5	81
Opponents	32	6425	804	1817	.442	359	503	.714	288	644	932	507	647	9	226	470	145	2129	66.5	89

3-pt. FG: Indiana 180-543 (.331) Catchings 76-193 (.394); McCray 21-66 (.318); Scott-Richardson 0-4 (.000); Williams(‡) 17-67 (.254); Thompson 7-29 (.241) Malcolm 12-41 (.293); Washington(*) 14-31 (.452); Washington(†) 22-52 (.423); Pettis 9-43 (.209); Schumacher 0-1 (.000) Ivey 19-50 (.380); Moore 0-1 (.000); Maxwell 5-17 (.294); Opponents 162-464 (.349).

LOS ANGELES SPARKS

Player	G	Min	FGM	FGA	Pct	FTM	FTA	Pct	Off	Def	Tot	Ast	PF	Dq	Stl	TO	Blk	Pts	Avg	Hi
									REBOUNDS									SCORING		
Lisa Leslie	31	1060	189	406	.466	133	183	.727	78	244	322	83	123	7	46	108	90	523	16.9	30
Mwadi Mabika	32	1050	188	444	.423	99	118	.839	32	135	167	92	90	1	38	62	9	539	16.8	32
DeLisha Milton	30	966	132	271	.487	77	104	.740	65	146	211	45	122	5	50	94	35	362	11.3	23
Tamecka Dixon	30	958	125	320	.391	49	59	.831	18	74	92	119	74	2	28	82	5	319	10.6	29
Latasha Byears	26	486	76	123	.618	30	53	.566	65	76	141	13	89	4	19	20	4	182	7.0	15
Nikki Teasley	32	882	67	166	.404	30	40	.750	17	67	84	140	63	1	25	68	9	204	6.4	18

Player	G	Min	FGM	FGA	Pct	FTM	FTA	Pct	Off	Def	Tot	Ast	PF	Dq	Stl	TO	Blk	Pts	Avg	Hi
Sophia Witherspoon ..31		358	49	118	.415	35	46	.761	9	20	29	29	27	0	13	22	2	161	5.2	19
Marlies Askamp(*)......20		215	26	55	.473	9	14	.643	24	25	49	4	25	0	11	11	4	61	3.1	12
Marlies Askamp(†) 26		287	30	65	.462	12	25	.480	30	30	60	7	34	0	12	12	5	72	2.8	12
Vedrana Grgin-Fonsec12		79	12	31	.387	2	3	.667	3	5	8	1	11	0	1	8	0	31	2.6	8
Vicki Hall 3		19	2	4	.500	3	4	.750	1	1	2	1	2	0	1	1	0	7	2.3	4
Nicky McCrimmon 32		356	20	49	.408	7	11	.636	9	14	23	53	22	0	22	24	3	51	1.6	7
Erika Desouza...........11		41	5	14	.357	2	10	.200	8	6	14	2	14	0	3	6	0	12	1.1	4
Katryna Gaither(‡).......1		5	0	1	.000	0	0	—	0	1	1	1	2	0	1	0	0	0	0.0	-
Los Angeles 32		6475	891	2002	.445	476	645	.738	329	814	1143	583	664	18	257	517	161	2452	76.6	102
Opponents 32		6475	796	2040	.390	480	649	.740	314	645	959	508	623	6	275	453	111	2235	69.8	94

3-pt. FG: Los Angeles 194-515 (.377) Leslie 12-37 (.324); Mabika 64-175 (.366); Milton 21-50 (.420); Dixon 20-57 (.351); Teasley 40-100 (.400); Askamp(*) 0-1 (.000) Witherspoon 28-67 (.418); Askamp(†) 0-1 (.000); Grgin-Fonseca 5-12 (.417); Hall 0-1 (.000); McCrimmon 4-15 (.267); Opponents 163-521 (.313).

MIAMI SOL

Player	G	Min	FGM	FGA	Pct	FTM	FTA	Pct	Off	Def	Tot	Ast	PF	Dq	Stl	TO	Blk	Pts	Avg	Hi
Sheri Sam.................32		1073	191	440	.434	55	89	.618	58	97	155	83	83	0	69	71	6	463	14.5	27
Betty Lennox(*) 26		581	110	307	.358	44	58	.759	18	55	73	47	79	2	25	62	5	310	11.9	24
Betty Lennox(†).........31		719	120	355	.338	50	68	.735	20	69	89	63	102	3	30	82	5	341	11.0	24
Sandy Brondello 30		763	97	266	.365	55	67	.821	7	34	41	46	40	0	26	40	4	263	8.8	23
Pollyanna Johns Kimb31		801	78	149	.523	61	97	.629	58	82	140	32	75	0	27	53	15	217	7.0	16
Ruth Riley 26		519	60	129	.465	28	46	.609	24	66	90	25	87	1	11	49	41	148	5.7	14
Tamara Moore(‡) 5		83	8	25	.320	10	10	1.000	3	4	7	10	16	0	7	11	0	28	5.6	22
Kristen Rasmussen 31		674	64	116	.552	39	46	.848	41	76	117	41	63	0	18	37	16	170	5.5	19
Debbie Black 32		800	64	160	.400	25	33	.750	41	82	123	137	75	1	59	32	5	153	4.8	14
Vanessa Nygaard 29		443	43	101	.426	10	13	.769	27	40	67	9	49	0	11	13	1	120	4.1	11
Iziane Castro Marque 19		182	24	72	.333	17	25	.680	7	10	17	7	22	0	7	18	0	66	3.5	11
Lindsey Yamasaki 15		147	19	43	.442	5	10	.500	3	12	15	9	20	0	4	10	1	52	3.5	12
Claudia Neves 20		194	11	31	.355	11	16	.688	0	7	7	25	18	0	8	13	0	37	1.9	9
Marlies Askamp(‡) 6		72	4	10	.400	3	11	.273	6	5	11	3	9	0	1	1	1	11	1.8	4
Trisha Stafford-Odom ..6		38	1	6	.167	6	8	.750	3	3	6	2	5	0	1	6	0	8	1.3	3
Carolyn Moos 2		6	0	1	.000	0	0	—	0	0	0	0	2	0	0	0	1	0	0.0	0
Miami 32		6475	774	1856	.417	369	529	.698	296	573	869	476	643	4	274	435	96	2046	63.9	86
Opponents 32		6475	745	1722	.433	469	614	.764	278	693	971	446	588	6	222	515	104	2088	65.3	81

3-pt. FG: Miami 129-389 (.332) Sam 26-76 (.342); Lennox(*) 46-131 (.351); Lennox(†) 51-154 (.331); Brondello 14-44 (.318); Moore(‡) 2-9 (.222); Black 0-3 (.000) Rasmussen 3-7 (.429); Nygaard 24-64 (.375); Castro Marques 1-17 (.059); Yamasaki 9-17 (.529); Neves 4-21 (.190); Opponents 129-382 (.338).

MINNESOTA LYNX

Player	G	Min	FGM	FGA	Pct	FTM	FTA	Pct	Off	Def	Tot	Ast	PF	Dq	Stl	TO	Blk	Pts	Avg	Hi
Katie Smith................31		1138	162	401	.404	126	153	.824	24	68	92	79	87	2	32	70	7	512	16.5	28
Svetlana Abrosimova...27		805	119	316	.377	56	116	.483	45	101	146	60	73	0	42	92	10	314	11.6	26
Tamika Williams 31		1023	124	221	.561	63	108	.583	96	133	229	51	57	0	44	74	13	314	10.1	19
Tamara Moore(*)........26		653	63	172	.366	44	53	.830	20	56	76	78	65	0	23	74	9	196	7.5	19
Tamara Moore(†) 31		736	71	197	.360	54	63	.857	23	60	83	88	81	0	30	85	9	224	7.2	22
Betty Lennox(‡).........5		138	10	48	.208	6	10	.600	2	14	16	16	23	1	5	20	0	31	6.2	13
Michele Van Gorp 22		352	41	90	.456	16	22	.727	29	35	64	14	53	2	6	20	11	100	4.5	18
Georgia Schweitzer....30		509	42	87	.483	26	30	.867	7	44	51	37	47	1	15	27	5	124	4.1	17
Lynn Pride 31		589	57	148	.385	8	17	.471	25	78	103	43	73	1	25	47	25	123	4.0	9
Kristi Harrower 27		481	37	95	.389	4	10	.400	9	37	46	54	24	0	12	28	0	96	3.6	9
Shaunzinski Gortman 29		369	35	97	.361	7	9	.778	16	45	61	21	42	0	13	25	6	91	3.1	14
Janell Burse 31		344	31	83	.373	21	36	.583	29	31	60	7	60	0	7	18	13	83	2.7	10
Val Whiting-Raymond ..6		52	4	13	.308	5	12	.417	3	6	9	5	10	0	2	4	2	13	2.2	6
Shanele Stires 9		22	2	4	.500	1	2	.500	4	2	6	3	3	0	2	1	0	6	0.7	5
Minnesota.................32		6475	727	1775	.410	383	578	.663	309	650	959	466	617	7	226	529	102	2003	62.6	85
Opponents 32		6475	747	1807	.413	469	613	.765	302	612	914	495	618	4	273	465	117	2104	65.8	87

3-pt. FG: Minnesota 166-500 (.332) Smith 62-188 (.330); Abrosimova 20-60 (.333); Williams 3-11 (.273); Moore(*) 26-68 (.382); Moore(†) 28-77 (.364); Burse 0-1 (.000) Lennox(‡) 5-23 (.217); Van Gorp 2-7 (.286); Schweitzer 14-33 (.424); Pride 1-10 (.100); Harrower 18-54 (.333); Stires 1-2 (.500) Gortman 14-43 (.326); Opponents 141-389 (.362).

NEW YORK LIBERTY

Player	G	Min	FGM	FGA	Pct	FTM	FTA	Pct	Off	Def	Tot	Ast	PF	Dq	Stl	TO	Blk	Pts	Avg	Hi
Tari Phillips 32		1009	183	373	.491	85	126	.675	69	154	223	41	113	2	58	93	14	451	14.1	23
Tamika Whitmore 32		977	148	310	.477	110	150	.733	43	98	141	23	102	1	27	49	43	406	12.7	28
Crystal Robinson........32		1068	126	302	.417	59	72	.819	22	70	92	81	101	0	48	52	12	378	11.8	24

Player	G	Min	FGM	FGA	Pct	FTM	FTA	Pct	Off	Def	Tot	Ast	PF	Dq	Stl	TO	Blk	Pts	Avg	Hi
Vickie Johnson 31		1028	139	305	.456	49	61	.803	42	67	109	86	60	0	27	45	4	359	11.6	21
Becky Hammon 32		659	87	197	.442	38	56	.679	18	50	68	54	49	0	25	55	0	256	8.0	22
Teresa Weatherspoon 32		954	39	114	.342	28	54	.519	23	63	86	181	88	2	42	78	3	108	3.4	10
Sue Wicks.................30		428	24	70	.343	18	27	.667	30	71	101	14	60	0	22	30	15	66	2.2	8
Korie Hlede 16		129	11	26	.423	4	9	.444	4	12	16	12	24	0	6	21	2	26	1.6	6
Camille Cooper 23		119	11	28	.393	5	8	.625	5	11	16	3	28	0	4	10	5	27	1.2	5
Bernadette Ngoyisa......7		12	3	5	.600	0	0	—	1	4	5	0	2	0	0	2	0	6	0.9	2
Linda Frohlich 16		67	1	10	.100	4	4	1.000	3	10	13	1	11	0	2	4	0	6	0.4	2
New York 32		6450	772	1740	.444	400	567	.705	260	610	870	496	638	5	261	458	100	2089	65.3	84
Opponents 32		6450	691	1733	.399	484	645	.750	312	649	961	410	597	2	228	478	88	2015	63.0	80

3-pt. FG: New York 145-400 (.363) Phillips 0-2 (.000); Whitmore 0-1 (.000); Robinson 67-181 (.370); Johnson 32-76 (.421); Hammon 44-114 (.386); Wicks 0-1 (.000) Weatherspoon 2-20 (.100); Hlede 0-1 (.000); Frohlich 0-4 (.000); Opponents 149-434 (.343).

ORLANDO MIRACLE

Player	G	Min	FGM	FGA	Pct	FTM	FTA	Pct	Off	Def	Tot	Ast	PF	Dq	Stl	TO	Blk	Pts	Avg	Hi
Shannon Johnson 31		1110	157	389	.404	164	214	.766	49	80	129	163	78	1	51	98	7	499	16.1	35
Nykesha Sales 32		1042	155	376	.412	84	106	.792	36	84	120	60	97	0	60	71	7	431	13.5	29
Wendy Palmer(*)........16		501	65	148	.439	27	39	.692	20	73	93	21	46	0	22	23	6	180	11.3	17
Wendy Palmer(†) 32		965	130	301	.432	62	92	.674	47	142	189	41	90	0	35	57	8	364	11.4	20
Katie Douglas 32		830	92	205	.449	58	67	.866	41	94	135	53	66	1	49	42	13	271	8.5	19
McWilliams-Franklin ..13		383	41	82	.500	27	31	.871	21	42	63	13	40	1	19	22	14	110	8.5	17
Jessie Hicks 31		471	73	153	.477	44	63	.698	60	42	102	23	77	1	19	51	25	190	6.1	18
Elaine Powell(‡) 15		308	35	99	.354	16	26	.615	7	25	32	30	31	0	20	30	4	88	5.9	13
Adrienne Johnson 32		602	68	181	.376	12	17	.706	14	32	46	22	40	0	15	26	2	166	5.2	12
C. Machanguana........29		428	61	114	.535	16	25	.640	26	38	64	17	61	0	12	33	4	138	4.8	14
Cintia dos Santos 26		260	26	53	.491	36	46	.783	15	20	35	10	48	1	4	20	13	88	3.4	18
Brooke Wyckoff........32		514	31	95	.326	5	7	.714	28	62	90	32	71	1	19	30	18	81	2.5	13
Carla McGhee 2		4	2	4	.500	1	1	1.000	1	0	1	0	0	0	0	0	0	5	2.5	3
Tiffany McCain 16		51	2	10	.200	3	4	.750	1	2	3	2	9	0	3	3	0	7	0.4	3
Davalyn Cunningham ..6		21	0	5	.000	0	0	—	1	1	2	0	5	0	2	1	0	0	0.0	0
Orlando....................32		6525	808	1914	.422	493	646	.763	320	595	915	446	669	6	295	456	113	2254	70.4	103
Opponents 32		6525	804	1862	.432	491	668	.735	362	684	1046	519	637	9	251	541	108	2255	70.5	99

3-pt. FG: Orlando 145-461 (.315) S. Johnson 21-77 (.273); Sales 37-115 (.322); Palmer(*) 23-60 (.383); Palmer(†) 42-120 (.350); Douglas 29-79 (.367) McWilliams-Frank 1-3 (.333); Powell(‡) 2-11 (.182); A. Johnson 18-61 (.295); dos Santos 0-1 (.000); Wyckoff 14-50 (.280) McCain 0-4 (.000); Opponents 156-422 (.370).

PHOENIX MERCURY

Player	G	Min	FGM	FGA	Pct	FTM	FTA	Pct	Off	Def	Tot	Ast	PF	Dq	Stl	TO	Blk	Pts	Avg	Hi
JJennifer Gillom 31		874	166	400	.415	105	131	.802	36	80	116	37	90	0	29	61	21	473	15.3	26
Gordana Grubin.........32		859	114	297	.384	60	79	.759	16	48	64	104	59	0	36	58	3	317	9.9	23
Lisa Harrison 32		899	120	242	.496	20	23	.870	43	83	126	40	62	0	31	45	3	262	8.2	22
Brandy Reed...............5		85	15	41	.366	8	11	.727	1	3	4	4	8	0	2	8	3	38	7.6	20
Adrain Williams.........32		878	79	169	.467	42	60	.700	64	156	220	35	88	0	48	63	29	200	6.3	15
Adriana Moises Pinto 32		619	63	164	.384	48	60	.800	15	45	60	79	53	0	30	72	3	193	6.0	20
Susanna Bonfiglio 22		306	43	89	.483	19	25	.760	16	21	37	23	35	0	12	18	0	105	4.8	12
Tracy Reid.................24		421	48	117	.410	17	28	.607	33	44	77	14	29	0	22	36	2	113	4.7	16
Kayte Christensen.....30		413	48	95	.505	24	35	.686	39	41	80	15	73	1	24	32	13	120	4.0	11
Jaynetta Saunders 27		302	39	103	.379	21	32	.656	10	28	38	23	23	0	9	20	4	99	3.7	12
Slobodanka Tuvic 26		320	30	77	.390	25	32	.781	11	52	63	11	53	0	9	31	9	86	3.3	11
Kristen Veal 23		361	24	79	.304	10	13	.769	6	21	27	41	41	0	14	42	2	71	3.1	11
Shea Mahoney 3		13	2	3	.667	1	1	1.000	2	0	2	1	4	0	0	1	0	5	1.7	5
Quacy Barnes 2		13	0	7	.000	3	4	.750	0	1	1	0	1	0	1	0	2	3	1.5	3
O. Zakaluzhnaya(*) 5		37	2	6	.333	2	4	.500	0	3	3	0	4	0	0	4	0	6	1.2	3
O. Zakaluzhnaya(†) 8		47	3	9	.333	2	4	.500	0	3	3	0	7	0	0	4	1	8	1.0	3
Phoenix....................32		6400	793	1889	.420	405	538	.753	292	626	918	427	623	1	267	501	94	2091	65.3	82
Opponents 32		6400	850	1870	.455	436	608	.717	309	692	1001	532	600	6	268	491	127	2291	71.6	91

3-pt. FG: Phoenix 100-328 (.305) Gillom 36-93 (.387); Grubin 29-92 (.315); Harrison 2-6 (.333); Reed 0-5 (.000); Moises Pinto 19-66 (.288); Bonfiglio 0-6 (.000) Reid 0-1 (.000); Christensen 0-1 (.000); Saunders 0-4 (.000); Tuvic 1-6 (.167); Veal 13-47 (.277); Mahoney 0-1 (.000); Opponents 155-388 (.399)

PORTLAND FIRE

Player	G	Min	FGM	FGA	Pct	FTM	FTA	Pct	Off	Def	Tot	Ast	PF	Dq	Stl	TO	Blk	Pts	Avg	Hi
DeMya Walker............31		848	139	287	.484	59	95	.621	55	99	154	51	97	1	26	90	33	339	10.9	21
Tamicha Jackson 32		692	122	291	.419	46	66	.697	20	39	59	95	59	0	55	64	1	314	9.8	21

Player	G	Min	FGM	FGA	Pct	FTM	FTA	Pct	Off	Def	Tot	Ast	PF	Dq	Stl	TO	Blk	Pts	Avg	Hi
LaQuanda Barksdale	17	285	36	101	.356	23	26	.885	18	22	40	12	31	0	8	23	7	100	5.9	13
Sylvia Crawley	32	819	114	284	.401	44	63	.698	46	88	134	47	90	0	18	62	37	279	8.7	18
Alisa Burras	32	633	117	186	.629	44	52	.846	52	95	147	7	58	0	10	49	7	278	8.7	19
Ukari Figgs	31	866	83	233	.356	59	65	.908	13	67	80	104	50	0	25	44	2	264	8.5	22
Jackie Stiles	21	382	43	135	.319	24	30	.800	7	11	18	20	38	0	4	21	0	125	6.0	18
Kristin Folkl	32	602	62	126	.492	31	35	.886	41	107	148	32	56	0	18	32	17	155	4.8	13
Stacey Thomas	32	621	51	148	.345	31	61	.508	34	60	94	67	62	0	42	36	12	143	4.5	12
Carolyn Young	19	186	26	74	.351	21	24	.875	5	9	14	12	18	0	4	18	0	83	4.4	11
Tully Bevilaqua	27	421	25	61	.410	19	29	.655	7	26	33	44	49	0	22	27	3	84	3.1	8
Amber Hall	20	104	11	24	.458	8	16	.500	8	18	26	1	12	0	7	12	1	30	1.5	6
Jenny Mowe	5	16	0	1	.000	1	2	.500	1	0	1	0	3	0	0	1	0	1	0.2	1
Portland	32	6475	829	1951	.425	410	564	.727	307	641	948	492	623	1	239	493	120	2195	68.6	87
Opponents	32	6475	819	1885	.434	463	647	.716	334	678	1012	486	616	6	272	508	139	2227	69.6	89

3-pt. FG: Portland 127-391 (.325) Walker 2-12 (.167); Jackson 24-76 (.316); Crawley 7-17 (.412); Figgs 39-120 (.325); Stiles 15-44 (.341); Barksdale 5-22 (.227) Folkl 0-3 (.000); Thomas 10-39 (.256); Young 10-22 (.455); Bevilaqua 15-36 (.417); Opponents 126-348 (.362)

SACRAMENTO MONARCHS

Player	G	Min	FGM	FGA	Pct	FTM	FTA	Pct	Off	Def	Tot	Ast	PF	Dq	Stl	TO	Blk	Pts	Avg	Hi
Yolanda Griffith	17	577	93	179	.520	102	127	.803	66	82	148	19	70	0	16	45	13	288	16.9	28
Tangela Smith	32	1063	184	435	.423	86	101	.851	56	132	188	40	126	4	27	59	46	469	14.7	27
Ruthie Bolton	32	737	125	316	.396	56	77	.727	31	63	94	37	74	0	45	35	2	349	10.9	21
Kedra Holland-Corn	32	902	102	299	.341	54	72	.750	28	62	90	63	74	1	41	81	5	296	9.3	28
Ticha Penicheiro	24	853	60	159	.377	75	103	.728	7	95	102	192	49	0	64	69	1	203	8.5	23
Lady Grooms	32	850	78	181	.431	71	83	.855	38	61	99	39	69	0	21	46	8	227	7.1	15
La'Keshia Frett	32	648	84	187	.449	14	17	.824	30	65	95	23	70	2	5	27	19	187	5.8	15
Edna Campbell	1	12	2	5	.400	0	0	—	0	1	1	0	0	0	1	0	0	4	4.0	4
Hamchetou Maiga	23	197	13	53	.245	14	30	.467	18	19	37	9	37	0	15	23	3	40	1.7	6
Cass Bauer-Bilodeau	25	233	17	57	.298	9	15	.600	14	27	41	1	34	0	2	25	5	43	1.7	6
Kara Wolters	14	78	9	28	.321	6	10	.600	8	15	23	3	18	0	0	6	3	24	1.7	6
Andrea Nagy	24	409	12	44	.273	7	16	.438	3	26	29	73	51	1	10	31	4	34	1.4	6
Stacey Ford	5	12	1	2	.500	0	2	.000	2	0	2	1	1	0	0	1	0	2	0.4	2
Monique Ambers	2	4	0	0	—	0	0	—	0	0	0	0	2	0	0	0	0	0	0.0	0
Sacramento	32	6575	780	1945	.401	494	653	.757	301	648	949	500	675	8	247	456	109	2166	67.7	86
Opponents	32	6575	815	1944	.419	515	681	.756	352	723	1075	493	633	8	233	496	128	2294	71.7	87

3-pt. FG: Sacramento 112-395 (.284) Smith 15-42 (.357); Bolton 43-132 (.326); Holland-Corn 38-157 (.242); Penicheiro 8-32 (.250); Grooms 0-1 (.000); Frett 5-15 (.333) Campbell 0-2 (.000); Nagy 3-14 (.214); Opponents 149-453 (.329)

SEATTLE STORM

Player	G	Min	FGM	FGA	Pct	FTM	FTA	Pct	Off	Def	Tot	Ast	PF	Dq	Stl	TO	Blk	Pts	Avg	Hi
Lauren Jackson	28	882	186	462	.403	68	90	.756	66	124	190	41	95	1	30	47	81	482	17.2	27
Sue Bird	32	1121	151	375	.403	102	112	.911	17	66	83	191	48	0	55	109	3	461	14.4	33
Kamila Vodichkova	32	817	114	245	.465	54	67	.806	61	115	176	47	96	1	36	55	18	295	9.2	20
Simone Edwards	32	694	84	158	.532	54	73	.740	46	95	141	19	66	0	21	44	12	223	7.0	18
Semeka Randall(‡)	21	458	47	133	.353	36	51	.706	38	30	68	29	33	0	20	36	1	134	6.4	21
Jamie Redd	10	112	17	34	.500	9	12	.750	8	5	13	7	17	0	2	7	0	52	5.2	14
Felicia Ragland	31	432	48	125	.384	23	28	.821	27	21	48	23	44	0	27	29	1	141	4.5	19
Amanda Lassiter(*)	24	554	47	130	.362	12	17	.706	23	40	63	55	58	1	27	49	19	126	5.3	14
Amanda Lassiter(†)	30	600	47	140	.336	13	19	.684	24	45	69	57	62	1	29	51	21	127	4.2	14
Adia Barnes	26	493	37	111	.333	15	29	.517	45	57	102	28	64	1	32	25	9	90	3.5	12
Kate Starbird(*)	9	186	20	44	.455	8	9	.889	3	16	19	12	19	0	6	11	4	53	5.9	13
Kate Starbird(†)	24	274	30	69	.435	12	16	.750	3	23	26	19	35	0	15	13	8	79	3.3	13
Michelle Marciniak	32	280	24	68	.353	22	29	.759	8	20	28	38	33	0	11	25	2	72	3.1	18
Sonja Henning(‡)	8	207	8	22	.364	2	4	.500	8	18	26	15	15	0	9	7	1	18	2.3	8
Takeisha Lewis	14	57	4	10	.400	10	18	.556	7	17	24	3	12	0	2	7	0	18	1.3	7
Kate Paye	19	114	7	19	.368	1	2	.500	2	5	7	5	18	1	3	8	0	21	1.1	11
Danielle McCulley	4	43	0	12	.000	2	2	1.000	3	4	7	1	5	0	1	2	0	2	0.5	2
Seattle	32	6450	794	1948	.408	418	543	.770	362	633	995	514	623	5	282	477	151	2188	68.4	90
Opponents	32	6450	783	1818	.431	435	587	.741	307	662	969	488	563	5	254	531	125	2103	65.7	82

3-pt. FG: Seattle 182-506 (.360) Jackson 42-120 (.350); Bird 57-142 (.401); Vodichkova 13-38 (.342); Edwards 1-1 (1.000); Randall(‡) 4-19 (.211); Redd 9-18 (.500) Ragland 22-55 (.400); Lassiter(*) 20-66 (.303); Lassiter(†) 20-71 (.282); Barnes 1-4 (.250); Starbird(*) 5-11 (.455); Starbird(†) 7-19 (.368); Marciniak 2-8 (.250); Henning(‡) 0-4 (.000); Lewis 0-1 (.000); Paye 6-16 (.375); McCulley 0-3 (.000); Opponents 102-342 (.298)

UTAH STARZZ

Player	G	Min	FGM	FGA	Pct	FTM	FTA	Pct	REBOUNDS			Ast	PF	Dq	Stl	TO	Blk	SCORING		
									Off	Def	Tot							Pts	Avg	Hi
Adrienne Goodson	32	1101	189	419	.451	117	157	.745	91	90	181	67	92	0	45	102	6	503	15.7	30
Marie Ferdinand	32	1065	176	371	.474	132	171	.772	19	88	107	91	86	0	51	89	7	489	15.3	27
Margo Dydek	30	876	139	319	.436	114	135	.844	52	210	262	71	99	2	25	96	107	394	13.1	27
Natalie Williams	31	1008	124	285	.435	98	132	.742	105	150	255	38	122	4	38	72	16	351	11.3	22
Jennifer Azzi	32	1151	91	198	.460	83	104	.798	15	54	69	158	102	0	27	67	14	306	9.6	19
Semeka Randall(*)	8	135	18	40	.450	22	29	.759	4	17	21	8	16	0	4	10	1	58	7.3	16
Semeka Randall(†)	29	593	65	173	.376	58	80	.725	42	47	89	37	49	0	24	46	2	192	6.6	21
LaTonya Johnson	28	269	25	76	.329	15	20	.750	8	11	19	10	36	1	7	15	2	75	2.7	10
Amy Herrig	28	269	23	53	.434	22	30	.733	15	42	57	4	35	0	9	21	14	68	2.4	11
LaNeishea Caufield	8	65	6	15	.400	2	2	1.000	3	2	5	1	13	0	7	8	0	19	2.4	8
A. Gardner-Combs	30	198	18	49	.367	21	38	.553	29	32	61	5	35	0	3	13	3	57	1.9	14
Kate Starbird(‡)	15	88	10	25	.400	4	7	.571	0	7	7	7	16	0	9	2	4	26	1.7	5
Danielle Crockrom	18	84	10	28	.357	9	12	.750	6	7	13	2	8	0	3	2	0	29	1.6	6
Elisa Aguilar	28	141	14	33	.424	4	7	.571	0	11	11	16	5	0	3	11	2	43	1.5	7
Utah	32	6450	843	1911	.441	643	844	.762	347	721	1068	478	665	7	228	522	178	2418	75.6	94
Opponents	32	6450	851	2067	.412	516	688	.750	361	645	1006	489	724	10	260	444	149	2344	73.3	102

3-pt. FG: Utah 89-247 (.360) Goodson 8-28 (.286); Ferdinand 5-34 (.147); Dydek 2-8 (.250); Williams 5-12 (.417); Azzi 41-92 (.446); Randall(*) 0-2 (.000) Randall(†) 4-21 (.190); Johnson 10-32 (.313); Caufield 5-9 (.556); Starbird(‡) 2-8 (.250); Crockrom 0-1 (.000); Aguilar 11-21 (.524); Opponents 126-377 (.334).

WASHINGTON MYSTICS

Player	G	Min	FGM	FGA	Pct	FTM	FTA	Pct	REBOUNDS			Ast	PF	Dq	Stl	TO	Blk	SCORING		
									Off	Def	Tot							Pts	Avg	Hi
Chamique Holdsclaw	20	634	149	330	.452	88	106	.830	54	178	232	45	50	0	20	45	6	397	19.9	32
S. Dales-Schuman	31	805	93	230	.404	74	100	.740	26	55	81	84	79	1	16	68	4	303	9.8	26
Coco Miller	32	904	114	263	.433	46	56	.821	44	72	116	82	84	0	33	59	2	298	9.3	22
Vicky Bullett	32	953	109	236	.462	34	41	.829	46	140	186	53	84	0	54	56	37	271	8.5	23
Asjha Jones	32	612	93	233	.399	20	33	.606	39	50	89	28	88	2	13	39	17	208	6.5	16
Murriel Page	32	750	88	195	.451	30	53	.566	55	100	155	37	79	0	14	45	15	208	6.5	20
Helen Luz	32	474	65	148	.439	15	19	.789	9	23	32	48	40	0	18	43	5	187	5.8	15
Annie Burgess	26	632	39	101	.386	35	45	.778	16	46	62	93	39	0	34	41	4	125	4.8	15
Tonya Washington	25	291	28	86	.326	11	13	.846	27	11	38	15	6	0	3	16	2	73	2.9	9
Audrey Sauret	15	165	10	24	.417	3	5	.600	3	8	11	18	12	0	8	15	2	24	1.6	9
Kiesha Brown	18	108	12	35	.343	3	3	1.000	4	8	12	6	10	0	5	5	0	28	1.6	8
Maren Walseth	18	104	6	25	.240	0	2	.000	7	14	21	7	8	0	2	9	0	13	0.7	4
Katryna Gaither(*)	1	1	0	0	—	0	0	—	0	0	0	0	1	0	0	0	0	0	0.0	0
Katryna Gaither(†)	2	6	0	1	.000	0	0	—	0	1	1	1	3	0	0	1	0	0	0.0	0
Tausha Mills	4	17	0	4	.000	0	2	.000	0	3	3	0	3	0	1	2	0	0	0.0	0
Washington	32	6450	806	1910	.422	359	478	.751	330	708	1038	516	583	3	221	455	94	2135	66.7	97
Opponents	32	6450	786	1903	.413	397	538	.738	309	680	989	442	570	3	237	441	101	2116	66.1	89

3-pt. FG: Washington 164-443 (.370) Holdsclaw 11-28 (.393); Dales-Schuman 43-109 (.394); Miller 24-64 (.375); Bullett 19-48 (.396); Jones 2-10 (.200); Page 2-4 (.500); Luz 42-106 (.396); Burgess 12-33 (.364); Washington 6-18 (.333); Sauret 1-5 (.200); Brown 1-11 (.091); Walseth 1-7 (.143); Opponents 147-446 (.330).

(*) Statistics with this team only (†) Totals with all teams (‡) Continued season with another team

2002 PLAYOFFS RESULTS

FIRST ROUND

New York defeats Indiana, 2-1

August 16	Indiana 73, New York 55
August 18	New York 84, Indiana 65
August 20	New York 75, Indiana 60

Washington defeats Charlotte, 2-0

August 15	Washington 74, Charlotte 62
August 17	Washington 62, Charlotte 59

Los Angeles defeats Seattle, 2-0

August 15	Los Angeles 78, Seattle 61
August 17	Los Angeles 69, Seattle 59

Utah defeats Houston, 2-1

August 16	Utah 66, Houston 59
August 18	Houston 83, Utah 77 (2OT)
August 20	Utah 75, Houston 72

CONFERENCE FINALS

New York defeats Washington, 2-1

August 22	Washington 79, New York 74
August 24	New York 96, Washington 79
August 25	New York 64, Washington 57

Los Angeles defeats Utah, 2-0

August 22	Los Angeles 75, Utah 67
August 24	Los Angeles 103, Utah 77

FINALS

Los Angeles defeats New York, 2-0

August 29	Los Angeles 71, New York 63
August 31	Los Angeles 69, New York 66

TEAM STANDINGS

OFFENSIVE

TEAM	G	FG	FGA	PCT	FG3	FG3A	PCT	FT	FTA	PCT	OFF	DEF	REB	AST	PF	DQ	STL	TO	BLK	PTS	AVG
L.A.	6	170	372	.457	34	88	.386	91	119	.765	53	148	201	119	128	2	62	78	29	465	77.5
Utah	5	133	307	.433	16	49	.327	80	111	.721	46	128	174	83	98	1	28	81	31	362	72.4
N.Y.	8	214	443	.483	42	108	.389	107	143	.748	60	154	214	132	130	0	45	87	14	577	72.1
Hou.	3	78	213	.366	15	48	.313	43	53	.811	38	65	103	41	57	0	27	30	14	214	71.3
Wash.	5	133	294	.452	26	72	.361	59	77	.766	44	89	133	94	85	0	32	47	14	351	70.2
Ind.	3	75	170	.441	19	54	.352	29	40	.725	34	58	92	46	52	1	11	46	4	198	66.0
Cha.	2	49	122	.402	12	43	.279	11	23	.478	20	43	63	28	34	0	14	27	5	121	60.5
Sea.	2	39	112	.348	10	37	.270	32	37	.865	15	34	49	28	35	0	20	36	8	120	60.0

DEFENSIVE

Team	FG	FGA	PCT	FG3	FG3A	PCT	FT	FTA	PCT	OFF	DEF	REB	AST	PF	DQ	STL	TO	BLK	PTS	AVG	DIFF
L.A.	137	355	.386	29	97	.299	90	116	.776	51	118	169	85	115	0	36	97	25	393	65.5	+12.0
Cha.	51	115	.443	10	30	.333	24	31	.774	17	42	59	38	26	0	19	22	4	136	68.0	-7.5
N.Y.	207	460	.450	44	122	.361	95	129	.736	80	156	236	138	155	2	38	98	24	553	69.1	+3.0
Wash.	133	279	.477	30	82	.366	59	84	.702	41	104	145	76	78	0	29	59	11	355	71.0	-0.8
Ind.	86	170	.506	12	34	.353	30	42	.714	22	55	77	59	49	0	21	33	3	214	71.3	-5.3
Hou.	79	180	.439	9	24	.375	51	72	.708	27	82	109	51	55	1	21	42	19	218	72.7	-1.3
Sea.	58	119	.487	8	23	.348	23	25	.920	11	53	64	38	41	1	23	33	5	147	73.5	-13.5
Utah	140	355	.394	32	87	.368	80	104	.769	61	109	170	86	100	0	52	48	28	392	78.4	-6.0
Avgs	111	254	.438	22	62	.349	57	75	.750	39	90	129	71	77	1	30	54	15	301	70.8	—
Totals	891	2033	—	174	499	—	452	603	—	310	719	1029	571	619	4	239	432	119	2408	—	—

TEAM COMPARISONS

TEAM	Points Per Game		Field Goal Percentage		Turnovers Per Game		Rebound Percentages			Below 70 Pts.		Overtime Games		3 PTS or Less		10 PTS or More	
	OWN	OPP	OWN	OPP	OWN	OPP	OFF	DEF	TOT	OWN	OPP	W	L	W	L	W	L
Charlotte	60.5	68.0	.402	.443	13.5	11.0	.323	.717	.520	2	1	0	0	0	1	0	1
Houston	71.3	72.7	.366	.439	10.0	14.0	.317	.707	.512	1	1	1	1	0	0	0	0
Indiana	66.0	71.3	.441	.506	15.3	11.0	.382*	.725	.554*	2	1	0	0	0	0	1	2
Los Angeles	77.5*	65.5*	.457	.386*	13.0	16.2	.310	.744	.527	2	5	0	0	1	0	3	0
New York	72.1	69.1	.483*	.450	10.9	12.3	.278	.658	.468	4	4	0	0	0	1	3	1
Seattle	60.0	73.5	.348	.487	18.0	16.5*	.221	.756*	.488	2	1	0	0	0	0	0	2
Utah	72.4	78.4	.433	.394	16.2	9.6	.297	.677	.487	2	1	0	1	1	0	0	1
Washington	70.2	71.0	.452	.477	9.4*	11.8	.297	.685	.491	2	3	0	0	1	0	1	1
COMPOSITE; 17 games	70.8		.438		12.7		.301	.699		17	1			3		8	

* - League Leader

REBOUND PERCENTAGES — OFF. - Percentage of a given team's missed shots which that team rebounds. DEF. - Percentage of opponents' missed shots which a given team rebounds. TOT. - Average of offensive and defensive rebound percentages.

INDIVIDUAL PLAYOFFS STATISTICS, TEAM BY TEAM

CHARLOTTE STING

Player	G	Min	FGM	FGA	Pct	FTM	FTA	Pct	REBOUNDS Off	Def	Tot	Ast	PF	Dq	Stl	TO	Blk	SCORING Pts	Avg	Hi
Andrea Stinson	2	65	12	25	.480	2	2	1.000	7	4	11	9	4	0	7	4	0	30	15.0	16
Erin Buescher	2	31	7	8	.875	2	4	.500	2	5	7	1	6	0	3	1	1	17	8.5	11
Dawn Staley	2	78	6	21	.286	3	6	.500	2	3	5	10	2	0	3	4	0	17	8.5	9
Allison Feaster	2	65	6	20	.300	0	0	—	3	12	15	7	1	0	2	4	0	15	7.5	15
Tammy Sutton-Brown	2	56	7	14	.500	1	6	.167	4	8	12	0	6	0	1	7	1	15	7.5	9
Charlotte Smith-Taylor	2	53	5	17	.294	2	2	1.000	0	7	7	0	7	0	1	2	2	12	6.0	10
Summer Erb	2	17	3	5	.600	1	1	1.000	0	1	1	0	3	0	0	1	0	7	3.5	5
Kelly Miller	2	13	2	4	.500	0	0	—	0	2	2	3	0	0	1	0		5	2.5	3
Tonya Edwards	2	19	1	5	.200	0	2	.000	0	1	1	1	2	0	1	0		3	1.5	3
Shalonda Enis	1	3	0	3	.000	0	0	—	2	0	2	0	0	0	0	0	0	0	0.0	—
Charlotte	2	400	49	122	.402	11	23	.478	20	43	63	28	34	0	14	27	5	121	60.5	62
Opponents	2	400	51	115	.443	24	31	.774	17	42	59	38	26	0	19	22	4	136	68.0	74

3-pt. FG: Charlotte 12-43 (.279) Stinson 4-7 (.571); Buescher 1-1 (1.000); Staley 2-10 (.200); Feaster 3-13 (.231); Smith-Taylor 0-7 (.000); Miller 1-1 (1.000) Edwards 1-3 (.333); Enis 0-1 (.000); Opponents 10-30 (.333)

HOUSTON COMETS

Player	G	Min	FGM	FGA	Pct	FTM	FTA	Pct	Off	Def	Tot	Ast	PF	Dq	Stl	TO	Blk	Pts	Avg	Hi
Sheryl Swoopes 3		127	25	63	.397	20	25	.800	10	12	22	17	7	0	12	8	2	73	24.3	28
Tina Thompson 3		128	16	44	.364	7	10	.700	9	15	24	4	12	0	6	2	3	43	14.3	18
Janeth Arcain 3		119	15	35	.429	7	8	.875	2	9	11	4	11	0	5	5	1	39	13.0	17
Rita Williams 3		69	8	25	.320	0	0	—	3	3	6	7	5	0	3	1	0	20	6.7	9
Michelle Snow 3		79	6	18	.333	7	8	.875	6	15	21	4	9	0	0	5	2	19	6.3	12
Kelley Gibson 2		22	4	8	.500	0	0	—	3	1	4	0	3	0	1	0	0	10	5.0	7
Tiffani Johnson 3		51	4	9	.444	0	0	—	2	7	9	1	8	0	0	4	6	8	2.7	4
Grace Daley 1		7	0	2	.000	2	2	1.000	2	0	2	0	0	0	0	1	0	2	2.0	2
Sonja Henning 3		48	0	9	.000	0	0	—	1	3	4	4	2	0	1	2	0	0	0.0	0
Houston 3		650	78	213	.366	43	53	.811	38	65	103	41	57	0	27	30	14	214	71.3	83
Opponents 3		650	79	180	.439	51	72	.708	27	82	109	51	55	1	21	42	19	218	72.7	77

3-pt. FG: Houston 15-48 (.313) Swoopes 3-9 (.333); Thompson 4-12 (.333); Arcain 2-7 (.286); Williams 4-14 (.286); Snow 0-1 (.000); Gibson 2-3 (.667) Henning 0-2 (.000); Opponents 9-24 (.375).

INDIANA FEVER

Player	G	Min	FGM	FGA	Pct	FTM	FTA	Pct	Off	Def	Tot	Ast	PF	Dq	Stl	TO	Blk	Pts	Avg	Hi
Tamika Catchings 3		103	22	45	.489	9	11	.818	12	20	32	7	7	0	4	11	1	61	20.3	29
Kelly Schumacher........3		52	13	20	.650	4	8	.500	6	3	9	3	6	0	2	2	2	32	10.7	17
Coquese Washington....3		110	9	27	.333	1	1	1.000	1	5	6	14	10	0	3	6	0	25	8.3	13
Nikki McCray 3		99	10	27	.370	3	5	.600	1	3	4	11	4	0	1	5	0	24	8.0	14
O. Scott-Richardson 3		99	8	16	.500	5	5	1.000	7	17	24	5	11	0	1	14	1	21	7.0	10
Nadine Malcolm 3		69	7	13	.538	2	3	.667	1	5	6	0	9	1	0	2	0	17	5.7	8
Bridget Pettis 3		43	5	15	.333	5	7	.714	6	3	9	2	0	0	4	0	0	16	5.3	6
Alicia Thompson 1		2	1	1	1.000	0	0	—	0	0	0	0	0	0	0	0	0	2	2.0	2
Niele Ivey 3		9	0	1	.000	0	0	—	0	1	1	3	2	0	1	0	0	0	0.0	0
Monica Maxwell 2		8	0	3	.000	0	0	—	0	0	0	1	0	0	1	0	0	0	0.0	0
Jackie Moore 2		6	0	2	.000	0	0	—	0	1	1	0	3	0	1	0	0	0	0.0	0
Indiana 3		600	75	170	.441	29	40	.725	34	58	92	46	52	1	11	46	4	198	66.0	73
Opponents 3		600	86	170	.506	30	42	.714	22	55	77	59	49	0	21	33	3	214	71.3	84

3-pt. FG: Indiana 19-54 (.352) Catchings 8-21 (.381); Schumacher 2-2 (1.000); Washington 6-16 (.375); McCray 1-6 (.167); Malcolm 1-4 (.250); Pettis 1-3 (.333) Ivey 0-1 (.000); Maxwell 0-1 (.000); Opponents 12-34 (.353)

LOS ANGELES SPARKS

Player	G	Min	FGM	FGA	Pct	FTM	FTA	Pct	Off	Def	Tot	Ast	PF	Dq	Stl	TO	Blk	Pts	Avg	Hi
Lisa Leslie 6		232	46	86	.535	19	26	.731	10	37	47	11	22	0	11	8	17	116	19.3	25
Mwadi Mabika 6		212	31	82	.378	18	26	.692	11	30	41	25	19	0	8	10	1	88	14.7	23
DeLisha Milton 6		204	27	60	.450	15	16	.938	9	32	41	8	22	0	10	11	9	78	13.0	19
Tamecka Dixon 5		147	25	44	.568	9	10	.900	2	18	20	17	15	1	12	13	0	61	12.2	15
Nikki Teasley..............6		184	14	42	.333	16	19	.842	3	10	13	47	22	1	9	22	1	49	8.2	11
Latasha Byears...........6		128	19	30	.633	4	11	.364	15	14	29	5	19	0	9	10	1	42	7.0	10
Erika Desouza..............1		3	0	1	.000	3	4	.750	1	0	1	0	0	0	0	0	0	3	3.0	3
Sophia Witherspoon ...6		39	5	14	.357	4	4	1.000	1	4	5	2	3	0	1	1	0	18	3.0	6
Nicky McCrimmon 5		22	3	7	.429	1	1	1.000	0	1	1	2	2	0	2	1	0	8	1.6	3
Marlies Askamp 4		24	0	5	.000	2	2	1.000	1	2	3	0	4	0	0	0	0	2	0.5	2
Vedrana Grgin-Fonsec..1		5	0	1	.000	0	0	—	0	0	0	2	0	0	0	0	0	0	0.0	0
Los Angeles 6		1200	170	372	.457	91	119	.765	53	148	201	119	128	2	62	78	29	465	77.5	103
Opponents 6		1200	137	355	.386	90	116	.776	51	118	169	85	115	0	36	97	25	393	65.5	77

3-pt. FG: Los Angeles 34-88 (.386) Leslie 5-8 (.625); Mabika 8-25 (.320); Milton 9-16 (.563); Dixon 2-4 (.500); Teasley 5-22 (.227); Witherspoon 4-11 (.364) McCrimmon 1-2 (.500); Opponents 29-97 (.299)

NEW YORK LIBERTY

Player	G	Min	FGM	FGA	Pct	FTM	FTA	Pct	Off	Def	Tot	Ast	PF	Dq	Stl	TO	Blk	Pts	Avg	Hi
Tamika Whitmore 8		271	51	93	.548	26	37	.703	8	28	36	10	20	0	3	9	4	129	16.1	24
Tari Phillips 8		249	45	91	.495	25	35	.714	16	31	47	10	26	0	9	19	4	115	14.4	23
Vickie Johnson 8		244	36	75	.480	12	16	.750	8	22	30	24	10	0	7	11	0	98	12.3	19
Becky Hammon 8		183	29	54	.537	7	8	.875	2	15	17	16	12	0	5	11	0	79	9.9	18
Crystal Robinson.........8		259	23	65	.354	9	9	1.000	8	16	24	14	17	0	8	5	2	67	8.4	20
Teresa Weatherspoon ..8		241	19	40	.475	15	18	.833	8	27	35	53	18	0	8	14	0	53	6.6	11
Bernadette Ngoyisa 3		10	3	5	.600	2	5	.400	1	2	3	0	2	0	0	1	0	8	2.7	5

Player	G	Min	FGM	FGA	Pct	FTM	FTA	Pct	Off	Def	Tot	Ast	PF	Dq	Stl	TO	Blk	Pts	Avg	Hi
									REBOUNDS									SCORING		
Sue Wicks	8	96	7	14	.500	6	7	.857	6	6	12	2	19	0	1	6	4	21	2.6	5
Korie Hlede	2	12	0	1	.000	3	4	.750	2	1	3	1	1	0	1	2	0	3	1.5	3
Camille Cooper	3	15	1	2	.500	1	2	.500	1	1	2	0	3	0	2	2	0	3	1.0	2
Linda Frohlich	3	20	0	3	.000	1	2	.500	0	5	5	2	2		1	3	0	1	0.3	1
New York	8	1600	214	443	.483	107	143	.748	60	154	214	132	130	0	45	87	14	577	72.1	96
Opponents	8	1600	207	460	.450	95	129	.736	80	156	236	138	155	2	38	98	24	553	69.1	79

3-pt. FG: New York 42-108 (.389) Whitmore 1-3 (.333); Phillips 0-3 (.000); Johnson 14-27 (.519); Hammon 14-33 (.424); Robinson 12-39 (.308); Wicks 1-1 (1.000) Weatherspoon 0-2 (.000); Opponents 44-122 (.361).

SEATTLE STORM

Player	G	Min	FGM	FGA	Pct	FTM	FTA	Pct	Off	Def	Tot	Ast	PF	Dq	Stl	TO	Blk	Pts	Avg	Hi
									REBOUNDS									SCORING		
Sue Bird	2	73	9	22	.409	7	7	1.000	0	0	0	12	6	0	5	5	0	28	14.0	17
Kamila Vodichkova	2	61	7	16	.438	10	11	.909	2	8	10	3	3	0	2	2	0	25	12.5	17
Lauren Jackson	2	68	9	26	.346	5	7	.714	5	5	10	3	9	0	3	4	6	23	11.5	19
Adia Barnes	2	50	4	9	.444	0	0	—	3	5	8	3	4	0	3	7	0	10	5.0	5
Amanda Lassiter	2	46	4	15	.267	0	0	—	0	7	7	4	4		3	5	1	10	5.0	6
Michelle Marciniak	2	29	1	5	.200	6	6	1.000	0	2	2	1	3	0	3	4	0	8	4.0	6
Felicia Ragland	2	19	3	9	.333	0	0	—	2	4	6	1	0	0	0	2	0	7	3.5	7
Kate Starbird	2	23	1	2	.500	2	2	1.000	1	2	3	1	2	0	1	4	1	5	2.5	3
Simone Edwards	2	31	1	8	.125	2	4	.500	2	1	3	0	4	0	0	2	0	4	2.0	3
Seattle	2	400	39	112	.348	32	37	.865	15	34	49	28	35	0	20	36	8	120	60.0	61
Opponents	2	400	58	119	.487	23	25	.920	11	53	64	38	41	1	23	33	5	147	73.5	78

3-pt. FG: Seattle 10-37 (.270) Bird 3-11 (.273); Vodichkova 1-2 (.500); Jackson 0-6 (.000); Barnes 2-4 (.500); Lassiter 2-9 (.222); Marciniak 0-1 (.000) Ragland 1-3 (.333); Starbird 1-1 (1.000); Opponents 8-23 (.348).

UTAH STARZZ

Player	G	Min	FGM	FGA	Pct	FTM	FTA	Pct	Off	Def	Tot	Ast	PF	Dq	Stl	TO	Blk	Pts	Avg	Hi
									REBOUNDS									SCORING		
Marie Ferdinand	5	186	25	56	.446	23	34	.676	4	18	22	13	16	0	10	20	0	74	14.8	22
Adrienne Goodson	5	190	29	74	.392	12	17	.706	9	18	27	8	11	0	7	21	0	72	14.4	20
Natalie Williams	5	186	25	47	.532	19	28	.679	21	25	46	7	16	1	5	8	7	70	14.0	25
Margo Dydek	5	171	22	55	.400	13	15	.867	3	41	44	12	17	0	1	16	17	60	12.0	16
Jennifer Azzi	5	186	13	33	.394	7	8	.875	2	11	13	34	20	0	4	8	5	40	8.0	16
Semeka Randall	5	62	8	22	.364	4	5	.800	3	9	12	5	9	0	1	3	0	20	4.0	8
LaTonya Johnson	5	40	7	14	.500	1	2	.500	2	2	4	2	2	0	1	0	1	17	3.4	9
Danielle Crockrom	1	2	1	2	.500	0	0	—	0	0	0	0	0	0	0	0	0	2	2.0	2
Andrea Gardner-Combs	3	14	2	3	.667	1	2	.500	1	3	4	0	5	0	1	1		5	1.7	3
Amy Herrig	2	9	1	1	1.000	0	0	—	1	1	2	0	1	0	1	1		2	1.0	2
Elisa Aguilar	2	4	0	0	—	0	0	—	0	0	0	2	1	0	0	0	0	0	0.0	0
Utah	5	1050	133	307	.433	80	111	.721	46	128	174	83	98	1	28	81	31	362	72.4	77
Opponents	5	1050	140	355	.394	80	104	.769	61	109	170	86	100	0	52	48	28	392	78.4	103

3-pt. FG: Utah 16-49 (.327) Ferdinand 1-5 (.200); Goodson 2-7 (.286); Williams 1-4 (.250); Dydek 3-5 (.600); Azzi 7-19 (.368); Johnson 2-9 (.222); Opponents 32-87 (.368).

WASHINGTON MYSTICS

Player	G	Min	FGM	FGA	Pct	FTM	FTA	Pct	Off	Def	Tot	Ast	PF	Dq	Stl	TO	Blk	Pts	Avg	Hi
									REBOUNDS									SCORING		
Chamique Holdsclaw	5	173	35	78	.449	22	30	.733	10	33	43	16	14	0	10	10	3	94	18.8	26
Coco Miller	5	163	21	50	.420	6	10	.600	7	8	15	12	13	0	2	7	0	54	10.8	21
Murriel Page	5	113	17	27	.630	14	15	.933	6	16	22	4	12	0	1	3	4	48	9.6	17
Stacey Dales-Schuman	5	98	13	30	.433	4	4	1.000	5	3	8	16	8	0	2	5	0	38	7.6	12
Annie Burgess	5	160	11	29	.379	6	9	.667	7	8	15	27	4	0	2	10	0	30	6.0	17
Vicky Bullett	5	110	11	27	.407	2	2	1.000	5	10	15	4	11	0	8	6	5	25	5.0	12
Tonya Washington	4	52	7	14	.500	4	5	.800	1	2	3	2	4	0	3	1	0	20	5.0	11
Helen Luz	4	46	7	12	.583	0	0	—	0	3	3	8	2	0	2	3	0	18	4.5	16
Asjha Jones	5	63	8	19	.421	1	2	.500	3	5	8	3	13	0	1	1	3	18	3.6	6
Kiesha Brown	2	15	3	6	.500	0	0	—	0	1	1	1	3	0	2	0	0	6	3.0	6
Maren Walseth	1	7	0	2	.000	0	0	—	0	0	0	1	1	0	1	1	0	0	0.0	0
Washington	5	1000	133	294	.452	59	77	.766	44	89	133	94	85	0	32	47	14	351	70.2	79
Opponents	5	1000	133	279	.477	59	84	.702	41	104	145	76	78	0	29	59	11	355	71.0	96

3-pt. FG: Washington 26-72 (.361) Holdsclaw 2-11 (.182); Miller 6-11 (.545); Dales-Schuman 8-18 (.444); Burgess 2-8 (.250); Bullett 1-7 (.143); Luz 4-8 (.500) Washington 2-5 (.400); Jones 1-2 (.500); Brown 0-2 (.000); Opponents 30-82 (.366).

2002 INDIVIDUAL FINALS STATISTICS, TEAM BY TEAM

LOS ANGELES SPARKS

Player	G	Min	FGM	FGA	Pct	FTM	FTA	Pct	REBOUNDS Off	Def	Tot	Ast	PF	Dq	Stl	TO	Blk	SCORING Pts	Avg	Hi
Lisa Leslie	2	80	12	24	.500	7	10	.700	2	14	16	3	8	0	1	3	4	32	16.0	17
Mwadi Mabika	2	76	9	27	.333	10	13	.769	4	9	13	7	5	0	2	4	0	32	16.0	20
DeLisha Milton	2	73	10	19	.526	4	5	.800	2	9	11	2	9	0	3	2	5	25	12.5	17
Nikki Teasley	2	76	6	18	.333	6	8	.750	1	4	5	22	6	0	3	11	0	19	9.5	11
Latasha Byears	2	65	7	14	.500	2	5	.400	10	12	22	1	8	0	3	2	1	16	8.0	10
Tamecka Dixon	1	14	3	3	1.000	0	0	—	0	2	2	1	6	1	2	4	0	6	6.0	6
Sophia Witherspoon	2	14	2	4	.500	2	2	1.000	0	1	1	0	1	0	0	0	0	8	4.0	5
Nicky McCrimmon	1	2	1	2	.500	0	0	—	0	0	0	0	1	0	0	0	0	2	2.0	2
Los Angeles	2	400	50	111	.450	31	43	.721	19	51	70	36	44	1	14	27	10	140	70.0	71
Opponents	2	400	44	116	.379	29	40	.725	17	38	55	25	37	0	9	22	5	129	64.5	66

3-pt. FG: Los Angeles 9-26 (.346) Leslie 1-2 (.500); Mabika 4-10 (.400); Milton 1-3 (.333); Teasley 1-8 (.125); Witherspoon 2-3 (.667); Opponents 12-35 (.343).

NEW YORK LIBERTY

Player	G	Min	FGM	FGA	Pct	FTM	FTA	Pct	REBOUNDS Off	Def	Tot	Ast	PF	Dq	Stl	TO	Blk	SCORING Pts	Avg	Hi
Becky Hammon	2	49	10	18	.556	2	2	1.000	1	4	5	4	5	0	1	2	0	27	13.5	18
Vickie Johnson	2	65	9	19	.474	3	5	.600	2	6	8	5	5	0	1	3	0	24	12.0	17
Tari Phillips	2	65	7	22	.318	10	14	.714	5	7	12	3	7	0	2	6	3	24	12.0	12
Tamika Whitmore	2	73	7	22	.318	8	11	.727	0	10	10	2	6	0	0	5	0	22	11.0	17
Crystal Robinson	2	62	5	18	.278	0	0	—	4	1	5	2	4	0	1	3	2	13	6.5	13
Teresa Weatherspoon	2	62	3	10	.300	6	8	.750	2	8	10	8	6	0	3	1	0	12	6.0	9
Sue Wicks	2	24	3	7	.429	0	0	—	3	2	5	1	4	0	1	1	0	7	3.5	5
New York	2	400	44	116	.379	29	40	.725	17	38	55	25	37	0	9	22	5	129	64.5	66
Opponents	2	400	50	111	.450	31	43	.721	19	51	70	36	44	1	14	27	10	140	70.0	71

3-pt. FG: New York 12-35 (.343) Hammon 5-12 (.417); Johnson 3-7 (.429); Phillips 0-2 (.000); Whitmore 0-1 (.000); Robinson 3-10 (.300); Weatherspoon 0-2 (.000) Wicks 1-1 (1.000); Opponents 9-26 (.346).

2002 FINALS BOX SCORES

GAME 1

At Madison Square Garden, August 29, 2002

OFFICIALS: Patty Broderick, Bob Trammell, Matthew Boland. TIME OF GAME: 2:02. ATTENDANCE: 17,666

SCORE BY PERIODS	1	2	FINAL
Los Angeles	35	36	71
New York	35	28	63

VISITORS: Los Angeles 5-0 Head Coach: Michael Cooper

No Player	MIN	FG	FGA	3P	3PA	FT	FTA	OR	DR	TOT	A	PF	ST	TO	TEC	PTS
8 DeLisha Milton	40	7	11	0	1	3	3	2	4	6	0	4	2	0	0	17
4 Mwadi Mabika	40	6	18	3	7	5	7	4	4	8	5	3	1	0	0	20
9 Lisa Leslie	40	6	12	1	1	2	2	1	8	9	2	4	1	2	0	15
42 Nikki Teasley	38	2	7	0	3	4	6	1	1	2	11	3	2	7	0	8
00 Latasha Byears	34	2	8	0	0	2	3	5	6	11	0	3	3	1	0	6
13 Sophia Witherspoon	6	1	3	1	2	0	0	0	1	1	1	0	1	0	0	3
10 Nicky McCrimmon	2	1	2	0	0	0	0	0	0	0	0	1	0	0	0	2
41 Marlies Askamp						Did not play.										
14 Erika Desouza						Did not play.										
21 Tamecka Dixon						Did not play.										
17 Grgin-Fonseca						Did not play.										
TOTALS	200	25	61	5	14	16	21	13	24	37	18	19	9	10	0	71

PERCENTAGES: 41.0 35.7 76.2   TM REB: 6   TOT TO: 11 (15 PTS)

HOME: New York 4-3 Head Coach: Richie Adubato

No Player	MIN	FG	FGA	3P	3PA	FT	FTA	OR	DR	TOT	A	PF	ST	TO	TEC	PTS
44 Tamika Whitmore	38	2	9	0	0	1	2	0	6	6	2	2	0	2	0	5
3 Crystal Robinson	36	5	12	3	7	0	0	2	0	2	1	3	0	3	0	13
24 Tari Phillips	35	4	13	0	2	4	6	1	3	4	3	3	0	3	0	12
55 Vickie Johnson	30	3	7	1	3	0	0	1	3	4	3	2	1	2	0	7

No Player	MIN	FG	FGA	3P	3PA	FT	FTA	OR	DR	TOT	A	PF	ST	TO	TEC	PTS
11 Weatherspoon	29	0	4	0	0	3	4	0	7	7	3	3	1	1	0	3
25 Becky Hammon	23	7	9	4	6	0	0	0	1	1	2	3	0	1	0	18
23 Sue Wicks	9	2	3	1	1	0	0	1	0	1	1	1	0	1	0	5
42 Camille Cooper						Did not play.										
31 Linda Frohlich						Did not play.										
7 Korie Hlede						Did not play.										
50 Bernadette Ngoyisa						Did not play.										
TOTALS	200	23	57	9	19	8	12	5	20	25	15	17	2	13	0	63

PERCENTAGES: 40.4 47.4 66.7   TM REB: 11   TOT TO: 13 (16 PTS)

BLOCKED SHOTS: Sparks 6: Milton 3, Leslie 3.   Liberty 4: Robinson 2, Phillips 2.
TECHNICAL FOULS: None.

	ILL	PTO	FBP	PIP	2PT
LA	0	16	2	24	18
NY	0	15	2	20	8

Flagrant Fouls: None.

GAME 2
At Staples Center, August 31, 2002

OFFICIALS: Roy Gulbeyan, June Courteau, Lisa Mattingly. TIME OF GAME: 2:07. ATTENDANCE: 13,493

SCORE BY PERIODS	1	2	FINAL
New York	24	42	66
Los Angeles	31	38	69

VISITORS: New York 4-4   Head Coach: Richie Adubato

No Player	MIN	FG	FGA	3P	3PA	FT	FTA	OR	DR	TOT	A	PF	ST	TO	TEC	PTS
44 Tamika Whitmore	35	5	13	0	1	7	9	0	4	4	0	4	0	3	0	17
3 Crystal Robinson	26	0	6	0	3	0	0	2	1	3	1	1	1	0	0	0
24 Tari Phillips	30	3	9	0	0	6	8	4	4	8	0	4	2	3	1	12
55 Vickie Johnson	35	6	12	2	4	3	5	1	3	4	2	3	0	1	0	17
11 Weatherspoon	33	3	6	0	2	3	4	2	1	3	5	3	2	0	0	9
25 Becky Hammon	26	3	9	1	6	2	2	1	3	4	2	2	1	1	0	9
23 Sue Wicks	15	1	4	0	0	0	2	2	2	4	0	3	1	0	0	2
42 Camille Cooper						Did not play.										
31 Linda Frohlich						Did not play.										
7 Korie Hlede						Did not play.										
50 Bernadette Ngoyisa						Did not play.										
TOTALS	200	21	59	3	16	21	28	12	18	30	10	20	7	8	2	66

PERCENTAGES: 35.6 18.8 75.0   TM REB: 8   TOT TO: 9 (3 PTS)

HOME: Los Angeles 6-0   Head Coach: Michael Cooper

No Player	MIN	FG	FGA	3P	3PA	FT	FTA	OR	DR	TOT	A	PF	ST	TO	TEC	PTS
8 DeLisha Milton	33	3	8	1	2	1	2	0	5	5	2	5	1	2	0	8
00 Latasha Byears	31	5	6	0	0	0	2	5	6	11	1	5	0	1	0	10
9 Lisa Leslie	40	6	12	0	1	5	8	1	6	7	1	4	0	1	1	17
42 Nikki Teasley	38	4	11	1	5	2	2	0	3	3	11	3	1	4	0	11
4 Mwadi Mabika	36	3	9	1	3	5	6	0	5	5	2	2	1	4	0	12
21 Tamecka Dixon	14	3	3	0	0	0	0	2	2	1	6	2	4	0	0	6
13 Sophia Witherspoon	8	1	1	1	1	2	2	0	0	0	0	0	0	0	0	5
41 Marlies Askamp						Did not play.										
14 Erika Desouza						Did not play.										
17 Grgin-Fonseca						Did not play.										
10 Nicky McCrimmon						Did not play.										
TOTALS	200	25	50	4	12	15	22	6	27	33	18	25	5	16	1	69

PERCENTAGES: 50.0 33.3 68.2   TM REB: 6   TOT TO: 16 (23 PTS)

BLOCKED SHOTS: Liberty 1. Phillips 1. Sparks 4. Milton 2, Adubato 1, Leslie 1.
TECHNICAL FOULS: Liberty 2. Byears 1, Leslie 1. Sparks 1. Phillips 1

	ILL	PTO	FBP	PIP	2PT
NY	0	23	2	28	13
LA	0	3	9	34	12

Flagrant Fouls: None.

At MCI Center, July 15, 2002

OFFICIALS: Teresa Dahlem, Tony Brown, Bob Trammell. TIME OF GAME: 1:58. ATTENDANCE: 19,487

SCORE BY PERIODS	1	2	FINAL
West	40	41	81
East	40	36	76

VISITORS: West   1-0   Head Coach: Michael Cooper

No Player	MIN	FG	FGA	3P	3PA	FT	FTA	OR	DR	TOT	A	PF	ST	TO	TEC	PTS
7 Tina Thompson	28	7	16	1	3	5	6	3	4	7	0	2	2	2	0	20
22 Sheryl Swoopes	23	4	12	0	1	3	4	5	1	6	3	1	2	2	0	11
9 Lisa Leslie	28	6	13	0	1	6	10	3	11	14	0	2	1	4	0	18
21 Ticha Penicheiro	22	1	1	0	0	0	0	0	1	1	2	2	2	2	0	2
10 Sue Bird	21	1	8	0	5	0	0	4	1	5	7	0	1	1	0	2
15 Lauren Jackson	20	6	11	2	3	1	1	2	4	6	0	4	1	0	0	15
4 Mwadi Mabika	16	1	5	0	3	0	0	1	5	6	1	1	0	1	0	2
21 Tamecka Dixon	13	2	6	1	3	0	0	0	1	1	0	0	0	2	0	5
30 Katie Smith	11	2	4	0	2	0	0	0	3	3	4	1	0	2	0	4
15 Adrienne Goodson	9	0	2	0	1	0	0	0	1	1	0	0	0	0	0	0
3 Marie Ferdinand	9	1	3	0	0	0	0	0	0	0	1	0	0	1	0	2
TOTALS	200	31	81	4	22	15	21	18	32	50	18	13	9	17	0	81

PERCENTAGES: 38.3 18.2 71.4   TM REB: 14   TOT TO: 17 (18 PTS)

HOME: East   0-1   Head Coach: Anne Donovan

No Player	MIN	FG	FGA	3P	3PA	FT	FTA	OR	DR	TOT	A	PF	ST	TO	TEC	PTS
24 Tamika Catchings	21	4	12	2	5	2	2	3	6	9	1	3	1	1	0	12
32 Andrea Stinson	20	3	10	1	4	2	2	0	1	1	2	3	1	1	0	9
24 Tari Phillips	22	1	9	0	0	2	2	5	5	10	0	6	0	5	0	4
11 Weatherspoon	21	2	3	0	1	0	0	0	2	2	2	1	2	4	0	4
5 Dawn Staley	18	2	5	0	0	0	0	1	3	4	5	0	1	1	0	4
14 Shannon Johnson	20	2	7	2	6	0	0	2	0	2	3	3	1	0	0	6
55 Sheri Sam	19	3	9	1	4	0	0	2	3	5	2	1	1	0	0	7
55 Tammy Sutton-Brown	17	3	5	0	0	3	4	1	3	4	1	1	0	0	0	9
14 Penny Taylor	17	4	8	0	2	1	1	1	2	3	0	0	2	0	0	9
42 Nykesha Sales	14	3	11	0	2	3	3	1	0	1	0	2	2	2	0	9
21 Dales-Schuman	11	1	5	1	3	0	0	1	2	3	0	0	0	0	0	3
1 Chamique Holdsclaw								Did not play.								
TOTALS	200	28	84	7	27	13	14	17	27	44	16	20	11	14	0	76

PERCENTAGES: 33.3 25.9 92.9   TM REB: 5   TOT TO: 14 (14 PTS)

BLOCKED SHOTS: Sparks: 7. Thompson 1, Leslie 4, Penicheiro 1, Jackson 1. Sting: 8. Catchings 4, Weatherspoon 1, Sutton-Brown 3.
TECHNICAL FOULS: None.

	ILL	PTO	FBP	PIP	2PT
West	0	14	14	28	18
East	0	18	11	32	15

Flagrant Fouls: None.
MVP-West, Lisa Leslie (2nd consecutive, third overall)
Chamique Holdsclaw (Washington) was elected to start, bue replaced due to injury.

Front Row (l. to r.)—Latasha Byears, Vedrana Grgin Fonseca, Lisa Leslie, President Johnny Buss, DeLisha Milton, Mwadi Mabika, Rhonda Mapp. Back Row (l. to r.)—Head Coach Michael Cooper, Coaches Assistant Rondre Jackson, Team Manager Karleen Thompson, Tamecka Dixon, Nicky McCrimmon, Wendi Willits, Nicole Levandusky, Ukari Figgs, Team Trainer Sandee Teruya, General Manager Penny Toler, Assistant Coach Glenn McDonald.

FINAL STANDINGS

EASTERN CONFERENCE

TEAM	W	L	PCT	GB	HOME	ROAD	LAST-10	STREAK
Cleveland	22	10	.687	-	14-2	8-8	5-5	Lost 3
New York	21	11	.656	1	13-3	8-8	5-5	Won 1
Miami	20	12	.625	2	10-6	10-6	7-3	Lost 1
Charlotte	18	14	.562	4	11-5	7-9	9-1	Won 7
Orlando	13	19	.406	9	10-6	3-13	4-6	Won 1
Detroit	10	22	.312	12	6-10	4-12	4-6	Won 1
Indiana	10	22	.312	12	7-9	3-13	3-7	Lost 1
Washington	10	22	.312	12	8-8	2-14	4-6	Lost 1

WESTERN CONFERENCE

TEAM	W	L	PCT	GB	HOME	ROAD	LAST-10	STREAK
Los Angeles	28	4	.875	-	16-0	12-4	9-1	Won 1
Sacramento	20	12	.625	8	12-4	8-8	7-3	Won 4
Utah	19	13	.594	9	9-7	10-6	8-2	Won 1
Houston	19	13	.594	9	11-5	8-8	4-6	Lost 1
Phoenix	13	19	.406	15	10-6	3-13	3-7	Won 2
Minnesota	12	20	.375	16	6-10	6-10	5-5	Lost 1
Portland	11	21	.344	17	6-10	5-11	0-10	Lost 10
Seattle	10	22	.312	18	5-11	5-11	2-8	Lost 3

TEAM STANDINGS
OFFENSIVE

TEAM	G	FG	FGA	PCT	FG3	FG3A	PCT	FT	FTA	PCT	OFF	DEF	REB	AST	PF	DQ	STL	TO	BLK	PTS	AVG
L.A.	32	916	2031	.451	160	436	.367	449	594	.756	350	755	1105	596	616	9	281	438	138	2441	76.3
Sac.	32	837	1974	.424	163	423	.385	457	618	.739	374	723	1097	558	588	4	276	494	158	2294	71.7
Utah	32	811	1849	.439	78	244	.320	507	675	.751	295	775	1070	524	622	7	202	493	156	2207	69.0
N.Y.	32	833	1828	.456	160	421	.380	336	500	.672	255	660	915	553	616	6	265	437	82	2162	67.6
Ind.	32	762	1822	.418	157	446	.352	472	591	.799	286	649	935	458	600	5	242	491	118	2153	67.3
Orl.	32	768	1914	.401	174	532	.327	430	587	.733	356	614	970	452	643	3	320	532	125	2140	66.9
Det.	32	774	1914	.404	143	405	.353	412	542	.760	324	621	945	469	602	3	225	498	82	2103	65.7
Port.	32	733	1891	.388	172	519	.331	450	612	.735	300	696	996	451	633	3	244	500	106	2088	65.3
Minn.	32	671	1810	.371	176	552	.319	559	727	.769	308	693	1001	437	695	9	210	507	127	2077	64.9
Phoe.	32	767	1894	.405	101	313	.323	429	587	.731	300	642	942	514	625	6	292	519	138	2064	64.5
Cha.	32	746	1780	.419	153	428	.357	410	528	.777	309	639	948	467	605	5	217	474	114	2055	64.2
Hou.	32	747	1908	.392	138	435	.317	415	539	.770	348	710	1058	426	509	2	251	436	95	2047	64.0
Clev.	32	763	1770	.431	106	335	.316	372	505	.737	297	662	959	503	532	1	267	444	83	2004	62.6
Miami	32	754	1826	.413	93	295	.315	356	469	.759	292	651	943	467	602	5	300	448	153	1957	61.2
Wash.	32	739	1915	.386	117	418	.280	333	504	.661	356	699	1055	424	537	3	257	495	127	1928	60.3
Sea.	32	689	1821	.378	128	412	.311	415	606	.685	306	585	891	412	605	6	273	431	127	1921	60.0

DEFENSIVE

Team	FG	FGA	PCT	FG3	FG3A	PCT	FT	FTA	PCT	OFF	DEF	REB	AST	PF	DQ	STL	TO	BLK	PTS	AVG	DIFF
Clev.	664	1745	.381	132	417	.317	328	444	.739	297	594	891	434	597	3	225	496	127	1788	55.9	+6.8
Miami	679	1725	.394	120	395	.304	420	588	.714	301	667	968	388	538	3	259	512	87	1898	59.3	+1.8
Hou.	740	1883	.393	152	456	.333	362	504	.718	297	685	982	452	561	3	248	433	120	1994	62.3	+1.7
Cha.	732	1846	.397	114	369	.309	431	562	.767	344	567	911	443	579	1	257	447	124	2009	62.8	+1.4
Sea.	753	1750	.430	125	325	.385	417	559	.746	296	756	1052	492	588	3	228	519	127	2048	64.0	-4.0
Wash.	791	1945	.407	146	408	.358	347	467	.743	331	737	1068	487	543	4	261	454	103	2075	64.8	-4.6
N.Y.	744	1759	.423	133	394	.338	461	640	.720	304	679	983	430	600	4	223	496	76	2082	65.1	+2.5
Sac.	804	2003	.401	116	400	.290	415	578	.718	343	662	1005	496	616	5	261	481	143	2139	66.8	+4.8
Minn.	752	1927	.390	153	472	.324	499	624	.800	328	688	1016	511	719	7	259	470	126	2156	67.4	-2.5
L.A.	779	1985	.392	192	603	.318	416	547	.761	294	627	921	538	591	8	234	453	114	2166	67.7	+8.6
Phoe.	785	1892	.415	137	391	.350	462	584	.791	333	698	1031	524	603	4	283	517	127	2169	67.8	-3.3
Utah	789	1976	.399	125	429	.291	489	660	.741	344	630	974	478	645	13	275	390	148	2192	68.5	+0.5
Port.	791	1944	.407	159	410	.388	461	656	.703	343	763	1106	501	643	6	293	474	144	2202	68.8	-3.6
Orl.	806	1831	.440	157	438	.358	436	605	.721	316	659	975	534	600	2	298	546	114	2205	68.9	-2.0
Ind.	853	1899	.449	131	367	.357	412	583	.707	306	660	966	565	616	6	256	466	140	2249	70.3	-3.0
Det.	848	1837	.462	127	340	.374	446	583	.765	279	702	981	438	591	5	262	483	109	2269	70.9	-5.2
Avg.	769	1872	.411	139	413	.336	425	574	.741	316	673	989	482	602	5	258	477	121	2103	65.7	—
Totals	12310			2219			6802			5056		15830	9630			4122		1929			
		29947			6614			9184			10774			7711		77		7637		33641	

TEAM COMPARISONS

TEAM	Points Per Game		Field Goal Percentage		Turnovers Per Game		Rebound Percentages			Below 70 Pts.		Overtime Games		3 PTS or Less		10 PTS or More	
	OWN	OPP	OWN	OPP	OWN	OPP	OFF	DEF	TOT	OWN	OPP	W	L	W	L	W	L
Charlotte	64.2	62.8	.419	.397	14.8	14.0	.353	.650	.501	22	22	0	3	3	3	6	5
Cleveland	62.6	55.9*	.431	.381*	13.9	15.5	.333	.690	.512	27	26	1	0	1	2	12	1
Detroit	65.7	70.9	.404	.462	15.6	15.1	.316	.690	.503	22	16	3	2	4	4	3	9
Houston	64.0	62.3	.392	.393	13.6	13.5	.337	.705	.521	20	26	0	1	3	3	9	6
Indiana	67.3	70.3	.418	.449	15.3	14.6	.302	.680	.491	21	15	1	2	1	4	3	8
Los Angeles	76.3*	67.7	.451	.392	13.7	14.2	.358	.720*	.539*	10	22	2	1	3	1	14	1
Miami	61.2	59.3	.413	.394	14.0	16.0	.304	.684	.494	24	29	3	4	3	2	10	5
Minnesota	64.9	67.4	.371	.390	15.8	14.7	.309	.679	.494	24	20	1	2	1	4	5	6
New York	67.6	65.1	.456*	.423	13.7	15.5	.273	.685	.479	19	25	0	0	5	0	11	7
Orlando	66.9	68.9	.401	.440	16.6	17.1*	.351	.660	.505	21	16	0	2	2	3	3	9
Phoenix	64.5	67.8	.405	.415	16.2	16.2	.301	.658	.480	22	19	0	2	3	3	6	11
Portland	65.3	68.8	.388	.407	15.6	14.8	.282	.670	.476	23	17	4	1	3	4	3	9
Sacramento	71.7	66.8	.424	.401	15.4	15.0	.361*	.678	.520	14	21	2	2	3	3	13	5
Seattle	60.0	64.0	.378	.430	13.5*	16.2	.288	.664	.476	25	23	2	1	2	4	3	11
Utah	69.0	68.5	.439	.399	15.4	12.2	.319	.693	.506	18	20	3	0	4	1	5	7
Washington	60.3	64.8	.386	.407	15.5	14.2	.326	.679	.502	27	22	1	0	3	3	4	10
COMPOSITE; 256 games	65.7		.411		14.9		.319	.681		339		23		44		110	

* - League Leader

REBOUND PERCENTAGES — OFF. - Percentage of a given team's missed shots which that team rebounds. DEF. - Percentage of opponents' missed shots which a given team rebounds. TOT. - Average of offensive and defensive rebound percentages.

SCORING AVERAGE

	G	FG	FT	PTS	AVG
Smith, Min.	32	204	246	739	23.1
Leslie, L.A.	31	221	142	606	19.5
Thompson, Hou.	30	199	137	579	19.3
Arcain, Hou.	32	217	135	591	18.5
Holdsclaw, Was.	29	187	101	486	16.8
Griffith, Sac.	32	192	134	518	16.2
Phillips, N.Y.	32	208	73	489	15.3
Jackson, Sea.	29	149	104	442	15.2
Stiles, Por.	32	156	116	478	14.9
Williams, Utah	31	171	97	439	14.2
Stinson, Cha.	32	179	63	450	14.1
Sam, Mia.	32	180	57	444	13.9
Sales, Orl.	32	166	58	433	13.5
Jones, Cle.	30	165	65	404	13.5
Abrosimova, Min.	26	114	96	343	13.2
Brondello, Mia.	29	142	57	367	12.7
McWilliams-Frank, Orl.	32	157	87	403	12.6
Gillom, Pho.	32	150	71	395	12.3
Goodson, Utah	28	138	62	343	12.3
Witherspoon, Por.	31	113	90	373	12.0

REBOUNDS PER GAME

	G	OFF	DEF	TOT	AVG
Griffith, Sac.	32	162	195	357	11.2
Williams, Utah	31	111	197	308	9.9
Leslie, L.A.	31	88	210	298	9.6
Holdsclaw, Was.	29	72	184	256	8.8
Phillips, N.Y.	32	89	168	257	8.0
Thompson, Hou.	30	84	149	233	7.8
Folkl, Por.	32	49	196	245	7.7
Dydek, Utah	32	29	214	243	7.6
McWilliams-Frank, Orl	32	114	129	243	7.6
Bullett, Was.	32	65	166	231	7.2
Palmer, Det.	22	38	116	154	7.0
Abrosimova, Min.	26	43	131	174	6.7
Jackson, Sea.	29	57	136	193	6.7
Crawley, Por.	32	63	140	203	6.3
Stepanova, Pho.	32	66	135	201	6.3
Baranova, Mia.	32	40	151	191	6.0
Byears, L.A.	32	80	103	183	5.7
Melvin, Cle.	27	66	88	154	5.7
Smith, Sac.	32	48	131	179	5.6
Page, Was.	32	74	103	177	5.5

ASSISTS PER GAME

	G	AST	AVG
Penicheiro, Sac.	23	172	7.5
Weatherspoon, N.Y.	32	203	6.3
Staley, Cha.	32	179	5.6
Azzi, Utah	32	171	5.3
Veal, Pho.	29	125	4.3
Timms, Pho.	21	87	4.1

	G	AST	AVG
Figgs, L.A.	32	126	3.9
Dixon, L.A.	29	114	3.9
Black, Mia.	32	123	3.8
Washington, Hou.	32	122	3.8
R. Williams, Ind.	32	114	3.6
Darling, Cle.	32	109	3.4
Bevilaqua, Por.	31	103	3.3
Andrade, Cle.	32	100	3.1
Mabika, L.A.	28	87	3.1
Powell, Orl.	32	98	3.1
Paye, Min.	32	97	3.0
Arcain, Hou.	32	94	2.9
Henning, Sea.	32	93	2.9
Burgess, Was.	31	88	2.8

FIELD GOAL PCT.

	FG	FGA	PCT
Byears, L.A.	133	221	.602
Wauters, Cle.	87	153	.569
Griffith, Sac.	192	368	.522
Brown, Cle.	101	195	.518
Phillips, N.Y.	208	410	.507
Stepanova, Pho.	143	282	.507
Ferdinand, Utah	143	290	.493
Fallon, Pho.	127	259	.490
Williams, Utah	171	349	.490
Stinson, Cha.	179	370	.484

3-PT FIELD GOAL PCT.

	3FG	3GA	PCT
Azzi, Utah	38	74	.514
Figgs, L.A.	54	117	.462
Campbell, Sac.	43	94	.457
Tornikidou, Det.	22	49	.449
Stinson, Cha.	29	65	.446
Stiles, Por.	50	116	.431
Robinson, N.Y.	70	168	.417
Malcolm, Ind.	23	56	.411
McCarty, Ind.	23	57	.404
Brondello, Mia.	26	66	.394

FREE THROW PCT.

	FT	FTA	PCT
Baranova, Mia.	66	71	.930
Feaster, Cha.	58	63	.921
Azzi, Utah	88	96	.917
Arcain, Hou.	135	150	.900
Staley, Cha.	51	57	.895
Smith, Min.	246	275	.895
Tornikidou, Det.	63	71	.887
Malcolm, Ind.	54	62	.871
Harrison, Pho.	51	59	.864
Vodichkova, Sea.	38	44	.864

STEALS PER GAME

	G	STL	AVG
Black, Mia.	32	82	2.56
R. Williams, Ind.	32	72	2.25
Sales, Orl.	32	70	2.19
Washington, Hou.	32	69	2.16
Griffith, Sac.	32	63	1.97
Bevilaqua, Por.	31	59	1.90
Arcain, Hou.	32	60	1.88
Jackson, Sea.	29	54	1.86
Holland-Corn, Sac.	32	56	1.75
Penicheiro, Sac.	23	40	1.74

BLOCKS PER GAME

	G	BLK	AVG
Dydek, Utah	32	113	3.53
Leslie, L.A.	31	71	2.29
Jackson, Sea.	29	64	2.21
Stepanova, Pho.	32	64	2.00
Bullett, Was.	32	58	1.81
Baranova, Mia.	32	57	1.78
Smith, Sac.	32	55	1.72
McWilliams-Frank, Orl.	32	50	1.56
Riley, Mia.	32	46	1.44
Sutton-Brown, Cha.	29	39	1.34

MINUTES PER GAME

	G	MIN	AVG
Smith, Min.	32	1234	38.6
Azzi, Utah	32	1205	37.7
Thompson, Hou.	30	1102	36.7
Arcain, Hou.	32	1154	36.1
Staley, Cha.	32	1152	36.0
Jackson, Sea.	29	1001	34.5
Sam, Mia.	32	1100	34.4
Williams, Utah	31	1064	34.3
Griffith, Sac.	32	1077	33.7
Holdsclaw, Was.	29	975	33.6

INDIVIDUAL STATISTICS, TEAM BY TEAM

CHARLOTTE STING

Player	G	Min	FGM	FGA	Pct	FTM	FTA	Pct	Off	Def	Tot	Ast	PF	Dq	Stl	TO	Blk	Pts	Avg	Hi
Andrea Stinson	32	1006	179	370	.484	63	79	.797	39	98	137	88	59	0	43	70	19	450	14.1	25
Allison Feaster	32	1007	126	336	.375	58	63	.921	55	98	153	46	86	1	29	59	10	365	11.4	23
Dawn Staley	32	1152	107	281	.381	51	57	.895	11	60	71	179	54	0	52	100	1	298	9.3	18
Tammy Sutton-Brown	29	602	72	147	.490	52	72	.722	51	78	129	11	84	1	21	40	39	196	6.8	20
Tonya Edwards(*)	22	372	34	100	.340	27	37	.730	11	32	43	30	49	0	14	40	6	100	4.5	16
Tonya Edwards(†)	32	580	60	171	.351	64	84	.762	16	46	62	48	79	1	19	62	7	194	6.1	17
Shalonda Enis	32	623	66	158	.418	45	63	.714	48	65	113	14	60	0	10	36	5	191	6.0	18
Charlotte Smith	30	678	57	146	.390	47	64	.734	36	65	101	50	73	1	16	41	13	171	5.7	13
C. Machaguana	30	580	63	126	.500	37	57	.649	34	87	121	17	95	2	16	41	16	163	5.4	14
Summer Erb	18	148	18	42	.429	18	21	.857	8	27	35	4	23	0	1	10	5	54	3.0	16
Kelly Miller	26	225	22	57	.386	4	5	.800	11	17	28	14	14	0	9	9	0	55	2.1	7
Keisha Anderson	18	102	2	16	.125	8	10	.800	3	12	15	14	8	0	6	17	0	12	0.7	10
Reshea Bristol	1	5	0	1	.000	0	0	—	2	0	2	0	0	0	0	1	0	0	0.0	0
Charlotte	32	6500	746	1780	.419	410	528	.777	309	639	948	467	605	5	217	474	114	2055	64.2	86
Opponents	32	6500	732	1846	.397	431	562	.767	344	567	911	443	579	1	257	447	124	2009	62.8	85

3-pt. FG: Charlotte 153-428 (.357) Stinson 29-65 (.446); Feaster 55-168 (.327); Staley 33-89 (.371); Edwards(*) 5-22 (.227); Edwards(!) 10-36 (.278) Enis 14-31 (.452); Smith 10-32 (.313); Miller 7-19 (.368); Anderson 0-2 (.000); Opponents 114-369 (.309)

CLEVELAND ROCKERS

Player	G	Min	FGM	FGA	Pct	FTM	FTA	Pct	Off	Def	Tot	Ast	PF	Dq	Stl	TO	Blk	Pts	Avg	Hi
Merlakia Jones	30	998	165	377	.438	65	82	.793	43	121	164	45	59	0	29	53	4	404	13.5	26
Chasity Melvin	27	754	102	215	.474	60	86	.698	66	88	154	50	81	0	24	45	16	266	9.9	22
Ann Wauters	24	622	87	153	.569	60	75	.800	35	79	114	35	55	0	17	50	13	234	9.8	19
Rushia Brown	30	760	101	195	.518	46	63	.730	49	83	132	37	73	1	44	37	10	249	8.3	20
Penny Taylor	32	561	86	225	.382	36	46	.783	36	76	112	44	46	0	35	38	11	230	7.2	21
Helen Darling	32	778	59	166	.355	55	72	.764	18	58	76	109	59	0	34	70	4	196	6.1	18
Mery Andrade	32	893	58	171	.339	30	45	.667	21	66	87	100	77	0	51	61	10	152	4.8	13
Vicki Hall(‡)	14	225	27	66	.409	4	8	.500	10	23	33	9	22	0	1	11	5	65	4.6	9
Eva Nemcova	8	113	13	38	.342	5	8	.625	1	9	10	8	9	0	2	6	5	34	4.3	10
Jennifer Rizzotti	32	476	42	110	.382	7	11	.636	2	28	30	51	30	0	25	41	2	119	3.7	9
Angelina Wolvert	1	5	1	3	.333	0	0	—	1	0	1	0	1	0	0	0	0	2	2.0	2
P. Johns Kimbrough	18	119	12	27	.444	4	9	.444	12	19	31	4	12	0	0	10	2	28	1.6	9
Tricia Bader Binford	19	114	8	20	.400	0	0	—	2	10	12	11	7	0	5	8	0	21	1.1	6
Paige Sauer	2	4	1	3	.333	0	0	—	1	1	2	0	1	0	0	1	1	2	1.0	2
Adia Barnes	3	3	1	1	1.000	0	0	—	0	1	1	1	0	0	0	0	0	2	0.7	2
Cleveland	32	6425	763	1770	.431	372	505	.737	297	662	959	503	532	1	267	444	83	2004	62.6	86
Opponents	32	6425	664	1745	.381	328	444	.739	297	594	891	434	597	3	225	496	127	1788	55.9	76

3-pt. FG: Cleveland 106-335 (.316) Jones 9-34 (.265); Melvin 2-2 (1.000); Wauters 0-2 (.000); Brown 1-1 (1.000); Taylor 22-73 (.301); Darling 23-70 (.329) Andrade 6-30 (.200); Hall(>) 7-22 (.318); Nemcova 3-15 (.200); Rizzotti 28-73 (.384); Bader Binford 5-13 (.385); Opponents 132-417 (.317)

DETROIT SHOCK

Player	G	Min	FGM	FGA	Pct	FTM	FTA	Pct	Off	Def	Tot	Ast	PF	Dq	Stl	TO	Blk	Pts	Avg	Hi
Astou Ndiaye-Diatta ..32	32	913	156	341	.457	59	76	.776	60	111	171	49	82	1	22	73	28	376	11.8	27
Wendy Palmer............22	22	651	91	215	.423	40	59	.678	38	116	154	23	64	0	23	48	4	233	10.6	17
Elena Tornikidou 32	32	777	111	249	.446	63	71	.887	28	49	77	56	59	0	19	59	14	307	9.6	22
Edwina Brown 32	32	800	85	232	.366	47	60	.783	31	70	101	87	83	1	33	68	7	237	7.4	19
Deanna Nolan...........27	27	545	64	194	.330	43	53	.811	16	37	53	30	43	0	17	35	6	192	7.1	15
Dominique Canty 32	32	625	70	193	.363	56	74	.757	45	38	83	70	69	0	31	55	1	197	6.2	20
Jae Kingi 29	29	625	55	142	.387	26	36	.722	20	43	63	74	42	0	31	53	8	169	5.8	25
Claudia M. das Neves 22	22	407	34	94	.362	8	8	1.000	3	26	29	34	21	0	21	28	0	95	4.3	16
Barbara Farris...........31	31	559	46	98	.469	37	58	.638	41	68	109	16	68	1	7	30	5	129	4.2	12
Kelly Santos 14	14	153	20	42	.476	12	18	.667	11	16	27	5	23	0	3	12	3	52	3.7	11
Carla Boyd 21	21	230	23	67	.343	18	20	.900	10	16	26	14	32	0	11	16	2	75	3.6	14
Rachael Sporn 23	23	265	19	47	.404	3	9	.333	21	31	52	11	16	0	7	13	4	41	1.8	9
Detroit 32	32	6550	774	1914	.404	412	542	.760	324	621	945	469	602	3	225	498	82	2103	65.7	89
Opponents 32	32	6550	848	1837	.462	446	583	.765	279	702	981	438	591	5	262	483	109	2269	70.9	98

3-pt. FG: Detroit 143-405 (.353) Ndiaye-Diatta 5-15 (.333); Palmer 11-33 (.333); Tornikidou 22-49 (.449); Brown 20-53 (.377); Nolan 21-73 (.288); Canty 1-5 (.200) Kingi 33-88 (.375); das Neves 19-52 (.365); Santos 0-1 (.000); Boyd 11-36 (.306); Opponents 127-340 (.374)

HOUSTON COMETS

Player	G	Min	FGM	FGA	Pct	FTM	FTA	Pct	Off	Def	Tot	Ast	PF	Dq	Stl	TO	Blk	Pts	Avg	Hi
Tina Thompson 30	30	1102	199	528	.377	137	163	.840	84	149	233	58	74	0	29	87	22	579	19.3	29
Janeth Arcain 32	32	1154	217	509	.426	135	150	.900	49	87	136	94	82	1	60	83	3	591	18.5	29
Coquese Washington..32	32	1013	63	177	.356	14	22	.636	20	98	118	122	63	1	69	57	9	169	5.3	12
Tiffani Johnson 32	32	672	62	138	.449	24	28	.857	44	94	138	22	67	0	12	42	15	148	4.6	14
Amanda Lassiter..........32	32	613	51	139	.367	10	15	.667	27	83	110	34	66	0	16	35	21	138	4.3	15
Trisha Stafford-Odom 30	30	365	39	106	.368	35	52	.673	37	48	85	16	42	0	12	26	2	113	3.8	11
Tynesha Lewis 29	29	419	39	92	.424	11	17	.647	21	41	62	15	26	0	11	26	4	97	3.3	11
Tammy Jackson 32	32	442	43	86	.500	18	40	.450	40	51	91	21	53	0	22	29	11	104	3.3	18
Kelley Gibson 28	28	288	13	57	.228	15	22	.682	6	23	29	13	20	0	8	15	6	44	1.6	10
Elena Shakirova 26	26	203	12	38	.316	14	23	.609	15	20	35	9	11	0	6	9	2	38	1.5	6
Nekeshia Henderson..23	23	179	9	38	.237	2	7	.286	5	16	21	22	5	0	6	16	0	26	1.1	11
Houston 32	32	6450	747	1908	.392	415	539	.770	348	710	1058	426	509	2	251	436	95	2047	64.0	87
Opponents 32	32	6450	740	1883	.393	362	504	.718	297	685	982	452	561	3	248	433	120	1994	62.3	78

3-pt. FG: Houston 138-435 (.317) Thompson 44-150 (.293); Arcain 22-66 (.333); Washington 29-81 (.358); Lassiter 26-67 (.388); Stafford-Odom 0-1 (.000) Lewis 8-20 (.400); Gibson 3-21 (.143); Shakirova 0-7 (.000); Henderson 6-22 (.273); Opponents 152-456 (.333)

INDIANA FEVER

Player	G	Min	FGM	FGA	Pct	FTM	FTA	Pct	Off	Def	Tot	Ast	PF	Dq	Stl	TO	Blk	Pts	Avg	Hi
Rita Williams..............32	32	1042	115	293	.392	109	130	.838	25	79	104	114	71	0	72	100	11	380	11.9	21
Jurgita Streimikyte 27	27	707	99	207	.478	48	57	.842	45	94	139	52	81	2	37	52	19	246	9.1	21
O. Scott-Richardson ..32	32	775	99	217	.456	82	111	.739	52	109	161	40	108	1	22	72	12	280	8.8	19
Alicia Thompson 22	22	381	76	174	.437	17	23	.739	21	42	63	25	24	0	9	22	7	186	8.5	17
Nadine Malcolm 31	31	705	90	212	.425	54	62	.871	31	60	91	26	75	2	13	48	3	257	8.3	25
Gordana Grubin..........27	27	481	62	167	.371	29	39	.744	18	31	49	33	30	0	7	34	0	170	6.3	23
Stephanie McCarty 30	30	504	52	137	.380	42	55	.764	13	42	55	58	50	0	26	38	14	169	5.6	20
Angie Braziel............23	23	341	50	115	.435	27	35	.771	21	56	77	7	27	0	9	20	13	127	5.5	14
Kelly Schumacher......28	28	380	46	93	.495	17	20	.850	23	47	70	10	41	0	5	21	29	112	4.0	10
Vicki Hall(*)...............13	13	123	14	34	.412	8	14	.571	5	11	16	4	11	0	4	7	0	36	2.8	8
Vicki Hall(†)...............27	27	348	41	100	.410	12	22	.545	15	34	49	13	33	0	5	18	5	101	3.7	9
Niele Ivey 32	32	708	38	102	.373	14	15	.933	16	39	55	70	51	0	33	35	5	115	3.6	13
Danielle McCulley 8	8	90	5	18	.278	17	18	.944	4	13	17	5	12	0	0	7	2	28	3.5	12
Monica Maxwell 15	15	238	16	53	.302	8	12	.667	12	26	38	14	19	0	5	22	3	47	3.1	11
Indiana 32	32	6475	762	1822	.418	472	591	.799	286	649	935	458	600	5	242	491	118	2153	67.3	86
Opponents 32	32	6475	853	1899	.449	442	583	.707	306	660	966	565	616	6	256	466	140	2249	70.3	86

3-pt. FG: Indiana 157-446 (.352) R. Williams 41-109 (.376); Streimikyte 0-9 (.000); Scott-Richardson 0-2 (.000); Thompson 17-43 (.395); Malcolm 23-56 (.411) Grubin 17-58 (.293); McCarty 23-57 (.404); Braziel 0-1 (.000); Schumacher 3-5 (.600); Hall(*) 0-3 (.000); Hall(!) 7-25 (.280) Ivey 25-70 (.357); McCulley 1-2 (.500); Maxwell 7-31 (.226); Opponents 131-367 (.357)

LOS ANGELES SPARKS

Player	G	Min	FGM	FGA	Pct	FTM	FTA	Pct	Off	Def	Tot	Ast	PF	Dq	Stl	TO	Blk	Pts	Avg	Hi
Lisa Leslie	31	1033	221	467	.473	142	193	.736	88	210	298	73	132	3	34	98	71	606	19.5	32
Tamecka Dixon	29	925	133	319	.417	68	86	.791	19	66	85	114	52	2	27	71	2	340	11.7	24
Mwadi Mabika	28	828	99	256	.387	68	79	.861	22	108	130	87	74	0	39	44	11	313	11.2	23
DeLisha Milton	32	938	134	296	.453	50	63	.794	71	98	169	68	101	0	49	58	29	330	10.3	20
Latasha Byears	32	739	133	221	.602	30	52	.577	80	103	183	29	112	4	42	38	13	297	9.3	17
Ukari Figgs	32	930	76	179	.425	51	63	.810	14	86	100	126	42	0	43	55	4	257	8.0	17
Rhonda Mapp	30	395	51	123	.415	24	32	.750	34	45	79	14	60	0	16	25	6	126	4.2	12
Vedrana Grgin Fonsec	24	223	28	65	.431	9	14	.643	13	22	35	12	21	0	4	15	1	71	3.0	12
Nicky McCrimmon	28	350	28	63	.444	3	7	.429	3	9	12	63	19	0	21	22	0	64	2.3	11
Nicole Levandusky	13	67	7	22	.318	1	1	1.000	5	4	9	7	3	0	5	5	1	20	1.5	6
Wendi Willits	13	47	6	20	.300	3	4	.750	1	4	5	3	0	0	1	2	0	17	1.3	5
Los Angeles	32	6475	916	2031	.451	449	594	.756	350	755	1105	596	616	9	281	438	138	2441	76.3	100
Opponents	32	6475	779	1985	.392	416	547	.761	294	627	921	538	591	8	234	453	114	2166	67.7	95

3-pt. FG: Los Angeles 160-436 (.367) Leslie 22-60 (.367); Dixon 6-34 (.176); Mabika 47-123 (.382); Milton 12-35 (.343); Byears 1-3 (.333); Figgs 54-117 (.462) Mapp 0-3 (.000); Grgin Fonseca 6-19 (.316); McCrimmon 5-12 (.417); Levandusky 5-17 (.294); Willits 2-13 (.154); Opponents 192-603 (.318)

MIAMI SOL

Player	G	Min	FGM	FGA	Pct	FTM	FTA	Pct	Off	Def	Tot	Ast	PF	Dq	Stl	TO	Blk	Pts	Avg	Hi
Sheri Sam	32	1100	180	417	.432	57	76	.750	41	96	137	88	67	0	55	87	8	444	13.9	26
Sandy Brondello	29	850	142	344	.413	57	70	.814	10	40	50	63	61	0	28	36	4	367	12.7	23
Elena Baranova	32	984	141	330	.427	66	71	.930	40	151	191	63	81	2	33	62	57	378	11.8	22
Ruth Riley	32	799	77	162	.475	64	83	.771	51	79	130	26	107	3	25	63	46	218	6.8	16
Debbie Black	32	946	70	187	.374	37	48	.771	43	83	126	123	69	0	82	51	2	180	5.6	15
Tracy Reid	21	278	32	63	.508	16	26	.615	10	27	37	13	28	0	15	25	5	80	3.8	12
Kristen Rasmussen	28	416	31	86	.360	12	16	.750	33	55	88	16	48	0	11	31	14	75	2.7	11
Marlies Askamp	30	431	28	58	.483	18	32	.563	35	52	87	15	62	0	12	19	11	74	2.5	6
Kisha Ford	30	395	26	80	.325	18	32	.563	19	46	65	21	43	0	17	18	5	71	2.4	7
Katrina Colleton	14	121	10	39	.256	6	10	.600	2	5	7	7	9	0	2	7	1	26	1.9	5
Marla Brumfield	27	247	17	60	.283	5	5	1.000	8	17	25	32	27	0	20	24	0	44	1.6	12
Levys Torres	2	8	0	0	—	0	0	—	0	0	0	0	0	0	0	2	0	0	0.0	0
Miami	32	6575	754	1826	.413	356	469	.759	292	651	943	467	602	5	300	448	153	1957	61.2	75
Opponents	32	6575	679	1725	.394	420	588	.714	301	667	968	388	538	3	259	512	87	1898	59.3	86

3-pt. FG: Miami 93-295 (.315) Sam 27-98 (.276); Brondello 26-66 (.394); Baranova 30-80 (.375); Black 3-20 (.150); Rasmussen 1-4 (.250); Ford 1-11 (.091) Colleton 0-1 (.000); Brumfield 5-15 (.333); Opponents 120-395 (.304)

MINNESOTA LYNX

Player	G	Min	FGM	FGA	Pct	FTM	FTA	Pct	Off	Def	Tot	Ast	PF	Dq	Stl	TO	Blk	Pts	Avg	Hi
Katie Smith	32	1234	204	519	.393	246	275	.895	40	82	122	70	94	0	23	87	5	739	23.1	46
Svetlana Abrosimova	26	846	114	293	.389	96	132	.727	43	131	174	53	70	2	42	85	9	343	13.2	27
Betty Lennox	11	241	41	110	.373	19	20	.950	13	41	54	16	29	0	10	25	4	121	11.0	18
Erin Buescher	32	725	64	184	.348	47	76	.618	42	76	118	62	101	2	27	65	29	183	5.7	16
Lynn Pride	32	713	68	174	.391	33	55	.600	47	99	146	28	77	2	28	46	20	170	5.3	13
Kristi Harrower	4	72	7	15	.467	4	4	1.000	1	3	4	11	4	0	3	3	0	21	5.3	13
Georgia Schweitzer	24	423	33	103	.320	13	17	.765	15	35	50	34	34	1	11	17	6	87	3.6	14
Val Whiting-Raymond	26	462	24	90	.267	40	54	.741	25	58	83	16	62	0	15	34	14	88	3.4	13
Maylana Martin	31	494	35	103	.340	19	31	.613	27	59	86	19	87	2	17	37	15	95	3.1	14
Kate Paye	32	652	30	78	.385	11	16	.688	7	54	61	97	55	0	21	46	0	91	2.8	11
Shanele Stires	18	201	20	53	.377	5	7	.714	10	17	27	14	26	0	8	19	4	51	2.8	9
Janell Burse	20	169	16	48	.333	15	20	.750	23	19	42	5	20	0	2	20	15	47	2.4	12
Michele VanGorp	22	243	15	40	.375	11	20	.550	15	19	34	12	36	0	3	18	6	41	1.9	8
Minnesota	32	6475	671	1810	.371	559	727	.769	308	693	1001	437	695	9	210	507	127	2077	64.9	95
Opponents	32	6475	752	1927	.390	499	624	.800	328	688	1016	511	719	7	259	470	126	2156	67.4	100

3-pt. FG: Minnesota 176-552 (.319) Smith 85-240 (.354); Abrosimova 19-76 (.250); Lennox 20-52 (.385); Buescher 8-29 (.276); Pride 1-4 (.250); Harrower 3-6 (.500) Schweitzer 8-43 (.186); Whiting-Raymond 0-1 (.000); Martin 6-18 (.333); Paye 20-56 (.357); Stires 6-25 (.240); Burse 0-1 (.000) VanGorp 0-1 (.000); Opponents 153-472 (.324)

NEW YORK LIBERTY

Player	G	Min	FGM	FGA	Pct	FTM	FTA	Pct	Off	Def	Tot	Ast	PF	Dq	Stl	TO	Blk	Pts	Avg	Hi
Tari Phillips	32	1049	208	410	.507	73	125	.584	89	168	257	34	110	0	48	84	17	489	15.3	27
Vickie Johnson	32	939	135	326	.414	53	70	.757	23	84	107	87	62	1	35	52	4	353	11.0	23
Crystal Robinson	32	980	123	267	.461	26	29	.897	23	69	92	83	86	1	32	28	8	342	10.7	18
Becky Hammon	32	619	90	197	.457	40	51	.784	10	42	52	51	46	0	27	48	1	262	8.2	21
Tamika Whitmore	32	752	96	222	.432	33	58	.569	29	68	97	19	70	0	17	33	10	226	7.1	23
Camille Cooper	4	51	8	12	.667	10	13	.769	7	4	11	1	6	0	0	3	2	26	6.5	10
Teresa Weatherspoon	32	974	72	167	.431	53	79	.671	29	89	118	203	83	1	55	81	4	207	6.5	16
Sue Wicks	30	602	61	130	.469	35	52	.673	36	102	138	37	86	2	36	43	30	157	5.2	14
Katarina Lazic	8	55	8	20	.400	1	2	.500	2	4	6	3	9	0	3	10	0	17	2.1	8
Stacey Ford	1	3	1	1	1.000	0	0	—	0	1	1	0	0	0	0	0	0	2	2.0	2
Grace Daley	15	66	10	21	.476	5	9	.556	3	5	8	10	12	0	8	7	1	25	1.7	7
Andrea Nagy	23	213	13	31	.419	2	4	.500	0	9	9	24	25	1	2	23	3	34	1.5	7
Rebecca Lobo	16	85	7	22	.318	2	4	.500	2	12	14	1	16	0	2	7	0	17	1.1	9
Hajdana Radunovic	4	9	1	2	.500	2	2	1.000	1	3	4	0	3	0	0	2	1	4	1.0	2
Mactabene Amachree	2	3	0	0	—	1	2	.500	1	0	1	0	2	0	0	1	1	1	0.5	1
New York	32	6400	833	1828	.456	336	500	.672	255	660	915	553	616	6	265	437	82	2162	67.6	95
Opponents	32	6400	744	1759	.423	461	640	.720	304	679	983	430	600	4	223	496	76	2082	65.1	86

3-pt. FG: New York 160-421 (.380) Phillips 0-4 (.000); Johnson 30-82 (.366); Robinson 70-168 (.417); Hammon 42-111 (.378); Whitmore 1-2 (.500); Wicks 0-7 (.000) Weatherspoon 10-26 (.385); Lazic 0-2 (.000); Daley 0-5 (.000); Nagy 6-12 (.500); Lobo 1-2 (.500); Opponents 133-394 (.338)

ORLANDO MIRACLE

Player	G	Min	FGM	FGA	Pct	FTM	FTA	Pct	Off	Def	Tot	Ast	PF	Dq	Stl	TO	Blk	Pts	Avg	Hi
Nykesha Sales	32	1039	166	379	.438	58	74	.784	57	115	172	58	109	0	70	72	6	433	13.5	21
T. McWilliams-Franklin	32	1059	157	331	.474	87	117	.744	114	129	243	69	74	1	52	80	50	403	12.6	23
Shannon Johnson	26	785	90	245	.367	84	111	.757	15	62	77	68	66	0	34	54	6	302	11.6	25
Elaine Powell	32	1055	119	296	.402	80	106	.755	32	66	98	98	64	0	49	79	7	357	11.2	20
Katie Douglas	22	439	51	141	.362	34	47	.723	16	35	51	39	34	0	37	44	7	154	7.0	18
Jessie Hicks	32	456	63	162	.389	43	66	.652	38	54	92	22	85	0	23	53	17	169	5.3	16
Brooke Wyckoff	32	648	41	125	.328	20	28	.714	48	74	122	37	91	2	26	50	15	108	3.4	8
Tiffany McCain	32	442	35	109	.321	6	9	.667	7	31	38	36	52	0	10	34	8	97	3.0	13
Jaclyn Johnson	17	139	14	25	.560	4	5	.800	10	13	23	9	21	0	4	17	3	35	2.1	11
Cintia dos Santos	10	65	7	19	.368	5	6	.833	1	5	6	2	18	0	3	7	5	19	1.9	8
Tawona Alhaleem	26	252	19	58	.328	7	14	.500	15	23	38	14	20	0	11	28	0	49	1.9	10
Carla McGhee	17	71	6	24	.250	2	4	.500	3	7	10	0	9	0	1	6	1	14	0.8	6
Orlando	32	6450	768	1914	.401	430	587	.733	356	614	970	452	643	3	320	532	125	2140	66.9	92
Opponents	32	6450	806	1831	.440	436	605	.721	316	659	975	534	600	2	298	546	114	2205	68.9	86

3-pt. FG: Orlando 174-532 (.327) Sales 43-137 (.314); McWilliams-Frank 2-10 (.200); S. Johnson 38-104 (.365); Powell 39-102 (.382); Douglas 18-57 (.316) Wyckoff 6-37 (.162); McCain 21-67 (.313); J. Johnson 3-7 (.429); Alhaleem 4-11 (.364); Opponents 157-438 (.358)

PHOENIX MERCURY

Player	G	Min	FGM	FGA	Pct	FTM	FTA	Pct	Off	Def	Tot	Ast	PF	Dq	Stl	TO	Blk	Pts	Avg	Hi
Jennifer Gillom	32	858	150	355	.423	71	96	.740	36	91	127	35	91	1	31	71	19	395	12.3	25
Maria Stepanova	32	815	143	282	.507	48	78	.615	66	135	201	41	110	3	43	50	64	334	10.4	20
Trisha Fallon	31	841	127	259	.490	53	65	.815	35	42	77	33	43	0	35	47	12	322	10.4	24
Tonya Edwards(‡)	10	208	26	71	.366	37	47	.787	5	14	19	18	30	1	5	22	1	94	9.4	17
Lisa Harrison	32	915	96	223	.430	51	59	.864	39	100	139	52	58	0	39	49	1	246	7.7	15
Adriana Moises Pinto	7	123	14	36	.389	9	12	.750	4	12	16	17	11	0	6	16	0	41	5.9	13
Bridget Pettis	32	497	53	159	.333	46	56	.821	30	30	60	50	47	1	28	38	4	172	5.4	26
Michele Timms	21	408	38	110	.345	8	10	.800	11	34	45	87	42	0	21	42	2	98	4.7	14
Kristen Veal	29	658	35	125	.280	32	42	.762	14	46	60	125	58	0	33	82	4	116	4.0	16
Adrain Williams	25	375	38	113	.336	20	28	.714	21	54	75	11	43	0	15	34	5	96	3.8	12
Brandy Reed	1	13	1	8	.125	1	1	1.000	0	3	3	0	0	0	0	0	0	3	3.0	3
Jaynetta Saunders	28	253	25	77	.325	17	25	.680	13	27	40	7	28	0	10	14	8	68	2.4	12
Slobodanka Tuvic	30	325	13	42	.310	28	59	.475	18	45	63	17	49	0	16	28	17	54	1.8	8
Ilona Korstine	12	75	7	25	.280	6	7	.857	6	5	11	5	4	0	3	9	0	21	1.8	6
Nicole Kubik	3	21	1	4	.250	0	0	—	0	2	2	5	7	0	4	3	0	2	0.7	2

Player	G	Min	FGM	FGA	Pct	FTM	FTA	Pct	REBOUNDS Off	Def	Tot	Ast	PF	Dq	Stl	TO	Blk	SCORING Pts	Avg	Hi
Michelle Cleary	4	49	0	3	.000	2	2	1.000	2	1	3	9	2	0	2	3	0	2	0.5	2
E.C. Hill	3	8	0	1	.000	0	0	—	0	0	0	1	2	0	1	0	0	0	0.0	0
Pat Luckey	1	8	0	1	.000	0	0	—	0	1	1	1	0	0	0	0	1	0	0.0	0
Phoenix	32	6450	767	1894	.405	429	587	.731	300	642	942	514	625	6	292	519	138	2064	64.5	89
Opponents	32	6450	785	1892	.415	462	584	.791	333	698	1031	524	603	4	283	517	127	2169	67.8	95

3-pt. FG: Phoenix 101-313 (.323) Gillom 24-70 (.343); Stepanova 0-2 (.000); Fallon 15-37 (.405); Edwards(>) 5-14 (.357); Harrison 3-9 (.333); Pettis 20-63 (.317) Moises Pinto 4-12 (.333); Timms 14-46 (.304); Veal 14-50 (.280); Saunders 1-3 (.333); Korstine 1-3 (.333); Kubik 0-1 (.000) Cleary 0-2 (.000); Hill 0-1 (.000); Opponents 137-391 (.350)

PORTLAND FIRE

Player	G	Min	FGM	FGA	Pct	FTM	FTA	Pct	REBOUNDS Off	Def	Tot	Ast	PF	Dq	Stl	TO	Blk	SCORING Pts	Avg	Hi
Jackie Stiles	32	1023	156	385	.405	116	149	.779	24	53	77	55	75	0	24	68	3	478	14.9	32
Sophia Witherspoon	31	862	113	358	.316	90	106	.849	20	54	74	54	59	0	30	72	8	373	12.0	26
Sylvia Crawley	32	921	120	267	.449	59	77	.766	63	140	203	54	85	3	19	61	26	299	9.3	19
Kristin Folkl	32	862	71	166	.428	33	40	.825	49	196	245	45	56	0	20	39	34	180	5.6	13
DeMya Walker	21	297	44	100	.440	23	40	.575	29	29	58	10	51	0	7	35	12	113	5.4	12
Tully Bevilaqua	31	788	39	119	.328	52	71	.732	27	61	88	103	102	0	59	52	6	153	4.9	13
Carolyn Young	23	279	37	99	.374	27	37	.730	10	24	34	15	27	0	14	27	1	111	4.8	13
Tamicha Jackson	32	497	55	169	.325	16	23	.696	10	34	44	50	35	0	28	45	0	132	4.1	12
Alisa Burras	26	272	44	83	.530	18	31	.581	22	37	59	10	30	0	5	30	3	106	4.1	18
Vanessa Nygaard	31	259	28	72	.389	1	3	.333	13	22	35	10	48	0	6	14	2	76	2.5	8
Stacey Thomas	32	413	22	60	.367	15	35	.429	31	39	70	41	57	0	30	40	10	59	1.8	8
LaQuanda Barksdale	5	35	1	10	.100	0	0	—	1	5	6	4	3	0	2	1	0	2	0.4	2
Jenny Mowe	5	17	3	3	1.000	0	0	—	1	2	3	0	5	0	0	2	1	6	1.2	2
Portland	32	6525	733	1891	.388	450	612	.735	300	696	996	451	633	3	244	500	106	2088	65.3	86
Opponents	32	6525	791	1944	.407	461	656	.703	343	763	1106	501	643	6	293	474	144	2202	68.8	90

3-pt. FG: Portland 172-519 (.331) Stiles 50-116 (.431); Witherspoon 57-182 (.313); Crawley 0-1 (.000); Folkl 5-12 (.417); Walker 2-3 (.667); Bevilaqua 23-73 (.315) Young 10-34 (.294); Jackson 6-39 (.154); Nygaard 19-49 (.388); Thomas 0-7 (.000); Barksdale 0-3 (.000); Opponents 159-410 (.388)

SACRAMENTO MONARCHS

Player	G	Min	FGM	FGA	Pct	FTM	FTA	Pct	REBOUNDS Off	Def	Tot	Ast	PF	Dq	Stl	TO	Blk	SCORING Pts	Avg	Hi
Yolanda Griffith	32	1077	192	368	.522	134	186	.720	162	195	357	54	114	1	63	75	37	518	16.2	30
Tangela Smith	32	912	148	352	.420	62	85	.729	48	131	179	41	106	2	34	66	55	358	11.2	27
Kedra Holland-Corn	32	874	111	251	.442	41	60	.683	33	42	75	69	62	0	56	66	5	322	10.1	26
Edna Campbell	32	854	92	244	.377	33	43	.767	11	74	85	74	45	0	19	64	9	260	8.1	21
Ruthie Bolton	31	582	73	216	.338	36	52	.692	34	59	93	55	55	0	28	39	1	222	7.2	21
Ticha Penicheiro	23	744	42	124	.339	49	64	.766	6	80	86	172	58	1	40	64	8	144	6.3	17
Kara Wolters	31	378	63	134	.470	25	31	.806	21	53	74	17	55	0	4	33	25	151	4.9	18
Lady Grooms	31	543	49	114	.430	43	58	.741	32	46	78	38	43	0	15	25	10	141	4.5	13
La'Keshia Frett	30	403	49	126	.389	30	35	.857	23	32	55	18	30	0	10	32	6	128	4.3	18
Cindy Blodgett	11	72	13	29	.448	0	0	—	1	8	9	6	6	0	6	11	1	34	3.1	19
Dana Wynne	1	3	0	0	—	2	2	1.000	1	0	1	0	2	0	0	1	2	2	2.0	2
Maren Walseth	4	8	1	2	.500	2	2	1.000	2	0	2	0	2	0	0	2	0	4	1.0	4
Stacy Clinesmith	16	75	4	14	.286	0	0	—	0	3	3	14	10	0	1	6	0	10	0.6	3
Sacramento	32	6525	837	1974	.424	457	618	.739	374	723	1097	558	588	4	276	494	158	2294	71.7	91
Opponents	32	6525	804	2003	.401	415	578	.718	343	662	1005	496	616	5	261	481	143	2139	66.8	83

3-pt. FG: Sacramento 163-423 (.385) Smith 0-2 (.000); Holland-Corn 59-150 (.393); Campbell 43-94 (.457); Bolton 40-110 (.364); Penicheiro 11-42 (.262) Blodgett 8-15 (.533); Clinesmith 2-10 (.200); Opponents 116-400 (.290)

SEATTLE STORM

Player	G	Min	FGM	FGA	Pct	FTM	FTA	Pct	REBOUNDS Off	Def	Tot	Ast	PF	Dq	Stl	TO	Blk	SCORING Pts	Avg	Hi
Lauren Jackson	29	1001	149	406	.367	104	143	.727	57	136	193	44	97	3	54	53	64	442	15.2	26
Semeka Randall	32	884	117	315	.371	66	100	.660	32	73	105	44	45	0	29	73	4	300	9.4	28
Simone Edwards	32	810	91	190	.479	55	83	.663	67	90	157	26	54	0	24	37	20	237	7.4	19
Jamie Redd	32	659	82	216	.380	45	66	.682	29	53	82	48	101	0	17	48	3	231	7.2	24
Kamila Vodichkova	29	405	51	122	.418	38	44	.864	25	46	71	23	56	0	16	34	7	150	5.2	14
Michelle Marciniak	27	392	51	139	.367	20	37	.541	17	21	38	47	49	0	30	30	2	132	4.9	15

Player	G	Min	FGM	FGA	Pct	FTM	FTA	Pct	Off	Def	Tot	Ast	PF	Dq	Stl	TO	Blk	Pts	Avg	Hi
									Rebounds									Scoring		
Katy Steding 26		393	35	94	.372	16	20	.800	9	26	35	24	23	1	16	22	9	102	3.9	16
Stacey Lovelace 22		211	27	71	.380	12	17	.706	14	18	32	9	23	0	8	18	5	76	3.5	14
Quacy Barnes 20		229	23	59	.390	21	27	.778	14	20	34	11	29	0	9	16	6	68	3.4	10
Sonja Henning 32		902	41	129	.318	18	35	.514	14	57	71	93	62	2	52	43	6	108	3.4	13
Charmin Smith 32		589	17	63	.270	13	21	.619	18	37	55	39	52	0	17	26	1	58	1.8	8
Michelle Edwards 3		13	1	3	.333	2	2	1.000	0	2	2	4	2	0	1	3	0	4	1.3	2
Alessandra Santos de 10		62	4	14	.286	5	11	.455	10	6	16	0	12	0	0	3	0	13	1.3	5
Seattle 32		6550	689	1821	.378	415	606	.685	306	585	891	412	605	6	273	431	127	1921	60.0	83
Opponents 32		6550	753	1750	.430	417	559	.746	296	756	1052	492	588	3	228	519	127	2048	64.0	85

3-pt. FG: Seattle 128-412 (.311) Jackson 40-129 (.310); Randall 0-4 (.000); Redd 22-77 (.286); Vodichkova 10-25 (.400); Marciniak 10-33 (.303); Barnes 1-1 (1.000) Steding 16-35 (.457); Lovelace 10-26 (.385); Henning 8-44 (.182); Smith 11-38 (.289); Opponents 125-325 (.385)

UTAH STARZZ

Player	G	Min	FGM	FGA	Pct	FTM	FTA	Pct	Off	Def	Tot	Ast	PF	Dq	Stl	TO	Blk	Pts	Avg	Hi
									REBOUNDS									SCORING		
Natalie Williams 31		1064	171	349	.490	97	133	.729	111	197	308	55	128	4	41	70	10	439	14.2	26
Adrienne Goodson......28		854	138	319	.433	62	89	.697	66	86	152	58	64	0	27	75	0	343	12.3	21
Marie Ferdinand 32		864	143	290	.493	69	113	.611	23	63	86	79	70	1	40	63	4	366	11.4	19
Margo Dydek 32		970	128	291	.440	87	109	.798	29	214	243	64	108	1	25	90	113	349	10.9	24
Jennifer Azzi 32		1205	75	184	.408	88	96	.917	10	88	98	171	89	1	22	69	10	276	8.6	19
Korie Hlede 27		455	55	141	.390	33	38	.868	15	25	40	43	56	0	25	42	1	151	5.6	20
Kate Starbird..........23		310	41	110	.373	22	27	.815	13	17	30	21	30	0	8	15	1	109	4.7	21
Amy Herrig 32		448	43	93	.462	35	46	.761	23	58	81	14	47	0	8	35	14	121	3.8	11
LaTonya Johnson 26		228	17	65	.262	11	14	.786	4	15	19	7	26	0	2	13	1	50	1.9	7
Cara Consuegra 15		50	0	5	.000	2	4	.500	1	5	6	10	4	0	4	11	0	2	0.1	1
Michaela Pavlikova ..10		21	0	2	.000	1	2	.500	0	6	6	1	0	0	0	1	2	1	0.1	1
Keitha Dickerson.........4		6	0	0	—	0	4	.000	0	1	1	1	0	0	0	0	0	0	0.0	0
Utah 32		6475	811	1849	.439	507	675	.751	295	775	1070	524	622	7	202	493	156	2207	69.0	87
Opponents 32		6475	789	1976	.399	489	660	.741	344	630	974	478	645	13	275	390	148	2192	68.5	87

3-pt. FG: Utah 78-244 (.320) Williams 0-4 (.000); Goodson 5-31 (.161); Ferdinand 11-42 (.262); Dydek 6-15 (.400); Azzi 38-74 (.514); Hlede 8-23 (.348) Starbird 5-23 (.217); Johnson 5-30 (.167); Consuegra 0-2 (.000); Opponents 125-429 (.291)

WASHINGTON MYSTICS

Player	G	Min	FGM	FGA	Pct	FTM	FTA	Pct	Off	Def	Tot	Ast	PF	Dq	Stl	TO	Blk	Pts	Avg	Hi
									REBOUNDS									SCORING		
Chamique Holdsclaw..29		975	187	467	.400	101	148	.682	72	184	256	66	49	0	44	94	14	486	16.8	31
Nikki McCray 32		828	119	290	.410	91	128	.711	22	34	56	47	68	1	26	73	0	351	11.0	25
Vicky Bullett 32		1073	112	286	.392	35	48	.729	65	166	231	41	86	0	53	53	58	278	8.7	24
Murriel Page 32		989	100	231	.433	21	36	.583	74	103	177	55	88	2	30	60	36	225	7.0	14
Helen Luz 32		489	55	136	.404	22	25	.880	10	27	37	55	47	0	28	43	5	164	5.1	15
Annie Burgess 31		731	47	141	.333	16	27	.593	27	49	76	88	45	0	26	60	2	124	4.0	13
Tonya Washington......30		336	41	114	.360	9	11	.818	19	24	43	10	5	0	4	14	2	101	3.4	12
Audrey Sauret............25		455	33	111	.297	7	24	.292	11	31	42	43	39	0	24	41	4	76	3.0	12
Tausha Mills 30		319	23	69	.333	18	31	.581	40	65	105	6	72	0	14	25	4	64	2.1	6
Coco Miller 20		137	13	40	.325	6	11	.545	5	4	9	8	10	0	6	13	0	34	1.7	6
Markita Aldridge 5		35	3	9	.333	1	1	1.000	2	0	2	2	5	0	0	4	0	7	1.4	4
Cass Bauer-Bilodeau..15		102	5	17	.294	5	10	.500	8	10	18	3	12	0	2	6	1	15	1.0	3
Tamara Stocks 3		11	1	3	.333	1	2	.500	0	2	2	0	3	0	0	0	0	3	1.0	3
Jennifer Whittle...........4		20	0	1	.000	0	2	.000	1	0	1	0	8	0	0	3	1	0	0.0	0
Washington...............32		6500	739	1915	.386	333	504	.661	356	699	1055	424	537	3	257	495	127	1928	60.3	80
Opponents 32		6500	791	1945	.407	347	467	.743	331	737	1068	487	543	4	261	454	103	2075	64.8	86

3-pt. FG: Washington 117-418 (.280) Holdsclaw 11-46 (.239); McCray 22-95 (.232); Bullett 19-64 (.297); Page 4-17 (.235); Luz 32-82 (.390); Burgess 14-47 (.298) Washington 10-29 (.345); Sauret 3-26 (.115); Mills 0-1 (.000); Miller 2-6 (.333); Aldridge 0-3 (.000); Bauer-Bilodeau 0-1 (.000); Whittle 0-1 (.000); Opponents 146-408 (.358)

(*) Statistics with this team only (†) Totals with all teams (‡) Continued season with another team

PLAYOFFS RESULTS

FIRST ROUND

Charlotte defeats Cleveland, 2-1
August 16	Charlotte 53, Cleveland 46
August 18	Cleveland 69, Charlotte 51
August 20	Charlotte 72, Cleveland 64

New York defeats Miami, 2-1
August 17	New York 62, Miami 46
August 19	Miami 53, New York 50
August 21	New York 72, Miami 61

Los Angeles defeats Houston, 2-0
August 18	Los Angeles 64, Houston 59
August 20	Los Angeles 70, Houston 58

Sacramento defeats Utah, 2-0
August 17	Sacramento 89, Utah 65
August 19	Sacramento 71, Utah 66

CONFERENCE FINALS

Charlotte defeats New York, 2-1
August 24	New York 61, Charlotte 57
August 26	Charlotte 62, New York 53
August 27	Charlotte 48, New York 44

Los Angeles defeats Sacramento, 2-1
August 24	Los Angeles 74, Sacramento 73
August 26	Sacramento 80, Los Angeles 60
August 27	Los Angeles 93, Sacramento 62

FINALS

Los Angeles defeats Charlotte, 2-0
August 30	Los Angeles 75, Charlotte 66
September 1	Los Angeles 82, Charlotte 54

TEAM STANDINGS

OFFENSIVE

TEAM	G	FG	FGA	PCT	FG3	FG3A	PCT	FT	FTA	PCT	OFF	DEF	REB	AST	PF	DQ	STL	TO	BLK	PTS	AVG
Sac.	5	125	324	.386	34	80	.425	91	112	.813	49	101	150	79	89	0	35	53	20	375	75.0
L.A.	7	195	439	.444	33	110	.300	95	130	.731	71	178	249	140	119	0	47	86	57	518	74.0
Utah	2	45	110	.409	2	19	.105	39	50	.780	18	46	64	25	47	2	13	30	13	131	65.5
Clev.	3	68	162	.420	9	33	.273	34	41	.829	36	48	84	53	54	0	24	35	12	179	59.7
Hou.	2	45	120	.375	9	36	.250	18	26	.692	17	50	67	23	33	0	9	26	9	117	58.5
Cha.	8	177	429	.413	39	103	.379	70	90	.778	67	146	213	112	143	0	49	112	31	463	57.9
N.Y.	6	134	323	.415	24	74	.324	50	75	.667	56	116	172	88	96	1	44	76	21	342	57.0
Miami	3	57	154	.370	11	34	.324	35	57	.614	30	55	85	35	50	1	18	38	7	160	53.3

DEFENSIVE

Team	FG	FGA	PCT	FG3	FG3A	PCT	FT	FTA	PCT	OFF	DEF	REB	AST	PF	DQ	STL	TO	BLK	PTS	AVG	DIFF
N.Y.	116	302	.384	28	72	.389	67	94	.713	52	115	167	74	100	1	39	83	18	327	54.5	+2.5
Clev.	67	159	.421	16	40	.400	26	36	.722	30	49	79	44	50	0	17	39	9	176	58.7	+1.0
Miami	72	167	.431	12	37	.324	28	45	.622	33	64	97	47	54	1	19	36	6	184	61.3	-8.0
Cha.	186	435	.428	28	96	.292	94	120	.783	77	144	221	137	131	0	61	96	43	494	61.8	-3.9
L.A.	172	446	.386	40	121	.331	68	90	.756	58	142	200	107	126	0	41	87	34	452	64.6	+9.4
Hou.	50	125	.400	8	31	.258	26	34	.765	21	54	75	33	28	0	15	20	10	134	67.0	-8.5
Sac.	134	307	.436	20	72	.278	70	97	.722	50	126	176	89	103	2	33	75	44	358	71.6	+3.4
Utah	49	120	.408	9	20	.450	53	65	.815	23	46	69	24	39	0	14	20	6	160	80.0	-14.5
Avg	106	258	.410	20	61	.329	54	73	.744	43	93	136	69	79	1	30	57	21	286	63.5	—
Totals	846	2061		161	489		432	581		344	740	1084	555	631	4	239	456	170	2285		

TEAM COMPARISONS

TEAM	Points Per Game		Field Goal Percentage		Turnovers Per Game		Rebound Percentages			Below 70 Pts.		Overtime Games		3 PTS or Less		10 PTS or More	
	OWN	OPP	OWN	OPP	OWN	OPP	OFF	DEF	TOT	OWN	OPP	W	L	W	L	W	L
Charlotte	57.9	61.8	.413	.428	14.0	12.0	.318	.655	.486	7	6	0	0	0	0	0	2
Cleveland	59.7	58.7	.420	.421	11.7	13.0	.424*	.615	.519	3	2	0	0	0	0	1	0
Houston	58.5	67.0	.375	.400	13.0	10.0	.239	.704	.472	2	1	0	0	0	0	0	1
Los Angeles	74.0	64.6	.444*	.386	12.3	12.4	.333	.754*	.544*	2	5	0	0	1	0	3	1
Miami	53.3	61.3	.370	.431	12.7	12.0	.319	.625	.472	3	2	0	0	1	0	0	2
New York	57.0	54.5*	.415	.384*	12.7	13.8	.327	.690	.509	5	6	0	0	0	1	2	0
Sacramento	75.0*	71.6	.386	.436	10.6*	15.0*	.280	.669	.474	1	3	0	0	0	1	2	1
Utah	65.5	80.0	.409	.408	15.0	10.0	.281	.667	.474	2	0	0	0	0	0	0	1
COMPOSITE; 18 games	63.5		.410		12.7		.317	.683		25	0			2		8	

* - League Leader

REBOUND PERCENTAGES — OFF. - Percentage of a given team's missed shots which that team rebounds. DEF. - Percentage of opponents' missed shots which a given team rebounds. TOT. - Average of offensive and defensive rebound percentages.

CHARLOTTE STING

Player	G	Min	FGM	FGA	Pct	FTM	FTA	Pct	Off	Def	Tot	Ast	PF	Dq	Stl	TO	Blk	Pts	Avg	Hi
Andrea Stinson	8	278	37	95	.389	17	21	.810	12	37	49	26	18	0	13	18	2	96	12.0	18
Dawn Staley	8	301	32	77	.416	17	21	.810	3	15	18	35	19	0	9	34	2	94	11.8	18
Allison Feaster	8	248	26	74	.351	1	1	1.000	8	26	34	14	18	0	9	9	4	64	8.0	14
Tammy Sutton-Brown	8	167	25	46	.543	10	14	.714	10	16	26	4	25	0	1	8	11	60	7.5	12
Charlotte Smith	8	224	16	54	.296	10	11	.909	13	19	32	14	24	0	6	7	8	47	5.9	10
Clarisse Machanguana	8	132	17	32	.531	4	6	.667	7	12	19	2	11	0	3	6	3	38	4.8	10
Shalonda Enis	8	101	11	22	.500	9	12	.750	6	9	15	4	16	0	2	7	1	34	4.3	12
Tonya Edwards	8	119	9	21	.429	2	2	1.000	6	10	16	12	8	0	5	11	0	22	2.8	15
Summer Erb	4	15	4	5	.800	0	0	—	2	2	4	0	3	0	0	3	0	8	2.0	6
Keisha Anderson	2	7	0	1	.000	0	0	—	0	0	0	1	1	0	1	1	0	0	0.0	0
Kelly Miller	2	8	0	2	.000	0	2	.000	0	0	0	0	0	0	0	0	0	0	0.0	0
Charlotte	8	1600	177	429	.413	70	90	.778	67	146	213	112	143	0	49	112	31	463	57.9	72
Opponents	8	1600	186	435	.428	94	120	.783	77	144	221	137	131	0	61	96	43	494	61.8	82

3-pt. FG: Charlotte 39-103 (.379) Stinson 5-13 (.385); Staley 13-26 (.500); Feaster 11-35 (.314); Smith 5-20 (.250); Enis 3-4 (.750); Edwards 2-4 (.500) Anderson 0-1 (.000); Opponents 28-96 (.292)

CLEVELAND ROCKERS

Player	G	Min	FGM	FGA	Pct	FTM	FTA	Pct	Off	Def	Tot	Ast	PF	Dq	Stl	TO	Blk	Pts	Avg	Hi
Merlakia Jones	3	103	15	32	.469	5	5	1.000	8	10	18	9	5	0	1	3	1	36	12.0	19
Ann Wauters	3	86	13	19	.684	8	9	.889	6	4	10	2	10	0	2	4	3	34	11.3	12
Rushia Brown	3	62	10	15	.667	5	6	.833	2	6	8	5	9	0	4	3	2	25	8.3	14
Chasity Melvin	3	81	8	16	.500	8	11	.727	6	6	12	6	5	0	2	6	2	24	8.0	11
Penny Taylor	3	59	8	25	.320	3	4	.750	2	7	9	3	4	0	6	5	1	21	7.0	10
Helen Darling	3	80	5	27	.185	5	6	.833	5	6	11	19	9	0	7	5	1	18	6.0	12
Mery Andrade	3	72	6	17	.353	0	0	—	5	4	9	1	9	0	2	7	2	13	4.3	7
Jennifer Rizzotti	3	45	2	6	.333	0	0	—	0	3	3	7	2	0	0	0	0	6	2.0	3
Paige Sauer	1	4	1	3	.333	0	0	—	0	1	1	0	0	0	0	1	0	2	2.0	2
Tricia Bader Binford	1	4	0	2	.000	0	0	—	1	0	1	0	0	0	0	0	0	0	0.0	0
P Johns Kimbrough	1	4	0	0	—	0	0	—	1	1	2	1	1	0	0	1	0	0	0.0	0
Cleveland	3	600	68	162	.420	34	41	.829	36	48	84	53	54	0	24	35	12	179	59.7	69
Opponents	3	600	67	159	.421	26	36	.722	30	49	79	44	50	0	17	39	9	176	58.7	72

3-pt. FG: Cleveland 9-33 (.273) Jones 1-3 (.333); Taylor 2-11 (.182); Darling 3-9 (.333); Andrade 1-2 (.500); Rizzotti 2-6 (.333); Bader Binford 0-2 (.000); Opponents 16-40 (.400).

HOUSTON COMETS

Player	G	Min	FGM	FGA	Pct	FTM	FTA	Pct	Off	Def	Tot	Ast	PF	Dq	Stl	TO	Blk	Pts	Avg	Hi
Janeth Arcain	2	71	13	34	.382	2	2	1.000	2	9	11	5	5	0	2	5	0	29	14.5	18
Tina Thompson	2	68	11	20	.550	4	5	.800	4	8	12	7	5	0	1	10	0	29	14.5	16
Amanda Lassiter	2	54	7	16	.438	2	2	1.000	1	8	9	0	4	0	0	2	3	19	9.5	17
Tiffani Johnson	2	71	7	17	.412	4	7	.571	4	13	17	3	5	0	0	4	3	18	9.0	13
Tammy Jackson	1	15	0	3	.000	4	6	.667	2	1	3	0	4	0	1	1	1	4	4.0	4
Kelley Gibson	2	23	3	7	.429	0	0	—	0	3	3	0	1	0	1	2	0	7	3.5	5
Coquese Washington	2	74	3	17	.176	0	0	—	2	7	9	5	5	0	2	2	0	7	3.5	7
Trisha Stafford-Odom	2	16	1	5	.200	2	4	.500	2	1	3	1	3	0	2	0	2	4	2.0	4
Nekeshia Henderson	1	1	0	0	—	0	0	—	0	0	0	0	0	0	0	0	0	0	0.0	0
Tynesha Lewis	2	6	0	1	.000	0	0	—	0	0	0	2	1	0	0	0	0	0	0.0	0
Elena Shakirova	1	1	0	0	—	0	0	—	0	0	0	0	0	0	0	0	0	0	0.0	0
Houston	2	400	45	120	.375	18	26	.692	17	50	67	23	33	0	9	26	9	117	58.5	59
Opponents	2	400	50	125	.400	26	34	.765	21	54	75	33	28	0	15	20	10	134	67.0	70

3-pt. FG: Houston 9-36 (.250) Arcain 1-8 (.125); Thompson 3-5 (.600); Lassiter 3-9 (.333); Jackson 0-1 (.000); Gibson 1-3 (.333); Washington 1-10 (.100); Opponents 8-31 (.258).

LOS ANGELES SPARKS

Player	G	Min	FGM	FGA	Pct	FTM	FTA	Pct	Off	Def	Tot	Ast	PF	Dq	Stl	TO	Blk	Pts	Avg	Hi
Lisa Leslie 7		260	58	118	.492	37	50	.740	28	58	86	21	22	0	12	26	31	156	22.3	35
Tamecka Dixon 7		253	40	83	.482	9	11	.818	5	12	17	29	14	0	9	20	2	95	13.6	19
DeLisha Milton 7		226	35	64	.547	13	19	.684	12	32	44	20	22	0	7	11	10	86	12.3	19
Mwadi Mabika 7		231	21	66	.318	11	14	.786	6	40	46	17	21	0	7	10	6	63	9.0	15
Ukari Figgs 7		239	18	53	.340	12	16	.750	3	12	15	41	14	0	4	6	4	58	8.3	12
Latasha Byears...........7		102	18	36	.500	9	14	.643	15	13	28	2	16	0	3	5	4	45	6.4	9
Rhonda Mapp 5		27	3	9	.333	0	0	—	1	6	7	3	5	0	0	2	0	6	1.2	4
Vedrana Grgin Fonsec..4		7	1	3	.333	2	2	1.000	0	1	1	0	0	0	0	0	0	4	1.0	4
Nicky McCrimmon 7		41	1	2	.500	2	4	.500	0	4	4	6	5	0	5	4	0	5	0.7	3
Nicole Levandusky 3		5	0	3	.000	0	0	—	0	0	0	0	0	0	0	0	0	0	0.0	0
Wendi Willits 4		9	0	2	.000	0	0	—	1	0	1	1	0	0	0	1	0	0	0.0	0
Los Angeles 7		1400	195	439	.444	95	130	.731	71	178	249	140	119	0	47	86	57	518	74.0	93
Opponents 7		1400	172	446	.386	68	90	.756	58	142	200	107	126	0	41	87	34	452	64.6	80

3-pt. FG: Los Angeles 33-110 (.300) Leslie 3-7 (.429); Dixon 6-13 (.462); Milton 3-8 (.375); Mabika 10-40 (.250); Figgs 10-36 (.278); Grgin Fonseca 0-1 (.000) McCrimmon 1-1 (1.000); Levandusky 0-2 (.000); Willits 0-2 (.000); Opponents 40-121 (.331)

MIAMI SOL

Player	G	Min	FGM	FGA	Pct	FTM	FTA	Pct	Off	Def	Tot	Ast	PF	Dq	Stl	TO	Blk	Pts	Avg	Hi
Elena Baranova...........3		105	15	33	.455	8	11	.727	7	11	18	7	9	0	2	9	2	44	14.7	18
Sandy Brondello 3		107	13	36	.361	5	6	.833	1	9	10	7	5	0	2	3	0	34	11.3	18
Sheri Sam...................3		109	10	31	.323	9	11	.818	4	6	10	4	11	1	5	8	0	31	10.3	17
Ruth Riley 3		110	8	19	.421	8	19	.421	5	11	16	3	12	0	1	3	4	24	8.0	12
Debbie Black 3		95	7	18	.389	0	0	—	7	9	16	11	7	0	5	4	1	14	4.7	6
Tracy Reid..................3		21	2	5	.400	0	4	.000	1	4	5	1	1	0	1	2	0	4	1.3	2
Marla Brumfield 2		4	1	2	.500	0	0	—	0	0	0	0	0	0	1	0	0	2	1.0	2
Katrina Colleton 2		3	0	0	—	2	2	1.000	1	0	1	0	1	0	0	0	0	2	1.0	2
Levys Torres 2		3	0	0	—	2	2	1.000	0	2	2	0	0	0	0	1	0	2	1.0	2
Kisha Ford 3		20	1	5	.200	0	0	—	1	0	1	2	3	0	0	1	0	2	0.7	2
Kristen Rasmussen......3		23	0	5	.000	1	2	.500	3	3	6	0	1	0	1	6	0	1	0.3	1
Miami 3		600	57	154	.370	35	57	.614	30	55	85	35	50	1	18	38	7	160	53.3	61
Opponents 3		600	72	167	.431	28	45	.622	33	64	97	47	54	1	19	36	6	184	61.3	72

3-pt. FG: Miami 11-34 (.324) Baranova 6-11 (.545); Brondello 3-10 (.300); Sam 2-9 (.222); Black 0-3 (.000); Brumfield 0-1 (.000); Opponents 12-37 (.324)

NEW YORK LIBERTY

Player	G	Min	FGM	FGA	Pct	FTM	FTA	Pct	Off	Def	Tot	Ast	PF	Dq	Stl	TO	Blk	Pts	Avg	Hi
Vickie Johnson 6		218	34	75	.453	15	15	1.000	7	20	27	28	11	0	13	14	2	89	14.8	22
Crystal Robinson.........6		223	27	54	.500	3	4	.750	7	16	23	8	15	0	8	14	2	69	11.5	16
Tari Phillips.................6		202	26	62	.419	16	34	.471	15	34	49	10	17	1	9	17	6	68	11.3	16
Tamika Whitmore 6		152	18	44	.409	6	10	.600	10	12	22	4	13	0	4	7	4	42	7.0	12
Sue Wicks..................6		118	12	27	.444	4	5	.800	10	10	20	5	17	0	2	8	6	28	4.7	9
Teresa Weatherspoon ..6		198	8	38	.211	4	4	1.000	7	15	22	28	16	0	7	5	0	23	3.8	10
Becky Hammon 6		48	6	17	.353	0	0	—	0	3	3	2	3	0	1	3	0	15	2.5	6
Andrea Nagy...............4		30	3	4	.750	2	3	.667	0	4	4	3	2	0	0	3	1	8	2.0	3
Camille Cooper 3		8	0	2	.000	0	0	—	0	1	1	0	2	0	0	0	0	0	0.0	0
Grace Daley 1		1	0	0	—	0	0	—	0	0	0	0	0	0	0	1	0	0	0.0	0
Katarina Lazic.............2		2	0	0	—	0	0	—	0	1	1	0	0	0	0	1	0	0	0.0	0
New York 6		1200	134	323	.415	50	75	.667	56	116	172	88	96	1	44	76	21	342	57.0	72
Opponents 6		1200	116	302	.384	67	94	.713	52	115	167	74	100	1	39	83	18	327	54.5	62

3-pt. FG: New York 24-74 (.324) Johnson 6-22 (.273); Robinson 12-29 (.414); Phillips 0-1 (.000); Whitmore 0-1 (.000); Weatherspoon 3-11 (.273); Hammon 3-10 (.300); Opponents 28-72 (.389)

SACRAMENTO MONARCHS

Player	G	Min	FGM	FGA	Pct	FTM	FTA	Pct	Off	Def	Tot	Ast	PF	Dq	Stl	TO	Blk	Pts	Avg	Hi
Yolanda Griffith 5		181	32	67	.478	42	55	.764	18	26	44	7	18	0	8	11	6	106	21.2	30
Kedra Holland-Corn......5		160	21	48	.438	14	16	.875	2	16	18	7	10	0	8	7	2	69	13.8	17
Ruthie Bolton 5		121	17	44	.386	12	13	.923	10	12	22	9	11	0	4	10	0	55	11.0	17
Tangela Smith..............5		164	23	60	.383	9	11	.818	8	16	24	8	16	0	5	4	5	55	11.0	17
Ticha Penicheiro 5		163	10	40	.250	4	4	1.000	3	16	19	33	9	0	3	9	4	31	6.2	19
Edna Campbell 5		115	11	31	.355	2	3	.667	4	7	11	11	9	0	5	5	1	28	5.6	15
Cindy Blodgett 2		7	2	4	.500	1	2	.500	0	2	2	1	1	0	0	1	0	6	3.0	4
Kara Wolters 4		37	5	14	.357	0	0	—	1	3	4	1	10	0	2	1	2	10	2.5	6
Lady Grooms 5		31	2	7	.286	5	6	.833	1	3	4	1	3	0	0	3	0	9	1.8	7
Dana Wynne 2		3	1	1	1.000	0	0	—	0	0	0	0	0	0	0	0	0	2	1.0	2
La'Keshia Frett 5		18	1	8	.125	2	2	1.000	2	0	2	1	2	0	0	1	0	4	0.8	4
Sacramento 5		1000	125	324	.386	91	112	.813	49	101	150	79	89	0	35	53	20	375	75.0	89
Opponents 5		1000	134	307	.436	70	97	.722	50	126	176	89	103	2	33	75	44	358	71.6	93

3-pt. FG: Sacramento 34-80 (.425) Holland-Corn 13-27 (.481); Bolton 9-23 (.391); Penicheiro 7-19 (.368); Campbell 4-9 (.444); Blodgett 1-2 (.500); Opponents 20-72 (.278)

UTAH STARZZ

Player	G	Min	FGM	FGA	Pct	FTM	FTA	Pct	Off	Def	Tot	Ast	PF	Dq	Stl	TO	Blk	Pts	Avg	Hi
Adrienne Goodson........2		71	13	29	.448	5	9	.556	6	10	16	3	7	0	3	4	2	31	15.5	18
Marie Ferdinand 2		69	7	16	.438	15	18	.833	2	6	8	7	4	0	3	2	0	29	14.5	15
Margo Dydek 2		69	9	21	.429	10	13	.769	1	13	14	3	10	1	1	4	7	28	14.0	15
Natalie Williams 2		57	8	16	.500	5	6	.833	7	9	16	0	10	1	3	5	1	21	10.5	17
Jennifer Azzi 2		75	3	12	.250	1	1	1.000	0	3	3	10	7	0	1	5	1	9	4.5	8
Cara Consuegra 1		2	1	1	1.000	1	1	1.000	0	1	1	0	0	0	1	1	0	3	3.0	3
Korie Hlede 2		17	2	5	.400	0	0	—	1	2	3	1	1	0	1	3	0	4	2.0	2
LaTonya Johnson 2		15	1	4	.250	2	2	1.000	0	1	1	0	4	0	0	3	1	4	2.0	4
Amy Herrig 2		21	1	5	.200	0	0	—	1	1	2	1	4	0	0	1	1	2	1.0	2
Michaela Pavlickova 1		2	0	0	—	0	0	—	0	0	0	0	0	0	0	0	0	0	0.0	0
Kate Starbird...............1		2	0	1	.000	0	0	—	0	0	0	0	0	0	0	0	0	0	0.0	0
Utah 2		400	45	110	.409	39	50	.780	18	46	64	25	47	2	13	30	13	131	65.5	66
Opponents 2		400	49	120	.408	53	65	.815	23	46	69	24	39	0	14	20	6	160	80.0	89

3-pt. FG: Utah 2-19 (.105) Goodson 0-4 (.000); Ferdinand 0-2 (.000); Azzi 2-7 (.286); Hlede 0-2 (.000); Johnson 0-3 (.000); Starbird 0-1 (.000); Opponents 9-20 (.450)

(*) Statistics with this team only

(†) Totals with all teams

(‡) Continued season with another team

INDIVIDUAL FINALS STATISTICS, TEAM BY TEAM

CHARLOTTE STING

Player	G	Min	FGM	FGA	Pct	FTM	FTA	Pct	Off	Def	Tot	Ast	PF	Dq	Stl	TO	Blk	Pts	Avg	Hi
Andrea Stinson 2		69	11	29	.379	2	4	.500	1	8	9	7	7	0	2	4	1	24	12.0	18
Dawn Staley 2		73	7	18	.389	4	5	.800	1	3	4	7	8	0	1	8	0	19	9.5	10
Allison Feaster 2		64	8	21	.381	0	0	—	1	7	8	6	3	0	6	3	3	18	9.0	11
Charlotte Smith...........2		59	7	19	.368	1	2	.500	5	5	10	3	10	0	0	1	3	18	9.0	10
Tammy Sutton-Brown ..2		37	5	13	.385	4	5	.800	3	3	6	1	5	0	0	2	4	14	7.0	12
Clarisse Machanguana 2		34	6	7	.857	0	0	—	0	3	3	0	3	0	0	1	0	12	6.0	10
Tonya Edwards 2		28	3	6	.500	1	1	1.000	3	5	8	4	2	0	2	3	0	7	3.5	5
Summer Erb 2		9	3	4	.750	0	0	—	1	1	2	0	2	0	0	3	0	6	3.0	6
Shalonda Enis..............2		21	1	2	.500	0	0	—	0	2	2	1	3	0	0	1	0	2	1.0	2

Player	G	Min	FGM	FGA	Pct	FTM	FTA	Pct	Rebounds Off	Def	Tot	Ast	PF	Dq	Stl	TO	Blk	Scoring Pts	Avg	Hi
Keisha Anderson..........1	3	0	1	.000	0	0	—	0	0	0	0	0	0	0	1	0	0	0.0	0
Kelly Miller 1	3	0	2	.000	0	0	—	0	0	0	0	0	0	0	0	0	0	0.0	0
Charlotte.....................2	400	51	122	.418	12	17	.706	15	37	52	29	43	0	11	28	11	120	60.0	66
Opponents 2	400	56	117	.479	38	49	.776	18	44	62	43	35	0	12	21	16	157	78.5	82

3-pt. FG: Charlotte 6-25 (.240) Stinson 0-1 (.000); Staley 1-4 (.250); Feaster 2-9 (.222); Smith 3-10 (.300); Anderson 0-1 (.000); Opponents 7-26 (.269)

LOS ANGELES SPARKS

Player	G	Min	FGM	FGA	Pct	FTM	FTA	Pct	REBOUNDS Off	Def	Tot	Ast	PF	Dq	Stl	TO	Blk	SCORING Pts	Avg	Hi
Lisa Leslie 2	76	16	35	.457	15	19	.789	6	15	21	10	5	0	2	7	9	48	24.0	24
DeLisha Milton 2	69	13	18	.722	7	10	.700	6	10	16	8	7	0	3	3	2	34	17.0	19
Tamecka Dixon 2	71	10	22	.455	4	4	1.000	0	2	2	10	6	0	2	5	2	25	12.5	13
Latasha Byears............2	23	7	12	.583	3	4	.750	3	0	3	1	2	0	1	0	2	17	8.5	9
Ukari Figgs 2	67	5	10	.500	2	4	.500	1	5	6	6	6	0	1	0	0	14	7.0	9
Mwadi Mabika 2	59	3	15	.200	6	6	1.000	1	9	10	5	6	0	2	4	1	14	7.0	12
Rhonda Mapp 1	11	2	4	.500	0	0	—	1	1	2	0	2	0	0	0	0	4	4.0	4
Nicky McCrimmon 2	16	0	0	—	1	2	.500	0	1	1	2	1	0	2	1	0	1	0.5	1
Vedrana Grgin Fonsec..1	3	0	0	—	0	0	—	0	1	1	0	0	0	0	0	0	0	0.0	0
Nicole Levandusky 1	2	0	1	.000	0	0	—	0	0	0	0	0	0	0	0	0	0	0.0	0
Wendi Willits................1	3	0	0	—	0	0	—	0	0	0	1	0	0	0	0	0	0	0.0	0
Los Angeles 2	400	56	117	.479	38	49	.776	18	44	62	43	35	0	12	21	16	157	78.5	82
Opponents 2	400	51	122	.418	12	17	.706	15	37	52	29	43	0	11	28	11	120	60.0	66

3-pt. FG: Los Angeles 7-26 (.269) Leslie 1-3 (.333); Milton 1-2 (.500); Dixon 1-3 (.333); Figgs 2-7 (.286); Mabika 2-10 (.200); Levandusky 0-1 (.000); Opponents 6-25 (.240)

(*) Statistics with this team only
(†) Totals with all teams
(‡) Continued season with another team

FINALS BOX SCORES

GAME 1
At Charlotte Coliseum, August 30, 2001

OFFICIALS: Melissa Barlow, Gary Zielinski, Michael Price. TIME OF GAME: 2:00. ATTENDANCE: 16,132

SCORE BY PERIODS	2	4	FINAL
Los Angeles...........................35	40	75	
Charlotte 39	27	66	

VISITORS: Los Angeles   Head Coach: Michael Cooper

No Player	MIN	FG	FGA	3P	3PA	FT	FTA	OR	DR	TOT	A	PF	ST	TO	TEC	PTS
8 DeLisha Milton 40	7	9	1	2	4	5	4	4	8	5	5	2	3	0	19
4 Mwadi Mabika 26	1	6	0	4	0	0	0	4	4	1	5	1	2	0	2
9 Lisa Leslie 39	9	16	0	0	6	9	1	7	8	4	2	1	4	0	24
21 Tamecka Dixon...............34	5	12	0	2	2	2	0	1	1	3	4	0	3	0	12
5 Ukari Figgs 33	3	5	1	3	2	4	0	2	2	4	2	1	0	0	9
00 Latasha Byears 18	4	9	0	0	0	0	2	0	2	1	2	0	1	0	8
10 Nicky McCrimmon 10	0	0	0	0	1	2	0	1	1	1	1	2	0	0	1
51 Rhonda Mapp.....................							Did not play.								
17 Vedrana Grgin Fonseca........							Did not play.								
40 Nicole Levandusky							Did not play.								
20 Wendi Willits......................							Did not play.								
TOTALS 200	29	57	2	9	15	22	7	19	26	19	21	7	13	0	75
PERCENTAGES:..................50.9	22.268.2		TM REB: 9		TOT TO: 13 (19 PTS)											

HOME: Charlotte   Head Coach: Anne Donovan

No Player	MIN	FG	FGA	3P	3PA	FT	FTA	OR	DR	TOT	A	PF	ST	TO	TEC	PTS
21 Allison Feaster 33	5	10	1	4	0	0	1	4	5	3	1	3	2	0	11
23 Charlotte Smith 31	3	8	3	6	1	2	0	2	2	1	5	0	0	0	10
55 Tammy Sutton-Brown......16	0	4	0	0	2	2	2	2	4	1	3	0	0	0	2

No Player	MIN	FG	FGA	3P	3PA	FT	FTA	OR	DR	TOT	A	PF	ST	TO	TEC	PTS
5 Dawn Staley	39	3	9	1	3	3	4	1	2	3	2	5	0	6	0	10
32 Andrea Stinson	35	8	17	0	1	2	4	1	3	4	5	4	2	3	0	18
33 Machanguana	22	5	6	0	0	0	0	0	3	3	0	1	0	0	0	10
13 Tonya Edwards	13	2	3	0	0	1	1	2	0	2	2	0	1	2	0	5
7 Shalonda Enis	9	0	0	0	0	0	0	0	1	1	1	2	0	0	0	0
3 Summer Erb	2	0	1	0	0	0	0	0	0	0	0	1	0	0	0	0
20 Keisha Anderson						Did not play.										
8 Kelly Miller						Did not play.										
TOTALS	200	26	58	5	14	9	13	7	17	24	15	22	6	14	0	66
PERCENTAGES:	44.8	35.7	69.2			TM REB: 12		TOT TO: 14 (15 PTS)									

BLOCKED SHOTS: Sparks: 6. Milton 1, Mabika 1, Leslie 2, Byears: 2. Sting: 5. Feaster 3, Smith 2.
TECHNICAL FOULS: None.

	ILL	PTO	FBP	PIP	2PT
LA	0	15	10	38	9
CHA	0	19	9	26	11

Flagrant Fouls: None.

GAME 2

At STAPLES Center, September 1, 2001

OFFICIALS: Patty Broderick, June Courteau, Bob Trammell. TIME OF GAME: 1:55. ATTENDANCE: 13,141

SCORE BY PERIODS	1	2	FINAL
Charlotte	30	24	54
Los Angeles	38	44	82

VISITORS: Charlotte   Head Coach: Anne Donovan

No Player	MIN	FG	FGA	3P	3PA	FT	FTA	OR	DR	TOT	A	PF	ST	TO	TEC	PTS
21 Allison Feaster	31	3	11	1	5	0	0	0	3	3	3	2	3	1	0	7
23 Charlotte Smith	28	4	11	0	4	0	0	5	3	8	2	5	0	1	0	8
55 Tammy Sutton-Brown	21	5	9	0	0	2	3	1	1	2	0	2	0	2	0	12
5 Dawn Staley	34	4	9	0	1	1	1	0	1	1	5	3	1	2	0	9
32 Andrea Stinson	34	3	12	0	0	0	0	0	5	5	2	3	0	1	0	6
13 Tonya Edwards	15	1	3	0	0	0	0	1	5	6	2	2	1	1	0	2
7 Shalonda Enis	12	1	2	0	0	0	0	0	1	1	0	1	0	1	0	2
33 Machanguana	12	1	1	0	0	0	0	0	0	0	2	0	0	1	0	2
3 Summer Erb	7	3	3	0	0	0	0	1	1	2	0	1	0	3	0	6
20 Keisha Anderson	3	0	1	0	1	0	0	0	0	0	0	0	0	1	0	0
8 Kelly Miller	3	0	2	0	0	0	0	0	0	0	0	0	0	0	0	0
TOTALS	200	25	64	1	11	3	4	8	20	28	14	21	5	14	0	54
PERCENTAGES:	39.1	9.1	75.0			TM REB: 8		TOT TO: 14 (17 PTS)									

HOME: Los Angeles   Head Coach: Michael Cooper

No Player	MIN	FG	FGA	3P	3PA	FT	FTA	OR	DR	TOT	A	PF	ST	TO	TEC	PTS
4 Mwadi Mabika	33	2	9	2	6	6	6	1	5	6	4	1	1	2	0	12
8 DeLisha Milton	29	6	9	0	0	3	5	2	6	8	3	2	1	0	0	15
9 Lisa Leslie	37	7	19	1	3	9	10	5	8	13	6	3	1	3	0	24
21 Tamecka Dixon	37	5	10	1	3	2	2	0	1	1	7	2	2	2	0	13
5 Ukari Figgs	34	2	5	1	4	0	0	1	3	4	2	4	0	0	0	5
51 Rhonda Mapp	11	2	4	0	0	0	0	1	1	2	0	2	0	0	0	4
10 Nicky McCrimmon	6	0	0	0	0	0	0	0	0	0	1	0	0	1	0	0
00 Latasha Byears	5	3	3	0	0	3	4	1	0	1	0	0	0	0	0	9
17 Grgin Fonseca	3	0	0	0	0	0	0	0	1	1	0	0	0	0	0	0
20 Wendi Willits	3	0	0	0	0	0	0	0	0	0	1	0	0	0	0	0
40 Nicole Levandusky	2	0	1	0	1	0	0	0	0	0	0	0	0	0	0	0
TOTALS	200	27	60	5	17	23	27	11	25	36	24	14	5	8	0	82
PERCENTAGES:	45.0	29.4	85.2													

TM REB: 5   TOT TO: 8 (8 PTS)

BLOCKED SHOTS: Sting: 6. Smith 1, Sutton-Brown 4, Stinson 1. Sparks: 10. Milton 1, Leslie 7, Dixon 2.
TECHNICAL FOULS: None.

	ILL	PTO	FBP	PIP	2PT
CHA	0	8	6	42	8
LA	0	17	21	32	10

Flagrant Fouls: None.

ALL-STAR GAME BOX SCORE

At TD Waterhouse Centre, July 16, 2001

OFFICIALS: Michael Price, Bonita Spence, Melissa Barlow. TIME OF GAME: 1:59. ATTENDANCE: 16,906

SCORE BY PERIODS	1	2	FINAL
West	40	40	80
East	30	42	72

VISITORS: West   Head Coach: Van Chancellor

No Player	MIN	FG	FGA	3P	3PA	FT	FTA	OR	DR	TOT	A	PF	ST	TO	TEC	PTS
6 Ruthie Bolton	20	3	8	0	3	0	0	0	4	4	3	2	6	1	0	6
7 Tina Thompson	19	2	12	0	2	0	0	1	2	3	0	5	3	3	0	4
33 Yolanda Griffith	18	7	8	0	0	3	4	3	4	7	0	2	2	2	0	17
21 Ticha Penicheiro	21	0	2	0	0	1	2	0	3	3	5	1	2	5	0	1
9 Janeth Arcain	20	2	7	1	2	2	2	1	0	1	0	0	0	2	0	7
9 Lisa Leslie	23	8	14	1	2	3	4	3	6	9	1	4	1	3	0	20
30 Katie Smith	20	1	5	0	3	0	0	0	2	2	0	1	1	1	0	2
10 Jackie Stiles	20	0	3	0	0	4	4	0	2	2	0	3	0	0	0	4
21 Tamecka Dixon	20	4	7	0	1	0	0	0	2	2	4	0	0	1	0	8
15 Lauren Jackson	19	4	9	2	4	1	1	2	1	3	1	3	3	1	0	11
24 Natalie Williams							Did not play.									
TOTALS	200	31	75	4	17	14	17	10	26	36	14	21	18	19	0	80
PERCENTAGES:		41.3	23.5	82.4												

TM REB: 12   TOT TO: 19 (14 PTS)

HOME: East   Head Coach: Richie Adubato

No Player	MIN	FG	FGA	3P	3PA	FT	FTA	OR	DR	TOT	A	PF	ST	TO	TEC	PTS
11 McWilliams-Franklin	26	4	7	0	0	2	4	2	2	4	1	3	2	1	0	10
55 Vickie Johnson	19	2	8	2	5	2	2	0	3	3	1	0	0	3	0	8
24 Tari Phillips	24	4	8	0	0	1	6	4	5	9	0	1	1	7	0	9
15 Nikki McCray	22	2	7	0	0	1	2	0	0	0	2	1	0	1	0	5
11 Weatherspoon	15	0	1	0	0	0	0	0	1	1	2	0	3	3	0	0
28 Elena Baranova	25	4	8	1	2	1	2	0	7	7	2	2	1	2	0	10
25 Merlakia Jones	18	4	8	0	1	4	6	1	5	6	1	3	1	1	0	12
32 Andrea Stinson	17	2	9	0	3	0	0	2	3	5	1	2	0	1	0	4
5 Dawn Staley	15	2	3	0	0	0	0	0	0	0	3	2	4	0	0	4
42 Nykesha Sales	10	4	8	1	3	1	2	0	1	1	0	1	0	1	0	10
23 Rita Williams	9	0	2	0	2	0	0	0	0	0	1	0	0	0	0	0
44 Chasity Melvin							Did not play.									
23 Chamique Holdsclaw							Did not play.									
TOTALS	200	28	69	4	16	12	24	9	27	36	14	15	12	21	0	72
PERCENTAGES:		40.6	25.0	50.0												

TM REB: 16 TOT TO: 21 (25 PTS)

BLOCKED SHOTS: West: 5. Griffith 1, Leslie 3, Smith 1. East: 5. McWilliams-Franklin 1, Baranova 4.
TECHNICAL FOULS: None.

	ILL	PTO	FBP	PIP	2PT
West	0	25	6	50	18
East	0	14	18	34	14

FLAGRANT FOUL: None.

Holdsclaw was voted to the starting lineup but replaced due to injury
Melvin was named to the team but replaced due to injury

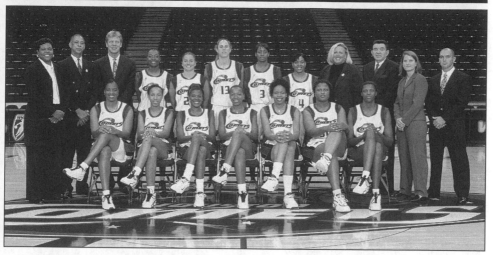

Front Row (l. to r.) - Tammy Jackson, Janeth Arcain, Sheryl Swoopes, Cynthia Cooper, Tina Thompson, Tiffani Johnson, Monica Lamb. Back Row (l. to r.) - Assistant Coach Alisa Scott, Video Coordinator Harold Liggans, Assistant Coach Kevin Cook, Nekeshia Henderson, Jennifer Rizzotti, Amaya Valdemoro, Kelley Gibson, Coquese Washington, Equipment Manager Jennie Vance, Head Coach & General Manager Van Chancellor, Trainer Michelle T. Leget, Strength & Conditioning Coach Anthony Falsone.

FINAL STANDINGS

EASTERN CONFERENCE

	CHA	CLE	DET	HOU	IND	LA	MIA	MIN	NY	ORL	PHO	POR	SAC	SEA	UTA	WAS	W	L	PCT	GB	Last-10	Streak
NY 3	2	1	1	3	0	2	1	--	2	1	1	0	1	1	1	20	12	.625	-	7-3	Lost 1
CLE 3	--	2	0	2	0	1	0	1	2	1	0	1	1	1	2	17	15	.531	3	4-6	Lost 2
ORL 3	1	3	0	2	0	2	0	1	--	0	0	1	1	1	1	16	16	.500	4	2-8	Lost 1
DET 2	1	--	0	3	0	2	0	2	0	0	0	1	2	1	0	14	18	.438	6	4-6	Won 2
WAS 1	1	3	0	2	0	2	0	2	2	0	0	0	1	0	--	14	18	.438	6	4-6	Won 1
MIA......2	2	1	0	1	0	--	0	1	1	0	1	0	2	1	1	13	19	.406	7	5-5	Won 3
IND......2	1	0	0	--	0	2	0	0	1	0	1	0	1	0	1	9	23	.281	11	3-7	Won 1
CHA....--	0	1	0	1	0	1	0	0	0	0	2	0	0	1	2	8	24	.250	12	3-7	Lost 2

WESTERN CONFERENCE

	CHA	CLE	DET	HOU	IND	LA	MIA	MIN	NY	ORL	PHO	POR	SAC	SEA	UTA	WAS	W	L	PCT	GB	Last-10	Streak
LA 1	1	2	3	1	--	1	3	2	1	3	2	2	2	2	2	28	4	.875	-	9-1	Lost 1
HOU 2	1	1	--	1	0	1	3	1	1	2	3	3	3	3	2	27	5	.844	1	8-2	Won 5
SAC 1	0	1	0	1	1	1	3	1	1	2	3	--	3	1	2	21	11	.656	7	8-2	Won 1
PHO 1	1	1	1	2	0	1	2	1	1	--	3	1	3	1	1	20	12	.625	8	6-4	Won 1
UTA 1	1	0	0	1	1	0	2	0	1	2	3	2	3	--	1	18	14	.563	10	6-4	Won 2
MIN 1	2	1	0	1	0	2	--	0	2	1	2	0	1	1	1	15	17	.469	13	5-5	Lost 1
POR 0	1	1	0	1	1	1	1	0	1	0	--	0	2	0	1	10	22	.313	18	3-7	Lost 4
SEA 1	0	0	0	1	1	0	2	0	0	0	1	0	--	0	0	6	26	.188	22	3-7	Lost 2

TEAM STANDINGS

OFFENSIVE

TEAM	G	FG	FGA	PCT	FG3	FG3A	PCT	FT	FTA	PCT	OFF	DEF	REB	AST	PF	DQ	STL	TO	BLK	PTS	AVG
Hou........	32	891	1894	.470	172	491	.350	521	634	.822	273	724	997	494	554	2	284	440	104	2475	77.3
L.A.	32	861	1956	.440	150	452	.332	545	693	.786	308	783	1091	586	704	13	271	466	156	2417	75.5
Utah........	32	858	1896	.453	88	262	.336	609	790	.771	348	732	1080	522	698	6	214	544	157	2413	75.4
Sac........	32	876	1993	.440	142	459	.309	449	650	.691	388	650	1038	567	571	5	332	458	157	2343	73.2
Det........	32	868	1981	.438	76	273	.278	519	699	.742	341	644	985	503	701	4	260	530	88	2331	72.8
Phoe........	32	803	1800	.446	124	394	.315	513	661	.776	275	619	894	465	630	5	285	429	91	2243	70.1
Ind.	32	796	1838	.433	193	521	.370	428	569	.752	285	647	932	501	642	9	271	518	126	2213	69.2
Orl.	32	833	1911	.436	145	424	.342	397	546	.727	319	606	925	473	583	5	255	486	130	2208	69.0
Minn........	32	770	1831	.421	204	571	.357	449	592	.758	258	612	870	495	690	11	237	497	63	2193	68.5
Cha........	32	812	1903	.427	131	386	.339	431	577	.747	305	630	935	551	713	8	222	496	90	2186	68.3
Clev.	32	809	1828	.443	141	407	.346	426	570	.747	331	603	934	539	647	7	259	538	91	2185	68.3
Wash.	32	832	1813	.459	109	335	.325	403	578	.697	300	646	946	521	597	3	245	506	126	2176	68.0
Port........	32	761	1828	.416	145	433	.335	488	697	.700	309	627	936	480	761	11	265	593	93	2155	67.3
N.Y.	32	792	1815	.436	135	396	.341	429	567	.757	288	652	940	477	617	7	246	474	102	2148	67.1
Miami	32	647	1774	.365	85	310	.274	452	664	.681	365	595	960	415	707	5	272	524	88	1831	57.2
Sea........	32	667	1741	.383	109	364	.299	379	561	.676	256	537	793	390	648	4	255	525	93	1822	56.9

DEFENSIVE

Team	FG	FGA	PCT	FG3	FG3A	PCT	FT	FTA	PCT	OFF	DEF	REB	AST	PF	DQ	STL	TO	BLK	PTS	AVG	DIFF
Miami ..715		1676	.427	117	315	.371	454	627	.724	275	648	923	416	661	10	247	528	118	2001	62.5	-5.3
N.Y. 741		1822	.407	116	420	.276	437	590	.741	320	647	967	462	645	5	223	479	94	2035	63.6	+3.5
Hou......786		1939	.405	124	418	.297	370	508	.728	290	612	902	473	648	3	233	480	85	2066	64.6	+12.8
Phoe.....773		1828	.423	135	416	.325	421	574	.733	334	635	969	486	698	8	224	531	91	2102	65.7	+4.4
Clev......774		1761	.440	119	368	.323	455	583	.780	277	596	873	540	693	9	305	552	95	2122	66.3	+2.0
L.A. 776		1963	.395	122	413	.295	495	692	.715	300	678	978	445	650	12	243	485	105	2169	67.8	+7.8
Sea.......778		1721	.452	117	334	.350	498	654	.761	288	721	1009	506	618	9	284	529	123	2171	67.8	-10.9
Sac.......811		1918	.423	144	418	.344	410	544	.754	320	631	951	503	600	2	226	524	116	2176	68.0	+5.2
Minn.....755		1758	.429	164	481	.341	514	702	.732	300	677	977	472	707	8	275	547	130	2188	68.4	+0.2
Wash......845		1875	.451	149	397	.375	382	555	.688	299	612	911	513	595	4	261	456	102	2221	69.4	-1.4
Orl. 851		1964	.433	153	450	.340	378	495	.764	348	669	1017	536	637	2	264	500	108	2233	69.8	-0.8
Ind. 839		1868	.449	109	358	.304	503	669	.752	321	633	954	528	612	5	267	476	75	2290	71.6	-2.4
Port......788		1847	.427	150	447	.336	577	766	.753	307	646	953	487	729	8	277	531	130	2303	72.0	-4.6
Utah......860		1964	.438	156	448	.348	531	721	.736	313	598	911	503	702	11	301	437	112	2407	75.2	+0.2
Det......905		1968	.460	136	372	.366	480	652	.736	331	640	971	513	672	9	284	543	148	2426	75.8	-3.0
Cha......879		1930	.455	138	423	.326	533	716	.744	326	664	990	596	596	1	259	426	123	2429	75.9	-7.6
Avg......805		1863	.432	134	405	.332	465	628	.740	309	644	954	499	654	7	261	502	110	2209	69.0	---
........12876				2149			7438			4949		15256		10463		4173		1755			
.... 29802				6478			10048			10307		7979		105		8024		35339			

TEAM COMPARISONS

TEAM	Points Per Game OWN	OPP	Field Goal Percentage OWN	OPP	Turnovers Per Game OWN	OPP	Rebound Percentages OFF	DEF	TOT	Below 70 Pts. OWN	OPP	Overtime Games W	L	3 PTS or Less W	L	10 PTS or More W	L
Charlotte	68.3	75.9	.427	.455	15.5	13.3	.315	.659	.487	17	8	2	1	3	5	1	14
Cleveland	68.3	66.3	.443	.440	16.8	17.3*	.357	.685	.521	16	18	3	1	4	2	11	10
Detroit	72.8	75.8	.438	.460	16.6	17.0	.348	.661	.504	15	9	0	1	4	2	5	12
Houston	77.3*	64.6	.470*	.405	13.8	15.0	.308	.714	.511	5	23	2	0	2	0	22	2
Indiana	69.2	71.6	.433	.449	16.2	14.9	.310	.668	.489	15	13	0	1	1	3	8	9
Los Angeles	75.5	67.8	.440	.395*	14.6	15.2	.312	.723*	.518	7	20	1	1	3	1	12	2
Miami..................	57.2	62.5*	.365	.427	16.4	16.5	.360	.684	.522	28	24	2	0	3	2	7	13
Minnesota	68.5	68.4	.421	.429	15.5	17.1	.276	.671	.473	18	17	1	0	2	1	8	9
New York	67.1	63.6	.436	.407	14.8	15.0	.308	.671	.489	20	23	0	1	1	4	12	6
Orlando	69.0	69.8	.436	.433	15.2	15.6	.323	.635	.479	20	15	0	3	4	3	6	7
Phoenix	70.1	65.7	.446	.423	13.4*	16.6	.302	.650	.476	19	21	1	0	3	3	12	6
Portland	67.3	72.0	.416	.427	18.5	16.6	.324	.671	.497	18	14	0	4	1	4	5	9
Sacramento	73.2	68.0	.440	.423	14.3	16.4	.381*	.670	.525	10	17	0	0	3	1	13	4
Seattle	56.9	67.8	.383	.452	16.4	16.5	.262	.651	.456	31	20	2	1	0	2	1	18
Utah	75.4	75.2	.453	.438	17.0	13.7	.368	.700	.534*	9	11	0	0	5	3	6	8
Washington	68.0	69.4	.459	.451	15.8	14.3	.329	.684	.506	18	13	0	0	2	5	8	8
COMPOSITE; 256 games																	
....	69.0		.432		15.7		.324	.676		266		14		41		137	

* - League Leader

REBOUND PERCENTAGES — OFF. - Percentage of a given team's missed shots which that team rebounds. DEF. - Percentage of opponents' missed shots which a given team rebounds. TOT. - Average of offensive and defensive rebound percentages.

SCORING AVERAGE

	G	FG	FT	PTS	AVG
Swoopes, Hou.	31	245	119	643	20.7
Smith, Min.	32	203	152	646	20.2
Reed, Pho.	32	231	128	608	19.0
Williams, Utah	29	179	182	543	18.7
Leslie, L.A.	32	197	169	570	17.8
Cooper, Hou.	31	180	147	550	17.7
Stinson, Cha.	32	214	99	565	17.7
Holdsclaw, Was.	32	232	87	561	17.5
Goodson, Utah	29	199	92	498	17.2
Lennox, Min.	32	201	84	541	16.9
Thompson, Hou.	32	191	103	540	16.9
Witherspoon, Por.	32	175	128	538	16.8
Griffith, Sac.	32	193	137	523	16.3
McCray, Was.	32	167	113	497	15.5
Palmer, Det.	32	167	95	441	13.8
Phillips, Por.-N.Y.	31	170	85	427	13.8
McWilliams-Franklin, Orl.	32	173	87	438	13.7
A. Johnson, Orl.	32	175	34	436	13.6
Sales, Orl.	32	170	43	430	13.4
Bolton-Holifield, Sac.	29	133	64	380	13.1

REBOUNDS PER GAME

	G	OFF	DEF	TOT	AVG
Williams, Utah	29	132	204	336	11.6
Griffith, Sac.	32	148	183	331	10.3
Leslie, L.A.	32	75	231	306	9.6
Phillips, Por.-N.Y.	31	86	161	247	8.0
Thompson, Hou.	32	68	177	245	7.7
McWilliams-Franklin, Orl.	32	90	154	244	7.6
Holdsclaw, Was.	32	57	183	240	7.5
Askamp, Mia.	32	96	135	231	7.2
Palmer, Det.	32	67	152	219	6.8
Mapp, Cha.	30	60	145	205	6.8
Page, Was.	32	79	129	208	6.5
Swoopes, Hou.	31	40	155	195	6.3
Milton, L.A.	32	55	139	194	6.1
Crawley, Por.	31	64	121	185	6.0
Ndiaye-Diatta, Det.	32	65	122	187	5.8
Reed, Pho.	32	59	128	187	5.8
Bullett, Was.	32	61	122	183	5.7
Goodson, Utah	29	69	95	164	5.7
Mabika, L.A.	32	45	134	179	5.6
Lennox, Min.	32	53	125	178	5.6

ASSISTS PER GAME

	G	AST	AVG
Penicheiro, Sac.	30	236	7.9
Weatherspoon, N.Y.	32	205	6.4
Staley, Cha.	32	190	5.9
S. Johnson, Orl.	32	169	5.3
Nagy, Was.	23	118	5.1
Cooper, Hou.	31	156	5.0

	G	AST	AVG
Figgs, L.A.	32	127	4.0
Swoopes, Hou.	31	119	3.8
Stinson, Cha.	32	121	3.8
McConnell Serio, Cle.	32	119	3.7
Cleary, Pho.	24	77	3.2
Thomas, Por.	32	101	3.2
R. Williams, Ind.	32	101	3.2
Dixon, L.A.	31	96	3.1
Black, Mia.	32	98	3.1
Mabika, L.A.	32	98	3.1
Hlede, Utah	31	92	3.0
Canty, Det.	28	82	2.9
Smith, Min.	32	90	2.8
Bevilaqua, Por.	32	89	2.8

FIELD GOAL PCT.

	FG	FGA	PCT
Page, Was.	131	222	.590
Wolters, Ind.	148	264	.561
Griffith, Sac.	193	361	.535
McWilliams-Franklin, Orl.	173	330	.524
Thompson, Ind.	131	255	.514
Milton, L.A.	150	293	.512
Reed, Pho.	231	456	.507
Tornikidou, Det.	122	241	.506
Swoopes, Hou.	245	484	.506
Brown, Cle.	93	187	.497

3-PT FIELD GOAL PCT.

	3FG	3GA	PCT
Hlede, Utah	25	58	.431
Thompson, Hou.	55	132	.417
Nemcova, Cle.	29	71	.408
Maxwell, Ind.	62	156	.397
Lennox, Min.	55	139	.396
Sales, Orl.	47	119	.395
McConnell Serio, Cle	38	97	.392
McCarty, Ind.	27	70	.386
Mabika, L.A.	61	159	.384
Johnson, N.Y.	27	71	.380

FREE THROW PCT.

	FT	FTA	PCT
Azzi, Utah	40	43	.930
Tornikidou, Det.	85	93	.914
Reed, Pho.	128	142	.901
Hammon, N.Y.	61	69	.884
Johnson, N.Y.	67	76	.882
Staley, Cha.	65	74	.878
Cooper, Hou.	147	168	.875
Witherspoon, Por.	128	147	.871
Smith, Min.	152	175	.869
Maxwell, Ind.	50	58	.862

REVIEW 2000 Regular Season

STEALS PER GAME

	G	STL	AVG
Swoopes, Hou.	31	87	2.81
Griffith, Sac.	32	83	2.59
R. Williams, Ind.	32	76	2.38
Penicheiro, Sac.	30	70	2.33
Reed, Pho.	32	66	2.06
Weatherspoon, N.Y.	32	65	2.03
Bullett, Was.	32	64	2.00
Henning, Sea.	32	61	1.91
Phillips, Por.-N.Y.	31	59	1.90
McWilliams-Franklin, Orl.	32	59	1.84

BLOCKS PER GAME

	G	BLK	AVG
Dydek, Utah	32	96	3.00
Leslie, L.A.	32	74	2.31
Smith, Sac.	32	64	2.00
dos Santos, Orl.	32	63	1.97
Griffith, Sac.	32	61	1.91
Wolters, Ind.	31	49	1.58
Bullett, Was.	32	47	1.47
Wicks, N.Y.	32	39	1.22
Barnes, Sea.	31	33	1.06
Swoopes, Hou.	31	33	1.06

MINUTES PER GAME

	G	MIN	AVG
Smith, Min.	32	1193	37.3
Azzi, Utah	15	559	37.3
Williams, Utah	29	1039	35.8
Holdsclaw, Was.	32	1131	35.3
S. Johnson, Orl.	32	1126	35.2
Swoopes, Hou.	31	1090	35.2
Stinson, Cha.	32	1123	35.1
Cooper, Hou.	31	1085	35.0
A. Johnson, Orl.	32	1100	34.4
Staley, Cha.	32	1099	34.3

INDIVIDUAL STATISTICS, TEAM BY TEAM

CHARLOTTE STING

Player	G	Min	FGM	FGA	Pct	FTM	FTA	Pct	Off	Def	Tot	Ast	PF	Dq	Stl	TO	Blk	Pts	Avg	Hi
Andrea Stinson	32	1123	214	463	.462	99	134	.739	35	101	136	121	77	0	55	86	23	565	17.7	33
Rhonda Mapp	30	856	138	300	.460	73	88	.830	60	145	205	64	112	3	30	59	24	357	11.9	25
Shalonda Enis	12	323	41	104	.394	46	60	.767	21	24	45	10	30	0	10	16	1	139	11.6	20
Dawn Staley	32	1099	94	253	.372	65	74	.878	21	56	77	190	80	1	37	91	1	282	8.8	19
Tracy Reid	29	620	86	180	.478	39	72	.542	45	55	100	29	47	1	14	51	9	211	7.3	21
Tiffany Travis	32	574	70	158	.443	21	28	.750	24	57	81	26	74	0	31	32	4	173	5.4	16
Charlotte Smith	30	659	56	159	.352	20	25	.800	29	77	106	55	88	2	15	48	17	156	5.2	17
Niesa Johnson	6	78	9	17	.529	6	6	1.000	0	4	4	11	3	0	4	9	0	26	4.3	10
Summer Erb	29	275	32	73	.438	28	43	.651	26	37	63	10	68	0	8	17	6	92	3.2	21
Cass Bauer	29	398	29	72	.403	18	21	.857	20	36	56	14	72	1	8	28	3	76	2.6	9
Angie Braziel	22	203	19	49	.388	13	19	.684	16	18	34	5	24	0	5	17	0	51	2.3	10
Larecha Jones	9	54	8	19	.421	1	2	.500	0	5	5	2	5	0	0	4	1	19	2.1	8
E.C. Hill	26	213	16	56	.286	2	5	.400	8	15	23	14	33	0	5	25	1	39	1.5	8
Charlotte	32	6475	812	1903	.427	431	577	.747	305	630	935	551	713	8	222	496	90	2186	68.3	87
Opponents	32	6475	879	1930	.455	533	716	.744	326	664	990	596	596	1	259	426	123	2429	75.9	96

3-pt. FG: Charlotte 131-386 (.339) Stinson 38-106 (.358); Mapp 8-22 (.364); Enis 11-32 (.344); Staley 29-88 (.330); Reid 0-2 (.000); Travis 12-25 (.480) Smith 24-76 (.316); Johnson 2-5 (.400); Erb 0-1 (.000); Bauer 0-1 (.000); Jones 2-6 (.333); Hill 5-22 (.227); Opponents 138-423 (.326)

CLEVELAND ROCKERS

Player	G	Min	FGM	FGA	Pct	FTM	FTA	Pct	Off	Def	Tot	Ast	PF	Dq	Stl	TO	Blk	Pts	Avg	Hi
Eva Nemcova	14	443	67	164	.409	22	24	.917	9	32	41	23	29	0	15	27	8	185	13.2	23
Chasity Melvin	32	904	136	289	.471	100	137	.730	69	103	172	61	113	4	29	62	18	373	11.7	28
Merlakia Jones	32	948	153	323	.474	32	47	.681	52	87	139	63	86	2	29	60	2	352	11.0	21
Rushia Brown	30	679	93	187	.497	66	78	.846	54	70	124	44	81	0	38	59	13	253	8.4	24
Mery Andrade	32	797	89	195	.456	60	80	.750	32	63	95	75	91	1	41	65	10	265	8.3	18
Ann Wauters	32	598	78	149	.523	43	58	.741	47	82	129	37	75	0	21	63	24	199	6.2	17
S. McConnell Serio	32	705	58	140	.414	19	25	.760	9	41	50	119	30	0	15	69	1	173	5.4	12
Helen Darling	32	556	47	150	.313	48	65	.738	24	39	63	65	52	0	37	67	5	155	4.8	17
Vicki Hall	32	577	59	158	.373	22	34	.647	24	68	92	24	60	0	17	25	8	150	4.7	19
Michelle Edwards(‡)	3	17	4	10	.400	0	0	---	0	2	2	1	3	0	0	4	0	8	2.7	6
Tricia Bader Binford	25	201	17	48	.354	5	6	.833	2	9	11	21	16	0	17	18	1	47	1.9	8
Adia Barnes	5	18	3	5	.600	2	4	.500	2	0	2	4	2	0	0	2	0	8	1.6	7

124

Player	G	Min	FGM	FGA	Pct	FTM	FTA	Pct	Off	Def	Tot	Ast	PF	Dq	Stl	TO	Blk	Pts	Avg	Hi
P. Johns Kimbrough ..12	57	5	10	.500	7	12	.583	7	7	14	2	9	0	0	8	1	17	1.4	4
Cleveland 32	6500	809	1828	.443	426	570	.747	331	603	934	539	647	7	259	538	91	2185	68.3	83
Opponents 32	6500	774	1761	.440	455	583	.780	277	596	873	540	693	8	305	552	95	2122	66.3	93

3-pt. FG: Cleveland 141-407 (.346) Nemcova 29-71 (.408); Melvin 1-7 (.143); Jones 14-45 (.311); Brown 1-2 (.500); Andrade 27-75 (.360); Wauters 0-2 (.000) McConnell Serio 38-97 (.392); Darling 13-38 (.342); Hall 10-42 (.238); Edwards(‡) 0-3 (.000); Bader Binford 8-24 (.333); Barnes 0-1 (.000); Opponents 119-368 (.323)

DETROIT SHOCK

Player	G	Min	FGM	FGA	Pct	FTM	FTA	Pct	Off	Def	Tot	Ast	PF	Dq	Stl	TO	Blk	Pts	Avg	Hi
Wendy Palmer............32	914	167	374	.447	95	135	.704	67	152	219	39	112	2	20	65	10	441	13.8	32
Astou Ndiaye-Diatta ..32	868	158	333	.474	29	51	.569	65	122	187	40	87	0	23	64	22	346	10.8	19
Elena Tornikidou 32	869	122	241	.506	85	93	.914	41	69	110	82	73	0	29	68	13	330	10.3	25
Dominique Canty 28	784	83	203	.409	91	131	.695	31	39	70	82	64	0	49	51	5	257	9.2	22
Tamicha Jackson 17	267	41	106	.387	26	35	.743	8	17	25	36	30	0	22	21	0	116	6.8	14
Claudia Maria das Ne 30	636	63	166	.380	25	30	.833	8	27	35	59	30	0	31	55	1	179	6.0	19
Edwina Brown 32	619	60	168	.357	67	80	.838	36	52	88	72	77	0	24	68	5	188	5.9	17
Anna DeForge............27	433	51	126	.405	25	32	.781	9	38	47	47	34	0	27	33	4	145	5.4	13
Oksana Zakaluzhnaya 23	258	38	73	.521	10	11	.909	15	31	46	2	45	0	5	19	13	89	3.9	15
O. Scott-Richardson ..28	369	37	89	.416	26	40	.650	28	52	80	28	83	2	12	45	10	100	3.6	16
Barbara Farris............14	130	15	30	.500	15	27	.556	16	16	32	2	30	0	6	14	1	45	3.2	9
Joy Holmes-Harris 29	271	33	70	.471	21	30	.700	17	28	45	14	36	0	11	16	4	91	3.1	11
Madinah Slaise............3	7	0	2	.000	4	4	1.000	0	1	1	0	0	0	1	0	0	4	1.3	4
Detroit 32	6425	868	1981	.438	519	699	.742	341	644	985	503	701	4	260	530	88	2331	72.8	111
Opponents 32	6425	905	1968	.460	480	652	.736	331	640	971	513	672	9	284	543	148	2426	75.8	108

3-pt. FG: Detroit 76-273 (.278) Palmer 12-48 (.250); Ndiaye-Diatta 1-6 (.167); Tornikidou 1-8 (.125); Canty 0-5 (.000); Jackson 8-32 (.250); Brown 1-4 (.250) das Neves 28-92 (.304); DeForge 18-56 (.321); Zakaluzhnaya 3-7 (.429); Scott-Richardson 0-2 (.000); Farris 0-1 (.000) Holmes-Harris 4-11 (.364); Slaise 0-1 (.000); Opponents 136-372 (.366)

HOUSTON COMETS

Player	G	Min	FGM	FGA	Pct	FTM	FTA	Pct	Off	Def	Tot	Ast	PF	Dq	Stl	TO	Blk	Pts	Avg	Hi
Sheryl Swoopes 31	1090	245	484	.506	119	145	.821	40	155	195	119	67	0	87	82	33	643	20.7	31
Cynthia Cooper 31	1085	180	392	.459	147	168	.875	17	68	85	156	61	0	39	99	6	550	17.7	28
Tina Thompson 32	1087	191	407	.469	103	123	.837	68	177	245	48	88	0	47	84	25	540	16.9	28
Janeth Arcain 32	977	109	233	.468	41	49	.837	36	83	119	60	66	1	42	53	3	268	8.4	18
Tiffani Johnson 31	687	48	100	.480	35	50	.700	59	88	147	10	86	1	10	17	16	131	4.2	10
Elen Chakirova 14	150	13	30	.433	29	33	.879	14	17	31	4	12	0	5	7	2	57	4.1	11
Tammy Jackson 29	339	35	61	.574	6	11	.545	18	43	61	11	62	0	12	24	9	76	2.6	8
Amaya Valdemoro......22	171	20	60	.333	6	6	1.000	3	18	21	13	21	0	8	13	4	57	2.6	10
Monica Lamb 13	140	10	20	.500	6	12	.500	5	21	26	3	23	0	2	4	4	26	2.0	5
Jennifer Rizzotti 32	437	21	55	.382	6	9	.667	6	30	36	44	38	0	15	26	2	60	1.9	10
Coquese Washington..25	236	12	33	.364	16	20	.800	3	16	19	24	19	0	16	19	0	43	1.7	7
Jawann Kelley-Gibson17	76	7	19	.368	7	8	.875	4	8	12	2	11	0	1	4	0	24	1.4	6
Houston 32	6475	891	1894	.470	521	634	.822	273	724	997	494	554	2	284	440	104	2475	77.3	107
Opponents 32	6475	786	1939	.405	370	508	.728	290	612	902	473	648	3	233	480	85	2066	64.6	90

3-pt. FG: Houston 172-491 (.350) Swoopes 34-91 (.374); Cooper 43-121 (.355); Thompson 55-132 (.417); Arcain 9-45 (.200); Chakirova 2-12 (.167) Valdemoro 11-29 (.379); Rizzotti 12-39 (.308); Washington 3-15 (.200); Kelley-Gibson 3-7 (.429); Opponents 124-418 (.297)

INDIANA FEVER

Player	G	Min	FGM	FGA	Pct	FTM	FTA	Pct	Off	Def	Tot	Ast	PF	Dq	Stl	TO	Blk	Pts	Avg	Hi
Kara Wolters 31	793	148	264	.561	74	100	.740	46	118	164	19	99	2	12	73	49	370	11.9	24
Rita Williams..............32	1014	112	274	.409	79	108	.731	22	73	95	101	69	1	76	69	3	352	11.0	21
Monica Maxwell 32	1029	110	285	.386	50	58	.862	40	120	160	63	92	0	49	64	16	332	10.4	29
Alicia Thompson 31	792	131	255	.514	30	42	.714	48	109	157	41	85	4	24	53	4	310	10.0	22
Gordana Grubin..........29	720	90	239	.377	31	40	.775	20	56	76	63	47	0	31	60	0	239	8.2	19
Stephanie McCarty 32	635	66	166	.398	71	86	.826	14	46	60	57	49	0	31	47	6	230	7.2	20
Danielle McCulley 29	456	63	153	.412	46	63	.730	45	37	82	19	63	1	16	37	22	175	6.0	17
Jurgita Streimikyte 27	424	46	117	.393	27	35	.771	25	46	71	44	67	1	16	32	23	121	4.5	15

125

Player	G	Min	FGM	FGA	Pct	FTM	FTA	Pct	Off	Def	Tot	Ast	PF	Dq	Stl	TO	Blk	Pts	Avg	Hi
									REBOUNDS									SCORING		
Chantel Tremitiere	25	318	18	51	.353	10	16	.625	6	25	31	51	30	0	0	30	1	50	2.0	12
Katryna Gaither(*)	6	24	3	8	.375	0	0	---	1	2	3	1	2	0	0	1	1	6	1.0	4
Katryna Gaither(†)	15	78	5	15	.333	10	10	1.000	8	12	20	5	10	0	4	5	1	20	1.3	4
Donna Harrington	8	67	1	6	.167	6	10	.600	4	5	9	5	16	0	2	11	1	8	1.0	2
Alessandra Santos de ..	3	11	1	1	1.000	1	6	.167	0	3	3	0	3	0	0	2	0	3	1.0	2
Texlin Quinney	17	118	6	14	.429	3	5	.600	11	5	16	15	12	0	4	10	0	15	0.9	2
Usha Gilmore	4	21	1	5	.200	0	0	---	3	2	5	2	6	0	0	4	0	2	0.5	2
Beverly Williams	1	3	0	0	---	0	0	---	0	0	0	0	2	0	0	0	0	0	0.0	0
Indiana	32	6425	796	1838	.433	428	569	.752	285	647	932	501	642	9	271	518	126	2213	69.2	87
Opponents	32	6425	839	1868	.449	503	669	.752	321	633	954	528	612	5	267	476	75	2290	71.6	111

3-pt. FG: Indiana 193-521 (.370) R. Williams 49-131 (.374); Maxwell 62-156 (.397); Thompson 18-40 (.450); Grubin 28-91 (.308); McCarty 27-70 (.386) McCulley 3-17 (.176); Streimikyte 2-6 (.333); Tremitiere 4-9 (.444); Gilmore 0-1 (.000); Opponents 109-358 (.304)

LOS ANGELES SPARKS

Player	G	Min	FGM	FGA	Pct	FTM	FTA	Pct	Off	Def	Tot	Ast	PF	Dq	Stl	TO	Blk	Pts	Avg	Hi
									REBOUNDS									SCORING		
Lisa Leslie	32	1028	197	430	.458	169	205	.824	75	231	306	60	134	7	31	103	74	570	17.8	30
Mwadi Mabika	32	940	130	335	.388	73	89	.820	45	134	179	98	117	2	58	51	18	394	12.3	26
DeLisha Milton	32	983	150	293	.512	76	102	.745	55	139	194	68	124	3	44	67	29	378	11.8	20
Tamecka Dixon	31	882	132	291	.454	62	77	.805	34	71	105	96	86	0	40	60	10	338	10.9	24
Ukari Figgs	32	803	66	153	.431	54	65	.831	14	41	55	127	53	0	21	43	3	215	6.7	15
Allison Feaster	32	469	60	167	.359	60	72	.833	36	49	85	33	46	0	23	35	2	202	6.3	18
C. Machanguana	31	421	48	83	.578	14	25	.560	20	52	72	18	66	1	13	19	4	110	3.5	10
Nicky McCrimmon	32	488	39	77	.506	7	14	.500	9	23	32	65	41	0	29	48	8	101	3.2	9
V. Grgin Fonseca	18	183	17	62	.274	14	23	.609	9	14	23	12	17	0	3	14	1	49	2.7	8
Paige Sauer	12	66	8	14	.571	4	5	.800	3	13	16	3	10	0	2	6	1	20	1.7	7
La'Keshia Frett	25	187	14	51	.275	12	16	.750	8	16	24	6	10	0	7	13	6	40	1.6	6
Los Angeles	32	6450	861	1956	.440	545	693	.786	308	783	1091	586	704	13	271	466	156	2417	75.5	94
Opponents	32	6450	776	1963	.395	495	692	.715	300	678	978	445	650	12	243	485	105	2169	67.8	89

3-pt. FG: Los Angeles 150-452 (.332) Leslie 7-32 (.219); Mabika 61-159 (.384); Milton 2-8 (.250); Dixon 12-34 (.353); Figgs 29-82 (.354); Feaster 22-85 (.259) Machanguana 0-1 (.000); McCrimmon 16-33 (.485); Grgin Fonseca 1-17 (.059); Frett 0-1 (.000); Opponents 122-413 (.295)

MIAMI SOL

Player	G	Min	FGM	FGA	Pct	FTM	FTA	Pct	Off	Def	Tot	Ast	PF	Dq	Stl	TO	Blk	Pts	Avg	Hi
									REBOUNDS									SCORING		
Sheri Sam	31	904	147	380	.387	67	100	.670	38	94	132	66	67	0	35	74	5	396	12.8	26
Katrina Colleton	32	873	103	293	.352	53	70	.757	15	48	63	50	65	0	27	65	7	264	8.3	19
Marlies Askamp	32	869	85	209	.407	80	117	.684	96	135	231	29	95	0	17	49	21	251	7.8	21
Kristen Rasmussen(*)	25	454	35	100	.350	54	64	.844	44	52	96	27	47	0	24	29	14	126	5.0	17
Kristen Rasmussen(†)	26	463	35	100	.350	54	64	.844	45	53	98	28	49	0	25	30	14	126	4.8	17
Debbie Black	32	820	57	150	.380	29	42	.690	23	69	92	98	86	0	58	50	1	152	4.8	13
Sharon Manning	24	403	44	92	.478	14	26	.538	41	59	100	17	59	1	23	39	4	103	4.3	13
Shantia Owens	31	605	51	131	.389	29	54	.537	47	50	97	21	95	3	11	54	26	131	4.2	12
Kisha Ford	28	424	33	108	.306	37	63	.587	32	30	62	21	65	1	32	27	1	104	3.7	14
Milena Flores	32	474	34	112	.304	26	42	.619	6	17	23	49	36	0	23	48	3	112	3.5	10
Jamie Cassidy	22	175	20	55	.364	30	43	.698	7	16	23	9	17	0	5	13	2	74	3.4	13
Umeki Webb	13	195	10	40	.250	21	25	.840	3	11	14	14	24	0	7	23	4	43	3.3	10
Jameka Jones	21	233	25	95	.263	11	16	.688	10	12	22	10	40	0	8	25	0	68	3.2	10
Tanja Kostic	5	46	3	9	.333	1	2	.500	3	2	5	4	6	0	2	7	0	7	1.4	4
Miami	32	6475	647	1774	.365	452	664	.681	365	595	960	415	707	5	272	524	88	1831	57.2	76
Opponents	32	6475	715	1676	.427	454	627	.724	275	648	923	416	661	10	247	528	118	2001	62.5	80

3-pt. FG: Miami 85-310 (.274) Sam 35-120 (.292); Colleton 5-21 (.238); Askamp 1-2 (.500); Rasmussen(*) 2-7 (.286); Rasmussen(†) 2-7 (.286); Black 9-42 (.214) Manning 1-2 (.500); K. Ford 1-4 (.250); Flores 18-61 (.295); Cassidy 4-8 (.500); Webb 2-8 (.250); Jones 7-35 (.200); Opponents 117-315 (.371)

MINNESOTA LYNX

Player	G	Min	FGM	FGA	Pct	FTM	FTA	Pct	Off	Def	Tot	Ast	PF	Dq	Stl	TO	Blk	Pts	Avg	Hi
Katie Smith	32	1193	203	482	.421	152	175	.869	28	65	93	90	71	0	44	76	7	646	20.2	34
Betty Lennox	32	984	201	471	.427	84	105	.800	53	125	178	82	112	4	53	97	9	541	16.9	31
Kristin Folkl	32	845	86	191	.450	66	94	.702	38	116	154	67	80	1	23	50	22	242	7.6	20
Grace Daley	30	577	57	147	.388	42	65	.646	32	40	72	57	49	0	12	50	0	173	5.8	17
Andrea Lloyd Curry	14	333	26	68	.382	12	17	.706	14	29	43	22	32	0	12	24	2	75	5.4	11
Keitha Dickerson	32	791	54	142	.380	34	45	.756	31	110	141	59	107	4	37	70	2	142	4.4	15
Maylana Martin	30	456	54	118	.458	19	32	.594	25	42	67	21	81	1	17	29	13	132	4.4	14
Marla Brumfield	32	613	47	101	.465	29	42	.690	22	38	60	42	70	1	22	40	2	124	3.9	14
Sonja Tate	8	94	10	22	.455	1	2	.500	6	7	13	5	13	0	3	7	0	27	3.4	13
Kate Paye	28	408	19	58	.328	6	9	.667	3	27	30	38	49	0	8	28	6	56	2.0	9
Shanele Stires	21	117	13	29	.448	4	6	.667	6	8	14	7	22	0	6	14	0	35	1.7	9
Angela Aycock(*)	3	6	0	0	---	0	0	---	0	3	3	4	1	0	0	0	0	0	0.0	0
Angela Aycock(†)	4	13	0	3	.000	0	0	---	1	4	5	4	3	0	0	0	0	0	0.0	0
Angie Potthoff	3	8	0	2	.000	0	0	---	0	2	2	1	3	0	0	0	0	0	0.0	0
Minnesota	32	6425	770	1831	.421	449	592	.758	258	612	870	495	690	11	237	497	63	2193	68.5	88
Opponents	32	6425	755	1758	.429	514	702	.732	300	677	977	472	707	8	275	547	130	2188	68.4	85

3-pt. FG: Minnesota 204-571 (.357) Smith 88-232 (.379); Lennox 55-139 (.396); Folkl 4-19 (.211); Daley 17-56 (.304); Lloyd Curry 11-32 (.344); Dickerson 0-2 (.000) Martin 5-19 (.263); Brumfield 1-9 (.111); Tate 6-11 (.545); Paye 12-41 (.293); Stires 5-10 (.500); Aycock(†) 0-2 (.000) Potthoff 0-1 (.000); Opponents 164-481 (.341)

NEW YORK LIBERTY

Player	G	Min	FGM	FGA	Pct	FTM	FTA	Pct	Off	Def	Tot	Ast	PF	Dq	Stl	TO	Blk	Pts	Avg	Hi
Tari Phillips	31	978	170	364	.467	85	130	.654	86	161	247	28	110	5	59	85	21	427	13.8	30
Vickie Johnson	31	1023	143	324	.441	67	76	.882	40	97	137	77	48	0	22	57	5	380	12.3	22
Becky Hammon	32	835	119	252	.472	61	69	.884	19	45	64	58	55	0	29	62	1	351	11.0	23
Crystal Robinson	27	722	86	201	.428	30	33	.909	26	42	68	48	74	0	23	33	10	238	8.8	19
Tamika Whitmore	32	689	109	253	.431	59	84	.702	34	71	105	20	102	1	17	53	17	277	8.7	17
Teresa Weatherspoon	32	1078	67	153	.438	60	81	.741	16	93	109	205	85	0	65	86	5	205	6.4	14
Sue Wicks	32	680	55	143	.385	45	62	.726	49	100	149	21	78	1	26	50	39	156	4.9	14
Venus Lacy	2	18	2	5	.400	2	4	.500	1	4	5	0	4	0	0	2	0	6	3.0	6
Marina Ferragut	23	154	23	53	.434	1	2	.500	4	13	17	4	34	0	0	11	2	50	2.2	10
Shea Mahoney	15	158	11	38	.289	4	8	.500	10	20	30	4	14	0	2	5	1	27	1.8	9
Olga Firsova	9	19	4	10	.400	4	5	.800	0	4	4	1	8	0	0	2	1	12	1.3	3
Jessica Bibby	17	69	3	18	.167	11	13	.846	3	2	5	11	9	0	3	12	0	19	1.1	7
Desiree Francis	1	2	0	1	.000	0	0	---	0	0	0	0	0	0	0	0	0	0	0.0	0
New York	32	6425	792	1815	.436	429	567	.757	288	652	940	477	617	7	246	474	102	2148	67.1	87
Opponents	32	6425	741	1822	.407	437	590	.741	320	647	967	462	645	5	223	479	94	2035	63.6	84

3-pt. FG: New York 135-396 (.341) Phillips 2-8 (.250); Johnson 27-71 (.380); Hammon 52-141 (.369); Robinson 36-102 (.353); Whitmore 0-3 (.000); Wicks 1-5 (.200) Weatherspoon 11-44 (.250); Ferragut 3-10 (.300); Mahoney 1-5 (.200); Firsova 0-1 (.000); Bibby 2-6 (.333); Opponents 116-420 (.276)

ORLANDO MIRACLE

Player	G	Min	FGM	FGA	Pct	FTM	FTA	Pct	Off	Def	Tot	Ast	PF	Dq	Stl	TO	Blk	Pts	Avg	Hi
McWilliams-Franklin	32	1098	173	330	.524	87	122	.713	90	154	244	54	86	0	59	83	31	438	13.7	23
Adrienne Johnson	32	1100	175	393	.445	34	38	.895	30	60	90	54	59	1	24	56	3	436	13.6	25
Nykesha Sales	32	995	170	383	.444	43	62	.694	43	96	139	69	92	2	47	67	12	430	13.4	25
Shannon Johnson	32	1126	122	309	.395	107	144	.743	53	102	155	169	83	0	58	102	7	381	11.9	23
Cintia dos Santos	32	820	94	222	.423	40	57	.702	35	89	124	38	111	2	16	54	63	228	7.1	17
Elaine Powell	20	347	26	66	.394	17	22	.773	17	33	50	42	21	0	12	30	1	72	3.6	9
Carla McGhee	32	408	30	83	.361	27	39	.692	27	37	64	23	58	0	21	31	5	87	2.7	9
Tiffany McCain	25	214	15	49	.306	16	18	.889	2	9	11	5	18	0	3	9	1	51	2.0	8

127

Player	G	Min	FGM	FGA	Pct	FTM	FTA	Pct	REBOUNDS Off	Def	Tot	Ast	PF	Dq	Stl	TO	Blk	SCORING Pts	Avg	Hi
LaCharlotte Smith........3	12	2	3	.667	1	1	1.000	1	1	2	1	2	0	2	0	0	5	1.7	5
Jannon Roland 21	173	13	37	.351	4	8	.500	7	10	17	8	16	0	6	19	0	33	1.6	5
Jessie Hicks 26	157	10	23	.435	18	29	.621	13	13	26	4	33	0	2	17	7	38	1.5	5
Cornelia Gayden 3	7	1	2	.500	0	0	---	0	0	0	1	0	0	0	0	0	2	0.7	2
Romana Hamzova......15	43	2	11	.182	3	6	.500	1	2	3	5	4	0	5	4	0	7	0.5	2
Orlando....................32	6500	833	1911	.436	397	546	.727	319	606	925	473	583	5	255	486	130	2208	69.0	92
Opponents 32	6500	851	1964	.433	378	495	.764	348	669	1017	536	637	2	264	500	108	2233	69.8	92

3-pt. FG: Orlando 145-424 (.342); McWilliams-Frank 5-17 (.294); A. Johnson 52-148 (.351); Sales 47-119 (.395); S. Johnson 30-90 (.333); dos Santos 0-1 (.000); Powell 3-9 (.333); McGhee 0-3 (.000); McCain 5-22 (.227); Smith 0-1 (.000); Roland 3-10 (.300); Gayden 0-1 (.000); Hamzova 0-3 (.000); Opponents 153-450 (.340)

PHOENIX MERCURY

Player	G	Min	FGM	FGA	Pct	FTM	FTA	Pct	REBOUNDS Off	Def	Tot	Ast	PF	Dq	Stl	TO	Blk	SCORING Pts	Avg	Hi
Brandy Reed..............32	1090	231	456	.507	128	142	.901	59	128	187	86	52	0	66	90	21	608	19.0	32
Jennifer Gillom 30	826	139	316	.440	79	106	.745	31	85	116	45	91	1	21	59	29	376	12.5	28
Tonya Edwards 32	926	112	298	.376	79	101	.782	19	57	76	58	80	0	36	63	9	338	10.6	19
Michelle Brogan 28	725	70	137	.511	63	79	.797	40	71	111	49	88	2	30	36	6	211	7.5	18
Lisa Harrison 31	750	81	154	.526	30	37	.811	38	83	121	36	62	0	30	22	4	200	6.5	22
Bridget Pettis 32	583	60	168	.357	49	61	.803	19	41	60	46	62	1	31	39	4	189	5.9	22
Maria Stepanova.......15	170	24	54	.444	9	15	.600	15	33	48	8	42	1	4	22	9	57	3.8	9
Michele Timms 8	176	11	30	.367	4	4	1.000	2	14	16	18	22	0	15	18	2	30	3.8	11
Rankica Sarenac........20	142	23	44	.523	17	27	.630	11	19	30	8	30	0	0	17	1	64	3.2	15
Adrain Williams..........28	351	29	72	.403	20	38	.526	24	47	71	16	42	0	14	29	4	78	2.8	12
Michelle Cleary..........24	509	14	45	.311	19	27	.704	12	25	37	77	36	0	34	14	2	57	2.4	12
Dena Head 17	149	8	22	.364	10	16	.625	5	13	18	15	17	0	4	11	0	27	1.6	6
Nicole Kubik 4	19	1	3	.333	4	4	1.000	0	2	2	2	4	0	0	3	0	6	1.5	4
Amanda Wilson...........3	9	0	1	.000	2	4	.500	0	1	1	1	2	0	0	0	0	2	0.7	2
Phoenix.....................32	6425	803	1800	.446	513	661	.776	275	619	894	465	630	5	285	429	91	2243	70.1	90
Opponents 32	6425	773	1828	.423	421	574	.733	334	635	969	486	698	8	224	531	91	2102	65.7	87

3-pt. FG: Phoenix 124-394 (.315); Reed 18-43 (.419); Gillom 19-69 (.275); Edwards 35-114 (.307); Brogan 8-25 (.320); Harrison 8-12 (.667); Pettis 20-75 (.267); Timms 4-17 (.235); Sarenac 1-1 (1.000); Cleary 10-30 (.333); Head 1-7 (.143); Kubik 0-1 (.000); Opponents 135-416 (.325)

PORTLAND FIRE

Player	G	Min	FGM	FGA	Pct	FTM	FTA	Pct	REBOUNDS Off	Def	Tot	Ast	PF	Dq	Stl	TO	Blk	SCORING Pts	Avg	Hi
Sophia Witherspoon ..32	1061	175	456	.384	128	147	.871	23	82	105	68	72	1	38	88	8	538	16.8	31
Sylvia Crawley 31	930	143	298	.480	71	102	.696	64	121	185	34	96	2	29	88	24	357	11.5	25
Vanessa Nygaard 32	843	91	209	.435	41	54	.759	50	71	121	30	98	2	17	38	5	253	7.9	18
Alisa Burras 21	314	64	109	.587	31	41	.756	20	54	74	6	36	0	3	36	7	159	7.6	22
Michelle Marciniak 32	537	58	154	.377	43	75	.573	11	48	59	73	79	2	37	67	6	177	5.5	13
Stacey Thomas 32	863	58	163	.356	44	74	.595	48	78	126	101	93	1	54	68	15	163	5.1	14
Tully Bevilaqua 32	796	40	112	.357	56	72	.778	19	76	95	89	93	1	41	66	6	153	4.8	11
Lynn Pride 32	462	41	118	.347	29	42	.690	22	39	61	40	59	1	16	33	9	114	3.6	9
Tara Williams 26	174	31	69	.449	4	8	.500	5	12	17	13	26	0	8	10	2	80	3.1	15
DeMya Walker............30	311	35	88	.398	22	47	.468	29	18	47	19	69	1	17	35	7	92	3.1	12
Michele VanGorp........28	199	25	50	.500	19	35	.543	16	26	42	5	37	0	3	30	4	69	2.5	16
Jamila Wideman 5	35	0	2	.000	0	0	---	2	2	4	2	3	0	2	6	0	0	0.0	0
Portland 32	6525	761	1828	.416	488	697	.700	309	627	936	480	761	11	265	593	93	2155	67.3	89
Opponents 32	6525	788	1847	.427	577	766	.753	307	646	953	487	729	8	277	531	130	2303	72.0	94

3-pt. FG: Portland 145-433 (.335); Witherspoon 60-163 (.368); Crawley 0-2 (.000); Nygaard 30-90 (.333); Marciniak 18-54 (.333); Thomas 3-12 (.250); Pride 3-9 (.333); Bevilaqua 17-60 (.283); Williams 14-41 (.341); Walker 0-2 (.000); Opponents 150-447 (.336)

SACRAMENTO MONARCHS

Player	G	Min	FGM	FGA	Pct	FTM	FTA	Pct	Off	Def	Tot	Ast	PF	Dq	Stl	TO	Blk	Pts	Avg	Hi
									REBOUNDS									SCORING		
Yolanda Griffith	32	1026	193	361	.535	137	194	.706	148	183	331	47	110	1	83	82	61	523	16.3	30
Ruthie Bolton	29	868	133	368	.361	64	84	.762	42	64	106	57	60	0	34	45	1	380	13.1	28
Tangela Smith	32	925	176	371	.474	36	46	.783	61	117	178	43	107	1	30	60	64	388	12.1	22
Kedra Holland-Corn	32	934	111	253	.439	46	66	.697	28	42	70	81	63	1	43	74	5	312	9.8	23
Ticha Penicheiro	30	936	68	185	.368	62	107	.579	12	77	89	236	71	1	70	71	6	208	6.9	17
Latasha Byears	32	521	75	143	.524	30	49	.612	42	80	122	21	72	1	30	35	5	181	5.7	17
Lady Grooms	30	401	39	88	.443	46	61	.754	27	17	44	13	27	0	10	21	3	124	4.1	16
Katy Steding	29	309	36	95	.379	2	7	.286	11	28	39	14	22	0	11	17	10	91	3.1	12
Cindy Blodgett	20	133	20	50	.400	4	6	.667	1	8	9	3	9	0	8	13	1	52	2.6	9
Stacy Clinesmith	26	285	20	57	.351	14	17	.824	7	23	30	49	19	0	12	25	1	66	2.5	10
Linda Burgess	5	41	3	15	.200	6	9	.667	7	10	17	2	8	0	1	4	0	12	2.4	6
Rhonda Banchero	9	21	2	7	.286	2	4	.500	2	1	3	1	3	0	0	2	0	6	0.7	2
Sacramento	32	6400	876	1993	.440	449	650	.691	388	650	1038	567	571	5	332	458	157	2343	73.2	108
Opponents	32	6400	811	1918	.423	410	544	.754	320	631	951	503	600	2	226	524	116	2176	68.0	96

3-pt. FG: Sacramento 142-459 (.309); Bolton-Holifield 50-160 (.313); Holland-Corn 44-122 (.361); Penicheiro 10-50 (.200); Byears 1-2 (.500); Hardmon 0-1 (.000); Steding 17-53 (.321); Blodgett 8-28 (.286); Clinesmith 12-41 (.293); Banchero 0-2 (.000); Opponents 144-418 (.344)

SEATTLE STORM

Player	G	Min	FGM	FGA	Pct	FTM	FTA	Pct	Off	Def	Tot	Ast	PF	Dq	Stl	TO	Blk	Pts	Avg	Hi
									REBOUNDS									SCORING		
Edna Campbell	16	510	84	215	.391	41	58	.707	8	26	34	37	35	0	19	40	4	222	13.9	22
Kamila Vodichkova	23	489	68	171	.398	60	78	.769	28	69	97	22	63	0	13	57	12	200	8.7	22
Robin Threatt	20	377	60	158	.380	23	35	.657	10	22	32	18	36	1	13	30	3	155	7.8	24
Simone Edwards	29	645	83	182	.456	50	80	.625	38	69	107	22	57	0	16	45	10	216	7.4	18
Quacy Barnes	31	705	89	213	.418	30	56	.536	27	57	84	33	103	2	19	62	33	209	6.7	17
Michelle Edwards(*)	20	455	51	143	.357	23	35	.657	7	27	34	40	29	0	14	38	5	131	6.6	20
Michelle Edwards(†)	23	472	55	153	.359	23	35	.657	7	29	36	41	32	0	14	42	5	139	6.0	20
Jamie Redd	26	387	49	125	.392	24	34	.706	18	27	45	16	53	0	19	35	1	140	5.4	19
Sonja Henning	32	980	53	151	.351	37	61	.607	22	64	86	79	73	1	61	54	3	168	5.3	19
Stacey Lovelace	23	324	36	103	.350	25	31	.806	19	38	57	16	42	0	13	35	2	99	4.3	13
Charisse Sampson	21	280	22	47	.468	25	28	.893	14	27	41	11	37	0	18	14	6	78	3.7	13
Andrea Garner	32	560	37	115	.322	24	38	.632	42	55	97	25	44	0	27	43	10	99	3.1	10
Katrina Hibbert	20	240	19	59	.322	7	9	.778	8	22	30	18	22	0	7	17	1	53	2.7	17
Charmin Smith	32	516	16	56	.286	10	18	.556	14	33	47	53	52	0	16	32	3	52	1.6	10
Angela Aycock(‡)	1	7	0	3	.000	0	0	---	1	1	2	0	2	0	0	0	0	0	0.0	0
Seattle	32	6475	667	1741	.383	379	561	.676	256	537	793	390	648	4	255	525	93	1822	56.9	78
Opponents	32	6475	778	1721	.452	498	654	.761	288	721	1009	506	618	9	284	529	123	2171	67.8	85

3-pt. FG: Seattle 109-364 (.299); Campbell 13-49 (.265); Vodichkova 4-20 (.200); Threatt 12-37 (.324); Barnes 1-9 (.111); M. Edwards(*) 6-32 (.188); M. Edwards(†) 6-35 (.171); Redd 18-52 (.346); Henning 25-66 (.379); Lovelace 2-9 (.222); Sampson 9-23 (.391); Garner 1-2 (.500); Hibbert 8-31 (.258); Smith 10-32 (.313); Aycock(‡) 0-2 (.000); Opponents 117-334 (.350)

UTAH STARZZ

Player	G	Min	FGM	FGA	Pct	FTM	FTA	Pct	Off	Def	Tot	Ast	PF	Dq	Stl	TO	Blk	Pts	Avg	Hi
									REBOUNDS									SCORING		
Natalie Williams	29	1039	179	365	.490	182	228	.798	132	204	336	51	124	3	35	79	18	543	18.7	30
Adrienne Goodson	29	929	199	415	.480	92	134	.687	69	95	164	69	67	0	41	81	7	498	17.2	29
Korie Hlede	31	867	118	260	.454	51	70	.729	25	68	93	92	84	1	38	76	4	312	10.1	20
Jennifer Azzi	15	559	47	104	.452	40	43	.930	5	36	41	92	43	0	12	28	5	144	9.6	20
Margo Dydek	32	775	105	236	.445	82	103	.796	29	146	175	51	114	1	18	82	96	294	9.2	19
LaTonya Johnson	29	481	52	129	.403	28	43	.651	14	38	52	26	65	0	12	34	2	144	5.0	14
Naomi Mulitauaopele	22	291	41	69	.594	15	20	.750	12	22	34	6	37	0	4	30	6	99	4.5	10
Kate Starbird	29	340	39	109	.358	34	42	.810	12	21	33	30	32	0	13	29	11	117	4.0	17

Player	G	Min	FGM	FGA	Pct	FTM	FTA	Pct	REBOUNDS Off	Def	Tot	Ast	PF	Dq	Stl	TO	Blk	SCORING Pts	Avg	Hi
Amy Herrig 25	341	36	75	.480	19	31	.613	26	33	59	20	41	1	7	29	5	91	3.6	14
Dalma Ivanyi.............27	489	30	96	.313	21	28	.750	12	42	54	63	67	0	25	50	3	93	3.4	9
Stacy Frese...............21	222	10	30	.333	33	36	.917	4	14	18	17	14	0	4	14	0	62	3.0	11
Katryna Gaither(‡)........9	54	2	7	.286	10	10	1.000	7	10	17	4	8	0	4	4	0	14	1.6	4
Kym Hope 3	4	0	1	.000	2	2	1.000	0	2	2	0	0	0	0	1	0	2	0.7	2
Kristen Rasmussen(‡)..1	9	0	0	---	0	0	---	1	1	2	1	2	0	1	1	0	0	0.0	0
Utah 32	6400	858	1896	.453	609	790	.771	348	732	1080	522	698	6	214	544	157	2413	75.4	96
Opponents 32	6400	860	1964	.438	531	721	.736	313	598	911	503	702	11	301	437	112	2407	75.2	107

3-pt. FG: Utah 88-262 (.336); Williams 3-5 (.600); Goodson 8-29 (.276); Hlede 25-58 (.431); Azzi 10-24 (.417); Dydek 2-14 (.143); Johnson 12-36 (.333); Mulitauaopele 2-3 (.667); Starbird 5-23 (.217); Herrig 0-1 (.000); Ivanyi 12-43 (.279); Frese 9-26 (.346); Opponents 156-448 (.348)

WASHINGTON MYSTICS

Player	G	Min	FGM	FGA	Pct	FTM	FTA	Pct	REBOUNDS Off	Def	Tot	Ast	PF	Dq	Stl	TO	Blk	SCORING Pts	Avg	Hi
Chamique Holdsclaw..32	1131	232	499	.465	87	128	.680	57	183	240	80	74	0	47	93	18	561	17.5	30
Nikki McCray 32	1046	167	385	.434	113	147	.769	22	34	56	85	79	0	45	89	5	497	15.5	26
Vicky Bullett 32	1094	143	294	.486	45	63	.714	61	122	183	42	88	0	64	58	47	342	10.7	22
Murriel Page 32	1046	131	222	.590	52	92	.565	79	129	208	64	103	2	23	63	32	314	9.8	20
Andrea Nagy..............23	694	31	79	.392	21	26	.808	10	53	63	118	55	0	17	55	8	97	4.2	10
Tausha Mills 31	295	46	105	.438	38	51	.745	39	41	80	9	71	1	10	37	8	130	4.2	17
Beth Cunningham 21	198	17	68	.250	16	19	.842	4	17	21	12	23	0	2	12	0	59	2.8	10
Keisha Anderson........30	434	29	68	.426	14	18	.778	12	34	46	75	53	0	25	47	3	75	2.5	13
Markita Aldridge 29	272	25	54	.463	7	22	.318	8	16	24	28	30	0	9	27	4	63	2.2	9
Renee Robinson 2	5	0	1	.000	4	4	1.000	0	0	0	0	3	0	1	1	0	4	2.0	4
Tonya Washington......19	103	8	29	.276	4	6	.667	6	8	14	5	4	0	2	4	0	26	1.4	6
Michelle Campbell 5	22	2	5	.400	2	2	1.000	0	2	2	1	2	0	0	3	1	6	1.2	4
Heather Owen............11	60	1	4	.250	0	0	---	2	7	9	2	12	0	0	3	0	2	0.2	2
Washington................32	6400	832	1813	.459	403	578	.697	300	646	946	521	597	3	245	506	126	2176	68.0	96
Opponents 32	6400	845	1875	.451	382	555	.688	299	612	911	513	595	4	261	456	102	2221	69.4	87

3-pt. FG: Washington 109-335 (.325); Holdsclaw 10-39 (.256); McCray 50-151 (.331); Bullett 11-34 (.324); Nagy 14-39 (.359); Cunningham 9-37 (.243); Anderson 3-8 (.375); Aldridge 6-12 (.500); Robinson 0-1 (.000); Washington 6-14 (.429); Opponents 149-397 (.375)

(*) Statistics with this team only
(†) Totals with all teams
(‡) Continued season with another team

PLAYOFFS RESULTS

FIRST ROUND

Cleveland defeats Orlando, 2-1

August 11	Orlando 62, Cleveland 55
August 13	Cleveland 63, Orlando 54
August 15	Cleveland 72, Orlando 43

New York defeats Washington, 2-0

| August 12 | New York 72, Washington 63 |
| August 14 | New York 78, Washington 57 |

Los Angeles defeats Phoenix, 2-0

| August 11 | Los Angeles 86, Phoenix 71 |
| August 13 | Los Angeles 101, Phoenix 76 |

Houston defeats Sacramento, 2-0

| August 12 | Houston 72, Sacramento 64 |
| August 14 | Houston 75, Sacramento 70 |

CONFERENCE FINALS

Houston defeats Los Angeles, 2-0

| August 17 | Houston 77, Los Angeles 56 |
| August 20 | Houston 74, Los Angeles 69 |

New York defeats Cleveland, 2-1

August 17	Cleveland 56, New York 43
August 20	New York 51, Cleveland 45
August 21	New York 81, Cleveland 67

CHAMPIONSHIP

Houston defeats New York, 2-0

| August 24 | Houston 59, New York 52 |
| August 26 | Houston 79, New York 73 (OT) |

TEAM STANDINGS

OFFENSIVE

TEAM	G	FG	FGA	PCT	FG3	FG3A	PCT	FT	FTA	PCT	OFF	DEF	REB	AST	PF	DQ	STL	TO	BLK	PTS	AVG
L.A.	4	112	250	.448	30	74	.405	58	72	.806	49	93	142	73	84	1	23	63	13	312	78.0
Phoe.	2	53	119	.445	11	40	.275	30	42	.714	12	36	48	34	45	1	11	23	10	147	73.5
Hou.	6	155	365	.425	34	90	.378	92	105	.876	63	122	185	70	83	0	54	74	13	436	72.7
Sac.	2	48	118	.407	11	32	.344	27	32	.844	19	44	63	31	34	1	15	24	4	134	67.0
N.Y.	7	171	390	.438	27	76	.355	81	100	.810	62	134	196	113	130	2	68	103	25	450	64.3
Wash.	2	47	101	.465	6	22	.273	20	32	.625	14	30	44	30	30	0	13	32	6	120	60.0
Clev.	6	136	340	.400	23	91	.253	63	89	.708	72	133	205	97	90	0	52	85	13	358	59.7
Orl.	3	64	169	.379	10	39	.256	21	30	.700	22	53	75	37	49	0	18	39	14	159	53.0

DEFENSIVE

Team	FG	FGA	PCT	FG3	FG3A	PCT	FT	FTA	PCT	OFF	DEF	REB	AST	PF	DQ	STL	TO	BLK	PTS	AVG	DIFF
Clev.	135	329	.410	20	72	.278	44	63	.698	41	113	154	90	105	0	50	85	27	334	55.7	+4.0
N.Y.	157	388	.405	27	95	.284	85	111	.766	75	136	211	97	112	0	59	107	21	426	60.9	+3.4
Orl.	76	179	.425	12	47	.255	26	42	.619	36	70	106	54	45	0	21	38	4	190	63.3	-10.3
Hou.	134	357	.375	34	101	.337	82	93	.882	66	122	188	89	117	4	41	93	18	384	64.0	+8.7
Sac.	51	115	.443	13	33	.394	32	36	.889	17	42	59	21	25	0	14	23	3	147	73.5	-6.5
L.A.	107	243	.440	22	68	.324	62	79	.785	33	73	106	59	66	1	36	46	14	298	74.5	+3.5
Wash.	58	114	.509	10	21	.476	24	28	.857	23	36	59	33	32	0	22	28	5	150	75.0	-15.0
Phoe.	68	127	.535	14	27	.519	37	50	.740	22	53	75	42	43	0	11	23	6	187	93.5	-20.0
Avg.	98	232	.424	19	58	.328	49	63	.781	39	81	120	61	68	1	32	55	12	265	66.1	---
	786	1852		152	464		392	502		313	645	958	485	545	5	254	443	98	2116		

TEAM COMPARISONS

TEAM	Points Per Game		Field Goal Percentage		Turnovers Per Game		Rebound Percentages			Below 70 Pts.		Overtime Games		3 PTS or Less		10 PTS or More	
	OWN	OPP	OWN	OPP	OWN	OPP	OFF	DEF	TOT	OWN	OPP	W	L	W	L	W	L
Cleveland	59.7	55.7*	.400	.410	14.2	14.2	.389	.764*	.577*	5	5	0	0	0	0	2	1
Houston	72.7	64.0	.425	.375*	12.3	15.5*	.341	.649	.495	1	4	1	0	0	0	1	0
Los Angeles	78.0*	74.5	.448	.440	15.8	11.5	.402*	.738	.570	2	0	0	0	0	0	2	1
New York	64.3	60.9	.438	.405	14.7	15.3	.313	.641	.477	3	6	0	1	0	0	2	1
Orlando	53.0	63.3	.379	.425	13.0	12.7	.239	.596	.417	3	2	0	0	0	0	0	1
Phoenix	73.5	93.5	.445	.535	11.5*	11.5	.185	.621	.403	0	0	0	0	0	0	0	2
Sacramento	67.0	73.5	.407	.443	12.0	11.5	.311	.721	.516	1	0	0	0	0	0	0	0
Washington	60.0	75.0	.465*	.509	16.0	14.0	.280	.566	.423	2	0	0	0	0	0	0	1
COMPOSITE;16 games	66.1		.424		13.8		.327	.673		17	1		0			7	

* - League Leader

REBOUND PERCENTAGES — OFF. - Percentage of a given team's missed shots which that team rebounds. DEF. - Percentage of opponents' missed shots which a given team rebounds. TOT. - Average of offensive and defensive rebound percentages.

INDIVIDUAL PLAYOFFS STATISTICS, TEAM BY TEAM

CLEVELAND ROCKERS

Player	G	Min	FGM	FGA	Pct	FTM	FTA	Pct	REBOUNDS Off	Def	Tot	Ast	PF	Dq	Stl	TO	Blk	SCORING Pts	Avg	Hi
Merlakia Jones	6	207	34	86	.395	9	12	.750	11	32	43	11	14	0	7	8	0	83	13.8	18
Rushia Brown	6	167	21	45	.467	21	24	.875	19	15	34	10	17	0	17	17	2	63	10.5	18
Chasity Melvin	6	183	20	38	.526	13	18	.722	16	24	40	11	20	0	5	11	3	53	8.8	14
Suzie McConnell Serio	6	147	14	45	.311	2	2	1.000	3	11	14	25	5	0	5	16	1	39	6.5	13
Helen Darling	6	106	9	28	.321	10	14	.714	7	13	20	13	5	0	7	6	0	33	5.5	15
Ann Wauters	6	107	13	27	.481	2	6	.333	5	13	18	5	7	0	3	8	3	28	4.7	12
Mery Andrade	6	166	8	33	.242	5	9	.556	5	12	17	14	17	0	6	11	3	21	3.5	7
Vicki Hall	6	69	10	24	.417	0	1	.000	5	10	15	4	4	0	2	1	0	21	3.5	8
P. Johns Kimbrough	4	6	3	3	1.000	1	2	.500	1	1	2	1	0	0	0	0	0	7	1.8	7
Tricia Bader Binford	5	36	3	9	.333	0	1	.000	0	1	1	1	1	0	2	1	0	8	1.6	8
Adia Barnes	4	6	1	2	.500	0	0	---	0	1	1	2	0	0	0	1	0	2	0.5	2
Cleveland	6	1200	136	340	.400	63	89	.708	72	133	205	97	90	0	52	85	13	358	59.7	72
Opponents	6	1200	135	329	.410	44	63	.698	41	113	154	90	105	0	50	85	27	334	55.7	81

3-pt. FG: Cleveland 23-91 (.253) Jones 6-20 (.300); Brown 0-1 (.000); Melvin 0-1 (.000); McConnell Serio 9-36 (.250); Darling 5-13 (.385); Wauters 0-2 (.000); Andrade 0-9 (.000); Hall 1-5 (.200); Bader Binford 2-3 (.667); Barnes 0-1 (.000); Opponents 20-72 (.278)

HOUSTON COMETS

Player	G	Min	FGM	FGA	Pct	FTM	FTA	Pct	REBOUNDS Off	Def	Tot	Ast	PF	Dq	Stl	TO	Blk	SCORING Pts	Avg	Hi
Cynthia Cooper	6	228	45	119	.378	35	39	.897	5	10	15	22	11	0	9	18	1	136	22.7	29
Sheryl Swoopes	6	220	41	87	.471	23	29	.793	9	25	34	19	11	0	17	12	0	113	18.8	31
Tina Thompson	6	233	25	62	.403	17	18	.944	17	31	48	10	19	0	5	10	5	76	12.7	21
Janeth Arcain	6	201	21	47	.447	6	7	.857	6	21	27	12	14	0	10	16	0	50	8.3	16
Tiffani Johnson	6	135	10	20	.500	2	2	1.000	12	17	29	1	15	0	3	7	2	22	3.7	6
Amaya Valdemoro	3	16	2	5	.400	4	4	1.000	1	3	4	0	0	0	1	0	0	9	3.0	6
Tammy Jackson	6	94	8	14	.571	0	0	---	9	8	17	0	9	0	4	2	4	16	2.7	12
Coquese Washington	6	92	3	9	.333	5	6	.833	4	7	11	6	4	0	5	8	1	14	2.3	6
Jawann Kelley-Gibson	1	3	0	1	.000	0	0	---	0	0	0	0	0	0	0	0	0	0	0.0	0
Jennifer Rizzotti	1	3	0	1	.000	0	0	---	0	0	0	0	0	0	0	0	0	0	0.0	0
Houston	6	1225	155	365	.425	92	105	.876	63	122	185	70	83	0	54	74	13	436	72.7	79
Opponents	6	1225	134	357	.375	82	93	.882	66	122	188	89	117	4	41	93	18	384	64.0	73

3-pt. FG: Houston 34-90 (.378) Cooper 11-32 (.344); Swoopes 8-17 (.471); Thompson 9-23 (.391); Arcain 2-7 (.286); Valdemoro 1-3 (.333); Washington 3-7 (.429); Rizzotti 0-1 (.000); Opponents 34-101 (.337)

LOS ANGELES SPARKS

Player	G	Min	FGM	FGA	Pct	FTM	FTA	Pct	REBOUNDS Off	Def	Tot	Ast	PF	Dq	Stl	TO	Blk	SCORING Pts	Avg	Hi
Lisa Leslie	4	139	28	57	.491	19	23	.826	10	31	41	8	14	0	1	13	5	75	18.8	29
Mwadi Mabika	4	136	25	46	.543	3	4	.750	6	15	21	4	14	0	6	5	4	70	17.5	21
DeLisha Milton	4	136	20	37	.541	10	12	.833	11	11	22	12	14	1	6	10	2	50	12.5	19
Tamecka Dixon	4	127	17	46	.370	8	9	.889	4	7	11	16	12	0	3	8	0	47	11.8	17
Ukari Figgs	4	106	7	23	.304	6	6	1.000	6	10	16	19	10	0	2	11	0	24	6.0	9
Allison Feaster	4	44	5	16	.313	2	2	1.000	3	6	9	3	11	0	2	5	1	15	3.8	8
Clarisse Machanguana	4	47	4	8	.500	4	6	.667	6	5	11	0	6	0	1	1	1	12	3.0	10
Nicky McCrimmon	4	49	3	12	.250	3	4	.750	3	4	7	10	2	0	1	5	0	10	2.5	7
La'Keshia Frett	3	7	2	3	.667	3	4	.750	0	0	0	0	0	0	0	0	0	7	2.3	5
Vedrana Grgin Fonseca	3	7	1	2	.500	0	2	.000	0	3	3	1	0	0	1	2	0	2	0.7	2
Paige Sauer	1	2	0	0	---	0	0	---	0	1	1	0	1	0	0	0	0	0	0.0	0
Los Angeles	4	800	112	250	.448	58	72	.806	49	93	142	73	84	1	23	63	13	312	78.0	101
Opponents	4	800	107	243	.440	62	79	.785	33	73	106	59	66	1	36	46	14	298	74.5	77

3-pt. FG: Los Angeles 30-74 (.405) Leslie 0-3 (.000); Mabika 17-32 (.531); Dixon 5-10 (.500); Figgs 4-11 (.364); Feaster 3-13 (.231); McCrimmon 1-4 (.250); Grgin Fonseca 0-1 (.000); Opponents 22-68 (.324)

NEW YORK LIBERTY

Player	G	Min	FGM	FGA	Pct	FTM	FTA	Pct	REBOUNDS Off	Def	Tot	Ast	PF	Dq	Stl	TO	Blk	SCORING Pts	Avg	Hi
Tari Phillips	7	222	48	95	.505	18	23	.783	16	37	53	8	26	1	12	16	6	114	16.3	24
Tamika Whitmore	7	196	31	65	.477	18	24	.750	9	18	27	6	22	0	3	15	9	81	11.6	19
Vickie Johnson	7	237	27	71	.380	12	14	.857	10	25	35	24	14	0	8	13	0	72	10.3	20
Becky Hammon	7	206	21	49	.429	17	19	.895	5	5	10	15	10	0	9	17	0	66	9.4	19
Crystal Robinson	7	150	16	39	.410	5	5	1.000	7	13	20	5	12	0	9	10	1	46	6.6	13
Teresa Weatherspoon	7	253	12	34	.353	7	11	.636	2	17	19	49	20	1	19	20	0	32	4.6	7
Sue Wicks	7	131	9	26	.346	4	4	1.000	11	16	27	3	21	0	7	5	9	23	3.3	7
Marina Ferragut	3	12	2	3	.667	0	0	---	0	3	3	1	4	0	1	0	0	6	2.0	3
Olga Firsova	3	6	3	4	.750	0	0	---	1	0	1	0	1	0	0	0	0	6	2.0	4
Jessica Bibby	3	8	2	2	1.000	0	0	---	0	0	0	2	0	0	0	2	0	4	1.3	2
Desiree Francis	2	4	0	2	.000	0	0	---	1	0	1	0	0	0	0	0	0	0	0.0	0
New York	7	1425	171	390	.438	81	100	.810	62	134	196	113	130	2	68	103	25	450	64.3	81
Opponents	7	1425	157	388	.405	85	111	.766	75	136	211	97	112	0	59	107	21	426	60.9	79

3-pt. FG: New York 27-76 (.355) Phillips 0-1 (.000); Whitmore 1-2 (.500); Johnson 6-22 (.273); Hammon 7-23 (.304); Robinson 9-19 (.474); Weatherspoon 1-5 (.200); Wicks 1-1 (1.000); Ferragut 2-2 (1.000); Francis 0-1 (.000); Opponents 27-95 (.284)

ORLANDO MIRACLE

Player	G	Min	FGM	FGA	Pct	FTM	FTA	Pct	REBOUNDS Off	Def	Tot	Ast	PF	Dq	Stl	TO	Blk	SCORING Pts	Avg	Hi
McWilliams-Franklin	3	107	18	38	.474	7	9	.778	6	17	23	5	8	0	2	5	3	43	14.3	16
Adrienne Johnson	3	111	14	42	.333	3	4	.750	3	1	4	8	7	0	1	7	1	34	11.3	17
Nykesha Sales	3	106	15	31	.484	0	2	.000	1	8	9	4	9	0	3	9	0	33	11.0	15

Player	G	Min	FGM	FGA	Pct	FTM	FTA	Pct	Off	Def	Tot	Ast	PF	Dq	Stl	TO	Blk	Pts	Avg	Hi
Cintia dos Santos 3	82	8	16	.500	2	2	1.000	3	5	8	3	9	0	2	5	7	18	6.0	12
Shannon Johnson 3	119	6	27	.222	4	8	.500	4	17	21	14	9	0	5	7	2	18	6.0	7
Tiffany McCain 2	11	2	3	.667	0	0	---	0	1	1	1	4	0	1	0	6	3.0	3
Carla McGhee 3	37	1	7	.143	3	3	1.000	4	1	5	1	3	0	4	3	0	5	1.7	3
Jannon Roland 3	26	0	5	.000	2	2	1.000	1	3	4	1	0	1	0	1	2	0.7	2
LaCharlotte Smith 1	1	0	0	---	0	0	---	0	0	0	0	0	0	0	0	0	0	0.0	0
Orlando.....................3	600	64	169	.379	21	30	.700	22	53	75	37	49	0	18	39	14	159	53.0	62
Opponents 3	600	76	179	.425	26	42	.619	36	70	106	54	45	0	21	38	4	190	63.3	72

3-pt. FG: Orlando 10-39 (.256) McWilliams-Frank 0-2 (.000); A. Johnson 3-10 (.300); Sales 3-10 (.300); S. Johnson 2-13 (.154); McCain 2-3 (.667); Roland 0-1 (.000); Opponents 12-47 (.255)

PHOENIX MERCURY

Player	G	Min	FGM	FGA	Pct	FTM	FTA	Pct	Off	Def	Tot	Ast	PF	Dq	Stl	TO	Blk	Pts	Avg	Hi
Brandy Reed................2	73	12	22	.545	3	4	.750	2	5	7	8	5	0	0	5	1	28	14.0	17
Jennifer Gillom 2	64	10	20	.500	5	10	.500	1	3	4	2	10	0	1	4	5	26	13.0	16
Lisa Harrison 2	68	12	17	.706	2	2	1.000	4	7	11	10	5	0	3	3	0	26	13.0	16
Michelle Brogan 2	52	5	13	.385	11	14	.786	0	9	9	1	5	0	1	3	1	22	11.0	13
Bridget Pettis 2	41	7	18	.389	2	2	1.000	1	4	5	6	7	0	1	3	0	21	10.5	14
Tonya Edwards 2	61	5	20	.250	4	6	.667	1	5	6	5	8	1	4	2	0	17	8.5	12
Adrain Williams 2	30	2	4	.500	1	2	.500	1	3	4	1	3	0	0	1	2	5	2.5	3
Nicole Kubik 2	5	0	2	.000	2	2	1.000	0	0	0	1	0	0	1	2	0	2	1.0	2
Dena Head 1	6	0	3	.000	0	0	---	2	0	2	1	0	0	1	1	1	0	0.0	0
Phoenix.....................2	400	53	119	.445	30	42	.714	12	36	48	34	45	1	11	23	10	147	73.5	76
Opponents 2	400	68	127	.535	37	50	.740	22	53	75	42	43	0	11	23	6	187	93.5	101

3-pt. FG: Phoenix 11-40 (.275) Reed 1-4 (.250); Gillom 1-5 (.200); Harrison 0-2 (.000); Brogan 1-4 (.250); Pettis 5-11 (.455); Edwards 3-13 (.231); Head 0-1 (.000); Opponents 14-27 (.519)

SACRAMENTO MONARCHS

Player	G	Min	FGM	FGA	Pct	FTM	FTA	Pct	Off	Def	Tot	Ast	PF	Dq	Stl	TO	Blk	Pts	Avg	Hi
R. Bolton-Holifield 2	70	13	34	.382	9	9	1.000	4	5	9	7	6	0	4	5	0	39	19.5	23
Yolanda Griffith 2	78	12	23	.522	5	8	.625	6	18	24	2	4	0	1	4	1	29	14.5	18
Tangela Smith..............2	59	9	22	.409	3	4	.750	0	8	8	1	5	0	2	2	1	21	10.5	13
Kedra Holland-Corn......2	60	7	16	.438	2	2	1.000	3	5	8	6	3	0	3	1	0	19	9.5	10
Ticha Penicheiro 2	77	4	16	.250	5	6	.833	2	5	7	14	10	1	4	6	0	16	8.0	12
Linda Burgess..............1	8	1	1	1.000	2	2	1.000	1	1	2	0	1	0	0	1	2	4	4.0	4
Stacy Clinesmith..........2	3	1	1	1.000	0	0	---	0	0	0	0	2	0	0	0	0	3	1.5	3
Lady Grooms 2	23	1	2	.500	1	1	1.000	0	2	2	0	3	0	1	0	1	3	1.5	3
Latasha Byears............2	12	0	1	.000	0	0	---	0	2	2	0	3	0	1	0	0	0	0.0	0
Katy Steding 2	10	0	2	.000	0	0	---	1	0	1	1	0	0	0	2	0	0	0.0	0
Sacramento 2	400	48	118	.407	27	32	.844	19	44	63	31	34	1	15	24	4	134	67.0	70
Opponents 2	400	51	115	.443	32	36	.889	17	42	59	21	25	0	14	23	3	147	73.5	75

3-pt. FG: Sacramento 11-32 (.344) Bolton-Holifield 4-14 (.286); Holland-Corn 3-9 (.333); Penicheiro 3-6 (.500); Clinesmith 1-1 (1.000); Steding 0-2 (.000); Opponents 13-33 (.394)

WASHINGTON MYSTICS

Player	G	Min	FGM	FGA	Pct	FTM	FTA	Pct	Off	Def	Tot	Ast	PF	Dq	Stl	TO	Blk	Pts	Avg	Hi
Vicky Bullett 2	69	10	20	.500	6	6	1.000	2	7	9	3	5	0	5	2	5	30	15.0	22
Chamique Holdsclaw ..2	75	13	29	.448	4	4	1.000	3	8	11	1	2	0	3	6	1	30	15.0	18
Nikki McCray 2	70	7	16	.438	0	0	---	2	4	6	13	6	0	1	10	0	15	7.5	15
Markita Aldridge 2	49	5	11	.455	4	8	.500	1	3	4	7	3	0	1	1	0	14	7.0	12
Tausha Mills 2	21	4	7	.571	3	8	.375	2	1	3	0	7	0	0	3	0	11	5.5	9
Murriel Page 2	69	4	9	.444	3	4	.750	2	4	6	1	5	0	2	4	0	11	5.5	7
Beth Cunningham 2	13	3	6	.500	0	0	---	0	0	0	0	0	0	1	1	0	7	3.5	7
Keisha Anderson..........2	30	1	3	.333	0	2	.000	2	3	5	5	1	0	4	0	0	2	1.0	2
Tonya Washington........1	4	0	0	---	0	0	---	0	0	0	0	1	0	0	1	0	0	0.0	0
Washington..................2	400	47	101	.465	20	32	.625	14	30	44	30	30	0	13	32	6	120	60.0	63
Opponents 2	400	58	114	.509	24	28	.857	23	36	59	33	32	0	22	28	5	150	75.0	78

3-pt. FG: Washington 6-22 (.273) Bullett 4-7 (.571); Holdsclaw 0-1 (.000); McCray 1-7 (.143); Aldridge 0-3 (.000); Cunningham 1-4 (.250); Opponents 10-21 (.476)

INDIVIDUAL FINALS STATISTICS, TEAM BY TEAM

HOUSTON COMETS

Player	G	Min	FGM	FGA	Pct	FTM	FTA	Pct	Off	Def	Tot	Ast	PF	Dq	Stl	TO	Blk	Pts	Avg	Hi
									REBOUNDS									SCORING		
Cynthia Cooper 2	82	15	44	.341	12	13	.923	3	4	7	12	4	0	3	6	1	45	22.5	25
Sheryl Swoopes 2	78	15	30	.500	10	13	.769	4	10	14	3	3	0	3	3	0	43	21.5	31
Tina Thompson 2	81	9	26	.346	4	4	1.000	5	11	16	3	6	0	3	4	3	26	13.0	15
Janeth Arcain 2	67	5	14	.357	0	0	---	4	7	11	5	8	0	2	8	0	10	5.0	8
Tiffani Johnson 2	47	4	7	.571	0	0	---	5	6	11	0	7	0	1	1	0	8	4.0	6
Tammy Jackson 2	41	2	4	.500	0	0	---	4	4	8	0	5	0	1	0	2	4	2.0	2
Coquese Washington....2	29	0	1	.000	2	2	1.000	0	1	1	1	4	0	2	6	0	2	1.0	2
Houston 2	425	50	126	.397	28	32	.875	25	43	68	24	37	0	15	28	6	138	69.0	79
Opponents 2	425	42	116	.362	34	39	.872	20	38	58	27	42	2	14	29	7	125	62.5	73

3-pt. FG: Houston 10-29 (.345) Cooper 3-10 (.300); Swoopes 3-6 (.500); Thompson 4-11 (.364); Arcain 0-1 (.000); Washington 0-1 (.000); Opponents 7-22 (.318)

NEW YORK LIBERTY

Player	G	Min	FGM	FGA	Pct	FTM	FTA	Pct	Off	Def	Tot	Ast	PF	Dq	Stl	TO	Blk	Pts	Avg	Hi
									REBOUNDS									SCORING		
Tari Phillips 2	74	17	38	.447	10	11	.909	6	16	22	1	9	1	4	8	3	44	22.0	24
Tamika Whitmore 2	59	5	18	.278	11	14	.786	0	5	5	2	8	0	1	4	1	22	11.0	15
Crystal Robinson.........2	56	6	14	.429	3	3	1.000	2	3	5	2	4	0	4	5	1	18	9.0	13
Vickie Johnson 2	76	5	20	.250	6	6	1.000	6	6	12	5	4	0	1	5	0	17	8.5	11
Teresa Weatherspoon ..2	79	5	11	.455	2	3	.667	1	5	6	13	9	1	3	2	0	13	6.5	7
Sue Wicks....................2	37	3	8	.375	0	0	---	4	3	7	0	5	0	1	2	2	7	3.5	7
Becky Hammon 2	44	1	7	.143	2	2	1.000	1	0	1	4	3	0	0	2	0	4	2.0	4
New York 2	425	42	116	.362	34	39	.872	20	38	58	27	42	2	14	29	7	125	62.5	73
Opponents 2	425	50	126	.397	28	32	.875	25	43	68	24	37	0	15	28	6	138	69.0	79

3-pt. FG: New York 7-22 (.318) Whitmore 1-2 (.500); Robinson 3-8 (.375); Johnson 1-6 (.167); Weatherspoon 1-2 (.500); Wicks 1-1 (1.000); Hammon 0-3 (.000); Opponents 10-29 (.345).

FINALS BOX SCORES

GAME 1
At Madison Square Garden, August 24, 2000

OFFICIALS: Gary Zielinski, Sally Bell, Dennis DeMayo. TIME OF GAME: 2:00. ATTENDANCE: 19,563

SCORE BY PERIODS	1	2	FINAL
Houston...............................29		30	59
New York..............................22		30	52

VISITORS: Houston. Head Coach: Van Chancellor.

No Player	MIN	FG	FGA	3P	3PA	FT	FTA	OR	DR	TOT	A	PF	ST	TO	TEC	PTS
7 Tina Thompson 38		5	12	3	6	2	2	1	7	8	2	3	2	1	0	15
22 Sheryl Swoopes 38		4	12	0	2	4	6	2	6	8	2	2	2	2	0	12
00 Tiffani Johnson 16		1	4	0	0	0	0	2	3	5	0	4	1	0	0	2
14 Cynthia Cooper 38		7	23	2	6	4	5	3	0	3	5	1	0	2	0	20
9 Janeth Arcain 35		4	8	0	0	0	0	2	5	7	4	3	2	5	0	8
23 Tammy Jackson 25		1	2	0	0	0	0	2	2	4	0	2	0	0	0	2
4 Coquese Washington......10		0	1	0	1	0	0	0	0	0	0	3	1	2	0	0
3 Jawann Kelley-Gibson........								Did not play.								
40 Monica Lamb								Did not play.								
21 Jennifer Rizzotti								Did not play.								
13 Amaya Valdemoro								Did not play.								
TOTALS 200		22	62	5	15	10	13	12	23	35	13	18	8	12	0	59

FG pct.: .355. 3PT pct.: .333. FT pct.: .769. Team Rebounds: 10. Total Turnovers: 12 (6 PTS).

HOME: New York. Head Coach: Richie Adubato.

No Player	MIN	FG	FGA	3P	3PA	FT	FTA	OR	DR	TOT	A	PF	ST	TO	TEC	PTS
55 Vickie Johnson 35		2	7	0	1	2	2	4	2	6	2	3	1	1	0	6
44 Tamika Whitmore 32		1	11	0	0	5	6	0	4	4	1	4	1	1	0	7

No Player	MIN	FG	FGA	3P	3PA	FT	FTA	OR	DR	TOT	A	PF	ST	TO	TEC	PTS
24 Tari Phillips	37	10	19	0	0	4	4	4	11	15	0	3	1	6	0	24
11 Teresa Weatherspoon	37	2	5	0	1	2	3	1	2	3	5	3	2	0	0	6
25 Becky Hammon	26	1	5	0	2	2	2	0	0	0	2	2	0	1	0	4
3 Crystal Robinson	22	2	8	0	4	1	1	1	3	4	0	1	2	3	0	5
23 Sue Wicks	11	0	1	0	0	0	0	1	1	2	0	2	0	0	0	0
42 Desiree Francis							Did not play.									
00 Olga Firsova							Did not play.									
22 Jessica Bibby							Did not play.									
13 Marina Ferragut							Did not play.									
TOTALS	200	18	56	0	8	16	18	11	23	34	10	18	7	13	0	52

FG pct.: .321. 3PT pct.: .000. FT pct. .889. Team Rebounds: 4. Total Turnovers: 13 (14 PTS).
Blocked Shots: Comets 3: Thompson 1, Cooper 1, Jackson 1. Liberty 2; Phillips 1, Robinson 1.
Technical Fouls: None.
Flagrant Fouls: None.
Points off Turnovers: Houston 14, New York 6.
Fast Break Points: Houston 4, New York 2.
Points in Paint: Houston 24, New York 22.
Second Chance Points: Houston 9, New York 10.

GAME 2
At Compaq Center, August 26, 2000

OFFICIALS: June Courteau, Michael Price, Courtney Kirkland. TIME OF GAME: 2:20. ATTENDANCE: 16,285.

SCORE BY PERIODS	1	2	FINAL	OT
New York	25	39	9	73
Houston	27	37	15	79

VISITORS: New York. Head Coach: Richie Adubato

No Player	MIN	FG	FGA	3P	3PA	FT	FTA	OR	DR	TOT	A	PF	ST	TO	TEC	PTS
55 Vickie Johnson	41	3	13	1	5	4	4	2	4	6	3	1	0	4	0	11
44 Tamika Whitmore	27	4	7	1	2	6	8	0	1	1	1	4	0	3	0	15
24 Tari Phillips	37	7	19	0	0	6	7	2	5	7	1	6	3	2	0	20
11 Teresa Weatherspoon	42	3	6	1	1	0	0	0	3	3	8	6	1	2	0	7
25 Becky Hammon	18	0	2	0	1	0	0	1	0	1	2	1	0	1	0	0
3 Crystal Robinson	34	4	6	3	4	2	2	1	0	1	2	3	2	2	0	13
23 Sue Wicks	26	3	7	1	1	0	0	3	2	5	0	3	1	2	0	7
42 Desiree Francis							Did not play.									
00 Olga Firsova							Did not play.									
22 Jessica Bibby							Did not play.									
13 Marina Ferragut							Did not play.									
TOTALS	225	24	60	7	14	18	21	9	15	24	17	24	7	16	0	73

FG pct.: .400. 3PT pct.: .500. FT pct.: .857. Team Rebounds: 12. Total Turnovers: 16 (14 PTS).

HOME: Houston. Head Coach: Van Chancellor.

No Player	MIN	FG	FGA	3P	3PA	FT	FTA	OR	DR	TOT	A	PF	ST	TO	TEC	PTS
7 Tina Thompson	43	4	14	1	5	2	2	4	4	8	1	3	1	3	0	11
22 Sheryl Swoopes	40	11	18	3	4	6	7	2	4	6	1	1	1	1	0	31
00 Tiffani Johnson	31	3	3	0	0	0	0	3	3	6	0	3	0	1	0	6
14 Cynthia Cooper	44	8	21	1	4	8	8	0	4	4	7	3	3	4	0	25
9 Janeth Arcain	32	1	6	0	1	0	0	2	2	4	1	5	0	3	0	2
4 Coquese Washington	19	0	0	0	0	2	2	0	1	1	1	1	1	4	0	2
23 Tammy Jackson	16	1	2	0	0	0	0	2	2	4	0	3	1	0	0	2
3 Jawann Kelley-Gibson							Did not play.									
40 Monica Lamb							Did not play.									
21 Jennifer Rizzotti							Did not play.									
13 Amaya Valdemoro							Did not play.									
TOTALS	225	28	64	5	14	18	19	13	20	33	11	19	7	16	0	79

FG pct.: .438. 3PT pct.: .357. FT pct.: .947. Team Rebounds: 7. Total Turnovers: 16 (23 PTS).
Blocked Shots: Liberty 5: Whitmore 1, Phillips 2, Wicks 2. Comets 3: Thompson 2, Jackson 1.
Technical Fouls: None. Flagrant Fouls: None.
Points off Turnovers: New York 23, Houston 14.
Fast Break Points: New York 0, Houston 6.
Points in Paint: New York 22, Houston 38.
Second Chance Points: New York 15, Houston 17.

ALL-STAR GAME BOX SCORE

At America West Arena, July 17, 2000

OFFICIALS: Barb Smith, Lisa Mattingly, Bill Stokes. TIME OF GAME: 1:57. ATTENDANCE: 17,717

SCORE BY PERIODS	1	2	FINAL
East	33	28	61
West	40	33	73

VISITORS: East. Head Coach: Richie Adubato.

No Player	MIN	FG	FGA	3P	3PA	FT	FTA	OR	DR	TOT	A	PF	ST	TO	TEC	PTS
23 Chamique Holdsclaw	25	4	11	0	0	1	2	1	3	4	1	0	0	1	0	9
23 Sue Wicks	16	1	6	0	0	0	0	0	3	3	0	0	0	0	0	2
11 Taj McWilliams-Franklin	24	4	8	0	0	2	2	7	2	9	0	2	2	0	0	10
11 Teresa Weatherspoon	20	1	4	0	1	0	0	1	2	3	3	3	3	4	0	2
15 Nikki McCray	19	1	11	1	6	2	2	0	0	0	1	0	3	3	0	5
24 Tari Phillips	22	5	14	0	2	0	3	8	1	9	1	4	0	2	0	10
14 Shannon Johnson	20	2	6	0	4	2	2	0	3	3	2	4	3	1	0	6
25 Merlakia Jones	14	3	8	0	0	0	0	1	1	2	0	1	0	1	0	6
3 Wendy Palmer	14	1	6	0	2	1	2	0	2	2	0	1	0	0	0	3
32 Andrea Stinson	13	1	6	0	1	1	1	1	1	2	2	0	1	3	0	3
42 Nykesha Sales	13	2	5	1	3	0	0	3	0	3	1	1	2	0	0	5
TOTALS	200	25	85	2	19	9	14	22	18	40	11	16	14	15	0	61

FG pct.: .294. 3PT pct.: .105. FT pct.: .643. Team Rebounds: 12 Total Turnovers: 15 (18 PTS).

HOME: West. Head Coach: Van Chancellor.

No Player	MIN	FG	FGA	3P	3PA	FT	FTA	OR	DR	TOT	A	PF	ST	TO	TEC	PTS
7 Tina Thompson	23	5	14	1	4	2	2	6	5	11	1	1	3	4	0	13
22 Sheryl Swoopes	21	3	7	0	1	0	0	1	5	6	3	1	0	2	0	6
9 Lisa Leslie	21	8	15	0	0	0	0	4	2	6	0	0	0	0	0	16
21 Ticha Penicheiro	25	1	2	0	1	1	2	0	2	2	4	0	1	7	0	3
30 Katie Smith	18	0	2	0	2	0	0	0	1	1	2	0	2	0	0	0
24 Natalie Williams	17	2	6	0	0	1	2	4	6	10	0	3	1	0	0	5
33 Yolanda Griffith	16	3	8	0	0	4	6	5	5	10	0	0	0	2	0	10
4 Mwadi Mabika	16	3	7	2	3	2	2	0	1	1	2	1	1	1	0	10
8 DeLisha Milton	16	2	2	0	0	0	0	3	1	4	3	0	0	0	0	4
23 Brandy Reed	14	1	11	0	2	1	2	0	4	4	0	1	2	3	0	3
22 Betty Lennox	13	1	3	1	2	0	0	2	3	5	1	1	0	4	0	3
14 Cynthia Cooper									Did not play.							
TOTALS	200	29	77	4	15	11	16	25	35	60	16	8	10	23	0	73

FG pct.: .377. 3PT pct.: .267. FT pct.: .688. Team Rebounds: 6. Total Turnovers: 23 (13 PTS).

Blocked Shots: East 5: Wicks 1, Phillips 3, S. Johnson 1. West 3: Thompson, Leslie, Griffith.

Technical Fouls: None.

Flagrant Fouls: None.

Points off Turnovers: East 13, West 18.

Fast Break Points: East 4, West 10.

Points in Paint: East 28, West 46.

Second Chance Points: East 12, West 25.

MVP: Tina Thompson.

Front Row (l. to r.) - Janeth Arcain, Tina Thompson, Sheryl Swoopes, Owner/President Leslie L. Alexander, Cynthia Cooper, Polina Tzekova, Sonja Henning. Back Row (l. to r.) - Assistant Coach Kevin Cook, Head Coach Van Chancellor, Assistant Coach Alisa Scott, Jennifer Rizzotti, Tammy Jackson, Kara Wolters, Mila Nikolich, Amaya Valdemoro, Video Coordinator Harold Liggans, Trainer Michelle T. Leget, Manager of Operations Shelly Patterson.

FINAL STANDINGS

EASTERN CONFERENCE

Team	CHA	CLE	DET	HOU	LA	MIN	NY	ORL	PHO	SAC	UTA	WAS	W	L	PCT	GB	Last-10	Streak
NY	2	3	2	1	1	0	—	4	1	1	2	1	18	14	.563	—	6-4	Lost 1
CHA	—	3	2	0	0	1	2	3	1	0	1	2	15	17	.469	3	3-7	Lost 5
DET	2	3	—	0	1	1	2	3	0	0	1	2	15	17	.469	3	5-5	Won 2
ORL	1	4	1	1	1	1	0	—	1	1	1	3	15	17	.469	3	6-4	Lost 1
WAS	2	2	2	0	1	1	3	1	0	0	0	—	12	20	.375	6	6-4	Lost 3
CLE	1	—	1	0	0	1	1	0	1	0	0	2	7	25	.219	11	2-8	Won 1

WESTERN CONFERENCE

Team	CHA	CLE	DET	HOU	LA	MIN	NY	ORL	PHO	SAC	UTA	WAS	W	L	PCT	GB	Last-10	Streak
HOU	2	2	2	—	2	4	1	1	3	3	4	2	26	6	.813	—	8-2	Won 1
LA	2	2	1	2	—	3	1	1	3	2	2	1	20	12	.625	6	4-6	Lost 1
SAC	2	2	2	1	2	2	1	1	3	—	1	2	19	13	.594	7	5-5	Lost 3
MIN	1	1	1	0	1	—	2	1	2	2	3	1	15	17	.469	11	3-7	Won 1
PHO	1	1	2	1	1	2	1	1	—	1	2	2	15	17	.469	11	5-5	Lost 2
UTA	1	2	1	0	2	1	0	1	2	3	—	2	15	17	.469	11	7-3	Won 2

TEAM STANDINGS
OFFENSIVE

TEAM	G	FG	FGA	PCT	FG3	FG3A	PCT	FT	FTA	PCT	OFF	DEF	REB	AST	PF	DQ	STL	TO	BLK	PTS	AVG
L.A.	32	890	2044	.435	163	476	.342	506	676	.749	342	725	1067	581	693	6	237	484	124	2449	76.5
Sac.	32	849	2006	.423	126	421	.299	568	847	.671	412	700	1112	500	614	4	329	508	123	2392	74.8
Utah	32	845	1949	.434	107	362	.296	570	742	.768	344	717	1061	552	740	5	240	560	158	2367	74.0
Hou.	32	841	1912	.440	176	547	.322	509	622	.818	303	682	985	499	586	4	272	452	139	2367	74.0
Det.	32	791	1972	.401	121	336	.360	536	764	.702	321	675	996	464	728	14	238	483	96	2239	70.0
Orl.	32	793	1869	.424	155	461	.336	465	672	.692	329	637	966	467	648	10	297	521	93	2206	68.9
Phoe.	32	762	1910	.399	134	456	.294	519	695	.747	343	659	1002	510	652	8	229	460	121	2177	68.0
N.Y.	32	800	1914	.418	175	473	.370	394	529	.745	319	625	944	522	700	9	297	482	91	2169	67.8
Cha.	32	793	1805	.439	108	369	.293	410	535	.766	268	685	953	568	560	3	233	469	97	2104	65.8
Wash.	32	759	1794	.423	100	345	.290	482	679	.710	312	701	1013	461	646	7	203	574	87	2100	65.6
Minn.	32	748	1925	.389	200	603	.332	339	470	.721	298	608	906	525	670	11	204	437	78	2035	63.6
Clev.	32	766	1852	.414	88	309	.285	394	545	.723	289	688	977	489	627	3	235	547	116	2014	62.9

DEFENSIVE

Team	FG	FGA	PCT	FG3	FG3A	PCT	FT	FTA	PCT	OFF	DEF	REB	AST	PF	DQ	STL	TO	BLK	PTS	AVG	DIFF
Hou.	763	1954	.390	125	442	.283	419	566	.740	350	621	971	459	633	3	216	491	78	2070	64.7	+9.3
N.Y.	720	1747	.412	109	405	.269	540	723	.747	299	682	981	451	584	3	252	557	89	2089	65.3	+2.5
Minn.	749	1763	.425	137	458	.299	476	641	.743	296	732	1028	507	614	3	194	492	92	2111	66.0	-2.4
Cha.	814	1920	.424	136	428	.318	378	522	.724	318	626	944	506	597	6	221	440	99	2142	66.9	-1.2
Phoe.	794	1911	.415	119	395	.301	475	637	.746	334	678	1012	494	676	15	234	479	108	2182	68.2	-0.2
Orl.	812	1892	.429	161	438	.368	431	608	.709	340	664	1004	537	660	9	257	534	124	2216	69.3	-0.3
Clev.	823	1939	.424	137	445	.308	434	616	.705	335	672	1007	536	608	3	314	477	113	2217	69.3	-6.3
Wash.	825	1986	.415	127	403	.315	469	650	.722	359	636	995	518	663	9	304	436	119	2246	70.2	-4.6
Sac.	829	1981	.418	161	474	.340	439	590	.744	310	665	975	535	718	8	226	569	152	2258	70.6	+4.2
Det.	830	1901	.437	114	338	.337	529	736	.719	293	769	1062	514	723	11	262	532	133	2303	72.0	-2.0
L.A.	818	1993	.410	147	445	.330	535	721	.742	335	696	1031	511	681	6	250	493	99	2318	72.4	+4.1
Utah	860	1965	.438	180	487	.370	567	766	.740	311	661	972	570	707	8	284	477	117	2467	77.1	-3.1
Avg	803	1913	.420	138	430	.320	474	648	.732	323	675	999	512	655	7	251	498	110	2218	69.3	---
Totals	9637			1653			5692			3880		11982		7864			3014		1323			
	22952			5158			7776			8102		6138		84			5977		26619		

TEAM COMPARISONS

TEAM	Points Per Game		Field Goal Percentage		Turnovers Per Game		Rebound Percentages			Below 70 Pts.		Overtime Games		3 PTS or Less		10 PTS or More	
	OWN	OPP	OWN	OPP	OWN	OPP	OFF	DEF	TOT	OWN	OPP	W	L	W	L	W	L
Charlotte	65.8	66.9	.439	.424	14.7	13.8	.300	.683	.491	23	20	1	0	1	3	6	8
Cleveland	62.9	69.3	.414	.424	17.1	14.9	.301	.673	.487	24	13	0	0	1	5	6	12
Detroit	70.0	72.0	.401	.437	15.1	16.6	.294	.697	.496	15	17	0	2	3	1	4	11
Houston	74.0	*64.7	*.440	*.390	14.1	15.3	.328	.661	.494	9	22	1	0	2	2	15	3
Los Angeles	76.5	72.4	.435	.410	15.1	15.4	.329	.684	.507	6	13	2	0	3	3	12	4
Minnesota	63.6	66.0	.389	.425	*13.7	15.4	.289	.673	.481	20	20	0	2	4	2	6	10
New York	67.8	65.3	.418	.412	15.1	17.4	.319	.676	.498	18	22	2	3	2	4	10	6
Orlando	68.9	69.3	.424	.429	16.3	16.7	.331	.652	.492	18	14	1	1	4	0	4	4
Phoenix	68.0	68.2	.399	.415	14.4	15.0	.336	.664	.500	18	16	0	0	1	2	9	9
Sacramento	74.8	70.6	.423	.418	15.9	*17.8	*.383	.693	*.538	9	14	0	0	1	2	14	4
Utah	74.0	77.1	.434	.438	17.5	14.9	.342	*.697	.520	11	10	1	2	2	1	6	10
Washington	65.6	70.2	.423	.415	17.9	13.6	.329	.661	.495	22	12	2	0	4	3	2	13
COMPOSITE; 192 games	69.3		.420		15.6		.324	.676		193		10		28		94	

* - League Leader

REBOUND PERCENTAGES

OFF. - Percentage of a given team's missed shots which that team rebounds.

DEF. - Percentage of opponents' missed shots which a given team rebounds.

TOT. - Average of offensive and defensive rebound percentages.

SCORING AVERAGE

	G	FG	FT	PTS	AVG
Cooper, Hou.	31	212	204	686	22.1
Griffith, Sac.	29	200	145	545	18.8
Swoopes, Hou.	32	226	100	585	18.3
Williams, Utah	28	180	144	504	18.0
McCray, Was.	32	193	129	561	17.5
Holdsclaw, Was.	31	202	116	525	16.9
Reed, Min.	25	168	53	402	16.1
Leslie, L.A.	32	182	114	500	15.6
Gillom, Pho.	32	163	141	485	15.2
Goodson, Utah	32	182	99	476	14.9
Edwards, Min.	32	165	79	475	14.8
S. Johnson, Orl.	32	151	105	447	14.0
Sales, Orl.	32	153	95	437	13.7
Bolton-Holifield, Sac.	31	143	75	421	13.6
Stinson, Cha.	32	174	65	434	13.6
Johnson, N.Y.	32	165	72	427	13.3
Brondello, Det.	32	152	83	424	13.3
McWilliams, Orl.	32	153	94	420	13.1
Dydek, Utah	32	141	114	403	12.6
Thompson, Hou.	32	142	68	391	12.2

REBOUNDS PER GAME

	G	OFF	DEF	TOT	AVG
Griffith, Sac.	29	141	188	329	11.3
Williams, Utah	28	109	148	257	9.2
Holdsclaw, Was.	31	74	172	246	7.9
Leslie, L.A.	32	72	176	248	7.8
McWilliams, Orl.	32	81	158	239	7.5
Askamp, Pho.	30	92	123	215	7.2
Wicks, N.Y.	32	76	147	223	7.0
Bullett, Cha.	32	60	159	219	6.8
Whiting, Det.	31	66	141	207	6.7
Page, Was.	32	68	145	213	6.7
Thompson, Hou.	32	67	139	206	6.4
Mapp, Cha.	30	48	145	193	6.4
Dydek, Utah	32	38	166	204	6.4
Swoopes, Hou.	32	48	154	202	6.3
Palmer, Utah-Det.	31	50	138	188	6.1
Reed, Min.	25	55	96	151	6.0
Gillom, Pho.	32	53	131	184	5.8
Hampton, N.Y.	32	61	118	179	5.6
Milton, L.A.	32	60	116	176	5.5
Enis, Was.	29	53	104	157	5.4

ASSISTS PER GAME

	G	AST	AVG
Penicheiro, Sac.	32	226	7.1
Weatherspoon, N.Y.	32	205	6.4
Staley, Cha.	32	177	5.5
Cooper, Hou.	31	162	5.2
Timms, Pho.	30	151	5.0
Black, Utah	32	161	5.0
Nagy, Was.	32	146	4.6

	G	AST	AVG
S. Johnson, Orl.	32	141	4.4
Swoopes, Hou.	32	127	4.0
Azzi, Det.	28	106	3.8
Mabika, L.A.	32	112	3.5
Johnson, N.Y.	32	106	3.3
Tate, Min.	32	100	3.1
Harrower, Pho.	32	96	3.0
Stinson, Cha.	32	93	2.9
Lloyd Curry, Min.	32	91	2.8
Sales, Orl.	32	91	2.8
Grubin, L.A.	32	90	2.8
Goodson, Utah	32	87	2.7
Edwards, Cle.	31	82	2.6

FIELD GOAL PCT.

	FG	FGA	PCT
Page, Was.	105	183	.574
Griffith, Sac.	200	370	.541
Burras, Cle.	103	191	.539
Byears, Sac.	130	242	.537
Milton, L.A.	125	236	.530
Williams, Utah	180	347	.519
Azzi, Det.	93	181	.514
Mapp, Cha.	118	236	.500
Dydek, Utah	141	283	.498
Bullett, Cha.	142	292	.486

3-PT FIELD GOAL PCT

	3FG	3GA	PCT
Azzi, Det.	30	58	.517
Brondello, Det.	37	76	.487
McWilliams, Orl.	20	45	.444
Robinson, N.Y.	76	174	.437
Grubin, L.A.	40	93	.430
Leslie, L.A.	22	52	.423
Baranova, Utah	20	48	.417
Hlede, Det.-Utah	21	53	.396
K. Smith, Min.	52	136	.382
Weatherspoon, N.Y.	31	82	.378

FREE THROW PCT.

	FT	FTA	PCT
Nemcova, Cle.	62	63	.984
Staley, Cha.	85	91	.934
Cooper, Hou.	204	229	.891
Hlede, Det.-Utah	72	82	.878
Toler, L.A.	39	45	.867
Dydek, Utah	114	133	.857
Brondello, Det.	83	98	.847
Robinson, N.Y.	49	58	.845
Johnson, N.Y.	72	86	.837
Congreaves, Orl.	44	53	.830

STEALS PER GAME

	G	STL	AVG
Griffith, Sac.	29	73	2.52

	G	STL	AVG
Weatherspoon, N.Y.	32	78	2.44
Black, Utah	32	77	2.41
Swoopes, Hou.	32	76	2.38
Sales, Orl.	32	69	2.16
Penicheiro, Sac.	32	67	2.09
Holland-Corn, Sac.	32	63	1.97
Bullett, Cha.	32	62	1.94
McWilliams, Orl.	32	57	1.78
S. Johnson, Orl.	32	54	1.69

BLOCKS PER GAME

	G	BLK	AVG
Dydek, Utah	32	77	2.41
Stepanova, Pho.	32	62	1.94
Griffith, Sac.	29	54	1.86
Leslie, L.A.	32	49	1.53
Swoopes, Hou.	32	46	1.44

	G	BLK	AVG
Bullett, Cha.	32	45	1.41
Wicks, N.Y.	32	43	1.34
Smith, Sac.	31	38	1.23
McWilliams, Orl.	32	38	1.19
Whiting, Det.	31	31	1.00

MINUTES PER GAME

	G	MIN	AVG
S. Johnson, Orl.	32	1147	35.8
Cooper, Hou.	31	1101	35.5
Penicheiro, Sac.	32	1120	35.0
Swoopes, Hou.	32	1100	34.4
Holdsclaw, Was.	31	1061	34.2
Gillom, Pho.	32	1095	34.2
Williams, Utah	28	954	34.1
Sam, Orl.	32	1088	34.0
Weatherspoon, N.Y.	32	1086	33.9
Johnson, N.Y.	32	1082	33.8

INDIVIDUAL STATISTICS, TEAM BY TEAM

CHARLOTTE STING

Player	G	Min	FGM	FGA	Pct	FTM	FTA	Pct	Off	Def	Tot	Ast	PF	Dq	Stl	TO	Blk	Pts	Avg	Hi
Andrea Stinson	32	1041	174	378	.460	65	88	.739	32	81	113	93	56	0	32	67	18	434	13.6	27
Vicky Bullett	32	1008	142	292	.486	75	97	.773	60	159	219	50	77	1	62	60	45	369	11.5	24
Dawn Staley	32	1065	125	301	.415	85	91	.934	12	60	72	177	71	0	38	90	3	368	11.5	23
Rhonda Mapp	30	790	118	236	.500	49	68	.721	48	145	193	56	102	0	25	60	13	286	9.5	22
Charlotte Smith	32	746	62	188	.330	41	58	.707	46	69	115	58	87	1	10	50	7	173	5.4	12
Stephanie McCarty	30	563	53	130	.408	30	33	.909	16	33	49	52	47	1	19	38	2	159	5.3	18
Tracy Reid	10	154	21	49	.429	6	14	.429	7	16	23	9	12	0	1	17	2	48	4.8	15
Sharon Manning	32	521	57	113	.504	24	46	.522	37	77	114	17	51	0	28	27	4	139	4.3	12
Angie Braziel	7	41	7	14	.500	10	12	.833	1	10	11	3	6	0	2	2	0	24	3.4	8
Christy Smith	4	19	3	4	.750	5	6	.833	0	1	1	1	3	0	1	1	0	13	3.3	10
Niesa Johnson	31	296	15	50	.300	11	12	.917	3	15	18	43	19	0	10	27	2	47	1.5	6
Cass Bauer	25	123	13	34	.382	7	8	.875	4	16	20	4	20	0	1	13	1	33	1.3	6
Sonia Chase	13	58	3	16	.188	2	2	1.000	2	3	5	5	9	0	4	2	0	11	0.8	6
Charlotte	32	6425	793	1805	.439	410	535	.766	268	685	953	568	560	3	233	469	97	2104	65.8	88
Opponents	32	6425	814	1920	.424	378	522	.724	318	626	944	506	597	6	221	440	99	2142	66.9	82

3-pt. FG: Charlotte 108-369 (.293) Stinson 21-68 (.309); Bullett 10-27 (.370); Staley 33-104 (.317); Mapp 1-9 (.111); Cha. Smith 8-56 (.143); McCarty 23-65 (.354) Reid 0-1 (.000); Manning 1-1 (1.000); Chr. Smith 2-3 (.667); Johnson 6-23 (.261); Bauer 0-1 (.000); Chase 3-11 (.273); Opponents 136-428 (.318)

CLEVELAND ROCKERS

Player	G	Min	FGM	FGA	Pct	FTM	FTA	Pct	Off	Def	Tot	Ast	PF	Dq	Stl	TO	Blk	Pts	Avg	Hi
Eva Nemcova	31	925	124	296	.419	62	63	.984	27	87	114	50	50	0	31	81	22	344	11.1	20
Merlakia Jones	32	853	141	325	.434	60	78	.769	47	75	122	51	81	1	41	66	5	347	10.8	27
Chasity Melvin	32	709	95	218	.436	68	98	.694	53	74	127	38	93	1	20	42	22	259	8.1	16
Michelle Edwards	31	745	88	245	.359	45	65	.692	6	66	72	82	58	0	26	72	8	236	7.6	17
Alisa Burras	31	563	103	191	.539	26	47	.553	40	84	124	17	47	0	17	38	10	232	7.5	20
S. McConnell Serio	18	511	36	98	.367	16	19	.842	4	39	43	76	31	0	10	54	2	108	6.0	15
Janice Braxton	26	476	52	113	.460	46	66	.697	26	85	111	33	53	0	19	34	13	151	5.8	12
Rushia Brown	30	434	53	124	.427	25	37	.676	31	56	87	20	60	1	19	34	10	131	4.4	13
Tracy Henderson	27	308	27	87	.310	17	29	.586	28	51	79	9	45	0	9	25	20	71	2.6	8
Mery Andrade	32	364	23	59	.390	18	26	.692	15	35	50	49	73	0	18	40	4	71	2.2	11

Player	G	Min	FGM	FGA	Pct	FTM	FTA	Pct	Off	Def	Tot	Ast	PF	Dq	Stl	TO	Blk	Pts	Avg	Hi
									REBOUNDS									SCORING		
Jamila Wideman 26	401	21	77	.273	11	17	.647	8	26	34	51	22	0	20	40	0	56	2.2	9	
Vanessa Nygaard 4	20	1	2	.500	0	0	---	1	2	3	1	4	0	2	2	0	3	0.8	3	
Tricia Bader(*)...........9	72	2	13	.154	0	0	---	3	8	11	11	8	0	3	3	0	5	0.6	3	
Tricia Bader(†)..........16	106	2	16	.125	2	2	1.000	3	10	13	12	20	0	6	7	1	7	0.4	3	
Jennifer Howard 4	15	0	4	.000	0	0	---	0	0	0	0	2	0	0	3	0	0	0.0	0	
Kellie Jolly Harper........1	4	0	0	---	0	0	---	0	0	0	1	0	0	0	2	0	0	0.0	0	
Cleveland 32	6400	766	1852	.414	394	545	.723	289	688	977	489	627	3	235	547	116	2014	62.9	85	
Opponents 32	6400	823	1939	.424	434	616	.705	335	672	1007	536	608	3	314	477	113	2217	69.3	87	

3-pt. FG: Cleveland 88-309 (.285) Nemcova 34-93 (.366); Jones 5-18 (.278); Melvin 1-1 (1.000); Edwards 15-69 (.217); McConnell Serio 20-60 (.333); Brown 0-1 (.000) Braxton 1-8 (.125); Andrade 7-24 (.292); Wideman 3-22 (.136); Nygaard 1-2 (.500); Bader(*) 1-8 (.125); Bader(†) 1-10 (.100) Howard 0-3 (.000); Opponents 137-445 (.308)

DETROIT SHOCK

Player	G	Min	FGM	FGA	Pct	FTM	FTA	Pct	Off	Def	Tot	Ast	PF	Dq	Stl	TO	Blk	Pts	Avg	Hi
									REBOUNDS									SCORING		
Sandy Brondello 32	1002	152	347	.438	83	98	.847	29	37	66	73	81	4	25	75	5	424	13.3	33	
Jennifer Azzi 28	838	93	181	.514	86	104	.827	5	56	61	106	103	3	24	56	4	302	10.8	27	
Wendy Palmer(*)........11	295	47	100	.470	42	55	.764	27	78	105	12	44	2	6	26	4	140	12.7	27	
Wendy Palmer(†) 31	741	104	241	.432	86	123	.699	50	138	188	42	101	3	9	58	12	307	9.9	27	
Dominique Canty 26	646	76	229	.332	94	136	.691	35	45	80	38	57	1	26	45	1	249	9.6	18	
Korie Hlede(‡) 21	408	67	172	.390	42	49	.857	24	31	55	25	49	1	22	32	2	184	8.8	22	
Cindy Brown(‡) 21	490	46	146	.315	45	65	.692	35	78	113	22	45	0	25	35	12	144	6.9	18	
Val Whiting 31	764	76	200	.380	50	110	.455	66	141	207	49	84	1	40	46	31	202	6.5	12	
Rachael Sporn 18	340	44	94	.468	18	28	.643	26	33	59	27	45	0	15	16	4	106	5.9	14	
Carla Porter 32	694	69	174	.397	17	27	.630	25	47	72	51	84	2	24	54	8	172	5.4	14	
Astou Ndiaye 31	438	70	160	.438	24	39	.615	25	74	99	17	51	0	11	32	18	164	5.3	14	
C. Maria das Neves....30	306	25	95	.263	12	19	.632	8	15	23	29	32	0	16	23	0	76	2.5	11	
O. Scott-Richardson(*) 8	52	6	18	.333	4	6	.667	3	9	12	3	14	0	5	3	16	2.0	6		
O. Scott-Richardson(†)12	88	9	28	.321	7	12	.583	8	12	20	5	21	0	1	8	3	25	2.1	9	
Wanda Guyton 11	98	4	17	.235	13	16	.813	8	18	26	2	21	0	2	10	2	21	1.9	7	
Elena Tornikidou 11	86	9	23	.391	2	6	.333	3	6	9	8	8	0	1	11	1	20	1.8	8	
Lesley Brown 13	43	7	16	.438	4	6	.667	2	7	9	2	10	0	1	6	1	19	1.5	9	
Detroit 32	6500	791	1972	.401	536	764	.702	321	675	996	464	728	14	238	483	96	2239	70.0	94	
Opponents 32	6500	830	1901	.437	529	736	.719	293	769	1062	514	723	11	262	532	133	2303	72.0	104	

3-pt. FG: Detroit 121-336 (.360) Brondello 37-76 (.487); Azzi 30-58 (.517); Palmer(*) 4-16 (.250); Palmer(†) 13-46 (.283); Canty 3-17 (.176); Hlede(‡) 8-24 (.333) C. Brown(‡) 7-30 (.233); Sporn 0-1 (.000); Porter 17-51 (.333); Ndiaye 0-1 (.000); das Neves 14-60 (.233); L. Brown 1-2 (.500); Opponents 114-338 (.337)

HOUSTON COMETS

Player	G	Min	FGM	FGA	Pct	FTM	FTA	Pct	Off	Def	Tot	Ast	PF	Dq	Stl	TO	Blk	Pts	Avg	Hi
									REBOUNDS									SCORING		
Cynthia Cooper 31	1101	212	458	.463	204	229	.891	17	70	87	162	61	0	43	104	11	686	22.1	42	
Sheryl Swoopes 32	1100	226	489	.462	100	122	.820	48	154	202	127	57	0	76	83	46	585	18.3	33	
Tina Thompson 32	1074	142	339	.419	68	87	.782	67	139	206	28	95	0	31	72	31	391	12.2	26	
Polina Tzekova 32	778	76	177	.429	31	40	.775	54	109	163	32	118	4	13	52	19	194	6.1	15	
Janeth Arcain 32	735	71	164	.433	34	41	.829	32	59	91	38	63	0	30	39	2	187	5.8	13	
Monica Lamb 3	36	4	10	.400	5	6	.833	3	3	6	0	6	0	0	1	2	13	4.3	6	
Sonja Henning 32	798	52	117	.444	11	18	.611	22	58	80	74	60	0	34	29	7	128	4.0	14	
Tammy Jackson 28	382	24	58	.414	25	35	.714	45	46	91	7	75	0	15	26	20	74	2.6	8	
Amaya Valdemoro 17	92	13	35	.371	12	16	.750	4	9	13	9	16	0	11	12	0	40	2.4	12	
Jennifer Rizzotti 25	242	14	40	.350	7	12	.583	2	25	27	19	21	0	18	16	1	42	1.7	9	
Kara Wolters 10	41	3	13	.231	10	12	.833	5	7	12	2	11	0	1	3	0	16	1.6	4	
Mila Nikolich 7	29	4	11	.364	1	2	.500	3	2	5	1	3	0	0	3	0	10	1.4	4	
Nyree Roberts(‡).........4	17	0	1	.000	1	2	.500	1	1	2	0	0	0	0	1	0	1	0.3	1	
Houston 32	6425	841	1912	.440	509	622	.818	303	682	985	499	586	4	272	452	139	2367	74.0	93	
Opponents 32	6425	763	1954	.390	419	566	.740	350	621	971	459	633	3	216	491	78	2070	64.7	84	

3-pt. FG: Houston 176-547 (.322) Cooper 58-173 (.335); Swoopes 33-98 (.337); Thompson 39-111 (.351); Tzekova 11-44 (.250); Arcain 11-44 (.250); Jackson 1-1 (1.000) Henning 13-41 (.317); Valdemoro 2-5 (.400); Rizzotti 7-26 (.269); Nikolich 1-4 (.250); Opponents 125-442 (.283)

LOS ANGELES SPARKS

Player	G	Min	FGM	FGA	Pct	FTM	FTA	Pct	Off	Def	Tot	Ast	PF	Dq	Stl	TO	Blk	Pts	Avg	Hi
Lisa Leslie	32	930	182	389	.468	114	156	.731	72	176	248	56	136	4	36	94	49	500	15.6	30
Mwadi Mabika	32	938	125	336	.372	56	78	.718	42	111	153	112	100	1	44	58	15	347	10.8	20
DeLisha Milton	32	835	125	236	.530	68	86	.791	60	116	176	50	112	0	47	71	17	318	9.9	20
Gordana Grubin	32	708	96	238	.403	52	68	.765	18	54	72	90	53	1	24	53	2	284	8.9	20
Tamecka Dixon	32	563	77	199	.387	48	65	.738	17	49	66	53	42	0	17	39	4	217	6.8	14
La'Keshia Frett	31	658	77	162	.475	34	43	.791	48	46	94	63	42	0	9	26	5	188	6.1	15
Allison Feaster	32	410	51	103	.495	39	57	.684	28	30	58	32	51	0	15	28	7	162	5.1	16
Penny Toler	30	427	51	150	.340	39	45	.867	12	31	43	66	36	0	13	40	0	143	4.8	21
Nina Bjedov	27	431	52	100	.520	9	18	.500	21	49	70	17	60	0	9	25	22	121	4.5	17
Ukari Figgs	22	330	30	82	.366	21	24	.875	8	27	35	33	27	0	15	31	0	95	4.3	15
C. Machanguana	28	245	24	49	.490	26	36	.722	16	36	52	9	34	0	8	14	3	74	2.6	8
Los Angeles	32	6475	890	2044	.435	506	676	.749	342	725	1067	581	693	6	237	484	124	2449	76.5	102
Opponents	32	6475	818	1993	.410	535	721	.742	335	696	1031	511	681	6	250	493	99	2318	72.4	89

3-pt. FG: Los Angeles 163-476 (.342) Leslie 22-52 (.423); Mabika 41-146 (.281); Milton 0-1 (.000); Grubin 40-93 (.430); Dixon 15-48 (.313); Feaster 21-57 (.368) Toler 2-13 (.154); Bjedov 8-19 (.421); Figgs 14-47 (.298); Opponents 147-445 (.330)

MINNESOTA LYNX

Player	G	Min	FGM	FGA	Pct	FTM	FTA	Pct	Off	Def	Tot	Ast	PF	Dq	Stl	TO	Blk	Pts	Avg	Hi
Brandy Reed	25	757	168	366	.459	53	70	.757	55	96	151	64	57	0	29	63	17	402	16.1	28
Tonya Edwards	32	1031	165	462	.357	79	98	.806	15	97	112	84	104	6	27	68	13	475	14.8	25
Katie Smith	30	971	113	292	.387	72	94	.766	42	46	88	60	106	3	19	55	10	350	11.7	27
A. Lloyd Curry	32	899	75	200	.375	34	45	.756	38	100	138	91	92	1	30	62	12	214	6.7	17
Kristin Folkl	32	518	67	140	.479	21	39	.538	41	75	116	23	68	0	14	23	12	157	4.9	21
Sonja Tate	32	828	52	147	.354	23	30	.767	48	79	127	100	84	0	36	65	3	143	4.5	19
Angela Potthoff	32	710	53	140	.379	18	33	.545	26	59	85	37	84	0	24	35	5	127	4.0	13
Trisha Fallon	26	281	24	80	.300	23	31	.742	9	13	22	22	30	1	11	16	6	77	3.0	13
Annie LaFleur	25	333	23	66	.348	2	8	.250	14	24	38	36	19	0	8	20	0	59	2.4	9
Adia Barnes	19	91	7	23	.304	6	12	.500	8	12	20	6	16	0	5	8	0	21	1.1	9
Charmin Smith	13	56	1	9	.111	8	10	.800	2	7	9	2	10	0	1	5	0	10	0.8	4
Minnesota	32	6475	748	1925	.389	339	470	.721	298	608	906	525	670	11	204	437	78	2035	63.6	86
Opponents	32	6475	749	1763	.425	476	641	.743	296	732	1028	507	614	3	194	492	92	2111	66.0	86

3-pt. FG: Minnesota 200-603 (.332) Reed 13-38 (.342); Edwards 66-192 (.344); K. Smith 52-136 (.382); Lloyd-Curry 30-90 (.333); Folkl 2-14 (.143); Tate 16-67 (.239) Potthoff 3-18 (.167); Fallon 6-17 (.353); LaFleur 11-24 (.458); Barnes 1-3 (.333); C. Smith 0-4 (.000); Opponents 137-458 (.299)

NEW YORK LIBERTY

Player	G	Min	FGM	FGA	Pct	FTM	FTA	Pct	Off	Def	Tot	Ast	PF	Dq	Stl	TO	Blk	Pts	Avg	Hi
Vickie Johnson	32	1082	165	394	.419	72	86	.837	43	99	142	106	77	0	44	66	1	427	13.3	26
Crystal Robinson	32	901	125	285	.439	49	58	.845	38	51	89	49	78	1	44	46	11	375	11.7	27
Kym Hampton	32	856	112	260	.431	68	91	.747	61	118	179	22	110	1	22	51	18	293	9.2	21
S. Witherspoon	32	581	97	245	.396	49	69	.710	20	27	47	37	54	0	33	48	2	271	8.5	22
Tamika Whitmore	27	573	80	184	.435	53	78	.679	43	53	96	18	78	1	16	56	6	214	7.9	20
T. Weatherspoon	32	1086	80	190	.421	38	56	.679	22	82	104	205	91	1	78	80	3	229	7.2	16
Sue Wicks	32	938	91	226	.403	32	52	.615	76	147	223	45	123	5	41	63	43	216	6.8	16
R. Hammon	30	202	27	64	.422	15	17	.882	2	17	19	17	27	0	6	24	0	80	2.7	16
Venus Lacy	17	111	10	24	.417	12	15	.800	7	13	20	1	24	0	3	14	4	32	1.9	8
Michele VanGorp	21	117	8	24	.333	4	5	.800	5	12	17	7	23	0	1	3	3	20	1.0	5
C. Washington	19	77	5	18	.278	2	2	1.000	1	6	7	15	15	0	9	13	0	12	0.6	4
Rebecca Lobo	1	1	0	0	---	0	0	---	1	0	1	0	0	0	0	1	0	0	0.0	0
New York	32	6525	800	1914	.418	394	529	.745	319	625	944	522	700	9	297	482	91	2169	67.8	88
Opponents	32	6525	720	1747	.412	540	723	.747	299	682	981	451	584	3	252	557	89	2089	65.3	91

3-pt. FG: New York 175-473 (.370) Johnson 25-71 (.352); Robinson 76-174 (.437); Hampton 1-2 (.500); Witherspoon 28-78 (.359); Whitmore 1-8 (.125); Wicks 2-15 (.133); Weatherspoon 31-82 (.378); Hammon 11-38 (.289); Washington 0-5 (.000); Opponents 109-405 (.269)

ORLANDO MIRACLE

Player	G	Min	FGM	FGA	Pct	FTM	FTA	Pct	Off	Def	Tot	Ast	PF	Dq	Stl	TO	Blk	Pts	Avg	Hi
Shannon Johnson 32		1147	151	338	.447	105	153	.686	44	106	150	141	79	0	54	121	12	447	14.0	31
Nykesha Sales 32		1039	153	397	.385	95	118	.805	44	91	135	91	97	2	69	69	8	437	13.7	29
Taj McWilliams..........32		1042	153	319	.480	94	141	.667	81	158	239	51	96	3	57	80	38	420	13.1	24
Sheri Sam................32		1088	134	345	.388	55	80	.688	39	107	146	77	112	4	41	64	9	364	11.4	22
A. Congreaves............32		812	75	150	.500	44	53	.830	40	61	101	34	84	1	24	49	7	209	6.5	16
Tari Phillips...............32		335	52	128	.406	26	54	.481	26	40	66	9	54	0	19	48	8	130	4.1	8
Elaine Powell 18		256	17	33	.515	12	22	.545	9	14	23	32	22	0	9	19	4	47	2.6	9
Adrienne Johnson 29		224	25	62	.403	6	9	.667	12	16	28	14	21	0	5	14	2	57	2.0	8
Carla McGhee............30		234	15	47	.319	15	18	.833	22	24	46	8	38	0	8	22	3	45	1.5	5
Yolanda Moore 23		114	10	21	.476	6	12	.500	4	9	13	1	21	0	4	13	0	26	1.1	5
Tora Suber 25		114	7	24	.292	5	10	.500	4	9	13	9	14	0	5	10	0	20	0.8	4
Kisha Ford 8		45	1	5	.200	2	2	1.000	4	2	6	0	10	0	2	1	2	4	0.5	2
Orlando....................32		6450	793	1869	.424	465	672	.692	329	637	966	467	648	10	297	521	93	2206	68.9	93
Opponents 32		6450	812	1892	.429	431	608	.709	340	664	1004	537	660	9	257	534	124	2216	69.3	86

3-pt. FG: Orlando 155-461 (.336) S. Johnson 40-110 (.364); Sales 36-109 (.330); McWilliams 20-45 (.444); Sam 41-125 (.328); Congreaves 15-41 (.366) Phillips 0-3 (.000); Powell 1-9 (.111); A. Johnson 1-8 (.125); Moore 0-1 (.000); Suber 1-9 (.111); Ford 0-1 (.000); Opponents 161-438 (.368)

PHOENIX MERCURY

Player	G	Min	FGM	FGA	Pct	FTM	FTA	Pct	Off	Def	Tot	Ast	PF	Dq	Stl	TO	Blk	Pts	Avg	Hi
Jennifer Gillom 32		1095	163	428	.381	141	177	.797	53	131	184	54	105	2	37	87	7	485	15.2	29
Edna Campbell 28		750	95	261	.364	40	56	.714	11	42	53	37	53	0	25	48	10	268	9.6	22
Marlies Askamp 30		781	95	197	.482	93	114	.816	92	123	215	25	98	1	22	37	18	283	9.4	23
C. Davis-Wrightsil 14		259	52	120	.433	16	24	.667	15	23	38	20	39	2	12	22	4	130	9.3	23
Maria Stepanova........32		554	96	198	.485	55	88	.625	62	102	164	24	86	1	13	43	62	248	7.8	19
Michele Timms 30		804	68	192	.354	38	49	.776	17	62	79	151	87	0	43	89	7	205	6.8	22
Lisa Harrison 32		828	81	170	.476	30	44	.682	47	83	130	52	65	1	23	35	5	193	6.0	21
Bridget Pettis 32		541	65	214	.304	29	47	.617	29	30	59	45	57	1	26	30	2	181	5.7	16
Kristi Harrower 32		666	36	99	.364	59	73	.808	9	54	63	96	45	0	25	45	4	143	4.5	20
Toni Foster 10		42	7	12	.583	11	16	.688	4	4	8	1	6	0	0	4	1	25	2.5	5
Amanda Wilson..........12		34	4	12	.333	3	3	1.000	4	2	6	2	3	0	1	2	1	12	1.0	6
Angela Aycock 8		30	0	4	.000	4	4	1.000	0	1	1	3	5	0	2	6	0	4	0.5	4
Andrea Kuklova............5		13	0	3	.000	0	0	---	0	0	0	0	2	0	0	1	0	0	0.0	0
M. Lange-Harris 1		3	0	0	---	0	0	---	0	2	2	0	1	0	0	0	0	0	0.0	0
Phoenix....................32		6400	762	1910	.399	519	695	.747	343	659	1002	510	652	8	229	460	121	2177	68.0	86
Opponents 32		6400	794	1911	.415	475	637	.746	334	678	1012	494	676	15	234	479	108	2182	68.2	96

3-pt. FG: Phoenix 134-456 (.294) Gillom 18-72 (.250); Campbell 38-101 (.376); Askamp 0-2 (.000); Davis-Wrightsil 10-33 (.303); Stepanova 1-1 (1.000) Timms 31-89 (.348); Harrison 1-9 (.111); Pettis 22-98 (.224); Harrower 12-43 (.279); Wilson 1-5 (.200); Aycock 0-3 (.000); Opponents 119-395 (.301)

SACRAMENTO MONARCHS

Player	G	Min	FGM	FGA	Pct	FTM	FTA	Pct	Off	Def	Tot	Ast	PF	Dq	Stl	TO	Blk	Pts	Avg	Hi
Yolanda Griffith 29		979	200	370	.541	145	235	.617	141	188	329	45	91	0	73	66	54	545	18.8	31
R. Bolton-Holifield 31		970	143	393	.364	75	94	.798	46	86	132	73	68	0	31	44	0	421	13.6	34
K. Holland-Corn..........32		1034	123	321	.383	76	108	.704	24	44	68	51	100	2	63	72	10	379	11.8	22
Latasha Byears 32		705	130	242	.537	35	62	.565	77	94	171	31	101	1	36	60	6	295	9.2	19
Tangela Smith............31		632	104	235	.443	47	72	.653	46	73	119	17	72	0	26	38	38	256	8.3	28
Ticha Penicheiro 32		1120	71	222	.320	87	131	.664	29	126	155	226	87	1	67	135	5	235	7.3	27
Linda Burgess............27		233	33	76	.434	31	41	.756	17	38	55	3	42	0	6	20	2	97	3.6	10
Lady Grooms 32		450	27	72	.375	44	63	.698	23	31	54	39	21	0	11	36	2	98	3.1	11
Kate Starbird..............24		215	12	55	.218	22	27	.815	9	14	23	14	23	0	13	17	4	48	2.0	5
Cindy Blodgett 12		34	3	13	.231	5	9	.556	0	1	1	1	4	0	1	5	0	11	0.9	5
Heather Quella 13		28	3	7	.429	1	5	.200	0	5	5	0	5	0	2	5	2	7	0.5	4

Player	G	Min	FGM	FGA	Pct	FTM	FTA	Pct	Off	Def	Tot	Ast	PF	Dq	Stl	TO	Blk	Pts	Avg	Hi
Sacramento	32	6400	849	2006	.423	568	847	.671	412	700	1112	500	614	4	329	508	123	2392	74.8	107
Opponents	32	6400	829	1981	.418	439	590	.744	310	665	975	535	718	8	226	569	152	2258	70.6	100

3-pt. FG: Sacramento 126-421 (.299) Griffith 0-1 (.000); Bolton-Holifield 60-187 (.321); Holland-Corn 57-167 (.341); Byears 0-1 (.000); Smith 1-2 (.500) Penicheiro 6-38 (.158); Burgess 0-1 (.000); Hardmon 0-2 (.000); Starbird 2-15 (.133); Blodgett 0-7 (.000) Opponents 161-474 (.340)

UTAH STARZZ

Player	G	Min	FGM	FGA	Pct	FTM	FTA	Pct	Off	Def	Tot	Ast	PF	Dq	Stl	TO	Blk	Pts	Avg	Hi
Natalie Williams	28	954	180	347	.519	144	191	.754	109	148	257	25	108	2	38	68	22	504	18.0	31
Adrienne Goodson	32	1068	182	427	.426	99	129	.767	71	67	138	87	76	0	27	98	8	476	14.9	25
Malgorzata Dydek	32	733	141	283	.498	114	133	.857	38	166	204	59	112	1	13	91	77	403	12.6	25
Korie Hlede(*)	11	277	44	95	.463	30	33	.909	7	23	30	28	34	0	8	22	1	131	11.9	21
Korie Hlede(†)	32	685	111	267	.416	72	82	.878	31	54	85	53	83	1	30	54	3	315	9.8	22
Wendy Palmer(‡)	20	446	57	141	.404	44	68	.647	23	60	83	30	57	1	3	32	8	167	8.4	22
LaTonya Johnson	31	718	66	181	.365	47	58	.810	14	40	54	50	65	1	21	40	8	203	6.5	19
Elena Baranova	29	572	60	148	.405	33	41	.805	25	73	98	45	58	0	20	44	23	173	6.0	20
Cindy Brown(*)	9	156	11	32	.344	11	16	.688	14	19	33	10	16	0	9	12	2	34	3.8	11
Cindy Brown(†)	30	646	57	178	.320	56	81	.691	49	97	146	32	61	0	34	47	14	178	5.9	18
Debbie Black	32	1014	62	163	.380	31	50	.620	31	80	111	161	116	0	77	67	6	163	5.1	10
Krystyna Lara	25	204	23	68	.338	6	6	1.000	1	12	13	23	29	0	10	36	2	62	2.5	17
O. Scott-Richardson(‡)	4	36	3	10	.300	3	6	.500	5	3	8	2	7	0	1	3	0	9	2.3	9
Chantel Tremitiere	20	191	9	29	.310	1	1	1.000	3	16	19	22	28	0	6	13	0	21	1.1	4
Michelle Campbell	8	30	3	10	.300	2	4	.500	0	6	6	2	4	0	0	4	0	8	1.0	4
Dalma Ivanyi	14	67	4	12	.333	3	4	.750	3	2	5	7	18	0	4	11	0	11	0.8	4
Tricia Bader(‡)	7	34	0	3	.000	2	2	1.000	0	2	2	1	12	0	3	4	1	2	0.3	2
Utah	32	6500	845	1949	.434	570	742	.768	344	717	1061	552	740	5	240	560	158	2367	74.0	104
Opponents	32	6500	860	1965	.438	567	766	.740	311	661	972	570	707	8	284	477	117	2467	77.1	107

3-pt. FG: Utah 107-362 (.296) Williams 0-2 (.000); Goodson 13-53 (.245); Dydek 7-20 (.350); Hlede(*) 13-29 (.448); Hlede(†) 21-53 (.396); Palmer(‡) 9-30 (.300) Johnson 24-82 (.293); Baranova 20-48 (.417); Brown(*) 1-10 (.100); Brown(†) 8-40 (.200); Black 8-40 (.200); Lara 10-33 (.303) Tremitiere 2-8 (.250); Campbell 0-1 (.000); Ivanyi 0-4 (.000); Bader(‡) 0-2 (.000); Opponents 180-487 (.370).

WASHINGTON MYSTICS

Player	G	Min	FGM	FGA	Pct	FTM	FTA	Pct	Off	Def	Tot	Ast	PF	Dq	Stl	TO	Blk	Pts	Avg	Hi
Nikki McCray	32	1043	193	455	.424	129	160	.806	35	51	86	78	86	1	34	107	1	561	17.5	26
C. Holdsclaw	31	1061	202	462	.437	116	150	.773	74	172	246	74	67	0	37	108	27	525	16.9	24
Murriel Page	32	916	105	183	.574	71	104	.683	68	145	213	28	103	4	24	49	30	281	8.8	19
Shalonda Enis	29	844	83	228	.364	39	57	.684	53	104	157	47	82	0	23	60	4	216	7.4	18
Andrea Nagy	32	947	54	132	.409	45	59	.763	11	67	78	146	111	2	31	83	3	162	5.1	12
A. Santos de Oliveira	13	216	22	39	.564	7	22	.318	19	23	42	1	25	0	1	16	2	51	3.9	16
Rita Williams	31	312	31	62	.500	23	36	.639	7	30	37	30	41	0	21	26	1	104	3.4	10
Markita Aldridge	31	379	29	94	.309	20	33	.606	12	25	37	33	35	0	15	41	7	81	2.6	10
Heather Owen	17	235	10	25	.400	16	23	.696	11	27	38	7	42	0	2	15	4	36	2.1	6
Monica Maxwell	20	141	11	50	.220	5	9	.556	3	19	22	10	9	0	5	11	1	34	1.7	9
Nyree Roberts(*)	8	62	6	10	.600	4	7	.571	2	8	10	1	5	0	5	10	1	16	2.0	6
Nyree Roberts(†)	12	79	6	11	.545	5	9	.556	3	9	12	1	5	0	5	11	1	17	1.4	6
Valerie Still	23	282	12	49	.245	7	19	.368	16	27	43	6	38	0	4	20	4	31	1.3	6
Penny Moore	4	19	1	3	.333	0	0	---	1	0	1	0	1	0	0	4	1	2	0.5	2
Jennifer Whittle	3	18	0	2	.000	0	0	---	0	3	3	0	1	0	1	5	1	0	0.0	0
Washington	32	6475	759	1794	.423	482	679	.710	312	701	1013	461	646	7	203	574	87	2100	65.6	83
Opponents	32	6475	825	1986	.415	469	650	.722	359	636	995	518	663	9	304	436	119	2246	70.2	88

3-pt. FG: Washington 100-345 (.290) McCray 46-153 (.301); Holdsclaw 5-29 (.172); Enis 11-40 (.275); Nagy 9-33 (.273); Williams 19-34 (.559); Aldridge 3-20 (.150) Maxwell 7-33 (.212); Still 0-3 (.000); Opponents 127-403 (.315)

(*) Statistics with this team only (†) Totals with all teams (‡) Continued season with another team

PLAYOFFS RESULTS

FIRST ROUND

August 24 — Charlotte 60, Detroit 54 at Detroit
August 24 — Los Angeles 71, Sacramento 58 at L.A.

CONFERENCE FINALS

Houston defeats Los Angeles, 2-1
August 26 — Los Angeles 75, Houston 60 at Los Angeles
August 29 — Houston 83, Los Angeles 55 at Houston
August 30 — Houston 72, Los Angeles 62 at Houston

New York defeats Charlotte, 2-1
August 27 — Charlotte 78, New York 67 at Charlotte
August 29 — New York 74, Charlotte 70 at New York
August 30 — New York 69, Charlotte 54 at New York

CHAMPIONSHIP

Houston defeats New York, 2-1
September 2 — Houston 73, New York 60 at New York
September 4 — New York 68, Houston 67 at Houston
September 5 — Houston 59, New York 47 at Houston

TEAM STATISTICS

OFFENSIVE

TEAM	G	FG	FGA	PCT	FG3	FG3A	PCT	FT	FTA	PCT	OFF	DEF	REB	AST	PF	DQ	STL	TO	BLK	PTS	AVG
Hou..........6		129	327	.394	30	94	.319	126	157	.803	55	127	182	73	92	1	52	74	28	414	69.0
L.A. 4		109	268	.407	13	56	.232	32	45	.711	44	88	132	76	77	3	38	51	17	263	65.8
Cha.........4		98	232	.422	14	46	.304	52	71	.732	39	85	124	65	59	0	32	41	11	262	65.5
N.Y. 6		147	339	.434	34	93	.366	57	86	.663	57	115	172	107	121	1	30	81	19	385	64.2
Sac..........1		23	66	.348	2	10	.200	10	16	.625	11	25	36	10	14	0	13	21	4	58	58.0
Det..........1		21	63	.333	3	17	.176	9	12	.750	13	23	36	10	18	0	8	13	5	54	54.0

DEFENSIVE

Team	FG	FGA	PCT	FG3	FG3A	PCT	FT	FTA	PCT	OFF	DEF	REB	AST	PF	DQ	STL	TO	BLK	PTS	AVG	DIFF
Det..........22	61	.361	1	9	.111	15	19	.789	12	29	41	16	14	0	10	13	5	60	60.0	-6.0
Hou. 142	364	.390	28	90	.311	55	80	.688	66	122	188	96	135	4	38	86	17	367	61.2	+7.8
Cha. 105	232	.453	19	61	.311	35	52	.673	38	77	115	74	67	0	23	44	13	264	66.0	-0.5
N.Y. 128	323	.396	26	79	.329	119	155	.768	58	117	175	79	91	0	55	64	16	401	66.8	-2.7
L.A. 100	241	.415	19	62	.306	54	70	.771	35	91	126	53	60	1	32	59	22	273	68.3	-2.5
Sac. 30	74	.405	3	15	.200	8	11	.727	10	27	37	23	14	0	15	15	11	71	71.0	-13.0
AVG.'S 88	216	.407	16	53	.304	48	65	.739	37	77	114	57	64	1	29	47	14	239	65.3	---
............527	1295		96	316		286	387		219	463	682	341	381	5	173	281	84	1436		

TEAM COMPARISONS

TEAM	Points Per Game		Field Goal Percentage		Turnovers Per Game		Rebound Percentages			Below 70 Pts.		Overtime Games		3 PTS or Less		10 PTS or More	
	OWN	OPP	OWN	OPP	OWN	OPP	OFF	DEF	TOT	OWN	OPP	W	L	W	L	W	L
Charlotte 65.5		66.0	.422	.453	10.3*	11.0	.336*	.691	.514	2	3	0	0	0	0	1	1
Detroit 54.0		60.0*	.333	.361*	13.0	13.0	.310	.657	.483	1	1	0	0	0	0	0	0
Houston 69.0*		61.2	.394	.390	12.3	14.3	.311	.658	.484	3	5	0	0	0	1	4	1
Los Angeles 65.8		68.3	.407	.415	12.8	14.8	.326	.715*	.521*	2	2	0	0	0	0	2	2
New York 64.2		66.8	.434*	.396	13.5	10.7	.328	.665	.496	5	3	0	0	1	0	1	3
Sacramento 58.0		71.0	.348	.405	21.0	15.0*	.289	.714	.502	1	0	0	0	0	0	0	1
COMPOSITE; 11 games																	
........................65.3		65.3	.407	.407	12.8	12.8	.321	.679		14		0	0	1	1	8	8

* - League Leader

REBOUND PERCENTAGES
OFF. - Percentage of a given team's missed shots which that team rebounds.
DEF. - Percentage of opponents' missed shots which a given team rebounds.
TOT. - Average of offensive and defensive rebound percentages.

INDIVIDUAL PLAYOFFS STATISTICS, TEAM BY TEAM

CHARLOTTE STING

Player	G	Min	FGM	FGA	Pct	FTM	FTA	Pct	REBOUNDS			Ast	PF	Dq	Stl	TO	Blk	SCORING		
									Off	Def	Tot							Pts	Avg	Hi
Andrea Stinson 4		153	32	64	.500	15	19	.789	6	24	30	17	8	0	11	5	1	83	20.8	27
Dawn Staley 4		157	13	40	.325	15	18	.833	2	3	5	23	7	0	3	11	1	48	12.0	16
Rhonda Mapp 4		121	17	32	.531	7	13	.538	9	19	28	4	14	0	1	8	0	42	10.5	16
Charlotte Smith...........4		106	13	31	.419	9	11	.818	8	10	18	3	11	0	4	7	0	36	9.0	10
Vicky Bullett 4		121	13	32	.406	2	4	.500	5	21	26	8	10	0	7	8	9	29	7.3	11
Sharon Manning 4		59	4	13	.308	3	4	.750	5	4	9	2	6	0	1	0	0	11	2.8	6
Angie Braziel...............4		19	4	10	.400	1	2	.500	2	1	3	0	1	0	0	0	1	9	2.3	4
Tracy Reid...................3		7	1	2	.500	0	0	---	1	0	1	0	0	0	1	1	0	2	0.7	2
Niesa Johnson 4		57	1	8	.125	0	0	---	1	3	4	8	2	0	4	1	0	2	0.5	2
Charlotte.....................4		800	98	232	.422	52	71	.732	39	85	124	65	59	0	32	41	11	262	65.5	78
Opponents 4		800	105	232	.453	35	52	.673	38	77	115	74	67	0	23	44	13	264	66.0	74

3-pt. FG: Charlotte 14-46 (.304) Stinson 4-14 (.286); Staley 7-16 (.438); Mapp 1-3 (.333); Cha. Smith 1-6 (.167); Bullett 1-3 (.333); Johnson 0-4 (.000); Opponents 19-61 (.311)

DETROIT SHOCK

Player	G	Min	FGM	FGA	Pct	FTM	FTA	Pct	Off	Def	Tot	Ast	PF	Dq	Stl	TO	Blk	Pts	Avg.	Hi
Wendy Palmer	1	37	4	11	.364	2	3	.667	4	5	9	2	3	0	1	1	1	10	10.0	10
Sandy Brondello	1	29	4	12	.333	0	0	---	2	1	3	0	2	0	2	1	1	9	9.0	9
Astou Ndiaye	1	16	4	5	.800	0	0	---	3	3	6	0	2	0	1	3	0	8	8.0	8
Val Whiting	1	27	2	7	.286	3	5	.600	3	3	6	1	4	0	2	2	1	7	7.0	7
Dominique Canty	1	21	2	6	.333	2	2	1.000	1	2	3	1	3	0	1	2	0	6	6.0	6
Jennifer Azzi	1	40	2	13	.154	0	0	---	0	5	5	3	3	0	0	2	1	5	5.0	5
Carla Porter	1	19	2	5	.400	0	0	---	0	2	2	2	1	0	0	2	1	5	5.0	5
C. Maria das Neves	1	11	1	4	.250	2	2	1.000	0	2	2	1	0	0	1	0	0	4	4.0	4
Detroit	1	200	21	63	.333	9	12	.750	13	23	36	10	18	0	8	13	5	54	54.0	54
Opponents	1	200	22	61	.361	15	19	.789	12	29	41	16	14	0	10	13	5	60	60.0	60

3-pt. FG: Detroit 3-17 (.176) Palmer 0-2 (.000); Brondello 1-4 (.250); Azzi 1-6 (.167); Porter 1-3 (.333); das Neves 0-2 (.000); Opponents 1-9 (.111)

HOUSTON COMETS

Player	G	Min	FGM	FGA	Pct	FTM	FTA	Pct	Off	Def	Tot	Ast	PF	Dq	Stl	TO	Blk	Pts	Avg	Hi
Cynthia Cooper	6	220	33	85	.388	45	52	.865	5	21	26	41	14	0	9	20	6	122	20.3	29
Sheryl Swoopes	6	216	29	81	.358	26	28	.929	7	15	22	7	9	0	14	12	3	88	14.7	23
Tina Thompson	6	208	21	57	.368	16	21	.762	6	24	30	4	24	1	5	13	7	67	11.2	15
Janeth Arcain	6	156	13	29	.448	10	16	.625	4	14	18	6	7	0	6	2	1	38	6.3	11
Tammy Jackson	6	115	13	24	.542	11	16	.688	18	24	42	1	15	0	7	7	7	37	6.2	11
Polina Tzekova	6	130	10	25	.400	10	12	.833	7	16	23	2	17	0	4	5	3	32	5.3	11
Sonja Henning	6	136	8	23	.348	2	6	.333	7	11	18	11	5	0	7	1	1	19	3.2	8
Amaya Valdemoro	2	4	1	1	1.000	2	2	1.000	0	0	0	0	1	0	0	1	0	5	2.5	5
Kara Wolters	2	5	1	1	1.000	2	2	1.000	1	0	1	0	0	0	0	1	0	4	2.0	4
Mila Nikolich	2	5	0	0	---	2	2	1.000	0	1	1	0	0	0	0	1	0	2	1.0	2
Jennifer Rizzotti	2	5	0	1	.000	0	0	---	0	1	1	1	0	0	0	0	0	0	0.0	0
Houston	6	1200	129	327	.394	126	157	.803	55	127	182	73	92	1	52	74	28	414	69.0	83
Opponents	6	1200	142	364	.390	55	80	.688	66	122	188	96	135	4	38	86	17	367	61.2	75

3-pt. FG: Houston 30-94 (.319) Cooper 11-34 (.324); Swoopes 4-13 (.308); Thompson 9-24 (.375); Arcain 2-9 (.222); Tzekova 2-3 (.667); Henning 1-9 (.111) Valdemoro 1-1 (1.000); Rizzotti 0-1 (.000); Opponents 28-90 (.311).

LOS ANGELES SPARKS

Player	G	Min	FGM	FGA	Pct	FTM	FTA	Pct	Off	Def	Tot	Ast	PF	Dq	Stl	TO	Blk	Pts	Avg	Hi
Lisa Leslie	4	145	29	60	.483	14	18	.778	6	28	34	11	12	0	4	14	6	76	19.0	23
DeLisha Milton	4	127	18	40	.450	3	7	.429	6	15	21	10	12	1	7	5	6	39	9.8	14
Mwadi Mabika	4	127	17	45	.378	0	1	.000	7	11	18	11	22	2	13	10	1	37	9.3	14
Gordana Grubin	4	119	13	37	.351	1	2	.500	3	9	12	23	9	0	5	8	0	31	7.8	13
La'Keshia Frett	4	121	11	30	.367	6	7	.857	12	9	21	13	6	0	2	3	2	28	7.0	11
C. Machanguana	1	7	2	3	.667	0	0	---	1	1	2	0	1	0	0	0	0	4	4.0	4
Tamecka Dixon	4	42	7	20	.350	1	1	1.000	4	4	8	5	4	0	3	5	0	15	3.8	6
Allison Feaster	4	32	4	15	.267	5	5	1.000	1	1	2	1	3	0	1	1	0	14	3.5	7
Penny Toler	4	42	4	12	.333	2	4	.500	1	5	6	2	4	0	2	3	0	10	2.5	4
Nina Bjedov	4	34	4	5	.800	0	0	---	2	5	7	0	4	0	1	2	2	9	2.3	7
Ukari Figgs	1	4	0	1	.000	0	0	---	1	0	1	0	0	0	0	0	0	0	0.0	0
Los Angeles	4	800	109	268	.407	32	45	.711	44	88	132	76	77	3	38	51	17	263	65.8	75
Opponents	4	800	100	241	.415	54	70	.771	35	91	126	53	60	1	32	59	22	273	68.3	83

3-pt. FG: Los Angeles 13-56 (.232) Leslie 4-13 (.308); Mabika 3-17 (.176); Grubin 4-16 (.250); Dixon 0-1 (.000); Feaster 1-5 (.200); Toler 0-1 (.000) Bjedov 1-2 (.500); Figgs 0-1 (.000); Opponents 19-62 (.306).

NEW YORK LIBERTY

Player	G	Min	FGM	FGA	Pct	FTM	FTA	Pct	Off	Def	Tot	Ast	PF	Dq	Stl	TO	Blk	Pts	Avg	Hi
Crystal Robinson	6	205	32	64	.500	7	7	1.000	7	11	18	13	20	1	6	10	2	86	14.3	21
Vickie Johnson	6	185	24	57	.421	9	14	.643	4	17	21	18	15	0	2	15	2	61	10.2	16
Kym Hampton	6	181	21	49	.429	11	17	.647	16	31	47	11	15	0	2	11	7	53	8.8	14
Teresa Weatherspoon	6	203	19	42	.452	6	8	.750	4	17	21	45	23	0	6	12	0	51	8.5	19
Sophia Witherspoon	6	86	17	38	.447	7	11	.636	7	6	13	2	13	0	4	8	0	45	7.5	18
Sue Wicks	6	174	17	46	.370	6	9	.667	14	27	41	10	17	0	6	4	6	42	7.0	11
Tamika Whitmore	6	114	15	31	.484	5	14	.357	5	5	10	3	14	0	4	10	2	35	5.8	11
Rebecca Hammon	6	50	2	12	.167	6	6	1.000	0	1	1	5	3	0	0	6	0	12	2.0	10
Venus Lacy	1	2	0	0	---	0	0	---	0	0	0	0	1	0	0	1	0	0	0.0	0
New York	6	1200	147	339	.434	57	86	.663	57	115	172	107	121	1	30	81	19	385	64.2	74

Player	G	Min	FGM	FGA	Pct	FTM	FTA	Pct	REBOUNDS Off	Def	Tot	Ast	PF	Dq	Stl	TO	Blk	SCORING Pts	Avg	Hi
Opponents	6	1200	128	323	.396	119	155	.768	58	117	175	79	91	0	55	64	16	401	66.8	78

3-pt. FG: New York 34-93 (.366) Robinson 15-39 (.385); Johnson 4-10 (.400); Hampton 0-1 (.000); Weatherspoon 7-19 (.368); Witherspoon 4-10 (.400) Wicks 2-5 (.400); Hammon 2-9 (.222); Opponents 26-79 (.329)

SACRAMENTO MONARCHS

Player	G	Min	FGM	FGA	Pct	FTM	FTA	Pct	REBOUNDS Off	Def	Tot	Ast	PF	Dq	Stl	TO	Blk	SCORING Pts	Avg	Hi
R. Bolton-Holifield........	1	32	6	15	.400	2	2	1.000	1	0	1	4	1	0	1	2	0	15	15.0	15
Tangela Smith..............	1	38	6	16	.375	2	6	.333	1	1	2	0	4	0	3	1	1	14	14.0	14
Linda Burgess.............	1	14	3	6	.500	2	2	1.000	1	3	4	0	2	0	2	2	0	8	8.0	8
Lady Grooms	1	25	3	7	.429	0	0	---	1	4	5	1	0	0	1	2	0	6	6.0	6
Ticha Penicheiro	1	20	1	5	.200	2	2	1.000	0	4	4	3	1	0	1	2	0	4	4.0	4
Cindy Blodgett	1	6	1	1	1.000	0	0	---	0	1	1	1	1	0	2	2	2	3	3.0	3
Heather Quella	1	4	1	2	.500	1	2	.500	0	2	2	0	1	0	1	1	0	3	3.0	3
Kedra Holland-Corn......	1	21	1	5	.200	0	0	---	2	3	5	1	2	0	2	4	0	2	2.0	2
Kate Starbird.............	1	16	1	5	.200	0	0	---	0	2	2	0	0	0	0	2	1	2	2.0	2
Latasha Byears............	1	24	0	4	.000	1	2	.500	5	5	10	0	2	0	1	3	0	1	1.0	1
Sacramento	1	200	23	66	.348	10	16	.625	11	25	36	10	14	0	13	21	4	58	58.0	58
Opponents	1	200	30	74	.405	8	11	.727	10	27	37	23	14	0	15	15	11	71	71.0	71

3-pt. FG: Sacramento 2-10 (.200) Bolton-Holifield 1-6 (.167); Burgess 0-1 (.000); Blodgett 1-1 (1.000); Holland-Corn 0-1 (.000); Starbird 0-1 (.000); Opponents 3-15 (.200)

(*) Statistics with this team only
(†) Totals with all teams
(‡) Continued season with another team

INDIVIDUAL FINALS STATISTICS, TEAM BY TEAM

HOUSTON COMETS

Player	G	Min	FGM	FGA	Pct	FTM	FTA	Pct	REBOUNDS Off	Def	Tot	Ast	PF	Dq	Stl	TO	Blk	SCORING Pts	Avg	Hi
Cynthia Cooper	3	109	14	38	.368	33	37	.892	4	9	13	13	7	0	8	12	0	65	21.7	29
Sheryl Swoopes	3	112	11	37	.297	16	17	.941	5	6	11	4	5	0	6	5	1	40	13.3	15
Tina Thompson	3	109	11	29	.379	12	15	.800	4	14	18	4	10	0	2	6	2	39	13.0	15
Janeth Arcain	3	78	5	12	.417	7	10	.700	3	7	10	5	4	0	4	2	1	17	5.7	10
Tammy Jackson	3	65	6	16	.375	4	8	.500	9	14	23	1	6	0	6	3	6	16	5.3	7
Polina Tzekova	3	60	2	9	.222	8	10	.800	2	6	8	0	10	0	2	0	0	13	4.3	11
Sonja Henning	3	67	3	11	.273	2	6	.333	4	5	9	3	4	0	5	4	0	9	3.0	8
Houston	3	600	52	152	.342	82	103	.796	31	61	92	30	46	0	33	36	10	199	66.3	73
Opponents	3	600	63	170	.371	31	46	.674	32	61	93	43	72	1	15	50	11	175	58.3	68

3-pt. FG: Houston 13-42 (.310) Cooper 4-13 (.308); Swoopes 2-7 (.286); Thompson 5-13 (.385); Arcain 0-2 (.000); Tzekova 1-1 (1.000); Henning 1-6 (.167); Opponents 18-49 (.367)

NEW YORK LIBERTY

Player	G	Min	FGM	FGA	Pct	FTM	FTA	Pct	REBOUNDS Off	Def	Tot	Ast	PF	Dq	Stl	TO	Blk	SCORING Pts	Avg	Hi
Crystal Robinson.........	3	99	12	31	.387	7	7	1.000	1	4	5	9	13	1	3	7	2	38	12.7	21
Vickie Johnson	3	88	13	27	.481	1	4	.250	3	9	12	5	10	0	2	11	2	29	9.7	16
Sophia Witherspoon	3	50	10	24	.417	6	9	.667	5	3	8	1	8	0	1	5	0	28	9.3	18
Sue Wicks..................	3	90	9	28	.321	3	4	.750	11	17	28	3	12	0	4	4	3	22	7.3	11
Teresa Weatherspoon ..	3	100	8	18	.444	1	1	1.000	2	10	12	17	11	0	3	8	0	21	7.0	8
Kym Hampton..............	3	89	7	24	.292	6	9	.667	8	14	22	6	8	0	1	5	3	20	6.7	10
Rebecca Hammon........	3	32	2	7	.286	6	6	1.000	0	1	1	2	2	0	3	0	0	12	4.0	10
Tamika Whitmore	3	52	2	11	.182	1	6	.167	2	3	5	0	8	0	1	3	1	5	1.7	4
New York	3	600	63	170	.371	31	46	.674	32	61	93	43	72	1	15	50	11	175	58.3	68
Opponents	3	600	52	152	.342	82	103	.796	31	61	92	30	46	0	33	36	10	199	66.3	73

3-pt. FG: New York 18-49 (.367) Robinson 7-23 (.304); Johnson 2-6 (.333); Witherspoon 2-5 (.400); Wicks 1-2 (.500); Weatherspoon 4-9 (.444); Hammon 2-4 (.500); Opponents 13-42 (.310)

GAME 1

At Madison Square Garden, September 2, 1999

OFFICIALS: Derek Collins, Gary Zielinski, Sally Bell. TIME OF GAME: 1:56. ATTENDANCE: 17,113.

SCORE BY PERIODS	1	2	FINAL
Houston	29	44	73
New York	20	40	60

VISITORS: Houston. Head Coach: Van Chancellor.

No Player	MIN	FG	FGA	3P	3PA	FT	FTA	OR	DR	TOT	A	PF	ST	TO	TEC	PTS
22 Sheryl Swoopes	37	5	13	0	2	5	5	0	2	2	1	2	1	2	0	15
7 Tina Thompson	36	3	6	2	4	3	4	0	7	7	3	3	1	2	0	11
15 Polina Tzekova	20	0	0	0	0	2	4	1	0	1	0	2	1	0	0	2
14 Cynthia Cooper	38	8	16	3	5	10	10	1	2	3	6	2	4	1	0	29
34 Sonja Henning	21	3	6	1	3	1	2	1	2	3	0	1	1	3	0	8
9 Janeth Arcain	26	1	3	0	1	1	2	2	2	4	4	0	2	1	0	3
23 Tammy Jackson	22	2	6	0	0	1	2	3	5	8	0	3	0	3	0	5
24 Mila Nikolich								Did not play.								
21 Jennifer Rizzotti								Did not play.								
13 Valdemoro Madari								Did not play.								
52 Kara Wolters								Did not play.								
TOTALS	200	22	50	6	15	23	29	8	20	28	14	13	10	13	0	73

FG pct.: .440. 3PT pct.: .400. FT pct.: .793. Team Rebounds: 7. Total Turnovers: 13 (13 PTS).

HOME: New York. Head Coach: Richie Adubato.

No Player	MIN	FG	FGA	3P	3PA	FT	FTA	OR	DR	TOT	A	PF	ST	TO	TEC	PTS
55 Vickie Johnson	28	7	12	1	4	1	4	1	0	1	1	1	1	3	0	16
23 Sue Wicks	26	1	7	0	1	1	2	4	7	11	1	4	4	0	0	3
34 Kym Hampton	27	1	8	0	0	0	0	3	4	7	3	1	1	1	0	2
11 Weatherspoon	38	2	5	0	1	1	1	0	4	4	10	3	0	2	0	5
3 Crystal Robinson	34	4	10	2	7	2	2	1	2	3	3	6	1	3	0	12
44 Tamika Whitmore	23	2	3	0	0	0	2	1	2	3	0	2	1	2	0	4
13 Sophia Witherspoon	21	7	13	2	4	2	4	1	1	2	0	1	0	2	0	18
25 Rebecca Hammon	3	0	1	0	1	0	0	0	0	0	0	0	0	0	0	0
5 Venus Lacy								Did not play.								
31 Michele VanGorp								Did not play.								
4 Coquese Washington								Did not play.								
TOTALS	200	24	59	5	18	7	15	11	20	31	18	18	8	16	1	60

FG pct.: .407. 3PT pct.: .278. FT pct. .467. Team Rebounds: 11. Total Turnovers: 16 (19 PTS).
Blocked Shots: Houston 1: Jackson. New York 2: Johnson, Wicks. Technical Fouls: New York: Adubato. Flagrant Fouls: None. Points off Turnovers: Houston 19, New York 13. Fast Break Points: Houston 11, New York 12. Points in Paint: Houston 24, New York 30. Second Chance Points: Houston 6, New York 7

GAME 2

At Compaq Center, September 4, 1999

OFFICIALS: June Courteau, Patty Broderick. Jason Phillips. TIME OF GAME: 2:14. ATTENDANCE: 16,285.

SCORE BY PERIODS	1	2	FINAL
New York	23	45	68
Houston	37	30	67

VISITORS: New York. Head Coach: Richie Adubato.

No Player	MIN	FG	FGA	3P	3PA	FT	FTA	OR	DR	TOT	A	PF	ST	TO	TEC	PTS
23 Sue Wicks	29	3	9	0	0	2	2	2	6	8	1	4	0	3	0	8
55 Vickie Johnson	24	2	8	0	1	0	0	2	3	5	3	5	1	4	0	4
34 Kym Hampton	33	4	10	0	0	2	4	4	5	9	1	3	0	2	0	10
3 Crystal Robinson	33	6	11	4	9	5	5	0	0	0	3	3	0	1	0	21
11 Weatherspoon	32	3	5	2	3	0	0	2	4	6	5	3	2	3	0	8
44 Tamika Whitmore	17	0	4	0	0	1	4	1	1	2	0	4	0	0	0	1
13 Sophia Witherspoon	17	2	5	0	0	2	3	2	1	3	1	3	1	1	0	6

No Player	MIN	FG	FGA	3P	3PA	FT	FTA	OR	DR	TOT	A	PF	ST	TO	TEC	PTS
25 Rebecca Hammon	15	2	4	2	3	4	4	0	1	1	1	1	0	3	0	10
5 Venus Lacy							Did not play.									
31 Michele VanGorp							Did not play.									
4 Coquese Washington							Did not play.									
TOTALS	200	22	56	8	16	16	22	13	21	34	15	26	4	18	0	68

FG pct.: .393. 3PT pct.: .500. FT pct.: .727. Team Rebounds: 10. Total Turnovers: 18 (14 PTS).

HOME: Houston. Head Coach: Van Chancellor.

No Player	MIN	FG	FGA	3P	3PA	FT	FTA	OR	DR	TOT	A	PF	ST	TO	TEC	PTS
22 Sheryl Swoopes	38	3	12	1	2	7	8	3	3	6	3	3	4	3	0	14
7 Tina Thompson	35	4	9	3	4	4	6	2	3	5	0	3	0	2	0	15
15 Polina Tzekova	28	2	7	1	1	6	6	1	5	6	0	5	1	0	0	11
14 Cynthia Cooper	37	1	10	0	4	10	12	1	3	4	6	1	1	5	0	12
34 Sonja Henning	13	0	1	0	0	1	4	0	1	1	1	0	2	0	0	1
9 Janeth Arcain	32	3	6	0	1	4	4	1	1	2	0	4	1	0	0	10
23 Tammy Jackson	17	2	5	0	0	0	2	1	3	4	0	2	3	0	0	4
24 Mila Nikolich							Did not play.									
21 Jennifer Rizzotti							Did not play.									
13 Valdemoro Madari							Did not play.									
52 Kara Wolters							Did not play.									
TOTALS	200	15	50	5	12	32	42	9	19	28	10	18	12	11	0	67

FG pct.: .300. 3PT pct.: .417. FT pct.: .762. Team Rebounds: 13. Total Turnovers: 11 (10 PTS).

Blocked Shots: New York 8:Hampton 3, Wicks 2, Robinson 2, Johnson. Houston: 4 Jackson 2, Swoopes, Thompson. Technical Fouls: None. Flagrant Fouls: None. Points off Turnovers: New York 10, Houston 14. Fast Break Points: New York 5, Houston 0. Points in Paint: New York 18, Houston 16. Second Chance Points: New York 8, Houston 10

GAME 3
At Compaq Center, September 5, 1999

OFFICIALS: Sally Bell, Michael Price, Stan Gaxiola. TIME OF GAME: 2:00. ATTENDANCE: 16,285.

SCORE BY PERIODS	1	2	FINAL
New York	25	22	47
Houston	33	26	59

VISITORS: New York. Head Coach: Richie Adubato.

No Player	MIN	FG	FGA	3P	3PA	FT	FTA	OR	DR	TOT	A	PF	ST	TO	TEC	PTS
55 Vickie Johnson	36	4	7	1	1	0	0	0	6	6	1	4	0	4	0	9
23 Sue Wicks	35	5	12	1	1	0	0	5	4	9	1	4	0	1	0	11
34 Kym Hampton	29	2	6	0	0	4	5	1	5	6	2	4	0	2	0	8
3 Crystal Robinson	32	2	10	1	7	0	0	0	2	2	3	4	2	3	0	5
11 Weatherspoon	30	3	8	2	5	0	0	0	2	2	2	5	1	3	0	8
25 Rebecca Hammon	14	0	2	0	0	2	2	0	0	0	1	1	0	0	0	2
44 Tamika Whitmore	12	0	4	0	0	0	0	0	0	0	0	2	0	1	0	0
13 Sophia Witherspoon	12	1	6	0	1	2	2	2	1	3	0	4	0	2	0	4
4 Coquese Washington							Did not play.									
5 Venus Lacy							Did not play.									
31 Michele VanGorp							Did not play.									
TOTALS	200	17	55	5	15	8	9	8	20	28	10	28	3	16	0	47

FG pct.: .309. 3PT pct.: .333. FT pct.: .889. Team Rebounds: 8. Total Turnovers: 16 (7 PTS).

HOME: Houston. Head Coach: Van Chancellor.

No Player	MIN	FG	FGA	3P	3PA	FT	FTA	OR	DR	TOT	A	PF	ST	TO	TEC	PTS
7 Tina Thompson	38	4	14	0	5	5	5	2	4	6	1	4	1	2	0	13
22 Sheryl Swoopes	37	3	12	1	3	4	4	2	1	3	0	0	1	0	0	11
15 Polina Tzekova	12	0	2	0	0	0	0	0	1	1	0	3	0	0	0	0
14 Cynthia Cooper	34	5	12	1	4	13	15	2	4	6	1	4	3	6	0	24
34 Sonja Henning	33	0	4	0	3	0	0	3	2	5	2	3	2	1	0	0
23 Tammy Jackson	26	2	5	0	0	3	4	5	6	11	1	1	3	0	0	7
9 Janeth Arcain	20	1	3	0	0	2	4	0	4	4	1	0	1	1	0	4
24 Mila Nikolich							Did not play.									
21 Jennifer Rizzotti							Did not play.									

No Player	MIN	FG	FGA	3P	3PA	FT	FTA	OR	DR	TOT	A	PF	ST	TO	TEC	PTS
13 Valdemoro Madari							Did not play.									
52 Kara Wolters							Did not play.									
TOTALS 200	15	52	2	15	27	32	14	22	36	6	15	11	12	0	59

FG pct.: .288. 3PT pct.: .133. FT pct.: .844. Team Rebounds:9. Total Turnovers: 12 (6 PTS).
Blocked Shots: New York 1: Whitmore. Houston 5: Jackson 3, Thompson, Arcain. Technical Fouls: None. Flagrant Fouls: None.
Points off Turnovers: New York 6, Houston 7. Fast Break Points: New York 2, Houston 12. Points in Paint: New York 22, Houston 24.
Second Chance Points: New York 8, Houston 9.

ALL-STAR GAME BOX SCORE

At Madison Square Garden, July 14, 1999

OFFICIALS: Sally Bell, Patty Broderick, June Courteau. TIME OF GAME: 1:49. ATTENDANCE: 18,649.

SCORE BY PERIODS	1	2	FINAL
West 43	43	36	79
East.....................................29	29	32	61

VISITORS: West. Head Coach: Van Chancellor.

No Player	MIN	FG	FGA	3P	3PA	FT	FTA	OR	DR	TOT	A	PF	ST	TO	TEC	PTS
22 Sheryl Swoopes 19	19	4	7	0	0	0	0	1	7	8	0	2	3	2	0	8
7 Tina Thompson 14	14	4	8	0	0	0	0	0	5	5	0	0	0	2	0	8
9 Lisa Leslie.....................17	17	5	11	0	1	3	4	3	2	5	1	2	1	0	0	13
7 Michele Timms 18	18	1	1	1	1	0	0	0	4	4	4	1	1	3	0	3
14 Cynthia Cooper 18	18	3	5	0	2	1	1	0	4	4	4	0	2	1	0	7
24 Natalie Williams..............21	21	3	4	0	0	8	10	4	4	8	3	0	1	1	0	14
33 Yolanda Griffith 21	21	5	10	0	0	0	0	2	3	5	1	2	1	3	0	10
6 Bolton-Holifield 20	20	1	7	0	4	0	0	1	2	3	1	0	1	0	0	2
21 Ticha Penicheiro 19	19	0	3	0	1	1	2	0	0	0	3	2	0	3	0	1
22 Jennifer Gillom 18	18	2	6	0	1	2	2	0	5	5	1	0	1	0	0	6
13 Tonya Edwards 15	15	3	8	1	4	0	0	0	1	1	1	1	0	2	0	7
TOTALS 200	200	31	70	2	14	15	19	11	37	48	19	10	11	17	0	79

FG pct.: .443. 3PT pct.: .143. FT pct.: .789. Team Rebounds: 6 Total Turnovers: 17 (0 PTS).

HOME: East. Head Coach: Linda Hill-MacDonald.

No Player	MIN	FG	FGA	3P	3PA	FT	FTA	OR	DR	TOT	A	PF	ST	TO	TEC	PTS
23 Vicky Bullett 25	25	2	6	0	1	0	0	1	4	5	1	5	0	2	0	4
23 Chamique Holdsclaw......11	11	2	6	0	0	1	1	0	5	5	0	0	0	2	0	5
34 Kym Hampton 21	21	2	6	0	0	1	2	1	2	3	0	2	2	0	0	5
11 Weatherspoon................17	17	1	6	1	2	0	0	0	2	2	4	2	1	3	0	3
15 Nikki McCray..................16	16	2	11	0	2	0	0	0	2	2	0	1	3	0	0	4
11 Taj McWilliams 31	31	2	5	1	1	3	4	2	5	7	1	2	2	2	0	8
14 Shannon Johnson 23	23	3	6	2	5	0	0	2	2	4	2	2	3	2	0	8
42 Nykesha Sales...............17	17	3	8	0	3	0	2	0	0	0	1	1	0	2	0	6
55 Vickie Johnson 15	15	3	8	0	3	0	0	0	2	2	3	0	0	2	0	6
25 Merlakia Jones 13	13	2	4	0	0	0	0	1	2	3	3	0	0	0	0	4
6 Sandy Brondello 11	11	4	8	0	1	0	0	2	1	3	1	0	0	0	0	8
50 Rebecca Lobo							Did not play.									
TOTALS 200	200	26	74	4	18	5	9	9	27	36	16	15	11	15	0	61

FG pct.: .351. 3PT pct.: .222. FT pct.: .556. Team Rebounds: 5. Total Turnovers: 15 (0 PTS).
Blocked Shots: West 3: Swoopes, Leslie, Griffith. East 4: Bullett 2, McWilliams, S. Johnson. Technical Fouls: None. Flagrant Fouls: None. Fast Break Points: West 25, East 4. Points in Paint: West 50, East 22. Second Chance Points: West 14, East 3.

1998 SEASON IN REVIEW

Front Row (l. to r.) Sheryl Swoopes, Tina Thompson, Kim Perrot, Coach Van Chancellor, Cynthia Cooper, Janeth Arcain, Monica Lamb. Back Row (l. to r.) Trainer Michelle T. Leget, Assistant Coach Alisa Scott, Tammy Jackson, Wanda Guyton, Tiffany Woosley, Amaya Valdemoro, Yolanda Moore, Nyree Roberts, Equipment Manager Stacey Johnson, Assistant Coach Kevin Cook.

FINAL STANDINGS

EASTERN CONFERENCE

Team	CHA	CLE	DET	HOU	LA	NY	PHO	SAC	UTA	WAS	W	L	PCT	GB	Last-10	Streak
CLE	3	—	2	1	1	3	0	3	3	4	20	10	.667	—	8-2	Won 4
CHA	—	1	3	0	1	3	2	2	2	4	18	12	.600	2	4-6	Won 1
NY	1	1	2	1	2	—	3	3	1	4	18	12	.600	2	7-3	Lost 2
DET	1	2	—	0	3	2	0	3	3	3	17	13	.567	3	6-4	Won 2
WAS	0	0	1	0	1	0	0	0	1	—	3	27	.100	17	1-9	Lost 5

WESTERN CONFERENCE

Team	CHA	CLE	DET	HOU	LA	NY	PHO	SAC	UTA	WAS	W	L	PCT	GB	Last-10	Streak
HOU	3	2	2	—	4	2	3	4	4	3	27	3	.900	—	8-2	Won 2
PHO	0	3	3	1	2	0	—	4	3	3	19	11	.633	8	7-3	Won 4
LA	2	1	0	0	—	1	2	1	3	2	12	18	.400	15	5-5	Lost 2
SAC	1	0	0	0	3	0	0	—	2	2	8	22	.267	19	2-8	Lost 2
UTA	1	0	0	0	1	1	1	2	—	2	8	22	.267	19	1-9	Lost 3

REVIEW 1998 Regular Season

TEAM STATISTICS
OFFENSIVE

TEAM	G	FG	FGA	PCT	FG3	FG3A	PCT	FT	FTA	PCT	OFF	DEF	REB	AST	PF	DQ	STL	TO	BLK	PTS	AVG
Hou........	30	795	1824	.436	177	523	.338	518	646	.802	297	630	927	428	510	3	332	435	81	2285	76.2
Phoe......	30	787	1856	.424	130	405	.321	513	709	.724	327	614	941	543	595	3	288	483	86	2217	73.9
Clev.	30	804	1719	.468	106	279	.380	483	631	.765	227	649	876	575	600	4	270	528	99	2197	73.2
L.A.	30	797	1914	.416	111	335	.331	443	609	.727	337	683	1020	472	675	7	229	511	148	2148	71.6
Cha........	30	798	1855	.430	105	377	.279	442	624	.708	304	677	981	512	507	4	273	457	96	2143	71.4
Utah.......	30	777	1837	.423	113	346	.327	426	608	.701	302	699	1001	481	638	9	221	543	170	2093	69.8
Det.	30	771	1875	.411	97	300	.323	448	638	.702	345	732	1077	432	602	3	197	490	81	2087	69.6
N.Y.	30	758	1784	.425	92	281	.327	450	629	.715	320	624	944	513	630	3	291	501	84	2058	68.6
Wash.	30	720	1821	.395	114	432	.264	400	620	.645	325	599	924	397	692	9	266	625	91	1954	65.1
Sac........	30	734	1802	.407	72	277	.260	376	560	.671	326	619	945	463	633	7	263	533	107	1916	63.9

DEFENSIVE

Team	FG	FGA	PCT	FG3	FG3A	PCT	FT	FTA	PCT	OFF	DEF	REB	AST	PF	DQ	STL	TO	BLK	PTS	AVG	DIFF
Hou.	729	1803	.404	110	369	.298	340	470	.723	324	630	954	450	637	6	206	560	102	1908	63.6	+12.6
N.Y.	709	1693	.419	103	325	.317	445	625	.712	272	620	892	420	610	4	261	538	81	1966	65.5	+3.1
Phoe.......	758	1747	.434	77	244	.316	432	601	.719	298	643	941	406	664	9	242	581	96	2025	67.5	+6.4
Cha.	780	1878	.415	113	381	.297	378	529	.715	305	663	968	470	601	5	242	501	108	2051	68.4	+3.1
Det.	768	1869	.411	113	375	.301	429	602	.713	282	667	949	445	635	8	249	447	114	2078	69.3	+0.3
Sac.........	733	1752	.418	107	366	.292	509	674	.755	307	646	953	493	556	5	239	500	134	2082	69.4	-5.5
Clev.	776	1835	.423	128	395	.324	430	625	.688	327	596	923	523	620	3	309	546	101	2110	70.3	+2.9
L.A.	780	1898	.411	119	372	.320	490	693	.707	337	663	1000	522	603	4	244	481	109	2169	72.3	-0.7
Utah	832	1942	.428	135	410	.329	495	680	.728	336	685	1021	539	559	7	304	441	94	2294	76.5	-6.7
Wash.	876	1870	.468	112	318	.352	551	775	.711	322	713	1035	548	597	1	334	511	104	2415	80.5	-15.4
AVG.'S	774	1829	.423	112	356	.314	450	627	.717	311	653	964	482	608	5	263	511	104	2110	70.3	---
....	7741	18287		1117	3555		4499	6274		3110	6526	9636	4816	6082	52	2630	5106	1043	21098		

TEAM COMPARISONS

	Points Per Game		Field Goal Percentage		Turnovers Per Game		Rebound Percentages			Below 70 Pts.		Overtime Games		3 PTS or Less		10 PTS or More	
TEAM	OWN	OPP	OWN	OPP	OWN	OPP	OFF	DEF	TOT	OWN	OPP	W	L	W	L	W	L
Charlotte	71.4	68.4	.430	.415	15.2	16.7	.314	.689	.502	13	20	0	0	3	2	6	6
Cleveland	73.2	70.3	.468*	.423	17.6	18.2	.276	.665	.470	12	14	1	1	3	2	12	8
Detroit	69.6	69.3	.411	.411	16.3	14.9	.341*	.722*	.531*	15	15	0	0	3	4	9	6
Washington	65.1	80.5	.395	.468	20.8	17.0	.313	.650	.482	21	4	0	1	1	2	1	23
Houston	76.2*	63.6*	.436	.404*	14.5*	18.7	.320	.660	.490	5	25	1	1	3	2	19	1
Los Angeles	71.6	72.3	.416	.411	17.0	16.0	.337	.670	.503	13	10	1	0	2	5	5	8
New York	68.6	65.5	.425	.419	16.7	17.9	.340	.696	.518	18	18	2	0	5	1	11	6
Phoenix	73.9	67.5	.424	.434	16.1	19.4*	.337	.673	.505	11	19	1	1	4	6	13	4
Sacramento	63.9	69.4	.407	.418	17.8	16.7	.335	.668	.502	19	14	0	1	1	3	3	11
Utah	69.8	76.5	.423	.428	18.1	14.7	.306	.675	.491	19	7	0	1	3	1	4	10
COMPOSITE; 150 games																	
....	70.3	70.3	.423	.423	17.0	17.0	.323	.677			146	6	6	28	28	83	83

* - League Leader

REBOUND PERCENTAGES

OFF. - Percentage of a given team's missed shots which that team rebounds.

DEF. - Percentage of opponents' missed shots which a given team rebounds.

TOT. - Average of offensive and defensive rebound percentages.

SCORING AVERAGE

	G	FG	FT	PTS	AVG
Cooper, Hou.	30	203	210	680	22.7
Gillom, Pho.	30	228	137	624	20.8
Leslie, L.A.	28	202	136	549	19.6
McCray, Was.	29	191	107	512	17.7
Dixon, L.A.	22	124	88	357	16.2
Swoopes, Hou.	29	173	71	453	15.6
Stinson, Cha.	30	173	75	450	15.0
Byears, Sac.	30	181	61	427	14.2
Brondello, Det.	30	157	96	426	14.2
Hlede, Det.	27	135	83	382	14.1
Reid, Cha.	30	151	111	413	13.8
Witherspoon, N.Y.	30	144	92	413	13.8
Fijalkowski, Cle.	28	146	87	383	13.7
Palmer, Utah	28	145	81	377	13.5
Bullett, Cha.	30	162	71	399	13.3
Baranova, Utah	20	92	59	258	12.9
Dydek, Utah	30	146	93	386	12.9
Thompson, Hou.	27	121	63	342	12.7
Johnson, N.Y.	30	146	63	376	12.5
Toler, L.A.	30	145	55	370	12.3

REBOUNDS PER GAME

	G	OFF	DEF	TOT	AVG
Leslie, L.A.	28	77	208	285	10.2
Brown, Det.	30	70	231	301	10.0
Baranova, Utah	20	61	125	186	9.3
Dydek, Utah	30	41	186	227	7.6
Gillom, Pho.	30	62	157	219	7.3
Thompson, Hou.	27	65	127	192	7.1
Page, Was.	30	81	127	208	6.9
Lobo, N.Y.	30	70	137	207	6.9
Fijalkowski, Cle.	28	59	133	192	6.9
Palmer, Utah	28	70	116	186	6.6
Byears, Sac.	30	85	114	199	6.6
Bullett, Cha.	30	62	132	194	6.5
Hampton, N.Y.	30	53	128	181	6.0
Braxton, Cle.	30	37	131	168	5.6
Manning, Cha.	30	60	106	166	5.5
Reid, Cha.	30	60	97	157	5.2
Hlede, Det.	27	39	102	141	5.2
Swoopes, Hou.	29	39	110	149	5.1
Mujanovic, Det.	30	54	100	154	5.1
Burgess, Sac.	30	53	93	146	4.9

ASSISTS PER GAME

	G	AST	AVG
Penicheiro, Sac.	30	224	7.5
Weatherspoon, N.Y.	30	191	6.4
McConnell Serio, Cle.	28	178	6.4
Timms, Pho.	30	158	5.3
Toler, L.A.	30	143	4.8
Perrot, Hou.	30	142	4.7
Stinson, Cha.	30	134	4.5

	G	AST	AVG
Cooper, Hou.	30	131	4.4
Tremitiere, Utah	28	102	3.6
Baranova, Utah	20	70	3.5
Brondello, Det.	30	98	3.3
McCray, Was.	29	90	3.1
Webb, Pho.	30	92	3.1
Chr. Smith, Cha.	24	71	3.0
Suber, Cha.	30	86	2.9
Edwards, Cle.	23	65	2.8
Hlede, Det.	27	73	2.7
Leslie, L.A.	28	70	2.5
Braxton, Cle.	30	74	2.5
Johnson, N.Y.	30	74	2.5

FIELD GOAL PCT.

	FG	FGA	PCT
Fijalkowski, Cle.	146	267	.547
Mujanovic, Det.	106	204	.520
Griffiths, Pho.	93	184	.505
Braxton, Cle.	108	218	.495
Reid, Cha.	151	310	.487
Lobo, N.Y.	136	281	.484
Dydek, Utah	146	303	.482
Page, Was.	104	217	.479
Leslie, L.A.	202	423	.478
Burgess, Sac.	90	189	.476

3-PT FIELD GOAL PCT.

	3FG	3GA	PCT
Nemcova, Cle.	28	62	.452
Toler, L.A.	25	60	.417
McConnell Serio, Cle	29	71	.408
Cooper, Hou.	64	160	.400
Hlede, Det.	29	74	.392
Gillom, Pho.	31	82	.378
Johnson, N.Y.	21	56	.375
Swoopes, Hou.	36	100	.360
Thompson, Hou.	37	103	.359
Price, Sac.	28	78	.359

FREE THROW PCT.

	FT	FTA	PCT
Brondello, Det.	96	104	.923
Nemcova, Cle.	67	75	.893
Pettis, Pho.	77	89	.865
Cooper, Hou.	210	246	.854
Thompson, Hou.	63	74	.851
Baranova, Utah	59	71	.831
Bullett, Cha.	71	86	.826
Swoopes, Hou.	71	86	.826
Fijalkowski, Cle.	87	106	.821
Hlede, Det.	83	103	.806

STEALS PER GAME

	G	STL	AVG
Weatherspoon, N.Y.	30	100	3.33

	G	STL	AVG
Perrot, Hou.	30	84	2.80
Swoopes, Hou.	29	72	2.48
Penicheiro, Sac.	30	67	2.23
Bullett, Cha.	30	66	2.20
Williams, Was.	30	63	2.10
Stinson, Cha.	30	54	1.80
McConnell Serio, Cle	28	49	1.75
Braxton, Cle.	30	51	1.70
Brown, Det.	30	51	1.70

BLOCKS PER GAME

	G	BLK	AVG
Dydek, Utah	30	114	3.80
Leslie, L.A.	28	60	2.14
Smith, Sac.	28	46	1.64
Bullett, Cha.	30	46	1.53
Baranova, Utah	20	30	1.50

	G	BLK	AVG
Lobo, N.Y.	30	33	1.10
Fijalkowski, Cle.	28	27	0.96
Thompson, Hou.	27	25	0.93
Brown, Was.	22	20	0.91
Rycraw, L.A.	20	18	0.90

MINUTES PER GAME

	G	MIN	AVG
Penicheiro, Sac.	30	1080	36.0
Cooper, Hou.	30	1051	35.0
Stinson, Cha.	30	1046	34.9
Hlede, Det.	27	912	33.8
Baranova, Utah	20	671	33.6
McCray, Was.	29	969	33.4
Weatherspoon, N.Y.	30	1002	33.4
Brondello, Det.	30	993	33.1
Perrot, Hou.	30	986	32.9
Nemcova, Cle.	30	972	32.4

INDIVIDUAL STATISTICS, TEAM BY TEAM

CHARLOTTE STING

Player	G	Min	FGM	FGA	Pct	FTM	FTA	Pct	Off	Def	Tot	Ast	PF	Dq	Stl	TO	Blk	Pts	Avg	Hi
Andrea Stinson	30	1046	173	414	.418	75	100	.750	29	109	138	134	72	0	54	77	15	450	15.0	25
Tracy Reid	30	966	151	310	.487	111	181	.613	60	97	157	46	59	1	40	71	12	413	13.8	22
Vicky Bullett	30	947	162	367	.441	71	86	.826	62	132	194	46	88	2	66	64	46	399	13.3	22
Rhonda Mapp	21	456	83	164	.506	45	60	.750	35	54	89	33	60	0	13	39	8	212	10.1	20
Tora Suber	30	682	58	185	.314	29	46	.630	12	41	53	86	55	1	30	44	1	181	6.0	14
Sharon Manning	30	575	59	134	.440	44	66	.667	60	106	166	30	62	0	32	43	7	162	5.4	14
Andrea Congreaves	24	372	35	81	.432	19	21	.905	18	53	71	36	37	0	11	23	5	104	4.3	23
Christy Smith	24	448	27	75	.360	17	20	.850	3	31	34	71	34	0	10	48	0	89	3.7	14
P. Johns Kimbrough	24	180	22	45	.489	18	28	.643	14	23	37	6	9	0	3	9	2	62	2.6	7
Sonia Chase	23	166	14	28	.500	6	6	1.000	5	9	14	13	16	0	5	13	0	34	1.5	8
Tia Paschal	20	110	11	37	.297	4	6	.667	4	11	15	9	12	0	8	11	0	27	1.4	5
Kelly Boucher	9	52	3	15	.200	3	4	.750	2	11	13	2	3	0	1	3	0	10	1.1	5
Charlotte	30	6000	798	1855	.430	442	624	.708	304	677	981	512	507	4	273	457	96	2143	71.4	105
Opponents	30	6000	780	1878	.415	378	529	.715	305	663	968	470	601	5	242	501	108	2051	68.4	86

3-pt. FG: Charlotte 105-377 (.279); Stinson 29-103 (.282); Reid 0-2 (.000); Bullett 4-26 (.154); Mapp 1-10 (.100); Suber 36-116 (.310); Manning 0-2 (.000); Congreaves 15-51 (.294); Chr. Smith 18-57 (.316); Paschal 1-4 (.250); Boucher 1-6 (.167); Opponents 113-381 (.297)

CLEVELAND ROCKERS

Player	G	Min	FGM	FGA	Pct	FTM	FTA	Pct	Off	Def	Tot	Ast	PF	Dq	Stl	TO	Blk	Pts	Avg	Hi
Isabelle Fijalkowski	28	806	146	267	.547	87	106	.821	59	133	192	58	115	3	17	81	27	383	13.7	25
Eva Nemcova	30	972	132	282	.468	67	75	.893	28	83	111	67	77	0	33	64	21	359	12.0	19
Janice Braxton	30	840	108	218	.495	77	102	.755	37	131	168	74	77	0	51	67	15	295	9.8	18
Merlakia Jones	30	683	109	235	.464	61	81	.753	28	67	95	39	69	0	32	52	3	286	9.5	19
S. McConnell Serio	28	882	80	176	.455	51	70	.729	8	54	62	178	48	0	49	104	5	240	8.6	19
Michelle Edwards	23	533	68	163	.417	31	50	.620	6	46	52	65	42	0	23	46	1	178	7.7	24
Rushia Brown	30	522	64	139	.460	66	85	.776	34	59	93	28	79	1	34	49	16	194	6.5	15
Adrienne Johnson	29	330	53	116	.457	13	18	.722	17	31	48	15	35	0	7	24	4	133	4.6	9
Cindy Blodgett	22	184	19	66	.288	15	24	.625	2	12	14	18	18	0	9	12	0	63	2.9	12
Tully Bevilaqua	12	126	9	16	.563	4	6	.667	2	8	10	24	14	0	12	9	2	23	1.9	7
Raegan Scott	22	167	14	38	.368	10	12	.833	5	24	29	7	24	0	3	9	5	38	1.7	10

Player	G	Min	FGM	FGA	Pct	FTM	FTA	Pct	Off	Def	Tot	Ast	PF	Dq	Stl	TO	Blk	Pts	Avg	Hi
									REBOUNDS									SCORING		
Tanja Kostic 5	30	2	3	.667	1	2	.500	1	1	2	2	2	0	0	3	0	5	1.0	5
Cleveland 30	6075	804	1719	.468	483	631	.765	227	649	876	575	600	4	270	528	99	2197	73.2	96
Opponents 30	6075	776	1835	.423	430	625	.688	327	596	923	523	620	3	309	546	101	2110	70.3	87

3-pt. FG: Cleveland 106-279 (.380); Fijalkowski 4-10 (.400); Nemcova 28-62 (.452); Braxton 2-6 (.333); Jones 7-20 (.350); McConnell Serio 29-71 (.408); Edwards 11-34 (.324); Brown 0-1 (.000); Johnson 14-33 (.424); Blodgett 10-37 (.270); Bevilaqua 1-3 (.333); Scott 0-2 (.000); Opponents 128-395 (.324).

DETROIT SHOCK

Player	G	Min	FGM	FGA	Pct	FTM	FTA	Pct	Off	Def	Tot	Ast	PF	Dq	Stl	TO	Blk	Pts	Avg	Hi
									Rebounds									Scoring		
Sandy Brondello 30	993	157	367	.428	96	104	.923	18	69	87	98	58	0	38	64	1	426	14.2	24
Korie Hlede 27	912	135	345	.391	83	103	.806	39	102	141	73	66	0	21	88	1	382	14.1	23
Cindy Brown 30	965	126	268	.470	82	114	.719	70	231	301	53	105	1	51	67	22	354	11.8	22
Razija Brcaninovic......30	695	106	204	.520	60	90	.667	54	100	154	29	86	1	9	64	26	272	9.1	25
Carla Porter 30	817	89	260	.342	48	76	.632	51	67	118	68	88	1	27	52	10	245	8.2	19
Rachael Sporn 30	535	60	147	.408	16	34	.471	51	57	108	38	58	0	8	34	12	136	4.5	12
Lynette Woodard........27	383	36	93	.387	23	40	.575	31	35	66	22	33	0	22	31	3	95	3.5	18
Gergana Branzova......26	204	29	65	.446	11	20	.550	13	29	42	7	42	0	3	21	4	69	2.7	11
Rhonda Blades 29	340	20	78	.256	14	29	.483	5	27	32	41	47	0	12	41	1	66	2.3	11
Tajama Abraham........12	44	5	14	.357	8	15	.533	2	5	7	0	8	0	2	5	1	18	1.5	5
Aneta Kausaite 10	58	5	20	.250	4	7	.571	8	3	11	1	4	0	3	3	0	14	1.4	5
Mfon Udoka 3	25	1	6	.167	2	4	.500	1	2	3	0	3	0	0	1	0	4	1.3	4
Angie Hamblin 6	29	2	8	.250	1	2	.500	2	5	7	2	4	0	1	7	0	6	1.0	3
Detroit 30	6000	771	1875	.411	448	638	.702	345	732	1077	432	602	3	197	490	81	2087	69.6	85
Opponents 30	6000	768	1869	.411	429	602	.713	282	667	949	445	635	8	249	447	114	2078	69.3	96

3-pt. FG: Detroit 97-300 (.323); Brondello 16-44 (.364); Hlede 29-74 (.392); Brown 20-61 (.328); Porter 19-63 (.302); Branzova 0-4 (.000); Blades 12-50 (.240); Kausaite 0-2 (.000); Hamblin 1-2 (.500); Opponents 113-375 (.301).

HOUSTON COMETS

Player	G	Min	FGM	FGA	Pct	FTM	FTA	Pct	Off	Def	Tot	Ast	PF	Dq	Stl	TO	Blk	Pts	Avg	Hi
									REBOUNDS									SCORING		
Cynthia Cooper 30	1051	203	455	.446	210	246	.854	25	85	110	131	65	0	48	95	11	680	22.7	34
Sheryl Swoopes 29	937	173	405	.427	71	86	.826	39	110	149	62	42	0	72	58	14	453	15.6	28
Tina Thompson 27	874	121	289	.419	63	74	.851	65	127	192	24	89	0	31	47	25	342	12.7	23
Kim Perrot 30	986	88	218	.404	49	70	.700	17	75	92	142	70	0	84	82	0	254	8.5	22
Janeth Arcain 30	657	83	195	.426	34	45	.756	43	65	108	26	48	0	25	38	3	205	6.8	14
Monica Lamb 30	649	66	122	.541	29	42	.690	62	80	142	9	87	3	24	27	21	161	5.4	16
Yolanda Moore 30	533	32	71	.451	33	41	.805	32	54	86	10	54	0	26	20	0	98	3.3	10
Amaya Valdemoro......16	61	8	16	.500	12	17	.706	2	8	10	7	8	0	7	17	1	30	1.9	10
Tammy Jackson(*) 19	160	8	21	.381	8	11	.727	6	15	21	6	31	0	4	14	5	24	1.3	6
Tammy Jackson(†) 21	174	10	24	.417	8	13	.615	7	18	25	6	34	0	4	14	5	28	1.3	6
Tiffany Woosley.........18	96	7	23	.304	5	7	.714	3	4	7	9	9	0	8	13	0	22	1.2	8
Nyree Roberts............14	55	6	7	.857	4	7	.571	3	7	10	2	3	0	1	4	0	16	1.1	9
Karen Booker 1	2	0	1	.000	0	0	---	0	0	0	0	0	0	1	0	0	0	0.0	0
Wanda Guyton 1	14	0	1	.000	0	0	---	0	0	0	0	4	0	1	2	1	0	0.0	0
Houston 30	6075	795	1824	.436	518	646	.802	297	630	927	428	510	3	332	435	81	2285	76.2	110
Opponents 30	6075	729	1803	.404	340	470	.723	324	630	954	450	637	6	206	560	102	1908	63.6	74

3-pt. FG: Houston 177-523 (.338); Cooper 64-160 (.400); Swoopes 36-100 (.360); Thompson 37-103 (.359); Perrot 29-108 (.269); Arcain 5-33 (.152); Moore 1-2 (.500); Valdemoro 2-5 (.400); Woosley 3-12 (.250); Opponents 110-369 (.298).

LOS ANGELES SPARKS

Player	G	Min	FGM	FGA	Pct	FTM	FTA	Pct	Off	Def	Tot	Ast	PF	Dq	Stl	TO	Blk	Pts	Avg	Hi
									REBOUNDS									SCORING		
Lisa Leslie 28	898	202	423	.478	136	177	.768	77	208	285	70	121	3	42	102	60	549	19.6	30

					REBOUNDS										SCORING		
Player	G	Min	FGM	FGA	Pct	FTM	FTA	Pct	Off	Def	Tot	Ast	PF	Dq	Stl	TO	Blk	Pts	Avg	Hi
Tamecka Dixon	22	710	124	283	.438	88	113	.779	13	43	56	54	67	2	24	57	8	357	16.2	26
Penny Toler	30	945	145	349	.415	55	74	.743	37	69	106	143	77	2	32	101	3	370	12.3	22
Mwadi Mabika	29	710	87	257	.339	30	43	.698	29	98	127	44	73	0	30	37	9	237	8.2	17
Haixia Zheng	6	98	20	32	.625	5	7	.714	8	18	26	3	11	0	0	6	1	45	7.5	19
Pamela McGee	30	570	80	183	.437	43	70	.614	62	83	145	13	104	0	23	54	24	203	6.8	18
A.a VanEmbricqs	28	470	43	89	.483	8	16	.500	34	41	75	16	57	0	24	19	9	94	3.4	9
Allison Feaster	3	41	3	14	.214	2	2	1.000	1	1	2	3	10	0	2	4	0	10	3.3	5
Erin Alexander(‡)	8	73	7	22	.318	2	2	1.000	8	7	15	6	11	0	2	7	0	22	2.8	10
Katrina Colleton	30	575	30	99	.303	15	18	.833	25	26	51	47	44	0	18	29	11	80	2.7	14
Octavia Blue	30	331	26	77	.338	15	24	.625	19	30	49	10	41	0	13	27	3	73	2.4	13
Eugenia Rycraw	20	226	15	32	.469	16	22	.727	17	33	50	4	27	0	7	14	18	46	2.3	8
Jamila Wideman	25	329	12	43	.279	21	29	.724	5	17	22	57	28	0	10	34	1	48	1.9	9
Michelle Reed	9	49	3	11	.273	7	12	.583	2	9	11	2	4	0	2	6	1	14	1.6	7
Los Angeles	30	6025	797	1914	.416	443	609	.727	337	683	1020	472	675	7	229	511	148	2148	71.6	89
Opponents	30	6025	780	1898	.411	490	693	.707	337	663	1000	522	603	4	244	481	109	2169	72.3	92

3-pt. FG: Los Angeles 111-335 (.331); Leslie 9-23 (.391); Dixon 21-59 (.356); Toler 25-60 (.417); Mabika 33-107 (.308); McGee 0-4 (.000); Feaster 2-10 (.200); Alexander(‡) 6-16 (.375); Colleton 5-19 (.263); Blue 6-21 (.286); Wideman 3-12 (.250); Reed 1-4 (.250); Opponents 119-372 (.320)

NEW YORK LIBERTY

					REBOUNDS										SCORING		
Player	G	Min	FGM	FGA	Pct	FTM	FTA	Pct	Off	Def	Tot	Ast	PF	Dq	Stl	TO	Blk	Pts	Avg	Hi
Sophia Witherspoon	30	898	144	359	.401	92	117	.786	33	58	91	57	54	0	40	73	4	413	13.8	26
Vickie Johnson	30	905	146	327	.446	63	82	.768	44	70	114	74	70	1	31	45	7	376	12.5	27
Rebecca Lobo	30	875	136	281	.484	66	93	.710	70	137	207	44	98	1	17	67	33	350	11.7	22
Kym Hampton	30	745	98	217	.452	78	109	.716	53	128	181	26	90	1	33	62	15	274	9.1	22
T. Weatherspoon	30	1002	73	188	.388	42	69	.609	20	100	120	191	85	0	100	96	0	204	6.8	15
Kisha Ford	30	471	60	138	.435	25	40	.625	23	14	37	23	68	0	32	16	2	147	4.9	19
Sue Wicks	30	444	46	107	.430	36	45	.800	40	43	83	36	66	0	16	48	10	128	4.3	12
Trena Trice	10	77	7	17	.412	7	11	.636	7	11	18	1	12	0	0	7	3	21	2.1	5
Albena Branzova	11	94	9	25	.360	3	4	.750	6	10	16	5	12	0	3	12	1	23	2.1	5
Coquese Washington	28	226	15	51	.294	18	26	.692	5	21	26	44	31	0	17	37	0	53	1.9	7
Elisabeth Cebrian	22	187	15	35	.429	8	14	.571	12	15	27	8	32	0	1	20	7	38	1.7	6
Alicia Thompson	19	126	9	39	.231	12	19	.632	7	17	24	4	12	0	1	8	2	31	1.6	7
New York	30	6050	758	1784	.425	450	629	.715	320	624	944	513	630	3	291	501	84	2058	68.6	92
Opponents	30	6050	709	1693	.419	445	625	.712	272	620	892	420	610	4	261	538	81	1966	65.5	82

3-pt. FG: New York 92-281 (.327); Witherspoon 33-96 (.344); Johnson 21-56 (.375); Lobo 12-39 (.308); Hampton 0-1 (.000); Weatherspoon 16-49 (.327); Ford 2-11 (.182); Wicks 0-3 (.000); Branzova 2-4 (.500); Washington 5-21 (.238); Thompson 1-1 (1.000); Opponents 103-325 (.317)

PHOENIX MERCURY

					REBOUNDS										SCORING		
Player	G	Min	FGM	FGA	Pct	FTM	FTA	Pct	Off	Def	Tot	Ast	PF	Dq	Stl	TO	Blk	Pts	Avg	Hi
Jennifer Gillom	30	962	228	492	.463	137	195	.703	62	157	219	42	94	1	50	89	10	624	20.8	36
Bridget Pettis	30	849	113	300	.377	77	89	.865	34	69	103	62	75	0	29	62	9	338	11.3	23
Michelle Griffiths	30	779	93	184	.505	78	98	.796	45	88	133	41	48	0	44	52	5	275	9.2	18
Michele Timms	30	934	71	223	.318	34	49	.694	18	56	74	158	76	0	38	69	4	207	6.9	15
Umeki Webb	30	846	59	161	.366	39	59	.661	47	69	116	92	105	2	47	41	21	161	5.4	15
Marlies Askamp	26	319	49	104	.471	41	62	.661	36	49	85	12	45	0	12	22	7	139	5.3	13
Brandy Reed	24	254	50	95	.526	22	31	.710	36	42	78	20	30	0	18	33	7	124	5.2	13
Toni Foster	16	218	28	60	.467	23	30	.767	10	20	30	19	20	0	14	15	5	79	4.9	14
Andrea Kuklova	29	340	38	95	.400	20	36	.556	19	18	37	31	40	0	18	40	4	97	3.3	10
Maria Stepanova	20	130	26	61	.426	14	22	.636	17	21	38	7	29	0	3	9	11	66	3.3	15
Pauline Jordan(‡)	6	30	5	8	.625	5	7	.714	1	4	5	4	4	0	0	1	0	15	2.5	9
Kristi Harrower	30	355	19	52	.365	21	28	.750	2	19	21	52	25	0	15	31	3	70	2.3	7

Player	G	Min	FGM	FGA	Pct	FTM	FTA	Pct	REBOUNDS Off	Def	Tot	Ast	PF	Dq	Stl	TO	Blk	SCORING Pts	Avg	Hi
Mikiko Hagiwara	10	59	8	21	.381	2	3	.667	0	2	2	3	4	0	0	5	0	22	2.2	8
Tiffani Johnson(*)	0	0	0	0	---	0	0	---	0	0	0	0	0	0	0	0	0	0	---	--
Tiffani Johnson(†)	6	32	0	6	.000	2	4	.500	3	7	10	0	5	0	2	3	0	2	0.3	1
Phoenix	30	6075	787	1856	.424	513	709	.724	327	614	941	543	595	3	288	483	86	2217	73.9	96
Opponents	30	6075	758	1747	.434	432	601	.719	298	643	941	406	664	9	242	581	96	2025	67.5	90

3-pt. FG: Phoenix 130-405 (.321); Gillom 31-82 (.378); Pettis 35-123 (.285); Griffiths 11-23 (.478); Timms 31-104 (.298); Webb 4-14 (.286); Reed 2-8 (.250); Kuklova 1-7 (.143); Harrower 11-32 (.344); Hagiwara 4-12 (.333); Opponents 77-244 (.316)

SACRAMENTO MONARCHS

Player	G	Min	FGM	FGA	Pct	FTM	FTA	Pct	REBOUNDS Off	Def	Tot	Ast	PF	Dq	Stl	TO	Blk	SCORING Pts	Avg	Hi
Latasha Byears	30	828	181	400	.453	61	92	.663	85	114	199	29	121	4	43	71	13	427	14.2	28
R. Bolton-Holifield	5	133	17	58	.293	17	28	.607	5	6	11	6	12	0	6	7	0	55	11.0	17
Tangela Smith	28	707	113	279	.405	40	54	.741	45	84	129	31	78	0	17	46	46	271	9.7	26
Adia Barnes	29	619	88	223	.395	29	39	.744	35	49	84	22	70	1	14	53	10	219	7.6	24
Linda Burgess	30	692	90	189	.476	45	59	.763	53	93	146	28	81	0	42	61	11	226	7.5	33
Lady Grooms	30	792	75	154	.487	63	94	.670	37	43	80	48	35	0	20	52	3	214	7.1	16
Ticha Penicheiro	30	1080	55	165	.333	70	109	.642	13	128	141	224	90	1	67	116	3	190	6.3	14
Franthea Price	26	379	43	115	.374	13	18	.722	7	37	44	35	29	0	20	32	2	127	4.9	14
Rehema Stephens	8	81	11	41	.268	2	4	.500	7	3	10	4	8	0	2	11	0	26	3.3	7
Pauline Jordan(*)	18	247	21	61	.344	17	28	.607	14	30	44	16	44	1	14	24	12	59	3.3	8
Pauline Jordan(†)	24	277	26	69	.377	22	35	.629	15	34	49	20	48	1	14	25	12	74	3.1	9
Nadine Domond	9	92	10	33	.303	4	4	1.000	6	3	9	9	13	0	7	11	1	27	3.0	7
Bridgette Gordon	22	253	24	63	.381	9	16	.563	11	19	30	9	27	0	8	30	0	57	2.6	12
Quacy Barnes	17	90	6	15	.400	4	11	.364	5	3	8	2	20	0	1	9	6	16	0.9	4
Tiffani Johnson(‡)	6	32	0	6	.000	2	4	.500	3	7	10	0	5	0	2	3	0	2	0.3	1
Sacramento	30	6025	734	1802	.407	376	560	.671	326	619	945	463	633	7	263	533	107	1916	63.9	82
Opponents	30	6025	733	1752	.418	509	674	.755	307	646	953	493	556	5	239	500	134	2082	69.4	88

3-pt. FG: Sacramento 72-277 (.260); Byears 4-18 (.222); Bolton-Holifield 4-26 (.154); Smith 5-14 (.357); A. Barnes 14-47 (.298); Burgess 1-8 (.125); Gordon 0-8 (.000); Hardmon 1-6 (.167); Penicheiro 10-43 (.233); Price 28-78 (.359); Stephens 2-12 (.167); Jordan(*) 0-1 (.000); Jordan(†) 0-1 (.000); Domond 3-16 (.188); Opponents 107-366 (.292)

UTAH STARZZ

Player	G	Min	FGM	FGA	Pct	FTM	FTA	Pct	REBOUNDS Off	Def	Tot	Ast	PF	Dq	Stl	TO	Blk	SCORING Pts	Avg	Hi
Wendy Palmer	28	761	145	307	.472	81	124	.653	70	116	186	30	75	1	18	56	5	377	13.5	31
Elena Baranova	20	671	92	219	.420	59	71	.831	61	125	186	70	44	1	21	55	30	258	12.9	22
Malgorzata Dydek	30	839	146	303	.482	93	127	.732	41	186	227	53	126	3	14	108	114	386	12.9	27
Kim Williams	30	543	91	223	.408	36	49	.735	24	34	58	46	74	1	43	66	6	227	7.6	19
Tammi Reiss	22	477	54	134	.403	19	29	.655	14	25	39	48	32	0	11	25	1	143	6.5	17
Chantel Tremitiere	28	709	48	132	.364	41	54	.759	13	49	62	102	53	0	22	42	2	155	5.5	16
LaTonya Johnson	28	490	58	145	.400	21	34	.618	14	40	54	20	42	0	11	42	1	151	5.4	15
O. Scott-Richardson	29	466	58	135	.430	37	65	.569	37	48	85	22	78	2	24	49	10	154	5.3	15
Fran Harris	18	353	28	79	.354	10	12	.833	14	25	39	30	33	0	13	17	1	71	3.9	10
Dena Head	30	467	36	85	.424	23	33	.697	14	38	52	37	40	0	30	44	0	108	3.6	13
Tricia Bader	22	206	16	53	.302	4	8	.500	0	10	10	20	34	1	13	26	1	46	2.1	10
Erin Alexander(*)	12	68	5	22	.227	2	2	1.000	0	3	3	3	7	0	1	5	0	17	1.4	6
Erin Alexander(†)	20	141	12	44	.273	4	4	1.000	8	10	18	9	18	0	3	12	0	39	2.0	10
Utah	30	6050	777	1837	.423	426	608	.701	302	699	1001	481	638	9	221	543	170	2093	69.8	99
Opponents	30	6050	832	1942	.428	495	680	.728	336	685	1021	539	559	7	304	441	94	2294	76.5	96

3-pt. FG: Utah 113-346 (.327); Palmer 6-17 (.353); Baranova 15-48 (.313); Dydek 1-7 (.143); Williams 9-28 (.321); Reiss 16-54 (.296); Tremitiere 18-49 (.367); Johnson 14-49 (.286); Scott-Richardson 1-5 (.200); Harris 5-16 (.313); Head 13-27 (.481); Bader 10-27 (.370); Alexander(*) 5-19 (.263); Alexander(†) 11-35 (.314); Opponents 135-410 (.329)

WASHINGTON MYSTICS

Player	G	Min	FGM	FGA	Pct	FTM	FTA	Pct	Off	Def	Tot	Ast	PF	Dq	Stl	TO	Blk	Pts	Avg	Hi
Nikki McCray 29		969	191	457	.418	107	143	.748	34	51	85	90	81	2	43	125	2	512	17.7	29
A. Santos de Oliveira..16		481	63	122	.516	50	108	.463	60	69	129	1	45	1	12	55	7	176	11.0	19
Murriel Page 30		955	104	217	.479	41	65	.631	81	127	208	40	97	1	19	57	13	249	8.3	19
Penny Moore...............29		756	93	271	.343	33	46	.717	35	73	108	46	58	0	44	61	20	238	8.2	18
Heidi Burge.................30		501	81	159	.509	37	62	.597	31	69	100	26	93	2	16	73	15	201	6.7	19
Marie Chaconas 30		397	44	148	.297	26	33	.788	7	17	24	38	52	2	13	49	0	144	4.8	17
Rita Williams..............30		712	41	127	.323	38	60	.633	13	55	68	69	51	0	63	69	2	132	4.4	11
Deborah Carter 29		434	39	144	.271	21	26	.808	20	45	65	23	57	0	16	40	4	111	3.8	12
Adrienne Shuler 25		363	31	84	.369	14	17	.824	12	40	52	48	52	0	23	41	3	89	3.6	14
Tammy Jackson(‡) 2		14	2	3	.667	0	2	.000	1	3	4	0	3	0	0	0	0	4	2.0	2
La'Shawn Brown 22		272	13	37	.351	17	33	.515	17	36	53	8	62	1	10	24	20	43	2.0	4
Margo Graham 10		49	8	19	.421	3	6	.500	8	5	13	1	14	0	1	8	1	19	1.9	10
Leila Sobral.................14		71	6	25	.240	9	13	.692	3	7	10	6	14	0	5	9	2	24	1.7	6
Angela Jackson 6		36	3	6	.500	4	6	.667	3	1	4	0	7	0	1	0	2	10	1.7	4
Leslie Johnson 7		15	1	2	.500	0	0	---	0	1	1	1	6	0	0	4	0	2	0.3	2
Washington.................30		6025	720	1821	.395	400	620	.645	325	599	924	397	692	9	266	625	91	1954	65.1	88
Opponents 30		6025	876	1870	.468	551	775	.711	322	713	1035	548	597	1	334	511	104	2415	80.5	110

3-pt. FG: Washington 114-432 (.264); McCray 23-73 (.315); Page 0-2 (.000); Moore 19-92 (.207); Burge 2-7 (.286); Chaconas 30-105 (.286); Williams 12-55 (.218); Carter 12-49 (.245); Shuler 13-38 (.342); Sobral 3-11 (.273); Opponents 112-318 (.352)
(*) Statistics with this team only (†) Totals with all teams (‡) Continued season with another team

PLAYOFFS RESULTS

SEMIFINALS

Houston defeats Charlotte, 2-0

August 22	Houston 85, Charlotte 71 at Charlotte
August 24	Houston 77, Charlotte 61 at Houston

Phoenix defeats Cleveland, 2-1

August 22	Phoenix 78, Cleveland 68 at Phoenix
August 24	Cleveland 67, Phoenix 66 at Cleveland
August 25	Phoenix 71, Cleveland 60 at Cleveland

CHAMPIONSHIP

Houston defeats Phoenix, 2-1

August 27	Phoenix 54, Houston 51 at Phoenix
August 29	Houston 74, Phoenix 69 (overtime) at Houston
September 1	Houston 80, Phoenix 71 at Houston

TEAM STATISTICS

OFFENSIVE

TEAM	G	FG	FGA	PCT	FG3	FG3A	PCT	FT	FTA	PCT	OFF	DEF	REB	AST	PF	DQ	STL	TO	BLK	PTS	AVG
Hou...........5		136	301	.452	25	84	.298	70	89	.787	40	125	165	83	77	0	41	71	21	367	73.4
Phoe..........6		156	369	.423	26	73	.356	71	92	.772	58	136	194	100	116	2	44	84	19	409	68.2
Cha..........2		55	131	.420	5	27	.185	17	30	.567	18	36	54	34	38	0	18	26	6	132	66.0
Clev. 3		72	186	.387	6	24	.250	45	55	.818	38	59	97	50	59	0	26	45	6	195	65.0

DEFENSIVE

Team	FG	FGA	PCT	FG3	FG3A	PCT	FT	FTA	PCT	OFF	DEF	REB	AST	PF	DQ	STL	TO	BLK	PTS	AVG	DIFF
Hou. 130	318	.409	18	68	.265	48	74	.649	46	106	152	77	94	1	37	68	20	326	65.2	+8.2	
Phoe.......149	370	.403	19	67	.284	83	104	.798	61	128	189	98	104	0	52	84	19	400	66.7	+1.5	
Clev. 81	182	.445	13	32	.406	40	48	.833	30	66	96	57	60	1	25	42	5	215	71.7	-6.7	
Cha. 59	117	.504	12	41	.293	32	40	.800	17	56	73	35	32	0	15	32	8	162	81.0	-15.0	
AVG.'S 105	247	.425	16	52	.298	51	67	.763	39	89	128	67	73	1	32	57	13	276	68.9	---	
.............419	987		62	208		203	266		154	356	510	267	290	2	129	226	52	1103			

TEAM COMPARISONS

	Points Per Game		Field Goal Percentage		Turnovers Per Game		Rebound Percentages			Below 70 Pts.		Overtime Games		3 PTS or Less		10 PTS or More	
TEAM	OWN	OPP	OWN	OPP	OWN	OPP	OFF	DEF	TOT	OWN	OPP	W	L	W	L	W	L
Charlotte 66.0		81.0	.420	.504	13.0*	16.0*	.243	.679	.461	1	0	0	0	0	0	0	2
Cleveland 65.0		71.7	.387	.445	15.0	14.0	.365*	.663	.514*	3	1	0	0	1	0	0	2

TEAM	Points Per Game		Field Goal Percentage		Turnovers Per Game		Rebound Percentages			Below 70 Pts.		Overtime Games		3 PTS or Less		10 PTS or More	
	OWN	OPP	OWN	OPP	OWN	OPP	OFF	DEF	TOT	OWN	OPP	W	L	W	L	W	L
Houston 73.4*	73.4*	65.2*	.452*	.409	14.2	13.6	.274	.731*	.502	1	3	1	0	0	1	2	0
Phoenix 68.2	68.2	66.7	.423	.403*	14.0	14.0	.312	.690	.501	3	4	0	1	1	1	2	0
COMPOSITE; 8 games 68.9	68.9	68.9	.425	.425	14.1	14.1	.302	.698		8		1	1	2	2	4	4

* - League Leader

REBOUND PERCENTAGES

OFF. - Percentage of a given team's missed shots which that team rebounds.

DEF. - Percentage of opponents' missed shots which a given team rebounds.

TOT. - Average of offensive and defensive rebound percentages.

INDIVIDUAL PLAYOFFS STATISTICS, TEAM BY TEAM

CHARLOTTE STING

Player	G	Min	FGM	FGA	Pct	FTM	FTA	Pct	Off	Def	Tot	Ast	PF	Dq	Stl	TO	Blk	Pts	Avg	Hi
Tracy Reid	2	74	14	25	.560	4	11	.364	5	5	10	0	2	0	2	5	1	32	16.0	18
Andrea Stinson	2	71	12	27	.444	3	5	.600	2	8	10	13	9	0	4	6	0	29	14.5	16
Rhonda Mapp	2	65	12	21	.571	3	3	1.000	5	9	14	2	10	0	0	2	1	27	13.5	16
Tora Suber	2	74	9	23	.391	2	3	.667	1	1	2	10	5	0	5	7	0	23	11.5	15
Vicky Bullett	2	69	6	24	.250	4	4	1.000	5	7	12	8	6	0	6	1	3	16	8.0	10
Christy Smith	2	19	1	6	.167	1	4	.250	0	1	1	1	4	0	0	0	0	3	1.5	2
Sharon Manning	2	22	1	4	.250	0	0	---	0	4	4	0	2	0	1	3	0	2	1.0	2
Andrea Congreaves	1	6	0	1	.000	0	0	---	0	1	1	0	0	0	0	2	1	0	0.0	0
Charlotte	2	400	55	131	.420	17	30	.567	18	36	54	34	38	0	18	26	6	132	66.0	71
Opponents	2	400	59	117	.504	32	40	.800	17	56	73	35	32	0	15	32	8	162	81.0	85

3-pt. FG: Charlotte 5-27 (.185); Stinson 2-7 (.286); Mapp 0-1 (.000); Suber 3-12 (.250); Bullett 0-2 (.000); Chr. Smith 0-4 (.000); Congreaves 0-1 (.000); Opponents 12-41 (.293)

CLEVELAND ROCKERS

Player	G	Min	FGM	FGA	Pct	FTM	FTA	Pct	Off	Def	Tot	Ast	PF	Dq	Stl	TO	Blk	Pts	Avg	Hi
Isabelle Fijalkowski	3	107	17	40	.425	19	22	.864	6	21	27	4	13	0	2	5	2	53	17.7	20
Janice Braxton	3	83	10	26	.385	12	14	.857	9	10	19	6	9	0	2	7	0	32	10.7	18
Michelle Edwards	3	95	12	33	.364	4	7	.571	4	6	10	10	5	0	6	8	0	29	9.7	18
Merlakia Jones	3	65	11	24	.458	4	4	1.000	5	7	12	1	7	0	0	3	0	27	9.0	10
Eva Nemcova	3	92	9	28	.321	2	2	1.000	4	5	9	14	10	0	2	8	2	21	7.0	9
S. McConnell Serio	3	99	7	14	.500	2	3	.667	3	4	7	15	9	0	8	9	1	19	6.3	8
Raegan Scott	3	26	4	12	.333	1	1	1.000	3	4	7	0	4	0	0	0	1	9	3.0	5
Rushia Brown	3	21	2	6	.333	1	2	.500	3	0	3	0	2	0	5	5	0	5	1.7	3
Adrienne Johnson	2	12	0	3	.000	0	0	---	1	2	3	0	0	0	1	0	0	0	0.0	0
Cleveland	3	600	72	186	.387	45	55	.818	38	59	97	50	59	0	26	45	6	195	65.0	68
Opponents	3	600	81	182	.445	40	48	.833	30	66	96	57	60	1	25	42	5	215	71.7	78

3-pt. FG: Cleveland 6-24 (.250); Fijalkowski 0-1 (.000); Braxton 0-1 (.000); Edwards 1-6 (.167); Jones 1-2 (.500); Nemcova 1-5 (.200); McConnell Serio 3-7 (.429); Johnson 0-2 (.000); Opponents 13-32 (.406)

HOUSTON COMETS

Player	G	Min	FGM	FGA	Pct	FTM	FTA	Pct	Off	Def	Tot	Ast	PF	Dq	Stl	TO	Blk	Pts	Avg	Hi
Cynthia Cooper	5	198	42	93	.452	38	45	.844	4	12	16	22	10	0	9	15	5	129	25.8	29
Sheryl Swoopes	5	188	27	61	.443	14	15	.933	7	43	50	26	10	0	9	16	7	73	14.6	18
Tina Thompson	5	186	20	49	.408	11	12	.917	12	34	46	6	19	0	7	8	4	58	11.6	18
Kim Perrot	5	182	15	40	.375	5	12	.417	5	11	16	25	8	0	8	17	1	41	8.2	13
Monica Lamb	5	107	14	25	.560	1	2	.500	5	13	18	0	16	0	2	8	4	29	5.8	12
Yolanda Moore	5	61	10	15	.667	1	3	.333	6	3	9	0	9	0	4	1	0	21	4.2	10
Janeth Arcain	5	92	8	18	.444	0	0	---	1	7	8	4	5	0	2	3	1	16	3.2	6
Tammy Jackson	3	11	0	0	---	0	0	---	0	2	2	0	0	0	0	0	0	0	0.0	0
Houston	5	1025	136	301	.452	70	89	.787	40	125	165	83	77	0	41	71	21	367	73.4	85
Opponents	5	1025	130	318	.409	48	74	.649	46	106	152	77	94	1	37	68	20	326	65.2	71

3-pt. FG: Houston 25-84 (.298); Cooper 7-28 (.250); Swoopes 5-18 (.278); Thompson 7-20 (.350); Perrot 6-16 (.375); Arcain 0-2 (.000); Opponents 18-68 (.265)

PHOENIX MERCURY

Player	G	Min	FGM	FGA	Pct	FTM	FTA	Pct	Off	Def	Tot	Ast	PF	Dq	Stl	TO	Blk	Pts	Avg	Hi
									REBOUNDS									SCORING		
Jennifer Gillom	6	214	36	95	.379	22	26	.846	8	39	47	2	18	0	8	17	7	102	17.0	27
Bridget Pettis	6	183	30	60	.500	15	19	.789	10	12	22	13	11	0	11	11	2	77	12.8	27
Michelle Griffiths	6	171	28	56	.500	13	20	.650	14	25	39	14	14	0	4	10	2	74	12.3	24
Michele Timms	6	208	19	54	.352	10	10	1.000	2	18	20	31	20	1	5	21	0	54	9.0	21
Kristi Harrower	6	78	12	20	.600	0	0	---	1	5	6	7	4	0	5	4	1	27	4.5	12
Brandy Reed	6	62	9	25	.360	2	2	1.000	7	10	17	5	6	0	2	6	1	20	3.3	8
Maria Stepanova	4	22	5	11	.455	1	2	.500	3	3	6	1	8	1	1	1	1	11	2.8	6
Umeki Webb	6	158	6	21	.286	3	5	.600	6	9	15	18	23	0	1	9	2	16	2.7	7
Andrea Kuklova	4	43	4	7	.571	0	0	---	1	1	2	3	2	0	3	0	2	9	2.3	7
Marlies Askamp	5	36	4	10	.400	1	4	.250	3	9	12	1	6	0	0	3	1	9	1.8	6
Toni Foster	6	50	3	10	.300	4	4	1.000	3	5	8	5	4	0	4	2	0	10	1.7	6
Phoenix	6	1225	156	369	.423	71	92	.772	58	136	194	100	116	2	44	84	19	409	68.2	78
Opponents	6	1225	149	370	.403	83	104	.798	61	128	189	98	104	0	52	84	19	400	66.7	80

3-pt. FG: Phoenix 26-73 (.356); Gillom 8-16 (.500); Pettis 2-10 (.200); Griffiths 5-11 (.455); Timms 6-22 (.273); Harrower 3-7 (.429); Reed 0-1 (.000); Webb 1-5 (.200); Kuklova 1-1 (1.000); Opponents 19-67 (.284).

INDIVIDUAL FINALS STATISTICS, TEAM BY TEAM

HOUSTON COMETS

Player	G	Min	FGM	FGA	Pct	FTM	FTA	Pct	Off	Def	Tot	Ast	PF	Dq	Stl	TO	Blk	Pts	Avg	Hi
									REBOUNDS									SCORING		
Cynthia Cooper	3	123	27	62	.435	21	27	.778	2	6	8	13	6	0	5	11	3	79	26.3	29
Sheryl Swoopes	3	117	13	37	.351	10	11	.909	4	25	29	17	3	0	6	10	5	38	12.7	16
Tina Thompson	3	109	13	31	.419	4	4	1.000	8	14	22	1	12	0	5	3	1	34	11.3	18
Monica Lamb	3	65	10	16	.625	0	0	---	3	8	11	0	10	0	1	3	3	20	6.7	12
Kim Perrot	3	109	6	24	.250	3	6	.500	4	8	12	14	4	0	4	9	0	18	6.0	13
Janeth Arcain	3	68	6	11	.545	0	0	---	1	6	7	3	5	0	2	1	1	12	4.0	6
Yolanda Moore	3	27	2	3	.667	0	1	.000	1	0	1	0	5	0	3	1	0	4	1.3	2
Tammy Jackson	2	7	0	0	---	0	0	---	0	2	2	0	0	0	0	0	0	0	0.0	0
Houston	3	625	77	184	.418	38	49	.776	23	69	92	48	45	0	26	39	13	205	68.3	80
Opponents	3	625	75	187	.401	31	44	.705	28	70	98	43	56	1	19	42	14	194	64.7	71

3-pt. FG: Houston 13-43 (.302); Cooper 4-14 (.286); Swoopes 2-9 (.222); Thompson 4-11 (.364); Perrot 3-9 (.333); Opponents 13-41 (.317).

PHOENIX MERCURY

Player	G	Min	FGM	FGA	Pct	FTM	FTA	Pct	Off	Def	Tot	Ast	PF	Dq	Stl	TO	Blk	Pts	Avg	Hi
									REBOUNDS									SCORING		
Jennifer Gillom	3	109	14	47	.298	12	15	.800	5	20	25	1	6	0	4	8	6	43	14.3	20
Michelle Griffiths	3	99	14	28	.500	9	14	.643	7	17	24	6	7	0	3	6	1	39	13.0	24
Michele Timms	3	109	12	34	.353	5	5	1.000	2	12	14	14	11	1	1	13	0	32	10.7	21
Bridget Pettis	3	86	12	25	.480	2	5	.400	3	5	8	4	7	0	5	6	1	26	8.7	13
Kristi Harrower	3	56	10	16	.625	0	0	---	1	3	4	2	4	0	3	3	1	23	7.7	12
Umeki Webb	3	65	4	13	.308	2	3	.667	4	5	9	6	14	0	0	2	1	11	3.7	7
Andrea Kuklova	3	39	4	6	.667	0	0	---	1	1	2	3	2	0	2	0	2	9	3.0	7
Maria Stepanova	3	13	2	6	.333	1	2	.500	2	2	4	0	2	0	0	1	0	5	1.7	3
Toni Foster	3	25	2	5	.400	0	0	---	1	3	4	5	1	0	0	0	0	4	1.3	7
Brandy Reed	3	17	1	6	.167	0	0	---	2	0	2	2	1	0	1	2	1	2	0.7	2
Marlies Askamp	2	7	0	1	.000	0	0	---	0	2	2	0	1	0	0	1	1	0	0.0	0
Phoenix	3	625	75	187	.401	31	44	.705	28	70	98	43	56	1	19	42	14	194	64.7	71
Opponents	3	625	77	184	.418	38	49	.776	23	69	92	48	45	0	26	39	13	205	68.3	80

3-pt. FG: Phoenix 13-41 (.317); Gillom 3-8 (.375); Griffiths 2-6 (.333); Timms 3-15 (.200); Pettis 0-2 (.000); Harrower 3-6 (.500); Webb 1-3 (.333); Kuklova 1-1 (1.000); Opponents 13-43 (.302).

1997 SEASON IN REVIEW

Front Row (l. to. r.) - Fran Harris, Kim Perrot, Tina Thompson, Wanda Guyton, Cynthia Cooper, Janeth Arcain, Sheryl Swoopes. Back Row (l. to r.) - Assistant Coach Kevin Cook, Equipment Manager Stacey Johnson, Assistant Coach Peggie Gillom, Nykeshia Henderson, Racquel Spurlock, Tammy Jackson, Catarina Pollini, Yolanda Moore, Pietra Gay, Tiffany Woosley, Trainer Michelle T. Leget, Head Coach Van Chancellor.

FINAL STANDINGS

EASTERN CONFERENCE

Team	CHA	CLE	HOU	LA	NY	PHO	SAC	UTA	W	L	PCT	GB	Last-10	Streak
HOU	3	2	--	3	1	3	3	3	18	10	.643	-	7-3	Lost 2
NY	2	3	3	2	--	2	3	2	17	11	.607	1	3-7	Won 1
CHA	--	2	1	3	2	2	2	3	15	13	.536	3	5-5	Won 1
CLE	2	--	2	2	1	2	2	4	15	13	.536	3	5-5	Lost 1

WESTERN CONFERENCE

Team	CHA	CLE	HOU	LA	NY	PHO	SAC	UTA	W	L	PCT	GB	Last-10	Streak
PHO	2	2	1	2	2	--	4	3	16	12	.571	-	7-3	Won 3
LA	1	2	1	--	2	2	3	3	14	14	.500	2	6-4	Lost 1
SAC	2	2	1	1	1	0	--	3	10	18	.357	6	5-5	Won 1
UTA	1	0	1	1	2	1	1	--	7	21	.250	9	2-8	Lost 2

TEAM STATISTICS

OFFENSIVE

TEAM	G	FG	FGA	PCT	FG3	FG3A	PCT	FT	FTA	PCT	OFF	DEF	REB	AST	PF	DQ	STL	TO	BLK	PTS	AVG
L.A.	28	794	1782	.446	65	242	.269	419	620	.676	290	683	973	495	601	6	259	528	138	2072	74.0
Hou.........	28	700	1660	.422	169	485	.348	441	592	.745	316	543	859	389	535	1	311	492	67	2010	71.8
Clev.	28	725	1633	.444	65	177	.367	450	623	.722	267	624	891	456	514	8	256	526	86	1965	70.2
Phoe.......	28	660	1768	.373	134	436	.307	484	634	.763	322	599	921	437	570	4	343	475	80	1938	69.2
N.Y.	28	707	1715	.412	93	339	.274	404	607	.666	320	600	920	484	556	4	289	536	116	1911	68.3
Sac.........	28	704	1732	.406	101	345	.293	393	536	.733	341	538	879	404	593	14	263	562	60	1902	67.9
Cha.........	28	719	1651	.435	110	321	.343	337	487	.692	279	635	914	485	465	0	219	496	116	1885	67.3
Utah........	28	666	1781	.374	106	349	.304	371	528	.703	339	612	951	425	567	4	252	520	123	1809	64.6

DEFENSIVE

Team	FG	FGA	PCT	FG3	FG3A	PCT	FT	FTA	PCT	OFF	DEF	REB	AST	PF	DQ	STL	TO	BLK	PTS	AVG	DIFF
Phoe.......	670	1622	.413	89	313	.284	397	589	.674	275	649	924	408	598	11	243	599	114	1826	65.2	+4.0
Hou.	679	1630	.417	91	305	.298	384	545	.705	296	557	853	405	558	4	237	537	102	1833	65.5	+6.3
N.Y.	661	1690	.391	106	320	.331	416	564	.738	327	604	931	397	563	3	278	570	87	1844	65.9	+2.4
Cha.	686	1707	.402	118	366	.322	359	513	.700	288	597	885	432	488	4	276	464	72	1849	66.0	+1.3
Clev.	709	1715	.413	122	356	.343	375	533	.704	306	563	869	464	599	6	303	494	96	1915	68.4	+1.8
L.A.	719	1812	.397	95	343	.277	477	649	.735	323	597	920	457	575	3	287	505	82	2010	71.8	+2.2
Utah	776	1808	.429	115	376	.306	436	606	.719	328	680	1008	498	501	6	278	458	119	2103	75.1	-10.5
Sac.........	775	1738	.446	107	315	.340	455	628	.725	331	587	918	514	519	4	290	508	114	2112	75.4	-7.5
AVG.'S	709	1715	.414	105	337	.313	412	578	.713	309	604	914	447	550	5	274	517	98	1937	69.2	---
....	5675	13722		843	2694		3299	4627		2474	4834	7308	3575	4401	41	2192	4135	786	15492		

TEAM COMPARISONS

TEAM	Points Per Game		Field Goal Percentage		Turnovers Per Game		Rebound Percentages			Below 70 Pts.		Overtime Games		3 PTS or Less		10 PTS or More	
	OWN	OPP	OWN	OPP	OWN	OPP	OFF	DEF	TOT	OWN	OPP	W	L	W	L	W	L
Charlotte	67.3	66.0	.435	.402	17.7	16.6	.318	.688*	.503	16	16	0	0	2	2	11	9
Cleveland	70.2	68.4	.444	.413	18.8	17.6	.322	.671	.496	11	15	0	2	2	2	11	7
Houston	71.8	65.5	.422	.417	17.6	19.2	.362	.647	.505	8	19	1	1	1	3	13	3
Los Angeles	74.0*	71.8	.446*	.397	18.9	18.0	.327	.679	.503	9	12	2	2	3	2	9	7
New York	68.3	65.9	.412	.391*	19.1	20.4	.346	.647	.497	16	18	3	0	3	3	9	5
Phoenix	69.2	65.2*	.373	.413	17.0*	21.4*	.332	.685	.508*	15	19	2	1	1	3	10	4
Sacramento	67.9	75.4	.406	.446	20.1	18.1	.367*	.619	.493	16	8	0	2	1	0	5	16
Utah	64.6	75.1	.374	.429	18.6	16.4	.333	.651	.492	21	5	1	1	2	0	2	19
COMPOSITE; 112 games																	
....	69.2	69.2	.414	.414	18.5	18.5	.339	.661			112	9	9	15	15	70	70

* - League Leader

REBOUND PERCENTAGES

OFF. - Percentage of a given team's missed shots which that team rebounds.

DEF. - Percentage of opponents' missed shots which a given team rebounds.

TOT. - Average of offensive and defensive rebound percentages.

SCORING AVERAGE

	G	FG	FT	PTS	AVG
Cooper, Hou.	28	191	172	621	22.2
Bolton-Holifield, Sac.	23	164	53	447	19.4
Leslie, L.A.	28	160	113	445	15.9
Palmer, Utah	28	157	117	443	15.8
Gillom, Pho.	28	163	94	440	15.7
Stinson, Cha.	28	177	60	439	15.7
Witherspoon, N.Y.	28	140	83	407	14.5
Nemcova, Cle.	28	138	71	384	13.7
Thompson, Hou.	28	133	67	370	13.2
Toler, L.A.	28	144	73	368	13.1
Gordon, Sac.	28	135	84	365	13.0
Bullett, Cha.	28	145	62	359	12.8
Pettis, Pho.	28	107	97	352	12.6
Lobo, N.Y.	28	133	64	348	12.4
Baranova, Utah	28	129	43	341	12.2
Timms, Pho.	27	99	79	326	12.1
Fijalkowski, Cle.	28	125	81	332	11.9
Dixon, L.A.	27	115	68	320	11.9
Mapp, Cha.	28	120	82	326	11.6
Braxton, Cle.	25	88	106	287	11.5

REBOUNDS PER GAME

	G	OFF	DEF	TOT	AVG
Leslie, L.A.	28	63	203	266	9.5
Palmer, Utah	28	76	149	225	8.0
Braxton, Cle.	25	38	151	189	7.6
Baranova, Utah	28	56	151	207	7.4
Lobo, N.Y.	28	62	141	203	7.3
Byears, Sac.	28	87	106	193	6.9
Thompson, Hou.	28	67	117	184	6.6
Bullett, Cha.	28	66	112	178	6.4
Foster, Pho.	28	64	108	172	6.1
Bolton-Holifield, Sac	23	31	103	134	5.8
Hampton, N.Y.	28	52	111	163	5.8
Fijalkowski, Cle.	28	62	94	156	5.6
Stinson, Cha.	28	48	107	155	5.5
Mapp, Cha.	28	53	101	154	5.5
Guyton, Hou.	25	76	60	136	5.4
Gillom, Pho.	28	45	106	151	5.4
Askamp, Pho.	28	66	80	146	5.2
Gordon, Sac.	28	67	68	135	4.8
Congreaves, Cha.	28	40	93	133	4.8
McGee, Sac.	27	54	66	120	4.4

ASSISTS PER GAME

	G	AST	AVG
Weatherspoon, N.Y.	28	172	6.1
Toler, L.A.	28	143	5.1
Timms, Pho.	27	137	5.1
Tremitiere, Sac.	28	135	4.8
Cooper, Hou.	28	131	4.7
Edwards, Cle.	20	89	4.5
Stinson, Cha.	28	124	4.4
Wideman, L.A.	28	103	3.7
Perrot, Hou.	28	88	3.1
Reiss, Utah	28	87	3.1
Gordon, Sac.	28	78	2.8
Pettis, Pho.	28	78	2.8
Levesque, Cha.	27	75	2.8
Leslie, L.A.	28	74	2.6
Bolton-Holifield, Sac.	23	59	2.6
Johnson, N.Y.	26	66	2.5
Fijalkowski, Cle.	28	68	2.4
Webb, Pho.	28	68	2.4
3 tied			2.4

FIELD GOAL PCT.

	FG	FGA	PCT
Zheng, L.A.	110	178	.618
Fijalkowski, Cle.	125	246	.508
Mapp, Cha.	120	244	.492
Nemcova, Cle.	138	292	.473
Hampton, N.Y.	99	210	.471
Cooper, Hou.	191	406	.470
Foster, Pho.	94	201	.468
McGee, Sac.	102	222	.459
Byears, Sac.	96	209	.459
Dixon, L.A.	115	252	.456

3-PT FIELD GOAL PCT.

	3FG	3GA	PCT
Nemcova, Cle.	37	85	.435
Dixon, L.A.	22	52	.423
Cooper, Hou.	67	162	.414
Suber, Cha.	23	58	.397
Baranova, Utah	40	106	.377
Thompson, Hou.	37	100	.370
Witherspoon, N.Y.	44	126	.349
Levesque, Cha.	23	66	.348
Timms, Pho.	49	142	.345
Bolton-Holifield, Sa	66	192	.344

FREE THROW PCT.

	FT	FTA	PCT
Pettis, Pho.	97	108	.898
Arcain, Hou.	76	85	.894
Cooper, Hou.	172	199	.864
Nemcova, Cle.	71	83	.855
Head, Utah	38	45	.844
Toler, L.A.	73	87	.839
Thompson, Hou.	67	80	.838
Fijalkowski, Cle.	81	103	.786
Gordon, Sac.	84	107	.785
Gillom, Pho.	94	121	.777

STEALS PER GAME

	G	STL	AVG
Weatherspoon, N.Y.	28	85	3.04
Timms, Pho.	27	71	2.63
Perrot, Hou.	28	69	2.46
Webb, Pho.	28	68	2.43
Bolton-Holifield, Sa.	23	54	2.35
Cooper, Hou.	28	59	2.11
Bullett, Cha.	28	54	1.93
Tremitiere, Sac.	28	54	1.93
Foster, Pho.	28	53	1.89
Dixon, L.A.	27	49	1.81

BLOCKS PER GAME

	G	BLK	AVG
Baranova, Utah	28	63	2.25
Leslie, L.A.	28	59	2.11
Bullett, Cha.	28	55	1.96
Lobo, N.Y.	28	51	1.82
Braxton, Cle.	25	28	1.12

	G	BLK	AVG
Thompson, Hou.	28	28	1.00
Foster, Pho.	28	21	0.75
Stinson, Cha.	28	21	0.75
Zheng, L.A.	28	20	0.71
Hampton, N.Y.	28	19	0.68

MINUTES PER GAME

	G	MIN	AVG
Tremitiere, Sac.	28	1051	37.5
Stinson, Cha.	28	1011	36.1
Timms, Pho.	27	966	35.8
Bolton-Holifield, Sac.	23	813	35.3
Cooper, Hou.	28	982	35.1
Gordon, Sac.	28	981	35.0
Nemcova, Cle.	28	944	33.7
Lobo, N.Y.	28	939	33.5
Palmer, Utah	28	936	33.4
Weatherspoon, N.Y.	28	924	33.0

INDIVIDUAL STATISTICS, TEAM BY TEAM

CHARLOTTE STING

Player	G	Min	FGM	FGA	Pct	FTM	FTA	Pct	Off	Def	Tot	Ast	PF	Dq	Stl	TO	Blk	Pts	Avg	Hi
Andrea Stinson	28	1011	177	396	.447	60	89	.674	48	107	155	124	55	0	43	99	21	439	15.7	29
Vicky Bullett	28	875	145	324	.448	62	80	.775	66	112	178	65	84	0	54	68	55	359	12.8	24
Rhonda Mapp	28	710	120	244	.492	82	106	.774	53	101	154	64	104	0	21	68	12	326	11.6	21
Andrea Congreaves	28	658	63	126	.500	43	56	.768	40	93	133	41	52	0	16	31	5	187	6.7	15
Sharon Manning	28	438	58	125	.464	21	50	.420	42	56	98	13	31	0	25	29	5	137	4.9	11
Penny Moore	28	539	57	159	.358	16	31	.516	15	57	72	28	35	0	16	44	11	135	4.8	13
Tora Suber	28	475	40	108	.370	28	41	.683	5	37	42	56	32	0	13	51	3	131	4.7	13
Nicole Levesque	27	622	36	98	.367	14	15	.933	5	42	47	75	47	0	21	71	3	109	4.0	12
Milica Vukadinovic	1	14	1	1	1.000	0	0	---	0	1	1	1	0	0	1	3	0	3	3.0	3
Debra Williams	10	116	11	43	.256	1	2	.500	3	10	13	9	9	0	2	6	0	27	2.7	5
S. Hopson-Shelton	6	29	7	11	.636	2	2	1.000	1	4	5	1	3	0	1	2	0	16	2.7	8
Katasha Artis	20	113	4	16	.250	8	15	.533	1	15	16	8	13	0	6	12	1	16	0.8	5
Charlotte	28	5600	719	1651	.435	337	487	.692	279	635	914	485	465	0	219	496	116	1885	67.3	87
Opponents	28	5600	686	1707	.402	359	513	.700	288	597	885	432	488	4	276	464	72	1849	66.0	81

3-pt. FG: Charlotte 110-321 (.343); Stinson 25-77 (.325); Bullett 7-23 (.304); Mapp 4-8 (.500); Congreaves 18-44 (.409); Moore 5-25 (.200); Suber 23-58 (.397); Levesque 23-66 (.348); Vukadinovic 1-1 (1.000); Williams 4-18 (.222); Artis 0-1 (.000); Opponents 118-366 (.322)

CLEVELAND ROCKERS

Player	G	Min	FGM	FGA	Pct	FTM	FTA	Pct	Off	Def	Tot	Ast	PF	Dq	Stl	TO	Blk	Pts	Avg	Hi
Eva Nemcova	28	944	138	292	.473	71	83	.855	23	87	110	67	53	0	39	78	8	384	13.7	23
Isabelle Fijalkowski	28	803	125	246	.508	81	103	.786	62	94	156	68	129	7	17	73	18	332	11.9	24
Janice Braxton	25	822	88	211	.417	106	138	.768	38	151	189	49	64	0	36	53	28	287	11.5	21
Michelle Edwards	20	622	76	170	.447	45	86	.523	13	57	70	89	40	1	34	77	3	203	10.2	17
Merlakia Jones	28	589	92	229	.402	40	56	.714	31	51	82	25	55	0	23	54	3	229	8.2	19
Lynette Woodard	28	712	87	218	.399	43	64	.672	37	79	116	67	44	0	46	69	10	217	7.8	20
Rushia Brown	28	511	64	123	.520	47	64	.734	48	65	113	20	72	0	34	27	14	175	6.3	17
Adrienne Johnson	25	194	22	59	.373	7	9	.778	8	14	22	9	12	0	5	27	1	53	2.1	11
Anita Maxwell	9	63	8	24	.333	3	8	.375	2	10	12	8	5	0	4	6	0	19	2.1	7
Tina Nicholson	24	273	18	44	.409	3	5	.600	2	8	10	42	28	0	10	28	1	48	2.0	9
Jenny Boucek	10	112	7	15	.467	4	7	.571	3	7	10	9	10	0	6	22	0	18	1.8	6

Player	G	Min	FGM	FGA	Pct	FTM	FTA	Pct	Off	Def	Tot	Ast	PF	Dq	Stl	TO	Blk	Pts	Avg	Hi
									REBOUNDS									SCORING		
Marcie Alberts.............5	30	0	2	.000	0	0	---	0	1	1	3	2	0	2	3	0	0	0.0	0
Cleveland 28	5675	725	1633	.444	450	623	.722	267	624	891	456	514	8	256	526	86	1965	70.2	95
Opponents 28	5675	709	1715	.413	375	533	.704	306	563	869	464	599	6	303	494	96	1915	68.4	87

3-pt. FG: Cleveland 65-177 (.367); Nemcova 37-85 (.435); Fijalkowski 1-4 (.250); Braxton 5-10 (.500); Edwards 6-26 (.231); Jones 5-12 (.417); Woodard 0-7 (.000); Johnson 2-4 (.500); Nicholson 9-24 (.375); Boucek 0-3 (.000); Alberts 0-2 (.000); Opponents 122-356 (.343)

HOUSTON COMETS

Player	G	Min	FGM	FGA	Pct	FTM	FTA	Pct	Off	Def	Tot	Ast	PF	Dq	Stl	TO	Blk	Pts	Avg	Hi
									REBOUNDS									SCORING		
Cynthia Cooper 28	982	191	406	.470	172	199	.864	33	78	111	131	68	0	59	109	6	621	22.2	44
Tina Thompson 28	885	133	318	.418	67	80	.838	67	117	184	32	107	1	21	62	28	370	13.2	24
Janeth Arcain 28	784	110	250	.440	76	85	.894	41	69	110	45	56	0	43	67	4	305	10.9	23
Sheryl Swoopes 9	129	25	53	.472	10	14	.714	6	9	15	7	5	0	7	4	4	64	7.1	20
Wanda Guyton 25	668	57	122	.467	38	68	.559	76	60	136	12	83	0	26	43	8	152	6.1	17
Kim Perrot 28	692	59	162	.364	15	37	.405	18	57	75	88	53	0	69	65	2	161	5.8	19
Fran Harris 25	369	37	107	.346	22	31	.710	16	40	56	25	27	0	17	29	3	104	4.2	13
Tammy Jackson 28	545	45	110	.409	25	41	.610	42	74	116	12	84	0	45	49	10	115	4.1	14
Tiffany Woosley..........26	397	29	88	.330	2	8	.250	8	20	28	29	19	0	18	30	1	76	2.9	9
Catarina Pollini 13	94	8	22	.364	6	12	.500	3	9	12	5	21	0	4	8	1	22	1.7	4
Yolanda Moore 13	93	5	20	.250	6	12	.500	6	7	13	1	9	0	1	7	0	16	1.2	4
Pietra Gay 5	12	1	2	.500	2	5	.400	0	3	3	2	3	0	1	4	0	4	0.8	2
Houston 28	5650	700	1660	.422	441	592	.745	316	543	859	389	535	1	311	492	67	2010	71.8	89
Opponents 28	5650	679	1630	.417	384	545	.705	296	557	853	405	558	4	237	537	102	1833	65.5	80

3-pt. FG: Houston 169-485 (.348); Cooper 67-162 (.414); Thompson 37-100 (.370); Arcain 9-33 (.273); Swoopes 4-16 (.250); Perrot 28-99 (.283); Harris 8-24 (.333); Jackson 0-1 (.000); Woosley 16-50 (.320); Opponents 91-305 (.298)

LOS ANGELES SPARKS

Player	G	Min	FGM	FGA	Pct	FTM	FTA	Pct	Off	Def	Tot	Ast	PF	Dq	Stl	TO	Blk	Pts	Avg	Hi
									REBOUNDS									SCORING		
Lisa Leslie 28	902	160	371	.431	113	189	.598	63	203	266	74	99	1	39	109	59	445	15.9	28
Penny Toler................28	907	144	338	.426	73	87	.839	25	69	94	143	66	3	36	107	3	368	13.1	19
Tamecka Dixon 27	715	115	252	.456	68	88	.773	22	59	81	55	76	0	49	58	5	320	11.9	25
Haixia Zheng..............28	557	110	178	.618	39	59	.661	32	91	123	17	77	0	11	46	20	259	9.3	28
Linda Burgess............28	492	73	135	.541	36	49	.735	46	71	117	9	46	0	20	47	13	183	6.5	20
Mwadi Mabika 21	325	53	136	.390	13	24	.542	22	32	54	22	48	0	23	27	6	126	6.0	12
Katrina Colleton 28	613	55	126	.437	17	30	.567	25	35	60	45	46	1	35	35	9	136	4.9	9
Heidi Burge................22	282	32	72	.444	23	45	.511	23	46	69	15	52	1	12	25	12	87	4.0	14
Jamila Wideman........28	633	25	106	.236	27	34	.794	16	41	57	103	44	0	24	51	1	84	3.0	16
Daedra Charles..........28	282	27	67	.403	10	15	.667	16	32	48	12	41	0	10	14	10	64	2.3	8
Travesa Gant...............2	13	0	1	.000	0	0	---	0	3	3	0	4	0	0	2	0	0	0.0	0
Kim Gessig 1	4	0	0	---	0	0	---	0	1	1	0	2	0	0	1	0	0	0.0	0
Los Angeles 28	5725	794	1782	.446	419	620	.676	290	683	973	495	601	6	259	528	138	2072	74.0	93
Opponents 28	5725	719	1812	.397	477	649	.735	323	597	920	457	575	3	287	505	82	2010	71.8	102

3-pt. FG: Los Angeles 65-242 (.269); Leslie 12-46 (.261); Toler 7-38 (.184); Dixon 22-52 (.423); Burgess 1-2 (.500); Mabika 7-38 (.184); Colleton 9-25 (.360); Burge 0-4 (.000); Wideman 7-36 (.194); Charles 0-1 (.000); Opponents 95-343 (.277)

NEW YORK LIBERTY

Player	G	Min	FGM	FGA	Pct	FTM	FTA	Pct	Off	Def	Tot	Ast	PF	Dq	Stl	TO	Blk	Pts	Avg	Hi
									REBOUNDS									SCORING		
Sophia Witherspoon ..28	867	140	345	.406	83	111	.748	30	54	84	64	62	0	49	77	7	407	14.5	27
Rebecca Lobo 28	939	133	354	.376	64	105	.610	62	141	203	53	73	1	26	88	51	348	12.4	27
Kym Hampton............28	663	99	210	.471	73	114	.640	52	111	163	38	68	1	39	49	19	271	9.7	21
Vickie Johnson 26	789	108	269	.401	27	35	.771	46	64	110	66	52	0	19	49	4	247	9.5	20
T. Weatherspoon 28	924	64	137	.467	65	100	.650	25	91	116	172	72	0	85	94	2	196	7.0	19
Trena Trice 28	340	51	92	.554	30	45	.667	32	36	68	2	65	0	9	40	9	134	4.8	17

Player	G	Min	FGM	FGA	Pct	FTM	FTA	Pct	Off	Def	Tot	Ast	PF	Dq	Stl	TO	Blk	Pts	Avg	Hi
									REBOUNDS									SCORING		
Kisha Ford 28		473	43	114	.377	27	44	.614	28	20	48	25	56	1	28	38	5	116	4.1	11
Sue Wicks.................28		332	38	107	.355	22	33	.667	36	58	94	29	52	0	17	46	18	100	3.6	9
Rhonda Blades 28		290	25	70	.357	13	20	.650	6	15	21	30	55	1	14	39	1	80	2.9	8
Jasmina Perazic-Gipe ..9		47	5	13	.385	0	0	---	2	9	11	4	1	0	3	7	0	10	1.1	2
C. Crumpton-Moorer 2		11	1	4	.250	0	0	---	1	1	2	1	0	0	0	1	0	2	1.0	2
New York 28		5675	707	1715	.412	404	607	.666	320	600	920	484	556	4	289	536	116	1911	68.3	80
Opponents 28		5675	661	1690	.391	416	564	.738	327	604	931	397	563	3	278	570	87	1844	65.9	87

3-pt. FG: New York 93-339 (.274); Witherspoon 44-126 (.349); Lobo 18-63 (.286); Hampton 0-1 (.000); Johnson 4-21 (.190); Weatherspoon 3-35 (.086); Trice 2-8 (.250) Ford 3-20 (.150); Wicks 2-7 (.286); Blades 17-54 (.315); Perazic-Gipe 0-3 (.000); Crumpton-Moorer 0-1 (.000); Opponents 106-320 (.331)

PHOENIX MERCURY

Player	G	Min	FGM	FGA	Pct	FTM	FTA	Pct	Off	Def	Tot	Ast	PF	Dq	Stl	TO	Blk	Pts	Avg	Hi
									REBOUNDS									SCORING		
Jennifer Gillom 28		874	163	376	.434	94	121	.777	45	106	151	21	93	0	37	58	15	440	15.7	29
Bridget Pettis 28		842	107	321	.333	97	108	.898	36	71	107	78	57	1	49	82	12	352	12.6	27
Michele Timms 27		966	99	295	.336	79	104	.760	23	76	99	137	95	0	71	80	3	326	12.1	24
Toni Foster 28		736	94	201	.468	57	81	.704	64	108	172	27	77	1	53	53	21	246	8.8	16
Marlies Askamp 28		517	70	178	.393	71	93	.763	66	80	146	23	59	0	21	46	9	211	7.5	16
Umeki Webb 28		775	47	158	.297	46	67	.687	42	75	117	68	92	2	68	55	8	141	5.0	9
Tara Williams 12		84	16	39	.410	0	0	---	1	7	8	3	9	0	3	4	0	37	3.1	9
Mikiko Hagiwara(*) 12		186	10	39	.256	5	10	.500	5	9	14	10	10	0	2	7	0	33	2.8	7
Mikiko Hagiwara(†) ...26		360	25	86	.291	9	16	.563	7	16	23	20	16	0	4	16	2	76	2.9	9
Tia Jackson 26		320	25	73	.342	21	25	.840	24	31	55	26	31	0	23	37	8	74	2.8	11
N. Lieberman-Cline 25		279	25	77	.325	8	10	.800	6	26	32	40	34	0	15	39	2	64	2.6	9
Monique Ambers........19		85	4	9	.444	6	15	.400	10	10	20	4	13	0	0	7	2	14	0.7	4
Ryneldi Becenti...........1		8	0	0	---	0	0	---	0	0	0	0	0	0	1	1	0	0	0.0	0
Molly Tuter 3		3	0	2	.000	0	0	---	0	0	0	0	0	0	0	0	0	0	0.0	0
Phoenix....................28		5675	660	1768	.373	484	634	.763	322	599	921	437	570	4	343	475	80	1938	69.2	84
Opponents 28		5675	670	1622	.413	397	589	.674	275	649	924	408	598	11	243	599	114	1826	65.2	86

3-pt. FG: Phoenix 134-436 (.307); Gillom 20-65 (.308); Pettis 41-134 (.306); Timms 49-142 (.345); Foster 1-6 (.167); Askamp 0-1 (.000); Webb 1-15 (.067); Williams 5-11 (.455); Hagiwara(*) 8-28 (.286); Hagiwara(†) 17-61 (.279); Jackson 3-8 (.375); Lieberman-Cline 6-26 (.231); Opponents 89-313 (.284)

SACRAMENTO MONARCHS

Player	G	Min	FGM	FGA	Pct	FTM	FTA	Pct	Off	Def	Tot	Ast	PF	Dq	Stl	TO	Blk	Pts	Avg	Hi
									REBOUNDS									SCORING		
R. Bolton-Holifield 23		813	164	408	.402	53	69	.768	31	103	134	59	71	3	54	58	1	447	19.4	34
Bridgette Gordon........28		981	135	312	.433	84	107	.785	67	68	135	78	58	0	39	83	9	365	13.0	23
Pamela McGee 27		691	102	222	.459	79	112	.705	54	66	120	20	113	5	27	73	14	285	10.6	23
Latasha Byears..........28		656	96	209	.459	51	69	.739	87	106	193	48	98	4	39	67	8	244	8.7	23
Chantel Tremitiere......28		1051	69	196	.352	67	90	.744	25	89	114	135	80	2	54	122	1	212	7.6	16
Judy Mosley-McAfee..12		265	22	48	.458	11	11	1.000	24	23	47	10	30	0	8	25	2	55	4.6	10
Tajama Abraham........28		422	48	126	.381	26	38	.684	32	35	67	13	70	0	12	49	12	122	4.4	13
Mikiko Hagiwara(‡) 14		174	15	47	.319	4	6	.667	2	7	9	10	6	0	2	9	2	43	3.1	9
Yvette Angel 5		90	7	16	.438	0	3	.000	2	7	9	11	6	0	4	8	1	14	2.8	6
Corissa Yasen 19		188	23	57	.404	6	12	.500	12	8	20	6	17	0	18	16	2	52	2.7	10
Laure Savasta...........14		157	11	45	.244	7	9	.778	1	5	6	12	14	0	4	21	1	33	2.4	8
Margold Clark.............5		46	3	8	.375	1	2	.500	0	6	6	1	10	0	1	2	1	7	1.4	2
Danielle Viglione 7		30	3	11	.273	0	0	---	1	3	4	1	5	0	1	0	0	7	1.0	3
Denique Graves 22		86	6	27	.222	4	8	.500	3	12	15	0	15	0	0	12	6	16	0.7	4
Sacramento 28		5650	704	1732	.406	393	536	.733	341	538	879	404	593	14	263	562	60	1902	67.9	93
Opponents 28		5650	775	1738	.446	455	628	.725	331	587	918	514	519	4	290	508	114	2112	75.4	93

3-pt. FG: Sacramento 101-345 (.293); Bolton-Holifield 66-192 (.344); Gordon 11-40 (.275); McGee 2-7 (.286); Byears 1-5 (.200); Tremitiere 7-37 (.189); Angel 0-5 (.000); Hagiwara(‡) 9-33 (.273); Yasen 0-1 (.000); Savasta 4-20 (.200); Clark 0-1 (.000); Viglione 1-4 (.250); Opponents 107-315 (.340)

UTAH STARZZ

Player	G	Min	FGM	FGA	Pct	FTM	FTA	Pct	Off	Def	Tot	Ast	PF	Dq	Stl	TO	Blk	Pts	Avg	Hi
									REBOUNDS									SCORING		
Wendy Palmer............	28	936	157	420	.374	117	173	.676	76	149	225	48	86	0	47	71	6	443	15.8	28
Elena Baranova..........	28	913	129	331	.390	43	62	.694	56	151	207	62	82	0	43	82	63	341	12.2	26
Kim Williams..............	28	608	88	229	.384	41	53	.774	34	47	81	60	83	2	38	57	7	226	8.1	17
Tammi Reiss..............	28	831	72	231	.312	42	55	.764	29	48	77	87	57	0	23	61	2	216	7.7	17
Dena Head	27	471	53	136	.390	38	45	.844	22	41	63	46	45	0	14	61	8	154	5.7	15
Lady Grooms	28	691	58	167	.347	36	55	.655	33	51	84	67	39	0	23	79	2	153	5.5	14
Deborah Carter	19	286	32	82	.390	10	14	.714	22	31	53	8	34	0	13	17	1	76	4.0	16
Greta Koss	13	268	15	29	.517	12	16	.750	12	25	37	10	15	0	9	18	4	44	3.4	12
Jessie Hicks	26	263	37	80	.463	9	16	.563	17	19	36	10	57	1	13	12	11	83	3.2	13
Karen Booker	26	321	20	60	.333	21	37	.568	34	46	80	24	62	1	24	49	15	61	2.3	8
Raegan Scott	8	43	5	13	.385	2	2	1.000	4	3	7	1	3	0	1	0	3	12	1.5	6
Megan Compain	4	19	0	3	.000	0	0	---	0	1	1	2	4	0	4	3	1	0	0.0	0
Utah	28	5650	666	1781	.374	371	528	.703	339	612	951	425	567	4	252	520	123	1809	64.6	102
Opponents	28	5650	776	1808	.429	436	606	.719	328	680	1008	498	501	6	278	458	119	2103	75.1	95

3-pt. FG: Utah 106-349 (.304); Palmer 12-48 (.250); Baranova 40-106 (.377); Williams 9-34 (.265); Reiss 30-101 (.297); Head 10-32 (.313); Hardmon 1-10 (.100); Carter 2-9 (.222); Koss 2-3 (.667); Hicks 0-1 (.000); Booker 0-3 (.000); Compain 0-2 (.000); Opponents 115-376 (.306)

(*) Statistics with this team only
(†) Totals with all teams
(‡) Continued season with another team

PLAYOFF RESULTS

SEMIFINALS			FINAL	
August 28	Houston 70, Charlotte 54 at Houston		August 30	Houston 65, New York 51 at Houston
August 28	New York 59, Phoenix 41 at Phoenix			

TEAM STATISTICS
OFFENSIVE

TEAM	G	FG	FGA	PCT	FG3	FG3A	PCT	FT	FTA	PCT	OFF	DEF	REB	AST	PF	DQ	STL	TO	BLK	PTS	AVG
Hou..........	2	45	115	.391	10	34	.294	35	49	.714	25	48	73	17	30	0	16	24	4	135	67.5
N.Y.	2	46	110	.418	2	12	.167	16	27	.593	20	57	77	28	42	0	14	34	10	110	55.0
Cha..........	1	21	55	.382	3	12	.250	9	12	.750	4	18	22	13	20	0	8	13	4	54	54.0
Phoe........	1	15	67	.224	1	11	.091	10	14	.714	14	18	32	9	17	0	11	13	3	41	41.0

DEFENSIVE

Team	FG	FGA	PCT	FG3	FG3A	PCT	FT	FTA	PCT	OFF	DEF	REB	AST	PF	DQ	STL	TO	BLK	PTS	AVG	DIFF
Hou.	44	115	.383	4	20	.200	13	22	.591	17	41	58	26	43	0	15	28	6	105	52.5	+15.0
N.Y.	37	121	.306	5	25	.200	27	39	.692	23	40	63	15	31	0	19	23	6	106	53.0	+2.0
Phoe........	23	50	.460	1	4	.250	12	17	.706	7	34	41	15	19	0	7	19	8	59	59.0	-18.0
Cha.	23	61	.377	6	20	.300	18	24	.750	16	26	42	11	16	0	8	14	1	70	70.0	-16.0
AVG.'S	32	87	.366	4	17	.232	18	26	.686	16	35	51	17	27	0	12	21	5	85	56.7	---
....	127	347		16	69		70	102		63	141	204	67	109	0	49	84	21	340		

TEAM COMPARISONS

TEAM	Points Per Game OWN	OPP	Field Goal Percentage OWN	OPP	Turnovers Per Game OWN	OPP	Rebound Percentages OFF	DEF	TOT	Below 70 Pts. OWN	OPP	Overtime Games W	L	3 PTS or Less W	L	10 PTS or More W	L
Charlotte	65.5	66.0	.422	.453	10.3*	11.0	.336*	.691	.514	2	3	0	0	0	0	1	1
Detroit	54.0	60.0*	.333	.361*	13.0	13.0	.310	.657	.483	1	1	0	0	0	0	0	0
Houston	69.0*	61.2	.394	.390	12.3	14.3	.311	.658	.484	3	5	0	0	0	1	4	1
Los Angeles	65.8	68.3	.407	.415	12.8	14.8	.326	.715*	.521*	2	2	0	0	0	0	2	2
New York	64.2	66.8	.434*	.396	13.5	10.7	.328	.665	.496	5	3	0	0	1	0	1	3
Sacramento	58.0	71.0	.348	.405	21.0	15.0*	.289	.714	.502	1	0	0	0	0	0	0	1
COMPOSITE; 11 games	65.3	65.3	.407	.407	12.8	12.8	.321	.679		14		0	0	1	1	8	8

* - League Leader
REBOUND PERCENTAGES
OFF. - Percentage of a given team's missed shots which that team rebounds.
DEF. - Percentage of opponents' missed shots which a given team rebounds.
TOT. - Average of offensive and defensive rebound percentages.

INDIVIDUAL PLAYOFFS STATISTICS, TEAM BY TEAM

CHARLOTTE STING

Player	G	Min	FGM	FGA	Pct	FTM	FTA	Pct	Off	Def	Tot	Ast	PF	Dq	Stl	TO	Blk	Pts	Avg	Hi
Andrea Congreaves	1	32	4	7	.571	2	4	.500	0	3	3	1	3	0	1	1	0	12	12.0	12
Rhonda Mapp	1	36	4	12	.333	4	4	1.000	1	6	7	3	5	0	1	2	0	12	12.0	12
Vicky Bullett	1	40	5	12	.417	0	0	---	2	7	9	2	3	0	3	3	4	10	10.0	10
Andrea Stinson	1	34	3	11	.273	2	2	1.000	0	0	0	3	4	0	0	3	0	8	8.0	8
Penny Moore	1	17	3	8	.375	1	2	.500	1	1	2	0	3	0	2	1	0	7	7.0	7
Nicole Levesque	1	30	1	2	.500	0	0	---	0	1	1	3	0	0	0	2	0	3	3.0	3
Sharon Manning	1	4	1	2	.500	0	0	---	0	0	0	0	0	1	0	1	0	2	2.0	2
Tora Suber	1	7	0	1	.000	0	0	---	0	0	0	1	2	0	1	0	0	0	0.0	0
Charlotte	1	200	21	55	.382	9	12	.750	4	18	22	13	20	0	8	13	4	54	54.0	54
Opponents	1	200	23	61	.377	18	24	.750	16	26	42	11	16	0	8	14	1	70	70.0	70

3-pt. FG: Charlotte 3-12 (.250); Congreaves 2-3 (.667); Bullett 0-1 (.000); Stinson 0-2 (.000); Moore 0-4 (.000); Levesque 1-2 (.500); Opponents 6-20 (.300)

HOUSTON COMETS

Player	G	Min	FGM	FGA	Pct	FTM	FTA	Pct	Off	Def	Tot	Ast	PF	Dq	Stl	TO	Blk	Pts	Avg	Hi
Cynthia Cooper	2	77	16	30	.533	20	27	.741	1	8	9	9	3	0	3	7	1	56	28.0	31
Tina Thompson	2	74	9	21	.429	6	10	.600	8	10	18	3	5	0	2	6	1	26	13.0	18
Janeth Arcain	2	70	9	27	.333	2	2	1.000	7	8	15	1	4	0	1	1	0	21	10.5	15
Kim Perrot	2	76	5	22	.227	3	4	.750	2	7	9	4	5	0	6	9	0	16	8.0	9
Tammy Jackson	2	60	5	8	.625	4	6	.667	4	11	15	0	7	0	4	0	1	14	7.0	7
Wanda Guyton	1	23	1	2	.500	0	0	---	2	2	4	0	4	0	0	0	0	2	2.0	2
Yolanda Moore	1	3	0	0	---	0	0	---	0	0	0	0	1	0	0	0	0	0	0.0	0
Sheryl Swoopes	2	14	0	5	.000	0	0	---	1	2	3	0	1	0	0	1	1	0	0.0	0
Tiffany Woosley	1	3	0	0	---	0	0	---	0	0	0	0	0	0	0	1	0	0	0.0	0
Houston	2	400	45	115	.391	35	49	.714	25	48	73	17	30	0	16	24	4	135	67.5	70
Opponents	2	400	44	115	.383	13	22	.591	17	41	58	26	43	0	15	28	6	105	52.5	54

3-pt. FG: Houston 10-34 (.294); Cooper 4-10 (.400); Thompson 2-5 (.400); Arcain 1-3 (.333); Perrot 3-14 (.214); Swoopes 0-2 (.000); Opponents 4-20 (.200)

NEW YORK LIBERTY

Player	G	Min	FGM	FGA	Pct	FTM	FTA	Pct	Off	Def	Tot	Ast	PF	Dq	Stl	TO	Blk	Pts	Avg	Hi
Kym Hampton	2	65	10	19	.526	7	10	.700	5	22	27	1	2	0	1	3	1	27	13.5	14
Rebecca Lobo	2	68	9	21	.429	7	12	.583	5	13	18	4	8	0	0	5	4	25	12.5	16
Vickie Johnson	2	68	11	26	.423	1	2	.500	5	7	12	4	6	0	2	2	1	23	11.5	12
Sophia Witherspoon	2	65	5	18	.278	0	0	---	2	8	10	5	7	0	3	5	2	12	6.0	7
Teresa Weatherspoon	2	75	5	10	.500	0	2	.000	1	2	3	10	6	0	4	12	0	10	5.0	6
Trena Trice	2	16	4	5	.800	1	1	1.000	1	1	2	0	5	0	1	2	1	9	4.5	6

Player	G	Min	FGM	FGA	Pct	FTM	FTA	Pct	Off	Def	Tot	Ast	PF	Dq	Stl	TO	Blk	Pts	Avg	Hi
									REBOUNDS									SCORING		
Sue Wicks...................2	11	2	6	.333	0	0	---	0	4	4	1	4	0	1	3	1	4	2.0	2
Rhonda Blades 1	13	0	0	---	0	0	---	0	0	0	2	1	0	0	2	0	0	0.0	0
Kisha Ford 2	19	0	5	.000	0	0	---	1	0	1	1	3	0	2	0	0	0	0.0	0
New York 2	400	46	110	.418	16	27	.593	20	57	77	28	42	0	14	34	10	110	55.0	59
Opponents 2	400	37	121	.306	27	39	.692	23	40	63	15	31	0	19	23	6	106	53.0	65

3-pt. FG: New York 2-12 (.167); Lobo 0-3 (.000); Johnson 0-1 (.000); Witherspoon 2-5 (.400); Weatherspoon 0-2 (.000); Ford 0-1 (.000); Opponents 5-25 (.200)

PHOENIX MERCURY

Player	G	Min	FGM	FGA	Pct	FTM	FTA	Pct	Off	Def	Tot	Ast	PF	Dq	Stl	TO	Blk	Pts	Avg	Hi
									REBOUNDS									SCORING		
Marlies Askamp 1	19	2	6	.333	5	5	1.000	1	1	2	1	3	0	0	0	1	9	9.0	9
Jennifer Gillom 1	31	4	11	.364	0	0	---	2	5	7	1	2	0	2	2	0	9	9.0	9
Toni Foster 1	29	3	9	.333	1	2	.500	2	3	5	1	2	0	3	1	0	7	7.0	7
Michele Timms 1	40	1	11	.091	3	5	.600	1	3	4	1	5	0	4	2	0	5	5.0	5
Umeki Webb 1	33	2	9	.222	1	2	.500	3	3	6	2	4	0	0	1	0	5	5.0	5
Bridget Pettis 1	27	2	15	.133	0	0	---	3	3	6	2	1	0	2	2	0	4	4.0	4
Mikiko Hagiwara 1	11	1	2	.500	0	0	---	0	0	0	0	0	0	3	1	2	2.0	2
Tia Jackson 1	8	0	4	.000	0	0	---	2	0	2	1	0	0	0	0	0	0	0.0	0
N. Lieberman-Cline......1	1	0	0	---	0	0	---	0	0	0	0	0	0	0	0	1	0	0.0	0
Tara Williams 1	1	0	0	---	0	0	---	0	0	0	0	0	0	0	0	0	0	0.0	0
Phoenix.......................1	200	15	67	.224	10	14	.714	14	18	32	9	17	0	11	13	3	41	41.0	41
Opponents 1	200	23	50	.460	12	17	.706	7	34	41	15	19	0	7	19	8	59	59.0	59

3-pt. FG: Phoenix 1-11 (.091); Gillom 1-3 (.333); Timms 0-2 (.000); Pettis 0-5 (.000); Hagiwara 0-1 (.000); Opponents 1-4 (.250)

INDIVIDUAL FINALS STATISTICS, TEAM BY TEAM

HOUSTON COMETS

Player	G	Min	FGM	FGA	Pct	FTM	FTA	Pct	Off	Def	Tot	Ast	PF	Dq	Stl	TO	Blk	Pts	Avg	Hi
									REBOUNDS									SCORING		
Cynthia Cooper 1	40	7	13	.538	11	15	.733	0	4	4	4	1	0	2	1	1	25	25.0	25
Tina Thompson 1	40	6	10	.600	5	8	.625	3	3	6	1	1	0	0	3	1	18	18.0	18
Kim Perrot 1	38	3	13	.231	0	0	---	2	3	5	0	3	0	3	5	0	9	9.0	9
Tammy Jackson 1	37	3	6	.500	1	2	.500	3	8	11	0	5	0	2	0	1	7	7.0	7
Janeth Arcain 1	37	3	11	.273	0	0	---	1	4	5	1	3	0	1	1	0	6	6.0	6
Yolanda Moore 1	3	0	0	---	0	0	---	0	0	0	0	1	0	0	0	0	0	0.0	0
Sheryl Swoopes 1	5	0	1	.000	0	0	---	0	0	0	0	0	0	0	0	0	0	0.0	0
Houston 1	200	22	54	.407	17	25	.680	9	22	31	6	14	0	8	10	3	65	65.0	65
Opponents 1	200	23	60	.383	4	10	.400	13	23	36	13	23	0	7	15	2	51	51.0	51

3-pt. FG: Houston 4-14 (.286); Cooper 0-2 (.000); Thompson 1-2 (.500); Perrot 3-9 (.333); Arcain 0-1 (.000); Opponents 1-8 (.125)

NEW YORK LIBERTY

Player	G	Min	FGM	FGA	Pct	FTM	FTA	Pct	Off	Def	Tot	Ast	PF	Dq	Stl	TO	Blk	Pts	Avg	Hi
									REBOUNDS									SCORING		
Kym Hampton 1	30	6	13	.462	1	4	.250	3	10	13	0	1	0	1	2	0	13	13.0	13
Vickie Johnson 1	34	6	16	.375	0	0	---	5	0	5	2	5	0	1	1	0	12	12.0	12
Rebecca Lobo.............1	34	3	8	.375	3	4	.750	1	8	9	0	3	0	0	1	1	9	9.0	9
Trena Trice 1	11	3	4	.750	0	0	---	1	0	1	0	2	0	0	1	1	6	6.0	6
Sophia Witherspoon 1	29	2	8	.250	0	0	---	1	2	3	3	4	0	0	2	0	5	5.0	5
Teresa Weatherspoon ..1	35	2	6	.333	0	2	.000	1	1	2	5	4	0	4	5	0	4	4.0	4
Sue Wicks...................1	5	1	3	.333	0	0	---	0	2	2	0	2	0	1	1	0	2	2.0	2
Rhonda Blades 1	13	0	0	---	0	0	---	0	0	0	2	1	0	0	2	0	0	0.0	0
Kisha Ford 1	9	0	2	.000	0	0	---	1	0	1	1	1	0	0	0	0	0	0.0	0
New York 1	200	23	60	.383	4	10	.400	13	23	36	13	23	0	7	15	2	51	51.0	51
Opponents 1	200	22	54	.407	17	25	.680	9	22	31	6	14	0	8	10	3	65	65.0	65

3-pt. FG: New York 1-8 (.125); Johnson 0-1 (.000); Lobo 0-1 (.000); Witherspoon 1-4 (.250); Weatherspoon 0-2 (.000); Opponents 4-14 (.286)

2006 PLAYER ACQUISITION SUMMARIES
NOVEMBER 16, 2005 - CHICAGO SKY EXPANSION DRAFT

PLAYER	WNBA TEAM
Jia Perkins	Charlotte Sting
Brooke Wyckoff	Connecticut Sun
Elaine Powell	Detroit Shock
Kiesha Brown	Houston Comets
Deanna Jackson	Indiana Fever
Laura Macchi	Los Angeles Sparks
Stacey Lovelace	Minnesota Lynx
DeTrina White	New York Liberty
Ashley Robinson	Phoenix Mercury
Chelsea Newton	Sacramento Monarchs
Bernadette Ngoyisa	San Antonio Silver Stars
Francesca Zara	Seattle Storm
Stacey Dales-Schuman	Washington Mystics

APRIL 5, 2006 - WNBA DRAFT

FIRST ROUND
1. Minnesota .... Seimone Augustus
2. Phoenix .... Cappie Pondexter
3. Charlotte .... Monique Currie
4. San Antonio .... Sophia Young
5. Los Angeles (from Washington) .... Lisa Willis
6. Chicago .... Candice Dupree
7. Minnesota (from Detroit) .... Shona Thorburn
8. Washington (from Los Angeles) .... Tamara James
9. Indiana (from New York) .... La'Tangela Atkinson
10. Charlotte (from Houston) .... Tye'sha Fluker
11. Seattle .... Barbara Turner
12. New York (from Indiana) .... Sherill Baker
13. Sacramento .... Kim Smith
14. Sacramento (from Connecticut from San Antonio) .... Scholanda Dorrell

SECOND ROUND
15. Houston (from Charlotte) .... Ann Strother*
16. San Antonio .... Shanna Zolman
17. Detroit (from Minnesota) .... Ambrosia Anderson**
18. Phoenix .... Liz Shimek*
19. Washington .... Nikki Blue
20. Chicago .... Jennifer Harris
21. Phoenix (from Detroit) .... Mistie Williams*
22. Los Angeles .... Willnett Crockett
23. New York .... Brooke Queenan
24. Houston .... Renae Camino
25. Seattle .... Dalila Eshe
26. Indiana .... Kasha Terry
27. Charlotte (from Sacramento) .... LaToya Bond
28. Connecticut .... Debbie Merrill

THIRD ROUND
29. Houston (from Charlotte) .... Tiffany Stansbury
30. San Antonio .... Khara Smith
31. Minnesota .... Megan Duffy
32. Phoenix .... Crystal Smith
33. Washington .... Mariam Sy
34. Chicago .... Kerri Gardin
35. Detroit .... Zane Teilane
36. Los Angeles .... Tiffany Porter-Talbert
37. New York .... Christelle N'Garsanet
38. Indiana (from Houston) .... Jessica Foley
39. Seattle .... Erin Grant
40. Indiana .... Marina Kuzina
41. Sacramento .... Lamisha Augustine
42. Connecticut .... Marita Payne

*—Houston traded the draft rights of Ann Strother to Phoenix in exchange for the draft rights of Liz Shimek and Mistie Williams.

**—Detroit traded the draft rights of Ambrosia Anderson and the Shock's second round pick in the 2007 WNBA Draft to Minnesota in exchange for Jacqueline Batteast and the Lynx's third round pick in the 2007 WNBA Draft.

2005 PLAYER ACQUISITION SUMMARIES
APRIL 16, 2005 - WNBA DRAFT

FIRST ROUND
1. Charlotte ....Janel McCarville
2. Indiana ....Tan White
3. Phoenix ....Sandora Irvin
4. San Antonio ....Kendra Wecker
5. Houston ....Sancho Lyttle
6. Washington ....Temeka Johnson
7. Detroit ....Kara Braxton
8. Connecticut ....Katie Feenstra*
9. Sacramento ....Kristin Haynie
10. New York ....Loree Moore
11. Minnesota ....Kristen Mann
12. Seattle ....Tanisha Wright
13. Detroit (from Washington from Los Angeles) ....Dionnah Jackson

SECOND ROUND
14. San Antonio ....Shyra Ely
15. Houston ....Roneeka Hodges
16. Indiana ....Yolanda Paige
17. Minnesota (from Charlotte) ....Jacqueline Batteast
18. Phoenix ....Angelina Williams
19. Washington ....Erica Taylor
20. Detroit ....Nikita Bell
21. Connecticut ....Erin Phillips
22. Sacramento ....Chelsea Newton
23. New York ....Tabitha Poole
24. Charlotte (from Minnesota) ....Jessica Moore
25. Seattle ....Ashley Battle
26. Los Angeles ....DeeDee Wheeler

THIRD ROUND
27. San Antonio ....Cathrine Kraayeveld
28. Houston ....Jenni Dant
29. Indiana ....Ashley Earley
30. Sacramento (from Charlotte) ....Anne O'Neil
31. Phoenix ....Jamie Carey
32. Washington ....Tashia Morehead
33. Detroit ....Jenni Lingor
34. Connecticut ....Megan Mahoney
35. Sacramento ....Cisti Greenwalt
36. New York ....Rebecca Richman
37. Minnesota ....Monique Bivins
38. Seattle ....Stephanie Blackmon
39. Los Angeles ....Heather Schreiber

*—Connecticut traded the draft rights of Katie Feenstra to San Antonio in exchange for Margo Dydek.

2004 PLAYER ACQUISITION SUMMARIES
JANUARY 6, 2004 - DISPERSAL DRAFT - CLEVELAND

1. Phoenix Mercury ....Penny Taylor
2. Washington Mystics ....Chasity Melvin
3. San Antonio Silver Stars ....LaToya Thomas
4. New York Liberty ....Ann Wauters
5. Indiana Fever ....Deanna Jackson
6. Seattle Storm ....Betty Lennox
7. Minnesota Lynx ....Helen Darling
8. Houston Comets (from Connecticut) ....Pollyanna Johns Kimbrough
9. Charlotte Sting ....Mery Andrade
10. Sacramento Monarchs ....Jennifer Butler
11. Houston Comets ....Lucienne Berthieu
12. Los Angeles Sparks ....Isabelle Fijalkowski
13. Detroit Shock ....Jennifer Rizzotti

FIRST ROUND

1. Phoenix Mercury .... Diana Taurasi
2. Washington Mystics .... Alana Beard
3. Charlotte Sting (from Indiana) .... Nicole Powell
4. Connecticut Sun (from San Antonio) .... Lindsay Whalen
5. New York Liberty .... Shameka Christon
6. Minnesota Lynx (from Seattle) .... Nicole Ohlde
7. Minnesota Lynx .... Vanessa Hayden
8. Phoenix Mercury (from Connecticut) .... Chandi Jones**
9. Indiana Fever (from Charlotte) .... Ebony Hoffman
10. Sacramento Monarchs .... Rebekkah Brunson
11. Detroit Shock (from Houston) .... Iciss Tillis
12. Los Angeles Sparks .... Christi Thomas
13. Detroit Shock .... Shereka Wright**

SECOND ROUND

14. Phoenix Mercury .... Ashley Robinson
15. Washington Mystics .... Kaayla Chones
16. Connecticut Sun (from San Antonio) .... Jessica Brungo
17. New York Liberty .... Amisha Carter
18. Charlotte Sting (from Indiana) .... Kelly Mazzante
19. Seattle Storm .... Catrina Frierson
20. Minnesota Lynx .... Tasha Butts
21. San Antonio Silver Stars (from Connecticut) .... Cindy Dallas
22. Charlotte Sting .... Jenni Benningfield
23. Detroit Shock (from Sacramento) .... Erika Valek**
24. Connecticut Sun (from Houston) .... Ugo Oha
25. Los Angeles Sparks .... Doneeka Hodges
26. Houston Comets (from Detroit) .... Lindsay Taylor*

THIRD ROUND

27. Phoenix Mercury .... Maria Villarroel*
28. Washington Mystics .... Evan Unrau
29. Connecticut Sun (from San Antonio) .... Candace Futrell
30. New York Liberty .... Cathy Joens
31. Indiana Fever .... Ieva Kublina
32. Detroit Shock (from Houston from Seattle) .... Jennifer Smith
33. Minnesota Lynx .... Amber Jacobs
34. San Antonio Silver Stars (from Connecticut) .... Toccara Williams
35. Charlotte Sting .... Jia Perkins
36. Sacramento Monarchs .... Nuria Martinez
37. Houston Comets .... Stacy Stephens
38. Minnesota Lynx (from Detroit) .... Kate Bulger

*—Houston traded the draft rights of Lindsay Taylor to Phoenix in exchange for the draft rights of Maria Villarroel.

**—Detroit traded the draft rights of Shereka Wright and Erika Valek and Sheila Lambert to Phoenix in exchange for the draft rights to Chandi Jones.

2003 PLAYER ACQUISITION SUMMARIES

APRIL 24, 2003 - DISPERSAL DRAFT - MIAMI AND PORTLAND

1. Detroit Shock .... Ruth Riley (Miami)
2. Minnesota Lynx .... Sheri Sam (Miami)
3. Cleveland Rockers .... Betty Lennox (Miami)
4. Phoenix Mercury .... Tamicha Jackson (Portland)

5.	Sacramento Monarchs	DeMya Walker (Portland)
6.	Connecticut Sun	Debbie Black (Miami)
7.	Indiana Fever	Sylvia Crawley (Portland)
8.	Washington Mystics	Jenny Mowe (Portland)
9.	Seattle Storm	Alisa Burras (Portland)
10.	Charlotte Sting	Pollyana Johns Kimbrough (Miami)
11.	New York Liberty	Elena Baranova (Miami)
12.	San Antonio Silver Stars	LaQuanda Quick (Portland)
13.	Houston Comets	Ukari Figgs (Portland)
14.	Los Angeles Sparks	Jackie Stiles (Portland)

APRIL 25, 2003 - WNBA DRAFT

FIRST ROUND
1.	Cleveland Rockers	LaToya Thomas
2.	Sacramento Monarchs	Chantelle Anderson
3.	Detroit Shock	Cheryl Ford
4.	Phoenix Mercury	Plenette Pierson
5.	Detroit Shock (from Connecticut)	Kara Lawson
6.	Indiana Fever	Gwen Jackson
7.	Washington Mystics	Aiysha Smith
8.	Seattle Storm	Jung Sun-min
9.	Charlotte Sting	Jocelyn Penn
10.	New York Liberty	Molly Creamer
11.	San Antonio Silver Stars	Coretta Brown
12.	Houston Comets	Allison Curtin

SECOND ROUND
13.	Connecticut Sun (from Detroit)	Courtney Coleman
14.	Minnesota Lynx	Teresa Edwards
15.	Cleveland Rockers	Jennifer Butler
16.	Phoenix Mercury	Petra Ujhelyi
17.	New York Liberty (from Sacramento)	Erin Thorn
18.	Minnesota Lynx (from Miami)	Jordan Adams
19.	Houston Comets (from Connecticut)	Lori Nero
20.	Indiana Fever	DeTrina White
21.	Washington Mystics	Zuzana Zirkova
22.	Seattle Storm	Suzy Batkovic
23.	Charlotte Sting	Dana Cherry
24.	New York Liberty	Sonja Mallory
25.	San Antonio Silver Stars	Ke-Ke Tardy
26.	New York Liberty (from Houston)	K.B. Sharp
27.	Los Angeles Sparks	Schuye LaRue

THIRD ROUND
28.	Detroit Shock	Syreeta Bromfield
29.	Minnesota Lynx	Carla Bennett
30.	Cleveland Rockers	Shaquala Williams
31.	Phoenix Mercury	Telisha Quarles
32.	Washington Mystics (from Sacramento)	Trish Juhline
33.	Phoenix Mercury (from Miami)	Marion Jones
34.	Connecticut Sun	Lindsey Wilson
35.	Indiana Fever	Ashley McElhiney
36.	Washington Mystics	Tamara Bowie
37.	Seattle Storm	Chrissy Floyd
38.	Houston Comets (from Charlotte)	Constance Jinks
39.	New York Liberty	Nicole Kaczmarski
40.	San Antonio Silver Stars	Brooke Armistead
41.	Houston Comets	Oksana Rakhmatulina
42.	Los Angeles Sparks	Mary Jo Noon

2002 PLAYER ACQUISITION SUMMARIES
APRIL 19, 2002 - WNBA DRAFT

FIRST ROUND
1. Seattle Storm .... Sue Bird
2. Detroit Shock .... Swin Cash
3. Washington Mystics .... Stacey Dales-Schuman
4. Washington Mystics .... Asjha Jones
5. Portland Fire .... Nikki Teasley*
6. Minnesota Lynx .... Tamika Williams
7. Charlotte Sting .... Sheila Lambert
8. Cleveland Rockers .... Deanna Jackson
9. Charlotte Sting .... Shaunzinski Gortman†
10. Houston Comets .... Michelle Snow
11. Utah Starzz .... Danielle Crockrom
12. Sacramento Monarchs .... Hamchétou Maïga
13. Indiana Fever .... Tawana McDonald
14. Utah Starzz .... LaNeishea Caufield
15. Miami Sol .... Tamara Moore
16. Los Angeles Sparks .... Rosalind Ross

SECOND ROUND
17. Indiana Fever .... Zuzi Klimesova
18. Detroit Shock .... Lenae Williams
19. Seattle Storm .... Lucienne Berthieu
20. Detroit Shock .... Ayana Walker
21. Detroit Shock .... Jill Chapman
22. Detroit Shock .... Kathy Wambe
23. Orlando Miracle .... Davalyn Cunningham
24. Cleveland Rockers .... Brandi McCain
25. Phoenix Mercury .... Tootie Shaw
26. New York Liberty .... Linda Fröhlich
27. Utah Starzz .... Andrea Gardner
28. Seattle Storm .... Felicia Ragland
29. Miami Sol .... Lindsey Yamasaki
30. Los Angeles Sparks .... Gergana Slavtcheva*
31. Cleveland Rockers .... Angie Welle
32. Los Angeles Sparks .... Jackie Higgins

THIRD ROUND
33. Washington Mystics .... LaNisha Cartwell
34. Indiana Fever .... Kelly Komara
35. Seattle Storm .... Takeisha Lewis
36. Washington Mystics .... Teresa Geter
37. Portland Fire .... Mandy Nightingale
38. Minnesota Lynx .... Lindsey Meder
39. Orlando Miracle .... Saundra Jackson
40. Phoenix Mercury .... Kayte Christensen
41. Charlotte Sting .... Edniesha Curry
42. Houston Comets .... Shondra Johnson
43. Utah Starzz .... Edmarie Lumbsley
44. Sacramento Monarchs .... Alayne Ingram
45. Miami Sol .... Jerica Watson
46. New York Liberty .... Tracy Gahan
47. Detroit Shock .... Ericka Haney
48. Los Angeles Sparks .... Rashana Barnes

FOURTH ROUND
49. Indiana Fever .... LaKeisha Taylor
50. Portland Fire .... Melody Johnson
51. Sacramento Monarchs .... Jermisha Dosty

52.	Indiana Fever	Jillian Danker
53.	Portland Fire	Monique Cardenas
54.	Minnesota Lynx	Shárron Francis
55.	Orlando Miracle	Tomeka Brown
56.	Phoenix Mercury	Amba Kongolo
57.	Charlotte Sting	Jessie Stomski
58.	Houston Comets	Cori Enghusen
59.	Utah Starzz	Jaclyn Winfield
60.	Sacramento Monarchs	Elizabeth Pickney
61.	Miami Sol	Jerkisha Dosty
62.	New York Liberty	Deedee Warley
63.	Cleveland Rockers	Marché Strickland
64.	Los Angeles Sparks	Tiffany Thompson

* — Portland traded Nikki Teasley and guard Sophia Witherspoon to Los Angeles for guards Gergana Slavtcheva and Ukari Figgs.

† — Shaunzinski Gortman was traded to Minnesota for forward Erin Buescher and center Maylana Martin.

2001 PLAYER ACQUISITION SUMMARIES
APRIL 20, 2001 - WNBA DRAFT

FIRST ROUND

1.	Seattle Storm	Lauren Jackson
2.	Charlotte Sting	Kelly Miller
3.	Indiana Fever	Tamika Catchings
4.	Portland Fire	Jackie Stiles
5.	Miami Sol	Ruth Riley
6.	Detroit Shock	Deanna Nolan
7.	Minnesota Lynx	Svetlana Abrosimova
8.	Utah Starzz	Marie Ferdinand
9.	Washington Mystics	Coco Miller
10.	Orlando Miracle	Katie Douglas
11.	Cleveland Rockers	Penny Taylor
12.	Portland Fire	LaQuanda Barksdale
13.	Phoenix Mercury	Kristen Veal
14.	Indiana Fever	Kelly Schumacher
15.	Houston Comets	Amanda Lassiter
16.	Los Angeles Sparks	Camille Cooper

SECOND ROUND

17.	Seattle Storm	Semeka Randall
18.	Charlotte Sting	Tammy Sutton-Brown
19.	Indiana Fever	Niele Ivey
20.	Portland Fire	Jenny Mowe
21.	Miami Sol	Georgia Schweitzer*
22.	Detroit Shock	Jae Kingi
23.	Minnesota Lynx	Erin Buescher
24.	Utah Starzz	Michaela Pavlickova
25.	Washington Mystics	Tamara Stocks
26.	Orlando Miracle	Brooke Wyckoff
27.	Cleveland Rockers	Jaynetta Saunders
28.	Minnesota Lynx	Janell Burse
29.	Phoenix Mercury	Ilona Korstine
30.	Sacramento Monarchs	Jackie Moore
31.	Houston Comets	Tynesha Lewis
32.	Los Angeles Sparks	Nicole Levandusky

THIRD ROUND

| 33. | Houston Comets | ShaRae Mansfield |

34.	Charlotte Sting	Jennifer Phillips
35.	Indiana Fever	Marlena Williams
36.	Portland Fire	Rasheeda Clark
37.	Miami Sol	Levys Torres
38.	Detroit Shock	Svetlana Volnaya
39.	Minnesota Lynx	Tombi Bell
40.	Utah Starzz	Shea Ralph
41.	Washington Mystics	Jamie Lewis
42.	Orlando Miracle	Jaclyn Johnson
43.	Cleveland Rockers	Angelina Wolvert
44.	Washington Mystics	Elena Karpova
45.	Phoenix Mercury	Tere Williams
46.	Sacramento Monarchs	Maren Walseth
47.	Houston Comets	Shala Crawford
48.	Los Angeles Sparks	Kelley Siemon

FOURTH ROUND

49.	Seattle Storm	Juana Brown
50.	Charlotte Sting	Reshea Bristol
51.	Indiana Fever	April Brown
52.	Portland Fire	Natasha Pointer
53.	Phoenix Mercury	Carolyn Moos
54.	Detroit Shock	Kelly Santos
55.	Minnesota Lynx	Megan Taylor
56.	Utah Starzz	Cara Consuegra
57.	New York Liberty	Taru Tuukkanen
58.	Orlando Miracle	Anne Thorius
59.	Cleveland Rockers	Erin Batth
60.	New York Liberty	Tara Mitchem
61.	Phoenix Mercury	Megan Franza
62.	Sacramento Monarchs	Katie Smrcka-Duffy
63.	Houston Comets	Kristen Clement
64.	Los Angeles Sparks	Beth Record

* — Traded to Minnesota for Marla Brumfield.

2000 PLAYER ACQUISITION SUMMARIES
DECEMBER 15, 1999 - EXPANSION DRAFT

FIRST ROUND

1.	Indiana Fever	Gordana Grubin	(Los Angeles)
2.	Seattle Storm	Edna Campbell	(Phoenix)
3.	Miami Sol	Kate Starbird	(Sacramento)*
4.	Portland Fire	Alisa Burras	(Cleveland)

SECOND ROUND

5.	Portland Fire	Sophia Witherspoon	(New York)†
6.	Miami Sol	Stephanie McCarty	(Charlotte)‡
7.	Seattle Storm	Sonja Henning	(Houston)
8.	Indiana Fever	Sandy Brondello	(Detroit)‡

THIRD ROUND

9.	Indiana Fever	Nyree Roberts	(Washington)∞
10.	Seattle Storm	Angela Aycock	(Minnesota)
11.	Miami Sol	Debbie Black	(Utah)
12.	Portland Fire	Tari Phillips	(Orlando)

FOURTH ROUND

13.	Portland Fire	Coquese Washington	(New York)†
14.	Miami Sol	Sharon Manning	(Charlotte)
15.	Seattle Storm	Nina Bjedov	(Los Angeles)
16.	Indiana Fever	Kara Wolters	(Houston)

FIFTH ROUND

17. Indiana Fever ....Rita Williams ....(Washington)
18. Seattle Storm ....Toni Foster ....(Phoenix)
19. Miami Sol...Lesley Brown ....(Detroit)
20. Portland Fire...Molly Goodenbour ....(Sacramento)

SIXTH ROUND

21. Portland Fire...Jamila Wideman ....(Cleveland)
22. Miami Sol...Yolanda Moore..(Orlando)
23. Seattle Storm ....Charmin Smith ....(Minnesota)
24. Indiana Fever ....Chantel Tremitiere ....(Utah)

* — Kate Starbird was traded with Miami's first-round draft pick (eighth overall) in the 2000 WNBA Draft to the Utah Starzz in exchange for Elena Baranova and Utah's second round pick (19th overall) in the 2000 WNBA Draft.

† — In exchange for selecting Sophia Witherspoon and Coquese Washington, Portland acquired Michele VanGorp from New York.

‡ — Stephanie McCarty was traded by Miami to Indiana for Sandy Brondello and Indiana's first-round pick (10th overall) in the 2000 WNBA Draft.

∞ — In exchange for selecting Nyree Roberts, Indiana acquired Monica Maxwell and a fourth-round pick in the 2000 WNBA Draft from Washington.

APRIL 25, 2000 - WNBA DRAFT

FIRST ROUND

1.   Cleveland Rockers..Ann Wauters
2.   Washington Mystics ....Tausha Mills
3.   Detriot Shock (from Utah) ....Edwina Brown
4.   Orlando Miracle...Cintia Dos Santos
5.   Minnesota Lynx (from Phoenix) ....Grace Daley
6.   Minnesota Lynx..Betty Lennox
7.   Portland Fire ....Lynn Pride
8.   Detroit Shock (from Utah/Miami) ....Tamicha Jackson
9.   Seattle Storm ....Kamila Vodichkova
10. Minnesota Lynx (from Miami/Indiana) ....Maylana Martin
11. Charlotte Sting ....Summer Erb
12. Utah Starzz (from Detroit) ....Naomi Mulitauaopele
13. New York Liberty ....Olga Firsova
14. Sacramento Monarchs ....Katy Steding
15. Los Angeles Sparks..Nicole Kubik
16. Houston Comets ....Elen Chakirova

SECOND ROUND

17. Cleveland Rockers...Helen Darling
18. Washington Mystics ....Tonya Washington
19. Miami Sol (from Utah) ....Jameka Jones
20. Orlando Miracle...Jannon Roland
21. Phoenix Mercury ....Adrain Williams
22. Minnesota Lynx..Marla Brumfield
23. Portland Fire ....Stacey Thomas
24. Minnesota Lynx (from Miami) ....Keitha Dickerson
25. Seattle Storm ....Charisse Sampson
26. Indiana Fever ....Jurgita Streimikyte
27. Charlotte Sting ....Tiffany Travis
28. Detroit Shock ....Madinah Slaise
29. New York Liberty ....Desiree Francis
30. Sacramento Monarchs ....Stacy Clinesmith
31. Los Angeles Sparks..Paige Sauer
32. Houston Comets ....Andrea Garner

THIRD ROUND

33. Cleveland Rockers...Monique Morehouse
34. Charlotte Sting (from Washington) ....Jill Morton

35.	Utah Starzz	Stacy Frese
36.	Orlando Miracle	Shawnetta Stewart
37.	Phoenix Mercury	Tauja Catchings
38.	Minnesota Lynx	Phylesha Whaley
39.	Portland Fire	Maxann Reese
40.	Miami Sol	Milena Flores
41.	Seattle Storm	Kirra Jordan
42.	Indiana Fever	Usha Gilmore
43.	Charlotte Sting	Peppi Browne
44.	Detroit Shock	Chavonne Hammond
45.	New York Liberty	Jessica Bibby
46.	Sacramento Monarchs	Rhonda Banchero
47.	Los Angeles Sparks	Marte Alexander
48.	Houston Comets	Latavia Coleman*

FOURTH ROUND

49.	Cleveland Rockers	Sophie Von Saldern
50.	Indiana Fever (from Washington)	Latina Davis*
51.	Utah Starzz	Kristi Rasmussen
52.	Orlando Miracle	Romana Hamzova
53.	Phoenix Mercury	Shantia Owens †
54.	Minnesota Lynx	Jana Lichnerova
55.	Portland Fire	Rhonda LaCher Smith
56.	Minnesota Lynx (from Miami)	Shanele Stires
57.	Seattle Storm	Katrina Hibbert
58.	Indiana Fever	Renee Robinson*
59.	Charlotte Sting	Shaka Massey
60.	Detroit Shock	Cal Bouchard
61.	New York Liberty	Natalie Porter
62.	Sacramento Monarchs	Jessica Zinobile
63.	Los Angeles Sparks	Nicky McCrimmon
64.	Houston Comets	Abbie Willenborg

* — Houston traded Latavia Coleman to Indiana in exchange for Latina Davis and Renee Robinson.

† — Phoenix traded Shantia Owens to Miami in exchange for a fourth-round pick in the 2001 WNBA Draft.

1999 PLAYER ACQUISITION SUMMARIES
SEPTEMBER 15, 1998 - PLAYER ALLOCATIONS

Minnesota Lynx — Kristin Folkl
Orlando Miracle — Nykesha Sales

APRIL 6, 1999 - EXPANSION DRAFT

Minnesota
1. Brandy Reed (Phoenix)
3. Kim Williams (Utah)
5. Octavia Blue (Los Angeles)
7. Adia Barnes (Sacramento)

Orlando
2. Andrea Congreaves (Charlotte)
4. Kisha Ford (New York)
6. Yolanda Moore (Houston)
8. Adrienne Johnson (Cleveland)

MAY 3, 1999 - PLAYER ALLOCATIONS

Minnesota Lynx — Katie Smith
Orlando Miracle — Shannon Johnson

MAY 4, 1999 - WNBA DRAFT

FIRST ROUND

1.	Washington Mystics	Chamique Holdsclaw
2.	Sacramento Monarchs	Yolanda Griffith
3.	Utah Starzz	Natalie Williams
4.	Los Angeles Sparks	DeLisha Milton
5.	Detroit Shock	Jennifer Azzi

6.	New York Liberty	Crystal Robinson
7.	Minnesota Lynx	Tonya Edwards
8.	Orlando Miracle	Tari Phillips
9.	Charlotte Sting	Dawn Staley
10.	Phoenix Mercury	Edna Campbell
11.	Cleveland Rockers	Chasity Melvin
12.	Houston Comets	Natalia Zasulskaya

SECOND ROUND

13.	Washington Mystics	Shalonda Enis
14.	Sacramento Monarchs	Kedra Holland-Corn
15.	Utah Starzz	Debbie Black
16.	Los Angeles Sparks	Clarisse Machanguana
17.	Detroit Shock	Val Whiting
18.	New York Liberty	Michele VanGorp
19.	Minnesota Lynx	Trisha Fallon
20.	Orlando Miracle	Sheri Sam
21.	Charlotte Sting	Stephanie McCarty
22.	Phoenix Mercury	Clarissa Davis-Wrightsil
23.	Cleveland Rockers	Mery Andrade
24.	Houston Comets	Sonja Henning

THIRD ROUND

25.	Washington Mystics	Andrea Nagy
26.	Sacramento Monarchs	Kate Starbird
27.	Utah Starzz	Adrienne Goodson
28.	Los Angeles Sparks	Ukari Figgs
29.	Detroit Shock	Dominique Canty
30.	New York Liberty	Tamika Whitmore
31.	Minnesota Lynx	Andrea Lloyd-Curry
32.	Orlando Miracle	Taj McWilliams
33.	Charlotte Sting	Charlotte Smith
34.	Phoenix Mercury	Lisa Harrison
35.	Cleveland Rockers	Tracy Henderson
36.	Houston Comets	Kara Wolters

FOURTH ROUND

37.	Washington Mystics	Jennifer Whittle
38.	Sacramento Monarchs	Amy Herrig
39.	Utah Starzz	Dalma Ivanyi
40.	Los Angeles Sparks	La'Keshia Frett
41.	Detroit Shock	Astou Ndiaye
42.	New York Liberty	Carolyn Jones-Young
43.	Minnesota Lynx	Sonja Tate
44.	Orlando Miracle	Carla McGhee
45.	Charlotte Sting	Angie Braziel
46.	Phoenix Mercury	Amanda Wilson
47.	Cleveland Rockers	Kellie Jolly Harper
48.	Houston Comets	Jennifer Rizzotti
49.	Minnesota Lynx	Angie Potthoff
50.	Orlando Miracle	Elaine Powel

1998 PLAYER ACQUISITION SUMMARIES
JANUARY 27, 1998 - PLAYER ALLOCATIONS

Detroit Shock	Cindy Brown, Razija Mujanivic
Washington Mystics	Nikki McCray, Alessandra Santos de Oliveira

FEBRUARY 18, 1998 - EXPANSION DRAFT

Detroit
1. Rhonda Blades (New York)
3. Tajama Abraham (Sacramento)

Washington
2. Heidi Burge (Los Angeles)
4. Penny Moore (Charlotte)

5. Tara Williams (Phoenix) 6. Deborah Carter (Utah)
7. Lynette Woodard (Cleveland) 8. Tammy Jackson (Houston)

APRIL 29, 1998 - WNBA DRAFT

FIRST ROUND
1. Utah Starzz ....Margo Dydek
2. Sacramento Monarchs ....Ticha Penicheiro
3. Washington Mystics ....Murriel Page
4. Detroit Shock ....Korie Hlede
5. Los Angeles Sparks...Allison Feaster
6. Cleveland Rockers..Cindy Blodgett
7. Charlotte Sting ....Tracy Reid
8. Phoenix Mercury ....Maria Stepanova
9. New York Liberty ....Alicia Thompson
10. Houston Comets ....Polina Tzekova

Second Round
11. Utah Starzz ....Olympia Scott
12. Sacramento Monarchs ....Tangela Smith
13. Washington Mystics ....Rita Williams
14. Detroit Shock ....Rachael Sporn
15. Los Angeles Sparks..Octavia Blue
16. Cleveland Rockers...Suzie McConnell Serio
17. Charlotte Sting ....Christy Smith
18. Phoenix Mercury ....Andrea Kuklova
19. New York Liberty ....Nadine Domond
20. Houston Comets ....Nyree Roberts

THIRD ROUND
21. Utah Starzz ....LaTonya Johnson
22. Sacramento Monarchs ....Quacy Barnes
23. Washington Mystics ....Angela Hamblin
24. Detroit Shock ....Gergana Branzova
25. Los Angeles Sparks..Rehema Stephens
26. Cleveland Rockers..Tanja Kostic
27. Charlotte Sting ....Pollyanna Johns
28. Phoenix Mercury ....Brandy Reed
29. New York Liberty ....Albena Branzova
30. Houston Comets ....Amaya Valdemoro

FOURTH ROUND
31. Utah Starzz ....Tricia Bader
32. Sacramento Monarchs ....Adia Barnes
33. Washington Mystics ....Angela Jackson
34. Detroit Shock ....Sandy Brondello
35. Los Angeles Sparks..Erica Kienast
36. Cleveland Rockers..Tammye Jenkins
37. Charlotte Sting ....Sonia Chase
38. Phoenix Mercury ....Karen Wilkins
39. New York Liberty ....Vanessa Nygaard
40. Houston Comets ....Monica Lamb

1997 PLAYER ACQUISITION SUMMARIES
JANUARY 22, 1997 - INITIAL PLAYER ALLOCATIONS
EASTERN CONFERENCE

Charlotte Sting Vicky Bullett, Andrea Stinson
Cleveland Rockers Janice Braxton, Michelle Edwards
Houston Comets Cynthia Cooper, Sheryl Swoopes
New York Liberty Rebecca Lobo, Teresa Weatherspoon

WESTERN CONFERENCE

Los Angeles Sparks	Lisa Leslie, Penny Toler
Phoenix Mercury	Jennifer Gillom, Michelle Timms
Sacramento Monarchs	Ruthie Bolton-Holifield, Bridgette Gordon
Utah Starzz	Elena Baranova, Lady Harmon

FEBRUARY 27, 1997 - WNBA ELITE DRAFT

FIRST ROUND
1. Utah Starzz ....Dena Head
2. Cleveland Rockers...Isabelle Fijalkowski
3. Charlotte Sting ....Rhonda Mapp
4. New York Liberty ....Kym Hampton
5. Houston Comets ....Wanda Guyton
6. Sacramento Monarchs ....Judy Mosley-McAfee
7. Phoenix Mercury ....Bridget Pettis
8. Los Angeles Sparks...Daedra Charles

SECOND ROUND
9. Utah Starzz ....Wendy Palmer
10. Cleveland Rockers...Lynette Woodard
11. Charlotte Sting ....Michi Atkins
12. New York Liberty ....Vickie Johnson
13. Houston Comets ....Janeth Arcain
14. Sacramento Monarchs ....Mikiko Hagiwara
15. Phoenix Mercury ....Nancy Lieberman-Cline
16. Los Angeles Sparks...Haixia Zheng

APRIL 28, 1997 - WNBA DRAFT

FIRST ROUND
1. Houston Comets ....Tina Thompson
2. Sacramento Monarchs ....Pamela McGee
3. Los Angeles Sparks...Jamila Wideman
4. Cleveland Rockers...Eva Nemcova
5. Utah Starzz ....Tammi Reiss
6. New York Liberty ....Sue Wicks
7. Charlotte Sting ....Tora Suber
8. Phoenix Mercury ....Toni Foster

SECOND ROUND
9. Phoenix Mercury ....Tia Jackson
10. Charlotte Sting ....Sharon Manning
11. New York Liberty ....Sophia Witherspoon
12. Utah Starzz ....Jessie Hicks
13. Cleveland Rockers...Merlakia Jones
14. Los Angeles Sparks...Tamecka Dixon
15. Sacramento Monarchs ....Denique Graves
16. Houston Comets ....Tammy Jackson

THIRD ROUND
17. Houston Comets ....Racquel Spurlock
18. Sacramento Monarchs ....Chantel Tremitiere
19. Los Angeles Sparks...Katrina Colleton
20. Cleveland Rockers...Tina Nicholson
21. Utah Starzz ....Raegan Scott
22. New York Liberty ....Trena Trice
23. Charlotte Sting ....Debra Williams
24. Phoenix Mercury ....Umeki Webb

FOURTH ROUND
25. Phoenix Mercury ....Monique Ambers

26.	Charlotte Sting	Andrea Congreaves
27.	New York Liberty	Kisha Ford
28.	Utah Starzz	Kim Williams
29.	Cleveland Rockers	Anita Maxwell
30.	Los Angeles Sparks	Travesa Gant
31.	Sacramento Monarchs	Tajama Abraham
32.	Houston Comets	Catarina Pollini

MAY 22, 1997 - FINAL ROSTER ALLOCATIONS

EASTERN CONFERENCE

Charlotte Sting	Katasha Artis, Milica Vukadinovic
Cleveland Rockers	Jenny Boucek, Donna Harrington
Houston Comets	Pietra Gay, Patty Jo Hedges-Ward, Nekeshia Henderson
New York Liberty	Rhonda Blades, Jasmina Perazic-Gipe

WESTERN CONFERENCE

Los Angeles Sparks	Linda Burgess, Mwadi Mabika
Phoenix Mercury	Marlies Askamp, Tara Williams
Sacramento Monarchs	Eliza Sokolowska, Corissa Yasen
Utah Starzz	Deborah Carter, Megan Compain

2005 WNBA Most Valuable Player

2005 Voting Results		Past Winners	
327	Sheryl Swoopes, Houston Comets	1997	Cynthia Cooper, Houston Comets
325	Lauren Jackson, Seattle Storm	1998	Cynthia Cooper, Houston Comets
238	Tamika Catchings, Indiana Fever	1999	Yolanda Griffith, Sacramento Monarchs
149	Yolanda Griffith, Sacramento Monarchs	2000	Sheryl Swoopes, Houston Comets
128	Taj McWilliams-Franklin, Connecticut Sun	2001	Lisa Leslie, Los Angeles Sparks
41	Nykesha Sales, Connecticut Sun	2002	Sheryl Swoopes, Houston Comets
21	Lisa Leslie, Los Angeles Sparks	2003	Lauren Jackson, Seattle Storm
18	Deanna Nolan, Detroit Shock	2004	Lisa Leslie, Los Angeles Sparks
17	Diana Taurasi, Phoenix Mercury		
17	Chamique Holdsclaw, Los Angeles Sparks		
11	Lindsay Whalen, Connecticut Sun		
7	Becky Hammon, New York Liberty		
1	Sue Bird, Seattle Storm		

WNBA Coach of the Year

2005 Voting Results		Past Winners	
25	John Whisenant, Sacramento Monarchs	1997	Van Chancellor, Houston Comets
19	Mike Thibault, Connecticut Sun	1998	Van Chancellor, Houston Comets
3	Van Chancellor, Houston Comets	1999	Van Chancellor, Houston Comets
1	Brian Winters, Indiana Fever	2000	Michael Cooper, Los Angeles Sparks
1	Carrie Graf, Phoenix Mercury	2001	Dan Hughes, Cleveland Rockers
1	Pat Coyle, New York Liberty	2002	Marianne Stanley, Washington Mystics
		2003	Bill Laimbeer, Detroit Shock
		2004	Suzie McConnell-Serio, Minnesota Lynx

WNBA Rookie of the Year

2005 Voting Results		Past Winners	
44	Temeka Johnson, Washington Mystics	1998	Tracy Reid, Charlotte Sting
3	Katie Feenstra, San Antonio Silver Stars	1999	Chamique Holdsclaw, Wash. Mystics
2	Tan White, Indiana Fever	2000	Betty Lennox, Minnesota Lynx
1	Suzy Batkovic, Seattle Storm	2001	Jackie Stiles, Portland Fire
		2002	Tamika Catchings, Indiana Fever
		2003	Cheryl Ford, Detroit Shock
		2004	Diana Taurasi, Phoenix Mercury

WNBA Defensive Player of the Year presented by Tampax

2005 Voting Results		Past Winners	
35	Tamika Catchings, Indiana Fever	1997	Teresa Weatherspoon, NY Liberty
7	Sheryl Swoopes, Houston Comets	1998	Teresa Weatherspoon, NY Liberty
3	Lisa Leslie, Los Angeles Sparks	1999	Yolanda Griffith, Sacramento Monarchs
2	Katie Douglas, Connecticut Sun	2000	Sheryl Swoopes, Houston Comets
2	Yolanda Griffith, Sacramento Monarchs	2001	Debbie Black, Miami Sol
1	Margo Dydek, Connecticut Sun	2002	Sheryl Swoopes, Houston Comets
		2003	Sheryl Swoopes, Houston Comets
		2004	Lisa Leslie, Los Angeles Sparks

WNBA Most Improved Player

2005 Voting Results		Past Winners	
20	Nicole Powell, Sacramento Monarchs	2000	Tari Phillips, New York Liberty
13	Janell Burse, Seattle Storm	2001	Janeth Arcain, Houston Comets
6	Ann Wauters, New York Liberty	2002	Coco Miller, Washington Mystics
2	Dominique Canty, Houston Comets	2003	Michelle Snow, Houston Comets
2	Kamila Vodichkova, Phoenix Mercury	2004	Kelly Miller, Indiana Fever
2	Taj McWilliams-Franklin, Connecticut Sun		
1	Alana Beard, Washington Mystics		
1	DeMya Walker, Sacramento Monarchs		
1	Lindsay Whalen, Connecticut Sun		
1	Michelle Snow, Houston Comets		

REVIEW Award Winners

WNBA Newcomer of the Year

1998	Suzie McConnell Serio, Cleveland Rockers
1999	Yolanda Griffith, Sacramento Monarchs

Kim Perrot Sportsmanship Award presented by Secret

1997	Haixia Zheng, Los Angeles Sparks
1998	Suzie McConnell-Serio, Cleveland Rockers
1999	Dawn Staley, Charlotte Sting
2000	Suzie McConnell-Serio, Cleveland Rockers
2001	Sue Wicks, New York Liberty
2002	Jennifer Gillom, Phoenix Mercury
2003	Edna Campbell, Sacramento Monarchs
2004	Teresa Edwards, Minnesota Lynx
2005	Taj McWilliams-Franklin, Connecticut Sun

American Express Small Business Service WNBA Entrepreneurial Award Winners

1999	Dawn Staley, Charlotte Sting
	Michele Petrillo, Ridgefield, N.J.
2000	Monica Lamb, Houston Comets
	Amy Cameron, Orlando, Fla.

WNBA Finals Most Valuable Player

1997	Cynthia Cooper, Houston Comets
1998	Cynthia Cooper, Houston Comets
1999	Cynthia Cooper, Houston Comets
2000	Cynthia Cooper, Houston Comets
2001	Lisa Leslie, Los Angeles Sparks
2002	Lisa Leslie, Los Angeles Sparks
2003	Ruth Riley, Detroit Shock
2004	Betty Lennox, Seattle Storm
2005	Yolanda Griffith, Sacramento Monarchs

WNBA All-Star Game Most Valuable Player

1999	Lisa Leslie, Los Angeles Sparks
2000	Tina Thompson, Houston Comets
2001	Lisa Leslie, Los Angeles Sparks
2002	Lisa Leslie, Los Angeles Sparks
2003	Nikki Teasley, Los Angeles Sparks
2004	No official All-Star Game
2005	Sheryl Swoopes, Houston Comets

ALL-WNBA TEAMS PRESENTED BY BUD LIGHT

1997

FIRST		SECOND	
Center	Lisa Leslie, Los Angeles Sparks	Center	Jennifer Gillom, Phoenix Mercury
Forward	Tina Thompson, Houston Comets	Forward	Wendy Palmer, Utah Starzz
Forward	Eva Nemcova, Cleveland Rockers	Forward	Rebecca Lobo, New York Liberty
Guard	Cynthia Cooper, Houston Comets	Guard	Teresa Weatherspoon, New York Liberty
Guard	Ruthie Bolton, Sacramento Monarchs	Guard	Andrea Stinson, Charlotte Sting

1998

FIRST		SECOND	
Center	Jennifer Gillom, Phoenix Mercury	Center	Lisa Leslie, Los Angeles Sparks
Forward	Tina Thompson, Houston Comets	Forward	Cindy Brown, Detroit Shock
Forward	Sheryl Swoopes, Houston Comets	Forward	Eva Nemcova, Cleveland Rockers
Guard	Cynthia Cooper, Houston Comets	Guard	Andrea Stinson, Charlotte Sting
Guard	Suzie McConnell Serio, Cle. Rockers	Guard	Teresa Weatherspoon, New York Liberty

FIRST

Center	Yolanda Griffith, Sacramento Monarchs
Forward	Natalie Williams, Utah Starzz
Forward	Sheryl Swoopes, Houston Comets
Guard	Ticha Penicheiro, Sacramento Monarchs
Guard	Cynthia Cooper, Houston Comets

FIRST

Center	Lisa Leslie, Los Angeles Sparks
Forward	Sheryl Swoopes, Houston Comets
Forward	Natalie Williams, Utah Starzz
Guard	Cynthia Cooper, Houston Comets
Guard	Ticha Penicheiro, Sacramento Monarchs

FIRST

Center	Lisa Leslie, Los Angeles Sparks
Forward	Katie Smith, Minnesota Lynx
Forward	Natalie Williams, Utah Starzz
Guard	Janeth Arcain, Houston Comets
Guard	Merlakia Jones, Cleveland Rockers

FIRST

Center	Lisa Leslie, Los Angeles Sparks
Forward	Sheryl Swoopes, Houston Comets
Forward	Tamika Catchings, Indiana Fever
Guard	Sue Bird, Seattle Storm
Guard	Mwadi Mabika, Los Angeles Sparks

FIRST

Center	Lisa Leslie, Los Angeles Sparks
Forward	Lauren Jackson, Seattle Storm
Forward	Tamika Catchings, Indiana Fever
Guard	Katie Smith, Minnesota Lynx
Guard	Sue Bird, Seattle Storm

FIRST

Center	Lisa Leslie, Los Angeles Sparks
Forward	Lauren Jackson, Seattle Storm
Forward	Tina Thompson, Houston Comets
Guard	Diana Taurasi, Phoenix Mercury
Guard	Sue Bird, Seattle Storm

FIRST

Center	Yolanda Griffith, Sacramento Monarchs
Forward	Sheryl Swoopes, Houston Comets
Forward	Lauren Jackson, Seattle Storm
Guard	Deanna Nolan, Detroit Shock
Guard	Sue Bird, Seattle Storm

1999
SECOND

Center	Lisa Leslie, Los Angeles Sparks
Forward	Chamique Holdsclaw, Wash. Mystics
Forward	Tina Thompson, Houston Comets
Guard	Teresa Weatherspoon, New York Liberty
Guard	Shannon Johnson, Orlando Miracle

2000
SECOND

Center	Yolanda Griffith, Sacramento Monarchs
Forward	Tina Thompson, Houston Comets
Forward	Katie Smith, Minnesota Lynx
Guard	Teresa Weatherspoon, New York Liberty
Guard	Betty Lennox, Minnesota Lynx
	Shannon Johnson, Orlando Miracle

2001
SECOND

Center	Yolanda Griffith, Sacramento Monarchs
Forward	Tina Thompson, Houston Comets
Forward	Chamique Holdsclaw, Wash. Mystics
Guard	Ticha Penicheiro, Sacramento Monarchs
Guard	Tamecka Dixon, Los Angeles Sparks

2002
SECOND

Center	Tari Phillips, New York Liberty
Forward	Chamique Holdsclaw, Wash.Mystics
Forward	Tina Thompson, Houston Comets
Guard	Shannon Johnson, Orlando Miracle
Guard	Katie Smith, Minnesota Lynx

2003
SECOND

Center	Cheryl Ford, Detroit Shock
Forward	Sheryl Swoopes, Houston Comets
Forward	Swin Cash, Detroit Shock
Guard	Nikki Teasley, Los Angeles Sparks
Guard	Deanna Nolan, Detroit Shock

2004
SECOND

Center	Yolanda Griffith, Sacramento Monarchs
Forward	Tamika Catchings, Indiana Fever
Forward	Swin Cash, Detroit Shock
Guard	Nikki Teasley, Los Angeles Sparks
Guard	Nykesha Sales, Connecticut Sun

2005
SECOND

Center	Lisa Leslie, Los Angeles Sparks
Forward	Tamika Catchings, Indiana Fever
Forward	Taj McWilliams-Franklin, Connecticut Sun
Guard	Becky Hammon, New York Liberty
Guard	Diana Taurasi, Phoenix Mercury

CHARLOTTE STING

Season	Coach	Finish	Regular Season W	L	Playoffs W	L
1997	Marynell Meadors	T3rd/East	15	13	0	1
1998	Marynell Meadors	T2nd/East	18	12	0	2
1999	Marynell Meadors (5-7)					
	Dan Hughes (10-10)	T2nd/East	15	17	2	2
2000	T.R. Dunn	8th/East	8	24	—	—
2001	Anne Donovan	4th/East	18	14	4	4
2002	Anne Donovan	T1st/East	18	14	0	2
2003	Trudi Lacey	T2nd/East	18	16	0	2
2004	Trudi Lacey	5th/East	16	18	—	—
2005	Trudi Lacey (3-21)					
	Muggsy Bogues (3-7)	6th/East	6	28	—	—
	Totals		132	156	6	13

CLEVELAND ROCKERS

Season	Coach	Finish	Regular Season W	L	Playoffs W	L
1997	Linda Hill-MacDonald	T3rd/East	15	13	—	—
1998	Linda Hill-MacDonald	1st/East	20	10	1	2
1999	Linda Hill-MacDonald	6th/East	7	25	—	—
2000	Dan Hughes	2nd/East	17	15	3	3
2001	Dan Hughes	1st/East	22	10	1	2
2002	Dan Hughes	7th/East	10	22	—	—
2003	Dan Hughes	4th/East	17	17	1	2
	Totals		108	112	6	9

CONNECTICUT SUN (formerly Orlando Miracle—1999-02)

Season	Coach	Finish	Regular Season W	L	Playoffs W	L
1999	Carolyn Peck	T2nd/East	15	17	—	—
2000	Carolyn Peck	3rd/East	16	16	1	2
2001	Carolyn Peck	5th/East	13	19	—	—
2002	Dee Brown	T4th/East	16	16	—	—
2003	Mike Thibault	T2nd/East	18	16	2	2
2004	Mike Thibault	T1st/East	18	16	5	3
2005	Mike Thibault	1st/East	26	8	5	3
	Totals		122	108	13	10

DETROIT SHOCK

Season	Coach	Finish	Regular Season W	L	Playoffs W	L
1998	Nancy Lieberman	4th/East	17	13	—	—
1999	Nancy Lieberman	T2nd/East	15	17	0	1
2000	Nancy Lieberman	T4th/East	14	18	—	—
2001	Greg Williams	T6th/East	10	22	—	—
2002	Greg Williams (0-10)					
	Bill Laimbeer (9-13)	8th/East	9	23	—	—
2003	Bill Lalmbeer	1st/East	25	9	6	2
2004	Bill Laimbeer	T3rd/East	17	17	1	2
2005	Bill Laimbeer	T4th/East	16	18	0	2
	Totals		123	137	7	7

HOUSTON COMETS

Season	Coach	Finish	Regular Season W	L	Playoffs W	L
1997	Van Chancellor	1st/East	18	10	2	0
1998	Van Chancellor	1st/West	27	3	4	1
1999	Van Chancellor	1st/West	26	6	4	2
2000	Van Chancellor	2nd/West	27	5	6	0
2001	Van Chancellor	T3rd/West	19	13	0	2

Season	Coach	Finish	Regular Season		Playoffs	
			W	L	W	L
2002	Van Chancellor	2nd/West	24	8	1	2
2003	Van Chancellor	2nd/West	20	14	1	2
2004	Van Chancellor	6th/West	13	21	—	—
2005	Van Chancellor	3rd/West	19	15	2	3
		Totals	193	95	20	12

INDIANA FEVER

Season	Coach	Finish	Regular Season		Playoffs	
			W	L	W	L
2000	Anne Donovan	7th/East	9	23	—	—
2001	Nell Fortner	T6th/West	10	22	—	—
2002	Nell Fortner	T4th/East	16	16	1	2
2003	Nell Fortner	T5th/East	16	18	—	—
2004	Brian Winters	6th/East	15	19	—	—
2005	Brian Winters	2nd/East	21	13	2	2
		Totals	87	111	3	4

LOS ANGELES SPARKS

Season	Coach	Finish	Regular Season		Playoffs	
			W	L	W	L
1997	Linda Sharp (4-7)					
	Julie Rousseau (10-7)	2nd/West	14	14	—	—
1998	Julie Rousseau (7-13)					
	Orlando Woolridge (5-5)	3rd/West	12	18	—	—
1999	Orlando Woolridge	2nd/West	20	12	2	2
2000	Michael Cooper	1st/West	28	4	2	2
2001	Michael Cooper	1st/West	28	4	6	1
2002	Michael Cooper	1st/West	25	7	6	0
2003	Michael Cooper	1st/West	24	10	5	4
2004	Michael Cooper (14-6)					
	Karleen Thompson (11-3)	1st/West	25	9	1	2
2005	Henry Bibby (13-16)					
	Joe Bryant (4-1)	4th/West	17	17	0	2
		Totals	193	95	22	13

MIAMI SOL

Season	Coach	Finish	Regular Season		Playoffs	
			W	L	W	L
2000	Ron Rothstein	6th/East	13	19	—	—
2001	Ron Rothstein	3rd/East	20	12	1	2
2002	Ron Rothstein	6th/East	15	17	—	—
		Totals	48	48	1	2

MINNESOTA LYNX

Season	Coach	Finish	Regular Season		Playoffs	
			W	L	W	L
1999	Brian Agler	T4th/West	15	17	—	—
2000	Brian Agler	6th/West	15	17	—	—
2001	Brian Agler	6th/West	12	20	—	—
2002	Brian Agler (6-13)					
	Heidi VanDerveer (4-9)	8th/West	10	22	—	—
2003	Suzie McConnell-Serio	T4th/West	18	16	1	2
2004	Suzie McConnell-Serio	T3rd/West	18	16	0	2
2005	Suzie McConnell-Serio	6th/West	14	20	—	—
		Totals	102	128	1	4

NEW YORK LIBERTY

Season	Coach	Finish	Regular Season		Playoffs	
			W	L	W	L
1997	Nancy Darsch	2nd/East	17	11	1	1
1998	Nancy Darsch	T2nd/East	18	12	—	—
1999	Richie Adubato	1st/East	18	14	3	3
2000	Richie Adubato	1st/East	20	12	4	3
2001	Richie Adubato	2nd/East	21	11	3	3
2002	Richie Adubato	T1st/East	18	14	4	4
2003	Richie Adubato	T5th/East	16	18	—	—
2004	Richie Adubato (7-9)					
	Pat Coyle (11-7)	T1st/East	18	16	2	3
2005	Pat Coyle	3rd/East	18	16	0	
		Totals	164	124	17	19

PHOENIX MERCURY

Season	Coach	Finish	Regular Season W	Regular Season L	Playoffs W	Playoffs L
1997	Cheryl Miller	1st/West	16	12	0	1
1998	Cheryl Miller	2nd/West	19	11	3	3
1999	Cheryl Miller	T4th/West	15	17	—	—
2000	Cheryl Miller	4th/West	20	12	0	2
2001	Cynthia Cooper	5th/West	13	19	—	—
2002	Cynthia Cooper (6-4) Linda Sharp (5-17)	7th/West	11	21	—	—
2003	John Shumate	7th/West	8	26	—	—
2004	Carrie Graf	7th/West	17	17	—	—
2005	Carrie Graf	5th/West	16	18	—	—
		Totals	135	153	3	6

PORTLAND FIRE

Season	Coach	Finish	Regular Season W	Regular Season L	Playoffs W	Playoffs L
2000	Linda Hargrove	7th/West	10	22	—	—
2001	Linda Hargrove	7th/West	11	21	—	—
2002	Linda Hargrove	5th/West	16	16	—	—
		Totals	37	59	—	—

SACRAMENTO MONARCHS

Season	Coach	Finish	Regular Season W	Regular Season L	Playoffs W	Playoffs L
1997	Mary Murphy (5-10) Heidi VanDerveer (5-8)	3rd/West	10	18	—	—
1998	Heidi VanDerveer	T4th/West	8	22	—	—
1999	Sonny Allen	3rd/West	19	13	0	1
2000	Sonny Allen	3rd/West	21	11	0	2
2001	Sonny Allen (6-6) Maura McHugh (14-6)	2nd/West	20	12	3	2
2002	Maura McHugh	6th/West	14	18	—	—
2003	Maura McHugh (7-11) John Whisenant (12-4)	3rd/West	19	15	3	3
2004	John Whisenant	T3rd/West	18	16	3	3
2005	John Whisenant	1st/West	25	9	7	1
		Totals	154	134	16	12

SAN ANTONIO SILVER STARS (formerly Utah Starzz—1997-02)

Season	Coach	Finish	Regular Season W	Regular Season L	Playoffs W	Playoffs L
1997	Denise Taylor	4th/West	7	21	—	—
1998	Denise Taylor (6-13) Frank Layden (2-9)	T4th/West	8	22	—	—
1999	Frank Layden (2-2) Fred Williams (13-15)	T4th/West	15	17	—	—
2000	Fred Williams	5th/West	18	14	—	—
2001	Fred Williams (5-8) Candi Harvey (14-5)	T3rd/West	19	13	0	2
2002	Candi Harvey	3rd/West	20	12	2	3
2003	Candi Harvey (6-16) Shell Dailey (6-6)	6th/West	12	22	—	—
2004	Dee Brown (6-18) Shell Dailey (3-7)	7th/West	9	25	—	—
2005	Dan Hughes	7th/West	7	27	—	—
		Totals	115	173	2	5

SEATTLE STORM

Season	Coach	Finish	Regular Season W	Regular Season L	Playoffs W	Playoffs L
2000	Lin Dunn	8th/West	6	26	—	—
2001	Lin Dunn	8th/West	10	22	—	—
2002	Lin Dunn	4th/West	17	15	0	2
2003	Anne Donovan	T4th/West	18	16	—	—
2004	Anne Donovan	2nd/West	20	14	6	2
2005	Anne Donovan	2nd/West	20	14	1	2
		Totals	91	107	7	6

WASHINGTON MYSTICS

Season	Coach	Finish	Regular Season		Playoffs	
			W	L	W	L
1998	Jim Lewis (2-16)					
	Cathy Parson (1-11)	5th/East	3	27	—	—
1999	Nancy Darsch	5th/East	12	20	—	—
2000	Nancy Darsch (9-11)					
	Darrell Walker (5-7)	T4th/East	14	18	0	2
2001	Tom Maher	T6th/East	10	22	—	—
2002	Marianne Stanley	3rd/East	17	15	3	2
2003	Marianne Stanley	7th/East	9	25	—	—
2004	Michael Adams	T4th/East	17	17	1	2
2005	Richie Adubato	T4th/East	16	18	—	—
		Totals	98	162	4	6

TEAM WINNING, LOSING STREAKS

Team	G	Winning Streak Dates	G	Losing Streak Dates
Charlotte	7	July 31-Aug. 14, 2001	10	July 12-Aug. 4, 2005
Connecticut	8	May 22-June 20, 2005	3	Last: July 30-Sept. 1, 2004
	*6	June 28-July 9, 2000	*7	July 21-Aug. 4, 2000
Detroit	8	June 5-27, 2003	13	May 30-June 28, 2002
Houston	15	June 27-July 30, 1998	5	June 30-July 14, 2004
Indiana	4	Aug. 14-23, 2005	10	June 18-July 8, 2000
		July 31-Aug. 7, 2002		
Los Angeles	18	June 26-Aug. 11, 2001	5	June 21-July 2, 1998
Minnesota	6	July 9-22, 2004	8	July 5-21, 2000
New York	7	June 21-July 5, 1997	6	June 11-24, 2004
				June 10-24, 2001
Phoenix	5	July 14-27, 2001	7	July 2-25, 2003
				July 29-Aug. 10, 2001
Sacramento	7	July 24-Aug. 7, 2005	9	July 16-Aug. 4, 1997
San Antonio	+8	July 24-Aug. 7, 2001	9	Aug. 2-26, 2005
	3	July 27-Aug. 1, 2003		July 18-Sept. 4, 2004
Seattle	6	July 15-31, 2005	8	June 15-July 3, 2000
		June 3-19, 2004		
Washington	6	June 4-18, 2002	11	June 13-July 9, 2003
		Aug. 2-14, 1999		July 13-Aug. 7, 1998

*Club located in Orlando. +Club located in Utah.

ALL-TIME TEAM STANDINGS

OVERALL

	W	L	PCT
Houston Comets	193	95	.670
Los Angeles Sparks	193	95	.670
New York Liberty	164	124	.569
Sacramento Monarchs	154	134	.535
Connecticut Sun	122	108	.530
Miami Sol	48	48	.500
Cleveland Rockers	108	112	.491
Detroit Shock	123	137	.473
Phoenix Mercury	135	153	.469
Seattle Storm	91	107	.460
Charlotte Sting	132	156	.458
Minnesota Lynx	102	128	.443
Indiana Fever	87	111	.439
San Antonio Silver Stars	115	173	.399
Portland Fire	37	59	.385
Washington Mystics	98	162	.377
Totals	1902	1902	.500

HOME

	W	L	PCT
Houston Comets	111	33	.771
Los Angeles Sparks	109	35	.757
New York Liberty	101	43	.701
Sacramento Monarchs	95	49	.660
Phoenix Mercury	93	51	.639
Connecticut Sun	73	42	.635
Cleveland Rockers	66	44	.600
Seattle Storm	59	40	.593
Charlotte Sting	84	60	.583
Miami Sol	28	20	.583
Indiana Fever	57	42	.576
Detroit Shock	72	58	.554
Minnesota Lynx	62	53	.530
San Antonio Silver Stars	74	70	.514
Portland Fire	21	27	.438
Washington Mystics	57	73	.438
Totals	1162	740	.610

ROAD

	W	L	PCT
Los Angeles Sparks	84	60	.583
Houston Comets	82	62	.569
New York Liberty	63	81	.438
Connecticut Sun	49	66	.426
Miami Sol	20	28	.417
Sacramento Monarchs	59	85	.410
Detroit Shock	51	79	.392
Cleveland Rockers	42	68	.382
Minnesota Lynx	40	75	.348
Charlotte Sting	48	96	.333
Portland Fire	16	32	.333
Seattle Storm	32	67	.323
Washington Mystics	41	89	.315
Indiana Fever	30	69	.303
Phoenix Mercury	42	102	.292
San Antonio Silver Stars	41	103	.285
Totals	740	1162	.390

ALL-TIME COACHING LEADERS

BY VICTORIES

COACH	W-L	PCT
Van Chancellor	193 - 95	.670
Michael Cooper	119 - 31	.793
Richie Adubato	116 - 96	.547
Anne Donovan	103 - 95	.520
Dan Hughes	83 - 101	.451
Cheryl Miller	70 - 52	.574
Bill Laimbeer	67 - 57	.540
Mike Thibault	62 - 40	.608
Nancy Darsch	56 - 54	.509
John Whisenant	55 - 29	.655
Suzie McConnell Serio	50 - 52	.490
Ron Rothstein	48 - 48	.500
Brian Agler	48 - 67	.417
Sonny Allen	46 - 30	.605
Nancy Lieberman-Cline	46 - 48	.489

BY GAMES

COACH	G
Van Chancellor	288
Richie Adubato	212
Anne Donovan	198
Dan Hughes	184
Michael Cooper	150
Bill Laimbeer	124
Cheryl Miller	122
Brian Agler	115
Nancy Darsch	110
Suzie McConnell Serio	102
Mike Thibault	102
Nell Fortner	98
Lin Dunn	96
Linda Hargrove	96
Carolyn Peck	96
Ron Rothstein	96

BY WINNING PERCENTAGE
(MIN: 75 GAMES)

COACH	PCT	W-L
Michael Cooper	.793	119 - 31
Van Chancellor	.670	193 - 95
John Whisenant	.655	55 - 29
Mike Thibault	.608	62 - 40
Sonny Allen	.605	46 - 30
Cheryl Miller	.574	70 - 52
Richie Adubato	.547	116 - 96
Bill Laimbeer	.540	67 - 57
Anne Donovan	.520	103 - 95
Nancy Darsch	.509	56 - 54
Ron Rothstein	.500	48 - 48
Suzie McConnell Serio	.490	50 - 52
Nancy Lieberman-Cline	.489	46 - 48
Linda Hill-MacDonald	.467	42 - 48
Carolyn Peck	.458	44 - 52

GAMES

Vickie Johnson	282
Lisa Leslie	273
Wendy Palmer-Daniel	272
Andrea Stinson	272
Tamecka Dixon	263
Murriel Page	259
Margo Dydek	255
Janeth Arcain	254
Mwadi Mabika	254
Tangela Smith	254
Teresa Weatherspoon	254

MINUTES

Vickie Johnson	8,950
Lisa Leslie	8,889
Tina Thompson	8,430
Andrea Stinson	8,056
Sheryl Swoopes	7,789
Ticha Penicheiro	7,719
Katie Smith	7,681
Janeth Arcain	7,638
Dawn Staley	7,511
Nykesha Sales	7,391

FIELD GOALS MADE

Lisa Leslie	1,743
Sheryl Swoopes	1,463
Tina Thompson	1,380
Chamique Holdsclaw	1,352
Andrea Stinson	1,310
Nykesha Sales	1,249
Tangela Smith	1,247
Vickie Johnson	1,244
Yolanda Griffith	1,189
Katie Smith	1,167

FIELD GOAL ATTEMPTS

Lisa Leslie	3,774
Tina Thompson	3,313
Sheryl Swoopes	3,289
Chamique Holdsclaw	3,091
Nykesha Sales	2,971
Tangela Smith	2,905
Andrea Stinson	2,905
Vickie Johnson	2,855
Katie Smith	2,835
Mwadi Mabika	2,657

FIELD GOAL PERCENTAGE
(Minimum: 400 FG)

	FG	FGA	PCT
Tamika Williams	441	759	.581
Ann Wauters	465	864	.538
Yolanda Griffith	1,189	2,308	.515
Latasha Byears	701	1,363	.514
Michelle Snow	427	854	.500

	FG	FGA	PCT
Tammy Sutton-Brown	516	1,065	.485
Taj McWilliams-Franklin	1,005	2,079	.483
Brandy Reed	465	966	.481
Rhonda Mapp	540	1127	.479
Natalie Williams	1,066	2,250	.474

FREE THROWS MADE

Lisa Leslie	1,137
Yolanda Griffith	928
Katie Smith	917
Shannon Johnson	780
Sheryl Swoopes	767
Chamique Holdsclaw	764
Cynthia Cooper	758
Natalie Williams	754
Tina Thompson	744
Margo Dydek	678

FREE THROW ATTEMPTS

Lisa Leslie	1,615
Yolanda Griffith	1,292
Katie Smith	1,073
Shannon Johnson	1,036
Natalie Williams	1,018
Chamique Holdsclaw	979
Sheryl Swoopes	915
Tina Thompson	912
Wendy Palmer-Daniel	889
Chasity Melvin	877

FREE THROW PERCENTAGE
(Minimum: 200 FT)

	FT	FTA	PCT
Eva Nemcova	227	253	.897
Sue Bird	295	335	.881
Cynthia Cooper	758	870	.871
Janeth Arcain	580	669	.867
Katie Smith	917	1,073	.855
Crystal Robinson	281	329	.854
Sandy Brondello	316	370	.854
Ukari Figgs	204	239	.854
Becky Hammon	408	481	.848
Elena Baranova	328	388	.845
Jennifer Azzi	348	412	.845

THREE-POINT FIELD GOALS

Katie Smith	478
Crystal Robinson	400
Tina Thompson	347
Allison Feaster	333
Mwadi Mabika	330
Ruthie Bolton	314
Nykesha Sales	297
Becky Hammon	294
Kedra Holland-Corn	279
Sophia Witherspoon	260

THREE-POINT FIELD GOAL ATTEMPTS

Katie Smith 1,294
Crystal Robinson 1,044
Mwadi Mabika 997
Ruthie Bolton 984
Tina Thompson 966
Allison Feaster 943
Nykesha Sales 839
Kedra Holland-Corn...................................817
Becky Hammon...801
Sophia Witherspoon 741

THREE-POINT PERCENTAGE
(Minimum: 100 FG3)

	3FG	3GA	PCT
Jennifer Azzi	158	345	.458
Sandy Brondello	114	278	.410
Sue Bird	215	531	.405
Kara Lawson	141	350	.403
Eva Nemcova	131	326	.402
Korie Hlede	104	262	.397
Nikki Teasley	207	524	.395
Elena Baranova	224	573	.391
Kelly Miller	136	348	.391
Edna Campbell	161	415	.388

OFFENSIVE REBOUNDS

Yolanda Griffith......................................818
Natalie Williams......................................733
Lisa Leslie...659
Taj McWilliams-Franklin 545
Tina Thompson.......................................518
Chasity Melvin..499
Adrienne Goodson 493
Murriel Page...480
Wendy Palmer-Daniel 477
Chamique Holdsclaw 466

DEFENSIVE REBOUNDS

Lisa Leslie...1,881
Margo Dydek..1,434
Chamique Holdsclaw 1,216
Wendy Palmer-Daniel 1,165
Tina Thompson.....................................1,138
Natalie Williams....................................1,099
Yolanda Griffith.....................................1,064
Elena Baranova.....................................1,037
Taj McWilliams-Franklin 963
Sheryl Swoopes 874

TOTAL REBOUNDS

Lisa Leslie...2,540
Yolanda Griffith....................................1,882
Natalie Williams....................................1,832
Margo Dydek..1,725
Chamique Holdsclaw 1,682
Tina Thompson.....................................1,656
Wendy Palmer-Daniel 1,642

Taj McWilliams-Franklin 1,508
Murriel Page...1,336
Elena Baranova......................................1,336

ASSISTS

Ticha Penicheiro...................................1,591
Teresa Weatherspoon 1,338
Dawn Staley...1,204
Shannon Johnson.................................1,031
Andrea Stinson..810
Vickie Johnson..787
Sheryl Swoopes 775
Sue Bird..772
Tamecka Dixon.......................................769
Mwadi Mabika...641

STEALS

Sheryl Swoopes 520
Ticha Penicheiro......................................481
Teresa Weatherspoon 465
Nykesha Sales 428
Yolanda Griffith.......................................409
Lisa Leslie...376
Vicky Bullett...353
Janeth Arcain...347
Andrea Stinson.......................................342
Sheri Sam...335
Shannon Johnson 335

PERSONAL FOULS

Lisa Leslie...1,090
Natalie Williams 847
Margo Dydek 804
Tangela Smith 783
DeLisha Milton-Jones...............................748
Wendy Palmer-Daniel 741
Mwadi Mabika 738
Murriel Page 712
Yolanda Griffith.......................................707
Chasity Melvin...701

DISQUALIFICATIONS

Lisa Leslie..35
Natalie Williams.......................................21
Latasha Byears 18
DeLisha Milton-Jones................................14
Ruth Riley..12
Kamila Vodichkova 12
Tari Phillips..11
Janell Burse 10
Isabelle Fijalkowski 10
Murriel Page...10
Tangela Smith 10

BLOCKED SHOTS

Margo Dydek..726
Lisa Leslie...635
Tangela Smith 338
Lauren Jackson.......................................338

Elena Baranova 320
Vicky Bullett 288
Yolanda Griffith 276
Ruth Riley..244
Taj McWilliams-Franklin. 236
Tammy Sutton-Brown.............................233

POINTS

Lisa Leslie..4,732
Sheryl Swoopes 3,894
Tina Thompson.....................................3,851
Katie Smith 3,729
Chamique Holdsclaw.............................3,521
Andrea Stinson.....................................3,351
Nykesha Sales......................................3,328
Yolanda Griffith.....................................3,306
Vickie Johnson......................................3,246

Tangela Smith 2,973

SCORING AVERAGE
(Minimum: 100 games)

	G	FG	FT	PTS	AVG
Cynthia Cooper	124	802	758	2,601	21.0
Lauren Jackson	155	1,015	616	2,853	18.4
Chamique Holdsclaw	195	1,352	764	3,521	18.1
Tamika Catchings	134	742	609	2,334	17.4
Lisa Leslie	273	1,743	1,137	4,732	17.3
Katie Smith..................	218	1,167	917	3,729	17.1
Sheryl Swoopes...........	228	1,463	767	3,894	17.1
Tina Thompson	247	1,380	744	3,851	15.6
Yolanda Griffith	212	1,189	928	3,306	15.6
Nykesha Sales	230	1,249	533	3,328	14.5

ALL-TIME TOP 50 SCORERS

PLAYER	G	MIN	FG	FGA	PCT	FT	FTA	PCT	REB	AST	STL	PF	BLK	PTS	AVG
Lisa Leslie	273	8889	1743	3774	.462	1137	1615	.704	2540	637	376	1090	635	4732	17.3
Sheryl Swoopes	228	7789	1463	3289	.445	767	915	.838	1134	775	520	379	188	3894	17.1
Tina Thompson	247	8430	1380	3313	.417	744	912	.816	1656	369	236	694	201	3851	15.6
Katie Smith	218	7681	1167	2835	.412	917	1073	.855	700	522	196	606	46	3729	17.1
Chamique Holdsclaw	195	6733	1352	3091	.437	764	979	.780	1682	514	259	475	114	3521	18.1
Andrea Stinson	272	8056	1310	2905	.451	524	712	.736	1127	810	342	511	117	3351	12.3
Nykesha Sales	230	7391	1249	2971	.420	533	689	.774	970	541	428	696	64	3328	14.5
Yolanda Griffith	212	6667	1189	2308	.515	928	1292	.718	1882	305	409	707	276	3306	15.6
Vickie Johnson	282	8950	1244	2855	.436	537	656	.819	1053	787	255	565	38	3246	11.5
Tangela Smith	254	7196	1247	2905	.429	440	576	.764	1280	315	266	783	338	2973	11.7
Mwadi Mabika	254	7165	1038	2657	.391	535	671	.797	1100	641	313	738	89	2941	11.6
Wendy Palmer-Daniel	272	7069	1085	2499	.434	624	889	.702	1642	302	206	741	60	2937	10.8
Jennifer Gillom	216	5886	1049	2464	.426	643	847	.759	968	255	221	629	104	2896	13.4
Natalie Williams	221	6879	1066	2250	.474	754	1018	.741	1832	308	270	847	122	2894	13.1
Lauren Jackson	155	5238	1015	2304	.441	616	772	.798	1210	255	189	491	338	2853	18.4
Tamecka Dixon	263	7315	1047	2451	.427	568	709	.801	788	769	280	639	47	2774	10.5
Sheri Sam	229	7211	1053	2603	.405	450	634	.710	996	575	335	594	42	2738	12.0
Adrienne Goodson	221	6475	1050	2398	.438	557	749	.744	1126	433	203	512	30	2705	12.2
Margo Dydek	255	6472	992	2148	.462	678	860	.788	1725	454	142	804	726	2682	10.5
Shannon Johnson	220	7333	835	2075	.402	780	1036	.753	818	1031	335	530	44	2653	12.1
Janeth Arcain	254	7638	997	2281	.437	580	669	.867	919	469	347	513	28	2652	10.4
Taj McWilliams-Franklin	211	6781	1005	2079	.483	555	777	.714	1508	364	315	575	236	2609	12.4
Cynthia Cooper	124	4363	802	1749	.459	758	870	.871	403	602	193	264	35	2601	21.0
Nikki McCray	241	6351	899	2172	.414	555	723	.768	480	448	231	515	13	2528	10.5
Chasity Melvin	225	6359	899	1946	.462	619	877	.706	1192	320	175	701	128	2431	10.8
DeLisha Milton-Jones	211	6481	883	1916	.461	510	659	.774	1232	384	319	748	179	2384	11.3
Merlakia Jones	251	6354	959	2283	.420	372	494	.753	944	360	239	510	26	2353	9.4
Tamika Catchings	134	4700	742	1829	.406	609	738	.825	1061	490	323	413	132	2334	17.4
Crystal Robinson	216	6608	810	1884	.430	281	329	.854	594	440	232	596	67	2301	10.7
Sophia Witherspoon	207	4862	735	1934	.380	489	610	.802	449	313	210	345	31	2219	10.7
Ruthie Bolton	218	5093	767	2088	.367	335	449	.746	676	353	254	437	7	2183	10.0
Allison Feaster	219	5697	690	1784	.387	407	487	.836	650	359	201	461	48	2120	9.7
Elena Baranova	209	5991	779	1836	.424	328	388	.845	1336	430	215	501	320	2110	10.1
Tari Phillips	205	5081	828	1822	.454	408	663	.615	1222	198	265	602	106	2067	10.1
Becky Hammon	205	4882	671	1487	.451	408	481	.848	456	494	215	340	7	2044	10.0

	G	MIN	FG	FGA	PCT	FT	FTA	PCT	REB	AST	STL	PF	BLK	PTS	AVG
Vicky Bullett	186	5950	813	1799	.452	322	415	.776	1191	297	353	507	288	2018	10.8
Dawn Staley	229	7511	669	1687	.397	437	523	.836	462	1204	303	501	12	1976	8.6
Betty Lennox	168	4224	724	1849	.392	313	384	.815	693	329	176	491	30	1965	11.7
Tamika Whitmore	224	5326	735	1649	.446	446	624	.715	810	164	157	635	117	1931	8.6
Marie Ferdinand	146	4553	657	1565	.420	536	705	.760	490	357	227	351	24	1912	13.1
Deanna Nolan	158	4654	653	1651	.396	375	469	.800	537	408	206	321	58	1853	11.7
Penny Taylor	158	4295	633	1456	.435	396	469	.844	698	368	200	359	57	1835	11.6
Kedra Holland-Corn	189	5141	613	1515	.405	293	410	.715	426	380	279	376	31	1798	9.5
Murriel Page	259	6904	739	1562	.473	287	454	.632	1336	320	168	712	175	1782	6.9
Sandy Brondello	155	4583	665	1606	.414	316	370	.854	300	349	148	298	16	1760	11.4
Sue Bird	130	4413	587	1363	.431	295	335	.881	374	772	183	189	15	1684	13.0
Swin Cash	118	3739	567	1293	.439	498	692	.720	711	383	136	289	89	1667	14.1
Latasha Byears	185	4007	701	1363	.514	245	388	.631	1030	173	209	605	51	1654	8.9
Ticha Penicheiro	240	7719	475	1410	.337	516	760	.679	891	1591	481	559	32	1557	6.5
Kamila Vodichkova	174	4114	555	1249	.444	366	470	.779	851	241	145	512	92	1507	8.7

INDIVIDUAL RECORDS

SEASONS

Most seasons
9 — By many

GAMES

Most games, career
282 — Vickie Johnson, New York, 1997-2005
273 — Lisa Leslie, Los Angeles, 1997-2005
272 — Andrea Stinson, Charlotte, 1997-2004;
Detroit, 2005
Wendy Palmer-Daniel, Utah, 1997-99; Detroit
1999-2002; Orlando 2002; Connecticut
2003-04; San Antonio, 2005

Most consecutive games, career
261 — Andrea Stinson, Charlotte-Detroit,
June 22, 1997-June 12, 2005
254 — Tangela Smith June 11, 1998-August 20, 2005
Janeth Arcain, Houston, June 21, 1997-
August 25, 2003, May 21, 2005-
August 27, 2005 (current)
Note: Arcain did not play in 2004
230 — Nykesha Sales, June 10, 1999-
August 27, 2005 (current)

Most games, season
36 — Katie Smith, Minnesota, 1999-2005;
Detroit, 2005
35 — Plenette Pierson, Phoenix, 2003-05;
Detroit, 2005
34 — By many

MINUTES

Most seasons leading league, minutes
2 — Tamika Catchings, Indiana, 2002-03
Katie Smith, Minnesota, 2000-01
1 — Sheryl Swoopes, Houston, 2005
Anna DeForge, Phoenix, 2004
Shannon Johnson, Orlando, 1999

Ticha Penicheiro, Sacramento, 1998
Chantel Tremitiere, Sacramento, 1997
Most minutes, career
8,950 — Vickie Johnson, New York, 1997-2005
8,889 — Lisa Leslie, Los Angeles, 1997-2005
8,430 — Tina Thompson, Houston, 1997-2005
Highest average, minutes per game, career
(Minimum 100 games)
35.2 — Katie Smith, Minnesota, 1999-2005;
Detroit 2005 (7681/218)
35.1 — Tamika Catchings, Indiana 2002-05
(4700/134)
35.2 — Cynthia Cooper, Houston, 1997-2000, 2003
(4363/124)
Most minutes, season
1,234 — Katie Smith, Minnesota, 2001
1,225 — Sheryl Swoopes, Houston, 2005
1,213 — Deanna Nolan, Detroit, 2005
Highest average, minutes per game, season
38.6 — Katie Smith, Minnesota, 2001 (1234/32)
37.7 — Jennifer Azzi, Utah, 2001 (1205/32)
37.5 — Chantel Tremitiere, Sacramento, 1997
(1051/28)
Most minutes, game
55 — Vicky Bullett, Washington at Seattle,
July 3, 2001 (4OT)
Lauren Jackson, Seattle vs. Washington,
July 3, 2001 (4OT)
54 — Chamique Holdsclaw, Washington at Seattle,
July 3, 2001 (4OT)
Audrey Sauret, Washington at Seattle,
July 3, 2001 (4OT)
53 — Chasity Melvin, Cleveland at Orlando,
June 8, 2002 (3OT)

COMPLETE GAMES

Most Complete Games, Season
13 — Jennifer Azzi, Utah, 2001

10 — Tamika Catchings, Indiana, 2002

9 — DeLisha Milton, Los Angeles, 2003

SCORING

Most seasons leading league

3 — Cynthia Cooper, Houston, 1997-99

2 — Sheryl Swoopes, Houston, 2000, 2005
   Lauren Jackson, Seattle, 2003-04

1 — Chamique Holdsclaw, Washington, 2002
   Katie Smith, Minnesota, 2001

Most points, lifetime

4,732 — Lisa Leslie, Los Angeles, 1997-2005

3,894 — Sheryl Swoopes, Houston, 1997-2000,
   2002-2005

3,851 — Tina Thompson, Houston, 1997-2005

Highest average, points per game, career
(Minimum 100 games)

21.0 — Cynthia Cooper, Houston, 1997-2000, 2003
   (2,601/124)

18.4 — Lauren Jackson, Seattle, 2001-2005
   (2,853/155)

18.1 — Chamique Holdsclaw, Washington, 1999-2004;
   Los Angeles, 2005 (2,960/162)

Most points, season

739 — Katie Smith, Minnesota, 2001

698 — Lauren Jackson, Seattle, 2003

686 — Cynthia Cooper, Houston, 1999

Highest average, points per game, season

23.1 — Katie Smith, Minnesota, 2001 (739/32)

22.7 — Cynthia Cooper, Houston, 1998 (680/30)

22.2 — Cynthia Cooper, Houston, 1997 (621/28)

Most points, game

46 — Katie Smith, Minnesota at Los Angeles,
   July 8, 2001 (OT)

44 — Cynthia Cooper, Houston at Sacramento,
   July 25, 1997

42 — Cynthia Cooper, Houston vs. Utah,
   August 16, 1999

Most games, 40 or more points, career

2 — Katie Smith, Minnesota, 1999-2005;
   Detroit 2005
   Cynthia Cooper, Houston 1997-2000, 2003

Most games, 30 or more points, career

16 — Cynthia Cooper, Houston, 1997-2000, 2003

12 — Katie Smith, Minnesota, 1999-2005;
   Detroit 2005

10 — Lisa Leslie, Los Angeles, 1997-2005

Most consecutive games, 30 or more points

3 — Cynthia Cooper, Houston, July 18-25, 1997

2 — Sheryl Swoopes, Houston, August 8-10, 2002
   Cynthia Cooper, Houston, August 5-7, 1997

Most games, 20 or more points, career

94 — Lisa Leslie, Los Angeles, 1997-2005

84 — Katie Smith, Minnesota, 1999-2005;
   Detroit 2005

82 — Sheryl Swoopes, Houston, 1997-2000,
   2002-2005

Most consecutive games, 20 or more points

11 — Cynthia Cooper, Houston, August 17, 1998-
   June 30, 1999

8 — Brandy Reed, Phoenix, July 13-28, 2000
   Sheryl Swoopes, Houston,
   May 29-June 12, 2000

7 — Chamique Holdsclaw, June 17-July 7, 2004
   Lauren Jackson, Seattle, July 17-31, 2003
   Ruthie Bolton-Holifield, Sacramento,
   June 23-July 10, 1997

Most consecutive games, 10 or more points

92 — Cynthia Cooper, June 21, 1997-June 1, 2000

84 — Lauren Jackson, June 26, 2002-
   September 18, 2004

54 — Lisa Leslie, June 17, 2000-August 8, 2001

Most points, one half

31 — Cynthia Cooper, Houston at Sacramento,
   July 25, 1997

29 — Katie Smith, Minnesota vs. Los Angeles,
   June 3, 2000

Most points, overtime period

12 — Deanna Nolan, Detroit vs. New York,
   June 3, 2005
   Sheryl Swoopes, Houston vs. Indiana,
   May 29, 2005
   Mwadi Mabika, Los Angeles vs. San Antonio,
   July 2, 2004

11 — Shannon Johnson, Orlando vs. Cleveland,
   June 8, 2002

FIELD GOAL PERCENTAGE

Most seasons leading league

2 — Murriel Page, Washington, 1999-00
   Tamika Williams, Minnesota, 2003-04

1 — Michelle Snow, Houston, 2005
   Alisa Burras, Portland, 2002
   Latasha Byears, Los Angeles, 2001
   Isabelle Fijalkowski, Cleveland, 1998
   Haixia Zheng, Los Angeles, 1997

Highest field goal percentage, career
(Minimum 400 field goals)

.581 — Tamika Williams, Minnesota, 2002-05
   (441/759)

.538 — Ann Wauters, Cleveland, 2000-02; New York
   2004-05 (465/864)

.515 — Yolanda Griffith, Sacramento, 1999-2005
   (1189/2308)

Highest field goal percentage, season (qualifiers)

.668 — Tamika Williams, Minnesota, 2003 (129/193)

.629 — Alisa Burras, Portland, 2002 (117/186)

.618 — Haixia Zheng, Los Angeles, 1997 (110/178)

Highest field goal percentage, game
(Minimum 10 field goals made)

.917 — Sheryl Swoopes, Houston at Portland,
   August 4, 2000 (11/12)

.909 — Kamila Vodichkova, Phoenix vs.

Los Angeles, July 26, 2005 (10/11)
LaToya Thomas, Cleveland vs. Indiana,
June 29, 2003 (10/11)
Vicky Bullett, Washington vs. Detroit,
July 18, 2002 (10/11)
Tracy Reid, Charlotte vs. Utah,
August 5, 2000 (10/11)
Kamila Vodichkova, Seattle vs. Detroit,
June 28, 2000 (10/11)
Haixia Zheng, Los Angeles vs. Sacramento,
August 22, 1997 (10/11)
.857 — Adrienne Goodson, Utah at Portland,
August 6, 2002 (12/14)
Tari Phillips, New York vs. Charlotte,
June 12, 2001 (12/14)

Most field goals, none missed, game
9 — Michelle Snow, Houston vs Indiana,
May 29, 2005 (2OT)
8 — Lisa Leslie, Los Angeles at Seattle,
July 31, 2005
Svetlana Abrosimova, Minnesota vs Detroit,
July 13, 2005
Kara Lawson, Sacramento at Connecticut,
July 9, 2004
Crystal Robinson, New York at Cleveland,
August 17, 2003
Becky Hammon, New York, at Phoenix,
June 21, 2001
7 — Natalie Williams, Indiana at Washington,
September 1, 2004
Tamika Williams, Minnesota vs. Phoenix,
June 5, 2004
Pollyan Johns Kimbrough, Miami vs. Phoenix,
July 3, 2002
Kara Wolters, Indiana at Portland,
July 28, 2000
Taj McWilliams, Orlando at Washington,
July 21, 2000

Most field goal attempts, none made, game
12 — Tina Thompson, Houston at Phoenix,
July 19, 1999
11 — Elena Baranova, New York vs. Detroit,
August 1, 2003
Slobodanka Tuvic, Phoenix at Seattle,
July 25, 2003
Kamila Vodichkova, Seattle vs. Portland,
August 9, 2002
10 — By Many

FIELD GOALS

Most seasons leading league
4 — Sheryl Swoopes, Houston, 1999-2000, 2002,
2005
2 — Lisa Leslie, Los Angeles, 2001, 2004
1 — Lauren Jackson, Seattle, 2003
Jennifer Gillom, Phoenix, 1998

Cynthia Cooper, Houston, 1997
Most field goals, career
1,743 — Lisa Leslie, Los Angeles, 1997-2005
1,463 — Sheryl Swoopes, Houston, 1997-2000,
2002-2005
1,380 — Tina Thompson, Houston, 1997-2005
Most field goals, season
254 — Lauren Jackson, Seattle, 2003
245 — Sheryl Swoopes, Houston, 2000
232 — Chamique Holdsclaw, Washington, 2000
Most consecutive field goals made
14 — Tammy Sutton-Brown, Charlotte,
June 1-8, 2002
13 — Tamika Whitmore, New York,
June 30-July 8, 2002
Tina Thompson, Houston, June 23-25, 2002
12 — Kelly Schumacher, Indiana, July 16-23, 2003
DeLisha Milton, Los Angeles,
August 20-21, 1999
Most field goals, game
17 — Lauren Jackson, Seattle vs. Los Angeles,
August 6, 2003
15 — Sheryl Swoopes, Houston at Seattle,
August 9, 2005
Cynthia Cooper, Houston at Charlotte,
August 11, 1997
14 — By many
Most field goals, one half
11 — Sheryl Swoopes, Houston at Seattle,
August 9, 2005
Lauren Jackson, Seattle vs. Los Angeles,
August 6, 2003
Linda Burgess, Sacramento vs. Utah,
August 15, 1998
10 — By many

FIELD GOAL ATTEMPTS

Most seasons leading league
3 — Sheryl Swoopes, Houston, 1999, 2002, 2005
1 — Diana Taurasi, Phoenix, 2004
Lauren Jackson, Seattle, 2003
Tina Thompson, Houston, 2001
Chamique Holdsclaw, Washington, 2000
Jennifer Gillom, Phoenix, 1998
Wendy Palmer, Utah, 1997
Most field goal attempts, career
3,774 — Lisa Leslie, Los Angeles, 1997-2005
3,313 — Tina Thompson, Houston, 1997-2005
3,289 — Sheryl Swoopes, Houston, 1997-2000,
2002-2005
Most field goal attempts, season
528 — Tina Thompson, Houston, 2001
526 — Lauren Jackson, Seattle, 2003
519 — Katie Smith, Minnesota, 2001
Most field goal attempts, game
31 — Wendy Palmer, Utah vs. Los Angeles,
August 16, 1997

29 — Lauren Jackson, Seattle vs. Washington,
July 3, 2001 (4OT)
Sheryl Swoopes, Houston at Los Angeles,
August 20, 1999
28 — Mwadi Mabika, Los Angeles at Sacramento,
July 29, 2004 (2OT)
Mwadi Mabika, Los Angeles vs. Phoenix,
July 15, 2003 (2OT)
Sandy Brondello, Detroit at Utah,
July 6, 1999 (2OT)
Cynthia Cooper, Houston at Utah,
June 30, 1998 (2OT)

Most field goal attempts, one half
20 — Wendy Palmer, Utah vs. Los Angeles,
August 16, 1997
19 — Chamique Holdsclaw, Washington vs. Los
Angeles, June 26, 2000
Sheryl Swoopes, Houston at Los Angeles,
August 20, 1999

THREE-POINT FIELD GOAL PERCENTAGE

Most seasons leading league
2 — Jennifer Azzi, Detroit, 1999; Utah, 2001
Eva Nemcova, Cleveland, 1997-98
1 — Laurie Koehn, 2005
Charlotte Smith-Taylor, 2004
Becky Hammon, New York, 2003
Kelly Miller, Charlotte, 2002
Korie Hlede, Utah, 2000

Highest three-point field goal percentage, career
(Minimum 100 three-point field goals)
.458 — Jennifer Azzi, Detroit, 1999; Utah, 2000-02;
San Antonio, 2003 (158/345)
.410 — Sandy Brondello, Detroit, 1998-99; Miami,
2001-02; Seattle, 2003 (114/278)
.405 — Sue Bird, Seattle, 2002-05 (215/531)

Highest three-point field goal percentage, season
(qualifiers)
.517 — Jennifer Azzi, Detroit, 1999 (30/58)
.514 — Jennifer Azzi, Utah, 2001 (38/74)
.500 — Charlotte Smith-Taylor, 2004 (29/58)

Most three-point field goals, none missed, game
6 — Tamika Catchings, Indiana at Orlando,
July 3, 2002 (OT)
5 — By many

Most three-point field goal attempts, none made, game
8 — Crystal Robinson, New York vs. Detroit,
May 22, 2005
Betty Lennox, Seattle at Los Angeles,
June 1, 2004
Crystal Robinson, New York vs. Cleveland,
August 4, 2001
Crystal Robinson, New York vs. Detroit,
June 21, 2000
Tina Thompson, Houston at Utah,
June 30, 1998 (2OT)

7 — By many

THREE-POINT FIELD GOALS

Most seasons leading league
3 — Katie Smith, Minnesota, 2000-01, 2003
2 — Cynthia Cooper, Houston, 1997-98
1 — Nicole Powell, Sacramento, 2005
Anna DeForge, Phoenix, 2004
Allison Feaster, Charlotte, 2002
Crystal Robinson, New York, 1999

Most three-point field goals, career
478 — Katie Smith, Minnesota, 1999-2005;
Detroit 2005
400 — Crystal Robinson, New York, 1999-2005
347 — Tina Thompson, Houston, 1997-2005

Most three-point field goals, season
88 — Katie Smith, Minnesota, 2000
85 — Katie Smith, Minnesota, 2001
79 — Allison Feaster, Charlotte, 2002

Most three-point field goals, game
7 — Deanna Nolan, Detroit vs. New York,
August 10, 2003 (OT)
Katie Smith, Minnesota at Seattle,
June 14, 2003
Sophia Witherspoon, Portland at Miami,
June 29, 2001 (OT)
Nykesha Sales, Orlando at Sacramento,
July 27, 2000
Crystal Robinson, New York at Los Angeles,
July 24, 1999 (OT)
Cynthia Cooper, Houston at Sacramento,
July 25, 1997
Elena Baranova, Utah at New York,
July 22, 1997
6 — By many

Most consecutive three-point field goals made
8 — Lauren Jackson, Seattle, July 10-22. 2004
Lisa Leslie, Los Angeles, June 5-16, 2001
Crystal Robinson, June 28, 1999-July 1, 1999
7 — By many

Most consecutive games, three-point field goals made
33 — Nikki Teasley, Los Angeles, June 5, 2004-
May 31, 2005
32 — Katie Smith, Minnesota, July 31, 2002-
August 2, 2003
25 — Katie Smith, Minnesota, June 22, 2000-
June 9, 2001

Most three-point field goals made, one half
5 — By many. Most recent:
Nikki Teasley, Los Angeles vs. Detroit,
September 9, 2004

THREE-POINT FIELD GOAL ATTEMPTS

Most seasons leading league
2 — Diana Taurasi, Phoenix, 2004-05
Katie Smith, Minnesota, 2000-01
1 — Allison Feaster, Charlotte, 2003

Tamika Catchings, Indiana, 2002
Tonya Edwards, Minnesota, 1999
Cynthia Cooper, Houston, 1998
Ruthie Bolton-Holifield, Sacramento, 1997
Most three-point field goal attempts, career
1,294 — Katie Smith, Minnesota, 1999-2005;
Detroit 2005
1,044 — Crystal Robinson, New York, 1999-2005
997 — Mwadi Mabika, Los Angeles, 1997-2005
Most three-point field goal attempts, season
240 — Katie Smith, Minnesota, 2001
232 — Katie Smith, Minnesota, 2000
205 — Allison Feaster, Charlotte, 2003
Most three-point field goal attempts, game
15 — Ruthie Bolton-Holifield, Sacramento at
Cleveland, July 10, 1997
14 — Crystal Robinson, New York at Los Angeles,
July 24, 1999 (OT)
Ruthie Bolton-Holifield, Sacramento vs. Utah,
July 2, 1997 (OT)
13 — Lauren Jackson, Seattle vs. Los Angeles,
May 21, 2005
Katie Smith, Minnesota vs. Los Angeles,
June 3, 2000
Cynthia Cooper, Houston at Utah,
August 4, 1998
Cynthia Cooper, Houston vs. Cleveland,
July 29, 1997
Most three-point field goal attempts, one half
10 — Cynthia Cooper, Houston vs. Cleveland,
July 29, 1997
9 — By Many

FREE THROW PERCENTAGE

Most seasons leading league
2 — Becky Hammon, New York, 2003, 2005
1 — Katie Smith, Minnesota, 2004
Sue Bird, Seattle, 2002
Elena Baranova, Miami, 2001
Jennifer Azzi, Utah, 2000
Eva Nemcova, Cleveland, 1999
Sandy Brondello, Detroit, 1998
Bridget Pettis, Phoenix, 1997
Highest free-throw percentage, career
(Minimum 200 free throws)
.897 — Eva Nemcova, Cleveland, 1997-2002 (227/253)
.881 — Sue Bird, Seattle, 2002-05 (295/335)
.871 — Cynthia Cooper, Houston, 1997-2000, 2003
(758/870)
Highest free-throw percentage, season (qualifiers)
.984 — Eva Nemcova, Cleveland, 1999 (62/63)
.951 — Becky Hammon, New York, 2003 (39/41)
.937 — Stephanie White, Indiana, 2003 (45/48)
Most free throws made, none missed, game
14 — Lisa Leslie, Los Angeles vs. Minnesota,
July 15, 2000

13 — Chamique Holdsclaw, Washington vs. Indiana,
July 24, 2003
Tina Thompson, Houston at Minnesota,
June 17, 2003
Sheryl Swoopes, Houston at Los Angeles,
August 8, 2002
Yolanda Griffith, Sacramento at Charlotte,
June 24, 2001 (OT)
12 — By Many
Most free throw attempts, none made, game
8 — Cheryl Ford, Detroit at Charlotte,
August 6, 2005 (2OT)
6 — Cheryl Ford, Detroit at Seattle,
September 8, 2004
Tara Phillips, New York vs. Seattle,
June 15, 2004
Swin Cash, Detroit at San Antonio,
June 7, 2003
Tangela Smith, Sacramento vs. Utah,
August 14, 1999
Wendy Palmer, Utah at Los Angeles,
June 28, 1999
5 — Cheryl Ford, Detroit vs. Sacramento,
July 1, 2005
Tammy Sutton-Brown, Charlotte vs. Minnesota,
September 11, 2004
Pollyan Johns Kimbrough, Miami vs. Phoenix,
July 3, 2002
Audrey Sauret, Washington vs. Portland,
August 3, 2001
Tammy Jackson, Houston at Miami,
July 20, 2001

FREE THROWS MADE

Most seasons leading league
3 — Cynthia Cooper, Houston, 1997-99
2 — Swin Cash, Detroit, 2002, 2004
1 — Sheryl Swoopes, Houston, 2005
Marie Ferdinand, San Antonio, 2003
Katie Smith, Minnesota, 2001
Natalie Williams, Utah, 2000
Most free throws made, career
1137 — Lisa Leslie, Los Angeles, 1997-2005
928 — Yolanda Griffith, Sacramento, 1999-2005
917 — Katie Smith, Minnesota, 1999-2005;
Detroit 2005
Most free throws made, season
246 — Katie Smith, Minnesota, 2001
210 — Cynthia Cooper, Houston, 1998
204 — Cynthia Cooper, Houston, 1999
Most consecutive free throws made
66 — Eva Nemcova, Cleveland, June 14, 1999-
June 5, 2000
47 — Cynthia Cooper, Houston, August 16, 1999-
June 1, 2000
46 — Lisa Leslie, Los Angeles, July 9-25, 2000

Most free throws made, game
22 — Cynthia Cooper, Houston vs. Sacramento,
July 3, 1998
18 — Katie Smith, Minnesota at Los Angeles,
July 8, 2001 (OT)
17 — Cynthia Cooper, Houston vs. Utah,
August 16, 1999
Most free throws made, one half
13 — Tamika Catchings, Indiana vs. Phoenix,
May 24, 2005
Yolanda Griffith, Sacramento at Charlotte,
June 24, 2001
Ruthie Bolton-Holifield, Sacramento at
Washington, July 2, 1999
12 — By many

FREE THROW ATTEMPTS

Most seasons leading league
2 — Cynthia Cooper, Houston, 1997-98
Swin Cash, Detroit, 2002, 2004
1 — Tamika Catchings, Indiana, 2005
Marie Ferdinand, San Antonio, 2003
Katie Smith, Minnesota, 2001
Natalie Williams, Utah, 2000
Yolanda Griffith, Sacramento, 1999
Most free throw attempts, career
1,615 — Lisa Leslie, Los Angeles, 1997-2005
1,292 — Yolanda Griffith, Sacramento, 1999-2005
1,073 — Katie Smith, Minnesota, 1999-2005;
Detroit 2005
Most free throw attempts, season
275 — Katie Smith, Minnesota, 2001
246 — Cynthia Cooper, Houston, 1998
235 — Yolanda Griffith, Sacramento, 1999
Most free throw attempts, game
24 — Cynthia Cooper, Houston vs. Sacramento,
uly 3, 1998
21 — Swin Cash, Detroit vs. Miami,
June 28, 2002 (OT)
19 — Plenette Pierson, Detroit at Washington,
August 27, 2005
Plenette Pierson, Phoenix vs. Los Angeles,
August 8, 2003
Lisa Leslie, Los Angeles vs. Utah,
August 4, 2002
Katie Smith, Minnesota at Los Angeles,
July 8, 2001 (OT)
Yolanda Griffith, Sacramento vs. Phoenix,
June 12, 1999
Most free throw attempts, one half
16 — Kayte Christensen, Phoenix vs. San Antonio,
August 22, 2003
Lisa Leslie, Los Angeles at New York,
June 25, 2000
14 — By many

REBOUNDS

Most seasons leading league
3 — Lisa Leslie, Los Angeles, 1997-98, 2004
2 — Chamique Holdsclaw, Washington, 2002-03
Yolanda Griffith, Sacramento, 1999, 2001
1 — Cheryl Ford, Detroit, 2005
Natalie Williams, Utah, 2000
Most rebounds, career
2,540 — Lisa Leslie, Los Angeles, 1997-2005
1,882 — Yolanda Griffith, Sacramento, 1999-2005
1,832 — Natalie Williams, Utah, 1999-2002; Indiana,
2003-05
Highest average, rebounds per game, career
(Minimum 100 games)
9.3 — Lisa Leslie, Los Angeles, 1997-2005
(2,540/273)
8.9 — Yolanda Griffith, Sacramento, 1999-2005
(1,882/212)
8.6 — Chamique Holdsclaw, Washington, 1999-2004;
Los Angeles, 2005 (1,682/195)
Most rebounds, season
357 — Yolanda Griffith, Sacramento, 2001
336 — Lisa Leslie, Los Angeles, 2004
Natalie Williams, Utah, 2000
334 — Cheryl Ford, Detroit, 2003
Highest average, rebounds per game, season (qualifiers)
11.60 — Chamique Holdsclaw, Washington, 2002
(232/20)
11.59 — Natalie Williams, Utah, 2000 (336/29)
11.30 — Yolanda Griffith, Sacramento, 1999 (329/29)
Most rebounds, game
24 — Chamique Holdsclaw, Washington at Charlotte,
May 23, 2003
22 — Cheryl Ford, Detroit at San Antonio,
May 22, 2004
21 — Cheryl Ford, Detroit at Connecticut,
June 22, 2003 (OT)
Lisa Leslie, Los Angeles vs. Orlando,
July 22, 2002
Chamique Holdsclaw, Washington at
Sacramento, June 25, 2002 (2OT)
Cindy Brown, Detroit at Utah, August 10, 1998
Lisa Leslie, Los Angeles vs. New York,
June 19, 1998
Most games, 10+ rebounds, career
127 — Lisa Leslie, Los Angeles, 1997-2005
85 — Yolanda Griffith, Sacramento, 1999-2005
75 — Natalie Williams, Utah, 1999-2002;
Indiana, 2003-05
Most consecutive games, 10+ rebounds
7 — Lisa Leslie, Los Angeles, August 13, 2002-
June 7, 2003
Lauren Jackson, Seattle, July 25-
August 12, 2003
Natalie Williams, Utah, July 15-August 2, 2000

Lisa Leslie, Los Angeles, August 22, 1997-
June 21, 1998
6 — Cheryl Ford, Detroit, May 22-June 12, 2005
Cindy Brown, Detroit, July 31-August 11, 1998
5 — By many
Most rebounds, one half
14 — Latasha Byears, Los Angeles vs. Houston,
August 11, 2001
Lisa Leslie, Los Angeles vs. New York,
June 19, 1998
13 — By Many

OFFENSIVE REBOUNDS

Most seasons leading league
4 — Yolanda Griffith, Sacramento, 1999-01, 2004
2 — Latasha Byears, Sacramento, 1997-98
Natalie Williams, Utah, 2002; Indiana, 2003
1 — Cheryl Ford, Detroit, 2005
Most offensive rebounds, career
818 — Yolanda Griffith, Sacramento, 1999-2005
733 — Natalie Williams, Utah, 1999-2002; Indiana,
2003-05
659 — Lisa Leslie, Los Angeles, 1997-2005
Highest average, offensive rebounds per game, career
(Minimum 100 games)
3.9 — Yolanda Griffith, Sacramento, 1999-2005
(818/212)
3.3 — Natalie Williams, Utah, 1999-2002; Indiana,
2003-05 (733/221)
2.6 — Tamika Williams, Minnesota, 2002-05 (346/133)
Most offensive rebounds, season
162 — Yolanda Griffith, Sacramento, 2001
148 — Yolanda Griffith, Sacramento, 2000
141 — Yolanda Griffith, Sacramento, 1999
Most offensive rebounds, game
12 — Cheryl Ford, Detroit at San Antonio,
May 22, 2004
11 — Yolanda Griffith, Sacramento vs. Houston,
August 6, 2000
Yolanda Griffith, Sacramento vs. Los Angeles,
June 26, 1999
10 — By many
Most offensive rebounds, one half
8 — Cheryl Ford, Detroit at San Antonio,
May 22, 2004
Tamika Williams, Minnesota at Phoenix,
June 23, 2002
Tausha Mills, Washington at Sacramento,
July 8, 2000
7 — By many

DEFENSIVE REBOUNDS

Most seasons leading league
4 — Lisa Leslie, Los Angeles, 1997, 2000, 2002,
2004
1 — Lauren Jackson, Seattle, 2005
5.9 — Sue Bird, Seattle, 2002-05 (772/130)

5.3 — Nikki Teasley, Los Angeles 2002-05 (631/119)
Most assists, season
236 — Ticha Penicheiro, Sacramento, 2000
229 — Ticha Penicheiro, Sacramento, 2003
226 — Ticha Penicheiro, Sacramento, 1999
Highest average, assists per game, season (qualifiers)
8.0 — Ticha Penicheiro, Sacramento, 2002 (192/24)
7.9 — Ticha Penicheiro, Sacramento, 2000 (236/30)
7.5 — Ticha Penicheiro, Sacramento, 2001 (172/23)
Most assists, game
16 — Ticha Penicheiro, Sacramento vs. Los Angeles,
August 3, 2002
Ticha Penicheiro, Sacramento at Cleveland,
July 29, 1998
15 — Ticha Penicheiro, Sacramento at Cleveland,
July 15, 2003
14 — By many
Most games, 10+ assists, career
49 — Ticha Penicheiro, Sacramento, 1998-2005
18 — Teresa Weatherspoon, New York, 1997-2003;
Los Angeles, 2004
14 — Sue Bird, Seattle, 2002-05
Most assists, one half
11 — Ticha Penicheiro, Sacramento vs. Los Angeles,
August 3, 2002
Ticha Penicheiro, Sacramento at Utah,
June 26, 2000
Ticha Penicheiro, Sacramento at Cleveland,
July 29, 1998
10 — Dawn Staley, Charlotte vs. Washington,
July 26, 2000
Michele Timms, Phoenix at Sacramento,
June 12, 1999
Ticha Penicheiro, Sacramento at Charlotte,
July 27, 1998

PERSONAL FOULS

Most seasons leading league
4 — Lisa Leslie, Los Angeles, 1999-01, 2004
1 — Cheryl Ford, Detroit, 2005
Natalie Williams, Indiana, 2003
Olympia Scott-Richardson, Indiana, 2002
Margo Dydek, Utah, 1998
Isabelle Fijalkowski, Cleveland, 1997
Most personal fouls, career
1,090 — Lisa Leslie, Los Angeles, 1997-2005
847 — Natalie Williams, Utah, 1999-2002; Indiana,
2003-05
804 — Margo Dydek, Utah, 1998-2002; San Antonio,
2003-04; Connecticut, 2005
Most personal fouls, season
143 — Cheryl Ford, Detroit, 2005
139 — Janell Burse, Seattle, 2005
138 — Tammy Sutton-Brown, Charlotte, 2005
Natalie Williams, Indiana, 2003

Most personal fouls, game
6 — By Many
Most personal fouls, one half
6 — By Many

DISQUALIFICATIONS

Most seasons leading league
3 — Lisa Leslie, Los Angeles 2000, 2002, 2004
2 — Latasha Byears, Sacramento, 1998;
  Los Angeles, 2001
  Kamila Vodichkova, Seattle, 2003-04
1 — Cheryl Ford, Detroit, 2005
  Janell Burse, Seattle, 2005
  Kayte Christensen, Phoenix, 2003
  Natalie Williams, Utah, 2001
  Tonya Edwards, Minnesota, 1999
  Isabelle Fijalkowski, Cleveland, 1997
Most disqualifications, career
35 — Lisa Leslie, Los Angeles, 1997-2005
21 — Natalie Williams, Utah, 1999-2002; Indiana,
  2003-05
18 — Latasha Byears, Sacramento, 1997-00;
  Los Angeles, 2001-03
Highest percentage, games disqualified, career
(Minimum 100 games)
12.8 — Lisa Leslie, Los Angeles, 1997-2005 (35/273)
9.7 — Latasha Byears, Sacramento, 1997-00;
  Los Angeles, 2001-03 (18/185)
9.5 — Natalie Williams, Utah, 1999-2002; Indiana,
  2003-05 (21/221)
Lowest percentage, games disqualified, career
(Minimum 100 games)
0.00 — By Many
Most disqualifications, season
7 — Lisa Leslie, Los Angeles, 2002
  Lisa Leslie, Los Angeles, 2000
  Isabelle Fijalkowski, Cleveland, 1997
6 — Cheryl Ford, Detroit, 2005
  Janell Burse, Seattle, 2005
  Tonya Edwards, Minnesota, 1999
5 — By many
Fewest minutes, disqualified, game
5 — Sharon Manning, Miami at Detroit,
  July 26, 2000
7 — Rushia Brown, Cleveland vs. Utah,
  July 24, 1999
8 — LaTonya Johnson, Utah vs. Los Angeles,
  August 9, 2002
  Asjha Jones, Washington at Portland,
  June 28, 2002

STEALS

Most seasons leading league
2 — Tamika Catchings, Indiana, 2002, 2005
  Yolanda Griffith, Sacramento, 1999, 2004
  Teresa Weatherspoon, New York, 1997-98
1 — Sheryl Swoopes, Houston, 2000, 2003

Debbie Black, Miami, 2001
Most steals, career
520 — Sheryl Swoopes, Houston, 1997-2000,
  2002-2005
481 — Ticha Penicheiro, Sacramento, 1998-2005
465 — Teresa Weatherspoon, New York, 1997-2003;
  Los Angeles, 2004
Highest average, steals per game, career
(Minimum 100 games)
2.41 — Tamika Catchings, Indiana 2002-05 (323/134)
2.28 — Sheryl Swoopes, Houston, 1997-2000,
  2002-05 (520/228)
2.00 — Ticha Penicheiro, Sacramento, 1998-2005
  (481/240)
Most steals, season
100 — Teresa Weatherspoon, New York, 1998
94 — Tamika Catchings, Indiana, 2002
90 — Tamika Catchings, Indiana, 2005
Highest average, steals per game, season (qualifiers)
3.33 — Teresa Weatherspoon, New York, 1998 (100/30)
3.04 — Teresa Weatherspoon, New York, 1997 (85/28)
2.94 — Tamika Catchings, Indiana, 2002 (94/32)
Most steals, game
10 — Ticha Penicheiro, Sacramento vs. San Antonio,
  July 10, 2003
9 — Tamika Catchings, Indiana vs. Minnesota,
  July 26, 2002
  Michelle Griffiths, Phoenix at Utah,
  July 27, 1998
8 — By Many
Most steals, one half
7 — Michelle Brogan, Phoenix at Utah,
  July 27, 1998
  Cynthia Cooper, Houston at Charlotte,
  August 11, 1997
6 — By many

BLOCKED SHOTS

Most seasons leading league
7 — Margo Dydek, Utah, 1998-2002; San Antonio,
  2003; Connecticut, 2005
2 — Lisa Leslie, Los Angeles, 2004-05
1 — Elena Baranova, Utah, 1997
Most blocked shots, career
726 — Margo Dydek, Utah, 1998-2002; San Antonio,
  2003-04; Connecticut, 2005
635 — Lisa Leslie, Los Angeles, 1997-2005
338 — Lauren Jackson, Seattle, 2001-05
  Tangela Smith, Sacramento, 1998-2004;
  Charlotte 2005
Highest average, blocked shots per game, career
(Minimum: 100 games)
2.85 — Margo Dydek, Utah, 1998-2002; San Antonio,
  2003-04; Connecticut, 2005 (726/255)
2.33 — Lisa Leslie, Los Angeles, 1997-2005
  (635/273)

2.18 — Lauren Jackson, Seattle, 2001-05 (338/155)

Most blocked shots, season

114 — Margo Dydek, Utah, 1998
113 — Margo Dydek, Utah, 2001
107 — Margo Dydek, Utah, 2002

Highest average, blocked shots per game, season (qualifiers)

3.80 — Margo Dydek, Utah, 1998 (114/30)
3.57 — Margo Dydek, Utah, 2002 (107/30)
3.53 — Margo Dydek, Utah, 2001 (113/32)

Most blocked shots, game

10 — Lisa Leslie, Los Angeles vs. Detroit,
September 9, 2004
Margo Dydek, Utah vs. Orlando, June 7, 2001

9 — Margo Dydek, Connecticut vs. San Antonio,
June 4, 2005
Margo Dydek, San Antonio vs. Minnesota,
May 26, 2004
Margo Dydek, Utah vs. Cleveland,
August 6, 1998

8 — By many

Most blocked shots, one half

7 — Margo Dydek, Connecticut vs. San Antonio,
June 4, 2005
Lisa Leslie, Los Angeles vs. Detroit,
September 9, 2004

6 — By many

TURNOVERS

Most turnovers, career

889 — Lisa Leslie, Los Angeles, 1997-2005
694 — Shannon Johnson, Orlando, 1999-2002:
Connecticut, 2003; San Antonio, 2004-2005
675 — Ticha Penicheiro, Sacramento, 1998-2005

Most turnovers, season

135 — Ticha Penicheiro, Sacramento, 1999
125 — Nikki McCray, Washington, 1998
122 — Chantel Tremitiere, Sacramento, 1997

Most turnovers, game

11 — Betty Lennox, Minnesota at Houston,
August 9, 2000
Chamique Holdsclaw, Washington vs. Utah,
July 8, 1999
Michelle Edwards, Cleveland vs. Sacramento,
August 2, 1997

10 — Becky Hammon, New York at Los Angeles,
June 29, 2004 (OT)
Nikki McCray, Washington vs. New York,
July 5, 1998 (OT)

9 — By many

TEAM OFFENSE

SCORING

Highest average, points per game, season

77.3 — Houston, 2000 (2,475/32)
76.6 — Los Angeles, 2002 (2,452/32)

76.5 — Los Angeles, 1999 (2,449/32)

Lowest average, points per game, season

56.9 — Seattle, 2000 (1,822/32)
57.2 — Miami, 2000 (1,831/32)
60.0 — Seattle, 2001 (1,921/32)

Most points, game

111 — Detroit vs. Indiana, June 18, 2000
110 — Houston at Washington, August 17, 1998
108 — Sacramento vs. Detroit, July 1, 2000

Fewest points, game

34 — Washington at Cleveland, May 31, 2001
35 — Miami vs. Cleveland, June 24, 2001
36 — Washington vs. Miami, August 8, 2001
Seattle vs. Cleveland, June 14, 2001

Most points, both teams, game

204 — Sacramento (108) vs. Detroit (96), July 1, 2000
202 — Orlando (103) vs. Cleveland (99),
June 8, 2002 (3OT)
198 — Utah (104) vs. Detroit (94), July 6, 1999 (2OT)

Fewest points, both teams, game

78 — Washington (36) vs. Miami (42), August 8, 2001
83 — Indiana (37) at Charlotte (46), June 26, 2004
86 — Seattle (38) at Charlotte (48), July 7, 2001

Largest margin of victory, game

45 — Houston (110) at Washington (65),
August 17, 1998
43 — New York (88) vs. Washington (45),
August 13, 1998
41 — Seattle (89) vs. Phoenix (48), July 19, 2002

BY HALF

Most points, first half

56 — Detroit vs. San Antonio, July 1, 2003
55 — Cleveland vs. Washington, July 26, 2003
Los Angeles at Connecticut, May 24, 2003
Los Angeles vs. Utah, August 4, 2002
54 — Houston vs. Indiana, July 6, 2001
Los Angeles vs. Sacramento, August 22, 1997

Fewest points, first half

8 — Detroit at Houston, July 6, 2002
11 — Minnesota vs. Houston, June 30, 2001
12 — Charlotte at Cleveland, July 21, 2001
Miami vs. Cleveland, June 24, 2001

Most points, both teams, first half

106 — Cleveland (53) at Detroit (53), June 15, 1998
103 — Detroit (56) vs. San Antonio (47), July 1, 2003
99 — Utah (50) vs. Los Angeles (49), June 23, 1997

Fewest points, both teams, first half

26 — Detroit (8) at Houston (18), July 6, 2002
31 — Miami (15) vs. Charlotte (16), August 14, 2001
33 — Minnesota (11) vs. Houston (22), June 30, 2001
Miami (12) vs. Cleveland (21), June 24, 2001
Washington (16) vs. Los Angeles (17),
August 14, 1999

Largest lead at halftime

31 — Sacramento at Minnesota, July 3, 2001
(led 46-15; won 91-52)

Houston vs. Miami, June 15, 2000 (led
44-13; won 77-53)
29 — Phoenix vs. San Antonio, August 19, 2005 (led
53-24; won 91-57)
28 — Houston vs. Indiana, July 6, 2001 (led 54-26;
won 79-64)
Cleveland vs. Charlotte, July 10, 1999 (led
47-19; won 82-56)
Phoenix vs. Washington, August 4, 1998 (led
48-20; won 88-59)
Cleveland vs. Phoenix, July 31, 1997 (led
43-15; won 79-67)

Largest deficit at halftime overcome to win game
19 — Detroit at Indiana, June 9, 2004
(trailed 51-32; won 83-79)
18 — Utah at Phoenix, August 20, 1999 (trailed
38-20; won 70-62)
17 — Los Angeles at San Antonio, June 26, 2003
(trailed 41-24; won 67-58)

Most points, second half
66 — Detroit vs. Indiana, June 18, 2000
63 — Washington vs. Utah, July 19, 1998
60 — Utah vs. Sacramento, June 26, 2000
Houston at Washington, August 17, 1998

Fewest points, second half
9 — Seattle vs. Cleveland, June 14, 2001
12 — Indiana at Charlotte, May 28, 2004
14 — Seattle at Phoenix, August 15, 2003

Most points, both teams, second half
115 — Washington (63) vs. Utah (52), July 19, 1998
111 — Utah (60) vs. Sacramento (51), June 26, 2000
108 — Sacramento (56) vs. Detroit (52), July 1, 2000

Fewest points, both teams, second half
35 — Washington (16) vs. Miami (19), August 8, 2001
37 — Miami (18) at Cleveland (19), July 25, 2001
Washington (15) at Seattle (22), July 3, 2001
Miami (18) vs. Cleveland (19), July 7, 2000
Utah (17) vs. Houston (20), June 30, 1998
39 — Charlotte (18) vs. New York (21),
August 24, 2003
Charlotte (18) at Washington (21),
July 29, 2001

OVERTIME

Most points, overtime period
19 — Washington vs. New York, August 23, 2005
Houston vs. Indiana, May 29, 2005
Los Angeles vs. Minnesota, July 8, 2001
18 — Detroit at Connecticut, June 22, 2003
Indiana vs. Phoenix, July 1, 2001
17 — New York vs. Indiana, September 16, 2004
Orlando vs. Cleveland, June 8, 2002
New York at Orlando, July 29, 1999

Fewest points, overtime period
0 — Houston at Minnesota, June 30, 2004
Miami at Cleveland, July 25, 2001
1 — Detroit at Utah, July 6, 1999

2 — By many

Most points, both teams, overtime period
33 — Los Angeles (19) vs. Minnesota (14),
July 8, 2001
30 — Houston (19) vs. Indiana (11), May 29, 2005
Orlando (17) vs. Cleveland (13), June 8, 2002
28 — New York (17) vs. Indiana (11),
September 16, 2004
Indiana (18) vs. Phoenix (10), July 1, 2001

Fewest points, both teams, overtime period
4 — Miami (0) at Cleveland (4), July 25, 2001
Seattle (2) vs. Washington (2), July 3, 2001
7 — Indiana (2) vs. Seattle (5), June 4, 2001
8 — Many times

Largest margin of victory, overtime period
13 — Washington (82) vs. New York (69),
August 23, 2005
11 — Detroit (82) vs. New York (71),
September 14, 2004
Miami (74) at Charlotte (63), June 3, 2000
10 — Washington (88) vs. Indiana (78), June 18, 2005
Seattle (78) vs. Minnesota (68), June 4, 2002
Seattle (69) vs. Los Angeles (59),
June 13, 2000
Utah (104) vs. Detroit (94), July 6, 1999

FIELD GOAL PERCENTAGE

Highest field-goal percentage, season
.470 — Houston, 2000 (891/1,894)
.468 — Cleveland, 1998 (804/1,719)
.459 — Washington, 2000 (832/1,813)

Lowest field-goal percentage, season
.365 — Miami, 2000 (647/1,774)
.371 — Minnesota, 2001 (671/1,810)
.373 — Phoenix, 1997 (660/1,768)

Highest field-goal percentage, game
.655 — Los Angeles vs. Houston, June 15, 2005 (36/55)
.654 — Houston at Washington, July 26, 2005 (34/52)
.636 — Phoenix vs. Seattle, August 3, 2000 (28/44)

Lowest field-goal percentage, game
.182 — Miami vs. Cleveland, June 24, 2001 (10/55)
.188 — Indiana at Charlotte, June 26, 2004 (9/48)
.196 — Washington vs. Miami, August 8, 2001 (10/51)

Highest field-goal percentage, both teams, game
.576 — Cleveland (.611) vs. Detroit (.547),
June 16, 2000 (68/118)
.573 — Houston (.654) at Washington (.490),
July 26, 2005 (59/103)
.563 — Cleveland (.593) at Los Angeles (.538),
July 23, 1997 (67/119)

Lowest field-goal percentage, both teams, game
.245 — Washington (.196) vs. Miami (.294),
August 8, 2001 (25/102)
.252 — Minnesota (.200) vs. Houston (.300),
July 23, 2001 (29/115)
.266 — Indiana (.188) at Charlotte (.348)
June 26, 2004 (25/94)

FIELD GOALS

Most field goals per game, season
28.6 — Los Angeles, 2001 (916/32)
28.4 — Los Angeles, 1997 (794/28)
27.8 — Los Angeles, 2002 (891/32)
Houston, 2000 (891/32)
Fewest field goals per game, season
20.2 — Miami, 2000 (647/32)
20.8 — Seattle, 2000 (667/32)
21.0 — Minnesota, 2001 (671/32)
Most field goals, game
41 — Houston at Washington, August 17, 1998
40 — Utah vs. Detroit, July 6, 1999 (2OT)
Charlotte at Washington, August 19, 1998
39 — Los Angeles at Detroit, June 26, 2001 (OT)
New York at Phoenix, June 21, 2001
Fewest field goals, game
9 — Indiana at Charlotte, June 26, 2004
10 — Washington vs. Miami, August 8, 2001
Miami vs. Cleveland, June 24, 2001
Miami vs. Seattle, July 10, 2000
11 — Minnesota vs. Houston, July 23, 2001
Most field goals, both teams, game
70 — Utah (40) vs. Detroit (30), July 6, 1999 (2OT)
69 — Seattle (35) vs. Connecticut (34), June 22, 2005
Sacramento (36) vs. Detroit (33), July 1, 2000
Utah (35) at Sacramento (34), August 14, 1999
Cleveland (38) at Detroit (31), June 15, 1998
68 — Orlando (35) vs. Cleveland (33),
June 8, 2002 (3OT)
Detroit (35) at Cleveland (33), June 16, 2000
Utah (35) vs. Charlotte (33), June 25, 1998
Fewest field goals, both teams, game
23 — Miami (10) vs. Seattle (13), July 10, 2000
25 — Indiana (9) at Charlotte (16), June 26, 2004
Washington (10) vs. Miami (15),
August 8, 2001
29 — Minnesota (11) vs. Houston (18), July 23, 2001
Most field goals, one half
23 — Portland at Utah, June 25, 2002
New York at Phoenix, June 21, 2001
Houston at Washington, August 17, 1998
22 — By many

FIELD GOAL ATTEMPTS

Most field goal attempts per game, season
64.4 — Washington, 2003 (2,191/34)
63.9 — Los Angeles, 1999 (2,044/32)
63.8 — Los Angeles, 1998 (1,914/30)
Fewest field goal attempts per game, season
51.3 — Charlotte, 2004 (1,744/34)
53.9 — San Antonio, 2005 (1833/34)
54.4 — New York, 2002 (1,740/32)
Seattle, 2000 (1,740/32)
Most field-goal attempts, game
94 — Detroit vs. Washington, July 10, 1999 (2OT)
93 — Phoenix at Los Angeles, July 15, 2003 (2 ot)

91 — Seattle vs. Washington, July 3, 2001 (4 ot)
Regulation Game:
84 — Connecticut vs. Los Angeles, May 24, 2003
Sacramento at Los Angeles, August 22, 1997
Fewest field goal attempts, game
36 — Minnesota at Miami, May 28, 2002
Portland vs. Miami, August 1, 2000
39 — New York vs. Miami, June 2, 2002
Washington at Cleveland, June 3, 2000
40 — Minnesota vs. Portland, July 10, 2002
Most field goal attempts, both teams, game
169 — Phoenix (93) at Los Angeles (76),
July 15, 2003 (2OT)
Utah (87) vs. Detroit (82), July 6, 1999 (2OT)
165 — Seattle (91) vs. Washington (74),
July 3, 2001 (4OT)
163 — Sacramento (86) vs. Los Angeles (77),
July 24, 2004 (2OT)
Regulation Game:
156 — Connecticut (84) vs. Los Angeles (72),
May 24, 2003
Fewest field goal attempts, both teams, game
84 — Miami (41) vs. Seattle (43), July 10, 2000
89 — New York (39) at Miami (50), June 2, 2002
90 — Washington (45) at Indiana (45),
August 18, 2005
Phoenix (46) at Charlotte (44), May 26, 2005
Seattle (42) at Charlotte (48), July 7, 2001
Portland (36) vs. Miami (54), August 1, 2000
Most field-goal attempts, one half
49 — Sacramento at Los Angeles, August 22, 1997
48 — Washington vs. Utah, July 19, 1998

THREE-POINT FIELD GOAL PERCENTAGE

Highest three-point field goal percentage, season
.400 — Charlotte, 2002 (211/527)
.387 — Detroit, 2003 (125/323)
.385 — Sacramento, 2001 (163/423)
Lowest three-point field goal percentage, season
.260 — Sacramento, 1998 (72/277)
.264 — Washington, 1998 (114/432)
.269 — Los Angeles, 1997 (65/242)
Most three-point field goals, none missed, game
9 — New York at Phoenix, June 21, 2001
3 — Houston vs. Seattle, June 28, 2005
Cleveland vs. Sacramento, August 2, 1997
2 — Utah vs. Charlotte, June 8, 2002
Most three-point field goal attempts, none made, game
17 — New York at Phoenix, July 7, 1997
16 — Washington vs. Miami, August 8, 2001
Washington at New York, August 13, 1998
15 — Indiana vs. Detroit, July 15, 2005
Minnesota at San Antonio May 26, 2004

THREE-POINT FIELD GOALS

Most three-point field goals per game, season
6.6 — Charlotte, 2002 (211/32)
6.38 — Minnesota, 2000 (204/32)

6.35 — New York, 2004 (216/34)

Fewest three-point field goals per game, season

    1.8 — Houston, 2005 (62/34)

        Detroit, 2004 (62/34)

    2.2 — Detroit, 2005 (76/34)

    2.3 — Cleveland, 1997 (65/28)

        Los Angeles, 1997 (65/28)

Most three-point field goals, game

    15 — Washington vs. Los Angeles, May 26, 2005

    14 — Sacramento at Minnesota, July 3, 2001

        Minnesota at Utah, June 26, 1999

    13 — Indiana at Washington, July 29, 2003 (OT)

        Charlotte at Detroit, July 3, 2003

        Seattle vs. Los Angeles, July 11, 2002

        Orlando at Sacramento, July 27, 2000

Fewest three-point field goals, game

    0 — By many

Most three-point field goals, both teams, game

    22 — Connecticut (12) vs. Indiana (10),

        June 26, 2003 (2OT)

    21 — Minnesota (11) vs. Sacramento (10),

        June 29, 1999

    20 — Orlando (13) at Sacramento (7), July 27, 2000

Fewest three-point field goals, both teams, game

    0 — Detroit vs. Houston, July 6, 2004

        Washington vs. Miami, August 8, 2001

    1 — By many

Most three-point field goals, one half

    10 — Washington vs. Los Angeles, May 26, 2005

    9 — Seattle vs. Los Angeles, July 11, 2002

        Washington vs. Utah, July 19, 1998

        Houston at New York, July 8, 1998

    8 — By Many

THREE-POINT FIELD GOAL ATTEMPTS

Most three-point field goal attempts per game, season

    18.8 — Minnesota, 1999 (603/32)

    18.1 — New York, 2004 (617/34)

    17.8 — Minnesota, 2000 (571/32)

Fewest three-point field goal attempts per game, season

    6.0 — Houston, 2005 (205/34)

    6.1 — Detroit, 2004 (209/34)

    6.3 — Cleveland, 1997 (177/28)

Most three-point field goal attempts, game

    32 — Seattle vs. Los Angeles, May 21, 2005

    31 — Phoenix vs. San Antonio, August 19, 2005

    30 — Indiana at Washington, July 29, 2003 (OT)

        Portland vs. Los Angeles, July 28, 2001

        Orlando at Sacramento, July 27, 2000

        Houston at Utah, June 30, 1998 (2OT)

Fewest three-point field goal attempts, game

    1 — Houston vs. Phoenix, June 4, 2005

        Charlotte vs. Phoenix, May 26, 2005

        Detroit at Charlotte, September 4, 2004

        San Antonio vs. Seattle, June 19, 2004

        Utah at Detroit, August 7, 2001

        Sacramento at Washington, July 26, 1998

New York vs. Detroit, July 6, 1998

        Los Angeles at New York, August 5, 1997

    2 — By many

Most three-point field goal attempts, both teams, game

    50 — Connecticut (27) vs. Indiana (23),

        June 26, 2003 (2OT)

    49 — Houston (30) at Utah (19), June 30, 1998 (2OT)

    48 — Indiana (28) at Washington (20),

        June 18, 2005 (2OT)

        Orlando (30) at Sacramento (18),

        July 27, 2000

Fewest three-point field goal attempts, both teams, game

    7 — Houston (2) at Charlotte (5), July 17, 2005

    8 — Miami (2) vs. Detroit (6), June 12, 2001 (ot)

    9 — Cleveland (3) vs. New York (6), July 14, 1997

Most three-point field goal attempts, one half

    23 — Washington vs. Utah, July 19, 1998

    20 — Indiana vs. San Antonio, September 10, 2004

        Minnesota at Cleveland, July 12, 1999

        Houston vs. Cleveland, July 29, 1997

FREE THROW PERCENTAGE

Highest free throw percentage, season

    .822 — Houston, 2000 (521/634)

    .819 — New York, 2005 (452/552)

    .818 — Houston, 1999 (509/622)

Lowest free throw percentage, season

    .645 — Washington, 1998 (400/620)

    .658 — Detroit, 2005 (509/774)

    .661 — Washington, 2001 (333/504)

Most free throws made, no misses, game

    27 — Los Angeles vs. Phoenix, July 24, 2003

        Portland vs. Los Angeles, July 28, 2001

    21 — Washington at New York, August 8, 2002

    20 — Minnesota vs. Phoenix, August 4, 2003

        Los Angeles at Minnesota, May 28, 2003

Lowest free-throw percentage, game

    .000 — Washington at Detroit, August 25, 2003 (0/1)

    .167 — Phoenix vs. Houston, August 14, 2001 (1/6)

    .200 — Minnesota at Portland, July 14, 2000 (1/5)

Highest free throw percentage, both teams, game

    1.000 — San Antonio (1.000) vs. Indiana (1.000),

        June 1, 2004 (22/22)

        Cleveland (1.000) vs. Washington (1.000),

        May 31, 2001 (11/11)

        Cleveland (1.000) vs. Orlando (1.000),

        June 22, 1999 (15/15)

    .958 — Orlando (1.000) at Houston (.941),

        August 3, 2002 (23/24)

        Washington (1.000) vs. Charlotte (.933),

        June 30, 2002 (23/24)

        Washington (1.000) vs. Charlotte (.875),

        July 12, 1999 (23/24)

    .952 — San Antonio (1.000) vs. Washington (0.900),

        June 7, 2005 (20/21)

Lowest free throw percentage, both teams, game

    .423 — Utah (.389) vs. Los Angeles (.500),

August 13, 2001 (OT) (11/26)
.435 — Minnesota (.200) at Portland (.500),
July 14, 2000 (10/23)
.448 — Washington (.313) vs. Portland (.615),
August 3, 2001 (13/29)

FREE THROWS MADE

Most free throws made per game, season
20.1 — Utah, 2002 (643/32)
19.0 — Utah, 2000 (609/32)
18.4 — Detroit, 2003 (624/34)
Fewest free throws made per game, season
10.4 — Washington, 2001 (333/32)
10.5 — New York, 2001 (336/32)
10.6 — Minnesota, 1999 (339/32)
Most free throws made, game
42 — Utah vs. Los Angeles, June 23, 1997
40 — Detroit vs. San Antonio, July 1, 2003
Detroit vs. Indiana, June 18, 2000
Los Angeles vs. Washington, August 3, 1998
38 — Miami vs. Seattle, July 10, 2000
Fewest free throws made, game
0 — Washington at Detroit, August 25, 2003
Washington vs. Charlotte, July 7, 2003
1 — Charlotte at New York September 2, 2004
Sacramento at Seattle, August 25, 2003
Indiana at Houston, July 8, 2003
Phoenix vs. Houston, August 14, 2001
Miami at Seattle, July 30, 2000
Minnesota at Portland, July 14, 2000
2 — By many
Most free throws made, both teams, game
61 — Detroit (40) vs. San Antonio (21), July 1, 2003
Sacramento (34) vs. Detroit (27), July 1, 2000
Los Angeles (33) vs. Houston (28),
June 20, 2000
60 — Minnesota (37) at Los Angeles (23),
July 8, 2001 (OT)
Utah (42) vs. Los Angeles (18), June 23, 1997
59 — Detroit (40) vs. Indiana (19), June 18, 2000
Fewest free throws made, both teams, game
7 — Indiana (1) at Houston (6), July 8, 2003
8 — Washington (0) vs. Charlotte (8), July 7, 2003
9 — Sacramento (4) at Washington (5),
June 26, 2005
New York (3) vs. Cleveland (6), August 8, 2000
Most free throws made, one half
30 — Los Angeles vs. Washington, August 3, 1998
28 — Connecticut vs. Detroit, July 30, 2005
Connecticut vs. Indiana, September 19, 2004
Utah vs. Los Angeles, June 23, 1997

FREE THROW ATTEMPTS

Most free throw attempts per game, season
26.5 — Sacramento, 1999 (847/32)
26.4 — Utah, 2002 (844/32)
25.9 — Detroit, 2003 (882/34)
Fewest free throw attempts per game, season

14.66— Miami, 2001 (469/32)
14.69— Minnesota, 1999 (470/32)
14.9 — Washington, 2003 (507/34)
Most free throw attempts, game
56 — Utah vs. Los Angeles, June 23, 1997
55 — Miami vs. Seattle, July 10, 2000
54 — Detroit vs. Indiana, June 18, 2000
Fewest free throw attempts, game
0 — Washington vs. Charlotte, July 7, 2003
1 — Washington at Detroit, August 25, 2003
Miami at Seattle, July 30, 2000
2 — Seattle at Phoenix, July 6, 2005
Charlotte at New York, September 2, 2004
Indiana at Houston, July 8, 2003
Washington vs. Connecticut, June 24, 2003
Phoenix at Washington, July 9, 2002
Sacramento at Phoenix, July 20, 1998
Most free throw attempts, both teams, game
88 — Detroit (54) vs. Indiana (34), June 18, 2000
87 — Phoenix (47) vs. San Antonio (40),
August 22, 2003
80 — Utah (56) vs. Los Angeles (24), June 23, 1997
Fewest free throw attempts, both teams, game
9 — Washington (0) vs. Charlotte (9), July 7, 2003
10 — New York (4) vs. Cleveland (6), August 8, 2000
11 — Indiana (2) at Houston (9), July 8, 2003
Cleveland (4) vs. Washington (7), May 31, 2001
Most free throw attempts, one half
39 — Miami vs. Seattle, July 10, 2000
Los Angeles vs. Washington, August 3, 1998
38 — Sacramento at Detroit, July 4, 1999

REBOUNDS

Most rebounds per game, season
36.2 — Detroit, 2003 (1,230/34)
35.9 — Detroit, 1998 (1,077/30)
35.7 — Detroit, 2005 (1,215/34)
Fewest rebounds per game, season
24.8 — Seattle, 2000 (793/32)
25.6 — Charlotte, 2004 (872/34)
26.9 — Phoenix, 2004 (916/34)
Most rebounds, game
54 — Utah vs. Detroit, July 6, 1999 (2 ot)
52 — Detroit at New York, May 22, 2005
51 — Sacramento vs. Los Angeles, July 29, 2004
Washington at Sacramento,
June 25, 2002 (2OT)
Houston vs. Orlando, August 3, 2001
Houston at Utah, June 30, 1998 (2OT)
Fewest rebounds, game
13 — Miami at Orlando, August 11, 2001
14 — Detroit vs. Utah, August 7, 2001
New York at Charlotte, July 30, 1999
15 — Indiana at Detroit, August 25, 2005
Charlotte at Los Angeles, June 9, 2004
Seattle at Sacramento, August 9, 2000

Most rebounds, both teams, game
- 97 — Sacramento (51) vs. Los Angeles (46), July 29, 2004 (2OT)
- 95 — Washington (50) at Seattle (45), July 3, 2001 (4OT)
- 94 — Houston (51) at Utah (43), June 30, 1998 (2OT)

Regulation Game:
- 89 — Connecticut (46) vs. Los Angeles (43), May 24, 2003
  - Sacramento (48) at Washington (41), June 5, 2001

Fewest rebounds, both teams, game
- 40 — New York (14) at Charlotte (26), July 30, 1999
- 41 — Charlotte (15) at Los Angele (26), June 9, 2004
  - Houston (19) vs. Indiana (22), July 8, 2003
  - Miami (13) at Orlando (28), August 11, 2001
- 42 — Washington (20) vs. Indiana (22), July 24, 2003
  - Phoenix (19) vs. Sacramento (23), July 27, 2002
  - Detroit (18) at Cleveland (24), August 8, 2001
  - Miami (20) at Phoenix (22), July 4, 2001

Most rebounds, one half
- 33 — Los Angeles vs. Houston, July 16, 1997
- 31 — Connecticut vs. Los Angeles, May 24, 2003

OFFENSIVE REBOUNDS

Most offensive rebounds per game, season
- 12.9 — Sacramento, 1999 (412/32)
- 12.2 — Sacramento, 1997 (341/28)
- 12.1 — Sacramento, 2000 (388/32)

Fewest offensive rebounds per game, season
- 7.1 — New York, 2005 (242/34)
- 7.5 — San Antonio, 2005 (256/34)
  - Charlotte, 2004 (256/34)
- 7.6 — Cleveland, 1998 (227/30)

Most offensive rebounds, game
- 23 — Cleveland vs. Los Angeles, August 7, 1997 (2OT)
- 22 — Detroit vs. Charlotte, July 3, 2003
  - Minnesota vs. Utah, May 25, 2002 (OT)
  - Houston vs. Orlando, August 3, 2001
  - Phoenix at Cleveland, July 31, 1997
- 21 — By many

Fewest offensive rebounds, game
- 1 — By Many
  - Most Recent: San Antonio vs. Seattle, June 30, 2005

Most offensive rebounds, both teams, game
- 37 — Sacramento (19) at Washington (18), June 5, 2001
- 35 — Orlando (19) at Miami (16), August 9, 2000 (2OT)
  - Phoenix (19) at New York (16), August 2, 1997
  - Sacramento (19) at Utah (16), June 21, 1997
- 34 — Houston (18) at Los Angeles (16), July 23, 2004
  - Charlotte (18) vs. New York (16), July 20, 2004 (OT)

- Detroit (21) at San Antonio (13), May 22, 2004

Fewest offensive rebounds, both teams, game
- 5 — New York (2) at Minnesota (3), July 6, 2001
- 7 — Washington (3) vs. Houston (4), July 26, 2005
  - Houston (2) vs. Indiana (5), July 8, 2003
- 8 — Los Angeles (3) vs. Washington (5), July 19, 2005
  - Los Angeles (3) at Connecticut (5), May 27, 2004
  - Seattle (2) at Houston (6), July 25, 2000
  - New York (1) at Charlotte (7), July 30, 1999

Most offensive rebounds, one half
- 16 — Phoenix at Seattle, August 27, 2005
  - Seattle at Utah, June 15, 2002
  - Phoenix at Cleveland, July 31, 1997
- 14 — By many

DEFENSIVE REBOUNDS

Most defensive rebounds per game, season
- 25.4 — Los Angeles, 2002 (814/32)
- 25.0 — Detroit, 2003 (851/34)
- 24.5 — Los Angeles, 2000 (783/32)

Fewest defensive rebounds per game, season
- 16.8 — Seattle, 2000 (537/32)
- 17.90 — Miami, 2002 (573/32)
- 17.91 — Charlotte, 2005 (609/34)

Most defensive rebounds, game
- 40 — Utah vs. Detroit, July 6, 1999 (2OT)
- 39 — San Antonio vs. Connecticut, June 1, 2003
- 38 — Los Angeles at Sacramento, July 27, 1997

Fewest defensive rebounds, game
- 6 — Houston at Los Angeles, June 15, 2005
- 8 — Miami vs. Minnesota, May 28, 2002
  - Washington at New York, August 13, 1998
- 9 — Charlotte vs. San Antonio, June 23, 2005

Most defensive rebounds, both teams, game
- 67 — Los Angeles (35) vs. Phoenix (32), July 15, 2003 (2OT)
- 66 — Detroit (36) at Connecticut (30), June 22, 2003 (OT)
  - San Antonio (39) vs. Connecticut (27), June 1, 2003
  - Washington (35) at Los Angeles (31), June 27, 2002
- 65 — Utah (40) vs. Detroit (25), July 6, 1999 (2OT)
  - Houston (33) at Utah (32), June 30, 1998 (2OT)

Fewest defensive rebounds, both teams, game
- 23 — Charlotte (9) vs. San Antonio (14), June 23, 2005
  - Seattle (11) at Cleveland (12), July 5, 2002
- 24 — Connecticut (11) vs. New York (13), September 17, 2004
- 25 — Cleveland (11) at Charlotte (14), June 25, 2003
  - New York (11) at Indiana (14), July 19, 2002

Most defensive rebounds, one half
- 22 — Seattle at San Antonio, August 23, 2005
  - San Antonio vs. Connecticut, June 1, 2003

Los Angeles vs. Portland, July 24, 2002
Los Angeles vs. New York, July 20, 2000
21 — Many times

ASSISTS

Most assists per game, season
19.2 — Cleveland, 1998 (575/30)
18.6 — Los Angeles, 2001 (596/32)
18.4 — Los Angeles, 2004 (626/34)
Fewest assists per game, season
12.2 — Seattle, 2000 (390/32)
12.5 — Charlotte, 2004 (426/34)
12.6 — San Antonio, 2003 (428/34)
Most assists, game
32 — New York at Phoenix, June 21, 2001
31 — Cleveland vs. Detroit, June 16, 2000
Charlotte at Washington, August 19, 1998
30 — Charlotte vs. Orlando, July 17, 2002
Fewest assists, game
3 — Minnesota at Seattle, August 8, 2003
Cleveland at Detroit, July 28, 2001
4 — Sacramento vs. Connecticut, June 24, 2005
Houston at Phoenix, June 24, 1998
5 — By many
Most assists, both teams, game
57 — Cleveland (31) vs. Detroit (26), June 16, 2000
53 — Cleveland (28) vs. Washington (25),
August 15, 1998
51 — Washington (28) at Charlotte (23),
July 26, 2000
Fewest assists, both teams, game
10 — Charlotte (5) vs. Indiana (5), June 26, 2004
11 — Seattle (5) at Miami (6), July 10, 2000
12 — Portland (5) at Houston (7), June 24, 2001
Most assists, one half
18 — Los Angeles vs. Utah, July 7, 2002
17 — By many

PERSONAL FOULS

Most personal fouls per game, season
23.8 — Portland, 2000 (761/32)
23.13— Utah, 1999 (740/32)
23.07— Washington, 1998 (692/30)
Fewest personal fouls per game, season
14.4 — Houston, 2003 (490/34)
14.6 — Houston, 2002 (467/32)
15.9 — Houston, 2001 (509/32)
Most personal fouls, game
39 — Indiana at Detroit, June 18, 2000
36 — San Antonio at Phoenix, August 22, 2003
Washington at Los Angeles, August 3, 1998
Los Angeles at Utah, June 23, 1997
35 — By many
Fewest personal fouls, game
5 — Indiana vs. New York, August 27, 2005
New York vs. Charlotte, September 02, 2004
6 — Seattle vs. Miami, July 30, 2000
7 — Detroit vs. Washington, August 25, 2003

Houston vs. Seattle, May 22, 2003
Houston vs. Minnesota, June 15, 2002
Most personal fouls, both teams, game
70 — Indiana (39) at Detroit (31), June 18, 2000
66 — Orlando (34) vs. Cleveland (32),
June 8, 2002 (3OT)
64 — San Antonio (36) at Phoenix (28),
August 22, 2003
Minnesota (34) at Utah (30), July 28, 2001 (OT)
Phoenix (35) at Sacramento (29),
June 12, 1999
Fewest personal fouls, both teams, game
20 — Orlando (8) vs. Washington (12),
August 15, 1999
21 — Indiana (5) vs. New York (16), August 27, 2005
Washington (9) vs. Detroit (12), July 18, 2002
Los Angeles (10) vs. Indiana (11),
August 6, 2001
Houston (8) at Orlando (13), July 18, 2001
Phoenix (9) at Los Angeles (12), July 5, 2001
Washington (10) vs. Cleveland (11),
August 9, 2000
22 — New York (8) vs. Seattle (14), August 6, 2005
San Antonio (9) at Houston (13), May 20, 2004
Charlotte (10) at Washington (12), July 7, 2003
Houston (7) vs. Minnesota (15), June 15, 2002
Most personal fouls, one half
25 — Portland at Miami, July 19, 2000
Indiana at Detroit, June 18, 2000
24 — Miami vs. Minnesota, June 10, 2000
Detroit vs. Sacramento, July 4, 1999

DISQUALIFICATIONS

Most disqualifications per game, season
.56 — Los Angeles, 2002 (18/32)
.50 — Sacramento, 1997 (14/28)
.44 — Detroit, 1999 (14/32)
Fewest disqualifications per game, season
0.00 — Charlotte, 1997 (0/28)
.03 — Connecticut, 2005 (1/34)
Sacramento, 2005 (1/34)
Connecticut, 2004 (1/34)
Washington, 2004 (1/34)
Most disqualifications, game
3 — Phoenix vs. Indiana, August 14, 2005
Indiana at New York, September 16, 2004 (OT)
Portland at Minnesota, July 23, 2000
Los Angeles at Seattle, June 13, 2000 (OT)
Charlotte vs. Miami, June 3, 2000 (OT)
Phoenix at Sacramento, June 12, 1999
Washington at Los Angeles, August 3, 1998
2 — By many
Most disqualifications, both teams, game
5 — Phoenix (3) at Sacramento (2), June 12, 1999
4 — Orlando (2) vs. Cleveland (2),
June 8, 2002 (3OT)
Los Angeles (3) at Seattle (1),

208

June 13, 2000 (OT)
  Detroit (2) vs. Washington (2),
  July 10, 1999 (2OT)
3 — By many

STEALS

Most steals per game, season
  12.3 — Phoenix, 1997 (343/28)
  11.11— Houston, 1997 (311/28)
  11.07— Houston, 1998 (332/30)
Fewest steals per game, season
  5.5 — San Antonio, 2003 (187/34)
  5.7 — San Antonio, 2005 (195/34)
  5.9 — Seattle, 2005 (201/34)
Most steals, game
  21 — Houston vs. Washington, June 29, 1998
  20 — Indiana vs. Detroit, July 6, 2003
     Detroit vs. Indiana, June 18, 2000
     Phoenix vs. Utah, August 17, 1997 (OT)
     Los Angeles at Cleveland, July 3, 1997
  19 — By many
Fewest steals, game
  0 — San Antonio vs. Connecticut, June 1, 2003
     Charlotte at Miami, August 14, 2001
     Indiana at New York, June 2, 2001
     Minnesota at Charlotte, July 21, 1999
  1 — By many
Most steals, both teams, game
  34 — Los Angeles (20) at Cleveland (14), July 3, 1997
  32 — Sacramento (19) at San Antonio (13),
     September 4, 2004
     New York (18) at Phoenix (14), July 7, 1997
  31 — Houston (19) vs. Minnesota (12),
     August 9, 2000
     Sacramento (16) at Indiana (15),
     June 21, 2000
     Houston (16) vs. Cleveland (15),
     August 1, 1998 (OT)
     Phoenix (20) vs. Utah (11),
     August 17, 1997 (OT)
Fewest steals, both teams, game
  2 — Connecticut (1) at Connecticut (1),
     June 22, 2005
     Indiana (0) at New York (2), June 2, 2001
     Minnesota (0) at Charlotte (2), July 21, 1999
  4 — Charlotte (0) at Miami (4), August 14, 2001
  5 — Connecticut (1) at New York (4), July 7, 2005
     Washington (2) vs. New York (3),
     September 9, 2004
     San Antonio (1) vs. Washington (4),
     July 19, 2003
     San Antonio (1) at Washington (4),
     June 10, 2003
     Seattle (2) at Charlotte (3), July 7, 2001
     Los Angeles (2) at Utah (3), August 16, 1997
Most steals, one half
  14 — New York at Phoenix, July 7, 1997
  13 — By many

BLOCKED SHOTS

Most blocked shots per game, season
  5.7 — Utah, 1998 (170/30)
  5.6 — Utah, 2002 (178/32)
  5.2 — Phoenix, 2005 (179/34)
Fewest blocked shots per game, season
  2.0 — Minnesota, 2000 (63/32)
  2.1 — Sacramento, 1997 (60/28)
  2.2 — Washington, 2005 (76/34)
Most blocked shots, game
  13 — Los Angeles at Phoenix, July 11, 2001
  12 — Phoenix vs. Seattle, July 6, 2005
     Los Angele vs. Detroit, September 9, 2004
     Seattle vs. Utah, August 11, 2002
     Utah vs. Sacramento, July 14, 2001
  11 — By many
Fewest blocked shots, game
  0 — By Many: Most Recent:
     Los Angeles at Houston, August 27, 2005
Most blocked shots, both teams, game
  21 — Los Angeles (13) at Phoenix (8), July 11, 2001
  18 — Indiana (9) vs. Phoenix (9), July 3, 2004
     Houston (10) at San Antonio (8), June 20, 2003
     Seattle (12) vs. Utah (6), August 11, 2002
     Sacramento (9) vs. Portland (9),
     June 16, 2001 (OT)
     Utah (10) vs. Portland (8), June 2, 2001
     Indiana (10) at Utah (8), July 29, 2000
     Utah (11) vs. Sacramento (7), August 12, 1998
  17 — Many times
Fewest blocked shots, both teams, game
  0 — Phoenix at Washington, June 21, 2005
     Houston vs. Connecticut, May 30, 2003
     Portland vs. Houston, July 19, 2002
     Portland vs. Houston, June 23, 2002
     Miami vs. Portland, June 29, 2001 (OT)
     Minnesota vs. Cleveland, May 31, 2000
     Houston vs. Cleveland, August 21, 1997
  1 — By Many
Most blocked shots, one half
  10 — Phoenix vs. Seattle, July 6, 2005
     Los Angeles at Phoenix, July 11, 2001
  9 — Indiana vs. Phoenix, July 3, 2004
     Detroit at Charlotte, July 10, 2003
     Los Angeles at Phoenix, June 21, 2003

TURNOVERS

Most turnovers per game, season
  20.8 — Washington, 1998 (625/30)
  20.1 — Sacramento, 1997 (562/28)
  19.1 — New York, 1997 (536/28)
Fewest turnovers per game, season
  12.47 — Washington, 2004 (424/34)
  12.50 — Houston, 2005 (425/34)
  12.75 — Charlotte, 2002 (408/32)
Most turnovers, game
  33 — Washington at Houston, June 29, 1998

Utah at Phoenix, August 17, 1997 (ot)
Utah at New York, July 17, 1997
30 — Utah at Los Angeles, June 28, 1999
Cleveland at New York, June 10, 1999
New York vs. Phoenix, August 11, 1998 (ot)
Fewest turnovers, game
4 — New York vs. Connecticut, July 7, 2005
Connecticut at Detroit, July 21, 2004
Orlando vs. Washington, August 15, 1999
5 — Seattle at Charlotte, June 30, 2003
Connecticut at San Antonio, June 1, 2003
Indiana vs. Utah, July 10, 2002
Miami vs. Indiana, June 30, 2002
Houston vs. Washington, June 27, 2001
6 — By Many
Most turnovers, both teams, game
56 — Houston (28) vs. New York (28),
June 26, 1997 (OT)
53 — New York (30) vs. Phoenix (23),
August 11, 1998 (OT)
51 — Washington (33) at Houston (18),
June 29, 1998
Fewest turnovers, both teams, game
12 — Houston (5) vs. Washington (7), June 27, 2001
13 — San Antonio (6) at New York (7), June 21, 2005
14 — Connecticut (6) at Seattle (8), June 22, 2005
Houston (6) at Los Angeles (8),
August 11, 2001
Most turnovers, one half
20 — Cleveland at New York, June 10, 1999

TEAM DEFENSE

POINTS

Fewest points allowed per game, season
55.9 — Cleveland, 2001 (1,788/32)
59.1 — Houston, 2002 (1,892/32)
59.3 — Miami, 2001 (1,898/32)
Most points allowed per game, season
80.5 — Washington, 1998 (2,415/30)
77.1 — Utah, 1999 (2,467/32)
76.5 — Utah, 1998 (2,294/30)

FIELD GOAL PERCENTAGE

Lowest opponents' field goal percentage, season
.375 — Houston, 2002 (705/1,880)
.381 — Cleveland, 2001 (664/1,745)
.389 — Los Angeles, 2004 (815/2,095)
Highest opponents' field goal percentage, season
.468 — Washington, 1998 (876/1,870)
.462 — Detroit, 2001 (848/1,837)
.460 — Detroit, 2000 (905/1,967)

TURNOVERS

Most opponents' turnovers per game, season
21.4 — Phoenix, 1997 (599/28)
20.4 — New York, 1997 (570/28)
19.4 — Phoenix, 1998 (581/30)
Fewest opponents' turnovers per game, season

12.1 — New York, 2005 (411/34)
12.2 — Utah, 2001 (390/32)
12.5 — San Antonio, 2003 (424/34)

TEAM MISCELLANEOUS

GAME WON AND LOST

Highest winning percentage, season
.900 — Houston, 1998 (27-3)
.875 — Los Angeles, 2001 (28-4)
Los Angeles, 2000 (28-4)
.844 — Houston, 2000 (27-5)
Lowest winning percentage, season
.100 — Washington, 1998 (3-27)
.176 — Charlotte 2005 (6-28)
.188 — Seattle, 2000 (6-26)
Most consecutive games won
18 — Los Angeles, June 26-August 11, 2001
15 — Houston, June 27-July 30, 1998
12 — Los Angeles, August 9, 2002-June 14, 2003
Los Angeles, July 14-August 8, 2000
Los Angeles, June 17-July 9, 2000
Most consecutive games won, one season
18 — Los Angeles, June 26-August 11, 2001
15 — Houston, June 27-July 30, 1998
12 — Los Angeles, July 14-August 8, 2000
Los Angeles, June 17-July 9, 2000
Most consecutive games won, start of season
9 — Los Angeles, May 24-June 14, 2003
Los Angeles, May 28-June 19, 2001
7 — Houston, June 10-25, 1999
New York, June 21-July 5, 1997
5 — Houston, June 13-21, 1998
Most consecutive games won, end of season
7 — Charlotte, July 31-August 14, 2001
5 — Los Angeles, August 14-25, 2003
Houston, August 1-9, 2000
4 — By Many
Most consecutive game lost
14 — Portland, July 27, 2001-June 3, 2002
13 — Detroit, May 30-June 28, 2002
11 — Washington, June 13-July 9, 2003
Washington, July 13-August 7, 1998
Most consecutive game lost, one season
13 — Detroit, May 30-June 28, 2002
11 — Washington, June 13-July 9, 2003
Washington, July 13-August 7, 1998
10 — Charlotte, July 12-August 4, 2005
Portland, July 27-August 14, 2001
Indiana, June 18-July 8, 2000
Most consecutive game lost, start of season
13 — Detroit, May 30-June 28, 2002
7 — Cleveland, June 10-25, 1999
5 — San Antonio, May 21-31, 2005
Miami, May 28-June 9, 2002
Indiana, May 31-June 9, 2001
Charlotte, June 1-10, 2000

Most consecutive game lost, end of season
   10 — Portland, July 27-August 14, 2001
   9 — San Antonio, August 2-26, 2005
   6 — Cleveland, August 3-13, 2002
   5 — Charlotte, August 9-20, 1999
      Washington, August 12-19, 1998
Highest winning percentage, home games, season
   1.000 — Los Angeles, 2001 (16-0)
   .938 — Los Angeles, 2000 (15-1)
      Houston, 1999 (15-1)
   .933 — Houston, 1998 (14-1)
Lowest winning percentage, home games, season
   .176 — Washington, 2003 (3-14)
   .200 — Washington, 1998 (3-12)
   .250 — Cleveland, 2002 (4-12)
      Seattle, 2000 (4-12)
Most consecutive home games won
   28 — Los Angeles, July 14, 2000-June 27, 2002
   16 — Cleveland, July 22, 2000-July 25, 2001
   13 — Indiana, July 22, 2002-July 10, 2003
      Houston, May 29-August 6, 2002
      Charlotte, July 14, 2001-July 1, 2002
      Houston, July 1, 1999-May 29, 2000
Most consecutive home games won, start of season
   16 — Los Angeles, June 5-August 11, 2001
      (entire season)
   12 — Cleveland, May 31-July 25, 2001
   10 — Connecticut, May 28-July 28, 2005
      Houston, June 13-July 30, 1998
Most consecutive home games won, end of season
   16 — Los Angeles, June 5-August 11, 2001
      (entire season)
   12 — Houston, July 1-August 18, 1999
   10 — New York, June 28-August 8, 2000
Most consecutive home games lost
   10 — Cleveland, June 30, 2002-May 27, 2003
   9 — Charlotte, August 20, 1999-July 1, 2000
   8 — Washington, August 9, 2003-June 11, 2004
      Indiana, June 10-July 8, 2000
      Washington, August 12, 1998-July 2, 1999
Most consecutive home games lost, start of season
   8 — Charlotte, June 3-July 1, 2000
   5 — Detroit, June 2-28, 2002
      Portland, May 31-June 20, 2000
      Washington, June 10-July 2, 1999
   4 — Washington, May 22-June 11, 2004
      Charlotte, June 2-24, 2001
      Cleveland, June 12-25, 1999
Most consecutive home games lost, end of season
   9 — Cleveland, June 30-August 13, 2002
   6 — San Antonio, August 2-26, 2005
      Washington, July 20-August 9, 2002
   5 — Portland, July 28-August 14, 2001
Highest winning percentage, road games, season
   .867 — Houston, 1998 (13-2)
   .813 — Los Angeles, 2002 (13-3)

      Los Angeles, 2000 (13-3)
      Houston, 2000 (13-3)
   .765 — Los Angeles, 2003 (13-4)
Lowest winning percentage, road games, season
   .000 — Washington, 1998 (0-15)
   .059 — Charlotte, 2005 (1-16)
   .063 — Phoenix, 2002 (1-15)
Most consecutive road games won
   12 — Los Angeles, June 17-August 8, 2000
   11 — Los Angeles, July 20, 2002-June 14, 2003
   9 — Houston, June 30-August 7, 1998
Most consecutive road games won, start of season
   6 — Los Angeles, May 24-June 14, 2003
   5 — Los Angeles, May 28-June 16, 2001
      Houston, June 10-30, 1999
      New York, June 21-July 5, 1997
   4 — By Many
Most consecutive road games won, end of season
   6 — Cleveland, August 1-17, 1998
   5 — Los Angeles, July 20-August 13, 2002
   4 — Charlotte, August 3-14, 2001
Most consecutive road games lost
   21 — Phoenix, July 29, 2001-August 6, 2002
   17 — Detroit, July 24, 2001-July 18, 2002
   16 — Washington, June 11, 1998-June 12, 1999
Most consecutive road games lost, start of season
   16 — Charlotte, May 22-August 20, 2005
   15 — Phoenix, May 29-August 6, 2002
      Washington, June 11-August 15, 1998
   12 — Detroit, May 30-July 18, 2002
Most consecutive road games lost, end of season
   15 — Washington, June 11-August 15, 1998
   10 — Houston, June 25-September 19, 2004
   9 — Seattle, July 6-August 9, 2000

OVERTIME GAMES

Most overtime games, season
   7 — Miami, 2001
   5 — Los Angeles, 2004
      Portland, 2001
      Detroit, 2001
      New York, 1999
   4 — By Many
Most consecutive overtime games, season
   3 — New York, July 24-29, 1999
   2 — By Many
Most overtime games won, season
   4 — Los Angeles, 2004
      Detroit, 2003
      Portland, 2001
   3 — Washington, 2005
      Orlando, 2002
      Detroit, 2001
      Miami, 2001
      Utah, 2001
      Cleveland, 2000
      New York, 1997

Most overtime games won, no losses, season
4 — Detroit, 2003
3 — Washington, 2005
    Orlando, 2002
    Utah, 2001
    New York, 1997
2 — By Many
Most consecutive overtime games won
6 — Utah-San Antonio, June 27, 2001-
    August 20, 2003
    New York, June 26, 1997-July 18, 1999
4 — Detroit, June 17-August 23, 2003
    Miami, July 27, 2001-July 7, 2002
    Washington, July 10, 1999-June 25, 2002
    Portland, June 4-29, 2001
Most overtime games lost, season
4 — Cleveland, 2002
    Miami, 2001
    Portland, 2000
3 — Sacramento, 2004
    Charlotte, 2001
    Orlando, 2000

    New York, 1999
2 — By Many
Most overtime games lost, no wins, season
4 — Cleveland, 2002
    Portland, 2000
3 — Sacramento, 2004
    Charlotte, 2001
    Orlando, 2000
2 — By Many
Most consecutive overtime games lost
6 — New York, August 11, 1999-June 29, 2004
5 — Orlando, June 7, 2000-July 27, 2001
4 — Connecticut, June 22, 2003-June 18, 2004
    Cleveland, June 1-July 28, 2002
    Sacramento, July 2, 1997-June 16, 2001
    Portland, May 31-August 6, 2000
Most overtime periods, game
4 — Washington (72) at Seattle (69), July 3, 2001
3 — Orlando (103) vs. Cleveland (99),
    June 8, 2002
2 — By Many

REGULAR-SEASON SINGLE-GAME BESTS

*Denotes number of overtime periods

POINTS

	FG	FT	PTS
Katie Smith, Minnesota at Los Angeles, July 8, 2001	11	23	*46
Cynthia Cooper, Houston at Sacramento, July 25, 1997	14	9	44
Cynthia Cooper, Houston vs. Utah, August 16, 1999	11	17	42
Katie Smith, Minnesota at Detroit, June 17, 2001	13	19	40
Cynthia Cooper, Houston at Charlotte, August 11, 1997	15	4	39
Jennifer Gillom, Phoenix at Cleveland, August 10, 1998	13	9	**36
Cynthia Cooper, Houston vs. Los Angeles, June 22, 1999	11	13	36
Katie Smith, Minnesota at Phoenix, August 1, 2001	11	16	36
Shannon Johnson, Orlando vs. Cleveland, June 8, 2002	11	11	***35
Tina Thompson, Houston at New York, May 23, 2004	12	10	35
Cynthia Cooper, Houston at Los Angeles, August 1, 1997	9	11	34
Cynthia Cooper, Houston vs. Phoenix, August 7, 1997	10	10	34
Ruthie Bolton-Holifield, Sacramento vs. Utah, August 8, 1997	11	7	34
Ruthie Bolton-Holifield, Sacramento vs. Cleveland, August 12, 1997	12	4	34
Cynthia Cooper, Houston vs. Sacramento, July 3, 1998	6	22	34
Cynthia Cooper, Houston at Detroit, August 7, 1998	13	4	34
Ruthie Bolton-Holifield, Sacramento at Washington, July 2, 1999	9	13	34
Katie Smith, Minnesota vs. Cleveland, May 31, 2000	9	10	34
Katie Smith, Minnesota vs. Connecticut, July 10, 2003	12	5	34
Chamique Holdsclaw, Washington vs. Indiana, July 24, 2003	10	13	34
Lauren Jackson, Seattle vs. Los Angeles, August 6, 2003	17	0	34
Katie Smith, Minnesota vs. Sacramento, July 11, 2004	12	4	*34
Deanna Nolan, Detroit vs. New York, June 3, 2005	9	13	*34
Sheryl Swoopes, Houston at Seattle, August 9, 2005	15	1	34

FIELD GOALS

	FG	FGA
Lauren Jackson, Seattle vs. Los Angeles, August 6, 2003	17	23
Cynthia Cooper, Houston at Charlotte, August 11, 1997	15	19

	FG	FGA
Sheryl Swoopes, Houston at Seattle, August, 9, 2005	15	24
Cynthia Cooper, Houston at Sacramento, July 25, 1997	14	21
Wendy Palmer, Utah vs. Chicago, July 8, 1998	14	20
Latasha Byears, Sacramento at Phoenix, July 20, 1998	14	20
Linda Burgess, Sacramento vs. Utah, August 15, 1998	14	20
Tangela Smith, Sacramento vs. Utah, August 14, 1999	14	23
Wendy Palmer, Detroit at Seattle, June 28, 2000	14	21
Lisa Leslie, Los Angeles vs. Seattle, August 1, 2002	14	17
Sheryl Swoopes, Houston vs. Seattle, June 18, 2004	14	25
Margo Dydek, Utah vs. Houston, June 30, 1998	**13	25
Cynthia Cooper, Houston at Detroit, August 7, 1998	13	21
Jennifer Gillom, Phoenix at Cleveland, August 10, 1998	**13	27
Sandy Brondello, Detroit at Utah, July 6, 1999	**13	28
Sheryl Swoopes, Houston at Utah, July 16, 1999	*13	21
Brandy Reed, Phoenix at Houston, June 3, 2000	13	18
Tari Phillips, New York vs. Indiana, June 30, 2000	13	19
Sheryl Swoopes, Houston vs. Charlotte, July 7, 2000	13	22
Yolanda Griffith, Sacramento vs. Utah, July 15, 2000	13	19
Tina Thompson, Houston at Detroit, June 2, 2001	13	18
Katie Smith, Minnesota at Detroit, June 17, 2001	13	19
Tamika Catchings, Indiana vs. Orlando, August 7, 2002	13	20

FREE THROWS

	FT	FTA
Cynthia Cooper, Houston vs. Sacramento, July 3, 1998	22	24
Katie Smith, Minnesota at Los Angeles, July 8, 2001	*18	19
Cynthia Cooper, Houston vs. Utah, August 16, 1999	17	18
Katie Smith, Minnesota at Utah, July 28, 2001	*16	18
Swin Cash, Detroit vs. Miami, June 28, 2002	*15	21
Lisa Leslie, Los Angeles vs. Utah, August 4, 2002	15	19
Tamika Catchings, Indiana vs. Phoenix, May 24, 2005	15	17
Katie Smith, Minnesota at Miami, June 10, 2000	14	16
Lisa Leslie, Los Angeles vs. Minnesota, July 15, 2000	14	14
Tina Thompson, Houston vs. Minnesota, August 9, 2000	14	16
Tamika Catchings, Indiana vs. New York, June 8, 2002	14	16
Sheryl Swoopes, Houston at Los Angeles, June 30, 2002	14	15
Lauren Jackson, Seattle vs. San Antonio, August 12, 2003	14	16
Lisa Leslie, Los Angeles vs. Washington, July 21, 2004	14	18

REBOUNDS

	REB
Chamique Holdsclaw, Washington at Charlotte, May 23, 2003	24
Cheryl Ford, Detroit at San Antonio, May 22, 2004	22
Lisa Leslie, Los Angeles vs. New York, June 19, 1998	21
Cindy Brown, Detroit at Utah, August 10, 1998	21
Chamique Holdsclaw, Washington at Sacramento, June 25, 2002	**21
Lisa Leslie, Los Angeles vs. Orlando, July 22, 2002	21
Cheryl Ford, Detroit at Connecticut, June 22, 2003	*21
Yolanda Griffith, Sacramento at Washington, June 5, 2001	20
Natalie Williams, Utah at Sacramento, June 22, 2002	20
Lauren Jackson, Seattle vs. Charlotte, July 31, 2003	20
Lisa Leslie, Los Angeles at Charlotte, June 20, 2004	**20
Yolanda Griffith, Sacramento vs. Cleveland, June 17, 1999	19
Yolanda Griffith, Sacramento at Utah, June 19, 1999	19
Yolanda Griffith, Sacramento vs. New York, July 22, 1999	19
Natalie Williams, Utah vs. Cleveland, July 26, 2000	19
Yolanda Griffith, Sacramento vs. Houston, August 6, 2000	19

ASSISTS

AST

Ticha Penicheiro, Sacramento at Cleveland, July 29, 1998...16
Ticha Penicheiro, Sacramento vs. Los Angeles, August 3, 2002 16
Ticha Penicheiro, Sacramento at Cleveland, July 15, 2003...15
Penny Toler, Los Angeles vs. Utah, August 14, 1998..14
Ticha Penicheiro, Sacramento vs. Minnesota, June 22, 1999 14
Ticha Penicheiro, Sacramento vs. Detroit, July 1, 2000 14
Ticha Penicheiro, Sacramento vs. Minnesota, August 7, 2001 14
Jennifer Rizzotti, Cleveland vs. New York, June 21, 2002...14
Ticha Penicheiro, Sacramento vs. Phoenix, May 30, 2003 14
Teresa Weatherspoon, New York at Los Angeles, July 21, 1998 13
Ticha Penicheiro, Sacramento vs. Washington, August 7, 1998 13
Ticha Penicheiro, Sacramento at Minnesota, June 29, 1999 13
Ticha Penicheiro, Sacramento at Houston, August 2, 1999..13
Teresa Weatherspoon, New York at Houston, May 29, 2000 13
Ticha Penicheiro, Sacramento at Utah, June 26, 2000 13
Dawn Staley, Charlotte vs. Washington, July 26, 2000 13
Ticha Penicheiro, Sacramento vs. Orlando, July 27, 2000 13
Ticha Penicheiro, Sacramento vs. Indiana, July 30, 2002 13
Nikki Teasley, Los Angeles at New York, June 14, 2003 13
Lindsay Whalen, Connecticut at Detroit, June 27, 2004...13
Shannon Johnson, San Antonio at Sacramento, August 18, 2005...13

STEALS

STL

Ticha Penicheiro, Sacramento vs. San Antonio, July 10, 2003..10
Michelle Griffiths, Phoenix at Utah, July 27, 1998 9
Tamika Catchings, Indiana vs. Minnesota, July 26, 2002 9
Janice Lawrence Braxton, Cleveland vs. Los Angeles, July 3, 1997 8
Michele Timms, Phoenix at Utah, July 3, 1997..8
Teresa Weatherspoon, New York vs. Charlotte, July 10, 1997...8
Cynthia Cooper, Houston at Charlotte, August 11, 1997 8
Michele Timms, Phoenix vs. Utah, August 17, 1997...*8
Yolanda Griffith, Sacramento vs. Washington, July 29, 1999 8
Chamique Holdsclaw, Washington vs. Indiana, July 20, 2000...8
Rita Williams, Indiana at Miami, August 10, 2001 ....*8
Semeka Randall, San Antonio vs. Charlotte, September 17, 2004 8
Tamika Catchings, Indiana vs. Connecticut, July 13, 2005 8

BLOCKED SHOTS

BLK

Margo Dydek, Utah vs. Orlando, June 7, 2001...10
Lisa Leslie, Los Angeles vs. Detroit, September 9, 2004...10
Margo Dydek, Utah vs. Cleveland, August 6, 1998...9
Margo Dydek, San Antonio vs. Minnesota, May 26, 2004 9
Margo Dydek, Connecticut vs. San Antonio, June 4, 2005 9
Margo Dydek, Utah at Detroit, July 17, 1998..8
Margo Dydek, Utah vs. Sacramento, August 12, 1998 8
Margo Dydek, Utah vs. Sacramento, July 14, 2001 8
Lauren Jackson, Seattle vs. Utah, August 11, 2002..8
Michelle Snow, Houston at San Antonio, June 20, 2003 8
Margo Dydek, Utah at Phoenix, August 8, 1998..7
Margo Dydek, Utah vs. Phoenix, August 13, 1999 7
Margo Dydek, Utah vs. Minnesota, June 1, 2000..7
Margo Dydek, Utah vs. Orlando, June 13, 2000..7
Margo Dydek, Utah vs. Charlotte, June 15, 2000..7

RECORDS Regular Season

	BLK
Lisa Leslie, Los Angeles at Utah, August 13, 2001	*7
Margo Dydek, Utah at Sacramento, July 12, 2001	7
Lisa Leslie, Los Angeles vs. New York, May 25, 2002	7
Margo Dydek, Utah vs. Detroit, July 8, 2002	7
Margo Dydek, Utah at Detroit, July 23, 2002	7
Margo Dydek, San Antonio at Minnesota, July 16, 2003	7
Margo Dydek, San Antonio vs. Houston, August 1, 2003	7
Lisa Leslie, Los Angeles at Charlotte, June 20, 2004	**7
Lisa Leslie, Los Angeles vs. Minnesota, June 18, 2005	*7

PLAYOFF RECORDS

ALL-TIME POSTSEASON STANDINGS

OVERALL

TEAM	W-L	PCT
Los Angeles Sparks	22 - 13	.629
Houston Comets	20 - 12	.625
Sacramento Monarchs	16 - 12	.571
Connecticut Sun	13 - 10	.565
Seattle Storm	7 - 6	.538
Detroit Shock	7 - 7	.500
New York Liberty	17 - 19	.472
Indiana Fever	3-4	.429
Cleveland Rockers	6 - 9	.400
Washington Mystics	4 - 6	.400
Miami Sol	1 - 2	.333
Phoenix Mercury	3 - 6	.333
Charlotte Sting	6 - 13	.316
San Antonio Silver Stars	2 - 5	.286
Minnesota Lynx	1 - 4	.200
Totals	128 - 128	.500

HOME

TEAM	W-L	PCT
Connecticut Sun	9 - 2	.818
Sacramento Monarchs	9 - 2	.818
Los Angeles Sparks	15 - 4	.789
Washington Mystics	3 - 1	.750
Houston Comets	13 - 6	.684
Cleveland Rockers	5 - 3	.625
Seattle Storm	5 - 3	.625
New York Liberty	11 - 9	.550
Detroit Shock	4 - 4	.500
Minnesota Lynx	1 - 1	.500
Phoenix Mercury	2 - 2	.500
Indiana Fever	1 - 2	.333
San Antonio Silver Stars	1 - 2	.333
Charlotte Sting	2 - 5	.286
Miami Sol	0 - 1	.000
Totals	82 - 46	.641

ROAD

TEAM	W-L	PCT
Houston Comets	7 - 6	.538
Detroit Shock	3 - 3	.500
Miami Sol	1 - 1	.500
Los Angeles Sparks	7 - 9	.438
Sacramento Monarchs	7 - 10	.412
Seattle Storm	2 - 3	.400

TEAM	W-L	PCT
New York Liberty	6 - 10	.375
Charlotte Sting	4 - 8	.333
Connecticut Sun	4 - 8	.333
Indiana Fever	1 - 3	.250
San Antonio Silver Stars	1 - 3	.250
Phoenix Mercury	1 - 4	.200
Washington Mystics	1 - 5	.167
Cleveland Rockers	1 - 6	.143
Minnesota Lynx	0 - 3	.000
Totals	46 - 82	.359

SERIES

TEAM	W-L	PCT
Houston Comets	10 - 4	.714
Los Angeles Sparks	10 - 5	.667
Seattle Storm	3 - 2	.600
Connecticut Sun	5 - 4	.556
Sacramento Monarchs	6 - 5	.545
New York Liberty	8 - 7	.533
Detroit Shock	3 - 3	.500
Charlotte Sting	3 - 6	.333
Indiana Fever	1 - 2	.333
San Antonio Silver Stars	1 - 2	.333
Phoenix Mercury	1 - 3	.250
Washington Mystics	1 - 3	.250
Cleveland Rockers	1 - 4	.200
Miami Sol	0 - 1	.000
Minnesota Lynx	0 - 2	.000
Totals	53 - 53	.500

WNBA ALL-TIME PLAYOFF LEADERS

GAMES

Vickie Johnson	36
Lisa Leslie	35
Becky Hammon	34
Tamecka Dixon	34
Crystal Robinson	34
Mwadi Mabika	33
Janeth Arcain	32
Tina Thompson	32
Tamika Whitmore	32
Teresa Weatherspoon	31

MINUTES

Lisa Leslie	1,280

Vickie Johnson	1,186
Tina Thompson	1,171
Mwadi Mabika	1,157
Sheryl Swoopes	1,064
Crystal Robinson	1,062
DeLisha Milton-Jones	1,031
Tina Thompson	1,003
Tamecka Dixon	997
Teresa Weatherspoon	980

FIELD GOALS MADE

Lisa Leslie	254
Sheryl Swoopes	177
Yolanda Griffith	164
Mwadi Mabika	164
Vickie Johnson	156
Tina Thompson	148
DeLisha Milton-Jones	147
Tamecka Dixon	142
Cynthia Cooper	136
Crystal Robinson	129

FIELD GOAL ATTEMPTS

Lisa Leslie	503
Sheryl Swoopes	430
Mwadi Mabika	406
Vickie Johnson	365
Tina Thompson	356
Yolanda Griffith	328
Cynthia Cooper	327
Tamecka Dixon	319
DeLisha Milton-Jones	307
Crystal Robinson	293

FIELD GOAL PERCENTAGE
(MINIMUM: 30 FG)

	FG	FGA	PCT
Latasha Byears	37	71	.521
Tammy Sutton-Brown	34	67	.507
Lisa Leslie	254	503	.505
Yolanda Griffith	164	328	.500
DeMya Walker	80	161	.497
Rushia Brwon	36	73	.493
Rhonda Mapp	36	74	.486
Tamika Whitmore	125	257	.486
Natalie Williams	50	103	.485
DeLisha Milton-Jones	147	307	.479

FREE THROWS MADE

Lisa Leslie	141
Cynthia Cooper	138
Yolanda Griffith	130
Sheryl Swoopes	115
Lindsay Whalen	80
Tina Thompson	77
DeLisha Milton-Jones	68
Vickie Johnson	66
Taj McWilliams-Franklin	65
Tari Phillips	62

Chasity Melvin	62
Tamika Whitmore	62

FREE THROW ATTEMPTS

Lisa Leslie	192
Yolanda Griffith	166
Cynthia Cooper	163
Sheryl Swoopes	134
Lindsay Whalen	101
Tina Thompson	97
Tari Phillips	96
Tamika Whitmore	95
DeLisha Milton-Jones	89
Chasity Melvin	84

FREE THROW PERCENTAGE
(MINIMUM: 20 FT)

	FT	FTA	PCT
Crystal Robinson	30	32	.938
Ruthie Bolton	26	28	.929
Deanna Nolan	35	38	.921
Kara Lawson	32	35	.914
Tamecka Dixon	60	66	.909
Betty Lennox	35	40	.875
Charlotte Smith-Taylor	21	24	.875
La'Keshia Frett	20	23	.870
Lauren Jackson	45	52	.865
Sheryl Swoopes	115	134	.858

THREE-POINT FIELD GOALS

Crystal Robinson	62
Mwadi Mabika	57
Tina Thompson	40
Becky Hammon	39
Nykesha Sales	34
Cynthia Cooper	33
Kara Lawson	32
Vickie Johnson	32
Kedra Holland-Corn	31
Dawn Staley	29
Katie Douglas	29

THREE-POINT FIELD GOAL ATTEMPTS

Mwadi Mabika	168
Crystal Robinson	166
Becky Hammon	115
Tina Thompson	112
Cynthia Cooper	104
Vickie Johnson	95
Nikki Teasley	93
Katie Douglas	87
Nykesha Sales	83
Sheryl Swoopes	83

THREE-POINT PERCENTAGE
(MINIMUM: 10 FG3)

	3FG	3GA	PCT
DeLisha Milton-Jones	22	42	.524
Kelly Miller	10	20	.500

	3FG	3GA	PCT
Lauren Jackson.	20	41	.488
Nicole Powell	20	42	.476
Kedra Holland-Corn.	31	69	.449
Dawn Staley	29	68	.426
Tamecka Dixon	17	40	.425
Kara Lawson	32	76	.421
Jennifer Gillom	10	24	.417
Nykesha Sales	34	83	.410

OFFENSIVE REBOUNDS

Yolanda Griffith.	90
Lisa Leslie.	84
Tina Thompson	69
DeLisha Milton-Jones	58
Taj McWilliams-Franklin	56
Tari Phillips	48
Vickie Johnson.	45
Sheryl Swoopes	44
Mwadi Mabika.	43
Sue Wicks	41
Natalie Williams	41

DEFENSIVE REBOUNDS

Lisa Leslie	243
Tina Thompson	151
Yolanda Griffith	146
Mwadi Mabika	141
Sheryl Swoopes	134
Taj McWilliams-Franklin	131
DeLisha Milton-Jones	127
Tari Phillips.	110
Vickie Johnson	108
Cheryl Ford.	89

TOTAL REBOUNDS

Lisa Leslie.	327
Yolanda Griffith	236
Tina Thompson	220
Taj McWilliams-Franklin	187
DeLisha Milton-Jones.	185
Mwadi Mabika...	184
Sheryl Swoopes..	178
Tari Phillips...	158
Vickie Johnson	153
Cheryl Ford	126

ASSISTS

Teresa Weatherspoon	186
Nikki Teasley.	148
Ticha Penicheiro	131
Vickie Johnson	121
Tamecka Dixon.	107
Sheryl Swoopes	101
Cynthia Cooper	94
Dawn Staley	89
Mwadi Mabika	88
Lisa Leslie	83

STEALS

Sheryl Swoopes	63
Mwadi Mabika	55
Nykesha Sales	49
DeLisha Milton-Jones	47
Lisa Leslie	46
Teresa Weatherspoon	45
Tamecka Dixon	44
Crystal Robinson	41
Janeth Arcain	40
Vickie Johnson	38
Yolanda Griffith	38

PERSONAL FOULS

Lisa Leslie	127
Mwadi Mabika	115
DeLisha Milton-Jones	110
Tina Thompson	108
Tamecka Dixon	88
Crystal Robinson	85
Teresa Weatherspoon	84
Tamika Whitmore	80
Sue Wicks	78
Tari Phillips	75

DISQUALIFICATIONS

DeLisha Milton-Jones	3
Tamecka Dixon	2
Mwadi Mabika	2
Tari Phillips	2
Crystal Robinson	2
Natalie Williams	2
Many tied	1

BLOCKED SHOTS

Lisa Leslie	98
DeLisha Milton-Jones	40
Margo Dydek.	37
Ruth Riley	32
Tina Thompson	32
Sue Wicks	26
Vicky Bullett	26
Yolanda Griffith.	23
Tangela Smith	22
Taj McWilliams-Franklin	22

POINTS

Lisa Leslie	662
Sheryl Swoopes	495
Yolanda Griffith	458
Cynthia Cooper	443
Tina Thompson	413
Vickie Johnson	410
DeLisha Milton-Jones	384
Tamecka Dixon	361
Crystal Robinson	350
Taj McWilliams-Franklin	318

SCORING AVERAGE
(MINIMUM: 10 GAMES)

	G	FG	FT	PTS	AVG
Cynthia Cooper	19	136	138	443	23.3

	G	FG	FT	PTS	AVG		G	FG	FT	PTS	AVG
Lisa Leslie	35	254	141	662	18.9	Andrea Stinson	19	108	48	282	14.8
Lauren Jackson	13	79	45	223	17.2	Swin Cash	10	47	50	146	14.6
Yolanda Griffith	27	164	130	458	17.0	Tari Phillips	21	119	59	297	14.1
Deanna Nolan	13	77	35	215	16.5	McWilliams-Franklin	23	125	65	318	13.8
Sheryl Swoopes	30	177	115	495	16.5						

TOP 25 CAREER PLAYOFF SCORERS

NAME	G	MIN	FG	FGA	PCT	FT	FTA	PCT	REB	AST	STL	PF	BLK	PTS	AVG
Lisa Leslie	35	1280	254	503	.505	141	192	.734	327	83	46	127	98	662	18.9
Sheryl Swoopes	30	1064	177	430	.412	115	134	.858	178	101	63	63	17	495	16.5
Yolanda Griffith	27	909	164	328	.500	130	166	.783	236	35	38	73	23	458	17.0
Mwadi Mabika	34	1168	165	410	.402	58	74	.784	184	88	55	115	14	445	13.1
Cynthia Cooper	19	723	136	327	.416	138	163	.847	66	94	30	38	13	443	23.3
Tina Thompson	32	1171	148	356	.416	77	97	.794	220	45	30	108	32	413	12.9
Vickie Johnson	36	1186	156	365	.427	66	81	.815	153	121	38	73	6	410	11.4
DeLisha Milton-Jones	30	1031	147	307	.479	68	89	.764	185	75	47	110	40	384	12.8
Tamecka Dixon	34	997	142	319	.445	60	66	.909	103	107	44	88	4	361	10.6
Crystal Robinson	34	1062	129	293	.440	30	32	.938	109	57	41	85	10	350	10.3
Taj McWilliams-Franklin	23	765	125	266	.470	65	82	.793	187	38	29	63	22	318	13.8
Tamika Whitmore	32	820	125	257	.486	62	95	.653	104	25	15	80	19	315	9.8
Nykesha Sales	23	767	113	274	.412	53	73	.726	97	43	49	63	17	313	13.6
Tari Phillips	26	726	124	260	.477	62	96	.646	158	29	31	75	16	310	11.9
Andrea Stinson	19	665	108	250	.432	48	58	.828	109	75	37	47	3	282	14.8
Janeth Arcain	32	954	107	254	.421	51	60	.850	114	41	40	56	3	274	8.6
Tangela Smith	20	622	105	257	.409	45	63	.714	111	28	24	59	22	262	13.1
Becky Hammon	34	741	87	203	.429	35	41	.854	51	59	21	48	0	248	7.3
Lauren Jackson	13	457	79	178	.444	45	52	.865	94	16	15	43	19	223	17.2
Deanna Nolan	13	455	77	178	.433	35	38	.921	51	35	17	30	4	215	16.5
Katie Douglas	20	672	64	163	.393	50	63	.794	79	52	24	45	2	207	10.4
Dawn Staley	21	719	63	168	.375	43	57	.754	37	89	28	43	2	198	9.4
DeMya Walker	18	508	80	161	.497	31	49	.633	65	45	10	48	11	191	10.6
Lindsay Whalen	15	475	49	122	.402	80	101	.792	42	64	17	34	4	185	12.3
Betty Lennox	14	390	68	154	.442	35	40	.875	50	32	14	37	1	184	3.1

INDIVIDUAL RECORDS

MINUTES

Most minutes, game
- 50 — Adrienne Goodson, Utah at Houston, August 18, 2002 (2OT)
- 48 — Tina Thompson, Houston vs. Utah, August 18, 2002 (2OT)
   Marie Ferdinand, Utah at Houston, August 18, 2002 (2OT)
   Margo Dydek, Utah at Houston, August 18, 2002 (2OT)
- 47 — Sheryl Swoopes, Houston vs. Utah, August 18, 2002 (2OT)
   Janeth Arcain, Houston vs. Utah, August 18, 2002 (2OT)

SCORING

Most points, game
- 35 — Lisa Leslie, Los Angeles vs. Sacramento, August 27, 2001
- 32 — Nykesha Sales, Connecticut at Seattle, October 10, 2004
- 31 — Lauren Jackson, Seattle at Sacramento, October 1, 2004 (OT)
   Sheryl Swoopes, Houston vs. New York, August 26, 2000 (OT)
   Cynthia Cooper, Houston vs. Charlotte, August 28, 1997

Most consecutive games, 20 or more points
- 7 — Cynthia Cooper, Houston, August 28, 1997-September 1, 1998
- 5 — Lisa Leslie, Los Angeles, August 27, 2001-August 17, 2002
- 4 — Lisa Leslie, Los Angeles, August 28-September 5, 2003
   Cynthia Cooper, Houston, August 17-26, 2000

Most consecutive games, 10 or more points
- 34 — Lisa Leslie, Los Angeles, August 24, 1999-August 31, 2005
- 20 — Yolanda Griffith, Sacramento, August 29, 2003-September 20, 2005 (current)
- 19 — Cynthia Cooper, Houston, August 28, 1997-August 26, 2000

RECORDS Playoffs

Most points, one half
- 22 — Lisa Leslie, Los Angeles vs. Sacramento,
  August 27, 2001
- 21 — Nykesha Sales, Connecticut at Seattle,
  October 10, 2004

Most points, overtime period
- 7 — Sheryl Swoopes, Houston vs. New York,
  August 26, 2000
- 6 — Tina Thompson, Houston vs. Utah,
  August 18, 2002

FIELD GOALS

Highest field-goal percentage, game
(Minimum: 8 field goals made)
- .846 — Tari Phillips, New York vs. Washington,
  August 24, 2002 (11/13)
- .833 — Tamika Whitmore, New York vs. Indiana,
  August 18, 2002 (10/12)
- .769 — Deanna Nolan, Detroit vs. Cleveland,
  September 2, 2003 (10/13)
  Tari Phillips, New York at Washington,
  August 22, 2002 (10/13)

Most field goals, none missed, game
- 7 — Taj McWilliams, Orlando vs. Cleveland,
  August 11, 2000
- 6 — Janell Burse, Seattle vs. Houston,
  September 1, 2005
  Tammy Sutton-Brown, Charlotte at Cleveland,
  August 20, 2001

Most field goals, game
- 15 — Lisa Leslie, Los Angeles vs. Sacramento,
  August 27, 2001
- 14 — Nykesha Sales, Connecticut at Seattle,
  October 10, 2004
- 12 — Lisa Leslie, Los Angeles vs. Phoenix,
  August 13, 2000

Most field goals, one half
- 9 — Nykesha Sales, Connecticut at Seattle,
  October 10, 2004
  Lisa Leslie, Los Angeles vs. Sacramento,
  August 27, 2001
- 8 — Yolanda Griffith, Sacramento at Connecticut,
  September 14, 2005

Most field goal attempts, game
- 24 — Merlakia Jones, Cleveland at Orlando,
  August 11, 2000
  Cynthia Cooper, Houston at Phoenix,
  August 27, 1998
- 23 — Sheryl Swoopes, Houson at Sacramento,
  September 10, 2005 (OT)
  Cynthia Cooper, Houston at New York,
  August 24, 2000
  Cynthia Cooper, Houston at Los Angeles,
  August 20, 2000

Most field goal attempts, none made, game
- 11 — Katie Douglas, Connecticut at Seattle,
  October 12, 2004
- 8 — Allison Feaster, Charlotte vs. Washington,
  August 17, 2002

Ticha Penicheiro, Sacramento at Los Angeles,
August 27, 2001
- 7 — Edna Campbell, Sacramento at Los Angeles,
  August 26, 2001
  Ticha Penicheiro, Sacramento vs. Utah,
  August 19, 2001
  Coquese Washington, Houston vs. Los Angeles,
  August 18, 2001

Most field goal attempts, one half
- 14 — Lisa Leslie, Los Angeles vs. Sacramento,
  August 27, 2001
  Adrienne Johnson, Orlando at Cleveland,
  August 13, 2000
  Cynthia Cooper, Houston at Phoenix,
  August 27, 1998
- 13 — By Many

THREE-POINT FIELD GOALS

Most three-point field goals, none missed, game
- 5 — Vickie Johnson, New York vs. Washington,
  August 24, 2002
- 4 — Kara Lawson, Sacramento vs. Houston,
  September 10, 2005 (OT)
  Kelly Miller, Indiana vs. Connecticut,
  September 8, 2005 (OT)
  Kedra Holland-Corn, Detroit at Connecticut,
  September 5, 2003
- 3 — Nykesha Sales, Connecticut at Seattle,
  October 10, 2004
  Tamecka Dixon, Los Angeles vs. Sacramento,
  August 27, 2001
  Edna Campbell, Sacramento vs. Los Angeles,
  August 24, 2001
  Michele Timms, Phoenix vs. Cleveland,
  August 22, 1998

Most three-point field goals, game
- 7 — Mwadi Mabika, Los Angeles at Houston,
  August 17, 2000
- 6 — Lauren Jackson, Seattle vs. Sacramento,
  October 5, 2004
  Deanna Nolan, Detroit vs. Cleveland,
  September 2, 2003
- 5 — Vickie Johnson, New York vs. Washington,
  August 24, 2002
  Ticha Penicheiro, Sacramento at Los Angeles,
  August 26, 2001

Most three-point field goals, one half
- 5 — Lauren Jackson, Seattle vs. Sacramento,
  October 5, 2004
- 4 — By Many

Most three-point field goal attempts, game
- 11 — Becky Hammon, New York vs. Detroit,
  September 28, 2004
  Crystal Robinson, New York vs. Detroit,
  September 28, 2004
  Mwadi Mabika, Los Angeles at Houston,
  August 17, 2000
- 10 — Nikki Teasley, Los Angeles vs. Detroit,
  September 12, 2003

Crystal Robinson, New York at Washington,
August 22, 2002

9 — By Many

Most three-point field goal attempts, none made, game

9 — Nikki Teasley, Los Angeles vs. Minnesota,
August 30, 2003

6 — Katie Douglas, Connecticut at Seattle,
October 12, 2004

Katie Douglas, Connecticut vs. New York,
October 3, 2004

Charlotte Smith, Charlotte at Washington,
August 15, 2002

5 — By Many

Most three-point field goal attempts, one half

7 — Shameka Christon, New York vs. Detroit,
September 26, 2004

Crystal Robinson, New York vs. Detroit,
September 26, 2004

Deanna Nolan, Detroit vs. Cleveland,
August 31, 2003

Stacey Dales-Schuman, Washington at
Charlotte, August 17, 2002

Kedra Holland-Corn, Sacramento vs.
Los Angeles, August 24, 2001

Bridget Pettis, Phoenix vs. Los Angeles,
August 11, 2000

6 — By Many

FREE THROWS

Most free throws made, none missed, game

10 — Yolanda Griffith, Sacramento at Los Angeles,
September 7, 2003

Nykesha Sales, Connecticut vs. Detroit,
September 5, 2003

Cynthia Cooper, Houston at New York,
September 2, 1999

9 — Taj McWilliams-Franklin, Connecticut at
Indiana, September 8, 2005 (OT)

Lauren Jackson, Seattle at Sacramento,
October 1, 2004 (OT)

8 — By Many

Most free throws made, game

18 — Yolanda Griffith, Sacramento vs. Utah,
August 19, 2001

15 — Lindsay Whalen, Connecticut vs. Detroit,
September 2, 2005

Lindsay Whalen, Connecticut vs. Washington,
September 27, 2004

13 — Cynthia Cooper, Houston vs. New York,
September 5, 1999

Most free throws made, one half

11 — Lindsay Whalen, Connecticut vs. Washington,
September 27, 2004

10 — Yolanda Griffith, Sacramento vs. Utah,
August 19, 2001

Most free throw attempts, game

24 — Yolanda Griffith, Sacramento vs. Utah,
August 19, 2001

17 — Lindsay Whalen, Connecticut vs. Detroit,
September 2, 2005

16 — Lindsay Whalen, Connecticut vs. Washington,
September 27, 2004

Most free throw attempts, one half

13 — Tamika Williams, Minnesota at Los Angeles,
August 30, 2003

Yolanda Griffith, Sacramento vs. Utah,
August 19, 2001

12 — Lindsay Whalen, Connecticut vs. Washington,
September 27, 2004

Chasity Melvin, Cleveland vs. Detroit,
August 29, 2003

Natalie Williams, Utah at Houston,
August 18, 2002

Cynthia Cooper, Houston vs. New York,
August 30, 1997

REBOUNDS

Most rebounds, game

18 — Lisa Leslie, Los Angeles vs. Houston,
August 20, 2001

17 — Yolanda Griffith, Sacramento at Houston,
September 2, 2003

16 — Taj McWilliams-Franklin, Connecticut vs.
Sacramento, September 15, 2005 (ot)

Lisa Leslie, Los Angeles vs. Sacramento,
August 27, 2001

Most rebounds, one half

14 — Lisa Leslie, Los Angeles vs. Sacramento,
August 27, 2001

12 — Cheryl Ford, Detroit vs. Cleveland,
September 2, 2003

Lisa Leslie, Los Angeles vs. Houston,
August 20, 2001

Most offensive rebounds, game

8 — Swin Cash, Detroit vs. Connecticut,
September 7, 2003

7 — Natalie Williams, Indiana at Connecticut,
September 10, 2005 (OT)

Cheryl Ford, Detroit vs. Los Angeles,
September 12, 2003

Tina Thompson, Houston vs. Utah,
August 18, 2002 (2OT)

Lisa Leslie, Los Angeles vs. Sacramento,
August 27, 2001

Yolanda Griffith, Sacramento vs. Utah,
August 19, 2001

6 — By Many

Most offensive rebounds, one half

5 — Tamika Catchings, Indiana vs. New York,
September 1, 2005

Simone Edwards, Seattle at Connecticut,
October 8, 2004

Lauren Jackson, Seattle at Sacramento,
October 1, 2004

Swin Cash, Detroit vs. Connecticut,
September 7, 2003

Michelle Snow, Houston vs. Sacramento,
September 2, 2003

Tamika Catchings, Indiana at New York,
August 18, 2002
Lisa Leslie, Los Angeles vs. Sacramento,
August 27, 2001
Yolanda Griffith, Sacramento vs. Utah,
August 19, 2001
Natalie Williams, Utah vs. Sacramento,
August 17, 2001
Janeth Arcain, Houston vs. Charlotte,
August 28, 1997
4 — By Many

Most defensive rebounds, game
14 — Tina Thompson, Houston vs. Charlotte,
August 24, 1998
13 — Cheryl Ford, Detroit vs. Cleveland,
September 2, 2003
Margo Dydek, Utah vs. Houston,
August 16, 2002
12 — By Many

Most defensive rebounds, one half
10 — Cheryl Ford, Detroit vs. Cleveland,
September 2, 2003
9 — Chamique Holdsclaw, Washington at Charlotte,
August 17, 2002
Lisa Leslie, Los Angeles vs. Sacramento,
August 27, 2001
Lisa Leslie, Los Angeles vs. Houston,
August 20, 2001

ASSISTS

Most assists, game
14 — Sue Bird, Seattle vs. Sacramento,
October 5, 2004
12 — Teresa Weatherspoon, New York vs.
Washington, August 24, 2002
Jennifer Azzi, Utah at Los Angeles,
August 24, 2002
Cynthia Cooper, Houston vs. Los Angeles,
August 30, 1999
11 — Nikki Teasley, Los Angeles vs. Detroit,
September 12, 2003
Nikki Teasley, Los Angeles vs. New York,
August 31, 2002
Nikki Teasley, Los Angeles at New York,
August 29, 2002
Nikki McCray, Washington vs. New York,
August 12, 2000
Teresa Weatherspoon, New York vs. Charlotte,
August 30, 1999

Most assists, one half
9 — Sheryl Swoopes, Houston at Seattle,
September 3, 2005
Teresa Weatherspoon, New York vs.
Washington, August 24, 2002
7 — By Many

PERSONAL FOULS

Most personal fouls, game
6 — By Many

Most personal fouls, one half
6 — Maria Stepanova, Phoenix at Cleveland,
August 25, 1998
5 — By Many

Most minutes played, no personal fouls, game
40 — Dawn Staley, Charlotte vs. Washington,
August 17, 2002
Cynthia Cooper, Houston vs. Los Angeles,
August 30, 1999
39 — Annie Burgess, Washington vs. New York,
August 22, 2002
Cynthia Cooper, Houston at Phoenix,
August 27, 1998
38 — Taj McWilliams-Franklin, Connecticut vs.
New York, October 3, 2004
Cheryl Ford, Detroit at New York,
September 28, 2004

DISQUALIFICATIONS

Fewest minutes played, disqualified player, game
9 — Maria Stepanova, Phoenix at Cleveland,
August 25, 1998
10 — Hamchetou Maiga, Sacramento vs. Houston,
September 10, 2005
14 — Tamecka Dixon, Los Angeles vs. New York,
August 31, 2002

STEALS

Most steals, game
7 — Nykesha Sales, Connecticut vs. Washington,
September 27, 2004
6 — Elaine Powell, Detroit at New York,
September 26, 2004
Tamecka Dixon, Los Angeles vs. Minnesota,
August 30, 2003
Sheryl Swoopes, Houston vs. Utah,
August 18, 2002 (2OT)
Vickie Johnson, New York at Charlotte,
August 24, 2001
Mwadi Mabika, Los Angeles vs. Sacramento,
August 24, 1999
5 — By Many

Most steals, one half
5 — Nykesha Sales, Connecticut vs. Washington,
September 27, 2004
4 — By Many

BLOCKED SHOTS

Most blocked shots, game
7 — Lisa Leslie, Los Angeles at Utah,
August 22, 2002
Lisa Leslie, Los Angeles vs. Charlotte,
September 1, 2001
Lisa Leslie, Los Angeles vs. Sacramento,
August 27, 2001
6 — Lisa Leslie, Los Angeles vs. Sacramento,
August 26, 2001
5 — By Many

Most blocked shots, one half
4 — Tangela Smith, Sacramento vs. Seattle,
October 1, 2004

Lisa Leslie, Los Angeles vs. Sacramento,
September 7, 2003
Lisa Leslie, Los Angeles at Sacramento,
September 5, 2003
Lisa Leslie, Los Angeles at Utah,
August 22, 2002
Lisa Leslie, Los Angeles vs. Charlotte,
September 1, 2001
Lisa Leslie, Los Angeles vs. Sacramento,
August 27, 2001
Lisa Leslie, Los Angeles vs. Sacramento,
August 26, 2001
Vicky Bullett, Washington vs. New York,
August 12, 2000
3 — By Many

TURNOVERS

Most turnovers, game
8 — Swin Cash, Detroit at Cleveland,
August 29, 2003
Olympia Scott-Richardson, Indiana at
New York, August 20, 2002
7 — Sheri Sam, Seattle vs. Sacramento,
October 3, 2004
Mwadi Mabika, Los Angeles at Minnesota,
August 28, 2003
Nikki Teasley, Los Angeles at New York,
August 29, 2002
Dawn Staley, Charlotte at New York,
August 26, 2001
Tina Thompson, Houston vs. Los Angeles,
August 18, 2001
Nikki McCray, Washington vs. New York,
August 12, 2000
Teresa Weatherspoon, New York at Phoenix,
August 28, 1997
6 — By Many
Most turnovers, one half
6 — Mwadi Mabika, Los Angeles at Minnesota,
August 28, 2003
5 — By Many

TEAM RECORDS

WON-LOST

Highest won-lost percentage, one postseason
1.000 — Los Angeles, 2002 (6-0)
Houston, 2000 (6-0)
Houston, 1997 (2-0)
.875 — Sacramento, 2005 (7-1)
.857 — Los Angeles, 2001 (6-1)
Most games, one postseason
9 — Los Angeles, 2003
8 — By Many
Most home games, one postseason
5 — Seattle, 2004
Detroit, 2003
Los Angeles, 2003
New York, 2002

4 — By Many
Most road games, one postseason
5 — Charlotte, 2001
4 — By Many
Most wins, one postseason
7 — Sacramento, 2005
6 — Seattle, 2004
Detroit, 2003
Los Angeles, 2002
Los Angeles, 2001
Houston, 2000
Most wins at home, one postseason
5 — Seattle, 2004
Los Angeles, 2003
4 — Sacramento, 2005
Connecticut, 2004
Detroit, 2003
New York, 2002
Most wins on road, one postseason
3 — Sacramento, 2005
Los Angeles, 2002
Los Angeles, 2001
Charlotte, 2001
Houston, 2000
2 — Connecticut, 2005
Houston, 2005
Detroit, 2003
New York, 2001
Sacramento, 2001
Most games lost, one postseason
4 — Los Angeles, 2003
New York, 2002
Charlotte, 2001
3 — By Many
Most games lost at home, one postseason
3 — New York, 2001
2 — Houston, 2005
Seattle, 2005
New York, 2004
Charlotte, 2001
Most games lost on road, one postseason
4 — Los Angeles, 2003
3 — Sacramento, 2004
Connecticut, 2004
Sacramento, 2003
New York, 2002
Cleveland, 2000
Phoenix, 1998
Most consecutive games won
9 — Los Angeles, 2001-02
7 — Houston, 1999-00
5 — Sacramento, 2005
Connecticut, 2004
Most consecutive games won, one postseason
6 — Los Angeles, 2002
Houston, 2000

5 — Sacramento, 2005
   Connecticut, 2004
4 — Connecticut, 2005
Most consecutive games won at home
   11 — Los Angeles, 2001-04
   7 — Houston, 1997-99
   6 — Connecticut, 2004-05
Most consecutive games won at home, one postseason
   5 — Seattle, 2004
      Los Angeles, 2003
   4 — Sacramento, 2005
      Connecticut, 2004
      Detroit, 2003
      New York, 2002
   3 — By Many
Most consecutive games won on road
   6 — Los Angeles, 2001-02
   4 — Houston, 1999-00
   3 — Sacramento, 2005
      Charlotte, 2001
Most consecutive games won on road, one postseason
   3 — Sacramento, 2005
      Los Angeles, 2002
      Los Angeles, 2001
      Charlotte, 2001
      Houston, 2000
   2 — Connecticut, 2005
      Houston, 2005
      Detroit, 2003
      New York, 2001
      Sacramento, 2001
   1 — By Many
Most consecutive games lost
   6 — Charlotte, 2001-03 (current)
   4 — New York, 2004-05 (current)
      Minnesota, 2003-04 (current)
      Phoenix, 1998, 2000 (current)
   3 — By Many
Most consecutive games lost, one postseason
   2 — By Many
Most consecutive games lost at home
   4 — Charlotte, 2001-03 (current)
   2 — By Many
Most consecutive games lost at home, one postseason
   2 — Houston, 2005
      Seattle, 2005
      Charlotte, 2001
      New York, 2001
   1 — By Many
Most consecutive games lost on road
   6 — Los Angeles, 2003-05 (current)
   5 — Cleveland, 1998, 2000-01
   4 — Washington, 2002, 2004 (current)
Most consecutive games lost on road, one postseason
   4 — Los Angeles, 2003
   3 — New York, 2002
      Cleveland, 2000
   2 — By Many

SCORING

Most points, game
   103 — Los Angeles vs. Utah, August 24, 2002
   101 — Los Angeles vs. Phoenix, August 13, 2000
   96 — New York vs. Washington, August 24, 2002
Fewest points, game
   41 — Phoenix vs. New York, August 28, 1997
   43 — New York at Cleveland, August 17, 2000
      Orlando at Cleveland, August 15, 2000
   44 — New York vs. Charlotte, August 27, 2001
Most points, both teams, game
   180 — Los Angeles (103) vs. Utah (77),
      August 24, 2002
   177 — Los Angeles (101) vs. Phoenix (76),
      August 13, 2000
   175 — New York (96) vs. Washington (79),
      August 24, 2002
Fewest points, both teams, game
   92 — New York (44) vs. Charlotte (48),
      August 27, 2001
   96 — Cleveland (45) at New York (51),
      August 20, 2000
   99 — Cleveland (46) at Charlotte (53),
      August 16, 2001
      New York (43) at Cleveland (56),
      August 17, 2000
Largest margin of victory, game
   31 — Los Angeles (93) vs. Sacramento (62),
      August 27, 2001
   29 — Cleveland (72) vs. Orlando (43),
      August 15, 2000
   28 — Los Angeles (82) vs. Charlotte (54),
      September 1, 2001
      Houston (83) vs. Los Angeles (55),
      August 29, 1999

BY HALF

Most points, first half
   50 — New York vs. Washington, August 24, 2002
   49 — Los Angeles at Minnesota, August 28, 2003
   48 — Detroit vs. Connecticut, September 7, 2003
Fewest points, first half
   15 — Orlando at Cleveland, August 13, 2000
   16 — New York at Indiana, September 1, 2005
   17 — New York vs. Connecticut, October 1, 2004
      Cleveland at New York, August 20, 2000
Most points, both teams, first half
   90 — Detroit (46) at Cleveland (44), August 29, 2003
   89 — New York (50) vs. Washington (39),
      August 24, 2002
   85 — Connecticut (45) at Indiana (40),
      September 8, 2005
      Detroit (48) vs. Connecticut (37),
      September 7, 2003
Fewest points, both teams, first half
   41 — Phoenix (18) vs. New York (23),
      August 28, 1997

42 — New York (21) vs. Charlotte (21),
August 27, 2001
43 — New York (16) at Indiana (27),
September 1, 2005
Largest lead at halftime
22 — Cleveland vs. Charlotte, August 18, 2001
(led 43-21; won 69-51)
21 — Los Angeles vs. Detroit, September 12, 2003
(led 42-21; won 75-63)
Cleveland vs. Orlando, August 13, 2000
(led 36-15; won 63-54)
20 — Los Angeles vs. Sacramento,
September 7, 2003 (led 46-26; won 79-54)
Largest deficit at halftime overcome to win game
17 — Minnesota vs. Los Angeles, August 28, 2003
(trailed 32-49; won 74-72)
14 — New York at Houston, September 4, 1999
(trailed 23-37; won 68-67)
13 — New York vs. Detroit, September 28, 2004
(trailed 37-24; won 66-64)
Most points, second half
59 — Los Angeles vs. Utah, August 24, 2002
Los Angeles vs. Phoenix, August 13, 2000
51 — Los Angeles vs. Sacramento, August 27, 2001
50 — Los Angeles vs. Sacramento, August 24, 1999
Fewest points, second half
15 — New York vs. Cleveland, August 20, 2000
17 — Miami vs. New York, August 17, 2001
18 — Cleveland at Charlotte, August 16, 2001
Most points, both teams, second half
107 — Los Angeles (59) vs. Utah (48), August 24, 2002
99 — Los Angeles (59) vs. Phoenix (40),
August 13, 2000
93 — Houston (48) vs. Phoenix (45),
September 1, 1998
Fewest points, both teams, second half
43 — New York (15) vs. Cleveland (28),
August 20, 2000
Phoenix (21) vs. Houston (22), August 27, 1998
46 — Cleveland (18) at Charlotte (28),
August 16, 2001
47 — Miami (17) vs. New York (30), August 17, 2001

OVERTIME PERIOD

Most points, overtime period
17 — Connecticut vs. Indiana, September 10, 2005
15 — Houston vs. New York, August 26, 2000
10 — Sacramento at Houston, September 8, 2005
Houston vs. Utah, August 18, 2002
Fewest points, overtime period
0 — Sacramento at Connecticut,
September 15, 2004
3 — Phoenix at Houston, August 29, 1998
4 — Utah at Houston, August 18, 2002
Most points, both teams, overtime period
24 — Connecticut (17) vs. Indiana (7),
September 10, 2005

Houston (15) vs. New York (9),
August 26, 2000
Fewest points, both teams, overtime period
7 — Sacramento (0) at Connecticut (7),
September 15, 2005
11 — Phoenix (3) at Houston (8), August 29, 1998

PLAYERS SCORING

Most players, 20 or more points, game
2 — By Many. Most Recent:
Los Angeles at Sacramento,
September 5, 2003
Most players, 20 or more points, both teams, game
3 — New York (2) at Washington (1),
August 22, 2002
Utah (2) at Houston (1), August 18, 2002 (2OT)
New York (2) vs. Indiana (1), August 18, 2002
Houston (2) vs. New York (1),
August 26, 2000 (OT)
Houston (2) vs. Los Angeles (1),
August 17, 2000
Houston (2) vs. Sacramento (1),
August 14, 2000
New York (2) at Washington (1),
August 12, 2000
Houston (2) vs. Los Angeles (1),
August 30, 1999
Phoenix (2) at Houston (1), September 1, 1998
Most players, 10 or more points, game
5 — By Many. Most Recent:
Connecticut vs. Indiana,
September 10, 2005 (OT)
Houston at Seattle, September 3, 2005
Fewest players, 10 or more points, game
0 — Phoenix vs. New York, August 28, 1997
Most players, 10 or more points, both teams, game
10 — Sacramento (5) vs. Los Angeles (5),
August 24, 2001
9 — Washington (5) at New York (4),
August 24, 2002
Los Angeles (5) vs. Phoenix (4),
August 13, 2000
Phoenix (5) vs. Los Angeles (4),
August 11, 2000
Houston (5) at Charlotte (4), August 22, 1998
8 — Many times
Fewest players, 10 or more points, both teams, game
2 — Houston (1) at Phoenix (1), August 27, 1998
3 — New York (1) vs. Indiana (2), August 30, 2005
Phoenix (0) vs. New York (3), August 28, 1997

FIELD GOAL PERCENTAGE

Highest field-goal percentage, game
.660 — New York vs. Washington, August 24, 2002
(35/53)
.630 — Sacramento at Los Angeles, August 31, 2005
(29/46)
.593 — New York vs. Indiana, August 18, 2002
(32/54)

Lowest field-goal percentage, game
  .224 — Phoenix vs. New York, August 28, 1997 (15/67)
  .268 — Sacramento vs. Utah, August 19, 2001 (15/56)
  .269 — Sacramento at Los Angeles,
        September 26, 2004 (18/67)
Highest field-goal percentage, both teams, game
  .569 — Sacramento (.630) at Los Angeles (.518),
        August 31, 2005 (58/102)
  .549 — New York (.660) vs. Washington (.450),
        August 24, 2002 (62/113)
  .500 — New York (.536) at Washington (.468),
        August 22, 2002 (59/118)
Lowest field-goal percentage, both teams, game
  .299 — Houston (.288) vs. New York (.309),
        September 5, 1999 (32/107)
  .314 — Indiana (.281) vs. New York (.354),
        September 1, 2005 (33/105)
  .325 — Phoenix (.224) vs. New York (.460),
        August 28, 1997 (38/117)

FIELD GOALS

Most field-goals, game
  38 — Los Angeles vs. Utah, August 24, 2002
  37 — Los Angeles vs. Sacramento, August 27, 2001
  35 — New York vs. Washington, August 24, 2002
Fewest field-goals, game
  14 — Charlotte at New York, August 27, 2001
  15 — Sacramento vs. Utah, August 19, 2001
       Houston vs. New York, September 5, 1999
       Houston vs. New York, September 4, 1999
       Phoenix vs. New York, August 28, 1997
  16 — Indiana vs. New York, September 1, 2005
       New York at Cleveland, August 17, 2000
       Orlando at Cleveland, August 15, 2000
Most field-goals, both teams, game
  69 — Los Angeles (38) vs. Utah (31), August 24, 2002
  62 — New York (35) vs. Washington (27),
       August 24, 2002
  61 — Los Angeles (34) at Phoenix (27),
       August 11, 2000
       Houston (31) at Charlotte (30),
       August 22, 1998
Fewest field-goals, both teams, game
  32 — Houston (15) vs. New York (17),
       September 5, 1999
  33 — Indiana (16) vs. New York (17),
       September 1, 2005
       Charlotte (14) at New York (19),
       August 27, 2001
  36 — Indiana (18) at New York (18), August 30, 2005
Most field goals, one half
  21 — Los Angeles at Minnesota, August 28, 2003
       New York vs. Indiana, August 20, 2002
       Los Angeles vs. Sacramento, August 24, 1999
  20 — Houston at Seattle, September 3, 2005
       Sacramento at Los Angeles, August 31, 2005
       Los Angeles vs. Sacramento,
       September 7, 2003

Los Angeles vs. Utah, August 24, 2002
New York vs. Washington, August 24, 2002
Los Angeles vs. Sacramento, August 27, 2001

FIELD GOAL ATTEMPTS

Most field-goal attempts, game
  79 — Houston vs. Utah, August 18, 2002 (2OT)
  74 — Seattle at Connecticut, October 8, 2004
       Detroit vs. Cleveland, September 2, 2003
       Los Angeles vs. Utah, August 24, 2002
       Los Angeles at Houston, August 29, 1999
       Los Angeles vs. Sacramento, August 24, 1999
  73 — Cleveland vs. Phoenix, August 24, 1998
Fewest field-goal attempts, game
  44 — Houston at Seattle, September 1, 2005
  45 — Charlotte at New York, August 27, 2001
  46 — Many times
Most field-goal attempts, both teams, game
  147 — Houston (79) vs. Utah (68),
        August 18, 2002 (2OT)
  140 — Los Angeles (74) vs. Sacramento (66),
        August 24, 1999
  139 — Detroit (70) at Los Angeles (69),
        September 12, 2003
        Los Angeles (74) vs. Utah (65),
        August 24, 2002
Fewest field-goal attempts, both teams, game
  92 — Indiana (46) at New York (46), August 30, 2005
  94 — Charlotte (45) at New York (49),
       August 27, 2001
  99 — Charlotte (48) vs. New York (51),
       August 24, 2001
Most field goal attempts, one half
  42 — Seattle at Connecticut, October 8, 2004
       Detroit vs. Cleveland, September 2, 2003
  41 — Los Angeles vs. Detroit, September 12, 2003
       Cleveland vs. Phoenix, August 24, 1998

THREE-POINT FIELD GOALS

Most three-point field goals, game
  12 — Seattle vs. Sacramento, October 5, 2004
  11 — Washington at New York, August 24, 2002
       Los Angeles vs. Utah, August 24, 2002
  10 — New York vs. Detroit, September 28, 2004
       New York vs. Detroit, September 26, 2004
       Sacramento at Los Angeles, August 26, 2001
Fewest three-point field goals, game
  0 — Houston at Seattle, September 1, 2005
      Utah vs. Sacramento, August 17, 2001
      New York vs. Houston, August 24, 2000
  1 — By Many
Most three-point field goals, both teams, game
  18 — Washington (11) at New York (7),
       August 24, 2002
  17 — Seattle (12) vs. Sacramento (5),
       October 5, 2004
  16 — Sacramento (10) at Los Angeles (6),
       August 26, 2001

225

Fewest three-point field goals, both teams, game
2 — New York (1) at Phoenix (1), August 28, 1997
3 — Houston (0) at Seattle (3), September 1, 2005
New York (1) vs. Cleveland (2),
August 20, 2000
4 — By Many
Most three-point field goals, one half
10 — Seattle vs. Sacramento, October 5, 2004
8 — Los Angeles vs. Utah, August 24, 2002

THREE-POINT FIELD GOAL ATTEMPTS
Most three-point field goal attempts, game
29 — New York Vs. Detroit, September 28, 2004
New York vs. Detroit, September 26, 2004
Charlotte at Washington, August 15, 2002
25 — Los Angeles vs. Houston, August 20, 2000
24 — Houston at Charlotte, August 22, 1998
Fewest three-point field goal attempts, game
3 — Detroit at New York, September 26, 2004
Washington vs. Connecticut,
September 25, 2004
4 — Detroit vs. New York, September 24, 2004
New York at Phoenix, August 28, 1997
5 — Houston at Seattle, September 1, 2005
Seattle vs. Connecticut, October 12, 2004
Most three-point field goal attempts, both teams, game
46 — Los Angeles (23) vs. Sacramento (23),
August 26, 2001
39 — Los Angeles (23) vs. Utah (16),
August 24, 2002
38 — Los Angeles (25) vs. Houston (13),
August 20, 2000
Fewest three-point field goal attempts, both teams, game
14 — Utah (6) at Sacramento (8), August 19, 2001
15 — New York (4) at Phoenix (11), August 28, 1997
16 — Houston (6) at Sacramento (10),
September 10, 2005 (OT)
Most three-point field goal attempts, one half
16 — Houston at Charlotte, August 22, 1998
Charlotte at Washington, August 15, 2002
15 — New York vs. Detroit, September 28, 2004
New York vs. Detroit, September 26, 2004
Washington at Charlotte, August 17, 2002

FREE THROW PERCENTAGE
Highest freethrow percentage, game
1.000 — By Many
Lowest free-throw percentage, game
.333 — New York vs. Charlotte, August 27, 2001 (2/6)
.400 — New York at Houston, August 30, 1997 (4/10)
.417 — New York vs. Charlotte, August 29, 1999 (5/12)
Highest free throw percentage, both teams, game
.970 — Phoenix (1.000) vs. Cleveland (.941),
August 22, 1998 (32/33)
.931 — Houston (.955) vs. Los Angeles (.857),
August 17, 2000 (27/29)
.930 — Connecticut (.938) vs. Washington (.917),
September 27, 2004 (52/56)

Lowest free throw percentage, both teams, game
.478 — Miami (.467) vs. New York (.500),
August 17, 2001 (11/23)
.567 — Cleveland (.444) vs. Orlando (.750),
August 15, 2000 (17/30)
.570 — New York (.462) vs. Detroit (.621),
September 28, 2004 (24/42)

FREE THROWS MADE
Most free throws made, game
39 — Sacramento vs. Utah, August 19, 2001
32 — Houston vs. New York, September 4, 1999
30 — Connecticut vs. Washington,
Septebmer 27, 2004
Fewest free throws made, game
2 — New York vs. Charlotte, August 27, 2001
3 — Charlotte at Los Angeles, September 1, 2001
4 — By Many
Most free throws made, both teams, game
59 — Sacramento (39) vs. Utah (20), August 19, 2001
52 — Connecticut (30) vs. Washington (22),
September 27, 2004
48 — Houston (32) vs. New York (16),
September 4, 1999
Fewest free throws made, both teams, game
11 — New York (4) at Miami (7), August 17, 2001
12 — New York (6) vs. Indiana (6), August 20, 2002
Charlotte (4) at New York (8), August 30, 1999
13 — Seattle (6) at Connecticut (7), October 8, 2004
Orlando (6) vs. Cleveland (7), August 11, 2000
Houston (6) at Phoenix (7), August 27, 1998
Most free throws made, one half
24 — Sacramento vs. Utah, August 19, 2001
23 — Los Angeles vs. Phoenix, August 13, 2000

FREE THROW ATTEMPTS
Most free throw attempts, game
47 — Sacramento vs. Utah, August 19, 2001
42 — Houston vs. New York, September 4, 1999
38 — Connecticut vs. Detroit, September 2, 2005
Fewest free throw attempts, game
4 — Charlotte at Los Angeles, September 1, 2001
5 — Seattle vs. Houston, September 1, 2005
Detroit vs. Los Angeles, September 14, 2003
6 — Sacramento at Houston, August 31, 2003
Los Angeles at Seattle, August 15, 2002
New York vs. Charlotte, August 27, 2001
Most free throw attempts, both teams, game
73 — Sacramento (47) vs. Utah (26),
August 19, 2001
64 — Houston (42) vs. New York (22),
September 4, 1999
62 — Sacramento (37) vs. Los Angeles (25),
September 2, 2005
Fewest free throw attempts, both teams, game
15 — Charlotte (7) at New York (8), August 30, 1999
17 — Charlotte (8) at New York (9), August 26, 2001
19 — Sacramento (8) vs. Los Angeles (11),

September 24, 2004
New York (9) vs. Indiana (10), August 20, 2002
Cleveland (7) at New York (12),
August 20, 2000
Houston (8) at Phoenix (11), August 27, 1998

Most free throw attempts, one half
29 — Sacramento vs. Utah, August 19, 2001
28 — Los Angeles vs. Phoenix, August 13, 2000

TOTAL REBOUNDS

Highest rebound percentage, game
.679 — Cleveland vs. Charlotte, August 18, 2001
.669 — Houston vs. Charlotte, August 28, 1997
.648 — Charlotte at Cleveland, August 20, 2001

Most rebounds, game
44 — Washington vs. Connecticut,
September 25, 2004
Houston vs. Utah, August 18, 2002 (2OT)
Los Angeles vs. Sacramento, August 27, 2001
43 — Houston vs. Los Angeles, August 29, 1999
42 — Seattle at Connecticut, October 8, 2004
Houston vs. Charlotte, August 28, 1997

Fewest rebounds, game
15 — Los Angeles vs. Sacramento, August 31, 2005
17 — Charlotte at Cleveland, August 18, 2001
19 — Washington at New York, August 24, 2002
Cleveland vs. Charlotte, August 20, 2001
Washington at New York, August 14, 2000

Most rebounds, both teams, game
81 — Houston (44) vs. Utah (37),
August 18, 2002 (2OT)
80 — Detroit (41) at Los Angeles (39),
September 12, 2003
78 — Houston (43) vs. Los Angeles (35),
August 29, 1999

Fewest rebounds, both teams, game
44 — Los Angeles (15) vs. Sacramento (29),
August 31, 2005
47 — New York (20) vs. Indiana (27), August 30, 2005
New York (21) at Charlotte (26),
August 24, 2001
48 — Seattle (24) at Houston (24),
September 1, 2005
Houston (24) vs. Phoenix (24),
September 1, 1998

Most rebounds, one half
26 — Cleveland vs. Orlando, August 13, 2000
25 — Detroit vs. Cleveland, September 2, 2003
Los Angeles vs. Sacramento, August 27, 2001
Cleveland vs. Orlando, August 15, 2000

OFFENSIVE REBOUNDS

Highest offensive rebound percentage, game
.630 — Charlotte at Cleveland, August 20, 2001 (17/27)
.538 — Detroit vs. Charlotte, September 7, 2003
(21/39)
.522 — New York vs. Charlotte, August 30, 1999
(12/23)

Most offensive rebounds, game
21 — Detroit vs. Connecticut, September 7, 2003
Cleveland vs. Phoenix, August 24, 1998
20 — Seattle at Connecticut, October 8, 2004
19 — Sacramento at Los Angeles,
September 26, 2004

Fewest offensive rebounds, game
2 — New York vs. Indiana, August 30, 2005
3 — Houston at Seattle, September 1, 2005
Los Angeles at Seattle, August 15, 2002
Houston vs. Phoenix, September 1, 1998

Most offensive rebounds, both teams, game
30 — Houston (18) vs. Utah (12),
August 18, 2002 (2OT)
29 — Sacramento (19) at Los Angeles (10),
September 26, 2004
Seattle (20) at Connecticut (9),
October 8, 2004
Detroit (21) vs. Connecticut (8),
September 7, 2003
28 — New York (14) vs. Miami (14), August 21, 2001
Los Angeles (16) at Houston (12),
August 29, 1999
Cleveland (21) vs. Phoenix (7),
August 24, 1998

Fewest offensive rebounds, both teams, game
8 — Houston (3) at Seattle (5), September 1, 2005
New York (2) vs. Indiana (6), August 30, 2005
Los Angeles (3) at Seattle (5),
August 15, 2002
10 — Connecticut (4) vs. Detroit (6),
September 5, 2003
Houston (3) vs. Phoenix (7),
September 1, 1998
11 — Sacramento (4) vs. Houston (7),
August 29, 2003
New York (5) vs. Washington (6),
August 24, 2002
New York (4) at Cleveland (7),
August 17, 2000

Most offensive rebounds, one half
16 — Cleveland vs. Phoenix, August 24, 1998
14 — Seattle at Connecticut, October 8, 2004

DEFENSIVE REBOUNDS

Highest defensive rebound percentage, game
.913 — Indiana at New York, August 30, 2005 (21/23)
.879 — Detroit at Connecticut, September 5, 2003
(29/33)
.875 — Detroit vs. Cleveland,
September 2, 2003 (28/42)

Most defensive rebounds, game
34 — New York at Phoenix, August 28, 1997
33 — Los Angeles vs. Sacramento, August 27, 2001
31 — By Many

Fewest defensive rebounds, game
9 — Los Angeles vs. Sacramento, August 31, 2005

10 — Cleveland vs. Charlotte, August 20, 2001

11 — Charlotte at New York, August 30, 1999

Most defensive rebounds, both teams, game

55 — Los Angeles (31) vs. Houston (24),
August 20, 2001

54 — Washington (31) vs. Connecticut (23),
September 25, 2004

Los Angeles (29) vs. Detroit (25),
September 12, 2003

Detroit (29) at Connecticut (25),
September 5, 2003

Cleveland (28) at Detroit (26), August 31, 2003

52 — Many times

Fewest defensive rebounds, both teams, game

28 — Cleveland (10) vs. Charlotte (18),
August 20, 2001

30— Washington (15) vs. New York (15),
August 22, 2002

31 — Indiana (13) at New York (18),
August 18, 2002

Charlotte (11) at New York (20),
August 30, 1999

Most defensive rebounds, one half

20 — Los Angeles vs. Sacramento,
September 7, 2003

19 — Washington vs. Connecticut,
September 25, 2004

Los Angeles vs. Houston, August 20, 2001

New York at Phoenix, August 28, 1997

ASSISTS

Most assists, game

31 — Los Angeles vs. Utah, August 24, 2002

26 — Los Angeles vs. Sacramento,
September 7, 2003

25 — Los Angeles vs. Minnesota, September 1, 2003

Los Angeles vs. Sacramento, August 27, 2001

New York vs. Cleveland, August 21, 2000

Fewest assists, game

6 — Washington at Connecticut,
September 27, 2004

Houston vs. New York, September 5, 1999

Houston vs. New York, August 30, 1997

7 — Connecticut at Sacramento,
September 18, 2005

Connecticut at Seattle, October 12, 2004

8 — Indiana at New York, August 30, 2005

Sacramento at Los Angeles,
September 26, 2004

Houston at Los Angeles, August 20, 2001

Cleveland at Detroit, September 2, 2003

Most assists, both teams, game

51 — Los Angeles (31) vs. Utah (20),
August 24, 2002

44 — Los Angeles (25) vs. Minnesota (19),
September 1, 2003

43 — Los Angeles (22) vs. Sacramento (21),
August 31, 2005

Charlotte (23) vs. New York (20),
August 27, 1999

Fewest assists, both teams, game

16 — Houston (6) vs. New York (10),
September 5, 1999

18 — Indiana (8) at New York (10), August 30, 2005

19 — New York (9) vs. Charlotte (10),
August 27, 2001

Houston (6) vs. New York (13),
August 30, 1997

Most assists, one half

17 — Los Angeles vs. Sacramento,
September 7, 2003

Los Angeles vs. Sacramento, August 27, 2001

16 — Los Angeles vs. Minnesota,
September 1, 2003

Los Angeles vs. Utah, August 24, 2002

New York vs. Washington, August 24, 2002

Los Angeles vs. Sacramento, August 24, 1999

PERSONAL FOULS

Most personal fouls, game

31 — Utah at Sacramento, August 19, 2001

30 — Los Angeles at Sacramento,
September 2, 2005

29 — Indiana at Connecticut,
September 10, 2005 (OT)

Fewest personal fouls, game

7 — Connecticut at New York, October 1, 2004

Houston vs. Los Angeles, August 17, 2000

9 — New York vs. Charlotte, August 26, 2001

10 — Sacramento at Connecticut,
September 14, 2005

Houston at Sacramento, August 12, 2000

Most personal fouls, both teams, game

52 — Los Angeles (30) at Sacramento (22),
September 2, 2005

51 — Utah (31) at Sacramento (20),
August 19, 2001

50 — Minnesota (26) at Los Angeles (24),
August 30, 2003

Fewest personal fouls, both teams, game

22 — Sacramento (10) at Connecticut (12),
September 14, 2005

New York (9) vs. Charlotte (13),
ugust 26, 2001

23 — Connecticut (7) at New York (16),
October 1, 2004

25 — Houston (10) at Sacramento (15),
August 12, 2000

Most personal fouls, one half

19 — Utah at Sacramento, August 19, 2001

17 — Detroit at Connecticut, September 2, 2005

Phoenix at Los Angeles, August 13, 2000

DISQUALIFICATIONS

Most disqualifications, game
2 — Detroit at Connecticut, September 2, 2005
New York at Houston, August 26, 2000 (ot)
Los Angeles at Houston, August 29, 1999
1 — By Many

Most disqualifications, both teams, game
2 — Detroit (2) at Connecticut (0),
September 2, 2005
New York (1) vs. Miami (1), August 21, 2001
New York (2) at Houston (0),
August 26, 2000 (OT)
Los Angeles (2) at Houston (0),
August 29, 1999
1 — By Many

STEALS

Most steals, game
15 — Connecticut vs. Seattle, October 8, 2004
Los Angeles vs. Minnesota, August 30, 2003
Houston vs. Los Angeles, August 17, 2000
Los Angeles vs. Sacramento, August 24, 1999
14 — By Many

Fewest steals, game
1 — Indiana at New York, August 18, 2002
2 — By Many

Most steals, both teams, game
28 — Los Angeles (15) vs. Sacramento (13),
August 24, 1999
25 — Utah (14) at Houston (11),
August 18, 2002 (2OT)
23 — New York (14) vs. Cleveland (9),
August 20, 2000

Fewest steals, both teams, game
5 — Indiana (1) at New York (4), August 18, 2002
6 — Phoenix (3) vs. Los Angeles (3),
August 11, 2000
7 — Los Angeles (3) vs. Sacramento (4),
August 27, 2001

Most steals, one half
12 — Los Angeles vs. Sacramento, August 24, 1999
10 — Detroit at New York, September 26, 2004
Minnesota vs. Los Angeles, August 28, 2003
New York vs. Cleveland, August 20, 2000
Houston vs. Los Angeles, August 17, 2000

BLOCKED SHOTS

Most blocked shots, game
13 — Los Angeles vs. Sacramento, August 27, 2001
11 — Los Angeles vs. Sacramento, August 24, 1999

10 — Sacramento vs. Seattle, October 1, 2004 (ot)
Los Angeles at Utah, August 22, 2002
Los Angeles vs. Charlotte, September 1, 2001

Fewest blocked shots, game
0 — By Many

Most blocked shots, both teams, game
19 — Los Angeles (10) at Utah (9), August 22, 2002
17 — Los Angeles (13) vs. Sacramento (4),
August 27, 2001
16 — Los Angeles (10) vs. Charlotte (6),
September 1, 2001

Fewest blocked shots, both teams, game
2 — By Many

Most blocked shots, one half
8 — Los Angeles vs. Sacramento, August 27, 2001
7 — Sacramento vs. Seattle, October 1, 2004
6 — By Many

TURNOVERS

Most turnovers, game
25 — Los Angeles at Houston, August 17, 2000
24 — Minnesota at Los Angeles, August 30, 2003
21 — Los Angeles vs. Sacramento,
September 28, 2004
Utah vs. Los Angeles, August 22, 2002
Indiana at New York, August 20, 2002
Sacramento at Los Angeles, August 24, 1999

Fewest turnovers, game
4 — Connecticut at Detroit, August 31, 2005
5 — Indiana at New York, August 30, 2005
New York at Charlotte, August 27, 1999
6 — By Many

Most turnovers, both teams, game
39 — Minnesota (24) at Los Angeles (15),
August 30, 2003
37 — Los Angeles (19) at Seattle (18),
August 15, 2002
Seattle (19) vs. Sacramento (18),
October 3, 2004
36 — New York (19) vs. Detroit (17),
September 26, 2004
Charlotte (20) vs. New York (16),
August 24, 2001
Sacramento (21) at Los Angeles (15),
August 24, 1999

Fewest turnovers, both teams, game
14 — New York (5) at Charlotte (9), August 27, 1999
15 — Indiana (5) at New York (10), August 30, 2005
16 — By Many

Most turnovers, one half
16 — Los Angeles at Houston, August 17, 2000
15 — Minnesota at Los Angeles, August 30, 2003

PLAYOFFS SINGLE-GAME BESTS
POINTS

	FG	FT	PTS
Lisa Leslie, Los Angeles vs. Sacramento, August 27, 2001	15	5	35
Nykesha Sales, Connecticut at Seattle, October 10, 2004	14	0	32
Cynthia Cooper, Houston vs. Charlotte, August 28, 1997	9	9	31
Sheryl Swoopes, Houston vs. New York, August 26, 2000	11	6	*31

* Denotes overtime. ** Denotes double overtime.

229

	FG	FT	PTS
Lauren Jackson, Seattle at Sacramento, October 1, 2004	9	9	*31
Yolanda Griffith, Sacramento vs. Utah, August 19, 2001	6	18	30
Cynthia Cooper, Houston at Phoenix, August 27, 1998	11	5	29
Cynthia Cooper, Houston at New York, September 2, 1999	8	10	29
Lisa Leslie, Los Angeles vs. Phoenix, August 13, 2000	12	5	29
Cynthia Cooper, Houston at Los Angeles, August 20, 2000	10	7	29
Tamika Catchings, Indiana vs. New York, August 16, 2002	11	3	29
Mwadi Mabika, Los Angeles at Detroit, September 16, 2003	11	5	29
Yolanda Griffith, Sacramento at Utah, August 17, 2001	10	8	28
Lisa Leslie, Los Angeles vs. Houston, August 20, 2001	8	10	28
Sheryl Swoopes, Houston vs. Utah, August 18, 2002	11	6	**28
Sheryl Swoopes, Houston vs. Utah, August 20, 2002	9	8	28
Cynthia Cooper, Houston at Charlotte, August 22, 1998	8	8	27
Jennifer Gillom, Phoenix at Cleveland, August 24, 1998	10	4	27
Bridget Pettis, Phoenix at Cleveland, August 25, 1998	9	8	27
Cynthia Cooper, Houston vs. Phoenix, August 29, 1998	7	11	*27
Andrea Stinson, Charlotte at New York, August 29, 1999	9	8	27
Sheryl Swoopes, Houston vs. Sacramento, August 14, 2000	9	8	27
Sheryl Swoopes, Houston at Sacramento, August 29, 2003	9	8	27
Yolanda Griffith, Sacramento at Houston, September 2, 2003	11	5	27
Ruth Riley, Detroit vs. Los Angeles, September 16, 2003	11	5	27
Lauren Jackson, Seattle vs. Sacramento, October 5, 2004	9	3	27
Betty Lennox, Seattle vs. Connecticut, October 10, 2004	11	5	27
Lindsay Whalen, Connecticut vs. Detroit, September 2, 2005	5	15	27

FIELD GOALS

	FG	FGA
Lisa Leslie, Los Angeles vs. Sacramento, August 27, 2001	15	22
Nykesha Sales, Connecticut at Seattle, October 10, 2004	14	22
Lisa Leslie, Los Angeles vs. Phoenix, August 13, 2000	12	17
Cynthia Cooper, Houston at Phoenix, August 27, 1998	11	24
Sheryl Swoopes, Houston vs. New York, August 26, 2000	*11	*18
Lisa Leslie, Los Angeles at Seattle, August 15, 2002	11	17
Tamika Catchings, Indiana vs. New York, August 16, 2002	11	19
Sheryl Swoopes, Houston vs. Utah, August 18, 2002	**11	**22
Natalie Williams, Utah at Houston, August 20, 2002	11	16
Tari Phillips, New York vs. Washington, August 24, 2002	11	13
Yolanda Griffith, Sacramento at Houston, September 2, 2003	11	15
Mwadi Mabika, Los Angeles at Detroit, September 16, 2003	11	20
Ruth Riley, Detroit vs. Los Angeles, September 16, 2003	11	19
Betty Lennox, Seattle vs. Connecticut, October 10, 2004	11	16
Chamique Holdsclaw, Los Angeles vs. Sacramento, August 31, 2005	11	15
Yolanda Griffith, Sacramento at Connecticut, September 14, 2005	11	17
Jennifer Gillom, Phoenix at Cleveland, August 24, 1998	10	19
Michelle Griffiths, Phoenix at Houston, September 1, 1998	10	16
Andrea Stinson, Charlotte at New York, August 30, 1999	10	19
Sheryl Swoopes, Houston vs. Los Angeles, August 30, 1999	10	19
Cynthia Cooper, Houston at Los Angeles, August 20, 2000	10	23
Tari Phillips, New York vs. Houston, August 24, 2000	10	19
Yolanda Griffith, Sacramento at Utah, August 17, 2001	10	17
Lisa Leslie, Los Angeles vs. Seattle, August 17, 2002	10	16
Tamika Whitmore, New York vs. Indiana, August 18, 2002	10	12
Tari Phillips, New York at Washington, August 22, 2002	10	13
Lisa Leslie, Los Angeles vs. Utah, August 24, 2002	10	17
Deanna Nolan, Detroit vs. Cleveland, September 2, 2003	10	13
Mwadi Mabika, Los Angeles vs. Sacramento, September 7, 2003	10	18
Lisa Leslie, Los Angeles vs. Sacramento, September 8, 2003	10	16
Lisa Leslie, Los Angeles vs. Detroit, September 12, 2003	10	18
Tangela Smith, Sacramento vs. Seattle, October 1, 2004	*10	*18

* Denotes overtime. ** Denotes double overtime.

FREE THROWS

	FT	FTA
Yolanda Griffith, Sacramento vs. Utah, August 19, 2001	18	24
Lindsay Whalen, Connecticut vs. Washington, September 27, 2004	15	16
Lindsay Whalen, Connecticut vs. Detroit, September 2, 2005	15	17
Cynthia Cooper, Houston vs. New York, September 5, 1999	13	15
Cynthia Cooper, Houston vs. New York, August 30, 1997	11	15
Cynthia Cooper, Houston vs. Phoenix, August 29, 1998	*11	14
Marie Ferdinand, Utah at Sacramento, August 19, 2001	11	14
Chasity Melvin, Cleveland at Detroit, September 2, 2003	11	14
Cynthia Cooper, Houston at New York, September 2, 1999	10	10
Cynthia Cooper, Houston vs. New York, September 4, 1999	10	12
Lisa Leslie, Los Angeles vs. Houston, August 20, 2001	10	12
Swin Cash, Detroit at Cleveland, August 29, 2003	10	13
Nykesha Sales, Connecticut vs. Detroit, September 5, 2003	10	10
Yolanda Griffith, Sacramento at Los Angeles, September 7, 2003	10	10
Cynthia Cooper, Houston vs. Charlotte, August 28, 1997	9	12
Cynthia Cooper, Houston vs. Charlotte, August 24, 1998	9	10
Sheryl Swoopes, Houston vs. Phoenix, September 1, 1998	9	10
Kedra Holland-Corn, Sacramento vs. Utah, August 19, 2001	9	10
Lisa Lesle, Los Angeles vs. Charlotte, September 1, 2001	9	10
Natalie Williams, Utah at Houston, August 18, 2002	**9	14
Chasity Melvin, Cleveland vs. Detroit, August 29, 2003	9	12
LaToya Thomas, Cleveland vs. Detroit, August 29, 2003	9	11
Tamika Williams, Minnesota at Los Angeles, August 30, 2003	9	13
Yolanda Griffith, Sacramento vs. Los Angeles, September 5, 2003	9	10
Lindsay Whalen, Connecticut vs. Washington, September 29, 2004	9	10
Lauren Jackson, Seattle at Sacramento, October 1, 2004	*9	9
Betty Lennox, Seattle vs. Connecticut, October 12, 2004	9	11
Betty Lennox, Seattle at Houston, August 30, 2005	9	10
Taj McWilliams-Franklin, Connecticut at Indiana, September 8, 2005	*9	9

REBOUNDS

	REB
Lisa Leslie, Los Angeles vs. Houston, August 20, 2001	18
Yolanda Griffith, Sacramento at Houston, September 2, 2003	17
Lisa Leslie, Los Angeles vs. Sacramento, August 27, 2001	16
Taj McWilliams-Franklin, Connecticut vs. Sacramento, September 15, 2005	*16
Tari Phillips, New York vs. Houston, August 24, 2000	15
Tari Phillips, New York vs. Miami, August 19, 2001	15
Cheryl Ford, Detroit vs. Cleveland, September 2, 2003	15
Michelle Snow, Houston vs. Sacramento, September 2, 2003	15
Lisa Leslie, Los Angeles at Detroit, September 14, 2003	15
Kym Hampton, New York at Phoenix, August 28, 1997	14
Tina Thompson, Houston vs. Charlotte, August 24, 1998	14
Andrea Stinson, Charlotte at Detroit, August 24, 1999	14
Yolanda Griffith, Sacramento vs. Houston, August 12, 2000	14
Tina Thompson, Houston vs. Sacramento, August 14, 2000	14
Lisa Leslie, Los Angeles vs. Houston, August 20, 2000	14
Yolanda Griffith, Sacramento vs. Utah, August 19, 2001	14
Olympia Scott-Richardson, Indiana vs. New York, August 16, 2002	14
Tina Thompson, Houston vs. Utah, August 18, 2002	**14
Tamika Catchings, Indiana at New York, August 18, 2002	14
Cheryl Ford, Detroit vs. Connecticut, September 7, 2003	14
Cheryl Ford, Detroit vs. New York, September 24, 2004	14

ASSISTS

	AST
Sue Bird, Seattle vs. Sacramento, October 5, 2004	14
Cynthia Cooper, Houston vs. Los Angeles, August 30, 1999	12
Jennifer Azzi, Utah at Los Angeles, August 24, 2002	12
Teresa Weatherspoon, New York vs. Washington, August 24, 2002	12
Teresa Weatherspoon, New York vs. Charlotte, August 30, 1999	11
Nikki McCray, Washington vs. New York, August 12, 2000	11
Nikki Teasley, Los Angeles at New York, August 29, 2002	11

* Denotes overtime. ** Denotes double overtime.

AST

Nikki Teasley, Los Angeles vs. New York, August 31, 2002 11
Nikki Teasley, Los Angeles vs. Detroit, September 12, 2003 11
Teresa Weatherspoon, New York vs. Houston, September 2, 1999 10
Ticha Penicheiro, Sacramento at Houston, August 14, 2000 10
Teresa Weatherspoon, New York vs. Washington, August 14, 2000 10
Vickie Johnson, New York vs. Cleveland, August 21, 2000 10
Helen Darling, Cleveland vs. Charlotte, August 20, 2001 10
Ukari Figgs, Los Angeles vs. Sacramento, August 27, 2001 10
Jennifer Azzi, Utah at Houston, August 20, 2002 10
Nikki Teasley, Los Angeles vs. Sacramento, September 7, 2003 10
Nikki Teasley, Los Angeles vs. Sacramento, September 8, 2003 10
Sheryl Swoopes, Houston at Seattle, September 3, 2005 10

STEALS

STL

Nykesha Sales, Connecticut vs. Washington, September 27, 2004 7
Mwadi Mabika, Los Angeles vs. Sacramento, August 24, 1999 6
Vickie Johnson, New York at Charlotte, August 24, 2001 6
Sheryl Swoopes, Houston vs. Utah, August 18, 2002 ....**6
Tamecka Dixon, Los Angeles vs. Minnesota, August 30, 2003 6
Elaine Powell, Detroit at New York, September 26, 2004 6
Andrea Stinson, Charlotte at Detroit, August 24, 1999 5
Sheryl Swoopes, Houston vs. Los Angeles, August 30, 1999 5
Sheryl Swoopes, Houston vs. Los Angeles, August 17, 2000 5
Helen Darling, Cleveland at Charlotte, August 16, 2001 5
Penny Taylor, Cleveland vs. Charlotte, August 18, 2001 5
Chamique Holdsclaw, Washington vs. Charlotte, August 15, 2002 5
Marie Ferdinand, Utah at Houston, August 18, 2002..**5
Adrienne Goodson, Utah at Houston, August 18, 2002 ....**5
Tamika Williams, Minnesota vs. Los Angeles, August 28, 2003..5
Sheri Sam, Minnesota at Los Angeles, September 1, 2003..5
Tanty Maiga, Sacramento at Los Angeles, September 28, 2004 5

BLOCKED SHOTS

BLK

Lisa Leslie, Los Angeles vs. Sacramento, August 27, 2001 7
Lisa Leslie, Los Angeles vs. Charlotte, September 1, 2001 7
Lisa Leslie, Los Angeles at Utah, August 22, 2002..7
Lisa Leslie, Los Angeles vs. Sacramento, August 26, 2001 6
DeLisha Milton, Los Angeles vs. Sacramento, August 24, 1999 5
Vicky Bullett, Washington vs. New York, August 12, 2000 5
Margo Dydek, Utah at Houston, August 18, 2002 ....**5
Lisa Leslie, Los Angeles vs. Minnesota, September 1, 2003 5
Lisa Leslie, Los Angeles vs. Sacramento, September 7, 2003...5
DeMya Walker, Sacramento vs. Seattle, October 1, 2004 ....*5
Vicky Bullett, Charlotte at Houston, August 28, 1997 4
Vicky Bullett, Charlotte at Detroit, August 24, 1999 4
Cintia Dos Santos, Orlando at Cleveland, August 13, 2000 4
Jennifer Gillom, Phoenix at Los Angeles, August 13, 2000..4
Margo Dydek, Utah vs. Sacramento, August 17, 2001 4
Lisa Leslie, Los Angeles at Sacramento, August 24, 2001 4
Tammy Sutton-Brown, Charlotte at Los Angeles, September 1, 2001 4
Margo Dydek, Utah vs. Houston, August 16, 2002 4
Tiffani Johnson, Houston vs. Utah, August 18, 2002 ....**4
Margo Dydek, Utah vs. Los Angeles, August 22, 2002 4
Lisa Leslie, Los Angeles at Sacramento, September 5, 2003..4
Ruth Riley, Detroit vs. Los Angeles, September 14, 2003...4
Lisa Leslie, Los Angeles at Sacramento, September 24, 2004 4
Alana Beard, Washington at Connecticut, September 29, 2004 4
Tangela Smith, Sacramento vs. Seattle, October 1, 2004 ....*4
Taj McWilliams-Franklin, Connecticut at Detroit, August 31, 2005 4
Margo Dydek, Connecticut vs. Sacramento, September 14, 2005..4

* Denotes overtime. ** Denotes double overtime.

RESULTS

Year	Dates	Winner (coach)	Loser (coach)	Games
1997	August 30	Houston (Van Chancellor)	New York (Nancy Darsch)	1-0
1998	Aug. 27-Sep. 1	Houston (Van Chancellor)	Phoenix (Cheryl Miller)	2-1
1999	Sep. 2-5	Houston (Van Chancellor)	New York (Richie Adubato)	2-1
2000	Aug. 24-26	Houston (Van Chancellor)	New York (Richie Adubato)	2-0
2001	Aug. 30-Sep. 1	Los Angeles (Michael Cooper)	Charlotte (Anne Donovan)	2-0
2002	Aug. 29-31	Los Angeles (Michael Cooper)	New York (Richie Adubato)	2-0
2003	Sept. 12-16	Detroit (Bill Laimbeer)	Los Angeles (Michael Cooper)	2-1
2004	Oct. 8-12	Seattle (Anne Donovan)	Connecticut (Mike Thibault)	2-1
2005	Sept. 14-20	Sacramento (John Whisenant)	Connecticut (Mike Thibault)	3-1

SERIES

TEAM	W-L	PCT
Detroit Shock	1 - 0	1.000
Houston Comets	4 - 0	1.000
Sacramento Monarchs	1 - 0	1.000
Seattle Storm	1 - 0	1.000
Los Angeles Sparks	2 - 1	.667
Connecticut Sun	0 - 2	.000
Charlotte Sting	0 - 1	.000
Phoenix Mercury	0 - 1	.000
New York Liberty	0 - 4	.000
Total	9 - 9	.500

HOME

TEAM	W-L	PCT
Los Angeles Sparks	3 - 0	1.000
Detroit Shock	2 - 0	1.000
Sacramento Monarchs	2 - 0	1.000
Seattle Storm	2 - 0	1.000
Phoenix Mercury	1 - 0	1.000
Houston Comets	5 - 1	.833
Connecticut Sun	2 - 1	.667
Charlotte Sting	0 - 1	.000
New York Liberty	0 - 3	.000
Total	17 - 6	.739

OVERALL

TEAM	W-L	PCT
Houston Comets	7 - 2	.778
Sacramento Monarchs	3 - 1	.750
Los Angeles Sparks	5 - 2	.714
Detroit Shock	2 - 1	.667
Seattle Storm	2 - 1	.667
Phoenix Mercury	1 - 2	.333
Connecticut Sun	2 - 5	.286
New York Liberty	1 - 7	.125
Charlotte Sting	0 - 2	.000
Total	23 - 23	.500

ROAD

TEAM	W-L	PCT
Houston Comets	2 - 1	.667
Los Angeles Sparks	2 - 2	.500
Sacramento Monarchs	1 - 1	.500
New York Liberty	1 - 4	.200
Charlotte Sting	0 - 1	.000
Detroit Shock	0 - 1	.000
Seattle Storm	0 - 1	.000
Phoenix Mercury	0 - 2	.000
Connecticut Sun	0 - 4	.000
Total	6 - 17	.261

ALL-TIME FINALS LEADERS

GAMES

Janeth Arcain	9
Cynthia Cooper	9
Sheryl Swoopes	9
Tina Thompson	9
Tammy Jackson	8
Vickie Johnson	8
Teresa Weatherspoon	8
Sue Wicks	8
Many tied	7

MINUTES

Cynthia Cooper	354
Tina Thompson	339
Sheryl Swoopes	312
Teresa Weatherspoon	276
Lisa Leslie	275
Vickie Johnson	263
DeLisha Milton-Jones	257

Mwadi Mabika	253
Janeth Arcain	250
Katie Douglas	240
Taj McWilliams-Franklin	240
Nykesha Sales	240

FIELD GOALS MADE

Cynthia Cooper	63
Lisa Leslie	49
Nykesha Sales	45
DeLisha Milton-Jones	41
Sheryl Swoopes	39
Tina Thompson	39
Taj McWilliams-Franklin	34
Vickie Johnson	33
Katie Douglas	30
Yolanda Griffith	28
Mwadi Mabika	28

RECORDS Finals

FIELD GOAL ATTEMPTS

Cynthia Cooper	157
Lisa Leslie	109
Sheryl Swoopes	105
Nykesha Sales	104
Tina Thompson	96
Mwadi Mabika	84
DeLisha Milton-Jones	84
Vickie Johnson	82
Taj McWilliams-Franklin	80
Katie Douglas	74

FIELD GOAL PERCENTAGE
(MINIMUM: 15 FG)

	FG	FGA	PCT
Betty Lennox	25	50	.500
Yolanda Griffith	28	57	.491
Asjha Jones	21	43	.488
DeLisha Milton-Jones	41	84	.488
Tamecka Dixon	26	56	.464
Lisa Leslie	49	109	.450
DeMya Walker	17	38	.447
NYkesha Sales	45	104	.433
Deanna Nolan	15	35	.429
Taj McWilliams-Franklin	34	80	.425

FREE THROWS MADE

Cynthia Cooper	77
Sheryl Swoopes	36
Lisa Leslie	34
DeLisha Milton-Jones	25
Tina Thompson	25
Mwadi Mabika	23
Tari Phillips	20
Tamika Whitmore	20
Nykesha Sales	19
Katie Douglas	18
Yolanda Griffith	18

FREE THROW ATTEMPTS

Cynthia Cooper	92
Lisa Leslie	45
Sheryl Swoopes	41
DeLisha Milton-Jones	31
Tina Thompson	31
Tamika Whitmore	31
Yolanda Griffith	27
Mwadi Mabika	26
Tari Phillips	25
Katie Douglas	24
Nykesha Sales	24

FREE THROW PERCENTAGE
(MINIMUM: 10 FT)

	FT	FTA	PCT
Tamecka Dixon	13	13	1.000
Kara Lawson	12	12	1.000
Becky Hammon	10	10	1.000
Deanna Nolan	10	10	1.000
Crystal Robinson	10	10	1.000
Mwadi Mabika	23	26	.885
Sheryl Swoopes	36	41	.878
Betty Lennox	14	16	.875
Sue Bird	11	13	.846
Cynthia Cooper	77	92	.837

THREE-POINT FIELD GOALS

Nykesha Sales	17
Tina Thompson	14
Nicole Powell	13
Crystal Robinson	13
Cynthia Cooper	11
Katie Douglas	11
Mwadi Mabika	9
DeLisha Milton-Jones.	8
Becky Hammon	7
Kedra Holland-Corn	7
Sheryl Swoopes	7

THREE-POINT FIELD GOAL ATTEMPTS

Crystal Robinson	41
Cynthia Cooper	39
Tina Thompson	37
Katie Douglas	35
Nykesha Sales	35
Mwadi Mabika	30
Nikki Teasley	27
Nicole Powell	25
Sheryl Swoopes	22
Vickie Johnson	20

THREE-POINT PERCENTAGE
(MINIMUM: 5 FG3)

	3FG	3GA	PCT
Kedra Holland-Corn	7	12	.583
DeLisha Milton-Jones	8	14	.571
Nicole Powell	13	25	.520
Kara Lawson	5	10	.500
Nykesha Sales	17	35	.486
Tina Thompson	14	37	.378
Deanna Nolan	6	16	.375
Becky Hammon	7	19	.368
Kim Perrot	6	18	.333
Sophia Witherspoon	5	15	.368
Teresa Weatherspoon	5	15	.333

OFFENSIVE REBOUNDS

Taj McWilliams-Franklin	21
Tina Thompson	20
Lisa Leslie	18
Sue Wicks	18
Yolanda Griffith	17
Tammy Jackson	16
Vickie Johnson	16
DeLisha Milton-Jones	15
Latasha Byears	13
Sheryl Swoopes.	13

DEFENSIVE REBOUNDS

Lisa Leslie	57
Taj McWilliams-Franklin	47
Tina Thompson	42
Sheryl Swoopes	41
Mwadi Mabika	34
DeLisha Milton-Jones	31
Tammy Jackson	28
Janeth Arcain	24
Kym Hampton	24
Teresa Weatherspoon	24
Sue Wicks	24

TOTAL REBOUNDS

Lisa Leslie	75
Taj McWilliams-Franklin	68
Tina Thompson	62
Sheryl Swoopes	54
DeLisha Milton-Jones	46
Tammy Jackson	44
Mwadi Mabika	42
Sue Wicks	42
Yolanda Griffith	39
Vickie Johnson	37

ASSISTS

Nikki Teasley	46
Teresa Weatherspoon	43
Cynthia Cooper	42
Lindsay Whalen	27
Sheryl Swoopes	24
Lisa Leslie	20
Mwadi Mabika	19
Tamecka Dixon	17
Vickie Johnson	17
DeLisha Milton-Jones	17
Swin Cash	16

STEALS

Cynthia Cooper	18
Nykesha Sales	17
Sheryl Swoopes	15
Katie Douglas	14
DeLisha Milton-Jones	13
Teresa Weatherspoon	13
Tina Thompson	10
Janeth Arcain	9
Tammy Jackson	9
Lisa Leslie	9
Mwadi Mabika	8
Taj McWilliams-Franklin	8
Crystal Robinson	8

PERSONAL FOULS

Teresa Weatherspoon	30
Tina Thompson	29
DeLisha Milton-Jones	28
Lisa Leslie	26
Vickie Johnson	24
Tamecka Dixon	23
Sue Wicks	23
Tamika Whitmore	22
Crystal Robinson	21
Janeth Arcain	20

DISQUALIFICATIONS

Tamecka Dixon	1
Lisa Leslie	1
Tari Phillips	1
Crystal Robinson	1
Michele Timms	1
Teresa Weatherspoon	1

BLOCKED SHOTS

Lisa Leslie	20
DeLisha Milton-Jones	12
Ruth Riley	10
Tammy Jackson	9
Taj McWilliams-Franklin	9
Margo Dydek	7
Nykesha Sales	7
Tina Thompson	7
Jennifer Gillom	6
Tari Phillips	6
Sheryl Swoopes	6

POINTS

Cynthia Cooper	214
Lisa Leslie	134
Nykesha Sales	121
Sheryl Swoopes	121
Tina Thompson	117
DeLisha Milton-Jones	115
Katie Douglas	89
Mwadi Mabika	88
Vickie Johnson	82
Taj McWilliams-Franklin	80

SCORING AVERAGE
(MINIMUM: 5 G)

	G	FG	FT	PTS	AVG
Cynthia Cooper	9	63	77	214	23.8
Lisa Leslie	7	49	34	134	19.1
Nykesha Sales	7	45	19	126	18.0
DeLisha Milton-Jones	7	41	25	115	16.4
Sheryl Swoopes	9	39	36	121	13.4
Tina Thompson	9	39	25	117	13.0
Katie Douglas	7	30	18	89	12.7
Mwadi Mabika	7	28	23	88	12.6
Taj McWilliams-Franklin	7	34	12	80	11.4
Tamecka Dixon	6	26	13	68	11.3

INDIVIDUAL RECORDS

MINUTES

Most minutes, game
44 — Cynthia Cooper, Houston vs. New York,
August 26, 2000 (OT)
Cynthia Cooper, Houston vs. Phoenix,
August 29, 1998 (OT)
41 — Taj McWilliams Franklin, Connecticut vs.
Sacramento, September 15, 2005 (OT)
Katie Douglas, Connecticut vs. Sacramento,
September 15, 2005 (OT)

Regulation game:
40 — By Many. Most recent:
Lauren Jackson, Seattle at Connecticut,
October 8, 2004

SCORING

Most points, game
32 — Nykesha Sales, Connecticut at Seattle,
October 10, 2004
31 — Sheryl Swoopes, Houston vs. New York,
August 26, 2000 (OT)

29 — Mwadi Mabika, Los Angeles at Detroit,
September 16, 2003
Cynthia Cooper, Houston at New York,
September 2, 1999
Cynthia Cooper, Houston at Phoenix,
August 27, 1998

Most consecutive games, 20 or more points
5 — Cynthia Cooper, Houston, August 30, 1997-
September 2, 1999
3 — Cynthia Cooper, Houston,
September 5, 1999-August 26, 2000
2 — Betty Lennox, Seattle, October 10-12, 2004
Lisa Leslie, Los Angeles, August 30-
September 1, 2001
Tari Phillips, New York, August 24-26, 2000

Most consecutive games, 10 or more points
9 — Cynthia Cooper, Houston, August 30, 1997-
August 26, 2000
7 — Lisa Leslie, Los Angeles, August 30, 2001-
September 16, 2003
Sheryl Swoopes, Houston, August 29, 1998-
August 26, 2000
Tina Thompson, Houston, August 29, 1998-
August 26, 2000
6 — Nykesha Sales, Connecticut, October 10, 2004-
September 20, 2005

Most points, one half
21 — Nykesha Sales, Connecticut at Seattle,
October 10, 2004
20 — Cynthia Cooper, Houston at New York,
September 2, 1999

Most points, overtime period
7 — Sheryl Swoopes, Houston vs. New York,
August 26, 2000
4 — By Many

FIELD GOALS

Highest field-goal percentage, game
(Minimum: 8 field goals made)
.688 — Betty Lennox, Seattle vs. Connecticut,
October 10, 2004 (11/16)
.667 — Asjha Jones, Connecticut at Sacramento,
September 20, 2005 (8/12)
.647 — Yolanda Griffith, Sacramento at Connecticut,
September 14, 2005 (11/17)

Most field goals, none missed, game
3 — Alicia Thompson, Seattle vs. Connecticut,
October 10, 2004
Tamecka Dixon, Los Angeles vs. New York,
August 31, 2002
Summer Erb, Charlotte at Los Angeles,
September 1, 2001
Latasha Byears, Los Angeles vs. Charlotte,
September 1, 2001
Tiffani Johnson, Houston vs. New York,
August 26, 2000 (OT)
2 — Tully Bevilaqua, Seattle at Connecticut,
October 8, 2004
Monica Lamb, Houston vs. Phoenix,
September 1, 1998

Most field goals, game
14 — Nykesha Sales, Connecticut at Seattle,
October 10, 2004
11 — Yolanda Griffith, Sacramento at Connecticut,
September 14, 2005
Betty Lennox, Seattle vs. Connecticut,
October 10, 2004
Ruth Riley, Detroit vs. Los Angeles,
September 16, 2003
Mwadi Mabika, Los Angeles at Detroit,
September 16, 2003
Sheryl Swoopes, Houston vs. New York,
August 26, 2000 (OT)
Cynthia Cooper, Houston at Phoenix,
August 27, 1998

Most field goals, one half
8 — Yolanda Griffith, Sacramento at Connecticut,
September 14, 2005
7 — Betty Lennox, Seattle vs. Connecticut,
October 10, 2004
Mwadi Mabika, Los Angeles at Detroit,
September 16, 2003
Lisa Leslie, Los Angeles vs. Detroit,
September 12, 2003
Tari Phillips, New York at Houston,
August 26, 2000
Tari Phillips, New York vs. Houston,
August 24, 2000
6 — By Many

Most field goal attempts, game
24 — Cynthia Cooper, Houston at Phoenix,
August 27, 1998
23 — Cynthia Cooper, Houston at New York,
August 24, 2000
22 — Nykesha Sales, Connecticut at Seattle,
October 10, 2004

Most field goal attempts, none made, game
11 — Katie Douglas, Connecticut at Seattle,
October 12, 2004
6 — Crystal Robinson, New York at Los Angeles,
August 31, 2002

Most field goal attempts, one half
14 — Cynthia Cooper, Houston at Phoenix,
August 27, 1998
13 — Nykesha Sales, Connecticut at Seattle,
October 10, 2004
Cynthia Cooper, Houston vs. New York,
August 26, 2000
Tari Phillips, New York at Houston,
August 26, 2000

THREE-POINT FIELD GOALS

Most three-point field goals, none missed, game
2 — Kara Lawson, Sacramento vs. Connecticut,
September 18, 2005
Alicia Thompson, Seattle vs. Connecticut,
October 10, 2004
Kristi Harrower, Phoenix at Houston,
August 29, 1998 (OT)
1 — By Many

Most three-point field goals, game
  4 — By Many. Most Recent:
      Nicole Powell, Sacramento vs. Connecticut,
      September 18, 2005
  3 — By Many
Most three-point field goals, one half
  3 — Nicole Powell, Sacramento vs. Connecticut,
      September 18, 2005
      Nykesha Sales, Connecticut vs. Sacramento,
      September 14, 2005
      Nykesha Sales, Connecticut at Seattle,
      October 12, 2004
      Nykesha Sales, Connecticut at Seattle,
      October 10, 2004
      Nikki Teasley, Los Angeles at Detroit,
      September 14, 2003
      Becky Hammon, New York vs. Los Angeles,
      August 29, 2002
      Crystal Robinson, New York vs. Los Angeles,
      August 29, 2002
      Crystal Robinson, New York at Houston,
      September 4, 1999
  2 — By Many
Most three-point field goal attempts, game
  10 — Nikki Teasley, Los Angeles vs. Detroit,
      September 12, 2003
  9 — Nicole Powell, Sacramento at Connecticut,
      September 15, 2005 (OT)
      Crystal Robinson, New York at Houston,
      September 4, 1999
      Kim Perrot, Houston vs. New York,
      August 30, 1997
  8 — Nicole Powell, Sacramento vs. Connecticut,
      September 18, 2005
      Michele Timms, Phoenix at Houston,
      August 29, 1998 (OT)
Most three-point field goal attempts, none made, game
  6 — Katie Douglas, Connecticut at Seattle,
      October 12, 2004
  5 — Tina Thompson, Houston vs. New York,
      September 5, 1999
  4 — By Many
Most three-point field goal attempts, one half
  6 — Crystal Robinson, New York at Houston,
      September 4, 1999
  5 — By Many

FREE THROWS

Most free throws made, none missed, game
  10 — Cynthia Cooper, Houston at New York,
      September 2, 1999
  8 — Cynthia Cooper, Houston vs. New York,
      August 26, 2000 (OT)
  6 — By Many
Most free throws made, game
  13 — Cynthia Cooper, Houston vs. New York,
      September 5, 1999
  11 — Cynthia Cooper, Houston vs. Phoenix,
      August 29, 1998 (OT)
      Cynthia Cooper, Houston vs. New York,
      August 30, 1997

  10 — Cynthia Cooper, Houston vs. New York,
      September 4, 1999
      Cynthia Cooper, Houston at New York,
      September 2, 1999
Most free throws made, one half
  9 — Sheryl Swoopes, Houston vs. Phoenix,
      September 1, 1998
  8 — Cynthia Cooper, Houston vs. New York,
      August 26, 2000
      Cynthia Cooper, Houston vs. New York,
      September 5, 1999
      Cynthia Cooper, Houston at New York,
      September 2, 1999
      Cynthia Cooper, Houston vs. New York,
      August 30, 1997
Most free throw attempts, game
  15 — Cynthia Cooper, Houston vs. New York,
      September 5, 1999
      Cynthia Cooper, Houston vs. New York,
      August 30, 1997
  14 — Cynthia Cooper, Houston vs. Phoenix,
      August 29, 1998 (OT)
  12 — Cynthia Cooper, Houston vs. New York,
      September 4, 1999
Most free throw attempts, one half
  12 — Cynthia Cooper, Houston vs. New York,
      August 30, 1997
  10 — Cynthia Cooper, Houston vs. New York,
      September 5, 1999
      Sheryl Swoopes, Houston vs. Phoenix,
      September 1, 1998

REBOUNDS

Most rebounds, game
  16 — Taj McWilliams-Franklin, Connecticut vs.
      Sacramento, September 15, 2005 (OT)
  15 — Lisa Leslie, Los Angeles at Detroit,
      September 14, 2003
      Tari Phillips, New York vs. Houston,
      August 24, 2000
  13 — Taj McWilliams-Franklin, Connecticut at
      Sacramento, September 18, 2005
      Lisa Leslie, Los Angeles vs. Charlotte,
      September 1, 2001
      Sheryl Swoopes, Houston vs. Phoenix,
      August 29, 1998 (OT)
      Kym Hampton, New York at Houston,
      August 30, 1997
Most rebounds, one half
  10 — Tari Phillips, New York vs. Houston,
      August 24, 2000
  9 — Lauren Jackson, Seattle vs. Connecticut,
      October 10, 2004
      Swin Cash, Detroit vs. Los Angeles,
      September 16, 2003
      Lisa Leslie, Los Angeles at Detroit,
      September 14, 2003
      Lisa Leslie, Los Angeles vs. Charlotte,
      September 1, 2001
      Tammy Jackson, Houston vs. New York,
      September 5, 1999
      Kym Hampton, New York at Houston,
      August 30, 1997

Most offensive rebounds, game
- 7 — Cheryl Ford, Detroit at Los Angeles,
September 12, 2003
- 6 — Yolanda Griffith, Sacramento at Connecticut,
September 15, 2005 (OT)
- 5 — By Many

Most offensive rebounds, one half
- 5 — Simone Edwards, Seattle vs. Connecticut,
October 8, 2004
- 4 — Lauren Jackson, Seattle at Connecticut,
October 8, 2004
  Cheryl Ford, Detroit at Los Angeles,
September 12, 2003
  Charlotte Smith, Charlotte at Los Angeles,
September 1, 2001
  Lisa Leslie, Los Angeles vs. Charlotte,
September 1, 2001
  Tammy Jackson, Houston vs. New York,
September 5, 1999
- 3 — By Many

Most defensive rebounds, game
- 12 — Taj McWilliams-Franklin, Connecticut vs.
Sacramento, September 15, 2005 (OT)
- 11 — Lisa Leslie, Los Angeles at Detroit,
September 14, 2003
  Tari Phillips, New York vs. Houston,
August 24, 2000
  Sheryl Swoopes, Houston vs. Phoenix,
August 29, 1998 (OT)
- 10 — Taj McWilliams-Franklin, Connecticut at
Sacramento, September 18, 2005
  Lisa Leslie, Los Angeles vs. Detroit,
September 12, 2003
  Kym Hampton, New York at Houston,
August 30, 1997

Most defensive rebounds, one half
- 7 — Lauren Jackson, Seattle vs. Connecticut,
October 10, 2004
  Swin Cash, Detroit vs. Los Angeles,
September 16, 2003
  Tari Phillips, New York vs. Houston,
August 24, 2000
  Kym Hampton, New York at Houston,
August 30, 1997
- 6 — By Many

ASSISTS

Most assists, game
- 11 — Nikki Teasley, Los Angeles vs. Detroit,
September 12, 2003
  Nikki Teasley, Los Angeles vs. New York,
August 31, 2002
  Nikki Teasley, Los Angeles at New York,
August 29, 2002
- 10 — Teresa Weatherspoon, New York vs. Houston,
September 2, 1999
- 9 — Lindsay Whalen, Connecticut vs. Seattle,
October 8, 2004
  Swin Cash, Detroit vs. Los Angeles,
September 16, 2003

Most assists, one half
- 7 — Nikki Teasley, Los Angeles at New York,
August 29, 2002
- 6 — Swin Cash, Detroit vs. Los Angeles,
September 16, 2003
  Nikki Teasley, Los Angeles vs. Detroit,
September 12, 2003
  Nikki Teasley, Los Angeles vs. New York,
August 31, 2002
  Teresa Weatherspoon, New York vs. Houston,
September 2, 1999

PERSONAL FOULS

Most personal fouls, game
- 6 — Lisa Leslie, Los Angeles at Detroit,
September 16, 2003
  Tamecka Dixon, Los Angeles vs. New York,
August 31, 2002
  Teresa Weatherspoon, New York at Houston,
August 26, 2000 (OT)
  Tari Phillips, New York at Houston,
August 26, 2000 (OT)
  Crystal Robinson, New York vs. Houston,
September 2, 1999
  Michele Timms, Phoenix at Houston,
August 29, 1998 (OT)
- 5 — By Many

Most personal fouls, one half
- 5 — Dawn Staley, Charlotte vs. Los Angeles,
August 30, 2001
  Teresa Weatherspoon, New York at Houston,
September 5, 1999
- 4 — By Many

Most minutes played, no personal fouls, game
- 39 — Cynthia Cooper, Houston at Phoenix,
August 27, 1998
- 37 — Sheryl Swoopes, Houston vs. New York,
September 5, 1999
- 35 — Nicole Powell, Sacramento vs. Connecticut,
September 18, 2005

DISQUALIFICATIONS

Fewest minutes played, disqualified player, game
- 14 — Tamecka Dixon, Los Angeles vs. New York,
August 31, 2002
- 34 — Crystal Robinson, New York vs. Houston,
September 2, 1999
- 37 — Tari Phillips, New York at Houston,
August 26, 2000 (OT)

STEALS

Most steals, game
- 4 — Nykesha Sales, Connecticut at Seattle,
October 10, 2004
  Nykesha Sales, Connecticut vs. Seattle,
October 8, 2004
  Taj McWilliams-Franklin, Connecticut vs.
Seattle, October 8, 2004
  Sheryl Swoopes, Houston vs. New York,
September 4, 1999
  Sue Wicks, New York vs. Houston,
September 2, 1999

Cynthia Cooper, Houston at New York,
September 2, 1999
Teresa Weatherspoon, New York at Houston,
August 30, 1997
3 — By Many
Most steals, one half
3 — Nykesha Sales, Connecticut at Seattle,
October 10, 2004
DeLisha Milton, Los Angeles at Detroit,
September 14, 2003
Allison Feaster, Charlotte at Los Angeles,
September 1, 2001
Cynthia Cooper, Houston vs. New York,
September 5, 1999
Tammy Jackson, Houston vs. New York,
September 5, 1999
Kim Perrot, Houston vs. New York,
August 30, 1997

BLOCKED SHOTS

Most blocked shots, game
7 — Lisa Leslie, Los Angeles vs. Charlotte,
September 1, 2001
4 — Margo Dydek, Connecticut vs. Sacramento,
September 14, 2005
Ruth Riley, Detroit vs. Los Angeles,
September 14, 2003
Tammy Sutton-Brown, Charlotte at
Los Angeles, September 1, 2001
3 — By Many
Most blocked shots, one half
4 — Lisa Leslie, Los Angeles vs. Charlotte,
September 1, 2001
3 — Lisa Leslie, Los Angeles vs. Detroit,
September 12, 2003
Lisa Leslie, Los Angeles vs. Charlotte,
September 1, 2001
Kym Hampton, New York at Houston,
September 4, 1999
2 — By Many

TURNOVERS

Most turnovers, game
7 — Nikki Teasley, Los Angeles at New York,
August 29, 2002
6 — Sue Bird, Seattle at Connecticut,
October 8, 2004
Dawn Staley, Charlotte vs. Los Angeles,
August 30, 2001
Tari Phillips, New York vs. Houston,
August 24, 2000
Cynthia Cooper, Houston vs. New York,
September 5, 1999
Cynthia Cooper, Houston vs. Phoenix,
September 1, 1998
Sheryl Swoopes, Houston vs. Phoenix,
August 29, 1998 (OT)
5 — By Many
Most turnovers, one half
5 — Sheryl Swoopes, Houston vs. Phoenix,
August 29, 1998
4 — By Many

WON-LOST

Most consecutive games won
5 — Los Angeles, 2001-03
3 — Houston, 1999-00 (current)
Houston, 1998-99
Most consecutive games won at home
3 — Los Angeles, 2001-03 (current)
Houston, 1997-98
2 — Sacramento, 2005 (current)
Seattle, 2004 (current)
Detroit, 2003 (current)
Houston, 1999-00 (current)
Most consecutive games won on road
2 — Los Angeles, 2001-02
Houston, 1999-00 (current)
1 — New York, 1999
Most consecutive games lost
5 — New York, 1999-00, 2002
3 — Connecticut, 2004-05
Most consecutive games lost at home
3 — New York, 1999-00, 2002 (current)
1 — Connecticut, 2005
Charlotte, 2001 (current)
Houston, 1999
Most consecutive games lost on road
4 — Connecticut, 2004-05 (current)
3 — New York, 1999-00, 2002 (current)

SCORING

Most points, game
83 — Detroit vs. Los Angeles, September 16, 2003
82 — Los Angeles vs. Charlotte, September 1, 2001
Fewest points, game
47 — New York at Houston, September 5, 1999
51 — Houston at Phoenix, August 27, 1998
New York at Houston, August 30, 1997
Most points, both teams, game
161 — Detroit (83) vs. Los Angeles (78),
September 16, 2003
152 — Houston (79) vs. New York (73),
August 26, 2000 (OT)
Fewest points, both teams, game
105 — Houston (51) at Phoenix (54),
August 27, 1998
106 — New York (47) at Houston (59),
September 5, 1999
Largest margin of victory, game
28 — Los Angeles (82) vs. Charlotte (54),
September 1, 2001
14 — Seattle (74) vs. Connecticut (60),
October 12, 2004
Houston (65) vs. New York (51),
August 30, 1997

BY HALF

Most points, first half
42 — Detroit vs. Los Angeles, September 16, 2003
Los Angeles vs. Detroit, September 12, 2003
39 — Sacramento at Connecticut,
September 15, 2005
Charlotte vs. Los Angeles, August 30, 2001

RECORDS Finals

Fewest points, first half
20 — New York vs. Houston, September 2, 1999
21 — Detroit at Los Angeles, September 12, 2003
Most points, both teams, first half
79 — Detroit (42) vs. Los Angeles (37),
September 16, 2003
77 — Sacramento (39) at Connecticut (38),
September 15, 2005
Fewest points, both teams, first half
49 — New York (20) vs. Houston (29),
September 2, 1999
51 — New York (22) vs. Houston (29),
August 24, 2000
Largest lead at halftime
21 — Los Angeles vs. Detroit, September 12, 2003
(led 42-21; won 75-63)
16 — Detroit vs. Los Angeles, September 14, 2003
(led 38-22; won 62-61)
Largest deficit at halftime overcome to win game
14 — New York at Houston, September 4, 1999
(trailed 23-37; won 68-67)
6 — Sacramento vs. Connecticut, September 20,
2005 (trailed 31-25; won 62-59)
Most points, second half
48 — Houston vs. Phoenix, September 1, 1998
45 — New York at Houston, September 4, 1999
Phoenix at Houston, September 1, 1998
Fewest points, second half
21 — Phoenix vs. Houston, August 27, 1998
22 — New York at Houston, September 5, 1999
Houston at Phoenix, August 27, 1998
Most points, both teams, second half
93 — Houston (48) vs. Phoenix (45),
September 1, 1998
84 — Houston (44) at New York (40),
September 2, 1999
Fewest points, both teams, second half
43 — Phoenix (21) vs. Houston (22),
August 27, 1998
48 — New York (22) at Houston (26),
September 5, 1999

OVERTIME PERIOD

Most points, overtime period
15 — Houston vs. New York, August 26, 2000
9 — New York at Houston, August 26, 2000
Fewest points, overtime period
0 — Sacramento at Connecticut,
September 15, 2005
3 — Phoenix at Houston, August 29, 1998
Most points, both teams, overtime period
24 — Houston (15) vs. New York (9),
August 26, 2000
Fewest points, both teams, overtime period
7 — Sacramento (0) at Connecticut (7),
September 15, 2005
11 — Phoenix (3) at Houston (8), August 29, 1998

PLAYERS SCORING

Most players, 20 or more points, game
2 — Phoenix at Houston, September 1, 1998
Houston vs. New York, August 26, 2000 (OT)
1 — By Many

Most players, 20 or more points, both teams, game
3 — Houston (2) vs. New York (1),
August 26, 2000 (OT)
Phoenix (2) at Houston (1), September 1, 1998
2 — Connecticut (1) vs. Sacramento (1),
September 14, 2005
Seattle (1) vs. Connecticut (1),
October 10, 2004
Detroit (1) vs. Los Angeles (1),
September 16, 2003
New York (1) vs. Houston (1), August 24, 2000
Houston (1) vs. Phoenix (1),
August 29, 1998 (OT)
Most players, 10 or more points, game
5 — Charlotte vs. Los Angeles, August 30, 2001
Houston vs. New York, September 4, 1999
4 — By Many
Most players, 10 or more points, both teams, game
8 — Detroit (4) vs. Los Angeles (4),
September 16, 2003
Charlotte (5) vs. Los Angeles (3),
August 30, 2001
Houston (5) vs. New York (3),
September 4, 1999
7 — By Many

FIELD GOAL PERCENTAGE

Highest field goal percentage, game
.519 — Houston vs. Phoenix, September 1, 1998
(28/54)
.509 — Los Angeles at Charlotte, August 30, 2001
(29/57)
Lowest field goal percentage, game
.286 — Detroit at Los Angeles, September 12, 2003
(20/70)
.288 — Houston vs. New York, September 5, 1999
(15/52)
Highest field goal percentage, both teams, game
.496 — Houston (.519) vs. Phoenix (.475),
September 1, 1998 (57/115)
.478 — Los Angeles (.509) at Charlotte (.448),
August 30, 2001 (55/115)
Lowest field goal percentage, both teams, game
.299 — Houston (.288) vs. New York (.309),
September 5, 1999 (32/107)
.336 — Houston (.323) at Phoenix (.349),
August 27, 1998 (43/128)

FIELD GOALS

Most field goals, game
29 — Los Angeles at Charlotte, August 30, 2001
Phoenix at Houston, September 1, 1998
28 — By Many
Fewest field goals, game
15 — Houston vs. New York, September 5, 1999
Houston vs. New York, September 4, 1999
17 — New York at Houston, September 5, 1999
Most field goals, both teams, game
57 — Phoenix (29) at Houston (28),
September 1, 1998
56 — Detroit (28) vs. Los Angeles (28),
September 16, 2003

Fewest field goals, both teams, game
  32 — Houston (15) vs. New York (17),
   September 5, 1999
  37 — Houston (15) vs. New York (22),
   September 4, 1999
Most field goals, one half
  19 — Phoenix at Houston, September 1, 1998
  17 — Sacramento at Connecticut,
   September 15, 2005
   Detroit vs. Los Angeles, September 14, 2003
   Los Angeles vs. Detroit, September 12, 2003
   New York vs. Houston, September 2, 1999

FIELD GOAL ATTEMPTS

Most field goal attempts, game
  74 — Seattle at Connecticut, October 8, 2004
  71 — Los Angeles at Detroit, September 16, 2003
Fewest field-goal attempts, game
  50 — Los Angeles vs. New York, August 31, 2002
   Houston vs. New York, September 4, 1999
   Houston at New York, September 2, 1999
  52 — Sacramento vs. Connecticut
   September 18, 2005
   Houston vs. New York, September 5, 1999
Most field goal attempts, both teams, game
  139 — Detroit (70) at Los Angeles (69),
   September 12, 2003
  135 — Seattle (74) at Connecticut (61),
   October 8, 2004
Fewest field-goal attempts, both teams, game
  106 — Houston (50) vs. New York (56),
   September 4, 1999
  107 — Houston (52) vs. New York (55),
   September 5, 1999
Most field goal attempts, one half
  42 — Seattle at Connecticut, October 8, 2004
  41 — Los Angeles vs. Detroit, September 12, 2003

THREE-POINT FIELD GOALS

Most three-point field goals, game
  9 — New York vs. Los Angeles, August 29, 2002
  8 — Connecticut vs. Sacramento,
   September 15, 2005 (OT)
   New York at Houston, September 4, 1999
Fewest three-point field goals, game
  0 — New York vs. Houston, August 24, 2000
  1 — Seattle vs. Connecticut, October 12, 2004
   Charlotte at Los Angeles, September 1, 2001
   New York at Houston, August 30, 1997
Most three-point field goals, both teams, game
  14 — New York (9) vs. Los Angeles (5),
   August 29, 2002
  13 — Connecticut (8) vs. Sacramento (5),
   September 15, 2005 (OT)
   New York (8) at Houston (5),
   September 4, 1999
Fewest three-point field goals, both teams, game
  4 — Seattle (1) vs. Connecticut (3),
   October 12,2004
  5 — New York (0) vs. Houston (5), August 24, 2000
   New York (1) at Houston (4), August 30, 1997

Most three-point field goals, one half
  7 — New York vs. Los Angeles, August 29, 2002
  6 — Connecticut vs Sacramento,
   September 15, 2005
   New York at Houston, September 4, 1999
   Phoenix at Houston, August 29, 1998

THREE-POINT FIELD-GOAL ATTEMPTS

Most three-point field goal attempts, game
  23 — Los Angeles vs. Detroit, September 12, 2003
  19 — New York vs. Los Angeles, August 29, 2002
Fewest three-point field goal attempts, game
  5 — Seattle vs. Connecticut, October 12, 2004
  6 — Seattle vs. Connecticut, October 10, 2004
Most three-point field goal attempts, both teams, game
  36 — Los Angeles (23) vs. Detroit (13),
   September 12, 2003
  33 — New York (19) vs. Los Angeles (14),
   August 29, 2002
   New York (18) vs. Houston (15),
   September 2, 1999
Fewest three-point field goal attempts, both teams, game
  19 — Seattle (6) vs. Connecticut (13),
   October 10, 2004
  21 — Sacramento (7) vs. Connecticut (14),
   September 20, 2005
   Seattle (5) vs. Connecticut (16),
   October 12, 2004
Most three-point, field goal attempts, one half
  14 — Los Angeles vs. Detroit, September 12, 2003
  12 — Connecticut at Seattle, October 12, 2004

FREE THROW PERCENTAGE

Highest free throw percentage, game
  .950 — Detroit at Los Angeles, September 12, 2003
   (19/20)
  .947 — Houston vs. New York, August 26, 2000 (OT)
   (18/19)
Lowest free throw percentage, game
  .400 — New York at Houston, August 30, 1997
   (4/10)
  .467 — New York vs. Houston, September 2, 1999
   (7/15)
Highest free throw percentage, both teams, game
  .917 — Detroit (.950) at Los Angeles (.875),
   September 12, 2003 (33/36)
  .900 — Houston (.947) vs. New York (.857),
   August 26, 2000 (OT) (36/40)
Lowest free throw percentage, both teams, game
  .600 — New York (.400) at Houston (.680),
   August 30, 1997 (21/35)
  .617 — Connecticut (.500) vs. Seattle (.857),
   October 8, 2004 (13/21)

FREE THROWS MADE

Most free throws made, game
  32 — Houston vs. New York, September 4, 1999
  27 — Houston vs. New York, September 5, 1999
Fewest free throws made, game
  3 — Charlotte at Los Angeles, September 1, 2001
  4 — Detroit vs. Los Angeles, September 14, 2003
   New York at Houston, August 30, 1997

Most free throws made, both teams, game
    48 — Houston (32) vs. New York (16),
        September 4, 1999
    40 — Detroit (23) vs. Los Angeles (17),
        September 16, 2003
Fewest free throws made, both teams, game
    13 — Seattle (6) at Connecticut (7),
        October 8, 2004
        Houston (6) at Phoenix (7), August 27, 1998
    17 — Detroit (4) vs. Los Angeles (13),
        September 14, 2003
Most free throws made, one half
    17 — Houston at New York, September 2, 1999
    16 — Houston vs. New York, September 4, 1999
        (both halves)

FREE THROW ATTEMPTS

Most free throw attempts, game
    42 — Houston vs. New York, September 4, 1999
    32 — Houston vs. New York, September 5, 1999
Fewest free throw attempts, game
    4 — Charlotte at Los Angeles, September 1, 2001
    5 — Detroit vs. Los Angeles, September 14, 2003
Most free throw attempts, both teams, game
    64 — Houston (42) vs. New York (22),
        September 4, 1999
    50 — New York (28) at Los Angeles (22),
        August 31, 2002
Fewest free throw attempts, both teams, game
    19 — Houston (8) at Phoenix (11), August 27, 1998
    21 — Seattle (7) at Connecticut (14),
        October 8, 2004
        Detroit (5) vs. Los Angeles (16),
        September 14, 2003
Most free throw attempts, one half
    21 — Houston vs. New York, September 4, 1999
        (both halves)
        Houston at New York, September 2, 1999
    19 — Houston vs. New York,
        September 5, 1999

TOTAL REBOUNDS

Highest rebound percentage, game
    .611 — Los Angeles at New York, August 29, 2002
    .582 — Seattle at Connecticut, October 8, 2004
Most rebounds, game
    42 — Seattle at Connecticut, October 8, 2004
    41 — Detroit at Los Angeles, September 12, 2003
        Phoenix vs. Houston, August 27, 1998
Fewest rebounds, game
    24 — Charlotte vs. Los Angeles, August 30, 2001
        New York at Houston, August 26, 2000 (OT)
        Phoenix at Houston, September 1, 1998
        Houston vs. Phoenix, September 1, 1998
    25 — New York vs. Los Angeles, August 29, 2002
Most rebounds, both teams, game
    80 — Detroit (41) at Los Angeles (39),
        September 12, 2003
    75 — Seattle (42) at Connecticut (33)
        October 8, 2004

Fewest rebounds, both teams, game
    48 — Houston (24) vs. Phoenix (24),
        September 1, 1998
    50 — Charlotte (24) vs. Los Angeles (26),
        August 30, 2001
Most rebounds, one half
    24 — Seattle at Connecticut, October 8, 2004
        Detroit at Los Angeles, September 12, 2003
    22 — Connecticut at Sacramento,
        September 20, 2005
        Los Angeles vs. Detroit, September 12, 2003

OFFENSIVE REBOUNDS

Highest offensive rebound percentage, game
    .464 — Houston vs. New York, August 26, 2000 (OT)
        (13/28)
    .455 — Seattle at Connecticut, October 8, 2004
        (20/44)
Most offensive rebounds, game
    20 — Seattle at Connecticut, October 8, 2004
    16 — Detroit at Los Angeles, September 12, 2003
Fewest offensive rebounds, game
    3 — Houston vs. Phoenix, September 1, 1998
    5 — Connecticut at Sacramento,
        September 18, 2005
        Detroit vs. Los Angeles, September 14, 2003
        New York vs. Los Angeles, August 29, 2002
Most offensive rebounds, both teams, game
    29 — Seattle (20) at Connecticut (9),
        October 8, 2004
    26 — Detroit (16) at Los Angeles (10),
        September 12, 2003
Fewest offensive rebounds, both teams, game
    10 — Houston (3) vs. Phoenix (7),
        September 1, 1998
    13 — Detroit (5) vs. Los Angeles (8),
        September 14, 2003
Most offensive rebounds, one half
    14 — Seattle at Connecticut, October 8, 2004
    10 — Los Angeles at Detroit, September 16, 2003
        Detroit at Los Angeles, September 12, 2003
        Houston vs. New York, September 5, 1999

DEFENSIVE REBOUNDS

Highest defensive rebound percentage, game
    .850 — Phoenix at Houston, September 1, 1998
        (17/20)
    .833 — Los Angeles at Detroit, September 14, 2003
        (25/30)
Most defensive rebounds, game
    29 — Seattle vs. Connecticut, October 12, 2004
        Los Angeles vs. Detroit, September 12, 2003
    28 — Phoenix vs. Houston, August 27, 1998
Fewest defensive rebounds, game
    15 — New York at Houston, August 26, 2000 (OT)
    17 — Charlotte vs. Los Angeles, August 30, 2001
        Phoenix at Houston, September 1, 1998
Most defensive rebounds, both teams, game
    54 — Los Angeles (29) vs. Detroit (25),
        September 12, 2003
    52 — Connecticut (26) vs. Sacramento (26),
        September 15, 2005 (OT)

Fewest defensive rebounds, both teams, game
    35 — New York (15) at Houston (20),
        August 26, 2000 (OT)
    36 — Charlotte (17) vs. Los Angeles (19),
        August 30, 2001
Most defensive rebounds, one half
    17 — Seattle vs. Connecticut, October 12, 2004
        Detroit vs. Los Angeles, September 14, 2003
    16 — Connecticut at Sacramento,
        September 20, 2005
        Los Angeles vs. Detroit, September 12, 2003
        Los Angeles vs. New York, August 31, 2002

ASSISTS

Most assists, game
    24 — Los Angeles vs. Charlotte,
        September 1, 2001
    22 — Los Angeles vs. Detroit, September 12, 2003
Fewest assists, game
    6 — Houston vs. New York, September 5, 1999
        Houston vs. New York, August 30, 1997
    7 — Connecticut at Sacramento,
        September 18, 2005
        Connecticut at Seattle, October 12, 2004
Most assists, both teams, game
    38 — Detroit (21) vs. Los Angeles (17),
        September 16, 2003
        Los Angeles (24) vs. Charlotte (14),
        September 1, 2001
    36 — Los Angeles (22) vs. Detroit (14),
        September 12, 2003
        Houston (18) vs. Phoenix (18),
        September 1, 1998
Fewest assists, both teams, game
    16 — Houston (6) vs. New York (10),
        September 5, 1999
    19 — Houston (6) vs. New York (13),
        August 30, 1997
Most assists, one half
    15 — Los Angeles vs. Charlotte, September 1, 2001
    14 — Detroit vs. Los Angeles, September 14, 2003

PERSONAL FOULS

Most personal fouls, game
    28 — New York at Houston, September 5, 1999
    26 — New York at Houston, September 4, 1999
Fewest personal fouls, game
    10 — Sacramento at Connecticut,
        September 14, 2005
    12 — Connecticut vs. Sacramento,
        September 14, 2005
        Los Angeles at Detroit, September 14, 2003
        Detroit at Los Angeles, September 12, 2003
        Houston vs. Phoenix, September 1, 1998
Most personal fouls, both teams, game
    45 — Los Angeles (25) vs. New York (20),
        August 31, 2002
    44 — New York (26) at Houston (18),
        September 4, 1999
Fewest personal fouls, both teams, game
    22 — Sacramento (10) at Connecticut (12),
        September 14, 2005

    26 — Los Angeles (12) at Detroit (14),
        September 14, 2003
Most personal fouls, one half
    16 — New York at Houston, September 5, 1999
    14 — New York at Houston, September 4, 1999
        New York at Houston, August 30, 1997

DISQUALIFICATIONS

Most disqualifications, game
    2 — New York at Houston, August 26, 2000 (OT)
    1 — Los Angeles at Detroit, September 16, 2003
        Los Angeles vs. New York, August 31, 2002
        New York vs. Houston, September 2, 1999
        Phoenix at Houston, August 29, 1998 (OT)
Most disqualifications, both teams, game
    2 — New York (2) at Houston (0),
        August 26, 2000 (OT)
    1 — Los Angeles (1) at Detroit (0),
        September 16, 2003
        Los Angeles (1) vs. New York (0),
        August 31, 2002
        New York (1) vs. Houston (0),
        September 2, 1999
        Phoenix (1) at Houston (0),
        August 29, 1998 (OT)

STEALS

Most steals, game
    15 — Connecticut vs. Seattle, October 8, 2004
    12 — Houston vs. New York, September 4, 1999
Fewest steals, game
    2 — New York vs. Los Angeles, August 29, 2002
    3 — New York at Houston, September 5, 1999
Most steals, both teams, game
    21 — Connecticut (15) vs. Seattle (6),
        October 8, 2004
    19 — Seattle (10) vs. Connecticut (9),
        October 10, 2004
Fewest steals, both teams, game
    10 — Los Angeles (5) vs. Charlotte (5),
        September 1, 2001
    11 — New York (2) vs. Los Angeles (9),
        August 29, 2002
        Phoenix (5) at Houston (6), September 1, 1998
Most steals, one half
    8 — Connecticut vs. Seattle, October 8, 2004
    7 — Connecticut vs. Seattle, October 8, 2004
        Houston vs. New York, September 4, 1999

BLOCKED SHOTS

Most blocked shots, game
    10 — Los Angeles vs. Charlotte,
        September 1, 2001
    8 — Connecticut at Sacramento,
        September 18, 2005
        New York at Houston, September 4, 1999
Fewest blocked shots, game
    1 — By Many
Most blocked shots, both teams, game
    16 — Los Angeles (10) vs. Charlotte (6),
        September 1, 2001
    13 — Detroit (7) at Los Angeles (6),
        September 12, 2003

Fewest blocked shots, both teams, game
- 3 — Houston (1) at New York (2),
  September 2, 1999
- 4 — Connecticut (1) at Seattle (3),
  October 12, 2004

Most blocked shots, one half
- 6 — Los Angeles vs. Detroit, September 12, 2003
  New York at Houston, September 4, 1999
- 5 — Connecticut at Sacramento,
  September 18, 2005
  Los Angeles vs. Charlotte,
  September 1, 2001 (both halves)

TURNOVERS

Most turnovers, game
- 18 — Seattle at Connecticut, October 8, 2004
  New York at Houston, September 4, 1999
- 16 — By Many

Fewest turnovers, game
- 6 — Sacramento vs. Connecticut,
  September 18, 2005
- 7 — Sacramento at Connecticut,
  September 14, 2005

Most turnovers, both teams, game
- 33 — Seattle (18) at Connecticut (15),
  October 8, 2004
- 32 — Seattle (16) vs. Connecticut (16),
  October 10, 2004
  Houston (16) vs. New York (16),
  August 26, 2000 (OT)

Fewest turnovers, both teams, game
- 20 — Los Angeles (9) at Detroit (11),
  September 16, 2003
- 21 — Sacramento (6) vs. Connecticut (15),
  September 18, 2005

FINALS SINGLE-GAME BESTS

POINTS

	FG	FT	PTS
Nykesha Sales, Connecticut at Seattle, October 10, 2004	14	0	32
Sheryl Swoopes, Houston vs. New York, August 26, 2000	11	6	*31
Cynthia Cooper, Houston at Phoenix, August 27, 1998	11	5	29
Cynthia Cooper, Houston at New York, September 2, 1999	8	10	29
Mwadi Mabika, Los Angeles at Detroit, September 16, 2003	11	5	29
Cynthia Cooper, Houston vs. Phoenix, August 29, 1998	7	11	*27
Ruth Riley, Detroit vs. Los Angeles, September 16, 2003	11	5	27
Betty Lennox, Seattle vs. Connecticut, October 10, 2004	11	5	27
Cynthia Cooper, Houston vs. New York, August 30, 1997	7	11	25
Cynthia Cooper, Houston vs. New York, August 26, 2000	8	8	*25
Yolanda Griffith, Sacramento at Connecticut, September 14, 2005	11	3	25
Michelle Griffiths, Phoenix at Houston, September 1, 1998	10	3	24
Cynthia Cooper, Houston vs. New York, September 5, 1999	5	13	24
Tari Phillips, New York vs. Houston, August 24, 2000	10	4	24
Lisa Leslie, Los Angeles at Charlotte, August 30, 2001	9	6	24
Lisa Leslie, Los Angeles vs. Charlotte, September 1, 2001	7	9	24
Taj McWilliams-Franklin, Connecticut vs. Sacramento, September 15, 2005	8	8	*24
Cynthia Cooper, Houston vs. Phoenix, September 1, 1998	9	5	23
Lisa Leslie, Los Angeles vs. Detroit, September 12, 2003	10	3	23
Betty Lennox, Seattle vs. Connecticut, October 12, 2004	7	9	23
Nykesha Sales, Connecticut vs. Sacramento, September 14, 2005	7	5	23
Michele Timms, Phoenix at Houston, August 29, 1998	7	5	*21
Crystal Robinson, New York at Houston, September 4, 1999	6	5	21
Ashja Jones, Connecticut at Sacramento, September 20, 2005	8	5	21

FIELD GOALS

	FG	FGA
Nykesha Sales, Connecticut at Seattle, October 10, 2004	14	22
Cynthia Cooper, Houston at Phoenix, August 27, 1998	11	24
Sheryl Swoopes, Houston vs. New York, August 26, 2000	*11	18
Mwadi Mabika, Los Angeles at Detroit, September 16, 2003	11	20
Ruth Riley, Detroit vs. Los Angeles, September 16, 2003	11	19
Betty Lennox, Seattle vs. Connecticut, October 10, 2004	11	16
Yolanda Griffith, Sacramento at Connecticut, September 14, 2005	11	17
Michelle Griffiths, Phoenix at Houston, September 1, 1998	10	16
Tari Phillips, New York vs. Houston, August 24, 2000	10	19
Lisa Leslie, Los Angeles vs. Detroit, September 12, 2003	10	18
Cynthia Cooper, Houston vs. Phoenix, September 1, 1998	9	20
Lisa Leslie, Los Angeles at Charlotte, August 30, 2001	9	16
Cynthia Cooper, Houston at New York, September 2, 1999	8	16
Cynthia Cooper, Houston vs. New York, August 26, 2000	*8	21

Andrea Stinson, Charlotte vs. Los Angeles, August 30, 2001 8   17
Asjha Jones, Connecticut at Sacramento, September 20, 2005...8   12
Taj McWilliams-Franklin, Connecticut vs. Sacramento, September 15, 2005....................*8   17

FREE THROWS

	FT	FTA
Cynthia Cooper, Houston vs. New York, September 5, 1999	13	15
Cynthia Cooper, Houston vs. New York, August 30, 1997	11	15
Cynthia Cooper, Houston vs. Phoenix, August 29, 1998	*11	14
Cynthia Cooper, Houston at New York, September 2, 1999	10	10
Cynthia Cooper, Houston vs. New York, September 4, 1999	10	12
Sheryl Swoopes, Houston vs. Phoenix, September 1, 1998	9	10
Lisa Leslie, Los Angeles vs. Charlotte, September 1, 2001	9	10
Betty Lennox, Seattle vs. Connecticut, October 12, 2004	9	11
Cynthia Cooper, Houston vs. New York, August 26, 2000	*8	8
Taj McWilliams-Franklin, Connecticut vs. Sacramento, September 15, 2005	*8	11
Yolanda Griffith, Sacramento vs. Connecticut, September 20, 2005	8	10
Sheryl Swoopes, Houston vs. New York, September 4, 1999	7	8
Tamika Whitmore, New York at Los Angeles, August 31, 2002	7	9

REBOUNDS

	REB
Taj McWilliams-Franklin, Connecticut vs. Sacramento, September 15, 2005	*16
Tari Phillips, New York vs. Houston, August 24, 2000	15
Lisa Leslie, Los Angeles at Detroit, September 14, 2003	15
Kym Hampton, New York at Houston, August 30, 1997	13
Sheryl Swoopes, Houston vs. Phoenix, August 29, 1998	*13
Lisa Leslie, Los Angeles vs. Charlotte, September 1, 2001	13
Taj McWilliams-Franklin, Connecticut at Sacramento, September 18, 2005	13
Michelle Griffiths, Phoenix vs. Houston, August 27, 1998	12
Tina Thompson, Houston vs. Phoenix, August 29, 1998	*12
Cheryl Ford, Detroit at Los Angeles, September 12, 2003	12
Lisa Leslie, Los Angeles vs. Detroit, September 12, 2003	12
Swin Cash, Detroit vs. Los Angeles, September 16, 2003	12
Tammy Jackson, Houston vs. New York, August 30, 1997	11
Sheryl Swoopes, Houston at Phoenix, August 27, 1998	11
Sue Wicks, New York vs. Houston, September 2, 1999	11
Tammy Jackson, Houston vs. New York, September 5, 1999	11
Latasha Byears, Los Angeles at New York, August 29, 2002	11
Latasha Byears, Los Angeles vs. New York, August 31, 2002	11
Chery Ford, Detroit vs. Los Angeles, September 16, 2003	11
Lisa Leslie, Los Angeles at Detroit, September 16, 2003	11
Lauren Jackson, Seattle vs. Connecticut, October 10, 2004	11
Yolanda Griffith, Sacramento vs. Connecticut, September 18, 2005	11

ASSISTS

	AST
Nikki Teasley, Los Angeles at New York, August 29, 2002	11
Nikki Teasley, Los Angeles vs. New York, August 31, 2002	11
Nikki Teasley, Los Angeles vs. Detroit, September 12, 2003	11
Teresa Weatherspoon, New York vs. Houston, September 2, 1999	10
Swin Cash, Detroit vs. Los Angeles, September 16, 2003	9
Lindsay Whalen, Connecticut vs. Seattle, October 8, 2004	9
Teresa Weatherspoon, New York at Houston, August 26, 2000	*8
Ticha Penicheiro, Sacramento at Connecticut, September 14, 2005	8
Michele Timms, Phoenix at Houston, September 1, 1998	7
Cynthia Cooper, Houston vs. New York, August 26, 2000	*7
Tamecka Dixon, Los Angeles vs. Charlotte, September 1, 2001	7
Nikki Teasley, Los Angeles at Detroit, September 16, 2003	7
Lindsay Whalen, Connecticut at Seattle, October 10, 2004	7
Kim Perrot, Houston at Phoenix, August 27, 1998	6
Sheryl Swoopes, Houston at Phoenix, August 27, 1998	6
Cynthia Cooper, Houston vs. Phoenix, August 29, 1998	*6
Cynthia Cooper, Houston vs. Phoenix, September 1, 1998	6
Sheryl Swoopes, Houston vs. Phoenix, September 1, 1998	6

Cynthia Cooper, Houston at New York, September 2, 1999 6
Cynthia Cooper, Houston vs. New York, September 4, 1999 6
Lisa Leslie, Los Angeles vs. Charlotte, September 1, 2001 6
Nikki Teasley, Los Angeles at Detroit, September 14, 2003 6
Sue Bird, Seattle vs. Connecticut, October 12, 2004..6

STEALS

STL

Teresa Weatherspoon, New York at Houston, August 30, 1997 4
Cynthia Cooper, Houston at New York, September 2, 1999 4
Sue Wicks, New York vs. Houston, September 2, 1999 4
Sheryl Swoopes, Houston vs. New York, September 4, 1999 4
Taj McWilliams-Franklin, Connecticut vs. Seattle, October 8, 2004 4
Nykesha Sales, Connecticut vs. Seattle, October 8, 2004 4
Nykesha Sales, Connecticut at Seattle, October 10, 2004 4
Kim Perrot, Houston vs. New York, August 30, 1997 3

STL

Cynthia Cooper, Houston vs. Phoenix, August 29, 1998..*3
Tammy Jackson, Houston vs. New York, September 4, 1999 3
Cynthia Cooper, Houston vs. New York, September 5, 1999..3
Tammy Jackson, Houston vs. New York, September 5, 1999 3
Cynthia Cooper, Houston vs. New York, August 26, 2000..*3
Tari Phillips, New York at Houston, August 26, 2000 ....*3
Allison Feaster, Charlotte vs. Los Angeles, August 30, 2001..3
Allison Feaster, Charlotte at Los Angeles, September 1, 2001 3
Latasha Byears, Los Angeles at New York, August 29, 2002..3
Kedra Holland-Corn, Detroit at Los Angeles, September 12, 2003 3
Lisa Leslie, Los Angeles at Detroit, September 14, 2003...3
DeLisha Milton, Los Angeles at Detroit, September 14, 2003..3
Deanna Nolan, Detroit vs. Los Angeles, September 14, 2003 3
Sue Bird, Seattle vs. Connecticut, October 10, 2004..3
Katie Douglas, Connecticut at Seattle, October 10, 2004...3
Katie Douglas, Connecticut vs. Sacramento, September 15, 2005 ....*3
Nykesha Sales, Connecticut vs. Sacramento, September 15, 2005 ....*3
Katie Douglas, Connecticut at Sacramento, September 20, 2005 3

BLOCKED SHOTS

BLK

Lisa Leslie, Los Angeles vs. Charlotte, September 1, 2001 7
Tammy Sutton-Brown, Charlotte at Los Angeles, September 1, 2001 4
Ruth Riley, Detroit vs. Los Angeles, September 14, 2003...4
Margo Dydek, Connecticut vs. Sacramento, September 14, 2005...4
Jennifer Gillom, Phoenix at Houston, August 29, 1998 ....*3
Kym Hampton, New York at Houston, September 4, 1999 3
Tammy Jackson, Houston vs. New York, September 5, 1999 3
Allison Feaster, Charlotte vs. Los Angeles, August 30, 2001..3
DeLisha Milton, Los Angeles at New York, August 29, 2002...3
Lisa Leslie, Los Angeles at New York, August 29, 2002 3
Cheryl Ford, Detroit at Los Angeles, September 12, 2003..3
Lisa Leslie, Los Angeles vs. Detroit, September 12, 2003..3
Ruth Riley, Detroit at Los Angeles, September 12, 2003..3
Ruth Riley, Detroit vs. Los Angeles, September 16, 2003...3
Taj McWilliams-Franklin, Connecticut at Sacramento, September 18, 2005...3

*Overtime

RESULTS

Year	Result	Winning coach	Losing coach	MVP
1999	West 79, East 61 at New York	Van Chancellor	Linda Hill-McDonald	Lisa Leslie, Los Angeles
2000	West 73, East 61 at Phoenix.	Van Chancellor	Richie Adubato	Tina Thompson, Houston
2001	West 80, East 72 at Orlando	Van Chancellor	Richie Adubato	Lisa Leslie, Los Angeles
2002	West 81, East 76 at Washington	Michael Cooper	Anne Donovan	Lisa Leslie, Los Angeles
2003	West 84, East 75 at New York.	Michael Cooper	Richie Adubato	Nikki Teasley, Los Angeles
2005	West 122, East 99 at Connecticut	Anne Donovan	Mike Thibault	Sheryl Swoopes, Houston

ALL-TIME ALL-STAR GAME LEADERS

GAMES

Lisa Leslie	6
Nykesha Sales	6
Yolanda Griffith	5
Katie Smith	5
Sheryl Swoopes	5
Teresa Weatherspoon	5
Taj McWilliams-Franklin	4
Chamique Holdsclaw	4
Lauren Jackson	4
Shannon Johnson	4
Ticha Penicheiro	4
Tari Phillips	4
Dawn Staley	4
Tina Thompson	4

MINUTES

Leslie Leslie	125
Sheryl Swoopes	109
Yolanda Griffith	99
Taj McWilliams-Franklin	98
Teresa Weatherspoon	89
Tari Phillips	88
Ticha Penicheiro	87
Nykesha Sales	85
Katie Smith	84
Tina Thompson	84

FIELD GOALS MADE

Lisa Leslie	36
Yolanda Griffith	26
Nykesha Sales	20
Sheryl Swoopes	18
Tina Thompson	18
Tamika Catchings	17
Lauren Jackson	16
Tari Phillips	16
Taj McWilliams-Franklin	12
Deanna Nolan	12

FIELD GOAL ATTEMPTS

Lisa Leslie	71
Tina Thompson	50
Nykesha Sales	48
Yolanda Griffith	44
Tari Phillips	43
Sheryl Swoopes	43
Tamika Catchings	38
Chamique Holdsclaw	37
Lauren Jackson	37
Deanna Nolan	31

FIELD GOAL PERCENTAGE
(MINIMUM: 8 FG)

	FG	FGA	PCT
Yolanda Griffith	26	44	.591
Natalie Williams	8	15	.533
Lisa Leslie	36	71	.507
Marie Ferdinand	9	18	.500

Taj McWilliams-Franklin	12	25	.480
Merlakia Jones	9	20	.450
Tamika Catchings	17	38	.447
Lauren Jackson	16	37	.432
Sheryl Swoopes	18	43	.419
Nykesha Sales	20	48	.417

FREE THROWS MADE

Lisa Leslie	19
Yolanda Griffith	11
Taj McWilliams-Franklin	11
Natalie Williams	9
Chamique Holdsclaw	8
Tamika Catchings	7
Tina Thompson	7
Lauren Jackson	6
Sheryl Swoopes	6
Sue Bird	5

FREE THROW ATTEMPTS

Lisa Leslie	27
Yolanda Griffith	17
Taj McWilliams-Franklin	15
Tari Phillips	12
Natalie Williams	12
Sheryl Swoopes	10
Tamika Catchings	9
Chamique Holdsclaw	9
Tina Thompson	8
Sue Bird	7
Lauren Jackson	7
Nykesha Sales	7

FREE THROW PERCENTAGE
(MINIMUM: 4 FT)

	FT	FTA	PCT
Katie Smith	4	4	1.000
Jackie Stiles	4	4	1.000
Nikki Teasley	4	4	1.000
Chamique Holdsclaw	8	9	.889
Tina Thompson	7	8	.875
Lauren Jackson	6	7	.857
Deanna Nolan	4	5	.800
Tamika Catchings	7	9	.778
Natalie Williams	9	12	.750
Taj McWilliams-Franklin	11	15	.733

THREE-POINT FIELD GOALS

Deanna Nolan	7
Tamika Catchings	6
Lauren Jackson	6
Shannon Johnson	4
Sue Bird	4

RECORDS All-Star Game

Becky Hammon 4
Nykesha Sales 4
Katie Smith 4
Many tied 2

THREE-POINT FIELD GOAL ATTEMPTS
Shannon Johnson 16
Nykesha Sales 16
Deanna Nolan 15
Tamika Catchings 13
Lauren Jackson 13
Katie Smith 13
Sue Bird 12
Tina Thompson 9
Vickie Johnson 8
Nikki McCray 8
Andrea Stinson 8

THREE-POINT PERCENTAGE
(MINIMUM: 2 FG3)

	3FG	3GA	PCT
Becky Hammon	4	6	.667
Deanna Nolan	7	15	.467
Tamika Catchings	6	13	.462
Lauren Jackson	6	13	.462
Nikki Teasley	2	5	.400
Sue Bird	4	12	.333
Mwadi Mabika	2	6	.333
Sheryl Swoopes	2	6	.333
Diana Taurasi	2	6	.333
Katie Smith	4	13	.308

OFFENSIVE REBOUNDS
Yolanda Griffith 19
Tari Phillips 19
Lisa Leslie 15
Natalie Williams 15
Taj McWilliams-Franklin 12
Tina Thompson 10
Sheryl Swoopes 8
Tamika Catchings 7
Lauren Jackson 7
Sue Bird 6
Nykesha Sales 6

DEFENSIVE REBOUNDS
Lisa Leslie 26
Yolanda Griffith 24
Sheryl Swoopes 20
Tari Phillips 16
Tina Thompson 16
Natalie Williams 14
Tamika Catchings 12
Chamique Holdsclaw 11
Lauren Jackson 10
Taj McWilliams-Franklin 10

TOTAL REBOUNDS
Yolanda Griffith 43
Lisa Leslie 41

Tari Phillips 35
Natalie Williams 29
Sheryl Swoopes 28
Tina Thompson 26
Taj McWilliams-Franklin 22
Tamika Catchings 19
Lauren Jackson 17
Chamique Holdsclaw 16

ASSISTS
Dawn Staley 19
Ticha Penicheiro 14
Teresa Weatherspoon 13
Sue Bird 12
Sheryl Swoopes 12
Shannon Johnson 9
Katie Smith 7
Nikki Teasley 6
Tamika Catchings 5
Tamecka Dixon 5
Taj McWilliams-Franklin 5
Andrea Stinson 5

STEALS
Teresa Weatherspoon 9
Tina Thompson 8
Ruthie Bolton 7
Lauren Jackson 7
Shannon Johnson 7
Taj McWilliams-Franklin 7
Nikki McCray 6
Nykesha Sales 6
Sheryl Swoopes 6
Many tied 5

PERSONAL FOULS
Tari Phillips 15
Lisa Leslie 12
Tamika Catchings 10
Shannon Johnson 10
Taj McWilliams-Franklin 9
Lauren Jackson 8
Nykesha Sales 8
Tina Thompson 8
May tied 7

DISQUALIFICATIONS
Tari Phillips 1

BLOCKED SHOTS
Lisa Leslie 9
Yolanda Griffith 6
Tari Phillips 5
Elena Baranova 4
Tamika Catchings 4
Lauren Jackson 4
Tammy Sutton-Brown 3

Vicky Bullett	2
Shannon Johnson	2
Taj McWilliams-Franklin	2
Tina Thompson	2

POINTS

Lisa Leslie	93
Yolanda Griffith	63
Nykesha Sales	48
Tamika Catchings	47
Tina Thompson	45
Lauren Jackson	44
Sheryl Swoopes	44
Taj McWilliams-Franklin	36
Tari Phillips	36
Deanna Nolan	35

SCORING AVERAGE
(MINIMUM: 3 G)

	G	FG	FT	PTS	AVG
Tamika Catchings	3	17	7	47	15.7
Lisa Leslie	6	36	19	93	15.5
Yolanda Griffith	5	26	11	63	12.6
Tina Thompson	4	18	7	45	11.3
Lauren Jacskon	4	16	6	44	11.0
Nykesha Sales	5	20	4	48	9.6
Sue Bird	3	9	5	27	9.0
Tari Phillips	4	16	4	36	9.0
Taj McWilliams-Franklin	4	12	11	36	9.0
Sheryl Swoopes	5	18	6	44	8.8

INDIVIDUAL RECORDS

Most minutes, game
31 — Taj McWilliams, 1999
30 — Tamika Catchings, 2003
28 — Lisa Leslie, 2002
Tina Thompson, 2002
Most points, game
20 — Deanna Nolan, 2005
Tina Thompson, 2002
Lisa Leslie, 2001
18 — Tamika Catchings, 2005
Becky Hammon, 2005
Lisa Leslie, 2002
17 — By Many
Most field goals, game
8 — Lisa Leslie, 2001
Lisa Leslie, 2000
7 — By Many
Most field goal attempts, game
21 — Deanna Nolan, 2005
16 — Tina Thompson, 2002
15 — Tamika Catchings, 2003
Lisa Leslie, 2000
Highest field goal percentage, game
(Minimum: 4 FG)
.875 — Yolanda Griffith, 2001 (7/8)
.833 — Sue Bird, 2005 (5/6)
.800 — Ruth Riley, 2005 (4/5)
Most free throws, game
8 — Natalie Williams, 1999
6 — Chamique Holdsclaw, 2005
Lisa Leslie, 2002
5 — Lisa Leslie, 2005
Tina Thompson, 2002
Most free throw attempts, game
10 — Lisa Leslie, 2002
Natalie Williams, 1999
7 — Lisa Leslie, 2005
6 — By Many
Most free throw made, no misses, game
6 — Chamique Holdsclaw, 2005
4 — Katie Smith, 2005
Nikki Teasley, 2003
Jackie Stiles, 2001
3 — Nykesha Sales, 2002

Most three-point field goals, game
4 — Katie Smith, 2005
Becky Hammon, 2005
Deanna Nolan, 2005
Tamika Catchings, 2003
3 — Sue Bird, 2005
Deanna Nolan, 2003
2 — By Many
Most three-point field goal attempts, game
8 — Deanna Nolan, 2005
7 — Deanna Nolan, 2003
6 — By Many
Most rebounds, game
14 — Yolanda Griffith, 2005
Lisa Leslie, 2002
11 — Natalie Williams, 2003
Tina Thompson, 2000
10 — Tari Phillips, 2002
Yolanda Griffith, 2000
Natalie Williams, 2000
Most offensive rebounds, game
8 — Tari Phillips, 2000
7 — Yolanda Griffith, 2005
Natalie Williams, 2003
Taj McWilliams, 2000
6 — Tina Thompson, 2000
Most defensive rebounds, game
11 — Lisa Leslie, 2002
7 — Yolanda Griffith, 2005
Elena Baranova, 2001
Sheryl Swoopes, 1999
6 — Nikki Teasley, 2003
Tamika Catchings, 2002
Lisa Leslie, 2001
Natalie Williams, 2000
Most assists, game
7 — Dawn Staley, 2003
Sue Bird, 2002
6 — Nikki Teasley, 2003
5 — Dawn Staley, 2002
Ticha Penicheiro, 2001

Most personal fouls, game
6 — Tari Phillips, 2002
5 — Tina Thompson, 2001
Vicky Bullett, 1999
4 — By Many
Most steals, game
6 — Ruthie Bolton-Holifield, 2001
5 — Nikki Teasley, 2003
4 — Dawn Staley, 2001
Most blocked shots, game
4 — Tamika Catchings, 2002
Lisa Leslie, 2002
Elena Baranova, 2001
3 — Lauren Jackson, 2003
Tammy Sutton-Brown, 2002
Lisa Leslie, 2001
Tari Phillips, 2000
Most turnovers, game
7 — Tari Phillips, 2001
Ticha Penicheiro, 2000
6 — Yolanda Griffith, 2003
5 — Tari Phillips, 2002
Ticha Penicheiro, 2001

TEAM RECORDS

SCORING
Most points, game
122 — West, 2005
99 — East, 2005
Fewest points, game
61 — East, 2000, 1999
72 — East, 2001
Most points, both teams, game
221 — West (122) vs. East (99), 2005
Fewest points, both teams, game
134 — East (61) vs. West (73), 2000
Most points, first half
52 — West, 2005
46 — East, 2003
Fewest points, first half
29 — East, 1999
30 — East, 2001
Most points, both teams, first half
95 — West (52) vs. East (43), 2005
Fewest points, both teams, first half
70 — East (30) vs. West (40), 2001
Most points, second half
70 — West, 2005
56 — East, 2005
Fewest points, second half
28 — East, 2000
29 — East, 2003
Most points, both teams, second half
126 — West (70) vs. East (56), 2005
Fewest points, both teams, second half
61 — East (28) vs. West (33), 2000
Most points, overtime period
None
Fewest points, overtime period
None
Most points, both teams, overtime period
None

FIELD GOALS
Most field goals, game
42 — West, 2005
38 — East, 2005
Fewest field goals, game
25 — East, 2000
26 — East, 1999
Most field goals, both teams, game
80 — West (42) vs. East (38), 2005
Fewest field goals, both teams, game
54 — East (25) vs. West (29), 2000

FIELD GOAL ATTEMPTS
Most field goal attempts, game
94 — East, 2005
90 — West, 2005
Fewest field goal attempts, game
65 — West, 2003
69 — East, 2001
Most field goal attempts, both teams, game
184 — East (94) vs. West (90), 2005
Fewest field goal attempts, both teams, game
144 — West (70) vs. East (74), 1999
East (69) vs. West (75), 2001

FIELD GOAL PERCENTAGE
Highest field goal percentage, game
.477 — West, 2003 (31/65)
.467 — West, 2005 (42/90)
Lowest field goal percentage, game
.294 — East, 2000 (25/85)
.333 — East, 2002 (28/84)
Highest field goal percentage, both teams, game
.435 — West (.467) vs. East (.404), 2005 (80/184)
Lowest field goal percentage, both teams, game
.333 — East (.294) vs. West (.377), 2000 (54/162)

THREE-POINT FIELD GOALS
Most three-point field goals, game
12 — West, 2005
9 — East, 2005, 2003
Fewest three-point field goals, game
2 — West, 1999
East, 2000
Most three-point field goals, both teams, game
21 — West (12) vs. East (9), 2005
Fewest three-point field goals, both teams, game
6 — East (2) vs. West (4), 2000
West (2) vs. East (4), 1999

THREE-POINT FIELD GOAL ATTEMPTS
Most three-point field goal attempts, game
28 — East, 2005
27 — East, 2002
Fewest three-point field goal attempts, game
14 — West, 1999
15 — West, 2003, 2000
Most three-point field goal attempts, both teams, game
52 — East (28) vs. West (24), 2005
Fewest three-point field goal attempts, both teams, game
32 — West (14) vs. East (18), 1999

FREE THROWS

Most free throws, game
26 — West, 2005
17 — West, 2003
Fewest free throws, game
5 — East, 1999
6 — East, 2003
Most free throws, both teams, game
40 — West (26) vs. East (14), 2005
Fewest free throws, both teams, game
20 — East (5) vs. West (15), 1999
East (9) vs. West (11), 2000

FREE THROW ATTEMPTS

Most free throw attempts, game
33 — West, 2005
24 — East, 2001
Fewest free throw attempts, game
9 — East, 1999
10 — East, 2003
Most free throw attempts, both teams, game
49 — West (33) vs. East (16), 2005
Fewest free throw attempts, both teams, game
28 — East (9) vs. West (19), 1999

REBOUNDS

Most rebounds, game
60 — West, 2000
50 — West, 2002
Fewest rebounds, game
36 — East, 1999, 2001
West, 2001
Most rebounds, both teams, game
100 — West (60) vs. East (40), 2000
Fewest rebounds, both teams, game
72 — East (36) vs. West (36), 2001

OFFENSIVE REBOUNDS

Most offensive rebounds, game
25 — West, 2000
22 — East, 2000
Fewest offensive rebounds, game
8 — West, 2003
9 — East, 2001, 1999
Most offensive rebounds, both teams, game
47 — West (25) vs. East (22), 2000
Fewest offensive rebounds, both teams, game
19 — East (9) vs. West (10), 2001

DEFENSIVE REBOUNDS

Most defensive rebounds, game
37 — West, 1999
35 — West, 2000
Fewest defensive rebounds, game
18 — East, 2000
25 — East, 2005
Most defensive rebounds, both teams, game
64 — West (37) vs. East (27), 1999
Fewest defensive rebounds, both teams, game
51 — East (25) vs. West (26), 2005

ASSISTS

Most assists, game
20 — East, 2005
19 — West, 1999
Fewest assists, game
11 — East, 2000
14 — East, 2001
West, 2001
Most assists, both teams, game
36 — East (20) vs. West (16), 2005
Fewest assists, both teams, game
27 — East (11) vs. West (16), 2000

PERSONAL FOULS

Most personal fouls, game
21 — West, 2001
20 — East, 2002
Fewest personal fouls, game
8 — West, 2000
10 — West, 1999
Most personal fouls, both teams, game
36 — West (21) vs. East (15), 2001
Fewest personal fouls, both teams, game
24 — West (8) vs. East (16), 2000

STEALS

Most steals, game
18 — West, 2001
14 — East, 2000
West, 2003
Fewest steals, game
5 — East, 2005
9 — West, 2005, 2002
Most steals, both teams, game
30 — West (18) vs. East (12), 2001
Fewest steals, both teams, game
14 — East (5) vs. West (9), 2005

BLOCKED SHOTS

Most blocked shots, game
8 — East, 2002
7 — West, 2002
Fewest blocked shots, game
2 — East, 2005
3 — West, 2005, 2000, 1999
Most blocked shots, both teams, game
15 — East (8) vs. West (7), 2002
Fewest blocked shots, both teams, game
5 — East (2) vs. West (3), 2005

DISQUALIFICATIONS

Most disqualifications, game
1 — East, 2002
Most disqualifications, both teams, game
1 — East (1) vs. West (0), 2002

TURNOVERS

Fewest turnovers, game
9 — West, 2005
14 — East, 2002
Most turnovers, game
23 — West, 2000
21 — East, 2001
Fewest turnovers, both teams, game
26 — West (9) vs. East (17), 2005
Most turnovers, both teams, game
40 — East (21) vs. West (19), 2001
East (20) vs. West (20), 2003

CHARLOTTE STING

REGULAR SEASON TEAM RECORDS

TEAM OFFENSE

SCORING

Highest average, points per game, season
71.4 — 1998 (2143/30)
70.0 — 2002 (2241/32)
Lowest average, points per game, season
61.5 — 2004 (2092/34)
61.6 — 2005 (2095/34)
Most points, game
105 — at Washington, August 19, 1998
94 — vs. Los Angeles, June 1, 2002 (OT)
Fewest points, game
41 — at Cleveland, July 21, 2001
42 — vs. Washington, May 21, 2005
at Washington, July 29, 2001
Largest margin of victory, game
36 — at Washington, August 19, 1998 (105-69)
30 — vs. Indiana, August 20, 2003 (80-50)
vs. Washington, July 17, 1998 (86-56)
Largest margin of defeat, game
33 — vs. Phoenix, June 22, 2000 (57-90)
32 — at Cleveland, August 17, 1997 (49-81)
at Seattle, August 1, 2004 (55-87)

BY HALF

Most points, first half
51 — at Washington, August 19, 1998
47 — vs. Phoenix, July 1, 2002
Fewest points, first half
12 — at Cleveland, July 21, 2001
15 — at Phoenix, August 15, 1999
Largest lead at halftime
20 — at Miami, July 5, 2002 (led 41-21;
won 72-68)
at Minnesota, August 3, 2001 (led 33-13;
won 72-64)
19 — at Washington, August 19, 1998 (led 51-32;
won 105-69)
Largest deficit at halftime overcome to win game
13 — vs. Detroit, August 3, 1998 (trailed 27-40;
won 71-68)
10 — vs. Connecticut, August 9, 2003
(trailed 30-40; won 69-68)
Most points, second half
55 — vs. New York, July 9, 1997
54 — at Washington, August 19, 1998
Fewest points, second half
18 — vs. New York, August 24, 2003
at Washington, July 29, 2001
vs. Utah, July 22, 1998
19 — at Washington, June 30, 2002
at Cleveland, June 25, 1999

OVERTIME

Most points, overtime period
14 — vs. Los Angeles, June 1, 2002
13 — at Cleveland, July 24, 2002
Fewest points, overtime period
3 — vs. New York, August 12, 2005
4 — vs. New York, July 20, 2004
vs. Miami, June 3, 2000
Largest margin of victory, overtime period
9 — vs. Detroit, August 6, 2005 (82-73)
7 — at Cleveland, July 24, 2002 (73-66)
vs. Los Angeles, June 1, 2002 (94-87)

FIELD GOAL PERCENTAGE

Highest field goal percentage, season
.439 — 1999 (793/1805)
.435 — 1997 (719/1651)
Lowest field goal percentage, season
.404 — 2005 (772/1913)
.418 — 2003 (787/1881)
Highest field goal percentage, game
.625 — at Washington, August 19, 1998 (40/64)
.603 — vs. Orlando, July 17, 2002 (35/58)
Lowest field goal percentage, game
.246 — at Detroit, June 29, 1998 (16/65)
.254 — at Washington, July 29, 2001 (15/59)

FIELD GOALS

Most field goals per game, season
26.6 — 1998 (798/30)
25.7 — 1997 (719/28)
Fewest field goals per game, season
21.9 — 2004 (745/34)
22.7 — 2005 (772/34)
Most field goals, game
40 — at Washington, August 19, 1998
35 — vs. Orlando, July 17, 2002
Fewest field goals, game
15 — vs. Indiana, July 23, 2005
vs. Washington, May 21, 2005
at Washington, July 29, 2001
16 — Many times

FIELD GOAL ATTEMPTS

Most field goal attempts per game, season
61.8 — 1998 (1855/30)
59.5 — 2000 (1903/32)
Fewest field goal attempts per game, season
51.3 — 2004 (1744/34)
55.3 — 2003 (1881/34)
Most field goal attempts, game
76 — vs. Detroit, August 6, 2005 (2OT)
75 — vs. Connecticut, August 27, 2005

Fewest field goal attempts, game
41 — at Indiana, August 20, 2005
at Phoenix, June 11, 2004
vs. Miami, July 31, 2001
43 — vs. Detroit, August 23, 2005
vs. Houston, July 17, 2005
at Indiana, June 5, 2004
vs. Indiana, May 28, 2004

THREE-POINT FIELD GOAL PERCENTAGE
Highest three-point field goal percentage, season
.400 — 2002 (211/527)
.362 — 2004 (166/459)
2003 (187/517)
Lowest three-point field goal percentage, season
.279 — 1998 (105/377)
.293 — 1999 (108/369)

THREE-POINT FIELD GOALS
Most three-point field goals per game, season
6.6 — 2002 (211/32)
5.5 — 2003 (187/34)
Fewest three-point field goals per game, season
3.1 — 2005 (104/34)
3.4 — 1999 (108/32)
Most three-point field goals, game
13 — at Detroit, July 3, 2003
12 — vs. Los Angeles, June 1, 2002 (OT)
Fewest three-point field goals, game
0 — vs. Cleveland, June 5, 2000
vs. Utah, July 22, 1998
at Los Angeles, June 24, 1998
1 — many times

THREE-POINT FIELD GOAL ATTEMPTS
Most three-point field goal attempts per game, season
16.5 — 2002 (527/32)
15.2 — 2003 (517/34)
Fewest three-point field goal attempts per game, season
8.85 — 2005 (301/34)
11.46 — 1997 (321/28)
Most three-point field goal attempts, game
24 — vs. Cleveland, July 6, 2002
23 — vs. New York, August 4, 2002
Fewest three-point field goal attempts, game
1 — vs. Phoenix, May 26, 2005
3 — at Sacramento, June 26, 1997

FREE THROW PERCENTAGE
Highest free throw percentage, season
.777 — 2001 (410/528)
.773 — 2003 (456/590)
Lowest free throw percentage, season
.692 — 1997 (337/487)
.708 — 1998 (442/624)
Highest free throw percentage, game
1.000 — vs. Detroit, June 23, 2004 (11/11)
at New York, June 12, 2001 (6/6)
vs. Sacramento, August 4, 1999 (11/11)

.955 — vs. Sacramento, June 27, 1998 (21/22)
Lowest free throw percentage, game
.412 — vs. Cleveland, August 14, 1998 (7/17)
.444 — at Cleveland, August 8, 1998 (4/9)

FREE THROWS MADE
Most free throws made per game, season
15.3 — 2002 (490/32)
14.7 — 1998 (442/30)
Fewest free throws made per game, season
12.0 — 1997 (337/28)
12.8 — 2001 (410/32)
1999 (410/32)
Most free throws made, game
33 — at Orlando, July 12, 2002
27 — vs. Connecticut, June 28, 2003
vs. Washington, July 26, 2000
Fewest free throws made, game
1 — at New York, September 2, 2004
3 — vs. San Antonio, June 23, 2005

FREE THROW ATTEMPTS
Most free throw attempts per game, season
20.8 — 1998 (624/30)
20.7 — 2002 (663/32)
Fewest free throw attempts per game, season
16.5 — 2001 (528/32)
16.7 — 1999 (535/32)
Most free throw attempts, game
44 — at Orlando, July 12, 2002
35 — vs. Washington, July 26, 2000
Fewest free throw attempts, game
2 — at New York, September 2, 2004
5 — vs. San Antonio, June 23, 2005
at Washington, July 15, 2004
at Seattle, June 18, 2001

REBOUNDS
Most rebounds per game, season
32.7 — 1998 (981/30)
32.6 — 1997 (914/28)
Fewest rebounds per game, season
25.6 — 2004 (872/34)
27.2 — 2005 (925/34)
Most rebounds, game
47 — vs. Cleveland, July 12, 1997
45 — vs. Phoenix, August 9, 1997
Fewest rebounds, game
15 — at Los Angeles, June 9, 2004
16 — at Cleveland, August 25, 2003

OFFENSIVE REBOUNDS
Most offensive rebounds per game, season
10.10 — 2003 (342/34)
1998 (304/30)
10.00 — 1997 (279/28)
Fewest offensive rebounds per game, season
7.5 — 2004 (256/34)
8.4 — 1999 (268/32)

253

Most offensive rebounds, game
- 19 — vs. Cleveland, August 14, 1998
- 18 — vs. Connecticut, August 27, 2005
  - vs. New York, July 20, 2004 (OT)
  - at New York, June 22, 2003

Fewest offensive rebounds, game
- 2 — at Indiana, June 5, 2004
  - vs. Sacramento, August 4, 1999
- 3 — Many times

DEFENSIVE REBOUNDS

Most defensive rebounds per game, season
- 22.7 — 1997 (635/28)
- 22.6 — 1998 (677/30)

Fewest defensive rebounds per game, season
- 17.9 — 2005 (609/34)
- 18.1 — 2004 (616/34)

Most defensive rebounds, game
- 35 — vs. Detroit, June 16, 2001 (2OT)
- 34 — at New York, July 26, 1999 (OT)

Fewest defensive rebounds, game
- 9 — vs. San Antonio, June 23, 2005
- 10 — vs. Seattle, June 12, 2005
  - at Orlando, June 9, 2001

ASSISTS

Most assists per game, season
- 17.8 — 1999 (568/32)
- 17.3 — 1997 (485/28)

Fewest assists per game, season
- 12.5 — 2004 (426/34)
- 14.5 — 2005 (493/34)

Most assists, game
- 31 — at Washington, August 19, 1998
- 30 — vs. Orlando, July 17, 2002

Fewest assists, game
- 5 — vs. Indiana, June 26, 2004
  - at Washington, July 29, 2001
- 6 — at Seattle, July 31, 2003
  - at Miami, July 18, 2001
  - at Detroit, July 6, 2001

PERSONAL FOULS

Most personal fouls per game, season
- 22.3 — 2000 (713/32)
- 21.4 — 2005 (727/34)

Fewest personal fouls per game, season
- 16.6 — 1997 (465/28)
- 16.9 — 1998 (507/30)

Most personal fouls, game
- 33 — at Detroit, September 19, 2004
- 32 — vs. Miami, June 3, 2000 (OT)

Fewest personal fouls, game
- 9 — vs. Sacramento, June 27, 1998
- 10 — at Washington, July 7, 2003

DISQUALIFICATIONS

Most disqualifications per game, season
- .29 — 2005 (10/34)
- .28 — 2002 (9/32)

Fewest disqualifications per game, season
- .00 — 1997 (0/28)
- .09 — 2003 (3/34)

Most disqualifications, game
- 3 — vs. Miami, June 3, 2000 (OT)
- 2 — vs Detroit August 6, 2005 (2OT)
  - at Indiana, July 22, 2002
  - at Utah, June 8, 2002
  - vs. Houston, June 15, 1998

STEALS

Most steals per game, season
- 9.1 — 1998 (273/30)
- 8.4 — 2005 (284/34)

Fewest steals per game, season
- 6.2 — 2004 (210/34)
- 6.8 — 2001 (217/32)

Most steals, game
- 17 — vs. Connecticut, August 27, 2005
  - vs. Washington, June 11, 1998
- 16 — vs. Detroit, July 10, 2003
  - vs. Seattle, June 9, 2000

Fewest steals, game
- 0 — at Miami, August 14, 2001
- 1 — vs. Houston, July 17, 2005
  - at Phoenix, June 11, 2004
  - at Cleveland, July 21, 2001
  - vs. Orlando, July 20, 2001

BLOCKED SHOTS

Most blocked shots per game, season
- 4.1 — 1997 (116/28)
- 3.9 — 2004 (134/34)

Most blocked shots per game, season
- 2.8 — 2000 (90/32)
- 3.0 — 1999 (97/32)

Most blocked shots, game
- 9 — at Seattle, July 29, 2005
  - at Indiana, July 28, 2004
  - vs. Washington, July 10, 2004
  - vs. Detroit, June 16, 2001 (2OT)
- 8 — at Washington, July 17, 2003
  - vs. Orlando, July 17, 2002

Fewest blocked shots, game
- 0 — Many times.

TURNOVERS

Most turnovers per game, season
- 17.7 — 1997 (496/28)
- 15.7 — 2005 (535/34)

Fewest turnovers per game, season
- 12.8 — 2002 (408/32)
- 14.1 — 2004 (479/34)

Most turnovers, game
    28 — at New York, July 26, 1997
    25 — at Detroit, August 9, 2005
        vs. Washington, May 21, 2005
Fewest turnovers, game
    6 — at New York, August 11, 2002
        vs. Cleveland, June 30, 2001
    8 — at Connecticut, July 26, 2003
        vs. Miami, June 22, 2002
        at Houston, June 11, 2002
        at New York, July 12, 1998
        vs. Sacramento, August 1, 1997

TEAM DEFENSE

POINTS

Fewest points allowed per game, season
    62.8 — 2001 (2009/32)
    63.8 — 2004 (2168/34)
Most points allowed per game, season
    75.9 — 2000 (2429/32)
    68.7 — 2005 (2335/34)
Fewest points allowed, game
    37 — vs. Indiana, June 26, 2004
    38 — vs. Seattle, July 7, 2001
Fewest points allowed, first half
    13 — at Minnesota, August 3, 2001
    15 — at Miami, August 14, 2001
Fewest points allowed, second half
    12 — vs. Indiana, May 28, 2004
    17 — vs. Washington, June 28, 2005
        vs. Indiana, June 26, 2004
Fewest points allowed, overtime period
    2 — vs. Detroit, August 6, 2005
    5 — at New York, July 26, 1999

FIELD GOAL PERCENTAGE

Lowest opponents' field goal percentage, season
    .397 — 2001 (732/1846)
    .402 — 1997 (686/1707)
Highest opponents' field goal percentage, season
    .455 — 2000 (879/1930)
    .451 — 2005 (851/1888)
Lowest opponents' field goal percentage, game
    .188 — vs. Indiana, June 26, 2004 (9/48)
    .254 — vs. Houston, August 4, 2001 (15/59)

TURNOVERS

Most opponents' turnovers per game, season
    16.7 — 1998 (501/30)
    16.6 — 1997 (464/28)
Fewest opponents' turnovers per game, season
    12.9 — 2004 (437/34)
    13.3 — 2002 (424/32)
Most opponents' turnovers, game
    26 — vs. Detroit, August 6, 2005 (2OT)
    25 — vs. Minnesota, September 11, 2004
        vs. Utah, July 22, 1998
        vs. Sacramento, June 27, 1998

TEAM MISCELLANEOUS

GAME WON AND LOST

Highest winning percentage, season
    .600 — 1998 (18-12)
    .563 — 2001 (18-14)
        2002 (18-14)
Lowest winning percentage, season
    .176 — 2005 (6-28)
    .250 — 2000 (8-24)
Most consecutive games won
    9 — July 31, 2001-June 3, 2002
    6 — June 27-July 7, 2001
        July 25-August 2, 1999
Most consecutive games won, one season
    7 — July 31-August 14, 2001
    6 — June 27-July 7, 2001
        July 25-August 2, 1999
Most consecutive games lost
    10 — July 12-August 4, 2005
        August 9, 1999-June 10, 2000
    7 — June 12-24, 2001
Most consecutive games lost, one season
    10 — July 12-August 4, 2005
    7 — June 12-24, 2001
Highest winning percentage, home games, season
    .857 — 1997 (12-2)
    .765 — 2003 (13-4)
Lowest winning percentage, home games, season
    .294 — 2005 (5-12)
    .313 — 2000 (5-11)
Most consecutive home games won
    13 — July 14, 2001-July 1, 2002
    6 — May 29-June 28, 2003
Most consecutive home games lost
    9 — August 20, 1999-July 1, 2000
    5 — August 8, 2000-June 24, 2001
Highest winning percentage, road games, season
    .600 — 1998 (9-6)
    .438 — 2002, 2001, 1999 (7-9)
Lowest winning percentage, road games, season
    .059 — 2005 (1-16)
    .188 — 2000 (3-13)
Most consecutive road games won
    4 — August 6, 2002-May 31, 2003
        August 3-14, 2001
        July 16-31, 1999
        June 13-25, 1998
    3 — June 11-July 3, 2004
        July 8-12, 1998
Most consecutive road games lost
    18 — September 17, 2004-August 20, 2005
    7 — July 22, 2000-June 7, 2001

OVERTIME GAMES

Most overtime games, season
    3 — 2005, 2004, 2001, 2000
    2 — 2002, 2003
Most consecutive overtime games, season
    2 — June 22-24, 2001
Most overtime games won, season
    2 — 2004, 2002, 2000
    1 — 2005, 2003,1999
Most overtime games won, no losses, season
    2 — 2002
    1 — 1999
Most consecutive overtime games won
    3 — August 24, 2003-June 20, 2004
    2 — June 1-July 24, 2002
        June 20-July 24, 2000
Most overtime games lost, season
    3 — 2001
    2 — 2005
Most overtime games lost, no wins, season
    3 — 2001
Most consecutive overtime games lost
    3 — June 16-24, 2001
Most overtime periods, game
    2 — vs. New York, August 12, 2005
        vs. Detroit, August 6, 2005
        vs. Los Angeles, June 20, 2004
        vs. Detroit, June 16, 2001

INDIVIDUAL RECORDS

SEASONS

Most seasons
    8 — Andrea Stinson
    7 — Dawn Staley
    6 — Charlotte Smith-Taylor

GAMES

Most games, career
    254 — Andrea Stinson
    219 — Dawn Staley
    185 — Charlotte Smith-Taylor
Most consecutive games, career
    254 — Andrea Stinson, June 22, 1997-September 19, 2004
    219 — Dawn Staley, June 10, 1999-July 29, 2005
    98 — Allison Feaster, June 2, 2001-August 25, 2003
Most games, season
    34 — By Many

MINUTES

Most minutes, career
    7,954 — Andrea Stinson
    7,290 — Dawn Staley
    4,777 — Allison Feaster
Highest average, minutes per game, career
(Minimum 100 games)
    33.3 — Dawn Staley (7290/219)
    31.4 — Allison Feaster (4777/152)
    31.3 — Andrea Stinson (7954/254)

Most minutes, season
    1,152 — Dawn Staley, 2001
    1,143 — Dawn Staley, 2004
    1,123 — Andrea Stinson, 2000
Highest average, minutes per game, season
    36.1 — Andrea Stinson, 1997 (1011/28)
    36.0 — Dawn Staley, 2001 (1152/32)
    35.1 — Andrea Stinson, 2000 (1123/32)
Most minutes, game
    48 — Sheri Sam, vs New York, August 12, 2005 (2OT)
        Helen Darling, vs New York, Aug. 12, 2005 (2OT)
    47 — Helen Darling, vs Detroit, Aug. 6, 2005 (2OT)
    46 — Sheri Sam, vs Detroit, August 6, 2005 (2OT)
        Tangela Smith, vs Detroit, Aug. 6, 2005 (2OT)

SCORING

Most points, lifetime
    3,329 — Andrea Stinson
    1,943 — Dawn Staley
    1,746 — Allison Feaster
Highest average, points per game, career
(Minimum 100 games)
    13.1 — Andrea Stinson (3329/254)
    11.5 — Allison Feaster (1746/152)
    10.8 — Rhonda Mapp (1181/109)
Most points, season
    565 — Andrea Stinson, 2000
    450 — Andrea Stinson, 2001
        Andrea Stinson, 1998
    439 — Andrea Stinson, 1997
Highest average, points per game, season
    17.7 — Andrea Stinson, 2000 (565/32)
    15.7 — Andrea Stinson, 1997 (439/28)
    15.0 — Andrea Stinson, 1998 (450/30)
Most points, game
    33 — Andrea Stinson, vs Washington, July 26, 2000
    29 — Shalonda Enis, at Detroit, July 3, 2003
        Andrea Stinson, vs New York, July 9, 1997
    27 — Andrea Stinson, vs Detroit, July 28, 1999
        Andrea Stinson, vs Washington, June 19, 2002
Most games, 30 or more points, career
    1 — Andrea Stinson
Most games, 20 or more points, career
    37 — Andrea Stinson
    12 — Allison Feaster
    8 — Vicky Bullett
Most consecutive games, 20 or more points
    2 — Many times
Most consecutive games, 10 or more points
    20 — Andrea Stinson, August 16, 1999-July 8, 2000
    19 — Andrea Stinson, July 12, 2000-June 14, 2001
    14 — Andrea Stinson, July 10-August 4, 1999

FIELD GOAL PERCENTAGE

Highest field goal percentage, career
(Minimum 400 field goals)
    .486 — Rhonda Mapp (459/944)
    .485 — Tammy Sutton-Brown (516/1065)
    .457 — Vicky Bullett (449/983)

Highest field goal percentage, season (qualifiers)
.531 — Tammy Sutton-Brown, 2002 (129/243)
.509 — Tammy Sutton-Brown, 2005 (111/218)
.500 — Rhonda Mapp 1999 (118/236)
Highest field goal percentage, game
(Minimum 8 field goals made)
.909 — Tracy Reid, vs. Utah, August 5, 2000 (10/11)
.889 — Andrea Stinson, vs. Houston, June 3, 2002 (8/9)
.833 — Rhonda Mapp, vs. Cleveland,
July 30, 1998 (10/12)
Most field goals, none missed, game
5 — Tammy Sutton-Brown, at Seattle, June 6, 2002
Tammy Sutton-Brown, vs Indiana,
June 13, 2002
Janel McCarville, vs Washington,
June 28, 2005 (OT)
4 — Summer Erb, vs Indiana, June 13, 2002
Erin Buescher, vs Detroit, July 27, 2002
Sharon Manning, at Detroit, July 25, 1999
Most field goal attempts, none made, game
10 — Charlotte Smith-Taylor, vs. Los Angeles,
June 20, 2004 (OT)
8 — Kelly Miller, vs. Detroit, July 10, 2003

FIELD GOALS

Most field goals, career
1,302 — Andrea Stinson
659 — Dawn Staley
576 — Allison Feaster
Most field goals, season
214 — Andrea Stinson, 2000
179 — Andrea Stinson, 2001
177 — Andrea Stinson, 1997
Most field goals, game
12 — Andrea Stinson, vs Washington, June 19, 2002
11 — Andrea Stinson, vs New York, July 9, 1997
Andrea Stinson, vs Phoenix, June 24, 1999
Andrea Stinson, vs Houston, August 16, 1997
Andrea Stinson, vs Washington, July 26, 2000
Vicky Bullett, at Los Angeles, June 24, 1998

FIELD GOAL ATTEMPTS

Most field goal attempts, career
2,882 — Andrea Stinson
1,659 — Dawn Staley
1,500 — Allison Feaster
Most field goal attempts, season
463 — Andrea Stinson, 2000
414 — Andrea Stinson, 1998
405 — Tangela Smith, 2005
Most field goal attempts, game
23 — Andrea Stinson, vs , August 14, 1998
Tangela Smith, at Houston, July 2, 2005
Andrea Stinson, vs Los Angeles, August 12, 1998
22 — Andrea Stinson, at Los Angeles, July 7, 1998

Vicky Bullett, at Los Angeles, June 24, 1998

THREE-POINT FIELD GOAL PERCENTAGE

Highest three-point field goal percentage, career
(Minimum 100 three-point field goals)
.367 — Dawn Staley (197/537)
.364 — Allison Feaster (288/791)
.341 — Andrea Stinson (205/601)
Highest three-point field goal percentage, season (qualifiers)
.500 — Charlotte Smith-Taylor, 2004 (29/58)
.471 — Kelly Miller, 2002 (24/51)
.446 — Andrea Stinson, 2001 (29/65)
Most three-point field goals, none missed, game
5 — Shalonda Enis, at Detroit, July 3, 2003
4 — Kelly Miller, vs Los Angeles, June 1, 2002 (OT)
Dawn Staley, vs New York, August 4, 2002
Most three-point field goal attempts, none made, game
6 — Allison Feaster, vs New York, August 4, 2002
5 — By Many

THREE-POINT FIELD GOALS

Most three-point field goals, career
288 — Allison Feaster
205 — Andrea Stinson
197 — Dawn Staley
Most three-point field goals, season
79 — Allison Feaster, 2002
72 — Allison Feaster, 2003
55 — Allison Feaster, 2001
Most three-point field goals, game
6 — Allison Feaster, vs Cleveland, July 6, 2002
5 — By Many
Most consecutive games, three-point field goals made
16 — Allison Feaster, June 30-August 3, 2002
15 — Allison Feaster, May 31-July 7, 2003
13 — Allison Feaster, July 17-August 20, 2003

THREE-POINT FIELD GOAL ATTEMPTS

Most three-point field goal attempts, career
791 — Allison Feaster
601 — Andrea Stinson
537 — Dawn Staley
Most three-point field goal attempts, season
205 — Allison Feaster, 2003
189 — Allison Feaster, 2002
168 — Allison Feaster, 2001
Most three-point field goal attempts, game
11 — Tora Suber, vs Cleveland, August 14, 1998
Allison Feaster, vs San Antonio, June 4, 2003
10 — By Many

FREE THROW PERCENTAGE

Highest free throw percentage, career
(Minimum 200 free throws)
.860 — Allison Feaster (306/356)
.834 — Dawn Staley (428/513)
.791 — Vicky Bullett (208/263)
Highest free throw percentage, season (qualifiers)
.934 — Dawn Staley, 1999 (85/91)
.921 — Allison Feaster, 2001 (58/63)

.895 — Dawn Staley, 2001 (51/57)
Most free throws made, none missed, game
    10 — Tammy Sutton-Brown, at Orlando,
        July 12, 2002
    8 — By Many
Most free throw attempts, none made, game
    5 — Tammy Sutton-Brown, vs Minnesota,
        September 11, 2004
    3 — Tracy Reid, vs Houston, July 25, 1998
        Tracy Reid, vs Houston, June 28, 2000
        Rhonda Mapp, vs New York, July 28, 2000
        Sheri Sam, at Washington, June 30, 2005
        Tracy Reid, vs Minnesota, July 21, 1999

FREE THROWS MADE

Most free throws made, career
    520 — Andrea Stinson
    475 — Tammy Sutton-Brown
    428 — Dawn Staley
Most free throws made, season
    124 — Tammy Sutton-Brown, 2002
    113 — Tammy Sutton-Brown, 2004
    111 — Tracy Reid, 1998
Most free throws made, game
    11 — Tracy Reid, at Phoenix, June 21, 1998
        Tangela Smith, at Detroit, August 9, 2005
        Andrea Stinson, vs Washington, July 26, 2000
    10 — By Many

FREE THROW ATTEMPTS

Most free throw attempts, career
    706 — Andrea Stinson
    680 — Tammy Sutton-Brown
    513 — Dawn Staley
Most free throw attempts, season
    181 — Tracy Reid, 1998
    174 — Tammy Sutton-Brown, 2002
    162 — Tammy Sutton-Brown, 2004
Most free throw attempts, game
    16 — Tracy Reid, at Phoenix, June 21, 1998
    14 — Tracy Reid, at Washington, July 21, 1998
        Andrea Stinson, at New York, July 12, 2000
    13 — Sheri Sam, vs Detroit, August 6, 2005 (2OT)
        Tracy Reid, at Los Angeles, June 24, 1998
        Tracy Reid, vs Los Angeles, August 12, 1998
        Andrea Stinson, vs Sacramento,
        June 24, 2001 (OT)

REBOUNDS

Most rebounds, career
    1115 — Andrea Stinson
    911 — Tammy Sutton-Brown
    642 — Charlotte Smith-Taylor
Highest average, rebounds per game, career
(Minimum 100 games)
    5.9 — Rhonda Mapp (641/109)
    5.6 — Tammy Sutton-Brown (911/163)
    4.4 — Andrea Stinson (1115/254)
Most rebounds, season
    219 — Vicky Bullett, 1999
    211 — Tammy Sutton-Brown, 2004

    205 — Rhonda Mapp, 2000
Highest average, rebounds per game, season (qualifiers)
    6.84 — Vicky Bullett, 1999 (219/32)
    6.83 — Rhonda Mapp, 2000 (205/30)
    6.5 — Vicky Bullett, 1998 (194/30)
Most rebounds, game
    18 — Rhonda Mapp, at New York, July 26, 1999 (OT)
    16 — Andrea Congreaves, vs Phoenix, July 30, 1997
    15 — By Many
Most games, 10+ rebounds, career
    16 — Vicky Bullett
    13 — Rhonda Mapp
    12 — Tammy Sutton-Brown
Most consecutive games, 10+ rebounds
    3 — Vicky Bullett, July 30-August 3, 1998
    2 — By Many

OFFENSIVE REBOUNDS

Most offensive rebounds, career
    327 — Tammy Sutton-Brown
    273 — Andrea Stinson
    223 — Charlotte Smith-Taylor
Highest average, offensive rebounds per game, career
(Minimum 100 games)
    2.0 — Tammy Sutton-Brown (327/163)
    1.8 — Rhonda Mapp (196/109)
    1.2 — Charlotte Smith-Taylor (223/185)
Most offensive rebounds, season
    76 — Tammy Sutton-Brown, 2002
    73 — Tammy Sutton-Brown, 2003
    66 — Vicky Bullett, 1997
Most offensive rebounds, game
    9 — Sharon Manning, at Los Angeles,
        June 24, 1998
    8 — Vicky Bullett, vs Detroit, August 3, 1998
    7 — By Many

DEFENSIVE REBOUNDS

Most defensive rebounds, career
    842 — Andrea Stinson
    584 — Tammy Sutton-Brown
    445 — Rhonda Mapp
Highest average, defensive rebounds per game, career
(Minimum 100 games)
    4.1 — Rhonda Mapp (445/109)
    3.6 — Tammy Sutton-Brown (584/163)
    3.3 — Andrea Stinson (842/254)
Most defensive rebounds, season
    159 — Vicky Bullett, 1999
    148 — Tammy Sutton-Brown, 2004
    145 — Rhonda Mapp, 1999
        Rhonda Mapp, 2000
Most defensive rebounds, game
    15 — Rhonda Mapp, at New York, July 26, 1999
    13 — Rhonda Mapp, at Detroit, June 12, 2000
    12 — Tammy Sutton-Brown, vs Indiana,
        June 26, 2004

ASSISTS

Most assists, career
    1176 — Dawn Staley
    797 — Andrea Stinson
    291 — Allison Feaster

Highest average, assists per game, career
(Minimum 100 games)
    5.4 — Dawn Staley (1176/219)
    3.1 — Andrea, Stinson (797/254)
    2.0 — Rhonda Mapp (217/109)
Most assists, season
    190 — Dawn Staley, 2000
    179 — Dawn Staley, 2001
    177 — Dawn Staley, 1999
Highest average, assists per game, season (qualifiers)
    5.9 — Dawn Staley, 2000 (190/32)
    5.6 — Dawn Staley, 2001 (179/32)
    5.5 — Dawn Staley, 1999 (177/32)
Most assists, game
    13 — Dawn Staley, vs Washington, July 26, 2000
    11 — Dawn Staley, vs Detroit, June 27, 2001
    10 — By Many
Most games, 10+ assists, career
    12 — Dawn Staley
    1 — Helen Darling
        Andrea Stinson

PERSONAL FOULS

Most personal fouls, career
    590 — Tammy Sutton-Brown
    524 — Charlotte Smith-Taylor
    505 — Andrea Stinson
Most personal fouls, season
    138 — Tammy Sutton-Brown, 2005
    132 — Tammy Sutton-Brown, 2003
    125 — Tammy Sutton-Brown, 2002
Most personal fouls, game
    6 — By Many

STEALS

Most steals, career
    339 — Andrea Stinson
    297 — Dawn Staley
    182 — Vicky Bullett
Highest average, steals per game, career
(Minimum 100 games)
    1.4 — Dawn Staley (297/219)
    1.3 — Andrea Stinson (339/254)
    1.1 — Allison Feaster (161/152)
Most steals, season
    66 — Vicky Bullett, 1998
    62 — Vicky Bullett, 1999
    55 — Andrea Stinson, 2000
Highest average, steals per game, season (qualifiers)
    2.2 — Vicky Bullett, 1998 (66/30)
    1.94 — Vicky Bullett, 1999 (62/32)
    1.93 — Vicky Bullett, 1997 (54/28)
Most steals, game
    7 — Helen Darling, vs New York, Aug. 12, 2005 (OT)
    6 — Andrea Stinson, vs Seattle, June 9, 2000

Dawn Staley, vs Washington, July 26, 2001
Andrea Stinson, at Washington, July 7, 2003
Tangela Smith, at Sacramento, July 26, 2005
Vicky Bullett, vs Connecticut, August 7, 1999

BLOCKED SHOTS

Most blocked shots, career
    233 — Tammy Sutton-Brown
    146 — Vicky Bullett
    117 — Andrea Stinson
Highest average, blocked shots per game, career
(Minimum: 100 games)
    1.4 — Tammy Sutton-Brown (233/163)
    .52 — Rhonda Mapp (57/109)
    .50 — Andrea Stinson (117/254)
Most blocked shots, season
    71 — Tammy Sutton-Brown, 2004
    55 — Vicky Bullett, 1997
    50 — Tammy Sutton-Brown, 2003
Highest average, blocked shots per game, season
(qualifiers)
    2.1 — Tammy Sutton-Brown, 2004 (71/34)
    2.0 — Vicky Bullett, 1997 (55/28)
    1.5 — Vicky Bullett, 1998 (46/30)
Most blocked shots, game
    6 — Tangela Smith, at Seattle, July 29, 2005
        Tammy Sutton-Brown, at Indiana,
        July 28, 2004
    5 — Tammy Sutton-Brown, at Cleveland,
        July 24, 2002 (OT)
        Vicky Bullett, vs New York, June 12, 1999
        Tammy Sutton-Brown, vs Indiana,
        May 28, 2004
        Andrea Stinson, at San Antonio,
        August 4, 1997
        Olympia Scott-Richardson, vs Washington,
        July 10, 2004

TURNOVERS

Most turnovers, career
    567 — Andrea Stinson
    555 — Dawn Staley
    288 — Tammy Sutton-Brown
Most turnovers, season
    100 — Sheri Sam, 2005
        Dawn Staley, 2001
    99 — Andrea Stinson, 1997
Most turnovers, game
    9 — Helen Darling, vs Sacramento, August 4, 2005
    8 — Andrea Stinson, vs Houston, August 11, 1997
        Nicole Levesque, at New York, July 26, 1997
    7 — By Many

CONNECTICUT SUN

Orlando Miracle (1999-2002)

REGULAR SEASON TEAM RECORDS

TEAM OFFENSE

SCORING

Highest average, points per game, season
72.7 — 2005 (2474/34)
70.4 — 2002 (2254/32)
Lowest average, points per game, season
66.9 — 2001 (2140/32)
68.7 — 2004 (2335/34)
Most points, game
103 — vs Cleveland, June 8, 2002 (3OT)
93 — vs Detroit, August 18, 1999
Fewest points, game
41 — vs Cleveland, June 27, 2001
45 — vs Washington, August 1, 2003
Largest margin of victory, game
34 — vs Washington, August 26, 2005 (81-47)
29 — vs Detroit, August 6, 2000 (92-63)
Largest margin of defeat, game
28 — at Cleveland, June 14, 2003 (56-84)
27 — at Charlotte, July 17, 2002 (62-89)

BY HALF

Most points, first half
50 — vs Seattle, June 7, 2005
49 — at Seattle, June 22, 2005
at Houston, May 30, 2003
Fewest points, first half
17 — vs Minnesota, June 8, 2000
18 — vs Seattle, July 17, 2003
Largest lead at half time
18 — vs Detroit, August 6, 2000 (led 43-25; won 92-63)
17 — vs Detroit, August 18, 1999 (led 46-29; won 93-81)
vs Washington, July 24, 2001 (led 40-23; won 71-63)
vs Washington, June 20, 2004 (led 43-26; won 75-65)
Largest deficit at halftime overcome to win game
12 — vs New York, July 6, 2003 (trailed 20-32; won 62-58)
11 — vs Los Angeles, June 15, 1999 (trailed 39-50; won 88-86)
Most points, second half
54 — vs New York, June 23, 2002
at Indiana, June 3, 2000
49 — at Phoenix, June 25, 2005
vs Charlotte, August 18, 2005
at San Antonio, June 1, 2003
vs Detroit, August 6, 2000
vs Los Angeles, June 15, 1999
Fewest points, second half
16 — at Detroit, July 8, 2003
18 — at Houston, July 17, 2004
at Cleveland, July 30, 2001

OVERTIME

Most points, overtime period
17 — vs Cleveland, June 8, 2002
16 — vs Indiana, July 3, 2002
Fewest points, overtime period
4 — vs Miami, July 10, 2001
6 — vs Cleveland, June 8, 2002
at Miami, July 27, 2001
at Cleveland, June 7, 2000
Largest margin of victory, overtime period
8 — vs Indiana, July 3, 2002 (79-71)
6 — at Cleveland, July 28, 2002 (76-70)

FIELD GOAL PERCENTAGE

Highest field goal percentage, season
.452 — 2005 (916/2025)
.436 — 2000 (833/1911)
Lowest field goal percentage, season
.401 — 2001 (768/1914)
.411 — 2003 (864/2102)
Highest field goal percentage, game
.600 — at Indiana, June 18, 2001 (30/50)
.577 — at Cleveland, June 7, 2000 (OT) (30/52)
Lowest field goal percentage, game
.238 — vs Washington, August 1, 2003 (15/63)
.263 — vs Cleveland, June 27, 2001 (15/57)

FIELD GOALS

Most field goals per game, season
26.9 — 2005 (916/34)
26.0 — 2000 (833/32)
Fewest field goals per game, season
24.0 — 2001 (768/32)
24.8 — 1999 (793/32)
Most field goals, game
37 — at Detroit, June 5, 2001
vs Detroit, July 19, 2000
35 — at Los Angeles, June 20, 2005
vs Cleveland, June 8, 2002 (3OT)
vs Detroit, August 6, 2000
Fewest field goals, game
15 — vs Washington, August 1, 2003
vs Cleveland, June 27, 2001
16 — vs Detroit, July 30, 2005

FIELD GOAL ATTEMPTS

Most field goal attempts per game, season
61.8 — 2003 (2102/34)
60.3 — 2004 (2051/34)
Fewest field goal attempts per game, season
58.4 — 1999 (1869/32)
59.6 — 2005 (2025/34)
Most field goal attempts, game
84 — vs Los Angeles, May 24, 2003
82 — vs Detroit, June 22, 2003 (OT)
at Utah, June 7, 2001
Fewest field goal attempts, game
43 — at Portland, July 30, 2000
44 — at Charlotte, August 9, 2003

THREE-POINT FIELD GOAL PERCENTAGE

Highest three-point field goal percentage, season
.349 — 2005 (130/373)
.342 — 2000 (145/424)
Lowest three-point field goal percentage, season
.315 — 2002 (145/461)
.319 — 2004 (149/467)

THREE-POINT FIELD GOALS

Most three-point field goals per game, season
5.4 — 2001 (174/32)
5.2 — 2003 (177/34)
Fewest three-point field goals per game, season
3.8 — 2005 (130/34)
4.4 — 2004 (149/34)
Most three-point field goals, game
13 — at Sacramento, July 27, 2000
12 — at Sacramento, June 12, 2004
vs Indiana, June 26, 2003 (2OT)
Fewest three-point field goals, game
0 — vs Houston, June 26, 2000
vs Phoenix, May 22, 2004
1 — Many Times

THREE-POINT FIELD GOAL ATTEMPTS

Most three-point field goal attempts per game, season
16.6 — 2001 (532/32)
16.2 — 2003 (549/34)
Fewest three-point field goal attempts per game, season
11.0 — 2005 (373/34)
13.3 — 2000 (424/32)
Most three-point field goal attempts, game
30 — at Sacramento, July 27, 2000
28 — at Utah, June 12, 1999
Fewest three-point field goal attempts, game
4 — vs Phoenix, May 28, 2005
vs New York, September 3, 2004
5 — at Washington, May 22, 2005

FREE THROW PERCENTAGE

Highest free throw percentage, season
.763 — 2002 (493/646)
.744 — 2005 (512/688)
Lowest free throw percentage, season
.692 — 1999 (465/672)
.727 — 2000 (397/546)
Highest free throw percentage, game
1.000 — at Minnesota, July 17, 2005 (5/5)
at Houston, August 3, 2002 (7/7)
at Cleveland, June 22, 1999 (10/10)
.955 — at Miami, June 30, 2000 (21/22)
Lowest free throw percentage, game
.412 — at Indiana, July 13, 2005 (7/17)
.455 — at Charlotte, July 17, 2002 (10/22)

FREE THROWS MADE

Most free throws made per game, season
15.4 — 2002 (493/32)
15.1 — 2005 (512/34)
Fewest free throws made per game, season
12.4 — 2000 (397/32)
12.8 — 2004 (434/34)
Most free throws made, game
35 — vs Indiana, September 19, 2004
vs Detroit, August 18, 1999
32 — at Phoenix, June 25, 2005

Fewest free throws made, game
2 — at Cleveland, July 30, 2001
3 — at Sacramento, July 27, 2000

FREE THROW ATTEMPTS

Most free throw attempts per game, season
21.0 — 1999 (672/32)
20.2 — 2005 (688/34)
Fewest free throw attempts per game, season
17.1 — 2000 (546/32)
17.4 — 2004 (590/34)
Most free throw attempts, game
47 — vs Detroit, August 18, 1999
43 — vs Indiana, September 19, 2004
Fewest free throw attempts, game
4 — at Cleveland, July 30, 2001
5 — at Sacramento, July 27, 2000

REBOUNDS

Most rebounds per game, season
32.7 — 2005 (1110/34)
32.2 — 2003 (1095/34)
Fewest rebounds per game, season
28.6 — 2002 (915/32)
28.9 — 2000 (925/32)
Most rebounds, game
46 — vs Los Angeles, May 24, 2003
45 — vs Detroit, June 22, 2003 (1 ot)
Fewest rebounds, game
16 — vs Charlotte, July 16, 1999
vs Seattle, July 8, 2000
18 — vs Utah, July 19, 2002

OFFENSIVE REBOUNDS

Most offensive rebounds per game, season
11.1 — 2001 (356/32)
10.3 — 1999 (329/32)
Fewest offensive rebounds per game, season
9.4 — 2004 (321/34)
9.5 — 2005 (322/34)
Most offensive rebounds, game
21 — at Charlotte, July 12, 2001
19 — at Miami, August 9, 2000 (2OT)
Fewest offensive rebounds, game
3 — vs Indiana, July 26, 2005
at Los Angeles, June 14, 2004 (OT)
at Indiana, August 25, 2003
at Los Angeles, July 22, 2002
at Indiana, June 18, 2001
at Seattle, June 12, 2001
4 — at Washington, May 22, 2005
vs Detroit, July 19, 2000
at Detroit, June 17, 1999

DEFENSIVE REBOUNDS

Most defensive rebounds per game, season
23.2 — 2005 (788/34)
22.4 — 2003 (762/34)
Fewest defensive rebounds per game, season
18.6 — 2002 (595/32)
18.9 — 2000 (606/32)
Most defensive rebounds, game
32 — vs Detroit, June 25, 2004 (OT)
vs Los Angeles, May 24, 2003

31 — at Charlotte, August 27, 2005
vs Washington, August 26, 2005
at Indiana, August 6, 2005
vs Seattle, June 7, 2005
vs New York, July 6, 2003

Fewest defensive rebounds, game
11 — vs New York, September 17, 2004
vs Charlotte, July 16, 1999
12 — vs Seattle, July 8, 2000

ASSISTS

Most assists per game, season
16.9 — 2005 (573/34)
16.8 — 2004 (572/34)

Fewest assists per game, season
13.9 — 2002 (446/32)
14.1 — 2001 (452/32)

Most assists, game
26 — at Minnesota, August 20, 1999 (OT)
25 — vs San Antonio, June 4, 2005

Fewest assists, game
5 — at Detroit, June 17, 1999
6 — vs Cleveland, June 27, 2001

PERSONAL FOULS

Most personal fouls per game, season
20.9 — 2002 (669/32)
20.3 — 1999 (648/32)

Fewest personal fouls per game, season
17.9 — 2004 (610/34)
18.2 — 2000 (583/32)

Most personal fouls, game
34 — vs Cleveland, June 8, 2002 (3OT)
at Utah, June 7, 2001
31 — at Detroit, June 17, 1999

Fewest personal fouls, game
8 — vs Washington, August 15, 1999
10 — vs New York, September 17, 2004

DISQUALIFICATIONS

Most disqualifications per game, season
.31 — 1999 (10/32)
.19 — 2002 (6/32)

Fewest disqualifications per game, season
.03 — 2005 (1/34)
.09 — 2001 (3/32)

Most disqualifications, game
2 — at Detroit, June 17, 1999
at Phoenix, July 23, 1999
at Detroit, August 21, 1999
at Phoenix, August 1, 2000
vs Cleveland, June 8, 2002 (3OT)
vs Indiana, June 26, 2003 (2OT)

STEALS

Most steals per game, season
10.0 — 2001 (320/32)
9.3 — 1999 (297/32)

Fewest steals per game, season
6.9 — 2005 (236/34)
7.9 — 2003 (270/34)

Most steals, game
17 — vs Los Angeles, June 1, 2001
16 — vs Miami, July 10, 2001 (OT)

Fewest steals, game
1 — at New York, July 7, 2005
at Seattle, June 22, 2005
2 — at Portland, July 30, 2000

BLOCKED SHOTS

Most blocked shots per game, season
4.1 — 2000 (130/32)
3.9 — 2001 (125/32)

Fewest blocked shots per game, season
2.8 — 2004 (96/34)
2.9 — 1999 (93/32)

Most blocked shots, game
10 — vs San Antonio, June 4, 2005
at Indiana, August 25, 2003
vs Detroit, July 19, 2000
vs Charlotte, June 24, 2000
9 — vs Sacramento, July 4, 2003

Fewest blocked shots, game
0 — Many Times

TURNOVERS

Most turnovers per game, season
16.6 — 2001 (532/32)
16.3 — 1999 (521/32)

Fewest turnovers per game, season
12.8 — 2003 (434/34)
13.3 — 2005 (452/34)

Most turnovers, game
27 — at Cleveland, June 7, 2000 (OT)
at Indiana, July 13, 2005
24 — vs Sacramento, July 17, 1999

Fewest turnovers, game
4 — at Detroit, July 21, 2004
vs Washington, August 15, 1999
5 — at San Antonio, June 1, 2003

TEAM DEFENSE

POINTS

Fewest points allowed per game, season
66.0 — 2005 (2244/34)
67.8 — 2004 (2304/34)

Most points allowed per game, season
70.9 — 2003 (2409/34)
70.5 — 2002 (2255/32)

Fewest points allowed, game
43 — vs New York, September 3, 2004
48 — vs Washington, August 1, 2003

Fewest points allowed, first half
20 — at Indiana, July 13, 2005
21 — vs Seattle, July 8, 2000
vs Washington, August 1, 2003
vs New York, August 12, 2003

Fewest points allowed, second half
19 — at Sacramento, June 24, 2005
vs New York, September 3, 2004
20 — vs Houston, June 7, 2003

Fewest points allowed, overtime period
5 — at Cleveland, July 28, 2002
6 — vs Miami, July 10, 2001
at Minnesota, August 20, 1999
vs Cleveland, June 8, 2002
vs Detroit, June 25, 2004

FIELD GOAL PERCENTAGE

Lowest opponents' field-goal percentage, season
.398 — 2005 (835/2100)
.411 — 2003 (864/2104)
Highest opponents' field-goal percentage, season
.440 — 2001 (806/1831)
.433 — 2000 (851/1964)
Lowest opponents' field-goal percentage, game
.254 — vs Minnesota, July 21, 2001 (16/63)
.280 — at Charlotte, August 27, 2005 (21/75)

TURNOVERS

Fewest opponents' turnovers per game, season
13.0 — 2005 (442/34)
14.0 — 2003 (476/34)
Most opponents' turnovers per game, season
17.1 — 2001 (546/32)
16.9 — 2002 (541/32)
Most opponents' turnovers, game
26 — at Los Angeles, June 14, 2004 (OT)
vs Detroit, May 30, 2002
25 — vs Washington, July 24, 2001
vs Miami, July 10, 2001 (OT)
vs Washington, July 8, 2002

TEAM MISCELLANEOUS

GAME WON AND LOST

Highest winning percentage, season
.765 — 2005 (26-8)
.529 — 2004 (18-16)
Lowest winning percentage, season
.406 — 2001 (13-19)
.469 — 1999 (15-17)
Most consecutive games won
8 — May 22-June 20, 2005
6 — August 2-18, 2005
June 20-July 6, 2004
June 28-July 9, 2000
Most consecutive games won, one season
8 — May 22-June 20, 2005
6 — August 2-18, 2005
June 20-July 6, 2004
June 28-July 9, 2000
Most consecutive games lost
7 — July 21-August 4, 2000
5 — June 7-16, 2001
Most consecutive games lost, one season
7 — July 21-August 4, 2000
5 — June 7-16, 2001
Highest winning percentage, home games, season
.824 — 2005 (14-3)
.688 — 2000 (11-5)
Lowest winning percentage, home games, season
.500 — 1999 (8-8)
.588 — 2003 (10-7)
.588 — 2004 (10-7)
Most consecutive home games won
11 — September 19, 2004-July 28, 2005
6 — July 18-August 7, 2001
Most consecutive home games lost
4 — July 12-29, 1999
2 — Many Times

Highest winning percentage, road games, season
.706 — 2005 (12-5)
.471 — 2004 (8-9)
.471 — 2003 (8-9)
Lowest winning percentage, road games, season
.188 — 2001 (3-13)
.313 — 2000 (5-11)
Most consecutive road games won
4 — May 22-June 20, 2005
August 2-27, 2005
June 4-21, 2002
June 22-July 19, 1999
3 — June 22-July 11, 2004
August 23, 2003-June 4, 2004
Most consecutive road games lost
8 — July 13, 2001-June 1, 2002
July 12-August 9, 2000
7 — June 26-July 22, 2002

OVERTIME GAMES

Most overtime games, season
4 — 2004
3 — 2002
2000
Most consecutive overtime games, season
2 — June 14-18, 2004
Most overtime games won, season
3 — 2002
2 — 2004
Most overtime games won, no losses, season
3 — 2002
Most overtime games lost, season
3 — 2000
2 — 2004, 2003, 2001
Most overtime games lost, no wins, season
3 — 2000
2 — 2003, 2001
Most overtime periods, game
3 — vs Cleveland, June 8, 2002
2 — at Miami, August 9, 2000
vs Indiana, June 26, 2003

INDIVIDUAL RECORDS

SEASONS

Most seasons
7 — Nykesha Sales
Taj McWilliams-Franklin
5 — By Many

GAMES

Most games, career
230 — Nykesha Sales
211 — Taj McWilliams-Franklin
155 — Shannon Johnson
Most games, season
34 — By Many
Most consecutive games, career
230 — Nykesha Sales, June 10, 1999-
August 27, 2005 (current)
109 — Taj McWilliams-Franklin, June 10, 1999-
June 29, 2002
102 — Taj McWilliams-Franklin, May 24, 2003-
August 27, 2005 (current)

Most minutes, career
  7,391 — Nykesha Sales
  6,781 — Taj McWilliams-Franklin
  5,275 — Shannon Johnson
Highest average, minutes per game, career
(Minimum 100 games)
  34.0 — Shannon Johnson (5275/155)
  32.1 — Taj McWilliams-Franklin (6781/211)
         Nykesha Sales (7391/230)
Most minutes, season
  1,147 — Shannon Johnson, 1999
  1,133 — Taj McWilliams-Franklin, 2004
  1,126 — Shannon Johnson, 2000
Highest average, minutes per game, season
  35.8 — Shannon Johnson, 1999 (1147/32)
         Shannon Johnson, 2002 (1110/31)
  35.2 — Shannon Johnson, 2000 (1126/32)
Most minutes, game
  51 — Shannon Johnson, vs Cleveland,
       June 8, 2002 (3OT)
  50 — Adrienne Johnson, at Miami,
       August 9, 2000 (2OT)
  49 — Shannon Johnson, at Miami,
       August 9, 2000 (2OT)

SCORING

Most points, lifetime
  3,328 — Nykesha Sales
  2,609 — Taj McWilliams-Franklin
  2,049 — Shannon Johnson
Highest average, points per game, career
(Minimum 100 games)
  14.5 — Nykesha Sales (3328/230)
  13.2 — Shannon Johnson (2049/155)
  12.4 — Taj McWilliams-Franklin (2609/211)
Most points, season
  548 — Nykesha Sales, 2003
  532 — Nykesha Sales, 2005
  517 — Nykesha Sales, 2004
Highest average, points per game, season
  16.1 — Nykesha Sales, 2003 (548/34)
         Shannon Johnson, 2002 (499/31)
  15.6 — Nykesha Sales, 2005 (532/34)
Most points, game
  35 — Shannon Johnson, vs Cleveland,
       June 8, 2002 (3OT)
  31 — Shannon Johnson, at Houston, May 30, 2003
       Nykesha Sales, vs New York, August 12, 2003
       Shannon Johnson, at Sacramento,
       July 24, 1999
  29 — Nykesha Sales, vs New York, June 23, 2002
       Nykesha Sales, at Charlotte, August 9, 2003
       Nykesha Sales, vs Los Angeles, June 15, 1999
Most games, 30 or more points, career
  3 — Shannon Johnson
  2 — Nykesha Sales
Most games, 20 or more points, career
  57 — Nykesha Sales
  27 — Shannon Johnson
  18 — Taj McWilliams-Franklin

Most consecutive games, 20 or more points
  3 — Nykesha Sales, August 9-16, 2003
      Shannon Johnson, June 5-13, 2003
      Nykesha Sales, May 30-June 5, 2003
      Shannon Johnson, July 19-22, 2002
  2 — By Many
Most consecutive games, 10 or more points
  15 — Nykesha Sales, August 7, 2002-June 24, 2003
       Taj McWilliams-Franklin, August 1, 2000-
       June 25, 2001
  14 — Shannon Johnson, July 12-August 8, 2002
  12 — Nykesha Sales, July 25, 2000-June 9, 2001
       Adrienne Johnson, July 14-August 9, 2000

FIELD GOAL PERCENTAGE

Highest field goal percentage, career
(Minimum 400 field goals)
  .483 — Taj McWilliams-Franklin (1005/2079)
  .420 — Nykesha Sales (1249/2971)
  .413 — Katie Douglas (507/1229)
Highest field goal percentage, season (qualifiers)
  .524 — Taj McWilliams-Franklin, 2000 (173/330)
  .495 — Taj McWilliams-Franklin, 2005 (180/364)
  .484 — Asjha Jones, 2005 (133/275)
Highest field goal percentage, game
(Minimum 8 field goals made)
  .900 — Taj McWilliams-Franklin, at San Antonio,
         July 15, 2004 (9/10)
  .889 — Elaine Powell, vs Washington, June 23, 2001
  (8/9)
         Lindsay Whalen, at New York,
         September 10, 2004 (8/9)
  .818 — Taj McWilliams-Franklin, vs Cleveland,
         June 22, 2000 (9/11)
         Lindsay Whalen, vs Charlotte,
         August 18, 2005 (9/11)
         Taj McWilliams-Franklin, vs Charlotte,
         June 9, 2001 (9/11)
Most field goals, none missed, game
  7 — Taj McWilliams-Franklin, at Washington,
      July 21, 2000
  4 — Many Times
Most field goal attempts, none made, game
  9 — Elaine Powell, at New York, June 30, 2001
  8 — Adrienne Johnson, at Portland, June 26, 2002
      Adrienne Johnson, at Detroit, July 8, 2003
      Nykesha Sales, at Los Angeles, July 27, 1999
  6 — By Many

FIELD GOALS

Most field goals, career
  1,249 — Nykesha Sales
  1,005 — Taj McWilliams-Franklin
  658 — Shannon Johnson
Most field goals, season
  210 — Nykesha Sales, 2004
  201 — Nykesha Sales, 2005
  194 — Nykesha Sales, 2003
Most field goals, game
  12 — Shannon Johnson, at Sacramento,
       July 24, 1999
       Nykesha Sales, at Charlotte,
       September 15, 2004

11 — Shannon Johnson, vs Cleveland,
　　June 8, 2002 (3OT)
　　Nykesha Sales, vs New York, August 12, 2003
　　Nykesha Sales, at Los Angeles, June 20, 2005
　　Taj McWilliams-Franklin, at Miami,
　　August 9, 2000
　　Katie Douglas, at Washington,
　　August 23, 2003

FIELD GOAL ATTEMPTS

Most field goal attempts, career
2,971 — Nykesha Sales
2,079 — Taj McWilliams-Franklin
1,600 — Shannon Johnson
Most field goal attempts, season
486 — Nykesha Sales, 2004
482 — Nykesha Sales, 2005
468 — Nykesha Sales, 2003
Most field goal attempts, game
23 — Taj McWilliams-Franklin, at Miami,
　　August 9, 2000 (2OT)
22 — Shannon Johnson, at Sacramento,
　　July 21, 2002
21 — Nykesha Sales, vs Charlotte, June 24, 2000
　　Nykesha Sales, at Sacramento, July 27, 2000
　　Nykesha Sales, at Sacramento, June 12, 2004

THREE-POINT FIELD GOAL PERCENTAGE

Highest three-point field goal percentage, career
(Minimum 100 three-point field goals)
.354 — Nykesha Sales (297/839)
.341 — Katie Douglas (178/522)
.326 — Shannon Johnson (148/454)
Highest three-point field goal percentage, season
(qualifiers)
.444 — Taj McWilliams-Franklin, 1999 (20/45)
.422 — Nykesha Sales, 2005 (49/116)
.395 — Nykesha Sales, 2000 (47/119)
Most three-point field goals, none missed, game
4 — Lindsay Whalen, vs Indiana, July 26, 2005
　　Elaine Powell, vs Washington, June 23, 2001
　　Katie Douglas, vs San Antonio, July 24, 2004
　　Andrea Congreaves, at Minnesota,
　　August 20, 1999 (OT)
3 — Sheri Sam, vs Phoenix, June 21, 1999
　　Nykesha Sales, at Phoenix, June 9, 2004
　　Brooke Wyckoff, vs Detroit, June 18, 2005
Most three-point field goal attempts, none made, game
6 — Katie Douglas, at Detroit, July 20, 2005
　　Katie Douglas, at Detroit, June 27, 2004
　　Katie Douglas, at Houston, August 3, 2002
5 — By Many

THREE-POINT FIELD GOALS

Most three-point field goals, career
297 — Nykesha Sales
178 — Katie Douglas
148 — Shannon Johnson
Most three-point field goals, season
53 — Katie Douglas, 2004
52 — Adrienne Johnson, 2000
49 — Nykesha Sales, 2005

Most three-point field goals, game
7 — Nykesha Sales, at Sacramento, July 27, 2000
6 — Katie Douglas, vs Houston, May 25, 2004
　　Katie Douglas, vs Indiana,
　　June 26, 2003 (2OT)
　　Nykesha Sales, at New York, July 1, 2003
5 — By Many
Most consecutive games, three-point field goals made
18 — Adrienne Johnson, June 30-August 9, 2000
15 — Nykesha Sales, July 17-August 25, 2003
14 — Nykesha Sales, June 4-July 15, 2005
　　Shannon Johnson, July 21, 2001-
　　June 1, 2002
　　Katie Douglas, July 2-August 9, 2003

THREE-POINT FIELD GOAL ATTEMPTS

Most three-point field goal attempts, career
839 — Nykesha Sales
522 — Katie Douglas
454 — Shannon Johnson
Most three-point field goal attempts, season
153 — Katie Douglas, 2004
148 — Adrienne Johnson, 2000
137 — Nykesha Sales, 2001
Most three-point field goal attempts, game
11 — Nykesha Sales, at Sacramento, July 27, 2000
10 — Sheri Sam, at Cleveland, June 22, 1999
　　Katie Douglas, vs Detroit, June 25, 2004 (OT)
　　Shannon Johnson, at Indiana, July 13, 2001
　　Nykesha Sales, at Sacramento, June 12, 2004
　　Adrienne Johnson, at Sacramento,
　　July 27, 2000
9 — By Many

FREE THROW PERCENTAGE

Highest free throw percentage, career
.778 — Katie Douglas (284/365)
.774 — Nykesha Sales (533/689)
.770 — Lindsay Whalen (214/278)
Highest free throw percentage, season (qualifiers)
.960 — Jessie Hicks, 2003 (24/25)
.866 — Katie Douglas, 2002 (58/67)
.854 — Asjha Jones, 2004 (41/48)
Most free throws made, none missed, game
10 — Shannon Johnson, at Miami, June 30, 2000
9 — Taj McWilliams-Franklin, vs Detroit,
　　July 8, 2001
　　Nykesha Sales, at New York, August 16, 2003
8 — By Many
Most free throw attempts, none made, game
4 — Sheri Sam, vs San Antonio, July 10, 1999
3 — Rebecca Lobo, at Los Angeles, July 20, 2003
　　Tari Phillips, vs San Antonio, July 10, 1999
　　Clarisse Machanguana, at Charlotte,
　　July 17, 2002
2 — By Many

FREE THROWS MADE

Most free throws made, career
585 — Shannon Johnson
555 — Taj McWilliams-Franklin
533 — Nykesha Sales

Most free throws made, season
164 — Shannon Johnson, 2002
125 — Lindsay Whalen, 2005
Shannon Johnson, 2003
116 — Nykesha Sales, 2003
Most free throws made, game
13 — Nykesha Sales, at Charlotte, August 9, 2003
12 — Lindsay Whalen, at Phoenix, June 25, 2005
Shannon Johnson, vs New York, June 23, 2002
Katie Douglas, vs Los Angeles, August 9, 2005
11 — Shannon Johnson, vs Cleveland,
June 8, 2002 (3OT)
Shannon Johnson, at Houston, May 30, 2003
Shannon Johnson, vs Minnesota,
July 23, 2003

FREE THROW ATTEMPTS

Most free throw attempts, career
793 — Shannon Johnson
777 — Taj McWilliams-Franklin
689 — Nykesha Sales
Most free throw attempts, season
214 — Shannon Johnson, 2002
171 — Shannon Johnson, 2003
156 — Lindsay Whalen, 2005
Most free throw attempts, game
16 — Nykesha Sales, at Charlotte, August 9, 2003
15 — Shannon Johnson, at Houston, May 30, 2003
Shannon Johnson, vs New York, June 23, 2002
14 — Shannon Johnson, at New York, June 18, 2002
Shannon Johnson, vs Minnesota,
July 23, 2003
Katie Douglas, vs Los Angeles, August 9, 2005
Taj McWilliams-Franklin, vs Detroit,
June 22, 2003 (OT)

REBOUNDS

Most rebounds, career
1508 — Taj McWilliams-Franklin
970 — Nykesha Sales
645 — Shannon Johnson
Highest average, rebounds per game, career
(Minimum 100 games)
7.2 — Taj McWilliams-Franklin (1508/211)
4.2 — Nykesha Sales (970/230)
Shannon Johnson (645/155)
Most rebounds, season
248 — Taj McWilliams-Franklin, 2005
244 — Taj McWilliams-Franklin, 2000
Taj McWilliams-Franklin, 2004
243 — Taj McWilliams-Franklln, 2001
Highest average, rebounds per game, season (qualifiers)
7.63— Taj McWilliams-Franklin, 2000 (244/32)
7.59— Taj McWilliams-Franklin, 2001 (243/32)
7.5 — Taj McWilliams-Franklin, 1999 (239/32)
7.3 — Taj McWilliams-Franklin, 2005 (248/34)
Most rebounds, game
15 — Taj McWilliams-Franklin, vs Cleveland,
August 12, 1999
14 — Margo Dydek, vs Seattle, June 7, 2005
Taj McWilliams-Franklin, at Indiana,
June 22, 2004

Taj McWilliams-Franklin, at Minnesota,
July 14, 2004
Taj McWilliams-Franklin, at New York,
August 4, 2000
Taj McWilliams-Franklin, al Sacramento,
June 24, 2005
13 — By Many
Most games, 10+ rebounds, career
42 — Taj McWilliams-Franklin
7 — Nykesha Sales
6 — Wendy Palmer
Most consecutive games, 10+ rebounds
2 — Taj McWilliams-Franklin, June 22-25, 2004
Taj McWilliams-Franklin, June 11-12, 2004
Taj McWilliams-Franklin, July 17-19, 2003
Taj McWilliams-Franklin, June 14-16, 2001
Taj McWilliams-Franklin, June 17-19, 1999

OFFENSIVE REBOUNDS

Most offensive rebounds, career
545 — Taj McWilliams-Franklin
276 — Nykesha Sales
200 — Shannon Johnson
Highest average, offensive rebounds per game, career
(Minimum 100 games)
2.6 — Taj McWilliams-Franklin (545/211)
1.3 — Shannon Johnson (200/155)
1.2 — Nykesha Sales (276/230)
Most offensive rebounds, season
114 — Taj McWilliams-Franklin, 2001
90 — Taj McWilliams-Franklin, 2000
83 — Taj McWilliams-Franklin, 2004
Most offensive rebounds, game
10 — Taj McWilliams-Franklin, vs Houston,
July 18, 2001
8 — Nykesha Sales, at Charlotte, July 12, 2001
Taj McWilliams-Franklin, at Detroit,
July 29, 2001
Taj McWilliams-Franklin, at Phoenix,
June 16, 2001
Taj McWilliams-Franklin, vs Washington,
July 24, 2001
7 — Taj McWilliams-Franklin, at Indiana,
June 22, 2004
Andrea Congreaves, vs Los Angeles,
June 15, 1999

DEFENSIVE REBOUNDS

Most defensive rebounds, career
963 — Taj McWilliams-Franklin
694 — Nykesha Sales
445 — Shannon Johnson
Highest average, defensive rebounds per game, career
(Minimum 100 games)
4.6 — Taj McWilliams-Franklin (963/211)
3.0 — Nykesha Sales (694/230)
2.9 — Shannon Johnson (445/155)
Most defensive rebounds, season
170 — Taj McWilliams-Franklin, 2005
168 — Margo Dydek, 2005
161 — Taj McWilliams-Franklin, 2004

Most defensive rebounds, game
    12 — Margo Dydek, vs Indiana, July 26, 2005
    11 — Margo Dydek, vs Seattle, June 7, 2005
        Taj McWilliams-Franklin, at Detroit,
        June 17, 1999
    10 — By Many

ASSISTS

Most assists, career
    737 — Shannon Johnson
    541 — Nykesha Sales
    364 — Taj McWilliams-Franklin
Highest average, assists per game, career
(Minimum 100 games)
    4.8 — Shannon Johnson (737/155)
    2.4 — Nykesha Sales (541/230)
    1.7 — Taj McWilliams-Franklin (364/211)
Most assists, season
    196 — Shannon Johnson, 2003
    172 — Lindsay Whalen, 2005
    169 — Shannon Johnson, 2000
Highest average, assists per game, season (qualifiers)
    5.8 — Shannon Johnson, 2003 (196/34)
    5.3 — Shannon Johnson, 2000 (169/32)
        Shannon Johnson, 2002 (163/31)
Most assists, game
    13 — Lindsay Whalen, at Detroit, June 27, 2004
    12 — Shannon Johnson, at San Antonio,
        June 13, 2000
        Shannon Johnson, vs San Antonio,
        July 19, 2002
    11 — Shannon Johnson, at Minnesota, July 10, 2003
Most games, 10+ assists, career
    8 — Shannon Johnson
    3 — Lindsay Whalen

PERSONAL FOULS

Most personal fouls, career
    696 — Nykesha Sales
    575 — Taj McWilliams-Franklin
    383 — Shannon Johnson
Most personal fouls, season
    112 — Sheri Sam, 1999
    109 — Nykesha Sales, 2001
        Brooke Wyckoff, 2003
    107 — Nykesha Sales, 2003
Most personal fouls, game
    6 — By Many

STEALS

Most steals, career
    428 — Nykesha Sales
    315 — Taj McWilliams-Franklin
    241 — Shannon Johnson
Highest average, steals per game, career
(Minimum 100 games)
    1.9 — Nykesha Sales (428/230)
    1.6 — Shannon Johnson (241/155)
    1.5 — Taj McWilliams-Franklin (315/211)
Most steals, season
    75 — Nykesha Sales, 2004
    70 — Nykesha Sales, 2001
    69 — Nykesha Sales, 1999

Highest average, steals per game, season (qualifiers)
    2.21 — Nykesha Sales, 2004 (75/34)
    2.20 — Nykesha Sales, 2001 (70/32)
    2.16 — Nykesha Sales, 1999 (69/32)
Most steals, game
    6 — Nykesha Sales, vs Phoenix, May 22, 2004
        Nykesha Sales, vs Detroit, August 18, 1999
        Nykesha Sales, vs Washington, June 19, 1999
        Nykesha Sales, at Los Angeles,
        June 14, 2004 (OT)
        Shannon Johnson, at New York, August 1, 1999
        Nykesha Sales, vs Seattle, September 12, 2004
    5 — By Many

BLOCKED SHOTS

Most blocked shots, career
    236 — Taj McWilliams-Franklin
    81 — Cintia dos Santos
    71 — Margo Dydek
Highest average, blocked shots per game, career
(Minimum: 100 games)
    1.118 — Taj McWilliams-Franklin (236/211)
    .500 — Jessie Hicks (58/116)
    .462 — Brooke Wyckoff (61/132)
Most blocked shots, season
    71 — Margo Dydek, 2005
    63 — Cintia dos Santos, 2000
    50 — Taj McWilliams-Franklin, 2001
Highest average, blocked shots per game, season
(qualifiers)
    2.3 — Margo Dydek, 2005 (71/31)
    2.0 — Cintia dos Santos, 2000 (63/32)
    1.6 — Taj McWilliams-Franklin, 2001 (50/32)
Most blocked shots, game
    9 — Margo Dydek, vs San Antonio, June 4, 2005
    5 — Margo Dydek, vs Seattle, June 7, 2005
        Margo Dydek, vs Indiana, July 26, 2005
        Cintia dos Santos, vs Detroit, July 19, 2000
        Cintia dos Santos, vs Indiana, June 17, 2000
        Taj McWilliams-Franklin, vs Detroit, July 8, 2001
        Taj McWilliams-Franklin, vs Indiana,
        August 3, 2003

TURNOVERS

Most turnovers, career
    492 — Nykesha Sales
    482 — Shannon Johnson
    451 — Taj McWilliams-Franklin
Most turnovers, season
    121 — Shannon Johnson, 1999
    107 — Shannon Johnson, 2003
    102 — Shannon Johnson, 2000
Most turnovers, game
    8 — Elaine Powell, at Miami, June 4, 2002
        Shannon Johnson, at Miami,
        August 9, 2000 (2OT)
        Shannon Johnson, at Cleveland,
        August 14, 1999
        Shannon Johnson, vs New York,
        August 13, 2002
    7 — Many Times

DETROIT SHOCK

REGULAR SEASON TEAM RECORDS

TEAM OFFENSE

SCORING

Highest average, points per game, season
75.1 — 2003 (2553/34)
72.8 — 2000 (2331/32)

Lowest average, points per game, season
65.7 — 2001 (2103/32)
66.0 — 2005 (2247/34)

Most points, game
111 — vs Indiana, June 18, 2000
103 — vs Connecticut, June 5, 2003

Fewest points, game
40 — at Houston, July 6, 2002
46 — at Houston, July 27, 1999

Largest margin of victory, game
37 — at Washington, June 14, 2003 (93-56)
vs Indiana, June 18, 2000 (111-74)
30 — vs Miami, July 14, 2000 (80-50)

Largest margin of defeat, game
40 — at Sacramento, July 24, 2005 (51-91)
39 — at Houston, July 27, 1999 (46-85)

BY HALF

Most points, first half
56 — vs San Antonio, July 1, 2003
53 — vs Cleveland, June 15, 1998

Fewest points, first half
8 — at Houston, July 6, 2002
16 — at Miami, July 14, 2001
at Minnesota, June 12, 1999

Largest lead at half time
19 — at Los Angeles, August 16, 1998 (led 42-23)
vs Cleveland, July 17, 1999 (led 42-23)
at Connecticut, August 5, 2003 (led 47-28)
17 — vs Miami, July 20, 2002 (led 36-19)

Largest deficit at halftime overcome to win game
19 — at Indiana, June 9, 2004 (trailed 32-51;
won 83-79)
15 — at Cleveland, June 27, 1998 (trailed 36-51;
won 84-73)

Most points, second half
66 — vs Indiana, June 18, 2000
58 — at Seattle, August 17, 2003

Fewest points, second half
15 — at Phoenix, August 16, 2005
18 — at New York, May 26, 2004

OVERTIME

Most points, overtime period
18 — at Connecticut, June 22, 2003
15 — vs New York, September 14, 2004
at Minnesota, August 23, 2003

Fewest points, overtime period
1 — at Utah, July 6, 1999

2 — at Seattle, July 24, 2001

Largest margin of victory, overtime period
11 — vs New York, September 14, 2004 (82-71)
9 — at Minnesota, August 23, 2003 (86-77)
at Connecticut, June 22, 2003 (82-73)
vs Los Angeles, June 17, 2003 (87-78)

FIELD GOAL PERCENTAGE

Highest field goal percentage, season
.450 — 2003 (902/2004)
.438 — 2000 (868/1980)

Lowest field goal percentage, season
.399 — 2002 (766/1919)
.401 — 1999 (791/1972)

Highest field goal percentage, game
.619 — at Phoenix, July 26, 2001 (26/42)
.593 — vs Indiana, June 18, 2000 (35/59)

Lowest field goal percentage, game
.259 — at Houston, July 6, 2002 (15/58)
.262 — at Houston, July 27, 1999 (17/65)

FIELD GOALS

Most field goals per game, season
27.1 — 2000 (868/32)
26.5 — 2003 (902/34)

Fewest field goals per game, season
23.9 — 2002 (766/32)
24.2 — 2001 (774/32)

Most field goals, game
36 — at Charlotte, June 25, 2000
35 — vs New York, July 30, 2004
vs Indiana, June 18, 2000
at Cleveland, June 16, 2000

Fewest field goals, game
15 — at Houston, July 6, 2002
16 — vs Orlando, June 21, 2002

FIELD GOAL ATTEMPTS

Most field goal attempts per game, season
62.5 — 1998 (1875/30)
61.9 — 2000 (1980/32)

Fewest field goal attempts per game, season
58.9 — 2003 (2004/34)
59.8 — 2001 (1914/32)

Most field goal attempts, game
94 — vs Washington, July 10, 1999
84 — at Portland, July 22, 2001

Fewest field goal attempts, game
42 — vs Charlotte, June 10, 2005
at Phoenix, July 26, 2001
45 — at Sacramento, August 11, 1998

THREE-POINT FIELD GOAL PERCENTAGE

Highest three-point field goal percentage, season
.387 — 2003 (125/323)
.360 — 1999 (121/336)
Lowest three-point field goal percentage, season
.278 — 2000 (76/273)
.297 — 2004 (62/209)

THREE-POINT FIELD GOALS

Most three-point field goals per game, season
4.5 — 2001 (143/32)
3.8 — 1999 (121/32)
Fewest three-point field goals per game, season
1.8 — 2004 (62/34)
2.2 — 2005 (76/34)
Most three-point field goals, game
10 — vs New York, August 10, 2003 (OT)
at Indiana, June 1, 2002
9 — vs New York, June 9, 2002
vs Los Angeles, June 26, 2001 (OT)
vs Orlando, June 5, 2001
at Orlando, August 18, 1999
Fewest three-point field goals, game
0 — Many Times

THREE-POINT FIELD GOAL ATTEMPTS

Most three-point field goal attempts per game, season
12.7 — 2001 (405/32)
11.4 — 2002 (364/32)
Fewest three-point field goal attempts per game, season
6.2 — 2004 (209/34)
7.0 — 2005 (238/34)
Most three-point field goal attempts, game
27 — vs Orlando, June 5, 2001
26 — at Indiana, June 1, 2002
Fewest three-point field goal attempts, game
1 — at Charlotte, September 4, 2004
2 — at Connecticut, July 30, 2005
vs Indiana, July 17, 2005
vs Sacramento, July 12, 2004

FREE THROW PERCENTAGE

Highest free throw percentage, season
.760 — 2001 (412/542)
.742 — 2000 (519/699)
Lowest free throw percentage, season
.658 — 2005 (509/774)
.702 — 2004 (556/792)
.702 — 1999 (536/764)
Highest free throw percentage, game
1.000 — at Charlotte, June 27, 2001 (8/8)
vs Houston, August 7, 1998 (4/4)
.952 — at Orlando, August 18, 1999 (20/21)
Lowest free throw percentage, game
.385 — at Washington, June 21, 1998 (5/13)
.400 — vs Orlando, July 9, 2000 (4/10)

FREE THROWS MADE

Most free throws made per game, season
18.4 — 2003 (624/34)
16.8 — 1999 (536/32)
Fewest free throws made per game, season
12.9 — 2001 (412/32)
14.8 — 2002 (472/32)

Most free throws made, game
40 — vs San Antonio, July 1, 2003
vs Indiana, June 18, 2000
30 — vs Connecticut, June 5, 2003
vs Miami, June 28, 2002 (OT)
Fewest free throws made, game
3 — at Phoenix, July 6, 2000
4 — at Indiana, June 1, 2002
vs Orlando, July 9, 2000
vs Houston, August 7, 1998

FREE THROW ATTEMPTS

Most free throw attempts per game, season
25.9 — 2003 (882/34)
23.9 — 1999 (764/32)
Fewest free throw attempts per game, season
16.9 — 2001 (542/32)
20.3 — 2002 (651/32)
Most free throw attempts, game
54 — vs Indiana, June 18, 2000
51 — vs San Antonio, July 1, 2003
Fewest free throw attempts, game
4 — vs Houston, August 7, 1998
5 — at Phoenix, July 6, 2000

REBOUNDS

Most rebounds per game, season
36.2 — 2003 (1230/34)
35.9 — 1998 (1077/30)
Fewest rebounds per game, season
29.5 — 2001 (945/32)
30.8 — 2000 (985/32)
Most rebounds, game
52 — at New York, May 22, 2005
48 — at Connecticut, June 22, 2003 (OT)
Fewest rebounds, game
14 — vs Utah, August 7, 2001
18 — at Cleveland, August 8, 2001

OFFENSIVE REBOUNDS

Most offensive rebounds per game, season
12.1 — 2005 (412/34)
11.7 — 2004 (397/34)
Fewest offensive rebounds per game, season
10.0 — 1999 (321/32)
10.1 — 2001 (324/32)
Most offensive rebounds, game
22 — vs Charlotte, July 3, 2003
21 — at Connecticut, June 18, 2005
at San Antonio, May 22, 2004
vs New York, June 9, 2002
Fewest offensive rebounds, game
4 — at Houston, July 15, 2004
vs Washington, June 22, 2004
at New York, June 27, 2003
at Cleveland, August 8, 2001
vs Utah, August 7, 2001
5 — Many Times

DEFENSIVE REBOUNDS

Most defensive rebounds per game, season
25.0 — 2003 (851/34)
24.4 — 1998 (732/30)
Fewest defensive rebounds per game, season
19.4 — 2001 (621/32)
20.1 — 2000 (644/32)
Most defensive rebounds, game
36 — at Connecticut, June 22, 2003 (OT)
35 — at New York, May 22, 2005
at Washington, June 14, 2003
Fewest defensive rebounds, game
10 — vs Utah, August 7, 2001
13 — at Charlotte, July 24, 2003
vs Charlotte, July 3, 2003
at Cleveland, July 28, 2000

ASSISTS

Most assists per game, season
16.6 — 2004 (564/34)
16.0 — 2003 (545/34)
Fewest assists per game, season
13.9 — 2005 (474/34)
14.4 — 1998 (432/30)
Most assists, game
28 — vs New York, July 30, 2004
26 — at Cleveland, June 16, 2000
Fewest assists, game
6 — at New York, June 12, 2005
at New York, May 22, 2005
vs Orlando, June 21, 2002
7 — vs Charlotte, August 9, 2005
at Houston, July 6, 2002
vs New York, August 13, 1999
vs Minnesota, August 4, 1999
vs Houston, June 24, 1999

PERSONAL FOULS

Most personal fouls per game, season
22.8 — 1999 (728/32)
22.4 — 2005 (761/34)
Fewest personal fouls per game, season
17.8 — 2003 (605/34)
18.8 — 2001 (602/32)
Most personal fouls, game
34 — at Orlando, August 18, 1999
32 — vs Sacramento, July 4, 1999
Fewest personal fouls, game
7 — vs Washington, August 25, 2003
11 — at Orlando, August 11, 2002
vs Seattle, July 28, 2002

DISQUALIFICATIONS

Most disqualifications per game, season
.44 — 1999 (14/32)
.32 — 2005 (11/34)

Fewest disqualifications per game, season
.03 — 2002 (1/32)
.09 — 2003 (3/34)
Most disqualifications, game
2 — at Utah, July 6, 1999 (2OT)
vs Washington, July 10, 1999 (2OT)
at Phoenix, August 11, 1999

STEALS

Most steals per game, season
8.2 — 2004 (277/34)
8.1 — 2000 (260/32)
Fewest steals per game, season
6.3 — 2002 (201/32)
6.6 — 1998 (197/30)
Most steals, game
20 — vs Indiana, June 18, 2000
18 — vs Washington, June 24, 2000
Fewest steals, game
1 — vs Charlotte, June 26, 2002
2 — at New York, July 24, 2004
at Cleveland, July 29, 2003
vs Utah, July 23, 2002
vs Cleveland, July 28, 2001
at Orlando, August 18, 1999
vs Sacramento, June 23, 1998

BLOCKED SHOTS

Most blocked shots per game, season
4.7 — 2003 (158/34)
4.6 — 2005 (155/34)
Fewest blocked shots per game, season
2.6 — 2001 (82/32)
2.7 — 1998 (81/30)
Most blocked shots, game
11 — at Charlotte, July 10, 2003
10 — at Charlotte, August 6, 2005 (2OT)
vs Indiana, August 2, 2003
at Indiana, July 16, 2003
Fewest blocked shots, game
0 — Many Times

TURNOVERS

Most turnovers per game, season
17.9 — 2003 (608/34)
16.9 — 2002 (541/32)
Fewest turnovers per game, season
15.1 — 2004 (513/34)
15.1 — 1999 (483/32)
Most turnovers, game
27 — at Minnesota, July 1, 2002 (OT)
26 — Many Times
Fewest turnovers, game
8 — at San Antonio, May 22, 2004
vs Utah, August 7, 2001
vs Washington, July 10, 1999 (2OT)
9 — vs Washington, August 21, 2005
vs Utah, July 23, 2002
vs Phoenix, June 29, 2001
vs Indiana, June 18, 2000
at Cleveland, June 14, 1999

POINTS

Fewest points allowed per game, season
    67.3 — 2005 (2287/34)
    69.3 — 1998 (2078/30)
Most points allowed per game, season
    75.8 — 2000 (2426/32)
    72.0 — 1999 (2303/32)
Fewest points allowed, game
    40 — vs Indiana, August 25, 2005
    41 — at Sacramento, August 11, 1998
Fewest points allowed, first half
    16 — at Sacramento, August 11, 1998
    18 — at Houston, July 6, 2002
Fewest points allowed, second half
    16 — vs Connecticut, July 8, 2003
    17 — vs Indiana, August 25, 2005
Fewest points allowed, overtime period
    2 — vs Los Angeles, June 17, 2003
    4 — vs Minnesota, August 11, 2005
        vs Washington, July 10, 1999
        vs New York, September 14, 2004

FIELD GOAL PERCENTAGE

Lowest opponents' field-goal percentage, season
    .399 — 2003 (911/2286)
    .403 — 2005 (784/1945)
Highest opponents' field-goal percentage, season
    .462 — 2001 (848/1837)
    .460 — 2000 (905/1967)
Lowest opponents' field-goal percentage, game
    .246 — vs Charlotte, June 29, 1998 (16/65)
    .257 — at San Antonio, June 7, 2003 (18/70))

TURNOVERS

Fewest opponents' turnovers per game, season
    13.8 — 2002 (443/32)
    14.6 — 2004 (496/34)
Most opponents' turnovers per game, season
    17.0 — 2000 (543/32)
    16.6 — 1999 (532/32)
Most opponents' turnovers, game
    28 — vs Indiana, June 18, 2000
        vs Washington, July 10, 1999 (2OT)
    25 — vs Charlotte, August 9, 2005

GAME WON AND LOST

Highest winning percentage, season
    .735 — 2003 (25-9)
    .567 — 1998 (17-13)
Lowest winning percentage, season
    .281 — 2002 (9-23)
    .313 — 2001 (10-22)
Most consecutive games won
    8 — June 5-27, 2003
    6 — June 21-July 1, 1998
Most consecutive games won, one season
    8 — June 5-27, 2003
    6 — June 21-July 1, 1998

Most consecutive games lost
    13 — May 30-June 28, 2002
    5 — June 17-27, 2001
        July 25-August 2, 1999
Most consecutive games lost, one season
    13 — May 30-June 28, 2002
    5 — June 17-June 27, 2001
        July 25-August 2, 1999
Highest winning percentage, home games, season
    .765 — 2003 (13-4)
    .733 — 1998 (11-4)
Lowest winning percentage, home games, season
    .375 — 2001 (6-10)
    .438 — 1999, 2000 (7-9)
Most consecutive home games won
    7 — July 20-August 25, 2005
    6 — July 17-August 5, 1998
Most consecutive home games lost
    5 — June 2-28, 2002
    4 — July 6-28, 2001
Highest winning percentage, road games, season
    .706 — 2003 (12-5)
    .529 — 2004 (9-8)
Lowest winning percentage, road games, season
    .125 — 2002 (2-14)
    .235 — 2005 (4-13)
Most consecutive road games won
    5 — June 6-23, 2004
    4 — June 7-27, 2003
Most consecutive road games lost
    17 — July 24-18, 2002
    5 — June 25-July 24, 2004

OVERTIME GAMES

Most overtime games, season
    5 — 2001
    4 — 2005, 2003
Most consecutive overtime games, season
    2 — July 6-10, 1999
        July 22-24, 2001
Most overtime games won, season
    4 — 2003
    3 — 2001
Most overtime games won, no losses, season
    4 — 2003
Most consecutive overtime games won, season
    4 — June 17-August 23, 2003
    2 — June 12-16, 2001
Most overtime games lost, season
    2 — 2005, 2002, 2001, 1999
    1 — 2004, 2000
Most overtime games lost, no wins, season
    2 — 1999, 2002
    1 — 2000
Most overtime periods, game
    2 — at Charlotte, August 6, 2005
        at Charlotte, June 16, 2001
        vs Washington, July 10, 1999

SEASONS

Most seasons
- 6 — Barbara Farris
- 5 — Astou Ndiaye-Diatta
  Deanna Nolan

GAMES

Most games, career
- 171 — Barbara Farris
- 158 — Deanna Nolan
- 138 — Astou Ndiaye-Diatta

Most consecutive games, career
- 108 — Astou Ndiaye-Diatta, July 28, 1999-
  August 13, 2002
- 101 — Ruth Riley, May 31,2003-August 25, 2005
- 83 — Barbara Farris, July 28, 2001-June 12, 2004

Most games, season
- 34 — By Many

MINUTES

Most minutes, career
- 4,654 — Deanna Nolan
- 3,739 — Swin Cash
- 3,065 — Astou Ndiaye-Diatta

Highest average, minutes per game, career
(Minimum 100 games)
- 31.7 — Swin Cash (3739/118)
- 29.5 — Deanna Nolan (4654/158)
- 28.6 — Ruth Riley (2887/101)

Most minutes, season
- 1,213 — Deanna Nolan, 2005
- 1,138 — Deanna Nolan, 2004
- 1,105 — Swin Cash, 2004

Highest average, minutes per game, season
- 36.7 — Deanna Nolan, 2005 (1213/33)
- 34.5 — Swin Cash, 2004 (1105/32)
- 33.8 — Korie Hlede, 1998 (912/27)

Most minutes, game
- 47 — Deanna Nolan, at Charlotte, Aug. 6, 2005 (2OT)
- 46 — Sandy Brondello, at Utah, July 6, 1999 (2OT)
- 45 — Deanna Nolan, vs New York, June 3, 2005 (OT)
  Swin Cash, at Connecticut, June 25, 2004
  Deanna Nolan, vs New York,
  September 14, 2004 (OT)

SCORING

Most points, lifetime
- 1,853 — Deanna Nolan
- 1,667 — Swin Cash
- 1,181 — Astou Ndiaye-Diatta

Highest average, points per game, career
(Minimum 100 games)
- 14.1 — Swin Cash (1667/118)
- 11.7 — Deanna Nolan (1853/158)
- 9.5 — Ruth Riley (956/101)

Most points, season
- 548 — Swin Cash, 2003
- 526 — Swin Cash, 2004

- 524 — Deanna Nolan, 2005

Highest average, points per game, season
- 16.6 — Swin Cash, 2003 (548/33)
- 16.4 — Swin Cash, 2004 (526/32)
- 15.8 — Deanna Nolan, 2005 (524/33)

Most points, game
- 34 — Deanna Nolan, vs New York, June 3, 2005 (OT)
- 33 — Sandy Brondello, at Utah, July 6, 1999 (2OT)
- 32 — Deanna Nolan, at Indiana, June 15, 2005 (OT)
  Wendy Palmer-Daniel, at Seattle, June 28,2000

Most games, 30 or more points, career
- 2 — Deanna Nolan
- 1 — Sandy Brondello
  Wendy Palmer-Daniel

Most games, 20 or more points, career
- 23 — Swin Cash
- 21 — Deanna Nolan
- 11 — Sandy Brondello

Most consecutive games, 20 or more points
- 3 — Deanna Nolan, August 2-7, 2005
  Swin Cash, June 12-22, 2004
- 2 — By Many

Most consecutive games, 10 or more points
- 24 — Sandy Brondello, July 31, 1998-July 16, 1999
- 20 — Swin Cash, July 8-August 23, 2003
- 15 — Swin Cash, May 29-July 10,2004

FIELD GOAL PERCENTAGE

Highest field goal percentage, career
(Minimum 400 field goals)
- .462 — Astou Ndiaye-Diatta (520/1125)
- .439 — Swin Cash (567/1293)
- .396 — Deanna Nolan (653/1651)

Highest field goal percentage, season (qualifiers)
- .520 — Razija Mujanovic 1998 (106/204)
- .514 — Jennifer Azzi 1999 (93/181)
- .506 — Elena Tornikidou, 2000 (122/241)

Highest field goal percentage, game
(Minimum 8 field goals made)
- .846 — Elena Tornikidou, at Charlotte,
  June 25, 2000 (11/13)
- .818 — Ruth Riley, vs Indiana, June 12, 2004 (9/11)
  Lynette Woodard, vs New York,
  Aug. 19, 1998 (9/11)
  Wendy Palmer-Daniel, vs Indiana,
  June 18, 2000 (9/11)
  Astou Ndiaye-Diatta, at Washington,
  Aug. 4, 2000 (9/11)

Most field goals, none missed, game
- 5 — Cheryl Ford, vs Connecticut, July 8, 2003
  Jennifer Azzi, at Minnesota, June 12, 1999
  Elaine Powell, vs San Antonio, May 24, 2005
  Elaine Powell, at Connecticut, August 5, 2003
- 4 — Carla Boyd, at Phoenix, July 26, 2001
  Plenette Pierson, vs Phoenix, July 31, 2005
  Dominique Canty, at Sacramento, July 1, 2000

Most field goal attempts, none made, game
10 — Dominique Canty, at Houston, July 27, 1999
9 — Astou Ndiaye-Diatta, vs Miami, July 14, 2000
    Dominique Canty, at Charlotte, August 20, 1999
8 — By Many

FIELD GOALS

Most field goals, career
653 — Deanna Nolan
567 — Swin Cash
520 — Astou Ndiaye-Diatta
Most field goals, season
195 — Swin Cash, 2003
184 — Deanna Nolan, 2005
180 — Swin Cash, 2004
Most field goals, game
14 — Wendy Palmer-Daniel, at Seattle, June 28, 2000
13 — Sandy Brondello, at Utah, July 6, 1999 (2OT)
11 — Swin Cash, at Cleveland, July 29, 2003
    Deanna Nolan, at Indiana, June 15, 2005 (OT)
    Astou Ndiaye-Diatta, vs Houston, June 2, 2001
    Elena Tornikidou, at Charlotte, June 25, 2000
    Astou Ndiaye-Diatta, at Seattle,
    July 24, 2001 (OT)

FIELD GOAL ATTEMPTS

Most field goal attempts, career
1,651 — Deanna Nolan
1,293 — Swin Cash
1,125 — Astou Ndiaye-Diatta
Most field goal attempts, season
462 — Deanna Nolan, 2005
435 — Deanna Nolan, 2004
430 — Swin Cash, 2003
Most field goal attempts, game
28 — Sandy Brondello, at Utah, July 6, 1999 (2OT)
23 — Astou Ndiaye-Diatta, vs Utah, August 7, 2001
22 — Dominique Canty, vs Washington,
    July 10, 1999 (2OT)

THREE-POINT FIELD GOAL PERCENTAGE

Highest three-point field goal percentage, career
(Minimum 100 three-point field goals)
.341 — Deanna Nolan (172/505)
Highest three-point field goal percentage, season
(qualifiers)
.517 — Jennifer Azzi, 1999 (30/58)
.487 — Sandy Brondello, 1999 (37/76)
.449 — Elena Tornikidou, 2001 (22/49)
Most three-point field goals, none missed, game
4 — Deanna Nolan, at Houston, August 2, 2005
    Katie Smith, vs Charlotte, August 9, 2005
    Jennifer Azzi, vs Orlando, August 21, 1999
3 — Many Times
Most three-point field goal attempts, none made, game
6 — Tamicha Jackson, vs Charlotte, June 12, 2000
    Kedra Holland-Corn, at Sacramento,
    Aug. 15, 2003
5 — Swin Cash, at Cleveland, June 6, 2002
    Korie Hlede, vs Houston, August 7, 1998

Katie Smith, vs New York, August 7, 2005
Claudia Neves, at Minnesota, June 12, 1999
Claudia Neves, at Washington, August 4, 2000

THREE-POINT FIELD GOALS

Most three-point field goals, career
172 — Deanna Nolan
61 — Claudia Neves
53 — Sandy Brondello
Most three-point field goals, season
50 — Kedra Holland-Corn, 2003
48 — Deanna Nolan, 2003
42 — Deanna Nolan, 2002
Most three-point field goals, game
7 — Deanna Nolan, vs New York, Aug. 10, 2003 (OT)
6 — Sandy Brondello, at Utah, July 6, 1999 (2OT)
5 — Jae Cross, vs Phoenix, June 29, 2001
    Deanna Nolan, at Indiana, June 1, 2002
    Claudia Neves, at Orlando, July 19, 2000
    Kedra Holland-Corn, at Washington, Aug. 6, 2003
Most consecutive games, three-point field goals made
10 — Deanna Nolan, May 31-June 28, 2003
8 — Katie Smith, August 9-25, 2005
    Deanna Nolan, July 15-30, 2004

THREE-POINT FIELD GOAL ATTEMPTS

Most three-point field goal attempts, career
505 — Deanna Nolan
204 — Claudia Neves
157 — Wendy Palmer-Daniel
Most three-point field goal attempts, season
124 — Kedra Holland-Corn, 2003
114 — Deanna Nolan, 2002
    Deanna Nolan, 2003
    Deanna Nolan, 2004
Most three-point field goal attempts, game
10 — Anna DeForge, vs Cleveland, July 31, 2000
    Deanna Nolan, at Indiana, June 1, 2002
    Deanna Nolan, vs New York, Aug. 10, 2003 (OT)
9 — Many Times

FREE THROW PERCENTAGE

Highest free throw percentage, career
.886 — Sandy Brondello (179/202)
.800 — Deanna Nolan (375/469)
.788 — Ruth Riley (216/274)
Highest free throw percentage, season (qualifiers)
.923 — Sandy Brondello, 1998 (96/104)
.914 — Elena Tornikidou, 2000 (85/93)
.887 — Elena Tornikidou, 2001 (63/71)
Most free throws made, none missed, game
11 — Wendy Palmer, at New York, August 15, 1999
10 — Wendy Palmer, at Orlando, August 18, 1999
    Wendy Palmer, vs Charlotte, July 29, 2000
9 — By Many
Most free throw attempts, none made, game
8 — Cheryl Ford, at Charlotte, August 6, 2005 (2OT)

6 — Swin Cash, at San Antonio, June 7, 2003
 Cheryl Ford, at Seattle, September 8, 2004
5 — Cheryl Ford, vs Sacramento, July 1, 2005

FREE THROWS MADE

Most free throws made, career
 498 — Swin Cash
 375 — Deanna Nolan
 296 — Dominique Canty
Most free throws made, season
 173 — Swin Cash, 2002
 158 — Swin Cash, 2004
 146 — Swin Cash, 2003
Most free throws made, game
 15 — Swin Cash, vs Miami, June 28, 2002 (OT)
 13 — Deanna Nolan, vs New York, June 3, 2005 (OT)
 Swin Cash, at Utah, July 8, 2002
 12 — Swin Cash, at New York, July 24, 2004
 Plenette Pierson, at Washington, Aug. 27,2005

FREE THROW ATTEMPTS

Most free throw attempts, career
 692 — Swin Cash
 469 — Deanna Nolan
 437 — Cheryl Ford
Most free throw attempts, season
 227 — Swin Cash, 2002
 219 — Swin Cash, 2004
 214 — Swin Cash, 2003
Most free throw attempts, game
 21 — Swin Cash, vs Miami, June 28, 2002
 19 — Plenette Pierson, at Washington, Aug. 27, 2005
 16 — Swin Cash, at New York, July 24, 2004
 Deanna Nolan, vs New York, June 3, 2005 (OT)

REBOUNDS

Most rebounds, career
 953 — Cheryl Ford
 711 — Swin Cash
 633 — Astou Ndiaye-Diatta
Highest average, rebounds per game, career
(Minimum 100 games)
 6.0 — Swin Cash (711/118)
 5.5 — Ruth Riley (556/101)
 4.6 — Astou Ndiaye-Diatta (633/138)
Most rebounds, season
 334 — Cheryl Ford, 2003
 322 — Cheryl Ford, 2005
 301 — Cindy Brown, 1998
Highest average, rebounds per game, season (qualifiers)
 10.4 — Cheryl Ford, 2003 (334/32)
 10.0 — Cindy Brown, 1998 (301/30)
 9.8 — Cheryl Ford, 2005 (322/33)
Most rebounds, game
 22 — Cheryl Ford, at San Antonio, May 22, 2004
 21 — Cheryl Ford, at Connecticut, June 22, 2003 (OT)
 Cindy Brown, at Utah, August 10, 1998
 18 — Cheryl Ford, at New York, May 22, 2005
 Cheryl Ford, at Washington, July 7, 2005

Most games, 10+ rebounds, career
 56 — Cheryl Ford
 21 — Cindy Brown
 17 — Wendy Palmer-Daniel
Most consecutive games, 10+ rebounds
 6 — Cheryl Ford, May 22-June 12, 2005
 Cindy Brown, July 31-August 11, 1998
 5 — Cheryl Ford, May 22-June 6, 2004
 Cheryl Ford, July 10-22, 2003
 Wendy Palmer, August 9-18, 1999

OFFENSIVE REBOUNDS

Most offensive rebounds, career
 316 — Cheryl Ford
 262 — Swin Cash
 199 — Astou Ndiaye-Diatta
Highest average, offensive rebounds per game, career
(Minimum 100 games)
 2.2 — Swin Cash (262/118)
 1.7 — Ruth Riley (170/101)
 1.4 — Astou Ndiaye-Diatta (199/138)
Most offensive rebounds, season
 113 — Cheryl Ford, 2005
 104 — Cheryl Ford, 2004
 99 — Cheryl Ford, 2003
Most offensive rebounds, game
 12 — Cheryl Ford, at San Antonio, May 22, 2004
 7 — Many Times

DEFENSIVE REBOUNDS

Most defensive rebounds, career
 637 — Cheryl Ford
 449 — Swin Cash
 434 — Astou Ndiaye-Diatta
Highest average, defensive rebounds per game, career
(Minimum 100 games)
 3.82 — Ruth Riley (386/101)
 3.81 — Swin Cash (449/118)
 3.2 — Astou Ndiaye-Diatta (434/138)
Most defensive rebounds, season
 235 — Cheryl Ford, 2003
 231 — Cindy Brown, 1998
 209 — Cheryl Ford, 2005
Most defensive rebounds, game
 18 — Cindy Brown, at Utah, August 10, 1998
 17 — Cheryl Ford, at Connecticut, June 22, 2003 (OT)
 14 — Cheryl Ford, vs Los Angeles, June 17, 2003 (OT)

ASSISTS

Most assists, career
 408 — Deanna Nolan
 400 — Elaine Powell
 383 — Swin Cash
Highest average, assists per game, career
(Minimum 100 games)
 3.7 — Elaine Powell (400/107)
 3.3 — Swin Cash (383/118)
 2.6 — Deanna Nolan (408/158)

Most assists, season
135 — Swin Cash, 2004
134 — Elaine Powell, 2004
129 — Elaine Powell, 2003
Highest average, assists per game, season (qualifiers)
4.5 — Elaine Powell, 2004 (134/30)
4.2 — Swin Cash, 2004 (135/32)
3.9 — Elaine Powell, 2003 (129/33)
Most assists, game
11 — Deanna Nolan, vs Connecticut, May 21, 2005
10 — Deanna Nolan, vs San Antonio, May 24, 2005
Elaine Powell, vs Connecticut, June 27, 2004
9 — Many Times
Most games, 10+ assists, career
2 — Deanna Nolan
1 — Elaine Powell

PERSONAL FOULS

Most personal fouls, career
380 — Ruth Riley
370 — Cheryl Ford
323 — Barbara Farris
Most personal fouls, season
143 — Cheryl Ford, 2005
131 — Ruth Riley, 2005
128 — Ruth Riley, 2003
Most personal fouls, game
6 — By Many

STEALS

Most steals, career
206 — Deanna Nolan
136 — Swin Cash
133 — Elaine Powell
Highest average, steals per game, career
(Minimum 100 games)
1.3 — Deanna Nolan (206/158)
1.24 — Elaine Powell (133/107)
1.20 — Swin Cash (136/118)
Most steals, season
66 — Deanna Nolan, 2004
55 — Deanna Nolan, 2005
51 — Cindy Brown, 1998
Highest average, steals per game, season (qualifiers)
1.9 — Deanna Nolan, 2004 (66/34)
1.8 — Dominique Canty, 2000 (49/28)
1.7 — Cindy Brown, 1998 (51/30)
Most steals, game
6 — Swin Cash, vs Houston, July 6, 2004
Deanna Nolan, at Indiana, June 9, 2004
Claudia Neves, vs Washington, June 24, 2000
5 — Many Times

BLOCKED SHOTS

Most blocked shots, career
157 — Ruth Riley
102 — Cheryl Ford
89 — Swin Cash
Highest average, blocked shots per game, career
(Minimum: 100 games)
1.6 — Ruth Riley (157/101)
.8 — Swin Cash (89/118)
.6 — Astou Ndiaye-Diatta (81/138)

Most blocked shots, season
58 — Ruth Riley, 2003
53 — Ruth Riley, 2004
46 — Ruth Riley, 2005
Cheryl Ford, 2005
Highest average, blocked shots per game, season
(qualifiers)
1.7 — Ruth Riley, 2003 (58/34)
1.6 — Ruth Riley, 2004 (53/34)
1.4 — Ruth Riley, 2005 (46/33)
Most blocked shots, game
5 — Ruth Riley, vs Seattle, July 10, 2004
Ayana Walker, vs Connecticut, July 8, 2003
4 — By Many

TURNOVERS

Most turnovers, career
355 — Deanna Nolan
336 — Swin Cash
236 — Astou Ndiaye-Diatta
Most turnovers, season
108 — Swin Cash, 2003
100 — Swin Cash, 2002
Deanna Nolan, 2005
90 — Deanna Nolan, 2004
Most turnovers, game
9 — Swin Cash, at New York, May 26, 2004
8 — Swin Cash, vs Indiana, June 24, 2003
Cheryl Ford, at Indiana, July 6, 2003
7 — By Many

HOUSTON COMETS

REGULAR SEASON TEAM RECORDS

TEAM OFFENSE

SCORING

Highest average, points per game, season
77.3 — 2000 (2475/32)
76.2 — 1998 (2285/30)
Lowest average, points per game, season
64.0 — 2004 (2177/34)
2001 (2047/32)
Most points, game
110 — at Washington, August 17, 1998
107 — vs Utah, June 12, 2000
Fewest points, game
38 — at Phoenix, August 14, 2001
45 — at Sacramento, August 7, 2005
Largest margin of victory, game
45 — at Washington, August 17, 1998 (110-65)
40 — vs Portland, June 30, 2000 (79-39)
Largest margin of defeat, game
25 — at Los Angeles, July 16, 1997 (52-77)
20 — vs Connecticut, June 10, 2005 (57-77)
at Sacramento, September 18, 2004 (48-68)

BY HALF

Most points, first half
54 — vs Indiana, July 6, 2001
53 — vs Utah, June 17, 1999
vs Sacramento, July 12, 1997
Fewest points, first half
16 — at Sacramento, August 7, 2005
at Miami, June 18, 2002
17 — at Miami, July 20, 2001
at Phoenix, August 14, 2001
Largest lead at half time
31 — vs Miami, June 15, 2000 (led 44-13)
28 — vs Indiana, July 6, 2001 (led 54-26)
Largest deficit at halftime overcome to win game
14 — vs Seattle, July 9, 2002 (trailed 27-41; won 67-59)
13 — at Detroit, August 7, 1998 (trailed 20-33; won 61-57)
Most points, second half
60 — at Washington, August 17, 1998
55 — vs Utah, June 12, 2000
Fewest points, second half
20 — at Connecticut, June 7, 2003
vs Detroit, August 2, 2005
at Phoenix, July 19, 1999
at Utah, June 30, 1998

OVERTIME

Most points, overtime period
19 — vs Indiana, May 29, 2005
14 — at Utah, July 16, 1999

Fewest points, overtime period
0 — at Minnesota, June 30, 2004
3 — vs Cleveland, August 1, 1998
at Minnesota, June 1, 2003
Largest margin of victory, overtime period
8 — vs Indiana, May 29, 2005 (86-78) (2OT)
5 — vs Los Angeles, June 30, 1997 (71-66)

FIELD GOAL PERCENTAGE

Highest field goal percentage, season
.470 — 2000 (891/1894)
.448 — 2005 (860/1920)
Lowest field goal percentage, season
.392 — 2001 (747/1908)
.413 — 2004 (798/1933)
Highest field goal percentage, game
.654 — at Washington, July 26, 2005 (34/52)
.609 — at Phoenix, August 7, 2000 (28/46)
Lowest field goal percentage, game
.236 — at Phoenix, August 14, 2001 (13/55)
.254 — at Charlotte, August 4, 2001 (15/59)

FIELD GOALS

Most field goals per game, season
27.8 — 2000 (891/32)
26.5 — 1998 (795/30)
Fewest field goals per game, season
23.3 — 2001 (747/32)
23.5 — 2004 (798/34)
Most field goals, game
41 — at Washington, August 17, 1998
36 — vs Portland, July 30, 2002
vs Washington, July 13, 1998
Fewest field goals, game
13 — at Phoenix, August 14, 2001
15 — at Charlotte, August 4, 2001

FIELD GOAL ATTEMPTS

Most field goal attempts per game, season
60.8 — 1998 (1824/30)
59.8 — 1999 (1912/32)
Fewest field goal attempts per game, season
55.6 — 2002 (1778/32)
56.4 — 2003 (1916/34)
Most field goal attempts, game
82 — at Portland, May 31, 2000 (2OT)
79 — vs Washington, June 12, 1999
Fewest field goal attempts, game
43 — vs Sacramento, May 30, 2004
44 — at Phoenix, June 1, 2004

THREE-POINT FIELD GOAL PERCENTAGE

Highest three-point field goal percentage, season
.350 — 2000 (172/491)

.348 — 1997 (169/485)
Lowest three-point field goal percentage, season
  .302 — 2005 (62/205)
  .317 — 2001 (138/435)

THREE-POINT FIELD GOALS

Most three-point field goals per game, season
  6.0 — 1997 (169/28)
  5.9 — 1998 (177/30)
Fewest three-point field goals per game, season
  1.8 — 2005 (62/34)
  3.4 — 2003 (115/34)
Most three-point field goals, game
    12 — at Sacramento, July 25, 1997
        at Phoenix, July 22, 1997
    11 — vs Los Angeles, August 12, 1999
        at Charlotte, July 25, 1998
        at Cleveland, July 6, 1998
Fewest three-point field goals, game
    0 — Many Times

THREE-POINT FIELD GOAL ATTEMPTS

Most three-point field goal attempts per game, season
  17.4 — 1998 (523/30)
  17.3 — 1997 (485/28)
Fewest three-point field goal attempts per game, season
  6.0 — 2005 (205/34)
  10.1 — 2003 (344/34)
Most three-point field goal attempts, game
    30 — at Utah, June 30, 1998 (2OT)
    28 — at Sacramento, July 8, 1999
Fewest three-point field goal attempts, game
    1 — vs Phoenix, June 4, 2005
    2 — at Charlotte, July 17, 2005
        vs San Antonio, June 25, 2005

FREE THROW PERCENTAGE

Highest free throw percentage, season
  .822 — 2000 (521/634)
  .818 — 1999 (509/622)
Lowest free throw percentage, season
  .745 — 1997 (441/592)
  .745 — 2004 (458/615)
  .764 — 2005 (527/690)
Highest free throw percentage, game
  1.000 — vs Detroit, August 2, 2005 (10/10)
        at Phoenix, June 10, 2001 (12/12)
        at Minnesota, July 9, 2000 (15/15)
        at Portland, August 4, 2000 (11/11)
        vs Phoenix, July 31, 1999 (11/11)
  .955 — at Phoenix, July 22, 1997 (21/22)
Lowest free throw percentage, game
  .417 — at Sacramento, June 25, 2004 (5/12)
  .455 — at Washington, June 13, 2002 (5/11)

FREE THROWS MADE

Most free throws made per game, season
  17.3 — 1998 (518/30)
  16.3 — 2000 (521/32)
Fewest free throws made per game, season
  13.0 — 2001 (415/32)

13.5 — 2004 (458/34)
Most free throws made, game
    33 — vs Sacramento, July 3, 1998
    31 — vs Utah, June 12, 2000
Fewest free throws made, game
    5 — Many Times

FREE THROW ATTEMPTS

Most free throw attempts per game, season
  21.5 — 1998 (646/30)
  21.1 — 1997 (592/28)
Fewest free throw attempts per game, season
  16.8 — 2001 (539/32)
  17.7 — 2003 (600/34)
Most free throw attempts, game
    39 — vs Utah, June 12, 2000
    37 — at Los Angeles, June 20, 2000
Fewest free throw attempts, game
    7 — vs San Antonio, May 20, 2004
        vs Washington, July 13, 1998
    8 — at Charlotte, June 6, 2003
        at Phoenix, July 11, 2002

REBOUNDS

Most rebounds per game, season
  33.1 — 2001 (1058/32)
  31.3 — 2002 (1001/32)
Fewest rebounds per game, season
  28.2 — 2005 (960/34)
  30.3 — 2003 (1030/34)
Most rebounds, game
    51 — vs Orlando, August 3, 2001
        at Utah, June 30, 1998 (2OT)
    47 — at Minnesota, July 23, 2001
        at Sacramento, July 10, 2001 (OT)
Fewest rebounds, game
    17 — vs Phoenix, June 4, 2005
    18 — at Los Angeles, June 15, 2005

OFFENSIVE REBOUNDS

Most offensive rebounds per game, season
  11.3 — 1997 (316/28)
  10.9 — 2001 (348/32)
Fewest offensive rebounds per game, season
  7.8 — 2003 (266/34)
  8.1 — 2005 (276/34)
Most offensive rebounds, game
    22 — vs Orlando, August 3, 2001
    19 — at Minnesota, July 23, 2001
Fewest offensive rebounds, game
    1 — at Phoenix, August 7, 2000
        at New York, August 8, 1999
    2 — vs Sacramento, May 30, 2004
        vs Indiana, July 8, 2003

DEFENSIVE REBOUNDS

Most defensive rebounds per game, season
  22.6 — 2000 (724/32)
  22.5 — 2003 (764/34)

Fewest defensive rebounds per game, season
    19.4 — 1997 (543/28)
    20.1 — 2005 (684/34)
Most defensive rebounds, game
    34 — at Phoenix, August 25, 2005
    33 — at Utah, June 30, 1998 (2OT)
Fewest defensive rebounds, game
    6 — at Los Angeles, June 15, 2005
    11 — vs Phoenix, June 4, 2005
        at Charlotte, August 16, 1997

ASSISTS

Most assists per game, season
    15.6 — 1999 (499/32)
    15.4 — 2000 (494/32)
Fewest assists per game, season
    13.3 — 2001 (426/32)
        2004 (451/34)
Most assists, game
    26 — at Washington, August 17, 1998
    24 — vs Charlotte, August 6, 1999
Fewest assists, game
    4 — at Phoenix, June 24, 1998
    5 — vs Seattle, August 19, 2003
        at New York, August 15, 1998

PERSONAL FOULS

Most personal fouls per game, season
    19.1 — 1997 (535/28)
    18.3 — 1999 (586/32)
Fewest personal fouls per game, season
    14.4 — 2003 (490/34)
    14.6 — 2002 (467/32)
Most personal fouls, game
    32 — at Los Angeles, June 20, 2000
    27 — Many Times
Fewest personal fouls, game
    7 — vs Seattle, May 22, 2003
        vs Minnesota, June 15, 2002
    8 — vs San Antonio, June 28, 2003
        at Orlando, July 18, 2001
        vs Sacramento, July 12, 2000

DISQUALIFICATIONS

Most disqualifications per game, season
    .15 — 2005 (5/34)
    .13 — 1999 (4/32)
Fewest disqualifications per game, season
    .03 — 2002 (1/32)
    .04 — 1997 (1/28)
Most disqualifications, game
    1 — Many Times

STEALS

Most steals per game, season
    11.11 — 1997 (311/28)
    11.07 — 1998 (332/30)
Fewest steals per game, season
    6.8 — 2003 (231/34)
    7.1 — 2004 (242/34)
Most steals, game
    21 — vs Washington, June 29, 1998
    19 — vs Detroit, July 15, 2004

        vs Minnesota, August 9, 2000
Fewest steals, game
    1 — vs Orlando, August 3, 2002
    2 — vs Washington, July 21, 2005
        vs Indiana, July 31, 2004
        vs Charlotte, July 3, 2004
        vs Orlando, August 3, 2001

BLOCKED SHOTS

Most blocked shots per game, season
    4.3 — 1999 (139/32)
    3.9 — 2002 (126/32)
Fewest blocked shots per game, season
    2.4 — 1997 (67/28)
    2.7 — 1998 (81/30)
Most blocked shots, game
    11 — at Utah, July 3, 2002
    10 — at San Antonio, June 20, 2003
        at Utah, June 5, 2001
Fewest blocked shots, game
    0 — Many Times

TURNOVERS

Most turnovers per game, season
    17.6 — 1997 (492/28)
    14.5 — 1998 (435/30)
Fewest turnovers per game, season
    12.5 — 2005 (425/34)
    13.2 — 2003 (450/34)
Most turnovers, game
    28 — vs New York, June 26, 1997 (OT)
    26 — vs New York, June 13, 1998
Fewest turnovers, game
    5 — vs Washington, June 27, 2001
    6 — vs Minnesota, May 22, 2005
        vs Minnesota, July 1, 2003
        at Los Angeles, August 11, 2001

TEAM DEFENSE

POINTS

Fewest points allowed per game, season
    59.1 — 2002 (1892/32)
    62.3 — 2001 (1994/32)
Most points allowed per game, season
    66.6 — 2005 (2263/34)
    65.5 — 1997 (1833/28)
Fewest points allowed, game
    39 — vs Portland, June 30, 2000
    40 — vs Detroit, July 6, 2002
Fewest points allowed, first half
    8 — vs Detroit, July 6, 2002
    11 — at Minnesota, June 30, 2001
Fewest points allowed, second half
    17 — vs Portland, June 30, 2000
        at Utah, June 30, 1998
    18 — vs Connecticut, July 17, 2004
        vs Sacramento, August 5, 2003
        vs Seattle, July 9, 2002

Fewest points allowed, overtime period
4 — vs Indiana, May 29, 2005
        at Cleveland, June 1, 2002
        vs Los Angeles, June 30, 1997
6 — Many Times

FIELD GOAL PERCENTAGE

Lowest opponents' field goal percentage, season
.375 — 2002 (705/1880)
.390 — 1999 (763/1954)
Highest opponents' field goal percentage, season
.436 — 2005 (848/1944)
.417 — 1997 (679/1630)
Lowest opponents' field goal percentage, game
.200 — at Minnesota, July 23, 2001 (11/55)
.217 — at Indiana, June 5, 2002 (13/60)

TURNOVERS

Fewest opponents' turnovers per game, season
12.7 — 2003 (430/34)
13.5 — 2001 (433/32)
Most opponents' turnovers per game, season
19.2 — 1997 (537/28)
18.7 — 1998 (560/30)
Most opponents' turnovers, game
33 — vs Washington, June 29, 1998
28 — vs Phoenix, June 4, 2005
        vs New York, June 26, 1997 (OT)

TEAM MISCELLANEOUS

GAME WON AND LOST

Highest winning percentage, season
.900 — 1998 (27-3)
.844 — 2000 (27-5)
Lowest winning percentage, season
.382 — 2004 (13-21)
.559 — 2005 (19-15)
Most consecutive games won
15 — June 27-July 30, 1998
10 — June 15-July 9, 2002
        June 23-July 12, 2000
Most consecutive games won, one season
15 — June 27-July 30, 1998
10 — June 15-July 9, 2002
        June 23-July 12, 2000
Most consecutive games lost
5 — June 30-July 14, 2004
4 — June 7-15, 2005
        August 21, 2003-May 20, 2004
        September 1-12, 2004
Most consecutive games lost, one season
5 — June 30-July 14, 2004
4 — June 7-June 15, 2005
        September 1-12, 2004

Highest winning percentage, home games, season
.938 — 1999 (15-1)
.933 — 1998 (14-1)
Lowest winning percentage, home games, season
.529 — 2004 (9-8)
.643 — 1997 (9-5)
Most consecutive home games won
13 — May 29-August 6, 2002
        July 1-May 29, 2000
11 — June 6-July 25, 2000
Most consecutive home games lost
3 — July 21-30, 2005
        July 8-28, 2001
2 — June 7-10, 2005
        July 3-10, 2004
        September 1-3, 2004
        August 21-24, 1997
Highest winning percentage, road games, season
.867 — 1998 (13-2)
.813 — 2000 (13-3)
Lowest winning percentage, road games, season
.235 — 2004 (4-13)
.353 — 2003 (6-11)
Most consecutive road games won
9 — June 30-August 7, 1998
7 — August 4, 2000-June 10, 2001
Most consecutive road games lost
10 — June 25-September 19, 2004
5 — August 5-21, 2005

OVERTIME GAMES

Most overtime games, season
2 — 1997, 1998, 2000, 2004, 2005
Most consecutive overtime games, season
1 — Many Times
Most overtime games won, season
2 — 2000
Most overtime games won, no losses, season
2 — 2000
Most overtime games lost, season
1 — 1997, 1998, 2001, 2003, 2004, 2005
Most overtime games lost, no wins, season
1 — 2001, 2003
Most overtime periods, game
2 — vs Indiana, May 29, 2005
        at Sacramento, July 10, 2001
        at Portland, May 31, 2000
        at Utah, June 30, 1998

INDIVIDUAL RECORDS

SEASONS

Most seasons
9 — Tina Thompson
8 — Janeth Arcain
        Sheryl Swoopes

GAMES

Most games, career
- 254 — Janeth Arcain
- 247 — Tina Thompson
- 228 — Sheryl Swoopes

Most consecutive games, career
- 220 — Janeth Arcain, June 21, 1997-August 25, 2003
- 88 — Cynthia Cooper, June 21, 1997-August 18, 1999
- 87 — Tina Thompson, August 10, 1998-July 18, 2001

Most games, season
- 34 — By Many

MINUTES

Most minutes, career
- 8,430 — Tina Thompson
- 7,789 — Sheryl Swoopes
- 7,638 — Janeth Arcain

Highest average, minutes per game, career
(Minimum 100 games)
- 35.2 — Cynthia Cooper (4363/124)
- 34.2 — Sheryl Swoopes (7789/228)
- 34.1 — Tina Thompson (8430/247)

Most minutes, season
- 1,225 — Sheryl Swoopes, 2005
- 1,154 — Janeth Arcain, 2001
  - Sheryl Swoopes, 2002

Highest average, minutes per game, season
- 37.1 — Sheryl Swoopes, 2005 (1225/33)
- 36.7 — Tina Thompson, 2001 (1102/30)
- 36.3 — Tina Thompson, 2002 (1052/29)

Most minutes, game
- 50 — Tina Thompson, at Utah, June 30, 1998 (2OT)
- 48 — Michelle Snow, vs Indiana, May 29, 2005 (2OT)
  - Sheryl Swoopes, vs Indiana, May 29, 2005 (2OT)
  - Cynthia Cooper, at Portland, May 31, 2000(2OT)
  - Sheryl Swoopes, at Portland, May 31, 2000(2OT)

SCORING

Most points, lifetime
- 3,894 — Sheryl Swoopes
- 3,851 — Tina Thompson
- 2,652 — Janeth Arcain

Highest average, points per game, career
(Minimum 100 games)
- 21.0 — Cynthia Cooper (2601/124)
- 17.1 — Sheryl Swoopes (3894/228)
- 15.6 — Tina Thompson (3851/247)

Most points, season
- 686 — Cynthia Cooper, 1999
- 680 — Cynthia Cooper, 1998
- 643 — Sheryl Swoopes, 2000

Highest average, points per game, season
- 22.7 — Cynthia Cooper, 1998 (680/30)
- 22.2 — Cynthia Cooper, 1997 (621/28)
- 22.1 — Cynthia Cooper, 1999 (686/31)

Most points, game
- 44 — Cynthia Cooper, at Sacramento, July 25, 1997
- 42 — Cynthia Cooper, vs Utah, August 16, 1999
- 39 — Cynthia Cooper, at Charlotte, August 11, 1997

Most games, 30 or more points, career
- 16 — Cynthia Cooper
- 8 — Sheryl Swoopes
- 5 — Tina Thompson

Most games, 20 or more points, career
- 84 — Sheryl Swoopes
- 72 — Cynthia Cooper
- 53 — Tina Thompson

Most consecutive games, 20 or more points
- 11 — Cynthia Cooper, August 17, 1998-June 30, 1999
- 8 — Sheryl Swoopes, May 29-June 12, 2000
- 6 — By Many

Most consecutive games, 10 or more points
- 92 — Cynthia Cooper, June 21, 1997-June 1, 2000
- 44 — Tina Thompson, July 6, 2000-August 13, 2001
- 39 — Tina Thompson, June 21, 2002-August 7, 2003

FIELD GOAL PERCENTAGE

Highest field goal percentage, career
(Minimum 400 field goals)
- .500 — Michelle Snow (427/854)
- .459 — Cynthia Cooper (802/1749)
- .445 — Sheryl Swoopes (1463/3289)

Highest field goal percentage, season (qualifiers)
- .551 — Michelle Snow, 2005 (152/276)
- .506 — Sheryl Swoopes, 2000 (245/484)
- .498 — Michelle Snow, 2003 (126/253)

Highest field goal percentage, game
(Minimum 8 field goals made)
- 1.000 — Michelle Snow, vs Indiana, May 29, 2005 (9/9)
- .917 — Sheryl Swoopes, at Portland, August 4, 2000(11/12)
- .800 — Michelle Snow, at Detroit, August 8, 2003 (8/10)

Most field goals, none missed, game
- 9 — Michelle Snow, vs Indiana, May 29, 2005 (2OT)
- 4 — By Many

Most field goal attempts, none made, game
- 12 — Tina Thompson, at Phoenix, July 19, 1999
- 10 — Sheryl Swoopes, at Los Angeles, June 21,1998
- 8 — Tina Thompson, at Los Angeles, July 18, 1999

FIELD GOALS

Most field goals, career
- 1,463 — Sheryl Swoopes
- 1,380 — Tina Thompson
- 997 — Janeth Arcain

Most field goals, season
- 245 — Sheryl Swoopes, 2000
- 226 — Sheryl Swoopes, 1999
- 221 — Sheryl Swoopes, 2002

Most field goals, game
- 15 — Sheryl Swoopes, at Seattle, August 9, 2005
  - Cynthia Cooper, at Charlotte, August 11, 1997
- 14 — Sheryl Swoopes, vs Seattle, June 18, 2004
  - Cynthia Cooper, at Sacramento, July 25, 1997

FIELD GOAL ATTEMPTS

Most field goal attempts, career
- 3,313 — Tina Thompson
- 3,289 — Sheryl Swoopes
- 2,281 — Janeth Arcain

Most field goal attempts, season
- 528 — Tina Thompson, 2001
- 509 — Janeth Arcain, 2001
  - Sheryl Swoopes, 2002
- 489 — Sheryl Swoopes, 1999

Most field goal attempts, game
- 29 — Sheryl Swoopes, at Los Angeles, August 20,1999
- 28 — Cynthia Cooper, at Utah, June 30, 1998 (2OT)
- 27 — Tina Thompson, vs Portland, July 2, 2001
  - Sheryl Swoopes, at Portland, May 31, 2000 (2OT)

THREE-POINT FIELD GOAL PERCENTAGE

Highest three-point field goal percentage, career
(Minimum 100 three-point field goals)
- .377 — Cynthia Cooper (239/634)
- .359 — Tina Thompson (347/966)
- .333 — Sheryl Swoopes (201/604)

Highest three-point field goal percentage, season (qualifiers)
- .417 — Tina Thompson, 2000 (55/132)
- .414 — Cynthia Cooper, 1997 (67/162)
- .407 — Tina Thompson, 2004 (44/108)

Most three-point field goals, none missed, game
- 5 — Tina Thompson, at Phoenix, August 7, 2000
- 4 — Tina Thompson, vs Indiana, July 31, 2004
  - Sheryl Swoopes, vs Phoenix, June 21, 2002
  - Tina Thompson, vs Sacramento, May 30, 2004

Most three-point field goal attempts, none made, game
- 8 — Tina Thompson, at Utah, June 30, 1998 (2OT)
- 7 — Cynthia Cooper, vs Cleveland, July 1, 1999
  - Kim Perrot, at Charlotte, June 15, 1998
  - Cynthia Cooper, vs Sacramento, August 24, 1997

THREE-POINT FIELD GOALS

Most three-point field goals, career
- 347 — Tina Thompson
- 239 — Cynthia Cooper
- 201 — Sheryl Swoopes

Most three-point field goals, season
- 67 — Cynthia Cooper, 1997
- 64 — Cynthia Cooper, 1998
- 58 — Cynthia Cooper, 1999

Most three-point field goals, game
- 7 — Cynthia Cooper, at Sacramento, July 25, 1997
- 6 — By Many

Most consecutive games, three-point field goals made
- 21 — Cynthia Cooper, July 25, 1998-June 30, 1999
- 15 — Tina Thompson, June 6-August 1, 2003
  - Cynthia Cooper, July 2-August 7, 1997
- 11 — Cynthia Cooper, June 28-July 25, 2000
  - Tina Thompson, June 6-28, 2000

THREE-POINT FIELD GOAL ATTEMPTS

Most three-point field goal attempts, career
- 966 — Tina Thompson
- 634 — Cynthia Cooper
- 604 — Sheryl Swoopes

Most three-point field goal attempts, season
- 173 — Cynthia Cooper, 1999
- 162 — Cynthia Cooper, 1997
- 160 — Cynthia Cooper, 1998

Most three-point field goal attempts, game
- 13 — Cynthia Cooper, vs Cleveland, July 29, 1997
  - Cynthia Cooper, at Utah, August 4, 1998
- 11 — Cynthia Cooper, at Portland, May 31, 2000 (2OT)
- 10 — By Many

FREE THROW PERCENTAGE

Highest free throw percentage, career
- .871 — Cynthia Cooper (758/870)
- .867 — Janeth Arcain (580/669)
- .838 — Sheryl Swoopes (767/915)

Highest free throw percentage, season (qualifiers)
- .900 — Janeth Arcain, 2001 (135/150)
- .894 — Janeth Arcain, 1997 (76/85)
- .891 — Cynthia Cooper, 1999 (204/229)

Most free throws made, none missed, game
- 13 — Sheryl Swoopes, at Los Angeles, Aug. 8, 2002
  - Tina Thompson, at Minnesota, June 17, 2003
- 12 — Cynthia Cooper, at Los Angeles, July 17, 1998
  - Cynthia Cooper, at Minnesota, June 19, 1999
  - Sheryl Swoopes, at Sacramento, July 19, 2003

Most free throw attempts, none made, game
- 5 — Tammy Jackson, at Miami, July 20, 2001
- 4 — Kim Perrot, vs Phoenix, August 7, 1997
  - Tari Phillips, vs Sacramento, July 19, 2005
  - Sheryl Swoopes, at Washington, June 13, 2002
  - Dominique Canty, at Sacramento, June 25, 2004
- 3 — Michelle Snow, at Minnesota, June 19, 2004
  - Tina Thompson, at Los Angeles, July 17, 1998

FREE THROWS MADE

Most free throws made, career
- 767 — Sheryl Swoopes
- 758 — Cynthia Cooper
- 744 — Tina Thompson

Most free throws made, season
- 210 — Cynthia Cooper, 1998
- 204 — Cynthia Cooper, 1999
- 172 — Cynthia Cooper, 1997

Most free throws made, game
- 22 — Cynthia Cooper, vs Sacramento, July 3, 1998
- 17 — Cynthia Cooper, vs Utah, August 16, 1999
- 14 — Tina Thompson, vs Minnesota, August 9, 2000
  - Sheryl Swoopes, at Los Angeles, June 30, 2002

FREE THROW ATTEMPTS

Most free throw attempts, career
- 915 — Sheryl Swoopes

912 — Tina Thompson
870 — Cynthia Cooper
Most free throw attempts, season
246 — Cynthia Cooper, 1998
229 — Cynthia Cooper, 1999
199 — Cynthia Cooper, 1997
Most free throw attempts, game
24 — Cynthia Cooper, vs Sacramento, July 3, 1998
18 — Cynthia Cooper, vs Utah, August 16, 1999
16 — Tina Thompson, vs Minnesota, August 9, 2000
Cynthia Cooper, at Utah, June 30, 1998 (2OT)

REBOUNDS

Most rebounds, career
1656 — Tina Thompson
1134 — Sheryl Swoopes
919 — Janeth Arcain
Highest average, rebounds per game, career
(Minimum 100 games)
6.7 — Tina Thompson (1656/247)
6.5 — Michelle Snow (846/130)
5.0 — Sheryl Swoopes (1134/228)
Most rebounds, season
263 — Michelle Snow, 2003
245 — Tina Thompson, 2000
239 — Michelle Snow, 2004
Highest average, rebounds per game, season (qualifiers)
7.8 — Tina Thompson, 2001 (233/30)
7.7 — Michelle Snow, 2003 (263/34)
Michelle Snow, 2004 (239/31)
Most rebounds, game
16 — Michelle Snow, at Phoenix, May 24, 2003
15 — Sheryl Swoopes, vs Detroit, July 27, 1999
Michelle Snow, at Minnesota, June 30, 2004 (OT)
Tiffani Johnson, at Detroit, July 21, 2000 (OT)
14 — By Many
Most games, 10+ rebounds, career
44 — Tina Thompson
23 — Michelle Snow
15 — Sheryl Swoopes
Most consecutive games, 10+ rebounds
4 — Michelle Snow, July 29-August 5, 2003
Tina Thompson, June 2-10, 2001
3 — Michelle Snow, May 22-30, 2003
Tina Thompson, August 4-7, 2000

OFFENSIVE REBOUNDS

Most offensive rebounds, career
518 — Tina Thompson
287 — Janeth Arcain
260 — Sheryl Swoopes
Highest average, offensive rebounds per game, career
(Minimum 100 games)
2.1 — Tina Thompson (518/247)
1.8 — Michelle Snow (237/130)
1.5 — Tiffani Johnson (225/150)
Most offensive rebounds, season
84 — Tina Thompson, 2001
76 — Wanda Guyton, 1997

Michelle Snow, 2003
73 — Tiffani Johnson, 2002
Most offensive rebounds, game
9 — Tiffani Johnson, at Detroit, July 21, 2000 (OT)
8 — Tina Thompson, vs Orlando, August 3, 2001
7 — Many Times

DEFENSIVE REBOUNDS

Most defensive rebounds, career
1138 — Tina Thompson
874 — Sheryl Swoopes
632 — Janeth Arcain
Highest average, defensive rebounds per game, career
(Minimum 100 games)
4.7 — Michelle Snow (609/130)
4.6 — Tina Thompson (1138/247)
3.8 — Sheryl Swoopes (874/228)
Most defensive rebounds, season
187 — Michelle Snow, 2003
177 — Michelle Snow, 2004
Tina Thompson, 2000
157 — Michelle Snow, 2005
Most defensive rebounds, game
15 — Michelle Snow, at Minnesota, June 30, 2004 (OT)
12 — Tina Thompson, at Detroit, July 21, 2000 (OT)
Sheryl Swoopes, at Phoenix, August 25, 2005
11 — Michelle Snow, at Detroit, July 6, 2004
Michelle Snow, at Phoenix, May 24, 2003
Sheryl Swoopes, vs Detroit, July 27, 1999
Michelle Snow, vs Phoenix, September 3, 2004

ASSISTS

Most assists, career
775 — Sheryl Swoopes
602 — Cynthia Cooper
Highest average, assists per game, career
(Minimum 100 games)
4.9 — Cynthia Cooper (602/124)
3.4 — Sheryl Swoopes (775/228)
1.9 — Janeth Arcain (469/254)
Most assists, season
162 — Cynthia Cooper, 1999
156 — Cynthia Cooper, 2000
142 — Kim Perrot, 1998
Highest average, assists per game, season (qualifiers)
5.2 — Cynthia Cooper, 1999 (162/31)
5.0 — Cynthia Cooper, 2000 (156/31)
4.7 — Kim Perrot, 1998 (142/30)
Most assists, game
10 — Sheryl Swoopes, vs Phoenix, June 3, 2003
Sheryl Swoopes, vs Detroit, July 27, 1999
Sheryl Swoopes, vs Seattle, July 23, 2002
Cynthia Cooper, at Charlotte, June 28, 2000
Cynthia Cooper, vs Utah, July 30, 1998
Cynthia Cooper, at Sacramento, Aug. 21,1999
9 — By Many

Most games, 10+ assists, career
- 4 — Sheryl Swoopes
- 3 — Cynthia Cooper

PERSONAL FOULS

Most personal fouls, career
- 694 — Tina Thompson
- 513 — Janeth Arcain
- 388 — Michelle Snow

Most personal fouls, season
- 120 — Michelle Snow, 2003
- Michelle Snow, 2005
- 118 — Polina Tzekova, 1999
- 107 — Tina Thompson, 1997

Most personal fouls, game
- 6 — By Many

STEALS

Most steals, career
- 520 — Sheryl Swoopes
- 347 — Janeth Arcain
- 236 — Tina Thompson

Highest average, steals per game, career
(Minimum 100 games)
- 2.3 — Sheryl Swoopes (520/228)
- 1.6 — Cynthia Cooper (193/124)

Most steals, season
- 88 — Sheryl Swoopes, 2002
- 87 — Sheryl Swoopes, 2000
- 84 — Kim Perrot, 1998

Highest average, steals per game, season (qualifiers)
- 2.81 — Sheryl Swoopes, 2000 (87/31)
- 2.80 — Kim Perrot, 1998 (84/30)
- 2.75 — Sheryl Swoopes, 2002 (88/32)

Most steals, game
- 8 — Cynthia Cooper, at Charlotte, August 11, 1997
- 7 — Sheryl Swoopes, vs Portland, June 30, 2000
- Kim Perrot, vs New York, June 13, 1998
- Kim Perrot, vs Washington, June 29, 1998
- Kim Perrot, vs Utah, July 14, 1997

BLOCKED SHOTS

Most blocked shots, career
- 201 — Tina Thompson
- 188 — Sheryl Swoopes
- 161 — Michelle Snow

Highest average, blocked shots per game, career
(Minimum: 100 games)
- 1.2 — Michelle Snow (161/130)
- .82 — Sheryl Swoopes (188/228)
- .81 — Tina Thompson (201/247)

Most blocked shots, season
- 62 — Michelle Snow, 2003
- 46 — Sheryl Swoopes, 1999
- 38 — Michelle Snow, 2005

Highest average, blocked shots per game, season
(qualifiers)
- 1.8 — Michelle Snow, 2003 (62/34)
- 1.4 — Sheryl Swoopes, 1999 (46/32)
- 1.2 — Michelle Snow, 2005 (38/33)

Most blocked shots, game
- 8 — Michelle Snow, at San Antonio, June 20, 2003
- 5 — Michelle Snow, vs San Antonio, August 2, 2003
- 4 — By Many

TURNOVERS

Most turnovers, career
- 615 — Tina Thompson
- 518 — Sheryl Swoopes
- 457 — Janeth Arcain

Most turnovers, season
- 109 — Cynthia Cooper, 1997
- 104 — Cynthia Cooper, 1999
- 99 — Cynthia Cooper, 2000

Most turnovers, game
- 8 — Cynthia Cooper, at Cleveland, June 21, 1997
- Tina Thompson, at Phoenix, June 10, 2001
- Cynthia Cooper, at Charlotte, July 25, 1998
- Sheryl Swoopes, vs Minnesota, June 15, 2002
- Janeth Arcain, at Orlando, July 18, 2001
- Cynthia Cooper, vs Sacramento, August 2, 1999
- 7 — By Many

INDIANA FEVER

TEAM OFFENSE

SCORING

Highest average, points per game, season
69.2 — 2000 (2213/32)
68.7 — 2003 (2337/34)
Lowest average, points per game, season
63.8 — 2005 (2170/34)
64.6 — 2004 (2198/34)
Most points, game
94 — at Connecticut, June 26, 2003 (2OT)
92 — at Washington, July 29, 2003 (OT)
Fewest points, game
37 — at Charlotte, June 26, 2004
40 — at Detroit, August 25, 2005
Largest margin of victory, game
34 — vs San Antonio, July 23, 2003 (81-47)
31 — vs Detroit, July 6, 2003 (85-54)
Largest margin of defeat, game
37 — at Detroit, June 18, 2000 (74-111)
31 — at Los Angeles, July 19, 2004 (51-82)

BY HALF

Most points, first half
51 — vs Detroit, June 9, 2004
48 — vs Connecticut, June 20, 2003
     at Orlando, June 17, 2000
     at Washington, July 20, 2000
Fewest points, first half
18 — at Seattle, June 10, 2003
19 — vs Charlotte, July 28, 2004
     at New York, June 25, 2002
     at Cleveland, July 15, 2000
Largest lead at half time
25 — vs New York, June 7, 2003 (led 46-21; won 86-66)
19 — vs Detroit, June 9, 2004 (led 51-32; lost 83-79)
Largest deficit at halftime overcome to win game
13 — at Miami, June 1, 2000 (trailed 20-33; won 57-54)
12 — at New York, June 11, 2004 (trailed 32-44; won 72-68)
Most points, second half
59 — at Portland, June 20, 2002
50 — vs Phoenix, May 24, 2005
     vs Cleveland, August 4, 2000
Fewest points, second half
12 — at Charlotte, May 28, 2004
17 — at Charlotte, June 26, 2004
     at Detroit, August 25, 2005

OVERTIME

Most points, overtime period
18 — vs Phoenix, July 1, 2001
14 — at Connecticut, June 26, 2003

Fewest points, overtime period
2 — vs Seattle, June 4, 2001
4 — at Houston, May 29, 2005
Largest margin of victory, overtime period
8 — vs Phoenix, July 1, 2001 (86-78)
5 — vs Detroit, June 15, 2005 (84-79)

FIELD GOAL PERCENTAGE

Highest field goal percentage, season
.433 — 2000 (796/1838)
.418 — 2001 (762/1822)
Lowest field goal percentage, season
.393 — 2004 (791/2011)
.400 — 2005 (784/1958)
Highest field goal percentage, game
.549 — at Sacramento, June 14, 2003 (28/51)
.544 — at Portland, July 28, 2000 (31/57)
     vs Cleveland, August 4, 2000 (31/57)
Lowest field goal percentage, game
.188 — at Charlotte, June 26, 2004 (9/48)
.217 — vs Houston, June 5, 2002 (13/60)

FIELD GOALS

Most field goals per game, season
24.9 — 2000 (796/32)
24.7 — 2003 (839/34)
Fewest field goals per game, season
22.8 — 2002 (731/32)
23.1 — 2005 (784/34)
Most field goals, game
33 — vs Detroit, July 16, 2004
     at Washington, July 29, 2003 (OT)
     vs Detroit, July 6, 2003
32 — at Connecticut, June 26, 2003 (2OT)
     vs New York, June 7, 2003
     vs Detroit, August 12, 2001
Fewest field goals, game
9 — at Charlotte, June 26, 2004
13 — vs Houston, June 5, 2002

FIELD GOAL ATTEMPTS

Most field goal attempts per game, season
59.2 — 2004 (2011/34)
       2003 (2011/34)
57.6 — 2005 (1958/34)
Fewest field goal attempts per game, season
56.9 — 2001 (1822/32)
57.0 — 2002 (1825/32)
Most field goal attempts, game
76 — vs San Antonio, September 10, 2004
73 — at Washington, June 18, 2005 (2OT)
     at Washington, July 1, 2004
     vs Utah, July 10, 2002

Fewest field goal attempts, game
43 — at Detroit, August 25, 2005
44 — at Portland, June 20, 2002
vs New York, June 8, 2002
at Detroit, June 2, 2002

THREE-POINT FIELD GOAL PERCENTAGE

Highest three-point field goal percentage, season
.370 — 2000 (193/521)
.352 — 2001 (157/446)
Lowest three-point field goal percentage, season
.321 — 2005 (150/468)
.331 — 2002 (180/543)

THREE-POINT FIELD GOALS

Most three-point field goals per game, season
6.2 — 2003 (210/34)
6.0 — 2000 (193/32)
Fewest three-point field goals per game, season
4.4 — 2005 (150/34)
4.9 — 2004 (166/34)
Most three-point field goals, game
13 — at Washington, July 29, 2003 (OT)
11 — at New York, July 20, 2003
vs Detroit, July 6, 2003
at Seattle, June 10, 2003
Fewest three-point field goals, game
1 — vs New York, June 10, 2005
vs Minnesota, July 8, 2004
vs Cleveland, August 23, 2003
at Charlotte, August 20, 2003
2 — Many Times

THREE-POINT FIELD GOAL ATTEMPTS

Most three-point field goal attempts per game, season
17.7 — 2003 (600/34)
17.0 — 2002 (543/32)
Fewest three-point field goal attempts per game, season
13.8 — 2005 (468/34)
13.9 — 2001 (446/32)
Most three-point field goal attempts, game
30 — at Washington, July 29, 2003 (OT)
28 — at Washington, June 18, 2005 (2OT)
at New York, July 20, 2003
Fewest three-point field goal attempts, game
5 — at Charlotte, July 23, 2005
vs Phoenix, May 24, 2005
6 — at Connecticut, August 23, 2005
at Miami, June 1, 2000

FREE THROW PERCENTAGE

Highest free throw percentage, season
.799 — 2001 (472/591)
.798 — 2003 (449/563)
Lowest free throw percentage, season
.752 — 2000 (428/569)
.760 — 2005 (452/595)
Highest free throw percentage, game
1.000 — Many Times
Lowest free throw percentage, game
.286 — at Seattle, July 22, 2004 (2/7)
.300 — at New York, July 31, 2005 (3/10)

FREE THROWS MADE

Most free throws made per game, season
14.8 — 2001 (472/32)
14.2 — 2002 (455/32)
Fewest free throws made per game, season
13.21 — 2003 (449/34)
13.24 — 2004 (450/34)
Most free throws made, game
34 — vs Phoenix, July 1, 2001 (OT)
31 — at Portland, June 20, 2002
Fewest free throws made, game
1 — at Houston, July 8, 2003
2 — at Seattle, July 22, 2004
at New York, July 20, 2003

FREE THROW ATTEMPTS

Most free throw attempts per game, season
18.5 — 2001 (591/32)
18.1 — 2002 (580/32)
Fewest free throw attempts per game, season
16.6 — 2003 (563/34)
17.1 — 2004 (580/34)
Most free throw attempts, game
39 — vs Phoenix, July 1, 2001 (OT)
38 — vs New York, June 8, 2002
vs Miami, June 5, 2000
Fewest free throw attempts, game
2 — at Houston, July 8, 2003
3 — at New York, July 20, 2003

REBOUNDS

Most rebounds per game, season
32.4 — 2004 (1101/34)
29.8 — 2005 (1012/34)
Fewest rebounds per game, season
29.1 — 2003 (988/34)
2000 (932/32)
29.2 — 2001 (935/32)
Most rebounds, game
43 — at Washington, June 18, 2005 (2OT)
at Connecticut, July 6, 2004 (OT)
vs San Antonio, July 23, 2003
vs Orlando, June 3, 2000
40 — at Connecticut, June 26, 2003 (2OT)
vs Detroit, June 1, 2002
Fewest rebounds, game
15 — at Detroit, August 25, 2005
17 — vs Minnesota, July 26, 2002

OFFENSIVE REBOUNDS

Most offensive rebounds per game, season
11.6 — 2004 (396/34)
10.0 — 2005 (341/34)
Fewest offensive rebounds per game, season
8.9 — 2000 (285/32)
2001 (286/32)
Most offensive rebounds, game
21 — vs Charlotte, August 20, 2005
19 — vs San Antonio, September 10, 2004
at Washington, July 1, 2004
Fewest offensive rebounds, game
1 — at Detroit, June 23, 2001
at Portland, July 28, 2000
3 — at Detroit, August 25, 2005

DEFENSIVE REBOUNDS

Most defensive rebounds per game, season
  20.7 — 2004 (705/34)
  20.3 — 2001 (649/32)
Fewest defensive rebounds per game, season
  19.2 — 2003 (654/34)
  19.7 — 2005 (671/34)
Most defensive rebounds, game
  34 — vs San Antonio, July 23, 2003
  31 — at Connecticut, June 26, 2003 (2OT)
Fewest defensive rebounds, game
  11 — vs Washington, August 12, 2003
  12 — at Detroit, August 25, 2005
       at Los Angeles, August 13, 2005
       at Seattle, June 10, 2003
       at Charlotte, June 13, 2002
       at Cleveland, July 15, 2000

ASSISTS

Most assists per game, season
  16.3 — 2004 (555/34)
  15.9 — 2003 (539/34)
Fewest assists per game, season
  14.0 — 2002 (447/32)
  14.3 — 2001 (458/32)
Most assists, game
  27 — vs Detroit, July 16, 2004
  26 — vs Washington, September 4, 2004
       at Washington, July 29, 2003 (OT)
Fewest assists, game
  5 — at Charlotte, June 26, 2004
      at Detroit, August 2, 2003
      at Miami, June 5, 2001
  6 — at Charlotte, August 20, 2003
      at Miami, August 10, 2001 (OT)

PERSONAL FOULS

Most personal fouls per game, season
  20.1 — 2000 (642/32)
  19.6 — 2005 (668/34)
         2003 (668/34)
Fewest personal fouls per game, season
  17.5 — 2002 (559/32)
  18.8 — 2001 (600/32)
Most personal fouls, game
  39 — at Detroit, June 18, 2000
  35 — at Houston, May 29, 2005 (2OT)
Fewest personal fouls, game
  5 — vs New York, August 27, 2005
  9 — vs Detroit, June 1, 2002

DISQUALIFICATIONS

Most disqualifications per game, season
  .28 — 2000 (9/32)
Fewest disqualifications per game, season
  .15 — 2003 (5/34)
Most disqualifications, game
  2 — at Washington, June 18, 2005 (2OT)
      vs Connecticut, August 25, 2003
      at Detroit, June 9, 2000

   at Detroit, June 18, 2000
  1 — Many Times

STEALS

Most steals per game, season
  9.9 — 2005 (336/34)
  8.8 — 2003 (299/34)
Fewest steals per game, season
  7.6 — 2001 (242/32)
  7.7 — 2004 (261/34)
Most steals, game
  20 — vs Detroit, July 6, 2003
  19 — vs Connecticut, July 13, 2005
Fewest steals, game
  0 — at New York, June 2, 2001
  2 — at Washington, September 1, 2004
      at Sacramento, June 14, 2003
      at Miami, June 30, 2002
      vs Orlando, June 3, 2000

BLOCKED SHOTS

Most blocked shots per game, season
  3.9 — 2004 (134/34)
        2000 (126/32)
Fewest blocked shots per game, season
  2.8 — 2005 (95/34)
  3.1 — 2002 (100/32)
Most blocked shots, game
  10 — at Utah, July 29, 2000
  9 — vs Phoenix, July 3, 2004
      vs Los Angeles, June 25, 2004
Fewest blocked shots, game
  0 — Many Times

TURNOVERS

Most turnovers per game, season
  16.2 — 2000 (518/32)
  15.3 — 2001 (491/32)
Fewest turnovers per game, season
  13.7 — 2002 (438/32)
  13.9 — 2003 (474/34)
Most turnovers, game
  28 — at Detroit, June 18, 2000
  26 — vs Cleveland, June 12, 2000
Fewest turnovers, game
  5 — vs Utah, July 10, 2002
  7 — vs Sacramento, June 28, 2002

TEAM DEFENSE

POINTS

Fewest points allowed per game, season
  62.7 — 2005 (2133/34)
  66.0 — 2004 (2245/34)
Most points allowed per game, season
  71.6 — 2000 (2290/32)
  70.3 — 2001 (2249/32)
Fewest points allowed, game
  42 — vs Washington, September 4, 2004
  45 — vs Washington, July 6, 2002
       vs Seattle, July 14, 2000

Fewest points allowed, first half
    19 — vs Seattle, July 14, 2000
    20 — vs Charlotte, August 3, 2002
        at Phoenix, July 31, 2002
Fewest points allowed, second half
    19 — vs Washington, September 4, 2004
        at Cleveland, August 13, 2002
        at Detroit, August 9, 2002
    20 — vs New York, August 27, 2005
        vs Connecticut, July 11, 2004
        vs San Antonio, July 23, 2003
        vs Washington, July 6, 2002
        vs Charlotte, August 9, 2000
Fewest points allowed, overtime period
    4 — vs Detroit, June 15, 2005
        at Houston, May 29, 2005
    5 — vs Seattle, June 4, 2001

FIELD GOAL PERCENTAGE

Lowest opponents' field goal percentage, season
    .431 — 2005 (775/1798)
        2004 (804/1865)
    .439 — 2003 (837/1908)
Highest opponents' field goal percentage, season
    .449 — 2001 (853/1899)
        2000 (839/1868)
Lowest opponents' field goal percentage, game
    .242 — vs San Antonio, July 23, 2003 (16/66)
    .273 — at Charlotte, July 23, 2005 (15/55)

TURNOVERS

Fewest opponents' turnovers per game, season
    13.7 — 2004 (466/34)
    14.6 — 2001 (466/32)
Most opponents' turnovers per game, season
    16.4 — 2005 (558/34)
    15.1 — 2003 (512/34)
Most opponents' turnovers, game
    26 — vs Detroit, July 6, 2003
    24 — at Detroit, July 17, 2005
        vs Connecticut, July 13, 2005

TEAM MISCELLANEOUS

GAME WON AND LOST

Highest winning percentage, season
    .618 — 2005 (21-13)
    .500 — 2002 (16-16)
Lowest winning percentage, season
    .281 — 2000 (9-23)
    .313 — 2001 (10-22)
Most consecutive games won
    4 — August 14-23, 2005
        July 31-August 7, 2002
    3 — May 22-26, 2005
        July 13-17, 2005
        June 10-16, 2005
        September 1-4, 2004
        June 14-20, 2003
Most consecutive games won, one season
    4 — August 14-23, 2005
        July 31-August 7, 2002

    3 — May 22-26, 2005
        July 13-17, 2005
        June 10-16, 2005
        September 1-4, 2004
        June 14-20, 2003
Most consecutive games lost
    10 — June 18-July 8, 2000
    6 — July 19-31, 2004
        August 2-12, 2003
Most consecutive games lost, one season
    10 — June 18-July 8, 2000
    6 — July 19-31, 2004
        August 2-12, 2003
Highest winning percentage, home games, season
    .824 — 2005 (14-3)
    .647 — 2003 (11-6)
Lowest winning percentage, home games, season
    .313 — 2000 (5-11)
    .438 — 2001 (7-9)
Most consecutive home games won
    13 — July 22, 2002-July 10, 2003
    6 — May 22-June 24, 2005
Most consecutive home games lost
    8 — June 10-July 8, 2000
    4 — July 26-August 12, 2003
        July 10-19, 2002
Highest winning percentage, road games, season
    .412 — 2005 (7-10)
    .375 — 2002 (6-10)
Lowest winning percentage, road games, season
    .188 — 2001 (3-13)
    .250 — 2000 (4-12)
Most consecutive road games won
    2 — August 14-23, 2005
        June 1-11, 2004
        September 1-3, 2004
        July 24-29, 2003
        July 31-August 6, 2002
        June 12-23, 2001
Most consecutive road games lost
    7 — July 1-31, 2004
    6 — June 21-July 30, 2002
        July 29, 2000-June 9, 2001

OVERTIME GAMES

Most overtime games, season
    3 — 2005, 2001
    2 — 2004, 2003
Most consecutive overtime games, season
    1 — Many Times
Most overtime games won, season
    2 — 2003
    1 — 2005, 2001
Most overtime games won, no losses, season
    2 — 2003
Most overtime games lost, season
    2 — 2005, 2004, 2001
    1 — 2002, 2000
Most overtime games lost, no wins, season
    2 — 2004
    1 — 2002, 2000

Most overtime periods, game
2 — at Washington, June 18, 2005
at Houston, May 29, 2005
at Connecticut, June 26, 2003

INDIVIDUAL RECORDS
SEASONS
Most seasons
5 — Kelly Schumacher
4 — Tamika Catchings
Niele Ivey
Stephanie White

GAMES
Most games, career
159 — Kelly Schumacher
134 — Tamika Catchings
112 — Stephanie White
Most consecutive games, career
134 — Tamika Catchings, June 1, 2002-
August. 27, 2005 (current)
102 — Natalie Williams, May 29, 2003-
August 27, 2005 (current)
68 — Kelly Miller, May 21, 2004-
August 27, 2005 (current)
Most games, season
34 — By Many

MINUTES
Most minutes, career
4,700 — Tamika Catchings
2,814 — Natalie Williams
2,540 — Rita Williams
Highest average, minutes per game, career
(Minimum 100 games)
35.1 — Tamika Catchings (4700/134)
27.6 — Natalie Williams (2814/102)
18.8 — Niele Ivey (1977/105)
Most minutes, season
1,210 — Tamika Catchings, 2003
1,174 — Tamika Catchings, 2005
1,167 — Tamika Catchings, 2002
Highest average, minutes per game, season
36.5 — Tamika Catchings, 2002 (1167/32)
35.6 — Tamika Catchings, 2003 (1210/34)
34.5 — Tamika Catchings, 2005 (1174/34)
Most minutes, game
45 — Rita Williams, vs Phoenix, July 1, 2001 (OT)
Tamika Catchings, at Washington,
July 29, 2003 (OT)
Tamika Catchings, at Washington,
June 18, 2005 (2OT)
Tamika Catchings, at Connecticut,
June 26, 2003 (2OT)
43 — Tamika Catchings, at Houston,
May 29, 2005 (2OT)

SCORING
Most points, lifetime
2,334 — Tamika Catchings
1,057 — Natalie Williams
852 — Rita Williams

Highest average, points per game, career
(Minimum 100 games)
17.4 — Tamika Catchings (2334/134)
10.4 — Natalie Williams (1057/102)
4.8 — Kelly Schumacher (768/159)
Most points, season
671 — Tamika Catchings, 2003
594 — Tamika Catchings, 2002
568 — Tamika Catchings, 2004
Highest average, points per game, season
19.7 — Tamika Catchings, 2003 (671/34)
18.6 — Tamika Catchings, 2002 (594/32)
16.7 — Tamika Catchings, 2004 (568/34)
Most points, game
32 — Tamika Catchings, vs New York, June 8, 2002
Tamika Catchings, at New York, August 22, 2003
Tamika Catchings, vs Orlando, August 7, 2002
31 — Tamika Catchings, vs New York, July 10, 2003
Olympia Scott-Richardson, vs Utah, July 10, 2002
Most games, 30 or more points, career
6 — Tamika Catchings
1 — Nikki McCray
Olympia Scott-Richardson
Most games, 20 or more points, career
55 — Tamika Catchings
5 — Rita Williams
4 — Nikki McCray
Natalie Williams
Most consecutive games, 20 or more points
4 — Tamika Catchings, August 7-12, 2003
Tamika Catchings, July 24-August 2, 2003
Tamika Catchings, August 6-11, 2002
3 — Tamika Catchings, July 8-16, 2003
Most consecutive games, 10 or more points
37 — Tamika Catchings, June 24, 2003-
June 25, 2004
17 — Natalie Williams, July 23, 2003-
May 23, 2004
15 — Tamika Catchings, June 7-July 10, 2002

FIELD GOAL PERCENTAGE
Highest field goal percentage, career
(Minimum 400 field goals)
.456 — Natalie Williams (412/904)
.406 — Tamika Catchings (742/1829)
Highest field goal percentage, season (qualifiers)
.561 — Kara Wolters, 2000 (148/264)
.514 — Alicia Thompson, 2000 (131/255)
.487 — Olympia Scott-Richardson, 2002 (113/232)
Highest field goal percentage, game
(Minimum 8 field goals made)
.846 — Nikki McCray, at Portland,
June 20, 2002 (11/13)
Natalie Williams, vs Phoenix, July 2, 2003 (11/13)
.818 — Tamika Catchings, vs Seattle,
August 4, 2005 (9/11)
Tamika Catchings, vs Washington,
August 18, 2005 (9/11)
.800 — Ebony Hoffman, vs Detroit, June 15, 2005 (8/10)
Nadine Malcolm, vs Minnesota,
June 16, 2001 (8/10)

Most field goals, none missed, game
- 7 — Kara Wolters, at Portland, July 28, 2000
  Natalie Williams, at Washington, Sept. 1, 2004
- 5 — Kelly Schumacher, at Seattle, June 21, 2002
  Kelly Schumacher, vs San Antonio, July 21, 2005
- 4 — Jackie Moore, at Charlotte, June 13, 2002
  Kelly Schumacher, at New York, July 20, 2003
  Kelly Schumacher, vs Charlotte, August 3, 2002

Most field goal attempts, none made, game
- 7 — Alicia Thompson, vs Houston, June 5, 2002
  Deanna Jackson, at Detroit, June 12, 2004
  Nadine Malcolm, vs Washington, August 1, 2001
  Natalie Williams, at San Antonio, August 11,2005
- 6 — Monica Maxwell, vs Washington, July 6, 2002
  Stephanie White, at Orlando, June 17, 2000

FIELD GOALS

Most field goals, career
- 742 — Tamika Catchings
- 412 — Natalie Williams
- 322 — Kelly Schumacher

Most field goals, season
- 221 — Tamika Catchings, 2003
- 184 — Tamika Catchings, 2002
- 180 — Tamika Catchings, 2004

Most field goals, game
- 13 — Tamika Catchings, vs Orlando, August 7, 2002
- 11 — Nikki McCray, at Portland, June 20, 2002
  Natalie Williams, vs Phoenix, July 2, 2003
  Tamika Catchings, vs New York, July 10, 2003
  Tamika Catchings, at New York,
  August 22, 2003
  Olympia Scott-Richardson, vs Utah,
  July 10, 2002
- 10 — By Many

FIELD GOAL ATTEMPTS

Most field goal attempts, career
- 1,829 — Tamika Catchings
- 904 — Natalie Williams
- 702 — Rita Williams

Most field goal attempts, season
- 512 — Tamika Catchings, 2003
- 468 — Tamika Catchings, 2004
- 439 — Tamika Catchings, 2002

Most field goal attempts, game
- 24 — Tamika Catchings, at Houston, July 31, 2004
- 22 — Tamika Catchings, at Detroit, August 9, 2002
- 21 — Tamika Catchings, at Washington,
  July 29, 2003 (OT)
  Tamika Catchings, at Connecticut,
  June 26, 2003 (2OT)

THREE-POINT FIELD GOAL PERCENTAGE

Highest three-point field goal percentage, career
(Minimum 100 three-point field goals)
- .358 — Tamika Catchings (241/674)

Highest three-point field goal percentage, season (qualifiers)
- .411 — Kelly Miller, 2004 (46/112)
  Nadine Malcolm, 2001 (23/56)
- .404 — Stephanie McCarty, 2001 (23/57)

Most three-point field goals, none missed, game
- 6 — Tamika Catchings, at Orlando, July 3, 2002 (OT)

4 — Alicia Thompson, vs Miami, July 28, 2001
  Niele Ivey, vs Washington, May 31, 2003
  Nadine Malcolm, at New York, July 9, 2001

Most three-point field goal attempts, none made, game
- 7 — Rita Williams, at Orlando, July 3, 2002 (OT)
- 6 — Tamika Catchings, vs Houston, June 5, 2002
  Tamika Catchings, vs New York, June 10, 2005
- 5 — By Many

THREE-POINT FIELD GOALS

Most three-point field goals, career
- 241 — Tamika Catchings
- 107 — Rita Williams
- 92 — Stephaine White

Most three-point field goals, season
- 76 — Tamika Catchings, 2002
- 74 — Tamika Catchings, 2003
- 62 — Monica Maxwell, 2000

Most three-point field goals, game
- 6 — Tamika Catchings, at Orlando, July 3, 2002 (OT)
- 5 — By Many

Most consecutive games, three-point field goals made
- 23 — Tamika Catchings, July 3, 2002-June 12, 2003
- 22 — Monica Maxwell, June 12-August 1, 2000
- 21 — Tamika Catchings, Aug. 20, 2004-July 6, 2004

THREE-POINT FIELD GOAL ATTEMPTS

Most three-point field goal attempts, career
- 674 — Tamika Catchings
- 307 — Rita Williams
- 250 — Stephanie White

Most three-point field goal attempts, season
- 193 — Tamika Catchings, 2002
- 191 — Tamika Catchings, 2003
- 167 — Tamika Catchings, 2004

Most three-point field goal attempts, game
- 12 — Tamika Catchings, at Washington, Aug. 6, 2002
- 11 — Tamika Catchings, vs Washington, July 6, 2002
  Tamika Catchings, at Washington,
  July 29, 2003 (OT)
- 10 — By Many

FREE THROW PERCENTAGE

Highest free throw percentage, career
- .825 — Tamika Catchings (609/738)
- .816 — Stephanie White (182/223)
- .783 — Rita Williams (213/272)

Highest free throw percentage, season (qualifiers)
- .938 — Stephanie White, 2003 (45/48)
- .877 — Kelly Miller, 2004 (50/57)
- .871 — Nadine Malcolm, 2001 (54/62)

Most free throws made, none missed, game
- 12 — Tamika Catchings, at Detroit, June 2, 2002
- 11 — Tamika Catchings, vs Minnesota, July 8, 2004
- 10 — Tamika Catchings, at Washington, July 1, 2004

Most free throw attempts, none made, game
- 4 — Alessandra Santos de Olive, at Detroit,
  June 18, 2000
- 2 — By Many

FREE THROWS MADE

Most free throws made, career
609 — Tamika Catchings
233 — Natalie Williams
213 — Rita Williams

Most free throws made, season
155 — Tamika Catchings, 2003
152 — Tamika Catchings, 2004
Tamika Catchings, 2005

Most free throws made, game
15 — Tamika Catchings, vs Phoenix, May 24, 2005
14 — Tamika Catchings, vs New York, June 8, 2002
13 — Rita Williams, vs Phoenix, July 1, 2001 (OT)

FREE THROW ATTEMPTS

Most free throw attempts, career
738 — Tamika Catchings
334 — Natalie Williams
272 — Rita Williams

Most free throw attempts, season
193 — Tamika Catchings, 2005
184 — Tamika Catchings, 2002
183 — Tamika Catchings, 2003

Most free throw attempts, game
17 — Tamika Catchings, vs Phoenix, May 24, 2005
16 — Tamika Catchings, vs New York, June 8, 2002
14 — Tamika Catchings, at Portland, June 20, 2002
Rita Williams, vs Phoenix, July 1, 2001 (OT)
Tamika Catchings, vs Detroit, July 15, 2005
Tamika Catchings, at Sacramento, June 7, 2005
Tamika Catchings, vs Connecticut,
August 25, 2003

REBOUNDS

Most rebounds, career
1061 — Tamika Catchings
676 — Natalie Williams
400 — Kelly Schumacher

Highest average, rebounds per game, career
(Minimum 100 games)
7.9 — Tamika Catchings (1061/134)
6.6 — Natalie Williams (676/102)
2.5 — Kelly Schumacher (400/159)

Most rebounds, season
276 — Tamika Catchings, 2002
272 — Tamika Catchings, 2003
264 — Tamika Catchings, 2005

Highest average, rebounds per game, season (qualifiers)
8.6 — Tamika Catchings, 2002 (276/32)
8.0 — Tamika Catchings, 2003 (272/34)
7.8 — Tamika Catchings, 2005 (264/34)

Most rebounds, game
17 — Natalie Williams, vs Charlotte, August 16, 2003
Olympia Scott-Richardson, vs Houston,
June 5, 2002
16 — Tamika Catchings, vs Detroit, June 15, 2005(OT)
Tamika Catchings, at Connecticut,
June 26, 2003 (2OT)
Tamika Catchings, vs Charlotte, Aug. 20, 2005

15 — By Many

Most games, 10+ rebounds, career
38 — Tamika Catchings
21 — Natalie Williams
8 — Olympia Scott-Richardson

Most consecutive games, 10+ rebounds
4 — Tamika Catchings, August 3-9, 2002
3 — Tamika Catchings, July 26-31, 2005
Natalie Williams, August 23-May 21, 2004
Natalie Williams, June 20-24, 2003
2 — By Many

OFFENSIVE REBOUNDS

Most offensive rebounds, career
322 — Tamika Catchings
276 — Natalie Williams
143 — Kelly Schumacher

Highest average, offensive rebounds per game, career
(Minimum 100 games)
2.7 — Natalie Williams (276/102)
2.4 — Tamika Catchings (322/134)
.9 — Kelly Schumacher (143/159)

Most offensive rebounds, season
109 — Natalie Williams, 2003
93 — Natalie Williams, 2004
92 — Tamika Catchings, 2002

Most offensive rebounds, game
10 — Tamika Catchings, vs Charlotte, August 20, 2005
9 — Tamika Catchings, vs Phoenix, July 3, 2004
Tamika Catchings, vs Washington,
August 12, 2003
Olympia Scott-Richardson, vs Houston,
June 5, 2002
8 — Natalie Williams, vs Charlotte, August 16, 2003
Olympia Scott-Richardson, vs Utah,
July 10, 2002

DEFENSIVE REBOUNDS

Most defensive rebounds, career
739 — Tamika Catchings
400 — Natalie Williams
257 — Kelly Schumacher

Highest average, defensive rebounds per game, career
(Minimum 100 games)
5.5 — Tamika Catchings (739/134)
3.9 — Natalie Williams (400/102)
1.6 — Kelly Schumacher (257/159)

Most defensive rebounds, season
195 — Tamika Catchings, 2005
190 — Tamika Catchings, 2003
184 — Tamika Catchings, 2002

Most defensive rebounds, game
13 — Tamika Catchings, at Washington,
June 18, 2005 (2OT)
11 — Tamika Catchings, vs Detroit,
June 15, 2005 (OT)
Tamika Catchings, vs Houston, August 7, 2003
Tamika Catchings, at Connecticut,
June 26, 2003 (2OT)
Tamika Catchings, vs Orlando, August 7, 2002
10 — Tamika Catchings, vs Detroit, June 1, 2002
Olympia Scott-Richardson, vs Miami,
July 12, 2002

ASSISTS

Most assists, career
490 — Tamika Catchings
258 — Rita Williams
225 — Stephanie White
Highest average, assists per game, career
(Minimum 100 games)
3.7 — Tamika Catchings (490/134)
2.0 — Stephanie White (225/112)
1.9 — Niele Ivey (198/105)
Most assists, season
143 — Tamika Catchings, 2005
118 — Tamika Catchings, 2002
115 — Tamika Catchings, 2004
Highest average, assists per game, season (qualifiers)
4.2 — Tamika Catchings, 2005 (143/34)
3.7 — Tamika Catchings, 2002 (118/32)
3.6 — Rita Williams, 2001 (114/32)
Most assists, game
11 — Coquese Washington, vs Orlando, August 7, 2002
10 — Tamika Catchings, at Cleveland, August 10, 2003
Rita Williams, vs Detroit, August 12, 2001
Stephanie White, vs Houston, July 14, 2004
Coquese Washington, at Washington,
July 24, 2003
9 — Rita Williams, vs Phoenix, July 1, 2001 (OT)
Most games, 10+ assists, career
2 — Coquese Washington
1 — Rita Williams
Stephanie White
Tamika Catchings

PERSONAL FOULS

Most personal fouls, career
413 — Tamika Catchings
365 — Natalie Williams
279 — Kelly Schumacher
Most personal fouls, season
138 — Natalie Williams, 2003
127 — Olympia Scott-Richardson, 2002
122 — Natalie Williams, 2004
Tamika Catchings, 2003
Most personal fouls, game
6 — By Many

STEALS

Most steals, career
323 — Tamika Catchings
169 — Rita Williams
118 — Natalie Williams
Highest average, steals per game, career
(Minimum 100 games)
2.4 — Tamika Catchings (323/134)
1.2 — Natalie Williams (118/102)
.8 — Niele Ivey (82/105)
Most steals, season
94 — Tamika Catchings, 2002
90 — Tamika Catchings, 2005
76 — Rita Williams, 2000
Highest average, steals per game, season (qualifiers)
2.9 — Tamika Catchings, 2002 (94/32)
2.6 — Tamika Catchings, 2005 (90/34)
2.4 — Rita Williams, 2001 (72/32)
Most steals, game
9 — Tamika Catchings, vs Minnesota, July 26, 2002

8 — Rita Williams, at Miami, August 10, 2001 (OT)
Tamika Catchings, vs Connecticut,
July 13, 2005
7 — Tamika Catchings, at Cleveland,
August 10, 2003
Rita Williams, at New York, June 30, 2000
Tamika Catchings, vs Houston, June 5, 2002
Tamika Catchings, vs Seattle, August 4, 2005

BLOCKED SHOTS

Most blocked shots, career
132 — Tamika Catchings
131 — Kelly Schumacher
56 — Natalie Williams
Highest average, blocked shots per game, career
(Minimum: 100 games)
.985 — Tamika Catchings (132/134)
.824 — Kelly Schumacher (131/159)
.549 — Natalie Williams (56/102)
Most blocked shots, season
49 — Kara Wolters, 2000
43 — Tamika Catchings, 2002
38 — Tamika Catchings, 2004
Highest average, blocked shots per game, season
(qualifiers)
1.6 — Kara Wolters, 2000 (49/31)
1.3 — Tamika Catchings, 2002 (43/32)
1.1 — Tamika Catchings, 2004 (38/34)
Most blocked shots, game
5 — Kara Wolters, vs Portland, July 3, 2000
Kara Wolters, vs Cleveland, August 4, 2000
Natalie Williams, vs Charlotte, June 17, 2003
4 — By Many

TURNOVERS

Most turnovers, career
352 — Tamika Catchings
198 — Rita Williams
191 — Natalie Williams
Most turnovers, season
102 — Tamika Catchings, 2003
100 — Rita Williams, 2001
91 — Tamika Catchings, 2005
Most turnovers, game
8 — Rita Williams, at Cleveland, July 27, 2001
Tamika Catchings, at Portland, June 20, 2002
Natalie Williams, at Detroit, June 24, 2003
Rita Williams, vs Sacramento, June 21, 2000
7 — By Many

LOS ANGELES SPARKS

TEAM OFFENSE

SCORING

Highest average, points per game, season
76.6 — 2002 (2452/32)
76.5 — 1999 (2449/32)
Lowest average, points per game, season
68.4 — 2005 (2326/34)
71.6 — 1998 (2148/30)
Most points, game
102 — vs Utah, July 7, 2002
vs Utah, June 28, 1999
100 — vs Minnesota, July 8, 2001 (OT)
vs Sacramento, June 10, 1999
Fewest points, game
51 — at Houston, August 27, 2005
at Connecticut, August 9, 2005
51 — at Sacramento, June 3, 2004
at San Antonio, August 9, 2003
Largest margin of victory, game
32 — vs Utah, June 28, 1999 (102-70)
31 — vs Indiana, July 19, 2004 (82-51)
Largest margin of defeat, game
36 — at Seattle, August 6, 2003 (56-92)
28 — at Sacramento, June 4, 2005 (53-81)

BY HALF

Most points, first half
55 — at Connecticut, May 24, 2003
vs Utah, August 4, 2002
54 — vs Sacramento, August 22, 1997
Fewest points, first half
16 — at Houston, August 27, 2005
at San Antonio, August 9, 2003
17 — at Washington, August 14, 1999
Largest lead at half time
26 — vs Minnesota, August 21, 2003 (led 50-24)
25 — vs Phoenix, July 21, 1999 (led 50-25)
Largest deficit at halftime overcome to win game
17 — at San Antonio, June 26, 2003 (trailed 24-41; won 67-58)
13 — at Minnesota, July 1, 1999 (trailed 28-41; won 81-77 in 2OT)
Most points, second half
53 — at Washington, July 9, 2003
at Sacramento, August 3, 2002
at Sacramento, July 19, 2001
vs Detroit, August 16, 1998
52 — vs San Antonio, May 31, 2005
Fewest points, second half
18 — at Sacramento, June 3, 2004
19 — vs Houston, August 1, 1997

OVERTIME

Most points, overtime period
19 — vs Minnesota, July 8, 2001

15 — at Sacramento, June 15, 2002
at Detroit, June 26, 2001
Fewest points, overtime period
2 — at Detroit, June 17, 2003
4 — at Seattle, June 13, 2000
at Houston, June 30, 1997
at Phoenix, August 24, 1997
at Utah, August 13, 2001
Largest margin of victory, overtime period
9 — at Detroit, June 26, 2001 (98-89)
8 — at Seattle, August 8, 2000 (60-52)

FIELD GOAL PERCENTAGE

Highest field goal percentage, season
.451 — 2001 (916/2031)
.446 — 1997 (794/1782)
Lowest field goal percentage, season
.416 — 1998 (797/1914)
.418 — 2003 (894/2140)
Highest field goal percentage, game
.655 — vs Houston, June 15, 2005 (36/55)
.607 — vs New York, July 20, 2000 (34/56)
Lowest field goal percentage, game
.257 — vs Houston, August 8, 2002 (19/74)
.279 — vs Detroit, August 9, 1999 (19/68)

FIELD GOALS

Most field goals per game, season
28.6 — 2001 (916/32)
28.4 — 1997 (794/28)
Fewest field goals per game, season
25.7 — 2005 (873/34)
26.3 — 2003 (894/34)
Most field goals, game
39 — at Detroit, June 26, 2001 (OT)
38 — vs Utah, July 7, 2002
Fewest field goals, game
16 — at San Antonio, August 9, 2003
at Seattle, July 11, 2002
17 — at Houston, August 12, 1999

FIELD GOAL ATTEMPTS

Most field goal attempts per game, season
63.9 — 1999 (2044/32)
63.8 — 1998 (1914/30)
Fewest field goal attempts per game, season
60.1 — 2005 (2042/34)
60.9 — 2004 (2069/34)
Most field goal attempts, game
82 — vs Minnesota, July 8, 2001 (OT)
78 — at Detroit, July 25, 1998
Fewest field goal attempts, game
45 — at Sacramento, June 30, 1998
48 — at Phoenix, June 18, 2004
at Miami, June 23, 2000

THREE-POINT FIELD GOAL PERCENTAGE

Highest three-point field goal percentage, season
.379 — 2004 (157/414)
.377 — 2002 (194/515)
Lowest three-point field goal percentage, season
.269 — 1997 (65/242)
.320 — 2005 (124/387)

THREE-POINT FIELD GOALS

Most three-point field goals per game, season
6.1 — 2002 (194/32)
5.1 — 2003 (174/34)
Fewest three-point field goals per game, season
2.3 — 1997 (65/28)
3.6 — 2005 (124/34)
Most three-point field goals, game
11 — at Sacramento, August 3, 2002
10 — Many Times
Fewest three-point field goals, game
0 — Many Times

THREE-POINT FIELD GOAL ATTEMPTS

Most three-point field goal attempts per game, season
16.1 — 2002 (515/32)
15.5 — 2003 (528/34)
Fewest three-point field goal attempts per game, season
8.6 — 1997 (242/28)
11.2 — 1998 (335/30)
Most three-point field goal attempts, game
25 — vs Miami, July 30, 2002
vs Orlando, July 22, 2002
at Utah, August 13, 2001 (OT)
at New York, June 18, 1999
23 — Many Times
Fewest three-point field goal attempts, game
1 — at New York, August 5, 1997
2 — vs Sacramento, August 22, 1997

FREE THROW PERCENTAGE

Highest free throw percentage, season
.792 — 2003 (537/678)
.786 — 2000 (545/693)
Lowest free throw percentage, season
.676 — 1997 (419/620)
.724 — 2005 (456/630)
Highest free throw percentage, game
1.000 — at Minnesota, May 28, 2003 (20/20)
vs Phoenix, July 24, 2003 (27/27)
vs Charlotte, August 2, 2003 (17/17)
at Minnesota, August 11, 2002 (8/8)
vs Minnesota, July 15, 2000 (16/16)
at Houston, August 19, 1998 (5/5)
.955 — vs Sacramento, June 27, 1997 (21/22)
Lowest free throw percentage, game
.375 — at Houston, June 21, 2001 (3/8)
.400 — vs Cleveland, July 5, 1999 (4/10)

FREE THROWS MADE

Most free throws made per game, season
17.0 — 2000 (545/32)
15.8 — 1999 (506/32)

Fewest free throws made per game, season
13.4 — 2005 (456/34)
14.0 — 2001 (449/32)
Most free throws made, game
40 — vs Washington, August 3, 1998
33 — vs Houston, June 20, 2000
Fewest free throws made, game
3 — vs Seattle, August 1, 2002
at Houston, June 21, 2001
4 — at Utah, August 13, 2001 (OT)
vs Cleveland, July 5, 1999

FREE THROW ATTEMPTS

Most free throw attempts per game, season
22.1 — 1997 (620/28)
21.7 — 2000 (693/32)
Fewest free throw attempts per game, season
18.5 — 2005 (630/34)
18.6 — 2001 (594/32)
Most free throw attempts, game
51 — vs Washington, August 3, 1998
42 — vs Utah, August 4, 2002
vs Houston, June 20, 2000
Fewest free throw attempts, game
5 — at Houston, August 19, 1998
7 — vs Houston, June 15, 2005
vs Seattle, August 1, 2002

REBOUNDS

Most rebounds per game, season
35.7 — 2002 (1143/32)
34.8 — 1997 (973/28)
Fewest rebounds per game, season
29.5 — 2005 (1004/34)
33.0 — 2004 (1121/34)
Most rebounds, game
50 — at Sacramento, July 27, 1997
vs Houston, July 16, 1997
48 — vs Seattle, August 4, 2001
Fewest rebounds, game
17 — at Utah, August 21, 1999
19 — at Detroit, August 2, 2000

OFFENSIVE REBOUNDS

Most offensive rebounds per game, season
11.2 — 1998 (337/30)
10.9 — 2001 (350/32)
Fewest offensive rebounds per game, season
9.2 — 2004 (312/34)
9.4 — 2005 (321/34)
Most offensive rebounds, game
20 — at Charlotte, May 28, 2005
19 — vs Seattle, June 24, 2005
vs Houston, July 16, 1997
Fewest offensive rebounds, game
3 — vs Washington, July 19, 2005
at San Antonio, July 31, 2004
at Connecticut, May 27, 2004
4 — Many Times

DEFENSIVE REBOUNDS

Most defensive rebounds per game, season
25.4 — 2002 (814/32)
24.5 — 2000 (783/32)

Fewest defensive rebounds per game, season
  20.1 — 2005 (683/34)
  22.7 — 1999 (725/32)
Most defensive rebounds, game
  38 — at Sacramento, July 27, 1997
  37 — vs Portland, July 24, 2002
Fewest defensive rebounds, game
  12 — at Sacramento, July 29, 2005
       at Utah, August 21, 1999
  13 — at Seattle, July 31, 2005
       at Detroit, August 2, 2000
       at Sacramento, July 15, 1997

ASSISTS

Most assists per game, season
  18.6 — 2001 (596/32)
  18.4 — 2004 (626/34)
Fewest assists per game, season
  15.7 — 1998 (472/30)
  16.2 — 2005 (551/34)
Most assists, game
  29 — vs Indiana, August 6, 2001
  28 — vs New York, July 20, 2000
Fewest assists, game
  6 — at San Antonio, August 9, 2003
      at New York, August 5, 1997
  7 — at Sacramento, June 4, 2005
      at Seattle, August 6, 2003
      at Detroit, July 25, 1998

PERSONAL FOULS

Most personal fouls per game, season
  22.5 — 1998 (675/30)
  22.0 — 2000 (705/32)
Fewest personal fouls per game, season
  19.3 — 2001 (616/32)
  20.1 — 2003 (682/34)
Most personal fouls, game
  36 — at Utah, June 23, 1997
  35 — at Portland, June 17, 2000
Fewest personal fouls, game
  10 — vs Indiana, August 6, 2001
  12 — vs Charlotte, June 25, 1997
       vs Phoenix, July 5, 2001
       at Houston, June 24, 2003

DISQUALIFICATIONS

Most disqualifications per game, season
  .56 — 2002 (18/32)
  .41 — 2000 (13/32)
Fewest disqualifications per game, season
  .18 — 2005 (6/34)
  .19 — 1999 (6/32)
Most disqualifications, game
  3 — at Seattle, June 13, 2000 (OT)
  2 — Many Times

STEALS

Most steals per game, season
  9.3 — 1997 (259/28)
  8.8 — 2001 (281/32)

Fewest steals per game, season
  7.1 — 2003 (242/34)
  7.4 — 1999 (237/32)
Most steals, game
  20 — at Cleveland, July 3, 1997
  17 — at San Antonio, July 31, 2004
       vs New York, June 29, 2004 (OT)
       at Portland, August 14, 2001
Fewest steals, game
  1 — vs New York, June 19, 1998
  2 — Many Times

BLOCKED SHOTS

Most blocked shots per game, season
  5.0 — 2002 (161/32)
  4.9 — 1998 (148/30)
Fewest blocked shots per game, season
  3.9 — 1999 (124/32)
  4.0 — 2005 (136/34)
Most blocked shots, game
  13 — at Phoenix, July 11, 2001
  12 — vs Detroit, September 9, 2004
Fewest blocked shots, game
  0 — Many Times

TURNOVERS

Most turnovers per game, season
  18.9 — 1997 (528/28)
  17.0 — 1998 (511/30)
Fewest turnovers per game, season
  13.7 — 2001 (438/32)
  13.8 — 2003 (470/34)
Most turnovers, game
  28 — at Sacramento, June 3, 2004
  27 — vs Portland, July 24, 2002
Fewest turnovers, game
  7 — vs Charlotte, June 9, 2004
      vs San Antonio, August 23, 2003
      vs Charlotte, June 19, 2001
  8 — Many Times

TEAM DEFENSE

POINTS

Fewest points allowed per game, season
  67.7 — 2001 (2166/32)
  67.8 — 2000 (2169/32)
Most points allowed per game, season
  72.4 — 1999 (2318/32)
  72.3 — 1998 (2169/30)
Fewest points allowed, game
  48 — at Phoenix, June 21, 2003
  49 — at New York, June 22, 2004
Fewest points allowed, first half
  16 — at Washington, August 14, 1999
  18 — vs Houston, July 16, 1997
Fewest points allowed, second half
  17 — at San Antonio, June 26, 2003
  19 — at Phoenix, June 21, 2003
       at Minnesota, August 6, 1999
Fewest points allowed, overtime period
  2 — at Seattle, August 8, 2000
      at Sacramento, July 29, 2004
  4 — at Phoenix, July 25, 1997

vs New York, June 29, 2004

FIELD GOAL PERCENTAGE

Lowest opponents' field goal percentage, season
.389 — 2004 (815/2095)
.390 — 2002 (796/2040)
Highest opponents' field goal percentage, season
.418 — 2005 (818/1955)
.411 — 1998 (780/1898)
Lowest opponents' field goal percentage, game
.237 — at Seattle, May 21, 2005 (18/76)
.258 — at New York, June 22, 2004 (16/62)

TURNOVERS

Fewest opponents' turnovers per game, season
13.8 — 2003 (468/34)
14.2 — 2002 (453/32)
2001 (453/32)
Most opponents' turnovers per game, season
18.0 — 1997 (505/28)
16.0 — 1998 (481/30)
Most opponents' turnovers, game
30 — vs Utah, June 28, 1999
28 — at Cleveland, July 3, 1999

TEAM MISCELLANEOUS

GAME WON AND LOST

Highest winning percentage, season
.875 — 2000, 2001 (28-4)
.781 — 2002 (25-7)
Lowest winning percentage, season
.400 — 1998 (12-18)
.500 — 2005 (17-17)
1997 (14-14)
Most consecutive games won
18 — June 26-August 11, 2001
12 — August 9, 2002-June 14, 2003
July 14-August 8, 2000
June 17-July 9, 2000
Most consecutive games won, one season
18 — June 26-August 11, 2001
12 — July 14-August 8, 2000
June 17-July 9, 2000
Most consecutive games lost
5 — June 21-July 2, 1998
4 — July 30-August 6, 2003
August 9-14, 1999
Most consecutive games lost, one season
5 — June 21-July 2, 1998
4 — July 30-August 6, 2003
August 9-14, 1999
Highest winning percentage, home games, season
1.000 — 2001 (16-0)
.938 — 2000 (15-1)
Lowest winning percentage, home games, season
.533 — 1998 (8-7)
.571 — 1997 (8-6)
Most consecutive home games won
28 — July 14, 2001-June 27, 2002
12 — August 16, 1999-July 9, 2000

Most consecutive home games lost
3 — June 21-July 2, 1998
2 — Many Times
Highest winning percentage, road games, season
.813 — 2000, 2002 (13-3)
.765 — 2003 (13-4)
Lowest winning percentage, road games, season
.267 — 1998 (4-11)
.353 — 2005 (6-11)
Most consecutive road games won
12 — June 17-August 8, 2000
11 — July 20, 2002-June 14, 2003
Most consecutive road games lost
7 — June 14-July 27, 1998
4 — August 10-21, 1999
July 5-21, 1997

OVERTIME GAMES

Most overtime games, season
5 — 2004
4 — 1997
Most consecutive overtime games, season
2 — June 29-July 2, 2004
Most overtime games won, season
4 — 2004
2 — 2003, 2002, 2001, 1999, 1997
Most overtime games won, no losses, season
2 — 1999
1 — 1998
Most overtime games lost, season
2 — 1997
1 — 2000, 2001, 2002, 2003, 2004
Most overtime games lost, no wins, season
none
Most overtime periods, game
2 — at Sacramento, July 29, 2004
at Charlotte, June 20, 2004
vs Phoenix, July 15, 2003
at Minnesota, July 1, 1999
at Cleveland, August 7, 1997

INDIVIDUAL RECORDS

SEASONS

Most seasons
9 — Lisa Leslie
Mwadi Mabika
Tamecka Dixon

GAMES

Most games, career
273 — Lisa Leslie
263 — Tamecka Dixon
254 — Mwadi Mabika
Most consecutive games, career
154 — DeLisha Milton-Jones, June 10, 1999-August 2, 2003
119 — Nikki Teasley, May 25, 2002-July 19, 2005
98 — Lisa Leslie, July 27, 1998-July 21, 2001
Most games, season
34 — By Many

MINUTES

Most minutes, career
  8,889 — Lisa Leslie
  7,315 — Tamecka Dixon
  7,165 — Mwadi Mabika
Highest average, minutes per game, career
(Minimum 100 games)
  32.6 — Lisa Leslie (8889/273)
  31.3 — Nikki Teasley (3727/119)
  30.4 — DeLisha Milton-Jones (5412/178)
Most minutes, season
  1,189 — Nikki Teasley, 2003
  1,183 — Chamique Holdsclaw, 2005
  1,150 — Lisa Leslie, 2004
Highest average, minutes per game, season
  35.8 — Chamique Holdsclaw, 2005 (1183/33)
  35.0 — Nikki Teasley, 2003 (1189/34)
          DeLisha Milton-Jones, 2003 (1086/31)
Most minutes, game
  50 — Nikki Teasley, vs Phoenix, July 15, 2003 (2OT)
  48 — Lisa Leslie, at Sacramento, July 29, 2004 (2OT)
  47 — Lisa Leslie, at Charlotte, June 20, 2004 (2OT)

SCORING

Most points, lifetime
  4,732 — Lisa Leslie
  2,941 — Mwadi Mabika
  2,774 — Tamecka Dixon
Highest average, points per game, career
(Minimum 100 games)
  17.3 — Lisa Leslie (4732/273)
  11.6 — Mwadi Mabika (2941/254)
  11.2 — DeLisha Milton-Jones (1990/178)
Most points, season
  606 — Lisa Leslie, 2001
  598 — Lisa Leslie, 2004
  570 — Lisa Leslie, 2000
Highest average, points per game, season
  19.6 — Lisa Leslie, 1998 (549/28)
  19.5 — Lisa Leslie, 2001 (606/31)
  18.4 — Lisa Leslie, 2003 (424/23)
Most points, game
  32 — Mwadi Mabika, at Portland, July 12, 2002 (OT)
        Lisa Leslie, vs Minnesota, July 8, 2001 (OT)
  31 — Lisa Leslie, at Portland, July 28, 2001
        Lisa Leslie, vs Phoenix, September 14, 2004
        Lisa Leslie, vs San Antonio, August 23, 2003
Most games, 30 or more points, career
  10 — Lisa Leslie
  1 — Mwadi Mabika
Most games, 20 or more points, career
  94 — Lisa Leslie
  36 — Mwadi Mabika
  21 — Tamecka Dixon
Most consecutive games, 20 or more points
  6 — Lisa Leslie, September 1-14, 2004
       Lisa Leslie, July 28-August 8, 2001
  4 — Mwadi Mabika, July 15-22, 2003
       Lisa Leslie, July 15-23, 2000
  3 — By Many

Most consecutive games, 10 or more points
  54 — Lisa Leslie, June 17, 2000-August 8, 2001
  40 — Lisa Leslie, August 16, 1997-June 24, 1999
  18 — Lisa Leslie, August 4, 2002-June 24, 2003

FIELD GOAL PERCENTAGE

Highest field goal percentage, career
(Minimum 400 field goals)
  .470 — DeLisha Milton-Jones (745/1585)
  .462 — Lisa Leslie (1743/3774)
  .427 — Tamecka Dixon (1047/2451)
Highest field goal percentage, season (qualifiers)
  .618 — Haixia Zheng, 1997 (110/178)
  .602 — Latasha Byears, 2001 (133/221)
  .530 — DeLisha Milton-Jones, 1999 (125/236)
Highest field goal percentage, game
(Minimum 8 field goals made)
  1.000 — Lisa Leslie, at Seattle, July 31, 2005 (8/8)
  .909 — Haixia Zheng, vs Sacramento,
           August 22, 1997 (10/11)
  .900 — Lisa Leslie, vs Seattle, August 4, 2001 (9/10)
Most field goals, none missed, game
  8 — Lisa Leslie, at Seattle, July 31, 2005
  6 — Latasha Byears, at Phoenix, June 28, 2002
  5 — Rhonda Mapp, vs Indiana, August 6, 2001
       Ukari Figgs, vs New York, July 20, 2000
       Linda Burgess, at Charlotte, July 5, 1997
       Vedrana Grgin Fonseca, at Cleveland,
       June 22, 2001
Most field goal attempts, none made, game
  7 — Tamecka Dixon, vs Cleveland, June 5, 2001
       Lisa Leslie, at Sacramento, June 4, 2005
       Jamila Wideman, vs Phoenix, July 13, 1997
       Mwadi Mabika, at Charlotte, August 12, 1998
       Nikki Teasley, at San Antonio, August 9, 2003
       Tamika Whitmore, vs Connecticut, June 20, 2005
  6 — By Many

FIELD GOALS

Most field goals, career
  1,743 — Lisa Leslie
  1,047 — Tamecka Dixon
  1,038 — Mwadi Mabika
Most field goals, season
  223 — Lisa Leslie, 2004
  221 — Lisa Leslie, 2001
  216 — Chamique Holdsclaw, 2005
Most field goals, game
  14 — Lisa Leslie, vs Seattle, August 1, 2002
  12 — Lisa Leslie, at Cleveland, June 12, 1999
        Lisa Leslie, at New York, June 14, 2003
        Lisa Leslie, vs San Antonio, August 23, 2003
  11 — Many Times

FIELD GOAL ATTEMPTS

Most field goal attempts, career
  3,774 — Lisa Leslie
  2,657 — Mwadi Mabika
  2,451 — Tamecka Dixon
Most field goal attempts, season
  467 — Lisa Leslie, 2001
  464 — Lisa Leslie, 2005
  451 — Lisa Leslie, 2004
Most field goal attempts, game
  28 — Mwadi Mabika, vs Phoenix, July 15, 2003 (2OT)
        Mwadi Mabika, at Sacramento,
        July 29, 2004 (2OT)

24 — Lisa Leslie, vs San Antonio, August 23, 2003
23 — By Many

THREE-POINT FIELD GOAL PERCENTAGE

Highest three-point field goal percentage, career
(Minimum 100 three-point field goals)
.395 — Nikki Teasley (207/524)
.331 — Mwadi Mabika (330/997)
.318 — Lisa Leslie (109/343)
Highest three-point field goal percentage, season
(qualifiers)
.462 — Ukari Figgs, 2001 (54/117)
.449 — Doneeka Hodges, 2005 (31/69)
.430 — Gordana Grubin, 1999 (40/93)
Most three-point field goals, none missed, game
5 — Nikki Teasley, at Houston, June 24, 2003
4 — Lisa Leslie, at Seattle, June 16, 2001
Nina Bjedov, at Utah, August 5, 1999
3 — By Many
Most three-point field goal attempts, none made, game
6 — Lisa Leslie, at Utah, August 13, 2001 (OT)
5 — Mwadi Mabika, vs Houston, July 23, 2004
Mwadi Mabika, vs Phoenix, July 11, 1999
Nikki Teasley, vs Sacramento, June 28, 2003
Allison Feaster, at Minnesota, July 31, 2000
Doneeka Hodges, vs Detroit,
September 9, 2004
4 — By Many

THREE-POINT FIELD GOALS

Most three-point field goals, career
330 — Mwadi Mabika
207 — Nikki Teasley
112 — Tamecka Dixon
Most three-point field goals, season
70 — Nikki Teasley, 2003
68 — Nikki Teasley, 2004
64 — Mwadi Mabika, 2002
Most three-point field goals, game
6 — Nikki Teasley, vs Detroit, September 9, 2004
5 — By Many
Most consecutive games, three-point field goals made
33 — Nikki Teasley, June 5, 2004-May 31, 2005
16 — Mwadi Mabika, June 11-July 14, 2000
Mwadi Mabika, June 8-July 20, 2002
15 — Mwadi Mabika, July 20, 2000-June 5, 2001
Ukari Figgs, July 8-August 13, 2001

THREE-POINT FIELD GOAL ATTEMPTS

Most three-point field goal attempts, career
997 — Mwadi Mabika
524 — Nikki Teasley
352 — Tamecka Dixon
Most three-point field goal attempts, season
175 — Mwadi Mabika, 2002
165 — Nikki Teasley, 2003
Nikki Teasley, 2004
Most three-point field goal attempts, game
11 — Mwadi Mabika, vs Miami, July 30, 2002
Mwadi Mabika, at Minnesota,
July 1, 1999 (2OT)
Mwadi Mabika, vs Houston, August 8, 2002
Sophia Witherspoon, vs Orlando, July 22, 2002

10 — Mwadi Mabika, vs Minnesota, July 30, 2001
Mwadi Mabika, at Sacramento, August 3, 2002
Nikki Teasley, at Sacramento, July 31, 2003

FREE THROW PERCENTAGE

Highest free throw percentage, career
.821 — Nikki Teasley (202/246)
.801 — Tamecka Dixon (568/709)
.797 — Mwadi Mabika (535/671)
Highest free throw percentage, season (qualifiers)
.883 — Tamecka Dixon, 2003 (83/94)
.875 — Nikki Teasley, 2003 (98/112)
.868 — Tamika Whitmore, 2005 (92/106)
Most free throws made, none missed, game
14 — Lisa Leslie, vs Minnesota, July 15, 2000
13 — Chamique Holdsclaw, at Washington,
May 26, 2005
12 — Tamika Whitmore, at Houston, July 23, 2005
Most free throw attempts, none made, game
4 — Sophia Witherspoon, at Miami, May 30, 2002
3 — Tamika Whitmore, at Houston, July 10, 2004
Vedrana Grgin Fonseca, at New York,
June 24, 2001
2 — By Many

FREE THROWS MADE

Most free throws made, career
1137 — Lisa Leslie
568 — Tamecka Dixon
535 — Mwadi Mabika
Most free throws made, season
169 — Lisa Leslie, 2000
146 — Lisa Leslie, 2004
142 — Lisa Leslie, 2001
Most free throws made, game
15 — Lisa Leslie, vs Utah, August 4, 2002
14 — Lisa Leslie, vs Minnesota, July 15, 2000
Lisa Leslie, vs Washington, July 21, 2004
13 — Lisa Leslie, vs San Antonio, September 1, 2004
Chamique Holdsclaw, at Washington,
May 26, 2005

FREE THROW ATTEMPTS

Most free throw attempts, career
1615 — Lisa Leslie
709 — Tamecka Dixon
671 — Mwadi Mabika
Most free throw attempts, season
205 — Lisa Leslie, 2000
Lisa Leslie, 2004
193 — Lisa Leslie, 2001
Most free throw attempts, game
19 — Lisa Leslie, vs Utah, August 4, 2002
18 — Lisa Leslie, vs Washington, July 21, 2004

REBOUNDS

Most rebounds, career
2540 — Lisa Leslie
1100 — Mwadi Mabika
1060 — DeLisha Milton-Jones
Highest average, rebounds per game, career
(Minimum 100 games)
9.3 — Lisa Leslie (2540/273)
6.0 — DeLisha Milton-Jones (1060/178)
4.3 — Mwadi Mabika (1100/254)

Most rebounds, season
   336 — Lisa Leslie, 2004
   322 — Lisa Leslie, 2002
   306 — Lisa Leslie, 2000
Highest average, rebounds per game, season (qualifiers)
   10.4 — Lisa Leslie, 2002 (322/31)
   10.2 — Lisa Leslie, 1998 (285/28)
   9.9 — Lisa Leslie, 2004 (336/34)
Most rebounds, game
   21 — Lisa Leslie, vs New York, June 19, 1998
       Lisa Leslie, vs Orlando, July 22, 2002
   20 — Lisa Leslie, at Charlotte, June 20, 2004 (2OT)
   18 — Lisa Leslie, vs Portland, June 3, 2002
       Lisa Leslie, at Cleveland, June 12, 1999
Most games, 10+ rebounds, career
   128 — Lisa Leslie
   18 — DeLisha Milton-Jones
   9 — Mwadi Mabika
Most consecutive games, 10+ rebounds
   7 — Lisa Leslie, August 22, 1997-June 21, 1998
      Lisa Leslie, August 13, 2002-June 7, 2003
   5 — Lisa Leslie, July 7-19, 2004
   4 — By Many

OFFENSIVE REBOUNDS

Most offensive rebounds, career
   659 — Lisa Leslie
   345 — DeLisha Milton-Jones
   273 — Mwadi Mabika
Highest average, offensive rebounds per game, career
(Minimum 100 games)
   2.4 — Lisa Leslie (659/273)
   1.9 — DeLisha Milton-Jones (345/178)
   1.1 — Mwadi Mabika (273/254)
Most offensive rebounds, season
   88 — Lisa Leslie, 2001
   86 — Chamique Holdsclaw, 2005
   80 — Latasha Byears, 2001
Most offensive rebounds, game
   10 — Latasha Byears, vs Sacramento, July 25, 2001
   8 — Lisa Leslie, at New York, June 24, 2001
      Chamique Holdsclaw, at Charlotte, May 28,2005
   7 — By Many

DEFENSIVE REBOUNDS

Most defensive rebounds, career
   1881 — Lisa Leslie
   827 — Mwadi Mabika
   715 — DeLisha Milton-Jones
Highest average, defensive rebounds per game, career
(Minimum 100 games)
   6.9 — Lisa Leslie (1881/273)
   4.0 — DeLisha Milton-Jones (715/178)
   3.3 — Mwadi Mabika (827/254)
Most defensive rebounds, season
   276 — Lisa Leslie, 2004
   244 — Lisa Leslie, 2002
   231 — Lisa Leslie, 2000

Most defensive rebounds, game
   16 — Lisa Leslie, vs New York, June 19, 1998
      Lisa Leslie, vs Orlando, July 22, 2002
   15 — Lisa Leslie, vs Portland, June 3, 2002
      Lisa Leslie, at Charlotte, June 20, 2004 (2OT)
      Lisa Leslie, vs Minnesota, June 11, 2004
   14 — Lisa Leslie, at Minnesota, June 9, 2001
      Lisa Leslie, vs Connecticut, June 14, 2004 (OT)

ASSISTS

Most assists, career
   769 — Tamecka Dixon
   641 — Mwadi Mabika
   637 — Lisa Leslie
Highest average, assists per game, career
(Minimum 100 games)
   2.9 — Tamecka Dixon (769/263)
   2.5 — Mwadi Mabika (641/254)
   2.3 — Lisa Leslie (637/273)
Most assists, season
   214 — Nikki Teasley, 2003
   207 — Nikki Teasley, 2004
   143 — Penny Toler, 1997
      Penny Toler, 1998
Highest average, assists per game, season (qualifiers)
   6.3 — Nikki Teasley, 2003 (214/34)
   6.1 — Nikki Teasley, 2004 (207/34)
   5.1 — Penny Toler, 1997 (143/28)
Most assists, game
   14 — Penny Toler, vs Utah, August 14, 1998
   13 — Nikki Teasley, at New York, June 14, 2003
   11 — Nikki Teasley, vs Cleveland, July 7, 2003
      Nikki Teasley, vs Indiana, June 12, 2003
      Nikki Teasley, at Minnesota, August 14, 2003
      Nikki Teasley, at Seattle, September 18, 2004
Most games, 10+ assists, career
   8 — Nikki Teasley
   2 — Penny Toler

PERSONAL FOULS

Most personal fouls, career
   1090 — Lisa Leslie
   738 — Mwadi Mabika
   639 — Tamecka Dixon
Most personal fouls, season
   136 — Lisa Leslie, 1999
   134 — Lisa Leslie, 2000
   132 — Lisa Leslie, 2001
Most personal fouls, game
   6 — By Many

STEALS

Most steals, career
   376 — Lisa Leslie
   313 — Mwadi Mabika
   280 — Tamecka Dixon
Highest average, steals per game, career
(Minimum 100 games)
   1.5 — DeLisha Milton-Jones (262/178)
   1.4 — Lisa Leslie (376/273)
   1.2 — Mwadi Mabika (313/254)

Most steals, season
   67 — Lisa Leslie, 2005
   58 — Mwadi Mabika, 2000
   50 — Lisa Leslie, 2004
       DeLisha Milton-Jones, 2002
Highest average, steals per game, season (qualifiers)
   2.0 — Lisa Leslie, 2005 (67/34)
   1.8 — Mwadi Mabika, 2000 (58/32)
       Tamecka Dixon, 1997 (49/27)
   1.6 — DeLisha Milton-Jones, 2003 (49/31)
Most steals, game
   6 — Lisa Leslie, vs Cleveland, July 12, 1998
      Latasha Byears, at Portland, July 28, 2001
      Lisa Leslie, at Indiana, June 25, 2004
      Mwadi Mabika, at Detroit, July 2, 1999
      Lisa Leslie, vs Utah, July 30, 1999
      Penny Toler, vs Washington, August 3, 1998
      Lisa Leslie, at Utah, August 1, 1998

8 — Lisa Leslie, at Sacramento, June 3, 2004
    Mwadi Mabika, vs Sacramento, June 5, 2003
    Tamecka Dixon, vs Detroit, September 9, 2004

BLOCKED SHOTS

Most blocked shots, career
   635 — Lisa Leslie
   161 — DeLisha Milton-Jones
    89 — Mwadi Mabika
Highest average, blocked shots per game, career
(Minimum: 100 games)
   2.3 — Lisa Leslie (635/273)
   .9 — DeLisha Milton-Jones (161/178)
   .4 — Mwadi Mabika (89/254)
Most blocked shots, season
   98 — Lisa Leslie, 2004
   90 — Lisa Leslie, 2002
   74 — Lisa Leslie, 2000
Highest average, blocked shots per game, season (qualifiers)
   2.90 — Lisa Leslie, 2002 (90/31)
   2.88 — Lisa Leslie, 2004 (98/34)
   2.7 — Lisa Leslie, 2003 (63/23)
Most blocked shots, game
   10 — Lisa Leslie, vs Detroit, September 9, 2004
   7 — Lisa Leslie, vs New York, May 25, 2002
      Lisa Leslie, at Charlotte, June 20, 2004 (2OT)
      Lisa Leslie, vs Minnesota, June 18, 2005
      Lisa Leslie, at Utah, August 13, 2001 (OT)
   6 — By Many

TURNOVERS

Most turnovers, career
   889 — Lisa Leslie
   547 — Tamecka Dixon
   417 — DeLisha Milton-Jones
Most turnovers, season
   110 — Lisa Leslie, 2004
   109 — Lisa Leslie, 1997
   108 — Lisa Leslie, 2002
       Nikki Teasley, 2003
Most turnovers, game
   9 — Nikki Teasley, vs Phoenix, July 15, 2003 (2OT)
      Nikki Teasley, vs Connecticut,
      June 14, 2004 (OT)

MINNESOTA LYNX

REGULAR SEASON TEAM RECORDS

TEAM OFFENSE

SCORING

Highest average, points per game, season
70.0 — 2003 (2380/34)
68.5 — 2000 (2193/32)
Lowest average, points per game, season
62.6 — 2002 (2003/32)
63.6 — 1999 (2035/32)
Most points, game
95 — at Los Angeles, July 8, 2001 (OT)
88 — vs Detroit, June 5, 2000
Fewest points, game
44 — at San Antonio, May 26, 2004
45 — at Phoenix, July 29, 2002
Largest margin of victory, game
27 — vs San Antonio, July 25, 2003 (81-54)
24 — vs Phoenix, August 2, 2002 (75-51)
vs Miami, July 28, 2000 (68-44)
vs Utah, June 14, 1999 (78-54)
Largest margin of defeat, game
39 — vs Sacramento, July 3, 2001 (52-91)
33 — at Phoenix, July 29, 1999 (46-79)

BY HALF

Most points, first half
48 — at Seattle, June 14, 2003
vs Utah, June 14, 1999
46 — vs Los Angeles, May 28, 2003
Fewest points, first half
11 — vs Houston, June 30, 2001
13 — vs Charlotte, August 3, 2001
Largest lead at half time
24 — at Orlando, June 8, 2000 (led 41-17; won 71-57)
23 — vs Utah, June 14, 1999 (led 48-25; won 78-54)
Largest deficit at halftime overcome to win game
12 — vs Phoenix, June 5, 2004 (trailed 31-43; won 76-68)
vs Phoenix, July 9, 2004 (trailed 22-34; won 61-59)
9 — at Sacramento, June 1, 2002 (trailed 26-35; won 63-61)
at Sacramento, May 22, 2004 (trailed 29-38; won 69-61)
vs Detroit, July 3, 2004 (trailed 31-40; won 78-70)
Most points, second half
52 — at Los Angeles, July 8, 2001
51 — vs Charlotte, August 3, 2001
Fewest points, second half
19 — vs Los Angeles, August 6, 1999
at Washington, August 21, 1999
20 — Many Times

OVERTIME

Most points, overtime period
14 — at Los Angeles, July 8, 2001
12 — vs Sacramento, July 11, 2004
Fewest points, overtime period
2 — at Utah, July 28, 2001
at Seattle, June 4, 2002
4 — at Detroit, August 11, 2005
Largest margin of victory, overtime period
10 — vs Sacramento, July 11, 2004 (83-73)
8 — vs Houston, June 30, 2004 (58-50)

FIELD GOAL PERCENTAGE

Highest field goal percentage, season
.442 — 2003 (875/1978)
.421 — 2000 (770/1831)
Lowest field goal percentage, season
.371 — 2001 (671/1810)
.389 — 1999 (748/1925)
Highest field goal percentage, game
.556 — at Miami, May 28, 2002 (20/36)
.548 — vs Seattle, July 20, 2003 (23/42)
Lowest field goal percentage, game
.200 — vs Houston, July 23, 2001 (11/55)
.254 — at Orlando, July 21, 2001 (16/63)

FIELD GOALS

Most field goals per game, season
25.7 — 2003 (875/34)
24.1 — 2000 (770/32)
Fewest field goals per game, season
21.0 — 2001 (671/32)
22.6 — 2004 (767/34)
Most field goals, game
32 — at Seattle, May 20, 2004
vs San Antonio, July 25, 2003
vs Connecticut, July 10, 2003
vs Indiana, August 6, 2000
vs Orlando, August 20, 1999 (ot)
31 — vs Phoenix, August 2, 2002
vs Utah, June 22, 2000
Fewest field goals, game
11 — vs Houston, July 23, 2001
14 — vs New York, July 6, 2001

FIELD GOAL ATTEMPTS

Most field goal attempts per game, season
60.2 — 1999 (1925/32)
58.2 — 2003 (1978/34)
Fewest field goal attempts per game, season
55.5 — 2002 (1775/32)
55.9 — 2004 (1900/34)
Most field goal attempts, game
77 — vs Detroit, August 23, 2003 (OT)
76 — vs Utah, May 25, 2002 (OT)
Fewest field goal attempts, game
36 — at Miami, May 28, 2002
40 — vs Portland, July 10, 2002

THREE-POINT FIELD GOAL PERCENTAGE

Highest three-point field goal percentage, season
.357 — 2000 (204/571)
.350 — 2005 (172/492)
Lowest three-point field goal percentage, season
.319 — 2001 (176/552)
.327 — 2004 (177/542)

THREE-POINT FIELD GOALS

Most three-point field goals per game, season
6.4 — 2000 (204/32)
6.3 — 1999 (200/32)
Fewest three-point field goals per game, season
5.1 — 2005 (172/34)
5.2 — 2002 (166/32)
Most three-point field goals, game
14 — at Utah, June 26, 1999
12 — at Los Angeles, July 8, 2001 (ot)
Fewest three-point field goals, game
0 — at San Antonio, May 26, 2004
at Phoenix, June 22, 2004
1 — Many Times

THREE-POINT FIELD GOAL ATTEMPTS

Most three-point field goal attempts per game, season
18.8 — 1999 (603/32)
17.8 — 2000 (571/32)
Fewest three-point field goal attempts per game, season
14.5 — 2005 (492/34)
15.4 — 2003 (524/34)
Most three-point field goal attempts, game
29 — vs Los Angeles, May 28, 2003
28 — vs New York, May 30, 2004
at Connecticut, July 23, 2003
vs Orlando, August 20, 1999 (OT)
at Utah, June 26, 1999
Fewest three-point field goal attempts, game
5 — at Phoenix, June 22, 2004
8 — vs Phoenix, June 22, 2005
vs Portland, July 10, 2002
vs Seattle, July 18, 2001
vs Detroit, June 12, 1999

FREE THROW PERCENTAGE

Highest free throw percentage, season
.769 — 2001 (559/727)
.758 — 2000 (449/592)
Lowest free throw percentage, season
.663 — 2002 (383/578)
.709 — 2004 (454/640)
Highest free throw percentage, game
1.000 — vs Sacramento, May 29, 2005 (15/15)
vs Phoenix, August 4, 2003 (20/20)
at Houston, August 9, 2000 (11/11)
vs Los Angeles, August 6, 1999 (6/6)
.957 — vs Orlando, June 15, 2000 (22/23)
Lowest free throw percentage, game
.200 — at Portland, July 14, 2000 (1/5)
.286 — at Los Angeles, August 18, 1999 (2/7)

FREE THROWS MADE

Most free throws made per game, season
17.5 — 2001 (559/32)
14.0 — 2000 (449/32)
Fewest free throws made per game, season
10.6 — 1999 (339/32)
12.0 — 2002 (383/32)
Most free throws made, game
37 — at Los Angeles, July 8, 2001 (OT)
31 — at Seattle, June 15, 2005 (OT)
Fewest free throws made, game
1 — at Portland, July 14, 2000
2 — at Los Angeles, August 18, 1999
at Phoenix, July 29, 1999

FREE THROW ATTEMPTS

Most free throw attempts per game, season
22.7 — 2001 (727/32)
18.8 — 2004 (640/34)
Fewest free throw attempts per game, season
14.7 — 1999 (470/32)
17.7 — 2005 (601/34)
Most free throw attempts, game
45 — at Sacramento, August 9, 2003
43 — at Los Angeles, July 8, 2001 (OT)
Fewest free throw attempts, game
4 — at Phoenix, July 29, 1999
5 — at Portland, July 14, 2000
vs Houston, July 25, 1999

REBOUNDS

Most rebounds per game, season
31.7 — 2003 (1079/34)
31.3 — 2001 (1001/32)
Fewest rebounds per game, season
27.2 — 2000 (870/32)
28.3 — 1999 (906/32)
Most rebounds, game
47 — vs Sacramento, August 5, 2001 (OT)
42 — at Connecticut, July 22, 2004
Fewest rebounds, game
18 — at Los Angeles, August 23, 2005
19 — vs Cleveland, August 16, 1999

OFFENSIVE REBOUNDS

Most offensive rebounds per game, season
10.6 — 2003 (361/34)
9.8 — 2004 (332/34)
Fewest offensive rebounds per game, season
8.1 — 2000 (258/32)
9.1 — 2005 (310/34)
Most offensive rebounds, game
22 — vs Utah, May 25, 2002 (ot)
19 — at Connecticut, July 23, 2003
at Utah, June 23, 2001
Fewest offensive rebounds, game
2 — at Sacramento, June 17, 2005
vs Los Angeles, August 6, 1999
3 — vs Sacramento, August 27, 2005
vs Indiana, July 19, 2005
vs New York, July 6, 2001
at Portland, July 14, 2000

DEFENSIVE REBOUNDS

Most defensive rebounds per game, season
21.7 — 2001 (693/32)
21.3 — 2004 (724/34)
Fewest defensive rebounds per game, season
19.0 — 1999 (608/32)
19.1 — 2000 (612/32)
Most defensive rebounds, game
33 — vs Sacramento, August 5, 2001 (OT)
31 — at Utah, July 28, 2001 (OT)
Fewest defensive rebounds, game
11 — vs Charlotte, August 3, 2001
12 — vs Los Angeles, June 27, 2004
vs New York, June 6, 2003

ASSISTS

Most assists per game, season
17.1 — 2003 (580/34)
16.4 — 1999 (525/32)
Fewest assists per game, season
13.7 — 2001 (437/32)
14.6 — 2002 (466/32)
Most assists, game
25 — vs Indiana, August 6, 2000
23 — Many Times
Fewest assists, game
3 — at Seattle, August 8, 2003
6 — vs Orlando, June 15, 2000

PERSONAL FOULS

Most personal fouls per game, season
21.7 — 2001 (695/32)
21.6 — 2000 (690/32)
Fewest personal fouls per game, season
18.4 — 2005 (624/34)
18.6 — 2003 (634/34)
Most personal fouls, game
34 — at Utah, July 28, 2001 (OT)
33 — at Utah, July 5, 2002
Fewest personal fouls, game
9 — vs San Antonio, June 28, 2005
vs Los Angeles, August 11, 2002
10 — vs Connecticut, July 17, 2005

DISQUALIFICATIONS

Most disqualifications per game, season
.34 — 1999 (11/32)
2000 (11/32)
Fewest disqualifications per game, season
.09 — 2005 (3/34)
.18 — 2003 (6/34)
Most disqualifications, game
2 — at Detroit, August 11, 2005 (OT)
at San Antonio, August 16, 2003
at Utah, July 28, 2001 (OT)
at Seattle, July 21, 2000
at Charlotte, July 21, 1999
1 — Many Times

STEALS

Most steals per game, season
7.59 — 2005 (258/34)
7.56 — 2004 (257/34)

Fewest steals per game, season
6.4 — 1999 (204/32)
6.6 — 2001 (210/32)
Most steals, game
15 — vs San Antonio, July 28, 2004
vs Cleveland, August 16, 1999
14 — vs Sacramento, July 8, 2003
at Houston, June 15, 2002
vs Orlando, June 15, 2000
Fewest steals, game
0 — at Charlotte, July 21, 1999
2 — at Charlotte, July 7, 2005
vs Sacramento, July 11, 2004 (ot)
vs Houston, June 19, 2004
at Indiana, July 26, 2003
at Houston, July 1, 2003

BLOCKED SHOTS

Most blocked shots per game, season
4.1 — 2004 (139/34)
4.0 — 2001 (127/32)
Fewest blocked shots per game, season
2.0 — 2000 (63/32)
2.4 — 1999 (78/32)
Most blocked shots, game
9 — vs Charlotte, June 4, 2005
vs Seattle, September 10, 2004
vs Phoenix, August 2, 2002
8 — vs San Antonio, August 9, 2005
at Connecticut, July 22, 2004
vs Washington, May 28, 2004
at Indiana, July 26, 2003
at Washington, June 29, 2003
at Los Angeles, July 8, 2001 (ot)
Fewest blocked shots, game
0 — Many Times

TURNOVERS

Most turnovers per game, season
18.0 — 2004 (613/34)
16.5 — 2002 (529/32)
Fewest turnovers per game, season
13.7 — 1999 (437/32)
15.5 — 2000 (497/32)
Most turnovers, game
27 — vs Phoenix, June 27, 2003
26 — vs Seattle, September 10, 2004
at Houston, August 9, 2000
Fewest turnovers, game
6 — at Charlotte, July 21, 1999
7 — vs Charlotte, July 31, 1999

TEAM DEFENSE

POINTS

Fewest points allowed per game, season
64.4 — 2004 (2190/34)
65.8 — 2002 (2104/32)
Most points allowed per game, season
69.7 — 2003 (2370/34)
68.4 — 2000 (2188/32)

Fewest points allowed, game
44 — vs Miami, July 28, 2000
45 — vs Indiana, July 19, 2005
at Washington, August 21, 1999
Fewest points allowed, first half
16 — vs Detroit, June 12, 1999
17 — at Miami, June 10, 2000
at Orlando, June 8, 2000
at New York, August 6, 2002
Fewest points allowed, second half
16 — vs Portland, June 13, 2002
19 — vs San Antonio, June 3, 2004
Fewest points allowed, overtime period
0 — vs Houston, June 30, 2004
2 — vs Sacramento, July 11, 2004

FIELD GOAL PERCENTAGE

Lowest opponents' field goal percentage, season
.390 — 2001 (752/1927)
.408 — 2004 (804/1972)
Highest opponents' field goal percentage, season
.429 — 2000 (755/1758)
.427 — 2005 (862/2019)
Lowest opponents' field goal percentage, game
.259 — vs San Antonio, June 3, 2004 (15/58)
.262 — at Washington, June 25, 2001 (16/61)

TURNOVERS

Fewest opponents' turnovers per game, season
13.9 — 2003 (471/34)
14.3 — 2005 (487/34)
Most opponents' turnovers per game, season
17.1 — 2000 (547/32)
15.4 — 1999 (492/32)
Most opponents' turnovers, game
28 — vs Portland, July 2, 2000
vs Utah, May 25, 2002 (OT)
27 — vs Detroit, July 1, 2002 (OT)

TEAM MISCELLANEOUS

GAME WON AND LOST

Highest winning percentage, season
.529 — 2003, 2004 (18-16)
.469 — 2000, 1999 (15-17)
Lowest winning percentage, season
.313 — 2002 (10-22)
.375 — 2001 (12-20)
Most consecutive games won
6 — July 9-22, 2004
5 — June 5-17, 2000
Most consecutive games won, one season
6 — July 9-22, 2004
5 — June 5-17, 2000
Most consecutive games lost
8 — July 5-21, 2000
7 — July 3-19, 2002
Most consecutive games lost, one season
8 — July 5-21, 2000
7 — July 3-19, 2002
Highest winning percentage, home games, season
.647 — 2005, 2004, 2003 (11-6)
.500 — 1999, 2000 (8-8)

Lowest winning percentage, home games, season
.375 — 2001 (6-10)
.438 — 2002 (7-9)
Most consecutive home games won
7 — July 8-August 4, 2003
6 — June 4-July 13, 2005
June 30-July 28, 2004
Most consecutive home games lost
4 — July 3-9, 2002
3 — Many Times
Highest winning percentage, road games, season
.438 — 2000, 1999 (7-9)
Lowest winning percentage, road games, season
.176 — 2005 (3-14)
.188 — 2002 (3-13)
Most consecutive road games won
3 — July 15-July 22, 2004
August 9-August 20, 2003
June 8-17, 2000
2 — Many Times
Most consecutive road games lost
12 — June 4-July 31, 2002
7 — July 26-August 23, 2005

OVERTIME GAMES

Most overtime games, season
3 — 2002, 2001
2 — 1999, 2003, 2004
Most consecutive overtime games, season
1 — Many Times
Most overtime games won, season
2 — 2004
1 — Many Times
Most overtime games won, no losses, season
2 — 2004
1 — 2000
Most overtime games lost, season
2 — 1999, 2001, 2002
Most overtime games lost, no wins, season
2 — 1999
Most overtime periods, game
2 — vs Los Angeles, July 1, 1999

INDIVIDUAL RECORDS

SEASONS

Most seasons
7 — Katie Smith
5 — Svetlana Abrosimova
4 — Michele Van Gorp

GAMES

Most games, career
205 — Katie Smith
136 — Svetlana Abrosimova
133 — Tamika Williams
Most consecutive games, career
118 — Tamika Williams, July 10, 2002-
August 27, 2005 (current)
94 — Katie Smith, June 19, 1999-August 13, 2001
Most games, season
34 — By Many

Most minutes, career
 7,287 — Katie Smith
 3,880 — Tamika Williams
 3,682 — Svetlana Abrosimova
Highest average, minutes per game, career
(Minimum 100 games)
 35.5 — Katie Smith (7287/205)
 29.2 — Tamika Williams (3880/133)
 27.1 — Svetlana Abrosimova (3682/136)
Most minutes, season
 1,234 — Katie Smith, 2001
 1,193 — Katie Smith, 2000
 1,185 — Katie Smith, 2003
Highest average, minutes per game, season
 38.6 — Katie Smith, 2001 (1234/32)
 37.3 — Katie Smith, 2000 (1193/32)
 36.7 — Katie Smith, 2002 (1138/31)
Most minutes, game
 49 — Sonja Tate, vs Los Angeles, July 1, 1999 (2OT)
 45 — Katie Smith, at Los Angeles, July 8, 2001
(OT)
 Katie Smith, vs Sacramento, Aug. 5, 2001 (OT)

SCORING
Most points, lifetime
 3,605 — Katie Smith
 1,425 — Svetlana Abrosimova
 1,068 — Tamika Williams
Highest average, points per game, career
(Minimum 100 games)
 17.6 — Katie Smith (3605/205)
 10.5 — Svetlana Abrosimova (1425/136)
 8.0 — Tamika Williams (1068/133)
Most points, season
 739 — Katie Smith, 2001
 646 — Katie Smith, 2000
 620 — Katie Smith, 2003
Highest average, points per game, season
 23.1 — Katie Smith, 2001 (739/32)
 20.2 — Katie Smith, 2000 (646/32)
 18.8 — Katie Smith, 2004 (432/23)
Most points, game
 46 — Katie Smith, at Los Angeles, July 8, 2001 (ot)
 40 — Katie Smith, at Detroit, June 17, 2001
 36 — Katie Smith, at Phoenix, August 1, 2001
Most games, 30 or more points, career
 12 — Katie Smith
 1 — Betty Lennox
Most games, 20 or more points, career
 83 — Katie Smith
 16 — Svetlana Abrosimova
 13 — Betty Lennox
Most consecutive games, 20 or more points
 6 — Katie Smith, July 1-17, 2003
 Katie Smith, June 16-28, 2001
 5 — Katie Smith, July 6-14, 2001
 Katie Smith, August 8, 2000-June 9, 2001
Most consecutive games, 10 or more points
 35 — Katie Smith, July 7, 2000-July 18, 2001
 18 — Katie Smith, July 23, 2001-June 13, 2002
 17 — Katie Smith, August 20, 1999-July 2, 2000

FIELD GOAL PERCENTAGE
Highest field goal percentage, career
(Minimum 400 field goals)
 .581 — Tamika Williams (441/759)
 .413 — Katie Smith (1127/2728)
 .384 — Svetlana Abrosimova (503/1309)
Highest field goal percentage, season (qualifiers)
 .668 — Tamika Williams, 2003 (129/193)
 .561 — Tamika Williams, 2002 (124/221)
 .540 — Tamika Williams, 2004 (102/189)
Highest field goal percentage, game
(Minimum 8 field goals made)
 1.000 — Svetlana Abrosimova, vs Detroit, July 13,2005 (8/8)
 .900 — Katie Smith, vs Phoenix, August 2, 2002 (9/10)
 .889 — Svetlana Abrosimova, vs Seattle, July 18,2001 (8/9)
Most field goals, none missed, game
 8 — Svetlana Abrosimova, vs Detroit, July 13, 2005
 7 — Tamika Williams, vs Phoenix, June 5, 2004
 6 — Stacey Lovelace, vs San Antonio, August 9,2005
Most field goal attempts, none made, game
 9 — Lynn Pride, vs Houston, July 23, 2001
 Erin Buescher, at Utah, June 23, 2001
 Andrea Lloyd-Curry, vs Houston, June 19,1999
 7 — Grace Daley, at Los Angeles, July 15, 2000
 Tamara Moore, at Sacramento, July 28, 2002
 Val Whiting-Raymond, at Utah, June 23, 2001

FIELD GOALS
Most field goals, career
 1,127 — Katie Smith
 503 — Svetlana Abrosimova
 441 — Tamika Williams
Most field goals, season
 208 — Katie Smith, 2003
 204 — Katie Smith, 2001
 203 — Katie Smith, 2000
Most field goals, game
 13 — Katie Smith, at Detroit, June 17, 2001
 12 — Brandy Reed, vs Washington, July 23, 1999
 Katie Smith, vs Sacramento, July 11, 2004(OT)
 Katie Smith, vs Connecticut, July 10, 2003
 11 — By Many

FIELD GOAL ATTEMPTS
Most field goal attempts, career
 2,728 — Katie Smith
 1,309 — Svetlana Abrosimova
 759 — Tamika Williams
Most field goal attempts, season
 519 — Katie Smith, 2001
 482 — Katie Smith, 2000
 471 — Betty Lennox, 2000
Most field goal attempts, game
 23 — Brandy Reed, vs Charlotte, July 31, 1999
 Katie Smith, at Los Angeles, July 8, 2001 (OT)
 Svetlana Abrosimova, at Los Angeles,
 July 30, 2001
 22 — Tonya Edwards, vs Houston, July 25, 1999

Katie Smith, vs Sacramento,
July 11, 2004 (OT)
Betty Lennox, vs Los Angeles, July 31, 2000
Betty Lennox, vs Utah, May 25, 2002 (OT)

THREE-POINT FIELD GOAL PERCENTAGE

Highest three-point field goal percentage, career
(Minimum 100 three-point field goals)
.371 — Katie Smith (460/1239)
.331 — Svetlana Abrosimova (117/353)
Highest three-point field goal percentage, season
(qualifiers)
.432 — Katie Smith, 2004 (60/139)
.413 — Stacey Lovelace, 2005 (26/63)
.402 — Svetlana Abrosimova, 2005 (33/82)
Most three-point field goals, none missed, game
5 — Svetlana Abrosimova, vs Detroit, July 13, 2005
Andrea Lloyd-Curry, at Sacramento,
June 22,1999
4 — Katie Smith, vs Miami, July 28, 2000
3 — By Many
Most three-point field goal attempts, none made, game
7 — Katie Smith, vs Miami, July 19, 2002
6 — Katie Smith, at Phoenix, July 29, 2002
Katie Smith, vs Phoenix, June 20, 2000
Teresa Edwards, vs Houston, June 1, 2003 (OT)
Andrea Lloyd-Curry, vs Washington, July 23,1999
5 — By Many

THREE-POINT FIELD GOALS

Most three-point field goals, career
460 — Katie Smith
117 — Svetlana Abrosimova
80 — Betty Lennox
Most three-point field goals, season
88 — Katie Smith, 2000
85 — Katie Smith, 2001
78 — Katie Smith, 2003
Most three-point field goals, game
7 — Katie Smith, at Seattle, June 14, 2003
6 — By Many
Most consecutive games, three-point field goals made
32 — Katie Smith, July 31, 2002-August 2, 2003
25 — Katie Smith, June 22, 2000-June 9, 2001
22 — Katie Smith, August 1, 2001-July 3, 2002

THREE-POINT FIELD GOAL ATTEMPTS

Most three-point field goal attempts, career
1239 — Katie Smith
353 — Svetlana Abrosimova
214 — Betty Lennox
Most three-point field goal attempts, season
240 — Katie Smith, 2001
232 — Katie Smith, 2000
200 — Katie Smith, 2003
Most three-point field goal attempts, game
13 — Katie Smith, vs Los Angeles, June 3, 2000
12 — Katie Smith, at Utah, June 23, 2001
Tonya Edwards, vs Charlotte, July 31, 1999
Betty Lennox, vs Utah, May 25, 2002 (OT)

FREE THROW PERCENTAGE

Highest free throw percentage, career
.858 — Katie Smith (891/1039)
.755 — Nicole Ohlde (241/319)
.649 — Svetlana Abrosimova (302/465)
Highest free throw percentage, season (qualifiers)
.899 — Katie Smith, 2004 (98/109)
.895 — Katie Smith, 2001 (246/275)
.881 — Katie Smith, 2003 (126/143)
Most free throws made, none missed, game
12 — Katie Smith, vs Orlando, June 15, 2000
Katie Smith, vs Washington, May 28, 2004
10 — Kristin Folkl, vs Detroit, June 5, 2000
Katie Smith, at Utah, June 23, 2001
Katie Smith, vs Washington, July 27, 2001
Katie Smith, vs Cleveland, July 5, 2003
Most free throw attempts, none made, game
4 — Maylana Martin, at Indiana, June 16, 2001
Janell Burse, vs Los Angeles, June 8, 2002
Tamika Williams, vs Houston,
June 30, 2004 (OT)
Svetlana Abrosimova, at Indiana, July 26, 2002
2 — By Many

FREE THROWS MADE

Most free throws made, career
891 — Katie Smith
302 — Svetlana Abrosimova
241 — Nicole Ohlde
Most free throws made, season
246 — Katie Smith, 2001
152 — Katie Smith, 2000
126 — Katie Smith, 2003
Katie Smith, 2002
Most free throws made, game
18 — Katie Smith, at Los Angeles, July 8, 2001 (OT)
16 — Katie Smith, at Utah, July 28, 2001 (OT)
14 — Katie Smith, at Miami, June 10, 2000

FREE THROW ATTEMPTS

Most free throw attempts, career
1039 — Katie Smith
465 — Svetlana Abrosimova
334 — Tamika Williams
Most free throw attempts, season
275 — Katie Smith, 2001
177 — Nicole Ohlde, 2004
175 — Katie Smith, 2000
Most free throw attempts, game
19 — Katie Smith, at Los Angeles, July 8, 2001
18 — Katie Smith, at Utah, July 28, 2001 (OT)
Svetlana Abrosimova, vs Utah,
May 25, 2002 (OT)
16 — Katie Smith, vs Portland, July 2, 2000
Katie Smith, at Miami, June 10, 2000
Svetlana Abrosimova, vs Houston,
July 23, 2001

REBOUNDS

Most rebounds, career
814 — Tamika Williams

672 — Katie Smith
642 — Svetlana Abrosimova
Highest average, rebounds per game, career
(Minimum 100 games)
  6.1 — Tamika Williams (814/133)
  4.7 — Svetlana Abrosimova (642/136)
  3.3 — Katie Smith (672/205)
Most rebounds, season
  229 — Tamika Williams, 2002
  209 — Tamika Williams, 2003
  205 — Tamika Williams, 2004
Highest average, rebounds per game, season (qualifiers)
  7.4 — Tamika Williams, 2002 (229/31)
  6.7 — Svetlana Abrosimova, 2001 (174/26)
  6.1 — Tamika Williams, 2003 (209/34)
Most rebounds, game
  15 — Svetlana Abrosimova, vs Sacramento,
      August 5, 2001 (OT)
  14 — Tamika Williams, at Seattle, August 18, 2005
  13 — Svetlana Abrosimova, vs Portland, June 13, 2002
      Brandy Reed, vs Charlotte, July 31, 1999
      Svetlana Abrosimova, at Seattle, August 10, 2001
Most games, 10+ rebounds, career
  13 — Tamika Williams
      Svetlana Abrosimova
  6 — Nicole Ohlde
Most consecutive games, 10+ rebounds
  3 — Svetlana Abrosimova, August 8-12, 2001
  2 — Svetlana Abrosimova, July 24-26, 2002
     Tamika Williams, July 10-16, 2003

OFFENSIVE REBOUNDS

Most offensive rebounds, career
  346 — Tamika Williams
  203 — Katie Smith
  178 — Svetlana Abrosimova
Highest average, offensive rebounds per game, career
(Minimum 100 games)
  2.6 — Tamika Williams (346/133)
  1.3 — Svetlana Abrosimova (178/136)
  1.0 — Katie Smith (203/205)
Most offensive rebounds, season
  96 — Tamika Williams, 2002
  92 — Tamika Williams, 2003
  83 — Nicole Ohlde, 2004
Most offensive rebounds, game
  10 — Tamika Williams, at Phoenix, June 23, 2002
  8 — Tamika Williams, at Connecticut, July 22, 2004
  7 — Tamika Williams, at Houston, June 15, 2002
     Tamika Williams, at Seattle, August 8, 2003
     Vanessa Hayden, vs San Antonio, August 9, 2005

DEFENSIVE REBOUNDS

Most defensive rebounds, career
  469 — Katie Smith
  468 — Tamika Williams
  464 — Svetlana Abrosimova
Highest average, defensive rebounds per game, career
(Minimum 100 games)
  3.5 — Tamika Williams (468/133)

  3.4 — Svetlana Abrosimova (464/136)
  2.3 — Katie Smith (469/205)
Most defensive rebounds, season
  133 — Tamika Williams, 2002
  131 — Nicole Ohlde, 2005
      Svetlana Abrosimova, 2001
  125 — Betty Lennox, 2000
Most defensive rebounds, game
  13 — Svetlana Abrosimova, vs Sacramento,
      August 5, 2001 (OT)
  11 — Kristin Folkl, at Seattle, July 21, 2000
  10 — Betty Lennox, at Potland, July 14, 2000
      Nicole Ohlde, vs Connecticut, July 14, 2004
      Svetlana Abrosimova, vs Utah, July 24, 2002

ASSISTS

Most assists, career
  496 — Katie Smith
  300 — Svetlana Abrosimova
  233 — Kristi Harrower
Highest average, assists per game, career
(Minimum 100 games)
  2.4 — Katie Smith (496/205)
  2.2 — Svetlana Abrosimova (300/136)
  1.3 — Tamika Williams (172/133)
Most assists, season
  148 — Teresa Edwards, 2003
  115 — Helen Darling, 2004
  100 — Sonja Tate, 1999
Highest average, assists per game, season (qualifiers)
  4.4 — Teresa Edwards, 2003 (148/34)
  3.5 — Helen Darling, 2004 (115/33)
  3.1 — Sonja Tate, 1999 (100—32)
Most assists, game
  11 — Andrea Lloyd-Curry, at Charlotte,
      July 21, 1999
  10 — Helen Darling, vs Seattle, September 10, 2004
  9 — Helen Darling, vs Detroit, July 3, 2004
     Svetlana Abrosimova, at San Antonio,
     May 30, 2003
Most games, 10+ assists, career
  1 — Helen Darling
  1 — Andrea Lloyd-Curry

PERSONAL FOULS

Most personal fouls, career
  579 — Katie Smith
  350 — Svetlana Abrosimova
  252 — Tamika Williams
Most personal fouls, season
  112 — Katie Smith, 2003
      Betty Lennox, 2000
  110 — Vanessa Hayden, 2005
  107 — Keitha Dickerson, 2000
Most personal fouls, game
  6 — By Many

STEALS

Most steals, career
  206 — Svetlana Abrosimova
  191 — Katie Smith
  147 — Tamika Williams

Highest average, steals per game, career
(Minimum 100 games)
    1.5 — Svetlana Abrosimova (206/136)
    1.1 — Tamika Williams (147/133)
    .9 — Katie Smith (191/205)
Most steals, season
    53 — Betty Lennox, 2000
    48 — Svetlana Abrosimova, 2005
    47 — Teresa Edwards, 2004
Highest average, steals per game, season (qualifiers)
    1.70 — Betty Lennox, 2000 (53/32)
    1.62 — Svetlana Abrosimova, 2001 (42/26)
    1.56 — Svetlana Abrosimova, 2002 (42/27)
Most steals, game
    6 — Sonja Tate, vs Cleveland, August 16, 1999
        Lynn Pride, vs Sacramento, Aug. 5, 2001 (OT)
        Tamika Williams, at Houston, June 15, 2002
        Teresa Edwards, vs Sacramento, July 8, 2003
    5 — Betty Lennox, at Cleveland, June 24, 2000 (OT)
        Svetlana Abrosimova, at Seattle,
        June 4, 2002 (OT)
        Helen Darling, vs San Antonio, July 28, 2004

BLOCKED SHOTS

Most blocked shots, career
    97 — Vanessa Hayden
    67 — Nicole Ohlde
    56 — Janell Burse
Highest average, blocked shots per game, career
(Minimum: 100 games)
    .279 — Svetlana Abrosimova (38/136)
    .226 — Tamika Williams (30/133)
    .210 — Katie Smith (43/205)
Most blocked shots, season
    68 — Vanessa Hayden, 2005
    45 — Nicole Ohlde, 2004
    29 — Erin Buescher, 2001
        Vanessa Hayden, 2004
Highest average, blocked shots per game, season (qualifiers)
    2.2 — Vanessa Hayden, 2005 (68/31)
    1.3 — Nicole Ohlde, 2004 (45/34)
    1.0 — Vanessa Hayden, 2004 (29/29)
Most blocked shots, game
    6 — Vanessa Hayden, vs Charlotte, June 4, 2005
    5 — Janell Burse, at Indiana, July 26, 2003
        Vanessa Hayden, vs Seattle, June 26, 2005
        Vanessa Hayden, at New York, July 15, 2005
        Nicole Ohlde, at Connecticut, July 22, 2004
        Vanessa Hayden, vs San Antonio,
        August 9, 2005

TURNOVERS

Most turnovers, career
    460 — Katie Smith
    390 — Svetlana Abrosimova
    239 — Tamika Williams
Most turnovers, season
    97 — Betty Lennox, 2000
    93 — Teresa Edwards, 2004
    92 — Teresa Edwards, 2003
        Svetlana Abrosimova, 2002

Most turnovers, game
    11 — Betty Lennox, at Houston, August 9, 2000
    9 — Svetlana Abrosimova, at Portland, August 8, 2001
        Teresa Edwards, at Seattle, May 20, 2004
        Keitha Dickerson, at Seattle, July 21, 2000
        Betty Lennox, vs Utah, May 25, 2002 (OT)

NEW YORK LIBERTY

TEAM OFFENSE

SCORING

Highest average, points per game, season
68.6 — 1998 (2058/30)
68.3 — 1997 (1911/28)
Lowest average, points per game, season
65.3 — 2002 (2089/32)
66.0 — 2003 (2243/34)
Most points, game
95 — at Phoenix, June 21, 2001
92 — at Los Angeles, July 21, 1998
Fewest points, game
41 — at Miami, August 6, 2000
43 — vs Cleveland, August 4, 2001
at Connecticut, September 3, 2004
Largest margin of victory, game
43 — vs Washington, August 13, 1998 (88-45)
35 — at Cleveland, July 8, 1999 (84-49)
Largest margin of defeat, game
26 — at Sacramento, July 1, 2004 (47-73)
25 — at Indiana, August 27, 2005 (50-75)
vs Houston, July 8, 1998 (54-79)

BY HALF

Most points, first half
52 — at Phoenix, June 21, 2001
50 — vs Charlotte, August 2, 1998
Fewest points, first half
13 — at Sacramento, July 1, 2004
15 — at Houston, July 3, 1999
Largest lead at half time
26 — at Phoenix, June 21, 2001 (52-26)
25 — vs Charlotte, August 2, 1998 (50-25)
Largest deficit at halftime overcome to win game
15 — vs Indiana, June 30, 2000 (trailed 25-40; won 72-70)
at Connecticut, August 12, 2003 (trailed 21-36; won 74-73)
14 — at Washington, August 21, 2003 (trailed 19-33; won 65-60)
Most points, second half
57 — vs Connecticut, July 7, 2005
53 — at Connecticut, August 12, 2003
Fewest points, second half
19 — at Connecticut, September 3, 2004
20 — at Indiana, August 27, 2005
vs Detroit, August 1, 2003

OVERTIME

Most points, overtime period
17 — vs Indiana, September 16, 2004
at Orlando, July 29, 1999
13 — vs Utah, July 18, 1999
Fewest points, overtime period
4 — at Washington, August 11, 1999

at Los Angeles, June 29, 2004
at Detroit, September 14, 2004
5 — vs Charlotte, July 26, 1999
Largest margin of victory, overtime period
8 — at Charlotte, August 12, 2005 (82-74)
at Orlando, July 29, 1999 (73-65)
7 — vs Cleveland, August 24, 1997 (79-72)

FIELD GOAL PERCENTAGE

Highest field goal percentage, season
.456 — 2001 (833/1828)
.445 — 2005 (828/1860)
Lowest field goal percentage, season
.412 — 1997 (707/1715)
.418 — 1999 (800/1914)
Highest field goal percentage, game
.621 — vs Connecticut, July 1, 2003 (36/58)
.600 — vs Orlando, August 10, 2001 (30/50)
Lowest field goal percentage, game
.219 — at Houston, July 3, 1999 (14/64)
.250 — at Washington, August 11, 1999 (16/64) (OT)

FIELD GOALS

Most field goals per game, season
26.0 — 2001 (833/32)
25.3 — 1998 (758/30)
Fewest field goals per game, season
24.2 — 2004 (819/34)
24.1 — 2002 (772/32)
Most field goals, game
39 — at Phoenix, June 21, 2001
36 — vs Connecticut, July 1, 2003
Fewest field goals, game
14 — at Houston, July 3, 1999
16 — at Washington, August 11, 1999 (OT)
at Phoenix, May 31, 2000
at Miami, July 23, 2002
at Cleveland, May 31, 2003
vs Los Angeles, June 22, 2004

FIELD GOAL ATTEMPTS

Most field goal attempts per game, season
61.3 — 1997 (1715/28)
59.8 — 1999 (1914/32)
Fewest field goal attempts per game, season
54.4 — 2002 (1740/32)
54.7 — 2005 (1860/34)
Most field goal attempts, game
79 — at Utah, August 19, 1997
78 — at Washington, July 5, 1998 (OT)
Fewest field goal attempts, game
39 — vs Miami, June 2, 2002
43 — at Charlotte, July 23, 1997

THREE-POINT FIELD GOAL PERCENTAGE

Highest three-point field goal percentage, season
.380 — 2001 (160/421)
.370 — 1999 (175/473)

Lowest three-point field goal percentage, season
.274 — 1997 (93/339)
.327 — 1998 (92/281)

THREE-POINT FIELD GOALS

Most three-point field goals per game, season
6.35 — 2004 (216/34)
6.12 — 2005 (208/34)
Fewest three-point field goals per game, season
3.1 — 1998 (92/30)
3.3 — 1997 (93/28)
Most three-point field goals, game
12 — at Connecticut, August 20, 2005
10 — vs Washington, August 16, 2005
at Detroit, August 7, 2005
vs Detroit, July 24, 2004
at Los Angeles, June 29, 2004 (OT)
vs Sacramento, June 17, 2003
vs Los Angeles, June 18, 1999
Fewest three-point field goals, game
0 — at Phoenix, July 7, 1997
at Washington, July 5, 1998 (OT)
at Detroit, July 18, 2001
vs Cleveland, August 4, 2001
1 — Many Times

THREE-POINT FIELD GOAL ATTEMPTS

Most three-point field goal attempts per game, season
18.1 — 2004 (617/34)
17.8 — 2005 (605/34)
Fewest three-point field goal attempts per game, season
9.4 — 1998 (281/30)
12.1 — 1997 (339/28)
Most three-point field goal attempts, game
28 — vs Detroit, July 24, 2004
27 — vs Detroit, May 22, 2005
vs Los Angeles, June 22, 2004
Fewest three-point field goal attempts, game
1 — vs Detroit, July 6, 1998
2 — at Phoenix, July 18, 1998

FREE THROW PERCENTAGE

Highest free throw percentage, season
.819 — 2005 (452/552)
.767 — 2003 (412/537)
Lowest free throw percentage, season
.666 — 1997 (404/607)
.672 — 2001 (336/500)
Highest free throw percentage, game
1.000 — at Connecticut, September 17, 2004 (4/4)
at Indiana, June 10, 2005 (6/6)
at Los Angeles, July 5, 2005 (14/14)
vs Sacramento, June 17, 2003 (8/8)
at Seattle, July 23, 2003 (7/7)
at Phoenix, July 29, 2003 (16/16)
vs Detroit, August 1, 2003 (3/3)
vs Minnesota, July 11, 1999 (9/9)
Lowest free throw percentage, game
.364 — at Charlotte, August 24, 2003 (4/11) (OT)
.375 — at Utah, July 26, 2001 (3/8)

FREE THROWS MADE

Most free throws made per game, season
15.0 — 1998 (450/30)
14.4 — 1997 (404/28)
Fewest free throws made per game, season
10.5 — 2001 (336/32)
11.7 — 2004 (398/34)
Most free throws made, game
30 — vs Cleveland, June 10, 2003
28 — vs Utah, June 3, 2000
Fewest free throws made, game
2 — at Indiana, August 27, 2005
3 — vs Detroit, August 1, 2003
at Houston, July 26, 2003
at Utah, July 26, 2001
at Cleveland, July 19, 2001
vs Cleveland, August 8, 2000
at Phoenix, August 6, 1999

FREE THROW ATTEMPTS

Most free throw attempts per game, season
21.7 — 1997 (607/28)
21.0 — 1998 (629/30)
Fewest free throw attempts per game, season
15.62 — 2004 (531/34)
15.63 — 2001 (500/32)
Most free throw attempts, game
41 — vs Cleveland, June 10, 2003
35 — vs Utah, June 3, 2000
Fewest free throw attempts, game
3 — vs Detroit, August 1, 2003
4 — at Indiana, August 27, 2005
at Connecticut, September 17, 2004
at Houston, July 26, 2003
vs Cleveland, August 8, 2000
at Phoenix, August 6, 1999

REBOUNDS

Most rebounds per game, season
32.9 — 1997 (920/28)
31.5 — 1998 (944/30)
Fewest rebounds per game, season
27.2 — 2002 (870/32)
28.1 — 2003 (957/34)
Most rebounds, game
43 — vs Washington, August 13, 1998
41 — at Charlotte, August 12, 2005 (2OT)
vs Houston, August 15, 1998
at Washington, July 5, 1998 (OT)
Fewest rebounds, game
14 — at Charlotte, July 30, 1999
17 — at Charlotte, July 23. 1997

OFFENSIVE REBOUNDS

Most offensive rebounds per game, season
11.4 — 1997 (320/28)
10.7 — 1998 (320/30)
Fewest offensive rebounds per game, season
7.1 — 2005 (242/34)
7.7 — 2004 (263/34)
Most offensive rebounds, game
20 — vs Charlotte, July 26, 1997
19 — vs Sacramento, June 9, 2000
at Cleveland, August 21, 1999

Fewest offensive rebounds, game
1 — vs Sacramento, June 17, 2003
vs Seattle, July 2, 2002
at Detroit, July 18, 2001
at Charlotte, July 30, 1999
2 — at San Antonio, June 5, 2004
2 — Many Times

DEFENSIVE REBOUNDS

Most defensive rebounds per game, season
21.8 — 2004 (741/34)
21.5 — 2005 (732/34)
Fewest defensive rebounds per game, season
19.1 — 2002 (610/32)
19.5 — 1999 (625/32)
Most defensive rebounds, game
33 — vs Charlotte, July 12, 2000
31 — vs Seattle, July 11, 2001
vs Cleveland, July 15, 1997
Fewest defensive rebounds, game
11 — at Detroit, August 9, 2000
at Indiana, July 19, 2002
12 — at Houston, June 13, 1998
vs Cleveland, August 17, 1998
vs Houston, August 18, 2003

ASSISTS

Most assists per game, season
17.3 — 2001 (553/32)
1997 (484/28)
17.1 — 1998 (513/30)
Fewest assists per game, season
14.6 — 2005 (498/34)
14.9 — 2000 (477/32)
Most assists, game
32 — at Phoenix, June 21, 2001
29 — vs Connecticut, July 1, 2003
Fewest assists, game
6 — vs Sacramento, June 9, 2000
at Houston, July 3, 1999
7 — at Washington, August 11, 1999 (OT)
at Miami, June 17, 2001
vs Los Angeles, June 22, 2004

PERSONAL FOULS

Most personal fouls per game, season
21.9 — 1999 (700/32)
21.0 — 1998 (630/30)
Fewest personal fouls per game, season
17.3 — 2003 (587/34)
2004 (587/34)
18.0 — 2005 (613/34)
Most personal fouls, game
32 — at Detroit, June 3, 2005 (OT)
at Los Angeles, July 24, 1999 (OT)
30 — at Washington, June 4, 2000
Fewest personal fouls, game
5 — vs Charlotte, September 2, 2004
8 — vs Seattle, August 6, 2005
at Washington, August 21, 2003

DISQUALIFICATIONS

Most disqualifications per game, season
.28 — 1999 (9/32)
.22 — 2000 (7/32)

Fewest disqualifications per game, season
.10 — 1998 (3/30)
.12 — 2005 (4/34)
Most disqualifications, game
2 — vs Connecticut, August 2, 2005
at Orlando, July 29, 1999 (OT)
vs Washington, June 14, 1999
at Detroit, August 19, 1998
1 — Many Times

STEALS

Most steals per game, season
10.3 — 1997 (289/28)
9.7 — 1998 (291/30)
Fewest steals per game, season
6.2 — 2004 (209/34)
6.3 — 2005 (214/34)
Most steals, game
18 — at Phoenix, July 7, 1997
17 — vs Los Angeles, June 24, 2001
vs Phoenix, August 11, 1998 (OT)
Fewest steals, game
2 — at Minnesota, July 24, 2005
vs Charlotte, September 2, 2004
at Cleveland, July 19, 2001
vs Indiana, June 2, 2001
3 — Many Times

BLOCKED SHOTS

Most blocked shots per game, season
4.1 — 1997 (116/28)
3.8 — 2003 (128/34)
Fewest blocked shots per game, season
2.6 — 2001 (82/32)
2.8 — 1998 (84/30)
Most blocked shots, game
8 — vs Phoenix, June 18, 2005
at Indiana, June 7, 2003
vs Phoenix, August 2, 1997
vs Sacramento, July 30, 1997 (OT)
at Houston, July 4, 1997
at Cleveland, August 21, 1999
7 — Many Times
Fewest blocked shots, game
0 — Many Times

TURNOVERS

Most turnovers per game, season
19.1 — 1997 (536/28)
16.7 — 1998 (501/30)
Fewest turnovers per game, season
13.6 — 2005 (462/34)
13.7 — 2001 (437/32)
Most turnovers, game
30 — vs Phoenix, August 11, 1998 (OT)
26 — vs Washington, August 13, 1998
at Phoenix, May 31, 2000
Fewest turnovers, game
6 — at Los Angeles, June 19, 1998
vs Detroit, July 24, 2004
7 — vs Washington, June 16, 2001

TEAM DEFENSE

POINTS

Fewest points allowed per game, season
63.0 — 2002 (2015/32)

63.6 — 2000 (2035/32)
Most points allowed per game, season
   67.6 — 2004 (2297/34)
   67.2 — 2005 (2285/34)
Fewest points allowed, game
   44 — vs Cleveland, August 8, 2000
   45 — vs Washington, August 13, 1998
        vs Portland, July 5, 2000
Fewest points allowed, first half
   17 — at Sacramento, June 18, 1998
   18 — at Miami, June 17, 2001
        vs Cleveland, July 22, 2002
Fewest points allowed, second half
   18 — vs Detroit, May 26, 2004
        at Charlotte, August 24, 2003
        vs Charlotte, September 2, 2004
   21 — vs Miami, June 2, 2002
        vs Portland, July 5, 2000
        vs Washington, August 13, 1998
Fewest points allowed, overtime period
   3 — at Charlotte, August 12, 2005
       vs Cleveland, August 24, 1997
   4 — at Houston, June 26, 1997
       vs Sacramento, July 30, 1997
       at Charlotte, July 20, 2004

FIELD GOAL PERCENTAGE

Lowest opponents' field goal percentage, season
   .391 — 1997 (661/1690)
   .399 — 2002 (691/1733)
Highest opponents' field goal percentage, season
   .427 — 2005 (859/2012)
   .423 — 2001 (744/1759)
Lowest opponents' field goal percentage, game
   .241 — at Cleveland, July 8, 1999 (14/58)
   .245 — vs Portland, July 5, 2000 (12/49)

TURNOVERS

Fewest opponents' turnovers per game, season
   12.1 — 2005 (411/34)
   12.7 — 2004 (430/34)
Most opponents' turnovers per game, season
   20.4 — 1997 (570/28)
   17.9 — 1998 (538/30)
Most opponents' turnovers, game
   33 — vs Utah, July 17, 1997
   30 — vs Cleveland, June 10, 1999

TEAM MISCELLANEOUS

GAME WON AND LOST

Highest winning percentage, season
   .656 — 2001 (21-11)
   .625 — 2000 (20-12)
Lowest winning percentage, season
   .471 — 2003 (16-18)
   .529 — 2004, 2005 (18-16)
Most consecutive games won
   7 — June 10-24, 2001
       June 21-July 5, 1997
   6 — Many Times
Most consecutive games won, one season
   7 — June 10-24, 2001
       June 21-July 5, 1997
   6 — Many Times

Most consecutive games lost
   6 — June 11-24, 2004
   5 — July 23-August 1, 2003
Most consecutive games lost, one season
   6 — June 11-24, 2004
   5 — July 23-August 1, 2003
Highest winning percentage, home games, season
   .813 — 2001 (13-3)
   .800 — 1998 (12-3)
Lowest winning percentage, home games, season
   .588 — 2005 (10-7)
   .625 — 2002 (10-6)
Most consecutive home games won
   11 — June 28, 2000-June 2, 2001
   8 — June 12-July 13, 2001
Most consecutive home games lost
   3 — June 11-22, 2004
       August 6-11, 2002
   2 — Many Times
Highest winning percentage, road games, season
   .500 — 1997 (7-7)
   .500 — 2000, 2001, 2002 (8-8)
Lowest winning percentage, road games, season
   .294 — 2003 (5-12)
   .375 — 1999 (6-10)
Most consecutive road games won
   5 — June 21-July 5, 1997
   4 — May 30-June 5, 2004
       June 10-21, 2001
       July 18-August 1, 1998
Most consecutive road games lost
   9 — June 7-August 7, 2003
   8 — August 10-June 15, 1998

OVERTIME GAMES

Most overtime games, season
   5 — 1999
   4 — 2005, 2004
Most consecutive overtime games, season
   3 — July 21-29, 1999
   2 — September 14-16, 2004
Most overtime games won, season
   3 — 1997
   2 — 1998, 1999, 2004, 2005
Most overtime games won, no losses, season
   3 — 1997
   2 — 1998
Most overtime games lost, season
   3 — 1999
   2 — 2003, 2004, 2005
Most overtime games lost, no wins, season
   2 — 2003
   1 — 2000, 2002
Most overtime periods, game
   2 — at Sacramento, June 13, 2002

INDIVIDUAL RECORDS

SEASONS

Most seasons
   9 — Vickie Johnson

7 — Becky Hammon
    Teresa Weatherspoon
    Crystal Robinson

GAMES

Most games, career
  282 — Vickie Johnson
  220 — Teresa Weatherspoon
  216 — Crystal Robinson

Most consecutive games, career
  220 — Teresa Weatherspoon, June 21, 1997-
    August 24, 2003
  149 — Sue Wicks, June 21, 1997-August 1, 2001
  124 — Tamika Whitmore, July 17, 1999-
    June 22, 2003

Most games, season
  34 — By Many

MINUTES

Most minutes, career
  8,950 — Vickie Johnson
  6,842 — Teresa Weatherspoon
  6,608 — Crystal Robinson

Highest average, minutes per game, career
(Minimum 100 games)
  31.7 — Vickie Johnson (8950/282)
  31.1 — Teresa Weatherspoon (6842/220)
    Tari Phillips (4380/141)

Most minutes, season
  1,180 — Becky Hammon, 2005
  1,130 — Becky Hammon, 2004
  1,119 — Vickie Johnson, 2004

Highest average, minutes per game, season
  34.7 — Becky Hammon, 2005 (1180/34)
  33.9 — Teresa Weatherspoon, 1999 (1086/32)
  33.8 — Vickie Johnson, 1999 (1082/32)

Most minutes, game
  46 — Becky Hammon, at Sacramento,
    June 13, 2002 (2OT)
    Becky Hammon, at Charlotte,
    August 12, 2005 (2OT)
  45 — Crystal Robinson, at Sacramento,
    June 13, 2002 (2OT)
    Teresa Weatherspoon, at Washington,
    July 5, 1998 (OT)

SCORING

Most points, lifetime
  3,246 — Vickie Johnson
  2,301 — Crystal Robinson
  2,044 — Becky Hammon

Highest average, points per game, career
(Minimum 100 games)
  13.0 — Tari Phillips (1826/141)
  11.5 — Vickie Johnson (3246/282)
  10.7 — Crystal Robinson (2301/216)

Most points, season
  489 — Tari Phillips, 2001
  473 — Becky Hammon, 2005
  460 — Becky Hammon, 2004

Highest average, points per game, season
  15.3 — Tari Phillips, 2001 (489/32)
  14.5 — Sophia Witherspoon, 1997 (407/28)
  14.1 — Tari Phillips, 2002 (451/32)

Most points, game

  33 — Becky Hammon, at Minnesota, June 6, 2003
  30 — Tari Phillips, vs Indiana, June 30, 2000
  28 — Becky Hammon, vs Cleveland, June 10, 2003
    Tamika Whitmore, vs Phoenix, July 8, 2002
    Becky Hammon, vs Indiana, September 16,
    2004 (OT)

Most games, 30 or more points, career
  1 — Becky Hammon
    Tari Phillips

Most games, 20 or more points, career
  23 — Becky Hammon
  21 — Vickie Johnson
  20 — Tari Phillips

Most consecutive games, 20 or more points
  3 — Tari Phillips, July 6-9, 2001
    Tari Phillips, June 28-July 1, 2000
    Vickie Johnson, July 1-5, 1999
    Sophia Witherspoon, July 26-August 2, 1997

Most consecutive games, 10 or more points
  23 — Tari Phillips, June 30, 2001-May 30, 2002
  19 — Vickie Johnson, July 6-August 18, 2003
  15 — Sophia Witherspoon, July 9-August 15, 1997

FIELD GOAL PERCENTAGE

Highest field goal percentage, career
(Minimum 400 field goals)
  .460 — Tari Phillips (736/1600)
  .451 — Becky Hammon (671/1487)
  .448 — Tamika Whitmore (543/1211)

Highest field goal percentage, season (qualifiers)
  .541 — Ann Wauters, 2005 (151/279)
  .507 — Tari Phillips, 2001 (208/410)
  .491 — Tari Phillips, 2002 (183/373)

Highest field goal percentage, game
(Minimum 8 field goals made)
  1.000 — Becky Hammon, at Phoenix, June 21, 2001
    (8/8)
    Crystal Robinson, at Cleveland,
    August 17, 2003 (8/8)
  .857 — Tari Phillips, vs Charlotte, June 12, 2001
    (12/14)
  .846 — Tamika Whitmore, vs Phoenix, July 8, 2002
    (11/13)

Most field goals, none missed, game
  8 — Crystal Robinson, at Cleveland,
    August 17, 2003
    Becky Hammon, at Phoenix, June 21, 2001
  6 — Tamika Whitmore, vs Seattle, July 2, 2002
    Tamika Whitmore, vs Houston,
    August 18, 2003
    Tamika Whitmore, vs Los Angeles,
    June 24, 2001

Most field goal attempts, none made, game
  11 — Elena Baranova, vs Detroit, August 1, 2003
  10 — Crystal Robinson, vs Detroit, May 22, 2005
  9 — Vickie Johnson, vs Charlotte, July 12, 1998

FIELD GOALS

Most field goals, career
  1,244 — Vickie Johnson
  810 — Crystal Robinson
  736 — Tari Phillips

Most field goals, season
208 — Tari Phillips, 2001
183 — Tari Phillips, 2002
170 — Tari Phillips, 2000
Most field goals, game
13 — Tari Phillips, vs Indiana, June 30, 2000
12 — Vickie Johnson, vs Cleveland, June 23, 1998
Becky Hammon, at Minnesota, June 6, 2003
Tari Phillips, vs Charlotte, June 12, 2001
Sophia Witherspoon, at Los Angeles,
August 20, 1997
11 — By Many

FIELD GOAL ATTEMPTS

Most field goal attempts, career
2,855 — Vickie Johnson
1,884 — Crystal Robinson
1,600 — Tari Phillips
Most field goal attempts, season
410 — Tari Phillips, 2001
394 — Vickie Johnson, 1999
373 — Tari Phillips, 2002
Most field goal attempts, game
21 — Tari Phillips, vs Detroit, June 27, 2003
20 — By Many
Most consecutive games, three-point field goals made
18 — Crystal Robinson, June 18-July 30, 1999
15 — Crystal Robinson, July 26-August 4, 2003
13 — Sophia Witherspoon, July 9-August 10, 1997

THREE-POINT FIELD GOAL PERCENTAGE

Highest three-point field goal percentage, career
(Minimum 100 three-point field goals)
.409 — Elena Baranova (119/291)
.383 — Crystal Robinson (400/1044)
.367 — Becky Hammon (294/801)
Highest three-point field goal percentage, season
(qualifiers)
.469 — Becky Hammon, 2003 (23/49)
.461 — Elena Baranova, 2004 (53/115)
.437 — Crystal Robinson, 1999 (76/174)
Most three-point field goals, none missed, game
5 — Becky Hammon, at Phoenix, June 21, 2001
Crystal Robinson, vs Phoenix, July 1, 1999
Becky Hammon, vs Connecticut, July 31, 2004
4 — Vickie Johnson, at Washington, June 1, 2005
Most three-point field goal attempts, none made, game
8 — Crystal Robinson, vs Cleveland, August 4, 2001
Crystal Robinson, vs Detroit, May 22, 2005
Crystal Robinson, vs Detroit, June 21, 2000
7 — Becky Hammon, vs Cleveland, July 29, 2000
Sophia Witherspoon, at Utah, August 19, 1997

THREE-POINT FIELD GOALS

Most three-point field goals, career
400 — Crystal Robinson
294 — Becky Hammon
221 — Vickie Johnson
Most three-point field goals, season
76 — Crystal Robinson, 1999
70 — Crystal Robinson, 2001
67 — Crystal Robinson, 2002
Most three-point field goals, game

7 — Crystal Robinson, at Los Angeles,
July 24, 1999 (OT)
6 — Becky Hammon, at Minnesota, June 6, 2003
Crystal Robinson, vs Indiana, June 25, 2002
Crystal Robinson, at Phoenix, August 6, 1999
Crystal Robinson, vs Charlotte,
July 26, 1999 (OT)
Sophia Witherspoon, at Detroit,
August 19, 1998

THREE-POINT FIELD GOAL ATTEMPTS

Most three-point field goal attempts, career
1044 — Crystal Robinson
801 — Becky Hammon
617 — Vickie Johnson
Most three-point field goal attempts, season
181 — Crystal Robinson, 202, 1999
178 — Becky Hammon, 2005
Most three-point field goal attempts, game
14 — Crystal Robinson, at Los Angeles,
July 24, 1999 (OT)
12 — Crystal Robinson, vs Charlotte,
July 26, 1999 (OT)
11 — Crystal Robinson, vs Portland, June 30, 2002
Becky Hammon, vs Detroit, May 22, 2005
Elena Baranova, vs Detroit, July 24, 2004

FREE THROW PERCENTAGE

Highest free throw percentage, career
.854 — Crystal Robinson (281/329)
.848 — Becky Hammon (408/481)
.819 — Vickie Johnson (537/656)
Highest free throw percentage, season (qualifiers)
.951 — Becky Hammon, 2003 (39/41)
.930 — Crystal Robinson, 2004 (40/43)
.925 — Elena Baranova, 2004 (49/53)
Most free throws made, none missed, game
10 — Becky Hammon, vs Los Angeles,
August 10, 2005
Vickie Johnson, vs Washington,
August 16, 2005
8 — Teresa Weatherspoon, vs Sacramento,
August 15, 1997
Most free throw attempts, none made, game
6 — Tari Phillips, vs Seattle, June 15, 2004
4 — Kym Hampton, vs Charlotte, July 26, 1997
3 — By Many

FREE THROWS MADE

Most free throws made, career
537 — Vickie Johnson
408 — Becky Hammon
351 — Tari Phillips
Most free throws made, season
118 — Becky Hammon, 2005
110 — Tamika Whitmore, 2002
97 — Becky Hammon, 2004
Most free throws made, game
11 — Becky Hammon, vs Utah, June 3, 2000
10 — Becky Hammon, vs Los Angeles, August 10,2005
Sophia Witherspoon, at Phoenix, July 18, 1998
Vickie Johnson, vs Washington, Aug. 16, 2005

Tamika Whitmore, vs Washington,
August 17,1999
9 — Vickie Johnson, vs Detroit, May 22, 2005
Tamika Whitmore, at Indiana, July 19, 2002
Crystal Robinson, at Washington,
August 11, 1999 (OT)

FREE THROW ATTEMPTS

Most free throw attempts, career
656 — Vickie Johnson
561 — Tari Phillips
481 — Becky Hammon
Most free throw attempts, season
150 — Tamika Whitmore, 2002
134 — Tari Phillips, 2003
131 — Becky Hammon, 2005
Most free throw attempts, game
12 — Tari Phillips, vs Phoenix, June 25, 2003
Becky Hammon, vs Utah, June 3, 2000
Kym Hampton, at Los Angeles, June 19, 1998
Tari Phillips, vs Sacramento, June 9, 2000
Becky Hammon, vs Indiana, September 16,2004 (OT)
Sophia Witherspoon, at Phoenix, July 18, 1998
Vickie Johnson, vs Washington,
August 16, 2005
Crystal Robinson, at Washington,
August 11,1999 (OT)
11 — By Many

REBOUNDS

Most rebounds, career
1077 — Tari Phillips
1053 — Vickie Johnson
788 — Sue Wicks
Highest average, rebounds per game, career
(Minimum 100 games)
7.6 — Tari Phillips (1077/141)
6.5 — Elena Baranova (654/100)
4.3 — Sue Wicks (788/182)
Most rebounds, season
280 — Tari Phillips, 2003
257 — Tari Phillips, 2001
247 — Tari Phillips, 2000
Highest average, rebounds per game, season (qualifiers)
8.5 — Tari Phillips, 2003 (280/33)
8.0 — Tari Phillips, 2000 (247/31)
Tari Phillips, 2001 (257/32)
Most rebounds, game
18 — Elena Baranova, at Connecticut, Aug. 20, 2005
16 — Tari Phillips, at Houston, July 26, 2003
Sue Wicks, at Washington, Aug. 11, 1999 (OT)
14 — Tari Phillips, at Portland, July 24, 2001
Tari Phillips, vs Indiana, July 9, 2001
Elena Baranova, vs Houston, May 23, 2004
Most games, 10+ rebounds, career
41 — Tari Phillips
17 — Elena Baranova
11 — Rebecca Lobo
Most consecutive games, 10+ rebounds
4 — Tari Phillips, July 6-20, 2003

3 — Tari Phillips, June 25-30, 2000
Tari Phillips, June 22-27, 2003
2 — Many Times

OFFENSIVE REBOUNDS

Most offensive rebounds, career
371 — Tari Phillips
342 — Vickie Johnson
267 — Sue Wicks
Highest average, offensive rebounds per game, career
(Minimum 100 games)
2.6 — Tari Phillips (371/141)
1.5 — Sue Wicks (267/182)
1.2 — Vickie Johnson (342/282)
Most offensive rebounds, season
99 — Tari Phillips, 2003
89 — Tari Phillips, 2001
86 — Tari Phillips, 2000
Most offensive rebounds, game
9 — Tari Phillips, vs Phoenix, June 25, 2003
8 — Tari Phillips, at Portland, July 24, 2001
Rebecca Lobo, vs Charlotte, July 26, 1997
Tari Phillips, at Charlotte, August 24, 2003(OT)
7 — Tari Phillips, at Charlotte, July 3, 2001
Tari Phillips, vs Washington, July 15, 2003

DEFENSIVE REBOUNDS

Most defensive rebounds, career
711 — Vickie Johnson
706 — Tari Phillips
596 — Teresa Weatherspoon
Highest average, defensive rebounds per game, career
(Minimum 100 games)
5.4 — Elena Baranova (537/100)
5.0 — Tari Phillips (706/141)
2.9 — Sue Wicks (521/182)
Most defensive rebounds, season
213 — Elena Baranova, 2004
188 — Elena Baranova, 2005
181 — Tari Phillips, 2003
Most defensive rebounds, game
17 — Elena Baranova, at Connecticut, August 20,2005
13 — Elena Baranova, vs Houston, May 23, 2004
12 — Tari Phillips, at Houston, July 26, 2003
Sue Wicks, at Washington, August 11, 1999(OT)
Tari Phillips, vs Orlando, June 30, 2001
Elena Baranova, vs Connecticut, July 31, 2004

ASSISTS

Most assists, career
1306 — Teresa Weatherspoon
787 — Vickie Johnson
494 — Becky Hammon
Highest average, assists per game, career
(Minimum 100 games)
5.9 — Teresa Weatherspoon (1306/220)
2.8 — Vickie Johnson (787/282)
2.4 — Becky Hammon (494/205)
Most assists, season
205 — Teresa Weatherspoon, 1999
Teresa Weatherspoon, 2000

203 — Teresa Weatherspoon, 2001
191 — Teresa Weatherspoon, 1998
Highest average, assists per game, season (qualifiers)
  6.4 — Teresa Weatherspoon, 1998 (191/30)
      Teresa Weatherspoon, 1999 (205/32)
      Teresa Weatherspoon, 2000 (205/32)
Most assists, game
  13 — Teresa Weatherspoon, at Houston, May 29, 2000
     Teresa Weatherspoon, at Los Angeles, July 21, 1998
  12 — Teresa Weatherspoon, vs Indiana, June 30, 2000
     Teresa Weatherspoon, at Sacramento,
     June 13, 2002 (2OT)
     Teresa Weatherspoon, at Los Angeles,
     July 24, 1999 (OT)
     Teresa Weatherspoon, at Los Angeles,
     August 20, 1997
  11 — By Many
Most games, 10+ assists, career
  18 — Teresa Weatherspoon
   2 — Becky Hammon

PERSONAL FOULS

Most personal fouls, career
  596 — Crystal Robinson
  565 — Vickie Johnson
  564 — Teresa Weatherspoon
Most personal fouls, season
  123 — Sue Wicks, 1999
  118 — Tari Phillips, 2003
  113 — Tari Phillips, 2002
Most personal fouls, game
   6 — By Many

STEALS

Most steals, career
  453 — Teresa Weatherspoon
  255 — Vickie Johnson
  235 — Tari Phillips
Highest average, steals per game, career
(Minimum 100 games)
  2.1 — Teresa Weatherspoon (453/220)
  1.7 — Tari Phillips (235/141)
  1.1 — Crystal Robinson (232/216)
Most steals, season
  100 — Teresa Weatherspoon, 1998
  85 — Teresa Weatherspoon, 1997
  78 — Teresa Weatherspoon, 1999
Highest average, steals per game, season (qualifiers)
  3.3 — Teresa Weatherspoon, 1998 (100/30)
  3.0 — Teresa Weatherspoon, 1997 (85/28)
  2.4 — Teresa Weatherspoon, 1999 (78/32)
Most steals, game
  8 — Teresa Weatherspoon, vs Charlotte, July 10, 1997
  7 — Teresa Weatherspoon, vs Phoenix,
    August 11, 1998 (OT)
    Teresa Weatherspoon, at Sacramento,
    July 24, 1998
  6 — By Many

BLOCKED SHOTS

Most blocked shots, career
  155 — Sue Wicks
  147 — Elena Baranova
  98 — Tamika Whitmore

Highest average, blocked shots per game, career
(Minimum: 100 games)
  1.5 — Elena Baranova (147/100)
   .9 — Sue Wicks (155/182)
   .6 — Tari Phillips (90/141)
Most blocked shots, season
  58 — Elena Baranova, 2004
  51 — Rebecca Lobo, 1997
  46 — Elena Baranova, 2005
Highest average, blocked shots per game, season
(qualifiers)
  1.8 — Rebecca Lobo, 1997 (51/28)
  1.7 — Elena Baranova, 2004 (58/34)
  1.4 — Elena Baranova, 2005 (46/33)
Most blocked shots, game
  5 — Sue Wicks, vs Sacramento, July 5, 1999
    Elena Baranova, vs Detroit, May 26, 2004
    Rebecca Lobo, at Utah, August 19, 1997
    Tamika Whitmore, vs Washington,
    August 8, 2002
  4 — By Many

TURNOVERS

Most turnovers, career
  577 — Teresa Weatherspoon
  484 — Vickie Johnson
  441 — Becky Hammon
Most turnovers, season
  118 — Becky Hammon, 2004
  107 — Becky Hammon, 2005
  96 — Teresa Weatherspoon, 1998
Most turnovers, game
  10 — Becky Hammon, at Los Angeles, June 29, 2004 (OT)
  8 — Ann Wauters, at Los Angeles, July 5, 2005
    Rebecca Lobo, at Sacramento, August 10, 1997
    Teresa Weatherspoon, at Phoenix, August 12, 1997
    Teresa Weatherspoon, at Utah, July 5, 1997
  7 — By Many

PHOENIX MERCURY

TEAM OFFENSE

SCORING

Highest average, points per game, season
73.9 — 1998 (2217/30)
70.1 — 2000 (2243/32)
Lowest average, points per game, season
61.7 — 2003 (2097/34)
64.5 — 2001 (2064/32)
Most points, game
96 — vs Utah, June 26, 1998
91 — vs San Antonio, August 19, 2005
Fewest points, game
45 — at Seattle, June 3, 2004
46 — at Houston, August 10, 2003
Largest margin of victory, game
34 — vs San Antonio, August 19, 2005 (91-57)
33 — at Charlotte, June 22, 2000 (90-57)
vs Seattle, June 7, 2000 (82-49)
vs Minnesota, July 29, 1999 (79-46)
vs Utah, June 26, 1998 (96-63)
Largest margin of defeat, game
41 — at Seattle, July 19, 2002 (48-89)
29 — at Seattle, July 25, 2003 (53-82)

BY HALF

Most points, first half
53 — vs San Antonio, August 19, 2005
52 — vs Utah, June 26, 1998
Fewest points, first half
14 — at Sacramento, July 29, 2001
15 — at Cleveland, July 31, 1997
Largest lead at half time
28 — vs Washington, August 4, 1998 (48-20)
23 — vs Houston, September 19, 2004 (50-27)
Largest deficit at halftime overcome to win game
14 — vs Utah, August 17, 1997 (trailed 21-35; won 71-63 in OT)
12 — at Detroit, July 8, 1998 (trailed 32-44; won 78-76)
at Washington, June 22, 1999 (trailed 32-44; won 79-76)
Most points, second half
57 — vs Sacramento, July 20, 1998
52 — vs San Antonio, June 15, 2005
vs Los Angeles, July 17, 1999
at Cleveland, July 31, 1997
Fewest points, second half
18 — at San Antonio, June 5, 2003
19 — vs Charlotte, June 12, 2003
vs Los Angeles, June 21, 2003
at Miami, August 3, 2001

OVERTIME

Most points, overtime period
11 — vs Utah, August 17, 1997
10 — at New York, August 11, 1998
at Indiana, July 1, 2001
Fewest points, overtime period
4 — vs Los Angeles, July 25, 1997
5 — at Washington, August 3, 2003
Largest margin of victory, overtime period
8 — vs Utah, August 17, 1997 (71-63)
5 — vs Los Angeles, August 24, 1997 (73-68)

FIELD GOAL PERCENTAGE

Highest field goal percentage, season
.446 — 2000 (803/1800)
.430 — 2004 (826/1922)
Lowest field goal percentage, season
.373 — 1997 (660/1768)
.382 — 2003 (801/2095)
Highest field goal percentage, game
.636 — vs Seattle, August 3, 2000 (28/44)
.582 — vs Charlotte, July 13, 2005 (32/55)
Lowest field goal percentage, game
.255 — at Sacramento, July 29, 2001 (14/55)
.264 — at Minnesota, June 22, 2005 (19/72)

FIELD GOALS

Most field goals per game, season
26.2 — 1998 (787/30)
25.1 — 2000 (803/32)
Fewest field goals per game, season
23.56— 2003 (801/34)
23.57— 1997 (660/28)
Most field goals, game
36 — vs San Antonio, July 21, 2004
34 — vs Utah, June 26, 1998
Fewest field goals, game
14 — at Sacramento, July 29, 2001
16 — at Charlotte, August 9, 1997

FIELD GOAL ATTEMPTS

Most field goal attempts per game, season
63.1 — 1997 (1768/28)
61.9 — 1998 (1856/30)
Fewest field goal attempts per game, season
56.3 — 2000 (1800/32)
56.5 — 2004 (1922/34)
Most field goal attempts, game
93 — at Los Angeles, July 15, 2003 (2OT)
81 — vs Utah, August 17, 1997 (OT)
Fewest field goal attempts, game
44 — vs Seattle, August 3, 2000
vs Minnesota, August 9, 1999
at Sacramento, August 20, 1997
45 — vs Los Angeles, August 8, 2003
at Miami, August 3, 2001

THREE-POINT FIELD GOAL PERCENTAGE

Highest three-point field goal percentage, season
.370 — 2004 (192/519)
.332 — 2003 (116/349)
Lowest three-point field goal percentage, season
.294 — 1999 (134/456)
.305 — 2002 (100/328)

THREE-POINT FIELD GOALS

Most three-point field goals per game, season
5.6 — 2004 (192/34)
5.2 — 2005 (178/34)
Fewest three-point field goals per game, season
3.1 — 2002 (100/32)
3.2 — 2001 (101/32)
Most three-point field goals, game
12 — vs San Antonio, August 19, 2005
11 — at Los Angeles, July 7, 2004
at Charlotte, July 1, 2004
vs Houston, June 1, 2004
Fewest three-point field goals, game
0 — Many Times

THREE-POINT FIELD GOAL ATTEMPTS

Most three-point field goal attempts per game, season
- 15.9 — 2005 (539/34)
- 15.6 — 1997 (436/28)

Fewest three-point field goal attempts per game, season
- 9.8 — 2001 (313/32)
- 10.3 — 2002 (328/32)

Most three-point field goal attempts, game
- 31 — vs San Antonio, August 19, 2005
- 29 — at Orlando, June 21, 1999

Fewest three-point field goal attempts, game
- 3 — at Seattle, July 28, 2000
- 4 — at Detroit, June 28, 2003
- vs Minnesota, June 23, 2002

FREE THROW PERCENTAGE

Highest free throw percentage, season
- .776 — 2000 (513/661)
- .766 — 2005 (531/693)

Lowest free throw percentage, season
- .682 — 2003 (379/556)
- .724 — 1998 (513/709)

Highest free throw percentage, game
- 1.000 — at Houston, September 3, 2004 (11/11)
  - vs Charlotte, June 11, 2004 (5/5)
  - at Houston, June 4, 2005 (10/10)
  - vs San Antonio, June 15, 2005 (16/16)
  - at Sacramento, August 23, 2003 (5/5)
  - at Washington, July 9, 2002 (2/2)
- .952 — at Minnesota, June 2, 2001 (20/21)

Lowest free throw percentage, game
- .167 — vs Houston, August 14, 2001 (1/6)
- .364 — vs Washington, September 17, 2004 (4/11)

FREE THROWS MADE

Most free throws made per game, season
- 17.3 — 1997 (484/28)
- 17.1 — 1998 (513/30)

Fewest free throws made per game, season
- 11.1 — 2003 (379/34)
- 12.7 — 2002 (405/32)

Most free throws made, game
- 35 — vs Sacramento, August 4, 1997
- 34 — vs Los Angeles, July 17, 1999

Fewest free throws made, game
- 1 — vs Houston, August 14, 2001
- 2 — at Washington, July 9, 2002

FREE THROW ATTEMPTS

Most free throw attempts per game, season
- 23.6 — 1998 (709/30)
- 22.6 — 1997 (634/28)

Fewest free throw attempts per game, season
- 16.4 — 2003 (556/34)
- 16.8 — 2002 (538/32)

Most free throw attempts, game
- 47 — vs San Antonio, August 22, 2003
- 45 — vs Sacramento, August 4, 1997

Fewest free throw attempts, game
- 2 — at Washington, July 9, 2002
- 4 — vs Sacramento, August 17, 1999

REBOUNDS

Most rebounds per game, season
- 32.9 — 1997 (921/28)

- 31.4 — 1998 (941/30)

Fewest rebounds per game, season
- 26.9 — 2004 (916/34)
- 27.9 — 2000 (894/32)

Most rebounds, game
- 48 — at Portland, June 4, 2001 (OT)
- 47 — at Los Angeles, July 15, 2003 (2OT)
  - vs New York, July 7, 1997

Fewest rebounds, game
- 17 — at Seattle, June 3, 2004
- 18 — at Minnesota, June 27, 2003

OFFENSIVE REBOUNDS

Most offensive rebounds per game, season
- 11.5 — 1997 (322/28)
- 10.9 — 1998 (327/30)

Fewest offensive rebounds per game, season
- 7.8 — 2004 (264/34)
- 8.6 — 2000 (275/32)

Most offensive rebounds, game
- 22 — at Cleveland, July 31, 1997
- 21 — at New York, June 29, 1997

Fewest offensive rebounds, game
- 1 — at Connecticut, May 22, 2004
- 3 — vs Los Angeles, September 8, 2004

DEFENSIVE REBOUNDS

Most defensive rebounds per game, season
- 21.4 — 1997 (599/28)
- 21.2 — 2005 (720/34)

Fewest defensive rebounds per game, season
- 18.9 — 2003 (643/34)
- 19.2 — 2004 (652/34)

Most defensive rebounds, game
- 33 — vs New York, July 7, 1997
  - vs Charlotte, June 22, 1997
- 32 — vs San Antonio, June 15, 2005
  - at Los Angeles, July 15, 2003 (2OT)
  - at Portland, June 4, 2001 (OT)

Fewest defensive rebounds, game
- 10 — vs Charlotte, June 11, 2004
  - at Minnesota, August 4, 2003
- 11 — at Seattle, June 3, 2004
  - vs Connecticut, July 19, 2003
  - at Minnesota, June 27, 2003
  - vs Detroit, July 26, 2001
  - at Utah, June 6, 2000

ASSISTS

Most assists per game, season
- 18.1 — 1998 (543/30)
- 16.1 — 2005 (549/34)

Fewest assists per game, season
- 13.3 — 2002 (427/32)
- 13.6 — 2003 (461/34)

Most assists, game
- 27 — vs Utah, June 26, 1998
- 25 — vs Minnesota, July 29, 1999
  - at Utah, July 3, 1997

Fewest assists, game
- 5 — at Seattle, July 25, 2003
- 7 — vs Minnesota, July 18, 2004
  - vs Los Angeles, August 13, 2002

PERSONAL FOULS

Most personal fouls per game, season
- 22.0 — 2004 (748/34)

20.5 — 2005 (697/34)
Fewest personal fouls per game, season
19.46 — 2002 (623/32)
19.52 — 2003 (664/34)
Most personal fouls, game
35 — at Sacramento, June 12, 1999
32 — at Indiana, July 1, 2001 (OT)
Fewest personal fouls, game
9 — at Los Angeles, July 5, 2001
at Minnesota, June 20, 2000
vs Sacramento, July 20, 1998
10 — vs Minnesota, July 29, 1999

DISQUALIFICATIONS
Most disqualifications per game, season
.35 — 2005 (12/34)
.25 — 1999 (8/32)
Fewest disqualifications per game, season
.03 — 2002 (1/32)
.10 — 1998 (3/30)
Most disqualifications, game
3 — vs Indiana, August 14, 2005
at Sacramento, June 12, 1999
2 — By Many

STEALS
Most steals per game, season
12.3 — 1997 (343/28)
9.6 — 1998 (288/30)
Fewest steals per game, season
7.15 — 2005 (243/34)
7.16 — 1999 (229/32)
Most steals, game
20 — vs Utah, August 17, 1997 (OT)
18 — at Minnesota, June 27, 2003
at Cleveland, July 31, 1997
Fewest steals, game
2 — vs Minnesota, August 9, 1999
3 — Many Times

BLOCKED SHOTS
Most blocked shots per game, season
5.3 — 2005 (179/34)
4.3 — 2001 (138/32)
Fewest blocked shots per game, season
2.8 — 2000 (91/32)
2.9 — 1997 (80/28)
Most blocked shots, game
12 — vs Seattle, July 6, 2005
10 — vs Detroit, August 16, 2005
Fewest blocked shots, game
0 — Many Times

TURNOVERS
Most turnovers per game, season
17.0 — 1997 (475/28)
16.2 — 2001 (519/32)
Fewest turnovers per game, season
13.4 — 2000 (429/32)
13.7 — 2004 (464/34)
Most turnovers, game
28 — at Houston, June 4, 2005
25 — at Sacramento, June 10, 2005
Fewest turnovers, game

6 — vs San Antonio, August 19, 2005
vs Los Angeles, August 5, 2000
7 — at Los Angeles, July 21, 1999

TEAM DEFENSE

POINTS
Fewest points allowed per game, season
65.2 — 1997 (1826/28)
65.7 — 2000 (2102/32)
2004 (2235/34)
Most points allowed per game, season
71.6 — 2002 (2291/32)
69.2 — 2005 (2354/34)
Fewest points allowed, game
38 — vs Houston, August 14, 2001
44 — at Miami, June 24, 2000
Fewest points allowed, first half
15 — vs Charlotte, August 15, 1999
16 — vs Minnesota, July 29, 1999
Fewest points allowed, second half
14 — vs Seattle, August 15, 2003
15 — vs Detroit, August 16, 2005
Fewest points allowed, overtime period
3 — vs Utah, August 17, 1997
4 — vs Los Angeles, August 24, 1997
at Washington, August 3, 2003

FIELD GOAL PERCENTAGE
Lowest opponents' field goal percentage, season
.413 — 1997 (670/1622)
.415 — 2001 (785/1892)
1999 (794/1911)
Highest opponents' field goal percentage, season
.455 — 2002 (850/1870)
.447 — 2003 (834/1867)
Lowest opponents' field goal percentage, game
.226 — at Miami, June 24, 2000 (14/62)
.236 — vs Houston, August 14, 2001 (13/55)

TURNOVERS
Fewest opponents' turnovers per game, season
14.2 — 2005 (483/34)
15.0 — 1999 (479/32)
Most opponents' turnovers per game, season
21.4 — 1997 (599/28)
19.3 — 1998 (581/30)
Most opponents' turnovers, game
33 — vs Utah, August 17, 1997 (OT)
30 — at New York, August 11, 1998 (OT)

TEAM MISCELLANEOUS

GAME WON AND LOST
Highest winning percentage, season
.633 — 1998 (19-11)
.625 — 2000, (20-12)
Lowest winning percentage, season
.235 — 2003 (8-26)

.344 — 2002 (11-21)

Most consecutive games won
6 — August 20-June 15, 1998
5 — July 14-27, 2001

Most consecutive games won, one season
5 — July 14-27, 2001
4 — Many Times

Most consecutive games lost
7 — July 2-25, 2003
July 29-August 10, 2001
6 — Many Times

Most consecutive games lost, one season
7 — July 2-25, 2003
July 29-August 10, 2001
6 — Many Times

Highest winning percentage, home games, season
.800 — 1998 (12-3)
.786 — 1997 (11-3)

Lowest winning percentage, home games, season
.353 — 2003 (6-11)
.588 — 2004 (10-7)

Most consecutive home games won
11 — July 17-August 17, 1999
9 — August 4, 1997-June 15, 1998

Most consecutive home games lost
4 — June 17-July 19, 2003
3 — August 13, 2002-May 24, 2003
August 5, 2000-May 30, 2001
July 22-28, 1997

Highest winning percentage, road games, season
.563 — 2000 (9-7)
.467 — 1998 (7-8)

Lowest winning percentage, road games, season
.063 — 2002 (1-15)
.118 — 2003 (2-15)

Most consecutive road games won
4 — June 13-24, 2000
3 — July 5-29, 2005
August 20, 1997-June 28, 1998

Most consecutive road games lost
21 — July 29-August 6, 2002
6 — Many Times

OVERTIME GAMES

Most overtime games, season
3 — 1997, 2003
2 — 1998, 2001

Most consecutive overtime games, season
2 — August 10-11, 1998

Most overtime games won, season
2 — 1997
1 — 1998, 2000, 2003

Most overtime games won, no losses, season
1 — 2000

Most overtime games lost, season
2 — 2001, 2003
1 — 1997, 1998, 2004

Most overtime games lost, no wins, season
2 — 2001

Most overtime periods, game
2 — at Washington, August 3, 2003
at Los Angeles, July 15, 2003
at Cleveland, August 10, 1998

SEASONS

Most seasons
6 — Lisa Harrison
Jennifer Gillom
5 — Bridgette Pettis
Adrian Williams
Michele Timms

GAMES

Most games, career
187 — Lisa Harrison
183 — Jennifer Gillom
154 — Bridgette Pettis

Most consecutive games, career
154 — Bridget Pettis, June 22, 1997-August 14, 2001
105 — Jennifer Gillom, June 22, 1997-July 2, 2000
104 — Lisa Harrison, June 24, 2000-July 15, 2003

Most games, season
34 — By Many

MINUTES

Most minutes, career
5,489 — Jennifer Gillom
4,527 — Lisa Harrison
3,348 — Anna DeForge

Highest average, minutes per game, career
(Minimum 100 games)
33.1 — Anna DeForge (3348/101)
30.0 — Jennifer Gillom (5489/183)
28.3 — Michele Timms (3288/116)

Most minutes, season
1,152 — Anna DeForge, 2004
1,131 — Anna DeForge, 2005
1,130 — Diana Taurasi, 2004

Highest average, minutes per game, season
35.8 — Michele Timms, 1997 (966/27)
34.2 — Anna DeForge, 2005 (1131/33)
Jennifer Gillom, 1999 (1095/32)

Most minutes, game
46 — Adrian Williams, at Los Angeles,
July 15, 2003 (2OT)
45 — Umeki Webb, at Cleveland, Aug. 10, 1998 (2OT)
44 — Jennifer Gillom, vs Portland, June 14, 2000 (OT)
Jennifer Gillom, at Cleveland,
August 10, 1998 (2OT)

SCORING

Most points, lifetime
2,793 — Jennifer Gillom
1,326 — Anna DeForge
1,232 — Bridgette Pettis

Highest average, points per game, career
(Minimum 100 games)
15.3 — Jennifer Gillom (2793/183)
13.1 — Anna DeForge (1326/101)
8.0 — Bridgette Pettis (1232/154)

Most points, season
624 — Jennifer Gillom, 1998
608 — Brandy Reed, 2000
578 — Diana Taurasi, 2004

Highest average, points per game, season
20.8 — Jennifer Gillom, 1998 (624/30)
19.0 — Brandy Reed, 2000 (608/32)
17.0 — Diana Taurasi, 2004 (578/34)

Most points, game
36 — Jennifer Gillom, at Cleveland, August 10,1998 (2OT)
32 — Brandy Reed, at Houston, June 3, 2000
    Brandy Reed, at Charlotte, June 22, 2000
31 — Diana Taurasi, at Seattle, August 27, 2005
    Anna DeForge, at New York, July 11, 2004
    Brandy Reed, vs Cleveland, July 24, 2000
    Brandy Reed, vs Utah, July 19, 2000
    Jennifer Gillom, at Utah, July 27, 1998

Most games, 30 or more points, career
4 — Brandy Reed
2 — Anna DeForge
   Jennifer Gillom
1 — Penny Taylor
   Diana Taurasi

Most games, 20 or more points, career
48 — Jennifer Gillom
21 — Diana Taurasi
19 — Brandy Reed

Most consecutive games, 20 or more points
8 — Brandy Reed, July 13-28, 2000
6 — Jennifer Gillom, July 21-August 4, 1998
5 — Jennifer Gillom, July 2-13, 1998
   Jennifer Gillom, August 10-17, 1998

Most consecutive games, 10 or more points
27 — Jennifer Gillom, June 29, 1998-June 21, 1999
22 — Jennifer Gillom, July 25, 1997-June 26, 1998
17 — Diana Taurasi, June 5, 2004-July 22, 2004
   Brandy Reed, July 6-August 9, 2000

FIELD GOAL PERCENTAGE

Highest field goal percentage, career
(Minimum 400 field goals)
.466 — Lisa Harrison (467/1002)
.426 — Jennifer Gillom (1009/2367)
.406 — Anna DeForge (454/1117)
Highest field goal percentage, season (qualifiers)
.507 — Brandy Reed, 2000 (231/456)
.507 — Maria Stepanova, 2001 (143/282)
.505 — Michelle Brogan, 1998 (93/184)
Highest field goal percentage, game
(Minimum 8 field goals made)
.909 — Kamila Vodichkova, vs Los Angeles,
    July 26,2005 (10/11)
.900 — Maria Stepanova, vs Detroit,
    July 26, 2001 (9/10)
.889 — Plenette Pierson, at San Antonio,
    June 29, 2004 (8/9)
Most field goals, none missed, game
6 — Lisa Harrison, at Seattle, May 31, 2001
4 — By Many
Most field goal attempts, none made, game
11 — Slobodanka Tuvic, at Seattle, July 25, 2003
10 — Umeki Webb, vs Utah, August 6, 1997
9 — Gordana Grubin, vs Seattle, June 14, 2002
   Tonya Edwards, vs Houston, August 7, 2000

FIELD GOALS

Most field goals, career
1,009 — Jennifer Gillom
467 — Lisa Harrison
454 — Anna DeForge
Most field goals, season
231 — Brandy Reed, 2000
228 — Jennifer Gillom, 1998
209 — Diana Taurasi, 2004
Most field goals, game
13 — Jennifer Gillom, at Cleveland, Aug.10,1998 (2OT)

Brandy Reed, at Houston, June 3, 2000
12 — By Many

FIELD GOAL ATTEMPTS

Most field goal attempts, career
2,367 — Jennifer Gillom
1,162 — Bridgette Pettis
1,117 — Anna DeForge
Most field goal attempts, season
503 — Diana Taurasi, 2004
492 — Jennifer Gillom, 1998
456 — Brandy Reed, 2000
Most field goal attempts, game
27 — Jennifer Gillom, at Cleveland,
    August 10, 1998 (2OT)
    Jennifer Gillom, vs Los Angeles,
    August 24, 1997 (OT)
25 — Anna DeForge, at New York, July 11, 2004
    Diana Taurasi, at Seattle, August 27, 2005
    Jennifer Gillom, at Utah, July 27, 1998
24 — Anna DeForge, at Los Angeles,
    July 15, 2003 (2OT)
    Diana Taurasi, vs San Antonio,
    June 26, 2004 (OT)
    Jennifer Gillom, vs Sacramento, Aug. 19, 1998

THREE-POINT FIELD GOAL PERCENTAGE

Highest three-point field goal percentage, career
(Minimum 100 three-point field goals)
.376 — Anna DeForge (178/473)
.328 — Jennifer Gillom (148/451)
.324 — Michele Timms (129/398)
Highest three-point field goal percentage, season (qualifiers)
.427 — Penny Taylor, 2004 (41/96)
.412 — Anna DeForge, 2003 (61/148)
.404 — Penny Taylor, 2005 (38/94)
Most three-point field goals, none missed, game
4 — Jennifer Gillom, at Cleveland, July 2, 1998
   Shereka Wright, vs Houston, June 1, 2004
   Anna DeForge, vs Minnesota, August 20, 2003
3 — Michele Timms, at Cleveland, June 28, 1997
   Anna DeForge, at New York, June 25, 2003
2 — By Many
Most three-point field goal attempts, none made, game
7 — Michele Timms, at Houston, August 6, 1998
6 — By Many

THREE-POINT FIELD GOALS

Most three-point field goals, career
178 — Anna DeForge
148 — Jennifer Gillom
138 — Bridgette Pettis
Most three-point field goals, season
70 — Anna DeForge, 2004
62 — Diana Taurasi, 2004
61 — Anna DeForge, 2003
Most three-point field goals, game
6 — Diana Taurasi, at Charlotte, July 1, 2004
   Penny Taylor, at Los Angeles, July 7, 2004
5 — By Many
Most consecutive games, three-point field goals made
15 — Anna DeForge, June 27-September 3, 2004
14 — Anna DeForge, September 8, 2004-June 10, 2005
   Diana Taurasi, September 1, 2004-June 2, 2005
13 — Anna DeForge, July 2-August 8, 2003

THREE-POINT FIELD GOAL ATTEMPTS

Most three-point field goal attempts, career
   493 — Bridgette Pettis
   473 — Anna DeForge
   451 — Jennifer Gillom
Most three-point field goal attempts, season
   188 — Diana Taurasi, 2004
   181 — Anna DeForge, 2004
   179 — Diana Taurasi, 2005
Most three-point field goal attempts, game
   11 — Diana Taurasi, vs Houston, August 25, 2005
      Anna DeForge, at San Antonio, July 30, 2004
      Diana Taurasi, at Houston, September 3, 2004
      Diana Taurasi, vs Los Angeles, June 18, 2004
      Bridget Pettis, at Utah, August 17, 1998
   10 — Anna DeForge, at Houston, September 3, 2004
      Diana Taurasi, at Los Angeles, June 8, 2005

FREE THROW PERCENTAGE

Highest free throw percentage, career
   .863 — Penny Taylor (195/226)
   .825 — Anna DeForge (240/291)
   .825 — Bridgette Pettis (298/361)
Highest free throw percentage, season (qualifiers)
   .901 — Brandy Reed, 2000 (128/142)
   .898 — Bridgette Pettis, 1997 (97/108)
   .870 — Lisa Harrison, 2002 (20/23)
Most free throws made, none missed, game
   12 — Jennifer Gillom, vs Portland, June 14, 2000 (OT)
      Kristi Harrower, vs Los Angeles, July 17, 1999
   10 — Bridgette Pettis, vs Sacramento, August 4,1997
      Jennifer Gillom, vs Sacramento, June 18, 2002
Most free throw attempts, none made, game
   4 — Michelle Brogan, vs Cleveland, July 10, 1998
     Tracy Reid, vs Detroit, June 13, 2002
     Marlies Askamp, vs New York, July 18, 1998
     Plenette Pierson, vs Indiana, July 24, 2004
     Maria Stepanova, vs Washington, July 7, 2001
   3 — By Many

FREE THROWS MADE

Most free throws made, career
   627 — Jennifer Gillom
   298 — Bridgette Pettis
   240 — Anna DeForge
Most free throws made, season
   141 — Jennifer Gillom, 1999
   137 — Jennifer Gillom, 1998
   128 — Brandy Reed, 2000
Most free throws made, game
   12 — Jennifer Gillom, vs Portland, June 14, 2000 (OT)
      Lisa Harrison, vs Minnesota, July 11, 2000
      Kristi Harrower, vs Los Angeles, July 17, 1999
      Plenette Pierson, vs Los Angeles, August 8,2003
   11 — By Many

FREE THROW ATTEMPTS

Most free throw attempts, career
   826 — Jennifer Gillom
   361 — Bridgette Pettis
   291 — Anna DeForge
Most free throw attempts, season
   195 — Jennifer Gillom, 1998
   177 — Jennifer Gillom, 1999
   151 — Diana Taurasi, 2005

Most free throw attempts, game
   19 — Plenette Pierson, vs Los Angeles, August 8, 2003
   16 — Diana Taurasi, vs Houston, August 5, 2005
      Kayte Christensen, vs San Antonio, Aug. 22, 2003
   15 — Jennifer Gillom, at Los Angeles, July 23,1998

REBOUNDS

Most rebounds, career
   913 — Jennifer Gillom
   673 — Lisa Harrison
   639 — Adrian Williams
Highest average, rebounds per game, career
(Minimum 100 games)
   5.0 — Jennifer Gillom (913/183)
   4.9 — Adrian Williams (639/130)
   4.7 — Maria Stepanova (531/114)
Most rebounds, season
   252 — Adrian Williams, 2003
   220 — Adrian Williams, 2002
   219 — Jennifer Gillom, 1998
Highest average, rebounds per game, season (qualifiers)
   7.4 — Adrian Williams, 2003 (252/34)
   7.3 — Jennifer Gillom, 1998 (219/30)
   7.2 — Marlies Askamp, 1999 (215/30)
Most rebounds, game
   16 — Adrian Williams, vs San Antonio, May 28,2003
   15 — Marlies Askamp, vs Cleveland, June 19, 1999
      Jennifer Gillom, vs Sacramento, June 14, 1999
      Adrian Williams, at Los Angeles, July 15,2003 (2OT)
   14 — Adrian Williams, vs Houston, June 14, 2003
      Kamila Vodichkova, at San Antonio, July 5,2005
      Adrian Williams, vs Los Angeles, August 13,2002
Most games, 10+ rebounds, career
   14 — Adrian Williams
   12 — Jennifer Gillom
   11 — Marlies Askamp
Most consecutive games, 10+ rebounds
   4 — Maria Stepanova, August 6-11, 1999
   3 — Kamila Vodichkova, August 23-27, 2005
   2 — By Many

OFFENSIVE REBOUNDS

Most offensive rebounds, career
   263 — Jennifer Gillom
   222 — Lisa Harrison
   194 — Marlies Askamp
Highest average, offensive rebounds per game, career
(Minimum 100 games)
   1.7 — Maria Stepanova (189/114)
   1.438 — Adrian Williams (187/130)
   1.437 — Jennifer Gillom (263/183)
Most offensive rebounds, season
   92 — Marlies Askamp, 1999
   68 — Adrian Williams, 2003
   66 — Maria Stepanova, 2001
      Marlies Askamp, 1997
Most offensive rebounds, game
   8 — Brandy Reed, at Charlotte, June 22, 2000
   7 — Marlies Askamp, at Minnesota, July 3, 1999
     Adrian Williams, vs San Antonio, May 28,2003
     Marlies Askamp, vs Los Angeles, July 17, 1999
   6 — By Many

DEFENSIVE REBOUNDS

Most defensive rebounds, career
- 650 — Jennifer Gillom
- 452 — Adrian Williams
- 451 — Lisa Harrison

Highest average, defensive rebounds per game, career
(Minimum 100 games)
- 3.6 — Jennifer Gillom (650/183)
- 3.5 — Adrian Williams (452/130)
- 3.0 — Maria Stepanova (342/114)

Most defensive rebounds, season
- 184 — Adrian Williams, 2003
- 157 — Jennifer Gillom, 1998
- 156 — Adrian Williams, 2002

Most defensive rebounds, game
- 12 — Adrian Williams, vs Houston, June 14, 2003
  - Jennifer Gillom, vs Sacramento, June 14, 1999
- 11 — Jennifer Gillom, at Houston, July 28, 1998
  - Adrian Williams, at Los Angeles, July 15, 2003 (2OT)
  - Adrian Williams, vs Los Angeles, August 13,2002
- 10 — By Many

ASSISTS

Most assists, career
- 551 — Michele Timms
- 282 — Diana Taurasi
- 281 — Bridgette Pettis

Highest average, assists per game, career
(Minimum 100 games)
- 4.8 — Michele Timms (551/116)
- 2.6 — Anna DeForge (259/101)
- 1.8 — Bridgette Pettis (281/154)

Most assists, season
- 158 — Michele Timms, 1998
- 151 — Michele Timms, 1999
- 150 — Diana Taurasi, 2005

Highest average, assists per game, season (qualifiers)
- 5.3 — Michele Timms, 1998 (158/30)
- 5.1 — Michele Timms, 1997 (137/27)
- 5.0 — Michele Timms, 1999 (151/30)

Most assists, game
- 12 — Michelle Cleary, vs Utah, July 19, 2000
- 10 — Kristen Veal, vs Houston, June 10, 2001
  - Michele Timms, at Sacramento, June 12,1999
  - Michele Timms, vs Sacramento, Aug. 17,1999
- 9 — By Many

Most games, 10+ assists, career
- 2 — Michele Timms
- 1 — Kristen Veal
- 1 — Michelle Cleary

PERSONAL FOULS

Most personal fouls, career
- 564 — Jennifer Gillom
- 338 — Lisa Harrison
- 322 — Michele Timms

Most personal fouls, season
- 117 — Diana Taurasi, 2004
- 115 — Slobodanka Tuvic, 2004
- 111 — Diana Taurasi, 2005

Most personal fouls, game
- 6 — By Many

STEALS

Most steals, career
- 205 — Jennifer Gillom
- 188 — Michele Timms
- 163 — Bridgette Pettis

Highest average, steals per game, career
(Minimum 100 games)
- 1.6 — Michele Timms (188/116)
- 1.4 — Anna DeForge (143/101)
- 1.1 — Jennifer Gillom (205/183)

Most steals, season
- 71 — Michele Timms, 1997
- 68 — Umeki Webb, 1997
- 66 — Brandy Reed, 2000

Highest average, steals per game, season (qualifiers)
- 2.6 — Michele Timms, 1997 (71/27)
- 2.4 — Umeki Webb, 1997 (68/28)
- 2.1 — Brandy Reed, 2000 (66/32)

Most steals, game
- 9 — Michelle Brogan, at Utah, July 27, 1998
- 8 — Michele Timms, at Utah, July 3, 1997
  - Michele Timms, vs Utah, Aug. 17, 1997 (OT)
- 7 — Brandy Reed, at Charlotte, June 22, 2000
  - Brandy Reed, vs Los Angeles, July 21, 2000

BLOCKED SHOTS

Most blocked shots, career
- 184 — Maria Stepanova
- 101 — Jennifer Gillom
- 78 — Slobodanka Tuvic

Highest average, blocked shots per game, career
(Minimum: 100 games)
- 1.6 — Maria Stepanova (184/114)
- .7 — Slobodanka Tuvic (78/106)
- .6 — Jennifer Gillom (101/183)

Most blocked shots, season
- 64 — Maria Stepanova, 2001
- 62 — Maria Stepanova, 1999
- 38 — Maria Stepanova, 2005

Highest average, blocked shots per game, season (qualifiers)
- 2.5 — Maria Stepanova, 2005 (38/15)
- 2.0 — Maria Stepanova, 2001 (64/32)
- 1.9 — Maria Stepanova, 1999 (62/32)

Most blocked shots, game
- 6 — Maria Stepanova, at Detroit, June 26, 1999
  - Plenette Pierson, at Los Angeles, June 8, 2005
- 5 — By Many

TURNOVERS

Most turnovers, career
- 425 — Jennifer Gillom
- 298 — Michele Timms
- 251 — Bridgette Pettis

Most turnovers, season
- 112 — Diana Taurasi, 2005
- 90 — Brandy Reed, 2000
  - Diana Taurasi, 2004

Most turnovers, game
- 9 — Diana Taurasi, at Sacramento, August 23, 2005
- 8 — Bridget Pettis, at Cleveland, June 28, 1997
  - Penny Taylor, vs Houston, August 5, 2005
  - Plenette Pierson, at Houston, June 4, 2005
- 7 — By Many

SACRAMENTO MONARCHS

REGULAR SEASON TEAM RECORDS

TEAM OFFENSE

SCORING

Highest average, points per game, season
74.8 — 1999 (2392/32)
73.2 — 2000 (2343/32)
Lowest average, points per game, season
63.9 — 1998 (1916/30)
67.6 — 2003 (2299/34)
Most points, game
108 — vs Detroit, July 1, 2000
107 — vs Utah, June 24, 1999
Fewest points, game
41 — vs Detroit, August 11, 1998
44 — vs Houston, July 18, 1998
Largest margin of victory, game
40 — vs Detroit, July 24, 2005 (91-51)
39 — at Minnesota, July 3, 2001 (91-52)
Largest margin of defeat, game
31 — vs Houston, July 18, 1998 (44-75)
28 — at Houston, July 12, 1997 (61-89)

BY HALF

Most points, first half
52 — vs Detroit, July 1, 2000
48 — vs Utah, June 24, 1999
vs Utah, August 14, 1999
vs Minnesota, June 28, 2000
Fewest points, first half
13 — vs Houston, July 18, 1998
16 — vs Detroit, August 11, 1998
Largest lead at half time
31 — at Minnesota, July 3, 2001 (led 46-15; won 91-52)
24 — vs Seattle, August 9, 2000 (led 47-23; won 79-46)
Largest deficit at halftime overcome to win game
11 — vs Phoenix, June 12, 1999 (trailed 39-50; won 96-85)
at Portland, July 7, 2000 (trailed 25-36; won 63-60)
8 — vs Utah, August 15, 1998 (trailed 30-38; won 82-55)
Most points, second half
59 — vs Utah, June 24, 1999
58 — vs Detroit, July 24, 2005
at Detroit, July 4, 1999
Fewest points, second half
18 — at Houston, August 5, 2003
19 — vs Connecticut, June 24, 2005

OVERTIME

Most points, overtime period
13 — at Charlotte, June 24, 2001
12 — Many Times

Fewest points, overtime period
2 — vs Portland, June 16, 2001
at Minnesota, July 11, 2004
4 — vs Utah, July 2, 1997
at New York, July 30, 1997
Largest margin of victory, overtime period
4 — at Phoenix, August 16, 2003 (65-61)
3 — at Charlotte, June 24, 2001 (85-82)

FIELD GOAL PERCENTAGE

Highest field goal percentage, season
.440 — 2000 (876/1993)
.430 — 2005 (853/1986)
Lowest field goal percentage, season
.401 — 2002 (780/1945)
.406 — 1997 (704/1732)
Highest field goal percentage, game
.600 — at San Antonio, August 7, 2003 (36/60)
.586 — vs Utah, August 14, 1999 (34/58)
Lowest field goal percentage, game
.273 — vs Houston, July 18, 1998 (18/66)
.281 — at Seattle, June 3, 2003 (18/64)

FIELD GOALS

Most field goals per game, season
27.4 — 2000 (876/32)
26.5 — 1999 (849/32)
Fewest field goals per game, season
24.4 — 2002 (780/32)
24.5 — 1998 (734/30)
Most field goals, game
36 — at San Antonio, August 7, 2003
vs Detroit, July 1, 2000
vs Utah, June 24, 1999
35 — at Connecticut, July 9, 2004
vs Washington, July 18, 2004
Fewest field goals, game
16 — at Charlotte, July 19, 2002
at New York, June 26, 1998
18 — Many Times

FIELD GOAL ATTEMPTS

Most field goal attempts per game, season
62.7 — 1999 (2006/32)
62.3 — 2000 (1993/32)
Fewest field goal attempts per game, season
58.4 — 2005 (1986/34)
60.1 — 1998 (1802/30)
Most field goal attempts, game
88 — at Los Angeles, July 15, 1998 (OT)
86 — vs Los Angeles, July 29, 2004 (2OT)
Fewest field goal attempts, game
43 — at Seattle, June 30, 2001
vs Cleveland, June 2, 2001
at New York, June 26, 1998
45 — vs Houston, July 18, 1997

THREE-POINT FIELD GOAL PERCENTAGE
Highest three-point field goal percentage, season
.385 — 2001 (163/423)
.358 — 2005 (129/360)
Lowest three-point field goal percentage, season
.260 — 1998 (72/277)
.284 — 2002 (112/395)

THREE-POINT FIELD GOALS
Most three-point field goals per game, season
5.1 — 2001 (163/32)
4.4 — 2000 (142/32)
Fewest three-point field goals per game, season
2.4 — 1998 (72/30)
3.5 — 2002 (112/32)
Most three-point field goals, game
14 — at Minnesota, July 3, 2001
10 — at Minnesota, June 29, 1999
vs Los Angeles, July 31, 2003
vs Los Angeles, July 2 9, 2004 (2OT)
Fewest three-point field goals, game
0 — Many Times

THREE-POINT FIELD GOAL ATTEMPTS
Most three-point field goal attempts per game, season
14.3 — 2000 (459/32)
13.9 — 2003 (473/34)
Fewest three-point field goal attempts per game, season
9.2 — 1998 (277/30)
10.6 — 2005 (360/34)
Most three-point field goal attempts, game
25 — at Los Angeles, July 25, 2001
24 — at Los Angeles, August 2, 2001
Fewest three-point field goal attempts, game
1 — at Washington, July 26, 1998
2 — at Charlotte, July 27, 1998

FREE THROW PERCENTAGE
Highest free throw percentage, season
.757 — 2002 (494/653)
.739 — 2001 (457/618)
Lowest free throw percentage, season
.671 — 1998 (376/560)
.671 — 1999 (568/847)
.679 — 2003 (425/626)
Highest free throw percentage, game
1.000 — at Charlotte, September 9, 2004 (12/12)
vs Connecticut, June 12, 2004 (12/12)
at Connecticut, June 28, 2005 (11/11)
at San Antonio, July 17, 2003 (15/15)
at San Antonio, August 7, 2003 (7/7)
at Los Angeles, July 25, 2001 (7/7)
at Phoenix, July 20, 1998 (2/2)
.958 — vs Utah, August 1, 2002 (23/24)
Lowest free throw percentage, game
.250 — at Seattle, August 25, 2003 (1/4)
.286 — at Minnesota, May 24, 2003 (2/7)

FREE THROWS MADE
Most free throws made per game, season
17.6 — 1999 (568/32)
15.4 — 2002 (494/32)

Fewest free throws made per game, season
12.50 — 2003 (425/34)
12.53 — 1998 (376/30)
Most free throws made, game
34 — vs Detroit, July 1, 2000
32 — at Washington, July 26, 1998
Fewest free throws made, game
1 — at Seattle, August 25, 2003
2 — at Minnesota, May 24, 2003
at Phoenix, July 20, 1998

FREE THROW ATTEMPTS
Most free throw attempts per game, season
26.5 — 1999 (847/32)
21.2 — 2005 (721/34)
Fewest free throw attempts per game, season
17.8 — 2004 (604/34)
18.4 — 2003 (626/34)
Most free throw attempts, game
48 — vs Phoenix, June 12, 1999
46 — vs Detroit, July 1, 2000
vs Utah, June 24, 1999
Fewest free throw attempts, game
2 — at Phoenix, July 20, 1998
4 — at Seattle, August 25, 2003

REBOUNDS
Most rebounds per game, season
34.8 — 1999 (1112/32)
34.3 — 2001 (1097/32)
Fewest rebounds per game, season
29.7 — 2002 (949/32)
30.1 — 2004 (1024/34)
Most rebounds, game
51 — vs Los Angeles, July 29, 2004 (2OT)
48 — vs Portland, June 16, 2001 (OT)
at Washington, June 5, 2001
Fewest rebounds, game
19 — vs Houston, July 18, 1997
20 — at Portland, June 6, 2002

OFFENSIVE REBOUNDS
Most offensive rebounds per game, season
12.9 — 1999 (412/32)
12.2 — 1997 (341/28)
Fewest offensive rebounds per game, season
9.4 — 2002 (301/32)
10.3 — 2003 (349/34)
Most offensive rebounds, game
21 — vs Los Angeles, June 30, 1998
20 — vs Los Angeles, July 29, 2004 (2OT)
at Los Angeles, July 15, 1998 (OT)
Fewest offensive rebounds, game
3 — vs Cleveland, June 2, 2001
4 — vs Houston, June 13, 2005
at Orlando, July 6, 2001
at Portland, July 7, 2000

DEFENSIVE REBOUNDS
Most defensive rebounds per game, season
22.6 — 2001 (723/32)
21.9 — 1999 (700/32)

Fewest defensive rebounds per game, season
  18.7 — 2004 (635/34)
  19.2 — 1997 (538/28)
Most defensive rebounds, game
  34 — vs Los Angeles, June 7, 2003
  33 — vs Phoenix, May 30, 2003
Fewest defensive rebounds, game
  10 — at Miami, July 7, 2001
  11 — at Cleveland, July 10, 1997

ASSISTS

Most assists per game, season
  17.7 — 2000 (567/32)
  17.4 — 2001 (558/32)
Fewest assists per game, season
  14.4 — 1997 (404/28)
  15.3 — 2004 (519/34)
Most assists, game
  27 — at Minnesota, May 24, 2003
  25 — at Los Angeles, July 25, 2001
Fewest assists, game
  4 — vs Connecticut, June 24, 2005
  6 — at Phoenix, August 19, 1998

PERSONAL FOULS

Most personal fouls per game, season
  21.2 — 1997 (593/28)
  21.1 — 1998 (633/30)
Fewest personal fouls per game, season
  17.8 — 2000 (571/32)
  18.4 — 2001 (588/32)
Most personal fouls, game
  32 — at Phoenix, August 4, 1997
  31 — vs Minnesota, August 9, 2003
Fewest personal fouls, game
  9 — vs Portland, July 27, 2001
      vs Detroit, July 21, 2001
  10 — vs Orlando, July 27, 2000

DISQUALIFICATIONS

Most disqualifications per game, season
  .50 — 1997 (14/28)
  .25 — 2002 (8/32)
Fewest disqualifications per game, season
  .03 — 2005 (1/34)
  .13 — 2001 (4/32)
        1999 (4/32)
Most disqualifications, game
  2 — Many times. Most recent:
      vs Minnesota, August 9, 2003

STEALS

Most steals per game, season
  10.4 — 2000 (332/32)
  10.3 — 1999 (329/32)
Fewest steals per game, season
  7.7 — 2002 (247/32)
  8.6 — 2001 (276/32)
Most steals, game
  19 — at San Antonio, September 4, 2004
       at Orlando, July 17, 1999
  18 — vs Seattle, July 26, 2003

Fewest steals, game
  3 — at Los Angeles, August 16, 2005
      at Houston, July 19, 2005
      vs Detroit, June 19, 2004
      vs Phoenix, July 29, 2001
  4 — Many Times

BLOCKED SHOTS

Most blocked shots per game, season
  4.94 — 2001 (158/32)
  4.91 — 2000 (157/32)
Fewest blocked shots per game, season
  2.1 — 1997 (60/28)
  3.2 — 2005 (108/34)
Most blocked shots, game
  11 — vs Los Angeles, July 31, 2003
       vs Portland, July 27, 2001
  10 — vs Cleveland, June 2, 2001
Fewest blocked shots, game
  0 — Many Times

TURNOVERS

Most turnovers per game, season
  20.1 — 1997 (562/28)
  17.8 — 1998 (533/30)
Fewest turnovers per game, season
  13.6 — 2003 (461/34)
  14.3 — 2002 (456/32)
Most turnovers, game
  26 — vs Cleveland, August 4, 1998
  25 — Many Times
Fewest turnovers, game
  6 — vs Seattle, August 20, 2005
      at Houston, September 16, 2004
      vs Cleveland, July 11, 2002
      vs Indiana, August 3, 2001
  7 — vs San Antonio, July 14, 2005
      vs Indiana, June 14, 2003
      vs Seattle, June 20, 2002
      vs Charlotte, June 17, 2000

TEAM DEFENSE

POINTS

Fewest points allowed per game, season
  61.6 — 2005 (2093/34)
  65.2 — 2003 (2216/34)
Most points allowed per game, season
  75.4 — 1997 (2112/28)
  71.7 — 2002 (2294/32)
Fewest points allowed, game
  45 — vs Houston, August 7, 2005
  46 — vs Seattle, August 9, 2000
Fewest points allowed, first half
  13 — vs New York, July 1, 2004
  14 — vs Phoenix, July 29, 2001
Fewest points allowed, second half
  17 — vs Utah, August 15, 1998
  18 — vs Los Angeles, June 3, 2004

Fewest points allowed, overtime period
6 — at Phoenix, August 16, 2003
vs Houston, July 10, 2001
vs New York, June 13, 2002
7 — vs Los Angeles, July 29, 2004
vs Houston, July 10, 2001

FIELD GOAL PERCENTAGE
Lowest opponents' field goal percentage, season
.401 — 2001 (804/2003)
.410 — 2003 (816/1991)
Highest opponents' field goal percentage, season
.446 — 1997 (775/1738)
.429 — 2004 (803/1872)
Lowest opponents' field goal percentage, game
.255 — vs Phoenix, July 29, 2001 (14/55)
.269 — vs Minnesota, August 7, 2001 (18/67)

TURNOVERS
Fewest opponents' turnovers per game, season
15.0 — 2001 (481/32)
15.5 — 2002 (496/32)
Most opponents' turnovers per game, season
18.3 — 2005 (622/34)
18.1 — 1997 (508/28)
Most opponents' turnovers, game
28 — vs Los Angeles, June 3, 2004
27 — vs Utah, July 2, 1997 (OT)

TEAM MISCELLANEOUS

GAME WON AND LOST
Highest winning percentage, season
.735 — 2005 (25-9)
.656 — 2000 (21-11)
Lowest winning percentage, season
.267 — 1998 (8-22)
.357 — 1997 (10-18)
Most consecutive games won
7 — July 24-August 7, 2005
6 — September 16, 2004-May 29, 2005
July 21-August 1, 2002
Most consecutive games won, one season
7 — July 24-August 7, 2005
6 — July 21-August 1, 2002
Most consecutive games lost
9 — July 16-August 4, 1997
8 — June 22-July 7, 2002
Most consecutive games lost, one season
9 — July 16-August 4, 1997
8 — June 22-July 7, 2002
Highest winning percentage, home games, season
.882 — 2005 (15-2)
.813 — 2000 (13-3)
Lowest winning percentage, home games, season
.333 — 1998 (5-10)
.500 — 1997 (7-7)
Most consecutive home games won
9 — July 31, 2004-June 17, 2005
8 — July 24-August 23, 2005

Most consecutive home games lost
5 — July 10-August 4, 1998
4 — July 18-27, 1997
Highest winning percentage, road games, season
.588 — 2005 (10-7)
.500 — 1999, 2000, 2001 (8-8)
Lowest winning percentage, road games, season
.200 — 1998 (3-12)
.214 — 1997 (3-11)
Most consecutive road games won
4 — September 16-May 29, 2005
July 12-September 4, 2004
July 26, 2000-June 4, 2001
June 24-July 6, 2001
3 — July 27-August 10, 2002
June 29-July 4, 1999
Most consecutive road games lost
10 — June 6-July 7, 2002
July 10-August 22, 1997
6 — July 29, 1998-June 10, 1999

OVERTIME GAMES
Most overtime games, season
4 — 2002, 2001
3 — 2004
Most consecutive overtime games, season
2 — June 13-15, 2002
Most overtime games won, season
2 — 2002, 2001
Most overtime games won, no losses, season
1 — 2003
Most overtime games lost, season
3 — 2004
2 — 1997, 2001, 2002
Most overtime games lost, no wins, season
3 — 2004
2 — 1997
Most overtime periods, game
2 — vs Portland, July 25, 2002
vs Washington, June 25, 2002
vs New York, June 13, 2002
vs Houston, July 10, 2001
vs Los Angeles, July 29, 2004

INDIVIDUAL RECORDS

SEASONS
Most seasons
8 — Ticha Penicheiro
Ruthie Bolton-Holyfield
7 — Tangela Smith
Yolanda Griffith
Lady Grooms

GAMES
Most games, career
240 — Ticha Penicheiro
223 — Tangela Smith
218 — Ruthie Bolton

Most consecutive games, career
   193 — Tangela Smith, June 17, 1999-Sept. 19, 2004
   128 — Kedra Holland-Corn, June 10, 1999-
       August 13, 2002
   122 — Latasha Byears, June 21, 1997-Aug. 9, 2000
Most games, season
   34 — By Many

MINUTES

Most minutes, career
  7,719 — Ticha Penicheiro
  6,667 — Yolanda Griffith
  6,133 — Tangela Smith
Highest average, minutes per game, career
(Minimum 100 games)
   32.2 — Ticha Penicheiro (7719/240)
   31.4 — Yolanda Griffith (6667/212)
   29.3 — Kedra Holland-Corn (3744/128)
Most minutes, season
  1,120 — Ticha Penicheiro, 1999
  1,089 — Ticha Penicheiro, 2003
  1,080 — Ticha Penicheiro, 1998
Highest average, minutes per game, season
   37.5 — Chantel Tremitiere, 1997 (1051/28)
   36.0 — Ticha Penicheiro, 1998 (1080/30)
   35.0 — Ticha Penicheiro, 1999 (1120/32)
Most minutes, game
   50 — La'Keshia Frett, vs New York,
      June 13, 2002 (2OT)
   49 — Andrea Nagy, vs Washington,
      June 25, 2002 (2OT)
   48 — Ticha Penicheiro, vs New York,
      June 13, 2002 (2OT)

SCORING

Most points, lifetime
  3,306 — Yolanda Griffith
  2,552 — Tangela Smith
  2,183 — Ruthie Bolton
Highest average, points per game, career
(Minimum 100 games)
   15.6 — Yolanda Griffith (3306/212)
   11.4 — Tangela Smith (2552/223)
   10.2 — Kedra Holland-Corn (1309/128)
Most points, season
   545 — Yolanda Griffith, 1999
   523 — Yolanda Griffith, 2000
   518 — Yolanda Griffith, 2001
Highest average, points per game, season
   19.4 — Ruthie Bolton, 1997 (447/23)
   18.8 — Yolanda Griffith, 1999 (545/29)
   16.3 — Yolanda Griffith, 2000 (523/32)
Most points, game
   34 — Ruthie Bolton, vs Cleveland, August 12, 1997
      Ruthie Bolton, at Washington, July 2, 1999
      Ruthie Bolton, vs Utah, August 8, 1997
   33 — Linda Burgess, vs Utah, August 15, 1998
   31 — Yolanda Griffith, vs Phoenix, June 12, 1999

Most games, 30 or more points, career
   4 — Yolanda Griffith
   3 — Ruthie Bolton
   1 — Linda Burgess
Most games, 20 or more points, career
   57 — Yolanda Griffith
   27 — Ruthie Bolton
   21 — Tangela Smith
Most consecutive games, 20 or more points
   7 — Ruthie Bolton-Holifield, June 23-July 10, 1997
   4 — Yolanda Griffith, July 16-22, 1999
   3 — By Many
Most consecutive games, 10 or more points
   25 — Ruthie Bolton-Holifield, June 21, 1997-
      June 16, 1998
   20 — Tangela Smith, June 18-August 1, 2002
   19 — Latasha Byears, June 30-August 11, 1998

FIELD GOAL PERCENTAGE

Highest field goal percentage, career
(Minimum 400 field goals)
   .515 — Yolanda Griffith (1189/2308)
   .485 — Latasha Byears (482/994)
   .431 — Tangela Smith (1078/2500)
Highest field goal percentage, season (qualifiers)
   .541 — Yolanda Griffith, 1999 (200/370)
   .537 — Latasha Byears, 1999 (130/242)
   .535 — Yolanda Griffith, 2000 (193/361)
Highest field goal percentage, game
(Minimum 8 field goals made)
  1.000 — Kara Lawson, at Connecticut, July 9, 2004 (8/8)
   .899 — Yolanda Griffith, at Seattle, August 14, 2001 (8/9)
   .833 — Tangela Smith, at Washington, June 23, 2000 (10/12)
Most field goals, none missed, game
   8 — Kara Lawson, at Connecticut, July 9, 2004
   5 — Latasha Byears, vs Phoenix, August 7, 1999
   4 — Latasha Byears, vs Cleveland, August 12, 1997
      Lady Grooms, at Phoenix, July 20, 1998
      DeMya Walker, vs Charlotte, August 3, 2003
      DeMya Walker, at Houston, September 16, 2004
      Ticha Penicheiro, vs San Antonio, July 14, 2005
Most field goal attempts, none made, game
   10 — Nicole Powell, vs Connecticut, June 24, 2005
   9 — Ticha Penicheiro, at New York, June 17, 2003
   8 — Chantel Tremitiere, vs Cleveland, August 12, 1997
      Ruthie Bolton, at Utah, June 19, 1999

FIELD GOALS

Most field goals, career
  1,189 — Yolanda Griffith
  1,078 — Tangela Smith
   767 — Ruthie Bolton
Most field goals, season
   200 — Yolanda Griffith, 1999
   193 — Yolanda Griffith, 2000
   192 — Yolanda Griffith, 2001
Most field goals, game
   14 — Latasha Byears, at Phoenix, July 20, 1998
      Linda Burgess, vs Utah, August 15, 1998
      Tangela Smith, vs Utah, August 14, 1999
   13 — Yolanda Griffith, vs Utah, July 15, 2000
   12 — Ruthie Bolton, vs Cleveland, August 12, 1997

Yolanda Griffith, vs Houston, July 10, 2001 (2OT)

FIELD GOAL ATTEMPTS

Most field goal attempts, career
2,500 — Tangela Smith
2,308 — Yolanda Griffith
2,088 — Ruthie Bolton

Most field goal attempts, season
435 — Tangela Smith, 2002
427 — Tangela Smith, 2003
408 — Ruthie Bolton, 1997

Most field goal attempts, game
24 — Ruthie Bolton, at Cleveland, July 10, 1997
Ruthie Bolton, vs Orlando, July 27, 2000
23 — By Many

THREE-POINT FIELD GOAL PERCENTAGE

Highest three-point field goal percentage, career
(Minimum 100 three-point field goals)
.427 — Edna Campbell (105/246)
.403 — Kara Lawson (141/350)
.332 — Kedra Holland-Corn (198/596)

Highest three-point field goal percentage, season
(qualifiers)
.457 — Edna Campbell, 2001 (43/94)
.444 — Kara Lawson, 2005 (36/81)
.415 — Nicole Powell, 2005 (66/159)

Most three-point field goals, none missed, game
5 — Kara Lawson, at Connecticut, July 9, 2004
Kara Lawson, vs Charlotte, August 3, 2003
4 — Kedra Holland-Corn, at Phoenix, July 13, 2000
3 — By Many

Most three-point field goal attempts, none made, game
7 — Ruthie Bolton, vs Los Angeles, July 27, 1997
6 — By Many

THREE-POINT FIELD GOALS

Most three-point field goals, career
314 — Ruthie Bolton
198 — Kedra Holland-Corn
141 — Kara Lawson

Most three-point field goals, season
66 — Nicole Powell, 2005
Ruthie Bolton, 1997
60 — Ruthie Bolton, 1999

Most three-point field goals, game
6 — By Many

Most consecutive games, three-point field goals made
20 — Ruthie Bolton, June 21-August 2, 2000
19 — Nicole Powell, July 1-August 25, 2005
18 — Kedra Holland-Corn, June 10-July 19, 1999
14 — Kedra Holland-Corn, August 11, 2001-
June 25, 2002

THREE-POINT FIELD GOAL ATTEMPTS

Most three-point field goal attempts, career
984 — Ruthie Bolton
596 — Kedra Holland-Corn
374 — Ticha Penicheiro

Most three-point field goal attempts, season
192 — Ruthie Bolton, 1997

187 — Ruthie Bolton, 1999
167 — Kedra Holland-Corn, 1999

Most three-point field goal attempts, game
15 — Ruthie Bolton, at Cleveland, July 10, 1997
14 — Ruthie Bolton, vs Utah, July 2, 1997 (OT)
12 — Ruthie Bolton, vs New York, June 23, 1997
Ruthie Bolton, vs Orlando, July 27, 2000

FREE THROW PERCENTAGE

Highest free throw percentage, career
.756 — Tangela Smith (357/472)
.753 — Lady Grooms (299/397)
.746 — Ruthie Bolton (335/449)

Highest free throw percentage, season (qualifiers)
.855 — Lady Grooms, 2002 (71/83)
.851 — Tangela Smith, 2002 (86/101)
.841 — Kara Lawson, 2004 (37/44)

Most free throws made, none missed, game
13 — Yolanda Griffith, at Charlotte, June 24, 2001(OT)
10 — Tangela Smith, vs Orlando, July 21, 2002
9 — Ticha Penicheiro, at Minnesota, June 11, 2002
Kara Lawson, vs Minnesota, September 19,2004

Most free throw attempts, none made, game
6 — Tangela Smith, vs Utah, August 14, 1999
4 — Pauline Jordan, at Detroit, July 31, 1998
Hamchetou Maiga, vs Minnesota, June 17,
2005
Ticha Penicheiro, vs New York, June 18, 1998
3 — Chantelle Anderson, vs Los Angeles, J
une 7, 2003

FREE THROWS MADE

Most free throws made, career
928 — Yolanda Griffith
516 — Ticha Penicheiro
357 — Tangela Smith

Most free throws made, season
147 — Yolanda Griffith, 2003
145 — Yolanda Griffith, 1999
140 — Yolanda Griffith, 2004

Most free throws made, game
13 — Ruthie Bolton, at Washington, July 2, 1999
Yolanda Griffith, at Phoenix, May 22, 2003
Yolanda Griffith, at Charlotte,
June 24, 2001 (OT)
Yolanda Griffith, vs Los Angeles, August 10,1999
12 — By Many

FREE THROW ATTEMPTS

Most free throw attempts, career
1,292 — Yolanda Griffith
760 — Ticha Penicheiro
472 — Tangela Smith

Most free throw attempts, season
235 — Yolanda Griffith, 1999
194 — Yolanda Griffith, 2000
190 — Yolanda Griffith, 2003

Most free throw attempts, game
19 — Yolanda Griffith, vs Phoenix, June 12, 1999
17 — Yolanda Griffith, vs Minnesota, August 7, 2001
16 — Yolanda Griffith, vs Los Angeles, Aug.10, 1999

REBOUNDS

Most rebounds, career
  1882 — Yolanda Griffith
  1118 — Tangela Smith
  891 — Ticha Penicheiro
Highest average, rebounds per game, career
(Minimum 100 games)
  8.9 — Yolanda Griffith (1882/212)
  5.6 — Latasha Byears (685/122)
  5.0 — Tangela Smith (1118/223)
Most rebounds, season
  357 — Yolanda Griffith, 2001
  331 — Yolanda Griffith, 2000
  329 — Yolanda Griffith, 1999
Highest average, rebounds per game, season (qualifiers)
  11.3 — Yolanda Griffith, 1999 (329/29)
  11.2 — Yolanda Griffith, 2001 (357/32)
  10.3 — Yolanda Griffith, 2000 (331/32)
Most rebounds, game
  20 — Yolanda Griffith, at Washington, June 5, 2001
  19 — Yolanda Griffith, vs Cleveland, June 17, 1999
       Yolanda Griffith, vs Houston, August 6, 2000
       Yolanda Griffith, at Utah, June 19, 1999
       Yolanda Griffith, vs New York, July 22, 1999
Most games, 10+ rebounds, career
  89 — Yolanda Griffith
  17 — Latasha Byears
  12 — Tangela Smith
Most consecutive games, 10+ rebounds
  5 — Yolanda Griffith, June 24-July 4, 1999
      Yolanda Griffith, June 12-21, 2001
  4 — Yolanda Griffith, July 8-16, 1999
      Yolanda Griffith, July 13-22, 2000
  3 — By Many

OFFENSIVE REBOUNDS

Most offensive rebounds, career
  818 — Yolanda Griffith
  363 — Tangela Smith
  291 — Latasha Byears
Highest average, offensive rebounds per game, career
(Minimum 100 games)
  3.9 — Yolanda Griffith (818/212)
  2.4 — Latasha Byears (291/122)
  1.6 — Tangela Smith (363/223)
Most offensive rebounds, season
  162 — Yolanda Griffith, 2001
  148 — Yolanda Griffith, 2000
  141 — Yolanda Griffith, 1999
Most offensive rebounds, game
  11 — Yolanda Griffith, vs Houston, August 6, 2000
       Yolanda Griffith, vs Los Angeles, June 26,1999
  10 — Yolanda Griffith, at Washington, June 5, 2001
  9 — By Many

DEFENSIVE REBOUNDS

Most defensive rebounds, career
  1,064 — Yolanda Griffith
  773 — Ticha Penicheiro
  755 — Tangela Smith

Highest average, defensive rebounds per game, career
(Minimum 100 games)
  5.0 — Yolanda Griffith (1064/212)
  3.4 — Tangela Smith (755/223)
  3.2 — Ticha Penicheiro (773/240)
Most defensive rebounds, season
  195 — Yolanda Griffith, 2001
  188 — Yolanda Griffith, 1999
  183 — Yolanda Griffith, 2000
Most defensive rebounds, game
  13 — Yolanda Griffith, vs Portland,
       June 16, 2001 (OT)
  12 — Yolanda Griffith, vs Cleveland, June 17, 1999
       Yolanda Griffith, at Phoenix, June 14, 1999
       Ticha Penicheiro, at Los Angeles, June 10,1999
       Ticha Penicheiro, vs Utah, August 15, 1998

ASSISTS

Most assists, career
  1591 — Ticha Penicheiro
  353 — Ruthie Bolton
  305 — Yolanda Griffith
Highest average, assists per game, career
(Minimum 100 games)
  6.6 — Ticha Penicheiro (1591/240)
  2.1 — Kendra Holland-Corn (264/128)
  1.6 — Ruthie Bolton (353/218)
Most assists, season
  236 — Ticha Penicheiro, 2000
  229 — Ticha Penicheiro, 2003
  226 — Ticha Penicheiro, 1999
Highest average, assists per game, season (qualifiers)
  8.0 — Ticha Penicheiro, 2002 (192/24)
  7.9 — Ticha Penicheiro, 2000 (236/30)
  7.5 — Ticha Penicheiro, 2001 (172/23)
Most assists, game
  16 — Ticha Penicheiro, at Cleveland, July 29, 1998
       Ticha Penicheiro, vs Los Angeles, August 3,2002
  15 — Ticha Penicheiro, at Cleveland, July 15, 2003
  14 — Ticha Penicheiro, vs Detroit, July 1, 2000
       Ticha Penicheiro, vs Phoenix, May 30, 2003
       Ticha Penicheiro, vs Minnesota, June 22, 1999
       Ticha Penicheiro, vs Minnesota, August 7,2001
Most games, 10+ assists, career
  49 — Ticha Penicheiro
  2 — Chantel Tremitiere
  1 — Andrea Nagy

PERSONAL FOULS

Most personal fouls, career
  707 — Yolanda Griffith
  678 — Tangela Smith
  559 — Ticha Penicheiro
Most personal fouls, season
  126 — Tangela Smith, 2002
  125 — Yolanda Griffith, 2003
  121 — Latasha Byears, 1998
Most personal fouls, game
  6 — By Many

STEALS

Most steals, career
  481 — Ticha Penicheiro
  409 — Yolanda Griffith
  254 — Ruthie Bolton

Highest average, steals per game, career
(Minimum 100 games)
    2.0 — Ticha Penicheiro (481/240)
    1.9 — Yolanda Griffith (409/212)
    1.6 — Kedra Holland-Corn (203/128)
Most steals, season
    83 — Yolanda Griffith, 2000
    75 — Yolanda Griffith, 2004
    73 — Yolanda Griffith, 1999
Highest average, steals per game, season (qualifiers)
    2.7 — Ticha Penicheiro, 2002 (64/24)
    2.6 — Yolanda Griffith, 2000 (83/32)
    2.5 — Yolanda Griffith, 1999 (73/29)
Most steals, game
    10 — Ticha Penicheiro, vs San Antonio, July 10, 2003
    8 — Yolanda Griffith, vs Washington, July 29, 1999
    7 — Ticha Penicheiro, at Houston, June 6, 2000
       Yolanda Griffith, at Detroit, June 3, 2000
       Ticha Penicheiro, vs Phoenix, August 6, 2002

BLOCKED SHOTS

Most blocked shots, career
    306 — Tangela Smith
    276 — Yolanda Griffith
    49 — DeMya Walker
Highest average, blocked shots per game, career
(Minimum: 100 games)
    1.4 — Tangela Smith (306/223)
    1.3 — Yolanda Griffith (276/212)
    .3 — Latasha Byears (32/122)
Most blocked shots, season
    64 — Tangela Smith, 2000
    61 — Yolanda Griffith, 2000
    55 — Tangela Smith, 2001
Highest average, blocked shots per game, season
(qualifiers)
    2.0 — Tangela Smith, 2000 (64/32)
    1.91 — Yolanda Griffith, 2000 (61/32)
    1.86 — Yolanda Griffith, 1999 (54/29)
Most blocked shots, game
    6 — Tangela Smith, vs Seattle, August 9, 2000
       Yolanda Griffith, vs Minnesota, July 20, 2000
       Yolanda Griffith, vs New York, July 22, 1999
       Yolanda Griffith, vs Orlando, July 24, 1999
    5 — By Many

TURNOVERS

Most turnovers, career
    675 — Ticha Penicheiro
    470 — Yolanda Griffith
    378 — Tangela Smith
Most turnovers, season
    135 — Ticha Penicheiro, 1999
    122 — Chantel Tremitiere, 1997
    116 — Ticha Penicheiro, 1998
Most turnovers, game
    8 — By Many

SAN ANTONIO SILVER STARS

REGULAR SEASON TEAM RECORDS

TEAM OFFENSE

SCORING

Highest average, points per game, season
75.6 — 2002 (2418/32)
75.4 — 2000 (2413/32)
Lowest average, points per game, season
62.9 — 2005 (2141/34)
64.4 — 2004 (2191/34)
Most points, game
104 — vs Detroit, July 6, 1999 (2OT)
102 — vs Los Angeles, June 23, 1997
Fewest points, game
44 — at Houston, June 25, 2005
46 — at Phoenix, August 6, 1997
Largest margin of victory, game
31 — vs Minnesota, July 5, 2002 (87-56)
28 — vs Charlotte, June 15, 2000 (96-68)
Largest margin of defeat, game
40 — at Seattle, June 22, 2003 (53-93)
38 — at Sacramento, June 24, 1999 (69-107)

BY HALF

Most points, first half
51 — vs Detroit, July 8, 2002
50 — vs Los Angeles, June 23, 1997
Fewest points, first half
17 — vs Seattle, June 25, 2001
18 — at Houston, June 9, 2004
    at Sacramento, June 24, 2003
    at Seattle, June 18, 2000
    vs Cleveland, August 11, 1997
Largest lead at half time
22 — at Washington, July 19, 1998 (led 47-25; won 99-88)
19 — vs Detroit, July 8, 2002 (led 51-32; won 94-76)
Largest deficit at halftime overcome to win game
18 — at Phoenix, August 20, 1999 (trailed 20-38; won 70-62)
14 — at Portland, July 8, 2001 (trailed 30-44; won 65-63)
Most points, second half
60 — vs Sacramento, June 26, 2000
54 — vs Charlotte, September 17, 2004
    at Detroit, July 23, 2002
    vs Charlotte, June 15, 2000
Fewest points, second half
17 — vs Los Angeles, June 26, 2003
    vs Houston, June 30, 1998
    at Sacramento, August 15, 1998
18 — at Phoenix, August 6, 1997

OVERTIME

Most points, overtime period
14 — at Phoenix, June 26, 2004
    vs Seattle, August 20, 2003
    vs Miami, July 31, 2002
13 — vs Detroit, July 6, 1999
Fewest points, overtime period
3 — at Phoenix, August 17, 1997
6 — vs Los Angeles, August 13, 2001
Largest margin of victory, overtime period
10 — vs Detroit, July 6, 1999 (104-94)
8 — at Phoenix, June 26, 2004 (80-72)
    vs Seattle, August 20, 2003 (78-70)
    vs Minnesota, July 28, 2001 (68-60)

FIELD GOAL PERCENTAGE

Highest field goal percentage, season
.453 — 2000 (858/1896)
.441 — 2002 (843/1911)
Lowest field goal percentage, season
.374 — 1997 (666/1781)
.383 — 2003 (792/2068)
Highest field goal percentage, game
.614 — vs Phoenix, July 14, 2000 (35/57)
.604 — at Indiana, July 10, 2002 (29/48)
Lowest field goal percentage, game
.242 — at Indiana, July 23, 2003 (16/66)
.250 — vs New York, July 5, 1997 (17/68)

FIELD GOALS

Most field goals per game, season
26.8 — 2000 (858/32)
26.4 — 1999 (845/32)
Fewest field goals per game, season
22.5 — 2005 (764/34)
23.3 — 2003 (792/34)
Most field goals, game
40 — vs Detroit, July 6, 1999 (2OT)
35 — vs Phoenix, July 14, 2000
    vs Charlotte, June 15, 2000
    at Sacramento, August 14, 1999
    vs Charlotte, June 25, 1998
Fewest field goals, game
14 — vs Phoenix, July 23, 2005
15 — at Minnesota, June 3, 2004
    vs New York, August 3, 1999

FIELD GOAL ATTEMPTS

Most field goal attempts per game, season
63.6 — 1997 (1781/28)
61.2 — 1998 (1837/30)
Fewest field goal attempts per game, season
53.9 — 2005 (1833/34)
57.1 — 2004 (1940/34)
Most field goal attempts, game
87 — vs Detroit, July 6, 1999 (2OT)
79 — vs Houston, June 30, 1998 (2OT)

Fewest field goal attempts, game
42 — at Houston, July 30, 2005
43 — at Indiana, July 21, 2005
vs New York, July 26, 2001

THREE-POINT FIELD GOAL PERCENTAGE
Highest three-point field goal percentage, season
.360 — 2002 (89/247)
.336 — 2000 (88/262)
Lowest three-point field goal percentage, season
.295 — 2003 (93/315)
.296 — 1999 (107/362)

THREE-POINT FIELD GOALS
Most three-point field goals per game, season
3.78 — 1997 (106/28)
3.76 — 1998 (113/30)
Fewest three-point field goals per game, season
2.3 — 2004 (79/34)
2.4 — 2001 (78/32)
Most three-point field goals, game
10 — vs Washington, June 13, 1998
9 — at Minnesota, August 2, 2000
Fewest three-point field goals, game
0 — Many Times

THREE-POINT FIELD GOAL ATTEMPTS
Most three-point field goal attempts per game, season
12.5 — 1997 (349/28)
11.5 — 1998 (346/30)
Fewest three-point field goal attempts per game, season
7.26 — 2004 (247/34)
7.62 — 2001 (244/32)
Most three-point field goal attempts, game
25 — vs Charlotte, August 21, 1997
20 — at Sacramento, July 10, 2003
Fewest three-point field goal attempts, game
1 — vs Seattle, June 19, 2004
at Detroit, August 7, 2001
2 — Many Times

FREE THROW PERCENTAGE
Highest free throw percentage, season
.777 — 2004 (488/628)
.771 — 2000 (609/790)
2005 (503/652)
Lowest free throw percentage, season
.701 — 1998 (426/608)
.703 — 1997 (371/528)
Highest free throw percentage, game
1.000 — at Detroit, May 24, 2005 (11/11)
vs Indiana, June 1, 2004 (13/13)
at Washington, June 17, 2004 (12/12)
vs Washington, June 7, 2005 (11/11)
at New York, June 21, 2005 (14/14)
at Sacramento, August 18, 2005 (9/9)
at Houston, July 11, 1998 (11/11)
vs Sacramento, July 7, 1997 (11/11)
Lowest free throw percentage, game
.364 — vs Charlotte, August 9, 1999 (4/11)
.389 — vs Los Angeles, August 13, 2001 (7/18) (OT)

FREE THROWS MADE
Most free throws made per game, season
20.1 — 2002 (643/32)
19.0 — 2000 (609/32)
Fewest free throws made per game, season
13.3 — 1997 (371/28)
14.2 — 1998 (426/30)
Most free throws made, game
42 — vs Los Angeles, June 23, 1997
33 — vs Orlando, June 7, 2001
Fewest free throws made, game
3 — at Phoenix, July 21, 2004
at Houston, June 28, 2003
4 — vs Charlotte, August 9, 1999

FREE THROW ATTEMPTS
Most free throw attempts per game, season
26.4 — 2002 (844/32)
24.7 — 2000 (790/32)
Fewest free throw attempts per game, season
18.5 — 2004 (628/34)
18.9 — 1997 (528/28)
Most free throw attempts, game
56 — vs Los Angeles, June 23, 1997
40 — at Phoenix, August 22, 2003
vs Orlando, June 7, 2001
vs Portland, August 7, 2000
Fewest free throw attempts, game
4 — at Houston, June 28, 2003
5 — at Phoenix, July 21, 2004

REBOUNDS
Most rebounds per game, season
34.0 — 1997 (951/28)
33.8 — 2000 (1080/32)
Fewest rebounds per game, season
27.8 — 2005 (946/34)
29.5 — 2004 (1003/34)
Most rebounds, game
54 — vs Detroit, July 6, 1999 (2OT)
47 — vs Charlotte, June 15, 2000
at Sacramento, July 2, 1997 (OT)
Fewest rebounds, game
17 — vs Indiana, June 1, 2004
19 — at Sacramento, August 18, 2005
at Phoenix, August 6, 1997

OFFENSIVE REBOUNDS
Most offensive rebounds per game, season
12.1 — 1997 (339/28)
10.9 — 2000 (348/32)
Fewest offensive rebounds per game, season
7.5 — 2005 (256/34)
8.9 — 2004 (302/34)
Most offensive rebounds, game
20 — vs Portland, May 30, 2002
vs Phoenix, June 6, 2000
vs New York, July 5, 1997
19 — vs Washington, July 19, 2003
at Houston, July 14, 1997
Fewest offensive rebounds, game
1 — vs Seattle, June 30, 2005
2 — at Phoenix, August 6, 1997

DEFENSIVE REBOUNDS

Most defensive rebounds per game, season
24.2 — 2001 (775/32)
23.4 — 2003 (795/34)
Fewest defensive rebounds per game, season
20.3 — 2005 (690/34)
20.6 — 2004 (701/34)
Most defensive rebounds, game
40 — vs Detroit, July 6, 1999 (2OT)
39 — vs Connecticut, June 1, 2003
Fewest defensive rebounds, game
11 — at Cleveland, July 19, 1997
12 — vs Sacramento, August 7, 2003
vs Sacramento, July 7, 1997

ASSISTS

Most assists per game, season
17.3 — 1999 (552/32)
16.4 — 2001 (524/32)
Fewest assists per game, season
12.6 — 2003 (428/34)
12.7 — 2005 (433/34)
Most assists, game
28 — vs Detroit, July 6, 1999 (2OT)
26 — at Seattle, July 1, 2000
Fewest assists, game
5 — vs Indiana, August 11, 2005
6 — at Miami, July 21, 2000

PERSONAL FOULS

Most personal fouls per game, season
23.1 — 1999 (740/32)
21.8 — 2000 (698/32)
Fewest personal fouls per game, season
18.5 — 2004 (628/34)
19.1 — 2005 (650/34)
Most personal fouls, game
36 — at Phoenix, August 22, 2003
35 — at Detroit, July 1, 2003
Fewest personal fouls, game
9 — at Houston, May 20, 2004
11 — vs Washington, June 7, 2005
vs Houston, September 9, 2004
at Washington, June 17, 2004
vs Miami, July 2, 2001

DISQUALIFICATIONS

Most disqualifications per game, season
.30 — 1998 (9/30)
.24 — 2003 (8/34)
Fewest disqualifications per game, season
.14 — 1997 (4/28)
.16 — 1999 (5/32)
Most disqualifications, game
2 — at Los Angeles, July 2, 2004 (OT)
at Seattle, August 12, 2003
vs Portland, July 12, 2000
vs Detroit, August 10, 1998
1 — Many Times

STEALS

Most steals per game, season
9.0 — 1997 (252/28)
8.0 — 2004 (272/34)
Fewest steals per game, season
5.5 — 2003 (187/34)
5.7 — 2005 (195/34)
Most steals, game
17 — at Los Angeles, July 11, 1997
14 — at Minnesota, June 3, 2004
vs Phoenix, June 5, 2003
vs Detroit, July 7, 2000
vs Detroit, July 13, 1998
vs New York, July 5, 1997
Fewest steals, game
0 — vs Connecticut, June 1, 2003
1 — vs Houston, June 18, 2005
vs Washington, July 19, 2003
at Washington, June 10, 2003
vs Detroit, June 7, 2003
at Indiana, July 10, 2002

BLOCKED SHOTS

Most blocked shots per game, season
5.7 — 1998 (170/30)
5.6 — 2002 (178/32)
Fewest blocked shots per game, season
2.6 — 2005 (90/34)
3.1 — 2004 (106/34)
Most blocked shots, game
12 — vs Sacramento, July 14, 2001
11 — vs Minnesota, May 26, 2004
vs Portland, June 25, 2002
vs Sacramento, July 31, 1999
vs Sacramento, June 19, 1999
vs Sacramento, August 12, 1998
Fewest blocked shots, game
0 — vs Houston, June 23, 2000
at Charlotte, August 5, 2000
at New York, August 8, 2001
at Houston, June 9, 2004
1 — Many Times

TURNOVERS

Most turnovers per game, season
18.6 — 1997 (520/28)
18.1 — 1998 (543/30)
Fewest turnovers per game, season
15.1 — 2004 (513/34)
2003 (513/34)
15.4 — 2001 (493/32)
Most turnovers, game
33 — at Phoenix, August 17, 1997
31 — at New York, July 17, 1997
Fewest turnovers, game
6 — at New York, June 21, 2005
at Phoenix, June 15, 2005
8 — vs Minnesota, July 26, 2005
at Seattle, August 12, 2003
at Los Angeles, July 30, 2003
vs Los Angeles, August 9, 2000
vs Los Angeles, June 23, 1997

TEAM DEFENSE

POINTS

Fewest points allowed per game, season
68.5 — 2001 (2192/32)
69.5 — 2004 (2364/34)
Most points allowed per game, season
77.1 — 1999 (2467/32)
76.5 — 1998 (2294/30)
Fewest points allowed, game
44 — vs Minnesota, May 26, 2004
49 — at Charlotte, June 23, 2005
Fewest points allowed, first half
16 — vs Los Angeles, August 9, 2003
17 — vs Minnesota, May 26, 2004
at New York, September 12, 2004
Fewest points allowed, second half
18 — vs Phoenix, June 5, 2003
at Charlotte, July 22, 1998
19 — at Portland, July 8, 2001
Fewest points allowed, overtime period
1 — vs Detroit, July 6, 1999
2 — at Miami, June 27, 2001
vs Minnesota, July 28, 2001

FIELD GOAL PERCENTAGE

Lowest opponents' field goal percentage, season
.398 — 2003 (867/2176)
.399 — 2001 (789/1976)
Highest opponents' field goal percentage, season
.443 — 2004 (888/2003)
.438 — 2000 (860/1964)
1999 (860/1965)
Lowest opponents' field goal percentage, game
.259 — vs Minnesota, July 28, 2001 (15/58) (OT)
.284 — vs Seattle, June 15, 2002 (19/67)

TURNOVERS

Fewest opponents' turnovers per game, season
12.2 — 2001 (390/32)
12.5 — 2003 (424/34)
Most opponents' turnovers per game, season
16.4 — 1997 (458/28)
14.9 — 1999 (477/32)
Most opponents' turnovers, game
26 — vs Detroit, July 7, 2000
24 — Many Times

TEAM MISCELLANEOUS

GAME WON AND LOST

Highest winning percentage, season
.625 — 2002 (20-12)
.594 — 2001 (19-13)
Lowest winning percentage, season
.206 — 2005 (7-27)
.250 — 1997 (7-21)
Most consecutive games won
8 — July 24-August 7, 2001
4 — Many Times

Most consecutive games won, one season
8 — July 24-August 7, 2001
4 — Many Times
Most consecutive games lost
9 — August 2-26, 2005
July 18-September 4, 2004
8 — June 1-19, 2004
Most consecutive games lost, one season
9 — August 2-26, 2005
July 18-September 4, 2004
8 — June 1-19, 2004
Highest winning percentage, home games, season
.750 — 2000, 2002 (12-4)
.688 — 1999 (11-5)
Lowest winning percentage, home games, season
.294 — 2005 (5-12)
.333 — 1998 (5-10)
Most consecutive home games won
7 — July 14, 2001-May 30, 2002
August 5, 1999-June 6, 2000
6 — July 5-31, 2002
July 12-August 9, 2000
Most consecutive home games lost
6 — August 2-26, 2005
4 — June 1-19, 2004
August 1-10, 1998
June 28-July 7, 1997
Highest winning percentage, road games, season
.625 — 2001 (10-6)
.500 — 2002 (8-8)
Lowest winning percentage, road games, season
.118 — 2005 (2-15)
.143 — 1997 (2-12)
Most consecutive road games won
5 — July 24-August 7, 2001
3 — May 30-June 27, 2001
Most consecutive road games lost
10 — July 30, 1997-June 26, 1998
9 — July 1-September 2, 2004
July 25, 1998-June 28, 1999

OVERTIME GAMES

Most overtime games, season
3 — 1999, 2001, 2004
2 — 1997, 2002
Most consecutive overtime games, season
2 — July 16-18, 1999
Most overtime games won, season
3 — 2001
2 — 2002
Most overtime games won, no losses, season
3 — 2001
2 — 2002
Most overtime games lost, season
2 — 1999, 2004
1 — 1997, 1998
Most overtime games lost, no wins, season
1 — 1998
Most overtime periods, game
2 — vs Detroit, July 6, 1999
vs Houston, June 30, 1998

SEASONS

Most seasons
    7 — Margo Dydek
    6 — Adrienne Goodson
        LaTonya Johnson

GAMES

Most games, career
    224 — Margo Dydek
    188 — Adrienne Goodson
    173 — LaTonya Johnson
Most consecutive games, career
    139 — Margo Dydek, June 11, 1998-June 30, 2002
    114 — Marie Ferdinand, May 30, 2001-July 2, 2004
    113 — Jennifer Azzi, July 7, 2000-August 23, 2003
Most games, season
    34 — By Many

MINUTES

Most minutes, career
    5,989 — Adrienne Goodson
    5,801 — Margo Dydek
    4,553 — Marie Ferdinand
Highest average, minutes per game, career
(Minimum 100 games)
    35.9 — Jennifer Azzi (4051/113)
    34.2 — Natalie Williams (4065/119)
    31.9 — Adrienne Goodson (5989/188)
Most minutes, season
    1,205 — Jennifer Azzi, 2001
    1,151 — Jennifer Azzi, 2002
    1,136 — Jennifer Azzi, 2003
Highest average, minutes per game, season
    37.7 — Jennifer Azzi, 2001 (1205/32)
    37.3 — Jennifer Azzi, 2000 (559/15)
    36.0 — Jennifer Azzi, 2002 (1151/32)
Most minutes, game
    46 — Adrienne Goodson, vs Detroit,
        July 6, 1999 (2OT)
    45 — Debbie Black, vs Houston, July 16, 1999 (OT)
        Natalie Williams, at New York,
        July 18, 1999 (OT)
        Jennifer Azzi, vs Los Angeles, Aug. 13,2001 (OT)

SCORING

Most points, lifetime
    2,563 — Adrienne Goodson
    2,457 — Margo Dydek
    1,912 — Marie Ferdinand
Highest average, points per game, career
(Minimum 100 games)
    15.4 — Natalie Williams (1837/119)
    13.6 — Adrienne Goodson (2563/188)
    13.1 — Marie Ferdinand (1912/146)
Most points, season
    543 — Natalie Williams, 2000
    504 — Natalie Williams, 1999
    503 — Adrienne Goodson, 2002
Highest average, points per game, season

18.7 — Natalie Williams, 2000 (543/29)
18.0 — Natalie Williams, 1999 (504/28)
17.2 — Adrienne Goodson, 2000 (498/29)
Most points, game
    31 — Natalie Williams, vs Detroit, July 6, 1999 (2OT)
        Wendy Palmer-Daniel, vs Sacramento,
        August 12, 1998
    30 — Adrienne Goodson, vs Portland, June 25, 2002
        Natalie Williams, vs Washington,
        June 17, 2000
        Wendy Palmer-Daniel, vs Charlotte,
        July 8, 1998
    29 — Adrienne Goodson, vs Indiana, July 29, 2000
        Natalie Williams, at Sacramento, July 15,2000
Most games, 30 or more points, career
    2 — Natalie Williams
        Wendy Palmer-Daniel
    1 — Adrienne Goodson
Most games, 20 or more points, career
    30 — Natalie Williams
    29 — Adrienne Goodson
    18 — Margo Dydek
        Marie Ferdinand
Most consecutive games, 20 or more points
    3 — Elena Baranova, July 19-26, 1997
        Wendy Palmer, August 10-14, 1998
        Natalie Williams, July 23-29, 2000
        Natalie Williams, August 5-9, 2000
    2 — By Many
Most consecutive games, 10 or more points
    36 — Adrienne Goodson, June 28,1999-June 17,2000
    23 — Natalie Williams, June 12-August 11, 1999
        Adrienne Goodson, July 24, 2001-
        June 25, 2002
    19 — Marie Ferdinand, June 9-July 24, 2002

FIELD GOAL PERCENTAGE

Highest field goal percentage, career
(Minimum 400 field goals)
    .486 — Natalie Williams (654/1346)
    .456 — Margo Dydek (905/1986)
    .440 — Adrienne Goodson (991/2254)
Highest field goal percentage, season (qualifiers)
    .519 — Natalie Williams, 1999 (180/347)
    .517 — Wendy Palmer-Daniel, 2005 (125/242)
    .498 — Margo Dydek, 1999 (141/283)
Highest field goal percentage, game
(Minimum 8 field goals made)
    .900 — Korie Hlede, at Minnesota,
        August 11, 1999 (9/10)
    .889 — Natalie Williams, vs Phoenix,
        July 14, 2000 (8/9)
    .857 — Adrienne Goodson, at Portland,
        August 6,2002 (12/14)
Most field goals, none missed, game
    6 — Margo Dydek, at New York, June 21, 1998
    5 — Tai Dillard, vs Los Angeles, July 9, 2004
        Wendy Palmer-Daniel, at Houston,
        July 30, 1998
    4 — Amy Herrig, at Minnesota, June 22, 2000

Bernadette Ngoyisa, at Houston, July 30, 2005

Most field goal attempts, none made, game

10 — Adrienne Goodson, vs Orlando, June 7, 2001

8 — Tammi Reiss, vs New York, July 5, 1997
Adrian Williams, at Phoenix, July 21, 2004
Marie Ferdinand, vs Phoenix, July 23, 2005
Natalie Williams, vs Seattle, June 15, 2002
Marie Ferdinand, vs Connecticut, June 1, 2003

7 — Tai Dillard, at Phoenix, August 22, 2003

FIELD GOALS

Most field goals, career

991 — Adrienne Goodson

905 — Margo Dydek

657 — Marie Ferdinand

Most field goals, season

199 — Adrienne Goodson, 2000

189 — Adrienne Goodson, 2002

182 — Adrienne Goodson, 1999

Most field goals, game

14 — Wendy Palmer-Daniel, vs Charlotte,
July 8, 1998

13 — Margo Dydek, vs Houston,
June 30, 1998 (2OT)

12 — Adrienne Goodson, at Portland, August 6, 2002
Marie Ferdinand, at Houston, May 20, 2004
Margo Dydek, at Los Angeles, August 23, 2003

FIELD GOAL ATTEMPTS

Most field goal attempts, career

2,254 — Adrienne Goodson

1,986 — Margo Dydek

1,565 — Marie Ferdinand

Most field goal attempts, season

427 — Adrienne Goodson, 1999

420 — Wendy Palmer-Daniel, 1997

419 — Adrienne Goodson, 2002

Most field goal attempts, game

31 — Wendy Palmer-Daniel, vs Los Angeles,
August16, 1997

25 — Margo Dydek, vs Houston, June 30, 1998 (2OT)

22 — Natalie Williams, vs Detroit, July 6, 1999 (2OT)

THREE-POINT FIELD GOAL PERCENTAGE

Highest three-point field goal percentage, career
(Minimum 100 three-point field goals)

.446 — Jennifer Azzi (128/287)

Highest three-point field goal percentage, season (qualifiers)

.514 — Jennifer Azzi, 2001 (38/74)

.446 — Jennifer Azzi, 2002 (41/92)

.431 — Korie Hlede, 2000 (25/58)

Most three-point field goals, none missed, game

3 — By Many

Most three-point field goal attempts, none made, game

6 — Marie Ferdinand, vs Houston, July 3, 2002

5 — Shannon Johnson, at Los Angeles,
May 31, 2005
Agnieszska Bibrzycka, at Connecticut,
July 24, 2004

4 — By Many

THREE-POINT FIELD GOALS

Most three-point field goals, career

128 — Jennifer Azzi

75 — Elena Baranova

71 — LaTonya Johnson

Most three-point field goals, season

41 — Jennifer Azzi, 2002

40 — Elena Baranova, 1997

39 — Jennifer Azzi, 2003

Most three-point field goals, game

7 — Elena Baranova, at New York, July 22, 1997

6 — LaQuanda Quick, at Sacramento, July 10, 2003

5 — Elena Baranova, at Cleveland, July 19, 1997
Jennifer Azzi, at Los Angeles, July 3, 2001

Most consecutive games, three-point field goals made

10 — Elena Baranova, August 2-21, 1997

8 — Shannon Johnson, June 25-July 21, 2005

7 — Jennifer Azzi, July 21-August 3, 2001
Jennifer Azzi, July 1-23, 2003

THREE-POINT FIELD GOAL ATTEMPTS

Most three-point field goal attempts, career

287 — Jennifer Azzi

252 — LaTonya Johnson

220 — Marie Ferdinand

Most three-point field goal attempts, season

106 — Elena Baranova, 1997

101 — Tammi Reiss, 1997

97 — Jennifer Azzi, 2003

Most three-point field goal attempts, game

10 — Jennifer Azzi, at Los Angeles, July 3, 2001
LaQuanda Quick, at Sacramento, July 10,2003

9 — Elena Baranova, at Cleveland, July 19, 1997
Elena Baranova, at New York, July 22, 1997
Elena Baranova, at Sacramento, August 8,1997

8 — By Many

FREE THROW PERCENTAGE

Highest free throw percentage, career

.851 — Jennifer Azzi (262/308)

.834 — Korie Hlede (186/223)

.802 — Shannon Johnson (195/243)

Highest free throw percentage, season (qualifiers)

.930 — Jennifer Azzi, 2000 (40/43)

.917 — Jennifer Azzi, 2001 (88/96)

.878 — Korie Hlede, 1999 (72/82)

Most free throws made, none missed, game

11 — Jennifer Azzi, at Seattle, August 12, 2003

10 — Margo Dydek, vs Houston, July 16, 1999 (OT)
Margo Dydek, at Seattle, June 18, 2000
Margo Dydek, at Minnesota,
May 25, 2002 (OT)
Marie Ferdinand, vs Miami, July 31, 2002 (OT)
LaToya Thomas, vs Houston,
September 9,2004

9 — Margo Dydek, vs Minnesota, June 26, 1999
Marie Ferdinand, vs Portland, May 30, 2002

Most free throw attempts, none made, game

6 — Wendy Palmer-Daniel, at Los Angeles,
June 28, 1999

4 — Dena Head, vs Phoenix, July 3, 1997
  Lady Hardmon, at Phoenix, Aug. 17, 1997 (OT)
  Semeka Randall, vs Charlotte, June 14, 2003
3 — By Many

FREE THROWS MADE

Most free throws made, career
628 — Margo Dydek
536 — Marie Ferdinand
535 — Adrienne Goodson
Most free throws made, season
182 — Natalie Williams, 2000
176 — Marie Ferdinand, 2003
144 — Natalie Williams, 1999
Most free throws made, game
13 — Kim Williams, vs Los Angeles, June 23, 1997
12 — By Many

FREE THROW ATTEMPTS

Most free throw attempts, career
795 — Margo Dydek
713 — Adrienne Goodson
705 — Marie Ferdinand
Most free throw attempts, season
228 — Natalie Williams, 2000
223 — Marie Ferdinand, 2003
191 — Natalie Williams, 1999
Most free throw attempts, game
18 — Wendy Palmer-Daniel, vs Los Angeles,
  June 23, 1997
16 — Natalie Williams, vs Los Angeles,
  August 9, 2000
15 — Kim Williams, vs Los Angeles, June 23, 1997

REBOUNDS

Most rebounds, career
1530 — Margo Dydek
1156 — Natalie Williams
1055 — Adrienne Goodson
Highest average, rebounds per game, career
(Minimum 100 games)
9.7 — Natalie Williams (1156/119)
6.8 — Margo Dydek (1530/224)
6.2 — Wendy Palmer-Daniel (687/110)
Most rebounds, season
336 — Natalie Williams, 2000
308 — Natalie Williams, 2001
262 — Margo Dydek, 2002
Highest average, rebounds per game, season (qualifiers)
11.6 — Natalie Williams, 2000 (336/29)
9.9 — Natalie Williams, 2001 (308/31)
9.3 — Elena Baranova, 1998 (186/20)
Most rebounds, game
20 — Natalie Williams, at Sacramento,
  June 22, 2002
19 — Natalie Williams, vs Cleveland, July 26, 2000
18 — Natalie Williams, vs Charlotte, June 15, 2000
Most games, 10+ rebounds, career
56 — Natalie Williams
49 — Margo Dydek
20 — Wendy Palmer-Daniel
Most consecutive games with 10+ rebounds

7 — Natalie Williams, July 15-August 2, 2000
5 — Elena Baranova, August 24, 1997-June 19,1998
  Natalie Williams, June 29-July 8, 2001
4 — By Many

OFFENSIVE REBOUNDS

Most offensive rebounds, career
460 — Adrienne Goodson
457 — Natalie Williams
264 — Margo Dydek
Highest average, offensive rebounds per game, career
(Minimum 100 games)
3.8 — Natalie Williams (457/119)
2.4 — Adrienne Goodson (460/188)
2.0 — Wendy Palmer-Daniel (222/110)
Most offensive rebounds, season
132 — Natalie Williams, 2000
111 — Natalie Williams, 2001
109 — Natalie Williams, 1999
Most offensive rebounds, game
10 — Gwen Jackson, vs Charlotte, June 14, 2003
  Natalie Williams, at Sacramento, June 22,2002
9 — Natalie Williams, vs Portland, July 12, 2000
  Natalie Williams, vs Charlotte, June 15, 2000
8 — Adrienne Goodson, vs Portland, May 30, 2002
  Natalie Williams, vs Indiana, July 29, 2000

DEFENSIVE REBOUNDS

Most defensive rebounds, career
1266 — Margo Dydek
699 — Natalie Williams
595 — Adrienne Goodson
Highest average, defensive rebounds per game, career
(Minimum 100 games)
5.9 — Natalie Williams (699/119)
5.7 — Margo Dydek (1266/224)
4.2 — Wendy Palmer-Daniel (465/110)
Most defensive rebounds, season
214 — Margo Dydek, 2001
210 — Margo Dydek, 2002
206 — Margo Dydek, 2003
Most defensive rebounds, game
15 — Margo Dydek, vs Phoenix, July 26, 2002
14 — Natalie Williams, vs Cleveland, July 26, 2000
13 — By Many

ASSISTS

Most assists, career
532 — Jennifer Azzi
416 — Margo Dydek
412 — Adrienne Goodson
Highest average, assists per game, career
(Minimum 100 games)
4.7 — Jennifer Azzi (532/113)
2.4 — Marie Ferdinand (357/146)
2.2 — Adrienne Goodson (412/188)
Most assists, season
171 — Jennifer Azzi, 2001
161 — Debbie Black, 1999
158 — Jennifer Azzi, 2002
  Shannon Johnson, 2005
Highest average, assists per game, season (qualifiers)
5.3 — Jennifer Azzi, 2001 (171/32)
5.0 — Debbie Black, 1999 (161/32)
4.9 — Jennifer Azzi, 2002 (158/32)

Most assists, game
13 — Shannon Johnson, at Sacramento, August 18,2005
12 — Shannon Johnson, vs Sacramento, May 28,2004
11 — Debbie Black, at Cleveland, July 24, 1999
Most games, 10+ assists, career
3 — Shannon Johnson
2 — Debbie Black
Jennifer Azzi

PERSONAL FOULS
Most personal fouls, career
742 — Margo Dydek
482 — Natalie Williams
472 — Adrienne Goodson
Most personal fouls, season
128 — Natalie Williams, 2001
126 — Margo Dydek, 1998
124 — Natalie Williams, 2000
Most personal fouls, game
6 — By Many

STEALS
Most steals, career
227 — Marie Ferdinand
192 — Adrienne Goodson
152 — Natalie Williams
Highest average, steals per game, career
(Minimum 100 games)
1.6 — Marie Ferdinand (227/146)
1.3 — Natalie Williams (152/119)
1.0 — Adrienne Goodson (192/188)
Most steals, season
77 — Debbie Black, 1999
58 — Marie Ferdinand, 2003
51 — Marie Ferdinand, 2002
Highest average, steals per game, season (qualifiers)
2.4 — Debbie Black, 1999 (77/32)
1.71 — Marie Ferdinand, 2003 (58/34)
1.68 — Wendy Palmer-Daniel, 1997 (47/28)
Most steals, game
8 — Semeka Randall, vs Charlotte, September 17,2004
7 — Debbie Black, at Washington, July 8, 1999
Wendy Palmer-Daniel, vs New York, July 5,1997
6 — Karen Booker, at Cleveland, June 26, 1997
Debbie Black, at Phoenix, July 27, 1999
Elena Baranova, at Los Angeles, July 11, 1997

BLOCKED SHOTS
Most blocked shots, career
655 — Margo Dydek
116 — Elena Baranova
66 — Natalie Williams
Highest average, blocked shots per game, career
(Minimum: 100 games)
2.9 — Margo Dydek (655/224)
.6 — Natalie Williams (66/119)
.3 — Jennifer Azzi (38/113)
Most blocked shots, season
114 — Margo Dydek, 1998
113 — Margo Dydek, 2001
107 — Margo Dydek, 2002

Highest average, blocked shots per game, season (qualifiers)
3.8 — Margo Dydek, 1998 (114/30)
3.6 — Margo Dydek, 2002 (107/30)
3.5 — Margo Dydek, 2001 (113/32)
Most blocked shots, game
10 — Margo Dydek, vs Orlando, June 7, 2001
9 — Margo Dydek, vs Cleveland, August 6, 1998
Margo Dydek, vs Minnesota, May 26, 2004
8 — Margo Dydek, at Detroit, July 17, 1998
Margo Dydek, vs Sacramento, July 14, 2001
Margo Dydek, vs Sacramento, August 12, 1998

TURNOVERS
Most turnovers, career
611 — Margo Dydek
508 — Adrienne Goodson
342 — Marie Ferdinand
Most turnovers, season
113 — Shannon Johnson, 2005
108 — Margo Dydek, 1998
102 — Adrienne Goodson, 2002
Most turnovers, game
9 — Adrienne Goodson, vs Los Angeles, June 26,2003
8 — By Many

SEATTLE STORM

TEAM OFFENSE

SCORING

Highest average, points per game, season
73.4 — 2005 (2498/34)
71.7 — 2004 (2437/34)
Lowest average, points per game, season
56.9 — 2000 (1822/32)
60.0 — 2001 (1921/32)
Most points, game
95 — vs Connecticut, June 22, 2005
93 — vs Los Angeles, May 22, 2004
vs San Antonio, June 22, 2003
Fewest points, game
36 — vs Cleveland, June 14, 2001
38 — at Charlotte, July 7, 2001
Largest margin of victory, game
41 — vs Phoenix, July 19, 2002 (89-48)
40 — vs San Antonio, June 22, 2003 (93-53)
Largest margin of defeat, game
33 — at Sacramento, August 9, 2000 (46-79)
at Phoenix, June 7, 2000 (49-82)
30 — at Houston, July 6, 2000 (50-80)
vs Houston, June 1, 2000 (47-77)

BY HALF

Most points, first half
49 — vs Sacramento, July 3, 2004
vs Sacramento, August 25, 2005
48 — vs Sacramento, July 3, 2005
at Phoenix, June 14, 2002
Fewest points, first half
17 — at Charlotte, July 7, 2001
at Miami, July 10, 2000
19 — at Sacramento, August 13, 2002
at Houston, July 6, 2000
at Indiana, July 14, 2000
Largest lead at half time
24 — vs Phoenix, July 19, 2002 (led 46-22; won 89-48)
23 — vs San Antonio, July 1, 2004 (led 43-20; won 76-52)
Largest deficit at halftime overcome to win game
9 — vs Washington, July 17, 2004 (trailed 31-40; won 85-83 in OT)
at Indiana, September 13, 2004 (trailed 30-39; won 76-70)
8 — vs Portland, August 6, 2000 (trailed 24-32; won 66-58 in OT)
vs Charlotte, June 6, 2002 (trailed 21-29; won 65-59)
Most points, second half
56 — vs Los Angeles, August 6, 2003
53 — vs Houston, May 27, 2005
vs Los Angeles, May 22, 2004
Fewest points, second half
9 — vs Cleveland, June 14, 2001
14 — at Phoenix, August 15, 2003

OVERTIME

Most points, overtime period
14 — vs Portland, August 6, 2000
vs Los Angeles, June 13, 2000
12 — vs Minnesota, June 4, 2002
Fewest points, overtime period
2 — vs Los Angeles, August 8, 2000
vs Washington, July 3, 2001
Largest margin of victory, overtime period
10 — vs Minnesota, June 4, 2002 (78-68)
vs Los Angeles, June 13, 2000 (69-59)
8 — vs Portland, August 6, 2000 (66-58)

FIELD GOAL PERCENTAGE

Highest field goal percentage, season
.439 — 2005 (906/2066)
.435 — 2003 (890/2045)
Lowest field goal percentage, season
.378 — 2001 (689/1821)
.383 — 2000 (667/1740)
Highest field goal percentage, game
.587 — at Sacramento, June 5, 2004 (27/46)
.569 — at Phoenix, June 14, 2002 (33/58)
Lowest field goal percentage, game
.237 — vs Los Angeles, May 21, 2005 (18/76)
.241 — vs Phoenix, July 27, 2001 (13/54)

FIELD GOALS

Most field goals per game, season
26.6 — 2005 (906/34)
26.2 — 2003 (890/34)
Fewest field goals per game, season
20.8 — 2000 (667/32)
21.5 — 2001 (689/32)
Most field goals, game
37 — vs Los Angeles, August 6, 2003
35 — vs Connecticut, June 22, 2005
Fewest field goals, game
13 — vs Phoenix, July 27, 2001
at Miami, July 10, 2000
14 — at Charlotte, July 7, 2001
at Portland, June 19, 2001
vs Cleveland, June 14, 2001

FIELD GOAL ATTEMPTS

Most field goal attempts per game, season
60.9 — 2002 (1948/32)
60.8 — 2005 (2066/34)
Fewest field goal attempts per game, season
54.4 — 2000 (1740/32)
56.9 — 2001 (1821/32)
Most field goal attempts, game
91 — vs Washington, July 3, 2001 (OT)
78 — vs Sacramento, August 14, 2001

Fewest field goal attempts, game
   42 — at Charlotte, July 7, 2001
   43 — at Sacramento, July 15, 2004
       vs Minnesota, July 21, 2000
       at Miami, July 10, 2000
       at Cleveland, June 10, 2000

THREE-POINT FIELD GOAL PERCENTAGE

Highest three-point field goal percentage, season
   .380 — 2004 (167/439)
   .360 — 2002 (182/506)
Lowest three-point field goal percentage, season
   .299 — 2000 (109/364)
   .311 — 2001 (128/412)

THREE-POINT FIELD GOALS

Most three-point field goals per game, season
   5.7 — 2002 (182/32)
   4.9 — 2004 (167/34)
Fewest three-point field goals per game, season
   3.4 — 2000 (109/32)
   4.0 — 2001 (128/32)
Most three-point field goals, game
   13 — vs Los Angeles, July 11, 2002
   11 — vs San Antonio, July 15, 2005
       vs Charlotte, August 1, 2004
Fewest three-point field goals, game
   0 — at Indiana, July 14, 2000
   1 — Many Times

THREE-POINT FIELD GOAL ATTEMPTS

Most three-point field goal attempts per game, season
   15.8 — 2002 (506/32)
   14.7 — 2003 (500/34)
Fewest three-point field goal attempts per game, season
   11.4 — 2000 (364/32)
   12.6 — 2005 (429/34)
Most three-point field goal attempts, game
   32 — vs Los Angeles, May 21, 2005
   27 — vs Houston, July 20, 2002
Fewest three-point field goal attempts, game
   3 — at Connecticut, September 12, 2004
   6 — at Charlotte, June 12, 2005
       at Detroit, June 8, 2005
       vs Indiana, June 4, 2005
       at Sacramento, July 15, 2004
       at Portland, July 4, 2001
       at Indiana, July 14, 2000

FREE THROW PERCENTAGE

Highest free throw percentage, season
   .791 — 2005 (544/688)
   .780 — 2003 (442/567)
Lowest free throw percentage, season
   .676 — 2000 (379/561)
   .685 — 2001 (415/606)
Highest free throw percentage, game
   1.000 — at Phoenix, July 6, 2005 (2/2)
           vs Cleveland, July 12, 2002 (8/8)
           at Houston, July 23, 2002 (6/6)
   .952 — at Minnesota, June 26, 2005 (20/21)
Lowest free throw percentage, game
   .400 — at Houston, August 19, 2003 (4/10)
   .412 — vs Minnesota, July 21, 2000 (14/34)

FREE THROWS MADE

Most free throws made per game, season
   16.0 — 2005 (544/34)
   15.4 — 2004 (524/34)
Fewest free throws made per game, season
   11.8 — 2000 (379/32)
   13.0 — 2001 (415/32)
Most free throws made, game
   31 — vs Indiana, June 4, 2005
   28 — vs Los Angeles, July 31, 2005
Fewest free throws made, game
   2 — at Phoenix, July 6, 2005
   3 — at New York, August 6, 2005

FREE THROW ATTEMPTS

Most free throw attempts per game, season
   20.2 — 2005 (688/34)
   19.9 — 2004 (676/34)
Fewest free throw attempts per game, season
   16.7 — 2003 (567/34)
   17.0 — 2002 (543/32)
Most free throw attempts, game
   37 — vs Los Angeles, July 31, 2005
       vs Indiana, June 4, 2005
   35 — vs Minnesota, May 20, 2004
Fewest free throw attempts, game
   2 — at Phoenix, July 6, 2005
   4 — at New York, August 6, 2005

REBOUNDS

Most rebounds per game, season
   32.3 — 2005 (1099/34)
   31.6 — 2003 (1074/34)
Fewest rebounds per game, season
   24.8 — 2000 (793/32)
   27.8 — 2001 (891/32)
Most rebounds, game
   49 — vs Phoenix, July 19, 2002
   48 — vs Portland, August 9, 2002
Fewest rebounds, game
   15 — at Sacramento, August 9, 2000
   16 — vs Sacramento, June 30, 2001

OFFENSIVE REBOUNDS

Most offensive rebounds per game, season
   11.3 — 2002 (362/32)
   10.3 — 2004 (350/34)
Fewest offensive rebounds per game, season
   8.0 — 2000 (256/32)
   9.5 — 2005 (323/34)
Most offensive rebounds, game
   20 — at San Antonio, June 30, 2005
       at Los Angeles, June 1, 2004
       vs Phoenix, July 19, 2002
   19 — at New York, June 15, 2004
       at Utah, June 15, 2002
Fewest offensive rebounds, game
   2 — at Los Angeles, July 27, 2000
       at Houston, July 25, 2000
   3 — at Sacramento, June 5, 2004
       at Miami, July 10, 2000

DEFENSIVE REBOUNDS

Most defensive rebounds per game, season
  22.8 — 2005 (776/34)
  21.5 — 2003 (732/34)
Fewest defensive rebounds per game, season
  16.8 — 2000 (537/32)
  18.3 — 2001 (585/32)
Most defensive rebounds, game
    36 — at San Antonio, August 23, 2005
    35 — vs Phoenix, July 25, 2003
Fewest defensive rebounds, game
    10 — at Sacramento, August 9, 2000
    11 — at Charlotte, June 30, 2003
        at Cleveland, July 5, 2002
        vs Utah, July 1, 2000

ASSISTS

Most assists per game, season
  16.2 — 2004 (552/34)
  16.1 — 2003 (548/34)
        2002 (514/32)
Fewest assists per game, season
  12.2 — 2000 (390/32)
  12.9 — 2001 (412/32)
Most assists, game
    24 — vs Sacramento, June 23, 2002
    22 — vs San Antonio, July 15, 2005
        vs Washington, July 3, 2003
        vs Indiana, June 10, 2003
        vs Phoenix, July 19, 2002
        vs Phoenix, May 31, 2001
Fewest assists, game
    5 — vs Phoenix, July 27, 2001
        at Miami, July 10, 2000
    6 — at Portland, June 19, 2001

PERSONAL FOULS

Most personal fouls per game, season
  20.3 — 2000 (648/32)
  19.6 — 2004 (665/34)
Fewest personal fouls per game, season
  18.91 — 2001 (605/32)
  18.94 — 2003 (644/34)
Most personal fouls, game
    35 — at Miami, July 10, 2000
    30 — at San Antonio, May 24, 2003
        at Portland, June 23, 2000
Fewest personal fouls, game
    6 — vs Miami, July 30, 2000
    9 — vs Sacramento, August 25, 2003
        at Phoenix, June 22, 2001

DISQUALIFICATIONS

Most disqualifications per game, season
  .29 — 2005 (10/34)
  .24 — 2003 (8/34)
Fewest disqualifications per game, season
  .13 — 2000 (4/32)
Most disqualifications, game
    2 — at Houston, June 28, 2005
        at Sacramento, June 21, 2003
        at Utah, June 9, 2001
    1 — Many Times

STEALS

Most steals per game, season
  8.9 — 2004 (302/34)
  8.8 — 2002 (282/32)
Fewest steals per game, season
  5.9 — 2005 (201/34)
  6.8 — 2003 (232/34)
Most steals, game
    16 — at Minnesota, September 10, 2004
        at Utah, June 25, 2001
    15 — vs Minnesota, May 20, 2004
        vs Houston, July 20, 2002
        at Sacramento, August 9, 2000
        vs Minnesota, July 21, 2000
Fewest steals, game
    1 — at Houston, June 28, 2005
        vs Connecticut, June 22, 2005
    2 — at Sacramento, August 20, 2005
        at Charlotte, July 7, 2001

BLOCKED SHOTS

Most blocked shots per game, season
  4.7 — 2002 (151/32)
  4.6 — 2005 (158/34)
Fewest blocked shots per game, season
  2.9 — 2000 (93/32)
  3.9 — 2004 (131/34)
Most blocked shots, game
    12 — vs Utah, August 11, 2002
    11 — at Indiana, September 13, 2004
Fewest blocked shots, game
    0 — Many Times

TURNOVERS

Most turnovers per game, season
  16.4 — 2000 (525/32)
  15.3 — 2005 (516/34)
Fewest turnovers per game, season
  13.5 — 2001 (431/32)
  13.7 — 2003 (465/34)
Most turnovers, game
    24 — vs Los Angeles, June 13, 2000 (ot)
    23 — at Sacramento, August 9, 2000
        at Sacramento, August 13, 2002
Fewest turnovers, game
    5 — at Charlotte, June 30, 2003
    6 — vs Houston, August 23, 2003
        vs Charlotte, June 6, 2002

TEAM DEFENSE

POINTS

Fewest points allowed per game, season
  64.0 — 2001 (2048/32)
  65.7 — 2002 (2103/32)
Most points allowed per game, season
  70.8 — 2005 (2407/34)
  67.8 — 2000 (2171/32)
Fewest points allowed, game
    45 — vs Phoenix, June 3, 2004
    47 — at Portland, June 2, 2002
        at Utah, June 25, 2001

Fewest points allowed, first half
17 — at Utah, June 25, 2001
18 — at Connecticut, July 17, 2003
at Miami, July 10, 2000
vs Utah, June 18, 2000
vs Indiana, June 10, 2003
Fewest points allowed, second half
15 — vs Washington, July 3, 2001
20 — vs Portland, August 6, 2000
Fewest points allowed, overtime period
2 — at Indiana, June 4, 2001
vs Detroit, July 24, 2001
vs Washington, July 3, 2001
vs Minnesota, June 4, 2002

FIELD GOAL PERCENTAGE
Lowest opponents' field goal percentage, season
.412 — 2005 (892/2163)
.414 — 2003 (844/2039)
Highest opponents' field goal percentage, season
.452 — 2000 (778/1721)
.431 — 2002 (783/1818)
Lowest opponents' field goal percentage, game
.244 — at Miami, July 10, 2000 (10/41)
.270 — vs Phoenix, July 25, 2003 (20/74)

TURNOVERS
Fewest opponents' turnovers per game, season
12.9 — 2005 (438/34)
13.5 — 2003 (459/34)
Most opponents' turnovers per game, season
16.6 — 2002 (531/32)
16.5 — 2000 (529/32)
Most opponents' turnovers, game
26 — vs Utah, June 18, 2000
at Minnesota, September 10, 2004
24 — at Utah, June 25, 2001

TEAM MISCELLANEOUS

GAME WON AND LOST
Highest winning percentage, season
.588 — 2005, 2004 (20-14)
.531 — 2002 (17-15)
Lowest winning percentage, season
.188 — 2000 (6-26)
.313 — 2001 (10-22)
Most consecutive games won
6 — July 15-31, 2005
June 3-19, 2004
5 — July 12-24, 2004
July 25-August 1, 2002
Most consecutive games won, one season
6 — July 15-31, 2005
June 3-19, 2004
5 — July 12-24, 2004
July 25-August 1, 2002
Most consecutive games lost
8 — June 15-July 3, 2000
7 — July 7-21, 2001
Most consecutive games lost, one season
8 — June 15-July 3, 2000
7 — July 7-21, 2001

Highest winning percentage, home games, season
.824 — 2005 (14-3)
.765 — 2004, 2003 (13-4)
Lowest winning percentage, home games, season
.250 — 2000 (4-12)
.313 — 2001 (5-11)
Most consecutive home games won
9 — July 15-August 27, 2005
8 — June 22-August 8, 2003
Most consecutive home games lost
7 — June 15-July 19, 2000
4 — June 30-July 20, 2001
Highest winning percentage, road games, season
.438 — 2002 (7-9)
.412 — 2004 (7-10)
Lowest winning percentage, road games, season
.125 — 2000 (2-14)
.294 — 2003 (5-12)
Most consecutive road games won
4 — June 5-19, 2004
July 25-August 1, 2002
2 — Many Times
Most consecutive road games lost
10 — July 6, 2000-June 3, 2001
9 — July 18, 2003-June 1, 2004

OVERTIME GAMES
Most overtime games, season
3 — 2000, 2001
Most consecutive overtime games, season
2 — August 6-8, 2000
Most overtime games won, season
2 — 2000, 2001
Most overtime games won, no losses, season
1 — 2004
Most overtime games lost, season
2 — 2003
Most overtime games lost, no wins, season
2 — 2003
Most overtime periods, game
4 — vs Washington, July 3, 2001

INDIVIDUAL RECORDS

SEASONS
Most seasons
6 — Simone Edwards
5 — Lauren Jackson
Kamila Vodichkova

GAMES
Most games, career
178 — Simone Edwards
155 — Lauren Jackson
146 — Kamila Vodichkova
Most consecutive games, career
119 — Simone Edwards, July 3, 2000-May 28, 2004
106 — Sue Bird, May 30, 2002-June 7, 2005
72 — Sonja Henning, May 31, 2000-June 15, 2002
Most games, season

34 — Many Times

MINUTES

Most minutes, career
5,238 — Lauren Jackson
4,413 — Sue Bird
3,293 — Kamila Vodichkova

Highest average, minutes per game, career
(Minimum 100 games)
33.9 — Sue Bird (4413/130)
33.8 — Lauren Jackson (5238/155)
22.6 — Kamila Vodichkova (3293/146)

Most minutes, season
1,176 — Lauren Jackson, 2005
1,136 — Sue Bird, 2004
Sue Bird, 2003
1,121 — Sue Bird, 2002

Highest average, minutes per game, season
35.0 — Sue Bird, 2002 (1121/32)
34.5 — Lauren Jackson, 2005 (1176/34)
Lauren Jackson, 2001 (1001/29)
Lauren Jackson, 2004 (1070/31)

Most minutes, game
54 — Lauren Jackson, vs Washington, July 3, 2001(4OT)
43 — Iziane Castro Marques, vs Minnesota, June15, 2005 (OT)
Lauren Jackson, vs Washington, July 17, 2004 (OT)
Sonja Henning, vs Minnesota, June 4, 2002(OT)
Sue Bird, vs Minnesota, June 4, 2002 (OT)
Semeka Randall, vs Washington, July 3,2001 (4OT)

SCORING

Most points, lifetime
2,853 — Lauren Jackson
1,684 — Sue Bird
1,202 — Kamila Vodichkova

Highest average, points per game, career
(Minimum 100 games)
18.4 — Lauren Jackson (2853/155)
13.0 — Sue Bird (1684/130)
8.2 — Kamila Vodichkova (1202/146)

Most points, season
698 — Lauren Jackson, 2003
634 — Lauren Jackson, 2004
597 — Lauren Jackson, 2005

Highest average, points per game, season
21.2 — Lauren Jackson, 2003 (698/33)
20.5 — Lauren Jackson, 2004 (634/31)
17.5 — Lauren Jackson, 2005 (597/34)

Most points, game
34 — Lauren Jackson, vs Los Angeles, Aug, 6, 2003
33 — Sue Bird, vs Portland, August 9, 2002
Lauren Jackson, vs Washington, July 17, 2004 (OT)
32 — Lauren Jackson, vs Sacramento, July 3, 2004
Lauren Jackson, vs San Antonio, August 12, 2003

Most games, 30 or more points, career
8 — Lauren Jackson

1 — Sue Bird

Most games, 20 or more points, career
66 — Lauren Jackson
18 — Sue Bird
6 — Betty Lennox

Most consecutive games, 20 or more points
7 — Lauren Jackson, July 17-31, 2003
4 — Lauren Jackson, September 12-18, 2004
Lauren Jackson, July 1-8, 2004
3 — Lauren Jackson, July 11-19, 2002
Lauren Jackson, June 3-10, 2003

Most consecutive games, 10 or more points
84 — Lauren Jackson, June 26, 2002-September 18, 2004
15 — Lauren Jackson, May 31-July 4, 2001
10 — Lauren Jackson, July 24, 2001-June 14,2002

FIELD GOAL PERCENTAGE

Highest field goal percentage, career
(Minimum 400 field goals)
.441 — Lauren Jackson (1015/2304)
.431 — Sue Bird (587/1363)
Kamila Vodichkova (428/992)

Highest field goal percentage, season (qualifiers)
.523 — Janell Burse, 2005 (127/243)
.483 — Lauren Jackson, 2003 (254/526)
.479 — Simone Edwards, 2001 (91/190)

Highest field goal percentage, game
(Minimum 8 field goals made)
.909 — Kamila Vodichkova, vs Detroit, June 28, 2000(10/11)
.889 — Sue Bird, vs Detroit, September 8, 2004 (8/9)
.846 — Janell Burse, vs Charlotte, July 29, 2005(11/13)

Most field goals, none missed, game
4 — Simone Edwards, at Minnesota, June 26, 2005
Felicia Ragland, vs Sacramento, June 23, 2002
Tully Bevilaqua, vs Sacramento, September1, 2004
3 — By Many

Most field goal attempts, none made, game
11 — Kamila Vodichkova, vs Portland, August 9,2002
9 — Stacey Lovelace, at Sacramento, August 9,2000
8 — Lauren Jackson, at New York, July 11, 2001

FIELD GOALS

Most field goals, career
1,015 — Lauren Jackson
587 — Sue Bird
428 — Kamila Vodichkova

Most field goals, season
254 — Lauren Jackson, 2003
220 — Lauren Jackson, 2004
206 — Lauren Jackson, 2005

Most field goals, game
17 — Lauren Jackson, vs Los Angeles, August 6,2003
12 — Betty Lennox, vs Connecticut, June 22, 2005
11 — By Many

FIELD GOAL ATTEMPTS

Most field goal attempts, career
2,304 — Lauren Jackson
1,363 — Sue Bird
992 — Kamila Vodichkova

Most field goal attempts, season

526 — Lauren Jackson, 2003
462 — Lauren Jackson, 2002
460 — Lauren Jackson, 2004
Most field goal attempts, game
  29 — Lauren Jackson, vs Washington,
     July 3, 2001 (4OT)
  23 — Lauren Jackson, vs Los Angeles, August 6,2003
     Lauren Jackson, vs Utah, August 11, 2002
  22 — Lauren Jackson, at San Antonio, June 30, 2005

THREE-POINT FIELD GOAL PERCENTAGE

Highest three-point field goal percentage, career
(Minimum 100 three-point field goals)
  .405 — Sue Bird (215/531)
  .342 — Lauren Jackson (207/605)
Highest three-point field goal percentage, season (qualifiers)
  .452 — Lauren Jackson, 2004 (52/115)
  .438 — Sue Bird, 2004 (64/146)
  .437 — Sue Bird, 2005 (45/103)
Most three-point field goals, none missed, game
  4 — Amanda Lassiter, vs New York, July 23, 2003
    Iziane Castro Marques, vs New York,
    July 19, 2005
  3 — By Many
Most three-point field goal attempts, none made, game
  8 — Betty Lennox, at Los Angeles, June 1, 2004
  7 — Lauren Jackson, vs Houston, August 8, 2001
  6 — Sue Bird, at Portland, June 2, 2002
    Edna Campbell, vs Portland, June 3, 2000
    Betty Lennox, vs New York, June 26, 2004
    Lauren Jackson, vs Minnesota, July 31, 2002

THREE-POINT FIELD GOALS

Most three-point field goals, career
  215 — Sue Bird
  207 — Lauren Jackson
  46 — Betty Lennox
Most three-point field goals, season
  64 — Sue Bird, 2004
  57 — Sue Bird, 2002
  52 — Lauren Jackson, 2004
Most three-point field goals, game
  6 — Sonja Henning, at Los Angeles, July 27, 2000
  5 — Sue Bird, at Detroit, July 10, 2004
    Sue Bird, at Los Angeles, July 5, 2003
    Lauren Jackson, at Houston, July 30, 2001
    Sue Bird, at Los Angeles, September 3, 2004
    Felicia Ragland, vs Los Angeles, July 11, 2002
  4 — By Many
Most consecutive games, three-point field goals made
  16 — Lauren Jackson, June 11-24, 2004
  13 — Lauren Jackson, June 27-July 28, 2002
  11 — Sue Bird, June 11-July 5, 2002

THREE-POINT FIELD GOAL ATTEMPTS

Most three-point field goal attempts, career
  605 — Lauren Jackson
  531 — Sue Bird

161 — Betty Lennox
Most three-point field goal attempts, season
  146 — Sue Bird, 2004
  142 — Sue Bird, 2002
  140 — Sue Bird, 2003
Most three-point field goal attempts, game
  13 — Lauren Jackson, vs Los Angeles, May 21, 2005
  10 — Sue Bird, at Detroit, July 10, 2004
    Sue Bird, vs Los Angeles, May 30, 2003 (OT)
    Betty Lennox, vs Los Angeles, May 21, 2005
    Sonja Henning, at Los Angeles, July 27, 2000
  9 — By Many

FREE THROW PERCENTAGE

Highest free throw percentage, career
  .881 — Sue Bird (295/335)
  .799 — Kamila Vodichkova (318/398)
  .798 — Lauren Jackson (616/772)
Highest free throw percentage, season (qualifiers)
  .911 — Sue Bird, 2002 (102/112)
  .884 — Sue Bird, 2003 (61/69)
  .874 — Betty Lennox, 2005 (76/87)
Most free throws made, none missed, game
  11 — Lauren Jackson, vs Phoenix, July 27, 2001
  8 — Kamila Vodichkova, vs Los Angeles,
    June 16, 2001
    Lauren Jackson, at Utah, June 25, 2001
    Lauren Jackson, vs Los Angeles,
    May 30,2003 (OT)
    Simone Edwards, vs San Antonio, June 22,2003
  7 — By Many
Most free throw attempts, none made, game
  4 — Semeka Randall, vs Phoenix, July 19, 2002
    Charmin Smith, vs Minnesota, July 21, 2000
    Quacy Barnes, vs Sacramento, June 15, 2000
  3 — Sonja Henning, vs Portland, June 3, 2000
    Simone Edwards, vs Phoenix, May 31, 2001

FREE THROWS MADE

Most free throws made, career
  616 — Lauren Jackson
  318 — Kamila Vodichkova
  295 — Sue Bird
Most free throws made, season
  151 — Lauren Jackson, 2003
    Lauren Jackson, 2005
  142 — Lauren Jackson, 2004
  104 — Lauren Jackson, 2001
Most free throws made, game
  14 — Lauren Jackson, vs San Antonio, August 12,2003
  13 — Lauren Jackson, vs Sacramento, July 3, 2004
  11 — Sue Bird, vs Minnesota, June 4, 2002 (ot)
    Lauren Jackson, vs Indiana, June 4, 2005
    Lauren Jackson, vs Phoenix, July 27, 2001
    Lauren Jackson, at Minnesota, July 20, 2003
    Lauren Jackson, vs Charlotte, July 31, 2003

FREE THROW ATTEMPTS

Most free throw attempts, career
  772 — Lauren Jackson
  398 — Kamila Vodichkova
  335 — Sue Bird
Most free throw attempts, season
  183 — Lauren Jackson, 2003

181 — Lauren Jackson, 2005
175 — Lauren Jackson, 2004
Most free throw attempts, game
16 — Lauren Jackson, vs San Antonio, August 12,2003
15 — Lauren Jackson, vs Charlotte, July 31, 2003
       Lauren Jackson, vs Sacramento, July 3, 2004
14 — Lauren Jackson, vs Los Angeles, July 31, 2005

REBOUNDS

Most rebounds, career
1,210 — Lauren Jackson
655 — Kamila Vodichkova
Highest average, rebounds per game, career
(Minimum 100 games)
7.8 — Lauren Jackson (1210/155)
4.5 — Kamila Vodichkova (655/146)
3.5 — Simone Edwards (625/178)
Most rebounds, season
313 — Lauren Jackson, 2005
307 — Lauren Jackson, 2003
207 — Lauren Jackson, 2004
Highest average, rebounds per game, season (qualifiers)
9.3 — Lauren Jackson, 2003 (307/33)
9.2 — Lauren Jackson, 2005 (313/34)
6.8 — Lauren Jackson, 2002 (190/28)
Most rebounds, game
20 — Lauren Jackson, vs Charlotte, July 31, 2003
18 — Lauren Jackson, vs San Antonio, August 12,2003
17 — Lauren Jackson, vs Connecticut, June 22, 2005
Most games, 10+ rebounds, career
42 — Lauren Jackson
8 — Kamila Vodichkova
5 — Janell Burse
Most consecutive games, 10+ rebounds
7 — Lauren Jackson, July 25-August 12, 2003
3 — Lauren Jackson, August 18-23, 2005
       Lauren Jackson, August 17-20, 2003
       Lauren Jackson, June 15-20, 2002

OFFENSIVE REBOUNDS

Most offensive rebounds, career
365 — Lauren Jackson
239 — Simone Edwards
234 — Kamila Vodichkova
Highest average, offensive rebounds per game, career
(Minimum 100 games)
2.4 — Lauren Jackson (365/155)
1.6 — Kamila Vodichkova (234/146)
1.3 — Simone Edwards (239/178)
Most offensive rebounds, season
96 — Lauren Jackson, 2005
82 — Lauren Jackson, 2003
81 — Janell Burse, 2005
Most offensive rebounds, game
8 — Semeka Randall, at Cleveland, July 5, 2002
       Janell Burse, vs New York, July 19, 2005
7 — Many Times

DEFENSIVE REBOUNDS

Most defensive rebounds, career

845 — Lauren Jackson
421 — Kamila Vodichkova
386 — Simone Edwards
Highest average, defensive rebounds per game, career
(Minimum 100 games)
5.5 — Lauren Jackson (845/155)
2.9 — Kamila Vodichkova (421/146)
2.2 — Sue Bird (292/130)
Most defensive rebounds, season
225 — Lauren Jackson, 2003
217 — Lauren Jackson, 2005
143 — Lauren Jackson, 2004
Most defensive rebounds, game
15 — Lauren Jackson, vs Charlotte, July 31, 2003
13 — Lauren Jackson, at Houston, August 19, 2003
12 — Lauren Jackson, vs Indiana, June 4, 2005
       Lauren Jackson, vs Connecticut,
       June 22, 2005
       Lauren Jackson, at Sacramento,
       August 20, 2005
       Lauren Jackson, vs Los Angeles,
       August 6, 2003

ASSISTS

Most assists, career
772 — Sue Bird
255 — Lauren Jackson
187 — Sonja Henning
Highest average, assists per game, career
(Minimum 100 games)
5.9 — Sue Bird (772/130)
1.6 — Lauren Jackson (255/155)
1.2 — Kamila Vodichkova (178/146)
Most assists, season
221 — Sue Bird, 2003
191 — Sue Bird, 2002
184 — Sue Bird, 2004
Highest average, assists per game, season (qualifiers)
6.5 — Sue Bird, 2003 (221/34)
6.0 — Sue Bird, 2002 (191/32)
5.9 — Sue Bird, 2005 (176/30)
Most assists, game
12 — Sue Bird, at Cleveland, July 5, 2002
       Sue Bird, at Cleveland, June 27, 2003
       Sue Bird, at Los Angeles, June 19, 2003
11 — Sue Bird, at Miami, July 7, 2002
       Sue Bird, at Indiana, June 28, 2003
       Sue Bird, at Orlando, July 25, 2002
Most games, 10+ assists, career
15 — Sue Bird

PERSONAL FOULS

Most personal fouls, career
491 — Lauren Jackson
426 — Kamila Vodichkova
270 — Simone Edwards
Most personal fouls, season
139 — Janell Burse, 2005
110 — Kamila Vodichkova, 2004
108 — Sheri Sam, 2004
Most personal fouls, game

6 — By Many

STEALS

Most steals, career
189 — Lauren Jackson
183 — Sue Bird
122 — Sonja Henning

Highest average, steals per game, career
(Minimum 100 games)
1.4 — Sue Bird (183/130)
1.2 — Lauren Jackson (189/155)
.8 — Kamila Vodichkova (117/146)

Most steals, season
61 — Sonja Henning, 2000
55 — Sue Bird, 2002
54 — Lauren Jackson, 2001

Highest average, steals per game, season (qualifiers)
1.91 — Sonja Henning, 2000 (61/32)
1.86 — Lauren Jackson, 2001 (54/29)
1.7 — Sue Bird, 2002 (55/32)

Most steals, game
6 — Sonja Henning, vs Portland, July 20, 2001
Adia Barnes, vs Houston, July 20, 2002
5 — By Many

BLOCKED SHOTS

Most blocked shots, career
338 — Lauren Jackson
76 — Janell Burse
70 — Kamila Vodichkova

Highest average, blocked shots per game, career
(Minimum: 100 games)
2.2 — Lauren Jackson (338/155)
.5 — Kamila Vodichkova (70/146)
.3 — Simone Edwards (56/178)

Most blocked shots, season
81 — Lauren Jackson, 2002
67 — Lauren Jackson, 2005
64 — Lauren Jackson, 2001
Lauren Jackson, 2003

Highest average, blocked shots per game, season
(qualifiers)
2.9 — Lauren Jackson, 2002 (81/28)
2.2 — Lauren Jackson, 2001 (64/29)
2.0 — Lauren Jackson, 2004 (62/31)

Most blocked shots, game
8 — Lauren Jackson, vs Utah, August 11, 2002
6 — Lauren Jackson, vs Houston, June 22, 2004
5 — By Many

TURNOVERS

Most turnovers, career
393 — Sue Bird
295 — Lauren Jackson
272 — Kamila Vodichkova

Most turnovers, season
110 — Sue Bird, 2003
109 — Sue Bird, 2002
87 — Sue Bird, 2004

Sue Bird, 2005

Most turnovers, game
8 — Sue Bird, at Phoenix, June 26, 2002
Sue Bird, at Phoenix, August 15, 2003
Sue Bird, vs Sacramento, June 3, 2003
7 — Sue Bird, at San Antonio, June 30, 2005
Betty Lennox, vs Minnesota, May 20, 2004
Sue Bird, at Sacramento, July 26, 2003
Sue Bird, vs Houston, July 20, 2002
Sonja Henning, at Orlando, July 8, 2000

WASHINGTON MYSTICS

REGULAR SEASON TEAM RECORDS

TEAM OFFENSE

SCORING

Highest average, points per game, season
68.5 — 2003 (2330/34)
68.4 — 2004 (2325/34)
Lowest average, points per game, season
60.3 — 2001 (1928/32)
65.1 — 1998 (1954/30)
Most points, game
97 — at Utah, June 4, 2002
96 — vs Detroit, August 4, 2000
Fewest points, game
34 — at Cleveland, May 31, 2001
36 — vs Miami, August 8, 2001
Largest margin of victory, game
35 — vs Cleveland, August 8, 1999 (80-45)
26 — vs Orlando, May 31, 2000 (92-66)
Largest margin of defeat, game
45 — vs Houston, August 17, 1998 (65-110)
43 — at New York, August 13, 1998 (45-88)

BY HALF

Most points, first half
50 — vs Orlando, June 1, 2002
vs Indiana, June 7, 2002
at Utah, June 13, 1998
49 — at Utah, June 4, 2002
Fewest points, first half
14 — vs Cleveland, June 6, 2003
16 — at Charlotte, July 24, 2004
at Cleveland, May 31, 2001
vs Los Angeles, August 14, 1999
Largest lead at half time
19 — vs Detroit, August 4, 2000 (led 45-26; won 96-72)
17 — vs Detroit, July 11, 1998 (led 41-24; won 78-53)
vs Indiana, June 7, 2002 (led 50-33; won 89-68)
Largest deficit at halftime overcome to win game
12 — vs Charlotte, June 30, 2002 (trailed 24-36; won 56-55)
11 — at Indiana, August 12, 2003 (trailed 29-40; won 84-80)
at Phoenix, September 17, 2004 (trailed 28-39; won 73-67)
Most points, second half
63 — vs Utah, July 19, 1998
55 — at Indiana, August 12, 2003
Fewest points, second half
15 — at Seattle, July 3, 2001
16 — vs Miami, August 8, 2001

OVERTIME

Most points, overtime period
19 — vs New York, August 23, 2005
15 — vs Indiana, June 18, 2005
Fewest points, overtime period
2 — at Seattle, July 3, 2001
4 — Many Times
Largest margin of victory, overtime period
13 — vs New York, August 23, 2005 (82-69)
10 — vs Indiana, June 18, 2005 (88-78)

FIELD GOAL PERCENTAGE

Highest field goal percentage, season
.459 — 2000 (832/1813)
.430 — 2005 (847/1968)
Lowest field goal percentage, season
.386 — 2001 (739/1915)
.395 — 1998 (720/1821)
Highest field goal percentage, game
.603 — vs Indiana, June 7, 2002 (35/58)
.588 — at Seattle, July 13, 2005 (30/51)
Lowest field goal percentage, game
.196 — vs Miami, August 8, 2001 (10/51)
.245 — at Cleveland, May 31, 2001 (13/53)

FIELD GOALS

Most field goals per game, season
26.4 — 2003 (896/34)
26.0 — 2000 (832/32)
Fewest field goals per game, season
23.1 — 2001 (739/32)
23.7 — 1999 (759/32)
Most field goals, game
38 — vs Orlando, May 31, 2000
35 — vs Indiana, June 7, 2002
vs Detroit, August 6, 2003
Fewest field goals, game
10 — vs Miami, August 8, 2001
13 — at Cleveland, May 31, 2001

FIELD GOAL ATTEMPTS

Most field goal attempts per game, season
64.44 — 2003 (2191/34)
61.41 — 2004 (2088/34)
Fewest field goal attempts per game, season
56.1 — 1999 (1794/32)
56.7 — 2000 (1813/32)
Most field goal attempts, game
84 — at Sacramento, June 25, 2002 (2OT)
79 — at Detroit, August 25, 2003
Fewest field goal attempts, game
39 — at Cleveland, June 3, 2000
42 — at New York, August 17, 1999

THREE-POINT FIELD GOAL PERCENTAGE

Highest three-point field goal percentage, season
.371 — 2004 (105/283)
.370 — 2002 (164/443)
Lowest three-point field goal percentage, season
.264 — 1998 (114/432)
.280 — 2001 (117/418)

THREE-POINT FIELD GOALS

Most three-point field goals per game, season
5.3 — 2005 (181/34)
5.1 — 2002 (164/32)
Fewest three-point field goals per game, season
3.08 — 2004 (105/34)
3.12 — 1999 (100/32)
Most three-point field goals, game
15 — vs Los Angeles, May 26, 2005
10 — vs Detroit, August 27, 2005
       at Utah, June 4, 2002
       vs Utah, July 19, 1998
Fewest three-point field goals, game
0 — Many Times

THREE-POINT FIELD GOAL ATTEMPTS

Most three-point field goal attempts per game, season
15.0 — 2005 (510/34)
14.9 — 2003 (505/34)
Fewest three-point field goal attempts per game, season
8.3 — 2004 (283/34)
10.5 — 2000 (335/32)
Most three-point field goal attempts, game
29 — vs Los Angeles, May 26, 2005
       vs Los Angeles, July 14, 2001
27 — vs Utah, July 19, 1998
Fewest three-point field goal attempts, game
2 — vs Minnesota, July 23, 2004
3 — at Charlotte, July 24, 2004
      at Charlotte, July 10, 2004
      vs Indiana, July 1, 2004

FREE THROW PERCENTAGE

Highest free throw percentage, season
.751 — 2002 (359/478)
         2003 (381/507)
Lowest free throw percentage, season
.645 — 1998 (400/620)
.661 — 2001 (333/504)
Highest free throw percentage, game
1.000 — Many Times
Lowest free throw percentage, game
.000 — at Detroit, August 25, 2003 (0/1)
.313 — vs Portland, August 3, 2001 (5/16)

FREE THROWS MADE

Most free throws made per game, season
15.1 — 1999 (482/32)
13.9 — 2004 (474/34)
Fewest free throws made per game, season
10.4 — 2001 (333/32)
11.2 — 2003 (381/34)

Most free throws made, game
30 — vs Detroit, August 4, 2000
       at New York, June 14, 1999
29 — at Utah, June 4, 2002
       vs Orlando, June 1, 2002
Fewest free throws made, game
0 — vs Charlotte, July 7, 2003
      at Detroit, August 25, 2003
2 — vs Connecticut, June 24, 2003
      at Houston, June 27, 2001

FREE THROW ATTEMPTS

Most free throw attempts per game, season
21.2 — 1999 (679/32)
20.7 — 1998 (620/30)
Fewest free throw attempts per game, season
14.91 — 2003 (507/34)
14.93 — 2002 (478/32)
Most free throw attempts, game
37 — vs Indiana, July 1, 2004
       vs Orlando, June 1, 2002
       vs Cleveland, July 21, 1999
       at New York, June 14, 1999
36 — at Utah, June 4, 2002
Fewest free throw attempts, game
0 — vs Charlotte, July 7, 2003
1 — at Detroit, August 25, 2003

REBOUNDS

Most rebounds per game, season
33.0 — 2001 (1055/32)
32.4 — 2002 (1038/32)
Fewest rebounds per game, season
27.7 — 2005 (943/34)
29.6 — 2000 (946/32)
Most rebounds, game
51 — at Sacramento, June 25, 2002 (2OT)
50 — at Seattle, July 3, 2001 (4OT)
Fewest rebounds, game
17 — at Charlotte, July 24, 2004
       at Detroit, June 14, 2001
       at Cleveland, June 3, 2000
18 — vs Houston, July 26, 2005

OFFENSIVE REBOUNDS

Most offensive rebounds per game, season
11.2 — 2003 (382/34)
11.1 — 2001 (356/32)
Fewest offensive rebounds per game, season
7.8 — 2005 (266/34)
9.4 — 2000 (300/32)
Most offensive rebounds, game
20 — vs Orlando, July 30, 2002
       at Minnesota, July 27, 2001
       at Orlando, June 19, 1999
19 — at Sacramento, July 2, 2003
       at Sacramento, June 25, 2002 (2OT)
       vs Detroit, August 4, 2000
Fewest offensive rebounds, game
1 — at Cleveland, June 3, 2000
3 — at Detroit, August 21, 2005
      vs San Antonio, July 28, 2005
      vs Houston, July 26, 2005
      at Orlando, August 15, 1999

DEFENSIVE REBOUNDS

Most defensive rebounds per game, season
22.1 — 2002 (708/32)
21.9 — 1999 (701/32)
Fewest defensive rebounds per game, season
19.9 — 2005 (677/34)
20.0 — 1998 (599/30)
Most defensive rebounds, game
37 — at Detroit, July 10, 1999 (2OT)
36 — at Seattle, July 3, 2001 (4OT)
Fewest defensive rebounds, game
8 — at New York, August 13, 1998
10 — at Indiana, September 4, 2004

ASSISTS

Most assists per game, season
16.7 — 2003 (568/34)
16.3 — 2000 (521/32)
Fewest assists per game, season
13.2 — 1998 (397/30)
13.3 — 2001 (424/32)
Most assists, game
29 — vs Detroit, August 6, 2003
28 — at Charlotte, July 26, 2000
vs Orlando, May 31, 2000
Fewest assists, game
5 — vs Miami, August 8, 2001
at Miami, August 5, 2001
at Charlotte, July 26, 2001
vs Orlando, July 19, 1999
7 — at Sacramento, July 18, 2004
at New York, August 13, 1998

PERSONAL FOULS

Most personal fouls per game, season
23.1 — 1998 (692/30)
20.5 — 2005 (697/34)
Fewest personal fouls per game, season
16.8 — 2001 (537/32)
18.2 — 2002 (583/32)
Most personal fouls, game
36 — at Los Angeles, August 3, 1998
33 — at Detroit, July 10, 1999 (2OT)
Fewest personal fouls, game
9 — vs Detroit, July 18, 2002
10 — vs Phoenix, July 9, 2002
vs Cleveland, August 9, 2000

DISQUALIFICATIONS

Most disqualifications per game, season
.30 — 1998 (9/30)
.22 — 1999 (7/32)
Fewest disqualifications per game, season
.09 — 2000, 2001, 2002 (3/32)
Most disqualifications, game
3 — at Los Angeles, August 3, 1998
2 — at Phoenix, June 15, 1998
vs Utah, July 19, 1998
at Detroit, July 10, 1999 (2OT)

STEALS

Most steals per game, season
8.9 — 1998 (266/30)
8.0 — 2001 (257/32)
Fewest steals per game, season
6.26 — 2003 (213/34)
6.34 — 1999 (203/32)
Most steals, game
19 — vs Cleveland, August 9, 2000
18 — at New York, August 13, 1998
Fewest steals, game
1 — at Miami, July 13, 2000
2 — Many Times

BLOCKED SHOTS

Most blocked shots per game, season
3.97 — 2001 (127/32)
3.94 — 2000 (126/32)
Fewest blocked shots per game, season
2.2 — 2005 (76/34)
2.7 — 1999 (87/32)
Most blocked shots, game
10 — vs Detroit, July 7, 2005
vs Detroit, July 28, 2004
9 — at Indiana, May 31, 2003
vs Sacramento, June 5, 2001
Fewest blocked shots, game
0 — Many Times

TURNOVERS

Most turnovers per game, season
20.8 — 1998 (625/30)
17.9 — 1999 (574/32)
Fewest turnovers per game, season
12.5 — 2004 (424/34)
12.8 — 2005 (435/34)
Most turnovers, game
33 — at Houston, June 29, 1998
28 — vs New York, July 5, 1998 (OT)
at Detroit, July 10, 1999 (2OT)
Fewest turnovers, game
6 — at New York, July 8, 2004
7 — vs Charlotte, July 15, 2004
vs San Antonio, June 10, 2003
at Houston, June 27, 2001

TEAM DEFENSE

POINTS

Fewest points allowed per game, season
64.8 — 2001 (2075/32)
66.1 — 2002 (2116/32)
Most points allowed per game, season
80.5 — 1998 (2415/30)
73.5 — 2003 (2498/34)
Fewest points allowed, game
42 — at Charlotte, May 21, 2005
vs Miami, August 8, 2001
vs Charlotte, July 29, 2001
45 — at Connecticut, August 1, 2003
vs Cleveland, June 23, 2002
vs Cleveland, August 8, 1999

Fewest points allowed, first half
17 — vs Los Angeles, August 14, 1999
vs New York, August 11, 1999
vs New York, July 5, 1998
18 — at Charlotte, May 21, 2005
Fewest points allowed, second half
18 — vs Charlotte, July 29, 2001
19 — vs Charlotte, June 30, 2002
vs Miami, August 8, 2001
vs Minnesota, August 21, 1999
Fewest points allowed, overtime period
2 — at Seattle, July 3, 2001
4 — Many Times

FIELD GOAL PERCENTAGE
Lowest opponents' field goal percentage, season
.407 — 2001 (791/1945)
.413 — 2002 (786/1903)
Highest opponents' field goal percentage, season
.468 — 1998 (876/1870)
.451 — 2000 (845/1875)
Lowest opponents' field goal percentage, game
.238 — at Connecticut, August 1, 2003 (15/63)
.250 — vs New York, August 11, 1999 (16/64) (OT)

TURNOVERS
Fewest opponents' turnovers per game, season
13.6 — 1999 (436/32)
13.8 — 2003 (468/34)
Most opponents' turnovers per game, season
17.0 — 1998 (511/30)
14.8 — 2005 (504/34)
Most opponents' turnovers, game
26 — at New York, August 13, 1998
25 — at Charlotte, May 21, 2005

TEAM MISCELLANEOUS

GAME WON AND LOST
Highest winning percentage, season
.531 — 2002 (17-15)
.500 — 2004 (17-17)
Lowest winning percentage, season
.100 — 1998 (3-27)
.265 — 2003 (9-25)
Most consecutive games won
6 — June 4-18, 2002
August 2-14, 1999
5 — September 7-17, 2004
Most consecutive games won, one season
6 — June 4-18, 2002
August 2-14, 1999
5 — September 7-17, 2004
Most consecutive games lost
11 — June 13-July 9, 2003
July 13-August 7, 1998
8 — June 21-July 8, 1998
June 10-27, 2001
Most consecutive games lost, one season
11 — June 13-July 9, 2003
July 13-August 7, 1998
8 — June 21-July 8, 1998
June 10-27, 2001

Highest winning percentage, home games, season
.647 — 2004 (11-6)
.588 — 2005 (10-7)
Lowest winning percentage, home games, season
.176 — 2003 (3-14)
.200 — 1998 (3-12)
Most consecutive home games won
9 — August 12, 2001-July 9, 2002
6 — June 13-July 23, 2004
Most consecutive home games lost
8 — August 9, 2003-June 11, 2004
August 12, 1998-July 2, 1999
7 — July 20, 2002-June 6, 2003
Highest winning percentage, road games, season
.500 — 2002 (8-8)
.438 — 2000 (7-9)
Lowest winning percentage, road games, season
.000 — 1998 (0-15)
.125 — 2001 (2-14)
Most consecutive road games won
3 — June 24-July 13, 2005
August 1-14, 2003
June 24-July 3, 2000
2 — Many Times
Most consecutive road games lost
16 — June 11 1998-June 12, 1998
7 — August 6-June 27, 2001
May 31-July 5, 2003

OVERTIME GAMES
Most overtime games, season
3 — 2005
2 — 2004, 2003, 1999
1 — 1998, 2001, 2002
Most consecutive overtime games, season
1 — Many Times
Most overtime games won, season
2 — 1999
1 — 2001, 2002, 2004
Most overtime games won, no losses, season
2 — 1999
1 — 2001, 2002
Most overtime games lost, season
2 — 2003
1 — 1998, 2004
Most overtime games lost, no wins, season
2 — 2003
1 — 1998
Most overtime periods, game
4 — at Seattle, July 3, 2001
2 — vs Indiana, June 18, 2005
at Sacramento, June 25, 2002
at Detroit, July 10, 1999

INDIVIDUAL RECORDS

SEASONS
Most seasons
8 — Murriel Page
6 — Chamique Holdsclaw
5 — Coco Miller

GAMES

Most games, career
    259 — Murriel Page
    162 — Chamique Holdsclaw
    152 — Coco Miller
Most consecutive games, career
    192 — Murriel Page, June 11, 1998-August 25, 2003
    111 — Nikki McCray, July 19, 1998-August 14, 2001
     96 — Vicky Bullett, May 31, 2000-August 13, 2002
Most games, season
     34 — By Many

MINUTES

Most minutes, career
    6,904 — Murriel Page
    5,550 — Chamique Holdsclaw
    3,886 — Nikki McCray
Highest average, minutes per game, career
(Minimum 100 games)
    34.3 — Chamique Holdsclaw (5550/162)
    31.1 — Nikki McCray (3886/125)
    26.7 — Murriel Page (6904/259)
Most minutes, season
    1,131 — Chamique Holdsclaw, 2000
    1,094 — Vicky Bullett, 2000
    1,076 — Coco Miller, 2003
Highest average, minutes per game, season
    35.3 — Chamique Holdsclaw, 2000 (1131/32)
    35.1 — Chamique Holdsclaw, 2003 (948/27)
    34.8 — Chamique Holdsclaw, 2004 (801/23)
Most minutes, game
     55 — Vicky Bullett, at Seattle, July 3, 2001 (4OT)
     54 — Audrey Sauret, at Seattle, July 3, 2001 (4OT)
           Chamique Holdsclaw, at Seattle,
           July 3, 2001 (4OT)
     49 — Nikki McCray, at Seattle, July 3, 2001 (4OT)

SCORING

Most points, lifetime
    2,960 — Chamique Holdsclaw
    1,921 — Nikki McCray
    1,782 — Murriel Page
Highest average, points per game, career
(Minimum 100 games)
    18.3 — Chamique Holdsclaw (2960/162)
    15.4 — Nikki McCray (1921/125)
     7.0 — Coco Miller (1058/152)
Most points, season
    561 — Nikki McCray, 1999
          Chamique Holdsclaw, 2000
    554 — Chamique Holdsclaw, 2003
    525 — Chamique Holdsclaw, 1999
Highest average, points per game, season
    20.5 — Chamique Holdsclaw, 2003 (554/27)
    19.9 — Chamique Holdsclaw, 2002 (397/20)
    19.0 — Chamique Holdsclaw, 2004 (437/23)
Most points, game
     34 — Chamique Holdsclaw, vs Indiana, July 24, 2003
     32 — Chamique Holdsclaw, vs Seattle, July 27, 2002

     31 — Chamique Holdsclaw, vs New York, June 10,2001
Most games, 30 or more points, career
      4 — Chamique Holdsclaw
      1 — Chasity Melvin
Most games, 20 or more points, career
     67 — Chamique Holdsclaw
     34 — Nikki McCray
     12 — Alana Beard
Most consecutive games, 20 or more points
      7 — Chamique Holdsclaw, June 17-July 7, 2004
      6 — Chamique Holdsclaw, July 9-24, 2003
           Alana Beard, September 7-19, 2004
      5 — Nikki McCray, August 5-14, 1999
Most consecutive games, 10 or more points
     24 — Chamique Holdsclaw, August 6, 2003-
           July 8,2004
     19 — Chamique Holdsclaw, August 1, 2001-
           June 27, 2002
     18 — Chamique Holdsclaw, May 23-July 29, 2003

FIELD GOAL PERCENTAGE

Highest field goal percentage, career
(Minimum 400 field goals)
    .473 — Murriel Page (739/1562)
    .434 — Coco Miller (439/1012)
    .430 — Chamique Holdsclaw (1136/2641)
Highest field goal percentage, season (qualifiers)
    .590 — Murriel Page, 2000 (131/222)
    .574 — Murriel Page, 1999 (105/183)
    .492 — Chasity Melvin, 2005 (150/305)
Highest field goal percentage, game
(Minimum 8 field goals made)
    .909 — Vicky Bullett, vs Detroit, July 18, 2002 (10/11)
    .889 — Elana Beard, vs Minnesota, July 23, 2004 (8/9)
    .818 — Temeka Johnson, vs Indiana,
           June 18, 2005 (9/11)
Most field goals, none missed, game
      5 — Murriel Page, at Miami, July 13, 2000
           Murriel Page, vs Utah, June 19, 1998
           Coco Miller, at San Antonio, September 15,2004
           Stacey Dales, at Indiana, August 12, 2003
      4 — Andrea Nagy, at Cleveland, June 26, 1999
           Murriel Page, vs Orlando, August 5, 1999
Most field goal attempts, none made, game
      8 — Coco Miller, at Sacramento, July 18, 2004
           Shalonda Enis, vs Orlando, July 19, 1999
      7 — Nikki McCray, vs Miami, August 8, 2001
           Stacey Dales-Schuman, at Indiana,
           September 4, 2004
      6 — By Many

FIELD GOALS

Most field goals, career
    1,136 — Chamique Holdsclaw
     739 — Murriel Page
     670 — Nikki McCray
Most field goals, season
    232 — Chamique Holdsclaw, 2000
    204 — Chamique Holdsclaw, 2003
    202 — Chamique Holdsclaw, 1999
Most field goals, game
     12 — Chamique Holdsclaw, vs Indiana, June 7, 2002
           Chasity Melvin, vs New York,

August 23, 2005 (OT)
Chamique Holdsclaw, vs Indiana,
July 20, 2000
Chamique Holdsclaw, vs New York,
June 10, 2001
Chamique Holdsclaw, vs Orlando,
May 31, 2000
11 — Many Times

FIELD GOAL ATTEMPTS

Most field goal attempts, career
2,641 — Chamique Holdsclaw
1,587 — Nikki McCray
1,562 — Murriel Page
Most field goal attempts, season
499 — Chamique Holdsclaw, 2000
480 — Chamique Holdsclaw, 2003
467 — Chamique Holdsclaw, 2001
Most field goal attempts, game
27 — Chamique Holdsclaw, at Sacramento,
June 25, 2002 (2OT)
Chamique Holdsclaw, vs Los Angeles,
June 26, 2000
26 — Chamique Holdsclaw, at Charlotte,
May 23, 2003
25 — Chamique Holdsclaw, vs Seattle,
July 27, 2002
Chamique Holdsclaw, vs Sacramento,
June 5, 2001

THREE-POINT FIELD GOAL PERCENTAGE

Highest three-point field goal percentage, career
(Minimum 100 three-point field goals)
.361 — Stacey Dales-Schuman (140/388)
.299 — Nikki McCray (141/472)
Highest three-point field goal percentage, season (qualifiers)
.467 — Laurie Koehn, 2005 (35/75)
.420 — Charlotte Smith-Taylor, 2005 (42/100)
.396 — Helen Luz, 2002 (42/106)
Most three-point field goals, none missed, game
4 — DeLisha Milton-Jones, at Seattle, July 13, 2005
3 — By Many
Most three-point field goal attempts, none made, game
6 — Stacey Dales, at New York, June 1, 2003
Penny Moore, vs Sacramento, July 26, 1998
5 — By Many

THREE-POINT FIELD GOALS

Most three-point field goals, career
141 — Nikki McCray
140 — Stacey Dales-Schuman
86 — Helen Luz
Most three-point field goals, season
57 — Stacey Dales-Schuman, 2003
50 — Nikki McCray, 2000
46 — Nikki McCray, 1999
Most three-point field goals, game
6 — Nikki McCray, at Cleveland, June 3, 2000
Nikki McCray, vs Orlando, May 31, 2000
5 — Keri Chaconas, vs Cleveland, July 1, 1998
Laurie Koehn, vs Detroit, August 27, 2005
Stacey Dales, vs Charlotte, July 17, 2003
Stacey Dales, at Connecticut, June 20, 2004

4 — By Many
Most consecutive games, three-point field goals made
13 — Nikki McCray, August 5, 1999-June 8, 2000
10 — Keri Chaconas, July 1-22, 1998
Charlotte Smith-Taylor, June 30-July 29,2005
8 — Helen Luz, June 4-21, 2002
Stacey Dales-Schuman, June 13-July 3, 2003
Stacey Dales-Schuman, July 7-26, 2003

THREE-POINT FIELD GOAL ATTEMPTS

Most three-point field goal attempts, career
472 — Nikki McCray
388 — Stacey Dales-Schuman
228 — Helen Luz
Most three-point field goal attempts, season
160 — Stacey Dales-Schuman, 2003
153 — Nikki McCray, 1999
151 — Nikki McCray, 2000
Most three-point field goal attempts, game
10 — Keri Chaconas, vs Cleveland, July 1, 1998
Nikki McCray, at Minnesota, July 27, 2001
Nikki McCray, vs Orlando, May 31, 2000
9 — Nikki McCray, at Charlotte, July 17, 1999
Nikki McCray, at Charlotte, July 26, 2000
Nikki McCray, vs Charlotte, July 15, 2000
Nikki McCray, vs Los Angeles, June 26, 2000

FREE THROW PERCENTAGE

Highest free throw percentage, career
.779 — Chamique Holdsclaw (638/819)
.761 — Nikki McCray (440/578)
.736 — Alana Beard (187/254)
Highest free throw percentage, season (qualifiers)
.903 — Chamique Holdsclaw, 2003 (140/155)
.830 — Chamique Holdsclaw, 2002 (88/106)
.821 — Coco Miller, 2002 (46/56)
Most free throws made, none missed, game
13 — Chamique Holdsclaw, vs Indiana,
July 24, 2003
10 — Chamique Holdsclaw, vs Seattle,
July 27, 2002
Chamique Holdsclaw, at New York,
August 8,2002
Chasity Melvin, at Charlotte, July 10, 2004
9 — Chamique Holdsclaw, at Cleveland,
June 20,2003
Most free throw attempts, none made, game
5 — Audrey Sauret, vs Portland, August 3, 2001
4 — Aiysha Smith, vs Phoenix, August 3, 2003 (2OT)
3 — Murriel Page, at New York, August 17, 1999

FREE THROWS MADE

Most free throws made, career
638 — Chamique Holdsclaw
440 — Nikki McCray
287 — Murriel Page
Most free throws made, season
140 — Chamique Holdsclaw, 2003
129 — Nikki McCray, 1999
116 — Chamique Holdsclaw, 1999
Most free throws made, game

13 — Chamique Holdsclaw, at Detroit,
June 22, 2004
Chamique Holdsclaw, vs Indiana,
July 24, 2003
Chamique Holdsclaw, at New York,
July 15, 2003
12 — Nikki McCray, vs Minnesota, July 29, 2000
Chamique Holdsclaw, at Connecticut,
June 20, 2004
11 — Chamique Holdsclaw, vs Indiana,
July 1, 2004
Stacey Dales-Schuman, vs Orlando,
June 1, 2002

FREE THROW ATTEMPTS

Most free throw attempts, career
819 — Chamique Holdsclaw
578 — Nikki McCray
454 — Murriel Page
Most free throw attempts, season
160 — Nikki McCray, 1999
155 — Chamique Holdsclaw, 2003
150 — Chamique Holdsclaw, 1999
Most free throw attempts, game
17 — Chamique Holdsclaw, at New York,
July 15, 2003
16 — Nikki McCray, vs Seattle, June 3, 2001
Nikki McCray, vs Minnesota, July 29, 2000
Chamique Holdsclaw, vs Indiana, July 1, 2004
14 — By Many

REBOUNDS

Most rebounds, career
1459 — Chamique Holdsclaw
1336 — Murriel Page
600 — Vicky Bullett
Highest average, rebounds per game, career
(Minimum 100 games)
9.0 — Chamique Holdsclaw (1459/162)
5.2 — Murriel Page (1336/259)
2.5 — Coco Miller (374/152)
Most rebounds, season
294 — Chamique Holdsclaw, 2003
256 — Chamique Holdsclaw, 2001
246 — Chamique Holdsclaw, 1999
Highest average, rebounds per game, season (qualifiers)
11.6 — Chamique Holdsclaw, 2002 (232/20)
10.9 — Chamique Holdsclaw, 2003 (294/27)
8.8 — Chamique Holdsclaw, 2001 (256/29)
Most rebounds, game
24 — Chamique Holdsclaw, at Charlotte, May 23,2003
21 — Chamique Holdsclaw, at Sacramento,
June 25, 2002 (2OT)
18 — Alessandra Santos de Oliveira, at Utah,
June 13, 1998
Most games, 10+ rebounds, career
65 — Chamique Holdsclaw
18 — Murriel Page
10 — Vicky Bullett

Most consecutive games, 10+ rebounds
5 — Chamique Holdsclaw, June 9-19, 2002
Chamique Holdsclaw, July 27-August 9, 2003
3 — Many Times

OFFENSIVE REBOUNDS

Most offensive rebounds, career
480 — Murriel Page
380 — Chamique Holdsclaw
172 — Vicky Bullett
Highest average, offensive rebounds per game, career
(Minimum 100 games)
2.3 — Chamique Holdsclaw (380/162)
1.9 — Murriel Page (480/259)
1.1 — Coco Miller (163/152)
Most offensive rebounds, season
82 — Chasity Melvin, 2005
81 — Murriel Page, 1998
79 — Murriel Page, 2000
Most offensive rebounds, game
9 — Tausha Mills, at Sacramento, July 8, 2000
8 — Chamique Holdsclaw, vs Cleveland,
August 12, 2001
Chasity Melvin, vs New York,
August 23,2005 (OT)
Alessandra Santos de Oliveira, at Houston,
July 13, 1998
7 — By Many

DEFENSIVE REBOUNDS

Most defensive rebounds, career
1079 — Chamique Holdsclaw
856 — Murriel Page
428 — Vicky Bullett
Highest average, defensive rebounds per game, career
(Minimum 100 games)
6.7 — Chamique Holdsclaw (1079/162)
3.3 — Murriel Page (856/259)
1.4 — Coco Miller (211/152)
Most defensive rebounds, season
222 — Chamique Holdsclaw, 2003
184 — Chamique Holdsclaw, 2001
183 — Chamique Holdsclaw, 2000
Most defensive rebounds, game
17 — Chamique Holdsclaw, at Charlotte,
May 23, 2003
14 — Chamique Holdsclaw, at Sacramento,
June 25, 2002 (2OT)
Chamique Holdsclaw, at Los Angeles,
July 22, 2003
13 — Chamique Holdsclaw, at Cleveland,
August 11, 2002
Chamique Holdsclaw, at Detroit,
July 10, 1999 (2OT)
Chamique Holdsclaw, at Los Angeles, J
June 27, 2002

ASSISTS

Most assists, career
410 — Chamique Holdsclaw

320 — Murriel Page
300 — Nikki McCray
Highest average, assists per game, career
(Minimum 100 games)
2.5 — Chamique Holdsclaw (410/162)
2.4 — Nikki McCray (300/125)
1.7 — Coco Miller (263/152)
Most assists, season
177 — Temeka Johnson, 2005
146 — Andrea Nagy, 1999
118 — Andrea Nagy, 2000
Highest average, assists per game, season (qualifiers)
5.2 — Temeka Johnson, 2005 (177/34)
5.1 — Andrea Nagy, 2000 (118/23)
4.6 — Andrea Nagy, 1999 (146/32)
Most assists, game
12 — Andrea Nagy, vs Charlotte, June 10, 1999
11 — Andrea Nagy, at Cleveland, August 7, 1999
Temeka Johnson, vs New York, June 1, 2005
Annie Burgess, at Connecticut, June 13, 2003
Keisha Anderson, at Charlotte, July 26, 2000
10 — By Many
Most games, 10+ assists, career
4 — Andrea Nagy
3 — Temeka Johnson
1 — Annie Burgess
Keisha Anderson
Stacey Dales-Schuman

PERSONAL FOULS
Most personal fouls, career
712 — Murriel Page
381 — Chamique Holdsclaw
314 — Nikki McCray
Most personal fouls, season
117 — DeLisha Milton-Jones, 2005
113 — Chasity Melvin, 2005
111 — Andrea Nagy, 1999
Most personal fouls, game
6 — Many Times

STEALS
Most steals, career
221 — Chamique Holdsclaw
171 — Vicky Bullett
168 — Murriel Page
Highest average, steals per game, career
(Minimum 100 games)
1.4 — Chamique Holdsclaw (221/162)
1.2 — Nikki McCray (148/125)
.8 — Coco Miller (122/152)
Most steals, season
69 — Alana Beard, 2004
64 — Vicky Bullett, 2000
63 — Rita Williams, 1998
Highest average, steals per game, season (qualifiers)
2.1 — Rita Williams, 1998 (63/30)
2.03 — Alana Beard, 2004 (69/34)
2.00 — Vicky Bullett, 2000 (64/32)
Most steals, game

8 — Chamique Holdsclaw, vs Indiana, July 20,2000
7 — Alana Beard, vs Detroit, July 28, 2004
Alana Beard, vs San Antonio, July 28, 2005
Rita Williams, vs Sacramento, July 26, 1998
5 — By Many

BLOCKED SHOTS
Most blocked shots, career
175 — Murriel Page
142 — Vicky Bullett
98 — Chamique Holdsclaw
Highest average, blocked shots per game, career
(Minimum: 100 games)
.676 — Murriel Page (175/259)
.605 — Chamique Holdsclaw (98/162)
.099 — Coco Miller (15/152)
Most blocked shots, season
58 — Vicky Bullett, 2001
47 — Vicky Bullett, 2000
37 — Vicky Bullett, 2002
Highest average, blocked shots per game, season
(qualifiers)
1.8 — Vicky Bullett, 2001 (58/32)
1.5 — Vicky Bullett, 2000 (47/32)
1.2 — Vicky Bullett, 2002 (37/32)
Most blocked shots, game
5 — Vicky Bullett, at Charlotte, July 1, 2000
Vicky Bullett, vs Minnesota, July 29, 2000
Vicky Bullett, at Orlando, July 24, 2001
LaShawn Brown, vs Sacramento, July 26,1998
4 — By Many

TURNOVERS
Most turnovers, career
469 — Chamique Holdsclaw
394 — Nikki McCray
368 — Murriel Page
Most turnovers, season
125 — Nikki McCray, 1998
108 — Chamique Holdsclaw, 1999
Most turnovers, game
11 — Chamique Holdsclaw, vs Utah, July 8, 1999
10 — Nikki McCray, vs New York, July 5, 1998
9 — Nikki McCray, at Utah, June 13, 199.8

OFFICIAL WNBA RULES

OFFICIAL WNBA RULES

OFFICIAL WNBA RULES

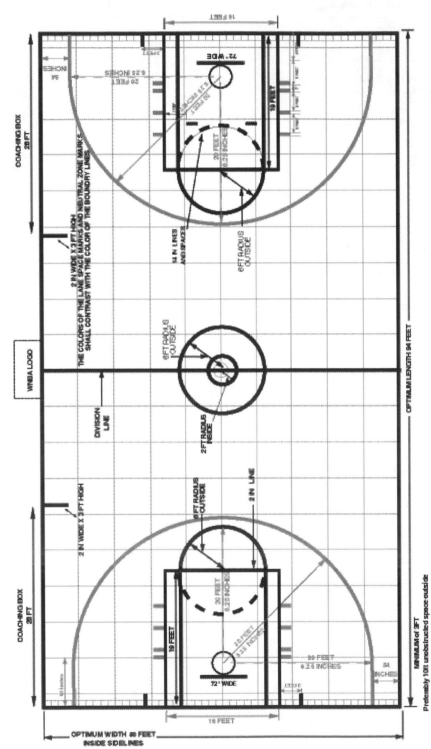

OFFICIAL WNBA COURT DIAGRAM

OFFICIAL RULES
RULE NO. 1—COURT DIMENSIONS—EQUIPMENT

SECTION I—COURT AND DIMENSIONS

a. The playing court shall be measured and marked as shown in the court diagram. (See page 10)

b. A free throw lane, shall be marked at each end of the court with dimensions and markings as shown on the court diagram. All boundary lines are part of the lane; lane space marks and neutral zones marks are not. The color of the lane space marks and neutral zones shall contrast with the color of the boundary lines. The areas identified by the lane space markings are 2" by 8" inches and the neutral zone marks are 12" by 8".

c. A free throw line shall be drawn (2" wide) across each of the circles indicated in the court diagram. It shall be parallel to the end line and shall be 15' from the plane of the face of the backboard.

d. The three-point field goal area has parallel lines 54" from the sidelines, extending 63" from the baseline and an arc of 20'61/4" from the middle of the basket which intersects the parallel lines.

e. Four hash marks shall be drawn (2" wide) perpendicular to the sideline on each side of the court and 28' from the baseline. These hash marks shall extend 3' onto the court.

f. Two hash marks shall be drawn (2" wide) perpendicular to the sideline, in front of the scorer's table, and 4' on each side of the midcourt line. This will designate the Substitution Box area.

g. Four hash marks shall be drawn (2" wide) perpendicular to the baseline on each side of the free throw lane line. These hash marks shall be 3' from the free throw lane line and extend 6" onto the court.

SECTION II—EQUIPMENT

a. The backboard shall be a rectangle measuring 6' horizontally and 31/2' vertically. The front surface shall be flat and transparent.

b. A transparent backboard shall be marked with a 2" white rectangle centered behind the ring. This rectangle shall have outside dimensions of 24" horizontally and 18" vertically.

c. Home management is required to have a spare board with supporting unit on hand for emergencies, and a steel tape or extension ruler and a level for use if necessary.

d. Each basket shall consist of a pressure-release WNBA approved metal safety ring 18" in inside diameter with a white cord net 15" to 18" in length. The cord of the net shall not be less than 30 thread nor more than 120 thread and shall be constructed to check the ball momentarily as it passes through the basket.

e. Each basket ring shall be securely attached to the backboard with its upper edge 10' above and parallel to the floor and equidistant from the vertical edges of the board. The nearest point of the inside edge of the ring shall be 6" from the plane of the face of the board. The ring shall be painted orange.

f. (1) The ball shall be an officially approved WNBA ball with a weight not less than 18 ounces nor more than 20 ounces. The circumference of the ball shall be within a maximum of 29 inches and a minimum of 28.5 inches. (2) Six balls must be made available to each team for pre-game warmup.

g. At least one electric light is to be placed behind the backboard, obvious to officials and synchronized to light up when the horn sounds at the expiration of time for each period. The electric light is to be "red."

SECTION I—THE GAME OFFICIALS

a. The game officials shall be a crew chief and two referees. They will be assisted by an official scorer and two trained timers. One timer will operate the game clock and the other will operate the 24-second clock. All officials shall be approved by the Operations Department.

b. The officials shall wear the uniform prescribed by the WNBA.

SECTION II—DUTIES OF THE OFFICIALS

a. The officials shall, prior to the start of the game, inspect and approve all equipment, including court, baskets, balls, backboards, timers and scorer's equipment.

b. The officials shall not permit players to play with any type of hand, arm, face, nose, ear, head or neck jewelry.

c. The officials shall not permit any player to wear equipment which, in his/her judgment, is dangerous to other players. Any equipment which is of hard substance (casts, splints, guards and braces) must be padded or foam covered and have no exposed sharp or cutting edge. All the face masks and eye or nose protectors must conform to the contour of the face and have no sharp or protruding edges. Approval is on a game-to-game basis.

d. All equipment used must be appropriate for basketball. Equipment that is unnatural and designed to increase a player's height or reach, or to gain an advantage, shall not be used.

e. The officials must check the game ball to see that it is properly inflated. The recommended ball pressure should be between 71/2 and 81/2 pounds.

f. The crew chief shall be the official in charge.

g. If a coach desires to discuss a rule or interpretation of a rule prior to the start of a game or between periods, it will be mandatory for the officials to ask the other coach to be present during the discussion. The same procedure shall be followed if the officials wish to discuss a game situation with either coach.

h. The designated official shall toss the ball at the start of the game. The crew chief shall decide whether or not a goal shall count if the officials disagree, and he/she shall decide matters upon which scorers and timers disagree.

i. All officials shall be present during the 20-minute pre-game warm-up period to observe and report to the Basketball Operations Department any infractions of Rule 12-A—Section IV-a (hanging on the basket ring) and to review scoring and timing procedures with table personnel. Officials should be in the tunnel by the 18-minute mark and may await the on-court arrival of the first team before entering the court.

j. Officials must meet with team captains prior to the start of the game.

k. Officials must report any atypical or unique incident to the Operations Department by E-mail. Flagrant, punching, fighting fouls or a team's failure to have eight players to begin the game must also be reported.

SECTION III—ELASTIC POWER

The officials shall have the power to make decisions on any point not specifically covered in the rules. The Operations Department will be advised of all such decisions at the earliest possible moment.

SECTION IV—DIFFERENT DECISIONS BY OFFICIALS

a. The crew chief shall have the authority to set aside or question decisions regarding a rule interpretation made by either of the other officials.

b. If the officials give conflicting signals as to who caused the ball to go out-of-bounds, a jump ball shall be called between the two players involved. However, if an official offers assistance, the calling official may change the call.

c. In the event that a violation and foul occur at the same time, the foul will take precedence.

d. Double Foul (See Rule 12-B—Section VI-f).

SECTION V—TIME AND PLACE FOR DECISIONS

a. The officials have the power to render decisions for infractions of rules committed inside or outside the boundary lines. This includes periods when the game may be stopped for any reason.

b. When a personal foul or violation occurs, an official will blow his/her whistle to terminate play. The whistle is the signal for the timer to stop the game clock. If a personal foul has occurred, the official (1) will indicate the number of the offender to the official scorer; (2) the type of foul committed; (3) the number of free throws, if any, to be attempted or indicate the spot of the throw-in. If a violation has occurred, the official will indicate: (1) the nature of the violation by giving the correct signal; (2) the number of the offender, if applicable; and (3) the direction in which the ball will be advanced.

c. When a team is entitled to a throw-in, an official shall clearly signal (1) the act which caused the ball to become dead (2) the spot of the throw-in (3) the team entitled to the throw-in, unless it follows a successful field goal or free throw.

d. When a whistle is erroneously sounded, whether the ball is in a possession or non-possession status, it is an inadvertent whistle and shall be interpreted as a suspension-of-play.

e. An official may suspend play for any unusual circumstance. (Rule 4—Section XV)

SECTION VI—CORRECTING ERRORS

A. FREE THROWS

Officials may correct an error if a rule is inadvertently set aside and results in the following:

(1) A team not shooting a merited free throw that will remain in play.

EXCEPTION: If the offensive team scores or shoots earned free throws as a result of a personal foul prior to possession by the defensive team the error shall be ignored if more than 24 seconds have expired.

(2) A team not shooting a merited free throw that will not remain in play. The error shall be corrected, all play shall stand and play will resume from the point of interruption with the clocks remaining the same.

(3) A team shooting an unmerited free throw.

(4) Permitting the wrong player to attempt a free throw.

a. Officials shall be notified of a possible error at the first dead ball.

b. Errors which occur in the first or third periods must be discovered and rectified prior to the start of the next period.

c. Errors which occur in the second period must be discovered and the scorer's table notified prior to the officials leaving the floor at the end of the period. The error(s) must be rectified prior to the start of the third period.

d. Errors which occur in the fourth period or overtime(s) must be discovered and rectified prior to the end of the period.

e. The ball is not in play on corrected free throw attempt(s). Play is resumed at the same spot and under the same conditions as would have prevailed had the error not been discovered.

f. All play that occurs is to be nullified if the error is discovered within a 24-second time period. The game clock shall be reset to the time that the error occurred.

EXCEPTION (1): Acts of unsportsmanlike conduct, flagrant fouls and points scored there from, shall not be nullified.

EXCEPTION (2): If the error to be corrected is for a free throw attempt, where there is to be no line-up of players on the free throw lane line (technical foul, flagrant foul, punching foul, clear-path-to-the-basket foul and away from the play foul in last one minute), the error shall be corrected, all play shall stand and play shall resume from the point of interruption with the clocks remaining the same.

B. LINEUP POSITIONS

In any jump ball situation, if the jumpers are lined up incorrectly and the error is discovered:

(1) After more than 24 seconds has elapsed, the teams will continue to shoot for that basket for the remainder of that half and/or overtime. If the error is discovered in the first half, teams will shoot at the proper basket as decided by the opening tap for the second half.

(2) If 24 seconds or less has elapsed, all play shall be nullified.

EXCEPTION: Acts of unsportsmanlike conduct, flagrant fouls and points scored therefrom, shall not be nullified and play will resume from the original jump ball with players facing the proper direction.

C. THROW-IN

If the second, third or fourth period or any throw-in begins with the wrong team being awarded possession or the teams are facing the wrong direction, and the error is discovered:

(1) After 24 seconds has elapsed, the error cannot be corrected.

(2) With 24 seconds or less having elapsed, all play shall be nullified.

EXCEPTION: Acts of unsportsmanlike conduct, all flagrant fouls, and points scored therefrom, shall not be nullified.

D. RECORD KEEPING

A record keeping error by the official scorer which involves the score, number of personal fouls and/or timeouts may be corrected by the officials at any time prior to the end of the fourth period. Any such error which occurs in overtime must be corrected prior to the end of that period.

SECTION VII—DUTIES OF SCORERS

a. The scorers shall record the field goals made, the free throws made and missed and shall keep a running summary of the points scored. They shall record the personal and technical fouls called on each player and shall notify the officials immediately when a sixth personal foul is called on any player. They shall record the timeouts charged to each team, shall notify a team and its coach through an official whenever that team is granted a team charged timeout and shall notify the nearest official when the team is granted a charged timeout in excess of the legal number. In case there is a question about an error in the scoring, the scorer shall check with the crew chief at once to find the discrepancy. If the error cannot be found, the official shall accept the record of the official scorer, unless he/she has knowledge that forces him/her to decide otherwise.

b. The scorers shall keep a record of the names, numbers and positions of the players who are to start the game and of all substitutes who enter the game. When there is an infraction of the rules pertaining to submission of the lineup, substitutions or numbers of players, they shall notify the nearest official immediately if the ball is dead, or as soon as it becomes dead if it is in play when the infraction is discovered. The scorer shall mark the time at which players are disqualified by reason of receiving six personal fouls, so that it may be easy to ascertain the order in which the players are eligible to go back into the game in accordance with Rule 3—Section I.

c. The scorers shall use a horn or other device unlike that used by the officials or timers to signal the officials. This may be used when the ball is dead or in certain specified situations when the ball is in control of a given team.

d. When a player is disqualified from the game, or whenever a penalty free throw is being awarded, a buzzer, siren or some other clearly audible sound must be used by the scorer or timer to notify the game officials. It is the duty of the scorekeeper to be certain the officials have acknowledged the sixth personal foul buzzer and the penalty shot buzzer.

e. The scorer shall not signal the officials while the ball is in play, except to notify them of the necessity to correct an error.

f. Should the scorer sound the horn while the ball is in play, it shall be ignored by the players on the court. The officials must use their judgment in stopping play to consult with the scorer's table.

g. Scorers shall record on the scoreboard the number of team fouls up to a total of five, which will indicate that the team is in a penalty situation.

h. Scorers shall immediately record the name of the team which secures first possession of the game.

SECTION VIII—DUTIES OF TIMERS

a. The timers shall note when each half is to start and shall notify the crew chief and both coaches five minutes before this time, or cause them to be notified at least five minutes before the half is to start. They shall signal the scorers two minutes before starting time. They shall record playing time and time of stoppages as provided in the rules. The official timer and the 24-second clock operator shall be provided with digital stop watches to be used with the timing of timeouts and in case the official game clock, 24-second clocks/game clocks located above the backboards fail to work properly.

b. At the beginning of the first period, any overtime period or whenever play is resumed by a jump ball, the game clock shall be started when the ball is legally tapped by either of the jumpers. No time will be removed from the game clock and/or 24-second clock if there is an illegal tap.

c. If the game clock has been stopped for a violation, successful field goal or free throw attempt and the ball is put in play by a throw-in, the game clock and the 24-second clock shall be started when the ball is legally touched by any player on the court. The starting of the game clock and the 24-second clock will be under the control of the official timer.

d. During an unsuccessful free throw attempt, the game clock will be started by the official timer when the ball is legally touched. The 24-second clock will be reset when player possession of the ball is obtained.

e. The game clock shall be stopped at the expiration of time for each period and when an official signals timeout. For a charged timeout, the timer shall start a digital stop watch and shall signal the official when it is time to resume play.

f. The game clock and the scoreboard will combine to cause a horn or buzzer to sound, automatically, when playing time for the period has expired. If the horn or buzzer fails to sound, or is not heard, the official timer shall use any other means to notify the officials immediately.

g. In a dead ball situation, if the clock shows :00.0, the period or game is considered to have ended although the buzzer may not have sounded.

EXCEPTION: See Rule 13—Section II–a(6).

h. Record only the actual playing time in the last minute of all four periods and any overtime periods..

RULE NO. 3—PLAYERS, SUBSTITUTES AND COACHES

SECTION I—TEAM

a. Each team shall consist of five players. No team may be reduced to less than five players. If a player in the game receives her sixth personal foul and all substitutes have already been disqualified, said player shall remain in the game and shall be charged with a personal and team foul. A technical foul also shall be assessed against her team. All subsequent personal fouls, including offensive fouls, shall be treated similarly. All players who have six or more personal fouls and remain in the game shall be treated similarly.

b. In the event that there are only five eligible players remaining and one of these players is injured and must leave the game or is ejected, she must be replaced by the last player who was disqualified by reason of receiving six personal fouls. Each subsequent requirement to replace an injured or ejected player will be treated in this inverse order.

Any such re-entry into a game by a disqualified player shall be penalized by a technical foul.

    c. In the event that a player becomes ill and must leave the court while the ball is in play, the official will stop play immediately when her team gains new possession. The player shall be replaced and no technical foul will be assessed. The opposing team is also permitted to substitute one player.

SECTION II—STARTING LINE-UPS

    At least ten minutes before the game is scheduled to begin, the scorer shall be supplied with the name and number of each player who may participate in the game. Starting line-ups will be indicated. Failure to comply with this provision shall be reported to the Basketball Operations Department.

SECTION III—THE CAPTAIN

    a. A team may have a captain and a co-captain numbering a maximum of two. The designated captain may be anyone on the squad who is in uniform, except a player-coach.

    b. The designated captain is the only player who may talk to an official during a regular or 20-second timeout charged to her team. She may not discuss a judgment decision.

    c. If the designated captain continues to sit on the bench, she remains the captain for the entire game.

    d. In the event that the captain is absent from the court and bench, her coach shall immediately designate a new captain.

SECTION IV—THE COACH AND OTHERS

    a. A coach's position may be on or off the bench from the 28' hash mark to the baseline. They are permitted between the 28' hash mark and the midcourt line to relay information to players but must return to the bench side of the 28' hash mark immediately or be called for a non-unsportsmanlike technical foul. A coach is not permitted to cross the midcourt line and violators will be assessed an unsportsmanlike technical foul immediately. All assistants and trainers must remain in the vicinity of the bench. Coaches and trainers are not permitted to go to the scorer's table, for any reason, except during a dead ball.

    b. A player-coach will have no special privileges. She is to conduct herself in the same manner as any other player.

    c. Any club personnel not seated on the bench must conduct themselves in a manner that would reflect favorably on the dignity of the game or that of the officials. Violations by any of the personnel indicated shall require a written report to the Basketball Operations Department for subsequent action.

    d. The bench shall be occupied only by a league-approved head coach, a maximum of two assistant coaches, players and trainer. During an altercation the head coach and assistant coaches are permitted on the court as "peace-makers."

    e. If a player, coach or assistant coach is suspended from a game or games, he/she shall not at any time before, during or after such game or games appear in any part of the arena or stands where his/her team is playing. A player, coach or assistant coach who is ejected may only remain in the dressing room of his/her team during the remainder of the game, or leave the building. A violation of this rule shall result in a fine.

SECTION V—SUBSTITUTES

    a. A substitute shall report to the scorer and position herself in the 8' Substitution Box located in front of the scorer's table. She shall inform the scorer whomshe is going to replace. The scorer shall sound the horn as soon as the ball is dead to indicate a substitution. The horn does not have to be sounded if the substitution occurs between periods or during timeouts. No substitute may enter the game after a successful field goal by either team, unless the ball is dead due to a personal foul, technical foul, timeout or violation. She may enter the game after the first of multiple free throws, whether made or missed.

    b. The substitute shall remain in the Substitution Box until she is beckoned onto the court by an official. If the ball is about to become live, the beckoning signal shall be withheld. Any player who enters the court prior to being beckoned by an official shall be assessed a non-unsportsmanlike technical foul.

    c. A substitute must be ready to enter the game when beckoned. No delays for removal of warm-up clothing will be permitted.

    d. The substitute shall not replace a free throw shooter or a player involved in a jump ball unless dictated to do so by an injury whereby she is selected by the opposing coach. At no time may she be allowed to attempt a free throw awarded as a result of a technical foul.

    e. A substitute shall be considered as being in the game when she is beckoned onto the court or recognized as being in the game by an official. Once a player is in the game, she cannot be removed until the ball is legally touched by a player on the court unless: (1) a personal foul or technical is called, (2) there is a change of possession, (3) administration of infection control rule.

    f. A substitute may be recalled from the scorer's table prior to being beckoned onto the court by an official.

    g. A player may be replaced and allowed to re-enter the game as a substitute during the same dead ball.

    h. A player must be in the Substitution Box at the time a violation occurs if the throw-in is to be administered in the backcourt. If a substitute fails to meet the requirement, she may not enter the game until the next legal opportunity.

EXCEPTION: In the last minute of each period or overtime, a reasonable amount of time will be allowed for a substitution.

i. Notification of all above infractions and ensuing procedures shall be in accordance with Rule 2—Section VII.

j. No substitutes are allowed to enter the game during an official's suspension-of-play for (1) a delay-of-game warning, (2) retrieving an errant ball (3) an inadvertent whistle or (4) any other unusual circumstance.

EXCEPTION: Suspension of play for a player bleeding. See Comments on the Rules—N.

SECTION VI—UNIFORMS (PLAYERS JERSEYS)

a. Each player shall be numbered on the front and back of her jersey with a number of solid color contrasting with the color of the shirt.

b. Each number must be not less than 3/4" in width and not less than 4" in height on both the front and back. Each player shall have her surname affixed to the back of her game jersey in letters at least 2" in height. If a team has more than one player with the same surname, each such player's first initial must appear before the surname on the back of the game jersey.

c. The home team shall wear light color jerseys and the visitors dark jerseys. For neutral court games and doubleheaders, the second team named in the official schedule shall be regarded as the home team and shall wear the light colored jerseys.

RULE NO. 4—DEFINITIONS

SECTION I—BASKET/BACKBOARD

a. A team's basket consists of the basket ring and net through which its players try to shoot the ball. The visiting team has the choice of baskets for the first half. The basket selected by the visiting team when it first enters onto the court shall be its basket for the first half.

b. The teams change baskets for the second half. All overtime periods are considered extensions of the second half.

c. Five sides of the backboard (front, two sides, bottom and top) are considered in play when contacted by the basketball. The back of the backboard and the area directly behind it are out of bounds.

SECTION II—BLOCKING

Blocking is illegal personal contact which impedes the progress of an opponent.

SECTION III—DRIBBLE

A dribble is movement of the ball, caused by a player in control, who throws or taps the ball to the floor.

a. The dribble ends when the dribbler:

    (1) Touches the ball simultaneously with both hands

    (2) Permits the ball to come to rest while she is in control of it

    (3) Tries for a field goal

    (4) Throws a pass

    (5) Touches the ball more than once while dribbling, before it touches the floor

    (6) Loses control

    (7) Allows the ball to become dead

SECTION IV—FOULS

a. A **common personal** foul is illegal physical contact which occurs with an opponent after the ball has become live, or before the horn sounds to end the period. If time expires before the personal foul occurs, the personal foul should be disregarded, unless it was unsportsmanlike.

EXCEPTION: If the foul is committed on or by a player in the act of shooting, and the shooter released the ball prior to the expiration of time on the game clock, then the foul should be administered in the same manner as with any similar play during the course of the game. See: Rule 13—Section II–a(6)

b. A **technical** foul is the penalty for unsportsmanlike conduct or violations by team members on the floor or seated on the bench. It may be assessed for illegal contact which occurs with an opponent before the ball becomes live.

c. A **double** foul is a situation in which two opponents commit personal or technical fouls against each other at approximately the same time.

d. An **offensive** foul is illegal contact, committed by an offensive player, after the ball is live and there is team control.

e. A **loose ball** foul is illegal contact, after the ball is live, when team control does not exist.

f. An **elbow** foul is making contact with the elbow in an unsportsmanlike manner, whether the ball is dead or alive.

g. A **flagrant** foul is unnecessary and/or excessive contact committed by a player against an opponent, whether the ball is dead or alive.

h. A **punching** foul is a punch by a player which makes contact with an opponent, whether the ball is dead or alive.

i. An **away-from-the-play** foul is illegal contact by the defense in the last minute of the game, and/or overtime, which occurs (1) deliberately away from the immediate area of the ball, and/or (2) prior to the ball being released on a throwin.

SECTION V—FREE THROW

A free throw is the privilege given a player to score one point by an unhindered attempt for the goal from a position directly behind the free throw line. This attempt must be made within 10 seconds.

SECTION VI—FRONTCOURT/BACKCOURT

a. A team's frontcourt consists of that part of the court between its endline and the nearer edge of the midcourt line, including the basket and inbounds part of the backboard.

b. A team's backcourt consists of the entire midcourt line and the rest of the court to include the opponent's basket and inbounds part of the backboard.

c. A ball being held by a player: (1) is in the frontcourt if neither the ball nor the player is touching the backcourt, (2) is in the backcourt if either the ball or the player is touching the backcourt.

d. A ball being dribbled is (1) in the frontcourt when the ball and both feet of the player are in the frontcourt, (2) in the backcourt if the ball or either foot of the player is in the backcourt.

e. The ball is considered in the frontcourt once it has broken the plane of the midcourt line and is not in player control.

f. The team on the offense must bring the ball across the midcourt line within 10 seconds.

EXCEPTION: (1) kicked ball, (2) punched ball, (3) personal or technical foul on the defensive team, (4) delay of game warning on the defensive team or (5) infection control.

g. Frontcourt/backcourt status is not attained until a player with the ball has established a positive position in either half during (1) a jump ball, (2) a steal by a defensive player or (3) any time the ball is loose.

h. The defensive team has no "frontcourt/backcourt."

SECTION VII—HELD BALL

A held ball occurs when two opponents have one or both hands firmly on the ball or anytime a defensive player touches the ball causing the offensive player to return to the floor with the ball in her continuous possession.

A held ball should not be called until both players have hands so firmly on the ball that neither can gain sole possession without undue roughness. If a player is lying or sitting on the floor, while in possession, she should have an opportunity to throw the ball, but a held ball should be called if there is danger of injury.

SECTION VIII—PIVOT

a. A pivot takes place when a player, who is holding the ball, steps once or more than once in any direction with the same foot, with the other foot (pivot foot) in contact with the floor.

b. If the player wishes to dribble after a pivot, the ball must be out of her hand before the pivot foot is raised off the floor.

c. If the player raises her pivot off the floor, she must pass or attempt a field goal before the foot is returned to the floor. If she fails to follow these guidelines, she has committed a traveling violation.

SECTION IX—TRAVELING

Traveling is progressing in any direction while in possession of the ball, which is in excess of prescribed limits as noted in Rule 4—Section VIII and Rule 10—Section XII.

SECTION X—SCREEN

A screen is the legal action of a player who, without causing undue contact, delays or prevents an opponent from reaching a desired position.

SECTION XI—FIELD GOAL ATTEMPT

A field goal attempt is a player's attempt to shoot the ball into her basket for a field goal. The act of shooting starts when, in the official's judgment, the player has started her shooting motion and continues until the shooting motion ceases and she returns to a normal floor position. It is not essential that the ball leave the shooter's hand. Her arm(s) might be held so that she cannot actually make an attempt.

The term is also used to include the flight of the ball until it becomes dead or is touched by a player. A tap during a jump ball or rebound is not considered a field goal attempt. However, anytime a live ball is in flight towards the rim from the playing court, the goal, if made, shall count, even if time expires or the official's whistle sounds. The field goal will not be scored if time on the game clock expires before the ball leaves the player's hand.

EXCEPTION: —Rule 5—Section III(2).

SECTION XII—THROW-IN

A throw-in is a method of putting the ball in play from out-of-bounds in accordance with Rule 8—Section III. The throw-in begins when the ball is at the disposal of the team or player entitled to it, and ends when the ball is released by the thrower-in.

SECTION XIII—LAST MINUTE

When the game clock shows 1:00, the game is considered to be in the oneminute period.

SECTION XIV—SUSPENSION OF PLAY

An official can suspend play for retrieving an errant ball, re-setting the timing devices, delay-of-game warning, inadvertent whistle, or any other unusual circumstance. During such a suspension, neither team is permitted to substitute and the defensive team may not be granted a timeout. Play shall be resumed from the point of interruption.

EXCEPTION: See Comments on Rules-N.

SECTION XV—POINT OF INTERRUPTION

Where the ball is located when the whistle sounds.

SECTION XVI—TEAM CONTROL

A team is in control when a player is holding, dribbling or passing the ball. Team control ends when the defensive team deflects the ball or there is a field goal attempt.

SECTION XVII—FUMBLE

A player who is holding the ball and fumbles it out of her control may recover the ball. If her pivot foot moves to recover the ball, she must then pass or shoot the ball. If she fumbles and recovers it without moving her pivot foot and before the ball touches the floor, she retains her status before the fumble.

SECTION XVIII—TEAM POSSESSION

A team is in possession when a player is holding, dribbling or passing the ball. Team possession ends when the defensive team gains possession or there is a field goal attempt which hits the rim.

RULE NO. 5—SCORING AND TIMING

SECTION I—SCORING

a. A legal field goal or free throw attempt shall be scored when a live ball from the playing area enters the basket from above and remains in or passes through the net.

b. A successful field goal attempt from the area on or inside the three-point field goal line shall count two points.

c. A successful field goal attempt from the area outside the three-point field goal line shall count three points.

(1) The shooter must have at least one foot on the floor outside the three-point field goal line prior to the attempt.

(2) The shooter may not be touching the floor on or inside the three-point field goal line.

(3) The shooter may contact the three-point field goal line, or land in the two-point field goal area, after the ball is released.

d. A field goal accidentally scored in an opponent's basket shall be added to the opponent's score, credited to the opposing player nearest the shooter and mentioned in a footnote.

e. It is a violation for a player to attempt a field goal at an opponent's basket. The ball shall be awarded to the opposing team out-of-bounds at the free throw line extended.

f. A successful free throw attempt shall count one point.

g. An unsuccessful free throw attempt which is tapped into the basket shall count two points and shall be credited to the player who tapped the ball in.

h. If there is a discrepancy in the score and it cannot be resolved, the running score shall be official.

SECTION II—TIMING

a. All periods of regulation play in the WNBA will be ten minutes.

b. All overtime periods of play will be five minutes.

c. Fifteen minutes will be permitted between halves of all games.

d. 120 seconds will be permitted for mandatory timeouts and between the first and second periods, the third and fourth periods and before any overtime period. 60 seconds will be permitted for all other full timeouts.

e. A team is permitted a total of 30 seconds to replace a disqualified player.

f. The game is considered to be in the one-minute period when the game clock shows 1:00 or less time remaining in the period.

g. The public address operator is required to announce that there is one minute remaining in each period.

h. The game clock shall be equipped to show tenths-of-a-second during the last minute of each period.

SECTION III—END OF PERIOD

a. Each period ends when time expires.

EXCEPTIONS:

(1) If a live ball is in flight toward the basket, the period ends when the goal is made, missed or touched by an offensive player.

(2) If the official's whistle sounds prior to the horn or :00.0 on the clock, the period is not over and time must be added to the clock.

(3) If a live ball is in flight toward the basket when the horn sounds ending a period, and it subsequently is touched by: (a) a defensive player, the goal, if successful, shall count; or (b) an offensive player, the period has ended.

(4) If a timeout request is made at approximately the instant time expires for a period, the period ends and the timeout shall not be granted.

(5) If there is a foul called on or by a player in the act of shooting, the period will end after the foul is penalized. (See Rule 13— Section II—a[6])

b. If the ball is dead and the game clock shows :00.0, the period has ended even though the horn may not have sounded.

EXCEPTION: See Rule 13—Section II—a(6).

SECTION IV—TIE SCORE—OVERTIME

If the score is tied at the end of the fourth period, play shall resume in 120 seconds without change of baskets for any of the overtime periods required. (See Rule 5—Section II—d for the amount of time between overtime periods.)

SECTION V—STOPPAGE OF TIMING DEVICES

a. The timing devices shall be stopped whenever the official's whistle sounds indicating one of the following:

(1) A personal or technical foul.

(2) A jump ball.

(3) A floor violation.

(4) An unusual delay.

(5) A suspension-of-play.

(6) A regular or 20-second timeout.

b. The timing devices shall be stopped during the last minute of each period and/or overtime(s) following a successful field goal attempt.

c. Officials may not use official time to permit a player to change or repair equipment.

SECTION VI—20-SECOND TIMEOUT

A player's request for a 20-second timeout shall be granted only when the ball is dead or in control by a player on the team making the request. A request at any other time shall be ignored.

EXCEPTION: The head coach may request a 20-second timeout if there is a suspension of play to administer Comments on the Rules—N—Guidelines for Infection Control.

a. Each team is entitled to one (1) 20-second timeout per half. 20-second timeouts not used in the first half will carryover to the second half.

b. For the overtime period, each team is entitled to one additional 20-second timeout plus one unused 20-second timeout carried over from the second half for a maximum of two 20-second timeouts per team.

c. During a 20-second timeout, both teams may have unlimited substitutions.

d. The official shall instruct the timer to record the 20 seconds and to inform him/her when the time has expired. A regular timeout will be charged if play is unable to resume at the expiration of that 20-second timeout limit.

EXCEPTIONS: No regular time-out remaining or an injured player is on the court.

e. This rule may be used for any reason, including a request for a rule interpretation. If the correction is sustained, no timeout shall be charged.

f. Players should say "20-second timeout" when requesting 20-second timeout.

g. If a 20-second timeout is awarded to the offensive team during the last minute of the fourth period and/or any overtime period and (1) the ball is out-of-bounds in the backcourt (except for a suspension of play after a team had advanced the ball), or (2) after securing the ball from a rebound in the backcourt and prior to any advance of the ball (3) after the offensive team secures the ball from a change of possession in the backcourt and prior to any advance of the ball, the timeout shall be granted. Upon resumption of play, the team granted the timeout shall have the option of putting the ball into play at the 28' hash mark in the frontcourt, with the ball having to be passed into the frontcourt, or at the designated spot out-of-bounds.

However, once the ball is (1) thrown in from out-of-bounds, or (2) dribbled or passed after receiving it from a rebound or a change of possession, the timeout shall be granted, and, upon resumption of play, the ball shall be inbounded on the sideline where play was interrupted. In the last minute of fourth period play and/or any overtime period, the official shall ask the head coach the type of time-out desired—(regular or 20-second)—prior to notifying the scorer's table. This applies only to a requested timeout.

The time on the game clock and the 24-second clock shall remain as when the timeout was called. In order for the option to be available under the conditions in Section VI(g), the offensive team must call two successive timeouts.

h. If a 20-second timeout has been granted and a mandatory timeout by the same team is due, only the mandatory timeout will be charged. If a 20-second timeout has been granted and a mandatory timeout by the other team is due, both the 20-second timeout and the mandatory timeout will be charged.

i. A 20-second timeout shall not be granted to the defensive team during an official's suspension-of-play for (1) delay-of-game warning, (2) retrieving an errant ball, (3) an inadvertent whistle or (4) any other unusual circumstance.

EXCEPTION: Suspension of play for a player bleeding. See Comments on the Rules—N.

SECTION VII—REGULAR TIMEOUTS–120/60 SECONDS

A player's request for a timeout shall be granted only when the ball is dead or in control by a player on the team making the request. A request at any other time shall be ignored.

a. There must be one (1) mandatory (120-second) timeout in the first and third period and two (2) mandatory (120-second) timeouts in the second and fourth period. Any regular timeout called by a team shall become the next mandatory timeout in that period (if any mandatory timeouts remain in that period) and shall be charged to the team that called the timeout. If neither team has called a regular timeout prior to 4:59 of the first or third period, it shall be mandatory for the Official Scorer to take a timeout at the first dead ball and charge it to neither team. If neither team has called a regular timeout prior to 5:59 of the second or fourth period, it shall be mandatory for the Official Scorer to take a timeout at the first dead ball and charge it to the home team (or to neither team if the first regular timeout of the first or third period was charged to one of the teams). If no subsequent regular timeouts are taken prior to 2:59 of the second or fourth period, it shall be mandatory for the Official Scorer to take a timeout at the first dead ball and charge it to the team not previously charged (or to neither team if both previously charged timeouts were charged to a team).

b. Each team is entitled to two (2) regular timeouts per half during regulation play. One (1) of those timeouts will generally be charged as a mandatory timeout (unless, due to the timing of called timeouts, the other team is charged with two (2) mandatory timeouts in a half, in which case such team will not be charged with any mandatory timeouts in such half). The first regular timeout in the first and third period and the first two regular timeouts in the second and fourth period shall be 120 seconds in length. All other regular timeouts shall be 60 seconds in length. Unused regular timeouts will not carryover from the first half to the second half.

c. In overtime periods, each team shall be allowed one (1) regular timeout plus one 20-second timeout. Unused regular timeouts from the 2nd half will not be carried over into overtime. However, unused 20-second timeouts can be carried over, with a maximum of two 20-second timeouts per team permitted in any overtime period. There is no restriction as to when a team must call its timeouts during any overtime period. No regular timeout shall be granted to the defensive team during an official's suspension-of-play for (1) a delay-of-game warning, (2) retrieving an errant ball, (3) an inadvertent whistle, or (4) any other unusual circumstance.

EXCEPTION: Suspension-of-play for player bleeding. See Comments on the Rules—N.

d. If a regular timeout is awarded to the offensive team during the last minute of the fourth period and/or any overtime period and (1) the ball is out-of-bounds in the backcourt (except for a suspension of play after the team had advanced the ball), or (2) after securing the ball from a rebound in the backcourt and prior to any advance of the ball, or (3) after securing the ball from a change of possession in the backcourt and prior to any advance of the ball, the timeout shall be granted. Upon resumption of play, the team granted the timeout shall have the option of putting the ball into play at the 28' hash mark in the frontcourt, with the ball having to be passed into the frontcourt, or at the designated spot out-of-bounds.

However, once the ball is (1) thrown in from out-of-bounds, or (2) dribbled or passed after receiving it from a rebound or a change of possession, the timeout shall be granted, and, upon resumption of play, the ball shall be inbounded on the sideline where play was interrupted. In the last minute of the second half and/or any overtime period, the official shall ask the head coach the type of timeout desired—(regular or 20-second)—prior to notifying the scorer's table. This applies only to a requested timeout.

The time on the game clock and the 24-second clock shall remain as when the timeout was called. In order for the option to be available under the conditions in Section VII(d), the offensive team must call two successive timeouts.

e. No timeout shall be charged if it is called to question a rule interpretation and the correction is sustained.

f. Requests for a timeout in excess of the authorized number shall be granted and a technical foul shall be assessed. Following the timeout, the ball will be awarded to the opposing team and play shall resume with a throw-in nearest the spot where play was interrupted. If a player is injured and cannot be removed from the playing court during stoppage of play, no excessive timeout will be charged and play will resume when playing conditions are safe.

g. During a regular timeout, both teams may have unlimited substitutions.

h. If a player is injured as a result of a player on the opposing team committing a flagrant foul or an unsportsmanlike act, play will resume when playing conditions are safe and no timeout will be charged as a result of any delay due to the player's injury.

SECTION VIII—TIMEOUT REQUESTS

a. If an official, upon receiving a timeout request (regular or 20-second) by the defensive team, inadvertently signals for a timeout while the play is in progress, play shall be suspended and the team in possession shall put the ball in play immediately at the sideline nearest where the ball was when the signal was given. The team in possession shall have only the time remaining of the original ten seconds in which to move the ball into the frontcourt. The 24-second clock shall remain the same.

b. If an official, upon receiving a timeout request (regular or 20-second) from the defensive team, inadvertently signals for a timeout during: (1) a successful field goal or free throw attempt, the point(s) shall be scored; (2) an unsuccessful field goal attempt, play shall be resumed with a jump ball at the center circle between any two opponents; (3) an unsuccessful free throw attempt, the official shall rule disconcerting and award a substitute free throw.

c. If an official inadvertently blows his/her whistle during (1) a successful field goal or free throw attempt, the points shall be scored, or (2) an unsuccessful field goal or free throw attempt, play shall be resumed with a jump ball at the center circle between any two opponents.

d. When a team is granted a regular or 20-second time-out, play shall not resume until the full 120 seconds, 60 seconds, or 20 seconds, as the case may be, have elapsed. The throw-in shall be nearest the spot where play was suspended. The throw-in shall be on the sideline, if the ball was in play when the request was granted.

e. A player shall not be granted a timeout (regular or 20-second) if both of her feet are in the air and any part of her body has broken the vertical plane of the boundary line (including the midcourt line).

f. If a player calls a timeout to stop play (or after a stoppage of play) due to an injury to herself or one of her teammates, a 20-second timeout will be charged to the team. If the team has exhausted its allotment of 20-second timeouts, a regular timeout will be charged. No more than one timeout (20-second or regular) will be charged during an injury timeout situation. Officials will not suspend play after an injury unless bleeding occurs. See Comments on the Rules—N—Guidelines for Infection Control.

SECTION IX—TIME-IN

a. After time has been out, the game clock shall be started when the ball is legally touched by any player within the playing area of the court. The timer is authorized to start the game clock if officials neglect to signal.

b. On a free throw that is unsuccessful and the ball continues in play, the game clock shall be started when the missed free throw is legally touched by any player.

c. If play is resumed by a throw-in from out-of-bounds, the game clock shall be started when the ball is legally touched by any player within the playing area of the court.

d. If play is resumed with a jump ball, the game clock shall be started when the ball is legally tapped.

RULE NO. 6—PUTTING THE BALL IN PLAY—LIVE/DEAD BALL

SECTION I—START OF GAMES/PERIODS AND OTHERS

a. The game and overtime(s) shall be started with a jump ball in the center circle.

b. The team which gains first possession of the game will put the ball into play at their opponent's endline to begin the fourth period. The other team will put the ball into play at their opponent's endline at the beginning of the second and third periods.

c. In putting the ball into play, the thrower-in may run along the endline or pass it to a teammate who is also out-of-bounds at the endline—as after a score.

d. After any dead ball, play shall be resumed by a jump ball, a throw-in or by placing the ball at the disposal of a free-thrower.

e. On the following infractions, the ball shall be awarded to the opposing team out-of-bounds on the nearest sideline at the free throw line extended:

(1) Three-seconds
(2) Ball entering basket from below
(3) Illegal assist in scoring
(4) Offensive screen set out-of-bounds
(5) Free throw violation by the offensive team
(6) Flagrant foul-penalty (1) or (2) and punching foul
(7) Jump ball violation at free throw circle
(8) Ball passing directly behind backboard
(9) Offensive basket interference
(10) Ball hitting horizontal basket support
(11) Loose ball fouls which occur inside the free throw line extended

f. On the following infractions, the ball shall be awarded to the opposing team on the baseline at the nearest spot outside the three-second area extended:

(1) Ball out-of-bounds on baseline
(2) Ball hitting vertical basket support

(3) Defensive goaltending (all privileges remain)

(4) During a throw-in violation on the baseline

g. On the following infractions, the ball shall be awarded to the opposing team on the sideline at the nearest spot but no nearer to the baseline than the free throw line extended:

(1) Traveling

(2) Double dribble

(3) Swinging of elbows

(4) 24-second violation

(5) Striking with fist or intentionally kicking the ball on any situation except a throw-in

h. If the ball is kicked or punched during any throw-in, the ball will be returned to the original throw-in spot with all privileges, if any, remaining.

i. Following a regular or 20-second timeout that was called while the ball was alive, the ball shall be awarded out-of-bounds on the sideline at the nearest spot. For all other timeouts, play shall resume where it was interrupted.

EXCEPTION: Rule 5—Section VII—f.

j. On a violation which requires putting the ball in play in the backcourt, the official will give the ball to the offensive player as soon as she is in a position out-of-bounds and ready to accept the ball.

EXCEPTION: In the last minute of each half or overtime, a reasonable amount of time shall be allowed for a substitution.

k. On any play where the ball goes out of bounds on the sideline, the ball shall be awarded to the opposing team at that spot.

SECTION II—LIVE BALL

a. The ball becomes live when:

(1) It is tossed by an official on any jump ball

(2) It is at the disposal of the offensive player for a throw-in

(3) It is placed at the disposal of a free throw shooter

SECTION III—BALL IS ALIVE

a. The ball becomes alive when:

(1) It is legally tapped by one of the participants of a jump ball

(2) It is released by the thrower-in

(3) It is released by the free throw shooter on a free throw which will remain in play

SECTION IV—DEAD BALL

The ball becomes dead and/or remains dead when the following occurs:

(1) Official blows his/her whistle

(2) Free throw which will not remain in play (free throw which will be followed by another free throw, technical, flagrant, etc.)

(3) Following a successful field goal or free throw that will remain in play, until player possession out-of-bounds. Contact which is not considered unsportsmanlike shall be ignored (See Rule 12A—Section V–i)

(4) Time expires at the end of any period

EXCEPTION: If a live ball is in flight, the ball becomes dead when the goal is made, missed or touched by an offensive player.

SECTION V—JUMP BALLS IN CENTER CIRCLE

a. The ball shall be put into play in the center circle by a jump ball between any two opponents:

(1) At the start of the game

(2) At the start of each overtime period

(3) A double free throw violation

(4) Double foul during a loose ball situation

(5) The ball becomes dead when neither team is in control and no field goal or infraction is involved

(6) The ball comes to rest on the basket flange or becomes lodged between the basket ring and the backboard

(7) A double foul which occurs as a result of a difference in opinion between officials

(8) A suspension of play occurs during a loose ball

(9) A fighting foul occurs during a loose ball situation

b. In all cases above, the jump ball shall be between any two opponents in the game at that time. If injury, ejection or disqualification makes it necessary for any player to be replaced, her substitute may not participate in the jump ball.

SECTION VI—OTHER JUMP BALLS

a. The ball shall be put into play by a jump ball at the circle which is closest to the spot where:

(1) A held ball occurs

(2) A ball out-of-bounds caused by both teams

(3) An official is in doubt as to who last touched the ball

b. The jump ball shall be between the two involved players unless injury or ejection precludes one of the jumpers from participation. If the injured or ejected player must leave the game, the coach of the opposing team shall select from his/her opponent's bench a player who will replace the injured or ejected player. The injured player will not be permitted to re-enter the game.

EXCEPTION: Excessive bleeding. See Comments on the Rules—N.

SECTION VII—RESTRICTIONS GOVERNING JUMP BALLS

a. Each jumper must have at least one foot on or inside that half of the jumping circle which is farthest from her own basket. Each jumper must have both feet within the restraining circle.

b. The ball must be tapped by one or both of the players participating in the jump ball after it reaches its highest point. If the ball falls to the floor without being tapped by at least one of the jumpers, the official off the ball shall whistle the ball dead and signal another toss.

c. Neither jumper may tap the tossed ball before it reaches its highest point.

d. Neither jumper may leave her half of the jumping circle until the ball has been tapped.

e. Neither jumper may catch the tossed or tapped ball until it touches one of the eight non-jumpers, the floor, the basket or the backboard.

f. Neither jumper is permitted to tap the ball more than twice on any jump ball.

g. The eight non-jumpers will remain outside the restraining circle until the ball has been tapped. Teammates may not occupy adjacent positions around the restraining circle if an opponent desires one of the positions. No player may position herself immediately behind an opponent on the restraining circle. Penalty for c., d., e., f., g.: Ball awarded out-of-bounds to the opponent.

h. Player position on the restraining circle is determined by the direction of a player's basket. The player whose basket is nearest shall have first choice of position, with position being alternated thereafter.

RULE NO. 7—24-SECOND CLOCK

SECTION I—DEFINITION

For the purpose of clarification, the 24-second device shall be referred to as "the 24-second clock."

SECTION II—STARTING AND STOPPING OF 24-SECOND CLOCK

a. The 24-second clock will start when a team gains new possession of a ball which is in play.

b. On a throw-in, the 24-second clock shall start when the ball is legally touched on the court by a player.

c. A team must attempt a field goal within 24 seconds after gaining possession of the ball. To constitute a legal field goal attempt, the following conditions must be complied with:

(1) The ball must leave the player's hand prior to the expiration of 24 seconds.

(2) After leaving the player's hand(s), the ball must make contact with the basket ring.

d. A team is considered in possession of the ball when holding, passing or dribbling. The team is considered in possession of the ball even though the ball has been batted away but the opponent has not gained possession.

e. Team possession ends when:

(1) There is a legal field goal attempt

(2) The opponent gains possession

f. If a ball is touched by a defensive player who does not gain possession of the ball, the 24-second clock shall continue to run.

g. If a defensive player causes the ball to go out-of-bounds or causes the ball to enter the basket ring from below, the 24-second clock is stopped and the offensive team shall be awarded the ball.The offensive team shall have only the unexpired time remaining on the 24-second clock in which to attempt a field goal. If the 24-second clock reads 0,a 24-second violation has occurred, even though the horn may not have sounded.

h. If during any period there are 24 seconds OR LESS left to play in the period, the 24-second clock shall not function following a change of possession.

i. If an official inadvertently blows his/her whistle and the 24-second clock buzzer sounds while the ball is in the air, play shall be suspended and play resumed by a jump ball between any two opponents at the center circle, if the shot hits the rim and is unsuccessful. If the shot does not hit the rim a 24-second violation has occurred. If the shot is successful, the goal shall count, and the ball shall be inbounded as after any successful field goal. It should be noted that even though the official blows his/her whistle, all provisions of the above rule apply.

j. If there is a question whether or not an attempt to score has been made within the 24 seconds allowed, the final decision shall be made by the officials.

k. Whenever the 24-second clock reads 0 and the ball is dead for any reason other than a kicking violation, punched ball violation, personal foul or a technical foul by the defensive team, a 24-second violation has occurred.

SECTION III—PUTTING BALL IN PLAY AFTER VIOLATION

If a team fails to attempt a field goal within the time allotted, a 24-second violation shall be called. The ball is awarded to the defensive team on the sideline nearest the spot where play was suspended, but no nearer to the baseline than the free throw line extended.

SECTION IV—RESETTING 24-SECOND CLOCK

a. The 24-second clock shall be reset when a special situation occurs which warrants such action.

b. The 24-second clock is never reset on technical fouls and/or delay-of-game warnings called on the offensive team.

c. The 24-second clock shall be reset to 24 seconds anytime the following occurs:

    (1) Change of possession

    (2) Personal foul that results in the ball being inbounded in the backcourt

    (3) Jump balls which are not the result of a held ball caused by the defense

    (4) Violation that results in the ball being inbounded in the backcourt

    (5) Ball from the playing court contacting the basket ring of the team which is in possession

    (6) All flagrant and punching fouls

d. The 24-second clock shall remain the same as when play was interrupted or reset to 14 seconds, whichever is greater, anytime the following occurs:

    (1) Personal foul by the defense that results in the ball being inbounded in the frontcourt

    (2) Technical foul and/or delay-of-game warnings on the defensive team

    (3) Kicked or punched ball by the defensive team that results in the ball being inbounded in the offensive team's frontcourt

    (4) Infection control

    (5) Jump balls retained by the offensive team as the result of any violation by the defensive team during a jump ball which results in a frontcourt throw-in

e. The 24-second clock shall remain the same as when play was stopped, or reset to 5 seconds, whichever is greater, on jump balls retained by the offensive team as a result of a held ball caused by the defense.

RULE NO. 8—OUT-OF-BOUNDS AND THROW-IN

SECTION I—PLAYER

The player is out-of-bounds when she touches the floor or any object on or outside a boundary. For location of a player in the air, her position is that from which she last touched the floor.

SECTION II—BALL

a. The ball is out-of-bounds when it touches a player who is out-of-bounds or any other person, the floor, or any object on, above or outside of a boundary or the supports or back of the backboard.

b. Any ball that rebounds or passes directly behind the backboard, in either direction, from any point is considered out-of-bounds.

c. The ball is caused to go out-of-bounds by the last player to touch it before it goes out, provided it is out-of-bounds because of touching something other than a player. If the ball is out-of-bounds because of touching a player who is on or outside a boundary, such player caused it to go out.

d. If the ball goes out-of-bounds and was last touched simultaneously by two opponents, both of whom are inbounds or out-of-bounds, or if the official is in doubt as to who last touched the ball, or if the officials disagree, play shall be resumed by a jump ball between the two involved players in the nearest restraining circle.

e. After the ball is out-of-bounds, the team shall designate a player to make the throw-in. She shall make the throw-in at the spot out-of-bounds nearest where the ball crossed the boundary. The designated thrower-in shall not be changed unless the offensive team makes a substitution or there is a regular or 20-second timeout.

f. If the ball is interfered with by an opponent seated on the bench or standing on the sideline (Rule 12A—Section II—a[7]), it shall be awarded to the offended team nearest the spot of the violation.

SECTION III—THE THROW-IN

a. The throw-in starts when the ball is at the disposal of a player entitled to the throw-in. She shall release the ball inbounds within 5 seconds from the time the throw-in starts. Until the passed ball has crossed the plane of the boundary, no player shall have any part of her person over the boundary line and teammates shall not occupy positions parallel or adjacent to the baseline if an opponent desires one of those positions. The defensive player shall have the right to be between her opponent and the basket.

b. On a throw-in which goes out of bounds and is not touched inbounds by a player, the ball is returned to the original throw-in spot.

c. After a score, field goal or free throw, the latter coming as the result of a personal foul, any player of the team not credited with the score shall put the ball into play from any point out-of-bounds at the endline of the court where the point(s) were scored. She may pass the ball to a teammate behind the endline; however, the five-second throw-in rule applies.

d. After a free throw violation by the shooter or her teammate, the throw-in is made from out-of-bounds at either end of the free throw line extended.

e. Any ball out-of-bounds in a team's frontcourt or at the midcourt line cannot be passed into the backcourt. On all backcourt and midcourt violations, the ball shall be awarded to the opposing team at the midcourt line, and must be passed into the frontcourt.

f. A throw-in which touches the floor, or any object on or outside the boundary line, or touches anything above the playing surface is a violation. The ball must be thrown directly inbounds.

EXCEPTION: Rule 8—Section III—c.

PENALTY: Violation of this rule is loss of possession, and the ball must be inbounded at the previous spot of the throw-in.

RULE NO. 9—FREE THROWS AND PENALTIES

SECTION I—POSITIONS AND VIOLATIONS

a. When a free throw is awarded, an official shall put the ball in play by placing it at the disposal of the free throw shooter. The shooter shall be above the free throw line and within the upper half of the free throw circle. She shall attempt the free throw within 10 seconds in such a way that the ball enters the basket or touches the ring.

PENALTY: If there is a violation and the free throw attempt is to remain in play, the opposing team shall inbound on either sideline at the free throw line extended. If both teams commit a violation during this free throw, a jump ball shall be administered at midcourt between any two opponents in the game. If the opponent's violation is disconcertion, then a substitute free throw shall be awarded.

If there is a violation and the free throw attempt is not to remain in play, then play will continue from that point. If an opponent also commits a violation (double violation), then play will also continue from that point. If the opponent's violation is disconcertion, then a substitute free throw shall be awarded.

b. The free throw shooter may not step over the plane of the free throw line until the ball touches the basket ring, backboard or the free throw ends.

PENALTY: This is a violation by the shooter on all free throw attempts and no point can be scored.

If there is a violation and the free throw attempt is to remain in play, the opposing team shall inbound on either sideline at the free throw line extended. If an opponent also commits a violation (double violation) during this free throw, a jump ball shall be administered at midcourt between any two opponents in the game.

If there is a violation and the free throw attempt is not to remain in play, then play will continue from that point. If an opponent also commits a violation (double violation), then play will also continue from that point.

c. The free throw shooter shall not purposely fake a free throw attempt.

PENALTY: This is a violation by the shooter on all free throw attempts and a double violation should not be called if an opponent violates any free throw rules.

If the free throw attempt is to remain in play, the opposing team shall inbound on either sideline at the free throw line extended. If the free throw attempt is not to remain in play, then play will continue from that point

d. During a free throw attempt for a personal foul, each of the spaces nearest the end-line must be occupied by an opponent of the free throw shooter. Teammates of the free throw shooter must occupy the next adjacent spaces on each side. Only one of the third spaces may be occupied by an opponent of the free throw shooter. It is not mandatory that either of the third spaces be occupied by an opponent but may not be occupied by a teammate. If there is a discrepancy, teammates of the free throw shooter will occupy the spaces first.

Players occupying lane spaces may not extend themselves over their space in front of an opponent or be touching the lane line or floor inside the line when the ball is released by the shooter. They may not vacate their lane space more than 3' from the lane line before the ball is released.

Players not occupying lane spaces must remain behind the free throw line and at least 3' from the three-point arc.

PENALTY: If the free throw attempt is to remain in play and a teammate of the shooter violates, no point can be scored and the opposing team will inbound on either sideline at the free throw line extended. If an opponent violates, the shooter shall receive a substitute free throw if her attempt is unsuccessful but shall be ignored if the attempt is successful. If a teammate and opponent both violate, a jump ball shall be administered at midcourt between any two opponents in the game.

If the free throw attempt is not to remain in play, no violation can occur regardless of which player or players violate since no advantage is gained unless there is a disconcertion violation by an opponent to which a substitute free throw will be awarded.

e. If the ball is to become dead after the last free throw attempt, players shall not occupy positions along the free throw lanes. All players must remain behind the three point line above the free throw line extended until the ball is released.

PENALTY: No violations can occur regardless of which player or players violate since no advantage is gained unless there is a disconcertion violation by an opponent to which a substitute free throw will be awarded.

f. During all free throw attempts, no opponent in the game shall disconcert the shooter once the ball is placed at her disposal. The following are acts of disconcertion:

(1) Raising her arms when positioned on the lane line on a free throw which will not remain in play.

(2) Waiving her arms or making a sudden movement when in the visual field of the shooter during any free throw attempt.

(3) Talking to the free throw shooter or talking in a loud disruptive manner during any free throw attempt.

PENALTY: No penalty is assessed if the free throw is successful. A substitute free throw will be administered if the attempt is unsuccessful.

g. A player shall not touch the ball or the basket ring when the ball is using the basket ring as its lower base nor touch the ball while it is in the imaginary cylinder above the ring after touching the basket ring or backboard.

PENALTY: If the free throw attempt is to remain in play and a teammate of the shooter violates, no point can be scored and the opposing team will inbound on either sideline at the free throw line extended. If an opponent violates, the shot shall be scored and play will continue as after any successful free throw with the official administering the throw-in.

If the free throw attempt is not remaining in play, no point can be scored if the violation is by a teammate and the shooter will attempt her next free throw. One point shall be scored if the violation is by an opponent and the shooter will attempt her next free throw.

h. No player shall touch the ball before it touches the basket ring or backboard.

PENALTY: If the free throw attempt is to remain in play and a teammate of the shooter violates, no point can be scored and the opposing team will inbound on either sideline at the free throw line extended. If an opponent violates, one point shall be scored and an additional free throw shall be awarded the same shooter.

If the free throw attempt is not remaining in play, no point can be scored if the violation is by a teammate and the shooter will attempt her next free throw. One point shall be scored if the violation is by an opponent and the shooter will attempt her next free throw.

i. During all free throw attempts, if an official suspends play before the free throw attempt is released, no violations can occur.

SECTION II—SHOOTING OF FREE THROW

a. The free throw(s) awarded because of a personal foul shall be attempted by the offended player.

EXCEPTIONS:

(1) If the offended player is injured or ejected from the game and cannot attempt the awarded free throw(s), the opposing coach shall select, from the opponents bench, the replacement player. That player will attempt the free throw(s) and the injured player will not be permitted to re-enter the game. The substitute must remain in the game until the ball is legally touched by a player on the court.

EXCEPTION: Rule 3—Section V–e.

(2) If the offended player is injured and unable to attempt the awarded free throw(s) due to any unsportsmanlike act, her coach may designate any eligible member of the squad to attempt the free throw(s). The injured player will be permitted to re-enter the game.

(3) If the offended player is disqualified and unable to attempt the awarded free throw(s), her coach shall designate an eligible substitute from the bench. That substitute will attempt the free throw(s) and cannot be removed until the ball is legally touched by a player on the court.

EXCEPTION: Rule 3—Section V–e.

(4) Away from play foul—Rule 12B—Section X–a(1).

b. A free throw attempt, personal or technical, shall be illegal if an official does not handle the ball and is in the free throw lane area during the actual attempt.

c. If multiple free throws are awarded, all those which remain must be attempted, if the first and/or second attempt is nullified by an offensive player's violation.

SECTION III—NEXT PLAY

After a successful free throw which is not followed by another free throw, the ball shall be put into play by a throw-in, as after any successful field goal.

EXCEPTION: After a free throw for a foul which occurs during a dead ball which immediately precedes any period, the ball shall be put into play by the team entitled to the throw-in in the period which follows. (See Rule 6—Section I–b).

This includes flagrant and punching fouls.

RULE NO. 10—VIOLATIONS AND PENALTIES

SECTION I—OUT-OF-BOUNDS

a. A player shall not cause the ball to go out-of-bounds.

PENALTY: Loss of ball. The ball is awarded to opponents at the boundary line nearest the spot of the violation.

EXCEPTION: On a throw-in which goes out of bounds and is not legally touched by a player in the game, the ball is returned to the original throw-in spot.

SECTION II—DRIBBLE

a. A player shall not run with the ball without dribbling it.

b. A player in control of a dribble who steps on or outside a boundary line, even though not touching the ball while on or outside that boundary line, shall not be allowed to return inbounds and continue her dribble. She may not even be the first player to touch the ball after she has re-established a position inbounds.

c. A player may not dribble a second time after she has voluntarily ended her first dribble.

d. A player may dribble a second time if she lost control of the ball because of:

(1) A field goal attempt at her basket, provided the ball touches the backboard or basket ring

(2) An opponent touching the ball

(3) A pass or fumble which touches her backboard, basket ring or is touched by another player

PENALTY: Loss of ball. Ball is awarded to the opposing team on the sideline nearest the spot of the violation but no nearer to the baseline than the free throw line extended.

SECTION III—THROWER-IN

a. A thrower-in shall not (1) carry the ball onto the court; (2) fail to release the ball within 5 seconds; (3) touch it on the court before it has touched another player; (4) leave the designated throw-in spot; (5) throw the ball so that it enters the basket before touching anyone on the court; (6) step on the court before the ball is released; (7) cause the ball to go out-of-bounds without being legally touched by a player in the game; (8) leave the playing surface to gain an advantage on a throw-in; (9) hand the ball to a player on the court.

EXCEPTION: After a field goal or free throw as a result of a personal foul, the thrower-in may run the end line or pass to a teammate behind the end line.

b. Once an official recognizes the designated player to throw the ball in, there shall be no change of the thrower-in unless the offensive team makes a substitution or uses a regular or 20-second timeout, or there is a suspension of play.

PENALTY: Loss of ball. The ball is awarded to the opponent at the original spot of the throw-in.

SECTION IV—STRIKE THE BALL

a. A player shall not kick the ball or strike it with the fist.

b. Kicking the ball or striking it with any part of the leg is a violation when it is an intentional act. The ball accidentally striking the foot, the leg or fist is not a violation.

c. A player may not use any part of her leg to intentionally move or secure the ball.

PENALTY: (1) If the violation is by the offense, the ball is awarded to the opponent nearest the spot of the violation but no nearer the baseline than the free throw line extended.

(2) If the violation is by the defense, the offensive team retains possession of the ball at the sideline nearest the spot of the violation but no nearer the baseline than the free throw line extended.

(3) If the violation occurs during a throw-in, the opposing team retains possession at the spot of the original throw-in with all privileges, if any, remaining.

SECTION V—JUMP BALL

a. A player shall not violate the jump ball rule (Rule 6—Section V).

b. During a jump ball, a personal foul committed prior to either team obtaining possession shall be ruled a "loose ball" foul. If the violation or foul occurs prior to the ball being legally tapped, neither the game clock or 24-second clock shall be started.

PENALTY: (1) In (a) above, the ball is awarded to the opponent on the sideline nearest the spot of the violation.

(2) In (a) above, if there is a violation by each team, or if the official makes a bad toss, the toss shall be repeated with the same jumpers. (3) In (b) above, free throws may or may not be awarded, consistent with whether the penalty is in effect (Rule 12B—Section VIII).

SECTION VI—THREE-SECOND RULE

a. An offensive player shall not remain for more than three seconds in that part of her free throw lane between the endline and extended 4' (imaginary) off the court and the farther edge of the free throw line while the ball is in control of her team.

b. Allowance may be made for a player who, having been in this area for less than three seconds, is in the act of shooting at the end of the third second. Under these conditions, the 3-second count is discontinued while her continuous motion is toward the basket. If that continuous motion ceases, the previous 3-second count is continued. This is also true if it is imminent the offensive player will exit this area.

c. The 3-second count shall not begin until the ball is in control in the offensive team's frontcourt. No violation can occur if the ball is batted away by an opponent.

PENALTY: Loss of ball. The ball is awarded to the opposing team at the sideline at the free throw line extended.

SECTION VII—TEN-SECOND RULE

A team shall not be in continuous possession of a ball which is in its backcourt for more than 10 consecutive seconds.

EXCEPTION (1): A new 10 seconds is awarded if the defense: (a) kicks or punches the ball with the fist, (b) is assessed a personal or technical foul, or (c) is issued a delay of game warning.

EXCEPTION (2): A new 10 seconds is awarded if play is suspended to administer Comments on the Rules—N—Infection Control and all jump balls.

PENALTY: Loss of ball. The ball is awarded to the opposing team at the midcourt line, with the ball having to be passed into the frontcourt.

SECTION VIII—BALL IN BACKCOURT

a. A player shall not be the first to touch a ball which she or a teammate caused to go from frontcourt to backcourt while her team was in control of the ball.

b. During a jump ball, a try for a goal, or a situation in which a player taps the ball away from a congested area, as during rebounding, in an attempt to get the ball out where player control may be secured, the ball is not in control of either team. Hence, the restriction on first touching does not apply.

PENALTY: Loss of ball. The ball is awarded to the opponent at the midcourt line, and the ball must be passed into the frontcourt.

SECTION IX—SWINGING OF ELBOWS

A player shall not be allowed excessive and/or a vigorous swinging motion of the elbows (no contact), when a defensive player is nearby and the offensive player has the ball.

PENALTY: Loss of ball. The ball is awarded to the opposing team on the side-line nearest the spot of the violation, but no nearer the baseline than the free throw line extended. If the violation occurs on a throw-in, the game clock shall not be started.

SECTION X—ENTERING BASKET FROM BELOW

A player shall not cause the ball to enter the basket from below.

PENALTY: Loss of ball. The ball is awarded to the opposing team at the sideline at the free throw line extended.

SECTION XI—ILLEGAL ASSIST IN SCORING

a. A player may not assist herself to score by using any part of the rim, net, backboard or basket support to lift, hold or raise herself.

b. A player may not assist a teammate to gain height while attempting to score.

PENALTY: Loss of ball. The ball is awarded to the opposing team at the free throw line extended.

SECTION XII—TRAVELING

a. A player who receives the ball while standing still may pivot, using either foot as the pivot foot.

b. A player who receives the ball while she is progressing or upon completion of a dribble, may use a two-count rhythm in coming to a stop, passing or shooting the ball. A player who receives the ball while she is progressing may use a two-count rhythm to start her dribble.

The first count occurs:

(1) As she receives the ball, if either foot is touching the floor at the time she receives it.

(2) As the foot touches the floor, or as both feet touch the floor simultaneously after she receives the ball, if both feet are off the floor when she receives it.

The second occurs:

(1) After the count of one when either foot touches the floor, or both feet touch the floor simultaneously.

A player who comes to a stop on the count of one when both feet are on the floor or touch the floor simultaneously may pivot using either foot as her pivot. If she alights with both feet, she must release the ball before either foot touches the floor.

A player who has one foot on the floor or lands with one foot first to the floor may only pivot with that foot. Once that foot is lifted from the floor it may not return until the ball is released.

A player who jumps off one foot on the count of one may land with both feet simultaneously for count two. In this situation, the player may not pivot with either foot and if one or both feet leave the floor the ball must be released before either returns to the floor.

c. In starting a dribble after (1) receiving the ball while standing still, or (2) coming to a legal stop, the ball must be out of the player's hand before the pivot foot is raised off the floor.

d. If a player, with the ball in her possession, raises her pivot foot off the floor, she must pass or shoot before her pivot foot returns to the floor. If she drops the ball while in the air, she may not be the first to touch the ball.

e. A player who falls to the floor while holding the ball, or while coming to a stop, may not gain an advantage by sliding.

f. A player who attempts a field goal may not be the first to touch the ball if it fails to touch the backboard, basket ring or another player.

g. A player may not be the first to touch her own pass unless the ball touches her backboard, basket ring or another player.

h. Upon ending her dribble or gaining control of the ball, a player may not touch the floor consecutively with the same foot (hop).

PENALTY: Loss of ball. The ball is awarded to the opponent at the sideline, nearest spot of the violation but no nearer the baseline than the free throw line extended.

SECTION XIII—OFFENSIVE SCREEN SET OUT-OF-BOUNDS

An offensive player shall not leave the playing area of the floor on the endline in the frontcourt for the purpose of setting a screen.

PENALTY: Loss of ball. The ball is awarded to the opponent at the sideline at the free throw line extended.

RULE NO. 11—BASKETBALL INTERFERENCE—GOALTENDING

SECTION I—A PLAYER SHALL NOT:

a. Touch the ball or the basket ring when the ball is using the basket ring as its lower base, or hang on the rim while the ball is passing through the net or bouncing on the rim.

EXCEPTION: If a player near her own basket has her hand(s) legally in contact with the ball, it is not a violation if her contact with the ball continues after the ball enters the cylinder, or if, in such action, she touches the basket.

b. Touch the ball when it is above the basket ring and within the imaginary cylinder.

c. During a field goal attempt, touch a ball after it has touched any part of the backboard above ring level, whether the ball is considered on its upward or downward flight.

d. During a field goal attempt, touch a ball after it has touched the backboard below the ring level and while the ball is on its upward flight.

e. Trap the ball against the face of the backboard after it has been released. (To be a trapped ball, three elements must exist simultaneously. The hand, the ball and the backboard must all occur at the same time. A batted ball against the backboard is not a trapped ball.)

f. Touch any live ball from within the playing area that is on its downward flight with an opportunity to score. This is considered to be a "field goal attempt" or trying for a goal.

g. Touch the ball at any time with a hand which is through the basket ring.

h. Vibrate the rim, net or backboard so as to cause the ball to make an unnatural bounce.

i. Touch the rim, net or ball while the ball is in the net preventing it from clearing the basket.

PENALTY: If the violation is at the opponent's basket, the offended team is awarded two points, if the attempt is from the two point zone and three points if it is from the three point zone. The crediting of the score and subsequent procedure is the same as if the awarded score has resulted from the ball having gone through the basket, except that the official shall hand the ball to a player of the team entitled to the throw-in. If the violation is at a team's own basket, no points can be scored and the ball is awarded to the offended team at the free throw line extended. If there is a violation by both teams, play shall be resumed by a jump ball between any two opponents at the center circle.

RULE NO. 12—FOULS AND PENALTIES

A. TECHNICAL FOUL

SECTION I—EXCESSIVE TIMEOUTS

a. Requests for a timeout in excess of the authorized number shall be granted and a technical foul shall be assessed. Following the timeout and free throw attempt, the ball will be awarded to the team which shot the free throw and play shall resume with a throw-in nearest the spot where play was interrupted.

b. If the excessive timeout is granted prior to free throw attempt(s), there will be no lineup for the remaining free throws and play shall resume with a throw-in at the point of interruption by the team which shot the technical foul.

c. If the excessive timeout is granted prior to a jump ball, the ball shall be awarded to the team shooting the technical foul at the point of interruption.

SECTION II—DELAY-OF-GAME

A delay-of-game shall be called for:

(1) Preventing the ball from being promptly put into play.

(2) Interfering with the ball after a successful field goal or free throw.

(3) Failing to immediately pass the ball to the nearest official when a personal foul or violation is assessed.

(4) Touching the ball before the throw-in has been released.

(5) A defender crossing the boundary line prior to the ball being released on a throw-in.

(6) A team preventing play from commencing at any time.

(7) Any player, coach or trainer interfering with a ball which has crossed the boundary line (Rule 8—Section II—f).

PENALTY: The first offense is a warning. A technical foul shall be assessed with each successive offense and charged to the team. An announcement will be made by the public address announcer. The 24-second clock shall remain the same or reset to 14, whichever is greater, if the violation is assessed against the defensive team. The offensive team shall be awarded a new 10 seconds to advance the ball if it is in the backcourt. If repeated acts become a travesty, the head coach shall be notified that he/she is being held responsible.

SECTION III—SUBSTITUTIONS

a. A substitute shall report to the official scorer while standing in the "substitution box."

b. A substitute shall not enter onto the court until she is beckoned by an official.

c. A substitute shall not be allowed to re-enter the game after being disqualified.

EXCEPTION: Rule 3—Section I—b.

d. It is the responsibility of each team to have the proper number of players on the court at all times. Failure to do so will result in a technical foul being assessed and charged to the team.

EXCEPTION: If the violation occurs on (1) a free throw attempt which is to be followed by another free throw attempt, or (2) a free throw attempt that is not going to remain in play, or (3) a throw-in before the ball is released.

SECTION IV—BASKET RING, BACKBOARD OR SUPPORT

a. An offensive player who deliberately hangs on her basket ring, net, backboard or support during the game shall be assessed a non-unsportsmanlike technical foul.

b. A defensive player who deliberately gains or maintains height or hangs on her opponent's basket ring, net, backboard or support, shall be assessed a non-unsportsmanlike technical foul. If she touches the ball during a field goal attempt, points shall be awarded consistent with the type of shot.

EXCEPTION: An offensive or defensive player may hang on the basket ring, backboard or support to prevent an injury to herself or another player, with no technical foul assessed.

c. Should a defensive player deliberately hang on the basket ring, backboard or support to successfully touch a ball which is in possession of an opponent, a non-unsportsmanlike technical foul shall be assessed.

SECTION V—CONDUCT

a. An official may assess a technical foul, without prior warning, at any time. A technical foul(s) may be assessed to any player on the court or anyone seated on the bench for conduct which, in the opinion of an official, is detrimental to the game. A technical foul cannot be assessed for physical contact when the ball is alive

EXCEPTION: Fighting fouls and/or taunting with physical contact.

b. A maximum of two technicals for unsportsmanlike acts may be assessed to any player, coach or trainer. Any of these offenders may be ejected for committing only one unsportsmanlike act, and they must be ejected for committing two unsportsmanlike acts.

c. A technical foul called for (1) delay of game, (2) coaches box violations, (3) having a team total of less or more than five players when the ball is alive, or (4) a player hanging on her basket ring or backboard, is not considered an act of unsportsmanlike conduct.

d. A technical foul shall be assessed for unsportsmanlike tactics such as:

(1) Disrespectfully addressing an official

(2) Physically contacting an official.

(3) Overt actions indicating resentment to a call

(4) Use of profanity

(5) A coach entering onto the court without permission of an official

(6) A deliberately-thrown elbow or any attempted physical act with no contact involved

(7) Taunting

e. Cursing or blaspheming an official shall not be considered the only cause for imposing technical fouls. Running tirades, continuous criticism or griping may be sufficient cause to assess a technical. Excessive misconduct shall result in ejection from the game.

f. Assessment of a technical foul shall be avoided whenever and wherever possible; but, when necessary they are to be assessed without delay or procrastination. Once a player has been ejected or the game is over, technicals cannot be assessed regardless of the provocation. Any additional unsportsmanlike conduct shall be reported by E-mail immediately to the Basketball Operations Department.

g. If a technical foul is assessed to a team following a personal foul on the same team, the free throw attempt for the technical foul shall be administered first.

h. The ball shall be awarded to the team which had possession at the time the technical foul was assessed, whether the free throw attempt is successful or not. Play shall be resumed by a throw-in nearest the spot where play was interrupted.

EXCEPTION: Rule 12A—Section I.

i. Anyone guilty of illegal contact which occurs during a dead ball may be assessed (1) a technical foul, if the contact is deemed to be unsportsmanlike in nature, or (2) a flagrant foul, if unnecessary and/or excessive contact occurs.

j. Free throws awarded for a technical foul must be attempted by a player in the game when the technical foul is assessed.

(1) If a substitute has been beckoned into the game or has been recognized by the officials as being in the game prior to a technical foul being assessed, she is eligible to attempt the free throw(s).

(2) If the technical foul is assessed before the opening tap, any player listed in the scorebook as a starter is eligible to attempt the free throw(s).

(3) If a technical foul is assessed before the starting lineup is indicated, any player on the squad may attempt the free throw(s).

k. A technical foul, unsportsmanlike act or flagrant foul must be called for a participant to be ejected. A player, coach or trainer may be ejected for:

(1) An elbow foul which makes contact shoulder level or below

(2) Any unsportsmanlike conduct where a technical foul is assessed

EXCEPTION: Rule 12A—Section V—1(5)

l. A player, coach or trainer must be ejected for:

(1) A punching foul

(2) A fighting foul

(3) An elbow foul which makes contact above shoulder level

(4) An attempted punch which does not make contact

(5) Deliberately entering the stands other than as a continuance of play

(6) Flagrant foul penalty 2

(7) Second flagrant foul penalty 1 in the same game

m. Eye guarding (placing a hand in front of the opponent's eyes when guarding from the rear) a player who does not have possession of the ball is illegal and an unsportsmanlike technical shall be assessed.

n. A free throw attempt is awarded when one technical foul is assessed.

o. No free throw attempts are awarded when a double technical foul is assessed. Technical fouls assessed to opposing teams during the same deadball and prior to the administering of any free throw attempt for the first technical foul shall be interpreted as a double technical foul.

p. The deliberate act of throwing the ball or any object at an official by a player, coach or trainer is a technical foul, and violators are subject to ejection from the game.

q. Elbow fouls, which make contact above shoulder level, and punching fouls, although recorded as both personal and team fouls, are unsportsmanlike acts. The player will be ejected immediately.

SECTION VI—FIGHTING FOULS

a. Technical fouls shall be assessed to players, coaches or trainers for fighting. No free throws will be attempted. The participants will be ejected immediately.

b. This rule applies whether play is in progress or the ball is dead.

c. If a fighting foul occurs with a team in possession of the ball, that team will retain possession on the sideline nearest the spot where play was interrupted but no nearer to the baseline than the free throw line extended.

d. If a fighting foul occurs with neither team in possession, play will be resumed with a jump ball between any two opponents who were in the game at the center circle.

e. A fine and/or suspension may be imposed upon such person(s) by the President at her sole discretion. Any fine imposed by the League Office upon a player who is involved in an altercation will be accompanied by a fine to that player's team.

SECTION VII—FINES

a. Recipients of technical fouls for unsportsmanlike conduct will be assessed a $150 fine for the first offense and an additional $150 for the second offense in any one given game, for a minimum total of $300. If a player is ejected on (1) the first technical foul for unsportsmanlike conduct, (2) a punching foul, (3) a fighting foul, (4) an elbow foul, or (5) a flagrant foul, she shall be fined a minimum of $300.

b. Whether or not said player(s) is ejected, a fine and/or suspension may be imposed upon such person(s) by the President at her sole discretion.

c. During an altercation, all players not participating in the game must remain in the immediate vicinity of their bench. Violators will be suspended, without pay, for a minimum of one game and fined a minimum of $500. Any such suspension will commence prior to the start of the player's next game.

A team must have a minimum of eight players dressed and ready to play in every game.

If four or more players leave the bench, the players will serve their suspensions alphabetically according to the letters of their last names.

If six bench players are suspended (assuming no participants are included), three of them will be suspended for the first game following the altercation. The remaining three will be suspended for the second game following the altercation.

d. A player, coach, or assistant coach, upon being notified by an official that he/she has been ejected from the game, must leave the playing area IMMEDIATELY and remain in the dressing room of his/her team during such suspension until completion of the game or leave the building. Violation of this rule shall result in an automatic fine of $250, an additional fine not to exceed $5,000, suspension, and possible forfeiture of the game. The use of messengers and/or telephones to transmit information from an ejected coach to the bench violates the spirit of this rule, and may result in appropriate penalties.

e. At halftime and the end of each game, the coach and his/her players are to leave the court and go directly to their dressing room without pause or delay. There is to be absolutely no talking to game officials.

f. Each player, when introduced prior to the start of the game, must be uniformly dressed.

g. Any player who is assessed a flagrant foul—penalty (2)—shall be ejected and will be fined a minimum of $300. The incident will be reported to the Basketball Operations Department.

B. PERSONAL FOUL

SECTION I—TYPES

a. A player shall not hold, push, charge into, impede the progress of an opponent by extending a hand, forearm, leg or knee or by bending the body into a position that is not normal. Contact that results in re-routing of an opponent is a foul which must be called immediately.

b. Contact initiated by a defensive player guarding a player with the ball is not legal. This contact includes, but is not limited to, forearms, hands or body check. EXCEPTIONS:

(1) A defender may apply contact with a forearm to an offensive player with the ball who has her back to the basket below the free throw line extended outside the Lower Defensive Box.

(2) A defender may apply contact with a forearm and/or one hand with a bent elbow to an offensive player in the post-up position with the ball in the Lower Defensive Box.

(3) A defender may apply contact with a forearm to an offensive player with the ball at any time in the Lower Defensive Box. The forearm in the above exceptions is solely for the purpose of maintaining a defensive position.

(4) A defender may position her leg between the legs of an offensive player in a post-up position in the lower Lower Defensive Box for the purpose of maintaining defensive position. If her foot leaves the floor in an attempt to dislodge her opponent, it is a foul immediately.

(5) Incidental contact with the hand against an offensive player shall be ignored if it does not affect a player's speed, quickness, balance and/or rhythm.

c. Any player whose actions against an opponent cause illegal contact with yet another opponent has committed the personal foul.

d. A personal foul committed by the offensive team during a throw-in shall be an offensive foul, regardless of whether the ball has been released.

e. Contact which occurs on the shooting hand of the offensive player, while that hand is in contact with the ball, is legal.

EXCEPTION: Flagrant, elbow and punching fouls.

PENALTIES: The offender is charged with a personal foul. The offended team is charged with a team foul if the illegal contact was caused by the defender. There is no team foul if there are personal fouls on one member of each team or the personal foul is against an offensive player. The offended team is awarded

(1) The ball out-of-bounds on the sideline at the spot nearest to where the play was interrupted but no nearer to the baseline than the free throw line extended, if an offensive foul is assessed.

(2) The ball out-of-bounds on the sideline nearest to where the play was interrupted but no nearer to the baseline than the free throw line extended if the personal foul is on the defender and if the penalty situation is not in effect.

(3) One free throw attempt if the personal foul is on the defender and there is a successful field goal or free throw on the play.

(4) Two/three free throw attempts if the personal foul is on the defender and the offensive player is in the

act of shooting an unsuccessful field goal.

(5) One free throw attempt plus a penalty free throw attempt if the personal foul is on the defender and the offensive player is not in the act of attempting a field goal if the penalty situation is in effect.

(6) One free throw attempt and possession of the ball on the sideline nearest the spot where play was interrupted if an offensive player, or a teammate is fouled while having a clear-path-to-the-basket. The ball and an offensive player must be positioned between the tip-ofcircle extended in the backcourt and the basket in the frontcourt, with no defender between the ball and the basket when the personal foul occurs. There must be team control and the new play must originate in the backcourt, including throw-ins, and the offended team must be deprived an opportunity to score an uncontested basket.

(7) Two free throw attempts shall be awarded if a personal foul is for illegal contact with an elbow. The elbow foul may be assessed whether the ball is dead or alive. Free throw attempts are awarded whether the ball is dead, alive, loose, or away-from-the-play in the last minute of regulation or overtime(s).

Contact must occur for an elbow foul to be assessed. It is an unsportsmanlike act whether or not there is contact. (See Rule 12A—Section V—d[6] for non-contact.)

If the deliberate elbow contact is above shoulder level, the player will be ejected. If the elbow contact is shoulder level or below, the player may be ejected at the discretion of the official.In all of the situations, the official has the discretion of assessing a flagrant foul-penalty (1) or (2).

(8) Two free throw attempts shall be awarded if a personal foul is committed by a defender prior to the ball being released on a throw-in.

EXCEPTION: Rule 12B—Section X

(9) Two free throw attempts are awarded if a personal foul is committed against an offensive player without the ball when her team has at least a one-woman advantage on a fast break and the defensive player takes a foul to stop play.

SECTION II—BY DRIBBLER

a. A dribbler shall not (1) charge into an opponent who has established a legal guarding position, or (2) attempt to dribble between two opponents, or (3) attempt to dribble between an opponent and a boundary, where sufficient space is not available for illegal contact to be avoided.

b. If a defender is able to establish a legal position in the straight line path of the dribbler, the dribbler must avoid contact by changing direction or ending her dribble.

c. The dribbler must be in control of her body at all times. If illegal contact occurs, the responsibility is on the dribbler.

PENALTY: The offender is assessed an offensive foul. There is no team foul. The ball is awarded to the offended team on the sideline nearest the spot where play was interrupted, but no nearer to the baseline than the free throw line extended.

EXCEPTION: Rule 3—Section I—a.

d. If a dribbler has sufficient space to have her head and shoulders in advance of her defender, the responsibility for illegal contact is on the defender.

e. If a dribbler has established a straight line path, a defender may not crowd her out of that path.

PENALTY: The defender shall be assessed a personal foul and a team foul. If the penalty is not in effect, the offended team is awarded the ball on the sideline nearest the spot where play was interrupted, but no nearer to the baseline than the free throw line extended. If the penalty is in effect, one free throw attempt plus a penalty free throw attempt is awarded.

SECTION III—BY SCREENING

A player who sets a screen shall not (1) assume a position nearer than a normal step from an opponent, if that opponent is stationary and unaware of the screener's position, or (2) make illegal contact with an opponent when she assumes a position at the side or front of an opponent, or (3) assume a position so near to a moving opponent that illegal contact cannot be avoided by the opponent without changing direction or stopping, or (4) move laterally or toward an opponent being screened, after having assumed a legal position. The screener maymove in the same direction and path of the opponent being screened.

In (3) above, the speed of the opponent being screened will determine what the screener's stationary position may be. This position will vary and may be one to two normal steps or strides from her opponent.

SECTION IV—FLAGRANT FOUL

a. If contact committed against a player, with or without the ball, is interpreted to be unnecessary, a flagrant foul—penalty 1 will be assessed. A personal foul is charged to the offender and a team foul is charged to the team.

PENALTY: (1) Two free throws shall be attempted and the ball awarded to the offended team on either side of the court at the free throw line extended. (2) If the offended player is injured and unable to attempt her free throws, the opposing coach will select any player from the bench to attempt the free throws. (3) This substitute may not be replaced until the ball is legally touched by a player on the court. (EXCEPTION: RULE 3—Section V—e.) (4) The injured player may notreturn to the game. (5) A player will be ejected if she commits two flagrant fouls in the same game.

b. If contact committed against a player, with or without the ball, is interpreted to be unnecessary and excessive, a flagrant foul—penalty 2 will be assessed. A personal foul is charged to the offender and a team foul is charged to the team.

PENALTY: (1) Two free throws shall be attempted and the ball awarded to the offended team on either side of the court at the free throw line extended. (2) If the offended player is injured and unable to attempt her free throws, her coach will select a substitute and any player from the team is eligible to attempt the free throws. (3) This substitute may not be replaced until the ball is legally touched by a player on the court. (EXCEPTION: RULE 3—Section V—e. (4) The injured player may return to the game at any time after the free throws are attempted. (5) This is an unsportsmanlike act and the offender is ejected.

c. A flagrant foul may be assessed whether the ball is dead or alive.

SECTION V—FREE THROW PENALTY SITUATIONS

a. Each team is limited to four team fouls per regulation period without additional penalties. Common fouls charged as team fouls, in excess of four, will be penalized by one free throw attempt plus a penalty free throw attempt.

(1) The first four common fouls committed by a team in any regulation period shall result in the ball being awarded to the opponent on the sideline nearest where play was interrupted but no nearer the baseline than the free throw line extended.

(2) The first three common fouls committed by a team in any overtime period, shall result in the ball being awarded to the opponent on the sideline nearest where play was interrupted but no nearer the baseline than the free throw line extended.

(3) If a team has not committed its quota of four team fouls during the first nine minutes of any regulation period, or its quota of three team fouls during the first four minutes of any overtime period, it shall be permitted to incur one team foul during the last minute without penalty.

(4) During any overtime period, common fouls charged as team fouls in excess of three will be penalized by one free throw plus a penalty free throw attempt.

(5) Personal fouls which are flagrant, punching, elbowing, away-from-the-play or clear-path-to-the-basket will carry their own separate penalties and are included in the team foul total.

(6) Personal fouls committed during a successful field goal attempt or free throw which result in one free throw attempt being awarded, will not result in an additional free throw attempt if the penalty situation exists.

b. A maximum of three points may be scored by the same team on a successful two-point field goal attempt.

c. A maximum of four points may be scored by the same team on a successful three-point field goal attempt.

SECTION VI—DOUBLE FOULS

a. No free throw attempts will be awarded on double fouls, whether they are personal or technical.

b. Double personal fouls shall add to a player's total, but not to the team total.

c. If a double foul occurs, the team in possession of the ball at the time of the call shall retain possession. Play is resumed on the sideline nearest the point where play was interrupted, but no nearer to the baseline than the free throw line extended. The 24-second clock is reset to 24 seconds if the ball is to be inbounded in the team's backcourt or stay the same or reset to 14, whichever is greater, if the ball is to be inbounded in the frontcourt.

d. If a double foul occurs with neither team in possession, or when the ball is in the air on an unsuccessful field goal or free throw attempt, play will be resumed with a jump ball at the center circle between any two opponents in the game at that time. If injury, ejection or disqualification makes it necessary for any player to be replaced, no substitute may participate in the jump ball. The jumper shall be selected from one of the remaining players in the game.

e. If a double foul occurs on a successful field goal or free throw attempt, the team that has been scored upon will inbound the ball at the baseline as after any other score.

f. If a double foul occurs as a result of a difference in opinion by the officials, no points can be scored and play shall resume with a jump ball at the center circle between any two opponents in the game at that time. No substitute may participate in the jump ball.

SECTION VII—OFFENSIVE FOULS

A personal foul assessed against an offensive player which is neither an elbow, punching or flagrant foul shall be penalized in the following manner:

(1) No points can be scored by the offensive team

(2) The offending player is charged with a personal foul

(3) The offending team is not charged with a team foul.

EXCEPTION: Rule 3—Section I—a. No penalty free throws are awarded.

(4) The ball is awarded to the offended team out-of-bounds on the sideline at the nearest spot where play was interrupted but no nearer the baseline than the free throw line extended.

b. A personal foul assessed against an offensive player which is elbow, punching or flagrant shall be penalized in the following manner:

(1) No points can be scored by the offensive team

(2) The offending player is charged with a personal foul

(3) The offending team is charged with a team foul

(4) Free throws are awarded consistent with the type of foul committed

(5) The ball would be put in play consistent with the type of foul committed.

SECTION VIII—LOOSE BALL FOULS

a. A personal foul, which is neither a punching, flagrant or an elbow foul, committed while there is no team control shall be administered in the following manner:

(1) Offending team is charged with a team foul

(2) Offending player is charged with a personal foul

(3) Offended team will be awarded possession at the sideline, nearest the spot of the foul, but no nearer to the baseline than the free throw line extended, if no penalty exists

(4) Offended player is awarded one free throw attempt plus a penalty free throw attempt if the offending team is in a penalty situation

b. If a "loose ball" foul called against the defensive team is then followed by a successful field goal, one free throw attempt will be awarded to the offended player, allowing for the three-point or four-point play. This interpretation applies:

(1) Regardless of which offensive player is fouled

(2) Whether or not the penalty situation exists. The ball can never be awarded to the scoring team out-of-bounds following a personal foul which occurs on the same play

c. If a "loose ball" foul called against the defensive team is followed by a successful free throw, one free throw will be awarded to the offended player whether or not the penalty is in effect.

d. If a "loose ball" foul called against the offensive team is then followed by a successful field goal attempt by the same offensive player, no points may be scored.

SECTION IX—PUNCHING FOULS

a. Illegal contact called on a player for punching is a personal foul and a team foul. One free throw attempt shall be awarded, regardless of the number of previous fouls in the period. The ball shall be awarded to the offended team out-of-bounds on either side of the court at the free throw line-extended, whether the free throw is successful or unsuccessful.

b. Any player who throws a punch, whether it connects or not, has committed an unsportsmanlike act. She will be ejected immediately and suspended for a minimum of one game.

c. This rule applies whether play is in progress or the ball is dead.

d. In the case where one punching foul is followed by another, all aspects of the rule are applied in both cases, and the team last offended is awarded possession on the sideline at the free throw line extended in the frontcourt.

SECTION X—AWAY-FROM-THE-PLAY FOUL

a. During the last minute of the fourth quarter or overtime period(s) with the offensive team in possession of the ball, all personal fouls which are assessed against the defensive team prior to the ball being released on a throw-in and/or away-from-the-play, shall be administered as follows:

(1) A personal foul and team foul shall be assessed and one free throw attempt shall be awarded. The free throw may be attempted by any player in the game at the time the personal foul was committed.

(2) If the foul occurs when the ball is inbounds, the offended team shall be awarded the ball at the nearest point where play was interrupted but no nearer to the baseline than the free throw line extended.

(3) If the foul occurs prior to the release on a throw-in, the offended team shall be awarded the ball at the original throw-in spot, with all privileges, if any, remaining.

EXCEPTION: Rule 12-B—Section X—b & c.

b. In the event that the personal foul committed is an elbow foul, the play shall be administered as follows:

(1) A personal foul and team foul shall be assessed and the free throw shooter shall be awarded two free throw attempts. The free throw(s) may be attempted by any player in the game at the time the personal foul was committed.

(2) In the event that the offended player is unable to participate in the game, the free throw shooter may be selected by her coach from any eligible player on the team. Any substitute must remain in the game until the ball is legally touched by a player on the court. (EXCEPTION: RULE 3—Section V—e.)

(3) The offended team shall be awarded the ball at the nearest point where play was interrupted with all privileges if any remaining.

c. In the event that the personal foul committed is a flagrant foul, the play shall be administered as follows:

(1) A personal foul and team foul shall be assessed and the free throw shooter shall be awarded two free throw attempts. The free throws may be attempted by any player in the game at the time the flagrant foul was committed.

(2) If a flagrant foul—penalty (1) is assessed and the offended player is unable to participate in the game, the substitute will be selected by her coach. The two free throws may be attempted by any of the four remaining players in the game. The ball will be awarded to the offended team at the free throw line extended in the frontcourt. The injured player may return to the game.

(3) If a flagrant foul—penalty (2) is assessed and the offended player is unable to participate in the game, the substitute will be selected by her coach. The two free throws may be attempted by the substitute or any of the four remaining players in the game. The ball will be awarded to the offended team at the free throw line extended in the frontcourt. The injured player may return to the game.

RULE NO. 13—INSTANT REPLAY

SECTION I—INSTANT REPLAY REVIEW TRIGGERS

a. Instant replay would be triggered automatically in the following situations:

(1) A field goal made with no time remaining on the clock (0:00) at the end of the fourth period or any overtime period that, if scored, would affect or potentially could affect, the outcome of the game.

(2) A field goal made with no time remaining on the clock (0:00) at the end of the first, second and third periods.

(3) A foul called with no time remaining on the clock (0:00) at the end of the fourth period or any overtime period, provided that it could affect the outcome of the game.

(4) A foul called with no time remaining on the clock (0:00) at the end of the first, second or third periods.

b. Instant replay would NOT be used to check a successful basket in 1 and 2 above if the throw-in, free throw attempt or jump ball started with .2 or .1 on the game clock. The officials will judge the legality of the basket in these situations based on the guidelines as set forth in Comments on the Rules L.

SECTION II—REVIEWABLE MATTERS

a. If an instant replay review is triggered as described in Section I-a (1) and (2) above, the officials would review the tape to determine only the following issues:

(1) Whether time on the game clock expired before the ball left the shooter's hand.

(2) If the shot was timely, whether the successful field goal was scored correctly as a two-point or three-point field goal.

(3) If the shot was timely, whether the shooter committed a boundary line violation. For purposes of this review, the officials would look only at the position of the shooter's feet at the moment they last touched the floor immediately prior to (or, if applicable, during) the release of the shot.

(4) Whether the 24-second clock expired before the ball left the shooter's hand.

(5) Whether a 10-second backcourt violation occurred before the ball left the shooter's hand.

b. If an instant replay review is triggered as described in Section I-a (3) and (4) above, the officials would review the tape to determine only the following issues:

(1) Whether a called foul that is not committed on or by a player in the act of shooting occurred prior to the expiration of time on the game clock.

(2) Whether a called foul that is committed on or by a player in the act of shooting, where the shooter releases the ball prior to expiration of time on the game clock, the foul should be administered regardless of whether it occurred prior to or after the expiration of time.

(3) Whether the shooter fouled was attempting a two or three point field goal.

(4) Whether a player fouled committed a boundary line violation prior to the foul. For purposes of this review, the official would look only at the position of the player's feet at the moment they last touched the floor immediately prior to (or, if applicable, during) the foul.

(5) Whether the 24-second clock expired before the foul occurred.

(6) Whether a 10-second backcourt violation occurred before the player was fouled.

NOTE: The officials would be permitted to utilize instant replay to determine whether (and how much) time should be put on the game clock but only when it is determined through replay that (i) the player committed a boundary line violation, (ii) a 24-second violation occurred, (iii) a 10-second backcourt violation occurred, or (iv) a called foul occurred prior to the expiration of time on the game clock.

SECTION III—REPLAY REVIEW PROCESS

a. All replay reviews would be conducted by the officials as a crew after gathering as much information as possible. In cases of conflict, the crew chief would make the final decision.

b. The call made by the game officials during play would be reversed only when the replay provides the officials with "clear and conclusive" visual evidence to do so.

c. The officials will use the following to make their final decision in the order listed below.

(1) Game clock or shot clock on top of backboard.

(2) LED lights.

(3) Game clock on the facades of the balcony.

(4) Game clock on score boards hanging from the ceilings.

(5) Superimposed TV clocks.

d. The officials will keep both teams on the court at the end of the second quarter if instant replay is being used to determine if a foul was called prior to expiration or if there is any question whether the shooter committed a 24-second violation, 10-second violation or boundary line violation where time may be added to the game clock.

e. The officials will keep both teams on the court anytime instant replay is used at the end of the fourth period or overtime period..

COMMENTS ON THE RULES

I. GUIDES FOR ADMINISTRATION AND APPLICATION OF THE RULES

Each official should have a definite and clear conception of his/her overall responsibilities. It is essential for them to know, understand and implement the rules as intended. If all officials possess the same conception there will be a guaranteed uniformity in the administration of all contests.

The restrictions placed upon the player by the rules are intended to create a balance of play, equal opportunity for the defense and the offense, provide reasonable safety and protection for all players and emphasize cleverness and skill without unduly limiting freedom of action of players or teams.

The purpose of penalties is to compensate a player who has been placed at a disadvantage through an illegal act of an opponent and to restrain players from committing acts which, if ignored, might lead to roughness even though they do not affect the immediate play. To implement this philosophy, there are times during a game where "degrees of certainty" are necessary to determine a foul during physical contact. This practice may be necessary throughout the game with a higher degree implemented during impact times when the intensity has risen, especially nearing the end of a game.

II. BASIC PRINCIPLES

A. CONTACT SITUATIONS

1. Incidental Contact

The mere fact that contact occurs does not necessarily constitute a foul. Contact which is incidental to an effort by a player to play an opponent, reach a loose ball, or perform normal defensive or offensive movements, should not be considered illegal. If, however, a player attempts to play an opponent from a position where she has no reasonable chance to perform without making contact with her opponent, the responsibility is on the player in this position.

The hand is considered "part of the ball" when it is in contact with the ball. Therefore, contact on that hand by a defender while it is in contact with the ball is not illegal.

2. Guarding an Opponent

In all guarding situations, a player is entitled to any spot on the court she desires, provided she legally gets to that spot first and without contact with an opponent. If a defensive or offensive player has established a position on the floor and her opponent initiates contact that results in dislodging, a foul should be called IMMEDIATELY.

During all throw-ins, the defensive player(s) must be allowed to take a position between her opponent and the basket.

A player may continue to move after gaining a guarding position in the path of an opponent provided she is not moving directly or obliquely toward her opponent when contact occurs. A player is never permitted to move into the path of an opponent after the opponent has jumped into the air.

A player who extends a hand, forearm, shoulder, hip or leg into the path of an opponent and thereby causes contact is not considered to have a legal position in the path of an opponent.

A player is entitled to a vertical position even to the extent of holding her arms above her shoulders, as in post play or when double-teaming in pressing tactics.

Any player who conforms to the above is absolved from responsibility for any contact by an opponent which may dislodge or tend to dislodge such player from the position which she has attained and is maintaining legally. If contact occurs, the official must decide whether the contact is incidental or a foul has been committed.

3. Screening

When a player screens in front of or at the side of a stationary opponent, she may be as close as she desires providing she does not make illegal contact. Her opponent can see her, and therefore, is expected to detour around the screen.

If she screens behind a stationary opponent, the opponent must be able to take a normal step backward without contact. Because the opponent is not expected to see a screener behind her, the player screened is given latitude of movement. The defender must be given an opportunity to change direction and avoid contact with the screener.

To screen a moving opponent, the player must stop soon enough to permit her opponent to stop or change direction. The distance between the player screening and her opponent will depend upon the speed at which the players are moving.

If two opponents are moving in the same direction and path, the player who is behind is responsible for contact. The player in front may stop or slow her pace, but she may not move backward or sideways into her opponent. The player in front may or may not have the ball. This situation assumes the two players have been moving in identically the same direction and path before contact.

4. The Dribble

If the dribbler's path is blocked, she is expected to pass or shoot; that is, she should not try to dribble by an opponent unless there is a reasonable chance of getting by without contact.nent unless there is a reasonable chance of getting by without contact.

B. FOULS: FLAGRANT—UNSPORTSMANLIKE

To be unsportsmanlike is to act in a manner unbecoming to the image of professional basketball. It consists of acts of deceit, disrespect of officials and profanity. The penalty for such action is a technical foul. Repeated acts shall result in expulsion from the game and potentially a fine.

A flagrant foul—penalty (1) is unnecessary contact committed by a player against an opponent.

A flagrant foul—penalty (2) is unnecessary and excessive contact committed by a player against an opponent. It is an unsportsmanlike act and the offender is ejected immediately.

The offender will be subject to a fine and/or suspension by the President.

See Rule 12B—Section IV for interpretation and penalties.

C. BLOCK-CHARGE

A defensive player is permitted to establish a legal guarding position in the path of a dribbler regardless of her speed and distance.

A defensive player is not permitted to move into the path of an offensive player once she has started her upward shooting motion with the ball.

A defensive player must allow a moving player the opportunity to stop or change direction when the offensive player receives a pass outside the lower defensive box. The lower defensive box is the area between the 3 ft. posted up marks, the bottom tip of the circle and the endline.

A defensive player must allow an alighted player the opportunity to land and then stop or change direction when the offensive player is outside the lower defensive box.

A defensive player is permitted to establish a legal guarding position in the path of an offensive player who receives a pass inside the lower defensive box regardless of her speed and distance.

A defensive player must allow an alighted player who received a pass the space to land when the offensive player is inside the lower defensive box.

A player must allow a moving opponent without the ball the opportunity to stop or change direction.

The speed of the player will determine the amount of distance an opponent must allow.

If a defensive player acquires a position directly under the basket/backboard on anything but a "baseline drive," she shall be responsible if contact occurs. An offensive foul should never be called under these conditions. The offensive player remains a shooter until she has regained a normal playing position on the floor. Many times this type of play is allowed to continue if the goal is successful.

The opposite is also true. If an offensive player causes contact with a defensive player who has established a legal position, an offensive foul shall be called, and no points may be scored. A defensive player may turn slightly to protect herself, but is never allowed to bend over and submarine an opponent.

On a "drive to the basket," if the defensive player has established a legal position in front of the basket/backboard, the offensive player shall be responsible for any illegal contact which occurs prior to her having regained her balance on the floor. An offensive foul shall be called and no points are to be awarded if the field goal is successful.

The mere fact that contact occurs on these type of plays, or any other similar play, does not necessarily mean that a personal foul has been committed. The officials must decide whether the contact is negligible and/or incidental, judging each situation separately.

D. GAME CANCELLATION

For the purpose of game cancellation, the officials' jurisdiction begins with the opening tipoff. Prior to this, it shall be the decision of the home team's management whether or not playing conditions are such to warrant postponement.

However, once the game begins, if because of extremely hazardous playing conditions the question arises whether or not the game should be canceled, the crew chief shall see that EVERY effort is made to continue the game before making the decision to terminate it.

E. PHYSICAL CONTACT—SUSPENSION

Any player or coach guilty of intentional physical contact with an official shall automatically be suspended without pay for one game. A fine and/or longer period of suspension will result if circumstances so dictate.

F. PROTEST

Protests are not permitted during the course of a game. In order to file a protest, a team must adhere to the following procedure:

(a) In order to protest against or appeal from the result of a game, notice thereof must be given to the President within forty-eight (48) hours after the conclusion of such game, by fax or E-mail, stating the grounds for protest. No protest may be filed in connection with any game played during the regular season after midnight of the day of the last game of the regular season schedule. A protest in connection with a playoff game must be filed not later than midnight of the day of the game protested. A game may be protested only by a Governor, Alternate Governor, or the Head Coach. The right of protest shall inure not only to the immediately allegedly aggrieved contestants, but to any other team who can show an interest in the grounds of protest and the results that might be attained if the protest were allowed. Each fax or e-mail of protest shall be immediately confirmed by letter, and no protest shall be valid unless the letter of confirmation is accompanied by a check in the sum of $5000 payable to the WNBA. If the team filing the protest prevails, the $5000 is to be refunded. If the team does not prevail, the $5000 is to be forfeited and retained by the WNBA.

(b) Upon receipt of a protest, the President shall at once notify the opposing team in the game protested and require both of said teams within five (5) days to file with her such evidence as she may desire bearing upon the issue. The President shall decide the question raised within five (5) days after receipt of such evidence.

G. SHATTERING BACKBOARDS

Any player whose contact with the basket ring or backboard causes the backboard to shatter will be penalized in the following manner:

(1) Pre-game and/or Half-time warm-ups—No penalty to be assessed by officials.

(2) During the game—Non-unsportsmanlike conduct technical foul. Under NO circumstances will that player be ejected from the game.

The President will review all actions and plays involved in the shattering of a backboard.

H. PLAYER/TEAM CONDUCT AND DRESS

(1) Each player when introduced, prior to the game, must be uniformly dressed.

(2) Players, coaches and trainers are to stand and line up in a dignified posture along the sidelines or on the foul line during the playing of the National Anthem.

(3) Coaches and assistant coaches must wear business attire or other apparel as may be designated by the WNBA.

(4) While playing, players must keep their uniform shirts untucked (worn outside of shorts), and no T-shirts are allowed.

(5) The only article bearing a commercial logo which can be worn by players is their shoes, subject to WNBA rules.

I. OFFENSIVE 3-SECONDS

The offensive player cannot be allowed in the 3-second lane for more than the allotted time. This causes the defensive player to "hand-check" because she cannot control the offensive player for that extended period of time.

If the offensive player is in the 3-second lane for less than three seconds and receives the ball, she must make a move toward the hoop for the official to discontinue his/her three second count. If she attempts to back the defensive player down to secure a better position in relation to the basket, offensive three seconds or an offensive foul must be called. If she passes off and immediately makes a move out of the lane, there should be no whistle.

J. PLAYER CONDUCT—SPECTATORS

Any coach, player or trainer who deliberately enters the spectator stands during the game will be automatically ejected and the incident reported via e-mail to the President. Entering the stands to keep a ball in play by a player or the momentum which carries the player into the stands is not considered deliberate. The first row of seats is considered the beginning of the stands.

K. PUNCHING, FIGHTING AND ELBOW FOULS

Violent acts of any nature on the court will not be tolerated. Players involved in altercations will be ejected, fined and/or suspended.

Officials have been instructed to eject a player who throws a punch, whether or not it connects, or an elbow which makes contact above shoulder level. If elbow contact is shoulder level or below, it shall be left to the discretion of the official as to whether the player is ejected. Even if a punch or an elbow goes undetected by the officials during the game, but is detected during a review of a videotape, that player will be penalized.

There is absolutely no justification for fighting in a WNBA game. The fact that a player believes she was provoked by another player is not an acceptable excuse. If a player takes it upon herself to retaliate, she can expect to be subject to appropriate penalties.

L. EXPIRATION OF TIME

NO LESS THAN :00.3 must expire on the game clock when a ball is thrown inbounds and then hit instantly out-of-bounds. If less than :00.3 expires in such a situation, the timer will be instructed to deduct AT LEAST :00.3 from the game clock. If, in the judgment of the official, the play took longer than :00.3, he/she will instruct the timer to deduct more time. If less than :00.3 remain on the game clock when this situation occurs, the period is over.

The game clock must show :00.3 or more in order for a player to secure possession of the ball on a rebound or throw-in to attempt a field goal. Instant replay shall be utilized if the basket is successful on this type of play and the clock runs to 0:00.

The only type of field goal which may be scored if the game clock is at :00.2 or :00.1 is a "tip-in" or "high lob."

A "tip-in" is defined as any action in which the ball is deflected, not controlled, by a player and then enters the basket ring. This type of action shall be deemed legal if :00.1 or more remains in a period.

A "high lob" is defined as a pass which is received by an offensive player while in mid-air, and is followed instantaneously by a field goal attempt. If the reception of the pass and the subsequent "slam dunk" is immediately adjacent to the basket ring, this type of action shall be deemed legal if :00.1 or more remains in a period. However, if the "high lob" attempt is a distance from the basket ring whereby the ball must be controlled in mid-air, either one-handed or two-handed, a minimum of :00.3 is necessary for a field goal to score if successful. Instant replay would NOT be used if the play starts with :00.2 or :00.1 on the game clock.

NO LESS than :00.3 must expire on the game clock when a player secures possession of an unsuccessful free throw attempt and immediately requests a timeout. If LESS than :00.3 expires in such a circumstance, the time on the game clock shall be reduced by at least :00.3. Therefore, if :00.3 OR LESS remain on the game clock when the above situation exists, and a player requests a timeout upon securing possession of the ball, the period is over.

During ANY regular or 20-second timeout taken during the FINAL minute of ANY period, the crew chief must meet with his/her fellow officials to discuss possible timing scenarios, fouls being taken if either team is under the penalty limit, number of timeouts, assistance by all officials on 3-point field goal attempts, rotation or away-from-the play foul.

Regardless of when the horn or red light operates to signify the end of period, the officials (as aided by instant replay, if required) will ultimately make the final decision whether to allow or disallow a successful field goal. THE CREW CHIEF MUST TAKE CHARGE OF THE SITUATION.

M. VERBAL FAN INTERFERENCE

Any spectator who verbally abuses players and/or coaches in a manner which, in the opinion of the game officials, interferes with the ability of a coach to communicate with his/her players during the game and/or huddles, will, at the direction of the crew chief, be given one warning by a building security officer. If the same spectator continues to behave in a like manner, the crew chief shall direct a building security officer to eject the spectator from the arena.

N. GUIDELINES FOR INFECTION CONTROL

If a player suffers a laceration or a wound where bleeding occurs, or if blood is visible on a player or her uniform, the officials shall suspend the game at the earliest appropriate time and allow a maximum of 30 seconds for treatment. After that time, the head coach shall be informed that she/he has the option to substitute for the player, call a regular timeout or a 20-second timeout. If a substitute replaces the player, the opposing team shall be allowed to substitute one player. The bleeding player may return to the game when she has received appropriate treatment by medical staff personnel.

If the player returns to the game, the officials shall make certain that any lesion, wound or dermatitis is covered with a dressing that will prevent contamination to and/or from other sources. A wrist or sweat band is not considered a suitable bandage.

If the bleeding player is awarded a free throw attempt(s) as a result of a personal foul, or is involved in a jump ball, the bleeding player will be given 30 seconds for treatment. If the treatment is not completed, play will resume and will then be suspended at the first appropriate time.

Mandatory timeouts shall not be granted during a suspension of play unless the offensive team calls a 20-second timeout. If the suspension of play is for a defensive player, a mandatory timeout shall not be granted if the defensive team calls a 20-second timeout.

If treatment is not completed within the allotted time, the head coach may call another timeout or substitute for the bleeding player. Substitutes are permitted consistent with existing rules on substitution.

If a team has no timeouts remaining when play is suspended, the officials will allow 30 seconds for appropriate treatment. If the treatment is not completed in accordance with paragraph one above, the bleeding player must be removed immediately. ONLY the bleeding player on that team may be removed from the game under these circumstances. If so, the opponent may also substitute one player.

The offensive team will receive a full ten seconds to advance the ball into the frontcourt. The 24 second clock will remain as is or reset to 14, whichever is greater.

O. DEAD BALL, LIVE BALL, BALL IS ALIVE

After the ball has been dead, it is put into play by a jump ball, throw-in or a free throw attempt. The game clock does not start until the ball is legally touched on the court by a player. However, any floor violation or personal foul which may occur will be penalized.

The ball is live when it is placed at the disposal of the thrower-in, free throw shooter or is tossed by the official on a jump ball. Illegal contact, which occurs prior to the ball becoming live, will be ignored if it is not unsportsmanlike.

The ball is alive when it is legally tapped by one of the participants of a jump ball, released by a thrower-in or released on a free throw attempt that will remain in play.

P. TAUNTING

If a player blatantly taunts an opponent, a technical foul shall be assessed. The opponent WILL NOT, automatically, be assessed a technical foul. Her behavior will be the determining factor.

Simultaneous taunting is a verbal altercation. Verbal altercations and unsportsmanlike conduct will be administered as a double technical foul and no free throws will be attempted.

Technical fouls assessed opponents during the same dead ball and prior to the administering of any free throw attempt for the first technical foul, shall be interpreted as a double technical foul.

A PLAYER(S) GUILTY OF TAUNTING MUST BE SINGLED OUT AND PENALIZED.

If a previous unsportsmanlike act has been committed and if this situation is BLATANT, a technical foul must be assessed and the guilty player(s) must be ejected.

A

ABROSIMOVA, SVETLANA   F   LYNX

PERSONAL: Born July 9, 1980, in St. Petersburg, Russia. ... 6-2/169. (1.88/76.7). ... Full name: Svetlana Olegovna Abrosimova
HIGH SCHOOL: Petrogradskoi N86 (St. Petersburg, Russia).
COLLEGE: Connecticut.
TRANSACTIONS/CAREER NOTES: Selected by Minnesota in first round (seventh overall) of WNBA Draft, April 20, 2001.

COLLEGE RECORD

NOTES: Member of NCAA Division I championship team (2000). ... Kodak All-American first team (1999, 2000).

Season Team	G	Min.	FGM	FGA	Pct.	FTM	FTA	Pct.	Reb.	Ast.	Pts.	RPG	APG	PPG
1997—Connecticut	37	972	191	372	.513	122	184	.663	235	114	538	6.4	3.1	14.5
1998—Connecticut	34	888	204	425	.480	118	186	.634	226	127	564	6.6	3.7	16.6
1999—Connecticut	37	1051	181	369	.491	91	122	.746	229	154	496	6.2	4.2	13.4
2000—Connecticut	19	466	100	186	.538	41	58	.707	124	78	267	6.5	4.1	14.1
Totals	127	3377	676	1352	.500	372	550	.676	814	473	1865	6.4	3.7	14.7

Three-point field goals: 1997-98, 34-for-80 (.425). 1998-99, 38-for-101 (.376). 1999-00, 43-for-108 (.398). 2000-01, 26-for-58 (.448). Totals, 141-for-347 (.406).

OLYMPICS RECORD

Season Team	G	Min.	FGM	FGA	Pct.	FTM	FTA	Pct.	Reb.	Ast.	Pts.	RPG	APG	PPG
2000—Russia	7	151	23	43	.535	8	15	.533	23	13	58	3.3	1.9	8.3
Totals	7	151	23	43	.535	8	15	.533	23	13	58	3.3	1.9	8.3

Three-point field goals: 2000-01, 4-for-10 (.400). Totals, 4-for-10 (.400).

WNBA REGULAR-SEASON RECORD

Season Team	G	Min.	FGM	FGA	Pct.	FTM	FTA	Pct.	Off.	Def.	Tot.	Ast.	St.	Blk.	TO	Pts.	RPG	APG	PPG
2001—Minnesota	26	846	114	293	.389	96	132	.727	43	131	174	53	42	9	85	343	6.7	2.0	13.2
2002—Minnesota	27	805	119	316	.377	56	116	.483	45	101	146	60	42	10	92	314	5.4	2.2	11.6
2003—Minnesota	30	792	112	285	.393	69	98	.704	44	97	141	82	44	11	90	318	4.7	2.7	10.6
2004—Minnesota	22	462	49	139	.353	28	46	.609	17	57	74	45	30	2	43	146	3.4	2.0	6.6
2005—Minnesota	31	777	109	276	.395	53	73	.726	29	78	107	60	48	6	80	304	3.5	1.9	9.8
Totals	136	3682	503	1309	.384	302	465	.649	178	464	642	300	206	38	390	1425	4.7	2.2	10.5

Three-point field goals: 2001-02, 19-for-76 (.250). 2002-03, 20-for-60 (.333). 2003-04, 25-for-82 (.305). 2004-05, 20-for-53 (.377). 2005-06, 33-for-82 (.402). Totals, 117-for-353 (.331).
Personal fouls/disqualifications: 2001-02, 70/2. 2002-03, 73/0. 2003-04, 79/0. 2004-05, 42/0. 2005-06, 86/0. Totals, 350/2.

WNBA PLAYOFF RECORD

Season Team	G	Min.	FGM	FGA	Pct.	FTM	FTA	Pct.	Off.	Def.	Tot.	Ast.	St.	Blk.	TO	Pts.	RPG	APG	PPG
2003—Minnesota	3	69	6	22	.273	8	8	1.000	1	4	5	4	4	1	8	23	1.7	1.3	7.7
2004—Minnesota	2	67	8	23	.348	2	4	.500	3	6	9	3	1	2	3	20	4.5	1.5	10.0
Totals	5	136	14	45	.311	10	12	.833	4	10	14	7	5	3	11	43	2.8	1.4	8.6

Three-point field goals: 2003-04, 3-for-7 (.429). 2004-05, 2-for-8 (.250). Totals, 5-for-15 (.333).
Personal fouls/disqualifications: 2003-04, 8/0. 2004-05, 7/0. Totals, 15/0.

AMACHREE, MACTABENE   F   MYSTICS

PERSONAL: Born January 30, 1978, in Nigeria. ... 6-2/172. (1.88/78.0).
TRANSACTIONS/CAREER NOTES: Signed by the WNBA and added by Phoenix, May 1, 2000. ... Waived by Phoenix, June 19, 2000. ... Added by New York, July 9, 2001. ... Signed by Seattle, July 14, 2003. ... Signed by Washington, April 11, 2005.
MISCELLANEOUS: Member of the Nigerian National Team.

WNBA REGULAR-SEASON RECORD

Season Team	G	Min.	FGM	FGA	Pct.	FTM	FTA	Pct.	Off.	Def.	Tot.	Ast.	St.	Blk.	TO	Pts.	RPG	APG	PPG
2001—New York	2	3	0	0	...	1	2	.500	1	0	1	0	0	1	1	1	0.5	0.0	0.5
2003—Seattle	7	47	3	10	.300	2	4	.500	4	10	14	0	5	2	9	8	2.0	0.0	1.1
2005—Washington	3	3	0	1	.000	2	2	1.000	0	0	0	0	0	0	0	2	0.0	0.0	0.7
Totals	12	53	3	11	.273	5	8	.625	5	10	15	0	5	3	10	11	1.3	0.0	0.9

Personal fouls/disqualifications: 2001-02, 2/0. 2003-04, 3/0. Totals, 5/0.

OLYMPICS RECORD

Season Team	G	Min.	FGM	FGA	Pct.	FTM	FTA	Pct.	Reb.	Ast.	Pts.	RPG	APG	PPG
2004—Nigeria	4	133	23	65	.354	9	17	.529	29	4	60	7.3	1.0	15.0
Totals	4	133	23	65	.354	9	17	.529	29	4	60	7.3	1.0	15.0

Three-point field goals: 2004-05, 5-for-20 (.250). Totals, 5-for-20 (.250).
Personal fouls/disqualifications: 2004-05, 12/0. Totals, 12/0.

ANDERSON, CHANTELLE   C   SILVER STARS

A

PERSONAL: Born January 22, 1981, in Loma Linda, Calif. ... 6-6/192. (1.98/87.1). ... Full name: Chantelle Denise Anderson
HIGH SCHOOL: Hudson Bay (Vancouver, Wash.).
COLLEGE: Vanderbilt.
TRANSACTIONS/CAREER NOTES: Selected by Sacramento in first round (second overall) of WNBA Draft, April 25, 2003.

COLLEGE RECORD

NOTES: AP All-American second team (2003). ... Top 20 finalist for the 2003 Naismith Award. ... All-SEC first team (2001, 2002, 2003). ... All-SEC second team (2000). ... Vanderbilt's all-time leading scorer (2,604). ... Led NCAA in field goal percentage (.723) in 2001. ... Led SEC in field goal percentage (.647) in 2002. ... NCAA Midwest Regional MVP (2002). ... SEC Tournament MVP (2001).

												AVERAGES		
Season Team	G	Min.	FGM	FGA	Pct.	FTM	FTA	Pct.	Reb.	Ast.	Pts.	RPG	APG	PPG
1999—Vanderbilt	34	935	216	367	.589	104	150	.693	190	25	536	5.6	0.7	15.8
2000—Vanderbilt	34	1034	292	404	.723	135	185	.730	215	37	722	6.3	1.1	21.2
2001—Vanderbilt	37	1106	295	456	.647	170	220	.773	250	54	765	6.8	1.5	20.7
2002—Vanderbilt	32	901	217	341	.636	147	196	.750	167	57	581	5.2	1.8	18.2
Totals	137	3976	1020	1568	.651	556	751	.740	822	173	2604	6.0	1.3	19.0

Three-point field goals: 1999-00, 0-for-1. 2000-01, 4-for-7 (.571). 2001-02, 5-for-13 (.385). Totals, 9-for-21 (.429).

WNBA REGULAR-SEASON RECORD

									REBOUNDS								AVERAGES		
Season Team	G	Min.	FGM	FGA	Pct.	FTM	FTA	Pct.	Off.	Def.	Tot.	Ast.	St.	Blk.	TO	Pts.	RPG	APG	PPG
2003—Sacramento	26	171	19	44	.432	4	12	.333	7	17	24	5	5	5	17	42	0.9	0.2	1.6
2004—Sacramento	30	231	25	64	.391	27	37	.730	14	20	34	5	3	6	25	77	1.1	0.2	2.6
2005—San Antonio	34	669	83	178	.466	37	46	.804	28	62	90	11	8	15	55	203	2.6	0.3	6.0
Totals	90	1071	127	286	.444	68	95	.716	49	99	148	21	16	26	97	322	1.6	0.2	3.6

Personal fouls/disqualifications: 2003-04, 33/1. 2004-05, 46/0. 2005-06, 106/5. Totals, 185/6.

WNBA PLAYOFF RECORD

									REBOUNDS								AVERAGES		
Season Team	G	Min.	FGM	FGA	Pct.	FTM	FTA	Pct.	Off.	Def.	Tot.	Ast.	St.	Blk.	TO	Pts.	RPG	APG	PPG
2003—Sacramento	5	29	3	5	.600	1	2	.500	0	3	3	0	0	2	4	7	0.6	0.0	1.4
2004—Sacramento	2	11	1	2	.500	0	0	...	0	2	2	1	0	0	1	2	1.0	0.5	1.0
Totals	7	40	4	7	.571	1	2	.500	0	5	5	1	0	2	5	9	0.7	0.1	1.3

Personal fouls/disqualifications: 2003-04, 7/0. 2004-05, 1/0. Totals, 8/0.

ARCAIN, JANETH   G   COMETS

PERSONAL: Born April 11, 1969, in Sao Paulo, Brazil. ... 5-11/147. (1.80/66.7).
HIGH SCHOOL: Minas Gerais (Sto Andres, Brazil).
TRANSACTIONS/CAREER NOTES: Selected by Houston in second round (12th overall) of the WNBA Elite Draft, February 27, 1997.
MISCELLANEOUS: Member of WNBA Championship Team (1997, 1998, 1999, 2000).

OLYMPICS RECORD

												AVERAGES		
Season Team	G	Min.	FGM	FGA	Pct.	FTM	FTA	Pct.	Reb.	Ast.	Pts.	RPG	APG	PPG
1992—Brazil	5	...	33	63	.524	19	24	.792	39	13	85	7.8	2.6	17.0
1996—Brazil	8	...	56	122	.459	29	37	.784	52	35	142	6.5	4.4	17.8
2000—Brazil	8	274	60	118	.508	43	53	.811	46	21	164	5.8	2.6	20.5
2004—Brazil	8	275	57	140	.407	28	36	.778	43	20	144	5.4	2.5	18.0
Totals	29	549	206	443	.465	119	150	.793	180	89	535	6.2	3.1	18.4

Three-point field goals: 1996-97, 1-for-7 (.143). 2000-01, 1-for-5 (.200). 2004-05, 2-for-15 (.133). Totals, 4-for-27 (.148).
Personal fouls/disqualifications: 2004-05, 20/0. Totals, 20/0.

WNBA REGULAR-SEASON RECORD

NOTES: WNBA Most Improved Player (2001). ... All-WNBA first team (2001).

									REBOUNDS								AVERAGES		
Season Team	G	Min.	FGM	FGA	Pct.	FTM	FTA	Pct.	Off.	Def.	Tot.	Ast.	St.	Blk.	TO	Pts.	RPG	APG	PPG
1997—Houston	28	784	110	250	.440	76	85	.894	41	69	110	45	43	4	67	305	3.9	1.6	10.9
1998—Houston	30	657	83	195	.426	34	45	.756	43	65	108	26	25	3	38	205	3.6	0.9	6.8
1999—Houston	32	735	71	164	.433	34	41	.829	32	59	91	38	30	2	39	187	2.8	1.2	5.8
2000—Houston	32	977	109	233	.468	41	49	.837	36	83	119	60	42	3	53	268	3.7	1.9	8.4
2001—Houston	32	1154	217	509	.426	135	150	.900	49	87	136	94	60	3	83	591	4.3	2.9	18.5
2002—Houston	32	1116	128	302	.424	98	111	.883	42	84	126	86	51	6	71	364	3.9	2.7	11.4
2003—Houston	34	1136	151	324	.466	79	94	.840	24	112	136	67	41	1	50	390	4.0	2.0	11.5
2005—Houston	34	1079	128	304	.421	83	94	.883	20	73	93	53	55	6	56	342	2.7	1.6	10.1
Totals	254	7638	997	2281	.437	580	669	.867	287	632	919	469	347	28	457	2652	3.6	1.8	10.4

Three-point field goals: 1997-98, 9-for-33 (.273). 1998-99, 5-for-33 (.152). 1999-00, 11-for-44 (.250). 2000-01, 9-for-45 (.200). 2001-02, 22-for-66 (.333). 2002-03, 10-for-37 (.270). 2003-04, 9-for-37 (.243). 2005-06, 3-for-16 (.188). Totals, 78-for-311 (.251).
Personal fouls/disqualifications: 1997-98, 56/0. 1998-99, 48/0. 1999-00, 63/0. 2000-01, 66/1. 2001-02, 82/1. 2002-03, 49/0. 2003-04, 64/0. 2005-06, 85/0. Totals, 513/2.

WNBA PLAYOFF RECORD

Season Team	G	Min.	FGM	FGA	Pct.	FTM	FTA	Pct.	REBOUNDS Off.	Def.	Tot.	Ast.	St.	Blk.	TO	Pts.	AVERAGES RPG	APG	PPG
1997—Houston	2	70	9	27	.333	2	2	1.000	7	8	15	1	1	0	1	21	7.5	0.5	10.5
1998—Houston	5	92	8	18	.444	0	0	...	1	7	8	4	2	1	3	16	1.6	0.8	3.2
1999—Houston	6	156	13	29	.448	10	16	.625	4	14	18	6	6	1	2	38	3.0	1.0	6.3
2000—Houston	6	201	21	47	.447	6	7	.857	6	21	27	12	10	0	16	50	4.5	2.0	8.3
2001—Houston	2	71	13	34	.382	2	2	1.000	2	9	11	5	2	0	5	29	5.5	2.5	14.5
2002—Houston	3	119	15	35	.429	7	8	.875	2	9	11	4	5	1	5	39	3.7	1.3	13.0
2003—Houston	3	107	12	31	.387	12	13	.923	6	8	14	3	8	0	7	37	4.7	1.0	12.3
2005—Houston	5	138	16	33	.485	12	12	1.000	1	9	10	6	6	0	2	44	2.0	1.2	8.8
Totals	**32**	**954**	**107**	**254**	**.421**	**51**	**60**	**.850**	**29**	**85**	**114**	**41**	**40**	**3**	**41**	**274**	**3.6**	**1.3**	**8.6**

Three-point field goals: 1997-98, 1-for-3 (.333). 1998-99, 0-for-2. 1999-00, 2-for-9 (.222). 2000-01, 2-for-7 (.286). 2001-02, 1-for-8 (.125). 2002-03, 2-for-7 (.286). 2003-04, 1-for-5 (.200). 2005-06, 0-for-1. Totals, 9-for-42 (.214).

Personal fouls/disqualifications: 1997-98, 4/0. 1998-99, 5/0. 1999-00, 7/0. 2000-01, 14/0. 2001-02, 5/0. 2002-03, 11/0. 2003-04, 5/0. 2005-06, 5/0. Totals, 56/0.

WNBA ALL-STAR GAME RECORD

Season Team	Min.	FGM	FGA	Pct.	FTM	FTA	Pct.	REBOUNDS Off.	Def.	Tot.	Ast.	PF	Dq.	St.	Blk.	TO	Pts.
2001—Houston..................	20	2	7	.286	2	2	1.000	1	0	1	0	0	0	0	0	2	7
Totals	**20**	**2**	**7**	**.286**	**2**	**2**	**1.000**	**1**	**0**	**1**	**0**	**0**	**0**	**0**	**0**	**2**	**7**

Three-point field goals: 2002, 1-for-2 (.500). Totals, 1-for-2 (.500).

BARANOVA, ELENA   F   LIBERTY

PERSONAL: Born January 28, 1972, in Bishkek, Kyrgyzstan. ... 6-5/182. (1.96/82.6).

TRANSACTIONS/CAREER NOTES: Signed by WNBA and assigned to Utah, January 22, 1997. ... Traded by Utah, along with a second-round pick in 2000 WNBA Draft, to Miami for G Kate Starbird and Miami's first-round pick in 2000 WNBA Draft, December 15, 1999.

OLYMPICS RECORD

Season Team	G	Min.	FGM	FGA	Pct.	FTM	FTA	Pct.	Reb.	Ast.	Pts.	AVERAGES RPG	APG	PPG
1996—Russia............................	8	...	62	177	.350	37	44	.841	105	10	162	13.1	1.3	20.3
2004—Russia............................	8	217	29	79	.367	28	32	.875	62	11	93	7.8	1.4	11.6
Totals.....................................	**16**	**217**	**91**	**256**	**.355**	**65**	**76**	**.855**	**167**	**21**	**255**	**10.4**	**1.3**	**15.9**

Three-point field goals: 1996-97, 1-for-11 (.091). 2004-05, 7-for-27 (.259). Totals, 8-for-38 (.211).
Personal fouls/disqualifications: 2004-05, 18/0. Totals, 18/0.

WNBA REGULAR-SEASON RECORD

NOTES: Bud Light Free Throw Shooting Champion (2001).

Season Team	G	Min.	FGM	FGA	Pct.	FTM	FTA	Pct.	REBOUNDS Off.	Def.	Tot.	Ast.	St.	Blk.	TO	Pts.	AVERAGES RPG	APG	PPG
1997—Utah................	28	913	129	331	.390	43	62	.694	56	151	207	62	43	63	82	341	7.4	2.2	12.2
1998—Utah................	20	671	92	219	.420	59	71	.831	61	125	186	70	21	30	55	258	9.3	3.5	12.9
1999—Utah................	29	572	60	148	.405	33	41	.805	25	73	98	45	20	23	44	173	3.4	1.6	6.0
2001—Miami	32	984	141	330	.427	66	71	.930	40	151	191	63	33	57	62	378	6.0	2.0	11.8
2003—New York.........	33	850	107	257	.416	31	35	.886	45	136	181	64	36	43	62	278	5.5	1.9	8.4
2004—New York.........	34	1048	146	315	.463	49	53	.925	33	213	246	67	37	58	80	394	7.2	2.0	11.6
2005—New York.........	33	953	104	236	.441	47	55	.855	39	188	227	59	25	46	59	288	6.9	1.8	8.7
Totals	**209**	**5991**	**779**	**1836**	**.424**	**328**	**388**	**.845**	**299**	**1037**	**1336**	**430**	**215**	**320**	**444**	**2110**	**6.4**	**2.1**	**10.1**

Three-point field goals: 1997-98, 40-for-106 (.377). 1998-99, 15-for-48 (.313). 1999-00, 20-for-48 (.417). 2001-02, 30-for-80 (.375). 2003-04, 33-for-91 (.363). 2004-05, 53-for-115 (.461). 2005-06, 33-for-85 (.388). Totals, 224-for-573 (.391).
Personal fouls/disqualifications: 1997-98, 82/0. 1998-99, 44/1. 1999-00, 58/0. 2001-02, 81/2. 2003-04, 69/0. 2004-05, 88/0. 2005-06, 79/1. Totals, 501/4.

WNBA PLAYOFF RECORD

Season Team	G	Min.	FGM	FGA	Pct.	FTM	FTA	Pct.	REBOUNDS Off.	Def.	Tot.	Ast.	St.	Blk.	TO	Pts.	AVERAGES RPG	APG	PPG
2001—Miami	3	105	15	33	.455	8	11	.727	7	11	18	7	2	2	9	44	6.0	2.3	14.7
2004—New York.........	5	154	15	38	.395	8	10	.800	7	27	34	10	4	9	12	42	6.8	2.0	8.4
2005—New York.........	2	59	3	10	.300	2	2	1.000	1	7	8	2	3	2	1	9	4.0	1.0	4.5
Totals	**10**	**318**	**33**	**81**	**.407**	**18**	**23**	**.783**	**15**	**45**	**60**	**19**	**9**	**13**	**22**	**95**	**6.0**	**1.9**	**9.5**

Three-point field goals: 2001-02, 6-for-11 (.545). 2004-05, 4-for-13 (.308). 2005-06, 1-for-3 (.333). Totals, 11-for-27 (.407).
Personal fouls/disqualifications: 2001-02, 9/0. 2004-05, 18/0. 2005-06, 4/0. Totals, 31/0.

WNBA ALL-STAR GAME RECORD

Season Team	Min.	FGM	FGA	Pct.	FTM	FTA	Pct.	REBOUNDS Off.	Def.	Tot.	Ast.	PF	Dq.	St.	Blk.	TO	Pts.
2001—Miami	25	4	8	.500	1	2	.500	0	7	7	2	2	0	1	4	2	10
Totals.........................	**25**	**4**	**8**	**.500**	**1**	**2**	**.500**	**0**	**7**	**7**	**2**	**2**	**0**	**1**	**4**	**2**	**10**

Three-point field goals: 2002, 1-for-2 (.500). Totals, 1-for-2 (.500).

BATKOVIC, SUZY   C   STORM

PERSONAL: Born December 17, 1980, in Lambton, NSW, Australia. ... 6-4. (1.93).

TRANSACTIONS/CAREER NOTES: Selected by Seattle in second round (22nd overall) of WNBA Draft, April 25, 2003.

MISCELLANEOUS: Played professionally in 2002/2003 season with Valenciennes (France and EuroLeague). ... 2001-02 season with Townsville Fire (Australia's WNBL). ... 1998-99 through 2000-01 with Sydney Panthers (WNBL). ... 1998-99 with Australian Institute of Sport (WNBL). ... Also played for Australian National Team (57 Senior Games).

B

WNBL RECORD

Season Team	G	Min.	FGM	FGA	Pct.	FTM	FTA	Pct.	Reb.	Ast.	Pts.	AVERAGES		
												RPG	APG	PPG
2001—Townsville	21	...	...	...	.490	...	...	.660	...	...	420	12.2	0.9	20.0
Totals	21	...	...	...	...	...	...	...	...	...	420	...	...	20.0

WNBA REGULAR-SEASON RECORD

Season Team	G	Min.	FGM	FGA	Pct.	FTM	FTA	Pct.	REBOUNDS			Ast.	St.	Blk.	TO	Pts.	AVERAGES		
									Off.	Def.	Tot.						RPG	APG	PPG
2005—Seattle	29	461	76	174	.437	45	58	.776	26	68	94	26	17	24	32	199	3.2	0.9	6.9
Totals	29	461	76	174	.437	45	58	.776	26	68	94	26	17	24	32	199	3.2	0.9	6.9

Three-point field goals: 2005-06, 2-for-7 (.286). Totals, 2-for-7 (.286).
Personal fouls/disqualifications: 2005-06, 85/1. Totals, 85/1.

WNBA PLAYOFF RECORD

Season Team	G	Min.	FGM	FGA	Pct.	FTM	FTA	Pct.	REBOUNDS			Ast.	St.	Blk.	TO	Pts.	AVERAGES		
									Off.	Def.	Tot.						RPG	APG	PPG
2005—Seattle	3	43	6	12	.500	2	5	.400	2	8	10	0	0	2	5	14	3.3	0.0	4.7
Totals	3	43	6	12	.500	2	5	.400	2	8	10	0	0	2	5	14	3.3	0.0	4.7

Personal fouls/disqualifications: 2005-06, 8/0. Totals, 8/0.

BATTEAST, JACQUELINE   F   SHOCK

PERSONAL: Born March 26, 1983, in South Bend, Ind. ... 6-2/175. (1.88/79.4). ... Full name: Jacqueline M. Batteast.
HIGH SCHOOL: Washington (South Bend, Ind.).
COLLEGE: Notre Dame.
TRANSACTIONS/CAREER NOTES: Selected by Minnesota in the second round (17th overall) of the WNBA Draft, April 16, 2005. ... Traded, along with a third-round pick in the 2007 draft, by Minnesota to Detroit for draft rights of Ambrosia Anderson and a second-round pick in the 2007 draft, April 5, 2006.

COLLEGE RECORD

NOTES: AP All-American third team (2005). ... AP All-American honorable mention (2004). ... All-Big East first team (2004, 2005). ... All-Big East second team (2002, 2003). ... USBWA national freshman of the year (2002). ... Big East rookie of the year (2002). ... Big East All-Freshman team (2002). ... NCAA East Regional All-Tournament team (2004). ... All-Big East academic team (2004).

Season Team	G	Min.	FGM	FGA	Pct.	FTM	FTA	Pct.	Reb.	Ast.	Pts.	AVERAGES		
												RPG	APG	PPG
2001—Notre Dame	26	718	132	327	.404	67	100	.670	165	44	462	6.3	1.7	17.8
2002—Notre Dame	32	1025	179	461	.388	78	116	.672	267	81	445	8.3	2.5	13.9
2003—Notre Dame	32	1052	204	451	.452	94	150	.627	276	73	512	8.6	2.3	16.0
2004—Notre Dame	33	1109	208	505	.412	127	162	.784	218	87	559	6.6	2.6	16.9
Totals	123	3904	723	1744	.415	366	528	.693	926	285	1978	7.5	2.3	16.1

WNBA REGULAR-SEASON RECORD

Season Team	G	Min.	FGM	FGA	Pct.	FTM	FTA	Pct.	REBOUNDS			Ast.	St.	Blk.	TO	Pts.	AVERAGES		
									Off.	Def.	Tot.						RPG	APG	PPG
2005—Minnesota	8	46	0	6	.000	0	0	...	0	5	5	3	0	1	3	0	0.6	0.4	0.0
Totals	8	46	0	6	.000	0	0	...	0	5	5	3	0	1	3	0	0.6	0.4	0.0

Personal fouls/disqualifications: 2005-06, 4/0. Totals, 4/0.

BATTLE, ASHLEY   F   LIBERTY

PERSONAL: Born May 31, 1982, in Pittsburgh. ... 6-0. (1.83). ... Full name: Ashley Michelle Battle
HIGH SCHOOL: The Linsly School (Pittsburgh).
COLLEGE: Connecticut.
TRANSACTIONS/CAREER NOTES: Selected by Seattle in the second round (25th overall) of the WNBA Draft, April 16, 2005. ... Signed by New York, February 7, 2006.
MISCELLANEOUS: Member of the gold medal-winning 2000 USA Junior World Championship Qualifying Team.

COLLEGE RECORD

NOTES: Big East defensive player of the year (2003).

Season Team	G	Min.	FGM	FGA	Pct.	FTM	FTA	Pct.	Reb.	Ast.	Pts.	AVERAGES		
												RPG	APG	PPG
2001—Connecticut	39	653	77	172	.448	50	74	.676	183	49	212	4.7	1.3	5.4
2002—Connecticut	37	828	118	245	.482	64	95	.674	198	70	307	5.4	1.9	8.3
2003—Connecticut	25	676	93	179	.520	63	76	.829	153	50	256	6.1	2.0	10.2
2004—Connecticut	33	673	95	229	.415	47	60	.783	148	59	258	4.5	1.8	7.8
Totals	134	2830	383	825	.464	224	305	.734	682	228	1033	5.1	1.7	7.7

WNBA REGULAR-SEASON RECORD

Season Team	G	Min.	FGM	FGA	Pct.	FTM	FTA	Pct.	REBOUNDS			Ast.	St.	Blk.	TO	Pts.	AVERAGES		
									Off.	Def.	Tot.						RPG	APG	PPG
2005—Seattle	2	8	1	2	.500	0	0	...	0	2	2	0	0	0	1	2	1.0	0.0	1.0
Totals	2	8	1	2	.500	0	0	...	0	2	2	0	0	0	1	2	1.0	0.0	1.0

Personal fouls/disqualifications: 2005-06, 1/0. Totals, 1/0.

BEARD, ALANA   G/F   MYSTICS

PERSONAL: Born May 14, 1982, in Shreveport, La. ... 5-11/160. (1.80/72.6). ... Full name: Alana Monique Beard
HIGH SCHOOL: Southwood (Shreveport, La.).
COLLEGE: Duke.
TRANSACTIONS/CAREER NOTES: Selected by Washington (second overall) in first round of the WNBA Draft, April 17, 2004.
MISCELLANEOUS: Member of the 2003 gold medal-winning USA Championship for Young Women Team. ... Member of the 2001 bronze medal-winning USA Junior World Championship Team. ... Member of the 2000 gold medal-winning USA Basketball Women's Junior World Championship qualifying team.

COLLEGE RECORD

NOTES: USBWA Player of the Year (2004). ... AP Player of the Year (2004). ... Wade Trophy Player of the Year (2004). ... AP All-American first team (2002, 2003, 2004). ... USBWA All-American (2002, 2003, 2004). ... Kodak All-American (2002, 2003, 2004). ... ACC Player of the Year (2002, 2003, 2004). ... All-ACC first team (2001, 2002, 2003, 2004). ... All-ACC Defensive Team (2002, 2003, 2004). ... NCAA Final Four All-Tournament Team (2003). ... USBWA, Sports Illustrated for Women, Sports Illustrated, CBS Sportsline and Women's Basketball Journal National Freshman of the Year (2001). ... ACC Freshman of the Year (2001). ... Duke's all-time leading scorer (2,687).

Season Team	G	Min.	FGM	FGA	Pct.	FTM	FTA	Pct.	Reb.	Ast.	Pts.	RPG	APG	PPG
2000—Duke	30	893	194	379	.512	111	141	.787	136	113	509	4.5	3.8	17.0
2001—Duke	35	1164	275	481	.572	119	158	.753	213	154	694	6.1	4.4	19.8
2002—Duke	37	1161	294	558	.527	201	259	.776	256	110	813	6.9	3.0	22.0
2003—Duke	34	1067	242	488	.496	151	194	.778	184	132	671	5.4	3.9	19.7
Totals	136	4285	1005	1906	.527	582	752	.774	789	509	2687	5.8	3.7	19.8

Three-point field goals: 2000-01, 10-for-51 (.196). 2001-02, 25-for-66 (.379). 2002-03, 24-for-85 (.282). 2003-04, 36-for-115 (.313). Totals, 95-for-317 (.300).

WNBA REGULAR-SEASON RECORD

NOTES: All-Defensive second team (2005).

Season Team	G	Min.	FGM	FGA	Pct.	FTM	FTA	Pct.	Off.	Def.	Tot.	Ast.	St.	Blk.	TO	Pts.	RPG	APG	PPG
2004—Washington	34	1025	159	380	.418	107	149	.718	28	115	143	91	69	34	80	446	4.2	2.7	13.1
2005—Washington	30	1015	155	408	.380	80	105	.762	25	105	130	90	45	9	63	422	4.3	3.0	14.1
Totals	64	2040	314	788	.398	187	254	.736	53	220	273	181	114	43	143	868	4.3	2.8	13.6

Three-point field goals: 2004-05, 21-for-56 (.375). 2005-06, 32-for-101 (.317). Totals, 53-for-157 (.338).
Personal fouls/disqualifications: 2004-05, 98/0. 2005-06, 87/0. Totals, 185/0.

WNBA PLAYOFF RECORD

Season Team	G	Min.	FGM	FGA	Pct.	FTM	FTA	Pct.	Off.	Def.	Tot.	Ast.	St.	Blk.	TO	Pts.	RPG	APG	PPG
2004—Washington	3	102	18	41	.439	13	13	1.000	2	13	15	9	6	8	10	50	5.0	3.0	16.7
Totals	3	102	18	41	.439	13	13	1.000	2	13	15	9	6	8	10	50	5.0	3.0	16.7

Three-point field goals: 2004-05, 1-for-4 (.250). Totals, 1-for-4 (.250).
Personal fouls/disqualifications: 2004-05, 8/0. Totals, 8/0.

WNBA ALL-STAR GAME RECORD

Season Team	Min.	FGM	FGA	Pct.	FTM	FTA	Pct.	Off.	Def.	Tot.	Ast.	PF	Dq.	St.	Blk.	TO	Pts.
2005—Washington	20	1	9	.111	0	0	...	1	4	5	2	0	0	0	1	3	2
Totals	20	1	9	.111	0	0	...	1	4	5	2	0	0	0	1	3	2

Three-point field goals: 2006, 0-for-4. Totals, 0-for-4 (.000).

BENNINGFIELD, JENNI   F   FEVER

PERSONAL: Born October 6, 1981, in Louisville, Ky. ... 6-3/185. (1.91/83.9). ... Full name: Jennifer Ann Benningfield
HIGH SCHOOL: Assumption (Louisville, Ky.).
COLLEGE: Vanderbilt.

COLLEGE RECORD

Season Team	G	Min.	FGM	FGA	Pct.	FTM	FTA	Pct.	Reb.	Ast.	Pts.	RPG	APG	PPG
2000—Vanderbilt	34	1070	113	266	.425	37	53	.698	241	107	319	7.1	3.1	9.4
2001—Vanderbilt	37	885	80	195	.410	19	27	.704	162	83	221	4.4	2.2	6.0
2002—Vanderbilt	32	992	212	381	.556	79	113	.699	253	91	528	7.9	2.8	16.5
2003—Vanderbilt	33	842	165	340	.485	93	138	.674	195	48	433	5.9	1.5	13.1
Totals	136	3789	570	1182	.482	228	331	.689	851	329	1501	6.3	2.4	11.0

Three-point field goals: 2000-01, 56-for-139 (.403). 2001-02, 42-for-102 (.412). 2002-03, 25-for-66 (.379). 2003-04, 10-for-34 (.294). Totals, 133-for-341 (.390).

WNBA REGULAR-SEASON RECORD

Season Team	G	Min.	FGM	FGA	Pct.	FTM	FTA	Pct.	Off.	Def.	Tot.	Ast.	St.	Blk.	TO	Pts.	RPG	APG	PPG
2005—Indiana	10	52	3	8	.375	3	4	.750	3	3	6	4	1	1	4	9	0.6	0.4	0.9
Totals	10	52	3	8	.375	3	4	.750	3	3	6	4	1	1	4	9	0.6	0.4	0.9

Three-point field goals: 2005-06, 0-for-2. Totals, 0-for-2 (.000).
Personal fouls/disqualifications: 2005-06, 5/0. Totals, 5/0.

BEVILAQUA, TULLY　　　　　G　　　　　　　FEVER

PERSONAL: Born July 19, 1972, in Australia. ... 5-7/140. (1.70/63.5).
TRANSACTIONS/CAREER NOTES: Signed by the WNBA and assigned to Cleveland, May 30, 1998. ... Waived by Cleveland, July 16, 1998. ... Signed by the WNBA and assigned to Portland, May 1, 2000. ... Signed by Indiana, February 24, 2005.
MISCELLANEOUS: Member of WNBA Championship Team (2004).

WNBA REGULAR-SEASON RECORD

NOTES: All-Defensive first team (2005).

Season Team	G	Min.	FGM	FGA	Pct.	FTM	FTA	Pct.	Off.	Def.	Tot.	Ast.	St.	Blk.	TO	Pts.	RPG	APG	PPG
									REBOUNDS								**AVERAGES**		
1998—Cleveland	12	126	9	16	.563	4	6	.667	2	8	10	24	12	2	9	23	0.8	2.0	1.9
2000—Portland	32	796	40	112	.357	56	72	.778	19	76	95	89	41	6	66	153	3.0	2.8	4.8
2001—Portland	31	788	39	119	.328	52	71	.732	27	61	88	103	59	6	52	153	2.8	3.3	4.9
2002—Portland	27	421	25	61	.410	19	29	.655	7	26	33	44	22	3	27	84	1.2	1.6	3.1
2003—Seattle	31	252	17	51	.333	16	21	.762	9	17	26	32	14	1	20	58	0.8	1.0	1.9
2004—Seattle	34	358	24	60	.400	20	29	.690	6	20	26	29	38	2	26	79	0.8	0.9	2.3
2005—Indiana	31	873	63	162	.389	24	44	.545	12	51	63	80	60	0	51	194	2.0	2.6	6.3
Totals	186	3488	208	565	.368	187	266	.703	80	251	331	377	234	18	242	721	1.8	2.0	3.9

Three-point field goals: 2000-01, 17-for-60 (.283). 2001-02, 23-for-73 (.315). 2002-03, 15-for-36 (.417). 2003-04, 8-for-21 (.381). 2004-05, 11-for-26 (.423). 2005-06, 44-for-116 (.379). Totals, 118-for-332 (.355).

Personal fouls/disqualifications: 2000-01, 93/1. 2001-02, 102/0. 2002-03, 49/0. 2003-04, 30/0. 2004-05, 48/0. 2005-06, 69/0. Totals, 391/1.

WNBA PLAYOFF RECORD

Season Team	G	Min.	FGM	FGA	Pct.	FTM	FTA	Pct.	Off.	Def.	Tot.	Ast.	St.	Blk.	TO	Pts.	RPG	APG	PPG
									REBOUNDS								**AVERAGES**		
2004—Seattle	8	111	8	17	.471	3	4	.750	3	13	16	11	8	1	9	22	2.0	1.4	2.8
2005—Indiana	4	152	8	25	.320	5	7	.714	1	8	9	11	7	1	10	27	2.3	2.8	6.8
Totals	12	263	16	42	.381	8	11	.727	4	21	25	22	15	2	19	49	2.1	1.8	4.1

Three-point field goals: 2004-05, 3-for-7 (.429). 2005-06, 6-for-14 (.429). Totals, 9-for-21 (.429).

Personal fouls/disqualifications: 2004-05, 12/0. 2005-06, 12/0. Totals, 24/0.

BIRD, SUE　　　　　　　G　　　　　　　STORM

PERSONAL: Born October 16, 1980, in Syosset, N.Y. ... 5-9/150. (1.75/68.0). ... Full name: Suzanne Brigit Bird
HIGH SCHOOL: Christ the King (Middle Village, N.Y.).
COLLEGE: Connecticut.
TRANSACTIONS/CAREER NOTES: Selected by Seattle in first round (first overall) of WNBA Draft, April 19, 2002.
MISCELLANEOUS: Member of WNBA Championship Team (2004).

COLLEGE RECORD

NOTES: Member of NCAA Division I Championship Team (2000, 2002). ... Naismith Award winner (2002). ... Wade Trophy recipient (2002). ... USBWA and AP National Player of the Year (2002). ... Kodak All-American first team (2002).

Season Team	G	Min.	FGM	FGA	Pct.	FTM	FTA	Pct.	Reb.	Ast.	Pts.	RPG	APG	PPG
												AVERAGES		
1998—Connecticut	8	160	16	41	.390	3	4	.750	16	25	41	2.0	3.1	5.1
1999—Connecticut	37	1052	140	279	.502	53	59	.898	94	160	405	2.5	4.3	10.9
2000—Connecticut	34	941	137	309	.443	35	45	.778	89	169	369	2.6	5.0	10.9
2001—Connecticut	39	1168	198	392	.505	98	104	.942	131	231	563	3.4	5.9	14.4
Totals	118	3321	491	1021	.481	189	212	.892	330	585	1378	2.8	5.0	11.7

Three-point field goals: 1998-99, 6-for-19 (.316). 1999-00, 72-for-145 (.497). 2000-01, 60-for-139 (.432). 2001-02, 69-for-148 (.466). Totals, 207-for-451 (.459).

WNBA REGULAR-SEASON RECORD

NOTES: All-WNBA first team (2002, 2003, 2004, 2005). ... Led WNBA in free throw percentage (.911) in 2002. ... Cascade Dish and Assist (2005). ... Led WNBA in assists (5.9 apg) in 2005.

Season Team	G	Min.	FGM	FGA	Pct.	FTM	FTA	Pct.	Off.	Def.	Tot.	Ast.	St.	Blk.	TO	Pts.	RPG	APG	PPG
									REBOUNDS								**AVERAGES**		
2002—Seattle	32	1121	151	375	.403	102	112	.911	17	66	83	191	55	3	109	461	2.6	6.0	14.4
2003—Seattle	34	1136	155	368	.421	61	69	.884	22	91	113	221	48	1	110	420	3.3	6.5	12.4
2004—Seattle	34	1136	151	326	.463	73	85	.859	22	84	106	184	51	5	87	439	3.1	5.4	12.9
2005—Seattle	30	1020	130	294	.442	59	69	.855	21	51	72	176	29	6	87	364	2.4	5.9	12.1
Totals	130	4413	587	1363	.431	295	335	.881	82	292	374	772	183	15	393	1684	2.9	5.9	13.0

Three-point field goals: 2002-03, 57-for-142 (.401). 2003-04, 49-for-140 (.350). 2004-05, 64-for-146 (.438). 2005-06, 45-for-103 (.437). Totals, 215-for-531 (.405).

Personal fouls/disqualifications: 2002-03, 48/0. 2003-04, 47/0. 2004-05, 48/0. 2005-06, 46/0. Totals, 189/0.

WNBA PLAYOFF RECORD

Season Team	G	Min.	FGM	FGA	Pct.	FTM	FTA	Pct.	Off.	Def.	Tot.	Ast.	St.	Blk.	TO	Pts.	RPG	APG	PPG
									REBOUNDS								**AVERAGES**		
2002—Seattle	2	73	9	22	.409	7	7	1.000	0	0	0	12	5	0	5	28	0.0	6.0	14.0
2004—Seattle	8	233	23	61	.377	16	21	.762	5	21	26	42	12	0	16	68	3.3	5.3	8.5
2005—Seattle	3	103	9	33	.273	7	8	.875	1	4	5	13	3	0	4	27	1.7	4.3	9.0
Totals	13	409	41	116	.353	30	36	.833	6	25	31	67	20	0	25	123	2.4	5.2	9.5

Three-point field goals: 2002-03, 3-for-11 (.273). 2004-05, 6-for-20 (.300). 2005-06, 2-for-15 (.133). Totals, 11-for-46 (.239).

B

Personal fouls/disqualifications: 2002-03, 6/0. 2004-05, 13/0. 2005-06, 6/0. Totals, 25/0.

WNBA ALL-STAR GAME RECORD

Season Team	Min.	FGM	FGA	Pct.	FTM	FTA	Pct.	REBOUNDS Off.	Def.	Tot.	Ast.	PF	Dq.	St.	Blk.	TO	Pts.
2002—Seattle	21	1	8	.125	0	0	...	4	1	5	7	0	0	1	0	1	2
2003—Seattle	21	3	8	.375	4	5	.800	1	3	4	2	1	0	0	0	2	11
2005—Seattle	19	5	6	.833	1	2	.500	1	3	4	3	0	0	1	0	0	14
Totals	61	9	22	.409	5	7	.714	6	7	13	12	1	0	2	0	3	27

Three-point field goals: 2003, 0-for-5. 2004, 1-for-4 (.250). 2006, 3-for-3 (1.000). Totals, 4-for-12 (.333).

OLYMPICS RECORD

Season Team	G	Min.	FGM	FGA	Pct.	FTM	FTA	Pct.	Reb.	Ast.	Pts.	AVERAGES RPG	APG	PPG
2004—United States	7	90	9	30	.300	0	0	...	6	8	20	0.9	1.1	2.9
Totals	7	90	9	30	.300	0	0	...	6	8	20	0.9	1.1	2.9

Three-point field goals: 2004-05, 2-for-16 (.125). Totals, 2-for-16 (.125).
Personal fouls/disqualifications: 2004-05, 3/0. Totals, 3/0.

BRAXTON, KARA   F   SHOCK

PERSONAL: Born February 18, 1983 ... 6-6/190. (1.98/86.2). ... Full name: Kara Liana Braxton
HIGH SCHOOL: Westview (Westview, Ore.).
COLLEGE: Georgia.
TRANSACTIONS/CAREER NOTES: Selected by Detroit in the first round (seventh overall) of the WNBA Draft, April 16, 2005.

COLLEGE RECORD

NOTES: All-SEC first team (2002). ... SEC Freshman of the Year (2002). ... SEC All-Freshman team (2002).

Season Team	G	Min.	FGM	FGA	Pct.	FTM	FTA	Pct.	Reb.	Ast.	Pts.	AVERAGES RPG	APG	PPG
2001—Georgia	30	734	198	367	.540	92	147	.626	205	68	489	6.8	2.3	16.3
2002—Georgia	21	500	134	243	.551	60	82	.732	153	52	330	7.3	2.5	15.7
2003—Georgia	20	488	108	226	.478	57	88	.648	160	23	274	8.0	1.2	13.7
Totals	71	1722	440	836	.526	209	317	.659	518	143	1093	7.3	2.0	15.4

Three-point field goals: 2001-02, 1-for-7 (.143). 2002-03, 2-for-7 (.286). 2003-04, 1-for-6 (.167). Totals, 4-for-20 (.200).

WNBA REGULAR-SEASON RECORD

NOTES: Named to WNBA All-Rookie team (2005).

Season Team	G	Min.	FGM	FGA	Pct.	FTM	FTA	Pct.	REBOUNDS Off.	Def.	Tot.	Ast.	St.	Blk.	TO	Pts.	AVERAGES RPG	APG	PPG
2005—Detroit	33	455	97	210	.462	33	60	.550	42	58	100	14	18	13	52	227	3.0	0.4	6.9
Totals	33	455	97	210	.462	33	60	.550	42	58	100	14	18	13	52	227	3.0	0.4	6.9

Three-point field goals: 2005-06, 0-for-1. Totals, 0-for-1 (.000).
Personal fouls/disqualifications: 2005-06, 78/0. Totals, 78/0.

WNBA PLAYOFF RECORD

Season Team	G	Min.	FGM	FGA	Pct.	FTM	FTA	Pct.	REBOUNDS Off.	Def.	Tot.	Ast.	St.	Blk.	TO	Pts.	AVERAGES RPG	APG	PPG
2005—Detroit	2	36	5	18	.278	5	6	.833	4	3	7	2	0	0	3	15	3.5	1.0	7.5
Totals	2	36	5	18	.278	5	6	.833	4	3	7	2	0	0	3	15	3.5	1.0	7.5

Personal fouls/disqualifications: 2005-06, 5/0. Totals, 5/0.

BROWN, CORETTA   G   FEVER

PERSONAL: Born October 21, 1980, in Statesboro, Ga. ... 5-9/150. (1.75/68.0). ... Full name: Coretta Renay Brown
HIGH SCHOOL: Southeast Bulloch (Brooklet, Ga.).
COLLEGE: North Carolina.
TRANSACTIONS/CAREER NOTES: Selected by San Antonio in first round (11th overall) of WNBA Draft, April 25, 2003. ... Traded by San Antonio with F Natalie Williams to Indiana for C Sylvia Crawley and F Gwen Jackson, May 1, 2003.

COLLEGE RECORD

NOTES: AP All-American Honorable Mention (2003). ... All-ACC first team (2002, 2003). ... Holds UNC record for career three-point percentage (.380). ... Set ACC record with 99 three-pointers made as a junior.

Season Team	G	Min.	FGM	FGA	Pct.	FTM	FTA	Pct.	Reb.	Ast.	Pts.	AVERAGES RPG	APG	PPG
1999—North Carolina	33	543	48	160	.300	26	41	.634	56	59	135	1.7	1.8	4.1
2000—North Carolina	29	1121	156	408	.382	99	145	.683	138	193	462	4.8	6.7	15.9
2001—North Carolina	35	1203	216	469	.461	67	93	.720	175	118	598	5.0	3.4	17.1
2002—North Carolina	34	1152	157	396	.396	90	108	.833	123	147	492	3.6	4.3	14.5
Totals	131	4019	577	1433	.403	282	387	.729	492	517	1687	3.8	3.9	12.9

Three-point field goals: 1999-00, 13-for-49 (.265). 2000-01, 51-for-138 (.370). 2001-02, 99-for-251 (.394). 2002-03, 88-for-223 (.395). Totals, 251-for-661 (.380).

WNBA REGULAR-SEASON RECORD

Season Team	G	Min.	FGM	FGA	Pct.	FTM	FTA	Pct.	REBOUNDS Off.	Def.	Tot.	Ast.	St.	Blk.	TO	Pts.	AVERAGES RPG	APG	PPG
2003—Indiana	30	522	61	164	.372	28	33	.848	11	30	41	31	21	4	36	186	1.4	1.0	6.2

Season Team	G	Min.	FGM	FGA	Pct.	FTM	FTA	Pct.	Off.	Def.	Tot.	Ast.	St.	Blk.	TO	Pts.	RPG	APG	PPG
2004—Indiana	26	398	37	108	.343	10	16	.625	10	24	34	41	7	1	31	104	1.3	1.6	4.0
2005—Indiana	6	23	2	5	.400	0	0	...	0	2	2	3	1	0	3	6	0.3	0.5	1.0
Totals	62	943	100	277	.361	38	49	.776	21	56	77	75	29	5	70	296	1.2	1.2	4.8

Three-point field goals: 2003-04, 36-for-100 (.360). 2004-05, 20-for-56 (.357). 2005-06, 2-for-5 (.400). Totals, 58-for-161 (.360).
Personal fouls/disqualifications: 2003-04, 30/0. 2004-05, 31/0. 2005-06, 1/0. Totals, 62/0.

BROWN, KIESHA G LIBERTY

B

PERSONAL: Born January 13, 1979 ... 5-10/134. (1.78/60.8).
COLLEGE: Georgia.
TRANSACTIONS/CAREER NOTES: Signed by the WNBA and added by Los Angeles, April 30, 2001. ... Waived by Los Angeles, May 24, 2001. ... Added by Washington, April 25, 2002. ... Signed by Houston, July 12, 2005. ... Selected by Chicago in WNBA Expansion Draft, November 16, 2005. ... Signed by New York, February 27, 2006.

COLLEGE RECORD

Season Team	G	Min.	FGM	FGA	Pct.	FTM	FTA	Pct.	Reb.	Ast.	Pts.	RPG	APG	PPG
1996—Georgia	8	...	19	41	.463	13	19	.684	20	36	52	2.5	4.5	6.5
1997—Georgia						Did not play—injured.								
1998—Georgia	34	...	65	147	.442	58	81	.716	102	109	196	3.0	3.2	5.8
1999—Georgia	36	...	36	100	.360	15	24	.625	68	55	87	1.9	1.5	2.4
2000—Georgia	33	...	53	159	.333	53	71	.746	102	93	160	3.1	2.8	4.8
Totals	111	...	173	447	.387	139	195	.713	292	293	495	2.6	2.6	4.5

Three-point field goals: 1996-97, 1-for-9 (.111). 1998-99, 8-for-34 (.235). 1999-00, 0-for-4. 2000-01, 1-for-12 (.083). Totals, 10-for-59 (.169).

WNBA REGULAR-SEASON RECORD

Season Team	G	Min.	FGM	FGA	Pct.	FTM	FTA	Pct.	Off.	Def.	Tot.	Ast.	St.	Blk.	TO	Pts.	RPG	APG	PPG
2002—Washington	18	108	12	35	.343	3	3	1.000	4	8	12	6	5	0	5	28	0.7	0.3	1.6
2003—Washington	27	269	24	72	.333	2	3	.667	6	26	32	28	13	1	22	60	1.2	1.0	2.2
2004—Washington	26	371	35	88	.398	21	24	.875	9	41	50	42	13	2	33	104	1.9	1.6	4.0
2005—Wash.-Houston	6	32	1	2	.500	0	0	...	0	1	1	2	3	0	4	2	0.2	0.3	0.3
Totals	77	780	72	197	.365	26	30	.867	19	76	95	78	34	3	64	194	1.2	1.0	2.5

Three-point field goals: 2002-03, 1-for-11 (.091). 2003-04, 10-for-33 (.303). 2004-05, 13-for-28 (.464). 2005-06, 0-for-1. Totals, 24-for-73 (.329).
Personal fouls/disqualifications: 2002-03, 10/0. 2003-04, 23/0. 2004-05, 21/0. 2005-06, 1/0. Totals, 55/0.

WNBA PLAYOFF RECORD

Season Team	G	Min.	FGM	FGA	Pct.	FTM	FTA	Pct.	Off.	Def.	Tot.	Ast.	St.	Blk.	TO	Pts.	RPG	APG	PPG
2002—Washington	2	15	3	6	.500	0	0	...	0	1	1	1	2	0	0	6	0.5	0.5	3.0
2004—Washington	2	3	1	1	1.000	0	0	...	0	0	0	0	0	0	0	3	0.0	0.0	1.5
2005—Houston	1	1	0	0	...	2	2	1.000	0	0	0	0	0	0	0	2	0.0	0.0	2.0
Totals	5	19	4	7	.571	2	2	1.000	0	1	1	1	2	0	0	11	0.2	0.2	2.2

Three-point field goals: 2002-03, 0-for-2. 2004-05, 1-for-1 (1.000). Totals, 1-for-3 (.333).
Personal fouls/disqualifications: 2002-03, 3/0. 2005-06, 1/0. Totals, 4/0.

BRUNGO, JESSICA F SUN

PERSONAL: Born April 16, 1982, in Plainview, N.Y. ... 6-1/165. (1.85/74.8). ... Full name: Jessica Kathryn Brungo
HIGH SCHOOL: North Allegheny (Allison Park, Pa.).
COLLEGE: Penn State.
TRANSACTIONS/CAREER NOTES: Selected by Connecticut in second round (16th overall) of WNBA Draft, April 17, 2004.

COLLEGE RECORD

NOTES: All-Big Ten honorable mention (coaches and media, 2004). ... All-Big Ten second team (media, 2003) ... All-Academic Big Ten (2002, 2003, 2004).

Season Team	G	Min.	FGM	FGA	Pct.	FTM	FTA	Pct.	Reb.	Ast.	Pts.	RPG	APG	PPG
2000—Penn State	29	415	60	143	.420	20	28	.714	86	28	167	3.0	1.0	5.8
2001—Penn State	35	675	95	227	.419	30	37	.811	142	42	233	4.1	1.2	6.7
2002—Penn State	35	1058	162	332	.488	38	47	.809	219	90	400	6.3	2.6	11.4
2003—Penn State	34	1083	128	330	.388	47	56	.839	202	57	343	5.9	1.7	10.1
Totals	133	3231	445	1032	.431	135	168	.804	649	217	1143	4.9	1.6	8.6

Three-point field goals: 2000-01, 27-for-62 (.435). 2001-02, 13-for-52 (.250). 2002-03, 38-for-113 (.336). 2003-04, 39-for-135 (.289). Totals, 117-for-362 (.323).

WNBA REGULAR-SEASON RECORD

Season Team	G	Min.	FGM	FGA	Pct.	FTM	FTA	Pct.	Off.	Def.	Tot.	Ast.	St.	Blk.	TO	Pts.	RPG	APG	PPG
2004—Connecticut	33	314	18	59	.305	4	5	.800	10	27	37	27	4	4	12	50	1.1	0.8	1.5
2005—Connecticut	12	47	1	9	.111	0	0	...	1	5	6	2	0	0	2	2	0.5	0.2	0.2
Totals	45	361	19	68	.279	4	5	.800	11	32	43	29	4	4	14	52	1.0	0.6	1.2

Three-point field goals: 2004-05, 10-for-38 (.263). 2005-06, 0-for-4. Totals, 10-for-42 (.238).

Personal fouls/disqualifications: 2004-05, 21/0. 2005-06, 4/0. Totals, 25/0.

WNBA PLAYOFF RECORD

Season Team	G	Min.	FGM	FGA	Pct.	FTM	FTA	Pct.	REBOUNDS Off.	Def.	Tot.	Ast.	St.	Blk.	TO	Pts.	AVERAGES RPG	APG	PPG
2004—Connecticut........	8	101	3	15	.200	0	0	...	5	8	13	5	1	0	2	8	1.6	0.6	1.0
Totals	8	101	3	15	.200	0	0	...	5	8	13	5	1	0	2	8	1.6	0.6	1.0

Three-point field goals: 2004-05, 2-for-10 (.200). Totals, 2-for-10 (.200).
Personal fouls/disqualifications: 2004-05, 5/0. Totals, 5/0.

BRUNSON, REBEKKAH   F   MONARCHS

PERSONAL: Born December 11, 1981, in Washington, D.C. ... 6-3/175. (1.91/79.4). ... Full name: Rebekkah Wright Brunson
HIGH SCHOOL: Oxon Hill (Oxon Hill, Md.).
COLLEGE: Georgetown.
TRANSACTIONS/CAREER NOTES: Selected by Sacramento in first round (10th overall) of WNBA Draft, April 17, 2004.
MISCELLANEOUS: Member of silver medal-winning Team USA at Pan American Games. ... Member of WNBA Championship team (2005).

COLLEGE RECORD

NOTES: AP All-American honorable mention (2004). ... Big East Defensive Player of the Year (2004). ... All-Big East first team (2003, 2004). ... All-Big East honorable mention (2001, 2002). ... Big East Rookie of the Year (2001). ... Georgetown's all-time leading rebounder (1,093). ... Georgetown's single-season rebound record holder (336 in 2004). ... Ranked first and second on Georgetown's single-season blocked shots list (51 in 2003, 50 in 2004).

Season Team	G	Min.	FGM	FGA	Pct.	FTM	FTA	Pct.	Reb.	Ast.	Pts.	AVERAGES RPG	APG	PPG
2000—Georgetown........................	32	1022	192	377	.509	90	160	.563	293	23	474	9.2	0.7	14.8
2001—Georgetown........................	18	567	102	212	.481	67	100	.670	153	11	272	8.5	0.6	15.1
2002—Georgetown........................	29	985	170	367	.463	134	200	.670	311	44	481	10.7	1.5	16.6
2003—Georgetown........................	28	1020	206	425	.485	121	199	.608	336	35	535	12.0	1.3	19.1
Totals	107	3594	670	1381	.485	412	659	.625	1093	113	1762	10.2	1.1	16.5

Three-point field goals: 2001-02, 1-for-12 (.083). 2002-03, 7-for-16 (.438). 2003-04, 2-for-11 (.182). Totals, 10-for-39 (.256).

WNBA REGULAR-SEASON RECORD

Season Team	G	Min.	FGM	FGA	Pct.	FTM	FTA	Pct.	REBOUNDS Off.	Def.	Tot.	Ast.	St.	Blk.	TO	Pts.	AVERAGES RPG	APG	PPG
2004—Sacramento	34	494	59	140	.421	33	46	.717	42	80	122	19	23	13	29	151	3.6	0.6	4.4
2005—Sacramento	34	722	105	246	.427	55	92	.598	75	112	187	16	28	15	42	265	5.5	0.5	7.8
Totals	68	1216	164	386	.425	88	138	.638	117	192	309	35	51	28	71	416	4.5	0.5	6.1

Personal fouls/disqualifications: 2004-05, 48/0. 2005-06, 61/0. Totals, 109/0.

WNBA PLAYOFF RECORD

Season Team	G	Min.	FGM	FGA	Pct.	FTM	FTA	Pct.	REBOUNDS Off.	Def.	Tot.	Ast.	St.	Blk.	TO	Pts.	AVERAGES RPG	APG	PPG
2004—Sacramento	6	80	7	20	.350	5	7	.714	8	9	17	3	2	4	3	19	2.8	0.5	3.2
2005—Sacramento	8	194	25	56	.446	5	11	.455	13	31	44	10	5	4	9	55	5.5	1.3	6.9
Totals	14	274	32	76	.421	10	18	.556	21	40	61	13	7	8	12	74	4.4	0.9	5.3

Personal fouls/disqualifications: 2004-05, 5/0. 2005-06, 27/0. Totals, 32/0.

BUESCHER, ERIN   G   MONARCHS

PERSONAL: Born June 5, 1979, in San Francisco. ... 6-2/181. (1.88/82.1). ... Full name: Erin Rebecca Buescher
HIGH SCHOOL: Rincon Valley Christian (Santa Rosa, Calif.).
COLLEGE: Master's College.
TRANSACTIONS/CAREER NOTES: Selected by Minnesota in second round (23rd overall) of WNBA Draft, April 20, 2001. ... Traded by Minnesota along with F Maylana Martin to Charlotte for G Shaunzinski Gortman, April 19, 2002. ... Traded by Charlotte along with G/F Nicole Powell and C/F Olympia Scott-Richardson to Sacramento in exchange for F/C Tangela Smith and the Monarchs' second-round pick in the 2006 WNBA Draft.
MISCELLANEOUS: Member of WNBA Championship team (2005).

COLLEGE RECORD

NOTES: NAIA All-American first team (2001).

Season Team	G	Min.	FGM	FGA	Pct.	FTM	FTA	Pct.	Reb.	Ast.	Pts.	AVERAGES RPG	APG	PPG
1997—UC-Santa Barbara	31	...	210	406	.517	89	131	.679	269	93	530	8.7	3.0	17.1
1998—UC-Santa Barbara	30	...	207	395	.524	140	195	.718	274	102	597	9.1	3.4	19.9
1999—UC-Santa Barbara	33	...	216	436	.495	119	183	.650	321	95	570	9.7	2.9	17.3
2000—Master's College................	25	700	158	323	.489	116	147	.789	233	77	439	9.3	3.1	17.6
Totals	119	700	791	1560	.507	464	656	.707	1097	367	2136	9.2	3.1	17.9

Three-point field goals: 1997-98, 21-for-54 (.389). 1998-99, 43-for-91 (.473). 1999-00, 19-for-71 (.268). 2000-01, 7-for-32 (.219). Totals, 90-for-248 (.363).

WNBA REGULAR-SEASON RECORD

Season Team	G	Min.	FGM	FGA	Pct.	FTM	FTA	Pct.	REBOUNDS Off.	Def.	Tot.	Ast.	St.	Blk.	TO	Pts.	AVERAGES RPG	APG	PPG
2001—Minnesota..........	32	725	64	184	.348	47	76	.618	42	76	118	62	27	29	65	183	3.7	1.9	5.7

Season Team	G	Min.	FGM	FGA	Pct.	FTM	FTA	Pct.	Off.	Def.	Tot.	Ast.	St.	Blk.	TO	Pts.	RPG	APG	PPG
2002—Charlotte	29	392	33	82	.402	25	36	.694	32	59	91	18	13	15	27	95	3.1	0.6	3.3
2003—Charlotte	14	44	3	8	.375	3	4	.750	2	2	4	3	0	0	2	9	0.3	0.2	0.6
2005—Sacramento	23	209	28	40	.700	20	34	.588	14	15	29	14	16	5	26	76	1.3	0.6	3.3
Totals	98	1370	128	314	.408	95	150	.633	90	152	242	97	56	49	120	363	2.5	1.0	3.7

Three-point field goals: 2001-02, 8-for-29 (.276). 2002-03, 4-for-11 (.364). Totals, 12-for-40 (.300).
Personal fouls/disqualifications: 2001-02, 101/2. 2002-03, 26/1. 2003-04, 61/1. 2005-06, 29/0. Totals, 197/3.

WNBA PLAYOFF RECORD

Season Team	G	Min.	FGM	FGA	Pct.	FTM	FTA	Pct.	Off.	Def.	Tot.	Ast.	St.	Blk.	TO	Pts.	RPG	APG	PPG
2002—Charlotte	2	31	7	8	.875	2	4	.500	2	5	7	1	0	1	3	17	3.5	0.5	8.5
2005—Sacramento	3	13	0	0	...	3	6	.500	1	3	4	2	0	1	1	3	1.3	0.7	1.0
Totals	5	44	7	8	.875	5	10	.500	3	8	11	3	0	2	4	20	2.2	0.6	4.0

Three-point field goals: 2002-03, 1-for-1 (1.000). Totals, 1-for-1 (1.000).
Personal fouls/disqualifications: 2002-03, 6/0. Totals, 6/0.

BURSE, JANELL   C   STORM

PERSONAL: Born May 19, 1979, in New Orleans. ... 6-5/199. (1.96/90.3). ... Full name: Janell Latrice Burse
HIGH SCHOOL: Redeemer-Seton (New Orleans).
COLLEGE: Tulane.
TRANSACTIONS/CAREER NOTES: Selected by Minnesota in second round (28th overall) of WNBA Draft, April 20, 2001.
MISCELLANEOUS: Member of WNBA Championship Team (2004).

COLLEGE RECORD

Season Team	G	Min.	FGM	FGA	Pct.	FTM	FTA	Pct.	Reb.	Ast.	Pts.	RPG	APG	PPG
1997—Tulane	22	186	37	78	.474	19	41	.463	66	5	93	3.0	0.2	4.2
1998—Tulane	30	455	133	237	.561	58	104	.558	148	10	324	4.9	0.3	10.8
1999—Tulane	32	913	233	392	.594	139	228	.610	315	26	605	9.8	0.8	18.9
2000—Tulane	32	905	233	391	.596	136	252	.540	342	30	603	10.7	0.9	18.8
Totals	116	2459	636	1098	.579	352	625	.563	871	71	1625	7.5	0.6	14.0

Three-point field goals: 2000-01, 1-for-1 (1.000). Totals, 1-for-1 (1.000).

WNBA REGULAR-SEASON RECORD

Season Team	G	Min.	FGM	FGA	Pct.	FTM	FTA	Pct.	Off.	Def.	Tot.	Ast.	St.	Blk.	TO	Pts.	RPG	APG	PPG
2001—Minnesota	20	169	16	48	.333	15	20	.750	23	19	42	5	2	15	20	47	2.1	0.3	2.4
2002—Minnesota	31	344	31	83	.373	21	36	.583	29	31	60	7	7	13	18	83	1.9	0.2	2.7
2003—Minnesota	29	438	76	155	.490	54	70	.771	40	68	108	19	13	28	42	206	3.7	0.7	7.1
2004—Seattle	29	514	51	119	.429	39	67	.582	51	45	96	19	23	36	41	141	3.3	0.7	4.9
2005—Seattle	34	859	127	243	.523	86	123	.699	81	118	199	23	19	40	78	340	5.9	0.7	10.0
Totals	143	2324	301	648	.465	215	316	.680	224	281	505	73	64	132	199	817	3.5	0.5	5.7

Three-point field goals: 2001-02, 0-for-1. 2002-03, 0-for-1. 2003-04, 0-for-2. Totals, 0-for-4 (.000).
Personal fouls/disqualifications: 2001-02, 20/0. 2002-03, 60/0. 2003-04, 81/2. 2004-05, 84/2. 2005-06, 139/6. Totals, 384/10.

WNBA PLAYOFF RECORD

Season Team	G	Min.	FGM	FGA	Pct.	FTM	FTA	Pct.	Off.	Def.	Tot.	Ast.	St.	Blk.	TO	Pts.	RPG	APG	PPG
2003—Minnesota	3	42	6	18	.333	4	6	.667	2	7	9	2	4	2	3	16	3.0	0.7	5.3
2004—Seattle	8	109	12	27	.444	3	4	.750	10	8	18	1	9	10	8	27	2.3	0.1	3.4
2005—Seattle	3	90	11	18	.611	6	6	1.000	8	6	14	3	3	1	2	28	4.7	1.0	9.3
Totals	14	241	29	63	.460	13	16	.813	20	21	41	6	16	13	13	71	2.9	0.4	5.1

Personal fouls/disqualifications: 2003-04, 3/0. 2004-05, 17/0. 2005-06, 11/0. Totals, 31/0.

CAMPBELL, EDNA   G   SILVER STARS

PERSONAL: Born November 26, 1968, in Philadelphia. ... 5-8/152. (1.73/68.9). ... Full name: Edna L. Campbell
HIGH SCHOOL: Allderdice (Pittsburgh).
COLLEGE: Texas.
TRANSACTIONS/CAREER NOTES: Selected by Phoenix in first round (10th overall) of WNBA Draft, May 4, 1999. ... Seleted by Seattle in first round (second overall) of WNBA Expansion Draft, December 15, 1999. ... Traded to Sacramento with a first-round pick in the 2002 WNBA Draft for F Katy Steding and a second-round pick in the 2002 WNBA Draft, April 24, 2001. ... Signed by San Antonio, February 17, 2005.

COLLEGE RECORD

Season Team	G	Min.	FGM	FGA	Pct.	FTM	FTA	Pct.	Reb.	Ast.	Pts.	RPG	APG	PPG
1986—Maryland	29	...	201	399	.504	64	87	.736	90	86	466	3.1	3.0	16.1
1987—Maryland	32	...	123	261	.471	41	56	.732	153	94	287	4.8	2.9	9.0
1989—Texas	29	...	180	318	.566	72	95	.758	107	57	432	3.7	2.0	14.9
1990—Texas	26	...	181	324	.559	69	86	.802	99	69	434	3.8	2.7	16.7
Totals	116	...	685	1302	.526	246	324	.759	449	306	1619	3.9	2.6	14.0

Three-point field goals: 1990-91, 3-for-7 (.429). Totals, 3-for-7 (.429).

ABL RECORD

Season Team	G	Min.	FGM	FGA	Pct.	FTM	FTA	Pct.	Reb.	Ast.	Pts.	AVERAGES RPG	APG	PPG
1996—Colorado	40	...	227	506	.449	62	78	.795	189	109	566	4.7	2.7	14.2
1997—Colorado	44	...	233	545	.428	80	94	.851	126	109	613	2.9	2.5	13.9
1998—Colorado	13	...	75	189	.397	38	41	.927	40	37	225	3.1	2.8	17.3
Totals	97	...	535	1240	.431	180	213	.845	355	255	1404	3.7	2.6	14.5

Three-point field goals: 1996-97, 50-for-124 (.403). 1997-98, 67-for-167 (.401). 1998-99, 37-for-85 (.435). Totals, 154-for-376 (.410).

NOTES: Kim Perrot Sportsmanship Award (2003).

WNBA REGULAR-SEASON RECORD

Season Team	G	Min.	FGM	FGA	Pct.	FTM	FTA	Pct.	REBOUNDS Off.	Def.	Tot.	Ast.	St.	Blk.	TO	Pts.	AVERAGES RPG	APG	PPG
1999—Phoenix	28	750	95	261	.364	40	56	.714	11	42	53	37	25	10	48	268	1.9	1.3	9.6
2000—Seattle	16	510	84	215	.391	41	58	.707	8	26	34	37	19	4	40	222	2.1	2.3	13.9
2001—Sacramento	32	854	92	244	.377	33	43	.767	11	74	85	74	19	9	64	260	2.7	2.3	8.1
2002—Sacramento	1	12	2	5	.400	0	0	...	0	1	1	0	1	0	0	4	1.0	0.0	4.0
2003—Sacramento	34	724	98	244	.402	25	33	.758	17	53	70	43	21	5	43	267	2.1	1.3	7.9
2004—Sacramento	22	332	29	76	.382	0	2	.000	3	16	19	16	5	2	15	74	0.9	0.7	3.4
2005—San Antonio	28	248	21	67	.313	1	1	1.000	2	12	14	14	7	0	15	48	0.5	0.5	1.7
Totals	161	3430	421	1112	.379	140	193	.725	52	224	276	221	97	30	225	1143	1.7	1.4	7.1

Three-point field goals: 1999-00, 38-for-101 (.376). 2000-01, 13-for-49 (.265). 2001-02, 43-for-94 (.457). 2002-03, 0-for-2. 2003-04, 46-for-111 (.414). 2004-05, 16-for-39 (.410). 2005-06, 5-for-19 (.263). Totals, 161-for-415 (.388).

Personal fouls/disqualifications: 1999-00, 53/0. 2000-01, 35/0. 2001-02, 45/0. 2003-04, 42/0. 2004-05, 24/0. 2005-06, 20/0. Totals, 219/0.

WNBA PLAYOFF RECORD

Season Team	G	Min.	FGM	FGA	Pct.	FTM	FTA	Pct.	REBOUNDS Off.	Def.	Tot.	Ast.	St.	Blk.	TO	Pts.	AVERAGES RPG	APG	PPG
2001—Sacramento	5	115	11	31	.355	2	3	.667	4	7	11	11	5	1	5	28	2.2	2.2	5.6
2003—Sacramento	6	148	17	36	.472	2	2	1.000	1	3	4	11	1	0	8	40	0.7	1.8	6.7
2004—Sacramento	6	102	10	25	.400	0	0	...	0	11	11	5	3	0	2	26	1.8	0.8	4.3
Totals	17	365	38	92	.413	4	5	.800	5	21	26	27	9	1	15	94	1.5	1.6	5.5

Three-point field goals: 2001-02, 4-for-9 (.444). 2003-04, 4-for-16 (.250). 2004-05, 6-for-14 (.429). Totals, 14-for-39 (.359).
Personal fouls/disqualifications: 2001-02, 9/0. 2003-04, 11/0. 2004-05, 6/0. Totals, 26/0.

CANTY, DOMINIQUE   G/F   COMETS

PERSONAL: Born March 2, 1977, in Chicago. ... 5-9/162. (1.75/73.5). ... Full name: Dominique Danyell Canty.
HIGH SCHOOL: Whitney Young (Chicago).
COLLEGE: Alabama.
TRANSACTIONS/CAREER NOTES: Selected by Detroit in third round (29th overall) of WNBA Draft, May 4, 1999.

COLLEGE RECORD

NOTES: AP All-American first team (1999). ... AP All-American second team (1998).

Season Team	G	Min.	FGM	FGA	Pct.	FTM	FTA	Pct.	Reb.	Ast.	Pts.	AVERAGES RPG	APG	PPG
1995—Alabama	31	...	176	332	.530	100	151	.662	210	75	452	6.8	2.4	14.6
1996—Alabama	31	...	177	345	.513	144	218	.661	226	90	498	7.3	2.9	16.1
1997—Alabama	34	...	262	506	.518	203	270	.752	241	164	732	7.1	4.8	21.5
1998—Alabama	31	...	213	445	.479	181	236	.767	232	130	612	7.5	4.2	19.7
Totals	127	...	828	1628	.509	628	875	.718	909	459	2294	7.2	3.6	18.1

Three-point field goals: 1995-96, null-for-7. 1996-97, null-for-5. 1997-98, 5-for-24 (.208). 1998-99, 5-for-16 (.313). Totals, 10-for-52 (.192).

WNBA REGULAR-SEASON RECORD

Season Team	G	Min.	FGM	FGA	Pct.	FTM	FTA	Pct.	REBOUNDS Off.	Def.	Tot.	Ast.	St.	Blk.	TO	Pts.	AVERAGES RPG	APG	PPG
1999—Detroit	26	646	76	229	.332	94	136	.691	35	45	80	38	26	1	45	249	3.1	1.5	9.6
2000—Detroit	28	784	83	203	.409	91	131	.695	31	39	70	82	49	5	51	257	2.5	2.9	9.2
2001—Detroit	32	625	70	193	.363	56	74	.757	45	38	83	70	31	1	55	197	2.6	2.2	6.2
2002—Detroit	28	625	52	154	.338	55	76	.724	24	45	69	83	21	4	56	160	2.5	3.0	5.7
2003—Houston	32	648	55	145	.379	62	93	.667	36	64	100	56	22	1	49	172	3.1	1.8	5.4
2004—Houston	32	770	63	150	.420	51	72	.708	40	44	84	64	32	1	45	177	2.6	2.0	5.5
2005—Houston	33	997	95	238	.399	80	110	.727	25	83	108	101	29	2	67	270	3.3	3.1	8.2
Totals	211	5095	494	1312	.377	489	692	.707	236	358	594	494	210	15	368	1482	2.8	2.3	7.0

Three-point field goals: 1999-00, 3-for-17 (.176). 2000-01, 0-for-5. 2001-02, 1-for-5 (.200). 2002-03, 1-for-5 (.200). 2003-04, 0-for-1. 2004-05, 0-for-2. 2005-06, 0-for-4. Totals, 5-for-39 (.128).
Personal fouls/disqualifications: 1999-00, 57/1. 2000-01, 64/0. 2001-02, 69/0. 2002-03, 59/0. 2003-04, 62/0. 2004-05, 61/0. 2005-06, 75/0. Totals, 447/1.

WNBA PLAYOFF RECORD

Season Team	G	Min.	FGM	FGA	Pct.	FTM	FTA	Pct.	REBOUNDS Off.	Def.	Tot.	Ast.	St.	Blk.	TO	Pts.	AVERAGES RPG	APG	PPG
1999—Detroit	1	21	2	6	.333	2	2	1.000	1	2	3	1	1	0	2	6	3.0	1.0	6.0
2003—Houston	3	48	3	9	.333	5	8	.625	7	4	11	5	1	0	3	11	3.7	1.7	3.7
2005—Houston	5	162	12	30	.400	16	20	.800	11	11	22	17	1	0	14	40	4.4	3.4	8.0
Totals	9	231	17	45	.378	23	30	.767	19	17	36	23	3	0	19	57	4.0	2.6	6.3

Personal fouls/disqualifications: 1999-00, 3/0. 2003-04, 7/0. 2005-06, 12/0. Totals, 22/0.

CAREY, JAMIE   G   SUN

PERSONAL: Born March 12, 1981, in Hutchinson, Kan. ... 5-6. (1.68). ... Full name: Jamie Leigh Carey
HIGH SCHOOL: Horizon (Thornton, Colo.).
COLLEGE: Texas.
TRANSACTIONS/CAREER NOTES: Selected by Phoenix in third round (31st overall) of WNBA Draft, April 16, 2005.
MISCELLANEOUS: Captain of the silver medal-winning USA Pan Am Games team (2003).

NOTES: All-Big 12 first team (2004, 2005). ... All-Big 12 academic first team (2004). ... CoSIDA Academic All-America third team (2004). ... NCAA West Regional All-Tournament team (2004). ... Jimmy V Foundation Comeback Award winner, given to a collegiate basketball player who has triumphed over adversity (2004).

COLLEGE RECORD

Season Team	G	Min.	FGM	FGA	Pct.	FTM	FTA	Pct.	Reb.	Ast.	Pts.	RPG	APG	PPG
												AVERAGES		
1999—Texas	29	896	104	248	.419	30	39	.769	63	88	319	2.2	3.0	11.0
2002—Texas	30	806	95	245	.388	76	94	.809	42	108	323	1.4	3.6	10.8
2003—Texas	35	1162	126	298	.423	55	69	.797	69	97	373	2.0	2.8	10.7
2004—Texas	31	1046	133	310	.429	42	53	.792	56	78	378	1.8	2.5	12.2
Totals	125	3910	458	1101	.416	203	255	.796	230	371	1393	1.8	3.0	11.1

WNBA REGULAR-SEASON RECORD

Season Team	G	Min.	FGM	FGA	Pct.	FTM	FTA	Pct.	Off.	Def.	Tot.	Ast.	St.	Blk.	TO	Pts.	RPG	APG	PPG
									REBOUNDS								AVERAGES		
2005—Connecticut	15	86	7	19	.368	0	0	...	2	4	6	7	2	0	4	18	0.4	0.5	1.2
Totals	15	86	7	19	.368	0	0	...	2	4	6	7	2	0	4	18	0.4	0.5	1.2

Three-point field goals: 2005-06, 4-for-13 (.308). Totals, 4-for-13 (.308).
Personal fouls/disqualifications: 2005-06, 9/0. Totals, 9/0.

WNBA PLAYOFF RECORD

Season Team	G	Min.	FGM	FGA	Pct.	FTM	FTA	Pct.	Off.	Def.	Tot.	Ast.	St.	Blk.	TO	Pts.	RPG	APG	PPG
									REBOUNDS								AVERAGES		
2005—Connecticut	6	71	2	9	.222	0	0	...	0	2	2	7	1	0	4	5	0.3	1.2	0.8
Totals	6	71	2	9	.222	0	0	...	0	2	2	7	1	0	4	5	0.3	1.2	0.8

Three-point field goals: 2005-06, 1-for-6 (.167). Totals, 1-for-6 (.167).
Personal fouls/disqualifications: 2005-06, 5/0. Totals, 5/0.

CARTER, AMISHA   F   LIBERTY

PERSONAL: Born June 21, 1982, in Oakland. ... 6-2/179. (1.88/81.2).
HIGH SCHOOL: McClymond (Oakland).
COLLEGE: Louisiana Tech.
TRANSACTIONS/CAREER NOTES: Selected by New York in the second round (20th overall) of the WNBA Draft, April 17, 2004.

COLLEGE RECORD

NOTES: AP All-American honorable mention (2004). ... WAC Player of the Year (2004). ... All-WAC first team (2004). ... WAC All-Defensive Team (2004). ... Louisiana Sports Writers Association All-Louisiana honorable mention (2003). ... NJCAA All-American honorable mention (2002). ... Region V first team (2002). ... NJCAA All-Tournament team (2001).

Season Team	G	Min.	FGM	FGA	Pct.	FTM	FTA	Pct.	Reb.	Ast.	Pts.	RPG	APG	PPG
												AVERAGES		
2002—Louisiana Tech	33	553	71	159	.447	57	89	.640	163	21	199	4.9	0.6	6.0
2003—Louisiana Tech	32	931	195	386	.505	152	231	.658	344	25	542	10.8	0.8	16.9
Totals	65	1484	266	545	.488	209	320	.653	507	46	741	7.8	0.7	11.4

Three-point field goals: 2003-04, null-for-1. Totals, null-for-1 (null).

WNBA REGULAR-SEASON RECORD

Season Team	G	Min.	FGM	FGA	Pct.	FTM	FTA	Pct.	Off.	Def.	Tot.	Ast.	St.	Blk.	TO	Pts.	RPG	APG	PPG
									REBOUNDS								AVERAGES		
2004—Detroit	2	13	0	0		1	2	.500	0	4	4	0	2	0	3	1	2.0	0.0	0.5
2005—New York	3	13	0	1	.000	0	0	...	0	2	2	0	0	0	1	0	0.7	0.0	0.0
Totals	5	26	0	1	.000	1	2	.500	0	6	6	0	2	0	4	1	1.2	0.0	0.2

Personal fouls/disqualifications: 2004-05, 5/0. 2005-06, 4/0. Totals, 9/0.

CASH, SWIN   F   SHOCK

PERSONAL: Born September 22, 1979, in McKeesport, Pa. ... 6-1/165. (1.85/74.8). ... Full name: Swintayla Marie Cash
HIGH SCHOOL: McKeesport (McKeesport, Pa.).
COLLEGE: Connecticut.
TRANSACTIONS/CAREER NOTES: Selected by Detroit in first round (second overall) of WNBA Draft, April 19, 2002.
MISCELLANEOUS: Member of WNBA Championship Team (2003).

COLLEGE RECORD

NOTES: Member of NCAA Division I Championship team (2000, 2002). ... Kodak All-American first team (2002).

Season Team	G	Min.	FGM	FGA	Pct.	FTM	FTA	Pct.	Reb.	Ast.	Pts.	RPG	APG	PPG
												AVERAGES		
1998—Connecticut	22	332	75	127	.591	59	92	.641	115	14	209	5.2	0.6	9.5
1999—Connecticut	37	768	141	265	.532	85	132	.644	196	24	367	5.3	0.6	9.9

C

Season Team	G	Min.	FGM	FGA	Pct.	FTM	FTA	Pct.	Reb.	Ast.	Pts.	RPG AVERAGES	APG	PPG
2000—Connecticut	35	832	162	292	.555	103	174	.592	263	51	427	7.5	1.5	12.2
2001—Connecticut	39	1085	220	401	.549	140	200	.700	336	86	580	8.6	2.2	14.9
Totals	133	3017	598	1085	.551	387	598	.647	910	175	1583	6.8	1.3	11.9

Three-point field goals: 2001-02, 0-for-1. Totals, 0-for-1 (.000).

WNBA REGULAR-SEASON RECORD

NOTES: All-WNBA second team (2003, 2004).

Season Team	G	Min.	FGM	FGA	Pct.	FTM	FTA	Pct.	REBOUNDS Off.	Def.	Tot.	Ast.	St.	Blk.	TO	Pts.	RPG AVERAGES	APG	PPG
2002—Detroit	32	1079	144	353	.408	173	227	.762	77	145	222	86	37	31	100	474	6.9	2.7	14.8
2003—Detroit	33	1097	195	430	.453	146	214	.682	65	128	193	119	43	23	108	548	5.8	3.6	16.6
2004—Detroit	32	1105	180	384	.469	158	219	.721	78	130	208	135	44	29	81	526	6.5	4.2	16.4
2005—Detroit	21	458	48	126	.381	21	32	.656	42	46	88	43	12	6	47	119	4.2	2.0	5.7
Totals	118	3739	567	1293	.439	498	692	.720	262	449	711	383	136	89	336	1667	6.0	3.2	14.1

Three-point field goals: 2002-03, 13-for-63 (.206). 2003-04, 12-for-40 (.300). 2004-05, 8-for-23 (.348). 2005-06, 2-for-10 (.200). Totals, 35-for-136 (.257).
Personal fouls/disqualifications: 2002-03, 85/0. 2003-04, 76/0. 2004-05, 84/0. 2005-06, 44/1. Totals, 289/1.

WNBA PLAYOFF RECORD

Season Team	G	Min.	FGM	FGA	Pct.	FTM	FTA	Pct.	REBOUNDS Off.	Def.	Tot.	Ast.	St.	Blk.	TO	Pts.	RPG AVERAGES	APG	PPG
2003—Detroit	8	289	43	104	.413	42	52	.808	24	27	51	35	4	5	28	130	6.4	4.4	16.3
2005—Detroit	2	51	4	13	.308	8	11	.727	5	4	9	7	3	2	4	16	4.5	3.5	8.0
Totals	10	340	47	117	.402	50	63	.794	29	31	60	42	7	7	32	146	6.0	4.2	14.6

Three-point field goals: 2003-04, 2-for-10 (.200). 2005-06, 0-for-1. Totals, 2-for-11 (.182).
Personal fouls/disqualifications: 2003-04, 21/0. 2005-06, 4/0. Totals, 25/0.

WNBA ALL-STAR GAME RECORD

Season Team	Min.	FGM	FGA	Pct.	FTM	FTA	Pct.	REBOUNDS Off.	Def.	Tot.	Ast.	PF	Dq.	St.	Blk.	TO	Pts.
2003—Detroit	19	3	13	.231	0	0	...	1	1	2	1	1	0	2	0	1	6
2005—Detroit	17	1	7	.143	0	0	...	3	2	5	1	0	0	0	0	1	2
Totals	36	4	20	.200	0	0	...	4	3	7	2	1	0	2	0	2	8

Three-point field goals: 2004, 0-for-4. 2006, 0-for-2. Totals, 0-for-6 (.000).

OLYMPICS RECORD

Season Team	G	Min.	FGM	FGA	Pct.	FTM	FTA	Pct.	Reb.	Ast.	Pts.	RPG AVERAGES	APG	PPG
2004—United States	7	101	16	35	.457	12	15	.800	31	2	44	4.4	0.3	6.3
Totals	7	101	16	35	.457	12	15	.800	31	2	44	4.4	0.3	6.3

Personal fouls/disqualifications: 2004-05, 8/0. Totals, 8/0.

CASTRO MARQUES, IZIANE G   STORM

PERSONAL: Born March 13, 1982, in Sao Luis, Brazil. ... 6-0/140. (1.83/63.5).
TRANSACTIONS/CAREER NOTES: Signed by the WNBA and added by Miami, April 25, 2002. ... Signed by Seattle, April 6, 2005.
MISCELLANEOUS: Member of Brazilian National Team.

WNBA REGULAR-SEASON RECORD

Season Team	G	Min.	FGM	FGA	Pct.	FTM	FTA	Pct.	REBOUNDS Off.	Def.	Tot.	Ast.	St.	Blk.	TO	Pts.	RPG AVERAGES	APG	PPG
2002—Miami	19	182	24	72	.333	17	25	.680	7	10	17	7	7	0	18	66	0.9	0.4	3.5
2003—Phoenix	16	178	25	71	.352	11	18	.611	6	6	12	9	6	1	10	69	0.8	0.6	4.3
2005—Seattle	33	879	93	242	.384	59	73	.808	23	74	97	49	18	4	59	269	2.9	1.5	8.2
Totals	68	1239	142	385	.369	87	116	.750	36	90	126	65	31	5	87	404	1.9	1.0	5.9

Three-point field goals: 2002-03, 1-for-17 (.059). 2003-04, 8-for-27 (.296). 2005-06, 24-for-72 (.333). Totals, 33-for-116 (.284).
Personal fouls/disqualifications: 2002-03, 22/0. 2003-04, 11/0. 2005-06, 73/0. Totals, 106/0.

WNBA PLAYOFF RECORD

Season Team	G	Min.	FGM	FGA	Pct.	FTM	FTA	Pct.	REBOUNDS Off.	Def.	Tot.	Ast.	St.	Blk.	TO	Pts.	RPG AVERAGES	APG	PPG
2005—Seattle	3	86	6	18	.333	4	4	1.000	0	3	3	4	2	0	8	17	1.0	1.3	5.7
Totals	3	86	6	18	.333	4	4	1.000	0	3	3	4	2	0	8	17	1.0	1.3	5.7

Three-point field goals: 2005-06, 1-for-6 (.167). Totals, 1-for-6 (.167).
Personal fouls/disqualifications: 2005-06, 12/0. Totals, 12/0.

OLYMPICS RECORD

Season Team	G	Min.	FGM	FGA	Pct.	FTM	FTA	Pct.	Reb.	Ast.	Pts.	RPG AVERAGES	APG	PPG
2004—Brazil	8	225	43	90	.478	26	35	.743	21	20	120	2.6	2.5	15.0
Totals	8	225	43	90	.478	26	35	.743	21	20	120	2.6	2.5	15.0

Three-point field goals: 2004-05, 8-for-24 (.333). Totals, 8-for-24 (.333).
Personal fouls/disqualifications: 2004-05, 11/0. Totals, 11/0.

CATCHINGS, TAMIKA　　　　F　　　　FEVER

PERSONAL: Born July 21, 1979, in Stratford, N.J. ... 6-1/167. (1.85/75.7). ... Full name: Tamika Devonne Catchings
HIGH SCHOOL: Duncanville (Duncanville, Texas).
COLLEGE: Tennessee.
TRANSACTIONS/CAREER NOTES: Selected by Indiana in first round (third overall) of WNBA Draft, April 20, 2001.

COLLEGE RECORD

NOTES: Member of NCAA Division I championship team (1998). ... Naismith Award winner (2000). ... Kodak All-American first team (1998, 1999, 2000, 2001).

Season Team	G	Min.	FGM	FGA	Pct.	FTM	FTA	Pct.	Reb.	Ast.	Pts.	RPG	APG	PPG
1997—Tennessee	39	1123	253	471	.537	165	217	.760	313	92	711	8.0	2.4	18.2
1998—Tennessee	34	991	205	400	.513	134	173	.775	249	95	563	7.3	2.8	16.6
1999—Tennessee	37	1143	209	440	.475	122	159	.767	292	101	580	7.9	2.7	15.7
2000—Tennessee	17	465	93	195	.477	50	62	.806	150	50	259	8.8	2.9	15.2
Totals	127	3722	760	1506	.505	471	611	.771	1004	338	2113	7.9	2.7	16.6

Three-point field goals: 1997-98, 40-for-110 (.364). 1998-99, 19-for-68 (.279). 1999-00, 40-for-121 (.331). 2000-01, 23-for-67 (.343). Totals, 122-for-366 (.333).

WNBA REGULAR-SEASON RECORD

NOTES: WNBA Rookie of the Year (2002). ... WNBA Defensive Player of the Year (2005). ... All-WNBA first team (2002, 2003). ... All-WNBA second team (2004, 2005). ... All-Defensive first team (2005). ... Led WNBA in steals in 2002 (2.94 spg) and 2005 (2.65 spg).

Season Team	G	Min.	FGM	FGA	Pct.	FTM	FTA	Pct.	REBOUNDS Off.	Def.	Tot.	Ast.	St.	Blk.	TO	Pts.	RPG	APG	PPG
2001—Indiana						Did not play due to injury.													
2002—Indiana	32	1167	184	439	.419	150	184	.815	92	184	276	118	94	43	82	594	8.6	3.7	18.6
2003—Indiana	34	1210	221	512	.432	155	183	.847	82	190	272	114	72	35	102	671	8.0	3.4	19.7
2004—Indiana	34	1149	180	468	.385	152	178	.854	79	170	249	115	67	38	77	568	7.3	3.4	16.7
2005—Indiana	34	1174	157	410	.383	152	193	.788	69	195	264	143	90	16	91	501	7.8	4.2	14.7
Totals	134	4700	742	1829	.406	609	738	.825	322	739	1061	490	323	132	352	2334	7.9	3.7	17.4

Three-point field goals: 2002-03, 76-for-193 (.394). 2003-04, 74-for-191 (.387). 2004-05, 56-for-167 (.335). 2005-06, 35-for-123 (.285). Totals, 241-for-674 (.358).
Personal fouls/disqualifications: 2002-03, 105/2. 2003-04, 122/2. 2004-05, 90/2. 2005-06, 96/1. Totals, 413/7.

WNBA PLAYOFF RECORD

Season Team	G	Min.	FGM	FGA	Pct.	FTM	FTA	Pct.	REBOUNDS Off.	Def.	Tot.	Ast.	St.	Blk.	TO	Pts.	RPG	APG	PPG
2002—Indiana	3	103	22	45	.489	9	11	.818	12	20	32	7	4	1	11	61	10.7	2.3	20.3
2005—Indiana	4	146	21	59	.356	22	28	.786	13	24	37	9	8	1	11	69	9.3	2.3	17.3
Totals	7	249	43	104	.413	31	39	.795	25	44	69	16	12	2	22	130	9.9	2.3	18.6

Three-point field goals: 2002-03, 8-for-21 (.381). 2005-06, 5-for-12 (.417). Totals, 13-for-33 (.394).
Personal fouls/disqualifications: 2002-03, 7/0. 2005-06, 13/1. Totals, 20/1.

WNBA ALL-STAR GAME RECORD

Season Team	Min.	FGM	FGA	Pct.	FTM	FTA	Pct.	REBOUNDS Off.	Def.	Tot.	Ast.	PF	Dq.	St.	Blk.	TO	Pts.
2002—Indiana	21	4	12	.333	2	2	1.000	3	6	9	1	3	0	1	4	1	12
2003—Indiana	30	6	15	.400	1	2	.500	2	2	4	2	4	0	2	0	5	17
2005—Indiana	24	7	11	.636	4	5	.800	2	4	6	2	3	0	2	0	1	18
Totals	75	17	38	.447	7	9	.778	7	12	19	5	10	0	5	4	7	47

Three-point field goals: 2003, 2-for-5 (.400). 2004, 4-for-6 (.667). 2006, 0-for-2. Totals, 6-for-13 (.462).

OLYMPICS RECORD

Season Team	G	Min.	FGM	FGA	Pct.	FTM	FTA	Pct.	Reb.	Ast.	Pts.	RPG	APG	PPG
2004—United States	8	198	19	47	.404	15	18	.833	43	3	55	5.4	0.4	6.9
Totals	8	198	19	47	.404	15	18	.833	43	3	55	5.4	0.4	6.9

Three-point field goals: 2004-05, 2-for-8 (.250). Totals, 2-for-8 (.250).
Personal fouls/disqualifications: 2004-05, 14/0. Totals, 14/0.

CHONES, KAAYLA　　　　C　　　　MYSTICS

PERSONAL: Born January 11, 1981, in Pepper Pike, Ohio. ... 6-3/180. (1.91/81.6).
HIGH SCHOOL: Eastlake North (Pepper Pike, Ohio).
COLLEGE: North Carolina State.
TRANSACTIONS/CAREER NOTES: Selected by Washington in second round (15th overall) of the WNBA Draft, April 17, 2004.
MISCELLANEOUS: Father Jim Chones was a first-round draft pick in the 1972 ABA Draft (New York Nets). He also played for the Carolina Cougars (ABA) and the NBA's Cleveland Cavaliers, Los Angeles Lakers and Washington Bullets. ... Sister Kareeda played at Marquette.

COLLEGE RECORD

Season Team	G	Min.	FGM	FGA	Pct.	FTM	FTA	Pct.	Reb.	Ast.	Pts.	RPG	APG	PPG
1999—North Carolina State	29	792	129	229	.563	72	128	.563	228	23	330	7.9	0.8	11.4
2001—North Carolina State	29	749	139	243	.572	79	125	.632	204	23	357	7.0	0.8	12.3

C

Season Team	G	Min.	FGM	FGA	Pct.	FTM	FTA	Pct.	Reb.	Ast.	Pts.	RPG	APG	PPG
												AVERAGES		
2002—North Carolina State	28	823	142	269	.528	103	168	.613	217	47	387	7.8	1.7	13.8
2003—North Carolina State	32	992	180	353	.510	104	161	.646	245	39	464	7.7	1.2	14.5
Totals	118	3356	590	1094	.539	358	582	.615	894	132	1538	7.6	1.1	13.0

WNBA REGULAR-SEASON RECORD

Season Team	G	Min.	FGM	FGA	Pct.	FTM	FTA	Pct.	REBOUNDS Off.	Def.	Tot.	Ast.	St.	Blk.	TO	Pts.	AVERAGES RPG	APG	PPG
2004—Washington	13	115	11	27	.407	6	11	.545	8	9	17	4	1	4	11	28	1.3	0.3	2.2
2005—Washington	12	61	6	14	.429	2	3	.667	2	4	6	1	1	0	4	14	0.5	0.1	1.2
Totals	25	176	17	41	.415	8	14	.571	10	13	23	5	2	4	15	42	0.9	0.2	1.7

Personal fouls/disqualifications: 2004-05, 13/0. 2005-06, 9/0. Totals, 22/0.

WNBA PLAYOFF RECORD

Season Team	G	Min.	FGM	FGA	Pct.	FTM	FTA	Pct.	REBOUNDS Off.	Def.	Tot.	Ast.	St.	Blk.	TO	Pts.	AVERAGES RPG	APG	PPG
2004—Washington	2	4	0	1	.000	0	0	...	0	0	0	0	0	1	0	0	0.0	0.0	0.0
Totals	2	4	0	1	.000	0	0	...	0	0	0	0	0	1	0	0	0.0	0.0	0.0

Personal fouls/disqualifications: 2004-05, 1/0. Totals, 1/0.

C

CHRISTENSEN, KAYTE   F   COMETS

PERSONAL: Born November 16, 1980, in Lakeview, Ore. ... 6-3/171. (1.91/77.6). ... Full name: Kayte Lauren Christensen
HIGH SCHOOL: Modoc (Modoc, Calif.).
COLLEGE: UC-Santa Barbara.
TRANSACTIONS/CAREER NOTES: Selected by Phoenix in third round (40th overall) of WNBA Draft, April 19, 2002. ... Signed by Houston, March 23, 2006.

COLLEGE RECORD

Season Team	G	Min.	FGM	FGA	Pct.	FTM	FTA	Pct.	Reb.	Ast.	Pts.	AVERAGES RPG	APG	PPG
1998—UC-Santa Barbara	30	508	87	158	.551	64	103	.621	167	12	239	5.6	0.4	8.0
1999—UC-Santa Barbara	18	367	78	138	.565	32	63	.508	113	7	188	6.3	0.4	10.4
2000—UC-Santa Barbara	31	786	163	297	.549	100	150	.667	236	27	426	7.6	0.9	13.7
2001—UC-Santa Barbara	32	834	184	339	.543	97	148	.655	291	27	465	9.1	0.8	14.5
Totals	111	2495	512	932	.549	293	464	.631	807	73	1318	7.3	0.7	11.9

Three-point field goals: 1998-99, 1-for-1 (1.000). 1999-00, 0-for-2. 2000-01, 0-for-4. 2001-02, 0-for-2. Totals, 1-for-9 (.111).

WNBA REGULAR-SEASON RECORD

Season Team	G	Min.	FGM	FGA	Pct.	FTM	FTA	Pct.	REBOUNDS Off.	Def.	Tot.	Ast.	St.	Blk.	TO	Pts.	AVERAGES RPG	APG	PPG
2002—Phoenix	30	413	48	95	.505	24	35	.686	39	41	80	15	24	13	32	120	2.7	0.5	4.0
2003—Phoenix	30	659	78	161	.484	50	83	.602	61	65	126	16	25	16	39	206	4.2	0.5	6.9
2004—Phoenix	32	407	19	49	.388	12	19	.632	27	42	69	23	21	7	26	50	2.2	0.7	1.6
2005—Phoenix	11	108	7	15	.467	4	7	.571	9	13	22	7	7	5	10	18	2.0	0.6	1.6
Totals	103	1587	152	320	.475	90	144	.625	136	161	297	61	77	41	107	394	2.9	0.6	3.8

Three-point field goals: 2002-03, 0-for-1. Totals, 0-for-1 (.000).
Personal fouls/disqualifications: 2002-03, 73/1. 2003-04, 104/4. 2004-05, 89/2. 2005-06, 25/1. Totals, 291/8.

CHRISTON, SHAMEKA   G/F   LIBERTY

PERSONAL: Born February 15, 1982, in Hot Springs, Ark. ... 6-1/175. (1.85/79.4). ... Full name: Shameka Delynn Christon
HIGH SCHOOL: Hot Springs (Hot Springs, Ark.).
COLLEGE: Arkansas.
TRANSACTIONS/CAREER NOTES: Selected by New York in first round (fifth overall) of the WNBA Draft, April 17, 2004.
MISCELLANEOUS: Member of the gold medal-winning 2002 USA World Championship team for Young Women. ... Member of the bronze medal-winning 2001 USA Junior World Championship team.

COLLEGE RECORD

NOTES: AP All-American third team (2004). ... SEC Player of the Year (2004). ... All-SEC first team (2004). ... All-SEC second team (2003). ... All-SEC Tournament team (2003). ... All-SEC Freshman team (2001). ... Second on Arkansas' all-time scoring list (1,951). ... Holds the Arkansas team record for most points scored in SEC play in a season (224).

Season Team	G	Min.	FGM	FGA	Pct.	FTM	FTA	Pct.	Reb.	Ast.	Pts.	AVERAGES RPG	APG	PPG
2000—Arkansas	32	765	117	289	.405	56	72	.778	132	20	327	4.1	0.6	10.2
2001—Arkansas	31	976	197	418	.471	92	133	.692	193	25	517	6.2	0.8	16.7
2002—Arkansas	32	1052	193	434	.445	81	117	.692	194	47	496	6.1	1.5	15.5
2003—Arkansas	28	931	219	500	.438	126	166	.759	195	49	611	7.0	1.8	21.8
Totals	123	3724	726	1641	.442	355	488	.727	714	141	1951	5.8	1.1	15.9

Three-point field goals: 2000-01, 37-for-113 (.327). 2001-02, 31-for-104 (.298). 2002-03, 29-for-81 (.358). 2003-04, 47-for-129 (.364). Totals, 144-for-427 (.337).

WNBA REGULAR-SEASON RECORD

Season Team	G	Min.	FGM	FGA	Pct.	FTM	FTA	Pct.	REBOUNDS Off.	Def.	Tot.	Ast.	St.	Blk.	TO	Pts.	AVERAGES RPG	APG	PPG
2004—New York	33	560	67	189	.354	33	51	.647	19	49	68	23	9	9	32	191	2.1	0.7	5.8

Season Team	G	Min.	FGM	FGA	Pct.	FTM	FTA	Pct.	REBOUNDS Off.	Def.	Tot.	Ast.	St.	Blk.	TO	Pts.	AVERAGES RPG	APG	PPG
2005—New York...........	34	809	111	270	.411	65	76	.855	25	67	92	41	33	19	50	311	2.7	1.2	9.1
Totals	67	1369	178	459	.388	98	127	.772	44	116	160	64	42	28	82	502	2.4	1.0	7.5

Three-point field goals: 2004-05, 24-for-82 (.293). 2005-06, 24-for-89 (.270). Totals, 48-for-171 (.281).
Personal fouls/disqualifications: 2004-05, 71/0. 2005-06, 100/1. Totals, 171/1.

WNBA PLAYOFF RECORD

Season Team	G	Min.	FGM	FGA	Pct.	FTM	FTA	Pct.	REBOUNDS Off.	Def.	Tot.	Ast.	St.	Blk.	TO	Pts.	AVERAGES RPG	APG	PPG
2004—New York...........	5	63	8	21	.381	6	9	.667	4	5	9	4	2	3	3	28	1.8	0.8	5.6
2005—New York...........	2	47	4	12	.333	1	2	.500	0	5	5	1	0	1	2	11	2.5	0.5	5.5
Totals	7	110	12	33	.364	7	11	.636	4	10	14	5	2	4	5	39	2.0	0.7	5.6

Three-point field goals: 2004-05, 6-for-14 (.429). 2005-06, 2-for-4 (.500). Totals, 8-for-18 (.444).
Personal fouls/disqualifications: 2004-05, 13/0. 2005-06, 7/0. Totals, 20/0.

CURRY, EDNIESHA　　　　　G　　　　　SPARKS

PERSONAL: Born July 9, 1979, in Panorama City, Calif. ... 5-6. (1.68).
HIGH SCHOOL: Palmdale (Palmdale, Calif.).
COLLEGE: Oregon.
TRANSACTIONS/CAREER NOTES: Selected by Charlotte in third round (41st overall) of WNBA Draft, April 19, 2002. ... Wiaved by Charlotte, May 24, 2002. ... Signed by Phoenix, April 30, 2003. ... Signed by Indiana, April 4, 2005.

COLLEGE RECORD

Season Team	G	Min.	FGM	FGA	Pct.	FTM	FTA	Pct.	Reb.	Ast.	Pts.	AVERAGES RPG	APG	PPG
1997—Cal State Northridge..........	28	964	167	439	.380	78	117	.667	131	118	477	4.7	4.2	17.0
1998—Cal State Northridge..........	29	876	186	444	.419	95	118	.805	108	92	533	3.7	3.2	18.4
1999—Cal State Northridge..........	16	507	89	241	.369	29	45	.644	56	67	244	3.5	4.2	15.3
2001—Oregon..............................	29	864	112	280	.400	56	79	.709	95	104	313	3.3	3.6	10.8
Totals	102	3211	554	1404	.395	258	359	.719	390	381	1567	3.8	3.7	15.4

Three-point field goals: 1997-98, 65-for-199 (.327). 1998-99, 66-for-170 (.388). 1999-00, 37-for-123 (.301). 2001-02, 33-for-117 (.282). Totals, 201-for-609 (.330).

WNBA REGULAR-SEASON RECORD

Season Team	G	Min.	FGM	FGA	Pct.	FTM	FTA	Pct.	REBOUNDS Off.	Def.	Tot.	Ast.	St.	Blk.	TO	Pts.	AVERAGES RPG	APG	PPG
2003—Phoenix..............	20	205	13	35	.371	2	3	.667	1	10	11	24	9	0	15	33	0.6	1.2	1.7
2005—Los Angeles	13	113	7	23	.304	3	6	.500	4	7	11	12	7	1	10	23	0.8	0.9	1.8
Totals	33	318	20	58	.345	5	9	.556	5	17	22	36	16	1	25	56	0.7	1.1	1.7

Three-point field goals: 2003-04, 5-for-22 (.227). 2005-06, 6-for-16 (.375). Totals, 11-for-38 (.289).
Personal fouls/disqualifications: 2003-04, 25/0. 2005-06, 16/0. Totals, 41/0.

WNBA PLAYOFF RECORD

Season Team	G	Min.	FGM	FGA	Pct.	FTM	FTA	Pct.	REBOUNDS Off.	Def.	Tot.	Ast.	St.	Blk.	TO	Pts.	AVERAGES RPG	APG	PPG
2005—Los Angeles	2	16	0	1	.000	0	0	...	0	1	1	1	1	0	5	0	0.5	0.5	0.0
Totals	2	16	0	1	.000	0	0	...	0	1	1	1	1	0	5	0	0.5	0.5	0.0

Three-point field goals: 2005-06, 0-for-1. Totals, 0-for-1 (.000).
Personal fouls/disqualifications: 2005-06, 3/0. Totals, 3/0.

DARLING, HELEN　　　　　G　　　　　STING

PERSONAL: Born August 29, 1978, in Columbus ... 5-6/164. (1.68/74.4). ... Full name: Helen Marie Darling
HIGH SCHOOL: Brookhaven (Columbus).
COLLEGE: Penn State.
TRANSACTIONS/CAREER NOTES: Selected by Cleveland in second round (17th overall) of WNBA Draft, April 25, 2000. ... Selected by Minnesota in dispersal draft, January 6, 2004. ... Traded by Minnesota along with the Lynx's second-round pick (24th overall) in the 2005 WNBA Draft to Charlotte in exchange for the Sting's second-round pick (17th overall) in the 2005 WNBA Draft.

COLLEGE RECORD

NOTES: Kodak All-American first team (2000). ... Naismith Award for small player of year (2000). ... Led NCAA in assists (7.8 apg) in 2000.

Season Team	G	Min.	FGM	FGA	Pct.	FTM	FTA	Pct.	Reb.	Ast.	Pts.	AVERAGES RPG	APG	PPG
1996—Penn State	27	...	60	199	.302	90	127	.709	118	119	210	4.4	4.4	7.8
1997—Penn State	34	...	114	288	.396	111	171	.649	178	172	343	5.2	5.1	10.1
1998—Penn State	30	...	113	289	.391	146	191	.764	175	226	373	5.8	7.5	12.4
1999—Penn State	35	...	111	280	.396	131	169	.775	201	274	368	5.7	7.8	10.5
Totals.....................................	126	...	398	1056	.377	478	658	.726	672	791	1294	5.3	6.3	10.3

Three-point field goals: 1996-97, 0-for-4. 1997-98, 4-for-15 (.267). 1998-99, 1-for-7 (.143). 1999-00, 15-for-52 (.288). Totals, 20-for-78 (.256).

WNBA REGULAR-SEASON RECORD

Season Team	G	Min.	FGM	FGA	Pct.	FTM	FTA	Pct.	REBOUNDS Off.	Def.	Tot.	Ast.	St.	Blk.	TO	Pts.	AVERAGES RPG	APG	PPG
2000—Cleveland	32	556	47	150	.313	48	65	.738	24	39	63	65	37	5	67	155	2.0	2.0	4.8

C

D

Season Team	G	Min.	FGM	FGA	Pct.	FTM	FTA	Pct.	Off.	Def.	Tot.	Ast.	St.	Blk.	TO	Pts.	RPG	APG	PPG
2001—Cleveland	32	778	59	166	.355	55	72	.764	18	58	76	109	34	4	70	196	2.4	3.4	6.1
2003—Cleveland	34	832	44	143	.308	30	41	.732	25	62	87	128	39	6	74	141	2.6	3.8	4.1
2004—Minnesota	33	707	43	130	.331	42	63	.667	11	56	67	115	30	4	74	140	2.0	3.5	4.2
2005—Charlotte	31	600	27	88	.307	43	58	.741	5	42	47	83	41	0	51	107	1.5	2.7	3.5
Totals	162	3473	220	677	.325	218	299	.729	83	257	340	500	181	19	336	739	2.1	3.1	4.6

Three-point field goals: 2000-01, 13-for-38 (.342). 2001-02, 23-for-70 (.329). 2003-04, 23-for-71 (.324). 2004-05, 12-for-55 (.218). 2005-06, 10-for-32 (.313). Totals, 81-for-266 (.305).
Personal fouls/disqualifications: 2000-01, 52/0. 2001-02, 59/0. 2003-04, 87/2. 2004-05, 83/0. 2005-06, 73/1. Totals, 354/3.

WNBA PLAYOFF RECORD

Season Team	G	Min.	FGM	FGA	Pct.	FTM	FTA	Pct.	Off.	Def.	Tot.	Ast.	St.	Blk.	TO	Pts.	RPG	APG	PPG
2000—Cleveland	6	106	9	28	.321	10	14	.714	7	13	20	13	7	0	6	33	3.3	2.2	5.5
2001—Cleveland	3	80	5	27	.185	5	6	.833	5	6	11	19	7	1	5	18	3.7	6.3	6.0
2003—Cleveland	3	83	2	13	.154	4	4	1.000	4	8	12	13	6	0	10	9	4.0	4.3	3.0
2004—Minnesota	2	44	2	9	.222	1	2	.500	2	1	3	3	3	0	11	7	1.5	1.5	3.5
Totals	14	313	18	77	.234	20	26	.769	18	28	46	48	23	1	32	67	3.3	3.4	4.8

Three-point field goals: 2000-01, 5-for-13 (.385). 2001-02, 3-for-9 (.333). 2003-04, 1-for-8 (.125). 2004-05, 2-for-3 (.667). Totals, 11-for-33 (.333).
Personal fouls/disqualifications: 2000-01, 5/0. 2001-02, 9/0. 2003-04, 11/0. 2004-05, 4/0. Totals, 29/0.

DEFORGE, ANNA   G   FEVER

PERSONAL: Born April 14, 1976, in Niagara, Wis. ... 5-10/160. (1.78/72.6).
COLLEGE: Nebraska.
TRANSACTIONS/CAREER NOTES: Signed by the WNBA and assigned to Detroit, May 3, 2000. ... Traded to Houston for G Jennifer Rizzotti, April 23, 2001. ... Waived by Houston, May 14, 2001. ... Assigned to Charlotte, April 25, 2002. ... Waived by Charlotte, May 20, 2002. ... Signed by Phoenix, May 9, 2003. ... Traded by Phoenix to Indiana for G Kelly Miller, April 3, 2006.

COLLEGE RECORD

Season Team	G	Min.	FGM	FGA	Pct.	FTM	FTA	Pct.	Reb.	Ast.	Pts.	RPG	APG	PPG
1994—Nebraska	27	...	128	311	.412	37	55	.673	185	86	339	6.9	3.2	12.6
1995—Nebraska	29	...	159	370	.430	73	89	.820	197	100	420	6.8	3.4	14.5
1996—Nebraska	28	...	185	402	.460	83	114	.728	162	86	489	5.8	3.1	17.5
1997—Nebraska	33	...	222	543	.409	117	151	.775	260	120	611	7.9	3.6	18.5
Totals	117	...	694	1626	.427	310	409	.758	804	392	1859	6.9	3.4	15.9

Three-point field goals: 1994-95, 46-for-138 (.333). 1995-96, 29-for-94 (.309). 1996-97, 30-for-78 (.385). 1997-98, 50-for-154 (.325). Totals, 155-for-464 (.334).

WNBA REGULAR-SEASON RECORD

Season Team	G	Min.	FGM	FGA	Pct.	FTM	FTA	Pct.	Off.	Def.	Tot.	Ast.	St.	Blk.	TO	Pts.	RPG	APG	PPG
2000—Detroit	27	433	51	126	.405	25	32	.781	9	38	47	47	27	4	33	145	1.7	1.7	5.4
2003—Phoenix	34	1065	147	357	.412	50	69	.725	32	73	105	72	51	12	53	405	3.1	2.1	11.9
2004—Phoenix	34	1152	165	396	.417	88	102	.863	23	100	123	107	51	8	68	488	3.6	3.1	14.4
2005—Phoenix	33	1131	142	364	.390	102	120	.850	31	83	114	80	41	7	81	433	3.5	2.4	13.1
Totals	128	3781	505	1243	.406	265	323	.820	95	294	389	306	170	31	235	1471	3.0	2.4	11.5

Three-point field goals: 2000-01, 18-for-56 (.321). 2003-04, 61-for-148 (.412). 2004-05, 70-for-181 (.387). 2005-06, 47-for-144 (.326). Totals, 196-for-529 (.371).
Personal fouls/disqualifications: 2000-01, 34/0. 2003-04, 61/0. 2004-05, 51/0. 2005-06, 66/0. Totals, 212/0.

DEREVJANIK, JEN   G   SUN

PERSONAL: Born March 29, 1982 ... 5-10. (1.78).
COLLEGE: George Mason.

WNBA REGULAR-SEASON RECORD

Season Team	G	Min.	FGM	FGA	Pct.	FTM	FTA	Pct.	Off.	Def.	Tot.	Ast.	St.	Blk.	TO	Pts.	RPG	APG	PPG
2004—Connecticut	23	140	7	26	.269	2	2	1.000	1	8	9	14	8	0	10	19	0.4	0.6	0.8
2005—Connecticut	34	359	8	22	.364	7	16	.438	10	20	30	40	11	2	26	24	0.9	1.2	0.7
Totals	57	499	15	48	.313	9	18	.500	11	28	39	54	19	2	36	43	0.7	0.9	0.8

Three-point field goals: 2004-05, 3-for-12 (.250). 2005-06, 1-for-7 (.143). Totals, 4-for-19 (.211).
Personal fouls/disqualifications: 2004-05, 20/0. 2005-06, 47/0. Totals, 67/0.

WNBA PLAYOFF RECORD

Season Team	G	Min.	FGM	FGA	Pct.	FTM	FTA	Pct.	Off.	Def.	Tot.	Ast.	St.	Blk.	TO	Pts.	RPG	APG	PPG
2004—Connecticut	1	1	0	0	...	0	0	...	0	0	0	0	0	0	0	0	0.0	0.0	0.0
2005—Connecticut	8	82	2	5	.400	2	4	.500	1	3	4	14	5	0	6	6	0.5	1.8	0.8
Totals	9	83	2	5	.400	2	4	.500	1	3	4	14	5	0	6	6	0.4	1.6	0.7

Three-point field goals: 2005-06, 0-for-1. Totals, 0-for-1 (.000).
Personal fouls/disqualifications: 2005-06, 4/0. Totals, 4/0.

DILLARD, TAI   G   SILVER STARS

PERSONAL: Born May 6, 1981 ... 5-9/154. (1.75/69.9).
COLLEGE: Texas.
TRANSACTIONS/CAREER NOTES: Signed by San Antonio, May 1, 2003.

COLLEGE RECORD

Season Team	G	Min.	FGM	FGA	Pct.	FTM	FTA	Pct.	Reb.	Ast.	Pts.	RPG	APG	PPG
1999—Texas	32	357	43	111	.387	18	24	.750	46	29	104	1.4	0.9	3.3
2000—Texas	25	724	112	288	.389	34	56	.607	114	80	259	4.6	3.2	10.4
2001—Texas	28	322	44	113	.389	5	8	.625	45	19	95	1.6	0.7	3.4
2002—Texas	35	969	121	326	.371	22	30	.733	164	83	266	4.7	2.4	7.6
Totals	120	2372	320	838	.382	79	118	.669	369	211	724	3.1	1.8	6.0

Three-point field goals: 1999-00, 0-for-2. 2000-01, 1-for-10 (.100). 2001-02, 2-for-5 (.400). 2002-03, 2-for-11 (.182). Totals, 5-for-28 (.179).

WNBA REGULAR-SEASON RECORD

Season Team	G	Min.	FGM	FGA	Pct.	FTM	FTA	Pct.	Off.	Def.	Tot.	Ast.	St.	Blk.	TO	Pts.	RPG	APG	PPG
2003—San Antonio	24	168	16	65	.246	5	6	.833	1	14	15	15	7	4	14	41	0.6	0.6	1.7
2004—San Antonio	23	205	16	54	.296	0	1	.000	2	12	14	19	4	1	14	37	0.6	0.8	1.6
2005—San Antonio	10	51	4	16	.250	1	4	.250	1	5	6	3	2	0	3	9	0.6	0.3	0.9
Totals	57	424	36	135	.267	6	11	.545	4	31	35	37	13	5	31	87	0.6	0.6	1.5

Three-point field goals: 2003-04, 4-for-23 (.174). 2004-05, 5-for-18 (.278). 2005-06, 0-for-3. Totals, 9-for-44 (.205).
Personal fouls/disqualifications: 2003-04, 22/0. 2004-05, 18/0. 2005-06, 5/0. Totals, 45/0.

DIXON, TAMECKA   G   COMETS

PERSONAL: Born December 14, 1975, in Linden, N.J. ... 5-9/148. (1.75/67.1). ... Full name: Tamecka Michele Dixon
HIGH SCHOOL: Linden (Linden, N.J.).
COLLEGE: Kansas.
TRANSACTIONS/CAREER NOTES: Selected by Los Angeles in second round (14th overall) of WNBA Draft, April 28, 1997. ... Signed by Houston, February 28, 2006.
MISCELLANEOUS: Member of WNBA Championship Team (2001, 2002).

D

NOTES: Kodak All-American first team (1997).

COLLEGE RECORD

Season Team	G	Min.	FGM	FGA	Pct.	FTM	FTA	Pct.	Reb.	Ast.	Pts.	RPG	APG	PPG
1993—Kansas	27	...	71	169	.420	39	75	.520	113	42	184	4.2	1.6	6.8
1994—Kansas	30	...	131	276	.475	71	111	.640	120	80	338	4.0	2.7	11.3
1995—Kansas	32	...	207	441	.469	123	159	.774	135	103	543	4.2	3.2	17.0
1996—Kansas	30	...	226	502	.450	152	205	.741	167	112	624	5.6	3.7	20.8
Totals	119	...	635	1388	.457	385	550	.700	535	337	1689	4.5	2.8	14.2

Three-point field goals: 1993-94, 3-for-16 (.188). 1994-95, 5-for-14 (.357). 1995-96, 6-for-30 (.200). 1996-97, 20-for-58 (.345). Totals, 34-for-118 (.288).

NOTES: All-WNBA second team (2001).

WNBA REGULAR-SEASON RECORD

Season Team	G	Min.	FGM	FGA	Pct.	FTM	FTA	Pct.	Off.	Def.	Tot.	Ast.	St.	Blk.	TO	Pts.	RPG	APG	PPG
1997—Los Angeles	27	715	115	252	.456	68	88	.773	22	59	81	55	49	5	58	320	3.0	2.0	11.9
1998—Los Angeles	22	710	124	283	.438	88	113	.779	13	43	56	54	24	8	57	357	2.5	2.5	16.2
1999—Los Angeles	32	563	77	199	.387	48	65	.738	17	49	66	53	17	4	39	217	2.1	1.7	6.8
2000—Los Angeles	31	882	132	291	.454	62	77	.805	34	71	105	96	40	10	60	338	3.4	3.1	10.9
2001—Los Angeles	29	925	133	319	.417	68	86	.791	19	66	85	114	27	2	71	340	2.9	3.9	11.7
2002—Los Angeles	30	958	125	320	.391	49	59	.831	18	74	92	119	28	5	82	319	3.1	4.0	10.6
2003—Los Angeles	30	1042	159	364	.437	83	94	.883	41	85	126	89	35	10	69	412	4.2	3.0	13.7
2004—Los Angeles	32	913	119	269	.442	68	87	.782	32	78	110	112	36	1	71	311	3.4	3.5	9.7
2005—Los Angeles	30	607	63	154	.409	34	40	.850	24	43	67	77	24	2	40	160	2.2	2.6	5.3
Totals	263	7315	1047	2451	.427	568	709	.801	220	568	788	769	280	47	547	2774	3.0	2.9	10.5

Three-point field goals: 1997-98, 22-for-52 (.423). 1998-99, 21-for-59 (.356). 1999-00, 15-for-48 (.313). 2000-01, 12-for-34 (.353). 2001-02, 6-for-34 (.176). 2002-03, 20-for-57 (.351). 2003-04, 11-for-52 (.212). 2004-05, 5-for-11 (.455). 2005-06, 0-for-5. Totals, 112-for-352 (.318).
Personal fouls/disqualifications: 1997-98, 76/0. 1998-99, 67/2. 1999-00, 42/0. 2000-01, 86/0. 2001-02, 52/2. 2002-03, 74/2. 2003-04, 83/0. 2004-05, 86/0. 2005-06, 73/0. Totals, 639/6.

WNBA PLAYOFF RECORD

Season Team	G	Min.	FGM	FGA	Pct.	FTM	FTA	Pct.	Off.	Def.	Tot.	Ast.	St.	Blk.	TO	Pts.	RPG	APG	PPG
1999—Los Angeles	4	42	7	20	.350	1	1	1.000	4	4	8	5	3	0	5	15	2.0	1.3	3.8
2000—Los Angeles	4	127	17	46	.370	8	9	.889	4	7	11	16	3	0	8	47	2.8	4.0	11.8
2001—Los Angeles	7	253	40	83	.482	9	11	.818	5	12	17	29	9	2	20	95	2.4	4.1	13.6
2002—Los Angeles	5	147	25	44	.568	9	10	.900	2	18	20	17	12	0	13	61	4.0	3.4	12.2
2003—Los Angeles	9	316	40	94	.426	26	27	.963	8	21	29	29	14	2	11	110	3.2	3.2	12.2
2004—Los Angeles	3	100	12	30	.400	7	8	.875	4	13	17	9	2	0	10	31	5.7	3.0	10.3
2005—Los Angeles	2	12	1	2	.500	0	0	...	0	1	1	2	1	0	1	2	0.5	1.0	1.0
Totals	34	997	142	319	.445	60	66	.909	27	76	103	107	44	4	68	361	3.0	3.1	10.6

Three-point field goals: 1999-00, 0-for-1. 2000-01, 5-for-10 (.500). 2001-02, 6-for-13 (.462). 2002-03, 2-for-4 (.500). 2003-04, 4-for-12 (.333). Totals, 17-for-40 (.425).

Personal fouls/disqualifications: 1999-00, 4/0. 2000-01, 12/0. 2001-02, 14/0. 2002-03, 15/1. 2003-04, 27/0. 2004-05, 12/1. 2005-06, 4/0. Totals, 88/2.

WNBA ALL-STAR GAME RECORD

Season Team	Min.	FGM	FGA	Pct.	FTM	FTA	Pct.	REBOUNDS Off.	Def.	Tot.	Ast.	PF	Dq.	St.	Blk.	TO	Pts.
2001—Los Angeles............	20	4	7	.571	0	0	...	0	2	2	4	0	0	0	0	1	8
2002—Los Angeles............	13	2	6	.333	0	0	...	0	1	1	0	0	0	0	0	2	5
2003—Los Angeles............	14	0	2	.000	0	0	...	1	2	3	1	0	0	0	0	2	0
Totals	47	6	15	.400	0	0	...	1	5	6	5	0	0	0	0	5	13

Three-point field goals: 2002, 0-for-1. 2003, 1-for-3 (.333). Totals, 1-for-4 (.250).

DOUGLAS, KATIE   G/F   SUN

PERSONAL: Born May 7, 1979, in Indianapolis. ... 6-0/165. (1.83/74.8). ... Full name: Kathryn Elizabeth Douglas
HIGH SCHOOL: Perry Meridian (Indianapolis).
COLLEGE: Purdue.
TRANSACTIONS/CAREER NOTES: Selected by Orlando in first round (10th overall) of WNBA Draft, April 20, 2001.

COLLEGE RECORD

NOTES: Member of NCAA Division I championship team (1999). ... Kodak All-American first team (2000, 2001).

Season Team	G	Min.	FGM	FGA	Pct.	FTM	FTA	Pct.	Reb.	Ast.	Pts.	AVERAGES RPG	APG	PPG
1997—Purdue	33	865	96	214	.449	92	122	.754	141	123	285	4.3	3.7	8.6
1998—Purdue	35	1178	175	376	.465	121	148	.818	217	124	493	6.2	3.5	14.1
1999—Purdue	30	1124	196	461	.425	188	227	.828	196	142	613	6.5	4.7	20.4
2000—Purdue	37	1187	188	421	.447	149	192	.776	173	137	574	4.7	3.7	15.5
Totals	135	4354	655	1472	.445	550	689	.798	727	526	1965	5.4	3.9	14.6

Three-point field goals: 1997-98, 1-for-4 (.250). 1998-99, 22-for-63 (.349). 1999-00, 33-for-102 (.324). 2000-01, 49-for-137 (.358). Totals, 105-for-306 (.343).

WNBA REGULAR-SEASON RECORD

NOTES: All-Defensive first team (2005).

Season Team	G	Min.	FGM	FGA	Pct.	FTM	FTA	Pct.	REBOUNDS Off.	Def.	Tot.	Ast.	St.	Blk.	TO	Pts.	AVERAGES RPG	APG	PPG
2001—Orlando	22	439	51	141	.362	34	47	.723	16	35	51	39	37	7	44	154	2.3	1.8	7.0
2002—Orlando	32	830	92	205	.449	58	67	.866	41	94	135	53	49	13	42	271	4.2	1.7	8.5
2003—Connecticut........	28	843	120	274	.438	49	68	.721	33	73	106	56	31	11	28	336	3.8	2.0	12.0
2004—Connecticut........	34	1120	125	321	.389	61	77	.792	33	99	132	90	50	13	52	364	3.9	2.6	10.7
2005—Connecticut........	32	998	119	288	.413	82	106	.774	45	85	130	94	48	4	54	351	4.1	2.9	11.0
Totals	148	4230	507	1229	.413	284	365	.778	168	386	554	332	215	48	220	1476	3.7	2.2	10.0

Three-point field goals: 2001-02, 18-for-57 (.316). 2002-03, 29-for-79 (.367). 2003-04, 47-for-123 (.382). 2004-05, 53-for-153 (.346). 2005-06, 31-for-110 (.282). Totals, 178-for-522 (.341).

Personal fouls/disqualifications: 2001-02, 34/0. 2002-03, 66/1. 2003-04, 38/0. 2004-05, 73/0. 2005-06, 57/0. Totals, 268/1.

WNBA PLAYOFF RECORD

Season Team	G	Min.	FGM	FGA	Pct.	FTM	FTA	Pct.	REBOUNDS Off.	Def.	Tot.	Ast.	St.	Blk.	TO	Pts.	AVERAGES RPG	APG	PPG
2003—Connecticut........	4	126	10	30	.333	6	7	.857	2	8	10	12	3	1	1	29	2.5	3.0	7.3
2004—Connecticut........	8	268	23	66	.348	25	27	.926	9	23	32	22	10	0	16	82	4.0	2.8	10.3
2005—Connecticut........	8	278	31	67	.463	19	29	.655	12	25	37	18	11	1	8	96	4.6	2.3	12.0
Totals	20	672	64	163	.393	50	63	.794	23	56	79	52	24	2	25	207	4.0	2.6	10.4

Three-point field goals: 2003-04, 3-for-12 (.250). 2004-05, 11-for-37 (.297). 2005-06, 15-for-38 (.395). Totals, 29-for-87 (.333).

Personal fouls/disqualifications: 2003-04, 9/0. 2004-05, 19/0. 2005-06, 17/0. Totals, 45/0.

DYDEK, MARGO   C   SUN

PERSONAL: Born April 28, 1974, in Warsaw, Poland. ... 7-2/223. (2.18/101.2).
TRANSACTIONS/CAREER NOTES: Selected by Utah in first round (first overall) of WNBA Draft, April 29, 1998. ... Traded by San Antonio to Connecticut for the draft rights to F Katie Feenstra and Connecticut's first-round pick in the 2006 WNBA Draft, April 16, 2005.

WNBA REGULAR-SEASON RECORD

NOTES: Led WNBA in blocked shots in 1998 (3.8 bpg), 1999 (2.41 bpg), 2000 (3.00 bpg), 2001 (3.53 bpg), 2002 (3.57 bpg), 2003 (2.94 bpg) and 2005 (2.29 bpg).

Season Team	G	Min.	FGM	FGA	Pct.	FTM	FTA	Pct.	REBOUNDS Off.	Def.	Tot.	Ast.	St.	Blk.	TO	Pts.	AVERAGES RPG	APG	PPG
1998—Utah	30	839	146	303	.482	93	127	.732	41	186	227	53	14	114	108	386	7.6	1.8	12.9
1999—Utah	32	733	141	283	.498	114	133	.857	38	166	204	59	13	77	91	403	6.4	1.8	12.6
2000—Utah	32	775	105	236	.445	82	103	.796	29	146	175	51	18	96	82	294	5.5	1.6	9.2
2001—Utah	32	970	128	291	.440	87	109	.798	29	214	243	64	25	113	90	349	7.6	2.0	10.9
2002—Utah	30	876	139	319	.436	114	135	.844	52	210	262	71	25	107	96	394	8.7	2.4	13.1
2003—San Antonio	34	926	156	346	.451	94	130	.723	45	206	251	58	19	100	80	406	7.4	1.7	11.9
2004—San Antonio	34	682	90	208	.433	44	58	.759	30	138	168	60	20	48	64	225	4.9	1.8	6.6
2005—Connecticut........	31	671	87	162	.537	50	65	.769	27	168	195	38	8	71	47	225	6.3	1.2	7.3
Totals	255	6472	992	2148	.462	678	860	.788	291	1434	1725	454	142	726	658	2682	6.8	1.8	10.5

D

Three-point field goals: 1998-99, 1-for-7 (.143). 1999-00, 7-for-20 (.350). 2000-01, 2-for-14 (.143). 2001-02, 6-for-15 (.400). 2002-03, 2-for-8 (.250). 2003-04, 0-for-1. 2004-05, 1-for-2 (.500). 2005-06, 1-for-2 (.500). Totals, 20-for-69 (.290).
Personal fouls/disqualifications: 1998-99, 126/3. 1999-00, 112/1. 2000-01, 114/1. 2001-02, 108/1. 2002-03, 99/2. 2003-04, 113/1. 2004-05, 70/0. 2005-06, 62/0. Totals, 804/9.

WNBA PLAYOFF RECORD

Season Team	G	Min.	FGM	FGA	Pct.	FTM	FTA	Pct.	Off.	Def.	Tot.	Ast.	St.	Blk.	TO	Pts.	RPG	APG	PPG
										REBOUNDS							AVERAGES		
2001—Utah	2	69	9	21	.429	10	13	.769	1	13	14	3	1	7	4	28	7.0	1.5	14.0
2002—Utah	5	171	22	55	.400	13	15	.867	3	41	44	12	1	17	16	60	8.8	2.4	12.0
2005—Connecticut	8	146	14	38	.368	7	11	.636	8	34	42	4	3	13	16	36	5.3	0.5	4.5
Totals	15	386	45	114	.395	30	39	.769	12	88	100	19	5	37	36	124	6.7	1.3	8.3

Three-point field goals: 2002-03, 3-for-5 (.600). 2005-06, 1-for-1 (1.000). Totals, 4-for-6 (.667).
Personal fouls/disqualifications: 2001-02, 10/1. 2002-03, 17/0. 2005-06, 19/0. Totals, 46/1.

WNBA ALL-STAR GAME RECORD

Season Team	Min.	FGM	FGA	Pct.	FTM	FTA	Pct.	Off.	Def.	Tot.	Ast.	PF	Dq.	St.	Blk.	TO	Pts.
									REBOUNDS								
2003—San Antonio	7	1	3	.333	0	0	...	1	1	2	0	0	0	1	0	1	2
Totals	7	1	3	.333	0	0	...	1	1	2	0	0	0	1	0	1	2

OLYMPICS RECORD

Season Team	G	Min.	FGM	FGA	Pct.	FTM	FTA	Pct.	Reb.	Ast.	Pts.	RPG	APG	PPG
													AVERAGES	
2000—Poland	7	245	49	110	.445	44	56	.786	85	10	143	12.1	1.4	20.4
Totals	7	245	49	110	.445	44	56	.786	85	10	143	12.1	1.4	20.4

Three-point field goals: 2000-01, 1-for-6 (.167). Totals, 1-for-6 (.167).

EDWARDS, SIMONE   C   STORM

PERSONAL: Born November 17, 1973, in Kingston, Jamaica. ... 6-4/164. (1.93/74.4). ... Full name: Simone Ann Marie Edwards
HIGH SCHOOL: Kingston Technical (Kingston, Jamaica).
COLLEGE: Iowa.
TRANSACTIONS/CAREER NOTES: Selected as developmental player and assigned to New York, May 27, 1997. ... Waived by New York, May 18, 1998. ... Signed by WNBA and assigned to Seattle Storm, May 2, 2000.
MISCELLANEOUS: Member of WNBA Championship team (2004).

COLLEGE RECORD

Season Team	G	Min.	FGM	FGA	Pct.	FTM	FTA	Pct.	Reb.	Ast.	Pts.	RPG	APG	PPG
													AVERAGES	
1993—Iowa	27	...	47	103	.456	8	22	.364	102	1	102	3.8	0.0	3.8
1995—Iowa	6	...	15	27	.556	7	14	.500	31	1	37	5.2	0.2	6.2
1996—Iowa	26	...	83	149	.557	18	46	.391	112	23	184	4.3	0.9	7.1
Totals	59	...	145	279	.520	33	82	.402	245	25	323	4.2	0.4	5.5

WNBA REGULAR-SEASON RECORD

Season Team	G	Min.	FGM	FGA	Pct.	FTM	FTA	Pct.	Off.	Def.	Tot.	Ast.	St.	Blk.	TO	Pts.	RPG	APG	PPG
										REBOUNDS							AVERAGES		
2000—Seattle	29	645	83	182	.456	50	80	.625	38	69	107	22	16	10	45	216	3.7	0.8	7.4
2001—Seattle	32	810	91	190	.479	55	83	.663	67	90	157	26	24	20	37	237	4.9	0.8	7.4
2002—Seattle	32	694	84	158	.532	54	73	.740	46	95	141	19	21	12	44	223	4.4	0.6	7.0
2003—Seattle	34	577	61	134	.455	35	56	.625	54	79	133	16	10	9	31	157	3.9	0.5	4.6
2004—Seattle	23	257	20	55	.364	8	19	.421	25	31	56	5	8	3	13	48	2.4	0.2	2.1
2005—Seattle	28	201	24	41	.585	7	12	.583	9	22	31	3	4	2	4	55	1.1	0.1	2.0
Totals	178	3184	363	760	.478	209	323	.647	239	386	625	91	83	56	174	936	3.5	0.5	5.3

Three-point field goals: 2002-03, 1-for-1 (1.000). Totals, 1-for-1 (1.000).
Personal fouls/disqualifications: 2000-01, 57/0. 2001-02, 54/0. 2002-03, 66/0. 2003-04, 55/0. 2004-05, 25/0. 2005-06, 13/0. Totals, 270/0.

WNBA PLAYOFF RECORD

Season Team	G	Min.	FGM	FGA	Pct.	FTM	FTA	Pct.	Off.	Def.	Tot.	Ast.	St.	Blk.	TO	Pts.	RPG	APG	PPG
										REBOUNDS							AVERAGES		
2002—Seattle	2	31	1	8	.125	2	4	.500	2	1	3	0	0	0	2	4	1.5	0.0	2.0
2004—Seattle	7	54	6	9	.667	0	0	...	7	7	14	1	0	1	2	12	2.0	0.1	1.7
2005—Seattle	2	5	0	1	.000	0	0	...	0	1	1	1	0	0	0	0	0.5	0.5	0.0
Totals	11	90	7	18	.389	2	4	.500	9	9	18	2	0	1	4	16	1.6	0.2	1.5

Personal fouls/disqualifications: 2002-03, 4/0. 2004-05, 5/0. Totals, 9/0.

ELY, SHYRA   F   SILVER STARS

PERSONAL: Born August 9, 1983, in Indianapolis. ... 6-2. (1.88). ... Full name: Shyra Quontae Ely
HIGH SCHOOL: Ben Davis (Indianapolis).
COLLEGE: Tennessee.
TRANSACTIONS/CAREER NOTES: Selected by San Antonio in the second round (14th overall) of the WNBA Draft, April 16, 2005.

COLLEGE RECORD

NOTES: AP All-American honorable mention (2005). ... Kodak All-American (2004). ... AP All-American third team (2004). ... NCAA All-Midwest Regional team (2004). ... NCAA All-Mideast Regional team (2003). ... All-SEC first team (2004, 2005).

Season Team	G	Min.	FGM	FGA	Pct.	FTM	FTA	Pct.	Reb.	Ast.	Pts.	AVERAGES RPG	APG	PPG
2001—Tennessee	33	691	123	251	.490	62	106	.585	177	36	308	5.4	1.1	9.3
2002—Tennessee	36	804	142	287	.495	67	94	.713	238	47	354	6.6	1.3	9.8
2003—Tennessee	35	1055	213	443	.481	82	121	.678	279	53	508	8.0	1.5	14.5
2004—Tennessee	36	1082	193	423	.456	112	155	.723	246	58	503	6.8	1.6	14.0
Totals	**140**	**3632**	**671**	**1404**	**.478**	**323**	**476**	**.679**	**940**	**194**	**1673**	**6.7**	**1.4**	**12.0**

WNBA REGULAR-SEASON RECORD

Season Team	G	Min.	FGM	FGA	Pct.	FTM	FTA	Pct.	REBOUNDS Off.	Def.	Tot.	Ast.	St.	Blk.	TO	Pts.	AVERAGES RPG	APG	PPG
2005—San Antonio	31	528	50	132	.379	30	39	.769	11	51	62	27	7	4	33	139	2.0	0.9	4.5
Totals	**31**	**528**	**50**	**132**	**.379**	**30**	**39**	**.769**	**11**	**51**	**62**	**27**	**7**	**4**	**33**	**139**	**2.0**	**0.9**	**4.5**

Three-point field goals: 2005-06, 9-for-31 (.290). Totals, 9-for-31 (.290).
Personal fouls/disqualifications: 2005-06, 42/0. Totals, 42/0.

FARRIS, BARBARA   F   LIBERTY

PERSONAL: Born September 10, 1976, in Harvey, La. ... 6-3/195. (1.91/88.5).
HIGH SCHOOL: St. Martin's (Harvey, La.).
COLLEGE: Tulane.
TRANSACTIONS/CAREER NOTES: Signed by the WNBA and assigned to Detroit, May 2, 2000. ... Signed by New York, February 27, 2006.
MISCELLANEOUS: Member of WNBA Championship Team (2003).

COLLEGE RECORD

NOTES: Kodak District IV All-American (1997). ... Finished second in NCAA in field goal percentage during her senior year at Tulane. ... All-Conference USA first team (1997). ... All-Conference USA second team (1998). ... Conference USA All-Tournament team (1997). ... Ranks in the top five on Tulane's all-time list in six different statistical categories.

Season Team	G	Min.	FGM	FGA	Pct.	FTM	FTA	Pct.	Reb.	Ast.	Pts.	AVERAGES RPG	APG	PPG
1994—Tulane	28	...	161	269	.599	116	198	.586	224	13	438	8.0	0.5	15.6
1995—Tulane	31	...	178	284	.627	109	194	.562	248	22	465	8.0	0.7	15.0
1996—Tulane	32	...	170	273	.623	97	161	.602	246	40	437	7.7	1.3	13.7
1997—Tulane	27	...	151	210	.719	86	131	.656	221	30	389	8.2	1.1	14.4
Totals	**118**	**...**	**660**	**1036**	**.637**	**408**	**684**	**.596**	**939**	**105**	**1729**	**8.0**	**0.9**	**14.7**

Three-point field goals: 1994-95, 0-for-1. 1997-98, 1-for-1 (1.000). Totals, 1-for-2 (.500).

ABL RECORD

Season Team	G	Min.	FGM	FGA	Pct.	FTM	FTA	Pct.	Reb.	Ast.	Pts.	AVERAGES RPG	APG	PPG
1998—New England	13	...	25	74	.338	45	65	.692	7	95	...	0.5	7.3	...
Totals	**13**	**...**	**25**	**74**	**.338**	**45**	**65**	**.692**	**7**	**95**	**...**	**0.5**	**7.3**	**...**

WNBA REGULAR-SEASON RECORD

Season Team	G	Min.	FGM	FGA	Pct.	FTM	FTA	Pct.	REBOUNDS Off.	Def.	Tot.	Ast.	St.	Blk.	TO	Pts.	AVERAGES RPG	APG	PPG
2000—Detroit	14	130	15	30	.500	15	27	.556	16	16	32	2	6	1	14	45	2.3	0.1	3.2
2001—Detroit	31	559	46	98	.469	37	58	.638	41	68	109	16	7	5	30	129	3.5	0.5	4.2
2002—Detroit	32	564	49	117	.419	45	61	.738	29	65	94	16	12	9	38	143	2.9	0.5	4.5
2003—Detroit	34	522	43	99	.434	41	63	.651	29	53	82	23	10	4	41	127	2.4	0.7	3.7
2004—Detroit	26	422	41	80	.513	36	54	.667	28	33	61	7	8	2	26	118	2.3	0.3	4.5
2005—Detroit	34	444	25	73	.342	33	54	.611	31	53	84	19	8	1	43	83	2.5	0.6	2.4
Totals	**171**	**2641**	**219**	**497**	**.441**	**207**	**317**	**.653**	**174**	**288**	**462**	**83**	**51**	**22**	**192**	**645**	**2.7**	**0.5**	**3.8**

Three-point field goals: 2000-01, 0-for-1. 2002-03, 0-for-1. Totals, 0-for-2 (.000).
Personal fouls/disqualifications: 2000-01, 30/0. 2001-02, 68/1. 2002-03, 62/0. 2003-04, 62/0. 2004-05, 46/0. 2005-06, 55/0. Totals, 323/1.

WNBA PLAYOFF RECORD

Season Team	G	Min.	FGM	FGA	Pct.	FTM	FTA	Pct.	REBOUNDS Off.	Def.	Tot.	Ast.	St.	Blk.	TO	Pts.	AVERAGES RPG	APG	PPG
2003—Detroit	8	133	10	25	.400	11	17	.647	8	12	20	4	1	0	10	31	2.5	0.5	3.9
2004—Detroit	3	78	6	17	.353	6	8	.750	8	7	15	2	1	0	5	18	5.0	0.7	6.0
2005—Detroit	2	12	0	1	.000	0	0	...	0	1	1	0	0	0	0	0	0.5	0.0	0.0
Totals	**13**	**223**	**16**	**43**	**.372**	**17**	**25**	**.680**	**16**	**20**	**36**	**6**	**2**	**0**	**15**	**49**	**2.8**	**0.5**	**3.8**

Three-point field goals: 2003-04, 0-for-1. Totals, 0-for-1 (.000).
Personal fouls/disqualifications: 2003-04, 14/0. 2004-05, 5/0. Totals, 19/0.

FEASTER, ALLISON   F   STING

PERSONAL: Born February 11, 1976, in Chester, S.C. ... 5-11/168. (1.80/76.2). ... Full name: Allison Sharlene Feaster
HIGH SCHOOL: Chester (Chester, S.C.).
COLLEGE: Harvard.
TRANSACTIONS/CAREER NOTES: Selected by Los Angeles in first round (fifth overall) of WNBA Draft, April 29, 1998. ... Traded by Los Angeles with C/F Clarisse Machanguana for C Rhonda Mapp and G E.C. Hill, October 10, 2000.

F

COLLEGE RECORD

NOTES: Kodak All-American first team (1998). ... Led NCAA in scoring with 28.5 ppg (1998).

Season Team	G	Min.	FGM	FGA	Pct.	FTM	FTA	Pct.	Reb.	Ast.	Pts.	AVERAGES RPG	APG	PPG
1994—Harvard	26	...	160	302	.530	113	145	.779	290	49	443	11.2	1.9	17.0
1995—Harvard	27	...	175	369	.474	110	146	.753	275	61	490	10.2	2.3	18.1
1996—Harvard	27	...	227	471	.482	87	114	.763	289	60	582	10.7	2.2	21.6
1997—Harvard	28	...	272	524	.519	195	245	.796	303	73	797	10.8	2.6	28.5
Totals	108		834	1666	.501	505	650	.777	1157	243	2312	10.7	2.3	21.4

Three-point field goals: 1994-95, 10-for-32 (.313). 1995-96, 30-for-84 (.357). 1996-97, 45-for-139 (.324). 1997-98, 58-for-143 (.406). Totals, 143-for-398 (.359).

WNBA REGULAR-SEASON RECORD

Season Team	G	Min.	FGM	FGA	Pct.	FTM	FTA	Pct.	REBOUNDS Off.	Def.	Tot.	Ast.	St.	Blk.	TO	Pts.	AVERAGES RPG	APG	PPG
1998—Los Angeles	3	41	3	14	.214	2	2	1.000	1	1	2	2	0	0	4	10	0.7	1.0	3.3
1999—Los Angeles	32	410	51	103	.495	39	57	.684	28	30	58	32	15	7	28	162	1.8	1.0	5.1
2000—Los Angeles	32	469	60	167	.359	60	72	.833	36	49	85	33	23	2	35	202	2.7	1.0	6.3
2001—Charlotte	32	1007	126	336	.375	58	63	.921	55	98	153	46	29	10	59	365	4.8	1.4	11.4
2002—Charlotte	32	956	115	292	.394	70	85	.824	37	81	118	61	39	12	40	379	3.7	1.9	11.8
2003—Charlotte	34	1096	142	378	.376	66	78	.846	37	76	113	73	52	9	72	422	3.3	2.1	12.4
2004—Charlotte	33	1052	132	332	.398	79	91	.868	22	62	84	60	27	6	68	388	2.5	1.8	11.8
2005—Charlotte	21	666	61	162	.377	33	39	.846	9	28	37	51	14	2	38	192	1.8	2.4	9.1
Totals	219	5697	690	1784	.387	407	487	.836	225	425	650	359	201	48	344	2120	3.0	1.6	9.7

Three-point field goals: 1998-99, 2-for-10 (.200). 1999-00, 21-for-57 (.368). 2000-01, 22-for-85 (.259). 2001-02, 55-for-168 (.327). 2002-03, 79-for-189 (.418). 2003-04, 72-for-205 (.351). 2004-05, 45-for-143 (.315). 2005-06, 37-for-86 (.430). Totals, 333-for-943 (.353).

Personal fouls/disqualifications: 1998-99, 10/0. 1999-00, 51/0. 2000-01, 47/0. 2001-02, 86/1. 2002-03, 79/0. 2003-04, 75/0. 2004-05, 61/0. 2005-06, 52/0. Totals, 461/1.

WNBA PLAYOFF RECORD

Season Team	G	Min.	FGM	FGA	Pct.	FTM	FTA	Pct.	REBOUNDS Off.	Def.	Tot.	Ast.	St.	Blk.	TO	Pts.	AVERAGES RPG	APG	PPG
1999—Los Angeles	4	32	4	15	.267	5	5	1.000	1	1	2	1	1	0	1	14	0.5	0.3	3.5
2000—Los Angeles	4	44	5	16	.313	2	2	1.000	3	6	9	3	2	1	5	15	2.3	0.8	3.8
2001—Charlotte	8	248	26	74	.351	1	1	1.000	8	26	34	14	9	4	9	64	4.3	1.8	8.0
2002—Charlotte	2	65	6	20	.300	0	0	...	3	12	15	7	2	0	4	15	7.5	3.5	7.5
2003—Charlotte	2	63	7	20	.350	3	4	.750	2	3	5	1	2	0	0	21	2.5	0.5	10.5
Totals	20	452	48	145	.331	11	12	.917	17	48	65	26	16	5	19	129	3.3	1.3	6.5

Three-point field goals: 1999-00, 1-for-5 (.200). 2000-01, 3-for-13 (.231). 2001-02, 11-for-35 (.314). 2002-03, 3-for-13 (.231). 2003-04, 4-for-10 (.400). Totals, 22-for-76 (.289).

Personal fouls/disqualifications: 1999-00, 3/0. 2000-01, 11/0. 2001-02, 18/0. 2002-03, 1/0. 2003-04, 5/0. Totals, 38/0.

FEENSTRA, KATIE   C   SILVER STARS

PERSONAL: Born November 17, 1982, in Grand Rapids, Mich. ... 6-8/240. (2.03/108.9). ... Full name: Katharen Ruth Feenstra
HIGH SCHOOL: Grand Rapids Baptist (Grand Rapids, Mich.).
COLLEGE: Liberty.
TRANSACTIONS/CAREER NOTES: Selected by Connecticut in the first round (eighth overall) of the WNBA Draft, April 16, 2005. ... Draft rights, along with a first-round pick in the 2006 WNBA Draft, traded by Connecticut to San Antonio for Margo Dydek, April 16, 2005.

COLLEGE RECORD

NOTES: AP All-American honorable mention (2004, 2005). ... Kodak/WBCA All-American Region II team (2004). ... Big South women's athlete of the year (2004). ... Big South Player of the Year (2003, 2004, 2005). ... All-Big South first team (2003, 2004, 2005). ... Big South All-Rookie team (2002). ... Big South Tournament MVP (2004). ... All-Big South Tournament team (2002, 2003, 2004). ... All-time Liberty and Big South leader in career blocks (246) and field goal percentage (.624).

Season Team	G	Min.	FGM	FGA	Pct.	FTM	FTA	Pct.	Reb.	Ast.	Pts.	AVERAGES RPG	APG	PPG
2001—Liberty	17	275	73	143	.510	32	57	.561	95	6	178	5.6	0.4	10.5
2002—Liberty	28	669	170	299	.569	84	124	.677	254	12	424	9.1	0.4	15.1
2003—Liberty	32	915	291	443	.657	92	161	.571	353	16	674	11.0	0.5	21.1
2004—Liberty	32	828	230	343	.671	109	162	.673	331	28	569	10.3	0.9	17.8
Totals	109	2687	764	1228	.622	317	504	.629	1033	62	1845	9.5	0.6	16.9

WNBA REGULAR-SEASON RECORD

NOTES: All-Rookie team (2005).

Season Team	G	Min.	FGM	FGA	Pct.	FTM	FTA	Pct.	REBOUNDS Off.	Def.	Tot.	Ast.	St.	Blk.	TO	Pts.	AVERAGES RPG	APG	PPG
2005—San Antonio	34	673	104	222	.468	90	128	.703	57	118	175	6	9	44	62	298	5.1	0.2	8.8
Totals	34	673	104	222	.468	90	128	.703	57	118	175	6	9	44	62	298	5.1	0.2	8.8

Personal fouls/disqualifications: 2005-06, 90/0. Totals, 90/0.

FEIFEI, SUI   G   MONARCHS

PERSONAL: Born January 29, 1979, in Qing Dao, China. ... 6-1/162. (1.85/73.5).
HIGH SCHOOL: Shan Dong Ji Nan Railway (Qing Dao, China).
TRANSACTIONS/CAREER NOTES: Played four years in the WBCA (Women's Chinese Basketball Association). ... Signed by Sacramento, April 2005.
MISCELLANEOUS: Member of WNBA Championship team (2005).

Season Team	G	Min.	FGM	FGA	Pct.	FTM	FTA	Pct.	Reb.	Ast.	Pts.	AVERAGES RPG	APG	PPG
2004—Baiyi	20	638	163	350	.466	67	91	.736	83	66	427	4.2	3.3	21.4
Totals	20	638	163	350	.466	67	91	.736	83	66	427	4.2	3.3	21.4

Three-point field goals: 2004-05, 34-for-92 (.370). Totals, 34-for-92 (.370).

WNBA REGULAR-SEASON RECORD

Season Team	G	Min.	FGM	FGA	Pct.	FTM	FTA	Pct.	REBOUNDS Off.	Def.	Tot.	Ast.	St.	Blk.	TO	Pts.	AVERAGES RPG	APG	PPG
2005—Sacramento	5	24	1	6	.167	4	4	1.000	0	1	1	3	0	0	2	7	0.2	0.6	1.4
Totals	5	24	1	6	.167	4	4	1.000	0	1	1	3	0	0	2	7	0.2	0.6	1.4

Three-point field goals: 2005-06, 1-for-1 (1.000). Totals, 1-for-1 (1.000).
Personal fouls/disqualifications: 2005-06, 3/0. Totals, 3/0.

FERDINAND, MARIE   G   SILVER STARS

PERSONAL: Born October 13, 1978, in Miami. ... 5-9/145. (1.75/65.8).
HIGH SCHOOL: Edison (Miami).
COLLEGE: Louisiana State.
TRANSACTIONS/CAREER NOTES: Selected by Utah in first round (eighth overall) of WNBA Draft, April 20, 2001.

COLLEGE RECORD

NOTES: Kodak All-American first team (2001).

Season Team	G	Min.	FGM	FGA	Pct.	FTM	FTA	Pct.	Reb.	Ast.	Pts.	AVERAGES RPG	APG	PPG
1997—Louisiana State	27	243	26	69	.377	14	24	.583	61	17	66	2.3	0.6	2.4
1998—Louisiana State	30	883	149	322	.463	69	104	.663	157	90	368	5.2	3.0	12.3
1999—Louisiana State	32	1138	240	479	.501	76	114	.667	148	170	560	4.6	5.3	17.5
2000—Louisiana State	31	1075	240	469	.512	173	234	.739	158	107	654	5.1	3.5	21.1
Totals	120	3339	655	1339	.489	332	476	.697	524	384	1648	4.4	3.2	13.7

Three-point field goals: 1998-99, 1-for-3 (.333). 1999-00, 4-for-13 (.308). 2000-01, 1-for-13 (.077). Totals, 6-for-29 (.207).

WNBA REGULAR-SEASON RECORD

Season Team	G	Min.	FGM	FGA	Pct.	FTM	FTA	Pct.	REBOUNDS Off.	Def.	Tot.	Ast.	St.	Blk.	TO	Pts.	AVERAGES RPG	APG	PPG
2001—Utah	32	864	143	290	.493	69	113	.611	23	63	86	79	40	4	63	366	2.7	2.5	11.4
2002—Utah	32	1065	176	371	.474	132	171	.772	19	88	107	91	51	7	89	489	3.3	2.8	15.3
2003—San Antonio	34	1116	139	384	.362	176	223	.789	28	99	127	90	58	6	85	470	3.7	2.6	13.8
2004—San Antonio	17	509	67	162	.414	55	64	.859	18	36	54	29	32	2	35	199	3.2	1.7	11.7
2005—San Antonio	31	999	132	358	.369	104	134	.776	40	76	116	68	46	5	70	388	3.7	2.2	12.5
Totals	146	4553	657	1565	.420	536	705	.760	128	362	490	357	227	24	342	1912	3.4	2.4	13.1

Three-point field goals: 2001-02, 11-for-42 (.262). 2002-03, 5-for-34 (.147). 2003-04, 16-for-52 (.308). 2004-05, 10-for-27 (.370). 2005-06, 20-for-65 (.308). Totals, 62-for-220 (.282).
Personal fouls/disqualifications: 2001-02, 70/1. 2002-03, 86/0. 2003-04, 87/0. 2004-05, 34/0. 2005-06, 74/0. Totals, 351/1.

WNBA PLAYOFF RECORD

Season Team	G	Min.	FGM	FGA	Pct.	FTM	FTA	Pct.	REBOUNDS Off.	Def.	Tot.	Ast.	St.	Blk.	TO	Pts.	AVERAGES RPG	APG	PPG
2001—Utah	2	69	7	16	.438	15	18	.833	2	6	8	7	3	0	2	29	4.0	3.5	14.5
2002—Utah	5	186	25	56	.446	23	34	.676	4	18	22	13	10	0	20	74	4.4	2.6	14.8
Totals	7	255	32	72	.444	38	52	.731	6	24	30	20	13	0	22	103	4.3	2.9	14.7

Three-point field goals: 2001-02, 0-for-2. 2002-03, 1-for-5 (.200). Totals, 1-for-7 (.143).
Personal fouls/disqualifications: 2001-02, 4/0. 2002-03, 16/0. Totals, 20/0.

WNBA ALL-STAR GAME RECORD

Season Team	Min.	FGM	FGA	Pct.	FTM	FTA	Pct.	REBOUNDS Off.	Def.	Tot.	Ast.	PF	Dq.	St.	Blk.	TO	Pts.
2002—Utah	9	1	3	.333	0	0	...	0	0	0	1	0	0	0	0	1	2
2003—San Antonio	19	3	7	.429	0	0	...	0	0	0	1	4	0	2	0	3	6
2005—San Antonio	13	5	8	.625	0	0	...	0	0	0	1	1	0	2	0	1	10
Totals	41	9	18	.500	0	0	...	0	0	0	3	5	0	4	0	5	18

Three-point field goals: 2004, 0-for-1. Totals, 0-for-1 (.000).

FORD, CHERYL   F   SHOCK

PERSONAL: Born June 6, 1981, in Homer, La. ... 6-3/215. (1.91/97.5). ... Daughter of Karl Malone, forward, Utah Jazz.
HIGH SCHOOL: Summerfield (Summerfield, La.).
COLLEGE: Louisiana Tech.
TRANSACTIONS/CAREER NOTES: Selected by Detroit in first round (third overall) of WNBA Draft, April 25, 2003.
MISCELLANEOUS: 1998 U.S. Olympic 17-under team member. ... Member of WNBA Championship Team (2003).

COLLEGE RECORD

NOTES: Associated Press All-American Honorable Mention (2003). ... Western Athletic Conference Player of the Year (2003, 2002). ... All-WAC first team (2003, 2002). ... Led the WAC in rebounding (8.7) as a junior.

F

Season Team	G	Min.	FGM	FGA	Pct.	FTM	FTA	Pct.	Reb.	Ast.	Pts.	RPG	APG	PPG
1999—Louisiana Tech	34	418	83	143	.580	56	84	.667	176	4	222	5.2	0.1	6.5
2000—Louisiana Tech	35	532	106	201	.527	75	125	.600	180	18	287	5.1	0.5	8.2
2001—Louisiana Tech	30	602	128	275	.465	82	140	.586	262	13	338	8.7	0.4	11.3
2002—Louisiana Tech	34	997	206	429	.480	121	192	.630	438	30	533	12.9	0.9	15.7
Totals	133	2549	523	1048	.499	334	541	.617	1056	65	1380	7.9	0.5	10.4

WNBA REGULAR-SEASON RECORD

NOTES: WNBA Rookie of the Year (2003). ... All-WNBA second team (2003). ... Bud Light Peak Performer, Rebounding (2005). ... Led WNBA in rebounding (9.8 rpg) in 2005.

Season Team	G	Min.	FGM	FGA	Pct.	FTM	FTA	Pct.	REBOUNDS Off.	Def.	Tot.	Ast.	St.	Blk.	TO	Pts.	AVERAGES RPG	APG	PPG
2003—Detroit	32	956	128	270	.474	88	129	.682	99	235	334	27	32	31	79	344	10.4	0.8	10.8
2004—Detroit	31	912	118	287	.411	93	158	.589	104	193	297	34	41	25	54	329	9.6	1.1	10.6
2005—Detroit	33	932	120	279	.430	73	150	.487	113	209	322	26	33	46	69	313	9.8	0.8	9.5
Totals	96	2800	366	836	.438	254	437	.581	316	637	953	87	106	102	202	986	9.9	0.9	10.3

Personal fouls/disqualifications: 2003-04, 109/1. 2004-05, 118/3. 2005-06, 143/6. Totals, 370/10.

WNBA PLAYOFF RECORD

Season Team	G	Min.	FGM	FGA	Pct.	FTM	FTA	Pct.	REBOUNDS Off.	Def.	Tot.	Ast.	St.	Blk.	TO	Pts.	AVERAGES RPG	APG	PPG
2003—Detroit	8	232	24	74	.324	19	23	.826	25	55	80	4	11	6	10	67	10.0	0.5	8.4
2004—Detroit	3	111	17	38	.447	14	22	.636	5	27	32	1	4	7	8	48	10.7	0.3	16.0
2005—Detroit	2	49	8	18	.444	3	5	.600	7	7	14	2	1	2	3	19	7.0	1.0	9.5
Totals	13	392	49	130	.377	36	50	.720	37	89	126	7	16	15	21	134	9.7	0.5	10.3

Personal fouls/disqualifications: 2003-04, 30/0. 2004-05, 3/0. 2005-06, 11/1. Totals, 44/1.

WNBA ALL-STAR GAME RECORD

Season Team	Min.	FGM	FGA	Pct.	FTM	FTA	Pct.	REBOUNDS Off.	Def.	Tot.	Ast.	PF	Dq.	St.	Blk.	TO	Pts.
2003—Detroit	9	0	2	.000	0	0	...	0	1	1	0	2	0	0	1	2	0
2005—Detroit	12	2	3	.667	0	0	...	1	4	5	0	3	0	0	0	1	4
Totals	21	2	5	.400	0	0	...	1	5	6	0	5	0	0	1	3	4

FRETT, LA'KESHIA   F   LIBERTY

PERSONAL: Born June 12, 1975, in Carmel, Calif. ... 6-3/170. (1.91/77.1).
HIGH SCHOOL: Phoebus (Hampton, Va.).
COLLEGE: Georgia.
TRANSACTIONS/CAREER NOTES: Seleted by Los Angeles in fourth round (40th overall) of WNBA Draft, May 4, 1999. ... Traded by Los Angeles to Sacramento for G/F Latasha Byears, October 11, 2000. ... Signed by New York, March 18, 2005.

NOTES: AP All-American third team (1997).

COLLEGE RECORD

Season Team	G	Min.	FGM	FGA	Pct.	FTM	FTA	Pct.	Reb.	Ast.	Pts.	RPG	APG	PPG
1993—Georgia	28	...	154	323	.477	85	111	.766	168	69	393	6.0	2.5	14.0
1994—Georgia	33	...	203	421	.482	116	155	.748	199	100	523	6.0	3.0	15.8
1995—Georgia	33	...	195	374	.521	90	107	.841	288	65	481	8.7	2.0	14.6
1996—Georgia	28	...	191	396	.482	70	90	.778	187	81	453	6.7	2.9	16.2
Totals	122	...	743	1514	.491	361	463	.780	842	315	1850	6.9	2.6	15.2

Three-point field goals: 1994-95, 1-for-2 (.500). 1995-96, 1-for-1 (1.000). 1996-97, 1-for-2 (.500). Totals, 3-for-5 (.600).

ABL RECORD

Season Team	G	Min.	FGM	FGA	Pct.	FTM	FTA	Pct.	Reb.	Ast.	Pts.	RPG	APG	PPG
1997—Philadelphia	44	...	160	338	.473	104	120	.867	200	47	427	4.5	1.1	9.7
1998—Philadelphia	14	...	40	106	.377	17	21	.810	48	15	97	3.4	1.1	6.9
Totals	58	...	200	444	.450	121	141	.858	248	62	524	4.3	1.1	9.0

Three-point field goals: 1997-98, 3-for-5 (.600). 1998-99, null-for-2. Totals, 3-for-7 (.429).

WNBA REGULAR-SEASON RECORD

Season Team	G	Min.	FGM	FGA	Pct.	FTM	FTA	Pct.	REBOUNDS Off.	Def.	Tot.	Ast.	St.	Blk.	TO	Pts.	AVERAGES RPG	APG	PPG
1999—Los Angeles	31	658	77	162	.475	34	43	.791	48	46	94	63	9	5	26	188	3.0	2.0	6.1
2000—Los Angeles	25	187	14	51	.275	12	16	.750	8	16	24	6	7	6	13	40	1.0	0.2	1.6
2001—Sacramento	30	403	49	126	.389	30	35	.857	23	32	55	18	10	6	32	128	1.8	0.6	4.3
2002—Sacramento	32	648	84	187	.449	14	17	.824	30	65	95	23	5	19	27	187	3.0	0.7	5.8
2003—Sacramento	24	150	17	47	.362	1	2	.500	9	14	23	12	2	3	10	36	1.0	0.5	1.5
2004—N.Y.-Charlotte	26	347	47	98	.480	23	37	.622	...	17	...	33	10	7	132	117	...	1.3	4.5
2005—New York	33	361	42	88	.477	14	19	.737	15	23	38	18	12	4	18	98	1.2	0.5	3.0
Totals	201	2754	330	759	.435	128	169	.757	133	213	329	173	55	50	258	794	1.6	0.9	4.0

Three-point field goals: 2000-01, 0-for-1. 2002-03, 5-for-15 (.333). 2003-04, 1-for-2 (.500). Totals, 6-for-18 (.333).
Personal fouls/disqualifications: 1999-00, 42/0. 2000-01, 10/0. 2001-02, 30/0. 2002-03, 70/2. 2003-04, 16/0. 2004-05, 29/0. 2005-06, 52/0. Totals, 249/2.

WNBA PLAYOFF RECORD

Season Team	G	Min.	FGM	FGA	Pct.	FTM	FTA	Pct.	REBOUNDS Off.	Def.	Tot.	Ast.	St.	Blk.	TO	Pts.	AVERAGES RPG	APG	PPG
1999—Los Angeles	4	121	11	30	.367	6	7	.857	12	9	21	13	2	2	3	28	5.3	3.3	7.0

Season Team	G	Min.	FGM	FGA	Pct.	FTM	FTA	Pct.	Off.	Def.	Tot.	Ast.	St.	Blk.	TO	Pts.	RPG	APG	PPG
2000—Los Angeles	3	7	2	3	.667	3	4	.750	0	0	0	0	0	0	0	7	0.0	0.0	2.3
2001—Sacramento	5	18	1	8	.125	2	2	1.000	2	0	2	1	0	0	1	4	0.4	0.2	0.8
2003—Sacramento	1	9	1	2	.500	0	0	...	0	0	0	0	0	0	1	2	0.0	0.0	2.0
2004—New York...........	5	116	20	48	.417	4	4	1.000	5	12	17	6	4	3	7	44	3.4	1.2	8.8
2005—New York...........	2	47	5	12	.417	5	6	.833	2	2	4	1	0	0	2	15	2.0	0.5	7.5
Totals	20	318	40	103	.388	20	23	.870	21	23	44	21	6	5	14	100	2.2	1.1	5.0

Three-point field goals: 2003-04, 0-for-1. 2004-05, 0-for-1. Totals, 0-for-2 (.000).
Personal fouls/disqualifications: 1999-00, 6/0. 2001-02, 2/0. 2003-04, 1/0. 2004-05, 12/0. 2005-06, 7/0. Totals, 28/0.

GOODSON, ADRIENNE   F   STING

PERSONAL: Born October 19, 1966, in Jersey City, N.J. ... 6-0/165. (1.83/74.8). ... Full name: Adrienne Maureen Goodson
HIGH SCHOOL: Bayonne (Bayonne, N.J.).
COLLEGE: Old Dominion.
TRANSACTIONS/CAREER NOTES: Selected by Utah in third round (27th overall) of WNBA Draft, May 4, 1999. ... Signed by Houston, April 19, 2005. ... Traded by Houston with F Kristen Rasmussen to Charlotte for G Dawn Staley, August 1, 2005.

COLLEGE RECORD

NOTES: Member of NCAA Championship team (1985).

Season Team	G	Min.	FGM	FGA	Pct.	FTM	FTA	Pct.	Reb.	Ast.	Pts.	RPG	APG	PPG
1984—Old Dominion..................	34	...	131	300	.437	61	90	.678	153	69	323	4.5	2.0	9.5
1985—Old Dominion..................	26	...	156	327	.477	62	88	.705	226	22	374	8.7	0.8	14.4
1986—Old Dominion..................	31	...	177	345	.513	77	116	.664	256	41	431	8.3	1.3	13.9
1987—Old Dominion..................	26	...	188	344	.547	70	107	.654	228	103	446	8.8	4.0	17.2
Totals.....................................	117	...	652	1316	.495	270	401	.673	863	235	1574	7.4	2.0	13.5

ABL RECORD

Season Team	G	Min.	FGM	FGA	Pct.	FTM	FTA	Pct.	Reb.	Ast.	Pts.	RPG	APG	PPG
1996—Philadelphia	40	...	250	515	.485	183	241	.759	291	100	690	7.3	2.5	17.3
1997—Philadelphia	43	...	288	582	.495	180	243	.741	376	98	761	8.7	2.3	17.7
1998—Chicago..........................	12	...	75	166	.452	53	66	.803	86	20	207	7.2	1.7	17.3
Totals.....................................	95	...	613	1263	.485	416	550	.756	753	218	1658	7.9	2.3	17.5

Three-point field goals: 1996-97, 7-for-24 (.292). 1997-98, 5-for-32 (.156). 1998-99, 4-for-19 (.211). Totals, 16-for-75 (.213).

WNBA REGULAR-SEASON RECORD

Season Team	G	Min.	FGM	FGA	Pct.	FTM	FTA	Pct.	Off.	Def.	Tot.	Ast.	St.	Blk.	TO	Pts.	RPG	APG	PPG
1999—Utah.................	32	1068	182	427	.426	99	129	.767	71	67	138	87	27	8	98	476	4.3	2.7	14.9
2000—Utah.................	29	929	199	415	.480	92	134	.687	69	95	164	69	41	7	81	498	5.7	2.4	17.2
2001—Utah.................	28	854	138	319	.433	62	89	.697	66	86	152	58	27	0	75	343	5.4	2.1	12.3
2002—Utah.................	32	1101	189	419	.451	117	157	.745	91	90	181	67	45	6	102	503	5.7	2.1	15.7
2003—San Antonio......	33	969	141	357	.395	81	102	.794	74	111	185	71	24	6	85	371	5.6	2.2	11.2
2004—San Antonio......	34	1068	142	317	.448	84	102	.824	89	146	235	60	28	2	67	372	6.9	1.8	10.9
2005—Hou.-Charlotte..	33	486	59	144	.410	22	36	.611	33	38	71	21	11	1	34	142	2.2	0.6	4.3
Totals	221	6475	1050	2398	.438	557	749	.744	493	633	1126	433	203	30	542	2705	5.1	2.0	12.2

Three-point field goals: 1999-00, 13-for-53 (.245). 2000-01, 8-for-29 (.276). 2001-02, 5-for-31 (.161). 2002-03, 8-for-28 (.286). 2003-04, 8-for-36 (.222). 2004-05, 4-for-16 (.250). 2005-06, 2-for-3 (.667). Totals, 48-for-196 (.245).
Personal fouls/disqualifications: 1999-00, 76/0. 2000-01, 67/0. 2001-02, 64/0. 2002-03, 92/0. 2003-04, 96/2. 2004-05, 77/1. 2005-06, 40/1. Totals, 512/4.

WNBA PLAYOFF RECORD

Season Team	G	Min.	FGM	FGA	Pct.	FTM	FTA	Pct.	Off.	Def.	Tot.	Ast.	St.	Blk.	TO	Pts.	RPG	APG	PPG
2001—Utah.................	2	71	13	29	.448	5	9	.556	6	10	16	3	3	2	4	31	8.0	1.5	15.5
2002—Utah.................	5	190	29	74	.392	12	17	.706	9	18	27	8	7	0	21	72	5.4	1.6	14.4
Totals	7	261	42	103	.408	17	26	.654	15	28	43	11	10	2	25	103	6.1	1.6	14.7

Three-point field goals: 2001-02, 0-for-4. 2002-03, 2-for-7 (.286). Totals, 2-for-11 (.182).
Personal fouls/disqualifications: 2001-02, 7/0. 2002-03, 11/0. Totals, 18/0.

WNBA ALL-STAR GAME RECORD

Season Team	Min.	FGM	FGA	Pct.	FTM	FTA	Pct.	Off.	Def.	Tot.	Ast.	PF	Dq.	St.	Blk.	TO	Pts.
2002—Utah......................	9	0	2	.000	0	0	...	0	1	1	0	0	0	0	0	0	0
Totals.........................	9	0	2	.000	0	0	...	0	1	1	0	0	0	0	0	0	0

Three-point field goals: 2003, 0-for-1. Totals, 0-for-1 (.000).

GRIFFITH, YOLANDA   C   MONARCHS

PERSONAL: Born March 1, 1970, in Chicago. ... 6-4/175. (1.93/79.4). ... Full name: Yolanda Evette Griffith
HIGH SCHOOL: George Washington Carver (Chicago).
COLLEGE: Florida Atlantic.
TRANSACTIONS/CAREER NOTES: Selected by Sacramento in first round (second overall) of WNBA Draft, May 4, 1999.
MISCELLANEOUS: Member of WNBA Championship team (2005).

COLLEGE RECORD

NOTES: Division II Kodak All-American (1993).

Season Team	G	Min.	FGM	FGA	Pct.	FTM	FTA	Pct.	Reb.	Ast.	Pts.	AVERAGES		
												RPG	APG	PPG
1992—Florida Atlantic	22	...	262	415	.631	97	164	.591	352	45	621	16.0	2.0	28.2
Totals	22	...	262	415	.631	97	164	.591	352	45	621	16.0	2.0	28.2

Three-point field goals: 1992-93, 0-for-1. Totals, 0-for-1 (.000).

ABL RECORD

NOTES: ABL Defensive Player of Year (1998).

Season Team	G	Min.	FGM	FGA	Pct.	FTM	FTA	Pct.	Reb.	Ast.	Pts.	AVERAGES		
												RPG	APG	PPG
1997—Chicago	44	...	310	573	.541	207	298	.695	493	65	827	11.2	1.5	18.8
1998—Chicago	12	...	62	145	.428	82	113	.726	147	31	206	12.3	2.6	17.2
Totals	56	...	372	718	.518	289	411	.703	640	96	1033	11.4	1.7	18.4

Three-point field goals: 1997-98, 0-for-2. 1998-99, 0-for-1. Totals, 0-for-3 (.000).

WNBA REGULAR-SEASON RECORD

NOTES: WNBA Most Valuable Player (1999). ... WNBA Newcomer of the Year (1999). ... WNBA Defensive Player of the Year (1999). ... All-WNBA first team (1999, 2005). ... All-WNBA second team (2000, 2001, 2004). ... All-Defensive first team (2005). ... Led WNBA in rebounds per game in 2001 (11.2 rpg) and 1999 (11.3 rpg). ... Led WNBA in steals per game in 1999 (2.52) and 2004 (2.21). ... Led WNBA in double-doubles in 2001 (18) and 1999 (17).

Season Team	G	Min.	FGM	FGA	Pct.	FTM	FTA	Pct.	REBOUNDS			Ast.	St.	Blk.	TO	Pts.	AVERAGES		
									Off.	Def.	Tot.						RPG	APG	PPG
1999—Sacramento	29	979	200	370	.541	145	235	.617	141	188	329	45	73	54	66	545	11.3	1.6	18.8
2000—Sacramento	32	1026	193	361	.535	137	194	.706	148	183	331	47	83	61	82	523	10.3	1.5	16.3
2001—Sacramento	32	1077	192	368	.522	134	186	.720	162	195	357	54	63	37	75	518	11.2	1.7	16.2
2002—Sacramento	17	577	93	179	.520	102	127	.803	66	82	148	19	16	13	45	288	8.7	1.1	16.9
2003—Sacramento	34	1015	161	332	.485	147	190	.774	92	156	248	46	57	39	75	469	7.3	1.4	13.8
2004—Sacramento	34	1031	177	341	.519	140	186	.753	122	124	246	42	75	41	59	494	7.2	1.2	14.5
2005—Sacramento	34	962	173	357	.485	123	174	.707	87	136	223	52	42	31	68	469	6.6	1.5	13.8
Totals	212	6667	1189	2308	.515	928	1292	.718	818	1064	1882	305	409	276	470	3306	8.9	1.4	15.6

Three-point field goals: 1999-00, 0-for-1. 2003-04, 0-for-2. 2004-05, 0-for-1. Totals, 0-for-4 (.000).

Personal fouls/disqualifications: 1999-00, 91/0. 2000-01, 110/1. 2001-02, 114/1. 2002-03, 70/0. 2003-04, 125/3. 2004-05, 99/2. 2005-06, 98/0. Totals, 707/7.

NOTES: WNBA Finals MVP (2005).

WNBA PLAYOFF RECORD

Season Team	G	Min.	FGM	FGA	Pct.	FTM	FTA	Pct.	REBOUNDS			Ast.	St.	Blk.	TO	Pts.	AVERAGES		
									Off.	Def.	Tot.						RPG	APG	PPG
2000—Sacramento	2	78	12	23	.522	5	8	.625	6	18	24	2	1	1	4	29	12.0	1.0	14.5
2001—Sacramento	5	181	32	67	.478	42	55	.764	18	26	44	7	8	6	11	106	8.8	1.4	21.2
2003—Sacramento	6	200	36	67	.537	31	34	.912	19	34	53	7	7	6	12	103	8.8	1.2	17.2
2004—Sacramento	6	204	31	63	.492	20	24	.833	20	29	49	8	12	6	12	82	8.2	1.3	13.7
2005—Sacramento	8	246	53	108	.491	32	45	.711	27	39	66	11	10	4	10	138	8.3	1.4	17.3
Totals	27	909	164	328	.500	130	166	.783	90	146	236	35	38	23	49	458	8.7	1.3	17.0

Personal fouls/disqualifications: 2000-01, 4/0. 2001-02, 18/0. 2003-04, 16/0. 2004-05, 15/0. 2005-06, 20/0. Totals, 73/0.

WNBA ALL-STAR GAME RECORD

Season Team	Min.	FGM	FGA	Pct.	FTM	FTA	Pct.	REBOUNDS			Ast.	PF	Dq.	St.	Blk.	TO	Pts.
								Off.	Def.	Tot.							
1999—Sacramento	21	5	10	.500	0	0	...	2	3	5	1	2	0	1	1	3	10
2000—Sacramento	16	3	8	.375	4	6	.667	5	5	10	0	0	0	0	1	2	10
2001—Sacramento	18	7	8	.875	3	4	.750	3	4	7	0	2	0	2	1	2	17
2003—Sacramento	25	6	8	.750	2	3	.667	2	5	7	1	3	0	2	2	6	14
2005—Sacramento	19	5	10	.500	2	4	.500	7	7	14	0	0	0	0	1	1	12
Totals	99	26	44	.591	11	17	.647	19	24	43	2	7	0	5	6	14	63

Three-point field goals: 2006, 0-for-1. Totals, 0-for-1 (.000).

OLYMPICS RECORD

Season Team	G	Min.	FGM	FGA	Pct.	FTM	FTA	Pct.	Reb.	Ast.	Pts.	AVERAGES		
												RPG	APG	PPG
2000—United States	8	168	37	54	.685	18	24	.750	70	3	92	8.8	0.4	11.5
2004—United States	8	138	26	43	.605	16	28	.571	53	1	68	6.6	0.1	8.5
Totals	16	306	63	97	.649	34	52	.654	123	4	160	7.7	0.3	10.0

Personal fouls/disqualifications: 2004-05, 21/1. Totals, 21/1.

G

GRUBIN, GORDANA   G   COMETS

PERSONAL: Born August 20, 1972, in Zrenjanin, Yugoslavia. ... 5-11/165. (1.80/74.8).

TRANSACTIONS/CAREER NOTES: Drafted by Los Angeles, June 10, 1999. ... Selected by Indiana in first round (first overall) of WNBA Expansion Draft, December 15, 1999. ... Traded by Indiana to Phoenix for G Bridget Pettis and a first-round pick in the 2002 WNBA Draft, March 4, 2002. ... Signed by Houston, March 1, 2004.

WNBA REGULAR-SEASON RECORD

Season Team	G	Min.	FGM	FGA	Pct.	FTM	FTA	Pct.	REBOUNDS			Ast.	St.	Blk.	TO	Pts.	AVERAGES		
									Off.	Def.	Tot.						RPG	APG	PPG
1999—Los Angeles	32	708	96	238	.403	52	68	.765	18	54	72	90	24	2	53	284	2.3	2.8	8.9

Season Team	G	Min.	FGM	FGA	Pct.	FTM	FTA	Pct.	REBOUNDS Off.	Def.	Tot.	Ast.	St.	Blk.	TO	Pts.	AVERAGES RPG	APG	PPG
2000—Indiana	29	720	90	239	.377	31	40	.775	20	56	76	63	31	0	60	239	2.6	2.2	8.2
2001—Indiana	27	481	62	167	.371	29	39	.744	18	31	49	33	7	0	34	170	1.8	1.2	6.3
2002—Phoenix	32	859	114	297	.384	60	79	.759	16	48	64	104	36	3	58	317	2.0	3.3	9.9
2004—Houston	5	24	0	3	.000	2	2	1.000	0	1	1	0	0	0	3	2	0.2	0.0	0.4
2005—Los Angeles	9	41	0	8	.000	1	4	.250	1	5	6	5	1	0	2	1	0.7	0.6	0.1
Totals	134	2833	362	952	.380	175	232	.754	73	195	268	295	99	5	210	1013	2.0	2.2	7.6

Three-point field goals: 1999-00, 40-for-93 (.430). 2000-01, 28-for-91 (.308). 2001-02, 17-for-58 (.293). 2002-03, 29-for-92 (.315). 2005-06, 0-for-2. Totals, 114-for-336 (.339).

Personal fouls/disqualifications: 1999-00, 53/1. 2000-01, 47/0. 2001-02, 30/0. 2002-03, 59/0. 2004-05, 2/0. 2005-06, 4/0. Totals, 195/1.

WNBA PLAYOFF RECORD

Season Team	G	Min.	FGM	FGA	Pct.	FTM	FTA	Pct.	REBOUNDS Off.	Def.	Tot.	Ast.	St.	Blk.	TO	Pts.	AVERAGES RPG	APG	PPG
1999—Los Angeles	4	119	13	37	.351	1	2	.500	3	9	12	23	5	0	8	31	3.0	5.8	7.8
Totals	4	119	13	37	.351	1	2	.500	3	9	12	23	5	0	8	31	3.0	5.8	7.8

Three-point field goals: 1999-00, 4-for-16 (.250). Totals, 4-for-16 (.250).
Personal fouls/disqualifications: 1999-00, 9/0. Totals, 9/0.

HAMMON, BECKY　　　　　　　G　　　　　　　LIBERTY

PERSONAL: Born March 11, 1977, in Rapid City, S.D. ... 5-6/136. (1.68/61.7). ... Full name: Rebecca Lynn Hammon
HIGH SCHOOL: Stevens (Rapid City, S.D.).
COLLEGE: Colorado State.
TRANSACTIONS/CAREER NOTES: Signed by WNBA and assigned to New York, May 12, 1999.

COLLEGE RECORD

NOTES: Kodak All-American first team (1999).

Season Team	G	Min.	FGM	FGA	Pct.	FTM	FTA	Pct.	Reb.	Ast.	Pts.	AVERAGES RPG	APG	PPG
1995—Colorado State	31	...	200	424	.472	106	131	.809	97	101	594	3.1	3.3	19.2
1996—Colorado State	28	...	219	476	.460	97	125	.776	111	102	618	4.0	3.6	22.1
1997—Colorado State	30	...	238	468	.509	148	167	.886	116	161	704	3.9	5.4	23.5
1998—Colorado State	36	...	261	526	.496	188	218	.862	138	171	824	3.8	4.8	22.9
Totals	125		918	1894	.485	539	641	.841	462	535	2740	3.7	4.3	21.9

Three-point field goals: 1995-96, 88-for-206 (.427). 1996-97, 83-for-209 (.397). 1997-98, 80-for-199 (.402). 1998-99, 114-for-274 (.416). Totals, 365-for-888 (.411).

WNBA REGULAR-SEASON RECORD

NOTES: All-WNBA second team (2005). ... Led the WNBA in three-point field goal percentage (.469) in 2003. ... Led the WNBA in free throw percentage in 2003 (.951) and 2005 (.901).

Season Team	G	Min.	FGM	FGA	Pct.	FTM	FTA	Pct.	REBOUNDS Off.	Def.	Tot.	Ast.	St.	Blk.	TO	Pts.	AVERAGES RPG	APG	PPG
1999—New York	30	202	27	64	.422	15	17	.882	2	17	19	17	6	0	24	80	0.6	0.6	2.7
2000—New York	32	835	119	252	.472	61	69	.884	19	45	64	58	29	1	62	351	2.0	1.8	11.0
2001—New York	32	619	90	197	.457	40	51	.784	10	42	52	51	27	1	48	262	1.6	1.6	8.2
2002—New York	32	659	87	197	.442	38	56	.679	18	50	68	54	25	0	55	256	2.1	1.7	8.0
2003—New York	11	257	50	87	.575	39	41	.951	1	20	21	18	10	1	27	162	1.9	1.6	14.7
2004—New York	34	1130	153	354	.432	97	116	.836	17	101	118	150	58	2	118	460	3.5	4.4	13.5
2005—New York	34	1180	145	336	.432	118	131	.901	20	94	114	146	60	2	107	473	3.4	4.3	13.9
Totals	205	4882	671	1487	.451	408	481	.848	87	369	456	494	215	7	441	2044	2.2	2.4	10.0

Three-point field goals: 1999-00, 11-for-38 (.289). 2000-01, 52-for-141 (.369). 2001-02, 42-for-111 (.378). 2002-03, 44-for-114 (.386). 2003-04, 23-for-49 (.469). 2004-05, 57-for-170 (.335). 2005-06, 65-for-178 (.365). Totals, 294-for-801 (.367).

Personal fouls/disqualifications: 1999-00, 27/0. 2000-01, 55/0. 2001-02, 46/0. 2002-03, 49/0. 2003-04, 13/0. 2004-05, 73/0. 2005-06, 77/0. Totals, 340/0.

WNBA PLAYOFF RECORD

Season Team	G	Min.	FGM	FGA	Pct.	FTM	FTA	Pct.	REBOUNDS Off.	Def.	Tot.	Ast.	St.	Blk.	TO	Pts.	AVERAGES RPG	APG	PPG
1999—New York	6	50	2	12	.167	6	6	1.000	0	1	1	5	0	0	6	12	0.2	0.8	2.0
2000—New York	7	206	21	49	.429	17	19	.895	5	5	10	15	9	0	17	66	1.4	2.1	9.4
2001—New York	6	48	6	17	.353	0	0	...	0	3	3	2	1	0	3	15	0.5	0.3	2.5
2002—New York	8	183	29	54	.537	7	8	.875	2	15	17	16	5	0	11	79	2.1	2.0	9.9
2004—New York	5	178	20	51	.392	2	5	.400	3	10	13	17	6	0	19	53	2.6	3.4	10.6
2005—New York	2	76	9	20	.450	3	3	1.000	0	7	7	4	0	0	10	23	3.5	2.0	11.5
Totals	34	741	87	203	.429	35	41	.854	10	41	51	59	21	0	66	248	1.5	1.7	7.3

Three-point field goals: 1999-00, 2-for-9 (.222). 2000-01, 7-for-23 (.304). 2001-02, 3-for-10 (.300). 2002-03, 14-for-33 (.424). 2004-05, 11-for-33 (.333). 2005-06, 2-for-7 (.286). Totals, 39-for-115 (.339).

Personal fouls/disqualifications: 1999-00, 3/0. 2000-01, 10/0. 2001-02, 3/0. 2002-03, 12/0. 2004-05, 12/0. 2005-06, 8/1. Totals, 48/1.

WNBA ALL-STAR GAME RECORD

Season Team	Min.	FGM	FGA	Pct.	FTM	FTA	Pct.	REBOUNDS Off.	Def.	Tot.	Ast.	PF	Dq.	St.	Blk.	TO	Pts.
2005—New York	21	7	14	.500	0	0	...	3	3	6	4	1	0	0	0	3	18
Totals	21	7	14	.500	0	0	...	3	3	6	4	1	0	0	0	3	18

Three-point field goals: 2006, 4-for-6 (.667). Totals, 4-for-6 (.667).

H

HARRISON, LISA   F   MERCURY

PERSONAL: Born January 2, 1971, in Louisville, Ky. ... 6-1/164. (1.85/74.4). ... Full name: Lisa Darlene Harrison
HIGH SCHOOL: Southern (Louisville, Ky.).
COLLEGE: Tennessee.
TRANSACTIONS/CAREER NOTES: Selected by Phoenix in third round (34th overall) of WNBA Draft, May 4, 1999.

COLLEGE RECORD

NOTES: Member of NCAA Divison I championship team (1991). ... Kodak All-American first team (1993).

Season Team	G	Min.	FGM	FGA	Pct.	FTM	FTA	Pct.	Reb.	Ast.	Pts.	RPG	APG	PPG
1989—Tennessee	33	...	107	229	.467	41	65	.631	159	51	255	4.8	1.5	7.7
1990—Tennessee	34	...	114	287	.397	31	61	.508	193	75	259	5.7	2.2	7.6
1991—Tennessee	31	...	75	193	.389	24	33	.727	162	64	174	5.2	2.1	5.6
1992—Tennessee	31	...	196	419	.468	54	87	.621	300	82	447	9.7	2.6	14.4
Totals	129	...	492	1128	.436	150	246	.610	814	272	1135	6.3	2.1	8.8

Three-point field goals: 1992-93, 1-for-2 (.500). Totals, 1-for-2 (.500).

ABL RECORD

Season Team	G	Min.	FGM	FGA	Pct.	FTM	FTA	Pct.	Reb.	Ast.	Pts.	RPG	APG	PPG
1996—Portland	40	...	168	382	.440	51	68	.750	176	79	393	4.4	2.0	9.8
1997—Portland	44	...	142	331	.429	33	52	.635	146	68	323	3.3	1.5	7.3
1998—Columbus	14	...	47	93	.505	23	27	.852	76	12	117	5.4	0.9	8.4
Totals	98	...	357	806	.443	107	147	.728	398	159	833	4.1	1.6	8.5

Three-point field goals: 1996-97, 6-for-21 (.286). 1997-98, 6-for-28 (.214). 1998-99, 0-for-1. Totals, 12-for-50 (.240).

WNBA REGULAR-SEASON RECORD

Season Team	G	Min.	FGM	FGA	Pct.	FTM	FTA	Pct.	Off.	Def.	Tot.	Ast.	St.	Blk.	TO	Pts.	RPG	APG	PPG
1999—Phoenix	32	828	81	170	.476	30	44	.682	47	83	130	52	23	5	35	193	4.1	1.6	6.0
2000—Phoenix	31	750	81	154	.526	30	37	.811	38	83	121	36	30	4	22	200	3.9	1.2	6.5
2001—Phoenix	32	915	96	223	.430	51	59	.864	39	100	139	52	39	1	49	246	4.3	1.6	7.7
2002—Phoenix	32	899	120	242	.496	20	23	.870	43	83	126	40	31	3	45	262	3.9	1.3	8.2
2003—Phoenix	33	838	74	179	.413	35	51	.686	42	76	118	36	29	6	34	183	3.6	1.1	5.5
2005—Phoenix	27	297	15	34	.441	11	14	.786	13	26	39	10	5	1	12	41	1.4	0.4	1.5
Totals	187	4527	467	1002	.466	177	228	.776	222	451	673	226	157	20	197	1125	3.6	1.2	6.0

Three-point field goals: 1999-00, 1-for-9 (.111). 2000-01, 8-for-12 (.667). 2001-02, 3-for-9 (.333). 2002-03, 2-for-6 (.333). 2003-04, 0-for-3. 2005-06, 0-for-1. Totals, 14-for-40 (.350).
Personal fouls/disqualifications: 1999-00, 65/1. 2000-01, 62/0. 2001-02, 58/0. 2002-03, 62/0. 2003-04, 58/0. 2005-06, 33/0. Totals, 338/1.

WNBA PLAYOFF RECORD

Season Team	G	Min.	FGM	FGA	Pct.	FTM	FTA	Pct.	Off.	Def.	Tot.	Ast.	St.	Blk.	TO	Pts.	RPG	APG	PPG
2000—Phoenix	2	68	12	17	.706	2	2	1.000	4	7	11	10	3	0	3	26	5.5	5.0	13.0
Totals	2	68	12	17	.706	2	2	1.000	4	7	11	10	3	0	3	26	5.5	5.0	13.0

Three-point field goals: 2000-01, 0-for-2. Totals, 0-for-2 (.000).
Personal fouls/disqualifications: 2000-01, 5/0. Totals, 5/0.

HARROWER, KRISTI   G   LYNX

PERSONAL: Born March 4, 1975, in Bendigo, Australia. ... 5-4/139. (1.63/63.0). ... Played for Australian team, 1998 FIBA Women's World Championship. ... Member of Australian National Team; named team's third MVP, 1997.
HIGH SCHOOL: Bendigo (Bendigo, Australia).
TRANSACTIONS/CAREER NOTES: Signed by WNBA and asigned to Phoenix, May 8, 1998. ... Traded by Phoenix to Minnesota with C Marlies Askamp and G Angela Aycock for F Adia Barnes, G Tonya Edwards and G/F Trisha Fallon, October 27, 1999.

WNBA REGULAR-SEASON RECORD

Season Team	G	Min.	FGM	FGA	Pct.	FTM	FTA	Pct.	Off.	Def.	Tot.	Ast.	St.	Blk.	TO	Pts.	RPG	APG	PPG
1998—Phoenix	30	355	19	52	.365	21	28	.750	2	19	21	52	15	3	31	70	0.7	1.7	2.3
1999—Phoenix	32	666	36	99	.364	59	73	.808	9	54	63	96	25	4	45	143	2.0	3.0	4.5
2000—Phoenix					Did not play due to injury.														
2001—Minnesota	4	72	7	15	.467	4	4	1.000	1	3	4	11	3	0	3	21	1.0	2.8	5.3
2002—Minnesota	27	481	37	95	.389	4	10	.400	9	37	46	54	12	0	28	96	1.7	2.0	3.6
2003—Minnesota	31	499	32	87	.368	8	13	.615	9	30	39	72	18	3	39	88	1.3	2.3	2.8
2005—Minnesota	34	832	53	151	.351	28	36	.778	11	71	82	96	38	1	54	156	2.4	2.8	4.6
Totals	158	2905	184	499	.369	124	164	.756	41	214	255	381	111	11	200	574	1.6	2.4	3.6

Three-point field goals: 1998-99, 11-for-32 (.344). 1999-00, 12-for-43 (.279). 2001-02, 3-for-6 (.500). 2002-03, 18-for-54 (.333). 2003-04, 16-for-43 (.372). 2005-06, 22-for-68 (.324). Totals, 82-for-246 (.333).
Personal fouls/disqualifications: 1998-99, 25/0. 1999-00, 45/0. 2001-02, 4/0. 2002-03, 24/0. 2003-04, 15/0. 2005-06, 37/0. Totals, 150/0.

WNBA PLAYOFF RECORD

Season Team	G	Min.	FGM	FGA	Pct.	FTM	FTA	Pct.	Off.	Def.	Tot.	Ast.	St.	Blk.	TO	Pts.	RPG	APG	PPG
1998—Phoenix	6	78	12	20	.600	0	0	...	1	5	6	7	5	1	4	27	1.0	1.2	4.5

H

Season Team	G	Min.	FGM	FGA	Pct.	FTM	FTA	Pct.	REBOUNDS			Ast.	St.	Blk.	TO	Pts.	AVERAGES		
									Off.	Def.	Tot.						RPG	APG	PPG
2003—Minnesota	3	65	4	11	.364	1	2	.500	1	6	7	5	1	0	3	11	2.3	1.7	3.7
Totals	9	143	16	31	.516	1	2	.500	2	11	13	12	6	1	7	38	1.4	1.3	4.2

Three-point field goals: 1998-99, 3-for-7 (.429). 2003-04, 2-for-7 (.286). Totals, 5-for-14 (.357).
Personal fouls/disqualifications: 1998-99, 4/0. 2003-04, 6/0. Totals, 10/0.

OLYMPICS RECORD

Season Team	G	Min.	FGM	FGA	Pct.	FTM	FTA	Pct.	Reb.	Ast.	Pts.	AVERAGES		
												RPG	APG	PPG
2000—Australia	8	195	17	47	.362	12	19	.632	23	30	50	2.9	3.8	6.3
2004—Australia	8	218	24	51	.471	9	14	.643	30	22	64	3.8	2.8	8.0
Totals	16	413	41	98	.418	21	33	.636	53	52	114	3.3	3.3	7.1

Three-point field goals: 2000-01, 4-for-18 (.222). 2004-05, 7-for-22 (.318). Totals, 11-for-40 (.275).
Personal fouls/disqualifications: 2004-05, 17/0. Totals, 17/0.

HAYDEN, VANESSA   C   LYNX

PERSONAL: Born June 5, 1982, in Orlando ... 6-4/224. (1.93/101.6). ... Full name: Vanessa L'asonya Hayden
HIGH SCHOOL: Boone (Orlando).
COLLEGE: Florida.
TRANSACTIONS/CAREER NOTES: Selected by Minnesota in first round (seventh overall) of WNBA Draft, April 17, 2004.
MISCELLANEOUS: USA Today high school All-American (2000). ... Gatorade Florida High School Player of the Year (2000).

COLLEGE RECORD

NOTES: AP All-American second team (2004). ... AP All-American honorable mention (2002, 2003). ... SEC Defensive Player of the Year (2004). ... All-SEC first team (2002, 2004). ... SEC All-Freshman team (2001). ... Led the nation in blocked shots per game (4.3 bpg) in 2002. ... Florida's all-time blocked shots leader (357).

Season Team	G	Min.	FGM	FGA	Pct.	FTM	FTA	Pct.	Reb.	Ast.	Pts.	AVERAGES		
												RPG	APG	PPG
2000—Florida	30	554	129	247	.522	54	115	.470	275	17	312	9.2	0.6	10.4
2001—Florida	29	799	200	395	.506	96	156	.615	343	41	496	11.8	1.4	17.1
2002—Florida	18	390	81	184	.440	35	58	.603	170	15	197	9.4	0.8	10.9
2003—Florida	30	823	235	450	.522	101	171	.591	317	38	571	10.6	1.3	19.0
Totals	107	2566	645	1276	.505	286	500	.572	1105	111	1576	10.3	1.0	14.7

WNBA REGULAR-SEASON RECORD

Season Team	G	Min.	FGM	FGA	Pct.	FTM	FTA	Pct.	REBOUNDS			Ast.	St.	Blk.	TO	Pts.	AVERAGES		
									Off.	Def.	Tot.						RPG	APG	PPG
2004—Minnesota	29	350	66	159	.415	21	38	.553	7	7	29	34	153	2.9	0.2	5.3			
2005—Minnesota	31	595	103	238	.433	40	72	.556	48	115	163	23	15	68	63	246	5.3	0.7	7.9
Totals	60	945	169	397	.426	61	110	.555	71	176	247	30	22	97	97	399	4.1	0.5	6.7

Personal fouls/disqualifications: 2004-05, 65/0. 2005-06, 110/2. Totals, 175/2.

WNBA PLAYOFF RECORD

Season Team	G	Min.	FGM	FGA	Pct.	FTM	FTA	Pct.	REBOUNDS			Ast.	St.	Blk.	TO	Pts.	AVERAGES		
									Off.	Def.	Tot.						RPG	APG	PPG
2004—Minnesota	2	16	2	7	.286	0	0	...	0	2	2	0	0	1	3	4	1.0	0.0	2.0
Totals	2	16	2	7	.286	0	0	...	0	2	2	0	0	1	3	4	1.0	0.0	2.0

Personal fouls/disqualifications: 2004-05, 2/0. Totals, 2/0.

HAYNIE, KRISTIN   G   MONARCHS

PERSONAL: Born June 17, 1983, in Lansing, Mich. ... 5-8/147. (1.73/66.7). ... Full name: Kristin Lynne Haynie
HIGH SCHOOL: Mason (Mason, Mich.).
COLLEGE: Michigan State.
TRANSACTIONS/CAREER NOTES: Selected by Sacramento in the first round (ninth overall) of the WNBA Draft, April 16, 2005.
MISCELLANEOUS: Member of WNBA Championship team (2005).

COLLEGE RECORD

NOTES: AP All-American honorable mention (2005). ... All-Big Ten first team (2005). ... All-Big Ten honorable mention (2003, 2004). ... Big Ten Tournament MVP (2005). ... All-Big Ten academic team (2003, 2004). ... All-Big Ten freshman team (2002). ... Michigan State all-time leader in career assists and steals.

Season Team	G	Min.	FGM	FGA	Pct.	FTM	FTA	Pct.	Reb.	Ast.	Pts.	AVERAGES		
												RPG	APG	PPG
2001—Michigan State	32	992	78	204	.382	70	93	.753	122	117	251	3.8	3.7	7.8
2002—Michigan State	29	999	103	239	.431	64	75	.853	108	144	293	3.7	5.0	10.1
2003—Michigan State	31	963	101	240	.421	62	74	.838	139	124	277	4.5	4.0	8.9
2004—Michigan State	35	1155	147	321	.458	64	78	.821	232	189	378	6.6	5.4	10.8
Totals	127	4109	429	1004	.427	260	320	.813	601	574	1199	4.7	4.5	9.4

WNBA REGULAR-SEASON RECORD

Season Team	G	Min.	FGM	FGA	Pct.	FTM	FTA	Pct.	REBOUNDS			Ast.	St.	Blk.	TO	Pts.	AVERAGES		
									Off.	Def.	Tot.						RPG	APG	PPG
2005—Sacramento	30	434	40	117	.342	19	23	.826	19	43	62	43	33	1	35	104	2.1	1.4	3.5
Totals	30	434	40	117	.342	19	23	.826	19	43	62	43	33	1	35	104	2.1	1.4	3.5

H

Three-point field goals: 2005-06, 5-for-32 (.156). Totals, 5-for-32 (.156).
Personal fouls/disqualifications: 2005-06, 41/0. Totals, 41/0.

WNBA PLAYOFF RECORD

Season Team	G	Min.	FGM	FGA	Pct.	FTM	FTA	Pct.	REBOUNDS Off.	Def.	Tot.	Ast.	St.	Blk.	TO	Pts.	AVERAGES RPG	APG	PPG
2005—Sacramento	8	103	7	19	.368	4	6	.667	4	10	14	8	8	0	4	18	1.8	1.0	2.3
Totals	8	103	7	19	.368	4	6	.667	4	10	14	8	8	0	4	18	1.8	1.0	2.3

Three-point field goals: 2005-06, 0-for-1. Totals, 0-for-1 (.000).
Personal fouls/disqualifications: 2005-06, 8/0. Totals, 8/0.

HODGES, RONEEKA   G   COMETS

PERSONAL: Born July 19, 1982, in New Orleans. ... 5-11/165. (1.80/74.8). ... Full name: Roneeka Rayshell Hodges
HIGH SCHOOL: O.P. Walker (New Orleans).
COLLEGE: Florida State.
TRANSACTIONS/CAREER NOTES: Selected by Houston in the second round (15th overall) of the WNBA Draft, April 16, 2005.

COLLEGE RECORD

NOTES: AP All-American Honorable Mention (2005). ... All-ACC first team (2005).

Season Team	G	Min.	FGM	FGA	Pct.	FTM	FTA	Pct.	Reb.	Ast.	Pts.	AVERAGES RPG	APG	PPG
2001—Louisiana State	30	631	100	214	.467	40	53	.755	124	40	253	4.1	1.3	8.4
2002—Louisiana State	30	723	106	236	.449	31	43	.721	159	41	266	5.3	1.4	8.9
2003—Louisiana State	34	974	125	306	.408	25	34	.735	81	89	323	2.4	2.6	9.5
2004—Florida State.....................	32	1103	236	504	.468	101	159	.635	179	47	615	5.6	1.5	19.2
Totals	126	3431	567	1260	.450	197	289	.682	543	217	1457	4.3	1.7	11.6

WNBA REGULAR-SEASON RECORD

Season Team	G	Min.	FGM	FGA	Pct.	FTM	FTA	Pct.	REBOUNDS Off.	Def.	Tot.	Ast.	St.	Blk.	TO	Pts.	AVERAGES RPG	APG	PPG
2005—Houston	26	188	13	47	.277	2	2	1.000	9	8	17	7	3	0	3	33	0.7	0.3	1.3
Totals	26	188	13	47	.277	2	2	1.000	9	8	17	7	3	0	3	33	0.7	0.3	1.3

Three-point field goals: 2005-06, 5-for-26 (.192). Totals, 5-for-26 (.192).
Personal fouls/disqualifications: 2005-06, 8/0. Totals, 8/0.

WNBA PLAYOFF RECORD

Season Team	G	Min.	FGM	FGA	Pct.	FTM	FTA	Pct.	REBOUNDS Off.	Def.	Tot.	Ast.	St.	Blk.	TO	Pts.	AVERAGES RPG	APG	PPG
2005—Houston	2	2	0	0	...	0	0	...	0	0	0	0	1	0	1	0	0.0	0.0	0.0
Totals	2	2	0	0	...	0	0	...	0	0	0	0	1	0	1	0	0.0	0.0	0.0

HODGES-LEWIS, DONEEKA   G   SPARKS

PERSONAL: Born July 19, 1982, in New Orleans. ... 5-9/160. (1.75/72.6). ... Full name: Doneeka Danyell Hodges-Lewis
HIGH SCHOOL: O.P. Walker (New Orleans).
COLLEGE: Louisiana State.

COLLEGE RECORD

Season Team	G	Min.	FGM	FGA	Pct.	FTM	FTA	Pct.	Reb.	Ast.	Pts.	AVERAGES RPG	APG	PPG
2000—Louisiana State	30	631	100	214	.467	40	53	.755	124	40	253	4.1	1.3	8.4
2001—Louisiana State	30	1106	157	373	.421	92	119	.773	134	106	459	4.5	3.5	15.3
2002—Louisiana State	34	974	125	306	.408	25	34	.735	81	89	323	2.4	2.6	9.5
2003—Louisiana State	35	1112	184	458	.402	56	73	.767	129	113	489	3.7	3.2	14.0
Totals	129	3823	566	1351	.419	213	279	.763	468	348	1524	3.6	2.7	11.8

Three-point field goals: 2000-01, 13-for-34 (.382). 2001-02, 53-for-139 (.381). 2002-03, 48-for-134 (.358). 2003-04, 64-for-193 (.332). Totals, 178-for-500 (.356).

WNBA REGULAR-SEASON RECORD

Season Team	G	Min.	FGM	FGA	Pct.	FTM	FTA	Pct.	REBOUNDS Off.	Def.	Tot.	Ast.	St.	Blk.	TO	Pts.	AVERAGES RPG	APG	PPG
2004—Los Angeles	24	245	16	52	.308	7	10	.700	3	19	22	16	10	2	17	43	0.9	0.7	1.8
2005—Los Angeles	32	669	65	157	.414	17	25	.680	8	39	47	77	18	7	48	178	1.5	2.4	5.6
Totals	56	914	81	209	.388	24	35	.686	11	58	69	93	28	9	65	221	1.2	1.7	3.9

Three-point field goals: 2004-05, 4-for-17 (.235). 2005-06, 31-for-69 (.449). Totals, 35-for-86 (.407).
Personal fouls/disqualifications: 2004-05, 9/0. 2005-06, 35/0. Totals, 44/0.

WNBA PLAYOFF RECORD

Season Team	G	Min.	FGM	FGA	Pct.	FTM	FTA	Pct.	REBOUNDS Off.	Def.	Tot.	Ast.	St.	Blk.	TO	Pts.	AVERAGES RPG	APG	PPG
2004—Los Angeles	3	29	2	5	.400	0	0	...	0	4	4	4	1	0	3	5	1.3	1.3	1.7
2005—Los Angeles	2	13	1	2	.500	0	0	...	0	1	1	2	1	0	2	3	0.5	1.0	1.5
Totals	5	42	3	7	.429	0	0	...	0	5	5	6	2	0	5	8	1.0	1.2	1.6

Three-point field goals: 2004-05, 1-for-1 (1.000). 2005-06, 1-for-2 (.500). Totals, 2-for-3 (.667).

H

HOFFMAN, EBONY — C — FEVER

PERSONAL: Born August 27, 1982, in Los Angeles. ... 6-2/210. (1.88/95.3). ... Full name: Ebony Vernice Hoffman
HIGH SCHOOL: Narbonne (Harbor City, Calif.).
COLLEGE: USC.
TRANSACTIONS/CAREER NOTES: Selected by Indiana in first round (ninth overall) of WNBA Draft, April 17, 2004.
MISCELLANEOUS: Member of gold medal-winning 2000 USA Junior World Championship qualifying team.

COLLEGE RECORD

NOTES: All-Pac-10 first team (2002, 2003, 2004). ... Pac-10 All-Freshman team (2001). ... First Pac-10 player to tally 1,500 points, 1,000 rebounds and 245 steals.

Season Team	G	Min.	FGM	FGA	Pct.	FTM	FTA	Pct.	Reb.	Ast.	Pts.	RPG	APG	PPG
2000—Southern Cal	28	768	128	285	.449	91	120	.758	223	58	350	8.0	2.1	12.5
2001—Southern Cal	28	815	159	352	.452	84	111	.757	250	44	416	8.9	1.6	14.9
2002—Southern Cal	31	952	177	384	.461	127	167	.760	303	70	504	9.8	2.3	16.3
2003—Southern Cal	28	820	149	343	.434	97	141	.688	227	53	417	8.1	1.9	14.9
Totals	115	3355	613	1364	.449	399	539	.740	1003	225	1687	8.7	2.0	14.7

Three-point field goals: 2000-01, 3-for-14 (.214). 2001-02, 14-for-44 (.318). 2002-03, 23-for-56 (.411). 2003-04, 22-for-59 (.373). Totals, 62-for-173 (.358).

WNBA REGULAR-SEASON RECORD

Season Team	G	Min.	FGM	FGA	Pct.	FTM	FTA	Pct.	REBOUNDS Off.	Def.	Tot.	Ast.	St.	Blk.	TO	Pts.	RPG	APG	PPG
2004—Indiana	30	334	26	83	.313	3	4	.750	34	53	87	21	15	5	27	60	2.9	0.7	2.0
2005—Indiana	33	497	47	116	.405	25	30	.833	34	63	97	16	21	10	23	120	2.9	0.5	3.6
Totals	63	831	73	199	.367	28	34	.824	68	116	184	37	36	15	50	180	2.9	0.6	2.9

Three-point field goals: 2004-05, 5-for-17 (.294). 2005-06, 1-for-2 (.500). Totals, 6-for-19 (.316).
Personal fouls/disqualifications: 2004-05, 51/1. 2005-06, 59/0. Totals, 110/1.

HOLDSCLAW, CHAMIQUE — F — SPARKS

PERSONAL: Born August 9, 1977, in Flushing, N.Y. ... 6-2/172. (1.88/78.0). ... Full name: Chamique Shaunta Holdsclaw
HIGH SCHOOL: Christ the King (Astoria, N.Y.).
COLLEGE: Tennessee.
TRANSACTIONS/CAREER NOTES: Selected by Washington in the first round (first overall) of WNBA Draft, May 4, 1999. ... Traded by Washington to Los Angeles for F DeLisha Milton-Jones and a first-round pick in the 2005 WNBA Draft, March 22, 2005.

COLLEGE RECORD

NOTES: Member of NCAA Championship team (1996, 1997, 1998). ... Naismith Player of the Year (1998). ... Kodak All-American first team (1996, 1997, 1998, 1999).

Season Team	G	Min.	FGM	FGA	Pct.	FTM	FTA	Pct.	Reb.	Ast.	Pts.	RPG	APG	PPG
1995—Tennessee	36	1057	237	507	.467	102	143	.713	326	75	583	9.1	2.1	16.2
1996—Tennessee	39	1296	332	667	.498	122	183	.667	367	114	803	9.4	2.9	20.6
1997—Tennessee	39	1168	370	678	.546	166	217	.765	328	117	915	8.4	3.0	23.5
1998—Tennessee	34	1061	294	567	.519	133	188	.707	274	80	724	8.1	2.4	21.3
Totals	148	4582	1233	2419	.510	523	731	.715	1295	386	3025	8.8	2.6	20.4

Three-point field goals: 1995-96, 7-for-30 (.233). 1996-97, 17-for-50 (.340). 1997-98, 9-for-41 (.220). 1998-99, 3-for-21 (.143). Totals, 36-for-142 (.254).

WNBA REGULAR-SEASON RECORD

NOTES: WNBA Rookie of Year (1999). ... All-WNBA second team (1999, 2001, 2002). ... Led WNBA in scoring (19.9 ppg) and rebounding (11.6 rpg) in 2002 and rebounding (10.9 rpg) in 2003. ... Bud Light Peak Performer, rebounding (2002, 2003), scoring (2002).

Season Team	G	Min.	FGM	FGA	Pct.	FTM	FTA	Pct.	REBOUNDS Off.	Def.	Tot.	Ast.	St.	Blk.	TO	Pts.	RPG	APG	PPG
1999—Washington	31	1061	202	462	.437	116	150	.773	74	172	246	74	37	27	108	525	7.9	2.4	16.9
2000—Washington	32	1131	232	499	.465	87	128	.680	57	183	240	80	47	18	93	561	7.5	2.5	17.5
2001—Washington	29	975	187	467	.400	101	148	.682	72	184	256	66	44	14	94	486	8.8	2.3	16.8
2002—Washington	20	634	149	330	.452	88	106	.830	54	178	232	45	20	6	45	397	11.6	2.3	19.9
2003—Washington	27	948	204	480	.425	140	155	.903	72	222	294	89	34	15	72	554	10.9	3.3	20.5
2004—Washington	23	801	162	403	.402	106	132	.803	51	140	191	56	39	18	57	437	8.3	2.4	19.0
2005—Los Angeles	33	1183	216	450	.480	126	160	.788	86	137	223	104	38	16	99	561	6.8	3.2	17.0
Totals	195	6733	1352	3091	.437	764	979	.780	466	1216	1682	514	259	114	568	3521	8.6	2.6	18.1

Three-point field goals: 1999-00, 5-for-29 (.172). 2000-01, 10-for-39 (.256). 2001-02, 11-for-46 (.239). 2002-03, 11-for-28 (.393). 2003-04, 6-for-35 (.171). 2004-05, 7-for-17 (.412). 2005-06, 3-for-13 (.231). Totals, 53-for-207 (.256).
Personal fouls/disqualifications: 1999-00, 67/0. 2000-01, 74/0. 2001-02, 49/0. 2002-03, 50/0. 2003-04, 74/0. 2004-05, 67/0. 2005-06, 94/2. Totals, 475/2.

WNBA PLAYOFF RECORD

Season Team	G	Min.	FGM	FGA	Pct.	FTM	FTA	Pct.	REBOUNDS Off.	Def.	Tot.	Ast.	St.	Blk.	TO	Pts.	RPG	APG	PPG
2000—Washington	2	75	13	29	.448	4	4	1.000	3	8	11	3	1	6	30	5.5	0.5	15.0
2002—Washington	5	173	35	78	.449	22	30	.733	10	33	43	16	10	3	10	94	8.6	3.2	18.8
2005—Los Angeles	2	78	14	27	.519	2	5	.400	3	7	10	2	4	0	6	31	5.0	1.0	15.5
Totals	9	326	62	134	.463	28	39	.718	16	48	64	19	17	4	22	155	7.1	2.1	17.2

Three-point field goals: 2000-01, 0-for-1. 2002-03, 2-for-11 (.182). 2005-06, 1-for-1 (1.000). Totals, 3-for-13 (.231).
Personal fouls/disqualifications: 2000-01, 2/0. 2002-03, 14/0. 2005-06, 6/0. Totals, 22/0.

H

WNBA ALL-STAR GAME RECORD

Season Team	Min.	FGM	FGA	Pct.	FTM	FTA	Pct.	REBOUNDS Off.	Def.	Tot.	Ast.	PF	Dq.	St.	Blk.	TO	Pts.
1999—Washington	11	2	6	.333	1	1	1.000	0	5	5	0	0	0	0	0	2	5
2000—Washington	25	4	11	.364	1	2	.500	1	3	4	1	0	0	0	0	1	9
2003—Washington	15	3	8	.375	0	0	...	0	1	1	0	0	0	1	1	0	6
2005—Los Angeles............	16	4	12	.333	6	6	1.000	4	2	6	1	1	0	0	0	1	14
Totals	67	13	37	.351	8	9	.889	5	11	16	2	1	0	1	1	4	34

Three-point field goals: 2004, 0-for-1. Totals, 0-for-1 (.000).

IRVIN, SANDORA   F   MERCURY

PERSONAL: Born February 23, 1982, in Fort Lauderdale, Fla. ... 6-3/185. (1.91/83.9). ... Full name: Sandora Lavett Irvin
HIGH SCHOOL: Fort Lauderdale (Fort Lauderdale, Fla.).
COLLEGE: Texas Christian.
TRANSACTIONS/CAREER NOTES: Selected by Phoenix in the first round (third overall) of the WNBA Draft, April 16, 2005.

COLLEGE RECORD

NOTES: AP All-American first team (2005). ... Kodak All-American (2005). ... USBWA All-American (2005). ... AP All-American honorable mention (2004). ... Kodak All-American honorable mention (2004). ... Conference USA player of the year (2005). ... All-Conference USA first team (2004, 2005). ... All-Conference USA second team (2003). ... All-Conference USA third team (2002). ... Conference USA Defensive Player of the Year (2003, 2004, 2005).

Season Team	G	Min.	FGM	FGA	Pct.	FTM	FTA	Pct.	Reb.	Ast.	Pts.	AVERAGES RPG	APG	PPG
2001—Texas Christian...............	31	818	120	282	.426	91	144	.632	294	36	335	9.5	1.2	10.8
2002—Texas Christian...............	33	881	134	320	.419	126	182	.692	320	37	396	9.7	1.1	12.0
2003—Texas Christian...............	30	886	195	382	.510	106	162	.654	366	44	504	12.2	1.5	16.8
2004—Texas Christian...............	33	1045	237	519	.457	159	217	.733	390	68	657	11.8	2.1	19.9
Totals	127	3630	686	1503	.456	482	705	.684	1370	185	1892	10.8	1.5	14.9

WNBA REGULAR-SEASON RECORD

Season Team	G	Min.	FGM	FGA	Pct.	FTM	FTA	Pct.	REBOUNDS Off.	Def.	Tot.	Ast.	St.	Blk.	TO	Pts.	AVERAGES RPG	APG	PPG
2005—Phoenix............	12	122	14	44	.318	12	15	.800	16	18	34	5	5	6	2	44	2.8	0.4	3.7
Totals	12	122	14	44	.318	12	15	.800	16	18	34	5	5	6	2	44	2.8	0.4	3.7

Three-point field goals: 2005-06, 4-for-8 (.500). Totals, 4-for-8 (.500).
Personal fouls/disqualifications: 2005-06, 20/0. Totals, 20/0.

IVANYI, DALMA   G   SILVER STARS

PERSONAL: Born March 18, 1976, in Bekescsaba, Hungary. ... 5-10/135. (1.78/61.2). ... Full name: Dalma Erika Ivanyi
HIGH SCHOOL: Janos Bolyai (Kecskemet, Hungary).
COLLEGE: Florida International.
TRANSACTIONS/CAREER NOTES: Selected by Utah in fourth round (39th overall) of WNBA Draft, May 4, 1999. ... Signed by Phoenix, May 20, 2003. ... Waived by Phonix, June 2, 2003. ... Signed by San Antonio, March 28, 2005.

NOTES: AP All-American third team (1999).

COLLEGE RECORD

Season Team	G	Min.	FGM	FGA	Pct.	FTM	FTA	Pct.	Reb.	Ast.	Pts.	AVERAGES RPG	APG	PPG
1995—Florida International............	28	...	148	359	.412	84	111	.757	158	186	398	5.6	6.6	14.2
1996—Florida International............	17	...	72	180	.400	37	47	.787	77	151	198	4.5	8.9	11.6
1997—Florida International............	31	...	170	360	.472	86	109	.789	159	294	453	5.1	9.5	14.6
1998—Florida International............	29	...	146	333	.438	95	111	.856	108	261	427	3.7	9.0	14.7
Totals	105	...	536	1232	.435	302	378	.799	502	892	1476	4.8	8.5	14.1

Three-point field goals: 1995-96, 18-for-67 (.269). 1996-97, 17-for-46 (.370). 1997-98, 27-for-84 (.321). 1998-99, 40-for-92 (.435). Totals, 102-for-289 (.353).

WNBA REGULAR-SEASON RECORD

Season Team	G	Min.	FGM	FGA	Pct.	FTM	FTA	Pct.	REBOUNDS Off.	Def.	Tot.	Ast.	St.	Blk.	TO	Pts.	AVERAGES RPG	APG	PPG
1999—Utah..................	14	67	4	12	.333	3	4	.750	3	2	5	7	4	0	11	11	0.4	0.5	0.8
2000—Utah..................	27	489	30	96	.313	21	28	.750	12	42	54	63	25	3	50	93	2.0	2.3	3.4
2003—Phoenix............	4	34	3	8	.375	0	0	...	2	2	4	2	0	1	2	6	1.0	0.5	1.5
2005—San Antonio	30	577	25	67	.373	5	8	.625	5	45	50	68	26	0	53	75	1.7	2.3	2.5
Totals	75	1167	62	183	.339	29	40	.725	22	91	113	140	55	4	116	185	1.5	1.9	2.5

Three-point field goals: 1999-00, 0-for-4. 2000-01, 12-for-43 (.279). 2003-04, 0-for-2. 2005-06, 20-for-45 (.444). Totals, 32-for-94 (.340).
Personal fouls/disqualifications: 1999-00, 18/0. 2000-01, 67/0. 2003-04, 4/0. 2005-06, 48/0. Totals, 137/0.

IVEY, NIELE   G   MERCURY

PERSONAL: Born September 24, 1977, in St. Louis. ... 5-7/149. (1.70/67.6).
HIGH SCHOOL: Cor Jesu (St. Louis).
COLLEGE: Notre Dame.
TRANSACTIONS/CAREER NOTES: Selected by Indiana in second round (19th overall) of WNBA Draft, April 20, 2001. ... Signed by Detroit as a restricted free agent, April 12, 2005.

COLLEGE RECORD

NOTES: Member of NCAA Division I Championship team (2001).

Season Team	G	Min.	FGM	FGA	Pct.	FTM	FTA	Pct.	Reb.	Ast.	Pts.	AVERAGES		
												RPG	APG	PPG
1996—Notre Dame	5	...	6	16	.375	3	4	.750	12	15	15	2.4	3.0	3.0
1997—Notre Dame	31	...	83	185	.449	63	80	.788	106	90	254	3.4	2.9	8.2
1998—Notre Dame	28	...	121	241	.502	80	92	.870	106	181	369	3.8	6.5	13.2
1999—Notre Dame	32	...	118	272	.434	61	81	.753	111	194	358	3.5	6.1	11.2
2000—Notre Dame	36	...	149	322	.463	79	111	.712	147	247	434	4.1	6.9	12.1
Totals	132	...	477	1036	.460	286	368	.777	482	727	1430	3.7	5.5	10.8

Three-point field goals: 1996-97, null-for-1. 1997-98, 25-for-67 (.373). 1998-99, 47-for-105 (.448). 1999-00, 61-for-167 (.365). 2000-01, 57-for-129 (.442). Totals, 190-for-469 (.405).

WNBA REGULAR-SEASON RECORD

Season Team	G	Min.	FGM	FGA	Pct.	FTM	FTA	Pct.	REBOUNDS			Ast.	St.	Blk.	TO	Pts.	AVERAGES		
									Off.	Def.	Tot.						RPG	APG	PPG
2001—Indiana	32	708	38	102	.373	14	15	.933	16	39	55	70	33	5	35	115	1.7	2.2	3.6
2002—Indiana	31	439	25	71	.352	17	21	.810	6	22	28	39	16	3	22	86	0.9	1.3	2.8
2003—Indiana	27	651	45	116	.388	12	17	.706	5	27	32	71	29	7	28	135	1.2	2.6	5.0
2004—Indiana	15	179	11	37	.297	4	6	.667	2	8	10	18	4	3	6	34	0.7	1.2	2.3
2005—Det.-Phoenix	26	254	13	47	.277	7	7	1.000	8	14	22	30	12	0	11	38	0.8	1.2	1.5
Totals	131	2231	132	373	.354	54	66	.818	37	110	147	228	94	18	102	408	1.1	1.7	3.1

Three-point field goals: 2001-02, 25-for-70 (.357). 2002-03, 19-for-50 (.380). 2003-04, 33-for-84 (.393). 2004-05, 8-for-24 (.333). 2005-06, 5-for-22 (.227). Totals, 90-for-250 (.360).
Personal fouls/disqualifications: 2001-02, 51/0. 2002-03, 31/0. 2003-04, 40/0. 2004-05, 20/0. 2005-06, 31/0. Totals, 173/0.

WNBA PLAYOFF RECORD

Season Team	G	Min.	FGM	FGA	Pct.	FTM	FTA	Pct.	REBOUNDS			Ast.	St.	Blk.	TO	Pts.	AVERAGES		
									Off.	Def.	Tot.						RPG	APG	PPG
2002—Indiana	3	9	0	1	.000	0	0	...	0	1	1	3	1	0	0	0	0.3	1.0	0.0
Totals	3	9	0	1	.000	0	0	...	0	1	1	3	1	0	0	0	0.3	1.0	0.0

Three-point field goals: 2002-03, 0-for-1. Totals, 0-for-1 (.000).
Personal fouls/disqualifications: 2002-03, 2/0. Totals, 2/0.

JACKSON, DEANNA   F   SKY

PERSONAL: Born December 15, 1979, in Selma, Ala. ... 6-2/159. (1.88/72.1). ... Full name: Deanna Renee Jackson
HIGH SCHOOL: T.R. Miller (Selma, Ala.).
COLLEGE: Alabama-Birmingham.
TRANSACTIONS/CAREER NOTES: Selected by Cleveland in first round (eighth overall) of WNBA Draft, April 19, 2002. ... Selected by Indiana in WNBA Dispersal Draft, January 6, 2004. ... Selected by Chicago in WNBA Expansion Draft, November 16, 2005.

COLLEGE RECORD

Season Team	G	Min.	FGM	FGA	Pct.	FTM	FTA	Pct.	Reb.	Ast.	Pts.	AVERAGES		
												RPG	APG	PPG
1998—Alabama-Birmingham	27	793	175	339	.516	84	118	.712	240	18	452	8.9	0.7	16.7
1999—Alabama-Birmingham	33	1182	250	524	.477	97	151	.642	385	43	...	11.7	1.3	...
2000—Alabama-Birmingham	31	1154	275	578	.476	180	242	.744	358	63	777	11.5	2.0	25.1
2001—Alabama-Birmingham	11	374	105	197	.533	67	91	.736	135	52	288	12.3	4.7	26.2
Totals	102	3503	805	1638	.491	428	602	.711	1118	176	1517	11.0	1.7	14.9

Three-point field goals: 1998-99, 18-for-65 (.277). 1999-00, 30-for-88 (.341). 2000-01, 47-for-118 (.398). 2001-02, 11-for-43 (.256). Totals, 106-for-314 (.338).

WNBA REGULAR-SEASON RECORD

Season Team	G	Min.	FGM	FGA	Pct.	FTM	FTA	Pct.	REBOUNDS			Ast.	St.	Blk.	TO	Pts.	AVERAGES		
									Off.	Def.	Tot.						RPG	APG	PPG
2002—Cleveland	18	143	19	46	.413	17	24	.708	10	17	27	6	2	1	9	55	1.5	0.3	3.1
2003—Cleveland	34	763	83	198	.419	50	70	.714	37	52	89	51	20	13	33	245	2.6	1.5	7.2
2004—Indiana	34	804	92	251	.367	52	73	.712	57	56	113	53	29	6	52	236	3.3	1.6	6.9
2005—Indiana	34	472	56	139	.403	50	68	.735	37	40	77	23	17	12	32	162	2.3	0.7	4.8
Totals	120	2182	250	634	.394	169	235	.719	141	165	306	133	68	32	126	698	2.6	1.1	5.8

Three-point field goals: 2002-03, 0-for-3. 2003-04, 29-for-70 (.414). 2004-05, 0-for-12. 2005-06, 0-for-3. Totals, 29-for-88 (.330).
Personal fouls/disqualifications: 2002-03, 11/0. 2003-04, 92/1. 2004-05, 82/3. 2005-06, 55/0. Totals, 240/4.

WNBA PLAYOFF RECORD

Season Team	G	Min.	FGM	FGA	Pct.	FTM	FTA	Pct.	REBOUNDS			Ast.	St.	Blk.	TO	Pts.	AVERAGES		
									Off.	Def.	Tot.						RPG	APG	PPG
2003—Cleveland	3	60	4	20	.200	4	6	.667	2	10	12	2	2	0	0	12	4.0	0.7	4.0
2005—Indiana	4	84	10	23	.435	14	17	.824	4	10	14	2	2	2	1	35	3.5	0.5	8.8
Totals	7	144	14	43	.326	18	23	.783	6	20	26	4	4	2	1	47	3.7	0.6	6.7

Three-point field goals: 2003-04, 0-for-2. 2005-06, 1-for-1 (1.000). Totals, 1-for-3 (.333).
Personal fouls/disqualifications: 2003-04, 7/0. 2005-06, 17/1. Totals, 24/1.

JACKSON, GWEN   F   MERCURY

PERSONAL: Born October 23, 1980 ... 6-3/182. (1.91/82.6). ... Full name: Gwendolyn Michelle Jackson
HIGH SCHOOL: Eufaula (Eufaula, Ala.).
COLLEGE: Tennessee.
TRANSACTIONS/CAREER NOTES: Selected by Indiana in first round (sixth overall) of WNBA Draft, April 25, 2003. ... Traded by San Antonio to Phoenix in exchange for Adrian Williams, July 20, 2004.

COLLEGE RECORD

NOTES: AP All-American honorable mention (2003). ... All-SEC first team (2001, 2003). ... NCAA Midwest Regional All-Tournament team (2002). ... All-SEC Freshman team (2000).

												AVERAGES		
Season Team	G	Min.	FGM	FGA	Pct.	FTM	FTA	Pct.	Reb.	Ast.	Pts.	RPG	APG	PPG
1999—Tennessee	37	601	71	155	.458	58	91	.637	165	20	204	4.5	0.5	5.5
2000—Tennessee	34	833	144	296	.486	93	118	.788	213	27	397	6.3	0.8	11.7
2001—Tennessee	28	634	105	223	.471	76	95	.800	174	27	295	6.2	1.0	10.5
2002—Tennessee	38	944	234	409	.572	118	156	.756	234	34	612	6.2	0.9	16.1
Totals	137	3012	554	1083	.512	345	460	.750	786	108	1508	5.7	0.8	11.0

Three-point field goals: 1999-00, 4-for-13 (.308). 2000-01, 16-for-34 (.471). 2001-02, 9-for-28 (.321). 2002-03, 26-for-65 (.400). Totals, 55-for-140 (.393).

WNBA REGULAR-SEASON RECORD

									REBOUNDS								AVERAGES		
Season Team	G	Min.	FGM	FGA	Pct.	FTM	FTA	Pct.	Off.	Def.	Tot.	Ast.	St.	Blk.	TO	Pts.	RPG	APG	PPG
2003—San Antonio	33	975	114	286	.399	56	88	.636	86	119	205	20	15	17	46	289	6.2	0.6	8.8
2005—Phoenix	11	121	13	26	.500	3	6	.500	8	15	23	3	0	3	10	31	2.1	0.3	2.8
Totals	44	1096	127	312	.407	59	94	.628	94	134	228	23	15	20	56	320	5.2	0.5	7.3

Three-point field goals: 2003-04, 5-for-30 (.167). 2005-06, 2-for-4 (.500). Totals, 7-for-34 (.206).
Personal fouls/disqualifications: 2003-04, 85/1. 2005-06, 12/0. Totals, 97/1.

JACKSON, LAUREN   F/C   STORM

PERSONAL: Born May 11, 1981, in Albury, Australia. ... 6-5/187. (1.96/84.8).
TRANSACTIONS/CAREER NOTES: Selected by Seattle in first round (first overall) of WNBA Draft, April 20, 2001.
MISCELLANEOUS: WNBL Co-MVP (2000) and MVP (1999). ... Played for WNBL Canberra 1999-2000 and 2000-01. ... WNBL All-Star Five selection (1999, 2000, 2001). ... WNBL All-Star Five selection (1999, 2000, 2001). ... Led WNBL in rebounding in 2000-01 (14.2 rpg) 1999-2000 (11.1 rpg). ... Led WNBL in blocks in 2000-01 (4.3 bpg) 1999-2000 (2.5 bpg). ... Led WNBL in scoring (1998-99). ... Member of WNBA Championship team (2004).

OLYMPICS RECORD

												AVERAGES		
Season Team	G	Min.	FGM	FGA	Pct.	FTM	FTA	Pct.	Reb.	Ast.	Pts.	RPG	APG	PPG
2000—Australia	8	207	49	101	.485	25	33	.758	67	8	127	8.4	1.0	15.9
2004—Australia	8	236	71	131	.542	29	36	.806	80	6	183	10.0	0.8	22.9
Totals	16	443	120	232	.517	54	69	.783	147	14	310	9.2	0.9	19.4

Three-point field goals: 2000-01, 4-for-14 (.286). 2004-05, 12-for-33 (.364). Totals, 16-for-47 (.340).
Personal fouls/disqualifications: 2004-05, 19/0. Totals, 19/0.

WBL RECORD

												AVERAGES		
Season Team	G	Min.	FGM	FGA	Pct.	FTM	FTA	Pct.	Reb.	Ast.	Pts.	RPG	APG	PPG
2000—Canberra	20	...	157	322	.488	103	127	.811	283	15	431	14.2	0.8	21.6
Totals	20	...	157	322	.488	103	127	.811	283	15	431	14.2	0.8	21.6

Three-point field goals: 2000-01, 14-for-36 (.389). Totals, 14-for-36 (.389).

WNBA REGULAR-SEASON RECORD

NOTES: WNBA Most Valuable Player (2003). ... All-WNBA first team (2003, 2004, 2005). ... All-Defensive second team (2005). ... Led WNBA in scoring in 2003 (21.2 ppg) and 2004 (20.5 ppg). ... Bud Light Peak Performer, Scoring (2003, 2004).

									REBOUNDS								AVERAGES		
Season Team	G	Min.	FGM	FGA	Pct.	FTM	FTA	Pct.	Off.	Def.	Tot.	Ast.	St.	Blk.	TO	Pts.	RPG	APG	PPG
2001—Seattle	29	1001	149	406	.367	104	143	.727	57	136	193	44	54	64	53	442	6.7	1.5	15.2
2002—Seattle	28	882	186	462	.403	68	90	.756	66	124	190	41	30	81	47	482	6.8	1.5	17.2
2003—Seattle	33	1109	254	526	.483	151	183	.825	82	225	307	62	38	64	69	698	9.3	1.9	21.2
2004—Seattle	31	1070	220	460	.478	142	175	.811	64	143	207	51	31	62	67	634	6.7	1.6	20.5
2005—Seattle	34	1176	206	450	.458	151	181	.834	96	217	313	57	36	67	59	597	9.2	1.7	17.6
Totals	155	5238	1015	2304	.441	616	772	.798	365	845	1210	255	189	338	295	2853	7.8	1.6	18.4

Three-point field goals: 2001-02, 40-for-129 (.310). 2002-03, 42-for-120 (.350). 2003-04, 39-for-123 (.317). 2004-05, 52-for-115 (.452). 2005-06, 34-for-118 (.288). Totals, 207-for-605 (.342).
Personal fouls/disqualifications: 2001-02, 97/3. 2002-03, 95/1. 2003-04, 106/1. 2004-05, 93/0. 2005-06, 100/2. Totals, 491/7.

WNBA PLAYOFF RECORD

									REBOUNDS								AVERAGES		
Season Team	G	Min.	FGM	FGA	Pct.	FTM	FTA	Pct.	Off.	Def.	Tot.	Ast.	St.	Blk.	TO	Pts.	RPG	APG	PPG
2002—Seattle	2	68	9	26	.346	5	7	.714	5	5	10	3	3	6	4	23	5.0	1.5	11.5
2004—Seattle	8	287	53	113	.469	35	39	.897	20	40	60	11	8	9	16	157	7.5	1.4	19.6
2005—Seattle	3	102	17	39	.436	5	6	.833	4	20	24	2	4	4	8	43	8.0	0.7	14.3
Totals	13	457	79	178	.444	45	52	.865	29	65	94	16	15	19	28	223	7.2	1.2	17.2

Three-point field goals: 2002-03, 0-for-6. 2004-05, 16-for-22 (.727). 2005-06, 4-for-13 (.308). Totals, 20-for-41 (.488).
Personal fouls/disqualifications: 2002-03, 9/0. 2004-05, 23/0. 2005-06, 11/0. Totals, 43/0.

WNBA ALL-STAR GAME RECORD

| Season Team | Min. | FGM | FGA | Pct. | FTM | FTA | Pct. | REBOUNDS | | | Ast. | PF | Dq. | St. | Blk. | TO | Pts. |
								Off.	Def.	Tot.							
2001—Seattle	19	4	9	.444	1	1	1.000	2	1	3	1	3	0	3	0	1	11
2002—Seattle	20	6	11	.545	1	1	1.000	2	4	6	0	4	0	1	1	0	15
2003—Seattle	19	3	7	.429	2	3	.667	1	3	4	0	0	0	0	3	0	9
2005—Seattle	20	3	10	.300	2	2	1.000	2	2	4	2	1	0	3	0	2	9
Totals	78	16	37	.432	6	7	.857	7	10	17	3	8	0	7	4	3	44

Three-point field goals: 2002, 2-for-4 (.500). 2003, 2-for-3 (.667). 2004, 1-for-2 (.500). 2006, 1-for-4 (.250). Totals, 6-for-13 (.462).

J

JACKSON, TAMICHA   G   MERCURY

PERSONAL: Born April 22, 1978, in Dallas. ... 5-6/118. (1.68/53.5). ... Full name: Tamicha Renia Jackson
HIGH SCHOOL: Lincoln (Dallas).
COLLEGE: Louisiana Tech.
TRANSACTIONS/CAREER NOTES: Selected by Detroit in first round (eighth overall) of WNBA Draft, April 25, 2000. ... Traded by Detroit with a fourth-round pick in the 2002 WNBA Draft to Portland for a second-round pick in the 2002 WNBA Draft, May 12, 2001. ... Phoenix traded Jackson to Washington, Washington traded F Ashja Jones to Connecticut, and Connecticut traded the eighth overall pick in the 2004 WNBA Draft to Phoenix, March 25, 2003.

COLLEGE RECORD

NOTES: Kodak All-American first team (2000).

| Season Team | G | Min. | FGM | FGA | Pct. | FTM | FTA | Pct. | Reb. | Ast. | Pts. | AVERAGES | | |
												RPG	APG	PPG
1996—Louisiana Tech	35	...	172	472	.364	36	59	.610	92	132	428	2.6	3.8	12.2
1997—Louisiana Tech	33	...	202	456	.443	20	33	.606	108	156	481	3.3	4.7	14.6
1998—Louisiana Tech	33	...	157	382	.411	34	42	.810	62	72	384	1.9	2.2	11.6
1999—Louisiana Tech	34	...	222	456	.487	39	53	.736	90	114	529	2.6	3.4	15.6
Totals	135	...	753	1766	.426	129	187	.690	352	474	1822	2.6	3.5	13.5

Three-point field goals: 1996-97, 48-for-145 (.331). 1997-98, 57-for-167 (.341). 1998-99, 36-for-134 (.269). 1999-00, 46-for-123 (.374). Totals, 187-for-569 (.329).

WNBA REGULAR-SEASON RECORD

| Season Team | G | Min. | FGM | FGA | Pct. | FTM | FTA | Pct. | REBOUNDS | | | Ast. | St. | Blk. | TO | Pts. | AVERAGES | | |
									Off.	Def.	Tot.						RPG	APG	PPG
2000—Detroit...............	17	267	41	106	.387	26	35	.743	8	17	25	36	22	0	21	116	1.5	2.1	6.8
2001—Portland	32	497	55	169	.325	16	23	.696	10	34	44	50	28	0	45	132	1.4	1.6	4.1
2002—Portland	32	692	122	291	.419	46	66	.697	20	39	59	95	55	1	64	314	1.8	3.0	9.8
2003—Phoenix..............	34	958	124	361	.343	17	21	.810	24	58	82	146	52	4	76	300	2.4	4.3	8.8
2004—Washington........	25	405	57	135	.422	11	16	.688	7	30	37	45	20	1	28	135	1.5	1.8	5.4
2005—Washington........	8	66	4	26	.154	0	2	.000	1	5	6	10	5	0	4	9	0.8	1.3	1.1
Totals	148	2885	403	1088	.370	116	163	.712	70	183	253	382	182	6	238	1006	1.7	2.6	6.8

Three-point field goals: 2000-01, 8-for-32 (.250). 2001-02, 6-for-39 (.154). 2002-03, 24-for-76 (.316). 2003-04, 35-for-99 (.354). 2004-05, 10-for-25 (.400). 2005-06, 1-for-9 (.111). Totals, 84-for-280 (.300).
Personal fouls/disqualifications: 2000-01, 30/0. 2001-02, 35/0. 2002-03, 59/0. 2003-04, 62/0. 2004-05, 21/0. 2005-06, 5/0. Totals, 212/0.

WNBA PLAYOFF RECORD

| Season Team | G | Min. | FGM | FGA | Pct. | FTM | FTA | Pct. | REBOUNDS | | | Ast. | St. | Blk. | TO | Pts. | AVERAGES | | |
									Off.	Def.	Tot.						RPG	APG	PPG
2004—Washington........	3	42	6	13	.462	2	2	1.000	0	1	1	4	0	0	2	17	0.3	1.3	5.7
Totals	3	42	6	13	.462	2	2	1.000	0	1	1	4	0	0	2	17	0.3	1.3	5.7

Three-point field goals: 2004-05, 3-for-5 (.600). Totals, 3-for-5 (.600).
Personal fouls/disqualifications: 2004-05, 7/0. Totals, 7/0.

JACOBS, AMBER   G   LYNX

PERSONAL: Born June 29, 1982, in Elkhart, Ind. ... 5-8/147. (1.73/66.7).
HIGH SCHOOL: Abington Heights (Clark Summit, Pa.).
COLLEGE: Boston College.
TRANSACTIONS/CAREER NOTES: Selected by Minnesota in third round (33rd overall) of WNBA Draft, April 17, 2004.
MISCELLANEOUS: Alternate on USA Basketball World Championships for Young Women team (2003).

COLLEGE RECORD

NOTES: AP All-American honorable mention (2004). ... All-Big East second team (2004). ... All-Big East Tournament team (2004). ... All-Big East honorable mention (2003). ... Big East All-Academic team (2003). ... Big East All-Rookie team (2001).

| Season Team | G | Min. | FGM | FGA | Pct. | FTM | FTA | Pct. | Reb. | Ast. | Pts. | AVERAGES | | |
												RPG	APG	PPG
2000—Boston College	29	1015	123	289	.426	55	72	.764	54	109	333	1.9	3.8	11.5
2001—Boston College	31	936	140	321	.436	40	56	.714	79	110	368	2.5	3.5	11.9
2002—Boston College	31	970	131	318	.412	62	68	.912	71	112	374	2.3	3.6	12.1
2003—Boston College	32	1053	150	310	.484	116	137	.847	93	138	469	2.9	4.3	14.7
Totals	123	3974	544	1238	.439	273	333	.820	297	469	1544	2.4	3.8	12.6

Three-point field goals: 2000-01, 32-for-103 (.311). 2001-02, 48-for-139 (.345). 2002-03, 50-for-127 (.394). 2003-04, 53-for-133 (.398). Totals, 183-for-502 (.365).

Season Team	G	Min.	FGM	FGA	Pct.	FTM	FTA	Pct.	REBOUNDS Off.	Def.	Tot.	Ast.	St.	Blk.	TO	Pts.	AVERAGES RPG	APG	PPG
2004—Minnesota.........	32	391	31	100	.310	20	22	.909	3	33	36	47	13	0	45	101	1.1	1.5	3.2
2005—Minnesota.........	33	478	40	104	.385	21	29	.724	4	15	19	68	19	4	46	121	0.6	2.1	3.7
Totals	65	869	71	204	.348	41	51	.804	7	48	55	115	32	4	91	222	0.8	1.8	3.4

Three-point field goals: 2004-05, 19-for-60 (.317). 2005-06, 20-for-53 (.377). Totals, 39-for-113 (.345).
Personal fouls/disqualifications: 2004-05, 36/0. 2005-06, 34/0. Totals, 70/0.

WNBA PLAYOFF RECORD

Season Team	G	Min.	FGM	FGA	Pct.	FTM	FTA	Pct.	REBOUNDS Off.	Def.	Tot.	Ast.	St.	Blk.	TO	Pts.	AVERAGES RPG	APG	PPG
2004—Minnesota.........	2	36	3	5	.600	1	2	.500	0	1	1	2	0	0	4	8	0.5	1.0	4.0
Totals	2	36	3	5	.600	1	2	.500	0	1	1	2	0	0	4	8	0.5	1.0	4.0

Three-point field goals: 2004-05, 1-for-2 (.500). Totals, 1-for-2 (.500).

J

JOHNSON, SHANNON   G   SILVER STARS

PERSONAL: Born August 18, 1974, in Hartsville, S.C. ... 5-7/152. (1.70/68.9). ... Full name: Shannon Regina Johnson
HIGH SCHOOL: Hartsville (Hartsville, S.C.).
COLLEGE: South Carolina.
TRANSACTIONS/CAREER NOTES: Signed by WNBA and allocated to Orlando, May 3, 1999. ... Traded by Connecticut with a second- and third-round pick in the 2004 WNBA Draft to San Antonio for a first-round, second-round and third-round pick in the 2004 WNBA Draft, January 28, 2004.

COLLEGE RECORD

Season Team	G	Min.	FGM	FGA	Pct.	FTM	FTA	Pct.	Reb.	Ast.	Pts.	AVERAGES RPG	APG	PPG
1992—South Carolina...................	27	...	89	212	.420	63	87	.724	98	83	259	3.6	3.1	9.6
1993—South Carolina...................	27	...	231	506	.457	128	187	.684	160	133	634	5.9	4.9	23.5
1994—South Carolina...................	27	...	214	497	.431	154	227	.678	172	138	...	6.4	5.1	...
1995—South Carolina...................	28	...	238	544	.438	133	179	.743	167	113	691	6.0	4.0	24.7
Totals	109	...	772	1759	.439	478	680	.703	597	467	1584	5.5	4.3	14.5

Three-point field goals: 1992-93, 18-for-50 (.360). 1993-94, 44-for-111 (.396). 1994-95, 64-for-182 (.352). 1995-96, 82-for-202 (.406). Totals, 208-for-545 (.382).

ABL RECORD

NOTES: ABL Eastern Conference All-Star (1998). ... Member of ABL Championship team (1997, 1998).

Season Team	G	Min.	FGM	FGA	Pct.	FTM	FTA	Pct.	Reb.	Ast.	Pts.	AVERAGES RPG	APG	PPG
1996—Columbus...........................	40	...	140	271	.517	60	74	.811	157	151	409	3.9	3.8	10.2
1997—Columbus...........................	44	...	153	357	.429	134	169	.793	210	215	484	4.8	4.9	11.0
1998—Columbus...........................	14	...	66	160	.413	56	72	.778	82	55	211	5.9	3.9	15.1
Totals	98	...	359	788	.456	250	315	.794	449	421	1104	4.6	4.3	11.3

Three-point field goals: 1996-97, 69-for-144 (.479). 1997-98, 44-for-127 (.346). 1998-99, 23-for-61 (.377). Totals, 136-for-332 (.410).

WNBA REGULAR-SEASON RECORD

NOTES: All-WNBA second team (1999, 2000, 2002). ... Led WNBA in minutes per game (35.8) in 1999.

Season Team	G	Min.	FGM	FGA	Pct.	FTM	FTA	Pct.	REBOUNDS Off.	Def.	Tot.	Ast.	St.	Blk.	TO	Pts.	AVERAGES RPG	APG	PPG
1999—Orlando	32	1147	151	338	.447	105	153	.686	44	106	150	141	54	12	121	447	4.7	4.4	14.0
2000—Orlando	32	1126	122	309	.395	107	144	.743	53	102	155	169	58	7	102	381	4.8	5.3	11.9
2001—Orlando	26	785	90	245	.367	84	111	.757	15	62	77	68	34	6	54	302	3.0	2.6	11.6
2002—Orlando	31	1110	157	389	.404	164	214	.766	49	80	129	163	51	7	98	499	4.2	5.3	16.1
2003—Connecticut........	34	1107	138	319	.433	125	171	.731	39	95	134	196	44	3	107	420	3.9	5.8	12.4
2004—San Antonio	31	954	89	234	.380	82	107	.766	14	68	82	136	48	4	99	287	2.6	4.4	9.3
2005—San Antonio	34	1104	88	241	.365	113	136	.831	17	74	91	158	46	5	113	317	2.7	4.6	9.3
Totals	220	7333	835	2075	.402	780	1036	.753	231	587	818	1031	335	44	694	2653	3.7	4.7	12.1

Three-point field goals: 1999-00, 40-for-110 (.364). 2000-01, 30-for-90 (.333). 2001-02, 38-for-104 (.365). 2002-03, 21-for-77 (.273). 2003-04, 19-for-73 (.260). 2004-05, 27-for-76 (.355). 2005-06, 28-for-90 (.311). Totals, 203-for-620 (.327).
Personal fouls/disqualifications: 1999-00, 79/0. 2000-01, 83/0. 2001-02, 66/0. 2002-03, 78/1. 2003-04, 77/0. 2004-05, 69/2. 2005-06, 78/1. Totals, 530/4.

WNBA PLAYOFF RECORD

Season Team	G	Min.	FGM	FGA	Pct.	FTM	FTA	Pct.	REBOUNDS Off.	Def.	Tot.	Ast.	St.	Blk.	TO	Pts.	AVERAGES RPG	APG	PPG
2000—Orlando	3	119	6	27	.222	4	8	.500	4	17	21	14	5	2	7	18	7.0	4.7	6.0
2003—Connecticut........	4	131	13	29	.448	14	18	.778	3	9	12	19	7	1	11	45	3.0	4.8	11.3
Totals	7	250	19	56	.339	18	26	.692	7	26	33	33	12	3	18	63	4.7	4.7	9.0

Three-point field goals: 2000-01, 2-for-13 (.154). 2003-04, 5-for-10 (.500). Totals, 7-for-23 (.304).
Personal fouls/disqualifications: 2000-01, 9/0. 2003-04, 11/0. Totals, 20/0.

WNBA ALL-STAR GAME RECORD

Season Team	Min.	FGM	FGA	Pct.	FTM	FTA	Pct.	REBOUNDS Off.	Def.	Tot.	Ast.	PF	Dq.	St.	Blk.	TO	Pts.
1999—Orlando	23	3	6	.500	0	0	...	2	2	4	2	2	0	3	1	2	8
2000—Orlando	20	2	6	.333	2	2	1.000	0	3	3	2	4	0	3	1	1	6
2002—Orlando	20	2	7	.286	0	0	...	2	0	2	3	3	0	1	0	0	6

Season Team	Min.	FGM	FGA	Pct.	FTM	FTA	Pct.	REBOUNDS Off.	Def.	Tot.	Ast.	PF	Dq.	St.	Blk.	TO	Pts.
2003—Connecticut............	12	0	5	.000	0	0	...	0	1	1	2	1	0	0	0	1	0
Totals	75	7	24	.292	2	2	1.000	4	6	10	9	10	0	7	2	4	20

Three-point field goals: 2000, 2-for-5 (.400). 2001, 0-for-4. 2003, 2-for-6 (.333). 2004, 0-for-1. Totals, 4-for-16 (.250).

OLYMPICS RECORD

Season Team	G	Min.	FGM	FGA	Pct.	FTM	FTA	Pct.	Reb.	Ast.	Pts.	AVERAGES RPG	APG	PPG
2004—United States....................	8	132	18	46	.391	9	9	1.000	20	15	49	2.5	1.9	6.1
Totals	8	132	18	46	.391	9	9	1.000	20	15	49	2.5	1.9	6.1

Three-point field goals: 2004-05, 4-for-11 (.364). Totals, 4-for-11 (.364).
Personal fouls/disqualifications: 2004-05, 19/0. Totals, 19/0.

JOHNSON, TEMEKA   G   SPARKS

PERSONAL: Born September 6, 1982, in New Orleans. ... 5-3/145. (1.60/65.8). ... Full name: Temeka Rochelle Johnson
HIGH SCHOOL: Bonnabel (New Orleans).
COLLEGE: LSU.
TRANSACTIONS/CAREER NOTES: Selected by Washington in the first round (6th overall) of the WNBA Draft, April 16, 2005. ... Traded by Washington with C Murriel Page to Los Angeles for G Nikki Teasley, March 1, 2006.
MISCELLANEOUS: Member of the gold medal-winning 2003 USA World Championship for Young Women team.

COLLEGE RECORD

NOTES: AP All-American second team (2005). ... USBWA All-American (2005). ... AP All-American honorable mention (2002, 2003, 2004). ... All-SEC first team (2004, 2005). ... All-SEC third team (2003). ... SEC Tournament MVP (2003). ... All-SEC Tournament team (2002, 2003). ... Broke LSU's career assist record, single-season assist record and tied her own single-game assist mark in 2004.

Season Team	G	Min.	FGM	FGA	Pct.	FTM	FTA	Pct.	Reb.	Ast.	Pts.	AVERAGES RPG	APG	PPG
2001—Louisiana State	24	858	96	190	.505	73	101	.723	115	179	266	4.8	7.5	11.1
2002—Louisiana State	34	964	133	263	.506	71	98	.724	124	199	339	3.6	5.9	10.0
2003—Louisiana State	35	1177	170	349	.487	102	126	.810	169	289	447	4.8	8.3	12.8
2004—Louisiana State	36	1125	145	303	.479	68	94	.723	119	278	374	3.3	7.7	10.4
Totals	129	4124	544	1105	.492	314	419	.749	527	945	1426	4.1	7.3	11.1

Three-point field goals: 2001-02, 1-for-7 (.143). 2002-03, 2-for-5 (.400). 2003-04, 5-for-16 (.313). 2004-05, 16-for-32 (.500). Totals, 24-for-60 (.400).

WNBA REGULAR-SEASON RECORD

NOTES: WNBA Rookie of the Year (2005). ... All-Rookie team (2005).

Season Team	G	Min.	FGM	FGA	Pct.	FTM	FTA	Pct.	REBOUNDS Off.	Def.	Tot.	Ast.	St.	Blk.	TO	Pts.	AVERAGES RPG	APG	PPG
2005—Washington........	34	973	125	273	.458	52	66	.788	13	91	104	177	44	1	88	315	3.1	5.2	9.3
Totals	34	973	125	273	.458	52	66	.788	13	91	104	177	44	1	88	315	3.1	5.2	9.3

Three-point field goals: 2005-06, 13-for-43 (.302). Totals, 13-for-43 (.302).
Personal fouls/disqualifications: 2005-06, 99/2. Totals, 99/2.

JOHNSON, VICKIE   G   SILVER STARS

PERSONAL: Born April 15, 1972, in Shreveport, La. ... 5-9/150. (1.75/68.0). ... Full name: Vickie Annette Johnson
HIGH SCHOOL: Coushatta (Coushatta, La.).
COLLEGE: Louisiana Tech.
TRANSACTIONS/CAREER NOTES: Selected by New York in second round (12th overall) of WNBA Elite Draft, February 27, 1997. ... Signed by San Antonio, February 9, 2006.

COLLEGE RECORD

NOTES: Kodak All-American first team (1995, 1996).

Season Team	G	Min.	FGM	FGA	Pct.	FTM	FTA	Pct.	Reb.	Ast.	Pts.	AVERAGES RPG	APG	PPG
1992—Louisiana Tech	31	...	165	372	.444	76	103	.738	194	70	417	6.3	2.3	13.5
1993—Louisiana Tech	35	...	209	418	.500	87	118	.737	244	76	517	7.0	2.2	14.8
1994—Louisiana Tech	33	...	224	421	.532	94	127	.740	227	91	542	6.9	2.8	16.4
1995—Louisiana Tech	26	...	169	313	.540	77	97	.794	166	68	415	6.4	2.6	16.0
Totals	125	...	767	1524	.503	334	445	.751	831	305	1891	6.6	2.4	15.1

Three-point field goals: 1992-93, 11-for-35 (.314). 1993-94, 12-for-38 (.316). 1994-95, 0-for-4. 1995-96, 0-for-2. Totals, 23-for-79 (.291).

WNBA REGULAR-SEASON RECORD

Season Team	G	Min.	FGM	FGA	Pct.	FTM	FTA	Pct.	REBOUNDS Off.	Def.	Tot.	Ast.	St.	Blk.	TO	Pts.	AVERAGES RPG	APG	PPG
1997—New York..........	26	789	108	269	.401	27	35	.771	46	64	110	66	19	4	49	247	4.2	2.5	9.5
1998—New York..........	30	905	146	327	.446	63	82	.768	44	70	114	74	31	7	45	376	3.8	2.5	12.5
1999—New York..........	32	1082	165	394	.419	72	86	.837	43	99	142	106	44	1	66	427	4.4	3.3	13.3
2000—New York..........	31	1023	143	324	.441	67	76	.882	40	97	137	77	22	5	57	380	4.4	2.5	12.3
2001—New York..........	32	939	135	326	.414	53	70	.757	23	84	107	87	35	4	52	353	3.3	2.7	11.0
2002—New York..........	31	1028	139	305	.456	49	61	.803	42	67	109	86	27	4	45	359	3.5	2.8	11.6
2003—New York..........	32	1042	158	345	.458	79	92	.859	30	65	95	75	29	7	55	430	3.0	2.3	13.4

Season Team	G	Min.	FGM	FGA	Pct.	FTM	FTA	Pct.	REBOUNDS Off.	Def.	Tot.	Ast.	St.	Blk.	TO	Pts.	AVERAGES RPG	APG	PPG
2004—New York	34	1119	121	293	.413	62	70	.886	37	84	121	124	25	4	71	321	3.6	3.6	9.4
2005—New York	34	1023	129	272	.474	65	84	.774	37	81	118	92	23	2	44	353	3.5	2.7	10.4
Totals	282	8950	1244	2855	.436	537	656	.819	342	711	1053	787	255	38	484	3246	3.7	2.8	11.5

Three-point field goals: 1997-98, 4-for-21 (.190). 1998-99, 21-for-56 (.375). 1999-00, 25-for-71 (.352). 2000-01, 27-for-71 (.380). 2001-02, 30-for-82 (.366). 2002-03, 32-for-76 (.421). 2003-04, 35-for-96 (.365). 2004-05, 17-for-60 (.283). 2005-06, 30-for-84 (.357). Totals, 221-for-617 (.358).

Personal fouls/disqualifications: 1997-98, 52/0. 1998-99, 70/1. 1999-00, 77/0. 2000-01, 48/0. 2001-02, 62/1. 2002-03, 60/0. 2003-04, 65/0. 2004-05, 75/0. 2005-06, 56/0. Totals, 565/2.

WNBA PLAYOFF RECORD

Season Team	G	Min.	FGM	FGA	Pct.	FTM	FTA	Pct.	REBOUNDS Off.	Def.	Tot.	Ast.	St.	Blk.	TO	Pts.	AVERAGES RPG	APG	PPG
1997—New York	2	68	11	26	.423	1	2	.500	5	7	12	4	2	1	2	23	6.0	2.0	11.5
1999—New York	6	185	24	57	.421	9	14	.643	4	17	21	18	2	2	15	61	3.5	3.0	10.2
2000—New York	7	237	27	71	.380	12	14	.857	10	25	35	24	8	0	13	72	5.0	3.4	10.3
2001—New York	6	218	34	75	.453	15	15	1.000	7	20	27	28	13	2	14	89	4.5	4.7	14.8
2002—New York	8	244	36	75	.480	12	16	.750	8	22	30	24	7	0	11	98	3.8	3.0	12.3
2004—New York	5	161	14	39	.359	11	12	.917	11	11	22	16	5	1	4	41	4.4	3.2	8.2
2005—New York	2	73	10	22	.455	6	8	.750	0	6	6	7	1	0	4	26	3.0	3.5	13.0
Totals	36	1186	156	365	.427	66	81	.815	45	108	153	121	38	6	63	410	4.3	3.4	11.4

Three-point field goals: 1997-98, 0-for-1. 1999-00, 4-for-10 (.400). 2000-01, 6-for-22 (.273). 2001-02, 6-for-22 (.273). 2002-03, 14-for-27 (.519). 2004-05, 2-for-10 (.200). 2005-06, 0-for-3. Totals, 32-for-95 (.337).

Personal fouls/disqualifications: 1997-98, 6/0. 1999-00, 15/0. 2000-01, 14/0. 2001-02, 11/0. 2002-03, 10/0. 2004-05, 10/0. 2005-06, 7/0. Totals, 73/0.

WNBA ALL-STAR GAME RECORD

Season Team	Min.	FGM	FGA	Pct.	FTM	FTA	Pct.	REBOUNDS Off.	Def.	Tot.	Ast.	PF	Dq.	St.	Blk.	TO	Pts.
1999—New York	15	3	8	.375	0	0	...	0	2	2	3	0	0	0	0	2	6
2001—New York	19	2	8	.250	2	2	1.000	0	3	3	1	0	0	0	0	3	8
Totals	34	5	16	.313	2	2	1.000	0	5	5	4	0	0	0	0	5	14

Three-point field goals: 2000, 0-for-3. 2002, 2-for-5 (.400). Totals, 2-for-8 (.250).

JONES, ASJHA   F/C   SUN

PERSONAL: Born August 1, 1980, in Piscataway, N.J. ... 6-2/198. (1.88/89.8). ... Full name: Asjha Takera Jones
HIGH SCHOOL: Piscataway (Piscataway, N.J.).
COLLEGE: Connecticut.
TRANSACTIONS/CAREER NOTES: Selected by Washington in first round (fourth overall) of WNBA Draft, April 19, 2002. ... Washington signed and traded Jones to Connecticut, Phoenix traded G Tamicha Jackson to Washington, and Connecticut traded the eighth overall pick inthe 2004 WNBA Draft to Phoenix, March 25, 2003.

COLLEGE RECORD

NOTES: Member of NCAA Division I Championship team (2002, 2000).

Season Team	G	Min.	FGM	FGA	Pct.	FTM	FTA	Pct.	Reb.	Ast.	Pts.	AVERAGES RPG	APG	PPG
1998—Connecticut	34	681	140	284	.493	52	73	.712	170	45	332	5.0	1.3	9.8
1999—Connecticut	36	632	127	251	.506	60	95	.632	177	33	319	4.9	0.9	8.9
2000—Connecticut	35	683	128	291	.440	44	73	.603	190	50	304	5.4	1.4	8.7
2001—Connecticut	39	961	247	445	.555	45	75	.600	257	66	547	6.6	1.7	14.0
Totals	144	2957	642	1271	.505	201	316	.636	794	194	1502	5.5	1.3	10.4

Three-point field goals: 1999-00, 5-for-10 (.500). 2000-01, 4-for-16 (.250). 2001-02, 8-for-25 (.320). Totals, 17-for-51 (.333).

WNBA REGULAR-SEASON RECORD

Season Team	G	Min.	FGM	FGA	Pct.	FTM	FTA	Pct.	REBOUNDS Off.	Def.	Tot.	Ast.	St.	Blk.	TO	Pts.	AVERAGES RPG	APG	PPG
2002—Washington	32	612	93	233	.399	20	33	.606	39	50	89	28	13	17	39	208	2.8	0.9	6.5
2003—Washington	34	748	121	279	.434	41	55	.745	62	73	135	52	16	25	63	290	4.0	1.5	8.5
2004—Connecticut	34	699	96	239	.402	41	48	.854	51	67	118	39	20	18	53	235	3.5	1.1	6.9
2005—Connecticut	33	705	133	275	.484	33	56	.589	54	67	121	40	10	7	51	301	3.7	1.2	9.1
Totals	133	2764	443	1026	.432	135	192	.703	206	257	463	159	59	67	206	1034	3.5	1.2	7.8

Three-point field goals: 2002-03, 2-for-10 (.200). 2003-04, 7-for-17 (.412). 2004-05, 2-for-6 (.333). 2005-06, 2-for-5 (.400). Totals, 13-for-38 (.342).
Personal fouls/disqualifications: 2002-03, 88/2. 2003-04, 109/1. 2004-05, 82/0. 2005-06, 70/0. Totals, 349/3.

WNBA PLAYOFF RECORD

Season Team	G	Min.	FGM	FGA	Pct.	FTM	FTA	Pct.	REBOUNDS Off.	Def.	Tot.	Ast.	St.	Blk.	TO	Pts.	AVERAGES RPG	APG	PPG
2002—Washington	5	63	8	19	.421	1	2	.500	3	5	8	3	0	1	1	18	1.6	0.6	3.6
2004—Connecticut	8	171	26	53	.491	7	11	.636	8	13	21	11	5	1	18	59	2.6	1.4	7.4
2005—Connecticut	8	178	29	60	.483	13	23	.565	8	20	28	7	2	4	11	71	3.5	0.9	8.9
Totals	21	412	63	132	.477	21	36	.583	19	38	57	21	7	6	30	148	2.7	1.0	7.0

Three-point field goals: 2002-03, 1-for-2 (.500). 2005-06, 0-for-2. Totals, 1-for-4 (.250).
Personal fouls/disqualifications: 2002-03, 13/0. 2004-05, 10/0. 2005-06, 23/0. Totals, 46/0.

JONES, CHANDI   G/F   LYNX

PERSONAL: Born March 25, 1982, in Wharton, Texas. ... 5-11/154. (1.80/69.9). ... Full name: Chandi Montrease Jones
HIGH SCHOOL: Bay City (Bay City, Texas).
COLLEGE: Houston.
TRANSACTIONS/CAREER NOTES: Selected by Phoenix in first round (eighth overall) of WNBA Draft, April 17, 2004. ... Traded by Phoenix to Detroit in exchange for G Shereka Wright and G Erika Valek, April 17, 2004. ... Traded by Detroit with F Stacey

Thomas to Minnesota for G Katie Smith, July 30, 2005.

MISCELLANEOUS: Member of gold medal-winning USA Junior World Championships team (2000).

COLLEGE RECORD

NOTES: Kodak All-American (2004). ... AP All-American second team (2004). ... USBWA All-American second team (2004). ... AP All-American honorable mention (2002, 2003). ... Conference USA Player of the Year (2002, 2003, 2004). ... All-Conference USA first team (2001, 2002, 2003, 2004). ... Conference USA Tournament MVP (2004). ... All-Conference USA Tournament team (2002, 2004). ... Conference USA Freshman of the Year (2001). ... Houston's all-time leading scorer (2,692).

Season Team	G	Min.	FGM	FGA	Pct.	FTM	FTA	Pct.	Reb.	Ast.	Pts.	RPG	APG	PPG
2000—Houston	20	674	156	346	.451	99	138	.717	113	49	429	5.7	2.5	21.5
2001—Houston	34	1221	277	604	.459	165	240	.688	196	91	766	5.8	2.7	22.5
2002—Houston	28	1020	275	563	.488	168	233	.721	228	68	770	8.1	2.4	27.5
2003—Houston	32	1139	255	607	.420	146	198	.737	177	77	727	5.5	2.4	22.7
Totals	114	4054	963	2120	.454	578	809	.714	714	285	2692	6.3	2.5	23.6

Three-point field goals: 2000-01, 18-for-71 (.254). 2001-02, 47-for-142 (.331). 2002-03, 52-for-141 (.369). 2003-04, 71-for-194 (.366). Totals, 188-for-548 (.343).

WNBA REGULAR-SEASON RECORD

Season Team	G	Min.	FGM	FGA	Pct.	FTM	FTA	Pct.	Off.	Def.	Tot.	Ast.	St.	Blk.	TO	Pts.	RPG	APG	PPG
2004—Detroit	31	397	37	103	.359	25	31	.806	8	26	34	45	18	5	40	107	1.1	1.5	3.5
2005—Det.-Minn.	31	610	75	196	.383	27	38	.711	18	46	64	53	26	5	40	206	2.1	1.7	6.6
Totals	62	1007	112	299	.375	52	69	.754	26	72	98	98	44	10	80	313	1.6	1.6	5.0

Three-point field goals: 2004-05, 8-for-32 (.250). 2005-06, 29-for-69 (.420). Totals, 37-for-101 (.366).
Personal fouls/disqualifications: 2004-05, 41/0. 2005-06, 68/0. Totals, 109/0.

WNBA PLAYOFF RECORD

Season Team	G	Min.	FGM	FGA	Pct.	FTM	FTA	Pct.	Off.	Def.	Tot.	Ast.	St.	Blk.	TO	Pts.	RPG	APG	PPG
2004—Detroit	2	10	1	4	.250	0	0	...	0	0	0	1	0	0	1	2	0.0	0.5	1.0
Totals	2	10	1	4	.250	0	0	...	0	0	0	1	0	0	1	2	0.0	0.5	1.0

Personal fouls/disqualifications: 2004-05, 2/0. Totals, 2/0.

KING BORCHARDT, SUSAN   G   LYNX

PERSONAL: Born July 27, 1981, in Richfield, Minn. ... 5-7. (1.70).
HIGH SCHOOL: Academy of Holy Angels (Richfield, Minn.).
COLLEGE: Stanford.
TRANSACTIONS/CAREER NOTES: Signed by Minnesota, April, 25, 2005.

COLLEGE RECORD

Season Team	G	Min.	FGM	FGA	Pct.	FTM	FTA	Pct.	Reb.	Ast.	Pts.	RPG	APG	PPG
2000—Stanford	9	284	36	77	.468	19	23	.826	25	46	102	2.8	5.1	11.3
2001—Stanford	2	45	2	9	.222	2	2	1.000	6	5	7	3.0	2.5	3.5
2002—Stanford	30	800	64	164	.390	30	37	.811	38	45	190	1.3	1.5	6.3
2003—Stanford	34	1013	101	211	.479	32	35	.914	42	89	289	1.2	2.4	2.6
2004—Stanford	26	629	82	156	.526	18	22	.818	45	48	227	1.7	1.8	8.7
Totals	101	2771	285	617	.462	101	119	.849	1564	233	815	1.5	2.3	8.1

Three-point field goals: 2000-01, 11-for-37 (.297). 2001-02, 1-for-4 (.250). 2002-03, 32-for-98 (.327). 2003-04, 55-for-126 (.437). 2004-05, 45-for-96 (.469). Totals, 144-for-361 (.399).

WNBA REGULAR-SEASON RECORD

Season Team	G	Min.	FGM	FGA	Pct.	FTM	FTA	Pct.	Off.	Def.	Tot.	Ast.	St.	Blk.	TO	Pts.	RPG	APG	PPG
2005—Minnesota	3	17	0	1	.000	3	4	.750	0	1	1	1	0	1	0	3	0.3	0.3	1.0
Totals	3	17	0	1	.000	3	4	.750	0	1	1	1	0	1	0	3	0.3	0.3	1.0

Personal fouls/disqualifications: 2005-06, 2/0. Totals, 2/0.

KOEHN, LAURIE   G   MYSTICS

PERSONAL: Born May 13, 1982, in Hesston, Kan. ... 5-8/143. (1.73/64.9). ... Full name: Laurie M. Koehn
HIGH SCHOOL: Moundridge (Newton, Kan.).
COLLEGE: Kansas State.

COLLEGE RECORD

NOTES: All-Big 12 second team (2004, 2005). ... Big 12 All-Academic first team (2005). ... CoSIDA Academic All-American (2004). ... Kansas State and Big 12's all-time leader in 3-pointers made (392).

Season Team	G	Min.	FGM	FGA	Pct.	FTM	FTA	Pct.	Reb.	Ast.	Pts.	RPG	APG	PPG
2001—Kansas State	34	1222	192	426	.451	94	105	.895	114	85	600	3.4	2.5	17.6
2002—Kansas State	24	745	106	251	.422	33	40	.825	82	44	317	3.4	1.8	13.2
2003—Kansas State	31	1036	140	307	.456	39	45	.867	75	41	419	2.4	1.3	13.5

K

Season Team	G	Min.	FGM	FGA	Pct.	FTM	FTA	Pct.	Reb.	Ast.	Pts.	AVERAGES RPG	APG	PPG
2004—Kansas State	32	985	136	333	.408	27	30	.900	91	48	397	2.8	1.5	12.4
Totals	121	3988	574	1317	.436	193	220	.877	362	218	1733	3.0	1.8	14.3

Three-point field goals: 2001-02, 122-for-289 (.422). 2002-03, 72-for-175 (.411). 2003-04, 100-for-230 (.435). 2004-05, 98-for-248 (.395). Totals, 392-for-942 (.416).

WNBA REGULAR-SEASON RECORD

NOTES: Led WNBA in three-point field goal percentage (.467) in 2005.

Season Team	G	Min.	FGM	FGA	Pct.	FTM	FTA	Pct.	REBOUNDS Off.	Def.	Tot.	Ast.	St.	Blk.	TO	Pts.	AVERAGES RPG	APG	PPG
2005—Washington	30	230	37	79	.468	4	5	.800	4	7	11	10	2	0	6	113	0.4	0.3	3.8
Totals	30	230	37	79	.468	4	5	.800	4	7	11	10	2	0	6	113	0.4	0.3	3.8

Three-point field goals: 2005-06, 35-for-75 (.467). Totals, 35-for-75 (.467).
Personal fouls/disqualifications: 2005-06, 15/0. Totals, 15/0.

KRAAYEVELD, CATHRINE   F   LIBERTY

PERSONAL: Born September 30, 1981, in Bellevue, Wash. ... 6-4/180. (1.93/81.6). ... Full name: Cathrine Helene Kraayeveld
HIGH SCHOOL: Lake Washington (Kirkland, Wash.).
COLLEGE: Oregon.
TRANSACTIONS/CAREER NOTES: Selected by San Antonio in the third round (27th overall) of the WNBA Draft, April 16, 2005.
MISCELLANEOUS: Redshirted the 2003-04 season.

COLLEGE RECORD

NOTES: All-Pac-10 first team (2005). ... All-Pac 10 honorable mention (2002, 2003). ... WNIT MVP (2002). ... Pac-10 academic all-district second team (2003).

Season Team	G	Min.	FGM	FGA	Pct.	FTM	FTA	Pct.	Reb.	Ast.	Pts.	AVERAGES RPG	APG	PPG
2000—Oregon	24	207	15	46	.326	17	21	.810	40	10	50	1.7	0.4	2.1
2001—Oregon	35	921	137	268	.511	72	97	.742	290	58	356	8.3	1.7	10.2
2002—Oregon	15	460	82	174	.471	36	53	.679	152	24	217	10.1	1.6	14.5
2004—Oregon	30	975	156	343	.455	90	117	.769	249	53	442	8.3	1.8	14.7
Totals	104	2563	390	831	.469	215	288	.747	731	145	1065	7.0	1.4	10.2

WNBA REGULAR-SEASON RECORD

Season Team	G	Min.	FGM	FGA	Pct.	FTM	FTA	Pct.	REBOUNDS Off.	Def.	Tot.	Ast.	St.	Blk.	TO	Pts.	AVERAGES RPG	APG	PPG
2005—New York	17	196	23	55	.418	14	15	.933	13	14	27	5	4	8	17	69	1.6	0.3	4.1
Totals	17	196	23	55	.418	14	15	.933	13	14	27	5	4	8	17	69	1.6	0.3	4.1

Three-point field goals: 2005-06, 9-for-24 (.375). Totals, 9-for-24 (.375).
Personal fouls/disqualifications: 2005-06, 21/0. Totals, 21/0.

WNBA PLAYOFF RECORD

Season Team	G	Min.	FGM	FGA	Pct.	FTM	FTA	Pct.	REBOUNDS Off.	Def.	Tot.	Ast.	St.	Blk.	TO	Pts.	AVERAGES RPG	APG	PPG
2005—New York	2	37	1	3	.333	5	6	.833	2	5	7	0	0	0	2	8	3.5	0.0	4.0
Totals	2	37	1	3	.333	5	6	.833	2	5	7	0	0	0	2	8	3.5	0.0	4.0

Three-point field goals: 2005-06, 1-for-1 (1.000). Totals, 1-for-1 (1.000).
Personal fouls/disqualifications: 2005-06, 6/0. Totals, 6/0.

LAMBERT, SHEILA   G   SHOCK

PERSONAL: Born July 21, 1980, in Seattle. ... 5-7/125. (1.70/56.7). ... Full name: Sheila Monique Lambert
HIGH SCHOOL: Chief Sealth (Seattle).
COLLEGE: Baylor.
TRANSACTIONS/CAREER NOTES: Selected by Charlotte in first round (seventh overall) of WNBA Draft, April 19, 2002.
MISCELLANEOUS: Member of WNBA Championship team (2003).

COLLEGE RECORD

NOTES: Kodak All-American first team (2002). ... Played first two seasons at Grayson County (Texas) Community College. ... NJCAA All-American first team (1999, 2000).

Season Team	G	Min.	FGM	FGA	Pct.	FTM	FTA	Pct.	Reb.	Ast.	Pts.	AVERAGES RPG	APG	PPG
2000—Baylor	30	1062	242	599	.404	148	196	.755	168	182	622	5.6	6.1	20.7
2001—Baylor	33	1109	253	516	.490	129	169	.763	145	216	653	4.4	6.5	19.8
Totals	63	2171	495	1115	.444	277	365	.759	313	398	1275	5.0	6.3	20.2

Three-point field goals: 2000-01, 30-for-118 (.254). 2001-02, 18-for-57 (.316). Totals, 48-for-175 (.274).

WNBA REGULAR-SEASON RECORD

Season Team	G	Min.	FGM	FGA	Pct.	FTM	FTA	Pct.	REBOUNDS Off.	Def.	Tot.	Ast.	St.	Blk.	TO	Pts.	AVERAGES RPG	APG	PPG
2002—Charlotte	3	16	1	3	.333	0	0	...	2	1	3	3	1	0	2	2	1.0	1.0	0.7
2003—Detroit	27	187	24	66	.364	32	41	.780	10	18	28	14	5	0	29	87	1.0	0.5	3.2

K
L

Season Team	G	Min.	FGM	FGA	Pct.	FTM	FTA	Pct.	REBOUNDS Off.	Def.	Tot.	Ast.	St.	Blk.	TO	Pts.	AVERAGES RPG	APG	PPG
2004—Houston	34	788	75	177	.424	40	51	.784	19	49	68	88	26	4	82	197	2.0	2.6	5.8
2005—Detroit.............	12	152	14	45	.311	4	5	.800	2	15	17	21	8	1	24	33	1.4	1.8	2.8
Totals	76	1143	114	291	.392	76	97	.784	33	83	116	126	40	5	137	319	1.5	1.7	4.2

Three-point field goals: 2003-04, 7-for-16 (.438). 2004-05, 7-for-27 (.259). 2005-06, 1-for-7 (.143). Totals, 15-for-50 (.300).
Personal fouls/disqualifications: 2002-03, 1/0. 2003-04, 15/0. 2005-06, 46/0. 2005-06, 11/0. Totals, 73/0.

WNBA PLAYOFF RECORD

Season Team	G	Min.	FGM	FGA	Pct.	FTM	FTA	Pct.	REBOUNDS Off.	Def.	Tot.	Ast.	St.	Blk.	TO	Pts.	AVERAGES RPG	APG	PPG
2003—Detroit.............	7	14	2	6	.333	0	0	...	0	2	2	1	0	0	4	5	0.3	0.1	0.7
Totals	7	14	2	6	.333	0	0	...	0	2	2	1	0	0	4	5	0.3	0.1	0.7

Three-point field goals: 2003-04, 1-for-3 (.333). Totals, 1-for-3 (.333).
Personal fouls/disqualifications: 2003-04, 3/0. Totals, 3/0.

LASSITER, AMANDA   F   SKY

PERSONAL: Born June 9, 1979, in San Francisco. ... 6-1/143. (1.85/64.9). ... Full name: Amanda D. Lassiter
HIGH SCHOOL: George Washington (San Francisco).
COLLEGE: Missouri.
TRANSACTIONS/CAREER NOTES: Selected by Houston in first round (15th overall) of WNBA Draft, April 20, 2001. ... Traded by Houston to Seattle for F Sonja Henning, June 17, 2002.

JUNIOR COLLEGE RECORD

Season Team	G	Min.	FGM	FGA	Pct.	FTM	FTA	Pct.	Reb.	Ast.	Pts.	AVERAGES RPG	APG	PPG
1997—Central Arizona College	32	...	165	324	.509	35	51	.686	205	114	407	6.4	3.6	12.7
1998—Central Arizona College	30	...	195	390	.500	24	43	.558	207	111	486	6.9	3.7	16.2
Totals	62	...	360	714	.504	59	94	.628	412	225	893	6.6	3.6	14.4

Three-point field goals: 1997-98, 14-for-52 (.269). 1998-99, 24-for-60 (.400). Totals, 38-for-112 (.339).

COLLEGE RECORD

NOTES: Member of NJCAA Division I Championship team (1998). ... Kodak and NJCAA All-American first team (1999). ... NJCAA Tournament MVP (1998).

Season Team	G	Min.	FGM	FGA	Pct.	FTM	FTA	Pct.	Reb.	Ast.	Pts.	AVERAGES RPG	APG	PPG
1999—Missouri	30	826	165	395	.418	53	69	.768	168	99	418	5.6	3.3	13.9
2000—Missouri	32	935	238	567	.420	69	97	.711	197	75	610	6.2	2.3	19.1
Totals	62	1761	403	962	.419	122	166	.735	365	174	1028	5.9	2.8	16.6

Three-point field goals: 1999-00, 35-for-95 (.368). 2000-01, 65-for-187 (.348). Totals, 100-for-282 (.355).

WNBA REGULAR-SEASON RECORD

Season Team	G	Min.	FGM	FGA	Pct.	FTM	FTA	Pct.	REBOUNDS Off.	Def.	Tot.	Ast.	St.	Blk.	TO	Pts.	AVERAGES RPG	APG	PPG
2001—Houston	32	613	51	139	.367	10	15	.667	27	83	110	34	16	21	35	138	3.4	1.1	4.3
2002—Hou.-Seattle.......	30	600	47	140	.336	13	19	.684	24	45	69	57	29	21	51	127	2.3	1.9	4.2
2003—Seattle	32	733	60	156	.385	19	30	.633	33	79	112	42	27	26	42	163	3.5	1.3	5.1
2004—Minnesota	33	563	47	135	.348	6	9	.667	15	65	80	37	21	22	40	127	2.4	1.1	3.8
2005—Minnesota	31	388	38	115	.330	7	11	.636	10	36	46	23	14	4	29	107	1.5	0.7	3.5
Totals	158	2897	243	685	.355	55	84	.655	109	308	417	193	107	94	197	662	2.6	1.2	4.2

Three-point field goals: 2001-02, 26-for-67 (.388). 2002-03, 20-for-71 (.282). 2003-04, 24-for-73 (.329). 2004-05, 27-for-89 (.303). 2005-06, 24-for-72 (.333). Totals, 121-for-372 (.325).
Personal fouls/disqualifications: 2001-02, 66/0. 2002-03, 62/1. 2003-04, 92/2. 2004-05, 74/0. 2005-06, 55/0. Totals, 349/3.

WNBA PLAYOFF RECORD

Season Team	G	Min.	FGM	FGA	Pct.	FTM	FTA	Pct.	REBOUNDS Off.	Def.	Tot.	Ast.	St.	Blk.	TO	Pts.	AVERAGES RPG	APG	PPG
2001—Houston	2	54	7	16	.438	2	2	1.000	1	8	9	0	0	3	2	19	4.5	0.0	9.5
2002—Seattle	2	46	4	15	.267	0	0	...	0	7	7	4	3	1	5	10	3.5	2.0	5.0
2004—Minnesota	2	30	3	7	.429	0	0	...	0	4	4	1	2	3	4	9	2.0	0.5	4.5
Totals	6	130	14	38	.368	2	2	1.000	1	19	20	5	5	7	11	38	3.3	0.8	6.3

Three-point field goals: 2001-02, 3-for-9 (.333). 2002-03, 2-for-9 (.222). 2004-05, 3-for-6 (.500). Totals, 8-for-24 (.333).
Personal fouls/disqualifications: 2001-02, 4/0. 2002-03, 4/0. 2004-05, 5/0. Totals, 13/0.

LAWSON, EDWIGE   G   STING

PERSONAL: Born May 14, 1979, in Ille-et-Cilaine, Rennes, France. ... 5-6. (1.68).
TRANSACTIONS/CAREER NOTES: Signed by New York, April 4, 2005.
MISCELLANEOUS: Played professionally in France for Bordeaux (1996-98), Aix-en-Provence (1998-2001) and US Valenciennes Olympic (2001-02).

FRENCH RECORD

Season Team	G	Min.	FGM	FGA	Pct.	FTM	FTA	Pct.	Reb.	Ast.	Pts.	AVERAGES RPG	APG	PPG
1996—Bordeaux..........................	22	642	69	141	.489	30	43	.698	43	36	176	2.0	1.6	8.0
1997—Bordeaux..........................	26	925	109	204	.534	36	47	.766	62	52	281	2.4	2.0	10.8

L

Season Team	G	Min.	FGM	FGA	Pct.	FTM	FTA	Pct.	Reb.	Ast.	Pts.	AVERAGES RPG	APG	PPG
1998—Aix-en-Provence	28	764	74	167	.443	53	64	.828	67	33	213	2.4	1.2	7.6
1999—Aix-en-Provence	28	857	97	212	.458	72	84	.857	64	84	281	2.3	3.0	10.0
2000—Aix-en-Provence	22	753	94	224	.420	34	50	.680	91	65	246	4.1	3.0	11.2
2001—US Valenciennes Olympic ...	28	...	115	281	.409	48	69	.696	119	80	306	4.3	2.9	10.9
Totals	154	3941	558	1229	.454	273	357	.765	446	350	1503	2.9	2.3	9.8

Three-point field goals: 1996-97, 8-for-26 (.308). 1997-98, 27-for-57 (.474). 1998-99, 12-for-28 (.429). 1999-00, 15-for-49 (.306). 2000-01, 24-for-63 (.381). 2001-02, 28-for-74 (.378). Totals, 114-for-297 (.384).

OLYMPICS RECORD

Season Team	G	Min.	FGM	FGA	Pct.	FTM	FTA	Pct.	Reb.	Ast.	Pts.	AVERAGES RPG	APG	PPG
1996—France	3	22	5	8	.625	3	4	.750	3	2	13	1.0	0.7	4.3
Totals	3	22	5	8	.625	3	4	.750	3	2	13	1.0	0.7	4.3

Three-point field goals: 1996-97, 0-for-2. Totals, 0-for-2 (.000).

WNBA REGULAR-SEASON RECORD

Season Team	G	Min.	FGM	FGA	Pct.	FTM	FTA	Pct.	REBOUNDS Off.	Def.	Tot.	Ast.	St.	Blk.	TO	Pts.	AVERAGES RPG	APG	PPG
2005—N.Y.-Houston	19	126	8	28	.286	6	6	1.000	1	8	9	4	2	1	12	27	0.5	0.2	1.4
Totals	19	126	8	28	.286	6	6	1.000	1	8	9	4	2	1	12	27	0.5	0.2	1.4

Three-point field goals: 2005-06, 5-for-15 (.333). Totals, 5-for-15 (.333).
Personal fouls/disqualifications: 2005-06, 7/0. Totals, 7/0.

WNBA PLAYOFF RECORD

Season Team	G	Min.	FGM	FGA	Pct.	FTM	FTA	Pct.	REBOUNDS Off.	Def.	Tot.	Ast.	St.	Blk.	TO	Pts.	AVERAGES RPG	APG	PPG
2005—Houston	1	1	0	0	...	0	0	...	0	0	0	0	0	0	0	0	0.0	0.0	0.0
Totals	1	1	0	0	...	0	0	...	0	0	0	0	0	0	0	0	0.0	0.0	0.0

LAWSON, KARA   G   MONARCHS

PERSONAL: Born February 14, 1981, in Alexandria, Va. ... 5-8/160. (1.73/72.6). ... Full name: Kara Marie Lawson
HIGH SCHOOL: West Springfield (Alexandria, Va.).
COLLEGE: Tennessee.
TRANSACTIONS/CAREER NOTES: Selected by Detroit in first round (fifth overall) of WNBA Draft, April 25, 2003. ... Traded by Detroit to Sacramento for G Kedra Holland-Corn and Detroit's second-round pick int he 2004 WNBA Draft, April 29, 2003.
MISCELLANEOUS: Captain of the gold medal-winning U.S. World University Games team (2001). ... Naismith High School Player of the Year (1999). ... Member of bronze medal-winning U.S. Women's World Youth Games team (1998). ... Member of WNBA Championship team (2005).

COLLEGE RECORD

NOTES: AP All-American second team (2003). ... All-SEC first team (2000, 2001, 2002, 2003). ... AP All-American third team (2002). ... USBWA All-American team (2002). ... SEC All-Freshman team (2000). ... Holds Tennessee career mark for three-pointers made (256). ... Led the SEC in three-point field goal percentage as a freshman (.436).

Season Team	G	Min.	FGM	FGA	Pct.	FTM	FTA	Pct.	Reb.	Ast.	Pts.	AVERAGES RPG	APG	PPG
1999—Tennessee	37	1036	168	367	.458	89	109	.817	152	102	504	4.1	2.8	13.6
2000—Tennessee	34	899	132	305	.433	60	70	.857	119	113	386	3.5	3.3	11.4
2001—Tennessee	34	1078	189	406	.466	96	115	.835	165	90	512	4.9	2.6	15.1
2002—Tennessee	38	1185	186	397	.469	99	112	.884	185	151	548	4.9	4.0	14.4
Totals	143	4198	675	1475	.458	344	406	.847	621	456	1950	4.3	3.2	13.6

Three-point field goals: 1999-00, 78-for-181 (.431). 2000-01, 62-for-150 (.413). 2001-02, 38-for-115 (.330). 2002-03, 77-for-171 (.450). Totals, 255-for-617 (.413).

WNBA REGULAR-SEASON RECORD

Season Team	G	Min.	FGM	FGA	Pct.	FTM	FTA	Pct.	REBOUNDS Off.	Def.	Tot.	Ast.	St.	Blk.	TO	Pts.	AVERAGES RPG	APG	PPG
2003—Sacramento	34	769	89	227	.392	31	40	.775	30	77	107	56	15	5	42	263	3.1	1.6	7.7
2004—Sacramento	34	827	103	245	.420	37	44	.841	12	65	77	68	21	8	53	294	2.3	2.0	8.6
2005—Sacramento	24	508	65	148	.439	26	31	.839	7	26	33	37	13	3	22	192	1.4	1.5	8.0
Totals	92	2104	257	620	.415	94	115	.817	49	168	217	161	49	16	117	749	2.4	1.8	8.1

Three-point field goals: 2003-04, 54-for-135 (.400). 2004-05, 51-for-134 (.381). 2005-06, 36-for-81 (.444). Totals, 141-for-350 (.403).
Personal fouls/disqualifications: 2003-04, 45/0. 2004-05, 41/0. 2005-06, 28/0. Totals, 114/0.

WNBA PLAYOFF RECORD

Season Team	G	Min.	FGM	FGA	Pct.	FTM	FTA	Pct.	REBOUNDS Off.	Def.	Tot.	Ast.	St.	Blk.	TO	Pts.	AVERAGES RPG	APG	PPG
2003—Sacramento	6	154	9	42	.214	7	8	.875	2	21	23	16	1	2	4	32	3.8	2.7	5.3
2004—Sacramento	6	153	20	54	.370	8	9	.889	3	12	15	11	8	1	5	58	2.5	1.8	9.7
2005—Sacramento	8	208	29	67	.433	17	18	.944	2	27	29	18	8	1	11	90	3.6	2.3	11.3
Totals	20	515	58	163	.356	32	35	.914	7	60	67	45	17	4	20	180	3.4	2.3	9.0

Three-point field goals: 2003-04, 7-for-23 (.304). 2004-05, 10-for-24 (.417). 2005-06, 15-for-29 (.517). Totals, 32-for-76 (.421).
Personal fouls/disqualifications: 2003-04, 8/0. 2004-05, 10/0. 2005-06, 9/0. Totals, 27/0.

LENNOX, BETTY G STORM

PERSONAL: Born December 4, 1976, in Oklahoma City. ... 5-8/143. (1.73/64.9). ... Full name: Betty Bernice Lennox
HIGH SCHOOL: Fort Osage (Independence, Mo.).
COLLEGE: Louisiana Tech.
TRANSACTIONS/CAREER NOTES: Selected by Minnesota in first round (sixth overall) of WNBA Draft, April 25, 2000. ... Traded by Minnesota with a first-round pick in the 2003 WNBA Draft to Miami for G Tamara Moore and a second-round pick, June 13, 2002. ... Selected by Seattle in WNBA Dispersal Draft, January 6, 2004.
MISCELLANEOUS: Member of WNBA Championship team (2004).

JUNIOR COLLEGE RECORD

Season Team	G	Min.	FGM	FGA	Pct.	FTM	FTA	Pct.	Reb.	Ast.	Pts.	AVERAGES RPG	APG	PPG
1996—Trinity Valley CC	35	...	261	...	...	115	...	...	...	...	820	...	...	23.4
Totals	35	...	261	...	...	115	...	...	...	...	820	...	...	23.4

COLLEGE RECORD

NOTES: AP All-American third team (2000). ... Member of NJCAA National Championship team (1997). ... NCAA Midwest Regional All-Tournament team (2000). ... NCAA West Regional All-Tournament team (1999). ... Sun Belt Conference Player of Year (2000). ... U.S. Basketball Writers Association All-American first team (2000). ... Women's Basketball News Service All-American first team (2000).

Season Team	G	Min.	FGM	FGA	Pct.	FTM	FTA	Pct.	Reb.	Ast.	Pts.	AVERAGES RPG	APG	PPG
1998—Louisiana Tech	33	...	137	335	.409	33	52	.635	136	59	333	4.1	1.8	10.1
1999—Louisiana Tech	34	...	232	526	.441	61	78	.782	199	116	587	5.9	3.4	17.3
Totals	67	...	369	861	.429	94	130	.723	335	175	920	5.0	2.6	13.7

Three-point field goals: 1998-99, 26-for-88 (.295). 1999-00, 62-for-163 (.380). Totals, 88-for-251 (.351).

WNBA REGULAR-SEASON RECORD

NOTES: All-WNBA second team (2000). ... WNBA Rookie of the Year (2000).

Season Team	G	Min.	FGM	FGA	Pct.	FTM	FTA	Pct.	REBOUNDS Off.	Def.	Tot.	Ast.	St.	Blk.	TO	Pts.	AVERAGES RPG	APG	PPG
2000—Minnesota	32	984	201	471	.427	84	105	.800	53	125	178	82	53	9	97	541	5.6	2.6	16.9
2001—Minnesota	11	241	41	110	.373	19	20	.950	13	41	54	16	10	4	25	121	4.9	1.5	11.0
2002—Minn.-Miami	31	719	120	355	.338	50	68	.735	20	69	89	63	30	5	82	341	2.9	2.0	11.0
2003—Cleveland	34	560	100	269	.372	26	36	.722	19	70	89	32	14	4	58	258	2.6	0.9	7.6
2004—Seattle	32	920	139	330	.421	58	68	.853	28	131	159	79	34	3	77	358	5.0	2.5	11.2
2005—Seattle	28	800	123	314	.392	76	87	.874	21	103	124	57	35	5	75	346	4.4	2.0	12.4
Totals	168	4224	724	1849	.392	313	384	.815	154	539	693	329	176	30	414	1965	4.1	2.0	11.7

Three-point field goals: 2000-01, 55-for-139 (.396). 2001-02, 20-for-52 (.385). 2002-03, 51-for-154 (.331). 2003-04, 32-for-103 (.311). 2004-05, 22-for-83 (.265). 2005-06, 24-for-78 (.308). Totals, 204-for-609 (.335).
Personal fouls/disqualifications: 2000-01, 112/4. 2001-02, 29/0. 2002-03, 102/3. 2003-04, 77/0. 2004-05, 89/0. 2005-06, 82/0. Totals, 491/7.

WNBA PLAYOFF RECORD

Season Team	G	Min.	FGM	FGA	Pct.	FTM	FTA	Pct.	REBOUNDS Off.	Def.	Tot.	Ast.	St.	Blk.	TO	Pts.	AVERAGES RPG	APG	PPG
2003—Cleveland	3	45	9	19	.474	1	2	.500	1	6	7	3	3	0	4	21	2.3	1.0	7.0
2004—Seattle	8	251	44	97	.454	21	24	.875	4	25	29	21	8	1	23	117	3.6	2.6	14.6
2005—Seattle	3	94	15	38	.395	13	14	.929	1	13	14	8	3	0	6	46	4.7	2.7	15.3
Totals	14	390	68	154	.442	35	40	.875	6	44	50	32	14	1	33	184	3.6	2.3	13.1

Three-point field goals: 2003-04, 2-for-5 (.400). 2004-05, 8-for-18 (.444). 2005-06, 3-for-12 (.250). Totals, 13-for-35 (.371).
Personal fouls/disqualifications: 2003-04, 7/0. 2004-05, 21/0. 2005-06, 9/0. Totals, 37/0.

WNBA ALL-STAR GAME RECORD

Season Team	Min.	FGM	FGA	Pct.	FTM	FTA	Pct.	REBOUNDS Off.	Def.	Tot.	Ast.	PF	Dq.	St.	Blk.	TO	Pts.
2000—Minnesota	13	1	3	.333	0	0	...	2	3	5	1	1	0	0	0	4	3
Totals	13	1	3	.333	0	0	...	2	3	5	1	1	0	0	0	4	3

Three-point field goals: 2001, 1-for-2 (.500). Totals, 1-for-2 (.500).

LESLIE, LISA C SPARKS

PERSONAL: Born July 7, 1972, in Gardena, Calif. ... 6-5/170. (1.96/77.1). ... Full name: Lisa DeShaun Leslie
HIGH SCHOOL: Morningside (Inglewood, Calif.).
COLLEGE: USC.
TRANSACTIONS/CAREER NOTES: Signed by WNBA and assigned to Los Angeles, January 22, 1997.
MISCELLANEOUS: Member of WNBA Championship team (2001, 2002). ... Recorded first dunk in WNBA history, July 22, 2002.

COLLEGE RECORD

NOTES: Naismith Award winner (1994). ... Kodak All-American (1994).

Season Team	G	Min.	FGM	FGA	Pct.	FTM	FTA	Pct.	Reb.	Ast.	Pts.	AVERAGES RPG	APG	PPG
1990—Southern Cal	30	...	241	504	.478	98	145	.676	299	20	582	10.0	0.7	19.4
1991—Southern Cal	31	...	262	476	.550	106	152	.697	261	46	632	8.4	1.5	20.4
1992—Southern Cal	29	...	211	378	.558	119	162	.735	285	59	543	9.8	2.0	18.7

Season Team	G	Min.	FGM	FGA	Pct.	FTM	FTA	Pct.	Reb.	Ast.	Pts.	RPG	APG	PPG
												AVERAGES		
1993—Southern Cal	30	...	259	464	.558	138	201	.687	369	83	657	12.3	2.8	21.9
Totals	120	...	973	1822	.534	461	660	.698	1214	208	2414	10.1	1.7	20.1

Three-point field goals: 1990-91, 2-for-8 (.250). 1991-92, 2-for-8 (.250). 1992-93, 2-for-8 (.250). 1993-94, 1-for-13 (.077). Totals, 7-for-37 (.189).

OLYMPICS RECORD

Season Team	G	Min.	FGM	FGA	Pct.	FTM	FTA	Pct.	Reb.	Ast.	Pts.	RPG	APG	PPG
												AVERAGES		
1996—United States....................	8	...	64	97	.660	28	44	.636	58	19	156	7.3	2.4	19.5
2000—United States....................	8	210	48	98	.490	27	39	.692	63	11	126	7.9	1.4	15.8
2004—United States....................	8	183	57	97	.588	11	15	.733	64	11	125	8.0	1.4	15.6
Totals	24	393	169	292	.579	66	98	.673	185	41	407	7.7	1.7	17.0

Three-point field goals: 1996-97, 0-for-1. 2000-01, 3-for-7 (.429). 2004-05, 0-for-2. Totals, 3-for-10 (.300).
Personal fouls/disqualifications: 2004-05, 20/0. Totals, 20/0.

WNBA REGULAR-SEASON RECORD

NOTES: WNBA MVP (2001, 2004). ... WNBA Defensive Player of the Year (2004). ... All-WNBA first team (1997, 2000, 2001, 2002, 2003, 2004). ... All-WNBA second team (1998, 1999, 2005). ... All-Defensive second team (2005). ... Led WNBA in rebounds in 1997 (9.5 rpg), 1998 (10.2 rpg) and 2004 (9.9 rpg). ... Led WNBA in blocked shots (2.88) in 2004. ... Led WNBA in double-doubles (16) in 1998. ... Bud Light Peak Performer, Rebounding (2003).

Season Team	G	Min.	FGM	FGA	Pct.	FTM	FTA	Pct.	Off.	Def.	Tot.	Ast.	St.	Blk.	TO	Pts.	RPG	APG	PPG
									REBOUNDS								**AVERAGES**		
1997—Los Angeles	28	902	160	371	.431	113	189	.598	63	203	266	74	39	59	109	445	9.5	2.6	15.9
1998—Los Angeles	28	898	202	423	.478	136	177	.768	77	208	285	70	42	60	102	549	10.2	2.5	19.6
1999—Los Angeles	32	930	182	389	.468	114	156	.731	72	176	248	56	36	49	94	500	7.8	1.8	15.6
2000—Los Angeles	32	1028	197	430	.458	169	205	.824	75	231	306	60	31	74	103	570	9.6	1.9	17.8
2001—Los Angeles	31	1033	221	467	.473	142	193	.736	88	210	298	73	34	71	98	606	9.6	2.4	19.5
2002—Los Angeles	31	1060	189	406	.466	133	183	.727	78	244	322	83	46	90	108	523	10.4	2.7	16.9
2003—Los Angeles	23	792	165	373	.442	82	133	.617	76	155	231	46	31	63	65	424	10.0	2.0	18.4
2004—Los Angeles	34	1150	223	451	.494	146	205	.712	60	276	336	88	50	98	110	598	9.9	2.6	17.6
2005—Los Angeles	34	1096	204	464	.440	102	174	.586	70	178	248	87	67	71	100	517	7.3	2.6	15.2
Totals	273	8889	1743	3774	.462	1137	1615	.704	659	1881	2540	637	376	635	889	4732	9.3	2.3	17.3

Three-point field goals: 1997-98, 12-for-46 (.261). 1998-99, 9-for-23 (.391). 1999-00, 22-for-52 (.423). 2000-01, 7-for-32 (.219). 2001-02, 22-for-60 (.367). 2002-03, 12-for-37 (.324). 2003-04, 12-for-37 (.324). 2004-05, 6-for-22 (.273). 2005-06, 7-for-34 (.206). Totals, 109-for-343 (.318).
Personal fouls/disqualifications: 1997-98, 99/1. 1998-99, 121/3. 1999-00, 136/4. 2000-01, 134/7. 2001-02, 132/3. 2002-03, 123/7. 2003-04, 93/3. 2004-05, 130/5. 2005-06, 122/2. Totals, 1090/35.

WNBA PLAYOFF RECORD

NOTES: WNBA Championship MVP (2001, 2002).

Season Team	G	Min.	FGM	FGA	Pct.	FTM	FTA	Pct.	Off.	Def.	Tot.	Ast.	St.	Blk.	TO	Pts.	RPG	APG	PPG
									REBOUNDS								**AVERAGES**		
1999—Los Angeles	4	145	29	60	.483	14	18	.778	6	28	34	11	4	6	14	76	8.5	2.8	19.0
2000—Los Angeles	4	139	28	57	.491	19	23	.826	10	31	41	8	1	5	13	75	10.3	2.0	18.8
2001—Los Angeles	7	260	58	118	.492	37	50	.740	28	58	86	21	12	31	26	156	12.3	3.0	22.3
2002—Los Angeles	6	232	46	86	.535	19	26	.731	10	37	47	11	11	17	8	116	7.8	1.8	19.3
2003—Los Angeles	9	327	74	137	.540	38	54	.704	22	58	80	23	12	28	24	187	8.9	2.6	20.8
2004—Los Angeles	3	110	14	31	.452	6	8	.750	4	22	26	2	1	8	8	34	8.7	0.7	11.3
2005—Los Angeles	2	67	5	14	.357	8	13	.615	4	9	13	7	5	3	2	18	6.5	3.5	9.0
Totals	35	1280	254	503	.505	141	192	.734	84	243	327	83	46	98	95	662	9.3	2.4	18.9

Three-point field goals: 1999-00, 4-for-13 (.308). 2000-01, 0-for-3. 2001-02, 3-for-7 (.429). 2002-03, 5-for-8 (.625). 2003-04, 1-for-3 (.333). Totals, 13-for-34 (.382).
Personal fouls/disqualifications: 1999-00, 12/0. 2000-01, 14/0. 2001-02, 22/0. 2002-03, 22/0. 2003-04, 39/1. 2004-05, 10/0. 2005-06, 8/0. Totals, 127/1.

WNBA ALL-STAR GAME RECORD

NOTES: WNBA All-Star MVP (1999, 2001, 2002).

Season Team	Min.	FGM	FGA	Pct.	FTM	FTA	Pct.	Off.	Def.	Tot.	Ast.	PF	Dq.	St.	Blk.	TO	Pts.
								REBOUNDS									
1999—Los Angeles............	17	5	11	.455	3	4	.750	3	2	5	1	2	0	1	1	0	13
2000—Los Angeles............	21	8	15	.533	0	0	...	4	2	6	0	0	0	0	1	0	16
2001—Los Angeles............	23	8	14	.571	3	4	.750	3	6	9	1	4	0	1	3	3	20
2002—Los Angeles............	28	6	13	.462	6	10	.600	3	11	14	0	2	0	1	4	4	18
2003—Los Angeles............	16	7	10	.700	2	2	1.000	1	2	3	0	2	0	1	0	2	17
2005—Los Angeles............	20	2	8	.250	5	7	.714	1	3	4	1	2	0	0	0	1	9
Totals	125	36	71	.507	19	27	.704	15	26	41	3	12	0	4	9	10	93

Three-point field goals: 2000, 0-for-1. 2002, 1-for-2 (.500). 2003, 0-for-1. 2004, 1-for-2 (.500). 2006, 0-for-1. Totals, 2-for-7 (.286).

LEWIS, TYNESHA   G/F   LYNX

PERSONAL: Born May 8, 1979, in Macclesfield, N.C. ... 5-10/150. (1.78/68.0). ... Full name: Tynesha Rashaun Lewis.
HIGH SCHOOL: Southwest Edgecomb (Pinetops, N.C.).
COLLEGE: North Carolina State.
TRANSACTIONS/CAREER NOTES: Selected by Houston in second round (31st overall) of WNBA Draft, April 20, 2001.

COLLEGE RECORD

Season Team	G	Min.	FGM	FGA	Pct.	FTM	FTA	Pct.	Reb.	Ast.	Pts.	RPG	APG	PPG
												AVERAGES		
1997—North Carolina State	32	860	146	321	.455	60	91	.659	128	80	376	4.0	2.5	11.8

Season Team	G	Min.	FGM	FGA	Pct.	FTM	FTA	Pct.	Reb.	Ast.	Pts.	RPG	APG	PPG
												AVERAGES		
1998—North Carolina State	29	954	176	408	.431	84	118	.712	197	92	480	6.8	3.2	16.6
1999—North Carolina State	29	932	117	324	.361	42	70	.600	147	71	318	5.1	2.4	11.0
2000—North Carolina State	33	1105	164	422	.389	87	117	.744	180	102	447	5.5	3.1	13.5
Totals	123	3851	603	1475	.409	273	396	.689	652	345	1621	5.3	2.8	13.2

Three-point field goals: 1997-98, 24-for-75 (.320). 1998-99, 44-for-145 (.303). 1999-00, 42-for-133 (.316). 2000-01, 32-for-109 (.294). Totals, 142-for-462 (.307).

WNBA REGULAR-SEASON RECORD

Season Team	G	Min.	FGM	FGA	Pct.	FTM	FTA	Pct.	Off.	Def.	Tot.	Ast.	St.	Blk.	TO	Pts.	RPG	APG	PPG
									REBOUNDS								**AVERAGES**		
2001—Houston	29	419	39	92	.424	11	17	.647	21	41	62	15	11	4	26	97	2.1	0.5	3.3
2002—Houston	17	145	13	30	.433	5	8	.625	6	12	18	9	3	3	9	34	1.1	0.5	2.0
2003—Charlotte	23	234	26	62	.419	11	12	.917	11	22	33	20	10	6	16	70	1.4	0.9	3.0
2004—Charlotte	34	617	91	210	.433	44	58	.759	23	34	57	44	27	7	44	246	1.7	1.3	7.2
2005—Charlotte.-Minn.	21	256	29	88	.330	15	25	.600	10	15	25	20	6	4	22	75	1.2	1.0	3.6
Totals	124	1671	198	482	.411	86	120	.717	71	124	195	108	57	24	117	522	1.6	0.9	4.2

Three-point field goals: 2001-02, 8-for-20 (.400). 2002-03, 3-for-8 (.375). 2003-04, 7-for-13 (.538). 2004-05, 20-for-50 (.400). 2005-06, 2-for-15 (.133). Totals, 40-for-106 (.377).
Personal fouls/disqualifications: 2001-02, 26/0. 2002-03, 18/0. 2003-04, 18/0. 2004-05, 47/1. 2005-06, 14/0. Totals, 123/1.

WNBA PLAYOFF RECORD

Season Team	G	Min.	FGM	FGA	Pct.	FTM	FTA	Pct.	Off.	Def.	Tot.	Ast.	St.	Blk.	TO	Pts.	RPG	APG	PPG
									REBOUNDS								**AVERAGES**		
2001—Houston	2	6	0	1	.000	0	0	...	0	0	0	2	0	0	0	0	0.0	1.0	0.0
2003—Charlotte	2	29	4	8	.500	5	6	.833	2	1	3	4	0	1	0	14	1.5	2.0	7.0
Totals	4	35	4	9	.444	5	6	.833	2	1	3	6	0	1	0	14	0.8	1.5	3.5

Three-point field goals: 2003-04, 1-for-1 (1.000). Totals, 1-for-1 (1.000).
Personal fouls/disqualifications: 2001-02, 1/0. 2003-04, 2/0. Totals, 3/0.

L

LI JIE, MIAO G MONARCHS

PERSONAL: Born June 6, 1981, in China. ... 5-11. (1.80).
MISCELLANEOUS: Member of WNBA Championship team (2005).

WNBA REGULAR-SEASON RECORD

Season Team	G	Min.	FGM	FGA	Pct.	FTM	FTA	Pct.	Off.	Def.	Tot.	Ast.	St.	Blk.	TO	Pts.	RPG	APG	PPG
									REBOUNDS								**AVERAGES**		
2005—Sacramento	18	135	9	30	.300	7	7	1.000	0	4	4	13	5	1	15	31	0.2	0.7	1.7
Totals	18	135	9	30	.300	7	7	1.000	0	4	4	13	5	1	15	31	0.2	0.7	1.7

Three-point field goals: 2005-06, 6-for-20 (.300). Totals, 6-for-20 (.300).
Personal fouls/disqualifications: 2005-06, 13/0. Totals, 13/0.

LOVELACE, STACEY F SKY

PERSONAL: Born December 5, 1974, in Detroit. ... 6-4/170. (1.93/77.1).
HIGH SCHOOL: St. Martin De Porres (Detroit).
COLLEGE: Purdue.
TRANSACTIONS/CAREER NOTES: Signed by the WNBA and assigned to Indiana, May 2, 2000. ... Waived by Indiana, May 24, 2000. ... Added by Seattle, June 8, 2000. ... Selected by Chicago in WNBA Expansion Draft, November 16, 2005.

COLLEGE RECORD

NOTES: Holds Purdue records for rebounds (876), blocked shots (220) double-doubles (27). ... Kodak All-American (1995). ... Big Ten Player of Year (1995). ... Big Ten Most Valuable Player (1995). ... WBCA College All-Star (1996). ... Ranks in top five on Purdue's all-time list in points, steals and scoring average. ... Ranks third on Big Ten career blocks list (220). ... Second in school history in rebounds per game and games played.

Season Team	G	Min.	FGM	FGA	Pct.	FTM	FTA	Pct.	Reb.	Ast.	Pts.	RPG	APG	PPG
												AVERAGES		
1992—Purdue	24	...	...	...	...	...	...	...	101	13	221	4.2	0.5	9.2
1993—Purdue	34	...	...	...	...	...	...	...	253	37	388	7.4	1.1	11.4
1994—Purdue	32	...	...	...	...	...	...	...	258	43	453	8.1	1.3	14.2
1995—Purdue	30	...	...	...	...	...	...	...	264	49	465	8.8	1.6	15.5
Totals	120	...	...	...	...	...	...	...	876	142	1527	7.3	1.2	12.7

ABL RECORD

NOTES: Played for ABL's Atlanta Glory from 1996-98 and ABL's New England Blizzard during 1998-99 season.

Season Team	G	Min.	FGM	FGA	Pct.	FTM	FTA	Pct.	Reb.	Ast.	Pts.	RPG	APG	PPG
												AVERAGES		
1996—Atlanta	39	...	196	368	.533	108	146	.740	237	35	503	6.1	0.9	12.9
1997—Atlanta	44	...	214	464	.461	186	231	.805	235	47	616	5.3	1.1	14.0
1998—New England	12	...	47	103	.456	28	39	.718	59	24	123	4.9	2.0	10.3
Totals	95	...	457	935	.489	322	416	.774	531	106	1242	5.6	1.1	13.1

Three-point field goals: 1996-97, 3-for-11 (.273). 1997-98, 2-for-14 (.143). 1998-99, 1-for-10 (.100). Totals, 6-for-35 (.171).

WNBA REGULAR-SEASON RECORD

Season Team	G	Min.	FGM	FGA	Pct.	FTM	FTA	Pct.	Off.	Def.	Tot.	Ast.	St.	Blk.	TO	Pts.	RPG	APG	PPG
2000—Indiana-Seattle...	23	324	36	103	.350	25	31	.806	19	38	57	16	13	2	35	99	2.5	0.7	4.3
2001—Seattle	22	211	27	71	.380	12	17	.706	14	18	32	9	8	5	18	76	1.5	0.4	3.5
2004—Minnesota	34	388	49	122	.402	20	24	.833	25	41	66	20	18	9	45	121	1.9	0.6	3.6
2005—Minnesota	34	594	70	173	.405	43	54	.796	35	72	107	31	24	11	37	209	3.1	0.9	6.1
Totals	113	1517	182	469	.388	100	126	.794	93	169	262	76	63	27	135	505	2.3	0.7	4.5

Three-point field goals: 2000-01, 2-for-9 (.222). 2001-02, 10-for-26 (.385). 2004-05, 3-for-17 (.176). 2005-06, 26-for-63 (.413). Totals, 41-for-115 (.357).
Personal fouls/disqualifications: 2000-01, 42/0. 2001-02, 23/0. 2004-05, 47/0. 2005-06, 57/0. Totals, 169/0.

WNBA PLAYOFF RECORD

Season Team	G	Min.	FGM	FGA	Pct.	FTM	FTA	Pct.	Off.	Def.	Tot.	Ast.	St.	Blk.	TO	Pts.	RPG	APG	PPG
2004—Minnesota	2	17	2	4	.500	2	4	.500	1	2	3	1	0	1	1	6	1.5	0.5	3.0
Totals	2	17	2	4	.500	2	4	.500	1	2	3	1	0	1	1	6	1.5	0.5	3.0

Three-point field goals: 2004-05, 0-for-1. Totals, 0-for-1 (.000).

LYTTLE, SANCHO   C   COMETS

PERSONAL: Born September 20, 1983, in St. Vincent, British West Indies. ... 6-4/175. (1.93/79.4). ... Full name: Sancho Tracy Lyttle
HIGH SCHOOL: St.Vincent Girls (St. Vincent, British West Indies).
JUNIOR COLLEGE: Clarendon.
COLLEGE: Houston.
TRANSACTIONS/CAREER NOTES: Selected by Houston in the first round (fifth overall) of the WNBA Draft, April 16, 2005.

COLLEGE RECORD

NOTES: AP All-American honorable mention (2005). ... All-Conference USA first team (2005). ... All-Conference USA second team (2004). ... All-Conference USA Tournament team (2005).

Season Team	G	Min.	FGM	FGA	Pct.	FTM	FTA	Pct.	Reb.	Ast.	Pts.	RPG	APG	PPG
2003—Houston.............................	32	948	227	432	.525	73	134	.545	299	35	527	9.3	1.1	16.5
2004—Houston.............................	30	1002	233	484	.481	99	144	.688	362	44	565	12.1	1.5	18.8
Totals	62	1950	460	916	.502	172	278	.619	661	79	1092	10.7	1.3	17.6

WNBA REGULAR-SEASON RECORD

Season Team	G	Min.	FGM	FGA	Pct.	FTM	FTA	Pct.	Off.	Def.	Tot.	Ast.	St.	Blk.	TO	Pts.	RPG	APG	PPG
2005—Houston	33	460	59	101	.584	22	40	.550	35	90	125	17	20	3	23	140	3.8	0.5	4.2
Totals	33	460	59	101	.584	22	40	.550	35	90	125	17	20	3	23	140	3.8	0.5	4.2

Personal fouls/disqualifications: 2005-06, 45/0. Totals, 45/0.

WNBA PLAYOFF RECORD

Season Team	G	Min.	FGM	FGA	Pct.	FTM	FTA	Pct.	Off.	Def.	Tot.	Ast.	St.	Blk.	TO	Pts.	RPG	APG	PPG
2005—Houston	5	34	3	5	.600	4	6	.667	2	10	12	0	2	0	0	10	2.4	0.0	2.0
Totals	5	34	3	5	.600	4	6	.667	2	10	12	0	2	0	0	10	2.4	0.0	2.0

Personal fouls/disqualifications: 2005-06, 5/0. Totals, 5/0.

MABIKA, MWADI   F   SPARKS

PERSONAL: Born July 27, 1976, in Kinshasa, Congo. ... 5-11/165. (1.80/74.8).
HIGH SCHOOL: Institute of Lemba (Kinshasa, Congo).
TRANSACTIONS/CAREER NOTES: Signed by WNBA and assigned to Los Angeles, May 22, 1997.
MISCELLANEOUS: Member of WNBA Championship team (2001, 2002).

OLYMPICS RECORD

Season Team	G	Min.	FGM	FGA	Pct.	FTM	FTA	Pct.	Reb.	Ast.	Pts.	RPG	APG	PPG
1996—Zaire	7	...	51	146	.349	9	15	.600	22	13	121	3.1	1.9	17.3
Totals	7	...	51	146	.349	9	15	.600	22	13	121	3.1	1.9	17.3

Three-point field goals: 1996-97, 10-for-29 (.345). Totals, 10-for-29 (.345).

NOTES: All-WNBA first team (2002).

WNBA REGULAR-SEASON RECORD

Season Team	G	Min.	FGM	FGA	Pct.	FTM	FTA	Pct.	Off.	Def.	Tot.	Ast.	St.	Blk.	TO	Pts.	RPG	APG	PPG
1997—Los Angeles......	21	325	53	136	.390	13	24	.542	22	32	54	22	23	6	27	126	2.6	1.0	6.0
1998—Los Angeles......	29	710	87	257	.339	30	43	.698	29	98	127	44	30	9	37	237	4.4	1.5	8.2
1999—Los Angeles......	32	938	125	336	.372	56	78	.718	42	111	153	112	44	15	58	347	4.8	3.5	10.8
2000—Los Angeles......	32	940	130	335	.388	73	89	.820	45	134	179	98	58	18	51	394	5.6	3.1	12.3
2001—Los Angeles......	28	828	99	256	.387	68	79	.861	22	108	130	87	39	11	44	313	4.6	3.1	11.2
2002—Los Angeles......	32	1050	188	444	.423	99	118	.839	32	135	167	92	38	9	62	539	5.2	2.9	16.8

Season Team	G	Min.	FGM	FGA	Pct.	FTM	FTA	Pct.	REBOUNDS Off.	Def.	Tot.	Ast.	St.	Blk.	TO	Pts.	AVERAGES RPG	APG	PPG
2003—Los Angeles	32	1042	158	388	.407	97	112	.866	34	107	141	82	30	18	74	441	4.4	2.6	13.8
2004—Los Angeles	31	965	159	383	.415	89	108	.824	39	83	122	75	36	3	48	445	3.9	2.4	14.4
2005—Los Angeles	17	367	39	122	.320	10	20	.500	8	19	27	29	15	0	14	99	1.6	1.7	5.8
Totals	254	7165	1038	2657	.391	535	671	.797	273	827	1100	641	313	89	415	2941	4.3	2.5	11.6

Three-point field goals: 1997-98, 7-for-38 (.184). 1998-99, 33-for-107 (.308). 1999-00, 41-for-146 (.281). 2000-01, 61-for-159 (.384). 2001-02, 47-for-123 (.382). 2002-03, 64-for-175 (.366). 2003-04, 28-for-106 (.264). 2004-05, 38-for-94 (.404). 2005-06, 11-for-49 (.224). Totals, 330-for-997 (.331).

Personal fouls/disqualifications: 1997-98, 48/0. 1998-99, 73/0. 1999-00, 100/1. 2000-01, 117/2. 2001-02, 74/0. 2002-03, 90/1. 2003-04, 105/3. 2004-05, 88/0. 2005-06, 43/0. Totals, 738/7.

WNBA PLAYOFF RECORD

Season Team	G	Min.	FGM	FGA	Pct.	FTM	FTA	Pct.	REBOUNDS Off.	Def.	Tot.	Ast.	St.	Blk.	TO	Pts.	AVERAGES RPG	APG	PPG
1999—Los Angeles	4	127	17	45	.378	0	1	.000	7	11	18	11	13	1	10	37	4.5	2.8	9.3
2000—Los Angeles	4	136	25	46	.543	3	4	.750	6	15	21	4	6	4	5	70	5.3	1.0	17.5
2001—Los Angeles	7	231	21	66	.318	11	14	.786	6	40	46	17	7	6	10	63	6.6	2.4	9.0
2002—Los Angeles	6	212	31	82	.378	18	26	.692	11	30	41	25	8	1	10	88	6.8	4.2	14.7
2003—Los Angeles	9	344	53	121	.438	11	13	.846	10	40	50	21	14	2	20	129	5.6	2.3	14.3
2004—Los Angeles	3	107	17	46	.370	15	16	.938	3	5	8	10	7	0	6	56	2.7	3.3	18.7
2005—Los Angeles	1	11	1	4	.250	0	0	...	0	0	0	0	0	0	2	2	0.0	0.0	2.0
Totals	34	1168	165	410	.402	58	74	.784	43	141	184	88	55	14	63	445	5.4	2.6	13.1

Three-point field goals: 1999-00, 3-for-17 (.176). 2000-01, 17-for-32 (.531). 2001-02, 10-for-40 (.250). 2002-03, 8-for-25 (.320). 2003-04, 12-for-34 (.353). 2004-05, 7-for-20 (.350). 2005-06, 0-for-2. Totals, 57-for-170 (.335).

Personal fouls/disqualifications: 1999-00, 22/2. 2000-01, 14/0. 2001-02, 21/0. 2002-03, 19/0. 2003-04, 29/0. 2004-05, 10/0. Totals, 115/2.

WNBA ALL-STAR GAME RECORD

Season Team	Min.	FGM	FGA	Pct.	FTM	FTA	Pct.	REBOUNDS Off.	Def.	Tot.	Ast.	PF	Dq.	St.	Blk.	TO	Pts.
2000—Los Angeles	16	3	7	.429	2	2	1.000	0	1	1	2	1	0	1	0	1	10
2002—Los Angeles	16	1	5	.200	0	0	...	1	5	6	1	1	0	0	0	1	2
Totals	32	4	12	.333	2	2	1.000	1	6	7	3	2	0	1	0	2	12

Three-point field goals: 2001, 2-for-3 (.667). 2003, 0-for-3. Totals, 2-for-6 (.333).

MACCHI, LAURA   F   SKY

PERSONAL: Born May 24, 1979 ... 6-1. (1.85).
TRANSACTIONS/CAREER NOTES: Selected by Chicago in WNBA Expansion Draft, November 16, 2005.

WNBA REGULAR-SEASON RECORD

Season Team	G	Min.	FGM	FGA	Pct.	FTM	FTA	Pct.	REBOUNDS Off.	Def.	Tot.	Ast.	St.	Blk.	TO	Pts.	AVERAGES RPG	APG	PPG
2004—Los Angeles	25	410	52	106	.491	41	55	.745	23	38	61	14	21	6	29	152	2.4	0.6	6.1
2005—Los Angeles	13	148	21	53	.396	12	17	.706	6	12	18	7	8	1	13	63	1.4	0.5	4.8
Totals	38	558	73	159	.459	53	72	.736	29	50	79	21	29	7	42	215	2.1	0.6	5.7

Three-point field goals: 2004-05, 7-for-26 (.269). 2005-06, 9-for-28 (.321). Totals, 16-for-54 (.296).
Personal fouls/disqualifications: 2004-05, 56/0. 2005-06, 23/0. Totals, 79/0.

WNBA PLAYOFF RECORD

Season Team	G	Min.	FGM	FGA	Pct.	FTM	FTA	Pct.	REBOUNDS Off.	Def.	Tot.	Ast.	St.	Blk.	TO	Pts.	AVERAGES RPG	APG	PPG
2004—Los Angeles	1	15	1	6	.167	0	0	...	1	3	4	1	1	0	3	2	4.0	1.0	2.0
2005—Los Angeles	2	9	2	4	.500	2	2	1.000	0	0	0	0	0	0	0	7	0.0	0.0	3.5
Totals	3	24	3	10	.300	2	2	1.000	1	3	4	1	1	0	3	9	1.3	0.3	3.0

Three-point field goals: 2004-05, 0-for-1. 2005-06, 1-for-1 (1.000). Totals, 1-for-2 (.500).
Personal fouls/disqualifications: 2004-05, 4/0. 2005-06, 1/0. Totals, 5/0.

MAIGA-BI, HAMCHETOU   G   MONARCHS

PERSONAL: Born April 25, 1978, in Bamako, Mali. ... 6-1/160. (1.85/72.6).
COLLEGE: Old Dominion.
TRANSACTIONS/CAREER NOTES: Selected by Sacramento in first round (12th overall) of WNBA Draft, April 19, 2002.
MISCELLANEOUS: Member of Mali National Team since 1994. ... Averaged 18 points, 10 rebounds, eight assists and three steals for Senegales champion Dakar Club in 1997-98. ... Named MVP of club play in Northwestern Africa and Senegal in 1998. ... Member of WNBA Championship team (2005).

COLLEGE RECORD

Season Team	G	Min.	FGM	FGA	Pct.	FTM	FTA	Pct.	Reb.	Ast.	Pts.	AVERAGES RPG	APG	PPG
1998—Old Dominion	32	...	81	158	.513	36	76	.474	130	...	199	4.1	...	6.2
1999—Old Dominion	34	...	201	336	.598	75	128	.586	256	...	477	7.5	...	14.0
2000—Old Dominion	30	...	168	293	.573	48	97	.495	223	...	410	7.4	...	13.7
2001—Old Dominion	34	939	174	305	.570	48	97	.495	276	117	397	8.1	3.4	11.7
Totals	130	939	624	1092	.571	207	398	.520	885	117	1483	6.8	0.9	11.4

Three-point field goals: 1998-99, 1-for-6 (.167). 2001-02, 1-for-3 (.333). Totals, 2-for-9 (.222).

Season Team	G	Min.	FGM	FGA	Pct.	FTM	FTA	Pct.	REBOUNDS Off.	Def.	Tot.	Ast.	St.	Blk.	TO	Pts.	AVERAGES RPG	APG	PPG
2002—Sacramento	23	197	13	53	.245	14	30	.467	18	19	37	9	15	3	23	40	1.6	0.4	1.7
2003—Sacramento	22	190	17	52	.327	8	20	.400	13	24	37	14	18	2	14	42	1.7	0.6	1.9
2004—Sacramento	34	480	62	132	.470	16	29	.552	35	36	71	25	29	6	49	140	2.1	0.7	4.1
2005—Sacramento	34	408	59	131	.450	11	35	.314	31	36	67	30	24	6	42	129	2.0	0.9	3.8
Totals	113	1275	151	368	.410	49	114	.430	97	115	212	78	86	17	128	351	1.9	0.7	3.1

Personal fouls/disqualifications: 2002-03, 37/0. 2003-04, 27/0. 2004-05, 63/0. 2005-06, 69/0. Totals, 196/0.

WNBA PLAYOFF RECORD

Season Team	G	Min.	FGM	FGA	Pct.	FTM	FTA	Pct.	REBOUNDS Off.	Def.	Tot.	Ast.	St.	Blk.	TO	Pts.	AVERAGES RPG	APG	PPG
2003—Sacramento	4	15	1	3	.333	0	0	...	1	2	3	2	0	0	5	2	0.8	0.5	0.5
2004—Sacramento	6	68	2	13	.154	1	4	.250	3	3	6	4	7	0	7	5	1.0	0.7	0.8
2005—Sacramento	8	82	13	26	.500	4	6	.667	5	8	13	4	5	3	8	30	1.6	0.5	3.8
Totals	18	165	16	42	.381	5	10	.500	9	13	22	10	12	3	20	37	1.2	0.6	2.1

Three-point field goals: 2004-05, 0-for-1. Totals, 0-for-1 (.000).
Personal fouls/disqualifications: 2003-04, 4/0. 2004-05, 11/0. 2005-06, 16/1. Totals, 31/1.

MANN, KRISTEN   F   LYNX

PERSONAL: Born August 10, 1983, in Lakewood, Calif. ... 6-2/180. (1.88/81.6). ... Full name: Kristen Cherie Mann
HIGH SCHOOL: Foothill (Santa Ana, Calif.).
COLLEGE: UC-Santa Barbara.
TRANSACTIONS/CAREER NOTES: Selected by Minnesota in the first round (11th overall) of the WNBA Draft, April 16, 2005.

COLLEGE RECORD

NOTES: AP All-American honorable mention (2005). ... Big West Player of the Year (2005). ... All-Big West first team (2003, 2004, 2005). ... All-Big West honorable mention (2002). ... Big West freshman of the year (2002).

Season Team	G	Min.	FGM	FGA	Pct.	FTM	FTA	Pct.	Reb.	Ast.	Pts.	AVERAGES RPG	APG	PPG
2001—UC-Santa Barbara	32	804	153	356	.430	73	101	.723	209	58	401	6.5	1.8	12.5
2002—UC-Santa Barbara	20	583	110	250	.440	46	63	.730	129	37	284	6.5	1.9	14.2
2003—UC-Santa Barbara	33	994	188	409	.460	41	63	.651	218	81	450	6.6	2.5	13.6
2004—UC-Santa Barbara	29	965	219	498	.440	95	139	.683	274	68	565	9.4	2.3	19.5
Totals	114	3346	670	1513	.443	255	366	.697	830	244	1700	7.3	2.1	14.9

WNBA REGULAR-SEASON RECORD

Season Team	G	Min.	FGM	FGA	Pct.	FTM	FTA	Pct.	REBOUNDS Off.	Def.	Tot.	Ast.	St.	Blk.	TO	Pts.	AVERAGES RPG	APG	PPG
2005—Minnesota	24	185	30	60	.500	11	16	.688	11	24	35	11	8	1	7	71	1.5	0.5	3.0
Totals	24	185	30	60	.500	11	16	.688	11	24	35	11	8	1	7	71	1.5	0.5	3.0

Three-point field goals: 2005-06, 0-for-9. Totals, 0-for-9 (.000).
Personal fouls/disqualifications: 2005-06, 16/0. Totals, 16/0.

MARTINEZ, NURIA   G   LYNX

PERSONAL: Born February 29, 1984 ... 5-9/145. (1.75/65.8).

OLYMPICS RECORD

Season Team	G	Min.	FGM	FGA	Pct.	FTM	FTA	Pct.	Reb.	Ast.	Pts.	AVERAGES RPG	APG	PPG
2004—Spain	7	95	8	22	.364	11	16	.688	10	6	31	1.4	0.9	4.4
Totals	7	95	8	22	.364	11	16	.688	10	6	31	1.4	0.9	4.4

Three-point field goals: 2004-05, 4-for-6 (.667). Totals, 4-for-6 (.667).
Personal fouls/disqualifications: 2004-05, 11/0. Totals, 11/0.

WNBA REGULAR-SEASON RECORD

Season Team	G	Min.	FGM	FGA	Pct.	FTM	FTA	Pct.	REBOUNDS Off.	Def.	Tot.	Ast.	St.	Blk.	TO	Pts.	AVERAGES RPG	APG	PPG
2005—Minnesota	1	2	0	1	.000	0	0	...	0	0	0	0	0	0	0	0	0.0	0.0	0.0
Totals	1	2	0	1	.000	0	0	...	0	0	0	0	0	0	0	0	0.0	0.0	0.0

Three-point field goals: 2005-06, 0-for-1. Totals, 0-for-1 (.000).

MASCIADRI, RAFFAELLA   F   SPARKS

PERSONAL: Born September 30, 1980 ... 6-0/169. (1.83/76.7).

M

WNBA REGULAR-SEASON RECORD

								REBOUNDS								AVERAGES		
Season Team	G	Min.	FGM	FGA	Pct.	FTM	FTA	Pct.	Off.	Def.	Tot.	Ast.	St.	Blk.	TO	Pts.	RPG	APG	PPG
2004—Los Angeles	17	116	10	25	.400	4	10	.400	1	4	5	8	1	0	5	28	0.3	0.5	1.6
2005—Los Angeles	33	463	44	104	.423	15	20	.750	20	27	47	23	15	1	21	122	1.4	0.7	3.7
Totals	50	579	54	129	.419	19	30	.633	21	31	52	31	16	1	26	150	1.0	0.6	3.0

Three-point field goals: 2004-05, 4-for-11 (.364). 2005-06, 19-for-46 (.413). Totals, 23-for-57 (.404).
Personal fouls/disqualifications: 2004-05, 23/0. 2005-06, 51/0. Totals, 74/0.

WNBA PLAYOFF RECORD

								REBOUNDS								AVERAGES		
Season Team	G	Min.	FGM	FGA	Pct.	FTM	FTA	Pct.	Off.	Def.	Tot.	Ast.	St.	Blk.	TO	Pts.	RPG	APG	PPG
2004—Los Angeles	1	2	0	0	...	0	0	...	0	0	0	0	0	0	0	0	0.0	0.0	0.0
2005—Los Angeles	2	47	8	17	.471	4	4	1.000	2	1	3	4	1	0	1	24	1.5	2.0	12.0
Totals	3	49	8	17	.471	4	4	1.000	2	1	3	4	1	0	1	24	1.0	1.3	8.0

Three-point field goals: 2005-06, 4-for-10 (.400). Totals, 4-for-10 (.400).
Personal fouls/disqualifications: 2004-05, 1/0. 2005-06, 6/0. Totals, 7/0.

MATTER, CAITY G STING

PERSONAL: Born August 22, 1982, in Bluffton, Ohio. ... 5-9/167. (1.75/75.7). ... Full name: Caitlyn Brooke Matter
HIGH SCHOOL: Bluffton (Bluffton, Ohio).
COLLEGE: Ohio State.
TRANSACTIONS/CAREER NOTES: Signed by Charlotte, April 2005.
MISCELLANEOUS: Medical redshirt during 2001-02 season.

COLLEGE RECORD

NOTES: AP All-American honorable mention (2005). ... All-Big Ten second team (2003, 2004, 2005). ... All-Big Ten Tournament team (2003). ... All-Big Ten Academic team (2003, 2004). ... Recipient of Edward S. Steitz Award, presented to the best three-point shooter in the country (2003).

											AVERAGES		
Season Team	G	Min.	FGM	FGA	Pct.	FTM	FTA	Pct.	Reb.	Ast.	Pts.	RPG	APG	PPG
2000—Ohio State	17	318	34	77	.442	22	25	.880	37	28	108	2.2	1.6	6.4
2002—Ohio State	32	993	169	348	.486	48	52	.923	114	45	492	3.6	1.4	15.4
2003—Ohio State	31	1001	157	256	.613	71	92	.772	117	61	458	3.8	2.0	14.8
2004—Ohio State	35	992	160	318	.503	72	80	.900	104	78	465	3.0	2.2	13.3
Totals	115	3304	520	999	.521	213	249	.855	372	212	1523	3.2	1.8	13.2

Three-point field goals: 2000-01, 18-for-49 (.367). 2002-03, 106-for-235 (.451). 2003-04, 72-for-209 (.344). 2004-05, 73-for-164 (.445). Totals, 269-for-657 (.409).

WNBA REGULAR-SEASON RECORD

								REBOUNDS								AVERAGES		
Season Team	G	Min.	FGM	FGA	Pct.	FTM	FTA	Pct.	Off.	Def.	Tot.	Ast.	St.	Blk.	TO	Pts.	RPG	APG	PPG
2005—Charlotte	10	56	3	13	.231	2	2	1.000	0	3	3	6	1	0	2	9	0.3	0.6	0.9
Totals	10	56	3	13	.231	2	2	1.000	0	3	3	6	1	0	2	9	0.3	0.6	0.9

Three-point field goals: 2005-06, 1-for-7 (.143). Totals, 1-for-7 (.143).
Personal fouls/disqualifications: 2005-06, 4/0. Totals, 4/0.

MAZZANTE, KELLY G STING

PERSONAL: Born February 2, 1982, in Williamsport, Pa. ... 6-0/155. (1.83/70.3). ... Full name: Kelly Anne Mazzante
HIGH SCHOOL: Montoursville (Montoursville, Pa.).
COLLEGE: Penn State.
TRANSACTIONS/CAREER NOTES: Selected by Charlotte in second round (18th overall) of WNBA Draft, April 17, 2004.
MISCELLANEOUS: Member of gold medal-winning 2002 USA World Championship for Young Women qualifying eam.

COLLEGE RECORD

NOTES: AP All-American first team (2003, 2004). ... Kodak All-American team (2002, 2003, 2004). ... USBWA All-American team (2002, 2003, 2004). ... AP All-American second team (2002). ... CoSIDA Academic All-American of the Year (2004). ... Big Ten Player of the Year (2003, 2004). ... All-Big Ten first team (2001, 2002, 2003, 2004). ... Big Ten Freshman of the Year (2001). ... Big Ten All-Freshman team (2001). ... Academic All-American first team (2004). ... Academic All-American second team (2002). ... Academic All-American third team (2001). ... All-Big Ten Tournament team (2002, 2004). ... Ranks ninth all-time in career points in NCAA Division I (2,919). ... Big Ten and Penn State's all-time leading scorer. ... Holds Penn State's single-season scoring record (872 in 2002).

											AVERAGES		
Season Team	G	Min.	FGM	FGA	Pct.	FTM	FTA	Pct.	Reb.	Ast.	Pts.	RPG	APG	PPG
2000—Penn State	29	881	203	434	.468	58	76	.763	123	47	529	4.2	1.6	18.2
2001—Penn State	35	1205	313	716	.437	144	177	.814	138	59	872	3.9	1.7	24.9
2002—Penn State	35	1262	292	647	.451	155	184	.842	161	76	837	4.6	2.2	23.9
2003—Penn State	34	1181	243	606	.401	103	125	.824	141	55	681	4.1	1.6	20.0
Totals	133	4529	1051	2403	.437	460	562	.819	563	237	2919	4.2	1.8	21.9

Three-point field goals: 2000-01, 65-for-176 (.369). 2001-02, 102-for-278 (.367). 2002-03, 98-for-284 (.345). 2003-04, 92-for-281 (.327). Totals, 357-for-1019 (.350).

Season Team	G	Min.	FGM	FGA	Pct.	FTM	FTA	Pct.	REBOUNDS Off.	Def.	Tot.	Ast.	St.	Blk.	TO	Pts.	AVERAGES RPG	APG	PPG
2004—Charlotte	34	339	31	92	.337	4	6	.667	9	24	33	9	7	2	20	79	1.0	0.3	2.3
2005—Charlotte	27	226	21	72	.292	8	10	.800	14	17	31	7	9	0	7	64	1.1	0.3	2.4
Totals	61	565	52	164	.317	12	16	.750	23	41	64	16	16	2	27	143	1.0	0.3	2.3

Three-point field goals: 2004-05, 13-for-52 (.250). 2005-06, 14-for-46 (.304). Totals, 27-for-98 (.276).
Personal fouls/disqualifications: 2004-05, 22/0. 2005-06, 9/0. Totals, 31/0.

MCCARVILLE, JANEL   C   STING

PERSONAL: Born November 3, 1982, in Stevens Point, Wis. ... 6-2/220. (1.88/99.8).
HIGH SCHOOL: Stevens Point Area (Stevens Point, Wis.).
COLLEGE: Minnesota.
TRANSACTIONS/CAREER NOTES: Selected by Charlotte in first round (first overall) of WNBA Draft, April 16, 2005.

COLLEGE RECORD

NOTES: AP All-American second team (2005). ... Kodak All-American (2005). ... USBWA All-American (2005). ... AP All-American honorable mention (2004). ... All-Big Ten first team (2003, 2004, 2005). ... Final Four All-Tournament team (2004). ... Big Ten All-Tournament team (2004).

Season Team	G	Min.	FGM	FGA	Pct.	FTM	FTA	Pct.	Reb.	Ast.	Pts.	AVERAGES RPG	APG	PPG
2001—Minnesota	30	747	138	238	.580	115	157	.732	241	60	391	8.0	2.0	13.0
2002—Minnesota	30	777	155	236	.657	78	106	.736	270	36	384	9.0	1.2	12.8
2003—Minnesota	34	1003	212	344	.616	124	158	.785	368	99	548	10.8	2.9	16.1
2004—Minnesota	32	984	202	402	.502	105	144	.729	338	119	512	10.6	3.7	16.0
Totals	126	3511	707	1220	.580	422	565	.747	1217	314	1835	9.7	2.5	14.6

WNBA REGULAR-SEASON RECORD

Season Team	G	Min.	FGM	FGA	Pct.	FTM	FTA	Pct.	REBOUNDS Off.	Def.	Tot.	Ast.	St.	Blk.	TO	Pts.	AVERAGES RPG	APG	PPG
2005—Charlotte	28	311	17	50	.340	16	25	.640	32	44	76	11	12	7	22	50	2.7	0.4	1.8
Totals	28	311	17	50	.340	16	25	.640	32	44	76	11	12	7	22	50	2.7	0.4	1.8

Personal fouls/disqualifications: 2005-06, 39/0. Totals, 39/0.

MCCRAY, NIKKI   G   SKY

PERSONAL: Born December 17, 1971, in Collierville, Tenn. ... 5-11/158. (1.80/71.7). ... Full name: Nikki Kesangane McCray
COLLEGE: Tennessee.
TRANSACTIONS/CAREER NOTES: Signed by WNBA and assigned to Washington, January 27, 1998. ... Traded by Washington with a second- and third-round pick in the 2002 WNBA Draft to Indiana for F Angie Braziel and a first-and third-round pick, December 5, 2001. ... Signed by San Antonio, April 19, 2005.

M

COLLEGE RECORD

Season Team	G	Min.	FGM	FGA	Pct.	FTM	FTA	Pct.	Reb.	Ast.	Pts.	AVERAGES RPG	APG	PPG
1991—Tennessee	31	...	87	174	.500	39	53	.736	114	25	215	3.7	0.8	6.9
1992—Tennessee	32	...	133	286	.465	83	115	.722	145	63	349	4.5	2.0	10.9
1993—Tennessee	33	...	213	421	.506	111	158	.703	231	81	537	7.0	2.5	16.3
1994—Tennessee	31	...	193	392	.492	83	122	.680	182	82	471	5.9	2.6	15.2
Totals	127	...	626	1273	.492	316	448	.705	672	251	1572	5.3	2.0	12.4

Three-point field goals: 1991-92, 2-for-10 (.200). 1994-95, 2-for-15 (.133). Totals, 4-for-25 (.160).

ABL RECORD

NOTES: Member of ABL Championship Team (1997). ... ABL MVP (1997).

Season Team	G	Min.	FGM	FGA	Pct.	FTM	FTA	Pct.	Reb.	Ast.	Pts.	AVERAGES RPG	APG	PPG
1996—Columbus	40	...	300	664	.452	33	91	.363	164	210	781	4.1	5.3	19.5
Totals	40	...	300	664	.452	33	91	.363	164	210	781	4.1	5.3	19.5

OLYMPICS RECORD

Season Team	G	Min.	FGM	FGA	Pct.	FTM	FTA	Pct.	Reb.	Ast.	Pts.	AVERAGES RPG	APG	PPG
1996—United States	8	...	28	43	.651	18	26	.692	28	9	75	3.5	1.1	9.4
2000—United States	8	147	16	40	.400	8	10	.800	7	9	41	0.9	1.1	5.1
Totals	24	147	72	126	.571	44	62	.710	63	27	191	2.6	1.1	8.0

Three-point field goals: 1996-97, 1-for-3 (.333). 1996-97, 1-for-3 (.333). 2000-01, 1-for-2 (.500). Totals, 3-for-8 (.375).

WNBA REGULAR-SEASON RECORD

Season Team	G	Min.	FGM	FGA	Pct.	FTM	FTA	Pct.	REBOUNDS Off.	Def.	Tot.	Ast.	St.	Blk.	TO	Pts.	AVERAGES RPG	APG	PPG
1998—Washington	29	969	191	457	.418	107	143	.748	34	51	85	90	43	2	125	512	2.9	3.1	17.7
1999—Washington	32	1043	193	455	.424	129	160	.806	35	51	86	78	34	1	107	561	2.7	2.4	17.5
2000—Washington	32	1046	167	385	.434	113	147	.769	22	34	56	85	45	5	89	497	1.8	2.7	15.5
2001—Washington	32	828	119	290	.410	91	128	.711	22	34	56	47	26	0	73	351	1.8	1.5	11.0

Season Team	G	Min.	FGM	FGA	Pct.	FTM	FTA	Pct.	REBOUNDS Off.	Def.	Tot.	Ast.	St.	Blk.	TO	Pts.	AVERAGES RPG	APG	PPG
2002—Indiana	32	1058	132	318	.415	84	103	.816	29	68	97	70	28	3	82	369	3.0	2.2	11.5
2003—Indiana	34	734	52	138	.377	20	24	.833	18	33	51	49	37	2	44	131	1.5	1.4	3.9
2004—Phoenix	27	371	30	67	.448	4	7	.571	10	19	29	13	7	0	18	69	1.1	0.5	2.6
2005—San Antonio	23	302	15	62	.242	7	11	.636	7	13	20	16	11	0	18	38	0.9	0.7	1.7
Totals	241	6351	899	2172	.414	555	723	.768	177	303	480	448	231	13	556	2528	2.0	1.9	10.5

Three-point field goals: 1998-99, 23-for-73 (.315). 1999-00, 46-for-153 (.301). 2000-01, 50-for-151 (.331). 2001-02, 22-for-95 (.232). 2002-03, 21-for-66 (.318). 2003-04, 7-for-32 (.219). 2004-05, 5-for-11 (.455). 2005-06, 1-for-20 (.050). Totals, 175-for-601 (.291).

Personal fouls/disqualifications: 1998-99, 81/2. 1999-00, 86/1. 2000-01, 79/0. 2001-02, 68/1. 2002-03, 73/2. 2003-04, 67/1. 2004-05, 35/0. 2005-06, 26/0. Totals, 515/7.

WNBA PLAYOFF RECORD

Season Team	G	Min.	FGM	FGA	Pct.	FTM	FTA	Pct.	REBOUNDS Off.	Def.	Tot.	Ast.	St.	Blk.	TO	Pts.	AVERAGES RPG	APG	PPG
2000—Washington	2	70	7	16	.438	0	0	...	2	4	6	13	1	0	10	15	3.0	6.5	7.5
2002—Indiana	3	99	10	27	.370	3	5	.600	1	3	4	11	1	0	5	24	1.3	3.7	8.0
Totals	5	169	17	43	.395	3	5	.600	3	7	10	24	2	0	15	39	2.0	4.8	7.8

Three-point field goals: 2000-01, 1-for-7 (.143). 2002-03, 1-for-6 (.167). Totals, 2-for-13 (.154).
Personal fouls/disqualifications: 2000-01, 6/0. 2002-03, 4/0. Totals, 10/0.

WNBA ALL-STAR GAME RECORD

Season Team	Min.	FGM	FGA	Pct.	FTM	FTA	Pct.	REBOUNDS Off.	Def.	Tot.	Ast.	PF	Dq.	St.	Blk.	TO	Pts.
1999—Washington	16	2	11	.182	0	0	...	0	2	2	0	1	0	3	0	0	4
2000—Washington	19	1	11	.091	2	2	1.000	0	0	0	1	0	0	3	0	3	5
2001—Washington	22	2	7	.286	1	2	.500	0	0	0	2	1	0	0	0	1	5
Totals	57	5	29	.172	3	4	.750	0	2	2	3	2	0	6	0	4	14

Three-point field goals: 2000, 0-for-2. 2001, 1-for-6 (.167). Totals, 1-for-8 (.125).

MCWILLIAMS-FRANKLIN, TAJ   F/C   SUN

PERSONAL: Born October 20, 1970, in El Paso, Texas. ... 6-2/184. (1.88/83.5). ... Full name: Taj Madona McWilliams-Franklin
HIGH SCHOOL: T.W. Josey (Augusta, Ga.).
COLLEGE: St. Edward's.
TRANSACTIONS/CAREER NOTES: Selected by Orlando in third round (32nd overall) of WNBA Draft, May 4, 1999.

COLLEGE RECORD

NOTES: Kodak NAIA All-American (1993). ... NAIA National Player of the Year (1993).

Season Team	G	Min.	FGM	FGA	Pct.	FTM	FTA	Pct.	Reb.	Ast.	Pts.	AVERAGES RPG	APG	PPG
1990—St. Edward's	31	...	184	322	.571	47	93	.505	243	12	415	7.8	0.4	13.4
1991—St. Edward's	32	...	278	485	.573	106	176	.602	342	33	662	10.7	1.0	20.7
1992—St. Edward's	31	...	336	521	.645	85	146	.582	365	34	760	11.8	1.1	24.5
Totals	94	...	798	1328	.601	238	415	.573	950	79	1837	10.1	0.8	19.5

ABL RECORD

NOTES: All-ABL second team (1997).

Season Team	G	Min.	FGM	FGA	Pct.	FTM	FTA	Pct.	Reb.	Ast.	Pts.	AVERAGES RPG	APG	PPG
1996—Richmond	40	...	203	376	.540	114	175	.651	340	42	521	8.5	1.1	13.0
1997—Philadelphia	44	...	173	358	.483	122	171	.713	356	53	471	8.1	1.2	10.7
1998—Philadelphia	14	...	75	142	.528	32	46	.696	112	13	184	8.0	0.9	13.1
Totals	98	...	451	876	.515	268	392	.684	808	108	1176	8.2	1.1	12.0

Three-point field goals: 1996-97, 1-for-8 (.125). 1997-98, 3-for-16 (.188). 1998-99, 2-for-3 (.667). Totals, 6-for-27 (.222).

WNBA REGULAR-SEASON RECORD

NOTES: Kim Perrot Sportsmanship Award (2005). ... All-WNBA second team (2005). ... All-Defensive second team (2005).

Season Team	G	Min.	FGM	FGA	Pct.	FTM	FTA	Pct.	REBOUNDS Off.	Def.	Tot.	Ast.	St.	Blk.	TO	Pts.	AVERAGES RPG	APG	PPG
1999—Orlando	32	1042	153	319	.480	94	141	.667	81	158	239	51	57	38	80	420	7.5	1.6	13.7
2000—Orlando	32	1098	173	330	.524	87	122	.713	90	154	244	54	59	31	83	438	7.6	1.7	13.7
2001—Orlando	32	1059	157	331	.474	87	117	.744	114	129	243	69	52	50	80	403	7.6	2.2	12.6
2002—Orlando	13	383	41	82	.500	27	31	.871	21	42	63	13	19	14	22	110	4.8	1.0	8.5
2003—Connecticut	34	983	133	301	.442	76	102	.745	78	149	227	49	43	33	54	354	6.7	1.4	10.4
2004—Connecticut	34	1133	168	352	.477	77	128	.602	83	161	244	63	48	45	73	413	7.2	1.9	12.1
2005—Connecticut	34	1083	180	364	.495	107	136	.787	78	170	248	65	37	25	59	471	7.3	1.9	13.9
Totals	211	6781	1005	2079	.483	555	777	.714	545	963	1508	364	315	236	451	2609	7.1	1.7	12.4

Three-point field goals: 1999-00, 20-for-45 (.444). 2000-01, 5-for-17 (.294). 2001-02, 2-for-10 (.200). 2002-03, 1-for-3 (.333). 2003-04, 12-for-43 (.279). 2004-05, 0-for-12. 2005-06, 4-for-18 (.222). Totals, 44-for-148 (.297).

Personal fouls/disqualifications: 1999-00, 96/3. 2000-01, 86/0. 2001-02, 74/1. 2002-03, 40/1. 2003-04, 103/1. 2004-05, 96/1. 2005-06, 80/1. Totals, 575/8.

WNBA PLAYOFF RECORD

Season Team	G	Min.	FGM	FGA	Pct.	FTM	FTA	Pct.	REBOUNDS Off.	Def.	Tot.	Ast.	St.	Blk.	TO	Pts.	AVERAGES RPG	APG	PPG
2000—Orlando	3	107	18	38	.474	7	9	.778	6	17	23	5	2	3	5	43	7.7	1.7	14.3
2003—Connecticut	4	122	24	47	.511	16	17	.941	9	21	30	5	6	2	6	65	7.5	1.3	16.3

Season Team	G	Min.	FGM	FGA	Pct.	FTM	FTA	Pct.	REBOUNDS Off.	Def.	Tot.	Ast.	St.	Blk.	TO	Pts.	AVERAGES RPG	APG	PPG
2004—Connecticut.......	8	252	35	87	.402	12	18	.667	19	40	59	15	12	6	13	83	7.4	1.9	10.4
2005—Connecticut.......	8	284	48	94	.511	30	38	.789	22	53	75	13	9	11	16	127	9.4	1.6	15.9
Totals	23	765	125	266	.470	65	82	.793	56	131	187	38	29	22	40	318	8.1	1.7	13.8

Three-point field goals: 2000-01, 0-for-2. 2003-04, 1-for-5 (.200). 2004-05, 1-for-2 (.500). 2005-06, 1-for-3 (.333). Totals, 3-for-12 (.250).
Personal fouls/disqualifications: 2000-01, 8/0. 2003-04, 10/0. 2004-05, 22/0. 2005-06, 23/0. Totals, 63/0.

WNBA ALL-STAR GAME RECORD

Season Team	Min.	FGM	FGA	Pct.	FTM	FTA	Pct.	REBOUNDS Off.	Def.	Tot.	Ast.	PF	Dq.	St.	Blk.	TO	Pts.
1999—Orlando	31	2	5	.400	3	4	.750	2	5	7	1	2	0	2	1	2	8
2000—Orlando	24	4	8	.500	2	2	1.000	7	2	9	0	2	0	2	0	0	10
2001—Orlando	26	4	7	.571	2	4	.500	2	2	4	1	3	0	2	1	1	10
2005—Connecticut............	17	2	5	.400	4	5	.800	1	1	2	3	2	0	1	0	1	8
Totals	98	12	25	.480	11	15	.733	12	10	22	5	9	0	7	2	4	36

Three-point field goals: 2000, 1-for-1 (1.000). 2006, 0-for-1. Totals, 1-for-2 (.500).

MELVIN, CHASITY   C   MYSTICS

PERSONAL: Born May 3, 1976, in Roseboro, N.C. ... 6-3/185. (1.91/83.9). ... Full name: Chasity Monique Melvin
HIGH SCHOOL: Lakewood (Roseboro, N.C.).
COLLEGE: North Carolina State.
TRANSACTIONS/CAREER NOTES: Selected by Cleveland in first round (11th overall) of WNBA Draft, May 4, 1999. ... Selected by Washington in WNBA Dispersal Draft, January 6, 2004.

COLLEGE RECORD

NOTES: Kodak All-American (1996).

Season Team	G	Min.	FGM	FGA	Pct.	FTM	FTA	Pct.	Reb.	Ast.	Pts.	AVERAGES RPG	APG	PPG
1994—North Carolina State	31	...	208	345	.603	92	163	.564	217	35	508	7.0	1.1	16.4
1995—North Carolina State	30	...	205	365	.562	79	147	.537	230	37	489	7.7	1.2	16.3
1996—North Carolina State	31	...	195	334	.584	110	182	.604	268	44	500	8.6	1.4	16.1
1997—North Carolina State	32	...	230	397	.579	85	147	.578	305	83	545	9.5	2.6	17.0
Totals	124	...	838	1441	.582	366	639	.573	1020	199	2042	8.2	1.6	16.5

Three-point field goals: 1996-97, 0-for-7. 1997-98, 0-for-4. Totals, 0-for-11 (.000).

ABL RECORD

Season Team	G	Min.	FGM	FGA	Pct.	FTM	FTA	Pct.	Reb.	Ast.	Pts.	AVERAGES RPG	APG	PPG
1998—Philadelphia.......................	14	...	65	117	.556	48	63	.762	78	8	178	5.6	0.6	12.7
Totals	14	...	65	117	.556	48	63	.762	78	8	178	5.6	0.6	12.7

Three-point field goals: 1998-99, 0-for-1. Totals, 0-for-1 (.000).

WNBA REGULAR-SEASON RECORD

Season Team	G	Min.	FGM	FGA	Pct.	FTM	FTA	Pct.	REBOUNDS Off.	Def.	Tot.	Ast.	St.	Blk.	TO	Pts.	AVERAGES RPG	APG	PPG
1999—Cleveland	32	709	95	218	.436	68	98	.694	53	74	127	38	20	22	42	259	4.0	1.2	8.1
2000—Cleveland	32	904	136	289	.471	100	137	.730	69	103	172	61	29	18	62	373	5.4	1.9	11.7
2001—Cleveland	27	754	102	215	.474	60	86	.698	66	88	154	50	24	16	45	266	5.7	1.9	9.9
2002—Cleveland	32	1055	153	330	.464	90	131	.687	84	110	194	57	28	18	74	399	6.1	1.8	12.5
2003—Cleveland	34	1061	159	333	.477	123	176	.699	82	133	215	52	28	22	67	444	6.3	1.5	13.1
2004—Washington	34	825	104	256	.406	85	111	.766	63	68	131	37	15	18	52	293	3.9	1.1	8.6
2005—Washington	34	1051	150	305	.492	93	138	.674	82	117	199	25	31	14	61	397	5.9	0.7	11.7
Totals	225	6359	899	1946	.462	619	877	.706	499	693	1192	320	175	128	403	2431	5.3	1.4	10.8

Three-point field goals: 1999-00, 1-for-1 (1.000). 2000-01, 1-for-7 (.143). 2001-02, 2-for-2 (1.000). 2002-03, 3-for-6 (.500). 2003-04, 3-for-11 (.273). 2005-06, 4-for-16 (.250). Totals, 14-for-43 (.326).
Personal fouls/disqualifications: 1999-00, 93/1. 2000-01, 113/4. 2001-02, 81/0. 2002-03, 104/2. 2003-04, 108/0. 2004-05, 89/0. 2005-06, 113/1. Totals, 701/8.

WNBA PLAYOFF RECORD

Season Team	G	Min.	FGM	FGA	Pct.	FTM	FTA	Pct.	REBOUNDS Off.	Def.	Tot.	Ast.	St.	Blk.	TO	Pts.	AVERAGES RPG	APG	PPG
2000—Cleveland	6	183	20	38	.526	13	18	.722	16	24	40	11	5	3	11	53	6.7	1.8	8.8
2001—Cleveland	3	81	8	16	.500	8	11	.727	6	6	12	6	2	2	6	24	4.0	2.0	8.0
2003—Cleveland	3	104	12	31	.387	26	34	.765	3	10	13	5	2	4	8	50	4.3	1.7	16.7
2004—Washington	3	104	13	31	.419	15	21	.714	7	18	25	6	1	4	2	41	8.3	2.0	13.7
Totals	15	472	53	116	.457	62	84	.738	32	58	90	28	10	13	27	168	6.0	1.9	11.2

Three-point field goals: 2000-01, 0-for-1. 2003-04, 0-for-1. Totals, 0-for-2 (.000).
Personal fouls/disqualifications: 2000-01, 20/0. 2001-02, 5/0. 2003-04, 10/0. 2004-05, 10/0. Totals, 45/0.

MILLER, COCO   G   MYSTICS

PERSONAL: Born September 6, 1978, in Rochester, Minn. ... 5-9/140. (1.75/63.5). ... Full name: Colleen Mary Miller
HIGH SCHOOL: Mayo (Rochester, Minn.).
COLLEGE: Georgia.
TRANSACTIONS/CAREER NOTES: Selected by Washington in first round (ninth overall) of WNBA Draft, April 20, 2001.

M

Season Team	G	Min.	FGM	FGA	Pct.	FTM	FTA	Pct.	Reb.	Ast.	Pts.	RPG	APG	PPG
												AVERAGES		
1997—Georgia	27	854	179	415	.431	50	74	.676	123	104	432	4.6	3.9	16.0
1998—Georgia	34	1046	263	536	.491	68	89	.764	132	77	626	3.9	2.3	18.4
1999—Georgia	36	1080	215	487	.441	76	98	.776	114	114	555	3.2	3.2	15.4
2000—Georgia	33	1017	207	452	.458	73	87	.839	134	101	518	4.1	3.1	15.7
Totals	130	3997	864	1890	.457	267	348	.767	503	396	2131	3.9	3.0	16.4

Three-point field goals: 1997-98, 24-for-61 (.393). 1998-99, 32-for-82 (.390). 1999-00, 49-for-122 (.402). 2000-01, 31-for-96 (.323). Totals, 136-for-361 (.377).

WNBA REGULAR-SEASON RECORD

NOTES: WNBA Most Improved Player (2002).

									REBOUNDS								AVERAGES		
Season Team	G	Min.	FGM	FGA	Pct.	FTM	FTA	Pct.	Off.	Def.	Tot.	Ast.	St.	Blk.	TO	Pts.	RPG	APG	PPG
2001—Washington	20	137	13	40	.325	6	11	.545	5	4	9	8	6	0	13	34	0.5	0.4	1.7
2002—Washington	32	904	114	263	.433	46	56	.821	44	72	116	82	33	2	59	298	3.6	2.6	9.3
2003—Washington	33	1076	172	382	.450	37	53	.698	55	72	127	86	39	7	53	413	3.8	2.6	12.5
2004—Washington	33	637	72	167	.431	11	14	.786	35	28	63	43	18	3	27	160	1.9	1.3	4.8
2005—Washington	34	500	68	160	.425	8	10	.800	24	35	59	44	26	3	28	153	1.7	1.3	4.5
Totals	152	3254	439	1012	.434	108	144	.750	163	211	374	263	122	15	180	1058	2.5	1.7	7.0

Three-point field goals: 2001-02, 2-for-6 (.333). 2002-03, 24-for-64 (.375). 2003-04, 32-for-89 (.360). 2004-05, 5-for-19 (.263). 2005-06, 9-for-24 (.375). Totals, 72-for-202 (.356).

Personal fouls/disqualifications: 2001-02, 10/0. 2002-03, 84/0. 2003-04, 95/1. 2004-05, 60/0. 2005-06, 53/0. Totals, 302/1.

WNBA PLAYOFF RECORD

									REBOUNDS								AVERAGES		
Season Team	G	Min.	FGM	FGA	Pct.	FTM	FTA	Pct.	Off.	Def.	Tot.	Ast.	St.	Blk.	TO	Pts.	RPG	APG	PPG
2002—Washington	5	163	21	50	.420	6	10	.600	7	8	15	12	2	0	7	54	3.0	2.4	10.8
2004—Washington	3	51	7	19	.368	2	2	1.000	3	4	7	2	5	0	2	16	2.3	0.7	5.3
Totals	8	214	28	69	.406	8	12	.667	10	12	22	14	7	0	9	70	2.8	1.8	8.8

Three-point field goals: 2002-03, 6-for-11 (.545). Totals, 6-for-11 (.545).
Personal fouls/disqualifications: 2002-03, 13/0. 2004-05, 2/0. Totals, 15/0.

MILLER, KELLY   G   MERCURY

PERSONAL: Born September 6, 1978, in Rochester, Minn. ... 5-10/140. (1.78/63.5). ... Full name: Kelly Marie Miller
HIGH SCHOOL: Mayo (Rochester, Minn.).
COLLEGE: Georgia.
TRANSACTIONS/CAREER NOTES: Selected by Charlotte in first round (second overall) of WNBA Draft, April 20, 2001. ... Traded by Charlotte along with a first-round pick in the 2004 WNBA Draft to Indiana for a first-round pick and a second-round pick in the 2004 WNBA Draft, February 5, 2004. ... Traded by Indiana to Phoenix for G Anna DeForge, April 3, 2006.

COLLEGE RECORD

NOTES: Kodak All-American first team (1999, 2001).

Season Team	G	Min.	FGM	FGA	Pct.	FTM	FTA	Pct.	Reb.	Ast.	Pts.	RPG	APG	PPG
												AVERAGES		
1997—Georgia	28	999	166	414	.401	118	144	.819	159	164	489	5.7	5.9	17.5
1998—Georgia	34	1119	219	477	.459	136	163	.834	205	150	628	6.0	4.4	18.5
1999—Georgia	36	1169	203	456	.445	94	115	.817	168	162	544	4.7	4.5	15.1
2000—Georgia	33	1079	193	378	.511	80	97	.825	179	163	516	5.4	4.9	15.6
Totals	131	4366	781	1725	.453	428	519	.825	711	639	2177	5.4	4.9	16.6

Three-point field goals: 1997-98, 39-for-110 (.355). 1998-99, 39-for-110 (.355). 1999-00, 44-for-122 (.361). 2000-01, 50-for-108 (.463). Totals, 172-for-450 (.382).

WNBA REGULAR-SEASON RECORD

NOTES: WNBA Co-Most Improved Player (2004).

									REBOUNDS								AVERAGES		
Season Team	G	Min.	FGM	FGA	Pct.	FTM	FTA	Pct.	Off.	Def.	Tot.	Ast.	St.	Blk.	TO	Pts.	RPG	APG	PPG
2001—Charlotte	26	225	22	57	.386	4	5	.800	11	17	28	14	9	0	9	55	1.1	0.5	2.1
2002—Charlotte	32	554	79	177	.446	29	38	.763	31	37	68	49	22	1	27	211	2.1	1.5	6.6
2003—Charlotte	34	523	68	167	.407	31	40	.775	20	33	53	47	18	2	35	189	1.6	1.4	5.6
2004—Indiana	34	1096	126	326	.387	50	57	.877	28	80	108	106	37	5	74	348	3.2	3.1	10.2
2005—Indiana	34	1057	122	278	.439	67	79	.848	26	60	86	81	40	2	53	348	2.5	2.4	10.2
Totals	160	3455	417	1005	.415	181	219	.826	116	227	343	297	126	10	198	1151	2.1	1.9	7.2

Three-point field goals: 2001-02, 7-for-19 (.368). 2002-03, 24-for-51 (.471). 2003-04, 22-for-52 (.423). 2004-05, 46-for-112 (.411). 2005-06, 37-for-114 (.325). Totals, 136-for-348 (.391).
Personal fouls/disqualifications: 2001-02, 14/0. 2002-03, 39/0. 2003-04, 44/0. 2004-05, 81/3. 2005-06, 81/1. Totals, 259/4.

WNBA PLAYOFF RECORD

									REBOUNDS								AVERAGES		
Season Team	G	Min.	FGM	FGA	Pct.	FTM	FTA	Pct.	Off.	Def.	Tot.	Ast.	St.	Blk.	TO	Pts.	RPG	APG	PPG
2001—Charlotte	2	8	0	2	.000	0	2	.000	0	0	0	0	0	0	0	0	0.0	0.0	0.0
2002—Charlotte	2	13	2	4	.500	0	0	...	0	2	2	0	0	1	5	1.0	0.0	2.5
2003—Charlotte	2	23	4	10	.400	0	0	...	0	1	1	2	0	0	1	8	0.5	1.0	4.0
2005—Indiana	4	155	12	39	.308	7	10	.700	0	7	7	10	5	0	5	40	1.8	2.5	10.0
Totals	10	199	18	55	.327	7	12	.583	0	10	10	12	5	0	7	53	1.0	1.2	5.3

Three-point field goals: 2002-03, 1-for-1 (1.000). 2003-04, 0-for-2. 2005-06, 9-for-17 (.529). Totals, 10-for-20 (.500).
Personal fouls/disqualifications: 2002-03, 3/0. 2003-04, 2/0. 2005-06, 13/0. Totals, 18/0.

MILLER, TEANA　　　　　　　　C　　　　　　　　STING

PERSONAL: Born October 5, 1980 ... 6-3. (1.91).
HIGH SCHOOL: East Duplin (Beulaville, N.C.).
COLLEGE: East Carolina, Tulane.

COLLEGE RECORD

NOTES: All-Conference USA second team (2002, 2003). ... Led Conference USA with 62.3 field-goal percentage (2002). ... Conference USA Sixth Player of the Year (2001).

Season Team	G	Min.	FGM	FGA	Pct.	FTM	FTA	Pct.	Reb.	Ast.	Pts.	AVERAGES RPG	APG	PPG
1998—East Carolina	19	299	72	132	.545	36	75	.480	105	6	180	5.5	0.3	9.5
2000—Tulane	32	600	103	189	.545	52	99	.525	168	22	258	5.3	0.7	8.1
2001—Tulane	35	916	235	377	.623	104	189	.550	260	25	574	7.4	0.7	16.4
2002—Tulane	29	792	149	262	.569	72	121	.595	206	52	372	7.1	1.8	12.8
Totals	115	2607	559	960	.582	264	484	.545	739	105	1384	6.4	0.9	12.0

Three-point field goals: 2002-03, 2-for-2 (1.000). Totals, 2-for-2 (1.000).

WNBA REGULAR-SEASON RECORD

Season Team	G	Min.	FGM	FGA	Pct.	FTM	FTA	Pct.	REBOUNDS Off.	Def.	Tot.	Ast.	St.	Blk.	TO	Pts.	AVERAGES RPG	APG	PPG
2003—Charlotte	31	341	41	78	.526	23	31	.742	37	54	91	6	14	24	27	105	2.9	0.2	3.4
2004—Charlotte	9	77	14	27	.519	7	14	.500	9	9	18	0	2	6	5	35	2.0	0.0	3.9
2005—Charlotte	31	362	44	91	.484	25	36	.694	29	36	65	7	14	18	26	113	2.1	0.2	3.6
Totals	71	780	99	196	.505	55	81	.679	75	99	174	13	30	48	58	253	2.5	0.2	3.6

Three-point field goals: 2003-04, 0-for-1. Totals, 0-for-1 (.000).
Personal fouls/disqualifications: 2003-04, 58/0. 2004-05, 21/0. 2005-06, 71/0. Totals, 150/0.

WNBA PLAYOFF RECORD

Season Team	G	Min.	FGM	FGA	Pct.	FTM	FTA	Pct.	REBOUNDS Off.	Def.	Tot.	Ast.	St.	Blk.	TO	Pts.	AVERAGES RPG	APG	PPG
2003—Charlotte	2	13	0	2	.000	0	0	...	2	0	2	0	0	1	0	0	1.0	0.0	0.0
Totals	2	13	0	2	.000	0	0	...	2	0	2	0	0	1	0	0	1.0	0.0	0.0

Personal fouls/disqualifications: 2003-04, 2/0. Totals, 2/0.

MILTON-JONES, DELISHA　　　F　　　　　　MYSTICS

PERSONAL: Born September 11, 1974, in Riceboro, Ga. ... 6-1/172. (1.85/78.0). ... Full name: DeLisha Lachell Milton-Jones
HIGH SCHOOL: Bradwell Institute (Hinesville, Ga.).
COLLEGE: Florida.
TRANSACTIONS/CAREER NOTES: Selected by Los Angeles in first round (fourth overall) of WNBA Draft, May 4, 1999. ... Traded, along with a first-round pick in the 2005 WNBA Draft, by Los Angeles to Washington in exchange for F Chamique Holdsclaw, March 22, 2005.
MISCELLANEOUS: Member of WNBA Championship team (2001, 2002).

COLLEGE RECORD

NOTES: Wade Trophy recipient (1997). ... Kodak All-American first team (1997).

Season Team	G	Min.	FGM	FGA	Pct.	FTM	FTA	Pct.	Reb.	Ast.	Pts.	AVERAGES RPG	APG	PPG
1993—Florida	29	...	134	275	.487	71	116	.612	334	31	339	11.5	1.1	11.7
1994—Florida	33	...	188	331	.568	68	110	.618	219	27	444	6.6	0.8	13.5
1995—Florida	30	...	182	380	.479	99	142	.697	262	47	462	8.7	1.6	15.4
1996—Florida	29	...	222	392	.566	119	158	.753	256	56	563	8.8	1.9	19.4
Totals	121	...	726	1378	.527	357	526	.679	1071	161	1808	8.9	1.3	14.9

Three-point field goals: 1994-95, 0-for-1. 1995-96, 0-for-7. Totals, 0-for-8 (.000).

ABL RECORD

Season Team	G	Min.	FGM	FGA	Pct.	FTM	FTA	Pct.	Reb.	Ast.	Pts.	AVERAGES RPG	APG	PPG
1997—Portland	44	...	163	326	.500	48	70	.686	217	99	376	4.9	2.3	8.5
1998—Portland	13	...	59	127	.465	36	46	.783	89	26	155	6.8	2.0	11.9
Totals	57	...	222	453	.490	84	116	.724	306	125	531	5.4	2.2	9.3

Three-point field goals: 1997-98, 2-for-12 (.167). 1998-99, 1-for-3 (.333). Totals, 3-for-15 (.200).

WNBA REGULAR-SEASON RECORD

Season Team	G	Min.	FGM	FGA	Pct.	FTM	FTA	Pct.	REBOUNDS Off.	Def.	Tot.	Ast.	St.	Blk.	TO	Pts.	AVERAGES RPG	APG	PPG
1999—Los Angeles	32	835	125	236	.530	68	86	.791	60	116	176	50	47	17	71	318	5.5	1.6	9.9
2000—Los Angeles	32	983	150	293	.512	76	102	.745	55	139	194	68	44	29	67	378	6.1	2.1	11.8
2001—Los Angeles	32	938	134	296	.453	50	63	.794	71	98	169	68	49	29	58	330	5.3	2.1	10.3
2002—Los Angeles	32	966	132	271	.487	77	104	.740	65	146	211	45	50	35	94	362	6.6	1.4	11.3
2003—Los Angeles	31	1086	139	328	.424	115	143	.804	59	161	220	64	49	41	79	416	7.1	2.1	13.4
2004—Los Angeles	19	604	65	161	.404	45	62	.726	35	55	90	31	23	10	48	186	4.7	1.6	9.8
2005—Washington	33	1069	138	331	.417	79	99	.798	45	127	172	58	57	18	75	394	5.2	1.8	11.9
Totals	211	6481	883	1916	.461	510	659	.774	390	842	1232	384	319	179	492	2384	5.8	1.8	11.3

Three-point field goals: 1999-00, 0-for-1. 2000-01, 2-for-8 (.250). 2001-02, 12-for-35 (.343). 2002-03, 21-for-50 (.420). 2003-04, 23-for-61 (.377). 2004-05, 11-for-37 (.297). 2005-06, 39-for-119 (.328). Totals, 108-for-311 (.347).
Personal fouls/disqualifications: 1999-00, 112/0. 2000-01, 124/3. 2001-02, 122/3. 2002-03, 122/3. 2003-04, 109/3. 2004-05, 63/1. 2005-06, 117/4. Totals, 748/14.

WNBA PLAYOFF RECORD

Season Team	G	Min.	FGM	FGA	Pct.	FTM	FTA	Pct.	REBOUNDS Off.	Def.	Tot.	Ast.	St.	Blk.	TO	Pts.	RPG	APG	PPG
1999—Los Angeles	4	127	18	40	.450	3	7	.429	6	15	21	10	7	6	5	39	5.3	2.5	9.8
2000—Los Angeles	4	136	20	37	.541	10	12	.833	11	11	22	12	6	2	10	50	5.5	3.0	12.5
2001—Los Angeles	7	226	35	64	.547	13	19	.684	12	32	44	20	7	10	11	86	6.3	2.9	12.3
2002—Los Angeles	6	204	27	60	.450	15	16	.938	9	32	41	8	10	9	11	78	6.8	1.3	13.0
2003—Los Angeles	9	338	47	106	.443	27	35	.771	20	37	57	25	17	13	20	131	6.3	2.8	14.6
Totals	30	1031	147	307	.479	68	89	.764	58	127	185	75	47	40	57	384	6.2	2.5	12.8

Three-point field goals: 2001-02, 3-for-8 (.375). 2002-03, 9-for-16 (.563). 2003-04, 10-for-18 (.556). Totals, 22-for-42 (.524).
Personal fouls/disqualifications: 1999-00, 12/1. 2000-01, 14/1. 2001-02, 22/0. 2002-03, 22/0. 2003-04, 40/1. Totals, 110/3.

WNBA ALL-STAR GAME RECORD

Season Team	Min.	FGM	FGA	Pct.	FTM	FTA	Pct.	REBOUNDS Off.	Def.	Tot.	Ast.	PF	Dq.	St.	Blk.	TO	Pts.
2000—Los Angeles	16	2	2	1.000	0	0	...	3	1	4	3	0	0	0	0	0	4
Totals	16	2	2	1.000	0	0	...	3	1	4	3	0	0	0	0	0	4

OLYMPICS RECORD

Season Team	G	Min.	FGM	FGA	Pct.	FTM	FTA	Pct.	Reb.	Ast.	Pts.	AVERAGES RPG	APG	PPG
2000—United States	8	91	16	31	.516	4	8	.500	19	0	36	2.4	0.0	4.5
Totals	8	91	16	31	.516	4	8	.500	19	0	36	2.4	0.0	4.5

MOORE, JESSICA   C   SPARKS

PERSONAL: Born July 9, 1982, in Fairbanks, Alaska. ... 6-3/175. (1.91/79.4). ... Full name: Jessica Alicia Moore
HIGH SCHOOL: Colony (Palmer, Alaska).
COLLEGE: Connecticut.
TRANSACTIONS/CAREER NOTES: Selected by Charlotte in the second round (24th overall) of the WNBA Draft, April 16, 2005. ... Signed by Los Angeles, July 15, 2005.

COLLEGE RECORD

NOTES: All-Big East honorable mention (2005). ... NCAA Final Four All-Tournament team (2004). ... NCAA Tournament East Regional All-Tournament team (2003). ... All-Big East Tournament team (2003).

Season Team	G	Min.	FGM	FGA	Pct.	FTM	FTA	Pct.	Reb.	Ast.	Pts.	AVERAGES RPG	APG	PPG
2001—Connecticut	39	719	81	139	.583	50	86	.581	154	33	212	3.9	0.8	5.4
2002—Connecticut	36	982	167	275	.607	69	106	.651	225	52	403	6.3	1.4	11.2
2003—Connecticut	35	882	141	228	.618	49	90	.544	247	41	332	7.1	1.2	9.5
2004—Connecticut	33	771	110	213	.516	55	79	.696	208	41	276	6.3	1.2	8.4
Totals	143	3354	499	855	.584	223	361	.618	834	167	1223	5.8	1.2	8.6

WNBA REGULAR-SEASON RECORD

Season Team	G	Min.	FGM	FGA	Pct.	FTM	FTA	Pct.	REBOUNDS Off.	Def.	Tot.	Ast.	St.	Blk.	TO	Pts.	RPG	APG	PPG
2005—Charlotte-L.A.	21	158	5	11	.455	1	2	.500	5	8	13	3	4	0	9	11	0.6	0.1	0.5
Totals	21	158	5	11	.455	1	2	.500	5	8	13	3	4	0	9	11	0.6	0.1	0.5

Personal fouls/disqualifications: 2005-06, 30/1. Totals, 30/1.

MOORE, LOREE   G   LIBERTY

PERSONAL: Born March 21, 1983, in Carson, Calif. ... 5-9. (1.75). ... Full name: Loree Marlowe Moore
HIGH SCHOOL: Narbonne (Carson, Calif.).
COLLEGE: Tennessee.
TRANSACTIONS/CAREER NOTES: Selected by New York in the first round (10th overall) of the WNBA Draft, April 16, 2005.
MISCELLANEOUS: Member of 2003 silver medal-winning USA Pan Am team.

COLLEGE RECORD

NOTES: All-SEC freshman team (2002).

Season Team	G	Min.	FGM	FGA	Pct.	FTM	FTA	Pct.	Reb.	Ast.	Pts.	AVERAGES RPG	APG	PPG
2001—Tennessee	34	726	71	151	.470	43	62	.694	93	133	194	2.7	3.9	5.7
2002—Tennessee	38	1029	95	202	.470	30	49	.612	129	145	244	3.4	3.8	6.4
2003—Tennessee	17	471	58	126	.460	9	17	.529	94	48	135	5.5	2.8	7.9
2004—Tennessee	29	792	56	166	.337	23	31	.742	132	96	148	4.6	3.3	5.1
Totals	118	3018	280	645	.434	105	159	.660	448	422	721	3.8	3.6	6.1

WNBA REGULAR-SEASON RECORD

Season Team	G	Min.	FGM	FGA	Pct.	FTM	FTA	Pct.	REBOUNDS Off.	Def.	Tot.	Ast.	St.	Blk.	TO	Pts.	RPG	APG	PPG
2005—New York	24	182	9	23	.391	4	9	.444	4	23	27	19	10	0	25	22	1.1	0.8	0.9
Totals	24	182	9	23	.391	4	9	.444	4	23	27	19	10	0	25	22	1.1	0.8	0.9

Three-point field goals: 2005-06, 0-for-2. Totals, 0-for-2 (.000).
Personal fouls/disqualifications: 2005-06, 12/0. Totals, 12/0.

M

WNBA PLAYOFF RECORD

| Season Team | G | Min. | FGM | FGA | Pct. | FTM | FTA | Pct. | REBOUNDS | | | Ast. | St. | Blk. | TO | Pts. | AVERAGES | | |
									Off.	Def.	Tot.						RPG	APG	PPG
2005—New York...........	1	1	0	0	...	0	0	...	0	0	0	0	0	0	0	0	0.0	0.0	0.0
Totals	1	1	0	0	...	0	0	...	0	0	0	0	0	0	0	0	0.0	0.0	0.0

MOORE, TAMARA   G/F   SPARKS

PERSONAL: Born April 11, 1980, in Minneapolis. ... 5-11/167. (1.80/75.7). ... Full name: Tamara Tennell Moore
HIGH SCHOOL: North Community (Minneapolis).
COLLEGE: Wisconsin.
TRANSACTIONS/CAREER NOTES: Selected by Miami in first round (15th overall) of WNBA Draft, April 19, 2002. ... Traded by Miami with a second-round pick in 2003 WNBA Draft to Minnesota for G Betty Lennox and a first-round pick, June 13, 2002. ... Traded by Minnesota to Detroit for Detroit's third-round pick in the 2004 WNBA Draft, May 19, 2003. ... Traded by Detroit to Phoenix for F Stacey Thomas, July 31, 2003.

COLLEGE RECORD

| Season Team | G | Min. | FGM | FGA | Pct. | FTM | FTA | Pct. | Reb. | Ast. | Pts. | AVERAGES | | |
												RPG	APG	PPG
1998—Wisconsin..........................	32	928	121	273	.443	86	106	.811	158	107	347	4.9	3.3	10.8
1999—Wisconsin..........................	33	999	152	329	.462	117	152	.770	167	108	445	5.1	3.3	13.5
2000—Wisconsin..........................	28	869	122	271	.450	89	122	.730	129	151	354	4.6	5.4	12.6
2001—Wisconsin..........................	31	1052	186	378	.492	95	114	.833	159	188	516	5.1	6.1	16.6
Totals	124	3848	581	1251	.464	387	494	.783	613	554	1662	4.9	4.5	13.4

Three-point field goals: 1998-99, 19-for-56 (.339). 1999-00, 24-for-69 (.348). 2000-01, 21-for-63 (.333). 2001-02, 49-for-135 (.363). Totals, 113-for-323 (.350).

WNBA REGULAR-SEASON RECORD

| Season Team | G | Min. | FGM | FGA | Pct. | FTM | FTA | Pct. | REBOUNDS | | | Ast. | St. | Blk. | TO | Pts. | AVERAGES | | |
									Off.	Def.	Tot.						RPG	APG	PPG
2002—Miami-Minn.	31	736	71	197	.360	54	63	.857	23	60	83	88	30	9	85	224	2.7	2.8	7.2
2003—Detroit................	26	176	19	42	.452	16	19	.842	6	22	28	12	9	6	16	54	1.1	0.5	2.1
2004—Phoenix..............	32	387	27	61	.443	25	29	.862	7	21	28	53	26	9	34	82	0.9	1.7	2.6
2005—New York...........	7	48	4	6	.667	2	2	1.000	0	7	7	6	0	0	4	11	1.0	0.9	1.6
Totals	96	1347	121	306	.395	97	113	.858	36	110	146	159	65	24	139	371	1.5	1.7	3.9

Three-point field goals: 2002-03, 28-for-77 (.364). 2003-04, 0-for-9. 2004-05, 3-for-10 (.300). 2005-06, 1-for-3 (.333). Totals, 32-for-99 (.323).
Personal fouls/disqualifications: 2002-03, 81/0. 2003-04, 14/0. 2004-05, 46/0. 2005-06, 6/0. Totals, 147/0.

NEWTON, CHELSEA   G   SKY

PERSONAL: Born February 17, 1983, in Monroe, La. ... 5-11/150. (1.80/68.0). ... Full name: Chelsea Marie Newton
HIGH SCHOOL: Carroll (Phoenix).
COLLEGE: Rutgers.
TRANSACTIONS/CAREER NOTES: Selected by Sacramento in the second round (22nd overall) of the WNBA Draft, April 16, 2005. ... Selected by Chicago in WNBA Expansion Draft, November 16, 2005.
MISCELLANEOUS: Member of WNBA Championship team (2005).

COLLEGE RECORD
NOTES: Big East Defensive Player of the Year (2005). ... All-Big East third team (2005).

| Season Team | G | Min. | FGM | FGA | Pct. | FTM | FTA | Pct. | Reb. | Ast. | Pts. | AVERAGES | | |
												RPG	APG	PPG
2001—Rutgers	21	477	50	129	.388	32	37	.865	103	25	136	4.9	1.2	6.5
2002—Rutgers	29	955	114	261	.437	67	93	.720	142	73	313	4.9	2.5	10.8
2003—Rutgers	21	593	90	190	.474	48	71	.676	61	66	230	2.9	3.1	11.0
2004—Rutgers	33	962	108	262	.412	83	106	.783	136	77	310	4.1	2.3	9.4
Totals	104	2987	362	842	.430	230	307	.749	442	241	989	4.3	2.3	9.5

WNBA REGULAR-SEASON RECORD
NOTES: All-Rookie team (2005).

| Season Team | G | Min. | FGM | FGA | Pct. | FTM | FTA | Pct. | REBOUNDS | | | Ast. | St. | Blk. | TO | Pts. | AVERAGES | | |
									Off.	Def.	Tot.						RPG	APG	PPG
2005—Sacramento......	34	715	60	149	.403	22	36	.611	32	34	66	55	24	9	37	148	1.9	1.6	4.4
Totals	34	715	60	149	.403	22	36	.611	32	34	66	55	24	9	37	148	1.9	1.6	4.4

Three-point field goals: 2005-06, 6-for-25 (.240). Totals, 6-for-25 (.240).
Personal fouls/disqualifications: 2005-06, 102/0. Totals, 102/0.

WNBA PLAYOFF RECORD

| Season Team | G | Min. | FGM | FGA | Pct. | FTM | FTA | Pct. | REBOUNDS | | | Ast. | St. | Blk. | TO | Pts. | AVERAGES | | |
									Off.	Def.	Tot.						RPG	APG	PPG
2005—Sacramento......	8	182	18	42	.429	8	12	.667	4	10	14	8	2	0	11	46	1.8	1.0	5.8
Totals	8	182	18	42	.429	8	12	.667	4	10	14	8	2	0	11	46	1.8	1.0	5.8

Three-point field goals: 2005-06, 2-for-4 (.500). Totals, 2-for-4 (.500).
Personal fouls/disqualifications: 2005-06, 19/0. Totals, 19/0.

M
N

NGOYISA, BERNADETTE   C   SKY

PERSONAL: Born August 26, 1982, in Congo. ... 6-4/195. (1.93/88.5).
TRANSACTIONS/CAREER NOTES: Signed by the WNBA and added by New York, April 25, 2002. ... Signed by San Antonio, April 15, 2005. ... Selected by Chicago in WNBA Expansion Draft, November 16, 2005.

WNBA REGULAR-SEASON RECORD

Season Team	G	Min.	FGM	FGA	Pct.	FTM	FTA	Pct.	REBOUNDS Off.	Def.	Tot.	Ast.	St.	Blk.	TO	Pts.	AVERAGES RPG	APG	PPG
2002—New York...........	7	12	3	5	.600	0	0	...	1	4	5	0	0	2	0	6	0.7	0.0	0.9
2005—San Antonio	26	251	46	81	.568	19	26	.731	17	44	61	5	5	2	25	111	2.3	0.2	4.3
Totals	33	263	49	86	.570	19	26	.731	18	48	66	5	5	4	25	117	2.0	0.2	3.5

Personal fouls/disqualifications: 2002-03, 2/0. 2005-06, 45/1. Totals, 47/1.

WNBA PLAYOFF RECORD

Season Team	G	Min.	FGM	FGA	Pct.	FTM	FTA	Pct.	REBOUNDS Off.	Def.	Tot.	Ast.	St.	Blk.	TO	Pts.	AVERAGES RPG	APG	PPG
2002—New York...........	3	10	3	5	.600	2	5	.400	1	2	3	0	0	0	1	8	1.0	0.0	2.7
Totals	3	10	3	5	.600	2	5	.400	1	2	3	0	0	0	1	8	1.0	0.0	2.7

Personal fouls/disqualifications: 2002-03, 2/0. Totals, 2/0.

NIEUWVEEN, MARLOUS   C

PERSONAL: Born April 12, 1980, in Leiden, Netherlands. ... 6-5/200. (1.96/90.7).
HIGH SCHOOL: Da Vinci College (Leiden, Netherlands).
COLLEGE: Valparaiso.

COLLEGE RECORD

Season Team	G	Min.	FGM	FGA	Pct.	FTM	FTA	Pct.	Reb.	Ast.	Pts.	AVERAGES RPG	APG	PPG
1998—Valparaiso	25	210	59	112	.527	15	30	.500	60	5	133	2.4	0.2	5.3
1999—Valparaiso	30	472	107	225	.476	58	89	.652	144	8	272	4.8	0.3	9.1
2000—Valparaiso	29	640	161	307	.524	87	119	.731	209	34	411	7.2	1.2	14.2
2001—Valparaiso	33	833	165	304	.543	71	107	.664	244	37	401	7.4	1.1	12.2
Totals	117	2155	492	948	.519	231	345	.670	657	84	1217	5.6	0.7	10.4

Three-point field goals: 1999-00, 0-for-1. 2000-01, 2-for-5 (.400). 2001-02, 0-for-6. Totals, 2-for-12 (.167).

WNBA REGULAR-SEASON RECORD

Season Team	G	Min.	FGM	FGA	Pct.	FTM	FTA	Pct.	REBOUNDS Off.	Def.	Tot.	Ast.	St.	Blk.	TO	Pts.	AVERAGES RPG	APG	PPG
2005—Los Angeles	7	16	2	3	.667	0	0	...	2	0	2	0	0	0	2	4	0.3	0.0	0.6
Totals	7	16	2	3	.667	0	0	...	2	0	2	0	0	0	2	4	0.3	0.0	0.6

Personal fouls/disqualifications: 2005-06, 5/0. Totals, 5/0.

NOLAN, DEANNA   G/F   SHOCK

PERSONAL: Born August 25, 1979, in Flint, Mich. ... 6-0/160. (1.83/72.6). ... Full name: Deanna Nicole Nolan
HIGH SCHOOL: Flint Northern (Flint, Mich.).
COLLEGE: Georgia.
TRANSACTIONS/CAREER NOTES: Selected by Detroit in the first round (sixth overall) of WNBA Draft, April 20, 2001.
MISCELLANEOUS: Member of WNBA Championship team (2003).

N

COLLEGE RECORD

Season Team	G	Min.	FGM	FGA	Pct.	FTM	FTA	Pct.	Reb.	Ast.	Pts.	AVERAGES RPG	APG	PPG
1998—Georgia	26	543	73	175	.417	36	57	.632	125	48	187	4.8	1.8	7.2
1999—Georgia	36	1008	178	325	.548	70	89	.787	164	126	436	4.6	3.5	12.1
2000—Georgia	24	614	126	278	.453	51	69	.739	94	78	321	3.9	3.3	13.4
Totals	86	2165	377	778	.485	157	215	.730	383	252	944	4.5	2.9	11.0

Three-point field goals: 1998-99, 5-for-32 (.156). 1999-00, 10-for-27 (.370). 2000-01, 18-for-55 (.327). Totals, 33-for-114 (.289).

WNBA REGULAR-SEASON RECORD

NOTES: All-WNBA first team (2005). ... All-WNBA second team (2003). ... All-Defensive second team (2005).

Season Team	G	Min.	FGM	FGA	Pct.	FTM	FTA	Pct.	REBOUNDS Off.	Def.	Tot.	Ast.	St.	Blk.	TO	Pts.	AVERAGES RPG	APG	PPG
2001—Detroit..............	27	545	64	194	.330	43	53	.811	16	37	53	30	17	6	35	192	2.0	1.1	7.1
2002—Detroit..............	32	804	103	248	.415	29	36	.806	17	70	87	62	27	12	61	277	2.7	1.9	8.7
2003—Detroit..............	32	954	136	312	.436	76	96	.792	12	95	107	83	41	14	69	396	3.3	2.6	12.4
2004—Detroit..............	34	1138	166	435	.382	99	124	.798	29	105	134	112	66	12	90	464	3.9	3.3	13.6
2005—Detroit..............	33	1213	184	462	.398	128	160	.800	31	125	156	121	55	14	100	524	4.7	3.7	15.9
Totals	158	4654	653	1651	.396	375	469	.800	105	432	537	408	206	58	355	1853	3.4	2.6	11.7

Three-point field goals: 2001-02, 21-for-73 (.288). 2002-03, 42-for-114 (.368). 2003-04, 48-for-114 (.421). 2004-05, 33-for-114 (.289). 2005-06, 28-for-90 (.311). Totals, 172-for-505 (.341).

Personal fouls/disqualifications: 2001-02, 43/0. 2002-03, 74/1. 2003-04, 65/0. 2004-05, 75/1. 2005-06, 64/0. Totals, 321/2.

Season Team	G	Min.	FGM	FGA	Pct.	FTM	FTA	Pct.	REBOUNDS Off.	Def.	Tot.	Ast.	St.	Blk.	TO	Pts.	AVERAGES RPG	APG	PPG
2003—Detroit.............	8	257	44	96	.458	15	16	.938	4	25	29	21	10	2	13	124	3.6	2.6	15.5
2004—Detroit.............	3	119	18	45	.400	14	15	.933	3	11	14	7	5	0	10	54	4.7	2.3	18.0
2005—Detroit.............	2	79	15	37	.405	6	7	.857	1	7	8	7	2	2	6	37	4.0	3.5	18.5
Totals	13	455	77	178	.433	35	38	.921	8	43	51	35	17	4	29	215	3.9	2.7	16.5

Three-point field goals: 2003-04, 21-for-47 (.447). 2004-05, 4-for-13 (.308). 2005-06, 1-for-4 (.250). Totals, 26-for-64 (.406).
Personal fouls/disqualifications: 2003-04, 21/0. 2004-05, 5/0. 2005-06, 4/0. Totals, 30/0.

WNBA ALL-STAR GAME RECORD

Season Team	Min.	FGM	FGA	Pct.	FTM	FTA	Pct.	REBOUNDS Off.	Def.	Tot.	Ast.	PF	Dq.	St.	Blk.	TO	Pts.
2003—Detroit....................	22	5	10	.500	2	3	.667	2	4	6	1	1	0	1	0	0	15
2005—Detroit....................	22	7	21	.333	2	2	1.000	2	2	4	1	2	0	1	0	3	20
Totals	44	12	31	.387	4	5	.800	4	6	10	2	3	0	2	0	3	35

Three-point field goals: 2004, 3-for-7 (.429). 2006, 4-for-8 (.500). Totals, 7-for-15 (.467).

OHLDE, NICOLE   F/C   LYNX

PERSONAL: Born March 12, 1982, in Clay Center, Kan. ... 6-5/180. (1.96/81.6). ... Full name: Nicole Katherine Ohlde
HIGH SCHOOL: Center (Clay Center, Kan.).
COLLEGE: Kansas State.
TRANSACTIONS/CAREER NOTES: Selected by Minnesota in first round (sixth overall) of WNBA Draft, April 17, 2004.
MISCELLANEOUS: Member of gold medal-winning USA Basketball World Championship for Young Women team (2002, 2003).

COLLEGE RECORD

NOTES: Kodak All-American (2003, 2004). ... AP All-American first team (2003, 2004). ... USBWA All-American (2003, 2004). ... Big 12 Conference Player of the Year (2003, 2004). ... All-Big 12 first team (2002, 2003, 2004). ... All-Big 12 third team (2001). ... Big 12 Freshman of the Year (2001). ... Academic All-Big 12 first team (2002, 2003, 2004). ... Kansas State's all-time leading scorer (2,161), rebounder (970) and shot blocker (201).

Season Team	G	Min.	FGM	FGA	Pct.	FTM	FTA	Pct.	Reb.	Ast.	Pts.	AVERAGES RPG	APG	PPG
2000—Kansas State	27	827	191	381	.501	82	122	.672	220	45	464	8.1	1.7	17.2
2001—Kansas State	34	1149	245	423	.579	120	184	.652	262	94	610	7.7	2.8	17.9
2002—Kansas State	34	1169	243	424	.573	138	205	.673	306	109	625	9.0	3.2	18.4
2003—Kansas State	31	958	203	356	.570	136	196	.694	207	119	542	6.7	3.8	17.5
Totals.................	126	4103	882	1584	.557	476	707	.673	995	367	2241	7.9	2.9	17.8

Three-point field goals: 2000-01, 0-for-2. 2001-02, 0-for-2. 2002-03, 1-for-5 (.200). Totals, 1-for-9 (.111).

WNBA REGULAR-SEASON RECORD

Season Team	G	Min.	FGM	FGA	Pct.	FTM	FTA	Pct.	REBOUNDS Off.	Def.	Tot.	Ast.	St.	Blk.	TO	Pts.	AVERAGES RPG	APG	PPG
2004—Minnesota	34	1018	136	308	.442	125	177	.706	83	111	194	60	16	45	74	397	5.7	1.8	11.7
2005—Minnesota	34	1038	133	292	.455	116	142	.817	63	131	194	78	21	22	84	382	5.7	2.3	11.2
Totals	68	2056	269	600	.448	241	319	.755	146	242	388	138	37	67	158	779	5.7	2.0	11.5

Three-point field goals: 2004-05, 0-for-2. 2005-06, 0-for-2. Totals, 0-for-4 (.000).
Personal fouls/disqualifications: 2004-05, 103/1. 2005-06, 92/1. Totals, 195/2.

WNBA PLAYOFF RECORD

Season Team	G	Min.	FGM	FGA	Pct.	FTM	FTA	Pct.	REBOUNDS Off.	Def.	Tot.	Ast.	St.	Blk.	TO	Pts.	AVERAGES RPG	APG	PPG
2004—Minnesota	2	74	11	23	.478	6	10	.600	4	6	10	9	1	0	6	28	5.0	4.5	14.0
Totals	2	74	11	23	.478	6	10	.600	4	6	10	9	1	0	6	28	5.0	4.5	14.0

Personal fouls/disqualifications: 2004-05, 5/0. Totals, 5/0.

PAGE, MURRIEL   C   SPARKS

PERSONAL: Born September 18, 1975, in Laurel, Miss. ... 6-2/160. (1.88/72.6).
COLLEGE: Florida.
TRANSACTIONS/CAREER NOTES: Selected by Washington in first round (third overall) of WNBA Draft, April 29, 1998. ... Traded by Washington with G Tameka Johnson to Los Angeles for G Nikki Teasley, March 1, 2006.

COLLEGE RECORD

NOTES: Kodak All-American first team (1998).

Season Team	G	Min.	FGM	FGA	Pct.	FTM	FTA	Pct.	Reb.	Ast.	Pts.	AVERAGES RPG	APG	PPG
1994—Florida	33	...	151	246	.614	47	90	.522	239	30	349	7.2	0.9	10.6
1995—Florida	30	...	172	354	.486	88	140	.629	271	48	432	9.0	1.6	14.4
1996—Florida	33	...	214	394	.543	94	157	.599	339	52	522	10.3	1.6	15.8
1997—Florida	32	...	253	443	.571	105	156	.673	402	70	612	12.6	2.2	19.1
Totals....................................	128	...	790	1437	.550	334	543	.615	1251	200	1915	9.8	1.6	15.0

Three-point field goals: 1997-98, 1-for-6 (.167). Totals, 1-for-6 (.167).

O
P

WNBA REGULAR-SEASON RECORD

NOTES: Bud Light Shooting Champion (1999, 2000).

Season Team	G	Min.	FGM	FGA	Pct.	FTM	FTA	Pct.	Off.	Def.	Tot.	Ast.	St.	Blk.	TO	Pts.	RPG	APG	PPG
1998—Washington	30	955	104	217	.479	41	65	.631	81	127	208	40	19	13	57	249	6.9	1.3	8.3
1999—Washington	32	916	105	183	.574	71	104	.683	68	145	213	28	24	30	49	281	6.7	0.9	8.8
2000—Washington	32	1046	131	222	.590	52	92	.565	79	129	208	64	23	32	63	314	6.5	2.0	9.8
2001—Washington	32	989	100	231	.433	21	36	.583	74	103	177	55	30	36	60	225	5.5	1.7	7.0
2002—Washington	32	750	88	195	.451	30	53	.566	55	100	155	37	14	15	45	208	4.8	1.2	6.5
2003—Washington	34	850	83	220	.377	42	56	.750	62	90	152	35	18	24	41	213	4.5	1.0	6.3
2004—Washington	33	809	81	175	.463	22	40	.550	40	100	140	36	25	16	30	184	4.2	1.1	5.6
2005—Washington	34	589	47	119	.395	8	8	1.000	21	62	83	25	15	9	23	108	2.4	0.7	3.2
Totals	259	6904	739	1562	.473	287	454	.632	480	856	1336	320	168	175	368	1782	5.2	1.2	6.9

Three-point field goals: 1998-99, 0-for-2. 2001-02, 4-for-17 (.235). 2002-03, 2-for-4 (.500). 2003-04, 5-for-12 (.417). 2004-05, 0-for-3. 2005-06, 6-for-22 (.273). Totals, 17-for-60 (.283).

Personal fouls/disqualifications: 1998-99, 97/1. 1999-00, 103/4. 2000-01, 103/2. 2001-02, 88/2. 2002-03, 79/0. 2003-04, 101/0. 2004-05, 85/1. 2005-06, 56/0. Totals, 712/10.

WNBA PLAYOFF RECORD

Season Team	G	Min.	FGM	FGA	Pct.	FTM	FTA	Pct.	Off.	Def.	Tot.	Ast.	St.	Blk.	TO	Pts.	RPG	APG	PPG
2000—Washington	2	69	4	9	.444	3	4	.750	2	4	6	1	2	0	4	11	3.0	0.5	5.5
2002—Washington	5	113	17	27	.630	14	15	.933	6	16	22	4	1	4	3	48	4.4	0.8	9.6
2004—Washington	3	90	5	16	.313	1	2	.500	3	11	14	4	0	1	3	11	4.7	1.3	3.7
Totals	10	272	26	52	.500	18	21	.857	11	31	42	9	3	5	10	70	4.2	0.9	7.0

Personal fouls/disqualifications: 2000-01, 5/0. 2002-03, 12/0. 2004-05, 5/0. Totals, 22/0.

PAIGE, YOLANDA   G   FEVER

PERSONAL: Born September 18, 1983, in Virginia Beach, Va. ... 5-6/145. (1.68/65.8). ... Full name: Yolanda Michelle Paige
HIGH SCHOOL: Bayside (Virginia Beach, Va.).
COLLEGE: West Virginia.
TRANSACTIONS/CAREER NOTES: Selected by Indiana in the second round (16th overall) of the WNBA Draft, April 16, 2005.

COLLEGE RECORD

NOTES: AP All-American honorable mention (2005). ... All-Big East second team (2005). ... All-Big East third team (2004). ... All-Big East Tournament team (2004). ... All-Big East rookie team (2002). ... Broke her own West Virginia single-season assists record in 2005 (287). ... Led the nation in assists per game in 2005 (9.0).

Season Team	G	Min.	FGM	FGA	Pct.	FTM	FTA	Pct.	Reb.	Ast.	Pts.	RPG	APG	PPG
2001—West Virginia	28	1046	113	267	.423	81	117	.692	135	153	319	4.8	5.5	11.4
2002—West Virginia	28	957	107	283	.378	63	85	.741	89	199	283	3.2	7.1	10.1
2003—West Virginia	32	1066	145	358	.405	88	116	.759	146	253	388	4.6	7.9	12.1
2004—West Virginia	32	1285	150	361	.416	83	109	.761	106	287	402	3.3	9.0	12.6
Totals	120	4354	515	1269	.406	315	427	.738	476	892	1392	4.0	7.4	11.6

WNBA REGULAR-SEASON RECORD

Season Team	G	Min.	FGM	FGA	Pct.	FTM	FTA	Pct.	Off.	Def.	Tot.	Ast.	St.	Blk.	TO	Pts.	RPG	APG	PPG
2005—Indiana	13	78	6	22	.273	3	4	.750	2	7	9	13	2	0	6	16	0.7	1.0	1.2
Totals	13	78	6	22	.273	3	4	.750	2	7	9	13	2	0	6	16	0.7	1.0	1.2

Three-point field goals: 2005-06, 1-for-5 (.200). Totals, 1-for-5 (.200).
Personal fouls/disqualifications: 2005-06, 1/0. Totals, 1/0.

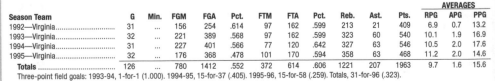

PALMER, WENDY   F   STORM

PERSONAL: Born August 12, 1974, in Timberlake, N.C. ... 6-2/165. (1.88/74.8). ... Full name: Wendy LaWan Palmer
COLLEGE: Virginia.
TRANSACTIONS/CAREER NOTES: Selected by Utah in second round (ninth overall) in WNBA Elite Draft, February 27, 1997. ... Traded by Utah with F Olympia Scott-Richardson to Detroit for G Korie Hlede and F Cindy Brown, July 29, 1999. ... Traded by Detroit with a second-round pick in 2003 WNBA Draft to Orlando for G Elaine Powell and a first-round pick, July 8, 2002. ... Signed by San Antonio, April 21, 2005. ... Signed by Seattle, February 24, 2006.

COLLEGE RECORD

NOTES: Kodak All-American first team (1995, 1996).

Season Team	G	Min.	FGM	FGA	Pct.	FTM	FTA	Pct.	Reb.	Ast.	Pts.	RPG	APG	PPG
1992—Virginia	31	...	156	254	.614	97	162	.599	213	21	409	6.9	0.7	13.2
1993—Virginia	32	...	221	389	.568	97	162	.599	323	60	540	10.1	1.9	16.9
1994—Virginia	31	...	227	401	.566	77	120	.642	327	63	546	10.5	2.0	17.6
1995—Virginia	32	...	176	368	.478	101	170	.594	358	63	468	11.2	2.0	14.6
Totals	126	...	780	1412	.552	372	614	.606	1221	207	1963	9.7	1.6	15.6

Three-point field goals: 1993-94, 1-for-1 (1.000). 1994-95, 15-for-37 (.405). 1995-96, 15-for-58 (.259). Totals, 31-for-96 (.323).

P

WNBA REGULAR-SEASON RECORD

NOTES: All-WNBA second team (1997). ... WNBA Co-Most Improved Player (2004).

Season Team	G	Min.	FGM	FGA	Pct.	FTM	FTA	Pct.	Off.	Def.	Tot.	Ast.	St.	Blk.	TO	Pts.	RPG	APG	PPG
1997—Utah	28	936	157	420	.374	117	173	.676	76	149	225	48	47	6	71	443	8.0	1.7	15.8
1998—Utah	28	761	145	307	.472	81	124	.653	70	116	186	30	18	5	56	377	6.6	1.1	13.5
1999—Utah-Detroit	31	741	104	241	.432	86	123	.699	50	138	188	42	9	12	58	307	6.1	1.4	9.9
2000—Detroit	32	914	167	373	.448	95	135	.704	67	152	219	39	20	10	65	441	6.8	1.2	13.8
2001—Detroit	22	651	91	215	.423	40	59	.678	38	116	154	23	23	4	48	233	7.0	1.0	10.6
2002—Detroit-Orlando	32	965	130	301	.432	62	92	.674	47	142	189	41	35	8	57	364	5.9	1.3	11.4
2003—Connecticut	32	433	58	147	.395	23	28	.821	29	77	106	16	11	3	35	149	3.3	0.5	4.7
2004—Connecticut	33	786	108	253	.427	68	85	.800	47	135	182	30	23	5	40	297	5.5	0.9	9.0
2005—San Antonio	34	882	125	242	.517	52	70	.743	53	140	193	33	20	7	42	326	5.7	1.0	9.6
Totals	272	7069	1085	2499	.434	624	889	.702	477	1165	1642	302	206	60	472	2937	6.0	1.1	10.8

Three-point field goals: 1997-98, 12-for-48 (.250). 1998-99, 6-for-17 (.353). 1999-00, 13-for-46 (.283). 2000-01, 12-for-48 (.250). 2001-02, 11-for-33 (.333). 2002-03, 42-for-120 (.350). 2003-04, 10-for-46 (.217). 2004-05, 13-for-41 (.317). 2005-06, 24-for-56 (.429). Totals, 143-for-455 (.314).

Personal fouls/disqualifications: 1997-98, 86/0. 1998-99, 75/1. 1999-00, 101/3. 2000-01, 112/2. 2001-02, 64/0. 2002-03, 90/0. 2003-04, 62/0. 2004-05, 77/0. 2005-06, 74/0. Totals, 741/6.

WNBA PLAYOFF RECORD

Season Team	G	Min.	FGM	FGA	Pct.	FTM	FTA	Pct.	Off.	Def.	Tot.	Ast.	St.	Blk.	TO	Pts.	RPG	APG	PPG
1999—Detroit	1	37	4	11	.364	2	3	.667	4	5	9	2	1	1	1	10	9.0	2.0	10.0
2003—Connecticut	4	64	13	22	.591	2	3	.667	1	11	12	3	0	0	7	29	3.0	0.8	7.3
2004—Connecticut	8	156	18	49	.367	5	8	.625	10	25	35	1	3	3	8	44	4.4	0.1	5.5
Totals	13	257	35	82	.427	9	14	.643	15	41	56	6	4	4	16	83	4.3	0.5	6.4

Three-point field goals: 1999-00, 0-for-2. 2003-04, 1-for-4 (.250). 2004-05, 3-for-12 (.250). Totals, 4-for-18 (.222).
Personal fouls/disqualifications: 1999-00, 3/0. 2003-04, 9/0. 2004-05, 11/0. Totals, 23/0.

WNBA ALL-STAR GAME RECORD

Season Team	Min.	FGM	FGA	Pct.	FTM	FTA	Pct.	Off.	Def.	Tot.	Ast.	PF	Dq.	St.	Blk.	TO	Pts.
2000—Detroit	14	1	6	.167	1	2	.500	0	2	2	0	1	0	0	0	0	3
Totals	14	1	6	.167	1	2	.500	0	2	2	0	1	0	0	0	0	3

Three-point field goals: 2001, 0-for-2. Totals, 0-for-2 (.000).

PENICHEIRO, TICHA   G   MONARCHS

PERSONAL: Born September 18, 1974, in Figueira da Foz, Portugal. ... 5-11/158. (1.80/71.7). ... Full name: Ticha Nunes Penicheiro
COLLEGE: Old Dominion.
TRANSACTIONS/CAREER NOTES: Selected by Sacramento in first round (second overall) of the WNBA Draft, April 29, 1998.
MISCELLANEOUS: Member of WNBA Championship team (2005).

COLLEGE RECORD

NOTES: Wade Trophy recipient (1998). ... Kodak All-American first team (1997, 1998).

Season Team	G	Min.	FGM	FGA	Pct.	FTM	FTA	Pct.	Reb.	Ast.	Pts.	RPG	APG	PPG
1994—Old Dominion	33	...	109	255	.427	48	87	.552	158	203	283	4.8	6.2	8.6
1995—Old Dominion	32	...	107	218	.491	57	85	.671	226	226	284	7.1	7.1	8.9
1996—Old Dominion	36	...	140	316	.443	87	134	.649	163	271	393	4.5	7.5	10.9
1997—Old Dominion	32	...	117	287	.408	88	140	.629	163	239	344	5.1	7.5	10.8
Totals	133	...	473	1076	.440	280	446	.628	710	939	1304	5.3	7.1	9.8

Three-point field goals: 1994-95, 17-for-51 (.333). 1995-96, 13-for-45 (.289). 1996-97, 26-for-84 (.310). 1997-98, 22-for-67 (.328). Totals, 78-for-247 (.316).

WNBA REGULAR-SEASON RECORD

NOTES: All-WNBA first team (1999, 2000). ... All-WNBA second team (2001). ... Led WNBA in assists in 1998 (7.5 apg), 1999 (7.1 apg), 2000 (7.9 apg), 2001 (7.5 apg), 2002 (8.0 apg) and 2003 (6.7 apg). ... Led WNBA in minutes (36.0 mpg) in 1998.

Season Team	G	Min.	FGM	FGA	Pct.	FTM	FTA	Pct.	Off.	Def.	Tot.	Ast.	St.	Blk.	TO	Pts.	RPG	APG	PPG
1998—Sacramento	30	1080	55	165	.333	70	109	.642	13	128	141	224	67	3	116	190	4.7	7.5	6.3
1999—Sacramento	32	1120	71	222	.320	87	131	.664	29	126	155	226	67	5	135	235	4.8	7.1	7.3
2000—Sacramento	30	936	68	185	.368	62	107	.579	12	77	89	236	70	6	71	208	3.0	7.9	6.9
2001—Sacramento	23	744	42	124	.339	49	64	.766	6	80	86	172	40	8	64	144	3.7	7.5	6.3
2002—Sacramento	24	853	60	159	.377	75	103	.728	7	95	102	192	64	1	69	203	4.3	8.0	8.5
2003—Sacramento	34	1089	62	205	.302	44	76	.579	29	90	119	229	61	1	81	183	3.5	6.7	5.4
2004—Sacramento	33	970	63	178	.354	50	70	.714	14	88	102	163	64	2	72	199	3.1	4.9	6.0
2005—Sacramento	34	927	54	172	.314	79	100	.790	8	89	97	149	48	6	67	195	2.9	4.4	5.7
Totals	240	7719	475	1410	.337	516	760	.679	118	773	891	1591	481	32	675	1557	3.7	6.6	6.5

Three-point field goals: 1998-99, 10-for-43 (.233). 1999-00, 6-for-38 (.158). 2000-01, 10-for-50 (.200). 2001-02, 11-for-42 (.262). 2002-03, 8-for-32 (.250). 2003-04, 15-for-60 (.250). 2004-05, 23-for-68 (.338). 2005-06, 8-for-41 (.195). Totals, 91-for-374 (.243).

Personal fouls/disqualifications: 1998-99, 90/1. 1999-00, 87/1. 2000-01, 71/1. 2001-02, 58/1. 2002-03, 49/0. 2003-04, 76/1. 2004-05, 64/0. 2005-06, 64/0. Totals, 559/5.

WNBA PLAYOFF RECORD

Season Team	G	Min.	FGM	FGA	Pct.	FTM	FTA	Pct.	Off.	Def.	Tot.	Ast.	St.	Blk.	TO	Pts.	RPG	APG	PPG
1999—Sacramento	1	20	1	5	.200	2	2	1.000	0	4	4	3	1	0	2	4	4.0	3.0	4.0

P

Season Team	G	Min.	FGM	FGA	Pct.	FTM	FTA	Pct.	REBOUNDS Off.	Def.	Tot.	Ast.	St.	Blk.	TO	Pts.	AVERAGES RPG	APG	PPG
2000—Sacramento	2	77	4	16	.250	5	6	.833	2	5	7	14	4	0	6	16	3.5	7.0	8.0
2001—Sacramento	5	163	10	40	.250	4	4	1.000	3	16	19	33	3	4	9	31	3.8	6.6	6.2
2003—Sacramento	6	143	8	24	.333	7	8	.875	1	13	14	18	6	3	7	25	2.3	3.0	4.2
2004—Sacramento	6	193	6	27	.222	11	16	.688	4	16	20	32	15	2	19	25	3.3	5.3	4.2
2005—Sacramento	6	162	10	31	.323	12	15	.800	2	22	24	31	6	1	14	32	4.0	5.2	5.3
Totals	26	758	39	143	.273	41	51	.804	12	76	88	131	35	10	57	133	3.4	5.0	5.1

Three-point field goals: 2000-01, 3-for-6 (.500). 2001-02, 7-for-19 (.368). 2003-04, 2-for-8 (.250). 2004-05, 2-for-15 (.133). 2005-06, 0-for-4. Totals, 14-for-52 (.269).

Personal fouls/disqualifications: 1999-00, 1/0. 2000-01, 10/1. 2001-02, 9/0. 2003-04, 12/0. 2004-05, 17/0. 2005-06, 9/0. Totals, 58/1.

WNBA ALL-STAR GAME RECORD

Season Team	Min.	FGM	FGA	Pct.	FTM	FTA	Pct.	REBOUNDS Off.	Def.	Tot.	Ast.	PF	Dq.	St.	Blk.	TO	Pts.
1999—Sacramento.............	19	0	3	.000	1	2	.500	0	0	0	3	2	0	0	0	3	1
2000—Sacramento.............	25	1	2	.500	1	2	.500	0	2	2	4	0	0	1	0	7	3
2001—Sacramento.............	21	0	2	.000	1	2	.500	0	3	3	5	1	0	2	0	5	1
2002—Sacramento.............	22	1	1	1.000	0	0	...	0	1	1	2	2	0	2	1	2	2
Totals	87	2	8	.250	3	6	.500	0	6	6	14	5	0	5	1	17	7

Three-point field goals: 2000, 0-for-1. 2001, 0-for-1. Totals, 0-for-2 (.000).

PERKINS, JIA   G   SKY

PERSONAL: Born February 23, 1982, in Newburgh, N.Y. ... 5-8/155. (1.73/70.3). ... Full name: Jia Dorene Perkins
HIGH SCHOOL: Granbury (Granbury, Texas).
COLLEGE: Texas Tech.
TRANSACTIONS/CAREER NOTES: Selected by Charlotte in the third round (35th overall) of the WNBA Draft, April 17, 2004. ... Selected by Chicago in WNBA Expansion Draft, November 16, 2005.

COLLEGE RECORD

Season Team	G	Min.	FGM	FGA	Pct.	FTM	FTA	Pct.	Reb.	Ast.	Pts.	AVERAGES RPG	APG	PPG
2000—Texas Tech	32	894	158	345	.458	95	118	.805	131	123	435	4.1	3.8	13.6
2001—Texas Tech	32	1015	217	509	.426	62	80	.775	161	121	513	5.0	3.8	16.0
2002—Texas Tech	35	1096	242	563	.430	71	91	.780	178	99	556	5.1	2.8	15.9
Totals	99	3005	617	1417	.435	228	289	.789	470	343	1504	4.7	3.5	15.2

Three-point field goals: 2000-01, 24-for-66 (.364). 2001-02, 17-for-73 (.233). 2002-03, 1-for-19 (.053). Totals, 42-for-158 (.266).

WNBA REGULAR-SEASON RECORD

Season Team	G	Min.	FGM	FGA	Pct.	FTM	FTA	Pct.	REBOUNDS Off.	Def.	Tot.	Ast.	St.	Blk.	TO	Pts.	AVERAGES RPG	APG	PPG
2004—Charlotte	4	17	0	5	.000	3	4	.750	1	2	3	1	3	0	1	3	0.8	0.3	0.8
2005—Charlotte	30	464	64	151	.424	19	30	.633	24	20	44	32	29	9	32	150	1.5	1.1	5.0
Totals	34	481	64	156	.410	22	34	.647	25	22	47	33	32	9	33	153	1.4	1.0	4.5

Three-point field goals: 2005-06, 3-for-9 (.333). Totals, 3-for-9 (.333).
Personal fouls/disqualifications: 2004-05, 2/0. 2005-06, 45/0. Totals, 47/0.

PHILLIPS, TARI   C   COMETS

PERSONAL: Born March 6, 1969, in Orlando ... 6-1/200. (1.85/90.7). ... Full name: Tari L. Phillips
HIGH SCHOOL: Edgewater (Orlando).
COLLEGE: Central Florida.
TRANSACTIONS/CAREER NOTES: Selected by Orlando in first round (eigth overall) of WNBA Draft, May 4, 1999. ... Selected by Portland in third round (12th overall) of WNBA Expansion Draft, December 15, 1999. ... Traded by Portland to New York for G Carolyn Jones-Young, May 28, 2000. ... Signed by Houston, February 16, 2005.

COLLEGE RECORD

Season Team	G	Min.	FGM	FGA	Pct.	FTM	FTA	Pct.	Reb.	Ast.	Pts.	AVERAGES RPG	APG	PPG
1986—Georgia	31	...	51	112	.455	24	37	.649	74	20	126	2.4	0.6	4.1
1987—Georgia	31	...	112	244	.459	53	85	.624	132	35	278	4.3	1.1	9.0
1988—Georgia	2	...	3	4	.750	...	...	...	1	...	6	0.5	...	3.0
1990—Central Florida....................	21	...	213	412	.517	93	151	.616	261	24	532	12.4	1.1	25.3
Totals	85	...	379	772	.491	170	273	.623	468	79	942	5.5	0.9	11.1

Three-point field goals: 1987-88, 1-for-6 (.167). 1990-91, 13-for-35 (.371). Totals, 14-for-41 (.341).

ABL RECORD

NOTES: ABL All-Star MVP (1997).

Season Team	G	Min.	FGM	FGA	Pct.	FTM	FTA	Pct.	Reb.	Ast.	Pts.	AVERAGES RPG	APG	PPG
1996—Seattle.............................	40	...	227	496	.458	99	186	.532	296	48	559	7.4	1.2	14.0
1997—Colorado...........................	44	...	247	492	.502	115	200	.575	360	37	610	8.2	0.8	13.9
1998—Colorado...........................	13	...	78	161	.484	26	45	.578	119	21	182	9.2	1.6	14.0
Totals	97	...	552	1149	.480	240	431	.557	775	106	1351	8.0	1.1	13.9

Three-point field goals: 1996-97, 6-for-27 (.222). 1997-98, 1-for-2 (.500). 1998-99, null-for-3. Totals, 7-for-32 (.219).

P

HONORS: WNBA Most Improved Player (2000). ... All-WNBA second team (2002).

Season Team	G	Min.	FGM	FGA	Pct.	FTM	FTA	Pct.	Off.	Def.	Tot.	Ast.	St.	Blk.	TO	Pts.	RPG	APG	PPG
1999—Orlando	32	335	52	128	.406	26	54	.481	26	40	66	9	19	8	48	130	2.1	0.3	4.1
2000—Portland-N.Y.	31	978	170	364	.467	85	130	.654	86	161	247	28	59	21	85	427	8.0	0.9	13.8
2001—New York	32	1049	208	410	.507	73	125	.584	89	168	257	34	48	17	84	489	8.0	1.1	15.3
2002—New York	32	1009	183	373	.491	85	126	.675	69	154	223	41	58	14	93	451	7.0	1.3	14.1
2003—New York	33	1033	142	358	.397	87	134	.649	99	181	280	56	56	28	92	372	8.5	1.7	11.3
2004—New York	13	311	33	95	.347	21	46	.457	28	42	70	16	14	10	33	87	5.4	1.2	6.7
2005—Houston	32	366	40	94	.426	31	48	.646	30	49	79	14	11	8	30	111	2.5	0.4	3.5
Totals	205	5081	828	1822	.454	408	663	.615	427	795	1222	198	265	106	465	2067	6.0	1.0	10.1

Three-point field goals: 1999-00, 0-for-3. 2000-01, 2-for-8 (.250). 2001-02, 0-for-4. 2002-03, 0-for-2. 2003-04, 1-for-5 (.200). Totals, 3-for-22 (.136). Personal fouls/disqualifications: 1999-00, 54/0. 2000-01, 110/5. 2001-02, 110/0. 2002-03, 113/2. 2003-04, 118/3. 2004-05, 41/1. 2005-06, 56/0. Totals, 602/11.

WNBA PLAYOFF RECORD

Season Team	G	Min.	FGM	FGA	Pct.	FTM	FTA	Pct.	Off.	Def.	Tot.	Ast.	St.	Blk.	TO	Pts.	RPG	APG	PPG
2000—New York	7	222	48	95	.505	18	23	.783	16	37	53	8	12	6	16	114	7.6	1.1	16.3
2001—New York	6	202	26	62	.419	16	34	.471	15	34	49	10	9	6	17	68	8.2	1.7	11.3
2002—New York	8	249	45	91	.495	25	35	.714	16	31	47	10	9	4	19	115	5.9	1.3	14.4
2005—Houston	5	53	5	12	.417	3	4	.750	1	8	9	1	1	0	4	13	1.8	0.2	2.6
Totals	26	726	124	260	.477	62	96	.646	48	110	158	29	31	16	56	310	6.1	1.1	11.9

Three-point field goals: 2000-01, 0-for-1. 2001-02, 0-for-1. 2002-03, 0-for-3. Totals, 0-for-5 (.000). Personal fouls/disqualifications: 2000-01, 26/1. 2001-02, 17/1. 2002-03, 26/0. 2005-06, 6/0. Totals, 75/2.

WNBA ALL-STAR GAME RECORD

Season Team	Min.	FGM	FGA	Pct.	FTM	FTA	Pct.	Off.	Def.	Tot.	Ast.	PF	Dq.	St.	Blk.	TO	Pts.
2000—New York	22	5	14	.357	0	3	.000	8	1	9	1	4	0	0	3	2	10
2001—New York	24	4	8	.500	1	6	.167	4	5	9	0	1	0	1	0	7	9
2002—New York	22	1	9	.111	2	2	1.000	5	5	10	0	6	1	0	0	5	4
2003—New York	20	6	12	.500	1	1	1.000	2	5	7	1	4	0	2	2	1	13
Totals	88	16	43	.372	4	12	.333	19	16	35	2	15	1	3	5	15	36

Three-point field goals: 2001, 0-for-2. Totals, 0-for-2 (.000).

PIERSON, PLENETTE   F/C   SHOCK

PERSONAL: Born August 31, 1981, in Houston. ... 6-2/170. (1.88/77.1). ... Full name: Plenette Michelle Pierson
HIGH SCHOOL: Kingwood (Kingwood, Texas).
COLLEGE: Texas Tech.
TRANSACTIONS/CAREER NOTES: Selected by Phoenix in first round (fourth overall) of WNBA Draft, April 25, 2003. ... Traded by Phoenix to Detroit for G Andrea Stinson, June 29, 2005.

COLLEGE RECORD

NOTES: AP All-American third team (2003). ... All-Big 12 first team (2003). ... All-Big 12 second team (2002). ... WBNS All-American second team (2002). ... Big 12 Conference Freshman of the Year (2000). ... NCAA Mideast Region team (2000).

Season Team	G	Min.	FGM	FGA	Pct.	FTM	FTA	Pct.	Reb.	Ast.	Pts.	RPG	APG	PPG
1999—Texas Tech	33	889	171	338	.506	107	188	.569	229	19	449	6.9	0.6	13.6
2000—Texas Tech	32	877	170	343	.496	131	205	.639	238	36	471	7.4	1.1	14.7
2001—Texas Tech	4	125	23	55	.418	12	18	.667	36	10	58	9.0	2.5	14.5
2002—Texas Tech	35	1000	238	467	.510	148	233	.635	284	51	624	8.1	1.5	17.8
Totals	104	2891	602	1203	.500	398	644	.618	787	116	1602	7.6	1.1	15.4

Three-point field goals: 2000-01, 0-for-1. 2002-03, 0-for-1. Totals, 0-for-2 (.000).

WNBA REGULAR-SEASON RECORD

Season Team	G	Min.	FGM	FGA	Pct.	FTM	FTA	Pct.	Off.	Def.	Tot.	Ast.	St.	Blk.	TO	Pts.	RPG	APG	PPG
2003—Phoenix	33	602	67	177	.379	64	101	.634	37	43	80	22	19	13	42	198	2.4	0.7	6.0
2004—Phoenix	31	803	112	253	.443	66	109	.606	46	85	131	26	26	17	49	290	4.2	0.8	9.4
2005—Phoenix-Det.	35	762	91	231	.394	87	125	.696	46	75	121	34	24	19	74	270	3.5	1.0	7.7
Totals	99	2167	270	661	.408	217	335	.648	129	203	332	82	69	49	165	758	3.4	0.8	7.7

Three-point field goals: 2003-04, 0-for-2. 2004-05, 0-for-3. 2005-06, 1-for-2 (.500). Totals, 1-for-7 (.143). Personal fouls/disqualifications: 2003-04, 87/1. 2004-05, 102/4. 2005-06, 93/2. Totals, 282/7.

WNBA PLAYOFF RECORD

Season Team	G	Min.	FGM	FGA	Pct.	FTM	FTA	Pct.	Off.	Def.	Tot.	Ast.	St.	Blk.	TO	Pts.	RPG	APG	PPG
2005—Detroit	2	20	2	5	.400	0	2	.000	3	3	6	0	1	0	0	4	3.0	0.0	2.0
Totals	2	20	2	5	.400	0	2	.000	3	3	6	0	1	0	0	4	3.0	0.0	2.0

Personal fouls/disqualifications: 2005-06, 5/0. Totals, 5/0.

POWELL, ELAINE   G   SKY

PERSONAL: Born August 9, 1975, in Monroe, La. ... 5-9/147. (1.75/66.7). ... Full name: Elaine Marie Powell
HIGH SCHOOL: Carroll (Monroe, La.).
COLLEGE: Louisiana State.
TRANSACTIONS/CAREER NOTES: Selected by Orlando in fourth round (50th overall) of WNBA Draft, May 4, 1999. ... Traded by Orlando with a first-round pick in 2003 WNBA Draft to Detroit for F Wendy Palmer and a second-round pick, July 8, 2002.

P

... Selected by Chicago in WNBA Expansion Draft, November 16, 2005.
MISCELLANEOUS: Member of WNBA Championship team (2003).

COLLEGE RECORD

Season Team	G	Min.	FGM	FGA	Pct.	FTM	FTA	Pct.	Reb.	Ast.	Pts.	AVERAGES RPG	APG	PPG
1995—Louisiana State	32	...	242	508	.476	125	167	.749	191	123	643	6.0	3.8	20.1
1996—Louisiana State	29	...	203	413	.492	92	133	.692	130	118	520	4.5	4.1	17.9
Totals	61	...	445	921	.483	217	300	.723	321	241	1163	5.3	4.0	19.1

Three-point field goals: 1995-96, 34-for-92 (.370). 1996-97, 22-for-59 (.373). Totals, 56-for-151 (.371).

ABL RECORD

Season Team	G	Min.	FGM	FGA	Pct.	FTM	FTA	Pct.	Reb.	Ast.	Pts.	AVERAGES RPG	APG	PPG
1997—Portland	44	...	183	439	.417	132	182	.725	166	164	539	3.8	3.7	12.3
1998—Portland	13	...	50	117	.427	22	36	.611	51	50	133	3.9	3.8	10.2
Totals	57	...	233	556	.419	154	218	.706	217	214	672	3.8	3.8	11.8

Three-point field goals: 1997-98, 41-for-107 (.383). 1998-99, 11-for-34 (.324). Totals, 52-for-141 (.369).

WNBA REGULAR-SEASON RECORD

Season Team	G	Min.	FGM	FGA	Pct.	FTM	FTA	Pct.	REBOUNDS Off.	Def.	Tot.	Ast.	St.	Blk.	TO	Pts.	AVERAGES RPG	APG	PPG
1999—Orlando	18	256	17	33	.515	12	22	.545	9	14	23	32	9	4	19	47	1.3	1.8	2.6
2000—Orlando	20	347	26	66	.394	17	22	.773	17	33	50	42	12	1	30	72	2.5	2.1	3.6
2001—Orlando	32	1055	119	296	.402	80	106	.755	32	66	98	98	49	7	79	357	3.1	3.1	11.2
2002—Orlando-Det.	30	705	89	220	.405	50	66	.758	33	62	95	90	43	12	71	236	3.2	3.0	7.9
2003—Detroit	33	938	105	233	.451	79	106	.745	43	63	106	129	45	9	79	296	3.2	3.9	9.0
2004—Detroit	30	760	52	138	.377	29	50	.580	31	53	84	134	36	8	61	133	2.8	4.5	4.4
2005—Detroit	29	671	62	142	.437	39	65	.600	25	55	80	77	29	4	51	163	2.8	2.7	5.6
Totals	192	4732	470	1128	.417	306	437	.700	190	346	536	602	223	45	390	1304	2.8	3.1	6.8

Three-point field goals: 1999-00, 1-for-9 (.111). 2000-01, 3-for-9 (.333). 2001-02, 39-for-102 (.382). 2002-03, 8-for-33 (.242). 2003-04, 7-for-20 (.350). 2005-06, 0-for-2. Totals, 58-for-175 (.331).
Personal fouls/disqualifications: 1999-00, 22/0. 2000-01, 21/0. 2001-02, 64/0. 2002-03, 50/0. 2003-04, 65/0. 2004-05, 67/0. 2005-06, 62/0. Totals, 351/0.

WNBA PLAYOFF RECORD

Season Team	G	Min.	FGM	FGA	Pct.	FTM	FTA	Pct.	REBOUNDS Off.	Def.	Tot.	Ast.	St.	Blk.	TO	Pts.	AVERAGES RPG	APG	PPG
2003—Detroit	8	219	16	46	.348	7	11	.636	6	24	30	38	7	4	13	41	3.8	4.8	5.1
2004—Detroit	3	97	7	14	.500	9	17	.529	4	2	6	21	10	0	8	23	2.0	7.0	7.7
2005—Detroit	2	32	0	0	...	0	0	...	2	5	7	5	3	0	2	0	3.5	2.5	0.0
Totals	13	348	23	60	.383	16	28	.571	12	31	43	64	20	4	23	64	3.3	4.9	4.9

Three-point field goals: 2003-04, 2-for-10 (.200). Totals, 2-for-10 (.200).
Personal fouls/disqualifications: 2003-04, 17/0. 2004-05, 7/0. 2005-06, 5/0. Totals, 29/0.

POWELL, NICOLE   G/F   MONARCHS

PERSONAL: Born June 22, 1982, in Sierra Vista, Ariz. ... 6-2/170. (1.88/77.1). ... Full name: Nicole Kristen Powell
HIGH SCHOOL: Mountain Pointe (Phoenix, Ariz.).
COLLEGE: Stanford.
TRANSACTIONS/CAREER NOTES: Selected by Charlotte in first round (third overall) of WNBA Draft, April 17, 2004. ... Traded by Charlotte along with Olympia Scott-Richardson and Erin Buesher to Sacramento in exchange for Tangela Smith and the Monarchs' second-round pick in the 2006 WNBA Draft.
MISCELLANEOUS: Member of silver medal-winning USA Pan American Games team. ... Member of bronze medal-winning 2001 FIBA Junior World Championships team. ... Member of gold medal-winning Women's Junior World Championship qualifying team. ... Member of WNBA Championship team (2005).

COLLEGE RECORD

NOTES: Kodak All-American (2002, 2003, 2004). ... AP All-American first team (2004). ... AP All-American second team (2002, 2003). ... USBWA All-American (2004). ... Pac-10 Player of the Year (2002, 2004). ... All-Pac-10 first team (2001, 2002, 2003, 2004). ... Pac-10 Tournament MVP (2002, 2003, 2004). ... All-Pac-10 Tournament team (2001, 2002, 2003, 2004). ... Set Stanford single-season record for rebounds (346 in 2004).

Season Team	G	Min.	FGM	FGA	Pct.	FTM	FTA	Pct.	Reb.	Ast.	Pts.	AVERAGES RPG	APG	PPG
2000—Stanford	30	1009	154	356	.433	75	102	.735	255	142	422	8.5	4.7	14.1
2001—Stanford	35	1128	195	398	.490	123	149	.826	327	220	581	9.3	6.3	16.6
2002—Stanford	23	710	149	310	.481	98	112	.875	215	88	432	9.3	3.8	18.8
2003—Stanford	31	1041	204	476	.429	161	188	.856	346	127	627	11.2	4.1	20.2
Totals	119	3888	702	1540	.456	457	551	.829	1143	577	2062	9.6	4.8	17.3

Three-point field goals: 2000-01, 39-for-106 (.368). 2001-02, 68-for-162 (.420). 2002-03, 36-for-89 (.404). 2003-04, 58-for-161 (.360). Totals, 201-for-518 (.388).

WNBA REGULAR-SEASON RECORD

NOTES: WNBA Most Improved Player (2005).

Season Team	G	Min.	FGM	FGA	Pct.	FTM	FTA	Pct.	REBOUNDS Off.	Def.	Tot.	Ast.	St.	Blk.	TO	Pts.	AVERAGES RPG	APG	PPG
2004—Charlotte	31	384	50	121	.413	8	10	.800	10	61	71	16	15	4	22	132	2.3	0.5	4.3
2005—Sacramento	34	988	120	317	.379	58	72	.806	32	92	124	62	39	16	44	364	3.6	1.8	10.7
Totals	65	1372	170	438	.388	66	82	.805	42	153	195	78	54	20	66	496	3.0	1.2	7.6

Three-point field goals: 2004-05, 24-for-58 (.414). 2005-06, 66-for-159 (.415). Totals, 90-for-217 (.415).
Personal fouls/disqualifications: 2004-05, 37/0. 2005-06, 83/0. Totals, 120/0.

P

WNBA PLAYOFF RECORD

Season Team	G	Min.	FGM	FGA	Pct.	FTM	FTA	Pct.	Off.	Def.	Tot.	Ast.	St.	Blk.	TO	Pts.	RPG	APG	PPG
									REBOUNDS								AVERAGES		
2005—Sacramento	8	257	30	78	.385	8	10	.800	2	18	20	15	7	1	12	88	2.5	1.9	11.0
Totals	8	257	30	78	.385	8	10	.800	2	18	20	15	7	1	12	88	2.5	1.9	11.0

Three-point field goals: 2005-06, 20-for-42 (.476). Totals, 20-for-42 (.476).
Personal fouls/disqualifications: 2005-06, 16/0. Totals, 16/0.

RAGLAND, FELICIA   G   COMETS

PERSONAL: Born February 3, 1980, in Tulare, Calif. ... 5-9/135. (1.75/61.2). ... Full name: Felicia Rae Ragland
HIGH SCHOOL: Tulare Western (Tulare, Calif.).
COLLEGE: Oregon State.
TRANSACTIONS/CAREER NOTES: Selected by Seattle in second round (28th overall) of WNBA Draft, April 19, 2002. ... Signed by Houston, March 3, 2004.

COLLEGE RECORD

Season Team	G	Min.	FGM	FGA	Pct.	FTM	FTA	Pct.	Reb.	Ast.	Pts.	RPG	APG	PPG
												AVERAGES		
1998—Oregon State	27	674	78	214	.364	31	47	.660	126	49	205	4.7	1.8	7.6
1999—Oregon State	30	928	146	391	.373	68	91	.747	186	86	388	6.2	2.9	12.9
2000—Oregon State	29	910	206	464	.444	97	129	.752	215	56	572	7.4	1.9	19.7
2001—Oregon State	32	1037	229	581	.394	111	134	.828	212	73	638	6.6	2.3	19.9
Totals	118	3549	659	1650	.399	307	401	.766	739	264	1803	6.3	2.2	15.3

Three-point field goals: 1998-99, 18-for-57 (.316). 1999-00, 28-for-105 (.267). 2000-01, 63-for-136 (.463). 2001-02, 69-for-199 (.347). Totals, 178-for-497 (.358).

WNBA REGULAR-SEASON RECORD

Season Team	G	Min.	FGM	FGA	Pct.	FTM	FTA	Pct.	Off.	Def.	Tot.	Ast.	St.	Blk.	TO	Pts.	RPG	APG	PPG
									REBOUNDS								AVERAGES		
2002—Seattle	31	432	48	125	.384	23	28	.821	27	21	48	23	27	1	29	141	1.5	0.7	4.5
2003—Phoenix	3	39	1	12	.083	2	2	1.000	0	2	2	2	2	0	3	5	0.7	0.7	1.7
2004—Houston	34	517	44	120	.367	11	13	.846	19	48	67	38	25	3	32	118	2.0	1.1	3.5
2005—Houston	4	9	0	1	.000	0	0	...	0	0	0	1	0	0	0	0	0.0	0.3	0.0
Totals	72	997	93	258	.360	36	43	.837	46	71	117	64	54	4	64	264	1.6	0.9	3.7

Three-point field goals: 2002-03, 22-for-55 (.400). 2003-04, 1-for-5 (.200). 2004-05, 19-for-49 (.388). Totals, 42-for-109 (.385).
Personal fouls/disqualifications: 2002-03, 44/0. 2003-04, 4/0. 2004-05, 48/0. 2005-06, 3/0. Totals, 99/0.

WNBA PLAYOFF RECORD

Season Team	G	Min.	FGM	FGA	Pct.	FTM	FTA	Pct.	Off.	Def.	Tot.	Ast.	St.	Blk.	TO	Pts.	RPG	APG	PPG
									REBOUNDS								AVERAGES		
2002—Seattle	2	19	3	9	.333	0	0	...	2	4	6	1	0	0	2	7	3.0	0.5	3.5
Totals	2	19	3	9	.333	0	0	...	2	4	6	1	0	0	2	7	3.0	0.5	3.5

Three-point field goals: 2002-03, 1-for-3 (.333). Totals, 1-for-3 (.333).

RASMUSSEN, KRISTEN   F   MERCURY

PERSONAL: Born November 1, 1978, in East Lansing, Mich. ... 6-2/172. (1.88/78.0).
HIGH SCHOOL: Okemos (Okemos, Mich.).
COLLEGE: Michigan State.
TRANSACTIONS/CAREER NOTES: Selected by Utah in fourth round (51st overall) of WNBA Draft, April 25, 2000. ... Waived by Utah, June 8, 2000. ... Added by Miami, June 13, 2000. ... Traded by Indiana to Houston for a third-round pick in the 2006 WNBA Draft, April 26, 2005. ... Traded by Houston with F Adrienne Goodson to Charlotte for G Dawn Staley, August 1, 2005. ... Signed by Phoenix, March 2, 2006.

NOTES: All-Big Ten first team (2000). ... All-Big Ten second team (1999). ... Holds MSU career blocks record (194). ... Led Big Ten in blocks in 1999 (1.84 bpg). ... Led Big Ten in rebounding (9.8 rpg) double-doubles (16) in 2000.

COLLEGE RECORD

Season Team	G	Min.	FGM	FGA	Pct.	FTM	FTA	Pct.	Reb.	Ast.	Pts.	RPG	APG	PPG
												AVERAGES		
1996—Michigan State	29	...	98	190	.516	46	67	.687	157	23	243	5.4	0.8	8.4
1997—Michigan State	27	...	124	245	.506	74	91	.813	217	45	322	8.0	1.7	11.9
1998—Michigan State	31	...	188	363	.518	87	109	.798	286	96	470	9.2	3.1	15.2
1999—Michigan State	31	...	185	347	.533	81	101	.802	304	85	458	9.8	2.7	14.8
Totals	118	...	595	1145	.520	288	368	.783	964	249	1493	8.2	2.1	12.7

Three-point field goals: 1996-97, 1-for-1 (1.000). 1997-98, null-for-2. 1998-99, 7-for-21 (.333). 1999-00, 7-for-15 (.467). Totals, 15-for-39 (.385).

WNBA REGULAR-SEASON RECORD

Season Team	G	Min.	FGM	FGA	Pct.	FTM	FTA	Pct.	Off.	Def.	Tot.	Ast.	St.	Blk.	TO	Pts.	RPG	APG	PPG
									REBOUNDS								AVERAGES		
2000—Utah-Miami	26	463	35	100	.350	54	64	.844	45	53	98	28	25	14	30	126	3.8	1.1	4.8
2001—Miami	28	416	31	86	.360	12	16	.750	33	55	88	16	11	14	31	75	3.1	0.6	2.7
2002—Miami	31	674	64	116	.552	39	46	.848	41	76	117	41	18	16	37	170	3.8	1.3	5.5
2003—Indiana	33	814	94	200	.470	31	39	.795	44	71	115	64	24	15	48	226	3.5	1.9	6.8
2004—Indiana	33	692	56	135	.415	30	38	.789	41	72	113	47	21	14	35	152	3.4	1.4	4.6

R

Season Team	G	Min.	FGM	FGA	Pct.	FTM	FTA	Pct.	REBOUNDS Off.	Def.	Tot.	Ast.	St.	Blk.	TO	Pts.	RPG	APG	PPG
2005—Hou.-Charlotte ...	27	551	49	102	.480	22	30	.733	28	53	81	24	14	16	20	127	3.0	0.9	4.7
Totals	178	3610	329	739	.445	188	233	.807	232	380	612	220	113	89	201	876	3.4	1.2	4.9

Three-point field goals: 2000-01, 2-for-7 (.286). 2001-02, 1-for-4 (.250). 2002-03, 3-for-7 (.429). 2003-04, 7-for-15 (.467). 2004-05, 10-for-27 (.370). 2005-06, 7-for-18 (.389). Totals, 30-for-78 (.385).
Personal fouls/disqualifications: 2000-01, 49/0. 2001-02, 48/0. 2002-03, 63/0. 2003-04, 65/0. 2004-05, 51/0. 2005-06, 64/0. Totals, 340/0.

WNBA PLAYOFF RECORD

Season Team	G	Min.	FGM	FGA	Pct.	FTM	FTA	Pct.	REBOUNDS Off.	Def.	Tot.	Ast.	St.	Blk.	TO	Pts.	RPG	APG	PPG
2001—Miami	3	23	0	5	.000	1	2	.500	3	3	6	0	1	0	6	1	2.0	0.0	0.3
Totals	3	23	0	5	.000	1	2	.500	3	3	6	0	1	0	6	1	2.0	0.0	0.3

Personal fouls/disqualifications: 2001-02, 1/0. Totals, 1/0.

RILEY, RUTH   C   SHOCK

PERSONAL: Born August 28, 1979, in Ranson, Kan. ... 6-5/195. (1.96/88.5).
HIGH SCHOOL: North Miami (Macy, Ind.).
COLLEGE: Notre Dame.
TRANSACTIONS/CAREER NOTES: Selected by Miami in first round (fifth overall) of WNBA Draft, April 20, 2001.
MISCELLANEOUS: Member of WNBA Championship team (2003). ... Member of silver medal-winning 1999 USA World University Games team.

COLLEGE RECORD

NOTES: Member of NCAA Division I Championship team (2001). ... Naismith Award winner (2001). ... AP Player of the Year (2001) . ... Kodak All-American first team (2001). ... NCAA Final Four Most Outstanding Player (2001). ... Led NCAA in field-goal percentage (.683) in 1998-99.

Season Team	G	Min.	FGM	FGA	Pct.	FTM	FTA	Pct.	Reb.	Ast.	Pts.	RPG	APG	PPG
1997—Notre Dame........................	32	...	141	235	.600	86	115	.748	233	21	368	7.3	0.7	11.5
1998—Notre Dame........................	31	...	198	290	.683	118	171	.690	260	40	514	8.4	1.3	16.6
1999—Notre Dame........................	32	...	193	314	.615	132	164	.805	233	41	518	7.3	1.3	16.2
2000—Notre Dame........................	36	...	245	390	.628	182	237	.768	281	70	672	7.8	1.9	18.7
Totals	131	...	777	1229	.632	518	687	.754	1007	172	2072	7.7	1.3	15.8

WNBA REGULAR-SEASON RECORD

Season Team	G	Min.	FGM	FGA	Pct.	FTM	FTA	Pct.	REBOUNDS Off.	Def.	Tot.	Ast.	St.	Blk.	TO	Pts.	RPG	APG	PPG
2001—Miami	32	799	77	162	.475	64	83	.771	51	79	130	26	25	46	63	218	4.1	0.8	6.8
2002—Miami	26	519	60	129	.465	28	46	.609	24	66	90	25	11	41	49	148	3.5	1.0	5.7
2003—Detroit...............	34	995	115	231	.498	97	127	.764	59	142	201	64	25	58	82	327	5.9	1.9	9.6
2004—Detroit...............	34	1037	153	343	.446	71	87	.816	68	131	199	50	31	53	82	378	5.9	1.5	11.1
2005—Detroit...............	33	855	100	267	.375	48	60	.800	43	113	156	39	23	46	68	251	4.7	1.2	7.6
Totals	159	4205	505	1132	.446	308	403	.764	245	531	776	204	115	244	344	1322	4.9	1.3	8.3

Three-point field goals: 2004-05, 1-for-2 (.500). 2005-06, 3-for-12 (.250). Totals, 4-for-14 (.286).
Personal fouls/disqualifications: 2001-02, 107/3. 2002-03, 87/1. 2003-04, 128/2. 2004-05, 121/2. 2005-06, 131/4. Totals, 574/12.

WNBA PLAYOFF RECORD

NOTES: WNBA Finals MVP (2003).

Season Team	G	Min.	FGM	FGA	Pct.	FTM	FTA	Pct.	REBOUNDS Off.	Def.	Tot.	Ast.	St.	Blk.	TO	Pts.	RPG	APG	PPG
2001—Miami	3	110	8	19	.421	8	19	.421	5	11	16	3	1	4	3	24	5.3	1.0	8.0
2003—Detroit...............	8	258	41	106	.387	21	26	.808	15	34	49	20	5	20	13	103	6.1	2.5	12.9
2004—Detroit...............	3	95	9	21	.429	11	15	.733	7	8	15	9	2	6	2	29	5.0	3.0	9.7
2005—Detroit...............	2	54	7	17	.412	0	0	...	3	8	11	0	1	2	5	17	5.5	0.0	8.5
Totals	16	517	65	163	.399	40	60	.667	30	61	91	32	9	32	23	173	5.7	2.0	10.8

Three-point field goals: 2005-06, 3-for-3 (1.000). Totals, 3-for-3 (1.000).
Personal fouls/disqualifications: 2001-02, 12/0. 2003-04, 26/0. 2004-05, 9/0. 2005-06, 10/1. Totals, 57/1.

WNBA ALL-STAR GAME RECORD

Season Team	Min.	FGM	FGA	Pct.	FTM	FTA	Pct.	REBOUNDS Off.	Def.	Tot.	Ast.	PF	Dq.	St.	Blk.	TO	Pts.
2005—Detroit....................	16	4	5	.800	2	2	1.000	0	1	1	1	3	0	0	0	0	10
Totals	16	4	5	.800	2	2	1.000	0	1	1	1	3	0	0	0	0	10

OLYMPICS RECORD

Season Team	G	Min.	FGM	FGA	Pct.	FTM	FTA	Pct.	Reb.	Ast.	Pts.	RPG	APG	PPG
2004—United States.....................	7	58	10	15	.667	4	5	.800	17	2	24	2.4	0.3	3.4
Totals	7	58	10	15	.667	4	5	.800	17	2	24	2.4	0.3	3.4

Personal fouls/disqualifications: 2004-05, 10/0. Totals, 10/0.

ROBINSON, ASHLEY   C   SKY

PERSONAL: Born August 12, 1982, in Dallas. ... 6-4/180. (1.93/81.6). ... Full name: Ashley Khristina Robinson
HIGH SCHOOL: South Grand Prairie (Grand Prairie, Texas).
COLLEGE: Tennessee.
TRANSACTIONS/CAREER NOTES: Selected by Phoenix in second round (14th overall) of WNBA Draft, April 17, 2004. Selected by Chicago in WNBA Expansion Draft, November 16, 2005.

MISCELLANEOUS: Member of gold medal-winning 2000 USA Junior World Championships qualifying team.

COLLEGE RECORD

NOTES: SEC All-Freshman team (2001). ... All-SEC honorable mention (media, 2001). ... Ranks third all-time on Tennessee blocked shots list (200).

Season Team	G	Min.	FGM	FGA	Pct.	FTM	FTA	Pct.	Reb.	Ast.	Pts.	RPG	APG	PPG
2000—Tennessee	34	749	124	252	.492	53	103	.515	181	26	301	5.3	0.8	8.9
2001—Tennessee	26	377	47	123	.382	27	51	.529	68	10	121	2.6	0.4	4.7
2002—Tennessee	37	800	87	208	.418	40	102	.392	198	20	215	5.4	0.5	5.8
2003—Tennessee	35	991	120	247	.486	42	106	.396	223	55	282	6.4	1.6	8.1
Totals	132	2917	378	830	.455	162	362	.448	670	111	919	5.1	0.8	7.0

Three-point field goals: 2000-01, 0-for-6. 2001-02, 0-for-1. 2002-03, 1-for-6 (.167). Totals, 1-for-13 (.077).

WNBA REGULAR-SEASON RECORD

Season Team	G	Min.	FGM	FGA	Pct.	FTM	FTA	Pct.	Off.	Def.	Tot.	Ast.	St.	Blk.	TO	Pts.	RPG	APG	PPG
2004—Phoenix	19	130	7	14	.500	3	7	.429	4	9	13	2	8	10	4	17	0.7	0.1	0.9
2005—Phoenix	34	659	42	129	.326	19	38	.500	48	70	118	31	20	34	38	103	3.5	0.9	3.0
Totals	53	789	49	143	.343	22	45	.489	52	79	131	33	28	44	42	120	2.5	0.6	2.3

Three-point field goals: 2004-05, 0-for-1. 2005-06, 0-for-1. Totals, 0-for-2 (.000).
Personal fouls/disqualifications: 2004-05, 22/0. 2005-06, 108/3. Totals, 130/3.

ROBINSON, CRYSTAL   F   MYSTICS

PERSONAL: Born January 22, 1974, in Atoka, Okla. ... 5-11/155. (1.80/70.3).
HIGH SCHOOL: Atoka (Atoka, Okla.).
COLLEGE: Southeastern Oklahoma State.
TRANSACTIONS/CAREER NOTES: Selected by New York in first round (sixth overall) of WNBA Draft, May 4, 1999. ... Signed by Washington, February 8, 2006.

COLLEGE RECORD

Season Team	G	Min.	FGM	FGA	Pct.	FTM	FTA	Pct.	Reb.	Ast.	Pts.	RPG	APG	PPG
1992—SE Oklahoma State	13	...	91	197	.462	54	75	.720	110	49	264	8.5	3.8	20.3
1993—SE Oklahoma State	28	...	307	609	.504	131	163	.804	289	120	830	10.3	4.3	29.6
1994—SE Oklahoma State	34	...	377	716	.527	162	185	.876	346	191	1032	10.2	5.6	30.4
1995—SE Oklahoma State	37	...	335	632	.530	123	153	.804	420	187	897	11.4	5.1	24.2
Totals	112	...	1110	2154	.515	470	576	.816	1165	547	3023	10.4	4.9	27.0

Three-point field goals: 1992-93, 28-for-72 (.389). 1993-94, 85-for-214 (.397). 1994-95, 116-for-260 (.446). 1995-96, 104-for-239 (.435). Totals, 333-for-785 (.424).

ABL RECORD

NOTES: ABL Rookie of the Year (1997).

Season Team	G	Min.	FGM	FGA	Pct.	FTM	FTA	Pct.	Reb.	Ast.	Pts.	RPG	APG	PPG
1996—Colorado	40	...	236	486	.486	122	142	.859	263	108	684	6.6	2.7	17.1
1997—Colorado	43	...	224	429	.522	92	114	.807	173	146	642	4.0	3.4	14.9
1998—Colorado	9	...	22	68	.324	8	14	.571	27	29	63	3.0	3.2	7.0
Totals	92	...	482	983	.490	222	270	.822	463	283	1389	5.0	3.1	15.1

Three-point field goals: 1996-97, 90-for-208 (.433). 1997-98, 102-for-219 (.466). 1998-99, 11-for-32 (.344). Totals, 203-for-459 (.442).

WNBA REGULAR-SEASON RECORD

Season Team	G	Min.	FGM	FGA	Pct.	FTM	FTA	Pct.	Off.	Def.	Tot.	Ast.	St.	Blk.	TO	Pts.	RPG	APG	PPG
1999—New York	32	901	125	285	.439	49	58	.845	38	51	89	49	44	11	46	375	2.8	1.5	11.7
2000—New York	27	722	86	201	.428	30	33	.909	26	42	68	48	23	10	33	238	2.5	1.8	8.8
2001—New York	32	980	123	267	.461	26	29	.897	23	69	92	83	32	8	28	342	2.9	2.6	10.7
2002—New York	32	1068	126	302	.417	59	72	.819	22	70	92	81	48	12	52	378	2.9	2.5	11.8
2003—New York	33	1078	143	326	.439	47	56	.839	13	57	70	63	40	13	43	395	2.1	1.9	12.0
2004—New York	28	890	122	279	.437	40	43	.930	19	64	83	58	24	8	33	339	3.0	2.1	12.1
2005—New York	32	969	85	224	.379	30	38	.789	29	71	100	58	21	5	38	234	3.1	1.8	7.3
Totals	216	6608	810	1884	.430	281	329	.854	170	424	594	440	232	67	273	2301	2.8	2.0	10.7

Three-point field goals: 1999-00, 76-for-174 (.437). 2000-01, 36-for-102 (.353). 2001-02, 70-for-168 (.417). 2002-03, 67-for-181 (.370). 2003-04, 62-for-168 (.369). 2004-05, 55-for-144 (.382). 2005-06, 34-for-107 (.318). Totals, 400-for-1044 (.383).
Personal fouls/disqualifications: 1999-00, 78/1. 2000-01, 74/0. 2001-02, 86/1. 2002-03, 101/0. 2003-04, 94/0. 2004-05, 77/2. 2005-06, 86/1. Totals, 596/5.

WNBA PLAYOFF RECORD

Season Team	G	Min.	FGM	FGA	Pct.	FTM	FTA	Pct.	Off.	Def.	Tot.	Ast.	St.	Blk.	TO	Pts.	RPG	APG	PPG
1999—New York	6	205	32	64	.500	7	7	1.000	7	11	18	13	6	2	10	86	3.0	2.2	14.3
2000—New York	7	150	16	39	.410	5	5	1.000	13	13	20	5	9	1	10	46	2.9	0.7	6.6
2001—New York	6	223	27	54	.500	3	4	.750	7	16	23	8	8	2	14	69	3.8	1.3	11.5
2002—New York	8	259	23	65	.354	9	9	1.000	8	16	24	14	8	2	5	67	3.0	1.8	8.4
2004—New York	5	175	29	58	.500	4	5	.800	4	12	16	13	9	2	8	75	3.2	2.6	15.0
2005—New York	2	50	2	13	.154	2	2	1.000	1	7	8	4	1	1	1	7	4.0	2.0	3.5
Totals	34	1062	129	293	.440	30	32	.938	34	75	109	57	41	10	48	350	3.2	1.7	10.3

Three-point field goals: 1999-00, 15-for-39 (.385). 2000-01, 9-for-19 (.474). 2001-02, 12-for-29 (.414). 2002-03, 12-for-39 (.308). 2004-05, 13-for-33 (.394). 2005-06, 1-for-7 (.143). Totals, 62-for-166 (.373).
Personal fouls/disqualifications: 1999-00, 20/1. 2000-01, 12/0. 2001-02, 15/0. 2002-03, 17/0. 2004-05, 16/1. 2005-06, 5/0. Totals, 85/2.

SALES, NYKESHA   F   SUN

PERSONAL: Born May 10, 1976, in Bloomfield, Conn. ... 6-0/175. (1.83/79.4). ... Full name: Nykesha Simone Sales
HIGH SCHOOL: Bloomfield (Bloomfield, Conn.).
COLLEGE: Connecticut.
TRANSACTIONS/CAREER NOTES: Signed by WNBA and assigned to Orlando, September 15, 1998.

COLLEGE RECORD

NOTES: Member of NCAA Division I Championship team (1995). ... Kodak All-American first team (1997, 1998).

												AVERAGES		
Season Team	G	Min.	FGM	FGA	Pct.	FTM	FTA	Pct.	Reb.	Ast.	Pts.	RPG	APG	PPG
1994—Connecticut	35	...	159	294	.541	45	77	.584	162	73	398	4.6	2.1	11.4
1995—Connecticut	38	...	237	459	.516	92	131	.702	168	101	596	4.4	2.7	15.7
1996—Connecticut	34	...	215	420	.512	97	128	.758	192	111	556	5.6	3.3	16.4
1997—Connecticut	30	...	241	426	.566	106	135	.785	166	86	628	5.5	2.9	20.9
Totals	137	...	852	1599	.533	340	471	.722	688	371	2178	5.0	2.7	15.9

Three-point field goals: 1994-95, 35-for-81 (.432). 1995-96, 30-for-89 (.337). 1996-97, 29-for-81 (.358). 1997-98, 40-for-105 (.381). Totals, 134-for-356 (.376).

WNBA REGULAR-SEASON RECORD

NOTES: Did not play during the 1998 WNBA season due to rehabilitation of Achilles tendon after rupture suffered on February 21, 1998. ... All-WNBA second team (2004).

									REBOUNDS								AVERAGES		
Season Team	G	Min.	FGM	FGA	Pct.	FTM	FTA	Pct.	Off.	Def.	Tot.	Ast.	St.	Blk.	TO	Pts.	RPG	APG	PPG
1999—Orlando	32	1039	153	397	.385	95	118	.805	44	91	135	91	69	8	69	437	4.2	2.8	13.7
2000—Orlando	32	995	170	383	.444	43	62	.694	43	96	139	69	47	12	67	430	4.3	2.2	13.4
2001—Orlando	32	1039	166	379	.438	58	74	.784	57	115	172	58	70	6	72	433	5.4	1.8	13.5
2002—Orlando	32	1042	155	376	.412	84	106	.792	36	84	120	60	60	7	71	431	3.8	1.9	13.5
2003—Connecticut	34	1106	194	468	.415	116	144	.806	27	118	145	92	46	13	73	548	4.3	2.7	16.1
2004—Connecticut	34	1096	210	486	.432	56	77	.727	33	102	135	97	75	8	76	517	4.0	2.9	15.2
2005—Connecticut	34	1074	201	482	.417	81	108	.750	36	88	124	74	61	10	64	532	3.6	2.2	15.6
Totals	230	7391	1249	2971	.420	533	689	.774	276	694	970	541	428	64	492	3328	4.2	2.4	14.5

Three-point field goals: 1999-00, 36-for-109 (.330). 2000-01, 47-for-119 (.395). 2001-02, 43-for-137 (.314). 2002-03, 37-for-115 (.322). 2003-04, 44-for-114 (.386). 2004-05, 41-for-129 (.318). 2005-06, 49-for-116 (.422). Totals, 297-for-839 (.354).

Personal fouls/disqualifications: 1999-00, 97/2. 2000-01, 92/2. 2001-02, 109/0. 2002-03, 97/0. 2003-04, 107/3. 2004-05, 98/0. 2005-06, 96/0. Totals, 696/7.

WNBA PLAYOFF RECORD

									REBOUNDS								AVERAGES		
Season Team	G	Min.	FGM	FGA	Pct.	FTM	FTA	Pct.	Off.	Def.	Tot.	Ast.	St.	Blk.	TO	Pts.	RPG	APG	PPG
2000—Orlando	3	106	15	31	.484	0	2	.000	1	8	9	4	3	0	9	33	3.0	1.3	11.0
2003—Connecticut	4	131	17	40	.425	13	18	.722	1	12	13	9	5	3	7	47	3.3	2.3	11.8
2004—Connecticut	8	260	44	102	.431	15	22	.682	12	31	43	11	25	6	20	118	5.4	1.4	14.8
2005—Connecticut	8	270	37	101	.366	25	31	.806	10	22	32	19	16	8	16	115	4.0	2.4	14.4
Totals	23	767	113	274	.412	53	73	.726	24	73	97	43	49	17	52	313	4.2	1.9	13.6

Three-point field goals: 2000-01, 3-for-10 (.300). 2003-04, 0-for-6. 2004-05, 15-for-29 (.517). 2005-06, 16-for-38 (.421). Totals, 34-for-83 (.410).
Personal fouls/disqualifications: 2000-01, 9/0. 2003-04, 12/0. 2004-05, 22/0. 2005-06, 20/0. Totals, 63/0.

WNBA ALL-STAR GAME RECORD

								REBOUNDS									
Season Team	Min.	FGM	FGA	Pct.	FTM	FTA	Pct.	Off.	Def.	Tot.	Ast.	PF	Dq.	St.	Blk.	TO	Pts.
1999—Orlando	17	3	8	.375	0	2	.000	0	0	0	1	1	0	0	0	2	6
2000—Orlando	13	2	5	.400	0	0	...	3	0	3	1	1	0	2	0	0	5
2001—Orlando	10	4	8	.500	1	2	.500	0	1	1	0	1	0	1	0	1	10
2002—Orlando	14	3	11	.273	3	3	1.000	1	0	1	0	2	0	2	0	2	9
2003—Connecticut	11	3	6	.500	0	0	...	0	1	1	0	1	0	1	0	1	7
2005—Connecticut	20	5	10	.500	0	0	...	2	2	4	2	2	0	1	0	1	11
Totals	85	20	48	.417	4	7	.571	6	4	10	4	8	0	6	0	7	48

Three-point field goals: 2000, 0-for-3. 2001, 1-for-3 (.333). 2002, 1-for-3 (.333). 2003, 0-for-2. 2004, 1-for-3 (.333). 2006, 1-for-2 (.500). Totals, 4-for-16 (.250).

SAM, SHERI   F   STING

PERSONAL: Born May 5, 1974, in Duson, La. ... 6-0/160. (1.83/72.6). ... Full name: Sheri Lynette Sam
HIGH SCHOOL: Acadiana (Lafayette, La.).
COLLEGE: Vanderbilt.
TRANSACTIONS/CAREER NOTES: Selected by Orlando in second round (20th overall) of WNBA Draft, May 4, 1999. ... Waived by Orlando, May 28, 2000. ... Signed by Miami, June 1, 2000. ... Signed by Charlotte as an unrestricted free agent, February 15, 2005.
MISCELLANEOUS: Member of WNBA Championship team (2004).

COLLEGE RECORD

NOTES: Kodak All-American first team (1996).

												AVERAGES		
Season Team	G	Min.	FGM	FGA	Pct.	FTM	FTA	Pct.	Reb.	Ast.	Pts.	RPG	APG	PPG
1992—Vanderbilt	24	...	32	61	.525	13	27	.481	50	11	77	2.1	0.5	3.2

Season Team	G	Min.	FGM	FGA	Pct.	FTM	FTA	Pct.	Reb.	Ast.	Pts.	AVERAGES RPG	APG	PPG
1993—Vanderbilt	33	...	125	240	.521	51	75	.680	206	64	304	6.2	1.9	9.2
1994—Vanderbilt	35	...	224	417	.537	88	118	.746	291	126	544	8.3	3.6	15.5
1995—Vanderbilt	30	...	244	427	.571	111	147	.755	215	105	612	7.2	3.5	20.4
Totals	122	...	625	1145	.546	263	367	.717	762	306	1537	6.2	2.5	12.6

Three-point field goals: 1993-94, 3-for-6 (.500). 1994-95, 8-for-25 (.320). 1995-96, 13-for-41 (.317). Totals, 24-for-72 (.333).

ABL RECORD

NOTES: ABL All-Star (1997, 1998).

Season Team	G	Min.	FGM	FGA	Pct.	FTM	FTA	Pct.	Reb.	Ast.	Pts.	AVERAGES RPG	APG	PPG
1996—San Jose	39	...	210	487	.431	105	146	.719	210	117	561	5.4	3.0	14.4
1997—San Jose	43	...	238	550	.433	98	154	.636	305	109	624	7.1	2.5	14.5
1998—San Jose	15	...	87	181	.481	19	34	.559	88	36	203	5.9	2.4	13.5
Totals	97	...	535	1218	.439	222	334	.665	603	262	1388	6.2	2.7	14.3

Three-point field goals: 1996-97, 36-for-117 (.308). 1997-98, 50-for-127 (.394). 1998-99, 10-for-35 (.286). Totals, 96-for-279 (.344).

WNBA REGULAR-SEASON RECORD

Season Team	G	Min.	FGM	FGA	Pct.	FTM	FTA	Pct.	REBOUNDS Off.	Def.	Tot.	Ast.	St.	Blk.	TO	Pts.	AVERAGES RPG	APG	PPG
1999—Orlando	32	1088	134	345	.388	55	80	.688	39	107	146	77	41	9	64	364	4.6	2.4	11.4
2000—Orlando-Miami	31	904	147	380	.387	67	100	.670	38	94	132	66	35	5	74	396	4.3	2.1	12.8
2001—Miami	32	1100	180	417	.432	57	76	.750	41	96	137	88	55	8	87	444	4.3	2.8	13.9
2002—Miami	32	1073	191	440	.434	55	89	.618	58	97	155	83	69	6	71	463	4.8	2.6	14.5
2003—Minnesota	34	953	138	360	.383	74	105	.705	46	96	142	88	38	6	48	374	4.2	2.6	11.0
2004—Seattle	34	1018	117	284	.412	65	76	.855	42	97	139	82	53	6	63	310	4.1	2.4	9.1
2005—Charlotte	34	1075	146	377	.387	77	108	.713	53	92	145	91	44	2	100	387	4.3	2.7	11.4
Totals	229	7211	1053	2603	.405	450	634	.710	317	679	996	575	335	42	507	2738	4.3	2.5	12.0

Three-point field goals: 1999-00, 41-for-125 (.328). 2000-01, 35-for-120 (.292). 2001-02, 27-for-98 (.276). 2002-03, 26-for-76 (.342). 2003-04, 24-for-73 (.329). 2004-05, 11-for-42 (.262). 2005-06, 18-for-56 (.321). Totals, 182-for-590 (.308).
Personal fouls/disqualifications: 1999-00, 112/4. 2000-01, 67/0. 2001-02, 67/0. 2002-03, 83/0. 2003-04, 70/0. 2004-05, 108/1. 2005-06, 87/1. Totals, 594/6.

WNBA PLAYOFF RECORD

Season Team	G	Min.	FGM	FGA	Pct.	FTM	FTA	Pct.	REBOUNDS Off.	Def.	Tot.	Ast.	St.	Blk.	TO	Pts.	AVERAGES RPG	APG	PPG
2001—Miami	3	109	10	31	.323	9	11	.818	4	6	10	4	5	0	8	31	3.3	1.3	10.3
2003—Minnesota	3	74	10	28	.357	6	8	.750	5	11	16	8	6	0	8	26	5.3	2.7	8.7
2004—Seattle	8	248	25	76	.329	6	9	.667	13	31	44	28	10	0	25	59	5.5	3.5	7.4
Totals	14	431	45	135	.333	21	28	.750	22	48	70	40	21	0	41	116	5.0	2.9	8.3

Three-point field goals: 2001-02, 2-for-9 (.222). 2003-04, 0-for-4. 2004-05, 3-for-12 (.250). Totals, 5-for-25 (.200).
Personal fouls/disqualifications: 2001-02, 11/1. 2003-04, 6/0. 2004-05, 21/0. Totals, 38/1.

WNBA ALL-STAR GAME RECORD

Season Team	Min.	FGM	FGA	Pct.	FTM	FTA	Pct.	REBOUNDS Off.	Def.	Tot.	Ast.	PF	Dq.	St.	Blk.	TO	Pts.
2002—Miami	19	3	9	.333	0	0	...	2	3	5	2	1	0	1	0	0	7
Totals	19	3	9	.333	0	0	...	2	3	5	2	1	0	1	0	0	7

Three-point field goals: 2003, 1-for-4 (.250). Totals, 1-for-4 (.250).

SANFORD, NAKIA — F/C — MYSTICS

PERSONAL: Born May 10, 1976, in Lithaonia, Ga. ... 6-2/182. (1.88/82.6).
HIGH SCHOOL: South Gwinnett (Atlanta).
COLLEGE: Kansas.
TRANSACTIONS/CAREER NOTES: Signed by Washington, April 30, 2003.

COLLEGE RECORD

Season Team	G	Min.	FGM	FGA	Pct.	FTM	FTA	Pct.	Reb.	Ast.	Pts.	AVERAGES RPG	APG	PPG
1995—Kansas	32	807	86	174	.494	37	74	.500	211	16	209	6.6	0.5	6.5
1996—Kansas	31	839	90	185	.486	45	93	.484	218	16	225	7.0	0.5	7.3
1997—Kansas	32	806	76	176	.432	60	109	.550	194	28	212	6.1	0.9	6.6
1998—Kansas	33	951	136	261	.521	51	96	.531	209	28	323	6.3	0.8	9.8
Totals	128	3403	388	796	.487	193	372	.519	832	88	969	6.5	0.7	7.6

WNBA REGULAR-SEASON RECORD

Season Team	G	Min.	FGM	FGA	Pct.	FTM	FTA	Pct.	REBOUNDS Off.	Def.	Tot.	Ast.	St.	Blk.	TO	Pts.	AVERAGES RPG	APG	PPG
2003—Washington	17	134	20	40	.500	9	20	.450	10	16	26	1	3	2	14	49	1.5	0.1	2.9
2004—Washington	31	653	63	126	.500	43	75	.573	53	101	154	18	18	16	37	169	5.0	0.6	5.5
2005—Washington	27	293	29	60	.483	30	62	.484	15	30	45	6	10	11	17	88	1.7	0.3	3.3
Totals	75	1080	112	226	.496	82	157	.522	78	147	225	25	31	29	68	306	3.0	0.3	4.1

Personal fouls/disqualifications: 2003-04, 35/0. 2004-05, 99/0. 2005-06, 50/0. Totals, 184/0.

WNBA PLAYOFF RECORD

Season Team	G	Min.	FGM	FGA	Pct.	FTM	FTA	Pct.	Off.	Def.	Tot.	Ast.	St.	Blk.	TO	Pts.	RPG	APG	PPG
										REBOUNDS								AVERAGES	
2004—Washington	3	62	4	12	.333	5	6	.833	8	11	19	0	2	1	7	13	6.3	0.0	4.3
Totals	3	62	4	12	.333	5	6	.833	8	11	19	0	2	1	7	13	6.3	0.0	4.3

Personal fouls/disqualifications: 2004-05, 12/0. Totals, 12/0.

SCHUMACHER, KELLY   C   LIBERTY

PERSONAL: Born October 14, 1977, in Cincinnati. ... 6-4/189. (1.93/85.7). ... Full name: Kelly Marie Schumacher.
HIGH SCHOOL: Pontiac (Guyon, Quebec, Canada).
COLLEGE: Connecticut.
TRANSACTIONS/CAREER NOTES: Selected by Indiana in first round (14th overall) of WNBA Draft, April 20, 2001. ... Traded by Indiana with the 12th overall pick in the 2006 WNBA Draft to New York for the 9th pick.
MISCELLANEOUS: Attended John Abbott College in Quebec. ... Canadian College Athletic Association Player of the Year (1997). ... Member of CCAA National Championship team (1996,1997).

COLLEGE RECORD

NOTES: Member of NCAA Division I Championship team (2000).

Season Team	G	Min.	FGM	FGA	Pct.	FTM	FTA	Pct.	Reb.	Ast.	Pts.	RPG	APG	PPG
													AVERAGES	
1997—Connecticut	35	408	70	117	.598	37	70	.529	103	19	177	2.9	0.5	5.1
1998—Connecticut	31	356	63	113	.558	46	70	.657	130	16	172	4.2	0.5	5.5
1999—Connecticut	37	577	80	144	.556	26	38	.684	141	27	186	3.8	0.7	5.0
2000—Connecticut	29	491	75	143	.524	30	39	.769	126	28	182	4.3	1.0	6.3
Totals	132	1832	288	517	.557	139	217	.641	500	90	717	3.8	0.7	5.4

Three-point field goals: 2000-01, 2-for-9 (.222). Totals, 2-for-9 (.222).

WNBA REGULAR-SEASON RECORD

Season Team	G	Min.	FGM	FGA	Pct.	FTM	FTA	Pct.	Off.	Def.	Tot.	Ast.	St.	Blk.	TO	Pts.	RPG	APG	PPG
										REBOUNDS								AVERAGES	
2001—Indiana	28	380	46	93	.495	17	20	.850	23	47	70	10	5	29	21	112	2.5	0.4	4.0
2002—Indiana	31	352	45	89	.506	18	26	.692	18	41	59	13	7	23	21	108	1.9	0.4	3.5
2003—Indiana	34	480	81	169	.479	23	27	.852	40	59	99	20	7	24	32	189	2.9	0.6	5.6
2004—Indiana	32	601	92	196	.469	35	45	.778	36	68	104	25	10	31	52	224	3.3	0.8	7.0
2005—Indiana	34	516	58	138	.420	17	21	.810	26	42	68	14	10	24	33	135	2.0	0.4	4.0
Totals	159	2329	322	685	.470	110	139	.791	143	257	400	82	39	131	159	768	2.5	0.5	4.8

Three-point field goals: 2001-02, 3-for-5 (.600). 2002-03, 0-for-1. 2003-04, 4-for-9 (.444). 2004-05, 5-for-13 (.385). 2005-06, 2-for-11 (.182). Totals, 14-for-39 (.359).
Personal fouls/disqualifications: 2001-02, 41/0. 2002-03, 49/0. 2003-04, 63/0. 2004-05, 67/0. 2005-06, 59/0. Totals, 279/0.

WNBA PLAYOFF RECORD

Season Team	G	Min.	FGM	FGA	Pct.	FTM	FTA	Pct.	Off.	Def.	Tot.	Ast.	St.	Blk.	TO	Pts.	RPG	APG	PPG
										REBOUNDS								AVERAGES	
2002—Indiana	3	52	13	20	.650	4	8	.500	6	3	9	3	0	2	2	32	3.0	1.0	10.7
2005—Indiana	4	42	9	19	.474	2	2	1.000	7	1	8	2	2	4	0	20	2.0	0.5	5.0
Totals	7	94	22	39	.564	6	10	.600	13	4	17	5	2	6	2	52	2.4	0.7	7.4

Three-point field goals: 2002-03, 2-for-2 (1.000). Totals, 2-for-2 (1.000).
Personal fouls/disqualifications: 2002-03, 6/0. 2005-06, 6/0. Totals, 12/0.

SCOTT, OLYMPIA   C   FEVER

PERSONAL: Born August 5, 1976, in Los Angeles. ... 6-2/175. (1.88/79.4). ... Full name: Olympia Ranee Scott
COLLEGE: Stanford.
TRANSACTIONS/CAREER NOTES: Selected by Utah in second round (11th overall) of WNBA Draft, April 29, 1998 . ... Traded by Utah with F Wendy Palmer to the Detroit Shock for G Korie Hlede and F Cindy Brown, July 29, 1999. ... Traded by Detroit with a third-round pick in the 2002 WNBA Draft to Indiana for a second-round pick in the 2002 WNBA Draft, May 27, 2001. ... Traded by Charlotte along with F Nicole Powell and G Erin Buescher to Sacramento in exchange for F/C Tangela Smith and the Monarchs' second-round pick in the 2006 WNBA Draft. ... Signed by Indiana, February 3, 2006.
MISCELLANEOUS: Member of WNBA Championship team (2005).

COLLEGE RECORD

Season Team	G	Min.	FGM	FGA	Pct.	FTM	FTA	Pct.	Reb.	Ast.	Pts.	RPG	APG	PPG
													AVERAGES	
1994—Stanford	23	...	55	118	.466	31	53	.585	106	18	141	4.6	0.8	6.1
1995—Stanford	32	...	131	267	.491	67	105	.638	163	23	329	5.1	0.7	10.3
1996—Stanford	36	...	226	411	.550	130	180	.722	281	37	582	7.8	1.0	16.2
1997—Stanford	27	...	177	307	.577	118	172	.686	203	39	472	7.5	1.4	17.5
Totals	118	...	589	1103	.534	346	510	.678	753	117	1524	6.4	1.0	12.9

Three-point field goals: 1997-98, 0-for-1. Totals, 0-for-1 (.000).

WNBA REGULAR-SEASON RECORD

Season Team	G	Min.	FGM	FGA	Pct.	FTM	FTA	Pct.	Off.	Def.	Tot.	Ast.	St.	Blk.	TO	Pts.	RPG	APG	PPG
										REBOUNDS								AVERAGES	
1998—Utah	29	466	58	135	.430	37	65	.569	37	48	85	22	24	10	49	154	2.9	0.8	5.3

Season Team	G	Min.	FGM	FGA	Pct.	FTM	FTA	Pct.	Off.	Def.	Tot.	Ast.	St.	Blk.	TO	Pts.	RPG	APG	PPG
1999—Utah-Detroit	12	88	9	28	.321	7	12	.583	8	12	20	5	1	3	8	25	1.7	0.4	2.1
2000—Detroit	28	369	37	89	.416	26	40	.650	28	52	80	28	12	10	45	100	2.9	1.0	3.6
2001—Indiana	32	775	99	217	.456	82	111	.739	52	109	161	40	22	12	72	280	5.0	1.3	8.8
2002—Indiana	31	975	113	232	.487	66	82	.805	80	131	211	52	38	13	69	292	6.8	1.7	9.4
2004—Charlotte	34	398	27	67	.403	19	32	.594	28	37	65	10	9	13	36	73	1.9	0.3	2.1
2005—Sacramento	18	170	14	39	.359	10	20	.500	17	16	33	5	4	2	22	38	1.8	0.3	2.1
Totals	184	3241	357	807	.442	247	362	.682	250	405	655	162	110	63	301	962	3.6	0.9	5.2

Three-point field goals: 1998-99, 1-for-5 (.200). 2000-01, 0-for-2. 2001-02, 0-for-2. 2002-03, 0-for-4. 2004-05, 0-for-1. Totals, 1-for-14 (.071).
Personal fouls/disqualifications: 1998-99, 78/2. 1999-00, 21/0. 2000-01, 83/2. 2001-02, 108/1. 2002-03, 127/2. 2004-05, 78/0. 2005-06, 27/0. Totals, 522/7.

WNBA PLAYOFF RECORD

Season Team	G	Min.	FGM	FGA	Pct.	FTM	FTA	Pct.	Off.	Def.	Tot.	Ast.	St.	Blk.	TO	Pts.	RPG	APG	PPG
2002—Indiana	3	99	8	16	.500	5	5	1.000	7	17	24	5	1	1	14	21	8.0	1.7	7.0
2005—Sacramento	7	38	4	8	.500	1	2	.500	2	5	7	5	0	1	3	9	1.0	0.7	1.3
Totals	10	137	12	24	.500	6	7	.857	9	22	31	10	1	2	17	30	3.1	1.0	3.0

Personal fouls/disqualifications: 2002-03, 11/0. 2005-06, 8/0. Totals, 19/0.

SMITH, CHARLOTTE   F   FEVER

PERSONAL: Born August 23, 1973, in Shelby, N.C. ... 6-0/148. (1.83/67.1). ... Full name: Charlotte D. Smith
COLLEGE: North Carolina.
TRANSACTIONS/CAREER NOTES: Selected by Charlotte in third round (33rd overall) of WNBA Draft, May 4, 1999. ... Signed by Washington, April 13, 2005. ... Signed by Indiana, February 3, 2006.

COLLEGE RECORD

NOTES: Consensus first team All-American (1995). ... NCAA Final Four MVP (1995). ... Member of NCAA National Championship team (1994). ... Holds record with 23 rebounds in NCAA championship game (1994).

Season Team	G	Min.	FGM	FGA	Pct.	FTM	FTA	Pct.	Reb.	Ast.	Pts.	RPG	APG	PPG
1991—North Carolina	31	...	175	360	.486	99	155	.639	251	...	251	8.1	...	8.1
1992—North Carolina	30	...	172	377	.456	96	157	.611	269	...	446	9.0	...	14.9
1993—North Carolina	33	...	196	390	.503	112	159	.704	304	...	513	9.2	...	15.5
1994—North Carolina	35	...	249	467	.533	174	267	.652	376	...	685	10.7	...	19.6
Totals	129	...	792	1594	.497	481	738	.652	1200	...	1895	9.3	...	14.7

Three-point field goals: 1991-92, 1-for-10 (.100). 1992-93, 6-for-21 (.286). 1993-94, 9-for-32 (.281). 1994-95, 13-for-46 (.283). Totals, 29-for-109 (.266).

ABL RECORD

Season Team	G	Min.	FGM	FGA	Pct.	FTM	FTA	Pct.	Reb.	Ast.	Pts.	RPG	APG	PPG
1996—Colorado	40	...	208	497	.419	182	234	.778	259	106	626	6.5	2.7	15.7
1997—San Jose	42	...	187	383	.488	135	183	.738	252	90	513	6.0	2.1	12.2
1998—San Jose	13	...	33	78	.423	29	37	.784	47	21	99	3.6	1.6	7.6
Totals	95	...	428	958	.447	346	454	.762	558	217	1238	5.9	2.3	13.0

Three-point field goals: 1996-97, 28-for-102 (.275). 1997-98, 4-for-28 (.143). 1998-99, 4-for-16 (.250). Totals, 36-for-146 (.247).

WNBA REGULAR-SEASON RECORD

NOTES: Led WNBA in three-point field goal percentage (.500) in 2004.

Season Team	G	Min.	FGM	FGA	Pct.	FTM	FTA	Pct.	Off.	Def.	Tot.	Ast.	St.	Blk.	TO	Pts.	RPG	APG	PPG
1999—Charlotte	32	746	62	188	.330	41	58	.707	46	69	115	58	10	7	50	173	3.6	1.8	5.4
2000—Charlotte	30	659	56	159	.352	20	25	.800	29	77	106	55	15	17	48	156	3.5	1.8	5.2
2001—Charlotte	30	678	57	146	.390	47	64	.734	36	65	101	50	16	13	41	171	3.4	1.7	5.7
2002—Charlotte	32	890	91	222	.410	40	54	.741	39	82	121	53	21	17	60	256	3.8	1.7	8.0
2003—Charlotte	27	443	31	98	.316	24	36	.667	23	37	60	18	10	2	24	95	2.2	0.7	3.5
2004—Charlotte	34	977	99	206	.481	53	73	.726	50	89	139	40	18	13	55	280	4.1	1.2	8.2
2005—Washington	34	1036	87	190	.458	30	46	.652	34	94	128	71	22	11	46	246	3.8	2.1	7.2
Totals	219	5429	483	1209	.400	255	356	.716	257	513	770	345	112	80	324	1377	3.5	1.6	6.3

Three-point field goals: 1999-00, 8-for-56 (.143). 2000-01, 24-for-76 (.316). 2001-02, 10-for-32 (.313). 2002-03, 34-for-91 (.374). 2003-04, 9-for-32 (.281). 2004-05, 29-for-58 (.500). 2005-06, 42-for-100 (.420). Totals, 156-for-445 (.351).
Personal fouls/disqualifications: 1999-00, 87/1. 2000-01, 88/2. 2001-02, 73/1. 2002-03, 113/3. 2003-04, 54/0. 2004-05, 109/1. 2005-06, 93/0. Totals, 617/8.

WNBA PLAYOFF RECORD

Season Team	G	Min.	FGM	FGA	Pct.	FTM	FTA	Pct.	Off.	Def.	Tot.	Ast.	St.	Blk.	TO	Pts.	RPG	APG	PPG
1999—Charlotte	4	106	13	31	.419	9	11	.818	8	10	18	3	4	0	7	36	4.5	0.8	9.0
2001—Charlotte	8	224	16	54	.296	10	11	.909	13	19	32	14	6	8	7	47	4.0	1.8	5.9
2002—Charlotte	2	53	5	17	.294	2	2	1.000	0	7	7	0	1	2	2	12	3.5	0.0	6.0
2003—Charlotte	2	7	1	1	1.000	0	0	...	1	0	1	1	0	0	0	2	0.5	0.5	1.0
Totals	16	390	35	103	.340	21	24	.875	22	36	58	18	11	10	16	97	3.6	1.1	6.1

Three-point field goals: 1999-00, 1-for-6 (.167). 2001-02, 5-for-20 (.250). 2002-03, 0-for-7. Totals, 6-for-33 (.182).
Personal fouls/disqualifications: 1999-00, 11/0. 2001-02, 24/0. 2002-03, 7/0. Totals, 42/0.

SMITH, JENNIFER   C   LIBERTY

PERSONAL: Born April 10, 1982, in Lansing, Mich. ... 6-3. (1.91). ... Full name: Jennifer Elaine Smith
HIGH SCHOOL: DeWitt (Lansing, Mich.).
COLLEGE: Michigan.

COLLEGE RECORD

Season Team	G	Min.	FGM	FGA	Pct.	FTM	FTA	Pct.	Reb.	Ast.	Pts.	RPG	APG	PPG
2000—Michigan	31	659	111	201	.552	70	86	.814	143	23	292	4.6	0.7	9.4
2001—Michigan	30	913	157	304	.516	97	122	.795	234	39	412	7.8	1.3	13.7
2002—Michigan	24	665	132	244	.541	79	94	.840	155	17	351	6.5	0.7	14.6
2003—Michigan	31	1084	213	446	.478	203	251	.809	220	25	642	7.1	0.8	20.7
Totals	116	3321	613	1195	.513	449	553	.812	752	104	1697	6.5	0.9	14.6

Three-point field goals: 2000-01, 0-for-1. 2001-02, 1-for-3 (.333). 2002-03, 8-for-20 (.400). 2003-04, 13-for-38 (.342). Totals, 22-for-62 (.355).

WNBA REGULAR-SEASON RECORD

Season Team	G	Min.	FGM	FGA	Pct.	FTM	FTA	Pct.	Off.	Def.	Tot.	Ast.	St.	Blk.	TO	Pts.	RPG	APG	PPG
2005—New York	2	7	0	1	.000	0	0	...	0	0	0	0	0	0	0	0	0.0	0.0	0.0
Totals	2	7	0	1	.000	0	0	...	0	0	0	0	0	0	0	0	0.0	0.0	0.0

SMITH, KATIE   G   SHOCK

PERSONAL: Born June 4, 1974, in Lancaster, Ohio. ... 5-11/175. (1.80/79.4). ... Full name: Katherine May Smith
HIGH SCHOOL: Logan (Logan, Ohio).
COLLEGE: Ohio State.
TRANSACTIONS/CAREER NOTES: Signed by WNBA and allocated to Minnesota Lynx, May 3, 1999. ... Traded by Minnesota to Detroit for G/F Chandi Jones and F Stacey Thomas, July 30, 2005.

COLLEGE RECORD

NOTES: Kodak All-American first team (1993, 1996).

Season Team	G	Min.	FGM	FGA	Pct.	FTM	FTA	Pct.	Reb.	Ast.	Pts.	RPG	APG	PPG
1992—Ohio State	32	...	189	375	.504	164	203	.808	186	104	578	5.8	3.3	18.1
1993—Ohio State	28	...	211	428	.493	149	182	.819	170	87	616	6.1	3.1	22.0
1994—Ohio State	30	...	196	433	.453	190	225	.844	174	108	639	5.8	3.6	21.3
1995—Ohio State	34	...	230	527	.436	205	235	.872	174	145	745	5.1	4.3	21.9
Totals	124	...	826	1763	.469	708	845	.838	704	444	2578	5.7	3.6	20.8

Three-point field goals: 1992-93, 36-for-80 (.450). 1993-94, 45-for-119 (.378). 1994-95, 57-for-155 (.368). 1995-96, 80-for-210 (.381). Totals, 218-for-564 (.387).

ABL RECORD

Season Team	G	Min.	FGM	FGA	Pct.	FTM	FTA	Pct.	Reb.	Ast.	Pts.	RPG	APG	PPG
1996—Columbus	40	...	214	459	.466	112	136	.824	134	102	633	3.4	2.6	15.8
1997—Columbus	44	...	243	523	.465	191	214	.893	149	108	764	3.4	2.5	17.4
1998—Columbus	2	...	14	32	.438	3	3	1.000	6	8	36	3.0	4.0	18.0
Totals	86	...	471	1014	.464	306	353	.867	289	218	1433	3.4	2.5	16.7

Three-point field goals: 1996-97, 91-for-218 (.417). 1997-98, 87-for-217 (.401). 1998-99, 5-for-11 (.455). Totals, 183-for-446 (.410).

WNBA REGULAR-SEASON RECORD

NOTES: All-WNBA first team (2001, 2003). ... All-WNBA second team (2000, 2002). ... Led WNBA in scoring (23.1 ppg) in 2001. ... Led WNBA in free throw percentage (.899) in 2004.

Season Team	G	Min.	FGM	FGA	Pct.	FTM	FTA	Pct.	Off.	Def.	Tot.	Ast.	St.	Blk.	TO	Pts.	RPG	APG	PPG
1999—Minnesota	30	971	113	292	.387	72	94	.766	42	46	88	60	19	10	55	350	2.9	2.0	11.7
2000—Minnesota	32	1193	203	482	.421	152	175	.869	28	65	93	90	44	7	76	646	2.9	2.8	20.2
2001—Minnesota	32	1234	204	519	.393	246	275	.895	40	82	122	70	23	5	87	739	3.8	2.2	23.1
2002—Minnesota	31	1138	162	401	.404	126	153	.824	24	68	92	79	32	7	70	512	3.0	2.5	16.5
2003—Minnesota	34	1185	208	455	.457	126	143	.881	40	98	138	84	25	6	67	620	4.1	2.5	18.2
2004—Minnesota	23	800	137	318	.431	98	109	.899	17	67	84	52	23	6	51	432	3.7	2.3	18.8
2005—Minn.-Detroit	36	1160	140	368	.380	97	124	.782	23	60	83	87	30	5	71	430	2.3	2.4	11.9
Totals	218	7681	1167	2835	.412	917	1073	.855	214	486	700	522	196	46	477	3729	3.2	2.4	17.1

Three-point field goals: 1999-00, 52-for-136 (.382). 2000-01, 88-for-232 (.379). 2001-02, 85-for-240 (.354). 2002-03, 62-for-188 (.330). 2003-04, 78-for-200 (.390). 2004-05, 60-for-139 (.432). 2005-06, 53-for-159 (.333). Totals, 478-for-1294 (.369).
Personal fouls/disqualifications: 1999-00, 106/3. 2000-01, 71/0. 2001-02, 94/0. 2002-03, 87/2. 2003-04, 112/2. 2004-05, 63/1. 2005-06, 73/0. Totals, 606/8.

WNBA PLAYOFF RECORD

Season Team	G	Min.	FGM	FGA	Pct.	FTM	FTA	Pct.	Off.	Def.	Tot.	Ast.	St.	Blk.	TO	Pts.	RPG	APG	PPG
2003—Minnesota	3	120	18	42	.429	11	12	.917	3	10	13	9	1	0	8	52	4.3	3.0	17.3
2005—Detroit	2	67	7	26	.269	5	5	1.000	2	4	6	1	2	0	2	21	3.0	0.5	10.5
Totals	5	187	25	68	.368	16	17	.941	5	14	19	10	3	0	10	73	3.8	2.0	14.6

Three-point field goals: 2003-04, 5-for-14 (.357). 2005-06, 2-for-10 (.200). Totals, 7-for-24 (.292).
Personal fouls/disqualifications: 2003-04, 11/0. 2005-06, 5/0. Totals, 16/0.

WNBA ALL-STAR GAME RECORD

Season Team	Min.	FGM	FGA	Pct.	FTM	FTA	Pct.	REBOUNDS Off.	Def.	Tot.	Ast.	PF	Dq.	St.	Blk.	TO	Pts.
2000—Minnesota	18	0	2	.000	0	0	...	0	1	1	2	0	0	2	0	0	0
2001—Minnesota	20	1	5	.200	0	0	...	0	2	2	0	1	0	1	1	1	2
2002—Minnesota	11	2	4	.500	0	0	...	0	3	3	4	1	0	0	0	2	4
2003—Minnesota	15	1	4	.250	0	0	...	0	0	0	0	1	0	0	0	1	2
2005—Minnesota	20	4	9	.444	4	4	1.000	1	3	4	1	1	0	1	0	0	16
Totals	84	8	24	.333	4	4	1.000	1	9	10	7	4	0	4	1	4	24

Three-point field goals: 2001, 0-for-2. 2002, 0-for-3. 2003, 0-for-2. 2006, 4-for-6 (.667). Totals, 4-for-13 (.308).

OLYMPICS RECORD

Season Team	G	Min.	FGM	FGA	Pct.	FTM	FTA	Pct.	Reb.	Ast.	Pts.	AVERAGES RPG	APG	PPG
2000—United States	8	155	20	39	.513	2	3	.667	5	9	54	0.6	1.1	6.8
2004—United States	3	13	0	2	.000	0	0	...	1	1	0	0.3	0.3	0.0
Totals	11	168	20	41	.488	2	3	.667	6	10	54	0.5	0.9	4.9

Three-point field goals: 2000-01, 12-for-20 (.600). Totals, 12-for-20 (.600).
Personal fouls/disqualifications: 2004-05, 1/0. Totals, 1/0.

SMITH, TANGELA   F/C   STING

PERSONAL: Born April 1, 1977, in Chicago. ... 6-4/160. (1.93/72.6). ... Full name: Tangela Nicole Smith
COLLEGE: Iowa.
TRANSACTIONS/CAREER NOTES: Selected by Sacramento in the second round (12th overall) of the WNBA Draft, April 29, 1998. ... Traded by Sacramento along with the Monarchs' second-round pick in the 2006 WNBA Draft to Charlotte in exchange for F Nicole Powell, F/C Olympia Scott-Richardson and G Erin Buesher, March 3, 2005.

COLLEGE RECORD

Season Team	G	Min.	FGM	FGA	Pct.	FTM	FTA	Pct.	Reb.	Ast.	Pts.	AVERAGES RPG	APG	PPG
1994—Iowa	28	...	102	225	.453	47	73	.644	211	20	251	7.5	0.7	9.0
1995—Iowa	31	...	172	365	.471	77	113	.681	218	25	422	7.0	0.8	13.6
1996—Iowa	30	...	149	280	.532	50	73	.685	186	37	348	6.2	1.2	11.6
1997—Iowa	29	...	240	429	.559	97	138	.703	244	39	577	8.4	1.3	19.9
Totals	118	...	663	1299	.510	271	397	.683	859	121	1598	7.3	1.0	13.5

Three-point field goals: 1994-95, 0-for-3. 1995-96, 1-for-9 (.111). 1996-97, 0-for-1. 1997-98, 0-for-2. Totals, 1-for-15 (.067).

WNBA REGULAR-SEASON RECORD

Season Team	G	Min.	FGM	FGA	Pct.	FTM	FTA	Pct.	REBOUNDS Off.	Def.	Tot.	Ast.	St.	Blk.	TO	Pts.	AVERAGES RPG	APG	PPG
1998—Sacramento	28	707	113	279	.405	40	54	.741	45	84	129	31	17	46	46	271	4.6	1.1	9.7
1999—Sacramento	31	632	104	235	.443	47	72	.653	46	73	119	17	26	38	38	256	3.8	0.5	8.3
2000—Sacramento	32	925	176	371	.474	36	46	.783	61	117	178	43	30	64	60	388	5.6	1.3	12.1
2001—Sacramento	32	912	148	352	.420	62	85	.729	48	131	179	41	34	55	66	358	5.6	1.3	11.2
2002—Sacramento	32	1063	184	435	.423	86	101	.851	56	132	188	40	27	46	59	469	5.9	1.3	14.7
2003—Sacramento	34	986	188	427	.440	41	58	.707	61	126	187	52	43	32	56	430	5.5	1.5	12.6
2004—Sacramento	34	908	165	401	.411	45	56	.804	46	92	138	50	38	25	53	380	4.1	1.5	11.2
2005—Charlotte	31	1063	169	405	.417	83	104	.798	45	117	162	41	51	32	84	421	5.2	1.3	13.6
Totals	254	7196	1247	2905	.429	440	576	.764	408	872	1280	315	266	338	462	2973	5.0	1.2	11.7

Three-point field goals: 1998-99, 5-for-14 (.357). 1999-00, 1-for-2 (.500). 2001-02, 0-for-2. 2002-03, 15-for-42 (.357). 2003-04, 13-for-49 (.265). 2004-05, 5-for-29 (.172). 2005-06, 0-for-7. Totals, 39-for-145 (.269).
Personal fouls/disqualifications: 1998-99, 78/0. 1999-00, 72/0. 2000-01, 107/1. 2001-02, 106/2. 2002-03, 126/4. 2003-04, 103/2. 2004-05, 86/0. 2005-06, 105/1. Totals, 783/10.

WNBA PLAYOFF RECORD

Season Team	G	Min.	FGM	FGA	Pct.	FTM	FTA	Pct.	REBOUNDS Off.	Def.	Tot.	Ast.	St.	Blk.	TO	Pts.	AVERAGES RPG	APG	PPG
1999—Sacramento	1	38	6	16	.375	2	6	.333	1	1	2	0	3	1	1	14	2.0	0.0	14.0
2000—Sacramento	2	59	9	22	.409	3	4	.750	0	8	8	1	2	1	2	21	4.0	0.5	10.5
2001—Sacramento	5	164	23	60	.383	9	11	.818	8	16	24	8	5	5	4	55	4.8	1.6	11.0
2003—Sacramento	6	176	29	73	.397	14	20	.700	9	37	46	11	5	3	11	77	7.7	1.8	12.8
2004—Sacramento	6	185	38	86	.442	17	22	.773	11	20	31	8	9	12	11	95	5.2	1.3	15.8
Totals	20	622	105	257	.409	45	63	.714	29	82	111	28	24	22	29	262	5.6	1.4	13.1

Three-point field goals: 2003-04, 5-for-15 (.333). 2004-05, 2-for-9 (.222). Totals, 7-for-24 (.292).
Personal fouls/disqualifications: 1999-00, 4/0. 2000-01, 5/0. 2001-02, 16/0. 2003-04, 17/0. 2004-05, 17/0. Totals, 59/0.

SNELL, BELINDA   G/F   MERCURY

PERSONAL: Born January 10, 1981, in Mirboo North, Victoria. ... 5-11.
MISCELLANEOUS: Played for WNBL's Sydney Uni Flames.

Season Team	G	Min.	FGM	FGA	Pct.	FTM	FTA	Pct.	REBOUNDS Off.	Def.	Tot.	Ast.	St.	Blk.	TO	Pts.	AVERAGES RPG	APG	PPG
2005—Phoenix..............	20	226	19	55	.345	16	18	.889	19	17	36	18	7	1	11	65	1.8	0.9	3.3
Totals	20	226	19	55	.345	16	18	.889	19	17	36	18	7	1	11	65	1.8	0.9	3.3

Three-point field goals: 2005-06, 11-for-37 (.297). Totals, 11-for-37 (.297).
Personal fouls/disqualifications: 2005-06, 31/0. Totals, 31/0.

SNOW, MICHELLE C COMETS

PERSONAL: Born March 20, 1980, in Pensacola, Fla. ... 6-5/158. (1.96/71.7). ... Full name: Donette JeMichelle Snow
HIGH SCHOOL: Pensacola (Pensacola, Fla.).
COLLEGE: Tennessee.
TRANSACTIONS/CAREER NOTES: Selected by Houston in first round (10th overall) of WNBA Draft, April 19, 2002.

COLLEGE RECORD

NOTES: Recorded her third dunk in 2002.

Season Team	G	Min.	FGM	FGA	Pct.	FTM	FTA	Pct.	Reb.	Ast.	Pts.	AVERAGES RPG	APG	PPG
1998—Tennessee........................	34	740	117	195	.600	56	108	.519	218	12	290	6.4	0.4	8.5
1999—Tennessee........................	37	919	181	326	.555	73	116	.629	232	16	290	6.3	0.4	7.8
2000—Tennessee........................	33	771	143	250	.572	79	130	.608	224	26	365	6.8	0.8	11.1
2001—Tennessee........................	33	823	144	286	.503	119	158	.753	214	17	407	6.5	0.5	12.3
Totals	137	3253	585	1057	.553	327	512	.639	888	71	1352	6.5	0.5	9.9

Three-point field goals: 1999-00, 0-for-1. Totals, 0-for-1 (.000).

WNBA REGULAR-SEASON RECORD

NOTES: WNBA Most Improved Player (2003). ... Led WNBA in field goal percentage (.551) in 2005.

Season Team	G	Min.	FGM	FGA	Pct.	FTM	FTA	Pct.	REBOUNDS Off.	Def.	Tot.	Ast.	St.	Blk.	TO	Pts.	AVERAGES RPG	APG	PPG
2002—Houston	32	480	45	96	.469	34	57	.596	31	88	119	13	12	26	22	125	3.7	0.4	3.9
2003—Houston	34	1025	126	253	.498	62	85	.729	76	187	263	42	35	62	68	314	7.7	1.2	9.2
2004—Houston	31	893	104	229	.454	68	113	.602	62	177	239	31	28	35	71	276	7.7	1.0	8.9
2005—Houston	33	966	152	276	.551	92	130	.708	68	157	225	40	20	38	65	396	6.8	1.2	12.0
Totals	130	3364	427	854	.500	256	385	.665	237	609	846	126	95	161	226	1111	6.5	1.0	8.5

Three-point field goals: 2002-03, 1-for-2 (.500). 2003-04, 0-for-1. Totals, 1-for-3 (.333).
Personal fouls/disqualifications: 2002-03, 59/0. 2003-04, 120/2. 2004-05, 89/0. 2005-06, 120/4. Totals, 388/6.

WNBA PLAYOFF RECORD

Season Team	G	Min.	FGM	FGA	Pct.	FTM	FTA	Pct.	REBOUNDS Off.	Def.	Tot.	Ast.	St.	Blk.	TO	Pts.	AVERAGES RPG	APG	PPG
2002—Houston	3	79	6	18	.333	7	8	.875	6	15	21	4	0	2	5	19	7.0	1.3	6.3
2003—Houston	3	89	10	25	.400	5	8	.625	12	17	29	5	4	4	5	25	9.7	1.7	8.3
2005—Houston	5	152	18	34	.529	16	23	.696	1	26	27	4	5	3	16	52	5.4	0.8	10.4
Totals	11	320	34	77	.442	28	39	.718	19	58	77	13	9	9	26	96	7.0	1.2	8.7

Three-point field goals: 2002-03, 0-for-1. Totals, 0-for-1 (.000).
Personal fouls/disqualifications: 2002-03, 9/0. 2003-04, 10/0. 2005-06, 15/0. Totals, 34/0.

WNBA ALL-STAR GAME RECORD

Season Team	Min.	FGM	FGA	Pct.	FTM	FTA	Pct.	REBOUNDS Off.	Def.	Tot.	Ast.	PF	Dq.	St.	Blk.	TO	Pts.
2005—Houston.................	14	3	3	1.000	2	2	1.000	2	1	3	1	1	0	0	1	0	8
Totals	14	3	3	1.000	2	2	1.000	2	1	3	1	1	0	0	1	0	8

STALEY, DAWN G COMETS

PERSONAL: Born May 4, 1970, in Philadelphia. ... 5-6/134. (1.68/60.8). ... Full name: Dawn Michelle Staley
HIGH SCHOOL: Dobbins Tech (Philadelphia).
COLLEGE: Virginia.
TRANSACTIONS/CAREER NOTES: Selected by Charlotte in first round (ninth overall) of WNBA Draft, May 4, 1999. ... Traded by Charlotte to Houston for F Kristen Rasmussen and F Adrienne Goodson, August 1, 2005.

COLLEGE RECORD

NOTES: Kodak All-American first team (1990, 1991, 1992).

Season Team	G	Min.	FGM	FGA	Pct.	FTM	FTA	Pct.	Reb.	Ast.	Pts.	AVERAGES RPG	APG	PPG
1988—Virginia..............................	31	...	197	431	.457	147	177	.831	158	144	574	5.1	4.6	18.5
1989—Virginia..............................	32	...	203	449	.452	132	169	.781	214	141	574	6.7	4.4	17.9
1990—Virginia..............................	34	...	176	391	.450	108	131	.824	209	235	495	6.1	6.9	14.6
1991—Virginia..............................	34	...	177	366	.484	118	146	.808	191	209	492	5.6	6.1	14.5
Totals	131	...	753	1637	.460	505	623	.811	772	729	2135	5.9	5.6	16.3

Three-point field goals: 1988-89, 33-for-93 (.355). 1989-90, 36-for-104 (.346). 1990-91, 35-for-108 (.324). 1991-92, 20-for-66 (.303). Totals, 124-for-371 (.334).

Season Team	G	Min.	FGM	FGA	Pct.	FTM	FTA	Pct.	Reb.	Ast.	Pts.	RPG	APG	PPG
1996—United States	8	...	6	18	.333	19	23	.826	5	28	33	0.6	3.5	4.1
2000—United States	8	140	9	19	.474	12	12	1.000	10	29	32	1.3	3.6	4.0
2004—United States	8	143	12	23	.522	8	9	.889	4	23	33	0.5	2.9	4.1
Totals	24	283	27	60	.450	39	44	.886	19	80	98	0.8	3.3	4.1

Three-point field goals: 1996-97, 2-for-5 (.400). 2000-01, 2-for-4 (.500). 2004-05, 1-for-5 (.200). Totals, 5-for-14 (.357).
Personal fouls/disqualifications: 2004-05, 17/0. Totals, 17/0.

WNBA REGULAR-SEASON RECORD

NOTES: WNBA Sportsmanship Award (1999). ... WNBA Entrepreneurial Award (1999).

Season Team	G	Min.	FGM	FGA	Pct.	FTM	FTA	Pct.	REBOUNDS Off.	Def.	Tot.	Ast.	St.	Blk.	TO	Pts.	RPG	APG	PPG
1999—Charlotte	32	1065	125	301	.415	85	91	.934	12	60	72	177	38	3	90	368	2.3	5.5	11.5
2000—Charlotte	32	1099	94	253	.372	65	74	.878	21	56	77	190	37	1	91	282	2.4	5.9	8.8
2001—Charlotte	32	1152	107	281	.381	51	57	.895	11	60	71	179	52	1	100	298	2.2	5.6	9.3
2002—Charlotte	32	1061	84	231	.364	77	101	.762	8	48	56	164	48	0	80	278	1.8	5.1	8.7
2003—Charlotte	34	1086	90	216	.417	61	73	.836	14	44	58	174	49	4	78	269	1.7	5.1	7.9
2004—Charlotte	34	1143	106	246	.431	66	87	.759	12	46	58	171	43	2	74	302	1.7	5.0	8.9
2005—Charlotte-Hou. ...	33	905	63	159	.396	32	40	.800	9	61	70	149	36	1	54	179	2.1	4.5	5.4
Totals	229	7511	669	1687	.397	437	523	.836	87	375	462	1204	303	12	567	1976	2.0	5.3	8.6

Three-point field goals: 1999-00, 33-for-104 (.317). 2000-01, 29-for-88 (.330). 2001-02, 33-for-89 (.371). 2002-03, 33-for-83 (.398). 2003-04, 28-for-72 (.389). 2004-05, 24-for-59 (.407). 2005-06, 21-for-56 (.375). Totals, 201-for-551 (.365).
Personal fouls/disqualifications: 1999-00, 71/0. 2000-01, 80/1. 2001-02, 54/0. 2002-03, 67/0. 2003-04, 76/0. 2004-05, 83/0. 2005-06, 70/1. Totals, 501/2.

WNBA PLAYOFF RECORD

Season Team	G	Min.	FGM	FGA	Pct.	FTM	FTA	Pct.	REBOUNDS Off.	Def.	Tot.	Ast.	St.	Blk.	TO	Pts.	RPG	APG	PPG
1999—Charlotte	4	157	13	40	.325	15	18	.833	2	3	5	23	3	0	11	48	1.3	5.8	12.0
2001—Charlotte	8	301	32	77	.416	17	21	.810	3	15	18	35	9	2	34	94	2.3	4.4	11.8
2002—Charlotte	2	78	6	21	.286	3	6	.500	2	3	5	10	3	0	4	17	2.5	5.0	8.5
2003—Charlotte	2	58	6	17	.353	2	5	.400	1	4	5	7	4	0	4	18	2.5	3.5	9.0
2005—Houston	5	125	6	13	.462	6	7	.857	0	4	4	14	9	0	7	21	0.8	2.8	4.2
Totals	21	719	63	168	.375	43	57	.754	8	29	37	89	28	2	60	198	1.8	4.2	9.4

Three-point field goals: 1999-00, 7-for-16 (.438). 2001-02, 13-for-26 (.500). 2002-03, 2-for-10 (.200). 2003-04, 4-for-8 (.500). 2005-06, 3-for-8 (.375). Totals, 29-for-68 (.426).
Personal fouls/disqualifications: 1999-00, 7/0. 2001-02, 19/0. 2002-03, 2/0. 2003-04, 6/0. 2005-06, 9/0. Totals, 43/0.

WNBA ALL-STAR GAME RECORD

Season Team	Min.	FGM	FGA	Pct.	FTM	FTA	Pct.	REBOUNDS Off.	Def.	Tot.	Ast.	PF	Dq.	St.	Blk.	TO	Pts.
2001—Charlotte	15	2	3	.667	0	0	...	0	0	0	3	2	0	4	0	0	4
2002—Charlotte	18	2	5	.400	0	0	...	1	3	4	5	0	0	1	0	1	4
2003—Charlotte	24	1	6	.167	2	2	1.000	0	4	4	7	1	0	0	0	4	5
2005—Charlotte	18	1	5	.200	0	0	...	1	1	2	4	3	0	0	0	2	2
Totals	75	6	19	.316	2	2	1.000	2	8	10	19	6	0	5	0	7	15

Three-point field goals: 2004, 1-for-4 (.250). 2006, 0-for-3. Totals, 1-for-7 (.143).

STEPANOVA, MARIA   C   MERCURY

PERSONAL: Born February 23, 1979, in Village Shpakovskoe, Russia. ... 6-8/187. (2.03/84.8). ... Full name: Maria Alexandrovna Stepanova
HIGH SCHOOL: St. Petersburg (St. Petersburg, Russia).
TRANSACTIONS/CAREER NOTES: Selected by Phoenix in first round (eighth overall) of the WNBA Draft, April 29, 1998.

OLYMPICS RECORD

Season Team	G	Min.	FGM	FGA	Pct.	FTM	FTA	Pct.	Reb.	Ast.	Pts.	RPG	APG	PPG
1996—Russia	8	...	5	10	.500	1	1	1.000	5	...	11	0.6	...	1.4
2000—Russia	7	86	24	32	.750	8	16	.500	23	7	56	3.3	1.0	8.0
2004—Russia	8	161	28	65	.431	8	11	.727	52	8	64	6.5	1.0	8.0
Totals	23	247	57	107	.533	17	28	.607	80	15	131	3.5	0.7	5.7

Personal fouls/disqualifications: 2004-05, 20/1. Totals, 20/1.

WNBA REGULAR-SEASON RECORD

Season Team	G	Min.	FGM	FGA	Pct.	FTM	FTA	Pct.	REBOUNDS Off.	Def.	Tot.	Ast.	St.	Blk.	TO	Pts.	RPG	APG	PPG
1998—Phoenix	20	130	26	61	.426	14	22	.636	17	21	38	7	3	11	9	66	1.9	0.4	3.3
1999—Phoenix	32	554	96	198	.485	55	88	.625	62	102	164	24	13	62	43	248	5.1	0.8	7.8
2000—Phoenix	15	170	24	54	.444	9	15	.600	15	33	48	8	4	9	22	57	3.2	0.5	3.8
2001—Phoenix	32	815	143	282	.507	48	78	.615	66	135	201	41	43	64	50	334	6.3	1.3	10.4
2005—Phoenix	15	409	68	144	.472	26	40	.650	29	51	80	23	20	38	22	162	5.3	1.5	10.8
Totals	114	2078	357	739	.483	152	243	.626	189	342	531	103	83	184	146	867	4.7	0.9	7.6

Three-point field goals: 1999-00, 1-for-1 (1.000). 2001-02, 0-for-2. Totals, 1-for-3 (.333).
Personal fouls/disqualifications: 1998-99, 29/0. 1999-00, 86/1. 2000-01, 42/1. 2001-02, 110/3. 2005-06, 33/0. Totals, 300/5.

WNBA PLAYOFF RECORD

Season Team	G	Min.	FGM	FGA	Pct.	FTM	FTA	Pct.	REBOUNDS Off.	Def.	Tot.	Ast.	St.	Blk.	TO	Pts.	AVERAGES RPG	APG	PPG
1998—Phoenix.............	4	22	5	11	.455	1	2	.500	3	3	6	1	1	1	1	11	1.5	0.3	2.8
Totals	4	22	5	11	.455	1	2	.500	3	3	6	1	1	1	1	11	1.5	0.3	2.8

Personal fouls/disqualifications: 1998-99, 8/1. Totals, 8/1.

STEVENSON, MANDISA   C   MERCURY

PERSONAL: Born February 4, 1982, in Decatur, Ga. ... 6-3/166. (1.91/75.3).
HIGH SCHOOL: Decatur (Decatur, Ga.).
JUNIOR COLLEGE: Gulf Coast.
COLLEGE: Auburn.
TRANSACTIONS/CAREER NOTES: Signed by Seattle, April 21, 2005.

WNBA REGULAR-SEASON RECORD

Season Team	G	Min.	FGM	FGA	Pct.	FTM	FTA	Pct.	REBOUNDS Off.	Def.	Tot.	Ast.	St.	Blk.	TO	Pts.	AVERAGES RPG	APG	PPG
2004—San Antonio	29	259	15	45	.333	7	8	.875	11	24	35	5	6	4	11	38	1.2	0.2	1.3
2005—Seattle	4	53	3	12	.250	0	0	...	2	4	6	1	2	0	4	6	1.5	0.3	1.5
Totals	33	312	18	57	.316	7	8	.875	13	28	41	6	8	4	15	44	1.2	0.2	1.3

Three-point field goals: 2004-05, 1-for-1 (1.000). 2005-06, 0-for-1. Totals, 1-for-2 (.500).
Personal fouls/disqualifications: 2004-05, 32/0. 2005-06, 3/0. Totals, 35/0.

STINSON, ANDREA   G   SHOCK

PERSONAL: Born November 25, 1967, in Mooresville, N.C. ... 5-10/158. (1.78/71.7). ... Full name: Andrea Maria Stinson
HIGH SCHOOL: North Mecklenburg (Charlotte, N.C.).
COLLEGE: North Carolina State.
TRANSACTIONS/CAREER NOTES: Signed by WNBA and assigned to Charlotte, January 22, 1997. ... Signed by Detroit, May 10, 2005. ... Traded by Detroit to Phoenix for F/C Plenette Pierson, June 29, 2005.

COLLEGE RECORD

NOTES: Kodak All-American first team (1990, 1991).

Season Team	G	Min.	FGM	FGA	Pct.	FTM	FTA	Pct.	Reb.	Ast.	Pts.	AVERAGES RPG	APG	PPG
1988—North Carolina State	31	...	320	605	.529	80	121	.661	141	113	733	4.5	3.6	23.6
1989—North Carolina State	30	...	283	514	.551	76	110	.691	197	149	651	6.6	5.0	21.7
1990—North Carolina State	33	...	314	577	.544	91	151	.603	208	140	752	6.3	4.2	22.8
Totals	94	...	917	1696	.541	247	382	.647	546	402	2136	5.8	4.3	22.7

Three-point field goals: 1988-89, 13-for-50 (.260). 1989-90, 9-for-23 (.391). 1990-91, 33-for-91 (.363). Totals, 55-for-164 (.335).

WNBA REGULAR-SEASON RECORD

NOTES: All-WNBA second team (1997, 1998).

Season Team	G	Min.	FGM	FGA	Pct.	FTM	FTA	Pct.	REBOUNDS Off.	Def.	Tot.	Ast.	St.	Blk.	TO	Pts.	AVERAGES RPG	APG	PPG
1997—Charlotte	28	1011	177	396	.447	60	89	.674	48	107	155	124	43	21	99	439	5.5	4.4	15.7
1998—Charlotte	30	1046	173	414	.418	75	100	.750	29	109	138	134	54	15	77	450	4.6	4.5	15.0
1999—Charlotte	32	1041	174	378	.460	65	88	.739	32	81	113	93	32	18	67	434	3.5	2.9	13.6
2000—Charlotte	32	1123	214	463	.462	99	134	.739	35	101	136	121	55	23	86	565	4.3	3.8	17.7
2001—Charlotte	32	1006	179	370	.484	63	79	.797	39	98	137	88	43	19	70	450	4.3	2.8	14.1
2002—Charlotte	32	950	159	349	.456	64	93	.688	37	140	177	91	37	9	52	411	5.5	2.8	12.8
2003—Charlotte	34	1000	147	321	.458	60	79	.759	28	112	140	97	48	5	75	377	4.1	2.9	11.1
2004—Charlotte	34	777	79	191	.414	34	44	.773	25	94	119	49	27	7	41	203	3.5	1.4	6.0
2005—Detroit..............	18	102	8	23	.348	4	6	.667	6	6	12	13	3	0	4	22	0.7	0.7	1.2
Totals	272	8056	1310	2905	.451	524	712	.736	279	848	1127	810	342	117	571	3351	4.1	3.0	12.3

Three-point field goals: 1997-98, 25-for-77 (.325). 1998-99, 29-for-103 (.282). 1999-00, 21-for-68 (.309). 2000-01, 38-for-106 (.358). 2001-02, 29-for-65 (.446). 2002-03, 29-for-70 (.414). 2003-04, 23-for-75 (.307). 2004-05, 11-for-37 (.297). 2005-06, 2-for-10 (.200). Totals, 207-for-611 (.339).
Personal fouls/disqualifications: 1997-98, 55/0. 1998-99, 72/0. 1999-00, 56/0. 2000-01, 77/0. 2001-02, 59/0. 2002-03, 56/0. 2003-04, 70/0. 2004-05, 60/1. 2005-06, 6/0. Totals, 511/1.

WNBA PLAYOFF RECORD

Season Team	G	Min.	FGM	FGA	Pct.	FTM	FTA	Pct.	REBOUNDS Off.	Def.	Tot.	Ast.	St.	Blk.	TO	Pts.	AVERAGES RPG	APG	PPG
1997—Charlotte	1	34	3	11	.273	2	2	1.000	0	0	0	3	0	0	3	8	0.0	3.0	8.0
1998—Charlotte	2	71	12	27	.444	3	5	.600	2	8	10	13	4	0	6	29	5.0	6.5	14.5
1999—Charlotte	4	153	32	64	.500	15	19	.789	6	24	30	17	11	1	5	83	7.5	4.3	20.8
2001—Charlotte	8	278	37	95	.389	17	21	.810	12	37	49	26	13	2	18	96	6.1	3.3	12.0
2002—Charlotte	2	65	12	25	.480	2	2	1.000	7	4	11	9	7	0	4	30	5.5	4.5	15.0
2003—Charlotte	2	64	12	28	.429	9	9	1.000	4	5	9	7	2	0	4	36	4.5	3.5	18.0
Totals	19	665	108	250	.432	48	58	.828	31	78	109	75	37	3	40	282	5.7	3.9	14.8

Three-point field goals: 1997-98, 0-for-2. 1998-99, 2-for-7 (.286). 1999-00, 4-for-14 (.286). 2001-02, 5-for-13 (.385). 2002-03, 4-for-7 (.571). 2003-04, 3-for-7 (.429). Totals, 18-for-50 (.360).
Personal fouls/disqualifications: 1997-98, 4/0. 1998-99, 9/0. 1999-00, 8/0. 2001-02, 18/0. 2002-03, 4/0. 2003-04, 4/0. Totals, 47/0.

466

WNBA ALL-STAR GAME RECORD

Season	Team	Min.	FGM	FGA	Pct.	FTM	FTA	Pct.	REBOUNDS Off.	Def.	Tot.	Ast.	PF	Dq.	St.	Blk.	TO	Pts.
2000	Charlotte	13	1	6	.167	1	1	1.000	1	1	2	2	0	0	1	0	3	3
2001	Charlotte	17	2	9	.222	0	0	...	2	3	5	1	2	0	0	0	1	4
2002	Charlotte	20	3	10	.300	2	2	1.000	0	1	1	2	3	0	1	0	1	9
Totals		50	6	25	.240	3	3	1.000	3	5	8	5	5	0	2	0	5	16

Three-point field goals: 2001, 0-for-1. 2002, 0-for-3. 2003, 1-for-4 (.250). Totals, 1-for-8 (.125).

STREIMIKYTE, JURGITA   F   FEVER

PERSONAL: Born May 14, 1972, in Lithuania. ... 6-3/165. (1.91/74.8).
TRANSACTIONS/CAREER NOTES: Selected by Indiana in second round (26th overall) of WNBA Draft, April 25, 2000. ... Signed by Indiana, March 17, 2005.
MISCELLANEOUS: Also played for USV Orchies (1997-98). ... Member of Euroleague Champion Pool Comense (1999). ... Member of European Champion Lithuanian National Team (1997).

WNBA REGULAR-SEASON RECORD

Season Team	G	Min.	FGM	FGA	Pct.	FTM	FTA	Pct.	REBOUNDS Off.	Def.	Tot.	Ast.	St.	Blk.	TO	Pts.	AVERAGES RPG	APG	PPG
2000—Indiana	27	424	46	117	.393	27	35	.771	25	46	71	44	16	23	32	121	2.6	1.6	4.5
2001—Indiana	27	707	99	207	.478	48	57	.842	45	94	139	52	37	19	52	246	5.1	1.9	9.1
2005—Indiana	34	686	82	178	.461	19	27	.704	37	64	101	32	29	11	36	186	3.0	0.9	5.5
Totals	88	1817	227	502	.452	94	119	.790	107	204	311	128	82	53	120	553	3.5	1.5	6.3

Three-point field goals: 2000-01, 2-for-6 (.333). 2001-02, 0-for-9. 2005-06, 3-for-6 (.500). Totals, 5-for-21 (.238).
Personal fouls/disqualifications: 2000-01, 67/1. 2001-02, 81/2. 2005-06, 75/0. Totals, 223/3.

WNBA PLAYOFF RECORD

Season Team	G	Min.	FGM	FGA	Pct.	FTM	FTA	Pct.	REBOUNDS Off.	Def.	Tot.	Ast.	St.	Blk.	TO	Pts.	AVERAGES RPG	APG	PPG
2005—Indiana	4	96	6	23	.261	6	6	1.000	10	8	18	5	5	1	6	18	4.5	1.3	4.5
Totals	4	96	6	23	.261	6	6	1.000	10	8	18	5	5	1	6	18	4.5	1.3	4.5

Personal fouls/disqualifications: 2005-06, 11/0. Totals, 11/0.

SUMMERTON, LAURA   C   SUN

PERSONAL: Born December 13, 1981 in Australia. ... 6-2.
MISCELLANEOUS: Played in the WNBL for Adelaide Quit Lightning (2002-04).

WNBA REGULAR-SEASON RECORD

Season Team	G	Min.	FGM	FGA	Pct.	FTM	FTA	Pct.	REBOUNDS Off.	Def.	Tot.	Ast.	St.	Blk.	TO	Pts.	AVERAGES RPG	APG	PPG
2005—Connecticut	11	43	3	9	.333	4	5	.800	5	5	10	3	2	0	4	10	0.9	0.3	0.9
Totals	11	43	3	9	.333	4	5	.800	5	5	10	3	2	0	4	10	0.9	0.3	0.9

Personal fouls/disqualifications: 2005-06, 11/0. Totals, 11/0.

WNBA PLAYOFF RECORD

Season Team	G	Min.	FGM	FGA	Pct.	FTM	FTA	Pct.	REBOUNDS Off.	Def.	Tot.	Ast.	St.	Blk.	TO	Pts.	AVERAGES RPG	APG	PPG
2005—Connecticut	2	2	0	0	...	0	0	...	0	0	0	0	0	0	0	0	0.0	0.0	0.0
Totals	2	2	0	0	...	0	0	...	0	0	0	0	0	0	0	0	0.0	0.0	0.0

SUTTON-BROWN, TAMMY   C   STING

PERSONAL: Born January 27, 1978, in Markham, Ontario, Canada. ... 6-4/199. (1.93/90.3). ... Full name: Tamara Kim Sutton-Brown
HIGH SCHOOL: Markham District (Markham, Ontario, Canada).
COLLEGE: Rutgers.
TRANSACTIONS/CAREER NOTES: Selected by Charlotte in second round (18th overall) of WNBA Draft, April 20, 2001.

COLLEGE RECORD

Season Team	G	Min.	FGM	FGA	Pct.	FTM	FTA	Pct.	Reb.	Ast.	Pts.	AVERAGES RPG	APG	PPG
1997—Rutgers	32	570	93	172	.541	40	89	.449	158	15	226	4.9	0.5	7.1
1998—Rutgers	35	745	132	196	.673	91	141	.645	205	16	355	5.9	0.5	10.1
1999—Rutgers	32	762	109	211	.517	75	118	.636	164	11	293	5.1	0.3	9.2
2000—Rutgers	31	736	137	237	.578	98	146	.671	158	10	372	5.1	0.3	12.0
Totals	130	2813	471	816	.577	304	494	.615	685	52	1246	5.3	0.4	9.6

Three-point field goals: 2000-01, 0-for-1. Totals, 0-for-1 (.000).

OLYMPICS RECORD

Season Team	G	Min.	FGM	FGA	Pct.	FTM	FTA	Pct.	Reb.	Ast.	Pts.	AVERAGES RPG	APG	PPG
2000—Canada	6	159	20	42	.476	22	30	.733	44	1	62	7.3	0.2	10.3
Totals	6	159	20	42	.476	22	30	.733	44	1	62	7.3	0.2	10.3

Season Team	G	Min.	FGM	FGA	Pct.	FTM	FTA	Pct.	REBOUNDS Off.	Def.	Tot.	Ast.	St.	Blk.	TO	Pts.	AVERAGES RPG	APG	PPG
2001—Charlotte	29	602	72	147	.490	52	72	.722	51	78	129	11	21	39	40	196	4.4	0.4	6.8
2002—Charlotte	32	885	129	243	.531	124	174	.713	76	115	191	15	29	36	49	382	6.0	0.5	11.9
2003—Charlotte	34	864	98	233	.421	90	131	.687	73	128	201	15	19	50	59	286	5.9	0.4	8.4
2004—Charlotte	34	970	106	224	.473	113	162	.698	63	148	211	15	31	71	71	325	6.2	0.4	9.6
2005—Charlotte	34	887	111	218	.509	96	141	.681	64	115	179	14	30	37	69	318	5.3	0.4	9.4
Totals	163	4208	516	1065	.485	475	680	.699	327	584	911	70	130	233	288	1507	5.6	0.4	9.2

Personal fouls/disqualifications: 2001-02, 84/1. 2002-03, 125/3. 2003-04, 132/2. 2004-05, 111/1. 2005-06, 138/5. Totals, 590/12.

WNBA PLAYOFF RECORD

Season Team	G	Min.	FGM	FGA	Pct.	FTM	FTA	Pct.	REBOUNDS Off.	Def.	Tot.	Ast.	St.	Blk.	TO	Pts.	AVERAGES RPG	APG	PPG
2001—Charlotte	8	167	25	46	.543	10	14	.714	10	16	26	4	1	11	8	60	3.3	0.5	7.5
2002—Charlotte	2	56	7	14	.500	1	6	.167	4	8	12	0	1	1	7	15	6.0	0.0	7.5
2003—Charlotte	2	32	2	7	.286	0	0	...	1	5	6	0	0	3	2	4	3.0	0.0	2.0
Totals	12	255	34	67	.507	11	20	.550	15	29	44	4	2	15	17	79	3.7	0.3	6.6

Personal fouls/disqualifications: 2001-02, 25/0. 2002-03, 6/0. 2003-04, 5/0. Totals, 36/0.

WNBA ALL-STAR GAME RECORD

Season Team	Min.	FGM	FGA	Pct.	FTM	FTA	Pct.	REBOUNDS Off.	Def.	Tot.	Ast.	PF	Dq.	St.	Blk.	TO	Pts.
2002—Charlotte	17	3	5	.600	3	4	.750	1	3	4	1	1	0	0	3	0	9
Totals	17	3	5	.600	3	4	.750	1	3	4	1	1	0	0	3	0	9

SWOOPES, SHERYL   F   COMETS

PERSONAL: Born March 25, 1971, in Brownfield, Texas. ... 6-0/145. (1.83/65.8). ... Full name: Sheryl Denise Swoopes.
HIGH SCHOOL: Brownfield (Brownfield, Texas).
COLLEGE: Texas Tech.
TRANSACTIONS/CAREER NOTES: Signed by WNBA and assigned to Houston, January 22, 1997.
MISCELLANEOUS: Member of WNBA Championship team (1997, 1998, 1999, 2000).

JUNIOR COLLEGE RECORD

Season Team	G	Min.	FGM	FGA	Pct.	FTM	FTA	Pct.	Reb.	Ast.	Pts.	AVERAGES RPG	APG	PPG
1989—South Plains College	35	...	361	758	.476	14	191	.073	404	182	770	11.5	5.2	22.0
1990—South Plains College	29	...	281	599	.469	123	179	.687	298	132	723	10.3	4.6	24.9
Totals	64	...	642	1357	.473	137	370	.370	702	314	1493	11.0	4.9	23.3

Three-point field goals: 1989-90, 34-for-121 (.281). 1990-91, 38-for-142 (.268). Totals, 72-for-263 (.274).

COLLEGE RECORD

NOTES: Member of NCAA Division I Championship team (1993). ... NCAA National Player of the Year (1993).

Season Team	G	Min.	FGM	FGA	Pct.	FTM	FTA	Pct.	Reb.	Ast.	Pts.	AVERAGES RPG	APG	PPG
1991—Texas Tech	32	1027	265	527	.503	135	167	.808	285	152	690	8.9	4.8	21.6
1992—Texas Tech	34	1153	365	652	.560	211	243	.868	312	139	973	9.2	4.1	28.6
Totals	66	2180	630	1179	.534	346	410	.844	597	291	1663	9.0	4.4	25.2

Three-point field goals: 1991-92, 25-for-61 (.410). 1992-93, 32-for-78 (.410). Totals, 57-for-139 (.410).

OLYMPICS RECORD

Season Team	G	Min.	FGM	FGA	Pct.	FTM	FTA	Pct.	Reb.	Ast.	Pts.	AVERAGES RPG	APG	PPG
1996—United States	8	...	40	66	.606	3	4	.750	28	31	104	3.5	3.9	13.0
1996—United States	8	...	40	66	.606	3	4	.750	28	31	104	3.5	3.9	13.0
2000—United States	8	232	46	89	.517	9	13	.692	37	24	107	4.6	3.0	13.4
2004—United States	8	195	29	71	.408	6	7	.857	32	13	73	4.0	1.6	9.1
Totals	32	427	155	292	.531	21	28	.750	125	99	388	3.9	3.1	12.1

Three-point field goals: 1996-97, 7-for-20 (.350). 1996-97, 7-for-20 (.350). 2000-01, 6-for-19 (.316). 2004-05, 9-for-21 (.429). Totals, 29-for-80 (.363).
Personal fouls/disqualifications: 2004-05, 13/0. Totals, 13/0.

WNBA REGULAR-SEASON RECORD

NOTES: WNBA MVP (2000, 2002, 2005). ... WNBA Defensive Player of the Year (2000, 2002, 2003). ... All-WNBA first team (1998, 1999, 2000, 2002, 2005). ... All-WNBA second team (2003). ... All-Defensive first team (2005). ... Led WNBA in scoring (20.8 ppg) and steals (2.81 spg) in 2000 and steals (2.48 spg) in 2003. ... Bud Light Peak Performer, Scoring (2005). ... Led WNBA in scoring in 2005 (18.6).

Season Team	G	Min.	FGM	FGA	Pct.	FTM	FTA	Pct.	REBOUNDS Off.	Def.	Tot.	Ast.	St.	Blk.	TO	Pts.	AVERAGES RPG	APG	PPG
1997—Houston	9	129	25	53	.472	10	14	.714	6	9	15	7	7	4	4	64	1.7	0.8	7.1
1998—Houston	29	937	173	405	.427	71	86	.826	39	110	149	62	72	14	58	453	5.1	2.1	15.6
1999—Houston	32	1100	226	489	.462	100	122	.820	48	154	202	127	76	46	83	585	6.3	4.0	18.3
2000—Houston	31	1090	245	484	.506	119	145	.821	40	155	195	119	87	33	82	643	6.3	3.8	20.7
2001—Houston							Did not play due to injury.												
2002—Houston	32	1154	221	509	.434	127	154	.825	30	128	158	107	88	23	87	592	4.9	3.3	18.5
2003—Houston	31	1084	175	434	.403	110	124	.887	32	111	143	121	77	26	73	484	4.6	3.9	15.6
2004—Houston	31	1070	181	429	.422	77	90	.856	38	115	153	91	47	16	59	459	4.9	2.9	14.8

Season Team	G	Min.	FGM	FGA	Pct.	FTM	FTA	Pct.	REBOUNDS Off.	Def.	Tot.	Ast.	St.	Blk.	TO	Pts.	AVERAGES RPG	APG	PPG
2005—Houston	33	1225	217	486	.447	153	180	.850	27	92	119	141	66	26	72	614	3.6	4.3	18.6
Totals	228	7789	1463	3289	.445	767	915	.838	260	874	1134	775	520	188	518	3894	5.0	3.4	17.1

Three-point field goals: 1997-98, 4-for-16 (.250). 1998-99, 36-for-100 (.360). 1999-00, 33-for-98 (.337). 2000-01, 34-for-91 (.374). 2002-03, 23-for-80 (.288). 2003-04, 24-for-79 (.304). 2004-05, 20-for-65 (.308). 2005-06, 27-for-75 (.360). Totals, 201-for-604 (.333).

Personal fouls/disqualifications: 1997-98, 5/0. 1998-99, 42/0. 1999-00, 57/0. 2000-01, 67/0. 2002-03, 50/0. 2003-04, 48/0. 2004-05, 56/0. 2005-06, 54/0. Totals, 379/0.

WNBA PLAYOFF RECORD

Season Team	G	Min.	FGM	FGA	Pct.	FTM	FTA	Pct.	REBOUNDS Off.	Def.	Tot.	Ast.	St.	Blk.	TO	Pts.	AVERAGES RPG	APG	PPG
1997—Houston	2	14	0	5	.000	0	0	...	1	2	3	0	0	1	0	0	1.5	0.0	0.0
1998—Houston	5	188	27	61	.443	14	15	.933	7	43	50	26	9	7	16	73	10.0	5.2	14.6
1999—Houston	6	216	29	81	.358	26	28	.929	7	15	22	7	14	3	12	88	3.7	1.2	14.7
2000—Houston	6	220	41	87	.471	23	29	.793	9	25	34	19	17	0	12	113	5.7	3.2	18.8
2002—Houston	3	127	25	63	.397	20	25	.800	10	12	22	17	12	2	8	73	7.3	5.7	24.3
2003—Houston	3	110	20	46	.435	15	16	.938	2	17	19	13	4	2	5	56	6.3	4.3	18.7
2005—Houston	5	189	35	87	.402	17	21	.810	8	20	28	19	7	2	15	92	5.6	3.8	18.4
Totals	30	1064	177	430	.412	115	134	.858	44	134	178	101	63	17	68	495	5.9	3.4	16.5

Three-point field goals: 1997-98, 0-for-2. 1998-99, 5-for-18 (.278). 1999-00, 4-for-13 (.308). 2000-01, 8-for-17 (.471). 2002-03, 3-for-9 (.333). 2003-04, 1-for-10 (.100). 2005-06, 5-for-14 (.357). Totals, 26-for-83 (.313).

Personal fouls/disqualifications: 1997-98, 1/0. 1998-99, 10/0. 1999-00, 9/0. 2000-01, 11/0. 2002-03, 7/0. 2003-04, 8/0. 2005-06, 17/0. Totals, 63/0.

WNBA ALL-STAR GAME RECORD

Season Team	Min.	FGM	FGA	Pct.	FTM	FTA	Pct.	REBOUNDS Off.	Def.	Tot.	Ast.	PF	Dq.	St.	Blk.	TO	Pts.
1999—Houston..................	19	4	7	.571	0	0	...	1	7	8	0	2	0	3	1	2	8
2000—Houston..................	21	3	7	.429	0	0	...	1	5	6	3	1	0	0	0	2	6
2002—Houston..................	23	4	12	.333	3	4	.750	5	1	6	3	1	0	2	0	2	11
2003—Houston..................	21	1	4	.250	2	4	.500	0	4	4	4	1	0	1	0	2	4
2005—Houston..................	25	6	13	.462	1	2	.500	1	3	4	2	2	0	0	0	1	15
Totals	109	18	43	.419	6	10	.600	8	20	28	12	7	0	6	1	9	44

Three-point field goals: 2001, 0-for-1. 2003, 0-for-1. 2004, 0-for-1. 2006, 2-for-3 (.667). Totals, 2-for-6 (.333).

TAURASI, DIANA   G   MERCURY

PERSONAL: Born June 11, 1982, in Glendale, Calif. ... 5-11/172. (1.80/78.0). ... Full name: Diana Lurena Taurasi
HIGH SCHOOL: Don Lugo (Chino, Calif.).
COLLEGE: Connecticut.
TRANSACTIONS/CAREER NOTES: Selected by Phoenix in the first round (first overall) of the WNBA Draft, April 17, 2004.
MISCELLANEOUS: Member of the bronze medal-winning 2001 USA Junior World Championship team. ... Member of the gold medal-winning 2000 USA Basketball Women's Junior World Championship qualifying team. ... Member of Division I NCAA Championship team (2002, 2003, 2004).

COLLEGE RECORD

NOTES: Naismith Player of the Year (2003, 2004). ... AP Player of the Year (2003). ... USBWA Player of the Year (2003). ... Wade Trophy Player of the Year (2003). ... Honda Broderick Player of the Year (2003). ... Kodak All-American (2002, 2003, 2004). ... USBWA All-American (2003, 2004). ... AP All-American first team (2003, 2004). ... AP All-American second team (2002). ... NCAA Final Four Most Outstanding Player (2003, 2004). ... East Regional Most Outstanding Player (2003). ... Big East Player of the Year (2003, 2004). ... All-Big East first team (2002, 2003, 2004). ... All-Big East Tournament team (2002, 2003). ... Big East Championship Most Outstanding Player (2001). ... Big East All-Rookie team (2001).

Season Team	G	Min.	FGM	FGA	Pct.	FTM	FTA	Pct.	Reb.	Ast.	Pts.	AVERAGES RPG	APG	PPG
2000—Connecticut....................	33	791	127	286	.444	36	41	.878	106	109	361	3.2	3.3	10.9
2001—Connecticut....................	39	1131	200	405	.494	72	87	.828	158	208	564	4.1	5.3	14.5
2002—Connecticut....................	37	1181	237	498	.476	119	146	.815	225	161	663	6.1	4.4	17.9
2003—Connecticut....................	34	1078	191	415	.460	85	107	.794	133	167	550	3.9	4.9	16.2
Totals	143	4181	755	1604	.471	312	381	.819	622	645	2138	4.3	4.5	15.0

Three-point field goals: 2000-01, 71-for-184 (.386). 2001-02, 92-for-209 (.440). 2002-03, 70-for-200 (.350). 2003-04, 83-for-211 (.393). Totals, 316-for-804 (.393).

OLYMPICS RECORD

Season Team	G	Min.	FGM	FGA	Pct.	FTM	FTA	Pct.	Reb.	Ast.	Pts.	AVERAGES RPG	APG	PPG
2004—United States..................	8	154	26	69	.377	5	7	.714	24	8	68	3.0	1.0	8.5
Totals	8	154	26	69	.377	5	7	.714	24	8	68	3.0	1.0	8.5

Three-point field goals: 2004-05, 11-for-33 (.333). Totals, 11-for-33 (.333).
Personal fouls/disqualifications: 2004-05, 16/0. Totals, 16/0.

WNBA REGULAR-SEASON RECORD

NOTES: WNBA Rookie of the Year (2004). ... All-WNBA first team (2004). ... All-WNBA second team (2005).

Season Team	G	Min.	FGM	FGA	Pct.	FTM	FTA	Pct.	REBOUNDS Off.	Def.	Tot.	Ast.	St.	Blk.	TO	Pts.	AVERAGES RPG	APG	PPG
2004—Phoenix............	34	1130	209	503	.416	98	129	.760	28	121	149	132	43	25	90	578	4.4	3.9	17.0
2005—Phoenix............	33	1089	175	427	.410	121	151	.801	22	116	138	150	38	28	112	527	4.2	4.5	16.0
Totals	67	2219	384	930	.413	219	280	.782	50	237	287	282	81	53	202	1105	4.3	4.2	16.5

Three-point field goals: 2004-05, 62-for-188 (.330). 2005-06, 56-for-179 (.313). Totals, 118-for-367 (.322).
Personal fouls/disqualifications: 2004-05, 117/4. 2005-06, 111/2. Totals, 228/6.

WNBA ALL-STAR GAME RECORD

Season Team	Min.	FGM	FGA	Pct.	FTM	FTA	Pct.	REBOUNDS Off.	Def.	Tot.	Ast.	PF	Dq.	St.	Blk.	TO	Pts.
2005—Phoenix	24	3	8	.375	2	2	1.000	1	1	2	4	0	0	1	0	2	10
Totals	24	3	8	.375	2	2	1.000	1	1	2	4	0	0	1	0	2	10

Three-point field goals: 2006, 2-for-6 (.333). Totals, 2-for-6 (.333).

TAYLOR, PENNY   F   MERCURY

PERSONAL: Born May 24, 1981, in Melbourne, Australia. ... 6-1/168. (1.85/76.2).
TRANSACTIONS/CAREER NOTES: Selected by Cleveland in first round (11th overall) of WNBA Draft, April 20, 2001. ... Selected by Phoenix in WNBA Dispersal Draft, January 6, 2004.
MISCELLANEOUS: WNBL MVP (2001). ... WNBL MVP (2001). ... Played for WNBL AIS (Australian Institute of Sports) in 1998-99. ... WNBL All-Star Five (2001). ... Led WNBL in scoring (25.5 ppg) steals (2.5 spg) in 2000-01. ... Member of WNBL Championship team (1999).

WNBA REGULAR-SEASON RECORD

Season Team	G	Min.	FGM	FGA	Pct.	FTM	FTA	Pct.	REBOUNDS Off.	Def.	Tot.	Ast.	St.	Blk.	TO	Pts.	AVERAGES RPG	APG	PPG
2001—Cleveland	32	561	86	225	.382	36	46	.783	36	76	112	44	35	11	38	230	3.5	1.4	7.2
2002—Cleveland	30	908	133	320	.416	87	102	.853	51	107	158	68	37	11	58	391	5.3	2.3	13.0
2003—Cleveland	34	898	143	340	.421	78	95	.821	44	104	148	80	38	10	60	398	4.4	2.4	11.7
2004—Phoenix	33	1076	150	310	.484	93	108	.861	51	109	160	82	52	14	81	434	4.8	2.5	13.2
2005—Phoenix	29	852	121	261	.464	102	118	.864	38	82	120	94	38	11	77	382	4.1	3.2	13.2
Totals	158	4295	633	1456	.435	396	469	.844	220	478	698	368	200	57	314	1835	4.4	2.3	11.6

Three-point field goals: 2001-02, 22-for-73 (.301). 2002-03, 38-for-111 (.342). 2003-04, 34-for-99 (.343). 2004-05, 41-for-96 (.427). 2005-06, 38-for-94 (.404). Totals, 173-for-473 (.366).
Personal fouls/disqualifications: 2001-02, 46/0. 2002-03, 66/0. 2003-04, 53/0. 2004-05, 108/1. 2005-06, 86/2. Totals, 359/3.

WNBA PLAYOFF RECORD

Season Team	G	Min.	FGM	FGA	Pct.	FTM	FTA	Pct.	REBOUNDS Off.	Def.	Tot.	Ast.	St.	Blk.	TO	Pts.	AVERAGES RPG	APG	PPG
2001—Cleveland	3	59	8	25	.320	3	4	.750	2	7	9	3	6	1	5	21	3.0	1.0	7.0
2003—Cleveland	3	99	16	36	.444	10	12	.833	1	12	13	3	6	1	6	45	4.3	1.0	15.0
Totals	6	158	24	61	.393	13	16	.813	3	19	22	6	12	2	11	66	3.7	1.0	11.0

Three-point field goals: 2001-02, 2-for-11 (.182). 2003-04, 3-for-10 (.300). Totals, 5-for-21 (.238).
Personal fouls/disqualifications: 2001-02, 4/0. 2003-04, 10/0. Totals, 14/0.

WNBA ALL-STAR GAME RECORD

Season Team	Min.	FGM	FGA	Pct.	FTM	FTA	Pct.	REBOUNDS Off.	Def.	Tot.	Ast.	PF	Dq.	St.	Blk.	TO	Pts.
2002—Cleveland	17	4	8	.500	1	1	1.000	1	2	3	0	0	0	2	0	0	9
Totals	17	4	8	.500	1	1	1.000	1	2	3	0	0	0	2	0	0	9

Three-point field goals: 2003, 0-for-2. Totals, 0-for-2 (.000).

OLYMPICS RECORD

Season Team	G	Min.	FGM	FGA	Pct.	FTM	FTA	Pct.	Reb.	Ast.	Pts.	AVERAGES RPG	APG	PPG
2004—Australia	8	192	43	84	.512	22	26	.846	43	13	118	5.4	1.6	14.8
Totals	8	192	43	84	.512	22	26	.846	43	13	118	5.4	1.6	14.8

Three-point field goals: 2004-05, 10-for-25 (.400). Totals, 10-for-25 (.400).
Personal fouls/disqualifications: 2004-05, 24/1. Totals, 24/1.

TEASLEY, NIKKI   G   MYSTICS

PERSONAL: Born March 22, 1979, in Washington, D.C. ... 6-0/169. (1.83/76.7). ... Full name: Michelle Nicole Teasley
HIGH SCHOOL: St. John's at Prospect Hall (Prospect Hall, Md.).
COLLEGE: North Carolina.
TRANSACTIONS/CAREER NOTES: Selected by Portland in first round (fifth overall) of WNBA Draft, April 19, 2002. ... Traded by Portland with G Sophia Witherspoon to Los Angeles for G Ukari Figgs & G Gergana Slavtcheva, April 19, 2002. ... Traded by Los Angeles to Washington for C Murriel Page and G Tameka Johnson, March 1, 2006.
MISCELLANEOUS: Member of WNBA Championship team (2002).

COLLEGE RECORD

Season Team	G	Min.	FGM	FGA	Pct.	FTM	FTA	Pct.	Reb.	Ast.	Pts.	AVERAGES RPG	APG	PPG
1997—North Carolina	30	896	131	316	.415	74	96	.771	104	166	387	3.5	5.5	12.9
1998—North Carolina	36	1189	193	467	.413	112	163	.687	169	211	555	4.7	5.9	15.4
1999—North Carolina	26	858	131	336	.390	66	81	.815	104	162	379	4.0	6.2	14.6
2000—North Carolina						Did not play.								
2001—North Carolina	33	1062	146	398	.367	132	153	.863	145	189	501	4.4	5.7	15.2
Totals	125	4005	601	1517	.396	384	493	.779	522	728	1822	4.2	5.8	14.6

Three-point field goals: 1997-98, 51-for-142 (.359). 1998-99, 57-for-182 (.313). 1999-00, 51-for-161 (.317). 2001-02, 77-for-209 (.368). Totals, 236-for-694 (.340).

WNBA REGULAR-SEASON RECORD

NOTES: All-WNBA second team (2003, 2004). ... Led WNBA in assists (6.1) in 2004.

Season Team	G	Min.	FGM	FGA	Pct.	FTM	FTA	Pct.	Off.	Def.	Tot.	Ast.	St.	Blk.	TO	Pts.	RPG	APG	PPG
									REBOUNDS								AVERAGES		
2002—Los Angeles	32	882	67	166	.404	30	40	.750	17	67	84	140	25	9	68	204	2.6	4.4	6.4
2003—Los Angeles	34	1189	112	288	.389	98	112	.875	30	145	175	214	39	15	108	392	5.1	6.3	11.5
2004—Los Angeles	34	1105	108	278	.388	52	68	.765	29	87	116	207	43	7	103	336	3.4	6.1	9.9
2005—Los Angeles	19	551	45	135	.333	22	26	.846	6	47	53	70	23	4	47	141	2.8	3.7	7.4
Totals	119	3727	332	867	.383	202	246	.821	82	346	428	631	130	35	326	1073	3.6	5.3	9.0

Three-point field goals: 2002-03, 40-for-100 (.400). 2003-04, 70-for-165 (.424). 2004-05, 68-for-165 (.412). 2005-06, 29-for-94 (.309). Totals, 207-for-524 (.395).

Personal fouls/disqualifications: 2002-03, 63/1. 2003-04, 68/0. 2004-05, 89/0. 2005-06, 38/0. Totals, 258/1.

WNBA PLAYOFF RECORD

Season Team	G	Min.	FGM	FGA	Pct.	FTM	FTA	Pct.	Off.	Def.	Tot.	Ast.	St.	Blk.	TO	Pts.	RPG	APG	PPG
									REBOUNDS								AVERAGES		
2002—Los Angeles	6	184	14	42	.333	16	19	.842	3	10	13	47	9	1	22	49	2.2	7.8	8.2
2003—Los Angeles	9	312	22	67	.328	16	20	.800	11	29	40	71	12	0	27	70	4.4	7.9	7.8
2004—Los Angeles	3	88	5	19	.263	4	4	1.000	1	2	3	16	2	1	14	19	1.0	5.3	6.3
2005—Los Angeles	2	61	7	21	.333	6	9	.667	2	3	5	14	3	0	3	22	2.5	7.0	11.0
Totals	20	645	48	149	.322	42	52	.808	17	44	61	148	26	2	66	160	3.1	7.4	8.0

Three-point field goals: 2002-03, 5-for-22 (.227). 2003-04, 10-for-45 (.222). 2004-05, 5-for-15 (.333). 2005-06, 2-for-11 (.182). Totals, 22-for-93 (.237).

Personal fouls/disqualifications: 2002-03, 22/1. 2003-04, 23/0. 2004-05, 10/0. 2005-06, 4/0. Totals, 59/1.

WNBA ALL-STAR GAME RECORD

NOTES: WNBA All-Star MVP (2003).

Season Team	Min.	FGM	FGA	Pct.	FTM	FTA	Pct.	Off.	Def.	Tot.	Ast.	PF	Dq.	St.	Blk.	TO	Pts.
								REBOUNDS									
2003—Los Angeles.............	24	2	6	.333	4	4	1.000	0	6	6	6	0	0	5	0	0	10
Totals	24	2	6	.333	4	4	1.000	0	6	6	6	0	0	5	0	0	10

Three-point field goals: 2004, 2-for-5 (.400). Totals, 2-for-5 (.400).

THOMAS, CHRISTI   F   SPARKS

PERSONAL: Born August 14, 1982, in Marietta, Ga. ... 6-3/185. (1.91/83.9). ... Full name: Christi Michelle Thomas
HIGH SCHOOL: Buford (Buford, Ga.).
COLLEGE: Georgia.
TRANSACTIONS/CAREER NOTES: Selected by Los Angeles in first round (12th overall) of WNBA Draft, April 17, 2004.
MISCELLANEOUS: Member of the gold medal-winning USA World Championship for Young Women team (2003).

COLLEGE RECORD

NOTES: AP All-American honorable mention (2004). ... All-SEC first team (coaches, 2004). ... All-SEC second team (coaches, 2003; media 2003, 2004). ... All-SEC Tournament team (2004). ... NCAA Tournament All-Midwest Regional team (2003).

Season Team	G	Min.	FGM	FGA	Pct.	FTM	FTA	Pct.	Reb.	Ast.	Pts.	RPG	APG	PPG
												AVERAGES		
2000—Georgia	29	623	130	255	.510	75	121	.620	188	18	338	6.5	0.6	11.7
2001—Georgia	30	664	122	237	.515	62	103	.602	187	27	311	6.2	0.9	10.4
2002—Georgia	30	850	180	335	.537	156	192	.712	241	22	481	8.0	0.7	16.0
2003—Georgia	35	935	173	321	.539	112	145	.772	290	28	463	8.3	0.8	13.2
Totals	124	3072	605	1148	.527	360	525	.686	906	95	1593	7.3	0.8	12.8

Three-point field goals: 2000-01, 3-for-16 (.188). 2001-02, 5-for-20 (.250). 2002-03, 10-for-37 (.270). 2003-04, 5-for-22 (.227). Totals, 23-for-95 (.242).

WNBA REGULAR-SEASON RECORD

Season Team	G	Min.	FGM	FGA	Pct.	FTM	FTA	Pct.	Off.	Def.	Tot.	Ast.	St.	Blk.	TO	Pts.	RPG	APG	PPG
									REBOUNDS								AVERAGES		
2004—Los Angeles	31	547	66	143	.462	28	41	.683	43	77	120	23	18	14	27	165	3.9	0.7	5.3
2005—Los Angeles	32	520	48	96	.500	22	32	.688	28	76	104	17	11	19	25	122	3.3	0.5	3.8
Totals	63	1067	114	239	.477	50	73	.685	71	153	224	40	29	33	52	287	3.6	0.6	4.6

Three-point field goals: 2004-05, 5-for-11 (.455). 2005-06, 4-for-12 (.333). Totals, 9-for-23 (.391).

Personal fouls/disqualifications: 2004-05, 80/0. 2005-06, 102/1. Totals, 182/1.

WNBA PLAYOFF RECORD

Season Team	G	Min.	FGM	FGA	Pct.	FTM	FTA	Pct.	Off.	Def.	Tot.	Ast.	St.	Blk.	TO	Pts.	RPG	APG	PPG
									REBOUNDS								AVERAGES		
2004—Los Angeles	3	100	12	22	.545	0	0	...	11	12	23	2	1	1	2	24	7.7	0.7	8.0
2005—Los Angeles	2	38	3	4	.750	1	1	1.000	1	1	2	2	0	2	2	8	1.0	1.0	4.0
Totals	5	138	15	26	.577	1	1	1.000	12	13	25	4	1	3	4	32	5.0	0.8	6.4

Three-point field goals: 2004-05, 0-for-1. 2005-06, 1-for-1 (1.000). Totals, 1-for-2 (.500).

Personal fouls/disqualifications: 2004-05, 14/0. 2005-06, 7/0. Totals, 21/0.

THOMAS, LATOYA   F   SILVER STARS

PERSONAL: Born July 6, 1981, in Greenville, Miss. ... 6-2/165. (1.88/74.8). ... Full name: LaToya Monique Thomas
HIGH SCHOOL: Greenville (Greenville, Miss.).
COLLEGE: Mississippi State.
TRANSACTIONS/CAREER NOTES: Selected by Cleveland in first round (first overall) of WNBA Draft, April 25, 2003. ... Selected by San Antonio in WNBA Dispersal Draft, January 6, 2004.

COLLEGE RECORD

NOTES: Kodak All-American first team (2000, 2001, 2002). ... AP All-American first team (2002). ... SEC Player of the Year (2003). ... All-SEC first team (2000, 2001, 2002, 2003). ... AP All-American second team (2001). ... SEC Freshman of the Year (2000). ... Led SEC in scoring as a freshman (21.0 ppg), sophomore (24.3 ppg) and junior (24.6 ppg). ... MSU's all-time career scoring leader (2,981). ... Broke her own single-season scoring records (763 points/24.6 ppg) as a junior.

Season Team	G	Min.	FGM	FGA	Pct.	FTM	FTA	Pct.	Reb.	Ast.	Pts.	RPG	APG	PPG
												AVERAGES		
1999—Mississippi State	32	967	260	456	.570	142	181	.785	254	50	672	7.9	1.6	21.0
2000—Mississippi State	31	978	276	504	.548	195	265	.736	265	42	752	8.5	1.4	24.3
2001—Mississippi State	31	1085	286	502	.570	190	245	.776	308	62	763	9.9	2.0	24.6
2002—Mississippi State	31	1066	297	562	.528	182	223	.816	281	49	794	9.1	1.6	25.6
Totals	125	4096	1119	2024	.553	709	914	.776	1108	203	2981	8.9	1.6	23.8

Three-point field goals: 1999-00, 10-for-35 (.286). 2000-01, 5-for-25 (.200). 2001-02, 1-for-8 (.125). 2002-03, 18-for-42 (.429). Totals, 34-for-110 (.309).

WNBA REGULAR-SEASON RECORD

Season Team	G	Min.	FGM	FGA	Pct.	FTM	FTA	Pct.	Off.	Def.	Tot.	Ast.	St.	Blk.	TO	Pts.	RPG	APG	PPG
									REBOUNDS								**AVERAGES**		
2003—Cleveland	32	852	137	296	.463	71	90	.789	63	101	164	37	28	13	42	345	5.1	1.2	10.8
2004—San Antonio	31	964	171	350	.489	95	113	.841	48	90	138	42	25	11	56	440	4.5	1.4	14.2
2005—San Antonio	21	505	69	161	.429	44	49	.898	18	50	68	22	7	8	33	185	3.2	1.0	8.8
Totals	84	2321	377	807	.467	210	252	.833	129	241	370	101	60	32	131	970	4.4	1.2	11.5

Three-point field goals: 2003-04, 0-for-6. 2004-05, 3-for-8 (.375). 2005-06, 3-for-7 (.429). Totals, 6-for-21 (.286).
Personal fouls/disqualifications: 2003-04, 62/1. 2004-05, 99/1. 2005-06, 42/0. Totals, 203/2.

WNBA PLAYOFF RECORD

Season Team	G	Min.	FGM	FGA	Pct.	FTM	FTA	Pct.	Off.	Def.	Tot.	Ast.	St.	Blk.	TO	Pts.	RPG	APG	PPG
									REBOUNDS								**AVERAGES**		
2003—Cleveland	3	100	14	32	.438	13	17	.765	6	17	23	4	1	4	6	41	7.7	1.3	13.7
Totals	3	100	14	32	.438	13	17	.765	6	17	23	4	1	4	6	41	7.7	1.3	13.7

Three-point field goals: 2003-04, 0-for-2. Totals, 0-for-2 (.000).
Personal fouls/disqualifications: 2003-04, 11/0. Totals, 11/0.

THOMAS, STACEY   F   STING

PERSONAL: Born August 29, 1978, in Flint, Mich. ... 5-10/154. (1.78/69.9). ... Full name: Stacey Latrice Thomas
HIGH SCHOOL: Flint Southwestern Academy (Flint, Mich.).
COLLEGE: Michigan.
TRANSACTIONS/CAREER NOTES: Selected by Portland in second round (23rd overall) of WNBA Draft, April 25, 2000. ... Traded by Phoenix to Detroit for G Tamara Moore, July 31, 2003. ... Signed by Detroit, April 19, 2005. ... Traded by Detroit with G/F Chandi Jones to Minnesota for G Katie Smith, July 30, 2005.
MISCELLANEOUS: Member of WNBA Championship team (2003).

COLLEGE RECORD

NOTES: All-Big Ten first team (coaches, 2000; media, 2000). ... All-Big Ten second team (coaches, 1998; 1999; media, 1999). ... Big Ten All-Freshman team (1997). ... Big Ten Defensive Player of the Year. ... Big Ten Freshman of the Year (1997). ... Holds Big Ten career steals record (372). ... Kodak/District 6 All-American (2000). ... Led Big Ten in steals 1998 (3.1 spg) 1999 (3.67 spg). ... Women's Basketball Journal Defensive All-American (2000).

Season Team	G	Min.	FGM	FGA	Pct.	FTM	FTA	Pct.	Reb.	Ast.	Pts.	RPG	APG	PPG
												AVERAGES		
1996—Michigan	26	...	140	275	.509	54	104	.519	171	50	336	6.6	1.9	12.9
1997—Michigan	29	...	131	303	.432	72	121	.595	213	53	338	7.3	1.8	11.7
1998—Michigan	30	...	189	421	.449	59	95	.621	235	56	446	7.8	1.9	14.9
1999—Michigan	30	...	162	425	.381	77	130	.592	232	64	436	7.7	2.1	14.5
Totals	115	...	622	1424	.437	262	450	.582	851	223	1556	7.4	1.9	13.5

Three-point field goals: 1996-97, 2-for-12 (.167). 1997-98, 4-for-23 (.174). 1998-99, 9-for-28 (.321). 1999-00, 35-for-124 (.282). Totals, 50-for-187 (.267).

WNBA REGULAR-SEASON RECORD

Season Team	G	Min.	FGM	FGA	Pct.	FTM	FTA	Pct.	Off.	Def.	Tot.	Ast.	St.	Blk.	TO	Pts.	RPG	APG	PPG
									REBOUNDS								**AVERAGES**		
2000—Portland	32	863	58	163	.356	44	74	.595	48	78	126	101	54	15	68	163	3.9	3.2	5.1
2001—Portland	32	413	22	60	.367	15	35	.429	31	39	70	41	30	10	40	59	2.2	1.3	1.8
2002—Portland	32	621	51	148	.345	31	61	.508	34	60	94	67	42	12	36	143	2.9	2.1	4.5
2003—Phoenix	30	269	20	62	.323	14	27	.519	15	28	43	15	20	9	16	61	1.4	0.5	2.0
2004—Detroit	1	1	0	0	...	0	0	...	0	0	0	0	0	0	0	0	0.0	0.0	0.0
2005—Detroit-Minn.	18	136	2	14	.143	8	20	.400	11	11	22	8	8	3	3	12	1.2	0.4	0.7
Totals	145	2303	153	447	.342	112	217	.516	139	216	355	232	154	49	163	438	2.4	1.6	3.0

Three-point field goals: 2000-01, 3-for-12 (.250). 2001-02, 0-for-7. 2002-03, 10-for-39 (.256). 2003-04, 7-for-27 (.259). 2005-06, 0-for-1. Totals, 20-for-86 (.233).
Personal fouls/disqualifications: 2000-01, 93/1. 2001-02, 57/0. 2002-03, 62/0. 2003-04, 24/0. 2005-06, 15/0. Totals, 251/1.

WNBA PLAYOFF RECORD

Season Team	G	Min.	FGM	FGA	Pct.	FTM	FTA	Pct.	Off.	Def.	Tot.	Ast.	St.	Blk.	TO	Pts.	RPG	APG	PPG
									REBOUNDS								**AVERAGES**		
2003—Detroit	4	13	0	1	.000	0	0	...	0	3	3	0	1	0	1	0	0.8	0.0	0.0
2004—Detroit	3	7	1	1	1.000	0	0	...	0	1	1	0	1	0	0	3	0.3	0.0	1.0
Totals	7	20	1	2	.500	0	0	...	0	4	4	0	2	0	1	3	0.6	0.0	0.4

Three-point field goals: 2004-05, 1-for-1 (1.000). Totals, 1-for-1 (1.000).
Personal fouls/disqualifications: 2003-04, 1/0. 2004-05, 1/0. Totals, 2/0.

THOMPSON, ALICIA   F   STORM

PERSONAL: Born June 30, 1976, in Big Lake, Texas. ... 6-1/180. (1.85/81.6).
HIGH SCHOOL: Reagan County (Big Lake, Texas).
COLLEGE: Texas Tech.
TRANSACTIONS/CAREER NOTES: Selected by New York in first round (ninth overall) of WNBA Draft, April 29, 1998. ... Waived by New York, June 7, 1999. ... Assigned to Indiana, May 2, 2000.
MISCELLANEOUS: Member of WNBA Championship team (2004).

COLLEGE RECORD

NOTES: AP All-American first team (1998). ... Kodak All-American (1998).

Season Team	G	Min.	FGM	FGA	Pct.	FTM	FTA	Pct.	Reb.	Ast.	Pts.	AVERAGES RPG	APG	PPG
1994—Texas Tech	35	...	76	137	.555	43	78	.551	104	15	195	3.0	0.4	5.6
1995—Texas Tech	32	...	226	482	.469	99	154	.643	295	77	556	9.2	2.4	17.4
1996—Texas Tech	29	...	264	546	.484	143	204	.701	279	41	686	9.6	1.4	23.7
1997—Texas Tech	31	...	299	551	.543	117	168	.696	275	62	719	8.9	2.0	23.2
Totals	127	...	865	1716	.504	402	604	.666	953	195	2156	7.5	1.5	17.0

Three-point field goals: 1995-96, 5-for-14 (.357). 1996-97, 15-for-43 (.349). 1997-98, 4-for-24 (.167). Totals, 24-for-81 (.296).

WNBA REGULAR-SEASON RECORD

Season Team	G	Min.	FGM	FGA	Pct.	FTM	FTA	Pct.	REBOUNDS Off.	Def.	Tot.	Ast.	St.	Blk.	TO	Pts.	AVERAGES RPG	APG	PPG
1998—New York	19	126	9	39	.231	12	19	.632	7	17	24	4	1	2	8	31	1.3	0.2	1.6
2000—Indiana	31	792	131	255	.514	30	42	.714	48	109	157	41	24	4	53	310	5.1	1.3	10.0
2001—Indiana	22	381	76	174	.437	17	23	.739	21	42	63	25	9	7	22	186	2.9	1.1	8.5
2002—Indiana	18	314	39	109	.358	12	17	.706	12	30	42	14	7	2	18	97	2.3	0.8	5.4
2004—Seattle	23	182	24	54	.444	1	2	.500	8	16	24	9	6	0	7	52	1.0	0.4	2.3
2005—Seattle	30	329	32	81	.395	12	16	.750	10	35	45	14	4	4	18	83	1.5	0.5	2.8
Totals	143	2124	311	712	.437	84	119	.706	106	249	355	107	51	19	126	759	2.5	0.7	5.3

Three-point field goals: 1998-99, 1-for-1 (1.000). 2000-01, 18-for-40 (.450). 2001-02, 17-for-43 (.395). 2002-03, 7-for-29 (.241). 2004-05, 3-for-16 (.188). 2005-06, 7-for-22 (.318). Totals, 53-for-151 (.351).
Personal fouls/disqualifications: 1998-99, 12/0. 2000-01, 85/4. 2001-02, 24/0. 2002-03, 20/0. 2004-05, 9/0. 2005-06, 17/0. Totals, 167/4.

WNBA PLAYOFF RECORD

Season Team	G	Min.	FGM	FGA	Pct.	FTM	FTA	Pct.	REBOUNDS Off.	Def.	Tot.	Ast.	St.	Blk.	TO	Pts.	AVERAGES RPG	APG	PPG
2002—Indiana	1	2	1	1	1.000	0	0	...	0	0	0	0	0	0	0	2	0.0	0.0	2.0
2004—Seattle	8	83	15	33	.455	3	3	1.000	6	9	15	6	2	1	7	39	1.9	0.8	4.9
2005—Seattle	1	10	1	4	.250	0	0	...	0	3	3	0	0	0	0	2	3.0	0.0	2.0
Totals	10	95	17	38	.447	3	3	1.000	6	12	18	6	2	1	7	43	1.8	0.6	4.3

Three-point field goals: 2004-05, 6-for-12 (.500). 2005-06, 0-for-1. Totals, 6-for-13 (.462).
Personal fouls/disqualifications: 2004-05, 6/0. Totals, 6/0.

THOMPSON, TINA   F   COMETS

PERSONAL: Born February 10, 1975, in Los Angeles. ... 6-2/178. (1.88/80.7). ... Full name: Tina Marie Thompson.
HIGH SCHOOL: Morningside (Inglewood, Calif.).
COLLEGE: USC.
TRANSACTIONS/CAREER NOTES: Selected by Houston in first round (first overall) of WNBA Draft, April 28, 1997.
MISCELLANEOUS: Member of WNBA Championship team (1997, 1998, 1999, 2000).

COLLEGE RECORD

NOTES: AP All-American second team (1997).

Season Team	G	Min.	FGM	FGA	Pct.	FTM	FTA	Pct.	Reb.	Ast.	Pts.	AVERAGES RPG	APG	PPG
1993—Southern Cal	30	...	163	327	.498	91	142	.641	316	25	427	10.5	0.8	14.2
1994—Southern Cal	28	...	193	372	.519	152	208	.731	294	24	545	10.5	0.9	19.5
1995—Southern Cal	27	...	229	452	.507	141	190	.742	252	42	623	9.3	1.6	23.1
1996—Southern Cal	29	...	222	445	.499	168	215	.781	306	59	653	10.6	2.0	22.5
Totals	114	...	807	1596	.506	552	755	.731	1168	150	2248	10.2	1.3	19.7

Three-point field goals: 1993-94, 10-for-28 (.357). 1994-95, 7-for-34 (.206). 1995-96, 24-for-76 (.316). 1996-97, 41-for-121 (.339). Totals, 82-for-259 (.317).

WNBA REGULAR-SEASON RECORD

NOTES: All-WNBA first team (1997, 1998, 2004). ... All-WNBA second team (1999, 2000, 2001, 2002).

Season Team	G	Min.	FGM	FGA	Pct.	FTM	FTA	Pct.	REBOUNDS Off.	Def.	Tot.	Ast.	St.	Blk.	TO	Pts.	AVERAGES RPG	APG	PPG
1997—Houston	28	885	133	318	.418	67	80	.838	67	117	184	32	21	28	62	370	6.6	1.1	13.2
1998—Houston	27	874	121	289	.419	63	74	.851	65	127	192	24	31	25	47	342	7.1	0.9	12.7
1999—Houston	32	1074	142	339	.419	68	87	.782	67	139	206	28	31	31	72	391	6.4	0.9	12.2
2000—Houston	32	1087	191	407	.469	103	123	.837	68	177	245	48	47	25	84	540	7.7	1.5	16.9
2001—Houston	30	1102	199	528	.377	137	163	.840	84	149	233	58	29	22	87	579	7.8	1.9	19.3
2002—Houston	29	1052	176	408	.431	93	113	.823	67	150	217	62	25	20	92	485	7.5	2.1	16.7
2003—Houston	28	974	176	426	.413	81	104	.779	39	126	165	47	18	23	69	472	5.9	1.7	16.9

Season Team	G	Min.	FGM	FGA	Pct.	FTM	FTA	Pct.	REBOUNDS Off.	Def.	Tot.	Ast.	St.	Blk.	TO	Pts.	AVERAGES RPG	APG	PPG
2004—Houston	26	943	180	448	.402	116	147	.789	44	113	157	48	22	23	70	520	6.0	1.8	20.0
2005—Houston	15	439	62	150	.413	16	21	.762	17	40	57	22	12	4	32	152	3.8	1.5	10.1
Totals	247	8430	1380	3313	.417	744	912	.816	518	1138	1656	369	236	201	615	3851	6.7	1.5	15.6

Three-point field goals: 1997-98, 37-for-100 (.370). 1998-99, 37-for-103 (.359). 1999-00, 39-for-111 (.351). 2000-01, 55-for-132 (.417). 2001-02, 44-for-150 (.293). 2002-03, 40-for-108 (.370). 2003-04, 39-for-114 (.342). 2004-05, 44-for-108 (.407). 2005-06, 12-for-40 (.300). Totals, 347-for-966 (.359).

Personal fouls/disqualifications: 1997-98, 107/1. 1998-99, 89/0. 1999-00, 95/0. 2000-01, 88/0. 2001-02, 74/0. 2002-03, 76/0. 2003-04, 65/0. 2004-05, 68/0. 2005-06, 32/0. Totals, 694/1.

WNBA PLAYOFF RECORD

Season Team	G	Min.	FGM	FGA	Pct.	FTM	FTA	Pct.	REBOUNDS Off.	Def.	Tot.	Ast.	St.	Blk.	TO	Pts.	AVERAGES RPG	APG	PPG
1997—Houston	2	74	9	21	.429	6	10	.600	8	10	18	3	2	1	6	26	9.0	1.5	13.0
1998—Houston	5	186	20	49	.408	11	12	.917	12	34	46	6	7	4	8	58	9.2	1.2	11.6
1999—Houston	6	208	21	57	.368	16	21	.762	6	24	30	4	5	7	13	67	5.0	0.7	11.2
2000—Houston	6	233	25	62	.403	17	18	.944	17	31	48	10	5	5	10	76	8.0	1.7	12.7
2001—Houston	2	68	11	20	.550	4	5	.800	4	8	12	7	1	0	10	29	6.0	3.5	14.5
2002—Houston	3	128	16	44	.364	7	10	.700	9	15	24	4	6	3	2	43	8.0	1.3	14.3
2003—Houston	3	106	18	46	.391	6	7	.857	3	11	14	5	2	6	6	45	4.7	1.7	15.0
2005—Houston	5	168	28	57	.491	10	14	.714	10	18	28	6	2	6	9	69	5.6	1.2	13.8
Totals	32	1171	148	356	.416	77	97	.794	69	151	220	45	30	32	64	413	6.9	1.4	12.9

Three-point field goals: 1997-98, 2-for-5 (.400). 1998-99, 7-for-20 (.350). 1999-00, 9-for-24 (.375). 2000-01, 9-for-23 (.391). 2001-02, 3-for-5 (.600). 2002-03, 4-for-12 (.333). 2003-04, 3-for-13 (.231). 2005-06, 3-for-10 (.300). Totals, 40-for-112 (.357).

Personal fouls/disqualifications: 1997-98, 5/0. 1998-99, 19/0. 1999-00, 24/1. 2000-01, 19/0. 2001-02, 5/0. 2002-03, 12/0. 2003-04, 9/0. 2005-06, 15/0. Totals, 108/1.

NOTES: WNBA All-Star MVP (2000).

WNBA ALL-STAR GAME RECORD

Season Team	Min.	FGM	FGA	Pct.	FTM	FTA	Pct.	REBOUNDS Off.	Def.	Tot.	Ast.	PF	Dq.	St.	Blk.	TO	Pts.
1999—Houston..................	14	4	8	.500	0	0	...	0	5	5	0	0	0	0	0	2	8
2000—Houston..................	23	5	14	.357	2	2	1.000	6	5	11	1	1	0	3	1	4	13
2001—Houston..................	19	2	12	.167	0	0	...	1	2	3	0	5	0	3	0	3	4
2002—Houston..................	28	7	16	.438	5	6	.833	3	4	7	0	2	0	2	1	2	20
Totals	84	18	50	.360	7	8	.875	10	16	26	1	8	0	8	2	11	45

Three-point field goals: 2001, 1-for-4 (.250). 2002, 0-for-2. 2003, 1-for-3 (.333). Totals, 2-for-9 (.222).

OLYMPICS RECORD

Season Team	G	Min.	FGM	FGA	Pct.	FTM	FTA	Pct.	Reb.	Ast.	Pts.	AVERAGES RPG	APG	PPG
2004—United States.....................	8	195	45	90	.500	17	22	.773	40	11	113	5.0	1.4	14.1
Totals	8	195	45	90	.500	17	22	.773	40	11	113	5.0	1.4	14.1

Three-point field goals: 2004-05, 6-for-18 (.333). Totals, 6-for-18 (.333).
Personal fouls/disqualifications: 2004-05, 13/0. Totals, 13/0.

THORN, ERIN   G   LIBERTY

PERSONAL: Born May 19, 1981, in Orem, Utah. ... 5-10/150. (1.78/68.0).
HIGH SCHOOL: Mountain View (Orem, Utah).
COLLEGE: Brigham Young.
TRANSACTIONS/CAREER NOTES: Selected by New York in second round (17th overall) of WNBA Draft, April 25, 2003.

COLLEGE RECORD

NOTES: Mountain West Conference MVP (2002). ... All-MWC first team (2001, 2002, 2003). ... All-MWC second team (2000). ... MWC Freshman of the Year (2000). ... Set a BYU single-game record with nine three-pointers (December 14, 2001).

Season Team	G	Min.	FGM	FGA	Pct.	FTM	FTA	Pct.	Reb.	Ast.	Pts.	AVERAGES RPG	APG	PPG
1999—Brigham Young	31	995	135	321	.421	48	59	.814	110	114	409	3.5	3.7	13.2
2000—Brigham Young	32	1044	173	415	.417	57	67	.851	143	101	496	4.5	3.2	15.5
2001—Brigham Young	33	1107	199	454	.438	66	79	.835	132	114	572	4.0	3.5	17.3
2002—Brigham Young	31	1084	199	447	.445	87	95	.916	129	176	584	4.2	5.7	18.8
Totals	127	4230	706	1637	.431	258	300	.860	514	505	2061	4.0	4.0	16.2

Three-point field goals: 1999-00, 91-for-210 (.433). 2000-01, 93-for-234 (.397). 2001-02, 108-for-264 (.409). 2002-03, 99-for-241 (.411). Totals, 391-for-949 (.412).

WNBA REGULAR-SEASON RECORD

Season Team	G	Min.	FGM	FGA	Pct.	FTM	FTA	Pct.	REBOUNDS Off.	Def.	Tot.	Ast.	St.	Blk.	TO	Pts.	AVERAGES RPG	APG	PPG
2003—New York...........	23	181	13	42	.310	10	10	1.000	3	8	11	16	4	1	13	44	0.5	0.7	1.9
2004—New York...........	17	156	12	45	.267	1	2	.500	0	8	8	4	1	9	34	0.5	0.5	2.0
2005—New York...........	21	203	21	54	.389	4	4	1.000	4	10	14	13	4	0	7	56	0.7	0.6	2.7
Totals	61	540	46	141	.326	15	16	.938	7	26	33	37	12	2	29	134	0.5	0.6	2.2

Three-point field goals: 2003-04, 8-for-33 (.242). 2004-05, 9-for-31 (.290). 2005-06, 10-for-29 (.345). Totals, 27-for-93 (.290).
Personal fouls/disqualifications: 2003-04, 8/0. 2004-05, 5/0. 2005-06, 12/0. Totals, 25/0.

Season Team	G	Min.	FGM	FGA	Pct.	FTM	FTA	Pct.	REBOUNDS Off.	Def.	Tot.	Ast.	St.	Blk.	TO	Pts.	AVERAGES RPG	APG	PPG
2004—New York...........	2	3	1	1	1.000	0	0	...	0	0	0	0	0	0	0	3	0.0	0.0	1.5
2005—New York...........	2	10	1	2	.500	0	0	...	0	0	0	0	0	0	0	2	0.0	0.0	1.0
Totals	4	13	2	3	.667	0	0	...	0	0	0	0	0	0	0	5	0.0	0.0	1.3

Three-point field goals: 2004-05, 1-for-1 (1.000). Totals, 1-for-1 (1.000).
Personal fouls/disqualifications: 2005-06, 1/0. Totals, 1/0.

VODICHKOVA, KAMILA　　　C　　　MERCURY

PERSONAL: Born December 19, 1972, in Czech Republic. ... 6-4/190. (1.93/86.2).
TRANSACTIONS/CAREER NOTES: Selected by Seattle in first round (ninth overall) of WNBA Draft, April 25, 2000. ... Signed by Phoenix, March 7, 2005.
MISCELLANEOUS: Member of Czech Republic National Team. ... Member of WNBA Championship team (2004).

WNBA REGULAR-SEASON RECORD

Season Team	G	Min.	FGM	FGA	Pct.	FTM	FTA	Pct.	REBOUNDS Off.	Def.	Tot.	Ast.	St.	Blk.	TO	Pts.	AVERAGES RPG	APG	PPG
2000—Seattle	23	489	68	171	.398	60	78	.769	28	69	97	22	13	12	57	200	4.2	1.0	8.7
2001—Seattle	29	405	51	122	.418	38	44	.864	25	46	71	23	16	7	34	150	2.4	0.8	5.2
2002—Seattle	32	817	114	245	.465	54	67	.806	61	115	176	47	36	18	55	295	5.5	1.5	9.2
2003—Seattle	28	709	101	213	.474	82	101	.812	55	88	143	31	20	21	53	284	5.1	1.1	10.1
2004—Seattle	34	873	94	241	.390	84	108	.778	65	103	168	55	32	12	73	273	4.9	1.6	8.0
2005—Phoenix...........	28	821	127	257	.494	48	72	.667	60	136	196	63	28	22	58	305	7.0	2.3	10.9
Totals	174	4114	555	1249	.444	366	470	.779	294	557	851	241	145	92	330	1507	4.9	1.4	8.7

Three-point field goals: 2000-01, 4-for-20 (.200). 2001-02, 10-for-25 (.400). 2002-03, 13-for-38 (.342). 2003-04, 0-for-5. 2004-05, 1-for-2 (.500). 2005-06, 3-for-7 (.429). Totals, 31-for-97 (.320).
Personal fouls/disqualifications: 2000-01, 63/0. 2001-02, 48/0. 2002-03, 96/1. 2003-04, 101/4. 2004-05, 110/5. 2005-06, 86/2. Totals, 512/12.

WNBA PLAYOFF RECORD

Season Team	G	Min.	FGM	FGA	Pct.	FTM	FTA	Pct.	REBOUNDS Off.	Def.	Tot.	Ast.	St.	Blk.	TO	Pts.	AVERAGES RPG	APG	PPG
2002—Seattle	2	61	7	16	.438	10	11	.909	2	8	10	3	2	0	2	25	5.0	1.5	12.5
2004—Seattle	8	204	19	47	.404	11	18	.611	13	17	30	6	7	7	13	49	3.8	0.8	6.1
Totals	10	265	26	63	.413	21	29	.724	15	25	40	9	9	7	15	74	4.0	0.9	7.4

Three-point field goals: 2002-03, 1-for-2 (.500). Totals, 1-for-2 (.500).
Personal fouls/disqualifications: 2002-03, 3/0. 2004-05, 16/0. Totals, 19/0.

V

W

VODOPYANOVA, NATALIA　　　F　　　STORM

PERSONAL: Born April 6, 1981 in St. Petersburg, Russia. ... 6/3
MISCELLANEOUS: Played for Dynamo Moscow (Russia League). ... Member of the bronze medal-winning Russian National Team (2004).

WNBA REGULAR-SEASON RECORD

Season Team	G	Min.	FGM	FGA	Pct.	FTM	FTA	Pct.	REBOUNDS Off.	Def.	Tot.	Ast.	St.	Blk.	TO	Pts.	AVERAGES RPG	APG	PPG
2005—Seattle	17	98	8	22	.364	8	12	.667	3	17	20	10	3	2	8	25	1.2	0.6	1.5
Totals	17	98	8	22	.364	8	12	.667	3	17	20	10	3	2	8	25	1.2	0.6	1.5

Three-point field goals: 2005-06, 1-for-5 (.200). Totals, 1-for-5 (.200).
Personal fouls/disqualifications: 2005-06, 9/0. Totals, 9/0.

WNBA PLAYOFF RECORD

Season Team	G	Min.	FGM	FGA	Pct.	FTM	FTA	Pct.	REBOUNDS Off.	Def.	Tot.	Ast.	St.	Blk.	TO	Pts.	AVERAGES RPG	APG	PPG
2005—Seattle	1	3	0	1	.000	0	0	...	0	0	0	0	0	0	0	0	0.0	0.0	0.0
Totals	1	3	0	1	.000	0	0	...	0	0	0	0	0	0	0	0	0.0	0.0	0.0

WALKER, AYANA　　　F　　　STING

PERSONAL: Born September 10, 1979, in Houston. ... 6-3/143. (1.91/64.9). ... Full name: Ayana D'Nay Walker
HIGH SCHOOL: Westbury (Houston).
COLLEGE: Louisiana Tech.
TRANSACTIONS/CAREER NOTES: Selected by Detroit in second round (20th overall) of WNBA Draft, April 19, 2002.
MISCELLANEOUS: USA Basketball Female Athlete of the Year (2001). ... Member of gold medal-winning USA Basketball Women's National Team (2001). ... Set USA single-game record with 19 rebounds in gold medal game. ... Member of WNBA Championship team (2003).

COLLEGE RECORD

Season Team	G	Min.	FGM	FGA	Pct.	FTM	FTA	Pct.	Reb.	Ast.	Pts.	AVERAGES RPG	APG	PPG
1998—Louisiana Tech................	33	524	70	141	.496	14	39	.359	123	9	154	3.7	0.3	4.7
1999—Louisiana Tech................	33	786	139	263	.529	54	75	.720	234	28	332	7.1	0.8	10.1

Season Team	G	Min.	FGM	FGA	Pct.	FTM	FTA	Pct.	Reb.	Ast.	Pts.	RPG	APG	PPG
2000—Louisiana Tech.............	36	1148	241	507	.475	94	135	.696	305	64	577	8.5	1.8	16.0
2001—Louisiana Tech.............	29	824	162	364	.445	67	98	.684	266	46	391	9.2	1.6	13.5
Totals	131	3282	612	1275	.480	229	347	.660	928	147	1454	7.1	1.1	11.1

Three-point field goals: 1998-99, 0-for-1. 1999-00, 0-for-1. 2000-01, 1-for-4 (.250). 2001-02, 0-for-1. Totals, 1-for-7 (.143).

WNBA REGULAR-SEASON RECORD

Season Team	G	Min.	FGM	FGA	Pct.	FTM	FTA	Pct.	REBOUNDS Off.	Def.	Tot.	Ast.	St.	Blk.	TO	Pts.	AVERAGES RPG	APG	PPG
2002—Detroit.............	32	548	63	167	.377	34	49	.694	56	62	118	17	12	34	29	162	3.7	0.5	5.1
2003—Detroit.............	34	271	24	70	.343	8	21	.381	34	37	71	10	10	11	19	56	2.1	0.3	1.6
2004—Detroit.............	18	148	8	28	.286	2	6	.333	10	16	26	6	1	4	5	18	1.4	0.3	1.0
2005—Det.-Charlotte...	21	333	29	68	.426	13	20	.650	20	45	65	19	8	12	19	71	3.1	0.9	3.4
Totals	105	1300	124	333	.372	57	96	.594	120	160	280	52	31	61	72	307	2.7	0.5	2.9

Three-point field goals: 2002-03, 2-for-9 (.222). Totals, 2-for-9 (.222).
Personal fouls/disqualifications: 2002-03, 56/0. 2003-04, 33/0. 2004-05, 13/0. 2005-06, 26/0. Totals, 128/0.

WNBA PLAYOFF RECORD

Season Team	G	Min.	FGM	FGA	Pct.	FTM	FTA	Pct.	REBOUNDS Off.	Def.	Tot.	Ast.	St.	Blk.	TO	Pts.	AVERAGES RPG	APG	PPG
2003—Detroit.............	4	24	1	5	.200	3	3	1.000	3	3	6	0	4	1	1	5	1.5	0.0	1.3
2004—Detroit.............	2	4	0	0	...	0	0	...	0	0	0	1	0	0	1	0	0.0	0.5	0.0
Totals	6	28	1	5	.200	3	3	1.000	3	3	6	1	4	1	2	5	1.0	0.2	0.8

Personal fouls/disqualifications: 2004-05, 1/0. Totals, 1/0.

WALKER, DEMYA　　　　　F　　　　　MONARCHS

PERSONAL: Born November 28, 1977, in Mount Holly, N.J. ... 6-4/168. (1.93/76.2). ... Full name: DeMya Chakheia Walker
HIGH SCHOOL: Rancocas Valley Regional (Mount Holly, N.J.).
COLLEGE: Virginia.
TRANSACTIONS/CAREER NOTES: Signed by WNBA and assigned to Detroit, May 2, 2000.
MISCELLANEOUS: Member of WNBA Championship team (2005).

COLLEGE RECORD

NOTES: All-ACC first team (1999). ... All-ACC Tournament second team (1999). ... Led ACC in blocked shots (1999). ... Only ACC player to be named a finalist for Naismith Player of the Year Award (1999). ... Women's Basketball Journal Defensive All-America second team (1999).

W

Season Team	G	Min.	FGM	FGA	Pct.	FTM	FTA	Pct.	Reb.	Ast.	Pts.	RPG	APG	PPG
1995—Virginia.............................	33	...	106	203	.522	38	73	.521	209	19	250	6.3	0.6	7.6
1996—Virginia.............................	31	...	165	276	.598	96	132	.727	232	44	426	7.5	1.4	13.7
1997—Virginia.............................	29	...	190	344	.552	91	144	.632	245	55	472	8.4	1.9	16.3
1998—Virginia.............................	29	...	168	306	.549	95	144	.660	246	80	435	8.5	2.8	15.0
Totals	122	...	629	1129	.557	320	493	.649	932	198	1583	7.6	1.6	13.0

Three-point field goals: 1995-96, null-for-1. 1996-97, null-for-1. 1997-98, 1-for-7 (.143). 1998-99, 4-for-14 (.286). Totals, 5-for-23 (.217).

WNBA REGULAR-SEASON RECORD

Season Team	G	Min.	FGM	FGA	Pct.	FTM	FTA	Pct.	REBOUNDS Off.	Def.	Tot.	Ast.	St.	Blk.	TO	Pts.	AVERAGES RPG	APG	PPG
2000—Portland	30	311	35	88	.398	22	47	.468	29	18	47	19	17	7	35	92	1.6	0.6	3.1
2001—Portland	21	297	44	100	.440	23	40	.575	29	29	58	10	7	12	35	113	2.8	0.5	5.4
2002—Portland	31	848	139	287	.484	59	95	.621	55	99	154	51	26	33	90	339	5.0	1.6	10.9
2003—Sacramento	34	740	111	242	.459	83	143	.580	61	88	149	47	25	23	69	307	4.4	1.4	9.0
2004—Sacramento	34	884	111	267	.416	62	103	.602	72	71	143	86	26	13	86	284	4.2	2.5	8.4
2005—Sacramento	22	598	125	234	.534	60	93	.645	47	70	117	48	28	13	69	311	5.3	2.2	14.1
Totals	172	3678	565	1218	.464	309	521	.593	293	375	668	261	129	101	384	1446	3.9	1.5	8.4

Three-point field goals: 2000-01, 0-for-2. 2001-02, 2-for-3 (.667). 2002-03, 2-for-12 (.167). 2003-04, 2-for-15 (.133). 2004-05, 0-for-10. 2005-06, 1-for-1 (1.000). Totals, 7-for-43 (.163).
Personal fouls/disqualifications: 2000-01, 69/1. 2001-02, 51/0. 2002-03, 97/1. 2003-04, 95/0. 2004-05, 109/1. 2005-06, 66/1. Totals, 487/4.

WNBA PLAYOFF RECORD

Season Team	G	Min.	FGM	FGA	Pct.	FTM	FTA	Pct.	REBOUNDS Off.	Def.	Tot.	Ast.	St.	Blk.	TO	Pts.	AVERAGES RPG	APG	PPG
2003—Sacramento	6	170	24	55	.436	11	20	.550	14	13	27	10	1	3	21	59	4.5	1.7	9.8
2004—Sacramento	6	173	30	54	.556	11	17	.647	11	9	20	14	6	8	18	71	3.3	2.3	11.8
2005—Sacramento	6	165	26	52	.500	9	12	.750	7	11	18	21	3	0	17	61	3.0	3.5	10.2
Totals	18	508	80	161	.497	31	49	.633	32	33	65	45	10	11	56	191	3.6	2.5	10.6

Personal fouls/disqualifications: 2003-04, 17/0. 2004-05, 12/0. 2005-06, 19/0. Totals, 48/0.

WNBA ALL-STAR GAME RECORD

Season　Team	Min.	FGM	FGA	Pct.	FTM	FTA	Pct.	REBOUNDS Off.	Def.	Tot.	Ast.	PF	Dq.	St.	Blk.	TO	Pts.
2005—Sacramento.............	10	2	3	.667	1	2	.500	0	1	1	0	2	0	1	1	0	5
Totals	10	2	3	.667	1	2	.500	0	1	1	0	2	0	1	1	0	5

WAUTERS, ANN   C   LIBERTY

PERSONAL: Born October 12, 1980, in Sint-Niklaas, Belgium. ... 6-4/193. (1.93/87.5).
HIGH SCHOOL: Heilige Familie (Sint-Niklaas, Belgium).
TRANSACTIONS/CAREER NOTES: Selected by Cleveland in first round (first overall) of WNBA Draft, April 25, 2000. ... Selected by New York in WNBA Dispersal Draft, January 6, 2004.

WNBA REGULAR-SEASON RECORD

Season Team	G	Min.	FGM	FGA	Pct.	FTM	FTA	Pct.	REBOUNDS Off.	Def.	Tot.	Ast.	St.	Blk.	TO	Pts.	AVERAGES RPG	APG	PPG
2000—Cleveland	32	598	78	149	.523	43	58	.741	47	82	129	37	21	24	63	199	4.0	1.2	6.2
2001—Cleveland	24	622	87	153	.569	60	75	.800	35	79	114	35	17	13	50	234	4.8	1.5	9.8
2002—Cleveland	28	802	120	217	.553	74	87	.851	45	95	140	39	16	21	59	314	5.0	1.4	11.2
2004—New York	13	271	29	66	.439	23	29	.793	10	30	40	21	4	8	21	82	3.1	1.6	6.3
2005—New York	28	879	151	279	.541	79	105	.752	47	137	184	41	18	23	71	383	6.6	1.5	13.7
Totals	125	3172	465	864	.538	279	354	.788	184	423	607	173	76	89	264	1212	4.9	1.4	9.7

Three-point field goals: 2000-01, 0-for-2. 2001-02, 0-for-2. 2002-03, 0-for-1. 2004-05, 1-for-3 (.333). 2005-06, 2-for-2 (1.000). Totals, 3-for-10 (.300).
Personal fouls/disqualifications: 2000-01, 75/0. 2001-02, 55/0. 2002-03, 74/0. 2004-05, 28/0. 2005-06, 91/1. Totals, 323/1.

WNBA PLAYOFF RECORD

Season Team	G	Min.	FGM	FGA	Pct.	FTM	FTA	Pct.	REBOUNDS Off.	Def.	Tot.	Ast.	St.	Blk.	TO	Pts.	AVERAGES RPG	APG	PPG
2000—Cleveland	6	107	13	27	.481	2	6	.333	5	13	18	5	3	3	8	28	3.0	0.8	4.7
2001—Cleveland	3	86	13	19	.684	8	9	.889	6	4	10	2	2	3	4	34	3.3	0.7	11.3
Totals	9	193	26	46	.565	10	15	.667	11	17	28	7	5	6	12	62	3.1	0.8	6.9

Three-point field goals: 2000-01, 0-for-2. Totals, 0-for-2 (.000).
Personal fouls/disqualifications: 2000-01, 7/0. 2001-02, 10/0. Totals, 17/0.

WNBA ALL-STAR GAME RECORD

Season Team	Min.	FGM	FGA	Pct.	FTM	FTA	Pct.	REBOUNDS Off.	Def.	Tot.	Ast.	PF	Dq.	St.	Blk.	TO	Pts.
2005—New York	13	1	4	.250	2	2	1.000	2	1	3	0	0	0	0	1	1	4
Totals	13	1	4	.250	2	2	1.000	2	1	3	0	0	0	0	1	1	4

WECKER, KENDRA   F   SILVER STARS

PERSONAL: Born December 16, 1982, in Marysville, Kan. ... 5-11/172. (1.80/78.0). ... Full name: Kendra Renee Wecker
HIGH SCHOOL: Marysville (Marysville, Kan.).
COLLEGE: Kansas State.
TRANSACTIONS/CAREER NOTES: Selected by San Antonio in the first round (fourth overall) of the WNBA Draft, April 16, 2005.

COLLEGE RECORD

NOTES: AP All-American first team (2005). ... AP All-American third team (2003, 2004). ... Kodak All-American (2004, 2005). ... USBWA All-American (2003, 2005). ... Big 12 player of the year (2005). ... All-Big 12 first team (2003, 2004, 2005). ... CoSIDA academic all-district second team (2003, 2004). ... All-Big 12 academic first team (2004, 2005).

Season Team	G	Min.	FGM	FGA	Pct.	FTM	FTA	Pct.	Reb.	Ast.	Pts.	AVERAGES RPG	APG	PPG
2001—Kansas State	34	1073	221	418	.529	86	101	.851	264	97	557	7.8	2.9	16.4
2002—Kansas State	34	1173	257	551	.466	76	88	.864	281	125	646	8.3	3.7	19.0
2003—Kansas State	31	965	217	440	.493	59	66	.894	250	83	521	8.1	2.7	16.8
2004—Kansas State	29	930	240	504	.476	89	104	.856	292	74	609	10.1	2.6	21.0
Totals	128	4141	935	1913	.489	310	359	.864	1087	379	2333	8.5	3.0	18.2

WNBA REGULAR-SEASON RECORD

Season Team	G	Min.	FGM	FGA	Pct.	FTM	FTA	Pct.	REBOUNDS Off.	Def.	Tot.	Ast.	St.	Blk.	TO	Pts.	AVERAGES RPG	APG	PPG
2005—San Antonio	1	11	2	6	.333	0	0	...	0	0	0	2	1	0	1	4	0.0	2.0	4.0
Totals	1	11	2	6	.333	0	0	...	0	0	0	2	1	0	1	4	0.0	2.0	4.0

Three-point field goals: 2005-06, 0-for-3. Totals, 0-for-3 (.000).

WHALEN, LINDSAY   G   SUN

PERSONAL: Born May 9, 1982, in Hutchinson, Minn. ... 5-8/150. (1.73/68.0). ... Full name: Lindsay Marie Whalen
HIGH SCHOOL: Hutchinson (Hutchinson, Minn.).
COLLEGE: Minnesota.
TRANSACTIONS/CAREER NOTES: Selected by Connecticut in first round (fourth overall) of WNBA Draft, April 17, 2004.
MISCELLANEOUS: Member of gold medal-winning USA World Championship for Young Women team (2003). ... Member of gold medal-winning USA World Championship for Young Women qualifying team (2002).

COLLEGE RECORD

NOTES: Kodak All-American (2003, 2004). ... AP All-American second team (2003, 2004). ... USBWA All-American (2003, 2004). ... AP All-American third team (2002). ... Kodak All-American honorable mention (2002). ... Big Ten Player of the Year (2002). ... All-Big Ten first team (2002, 2003, 2004).

Season Team	G	Min.	FGM	FGA	Pct.	FTM	FTA	Pct.	Reb.	Ast.	Pts.	RPG	APG	PPG
2000—Minnesota	25	895	149	313	.476	111	151	.735	100	82	425	4.0	3.3	17.0
2001—Minnesota	30	1016	245	437	.561	147	191	.770	166	159	667	5.5	5.3	22.2
2002—Minnesota	31	1019	225	412	.546	155	183	.847	155	192	639	5.0	6.2	20.6
2003—Minnesota	27	888	185	360	.514	144	173	.832	138	145	554	5.1	5.4	20.5
Totals	113	3818	804	1522	.528	557	698	.798	559	578	2285	4.9	5.1	20.2

Three-point field goals: 2000-01, 16-for-53 (.302). 2001-02, 30-for-86 (.349). 2002-03, 34-for-105 (.324). 2003-04, 40-for-100 (.400). Totals, 120-for-344 (.349).

WNBA REGULAR-SEASON RECORD

Season Team	G	Min.	FGM	FGA	Pct.	FTM	FTA	Pct.	Off.	Def.	Tot.	Ast.	St.	Blk.	TO	Pts.	RPG	APG	PPG
2004—Connecticut	31	946	83	183	.454	89	122	.730	21	69	90	148	39	0	94	275	2.9	4.8	8.9
2005—Connecticut	34	1047	135	290	.466	125	156	.801	29	99	128	172	42	2	89	411	3.8	5.1	12.1
Totals	65	1993	218	473	.461	214	278	.770	50	168	218	320	81	2	183	686	3.4	4.9	10.6

Three-point field goals: 2004-05, 20-for-57 (.351). 2005-06, 16-for-46 (.348). Totals, 36-for-103 (.350).
Personal fouls/disqualifications: 2004-05, 72/0. 2005-06, 90/0. Totals, 162/0.

WNBA PLAYOFF RECORD

Season Team	G	Min.	FGM	FGA	Pct.	FTM	FTA	Pct.	Off.	Def.	Tot.	Ast.	St.	Blk.	TO	Pts.	RPG	APG	PPG
2004—Connecticut	8	255	30	65	.462	43	53	.811	5	13	18	41	11	3	17	107	2.3	5.1	13.4
2005—Connecticut	7	220	19	57	.333	37	48	.771	6	18	24	23	6	1	20	78	3.4	3.3	11.1
Totals	15	475	49	122	.402	80	101	.792	11	31	42	64	17	4	37	185	2.8	4.3	12.3

Three-point field goals: 2004-05, 4-for-11 (.364). 2005-06, 3-for-15 (.200). Totals, 7-for-26 (.269).
Personal fouls/disqualifications: 2004-05, 23/0. 2005-06, 11/0. Totals, 34/0.

WHITE, DETRINA   F   SKY

PERSONAL: Born April 3, 1980, in Lafayette, La. ... 5-11/180. (1.80/81.6). ... Full name: DeTrina Mary White
HIGH SCHOOL: Acadiana (Lafayette, La.).
COLLEGE: Louisiana State.
TRANSACTIONS/CAREER NOTES: Selected by Indiana in second round (20th overall) of WNBA Draft, April 25, 2003. ... Selected by Chicago in WNBA Expansion Draft, November 16, 2005.
MISCELLANEOUS: Won Louisiana state titles in shot put, javelin and discus as a high school senior.

COLLEGE RECORD

NOTES: All-SEC second team (coaches/media: 2000, 1999). ... WBNS National Freshman of the Year (1999). ... SEC Freshman/Newcomer of the Year (1999). ... Holds LSU record for double-doubles (28). ... Led SEC in field-goal percentage as a freshman (.621) and sophomore (.617). ... Also led SEC in double-doubles as a freshman (12) and sophomore (11).

Season Team	G	Min.	FGM	FGA	Pct.	FTM	FTA	Pct.	Reb.	Ast.	Pts.	RPG	APG	PPG
1998—Louisiana State	30	844	159	256	.621	74	132	.561	247	31	392	8.2	1.0	13.1
1999—Louisiana State	32	903	163	264	.617	57	110	.518	283	26	383	8.8	0.8	12.0
2000—Louisiana State	20	517	78	128	.609	34	53	.642	149	19	190	7.5	1.0	9.5
2001—Louisiana State						Did not play—injured.								
2002—Louisiana State	25	532	84	144	.583	34	46	.739	161	19	202	6.4	0.8	8.1
Totals	107	2796	484	792	.611	199	341	.584	840	95	1167	7.9	0.9	10.9

WNBA REGULAR-SEASON RECORD

Season Team	G	Min.	FGM	FGA	Pct.	FTM	FTA	Pct.	Off.	Def.	Tot.	Ast.	St.	Blk.	TO	Pts.	RPG	APG	PPG
2004—New York	31	420	37	68	.544	8	17	.471	51	67	118	9	8	10	36	82	3.8	0.3	2.6
2005—New York	13	90	4	11	.364	8	12	.667	9	13	22	0	4	3	3	16	1.7	0.0	1.2
Totals	44	510	41	79	.519	16	29	.552	60	80	140	9	12	13	39	98	3.2	0.2	2.2

Personal fouls/disqualifications: 2004-05, 37/0. 2005-06, 15/0. Totals, 52/0.

WNBA PLAYOFF RECORD

Season Team	G	Min.	FGM	FGA	Pct.	FTM	FTA	Pct.	Off.	Def.	Tot.	Ast.	St.	Blk.	TO	Pts.	RPG	APG	PPG
2004—New York	5	34	1	5	.200	0	0	...	3	3	6	1	2	0	4	2	1.2	0.2	0.4
Totals	5	34	1	5	.200	0	0	...	3	3	6	1	2	0	4	2	1.2	0.2	0.4

Personal fouls/disqualifications: 2004-05, 6/0. Totals, 6/0.

WHITE, TAN   G   FEVER

PERSONAL: Born September 27, 1982, in Tupelo, Miss. ... 5-7/155. (1.70/70.3). ... Full name: LaTanya Chantella White
HIGH SCHOOL: Tupelo (Tupelo, Miss.).
COLLEGE: Mississippi State.
TRANSACTIONS/CAREER NOTES: Selected by Indiana in the first round (second overall) of the WNBA Draft, April 16, 2005.

COLLEGE RECORD

NOTES: AP All-American second team (2005). ... Kodak All-American (2005). ... All-SEC first team (2002, 2004). ... All-SEC second team (2003). ... WomensCollegeHoops.com All-American honorable mention (2003). ... SEC newcomer of the year (2002). ... All-SEC freshman team (2002). ... WomensCollegeHoops.com first team All-American (2002).

W

Season Team	G	Min.	FGM	FGA	Pct.	FTM	FTA	Pct.	Reb.	Ast.	Pts.	RPG	APG	PPG
												AVERAGES		
2001—Mississippi State	31	1070	227	533	.426	68	109	.624	223	134	575	7.2	4.3	18.5
2002—Mississippi State	32	1066	220	510	.431	78	106	.736	217	124	580	6.8	3.9	18.1
2003—Mississippi State	29	972	205	493	.416	129	158	.816	182	99	585	6.3	3.4	20.2
2004—Mississippi State	29	1036	241	566	.426	138	184	.750	222	100	681	7.7	3.4	23.5
Totals	121	4144	893	2102	.425	413	557	.741	844	457	2421	7.0	3.8	20.0

NOTES: WNBA All-Rookie team (2005).

WNBA REGULAR-SEASON RECORD

Season Team	G	Min.	FGM	FGA	Pct.	FTM	FTA	Pct.	REBOUNDS Off.	Def.	Tot.	Ast.	St.	Blk.	TO	Pts.	AVERAGES RPG	APG	PPG
2005—Indiana	34	693	85	254	.335	47	58	.810	21	32	53	53	30	7	70	242	1.6	1.6	7.1
Totals	34	693	85	254	.335	47	58	.810	21	32	53	53	30	7	70	242	1.6	1.6	7.1

Three-point field goals: 2005-06, 25-for-81 (.309). Totals, 25-for-81 (.309).
Personal fouls/disqualifications: 2005-06, 62/1. Totals, 62/1.

WNBA PLAYOFF RECORD

Season Team	G	Min.	FGM	FGA	Pct.	FTM	FTA	Pct.	REBOUNDS Off.	Def.	Tot.	Ast.	St.	Blk.	TO	Pts.	AVERAGES RPG	APG	PPG
2005—Indiana	4	16	0	8	.000	0	0	...	2	0	2	1	0	0	0	0	0.5	0.3	0.0
Totals	4	16	0	8	.000	0	0	...	2	0	2	1	0	0	0	0	0.5	0.3	0.0

Three-point field goals: 2005-06, 0-for-1. Totals, 0-for-1 (.000).
Personal fouls/disqualifications: 2005-06, 1/0. Totals, 1/0.

WHITMORE, TAMIKA   F   FEVER

PERSONAL: Born June 5, 1977, in Tupelo, Miss. ... 6-2/190. (1.88/86.2).
HIGH SCHOOL: Tupelo (Tupelo, Miss.).
COLLEGE: Memphis.
TRANSACTIONS/CAREER NOTES: Selected by New York in the third round (30th overall) of the 1999 WNBA Draft, May 4, 1999. ... Signed by Indiana, March 17, 2006.

NOTES: Led NCAA in scoring in 1999 (26.3 ppg).

COLLEGE RECORD

Season Team	G	Min.	FGM	FGA	Pct.	FTM	FTA	Pct.	Reb.	Ast.	Pts.	AVERAGES RPG	APG	PPG
1995—Memphis	30	...	119	206	.578	68	101	.673	152	25	312	5.1	0.8	10.4
1996—Memphis	29	...	230	381	.604	116	162	.716	244	24	579	8.4	0.8	20.0
1997—Memphis	29	...	300	464	.647	151	212	.712	288	39	754	9.9	1.3	26.0
1998—Memphis	32	...	325	556	.585	163	218	.748	268	37	843	8.4	1.2	26.3
Totals	120	...	974	1607	.606	498	693	.719	952	125	2488	7.9	1.0	20.7

Three-point field goals: 1995-96, 6-for-21 (.286). 1996-97, 3-for-17 (.176). 1997-98, 3-for-12 (.250). 1998-99, 30-for-64 (.469). Totals, 42-for-114 (.368).

WNBA REGULAR-SEASON RECORD

Season Team	G	Min.	FGM	FGA	Pct.	FTM	FTA	Pct.	REBOUNDS Off.	Def.	Tot.	Ast.	St.	Blk.	TO	Pts.	AVERAGES RPG	APG	PPG
1999—New York	27	573	80	184	.435	53	78	.679	43	53	96	18	16	6	56	214	3.6	0.7	7.9
2000—New York	32	689	109	253	.431	59	84	.702	34	71	105	20	17	17	53	277	3.3	0.6	8.7
2001—New York	32	752	96	222	.432	33	58	.569	29	68	97	19	17	10	33	226	3.0	0.6	7.1
2002—New York	32	977	148	310	.477	110	150	.733	43	98	141	23	27	43	49	406	4.4	0.7	12.7
2003—New York	33	823	110	242	.455	50	76	.658	38	84	122	25	35	22	57	271	3.7	0.8	8.2
2004—Los Angeles	34	595	77	173	.445	49	72	.681	38	68	106	17	12	5	34	210	3.1	0.5	6.2
2005—Los Angeles	34	917	115	265	.434	92	106	.868	54	89	143	42	33	14	57	327	4.2	1.2	9.6
Totals	224	5326	735	1649	.446	446	624	.715	279	531	810	164	157	117	339	1931	3.6	0.7	8.6

Three-point field goals: 1999-00, 1-for-8 (.125). 2000-01, 0-for-3. 2001-02, 1-for-2 (.500). 2002-03, 0-for-1. 2003-04, 1-for-3 (.333). 2004-05, 7-for-16 (.438). 2005-06, 5-for-19 (.263). Totals, 15-for-52 (.288).
Personal fouls/disqualifications: 1999-00, 78/1. 2000-01, 102/1. 2001-02, 70/0. 2002-03, 102/1. 2003-04, 100/1. 2004-05, 73/0. 2005-06, 110/1. Totals, 635/5.

WNBA PLAYOFF RECORD

Season Team	G	Min.	FGM	FGA	Pct.	FTM	FTA	Pct.	REBOUNDS Off.	Def.	Tot.	Ast.	St.	Blk.	TO	Pts.	AVERAGES RPG	APG	PPG
1999—New York	6	114	15	31	.484	5	14	.357	5	5	10	3	4	2	10	35	1.7	0.5	5.8
2000—New York	7	196	31	65	.477	18	24	.750	9	18	27	6	3	9	15	81	3.9	0.9	11.6
2001—New York	6	152	18	44	.409	6	10	.600	10	12	22	4	4	4	7	42	3.7	0.7	7.0
2002—New York	8	271	51	93	.548	26	37	.703	8	28	36	10	3	4	9	129	4.5	1.3	16.1
2004—Los Angeles	3	39	4	10	.400	2	2	1.000	0	6	6	1	0	0	3	10	2.0	0.3	3.3
2005—Los Angeles	2	48	6	14	.429	5	8	.625	2	1	3	1	1	0	7	18	1.5	0.5	9.0
Totals	32	820	125	257	.486	62	95	.653	34	70	104	25	15	19	51	315	3.3	0.8	9.8

Three-point field goals: 2000-01, 1-for-2 (.500). 2001-02, 0-for-1. 2002-03, 1-for-3 (.333). 2004-05, 0-for-2. 2005-06, 1-for-1 (1.000). Totals, 3-for-9 (.333).
Personal fouls/disqualifications: 1999-00, 14/0. 2000-01, 22/0. 2001-02, 13/0. 2002-03, 20/0. 2004-05, 4/0. 2005-06, 7/0. Totals, 80/0.

WILLIAMS, ANGELINA   F   MERCURY

PERSONAL: Born July 21, 1983, in Chicago. ... 6-0. (1.83). ... Full name: Angelina Danielle Williams
HIGH SCHOOL: George Washington (Chicago).
COLLEGE: Illinois.
TRANSACTIONS/CAREER NOTES: Selected by Phoenix in the second round (18th overall) of the WNBA Draft, April 16, 2005.

W

COLLEGE RECORD

NOTES: All-Big Ten second team (2005). ... All-Big Ten third team (2004). ... All-Big Ten freshman team (2002).

Season Team	G	Min.	FGM	FGA	Pct.	FTM	FTA	Pct.	Reb.	Ast.	Pts.	RPG	APG	PPG
2001—Illinois	29	618	96	220	.436	32	41	.780	119	41	235	4.1	1.4	8.1
2002—Illinois	29	860	181	399	.454	58	78	.744	125	78	446	4.3	2.7	15.4
2003—Illinois	27	895	175	417	.420	62	85	.729	140	74	425	5.2	2.7	15.7
2004—Illinois	30	941	217	488	.445	62	85	.729	137	81	533	4.6	2.7	17.8
Totals	115	3314	669	1524	.439	214	289	.740	521	274	1639	4.5	2.4	14.3

WNBA REGULAR-SEASON RECORD

Season Team	G	Min.	FGM	FGA	Pct.	FTM	FTA	Pct.	Off.	Def.	Tot.	Ast.	St.	Blk.	TO	Pts.	RPG	APG	PPG
2005—Phoenix	16	149	15	50	.300	6	7	.857	9	14	23	9	4	7	11	40	1.4	0.6	2.5
Totals	16	149	15	50	.300	6	7	.857	9	14	23	9	4	7	11	40	1.4	0.6	2.5

Three-point field goals: 2005-06, 4-for-18 (.222). Totals, 4-for-18 (.222).

Personal fouls/disqualifications: 2005-06, 17/0. Totals, 17/0.

WILLIAMS, NATALIE   F   FEVER

PERSONAL: Born November 30, 1970, in Long Beach, Calif. ... 6-2/210. (1.88/95.3). ... Full name: Natalie Jean Williams
HIGH SCHOOL: Taylorsville (Salt Lake City).
COLLEGE: UCLA.
TRANSACTIONS/CAREER NOTES: Selected by Utah in the first round (third overall) of the 1999 WNBA Draft, May 4, 1999. ... Traded by San Antonio with G Coretta Brown to Indiana for C Sylvia Crawley and F Gwen Jackson, May 1, 2003.

COLLEGE RECORD

NOTES: Kodak All-American first team (1994).

Season Team	G	Min.	FGM	FGA	Pct.	FTM	FTA	Pct.	Reb.	Ast.	Pts.	RPG	APG	PPG
1990—UCLA	19	...	104	208	.500	61	91	.670	195	14	269	10.3	0.7	14.2
1991—UCLA	23	...	197	352	.560	101	160	.631	318	29	495	13.8	1.3	21.5
1992—UCLA	23	...	201	425	.473	86	115	.748	310	107	488	13.5	4.7	21.2
1993—UCLA	24	...	243	426	.570	75	145	.517	314	31	561	13.1	1.3	23.4
Totals	89	...	745	1411	.528	323	511	.632	1137	181	1813	12.8	2.0	20.4

ABL RECORD

NOTES: ABL MVP (1998).

Season Team	G	Min.	FGM	FGA	Pct.	FTM	FTA	Pct.	Reb.	Ast.	Pts.	RPG	APG	PPG
1996—Portland	32	...	215	412	.522	125	186	.672	400	50	555	12.5	1.6	17.3
1997—Portland	44	...	351	633	.555	261	359	.727	508	84	964	11.5	1.9	21.9
1998—Portland	13	...	94	162	.580	70	95	.737	129	29	258	9.9	2.2	19.8
Totals	89	...	660	1207	.547	456	640	.713	1037	163	1777	11.7	1.8	20.0

Three-point field goals: 1997-98, 1-for-5 (.200). Totals, 1-for-5 (.200).

WNBA REGULAR-SEASON RECORD

NOTES: All-WNBA first team (1999, 2000, 2001). ... Led WNBA in rebounding (11.6 rpg) in 2000.

Season Team	G	Min.	FGM	FGA	Pct.	FTM	FTA	Pct.	Off.	Def.	Tot.	Ast.	St.	Blk.	TO	Pts.	RPG	APG	PPG
1999—Utah	28	954	180	347	.519	144	191	.754	109	148	257	25	38	22	68	504	9.2	0.9	18.0
2000—Utah	29	1039	179	365	.490	182	228	.798	132	204	336	51	35	18	79	543	11.6	1.8	18.7
2001—Utah	31	1064	171	349	.490	97	133	.729	111	197	308	55	41	10	70	439	9.9	1.8	14.2
2002—Utah	31	1008	124	285	.435	98	132	.742	105	150	255	38	38	16	72	351	8.2	1.2	11.3
2003—Indiana	34	1054	176	363	.485	105	148	.709	109	146	255	46	43	21	70	457	7.5	1.4	13.4
2004—Indiana	34	956	133	293	.454	83	119	.697	93	142	235	62	40	23	65	349	6.9	1.8	10.3
2005—Indiana	34	804	103	248	.415	45	67	.672	74	112	186	31	35	12	56	251	5.5	0.9	7.4
Totals	221	6879	1066	2250	.474	754	1018	.741	733	1099	1832	308	270	122	480	2894	8.3	1.4	13.1

Three-point field goals: 1999-00, 0-for-2. 2000-01, 3-for-5 (.600). 2001-02, 0-for-4. 2002-03, 5-for-12 (.417). 2003-04, 0-for-1. 2004-05, 0-for-4. Totals, 8-for-28 (.286).

Personal fouls/disqualifications: 1999-00, 108/2. 2000-01, 124/3. 2001-02, 128/4. 2002-03, 122/4. 2003-04, 138/2. 2004-05, 122/3. 2005-06, 105/3. Totals, 847/21.

WNBA PLAYOFF RECORD

Season Team	G	Min.	FGM	FGA	Pct.	FTM	FTA	Pct.	Off.	Def.	Tot.	Ast.	St.	Blk.	TO	Pts.	RPG	APG	PPG
2001—Utah	2	57	8	16	.500	5	6	.833	7	9	16	0	3	1	5	21	8.0	0.0	10.5
2002—Utah	5	186	25	47	.532	19	28	.679	21	25	46	7	5	7	8	70	9.2	1.4	14.0
2005—Indiana	4	134	17	40	.425	13	16	.813	13	17	30	6	5	2	1	47	7.5	1.5	11.8
Totals	11	377	50	103	.485	37	50	.740	41	51	92	13	13	10	14	138	8.4	1.2	12.5

Three-point field goals: 2002-03, 1-for-4 (.250). 2005-06, 0-for-1. Totals, 1-for-5 (.200).

Personal fouls/disqualifications: 2001-02, 10/1. 2002-03, 16/1. 2005-06, 14/0. Totals, 40/2.

W

WNBA ALL-STAR GAME RECORD

NOTES: Winner of America Online NBA All-Star 2ball with Jeff Hornacek, Utah Jazz, at All-Star 2000 in Oakland.

Season Team	Min.	FGM	FGA	Pct.	FTM	FTA	Pct.	REBOUNDS Off.	Def.	Tot.	Ast.	PF	Dq.	St.	Blk.	TO	Pts.
1999—Utah	21	3	4	.750	8	10	.800	4	4	8	3	0	0	1	0	1	14
2000—Utah	17	2	6	.333	1	2	.500	4	6	10	0	3	0	1	0	0	5
2003—Indiana	22	3	5	.600	0	0	...	7	4	11	1	1	0	3	0	1	6
Totals	60	8	15	.533	9	12	.750	15	14	29	4	4	0	5	0	2	25

OLYMPICS RECORD

Season Team	G	Min.	FGM	FGA	Pct.	FTM	FTA	Pct.	Reb.	Ast.	Pts.	AVERAGES RPG	APG	PPG
2000—United States	8	121	22	39	.564	17	25	.680	47	8	61	5.9	1.0	7.6
Totals	8	121	22	39	.564	17	25	.680	47	8	61	5.9	1.0	7.6

WILLIAMS, TAMIKA   C   LYNX

PERSONAL: Born April 12, 1980, in Dayton, Ohio. ... 6-2/205. (1.88/93.0). ... Full name: Tamika Maria Williams
HIGH SCHOOL: Chaminade-Julienne (Dayton, Ohio).
COLLEGE: Connecticut.
TRANSACTIONS/CAREER NOTES: Selected by Minnesota in first round (sixth overall) of WNBA Draft, April 19, 2002.

COLLEGE RECORD

NOTES: Member of NCAA Division I Championship team (2000, 2002).

Season Team	G	Min.	FGM	FGA	Pct.	FTM	FTA	Pct.	Reb.	Ast.	Pts.	AVERAGES RPG	APG	PPG
1998—Connecticut	33	738	173	263	.658	98	151	.649	226	27	444	6.8	0.8	13.5
1999—Connecticut	31	509	115	161	.714	51	71	.718	111	24	281	3.6	0.8	9.1
2000—Connecticut	33	656	132	174	.759	60	97	.619	186	25	324	5.6	0.8	9.8
2001—Connecticut	35	766	140	199	.704	73	112	.652	240	44	353	6.9	1.3	10.1
Totals	132	2669	560	797	.703	282	431	.654	763	120	1402	5.8	0.9	10.6

Three-point field goals: 1998-99, 0-for-2. 2000-01, 0-for-1. Totals, 0-for-3 (.000).

WNBA REGULAR-SEASON RECORD

NOTES: Led the WNBA in field goal percentage in 2003 (.668) and 2004 (.540).

Season Team	G	Min.	FGM	FGA	Pct.	FTM	FTA	Pct.	REBOUNDS Off.	Def.	Tot.	Ast.	St.	Blk.	TO	Pts.	AVERAGES RPG	APG	PPG
2002—Minnesota	31	1023	124	221	.561	63	108	.583	96	133	229	51	44	13	74	314	7.4	1.6	10.1
2003—Minnesota	34	1121	129	193	.668	45	93	.484	92	117	209	44	34	10	58	303	6.1	1.3	8.9
2004—Minnesota	34	978	102	189	.540	49	87	.563	82	123	205	38	39	5	66	254	6.0	1.1	7.5
2005—Minnesota	34	758	86	156	.551	25	46	.543	76	95	171	39	30	2	41	197	5.0	1.1	5.8
Totals	133	3880	441	759	.581	182	334	.545	346	468	814	172	147	30	239	1068	6.1	1.3	8.0

Three-point field goals: 2002-03, 3-for-11 (.273). 2003-04, 0-for-2. 2004-05, 1-for-4 (.250). 2005-06, 0-for-3. Totals, 4-for-20 (.200).
Personal fouls/disqualifications: 2002-03, 57/0. 2003-04, 78/0. 2004-05, 65/0. 2005-06, 52/0. Totals, 252/0.

WNBA PLAYOFF RECORD

Season Team	G	Min.	FGM	FGA	Pct.	FTM	FTA	Pct.	REBOUNDS Off.	Def.	Tot.	Ast.	St.	Blk.	TO	Pts.	AVERAGES RPG	APG	PPG
2003—Minnesota	3	116	17	28	.607	16	24	.667	12	10	22	3	7	1	4	50	7.3	1.0	16.7
2004—Minnesota	2	72	10	16	.625	4	4	1.000	5	12	17	6	1	0	1	24	8.5	3.0	12.0
Totals	5	188	27	44	.614	20	28	.714	17	22	39	9	8	1	5	74	7.8	1.8	14.8

Three-point field goals: 2004-05, 0-for-2. Totals, 0-for-2 (.000).
Personal fouls/disqualifications: 2003-04, 5/0. 2004-05, 4/0. Totals, 9/0.

WILLINGHAM, LE'COE   F   SUN

PERSONAL: Born February 10, 1981, in Augusta, Ga. ... 6-0/200. (1.83/90.7).
HIGH SCHOOL: Hephzibah (Augusta, Ga.).
COLLEGE: Auburn.
TRANSACTIONS/CAREER NOTES: Signed by Connecticut, April 27, 2004.

COLLEGE RECORD

NOTES: All SEC first team (2000, 2004). ... All-SEC second team (2002). ... All-SEC freshman team (2000). ... Redshirted 2000-01 season.

Season Team	G	Min.	FGM	FGA	Pct.	FTM	FTA	Pct.	Reb.	Ast.	Pts.	AVERAGES RPG	APG	PPG
1999—Auburn	27	696	113	228	.496	79	108	.731	206	29	305	7.6	1.1	11.3
2001—Auburn	29	893	134	272	.493	79	126	.627	235	31	348	8.1	1.1	12.0
2002—Auburn	33	823	113	234	.483	71	100	.710	205	44	316	6.2	1.3	9.6
2004—Auburn	31	928	192	3416	.056	117	153	.765	281	51	506	9.1	1.6	16.3
Totals	120	3340	552	4150	.133	346	487	.710	927	155	1475	7.7	1.3	12.3

Three-point field goals: 1999-00, 0-for-3. 2001-02, 1-for-2 (.500). 2002-03, 19-for-60 (.317). 2004-05, 5-for-15 (.333). Totals, 25-for-80 (.313).

WNBA REGULAR-SEASON RECORD

Season Team	G	Min.	FGM	FGA	Pct.	FTM	FTA	Pct.	REBOUNDS Off.	Def.	Tot.	Ast.	St.	Blk.	TO	Pts.	AVERAGES RPG	APG	PPG
2004—Connecticut	23	175	24	38	.632	20	26	.769	22	21	43	7	8	2	12	68	1.9	0.3	3.0
2005—Connecticut	18	91	7	17	.412	10	20	.500	10	7	17	3	2	0	14	24	0.9	0.2	1.3
Totals	41	266	31	55	.564	30	46	.652	32	28	60	10	10	2	26	92	1.5	0.2	2.2

Three-point field goals: 2004-05, 0-for-1. Totals, 0-for-1 (.000).
Personal fouls/disqualifications: 2004-05, 16/0. 2005-06, 16/0. Totals, 32/0.

W

WNBA PLAYOFF RECORD

Season Team	G	Min.	FGM	FGA	Pct.	FTM	FTA	Pct.	REBOUNDS Off.	Def.	Tot.	Ast.	St.	Blk.	TO	Pts.	AVERAGES RPG	APG	PPG
2005—Connecticut........	3	10	0	2	.000	2	2	1.000	0	1	1	0	0	1	1	2	0.3	0.0	0.7
Totals	3	10	0	2	.000	2	2	1.000	0	1	1	0	0	1	1	2	0.3	0.0	0.7

WRIGHT, SHEREKA   F   MERCURY

PERSONAL: Born September 21, 1981, in Fort Riley, Kan. ... 5-10/155. (1.78/70.3). ... Full name: Shereka Monique Wright
HIGH SCHOOL: Copperas Cove (Copperas Cove, Texas).
COLLEGE: Purdue.
TRANSACTIONS/CAREER NOTES: Selected by Detroit in first round (13th overall) of WNBA Draft, April 17, 2004. ... Traded by Detroit along with G Erika Valek to Phoenix in exchange for G Chandi Jones, April 17, 2004.
MISCELLANEOUS: Member of the gold medal-winning USA World University Games team (2001).

COLLEGE RECORD

NOTES: AP All-American second team (2004). ... USBWA All-American (2004). ... Kodak All-American honorable mention (2003). ... AP All-American third team (2003). ... All-Big Ten first team (2002, 2003, 2004). ... Big Ten Tournament MVP (2004). ... Big Ten All-Freshman team (2001).

Season Team	G	Min.	FGM	FGA	Pct.	FTM	FTA	Pct.	Reb.	Ast.	Pts.	AVERAGES RPG	APG	PPG
2000—Purdue	38	900	111	244	.455	135	203	.665	177	67	377	4.7	1.8	9.9
2001—Purdue	30	1075	176	363	.485	205	279	.735	199	58	569	6.6	1.9	19.0
2002—Purdue	34	1134	199	426	.467	231	311	.743	215	91	643	6.3	2.7	18.9
2003—Purdue	33	995	22	449	.049	205	278	.737	202	75	662	6.1	2.3	20.1
Totals	135	4104	508	1482	.343	776	1071	.725	793	291	2251	5.9	2.2	16.7

Three-point field goals: 2000-01, 20-for-39 (.513). 2001-02, 12-for-51 (.235). 2002-03, 14-for-44 (.318). 2003-04, 13-for-36 (.361). Totals, 59-for-170 (.347).

WNBA REGULAR-SEASON RECORD

Season Team	G	Min.	FGM	FGA	Pct.	FTM	FTA	Pct.	REBOUNDS Off.	Def.	Tot.	Ast.	St.	Blk.	TO	Pts.	AVERAGES RPG	APG	PPG
2004—Phoenix.............	24	243	13	42	.310	25	32	.781	17	10	27	8	3	1	15	57	1.1	0.3	2.4
2005—Phoenix.............	25	346	24	59	.407	35	52	.673	18	32	50	23	14	3	28	94	2.0	0.9	3.8
Totals	49	589	37	101	.366	60	84	.714	35	42	77	31	17	4	43	151	1.6	0.6	3.1

Three-point field goals: 2004-05, 6-for-13 (.462). 2005-06, 11-for-35 (.314). Totals, 17-for-48 (.354).
Personal fouls/disqualifications: 2004-05, 19/0. 2005-06, 13/0. Totals, 32/0.

WRIGHT, TANISHA   G   STORM

PERSONAL: Born November 29, 1983, in Brooklyn, N.Y. ... 5-11/165. (1.80/74.8). ... Full name: Tanisha L. Wright
HIGH SCHOOL: West Mifflin (West Mifflin, Pa.).
COLLEGE: Penn State.
TRANSACTIONS/CAREER NOTES: Selected by Seattle in the first round (12th overall) of the WNBA Draft, April 16, 2005.

COLLEGE RECORD

NOTES: AP All-American third team (2005). ... USBWA All-American (2005). ... AP All-American honorable mention (2004). ... All-Big Ten first team (2004, 2005). ... Big Ten defensive player of the year (2003, 2004, 2005).

Season Team	G	Min.	FGM	FGA	Pct.	FTM	FTA	Pct.	Reb.	Ast.	Pts.	AVERAGES RPG	APG	PPG
2001—Penn State	35	916	137	302	.454	79	109	.725	139	97	355	4.0	2.8	10.1
2002—Penn State	35	1155	224	442	.507	109	143	.762	189	139	560	5.4	4.0	16.0
2003—Penn State	34	1124	196	406	.483	104	125	.832	159	140	502	4.7	4.1	14.8
2004—Penn State	30	1055	214	517	.414	147	183	.803	134	108	578	4.5	3.6	19.3
Totals	134	4250	771	1667	.463	439	560	.784	621	484	1995	4.6	3.6	14.9

WNBA REGULAR-SEASON RECORD

Season Team	G	Min.	FGM	FGA	Pct.	FTM	FTA	Pct.	REBOUNDS Off.	Def.	Tot.	Ast.	St.	Blk.	TO	Pts.	AVERAGES RPG	APG	PPG
2005—Seattle	34	528	49	106	.462	24	36	.667	20	37	57	53	18	3	40	122	1.7	1.6	3.6
Totals	34	528	49	106	.462	24	36	.667	20	37	57	53	18	3	40	122	1.7	1.6	3.6

Three-point field goals: 2005-06, 0-for-1. Totals, 0-for-1 (.000).
Personal fouls/disqualifications: 2005-06, 60/1. Totals, 60/1.

WNBA PLAYOFF RECORD

Season Team	G	Min.	FGM	FGA	Pct.	FTM	FTA	Pct.	REBOUNDS Off.	Def.	Tot.	Ast.	St.	Blk.	TO	Pts.	AVERAGES RPG	APG	PPG
2005—Seattle	3	38	1	5	.200	7	7	1.000	1	4	5	7	3	0	2	9	1.7	2.3	3.0
Totals	3	38	1	5	.200	7	7	1.000	1	4	5	7	3	0	2	9	1.7	2.3	3.0

Personal fouls/disqualifications: 2005-06, 6/0. Totals, 6/0.

WYCKOFF, BROOKE   F   SKY

PERSONAL: Born March 30, 1980, in Lake Forest, Ill. ... 6-1/183. (1.85/83.0). ... Full name: Brooke Elizabeth Wyckoff
HIGH SCHOOL: Lakota (West Chester, Ohio).
COLLEGE: Florida State.
TRANSACTIONS/CAREER NOTES: Selected by Orlando in second round (26th overall) of WNBA Draft, April 20, 2001. ... Selected by Chicago in WNBA Expansion Draft, November 16, 2005.

W

COLLEGE RECORD

												AVERAGES		
Season Team	G	Min.	FGM	FGA	Pct.	FTM	FTA	Pct.	Reb.	Ast.	Pts.	RPG	APG	PPG
1997—Florida State	27	...	96	204	.471	70	113	.619	216	53	268	8.0	2.0	9.9
1998—Florida State	27	...	136	314	.433	93	140	.664	214	40	370	7.9	1.5	13.7
1999—Florida State	24	...	92	225	.409	59	79	.747	170	61	259	7.1	2.5	10.8
2000—Florida State	31	...	161	362	.445	98	125	.784	204	75	453	6.6	2.4	14.6
Totals	109	...	485	1105	.439	320	457	.700	804	229	1350	7.4	2.1	12.4

Three-point field goals: 1997-98, 6-for-25 (.240). 1998-99, 5-for-18 (.278). 1999-00, 16-for-54 (.296). 2000-01, 33-for-100 (.330). Totals, 60-for-197 (.305).

WNBA REGULAR-SEASON RECORD

									REBOUNDS								AVERAGES		
Season Team	G	Min.	FGM	FGA	Pct.	FTM	FTA	Pct.	Off.	Def.	Tot.	Ast.	St.	Blk.	TO	Pts.	RPG	APG	PPG
2001—Orlando	32	648	41	125	.328	20	28	.714	48	74	122	37	26	15	50	108	3.8	1.2	3.4
2002—Orlando	32	514	31	95	.326	5	7	.714	28	62	90	32	19	18	30	81	2.8	1.0	2.5
2003—Connecticut	34	755	55	142	.387	26	36	.722	48	98	146	35	33	19	39	156	4.3	1.0	4.6
2005—Connecticut	34	596	35	88	.398	13	20	.650	25	70	95	35	13	9	28	105	2.8	1.0	3.1
Totals	132	2513	162	450	.360	64	91	.703	149	304	453	139	91	61	147	450	3.4	1.1	3.4

Three-point field goals: 2001-02, 6-for-37 (.162). 2002-03, 14-for-50 (.280). 2003-04, 20-for-70 (.286). 2005-06, 22-for-52 (.423). Totals, 62-for-209 (.297).
Personal fouls/disqualifications: 2001-02, 91/2. 2002-03, 71/1. 2003-04, 109/1. 2005-06, 82/0. Totals, 353/4.

WNBA PLAYOFF RECORD

									REBOUNDS								AVERAGES		
Season Team	G	Min.	FGM	FGA	Pct.	FTM	FTA	Pct.	Off.	Def.	Tot.	Ast.	St.	Blk.	TO	Pts.	RPG	APG	PPG
2003—Connecticut	4	89	7	16	.438	3	4	.750	3	9	12	5	2	1	2	18	3.0	1.3	4.5
2005—Connecticut	8	109	5	12	.417	4	6	.667	3	12	15	3	1	2	5	18	1.9	0.4	2.3
Totals	12	198	12	28	.429	7	10	.700	6	21	27	8	3	3	7	36	2.3	0.7	3.0

Three-point field goals: 2003-04, 1-for-6 (.167). 2005-06, 4-for-10 (.400). Totals, 5-for-16 (.313).
Personal fouls/disqualifications: 2003-04, 11/0. 2005-06, 13/0. Totals, 24/0.

ZARA, FRANCESCA   G   SKY

PERSONAL: Born December 8, 1976, in Italy. ... 5-10. (1.78).
TRANSACTIONS/CAREER NOTES: Selected by Chicago in WNBA Expansion Draft, November 16, 2005.

WNBA REGULAR-SEASON RECORD

									REBOUNDS								AVERAGES		
Season Team	G	Min.	FGM	FGA	Pct.	FTM	FTA	Pct.	Off.	Def.	Tot.	Ast.	St.	Blk.	TO	Pts.	RPG	APG	PPG
2005—Seattle	34	413	34	85	.400	17	21	.810	11	28	39	51	16	1	41	90	1.1	1.5	2.6
Totals	34	413	34	85	.400	17	21	.810	11	28	39	51	16	1	41	90	1.1	1.5	2.6

Three-point field goals: 2005-06, 5-for-22 (.227). Totals, 5-for-22 (.227).
Personal fouls/disqualifications: 2005-06, 29/0. Totals, 29/0.

WNBA PLAYOFF RECORD

									REBOUNDS								AVERAGES		
Season Team	G	Min.	FGM	FGA	Pct.	FTM	FTA	Pct.	Off.	Def.	Tot.	Ast.	St.	Blk.	TO	Pts.	RPG	APG	PPG
2005—Seattle	3	26	4	6	.667	2	2	1.000	0	0	0	2	0	0	5	11	0.0	0.7	3.7
Totals	3	26	4	6	.667	2	2	1.000	0	0	0	2	0	0	5	11	0.0	0.7	3.7

Three-point field goals: 2005-06, 1-for-1 (1.000). Totals, 1-for-1 (1.000).

Z

INDIVIDUAL CAREER HIGHS
WNBA REGULAR SEASON SINGLE-GAME HIGHS

(Includes 2005 Season)

Player	FGM	FGA	FTM	FTA	REB	AST	STL	BLK	PTS
Abrosimova, Svetlana	10	23	12	18	15	9	5	2	27
Amachree, Mactabene	2	3	2	4	4	0	3	1	4
Anderson, Chantelle	7	12	6	8	7	2	3	2	16
Arcain, Janeth	12	22	10	10	9	9	6	2	29
Baranova, Elena	10	18	10	11	18	8	6	6	27
Batkovic, Suzy	6	10	5	6	9	5	2	3	16
Batteast, Jacqueline	0	2	0	0	3	2	0	1	0
Battle, Ashley	1	2	0	0	1	0	0	0	2
Beard, Alana	11	22	9	12	10	7	7	4	27
Benningfield, Jenni	1	3	2	2	2	1	1	1	4
Bevilaqua, Tully	7	11	9	12	8	8	6	2	19
Bird, Sue	11	20	11	12	8	12	5	2	33
Braxton, Kara	9	12	4	10	9	2	5	2	20
Brown, Coretta	8	14	5	6	6	5	3	1	26
Brown, Kiesha	5	9	4	6	6	7	2	1	13
Brungo, Jessica	2	6	2	2	4	3	1	1	6
Brunson, Rebekkah	7	17	6	11	14	2	4	3	17
Buescher, Erin	6	12	5	7	11	4	3	4	16
Burse, Janell	11	17	7	13	12	4	4	5	27
Campbell, Edna	10	21	8	12	7	8	3	3	22
Canty, Dominique	8	22	10	14	11	8	6	2	22
Carey, Jaime	2	3	0	0	1	2	1	0	5
Carter, Amisha	0	1	1	2	4	0	2	0	1
Cash, Swin	11	18	15	21	15	9	6	4	29
Castro Marques, Iziane	8	13	6	7	9	5	2	1	20
Catchings, Tamika	13	24	15	17	16	10	9	4	32
Chones, Kaayla	3	5	3	4	6	1	1	2	7
Christensen, Kayte	6	9	10	16	12	4	3	3	16
Christon, Shameka	7	14	8	9	7	7	3	2	19
Curry, Edniesha	3	5	2	3	3	3	4	1	8
Darling, Helen	6	12	8	8	6	10	7	3	18
DeForge, Anna	11	25	8	10	9	9	5	2	31
Derevjanik, Jennifer	2	7	2	2	5	3	3	1	6
Dillard, Tai	5	10	2	4	5	5	2	1	11
Dixon, Tamecka	11	23	11	12	9	8	5	3	28
Douglas, Katie	11	18	12	14	12	7	5	3	28
Dydek, Margo	13	25	10	11	16	7	3	10	27
Edwards, Simone	8	15	8	8	14	3	3	4	19
Ely, Shyra	4	11	4	5	8	3	1	1	13
Farris, Barbara	6	13	8	10	10	3	2	2	15
Feaster, Allison	9	17	11	14	11	6	4	2	24
Feenstra, Katie	6	12	7	9	12	2	3	3	17
Ferdinand, Marie	12	20	11	14	8	7	5	2	27
Ford, Cheryl	8	19	9	12	22	5	4	4	21

Player	FGM	FGA	FTM	FTA	REB	AST	STL	BLK	PTS
Frett, La'Keshia	7	14	5	8	13	8	3	3	18
Goodson, Adrienne	12	21	11	13	12	6	5	2	30
Griffith, Yolanda	13	22	13	19	20	5	8	6	31
Grubin, Gordana	8	19	9	10	7	8	5	1	23
Hammon, Becky	12	19	11	12	8	10	6	1	33
Harrison, Lisa	10	15	12	13	12	5	4	2	22
Harrower, Kristi	5	11	12	12	7	9	5	1	20
Hayden, Vanessa	8	18	5	7	11	2	3	6	18
Haynie, Kristin	4	10	3	4	6	4	5	1	10
Hodges, Doneeka	6	12	5	6	5	8	3	2	17
Hodges, Roneeka	2	6	2	2	3	2	1	0	5
Hoffman, Ebony	8	10	5	6	8	3	3	2	16
Holdsclaw, Chamique	12	27	13	17	24	7	8	4	34
Irvin, Sandora	6	10	6	6	7	2	2	4	13
Ivanyi, Dalma	4	9	4	5	7	7	5	1	14
Ivey, Niele	5	9	6	6	6	7	4	1	14
Jackson, Deanna	11	14	7	8	12	5	3	3	30
Jackson, Gwen	7	20	6	8	14	3	3	2	17
Jackson, Lauren	17	29	14	16	20	5	5	8	34
Jackson, Tamicha	9	21	8	10	7	9	6	1	21
Jacobs, Amber	4	9	6	6	4	5	4	1	11
Johnson, Shannon	12	22	12	15	11	13	6	2	35
Johnson, Temeka	9	15	6	6	6	11	3	1	21
Johnson, Vickie	12	19	10	12	12	9	5	2	27
Jones, Asjha	9	18	8	8	12	7	3	3	22
Jones, Chandi	7	17	5	8	7	6	3	2	17
King Borchardt, Susan	0	1	2	2	1	1	0	1	2
Koehn, Laurie	5	8	3	3	3	2	1	0	15
Kraayeveld, Cathrine	5	10	4	4	5	1	1	3	14
Lambert, Sheila	7	12	8	9	11	9	3	2	19
Lassiter, Amanda	7	13	4	8	13	7	4	3	16
Lawson, Edwige	3	5	2	2	1	2	1	1	10
Lawson, Kara	8	15	9	9	11	8	3	2	24
Lennox, Betty	12	22	9	10	12	8	5	2	31
Leslie, Lisa	14	24	15	19	21	9	6	10	32
Lewis, Tynesha	6	13	5	6	8	4	4	2	19
Lovelace, Stacey	6	14	7	8	10	6	4	2	17
Lyttle, Sancho	5	10	3	6	10	2	3	1	13
Mabika, Mwadi	11	28	11	11	12	9	6	3	32
Macchi, Laura	6	11	6	6	13	2	4	1	16
Maiga, Hamchetou	7	11	4	6	8	3	4	2	17
Mann, Kristen	5	10	2	4	9	3	3	1	11
Martinez, Nuria	0	1	0	0	0	0	0	0	0
Masciadri, Raffaella	4	6	3	6	4	3	3	1	10
Matter, Caity	2	4	2	2	3	4	1	0	5
Mazzante, Kelly	5	8	2	3	5	2	2	1	15
McCarville, Janel	5	5	5	8	7	2	2	1	11
McCray, Nikki	11	23	12	16	9	9	5	2	30

Player	FGM	FGA	FTM	FTA	REB	AST	STL	BLK	PTS
McWilliams-Franklin, Taj	11	23	11	14	15	6	5	5	28
Melvin, Chasity	12	19	10	13	12	7	3	4	30
Miao, Li jie	2	5	2	2	1	3	1	1	6
Miller, Coco	10	21	7	9	8	7	5	2	23
Miller, Kelly	8	15	6	7	7	7	4	2	23
Miller, Teana	7	9	4	8	9	2	2	3	15
Milton-Jones, DeLisha	10	19	10	12	14	7	5	5	23
Moore, Jessica	1	2	1	2	3	1	2	0	3
Moore, Loree	2	4	2	2	4	3	2	0	4
Moore, Tamara	7	13	8	8	7	7	3	2	22
Newton, Chelsea	4	10	4	4	5	6	3	3	9
Ngoyisa, Bernadette	7	9	4	6	7	1	2	2	17
Nieuwveen, Marlous	1	2	0	0	2	0	0	0	2
Nolan, Deanna	11	21	13	16	10	11	6	3	34
Ohlde, Nicole	8	18	10	14	11	5	2	5	21
Page, Murriel	9	16	7	10	15	7	4	4	20
Paige, Yolanda	2	7	2	2	3	4	1	0	4
Palmer-Daniel, Wendy	14	31	12	18	16	6	7	3	32
Penicheiro, Ticha	9	17	12	15	14	16	10	3	27
Perkins, Jia	10	21	4	4	5	6	3	2	21
Phillips, Tari	13	21	8	12	16	6	5	3	30
Pierson, Plenette	11	20	12	19	11	5	3	6	26
Powell, Elaine	8	15	8	10	11	10	5	3	20
Powell, Nicole	10	18	5	6	7	6	3	3	25
Ragland, Felicia	7	14	4	5	8	6	3	1	19
Rasmussen, Kristen	8	11	11	12	9	6	4	3	19
Riley, Ruth	9	21	8	10	13	5	3	5	26
Robinson, Ashley	4	11	6	8	9	4	3	5	10
Robinson, Crystal	10	19	9	12	10	6	5	3	27
Sales, Nykesha	12	21	13	16	10	8	6	3	31
Sam, Sheri	12	26	10	13	12	8	6	2	27
Sanford, Nakia	7	9	6	10	13	4	3	2	17
Schumacher, Kelly	8	18	7	8	9	3	3	4	22
Scott-Richardson, Olympia	11	17	9	14	17	5	4	5	31
Smith, Jennifer	0	1	0	0	0	0	0	0	0
Smith, Katie	13	23	18	19	10	8	5	3	46
Smith, Tangela	14	23	11	12	13	5	6	6	28
Smith-Taylor, Charlotte	8	15	6	10	11	6	3	4	18
Snell, Belinda	5	8	4	4	6	3	2	1	16
Snow, Michelle	9	15	7	11	16	4	4	8	23
Staley, Dawn	10	17	10	12	9	13	6	1	23
Stepanova, Maria	9	17	6	11	13	5	5	6	20
Stevenson, Mandisa	4	7	2	2	6	1	2	2	9
Stinson, Andrea	12	23	11	14	12	10	6	5	33
Streimikyte, Jurgita	7	13	4	6	9	3	3	2	14
Sui, FeiFei	1	3	2	2	1	1	0	0	3
Summerton, Laura	2	3	2	2	5	1	1	0	4
Sutton-Brown, Tammy	10	16	10	12	13	4	4	6	22

Player	FGM	FGA	FTM	FTA	REB	AST	STL	BLK	PTS
Swoopes, Sheryl	15	29	14	15	15	10	7	4	34
Taurasi, Diana	11	25	11	16	11	8	4	4	31
Taylor, Penny	11	23	11	13	11	7	5	2	33
Teasley, Nikki	8	20	10	10	11	13	3	2	25
Thomas, Christi	5	11	6	8	10	3	2	2	14
Thomas, LaToya	11	21	10	10	13	5	3	3	26
Thomas, Stacey	6	13	7	8	8	9	7	4	14
Thompson, Alicia	10	18	5	6	15	6	3	2	22
Thompson, Tina	13	27	14	16	14	6	4	4	35
Thorn, Erin	4	9	2	2	3	3	1	1	12
Vodichkova, Kamila	10	16	9	10	14	4	4	4	24
Vodopyanova, Natalia	3	5	3	4	3	3	2	1	7
Walker, Ayana	6	12	5	7	11	3	4	5	16
Walker, DeMya	11	18	8	12	14	7	4	4	24
Wauters, Ann	10	16	8	10	13	8	3	4	24
Wecker, Kendra	2	6	0	0	0	2	1	0	4
Whalen, Lindsay	9	15	12	13	9	13	5	1	28
White, DeTrina	4	5	4	6	13	2	2	3	10
White, Tan	10	19	11	13	6	4	3	2	26
Whitmore, Tamika	11	16	12	13	13	5	4	5	28
Williams, Angelina	3	8	5	6	4	3	2	4	11
Williams, Natalie	11	22	12	16	20	6	4	5	31
Williams, Tamika	9	15	8	11	14	5	6	2	22
Willingham, Le'Coe	6	9	6	7	6	2	2	1	12
Wright, Shereka	5	10	8	10	7	3	2	2	17
Wright, Tanisha	6	9	5	6	6	7	3	1	17
Wyckoff, Brooke	7	10	3	4	12	5	3	3	17
Zara, Francesca	4	7	2	3	4	5	2	1	9

WNBA POSTSEASON SINGLE-GAME HIGHS

(Includes 2005 Season)

Player	FGM	FGA	FTM	FTA	REB	AST	STL	BLK	PTS
Arcain, Janeth	9	19	6	6	10	4	3	1	18
Baranova, Elena	6	12	4	5	11	6	2	3	18
Batkovic, Suzy	3	5	1	4	4	0	0	2	7
Bevilaqua, Tully	4	9	3	5	5	4	4	1	14
Bird, Sue	6	15	6	7	6	14	3	0	17
Braxton, Kara	3	9	3	4	4	2	0	0	9
Brown, Kiesha	2	3	2	2	1	1	2	0	4
Brunson, Rebekkah	5	10	2	3	11	3	2	2	12
Buescher, Erin	4	5	2	4	4	1	0	1	11
Burse, Janell	6	6	4	4	8	2	3	3	12
Canty, Dominique	5	10	6	8	7	4	1	0	15
Carey, Jamie	1	3	0	0	1	4	1	0	3
Cash, Swin	8	15	10	13	12	9	3	2	26
Castro Marques, Iziane	2	8	2	2	2	3	1	0	6
Catchings, Tamika	11	19	7	8	14	5	4	1	29
Christon, Shameka	4	7	3	4	5	2	1	2	13

INDIVIDUAL CAREER HIGHS

Player	FGM	FGA	FTM	FTA	REB	AST	STL	BLK	PTS
Curry, Edniesha	0	1	0	0	1	1	1	0	0
Derevjanik, Jennifer	1	2	1	2	2	4	2	0	3
Dixon, Tamecka	8	15	6	6	9	8	6	2	19
Douglas, Katie	7	15	6	8	8	6	3	1	18
Dydek, Margo	5	13	6	7	13	4	1	5	16
Edwards, Simone	3	5	1	2	8	1	0	1	6
Farris, Barbara	3	9	5	6	9	3	1	0	11
Ford, Cheryl	7	15	7	10	15	2	2	3	21
Frett, La'Keshia	9	18	5	6	7	4	1	2	20
Griffith, Yolanda	11	18	18	24	17	3	3	3	30
Hammon, Becky	8	17	5	7	5	5	4	0	20
Haynie, Kristin	4	5	2	2	3	3	2	0	8
Hodges, Doneeka	2	4	0	0	3	2	1	0	5
Hodges, Roneeka	0	0	0	0	0	0	1	0	0
Holdsclaw, Chamique	11	20	8	10	13	6	5	2	26
Jackson, Deanna	5	10	6	6	5	2	1	2	12
Jackson, Lauren	9	19	9	9	13	3	3	3	31
Johnson, Vickie	8	16	8	8	8	10	6	1	22
Jones, Asjha	8	13	5	7	5	3	2	2	21
Kraayeveld, Cathrine	1	2	4	4	4	0	0	0	7
Lawson, Edwige	0	0	0	0	0	0	0	0	0
Lawson, Kara	6	13	6	6	9	7	3	1	18
Lennox, Betty	11	20	9	11	8	4	3	1	27
Leslie, Lisa	15	22	10	12	18	6	4	7	35
Lyttle, Sancho	1	3	2	3	5	0	1	0	4
Mabika, Mwadi	11	20	7	10	11	6	6	3	29
Macchi, Laura	1	6	2	2	4	1	1	0	5
Maiga, Hamchetou	4	7	2	4	3	2	5	2	10
Masciadri, Raffaella	4	10	2	2	2	3	1	0	13
McWilliams-Franklin, Taj	8	17	9	11	16	3	4	4	24
Miller, Kelly	5	12	3	4	4	4	2	0	14
Moore, Loree	0	0	0	0	0	0	0	0	0
Newton, Chelsea	4	8	4	6	3	3	1	0	9
Nolan, Deanna	10	20	6	6	8	5	3	2	26
Penicheiro, Ticha	7	12	5	6	6	10	4	2	19
Phillips, Tari	11	19	7	8	15	3	3	3	24
Pierson, Plenette	2	5	0	2	4	0	1	0	4
Powell, Elaine	3	10	4	9	8	9	6	1	10
Powell, Nicole	6	15	4	4	6	3	2	1	18
Riley, Ruth	11	19	7	10	9	5	2	4	27
Robinson, Crystal	7	15	5	5	6	4	3	2	21
Sales, Nykesha	14	22	10	10	12	4	7	2	32
Schumacher, Kelly	6	11	3	5	4	2	1	3	17
Scott-Richardson, Olympia	5	6	3	3	14	4	1	1	10
Smith, Katie	8	16	5	5	5	4	2	0	23
Snow, Michelle	7	14	7	9	15	3	3	2	21
Staley, Dawn	6	16	6	8	5	9	4	2	18
Streimikyte, Jurgita	2	7	4	4	8	4	4	1	6

488

Player	FGM	FGA	FTM	FTA	REB	AST	STL	BLK	PTS
Summerton, Laura	0	0	0	0	0	0	0	0	0
Swoopes, Sheryl	11	23	9	10	13	10	6	2	31
Teasley, Nikki	5	14	6	6	8	11	3	1	16
Thomas, Christi	6	9	1	1	9	2	1	1	12
Thompson, Alicia	4	7	2	2	3	2	1	1	10
Thompson, Tina	8	18	6	8	14	5	4	3	21
Thorn, Erin	1	2	0	0	0	0	0	0	3
Vodopyanova, Natalia	0	1	0	0	0	0	0	0	0
Walker, DeMya	7	11	6	9	6	6	2	5	17
Whalen, Lindsay	5	11	15	17	7	9	3	2	27
White, Tan	0	5	0	0	2	1	0	0	0
Whitmore, Tamika	10	15	7	9	8	2	1	2	24
Williams, Natalie	11	16	9	14	12	3	2	3	25
Willingham, Le'Coe	2	5	2	3	6	1	0	1	6
Wright, Tanisha	1	3	5	5	2	4	2	0	7
Wyckoff, Brooke	3	6	3	4	6	2	1	1	9
Zara, Francesca	2	3	2	2	0	1	0	0	5

ROOKIES & NEWCOMERS

ANDERSON, AMBROSIA   F   LYNX

PERSONAL: Born March 14, 1984, in Colorado Springs, Colo. ... 6-1. (1.85).
HIGH SCHOOL: Doherty (Colorado Springs, Colo.) .
COLLEGE: BYU.
TRANSACTIONS/CAREER NOTES: Selected by Detroit in the second round (17th overall) of the WNBA Draft, April 5, 2006. ... Draft rights, along with a second-round pick in the 2007 draft, traded by Detroit to Minnesota for F Jacqueline Batteast and a third-round pick in the 2007 draft, April 5, 2006.

COLLEGE RECORD

NOTES: AP All-American honorable mention (2006). ... MWC Co-Player of the Year (2006). ... All-MWC first team (2006). ... All-MWC honorable mention (2004).

Season Team	G	Min.	FGM	FGA	Pct.	FTM	FTA	Pct.	Reb.	Ast.	Pts.	AVERAGES RPG	APG	PPG
2002—Brigham Young	31	348	55	154	.357	8	12	.667	96	19	133	3.1	0.6	4.3
2003—Brigham Young	28	551	100	244	.410	46	60	.767	157	48	267	5.6	1.7	10.7
2004—Brigham Young	29	624	119	282	.422	44	61	.721	141	45	312	4.9	1.6	10.8
2005—Brigham Young	32	980	220	533	.413	69	107	.645	240	64	573	7.5	2.0	17.9
Totals	120	2503	494	1213	.407	167	240	.696	634	176	1285	5.3	1.5	10.7

Three-point field goals: 2002-03, 15-for-45 (.333). 2003-04, 21-for-59 (.356). 2004-05, 30-for-98 (.306). 2005-06, 64-for-176 (.364). Totals, 130-for-378 (.344).

ATKINSON, LA'TANGELA   G/F   FEVER

PERSONAL: Born March 22, 1984, in Bishopville, S.C. ... 6-2. (1.88).
HIGH SCHOOL: Lee Central (Bishopville, S.C.).
COLLEGE: North Carolina.
TRANSACTIONS/CAREER NOTES: Selected by Indiana in the first round (ninth overall) of the WNBA Draft, April 5, 2006.

COLLEGE RECORD

NOTES: AP All-American honorable mention (2006). ... All-ACC third team (2004). ... ACC Rookie of the Year (2003). ... ACC All-Freshman team (2003). ... All-ACC honorable mention (2003).

Season Team	G	Min.	FGM	FGA	Pct.	FTM	FTA	Pct.	Reb.	Ast.	Pts.	AVERAGES RPG	APG	PPG
2002—North Carolina	34	905	126	280	.450	75	149	.503	281	90	331	8.3	2.6	9.7
2003—North Carolina	31	882	123	246	.500	50	75	.667	251	89	306	8.1	2.9	9.9
2004—North Carolina	34	903	113	245	.461	43	68	.632	250	88	281	7.4	2.6	8.3
2005—North Carolina	35	916	135	244	.553	40	64	.625	230	107	317	6.6	3.1	9.1
Totals	134	3606	497	1015	.490	208	356	.584	1012	374	1235	7.6	2.8	9.2

Three-point field goals: 2002-03, 4-for-17 (.235). 2003-04, 10-for-34 (.294). 2004-05, 12-for-49 (.245). 2005-06, 7-for-34 (.206). Totals, 33-for-134 (.246).

AUGUSTINE, LAMISHA   F   MONARCHS

PERSONAL: Born February 7, 1982, in Fresno, Calif. ... 6-1. (1.85). ... Full name: Lamisha Lechic Augustine
HIGH SCHOOL: Roosevelt (Fresno, Calif.) .
COLLEGE: San Jose State.
TRANSACTIONS/CAREER NOTES: Selected by Sacramento in the third round (41st overall) of the WNBA Draft, April 5, 2006.

COLLEGE RECORD

NOTES: All-WAC first team (2006, 2005).

Season Team	G	Min.	FGM	FGA	Pct.	FTM	FTA	Pct.	Reb.	Ast.	Pts.	AVERAGES RPG	APG	PPG
2002—San Jose State	28	525	46	140	.329	11	17	.647	93	12	103	3.3	0.4	3.7
2003—San Jose State	29	719	87	232	.375	32	53	.604	131	26	208	4.5	0.9	7.2
2004—San Jose State	30	821	143	391	.366	49	68	.721	174	47	335	5.8	1.6	11.2
2005—San Jose State	28	1024	178	455	.391	118	157	.752	238	47	486	8.5	1.7	17.4
Totals	115	3089	454	1218	.373	210	295	.712	636	132	1132	5.5	1.1	9.8

Three-point field goals: 2002-03, 0-for-1. 2003-04, 2-for-3 (.667). 2004-05, 0-for-4. 2005-06, 12-for-29 (.414). Totals, 14-for-37 (.378).

AUGUSTUS, SEIMONE   G   LYNX

PERSONAL: Born April 30, 1984, in Baton Rouge, La. ... 6-1. (1.85).
HIGH SCHOOL: Capitol (Baton Rouge, La.).
COLLEGE: Louisiana State.
TRANSACTIONS/CAREER NOTES: Selected by Minnesota in the first round (first overall) of the WNBA Draft, April 5, 2006.

COLLEGE RECORD

NOTES: AP Player of the Year (2006, 2005). ... Kodak/WBCA Player of the Year (2006). ... Naismith Player of the Year (2005). ... USBWA Player of the Year (2005). ... Wade Trophy recipient (2005). ... Honda Broderick Player of the Year (2005). ... AP All-American first team (2006, 2005). ...

Kodak/WBCA All-American team (2006, 2005, 2004). ... AP All-American third team (2004, 2003). ... SEC Player of the Year (2006, 2005). ... All-SEC first team (2006, 2005, 2004). ... Consensus Freshman of the Year (2003).

Season Team	G	Min.	FGM	FGA	Pct.	FTM	FTA	Pct.	Reb.	Ast.	Pts.	AVERAGES		
												RPG	APG	PPG
2002—Louisiana State	34	1063	212	386	.549	79	89	.888	187	64	504	5.5	1.9	14.8
2003—Louisiana State	35	1199	285	540	.528	100	111	.901	210	72	679	6.0	2.1	19.4
2004—Louisiana State	36	1176	303	562	.539	113	130	.869	166	76	724	4.6	2.1	20.1
2005—Louisiana State	35	1169	334	595	.561	109	138	.790	165	64	795	4.7	1.8	22.7
Totals	140	4607	1134	2083	.544	401	468	.857	728	276	2702	5.2	2.0	19.3

Three-point field goals: 2002-03, 1-for-3 (.333). 2003-04, 9-for-24 (.375). 2004-05, 5-for-18 (.278). 2005-06, 18-for-40 (.450). Totals, 33-for-85 (.388).

BAKER, SHERILL   G   LIBERTY

PERSONAL: Born December 3, 1982, in Stone Mountain, Ga. ... 5-8. (1.73).
HIGH SCHOOL: Greater Atlanta Christian School (Stone Mountain, Ga.).
COLLEGE: Georgia.
TRANSACTIONS/CAREER NOTES: Selected by New York in the first round (12th overall) of the WNBA Draft, April 5, 2006.

COLLEGE RECORD

NOTES: AP All-American honorable mention (2006). ... All-SEC first team (2006).

Season Team	G	Min.	FGM	FGA	Pct.	FTM	FTA	Pct.	Reb.	Ast.	Pts.	AVERAGES		
												RPG	APG	PPG
2002—Georgia	30	877	115	307	.375	51	72	.708	129	83	289	4.3	2.8	9.6
2003—Georgia	35	1139	157	381	.412	62	86	.721	133	120	390	3.8	3.4	11.1
2004—Georgia	34	1113	162	375	.432	57	74	.770	158	93	388	4.6	2.7	11.4
2005—Georgia	31	1134	238	448	.531	99	124	.798	141	102	579	4.5	3.3	18.7
Totals	130	4263	672	1511	.445	269	356	.756	561	398	1646	4.3	3.1	12.7

Three-point field goals: 2002-03, 8-for-29 (.276). 2003-04, 14-for-40 (.350). 2004-05, 7-for-38 (.184). 2005-06, 4-for-15 (.267). Totals, 33-for-122 (.270).

BLUE, NIKKI   MYSTICS

PERSONAL: Born March 29, 1984, in Bakersfield, Calif. ... 5-8. (1.73). ... Full name: Anitra Necole Blue
HIGH SCHOOL: West (Bakersfield, Calif.) .
COLLEGE: UCLA.
TRANSACTIONS/CAREER NOTES: Selected by Washington in the second round (19th overall) of the WNBA Draft, April 5, 2006.

COLLEGE RECORD

NOTES: AP All-American honorable mention (2006, 2005). ... All-Pac-10 first team (2006, 2005, 2004, 2003). ... Pac-10 All-Tournament team (2005, 2004, 2003). ... Pac-10 All-Freshman team (2003).

Season Team	G	Min.	FGM	FGA	Pct.	FTM	FTA	Pct.	Reb.	Ast.	Pts.	AVERAGES		
												RPG	APG	PPG
2002—UCLA	29	857	181	447	.405	95	135	.704	160	103	481	5.5	3.5	16.6
2003—UCLA	30	1012	156	394	.396	121	167	.725	169	148	457	5.6	4.9	15.2
2004—UCLA	27	949	147	353	.416	136	189	.720	136	162	458	5.0	6.0	16.9
2005—UCLA	32	1079	130	328	.396	103	146	.705	151	189	401	4.7	5.9	12.5
Totals	118	3897	614	1522	.403	455	637	.714	616	602	1797	5.2	5.1	15.2

Three-point field goals: 2002-03, 24-for-86 (.279). 2003-04, 24-for-64 (.375). 2004-05, 28-for-80 (.350). 2005-06, 38-for-91 (.418). Totals, 114-for-321 (.355).

BOND, LATOYA   G   STING

PERSONAL: Born February 13, 1984, in Urbana, Ill. ... 5-7. (1.70).
HIGH SCHOOL: Urbana (Urbana, Ill.).
COLLEGE: Missouri.
TRANSACTIONS/CAREER NOTES: Selected by Charlotte in the second round (27th overall) of the WNBA Draft, April 5, 2006.

COLLEGE RECORD

NOTES: All-Big 12 first team (2006).

Season Team	G	Min.	FGM	FGA	Pct.	FTM	FTA	Pct.	Reb.	Ast.	Pts.	AVERAGES		
												RPG	APG	PPG
2002—Missouri	29	280	33	88	.375	20	31	.645	19	21	93	1.3	0.7	3.2
2003—Missouri	21	636	74	176	.420	54	68	.794	76	95	214	3.6	4.5	10.2
2004—Missouri	29	1027	118	267	.442	85	114	.746	143	116	346	4.9	4.0	11.9
2005—Missouri	30	1007	182	355	.513	113	137	.825	114	94	520	3.8	3.1	17.3
Totals	109	2950	407	886	.459	272	350	.777	352	326	1173	3.2	3.0	10.8

Three-point field goals: 2002-03, 7-for-20 (.350). 2003-04, 12-for-47 (.255). 2004-05, 25-for-76 (.329). 2005-06, 43-for-109 (.394). Totals, 87-for-252 (.345).

BUTLER, JENNIFER   C   SPARKS

PERSONAL: Born April 21, 1981, in Brooklyn, N.Y. ... 6-3/175. (1.91/79.4). ... Full name: Jennifer Ruth Butler
HIGH SCHOOL: Murry Bergtraum (Brooklyn, N.Y.).
COLLEGE: Massachusetts.
TRANSACTIONS/CAREER NOTES: Selected by Cleveland in second round (15th overall) of WNBA Draft, April 25, 2003. ... Selected by Sacramento in dispersal draft, January 6, 2004.

COLLEGE RECORD

NOTES: Atlantic 10 First Team All-Conference (2003). ... 2002-03 Atlanta 10 Defensive Player of the Year (2003). ... First in the nation averaging 14.7 rebounds per game in 2002-03. ... First player in school history to eclipse 1,000-point and 1,000-rebound plateau.

Season Team	G	Min.	FGM	FGA	Pct.	FTM	FTA	Pct.	Reb.	Ast.	Pts.	RPG	APG	PPG
1999—Massachusetts	28	746	99	205	.483	51	116	.440	294	22	249	10.5	0.8	8.9
2000—Massachusetts	28	871	125	318	.393	106	183	.579	269	22	356	9.6	0.8	12.7
2001—Massachusetts	30	965	152	350	.434	92	178	.517	353	26	396	11.8	0.9	13.2
2002—Massachusetts	28	990	179	389	.460	131	211	.621	412	53	489	14.7	1.9	17.5
Totals	114	3572	555	1262	.440	380	688	.552	1328	123	1490	11.6	1.1	13.1

Three-point field goals: 2000-01, 0-for-1. 2001-02, 0-for-1. Totals, 0-for-2 (.000).

CAMINO, RENAE G COMETS

PERSONAL: Born November 19, 1986, in Australia. ... 5-9. (1.75).
TRANSACTIONS/CAREER NOTES: Selected by Houston in the second round (24th overall) of the WNBA Draft, April 5, 2006.
MISCELLANEOUS: Competed in the WNBL in Australia (2003-06).

WNBL RECORD

Season Team	G	Min.	FGM	FGA	Pct.	FTM	FTA	Pct.	Reb.	Ast.	Pts.	RPG	APG	PPG
2004—AIS	21	—	143	294	.490	66	103	.640	199	33	362	9.5	1.6	17.2
Totals	21	—	143	294	.490	66	103	.640	199	33	362	9.5	1.6	17.2

Three-point field goals: 2004-05, 10-for-42 (.240). Totals, 10-for-42 (.240).

COLEMAN, RYAN G SHOCK

PERSONAL: Born July 2, 1983, in Detroit. ... 5-8. (1.73). ... Full name: Ryan-Rebekah Sharon Coleman
HIGH SCHOOL: Communication and Media Arts (Detroit).
COLLEGE: Eastern Michigan.

COLLEGE RECORD

NOTES: Kodak/WBCA All-America honorable mention (2005). ... All-Mid American Conference first team (2006, 2005, 2004). ... All-Mid-American Conference second team (2003).

Season Team	G	Min.	FGM	FGA	Pct.	FTM	FTA	Pct.	Reb.	Ast.	Pts.	RPG	APG	PPG
2002—Eastern Michigan	29	955	147	352	.418	89	109	.817	198	73	417	6.8	2.5	14.4
2003—Eastern Michigan	30	899	136	330	.412	88	118	.746	196	86	400	6.5	2.9	13.3
2004—Eastern Michigan	31	1077	204	440	.464	78	97	.804	208	114	554	6.7	3.7	17.9
2005—Eastern Michigan	24	892	161	346	.465	59	74	.797	140	101	412	5.8	4.2	17.2
Totals	114	3823	648	1468	.441	314	398	.789	742	374	1783	6.5	3.3	15.6

Three-point field goals: 2002-03, 34-for-97 (.351). 2003-04, 40-for-106 (.377). 2004-05, 68-for-160 (.425). 2005-06, 31-for-90 (.344). Totals, 173-for-453 (.382).

CROCKETT, WILLNETT F/C SPARKS

PERSONAL: Born July 5, 1984, in Harbor City, Calif. ... 6-2. (1.88). ... Full name: Willnett Via'Tonda Crockett
HIGH SCHOOL: Narbonne (Harbor City, Calif.).
COLLEGE: Connecticut.
TRANSACTIONS/CAREER NOTES: Selected by Los Angeles in the second round (32nd overall) of the WNBA Draft, April 5, 2006.

COLLEGE RECORD

Season Team	G	Min.	FGM	FGA	Pct.	FTM	FTA	Pct.	Reb.	Ast.	Pts.	RPG	APG	PPG
2002—Connecticut	26	569	71	145	.490	63	97	.649	167	22	206	4.6	0.8	5.7
2003—Connecticut	27	369	42	65	.646	28	48	.583	86	12	112	3.2	0.4	4.1
2004—Connecticut	31	508	62	104	.596	30	50	.600	142	23	154	4.6	0.7	5.0
2005—Connecticut	37	646	52	101	.515	26	41	.634	188	25	130	5.1	0.7	3.5
Totals	121	2092	227	415	.547	147	236	.623	583	82	602	4.8	0.7	5.0

Three-point field goals: 2002-03, 1-for-3 (.500). Totals, 1-for-3 (.333).

CURRIE, MONIQUE G/F STING

PERSONAL: Born February 25, 1983, in Washington D.C. ... 6-0. (1.83). ... Full name: Monique Paulette Currie
HIGH SCHOOL: The Bullis School (Washington D.C.).
COLLEGE: Duke.
TRANSACTIONS/CAREER NOTES: Selected by Charlotte in the first round (third overall) of the WNBA Draft, April 5, 2006.
MISCELLANEOUS: Redshirted 2002-03 season due to injury.

COLLEGE RECORD

NOTES: AP All-American first team (2005). ... AP All-American second team (2006). ... Kodak/WBCA All-American team (2006, 2005). ... USBWA All-American (2005). ... ACC Player of the Year (2005). ... All-ACC first team (2006, 2005). ... All-ACC second team (2004, 2002). ... ACC All-Freshman team (2002). ... ACC Tournament MVP (2002). ... ACC All-Tournament team (2004, 2002).

Season Team	G	Min.	FGM	FGA	Pct.	FTM	FTA	Pct.	Reb.	Ast.	Pts.	RPG	APG	PPG
2001—Duke	35	971	178	360	.494	138	179	.771	209	90	502	6.0	2.6	14.3
2003—Duke	34	943	151	318	.475	105	139	.755	208	101	417	6.1	3.0	12.3

Season Team	G	Min.	FGM	FGA	Pct.	FTM	FTA	Pct.	Reb.	Ast.	Pts.	AVERAGES RPG	APG	PPG
2004—Duke	36	1127	218	489	.446	168	215	.781	254	123	630	7.1	3.4	17.5
2005—Duke	35	972	202	425	.475	127	155	.819	203	99	573	5.8	2.8	16.4
Totals	140	4013	749	1592	.470	538	688	.782	874	413	2122	6.2	3.0	15.2

Three-point field goals: 2001-02, 8-for-34 (.235). 2003-04, 10-for-42 (.238). 2004-05, 26-for-82 (.317). 2005-06, 42-for-100 (.420). Totals, 86-for-258 (.333).

DORRELL, SCHOLANDA   G   MONARCHS

PERSONAL: Born January 9, 1983, in Miami. ... 5-10. (1.78). ... Full name: Scholanda Michelle Dorrell
HIGH SCHOOL: Miami Edison (Miami).
COLLEGE: Louisiana State.
TRANSACTIONS/CAREER NOTES: Selected by Sacramento in the first round (14th overall) of the WNBA Draft, April 5, 2006.

COLLEGE RECORD

Season Team	G	Min.	FGM	FGA	Pct.	FTM	FTA	Pct.	Reb.	Ast.	Pts.	AVERAGES RPG	APG	PPG
2002—Louisiana State	29	885	108	242	.446	83	116	.716	122	48	308	4.2	2.1	10.6
2003—Louisiana State	35	642	113	253	.447	47	70	.671	82	22	298	2.3	0.6	8.5
2004—Louisiana State	36	1008	117	307	.381	42	61	.689	91	74	322	2.5	2.1	8.9
2005—Louisiana State	35	947	107	261	.410	47	59	.797	88	78	301	2.5	2.2	8.6
Totals	135	3482	445	1063	.419	219	306	.716	383	222	1229	2.8	1.6	9.1

Three-point field goals: 2002-03, 9-for-39 (.231). 2003-04, 25-for-61 (.410). 2004-05, 46-for-132 (.348). 2005-06, 40-for-114 (.351). Totals, 120-for-346 (.347).

DUFFY, MEGAN   G   LYNX

PERSONAL: Born July 13, 1984, in Kettering, Ohio. ... 5-7. (1.70).
HIGH SCHOOL: Chaminade-Julienne (Dayton, Ohio).
COLLEGE: Notre Dame.
TRANSACTIONS/CAREER NOTES: Selected by Minnesota in the third round (31st overall) of the WNBA Draft, April 5, 2006.

COLLEGE RECORD

NOTES: AP All-American honorable mention (2006, 2005). ... All-Big East first team (2006, 2005). ... All-Big East honorable mention (2004). ... Big East All-Tournament team (2005). ... Big East Most Improved Player (2004). ... Big East All-Academic team (2005, 2004, 2003).

Season Team	G	Min.	FGM	FGA	Pct.	FTM	FTA	Pct.	Reb.	Ast.	Pts.	AVERAGES RPG	APG	PPG
2002—Notre Dame	32	747	22	91	.242	45	59	.763	60	73	96	1.9	2.3	3.0
2003—Notre Dame	32	1066	93	231	.403	86	105	.819	93	125	318	2.9	3.9	9.9
2004—Notre Dame	33	1222	110	252	.437	137	153	.895	101	178	407	3.1	5.4	12.3
2005—Notre Dame	30	1152	138	346	.399	135	152	.888	116	124	469	3.9	4.1	15.6
Totals	127	4187	363	920	.395	403	469	.859	370	500	1290	2.9	3.9	10.2

Three-point field goals: 2002-03, 7-for-35 (.200). 2003-04, 46-for-114 (.404). 2004-05, 50-for-125 (.400). 2005-06, 58-for-167 (.347). Totals, 161-for-441 (.365).

DUPREE, CANDICE   F/C   SKY

PERSONAL: Born August 16, 1984, in Tampa, Fla. ... 6-2. (1.88).
HIGH SCHOOL: Wharton (Tampa, Fla.).
COLLEGE: Temple.
TRANSACTIONS/CAREER NOTES: Selected by Chicago in the first round (sixth overall) of the WNBA Draft, April 5, 2006.

COLLEGE RECORD

NOTES: AP All-American third team (2006). ... AP All-American honorable mention (2005). ... Atlantic 10 Player of the Year (2006, 2005). ... Atlantic 10 Defensive Player of the Year (2006, 2005). ... All-Atlantic 10 first team (2006, 2005). ... All-Atlantic 10 second team (2004). ... Most Outstanding Player of Atlantic 10 Tournament (2005, 2004). ... Atlantic 10 All-Tournament team (2005, 2004).

Season Team	G	Min.	FGM	FGA	Pct.	FTM	FTA	Pct.	Reb.	Ast.	Pts.	AVERAGES RPG	APG	PPG
2002—Temple	18	555	82	190	.432	24	46	.522	136	23	188	7.6	1.3	10.4
2003—Temple	31	986	179	327	.547	73	138	.529	235	25	431	7.6	0.8	13.9
2004—Temple	32	1033	207	384	.539	107	160	.669	290	55	521	9.1	1.7	16.3
2005—Temple	32	1107	228	451	.506	99	137	.723	279	67	558	8.7	2.1	17.4
Totals	113	3681	696	1352	.515	303	481	.630	940	170	1698	8.3	1.5	15.0

Three-point field goals: 2003-04, 0-for-1. 2005-06, 3-for-17 (.176). Totals, 3-for-18 (.167).

ESHE, DALILA   F   STORM

PERSONAL: Born in Tallahassee, Fla. ... 6-3. (1.91).
COLLEGE: Florida.
TRANSACTIONS/CAREER NOTES: Selected by Seattle in the second round (25th overall) of the WNBA Draft, April 5, 2006.

NOTES: All-SEC first team (2006).

Season Team	G	Min.	FGM	FGA	Pct.	FTM	FTA	Pct.	Reb.	Ast.	Pts.	AVERAGES RPG	APG	PPG
2002—Florida	28	484	51	127	.402	37	49	.755	135	6	139	4.8	0.2	5.0
2003—Florida	29	299	22	55	.400	22	30	.733	80	6	66	2.8	0.2	2.3
2004—Florida	29	510	50	114	.439	43	57	.754	133	18	143	4.6	0.6	4.9
2005—Florida	30	959	143	324	.441	121	142	.852	213	38	427	7.1	1.3	14.2
Totals	116	2252	266	620	.429	223	278	.802	561	68	775	4.8	0.6	6.7

Three-point field goals: 2002-03, 0-for-8. 2003-04, 0-for-5. 2005-06, 20-for-52 (.385). Totals, 20-for-65 (.308).

EUN-JOO, HA   C   SPARKS

PERSONAL: ... 6-8. (2.03).
TRANSACTIONS/CAREER NOTES: Signed by Los Angeles, February 6, 2006.

FLUKER, TYE'SHA   C   STING

PERSONAL: Born December 27, 1984, in Pasadena, Calif. ... 6-5. (1.96). ... Full name: Tye'sha Nikcole Fluker
HIGH SCHOOL: John Muir (Pasadena, Calif.) .
COLLEGE: Tennessee.
TRANSACTIONS/CAREER NOTES: Selected by Charlotte in the first round (10th overall) of the WNBA Draft, April 5, 2006.

NOTES: SEC All-Academic team (2005, 2004).

Season Team	G	Min.	FGM	FGA	Pct.	FTM	FTA	Pct.	Reb.	Ast.	Pts.	AVERAGES RPG	APG	PPG
2002—Tennessee	36	359	46	115	.400	16	28	.571	91	12	110	2.5	0.3	3.1
2003—Tennessee	35	452	77	159	.484	34	54	.630	109	12	188	3.1	0.3	5.4
2004—Tennessee	33	628	101	219	.461	41	64	.641	178	17	243	5.4	0.5	7.4
2005—Tennessee	36	779	133	250	.532	68	104	.654	177	22	334	4.9	0.6	9.3
Totals	140	2218	357	743	.480	159	250	.636	555	63	875	4.0	0.5	6.3

Three-point field goals: 2002-03, 2-for-9 (.222). 2004-05, 0-for-1. 2005-06, 0-for-1. Totals, 2-for-11 (.182).

FOLEY, JESSICA   G   FEVER

PERSONAL: Born April 20, 1983, in Bega, New South Wales. ... 6-0. (1.83). ... Full name: Jessica Mary-Ellen Foley
HIGH SCHOOL: Catholic College Wodonga (Victory, Australia).
COLLEGE: Duke.
TRANSACTIONS/CAREER NOTES: Selected by Indiana in the third round (38th overall) of the WNBA Draft, April 5, 2006.

NOTES: All-ACC third team (2005).

Season Team	G	Min.	FGM	FGA	Pct.	FTM	FTA	Pct.	Reb.	Ast.	Pts.	AVERAGES RPG	APG	PPG
2002—Duke	32	426	61	147	.415	22	26	.846	67	62	174	2.1	1.9	5.4
2003—Duke	34	563	66	190	.347	17	20	.850	66	67	187	1.9	2.0	5.5
2004—Duke	34	1036	124	318	.390	55	69	.797	137	122	371	4.0	3.6	10.9
2005—Duke	35	565	71	160	.444	16	19	.842	57	59	197	1.6	1.7	5.6
Totals	135	2590	322	815	.395	110	134	.821	327	310	929	2.4	2.3	6.9

Three-point field goals: 2002-03, 30-for-86 (.349). 2003-04, 38-for-116 (.328). 2004-05, 68-for-191 (.356). 2005-06, 39-for-97 (.402). Totals, 175-for-490 (.357).

GARDIN, KERRI   F   SKY

PERSONAL: Born May 19, 1984, in Burke County, N.C. ... 6-1. (1.85).
HIGH SCHOOL: Freedom (Morganton, N.C.).
COLLEGE: Virginia Tech.
TRANSACTIONS/CAREER NOTES: Selected by Chicago in the third round (34th overall) of the WNBA Draft, April 5, 2006.

NOTES: All-ACC honorable mention (2005).

Season Team	G	Min.	FGM	FGA	Pct.	FTM	FTA	Pct.	Reb.	Ast.	Pts.	AVERAGES RPG	APG	PPG
2002—Virginia Tech	30	546	53	132	.402	24	38	.632	96	52	130	3.2	1.7	4.3
2003—Virginia Tech	31	799	88	256	.344	64	95	.674	167	90	242	5.4	2.9	7.3
2004—Virginia Tech	29	750	128	285	.449	59	96	.615	232	48	322	8.0	1.7	11.1
2005—Virginia Tech	29	822	150	333	.450	61	103	.592	289	69	367	10.0	2.4	12.7
Totals	119	2917	419	1006	.417	208	332	.627	784	259	1061	6.6	2.2	8.9

Three-point field goals: 2003-04, 2-for-6 (.333). 2004-05, 7-for-29 (.241). 2005-06, 6-for-17 (.353). Totals, 15-for-52 (.288).

GRANT, ERIN   G   STORM

PERSONAL: Born June 13, 1984, in Arlington, Texas. ... 5-8. (1.73). ... Full name: Erin Alyssa Grant
HIGH SCHOOL: Mansfield (Arlington, Texas).
COLLEGE: Texas Tech.
TRANSACTIONS/CAREER NOTES: Selected by Seattle in the third round (39th overall) of the WNBA Draft, April 5, 2006.

COLLEGE RECORD

NOTES: AP All-American honorable mention (2006). ... All-Big Ten first team (2006, 2005). ... All-Big Ten second team (2004). ... Co-Big Ten Freshman of the Year (2003). ... Big Ten All-Freshman team (2003). ... Big Ten All-Academic first team (2005, 2004).

Season Team	G	Min.	FGM	FGA	Pct.	FTM	FTA	Pct.	Reb.	Ast.	Pts.	RPG	APG	PPG
2002—Texas Tech	35	1076	92	192	.479	50	65	.769	124	228	234	3.5	6.5	6.7
2003—Texas Tech	33	1008	91	225	.404	81	96	.844	145	215	273	4.4	6.5	8.3
2004—Texas Tech	31	1019	93	210	.443	46	57	.807	89	218	253	2.9	7.0	8.2
2005—Texas Tech	29	1036	118	301	.392	94	120	.783	115	183	348	4.0	6.3	12.0
Totals	128	4139	394	928	.425	271	338	.802	473	844	1108	3.7	6.6	8.7

Three-point field goals: 2002-03, 0-for-1. 2003-04, 10-for-32 (.313). 2004-05, 21-for-49 (.429). 2005-06, 18-for-49 (.367). Totals, 49-for-131 (.374).

HARRIS, JENNIFER   G   SKY

PERSONAL: Born August 9, 1984, in Morristown, N.J. ... 5-10. (1.78). ... Full name: Jennifer Nakia Harris
HIGH SCHOOL: Morristown.
JUNIOR COLLEGE: Trinity.
COLLEGE: Washburn University.
TRANSACTIONS/CAREER NOTES: Selected by Chicago in the second round (20th overall) of WNBA Draft, April 5, 2006.

COLLEGE RECORD

NOTES: NCAA Division II Player of the Year (2006, 2005).

Season Team	G	Min.	FGM	FGA	Pct.	FTM	FTA	Pct.	Reb.	Ast.	Pts.	RPG	APG	PPG
2004—Washburn University	36	941	189	446	.424	88	117	.752	169	140	517	4.7	3.9	14.4
2005—Washburn University	33	1023	295	661	.446	150	203	.739	193	168	797	5.8	5.1	24.2
Totals	69	1964	484	1107	.437	238	320	.744	362	308	1314	5.2	4.5	19.0

JAMES, TAMARA   G/F   MYSTICS

PERSONAL: Born June 13, 1984, in Dania, Fla. ... 5-10. (1.78).
HIGH SCHOOL: South Broward (Dania, Fla.).
COLLEGE: Miami.
TRANSACTIONS/CAREER NOTES: Selected by Washington in the first round (8th overall) of the WNBA Draft, April 5, 2006.

COLLEGE RECORD

NOTES: AP All-American honorable mention (2006, 2005, 2003). ... Kodak All-American team (2003). ... WBCA All-American honorable mention (2005). ... All-ACC first team (2006, 2005). ... All-Big East first team (2004). ... All-Big East second team (2003). ... All-Big East All-Rookie team (2003). ... Big East All-Tournament team (2003).

Season Team	G	Min.	FGM	FGA	Pct.	FTM	FTA	Pct.	Reb.	Ast.	Pts.	RPG	APG	PPG
2002—Miami	31	1031	238	461	.516	155	204	.760	244	49	650	7.9	1.6	21.0
2003—Miami	29	983	170	340	.500	85	111	.766	129	72	464	4.6	2.5	16.6
2004—Miami	29	1046	242	504	.480	124	161	.770	199	57	647	6.9	2.0	22.3
2005—Miami	28	908	201	406	.495	132	158	.835	214	64	582	7.6	2.3	20.8
Totals	117	3968	851	1711	.497	496	634	.782	786	242	2343	6.7	2.1	20.0

Three-point field goals: 2002-03, 19-for-58 (.328). 2003-04, 39-for-103 (.379). 2004-05, 39-for-119 (.328). 2005-06, 48-for-126 (.381). Totals, 145-for-406 (.357).

KENDRICK, ALEXIS   G   STING

PERSONAL: Born January 3, 1984, in Inglewood, Calif. ... 5-7. (1.70).
HIGH SCHOOL: St. Bernard Catholic (Inglewood, Calif.).
COLLEGE: Georgia.

COLLEGE RECORD

NOTES: All-SEC third team (2004). ... SEC All-Freshman team (2003). ... WomensCollegeHoops.com first team Freshman All-American (2003).

Season Team	G	Min.	FGM	FGA	Pct.	FTM	FTA	Pct.	Reb.	Ast.	Pts.	RPG	APG	PPG
2002—Georgia	31	982	121	320	.378	89	105	.848	112	158	383	3.6	5.1	12.4
2003—Georgia	35	1114	110	314	.350	62	75	.827	137	155	323	3.9	4.4	9.2
2004—Georgia	34	859	74	199	.372	54	71	.761	135	117	228	4.0	3.4	6.7

Season Team	G	Min.	FGM	FGA	Pct.	FTM	FTA	Pct.	Reb.	Ast.	Pts.	AVERAGES		
												RPG	APG	PPG
2005—Georgia	31	863	76	177	.429	47	62	.758	116	113	220	3.7	3.6	7.1
Totals	131	3818	381	1010	.377	252	313	.805	500	543	1154	3.8	4.1	8.8

Three-point field goals: 2002-03, 52-for-143 (.364). 2003-04, 41-for-157 (.261). 2004-05, 26-for-99 (.263). 2005-06, 21-for-63 (.333). Totals, 140-for-462 (.303).

KUZINA, MARINA   C   FEVER

PERSONAL: Born July 19, 1985, in Moscow, Russia. ... 6-5. (1.96).
TRANSACTIONS/CAREER NOTES: Selected by Indiana in the third round (40th overall) of the WNBA Draft, April 5, 2006.

RUSSIAN SUPERLEAGUE RECORD

Season Team	G	Min.	FGM	FGA	Pct.	FTM	FTA	Pct.	Reb.	Ast.	Pts.	AVERAGES		
												RPG	APG	PPG
2003—Russian Superleague	30	410	84	197	.426	55	70	.786	120	4	241	4.0	0.1	8.0
2004—Russian Superleague	36	890	180	394	.457	134	173	.775	253	7	524	7.0	0.2	14.5
2005—Russian Superleague	27	668	142	299	.475	92	121	.760	188	6	397	7.0	0.2	14.7
Totals	93	1968	406	890	.456	281	364	.772	561	17	1162	6.0	0.2	12.5

Three-point field goals: 2003-04, 6-for-23 (.261). 2004-05, 10-for-23 (.435). 2005-06, 7-for-20 (.350). Totals, 23-for-66 (.348).

EUROCUP RECORD

Season Team	G	Min.	FGM	FGA	Pct.	FTM	FTA	Pct.	Reb.	Ast.	Pts.	AVERAGES		
												RPG	APG	PPG
2004—Eurocup	13	376	83	158	.525	41	51	.804	86	6	207	6.6	0.5	15.9
2005—Eurocup	12	307	76	140	.543	38	46	.826	76	6	199	6.3	0.5	16.6
Totals	25	683	159	298	.534	79	97	.814	162	12	406	6.5	0.5	16.2

Three-point field goals: 2004-05, 0-for-12. 2005-06, 3-for-6 (.500). Totals, 3-for-18 (.167).

MERRILL, DEBBIE   F/C   SUN

PERSONAL: Born in Cumberland City, Tenn. ... 6-1. (1.85).
HIGH SCHOOL: Montgomery (Cumberland City, Tenn.).
COLLEGE: Ohio State.
TRANSACTIONS/CAREER NOTES: Selected in the second round (28th overall) of the WNBA Draft, April 5, 2006.
MISCELLANEOUS: Redshirted 2004-05 season after transferring from the University of Cincinnati.

COLLEGE RECORD

NOTES: Kodak All-American (2003). ... WBCA All-American (2003). ... All-Conference USA first team (2003). ... Conference USA All-Tournament team (2003, 2002). ... Conference USA Freshman of the Year (2002).

Season Team	G	Min.	FGM	FGA	Pct.	FTM	FTA	Pct.	Reb.	Ast.	Pts.	AVERAGES		
												RPG	APG	PPG
2001—Cincinnati	32	816	178	354	.503	108	157	.688	251	35	469	7.8	1.1	14.7
2002—Cincinnati	31	959	215	425	.506	128	195	.656	263	59	558	8.5	1.9	18.0
2003—Cincinnati	25	788	155	335	.463	68	92	.739	187	55	381	7.5	2.2	15.2
2005—Ohio State	32	931	137	272	.504	46	73	.630	182	103	332	5.7	3.2	10.4
Totals	120	3494	685	1386	.494	350	517	.677	883	252	1740	7.4	2.1	14.5

Three-point field goals: 2001-02, 5-for-25 (.200). 2002-03, 0-for-6. 2003-04, 3-for-7 (.429). 2005-06, 12-for-32 (.375). Totals, 20-for-70 (.286).

MOODY, MEGAN   G/F   COMETS

PERSONAL: Born November 3, 1893, in Frankston, Victoria, Australia. ... 6-2. (1.88). ... Full name: Megan Janelle Moody
HIGH SCHOOL: Frankston (Frankston, Victoria, Australia).
COLLEGE: Tulsa.

COLLEGE RECORD

NOTES: All-Conference USA second team (2006).

Season Team	G	Min.	FGM	FGA	Pct.	FTM	FTA	Pct.	Reb.	Ast.	Pts.	AVERAGES		
												RPG	APG	PPG
2002—Tulsa	27	246	24	77	.312	4	8	.500	33	4	66	1.2	0.2	2.4
2003—Tulsa	31	878	119	290	.410	24	39	.615	125	48	308	4.0	1.5	9.9
2004—Tulsa	30	975	122	337	.362	38	53	.717	152	66	331	5.1	2.2	11.0
2005—Tulsa	31	1023	146	372	.392	48	59	.814	145	71	395	4.7	2.3	12.7
Totals	119	3122	411	1076	.382	114	159	.717	455	189	1100	3.8	1.6	9.2

Three-point field goals: 2002-03, 14-for-50 (.280). 2003-04, 46-for-144 (.319). 2004-05, 49-for-180 (.272). 2005-06, 55-for-158 (.348). Totals, 164-for-532 (.308).

N'GARSANET, CHRISTELLE   C   LIBERTY

PERSONAL: Born June 23, 1983, in Abidjan, Ivory Coast. ... 6-3. (1.91).
JUNIOR COLLEGE: Illinois Central College.
COLLEGE: Missouri.
TRANSACTIONS/CAREER NOTES: Selected by New York in the third round (37th overall) of the WNBA Draft, April 5, 2006.

COLLEGE RECORD

Season Team	G	Min.	FGM	FGA	Pct.	FTM	FTA	Pct.	Reb.	Ast.	Pts.	AVERAGES RPG	APG	PPG
2002—Illinois Central College	35	527	68	192	.354	31	53	.585	216	23	167	6.2	0.7	4.8
2003—Missouri	28	298	39	86	.453	23	50	.460	81	12	101	2.9	0.4	3.6
2004—Missouri	29	819	147	316	.465	70	146	.479	189	51	364	6.5	1.8	12.6
2005—Missouri	30	901	159	353	.450	81	179	.453	261	66	901	8.7	2.2	13.3
Totals	122	2545	413	947	.436	205	428	.479	747	152	1533	6.1	1.2	12.6

Three-point field goals: 2002-03, 0-for-1. 2005-06, 0-for-1. Totals, 0-for-2 (.000).

PAYNE, MARITA   C   SUN

PERSONAL: Born November 25, 1981, in Melbourne, Australia. ... 6-5. (1.96).
HIGH SCHOOL: John Paul College (Melbourne, Australia).
COLLEGE: Auburn.
TRANSACTIONS/CAREER NOTES: Selected by Connecticut in the third round (42nd overall) of the WNBA Draft, April 5, 2006.

COLLEGE RECORD

Season Team	G	Min.	FGM	FGA	Pct.	FTM	FTA	Pct.	Reb.	Ast.	Pts.	AVERAGES RPG	APG	PPG
2002—Auburn	34	384	69	154	.448	19	27	.704	110	7	157	3.2	0.2	4.6
2003—Auburn	21	451	82	158	.519	22	37	.595	106	11	186	3.4	0.5	6.0
2004—Auburn	28	844	110	235	.468	19	26	.731	225	33	239	8.0	5.0	8.5
2005—Auburn	29	846	101	192	.526	26	33	.788	189	35	228	6.5	1.2	7.9
Totals	112	2525	362	739	.490	86	123	.699	630	86	810	5.6	0.8	7.2

PONDEXTER, CAPPIE   G   MERCURY

PERSONAL: Born January 7, 1983, in Chicago. ... 5-9. (1.75). ... Full name: Cappie Marie Pondexter
HIGH SCHOOL: John Marshall (Chicago).
COLLEGE: Rutgers.
TRANSACTIONS/CAREER NOTES: Selected by Phoenix in the first round (second overall) of the WNBA Draft, April 5, 2006.

NOTES: AP All-American first team (2006). ... AP All-American third team (2004). ... AP All-American honorable mention (2005, 2003). ... Kodak/WBCA All-American team (2006). ... Kodak All-American honorable mention (2005, 2004, 2003). ... Big East Player of the Year (2006). ... All-Big East first team (2006, 2005, 2004, 2003). ... Big East All-Tournament team (2005). ... Big East Rookie of the Year (2003). ... Big East All-Rookie team (2003).

Season Team	G	Min.	FGM	FGA	Pct.	FTM	FTA	Pct.	Reb.	Ast.	Pts.	AVERAGES RPG	APG	PPG
2002—Rutgers	29	1043	200	419	.477	103	129	.798	147	142	532	5.1	4.9	18.3
2003—Rutgers	33	1186	216	518	.417	120	156	.769	151	141	592	4.6	4.3	17.9
2004—Rutgers	27	771	148	322	.460	68	86	.791	94	84	397	3.5	3.1	14.7
2005—Rutgers	32	1183	246	509	.483	136	168	.810	135	103	690	4.2	3.2	21.6
Totals	121	4183	810	1768	.458	427	539	.792	527	470	2211	4.4	3.9	18.3

Three-point field goals: 2002-03, 29-for-81 (.358). 2003-04, 40-for-105 (.381). 2004-05, 33-for-72 (.458). 2005-06, 62-for-127 (.488). Totals, 164-for-385 (.426).

PORTER-TALBERT, TIFFANY   G   SPARKS

PERSONAL: Born October 21, 1984, in Inglewood, Calif. ... 5-7. (1.70).
HIGH SCHOOL: Mira Costa (Manhattan Beach, Calif.) .
COLLEGE: Western Kentucky.
TRANSACTIONS/CAREER NOTES: Selected by Los Angeles in the third round (36th overall) of the WNBA Draft, April 5, 2006.

COLLEGE RECORD

NOTES: Sun Belt Player of the Year (2005). ... All-Sun Belt first team (2006, 2005, 2004). ... All-Sun Belt Conference Tournament team (2005, 2004, 2003).

Season Team	G	Min.	FGM	FGA	Pct.	FTM	FTA	Pct.	Reb.	Ast.	Pts.	AVERAGES RPG	APG	PPG
2002—Western Kentucky	31	1054	135	290	.466	114	168	.679	240	123	384	7.7	4.0	12.4
2003—Western Kentucky	34	1065	237	465	.510	109	169	.645	288	82	583	8.5	2.4	17.1
2004—Western Kentucky	30	989	221	413	.535	95	143	.664	220	78	537	7.3	2.6	17.9
2005—Western Kentucky	32	1028	202	438	.461	119	161	.739	247	95	524	7.7	3.0	16.4
Totals	127	4136	795	1606	.495	437	641	.682	995	378	2028	7.8	3.0	16.0

Three-point field goals: 2002-03, 0-for-3. 2003-04, 0-for-2. 2004-05, 0-for-1. 2005-06, 1-for-4 (.250). Totals, 1-for-10 (.100).

QUEENAN, BROOKE   F   LIBERTY

PERSONAL: Born April 10, 1984, in Abington, Pa. ... 6-2. (1.88).
HIGH SCHOOL: West Chester (West Chester, Pa.) .
COLLEGE: Boston College.
TRANSACTIONS/CAREER NOTES: Selected by New York in the second round (23rd overall) of the WNBA Draft, April 5, 2006.

COLLEGE RECORD

NOTES: All-ACC first team (2006). ... Big East Academic All-Star (2005, 2004, 2003).

Season Team	G	Min.	FGM	FGA	Pct.	FTM	FTA	Pct.	Reb.	Ast.	Pts.	AVERAGES RPG	APG	PPG
2002—Boston College	14	104	7	23	.304	6	8	.750	21	5	20	1.5	0.4	1.4
2003—Boston College	34	618	58	123	.472	21	28	.750	108	38	139	3.2	1.1	4.1
2004—Boston College	30	772	119	236	.504	79	100	.790	165	48	331	5.5	1.6	11.0
2005—Boston College	33	940	196	393	.499	84	104	.808	266	52	497	8.1	1.6	15.1
Totals	111	2434	380	775	.490	190	240	.792	560	143	987	5.0	1.3	8.9

Three-point field goals: 2002-03, 0-for-1. 2003-04, 2-for-10 (.200). 2004-05, 14-for-29 (.483). 2005-06, 21-for-74 (.284). Totals, 37-for-114 (.325).

SCOTT, CHAMEKA G MONARCHS

PERSONAL: Born May 9, 1984, in Houston. ... 6-0. (1.83). ... Full name: Chameka Nicole Vanelle Scott
HIGH SCHOOL: Clear Brook (Friendswood, Texas).
COLLEGE: Baylor.

COLLEGE RECORD

NOTES: All-Big 12 honorable mention (2006).

Season Team	G	Min.	FGM	FGA	Pct.	FTM	FTA	Pct.	Reb.	Ast.	Pts.	AVERAGES RPG	APG	PPG
2002—Baylor	21	203	21	67	.313	4	13	.308	49	15	57	2.3	0.7	2.7
2003—Baylor	34	489	59	143	.413	20	27	.741	126	39	154	3.7	1.6	4.5
2004—Baylor	36	934	104	246	.423	23	38	.605	153	76	280	4.3	2.1	7.8
2005—Baylor	33	1008	107	288	.372	25	33	.758	210	57	286	6.4	1.7	8.7
Totals	124	2634	291	744	.391	72	111	.649	538	187	777	4.3	1.5	6.3

Three-point field goals: 2002-03, 11-for-32 (.344). 2003-04, 16-for-54 (.296). 2004-05, 49-for-128 (.383). 2005-06, 47-for-148 (.318). Totals, 123-for-362 (.340).

SHIMEK, LIZ F COMETS

PERSONAL: Born May 25, 1984, in Empire, Mich. ... 6-1. (1.85).
HIGH SCHOOL: Maple City-Glen Lake (Empire, Mich.).
COLLEGE: Michigan State.
TRANSACTIONS/CAREER NOTES: Selected by Phoenix in the second round (18th overall) of the WNBA Draft, April 5, 2006. ... Draft rights, along with draft rights of Mistie Williams, traded by Phoenix to Houston for the draft rights of Ann Strother, April 5, 2006.

COLLEGE RECORD

NOTES: AP All-American honorable mention (2006, 2005). ... Kodak All-American honorable mention (2005). ... WBCA All-American honorable mention (2005). ... All-Big Ten second team (2005). ... All-Big Ten third team (2004). ... All-Big Ten honorable mention (2003). ... Co-Freshman of the Year (2003). ... Academic All-Big Ten (2004).

Season Team	G	Min.	FGM	FGA	Pct.	FTM	FTA	Pct.	Reb.	Ast.	Pts.	AVERAGES RPG	APG	PPG
2002—Michigan State	29	959	120	260	.462	62	82	.756	263	28	302	9.1	1.0	10.4
2003—Michigan State	31	966	133	286	.465	50	72	.694	252	31	335	8.1	1.0	10.8
2004—Michigan State	37	1251	217	433	.501	97	132	.735	335	74	546	9.1	2.0	14.8
2005—Michigan State	34	1135	249	460	.541	88	106	.830	280	67	597	8.2	2.0	17.6
Totals	131	4311	719	1439	.500	297	392	.758	1130	200	1780	8.6	1.5	13.6

Three-point field goals: 2002-03, 0-for-2. 2003-04, 19-for-47 (.404). 2004-05, 15-for-48 (.313). 2005-06, 11-for-38 (.289). Totals, 45-for-135 (.333).

SMITH, CRYSTAL G MERCURY

PERSONAL: Born March 12, 1984, in Shreveport, La. ... 5-6. (1.68).
HIGH SCHOOL: Haughton (Haughton, La.).
COLLEGE: Iowa.
TRANSACTIONS/CAREER NOTES: Selected by Phoenix in the third round (32nd overall) of the WNBA Draft, April 5, 2006.

COLLEGE RECORD

NOTES: All-Big Ten first team (2006). ... All-Big Ten third team (2005). ... WNIT All-Tournament team (2005).

Season Team	G	Min.	FGM	FGA	Pct.	FTM	FTA	Pct.	Reb.	Ast.	Pts.	AVERAGES RPG	APG	PPG
2002—Iowa	21	116	6	24	.250	10	12	.833	16	3	24	0.8	0.1	1.1
2003—Iowa	29	479	44	110	.400	11	14	.786	65	33	114	2.2	1.1	3.9
2004—Iowa	33	1133	207	407	.509	93	121	.769	111	96	556	3.4	2.9	16.8
2005—Iowa	29	975	162	379	.427	125	147	.850	97	98	499	3.3	3.4	17.2
Totals	112	2703	419	920	.455	239	294	.813	289	230	1193	2.6	2.1	10.7

Three-point field goals: 2002-03, 2-for-13 (.154). 2003-04, 15-for-49 (.306). 2004-05, 49-for-136 (.360). 2005-06, 50-for-148 (.338). Totals, 116-for-346 (.335).

SMITH, KHARA   F   SILVER STARS

PERSONAL: Born November 20, 1982, in Hillside, Ill. ... 6-2. (1.88).
HIGH SCHOOL: Proviso West (Hillside, Ill.).
COLLEGE: DePaul.
TRANSACTIONS/CAREER NOTES: Selected by San Antonio in the third round (30th overall) of the WNBA Draft, April 5, 2006.

COLLEGE RECORD

NOTES: AP All-American third team (2006, 2005). ... All-Big East first team (2006). ... All-Conference USA first team (2005, 2004). ... All-Conference USA third team (2003). ... Conference USA All-Tournament team (2005). ... Conference USA Freshman of the Year (2003). ... Conference USA All-Freshman team (2003).

Season Team	G	Min.	FGM	FGA	Pct.	FTM	FTA	Pct.	Reb.	Ast.	Pts.	AVERAGES RPG	APG	PPG
2002—DePaul	32	702	181	301	.601	73	113	.646	263	40	440	8.2	1.3	13.8
2003—DePaul	30	884	261	430	.607	83	131	.634	351	44	611	11.7	1.5	20.4
2004—DePaul	31	876	232	386	.601	109	145	.752	364	81	576	11.7	2.6	18.6
2005—DePaul	34	966	237	421	.563	126	170	.741	385	61	604	11.3	1.8	17.8
Totals	127	3428	911	1538	.592	391	559	.699	1363	226	2231	10.7	1.8	17.6

Three-point field goals: 2002-03, 5-for-22 (.227). 2003-04, 6-for-24 (.250). 2004-05, 3-for-13 (.231). 2005-06, 4-for-14 (.286). Totals, 18-for-73 (.247).

SMITH, KIM   F   MONARCHS

PERSONAL: Born May 7, 1984, in Surrey, British Columbia. ... 6-1. (1.85).
HIGH SCHOOL: Heritage Park Secondary (Mission, British Columbia.
COLLEGE: Utah.
TRANSACTIONS/CAREER NOTES: Selected by Sacramento in the first round (13th overall) of the WNBA Draft, April 5, 2006.

COLLEGE RECORD

NOTES: AP All-American third team (2006). ... AP All-American honorable mention (2005). ... Kodak All-America honorable mention (2005, 2004, 2003). ... MWC Co-Player of the Year (2006, 2005). ... MWC Player of the Year (2004, 2003). ... All-MWC first team (2006, 2005, 2004, 2003). ... MWC Newcomer of the Year (2003).

Season Team	G	Min.	FGM	FGA	Pct.	FTM	FTA	Pct.	Reb.	Ast.	Pts.	AVERAGES RPG	APG	PPG
2002—Utah	31	1076	177	372	.476	113	139	.813	196	48	540	6.3	1.5	17.4
2003—Utah	31	1108	180	361	.499	72	104	.692	234	51	480	7.5	1.6	15.5
2004—Utah	34	1292	227	452	.502	100	119	.840	205	89	606	8.9	2.6	17.8
2005—Utah	34	1222	247	471	.524	114	153	.745	283	101	655	8.3	3.0	19.3
Totals	130	4698	831	1656	.502	399	515	.775	918	289	2281	7.1	2.2	17.5

Three-point field goals: 2002-03, 73-for-169 (.432). 2003-04, 48-for-130 (.369). 2004-05, 52-for-139 (.374). 2005-06, 47-for-141 (.333). Totals, 220-for-579 (.380).

STANSBURY, TIFFANY   F/C   COMETS

PERSONAL: Born in Philadelphia. ... 6-3. (1.91). ... Full name: Tiffany Renee Stansbury
HIGH SCHOOL: Riverdale Baptist (Philadelphia).
JUNIOR COLLEGE: Gulf Coast Community College.
COLLEGE: N.C. State.
TRANSACTIONS/CAREER NOTES: Selected by Houston in the third round (29th overall) of the WNBA Draft, April 5, 2006.
MISCELLANEOUS: Transferred from Gulf Coast Community College.

COLLEGE RECORD

NOTES: All-ACC second team (2005).

Season Team	G	Min.	FGM	FGA	Pct.	FTM	FTA	Pct.	Reb.	Ast.	Pts.	AVERAGES RPG	APG	PPG
2002—Gulf Coast CC	22	...	110	192	.573	21	...	...	179	...	242	8.1	...	11.0
2003—Gulf Coast CC	36	...	208	410	.507	83	...	...	403	...	499	11.2	...	13.9
2004—NC State	29	803	151	296	.510	33	65	.508	204	27	335	7.0	0.9	11.6
2005—NC State	30	706	147	279	.527	51	95	.537	197	32	345	6.6	1.1	11.5
Totals	117	1509	616	1177	.523	188	160	1.175	983	59	1421	8.4	0.5	12.1

STROM, JESS   G   LYNX

PERSONAL: Born April 29, 1983, in Pittsburgh. ... 5-7/135. (1.70/61.2). ... Full name: Jessica Elizabeth Strom
HIGH SCHOOL: Steel Valley (Pittsburgh).
COLLEGE: Penn State.
TRANSACTIONS/CAREER NOTES: Signed by Connecticut, April 2005.

COLLEGE RECORD

NOTES: All-Big Ten first team (2005). ... All-Big Ten third team (2003, 2004). ... All-Big Ten honorable mention (2002). ... Big Ten All-Freshman team (2002). ... All-Big Ten Tournament team (2004). ... Ranked second in the Big Ten in steals and assists (2004).

Season Team	G	Min.	FGM	FGA	Pct.	FTM	FTA	Pct.	Reb.	Ast.	Pts.	AVERAGES RPG	APG	PPG
2001—Penn State	35	1244	90	220	.409	80	100	.800	125	235	302	3.6	6.7	8.6
2002—Penn State	35	1277	113	278	.406	71	81	.877	85	222	343	2.4	6.3	9.8
2003—Penn State	34	1268	109	263	.414	107	131	.817	126	184	370	3.7	5.4	10.9
2004—Penn State	29	1090	132	345	.383	129	148	.872	35	135	451	1.2	4.7	15.6
Totals	133	4879	444	1106	.401	387	460	.841	371	776	1466	2.8	5.8	11.0

Three-point field goals: 2001-02, 42-for-106 (.396). 2002-03, 46-for-142 (.324). 2003-04, 45-for-127 (.354). 2004-05, 58-for-150 (.387). Totals, 191-for-525 (.364).

ROOKIES & NEWCOMERS

STROTHER, ANN G/F MERCURY

PERSONAL: Born December 11, 1983, in Castle Rock, Colo. ... 6-3. (1.91). ... Full name: Ann Elise Strother
HIGH SCHOOL: Highlands Ranch (Castle Rock, Colo.).
COLLEGE: Connecticut.
TRANSACTIONS/CAREER NOTES: Selected by Houston in the second round (15th overall) of the WNBA Draft, April 5, 2006. ... Draft rights traded by Houston to Phoenix for the draft rights of Liz Shimek and Mistie Williams, April 5, 2006.

COLLEGE RECORD

NOTES: AP All-American honorable mention (2006). ... All-Big East first team (2006, 2005). ... All-Big East third team (2004, 2003). ... Big East All-Rookie team (2003). ... NCAA Final Four All-Tournament team (2003). ... Big East All-Tournament team (2005).

Season Team	G	Min.	FGM	FGA	Pct.	FTM	FTA	Pct.	Reb.	Ast.	Pts.	AVERAGES RPG	APG	PPG
2002—Connecticut	38	1196	137	330	.415	52	64	.813	173	117	384	4.6	3.1	10.1
2003—Connecticut	25	1019	139	318	.437	45	57	.789	150	82	384	4.3	2.3	11.0
2004—Connecticut	33	1030	144	344	.419	54	76	.711	110	106	427	3.3	3.2	12.9
2005—Connecticut	37	1205	182	427	.426	54	66	.818	181	113	504	4.9	3.1	13.6
Totals	133	4450	602	1419	.424	205	263	.779	614	418	1699	4.6	3.1	12.8

Three-point field goals: 2002-03, 58-for-156 (.372). 2003-04, 61-for-161 (.379). 2004-05, 43-for-110 (.391). 2005-06, 86-for-235 (.366). Totals, 248-for-662 (.375).

SY, MARIAM C MYSTICS

PERSONAL: Born September 13, 1979, in Mali, West Africa. ... 6-4. (1.93).
HIGH SCHOOL: : E.C.I.C.A (Mali, West Africa).
JUNIOR COLLEGE: Utah Valley State.
COLLEGE: Oklahoma City University.
TRANSACTIONS/CAREER NOTES: Selected by Washington in the third round (33rd overall) of the WNBA Draft, April 5, 2006.

COLLEGE RECORD

NOTES: NAIA All-American first team (2006). ... NAIA All-American second team (2005).

Season Team	G	Min.	FGM	FGA	Pct.	FTM	FTA	Pct.	Reb.	Ast.	Pts.	AVERAGES RPG	APG	PPG
2001—Utah Valley St. JC	33	399	92	155	.594	52	98	.531	160	14	236	4.8	0.4	7.2
2002—Utah Valley St. JC	16	364	111	190	.584	64	103	.621	167	15	286	10.4	0.9	17.9
2004—Oklahoma City University	24	706	164	314	.522	68	121	.562	217	36	398	9.0	1.5	16.6
2005—Oklahoma City University	35	966	302	530	.570	179	283	.633	339	44	784	9.7	1.3	22.4
Totals	108	2435	669	1189	.563	363	605	.600	883	109	1704	8.2	1.0	15.8

Three-point field goals: 2004-05, 2-for-4 (.500). 2005-06, 1-for-1 (1.000). Totals, 3-for-5 (.600).

TEILANE, ZANE C SHOCK

PERSONAL: Born September 24, 1983, in Riga, Latvia. ... 6-7. (2.01).
HIGH SCHOOL: Agenskalna Gimnazija (Riga, Latvia).
COLLEGE: Western Illinois.
TRANSACTIONS/CAREER NOTES: Selected by Detroit in the third round (35th overall) of the WNBA Draft, April 5, 2006.

COLLEGE RECORD

NOTES: Mid-Continent Player of the Year (2006, 2005). ... Mid-Continent Defensive Player of the Year (2006, 2005). ... All-Mid Continent first team (2006, 2005, 2004). ... Mid-Continent All-Tournament team (2004, 2003).

Season Team	G	Min.	FGM	FGA	Pct.	FTM	FTA	Pct.	Reb.	Ast.	Pts.	AVERAGES RPG	APG	PPG
2002—Western Illinois	19	438	81	133	.609	50	80	.625	116	21	212	6.1	1.1	11.2
2003—Western Illinois	29	823	165	290	.569	75	105	.714	273	44	405	9.4	1.5	14.7
2004—Western Illinois	28	741	164	314	.522	110	133	.827	260	60	438	9.3	2.1	15.6
2005—Western Illinois	30	943	189	395	.478	114	146	.781	320	95	492	10.7	3.2	16.4
Totals	106	2945	599	1132	.529	349	464	.752	969	220	1547	9.1	2.1	14.6

Three-point field goals: 2002-03, 0-for-1. 2004-05, 0-for-1. 2005-06, 0-for-1. Totals, 0-for-3 (.000).

TERRY, KASHA F/C FEVER

PERSONAL: Born October 21, 1983, in Douglasville, Ga. ... 6-3. (1.91). ... Full name: Kasha NiCarra Terry
HIGH SCHOOL: Douglas County (Douglasville, Ga.).
COLLEGE: Georgia Tech.
TRANSACTIONS/CAREER NOTES: Selected by Indiana in the second round (26th overall) of the WNBA Draft, April 5, 2006.

COLLEGE RECORD

NOTES: All-ACC Tournament team (2005) ... All-ACC Rookie team honorable mention (2003).

Season Team	G	Min.	FGM	FGA	Pct.	FTM	FTA	Pct.	Reb.	Ast.	Pts.	AVERAGES RPG	APG	PPG
2002—Georgia Tech	30	550	60	147	.408	21	51	.412	143	19	141	4.8	0.6	4.7
2003—Georgia Tech	28	547	71	161	.441	25	66	.379	128	12	167	4.6	0.4	6.0
2004—Georgia Tech	12	251	30	66	.455	18	29	.621	69	10	78	5.8	0.8	6.5
2005—Georgia Tech	29	623	87	182	.478	26	56	.464	167	13	200	5.8	0.4	6.9
Totals	99	1971	248	556	.446	90	202	.446	507	54	586	5.1	0.5	5.9

THORBURN, SHONA   G   LYNX

PERSONAL: Born August 7, 1982, in Oxford, England. ... 5-10. (1.78).
HIGH SCHOOL: Westdale (Hamilton, Ontario, Canada) .
COLLEGE: Utah.
TRANSACTIONS/CAREER NOTES: Selected by Minnesota in the first round (seventh overall) of the WNBA Draft, April 5, 2006.

COLLEGE RECORD

NOTES: AP All-American honorable mention (2006). ... MWC Co-Player of the Year (2005). ... WBCA All-American (2005). ... All-MWC first team (2006, 2005). ... All-MWC second team (2004, 2003). ... MWC All-Tournament team 2004).

Season Team	G	Min.	FGM	FGA	Pct.	FTM	FTA	Pct.	Reb.	Ast.	Pts.	AVERAGES RPG	APG	PPG
2002—Utah	31	1131	146	389	.375	96	118	.814	180	102	453	5.8	3.3	14.6
2003—Utah	31	1160	130	344	.378	67	105	.638	167	123	372	5.4	4.0	12.0
2004—Utah	34	1309	166	409	.406	125	191	.654	212	221	505	6.2	6.2	14.9
2005—Utah	34	1259	126	349	.361	122	165	.739	218	242	405	6.4	7.1	11.9
Totals	130	4859	568	1491	.381	410	579	.708	777	688	1735	6.0	5.3	13.3

Three-point field goals: 2002-03, 65-for-198 (.328). 2003-04, 45-for-136 (.331). 2004-05, 48-for-136 (.353). 2005-06, 31-for-113 (.274). Totals, 189-for-583 (.324).

TURNER, BARBARA   G/F   STORM

PERSONAL: Born June 8, 1984, in Cleveland. ... 6-0. (1.83).
HIGH SCHOOL: East Technical (Cleveland).
COLLEGE: Connecticut.
TRANSACTIONS/CAREER NOTES: Selected by Seattle in the first round (11th overall) of the WNBA Draft, April 5, 2006.

COLLEGE RECORD

NOTES: All-Big East second team (2004). ... All-Big East honorable mention (2005). ... Most Outstanding Player of Big East Tournament (2005). ... Big East All-Tournament team (2005). ... Big East All-Rookie team (2003).

Season Team	G	Min.	FGM	FGA	Pct.	FTM	FTA	Pct.	Reb.	Ast.	Pts.	AVERAGES RPG	APG	PPG
2002—Connecticut	38	795	134	269	.498	102	149	.685	220	45	379	5.8	1.2	10.0
2003—Connecticut	35	933	177	330	.536	105	158	.665	167	105	478	4.8	3.0	13.7
2004—Connecticut	29	638	126	241	.523	63	95	.663	140	44	320	4.8	1.5	11.0
2005—Connecticut	36	973	170	312	.545	100	140	.714	270	85	452	7.5	2.4	12.6
Totals	138	3339	607	1152	.527	370	542	.683	797	279	1629	5.8	2.0	11.8

Three-point field goals: 2002-03, 9-for-30 (.300). 2003-04, 19-for-47 (.404). 2004-05, 5-for-21 (.238). 2005-06, 12-for-40 (.300). Totals, 45-for-138 (.326).

VOLNAYA, SVETLANA   G/F   LIBERTY

PERSONAL: Born April 11, 1979, in Minsk, Belarus. ... 6-1/163. (1.85/73.9). ... Full name: Svetlana Vladimirovna Volnaya
HIGH SCHOOL: Math Oriented School #50 (Minsk, Belarus).
COLLEGE: Virginia.
TRANSACTIONS/CAREER NOTES: Selected by Detroit in third round (38th overall) of WNBA Draft, April 20, 2001.
MISCELLANEOUS: Member of Belarussian national team since 1998.

COLLEGE RECORD

NOTES: Attended Independence (Kan.) Community College in 1997-98. ... NJCAA All-America third team selection (1998), averaging 19.0 points, 6.8 rebounds and 2.6 assists, and shooting .450 from the field and .750 from the free throw line .

Season Team	G	Min.	FGM	FGA	Pct.	FTM	FTA	Pct.	Reb.	Ast.	Pts.	AVERAGES RPG	APG	PPG
1998—Virginia	29	540	65	186	.349	35	50	.700	99	28	186	3.4	1.0	6.4
1999—Virginia	33	984	149	335	.445	105	139	.755	134	51	457	4.1	1.5	13.8
2000—Virginia	31	906	132	304	.434	78	122	.639	125	49	391	4.0	1.6	12.6
Totals	93	2430	346	825	.419	218	311	.701	358	128	1034	3.8	1.4	11.1

Three-point field goals: 1998-99, 21-for-80 (.263). 1999-00, 54-for-126 (.429). 2000-01, 49-for-109 (.450). Totals, 124-for-315 (.394).

WILKINS, BRITTANY   F/C   MONARCHS

PERSONAL: Born June 15, 1983, in Arlington, Neb. ... 6-3. (1.91). ... Full name: Brittany Rae Wilkins
HIGH SCHOOL: Arlington.
COLLEGE: Iowa State.

COLLEGE RECORD

NOTES: All-Big 12 Conference first team (2005, 2003). ... All-Big 12 Conference second team (2004). ... Cyclone Classic All-Tournament team (2004).

Season Team	G	Min.	FGM	FGA	Pct.	FTM	FTA	Pct.	Reb.	Ast.	Pts.	AVERAGES RPG	APG	PPG
2002—Iowa State	28	375	41	84	.488	24	30	.800	73	9	109	2.6	0.3	3.9
2003—Iowa State	33	579	102	188	.543	38	54	.704	121	11	247	3.7	0.3	7.5
2004—Iowa State	24	212	35	62	.565	24	28	.857	43	4	100	1.8	0.2	4.2
2005—Iowa State	31	959	197	383	.514	76	94	.809	275	22	498	3.6	0.7	16.1
Totals	116	2125	375	717	.523	162	206	.786	512	46	954	4.4	0.4	8.2

Three-point field goals: 2002-03, 2-for-7 (.286). 2003-04, 5-for-13 (.385). 2005-06, 28-for-76 (.368). Totals, 35-for-96 (.365).

WILLIAMS, MISTIE — F — COMETS

PERSONAL: Born December 2, 1983, in Janesville, Wisc. ... 6-3. (1.91). ... Full name: Mistie McCray Williams
HIGH SCHOOL: Parker (Janesville, Wisc.).
COLLEGE: Duke.
TRANSACTIONS/CAREER NOTES: Selected by Phoenix in the second round (21st overall) in the WNBA Draft, April 5, 2006. ... Draft rights, along with draft rights of Liz Shimek, traded by Phoenix to Houston for the draft rights of Ann Strother, April 5, 2006.

COLLEGE RECORD

NOTES: All-ACC second team (2006). ... All-ACC third team (2005, 2004). ... All-ACC Tournament second team (2004). ... ACC All-Freshman team (2003).

Season Team	G	Min.	FGM	FGA	Pct.	FTM	FTA	Pct.	Reb.	Ast.	Pts.	RPG	APG	PPG
2002—Duke	37	594	89	181	.492	78	115	.678	138	28	256	3.7	0.8	6.9
2003—Duke	34	776	132	216	.611	77	122	.631	182	26	341	5.4	0.8	10.0
2004—Duke	36	975	176	327	.538	68	111	.613	258	64	420	7.2	1.8	11.7
2005—Duke	35	867	160	259	.618	72	111	.649	222	57	392	6.3	1.6	11.2
Totals	142	3212	557	983	.567	295	459	.643	800	175	1409	5.6	1.2	9.9

Three-point field goals: 2004-05, 0-for-1. Totals, 0-for-1 (.000).

WILLIS, LISA — G — SPARKS

PERSONAL: Born June 13, 1984, in Long Beach, Calif. ... 5-11. (1.80). ... Full name: Lisa Camille Willis
HIGH SCHOOL: Narbonne (Long Beach, Calif.).
COLLEGE: UCLA.
TRANSACTIONS/CAREER NOTES: Selected by Los Angeles in the first round (fifth overall) of the WNBA Draft, April 5, 2006.

COLLEGE RECORD

NOTES: AP All-American honorable mention (2006). ... All-Pac-10 first team (2006, 2005). ... All-Pac-10 honorable mention (2004). ... First Bruin player to record back-to-back 100 steals seasons.

Season Team	G	Min.	FGM	FGA	Pct.	FTM	FTA	Pct.	Reb.	Ast.	Pts.	RPG	APG	PPG
2002—UCLA	28	470	79	215	.367	29	27	1.074	104	22	224	3.6	0.8	7.7
2003—UCLA	30	956	157	365	.430	44	62	.710	162	64	428	5.4	2.1	14.3
2004—UCLA	28	966	158	392	.403	69	86	.802	192	65	455	6.9	2.3	16.3
2005—UCLA	32	1086	216	471	.459	68	90	.756	187	100	570	5.8	3.1	17.8
Totals	118	3478	610	1443	.423	210	265	.792	645	251	1677	5.5	2.1	14.2

Three-point field goals: 2002-03, 46-for-134 (.343). 2003-04, 70-for-189 (.370). 2004-05, 70-for-194 (.361). 2005-06, 70-for-193 (.363). Totals, 256-for-710 (.361).

YOUNG, SOPHIA — F — SILVER STARS

PERSONAL: Born December 15, 1983, in St. Vincent, The Grenadines, West Indies. ... 6-1.
HIGH SCHOOL: Evangel Christian Academy (Shreveport, La.).
COLLEGE: Baylor.
TRANSACTIONS/CAREER NOTES: Selected by San Antonio in the first round (fourth overall) of the WNBA Draft, April 5, 2006.

COLLEGE RECORD

NOTES: Big 12 Player of the Year (2006). ... AP All-American second team (2005). Kodak/WBCA All-American team (2005). NCAA Final Four Most Outstanding Player (2005). ... Big 12 Tournament MVP (2005). ... All-Big 12 first team (2006, 2005, 2004). ... All-Big 12 honorable mention (2003).

Season Team	G	Min.	FGM	FGA	Pct.	FTM	FTA	Pct.	Reb.	Ast.	Pts.	RPG	APG	PPG
2002—Baylor	35	974	218	387	.563	61	113	.540	351	55	497	10.0	1.6	14.2
2003—Baylor	35	1003	249	449	.555	88	145	.607	302	75	586	8.6	2.1	16.0
2004—Baylor	36	1175	266	506	.526	129	183	.705	334	103	661	9.3	2.9	18.4
2005—Baylor	33	1112	301	551	.546	134	190	.705	329	70	736	10.0	2.1	22.3
Totals	139	4264	1034	1893	.546	412	631	.653	1316	303	2480	9.5	2.2	17.8

Three-point field goals: 2003-04, 0-for-1 (.000). 2005-06, 0-for-1 (.000). Totals, 0-for-2 (.000).

ZOLMAN, SHANNA — G — SILVER STARS

PERSONAL: Born September 7, 1983, in Syracuse, Ind. ... 5-10. (1.78). ... Full name: Shanna Anette Zolman
HIGH SCHOOL: Wawasee (Syracuse, Ind.).
COLLEGE: Tennessee.
TRANSACTIONS/CAREER NOTES: Selected by San Antonio in the second round (16th overall) in the WNBA Draft, April 5, 2006.

COLLEGE RECORD

NOTES: AP All-American honorable mention (2006). ... All-SEC first team (2006). ... All-SEC second team (2005, 2004). ... SEC All-Tournament Team (2005). ... SEC All-Academic team (2005, 2004). ... SEC All-Freshman team (2003).

Season Team	G	Min.	FGM	FGA	Pct.	FTM	FTA	Pct.	Reb.	Ast.	Pts.	RPG	APG	PPG
2002—Tennessee	38	693	95	227	.419	58	65	.892	78	64	285	2.1	1.7	7.5
2003—Tennessee	35	1055	142	325	.437	88	92	.957	99	71	430	2.8	2.0	12.3
2004—Tennessee	35	968	147	333	.441	75	87	.862	81	63	437	2.3	1.8	12.5
2005—Tennessee	36	1203	183	423	.433	85	90	.944	104	114	554	2.9	2.9	15.4
Totals	144	3919	567	1308	.433	306	334	.916	362	312	1706	2.5	2.2	11.8

Three-point field goals: 2002-03, 37-for-96 (.385). 2003-04, 58-for-136 (.426). 2004-05, 68-for-156 (.436). 2005-06, 103-for-238 (.433). Totals, 266-for-626 (.425).

HEAD COACHES

ADUBATO, RICHIE — MYSTICS

PERSONAL: Born November 23, 1937, in East Orange, N.J. ... Full Name: Richard Adam Adubato.
HIGH SCHOOL: East Orange (N.J.).
COLLEGE: William Paterson College (N.J.).

HEAD COACHING RECORD

BACKGROUND: Led the Liberty to the playoffs in each of his four seasons as head coach. ... Won three Eastern Conference titles (1999, 2000, 2002) and guided the Liberty to the WNBA Championship Series. ... Spent six of his 19-year NBA coaching career at the helm of teams including Detroit, Dallas and Orlando. ... Prior to the NBA, spent 18 years as a high school and college coach in New Jersey, compiling an overall record of 290-85 (.771).

COLLEGIATE COACHING RECORD

Season Team	W	L	Pct.	Finish
72-73—Upsala College	15	9	.625	—
73-74—Upsala College	17	10	.630	—
74-75—Upsala College	18	11	.621	—
75-76—Upsala College	20	9	.690	—
76-77—Upsala College	11	14	.440	—
77-78—Upsala College	19	9	.679	—
Totals (6 years)	100	62	.617	

NBA COACHING RECORD

Season Team	W	L	Pct.	Finish	W	L	Pct.
79-80—Detroit	12	58	.171	6th/Central Division	—	—	—
89-90—Dallas	42	29	.592	3rd/Midwest Division	0	3	.000
90-91—Dallas	28	54	.341	6th/Midwest Division	—	—	—
91-92—Dallas	22	60	.268	5th/Midwest Division	—	—	—
96-97—Orlando	21	12	.636	3rd/Atlantic Division	2	3	.400
Totals (5 years)	125	213	.370		2	6	.250

NOTES:
1990—Lost to Portland in Western Conference first round.
1997—Replaced Brian Hill as Orlando head coach (February 18), with record of 24-25 and club in third place. Lost to Miami in Eastern Conference first round.

WNBA COACHING RECORD

Season Team	W	L	Pct.	Finish	W	L	Pct.
1999—New York	18	14	.563	1st/Eastern Conference	3	3	.500
2000—New York	20	12	.625	1st/East	4	3	.571
2001—New York	21	11	.656	2nd/East	3	3	.500
2002—New York	18	14	.563	T1st/East	4	4	.500
2003—New York	16	18	.471	T6th/East	—	—	—
2004—New York	7	9	.438	—	—	—	—
2005—Washington	16	18	.471	T4th/East	—	—	—
Totals (7 years)	116	96	.547		14	13	.519

NOTES:
2000—Defeated Charlotte, 2-1, in Eastern Conference Finals; lost to Houston, 2-1, in the Championship Series.
2001—Defeated Washington, 2-0 in first round; defeated Cleveland, 2-1 in Eastern Conference Finals; lost to Houston, 2-0 in WNBA Championship Series.
2002—Defeated Miami, 2-1 in first round; lost to Charlotte, 2-1 in Eastern Conference Finals.
2003—Defeated Indiana, 2-1 in first round; defeated Washington, 2-1 in Eastern Conference Finals; lost to Los Angeles, 2-0 in WNBA Championship Series.

BOGUES, MUGGSY — STING

PERSONAL: Born January 9, 1965, in Baltimore. ... 5-3/141. (1,60/64,0). ... Full Name: Tyrone Curtis Bogues. ... Name pronounced: rhymes with rogues.
HIGH SCHOOL: Dunbar (Baltimore).
COLLEGE: Wake Forest.
TRANSACTIONS/CAREER NOTES: Selected by Washington Bullets in first round (12th pick overall) of 1987 NBA Draft. ... Played in United States Basketball League with Rhode Island Gulls (1987). ... Selected by Charlotte Hornets from Bullets in NBA Expansion Draft (June 23, 1988). ... Traded by Hornets with G Tony Delk to Golden State Warriors for G B.J. Armstrong (November 7, 1997). ... Signed as free agent by Toronto Raptors (September 23, 1999). ... Traded by Raptors with G Mark Jackson to New York Knicks for G Chris Childs and 2001 first-round draft choice (February 22, 2001). ... Traded by Knicks to Dallas Mavericks as part of three-team trade in which Knicks acquired F Shandon Anderson from Houston Rockets and G Howard Eisley from Mavericks and Rockets acquired F Glen Rice from Knicks and draft rights to G Kyle Hill from Mavericks (August 10, 2001).
MISCELLANEOUS: Member of gold medal-winning U.S. World Championship team (1986). ... Charlotte Hornets all-time assists leader with 5,557 and all-time steals leader with 1,067 (1988-89 through 1997-98).

WNBA COACHING RECORD

Season Team	W	L	Pct.	Finish	W	L	Pct.
2005—Charlotte	3	7	.300	6th/East	—	—	—

COLLEGIATE RECORD

NOTES: Frances Pomeroy Naismith Award winner (1987).

Season Team	G	Min.	FGM	FGA	Pct.	FTM	FTA	Pct.	Reb.	Ast.	Pts.	AVERAGES RPG	APG	PPG
83-84—Wake Forest	32	312	14	46	.304	9	13	.692	21	53	37	0.7	1.7	1.2

Season Team	G	Min.	FGM	FGA	Pct.	FTM	FTA	Pct.	Reb.	Ast.	Pts.	RPG	APG	PPG
84-85—Wake Forest	29	1025	81	162	.500	30	44	.682	69	207	192	2.4	7.1	6.6
85-86—Wake Forest	29	1101	132	290	.455	65	89	.730	90	245	329	3.1	8.4	11.3
86-87—Wake Forest	29	1130	159	318	.500	75	93	.806	110	276	428	3.8	9.5	14.8
Totals	119	3568	386	816	.473	179	239	.749	290	781	986	2.4	6.6	8.3

Three-point field goals: 1986-87, 35-for-79 (.443).

NBA REGULAR-SEASON RECORD

Season Team	G	Min.	FGM	FGA	Pct.	FTM	FTA	Pct.	REBOUNDS Off.	Def.	Tot.	Ast.	St.	Blk.	TO	Pts.	AVERAGES RPG	APG	PPG
87-88—Washington	79	1628	166	426	.390	58	74	.784	35	101	136	404	127	3	101	393	1.7	5.1	5.0
88-89—Charlotte	79	1755	178	418	.426	66	88	.750	53	112	165	620	111	7	124	423	2.1	7.8	5.4
89-90—Charlotte	81	2743	326	664	.491	106	134	.791	48	159	207	867	166	3	146	763	2.6	10.7	9.4
90-91—Charlotte	81	2299	241	524	.460	86	108	.796	58	158	216	669	137	3	120	568	2.7	8.3	7.0
91-92—Charlotte	82	2790	317	671	.472	94	120	.783	58	177	235	743	170	6	156	730	2.9	9.1	8.9
92-93—Charlotte	81	2833	331	730	.453	140	168	.833	51	247	298	711	161	5	154	808	3.7	8.8	10.0
93-94—Charlotte	77	2746	354	751	.471	125	155	.806	78	235	313	780	133	2	171	835	4.1	10.1	10.8
94-95—Charlotte	78	2629	348	730	.477	160	180	.889	51	206	257	675	103	0	132	862	3.3	8.7	11.1
95-96—Charlotte	6	77	6	16	.375	2	2	1.000	6	1	7	19	2	0	6	14	1.2	3.2	2.3
96-97—Charlotte	65	1880	204	443	.460	54	64	.844	25	116	141	469	82	2	108	522	2.2	7.2	8.0
97-98—Char.-G.S.	61	1570	141	323	.437	61	68	.897	30	102	132	331	67	3	105	347	2.2	5.4	5.7
98-99—Golden State	36	714	76	154	.494	31	36	.861	16	57	73	134	43	1	47	183	2.0	3.7	5.1
99-00—Toronto	80	1731	157	358	.439	79	87	.908	25	110	135	299	65	4	59	410	1.7	3.7	5.1
00-01—Tor.-N.Y.	3	34	0	2	.000	0	0	.000	0	3	3	5	2	0	4	0	1.0	1.7	0.0
Totals	889	25429	2845	6210	.458	1062	1284	.827	534	1784	2318	6726	1369	39	1433	6858	2.6	7.5	7.7

Three-point field goals: 1987-88, 3-for-16 (.188). 1988-89, 1-for-13 (.077). 1989-90, 5-for-26 (.192). 1990-91, 0-for-12. 1991-92, 2-for-27 (.074). 1992-93, 6-for-26 (.231). 1993-94, 2-for-12 (.167). 1994-95, 6-for-30 (.200). 1995-96, 0-for-1. 1996-97, 60-for-144 (.417). 1997-98, 4-for-16 (.250). 1998-99, 0-for-6. 1999-00, 17-for-51 (.333). 2000-01, 0-for-1. Totals, 106-for-381 (.278).

Personal fouls/disqualifications: 1987-88, 138/1. 1988-89, 141/1. 1989-90, 168/1. 1990-91, 160/2. 1991-92, 156/0. 1992-93, 179/0. 1993-94, 147/1. 1994-95, 151/0. 1995-96, 4/0. 1996-97, 114/0. 1997-98, 58/0. 1998-99, 44/0. 1999-00, 119/0. 2000-01, 3/0. Totals, 1582/6.

NBA PLAYOFF RECORD

Season Team	G	Min.	FGM	FGA	Pct.	FTM	FTA	Pct.	REBOUNDS Off.	Def.	Tot.	Ast.	St.	Blk.	TO	Pts.	AVERAGES RPG	APG	PPG
87-88—Washington	1	2	0	0	...	0	0	...	0	0	0	2	0	0	1	0	0.0	2.0	0.0
92-93—Charlotte	9	346	39	82	.476	10	14	.714	6	30	36	70	24	0	17	88	4.0	7.8	9.8
94-95—Charlotte	4	145	14	45	.311	5	5	1.000	3	3	6	25	4	0	9	34	1.5	6.3	8.5
96-97—Charlotte	2	58	11	19	.579	4	4	1.000	1	2	3	5	1	0	6	32	1.5	2.5	16.0
99-00—Toronto	3	87	6	21	.286	1	3	.333	3	3	6	5	4	0	4	16	2.0	1.7	5.3
Totals	19	638	70	167	.419	20	26	.769	13	38	51	107	33	0	37	170	2.7	5.6	8.9

Three-point field goals: 1992-93, 0-for-2. 1994-95, 1-for-3 (.333). 1996-97, 6-for-7 (.857). 1999-00, 3-for-9 (.333). Totals, 10-for-21 (.476).
Personal fouls/disqualifications: 1992-93, 21/0. 1994-95, 8/0. 1996-97, 3/0. 1999-00, 4/0. Totals, 36/0.

BRYANT, JOE — SPARKS

PERSONAL: Born October 18, 1954, in Philadelphia.
HIGH SCHOOL: John Batram (Philadelphia).
COLLEGE: LaSalle.
TRANSACTIONS/CAREER NOTES: Selected by Golden State as hardship case in the first round (14th overall) of NBA Draft, 1975. ... Draft rights sold by Golden State to Philadelphia, September 12, 1975. ... Traded by Philadelphia to San Diego for a first-round pick in the 1986 draft, October 5, 1979. ... Traded by San Diego, along with a second-round pick in the 1982 draft, to Houston for a second-round pick in the 1982 draft, June 28, 1982.

WNBA COACHING RECORD

Season Team	W	L	Pct.	Finish	W	L	Pct.
2005—Los Angeles	4	1	.800	4th/West	0	2	.000

NOTES:
2005—Lost to Sacramento, 2-0, in the first round.

COLLEGIATE RECORD

Season Team	G	Min.	FGM	FGA	Pct.	FTM	FTA	Pct.	Reb.	Ast.	Pts.	RPG	APG	PPG
72-73—LaSalle						did not play—ineligible								
73-74—LaSalle	26	...	200	440	.455	86	123	.699	282	...	486	...	...	18.7
74-75—LaSalle	29	...	256	495	.517	120	165	.727	330	...	632	...	...	21.8
Totals	55	...	456	935	.488	206	289	.713	612	...	118	...	...	20.3

NBA REGULAR-SEASON RECORD

Season Team	G	Min.	FGM	FGA	Pct.	FTM	FTA	Pct.	REBOUNDS Off.	Def.	Tot.	Ast.	St.	Blk.	TO	Pts.	AVERAGES RPG	APG	PPG
75-76—Philadelphia	75	1203	233	552	.297	92	147	.385	97	181	278	61	44	23	—	558	3.7	0.8	7.4
76-77—Philadelphia	61	612	107	240	.308	53	70	.431	45	72	117	48	36	13	—	267	1.9	0.8	4.4
77-78—Philadelphia	81	1236	190	436	.304	111	144	.435	103	177	280	129	56	24	115	491	3.5	1.6	6.1
78-79—Philadelphia	70	1064	205	478	.301	123	170	.420	96	163	259	103	49	9	114	533	3.7	1.5	7.6

Season Team	G	Min.	FGM	FGA	Pct.	FTM	FTA	Pct.	REBOUNDS Off.	Def.	Tot.	Ast.	St.	Blk.	TO	Pts.	AVERAGES RPG	APG	PPG
79-80—San Diego	81	2328	294	682	.301	161	217	.426	171	345	516	144	102	39	170	754	6.4	1.8	9.3
80-81—San Diego	82	2359	379	791	.324	193	244	.442	146	294	440	189	72	34	176	953	5.4	2.3	11.6
81-82—San Diego	75	1988	341	701	.327	194	247	.440	79	195	274	189	78	29	183	884	3.7	2.5	11.8
82-83—Houston	81	2055	344	768	.309	116	165	.413	88	189	277	186	82	30	177	812	3.4	2.3	10.0
Totals	606	12845	2093	4648	.310	1043	1404	.426	825	1616	2441	1049	519	201	935	5252	4.0	1.7	8.7

NBA PLAYOFF RECORD

Season Team	G	Min.	FGM	FGA	Pct.	FTM	FTA	Pct.	REBOUNDS Off.	Def.	Tot.	Ast.	St.	Blk.	TO	Pts.	AVERAGES RPG	APG	PPG
75-76—Philadelphia	3	43	9	12	.750	5	7	.714	3	10	13	1	1	1	—	23	4.3	0.3	7.7
76-77—Philadelphia	10	74	12	31	.387	5	8	.625	2	13	15	7	6	2	—	29	1.5	0.7	2.9
77-78—Philadelphia	10	122	21	47	.447	8	11	.727	7	18	25	9	6	1	—	50	2.5	0.9	5.0
78-79—Philadelphia	7	35	10	26	.385	1	2	.500	0	1	1	4	1	0	—	21	0.1	0.6	3.0
Totals	30	274	52	116	.448	19	28	.679	12	42	54	21	14	4	—	123	1.8	0.7	4.1

CHANCELLOR, VAN   COMETS

PERSONAL: Born September 17, 1943, in Louisville, Miss. ... Full Name: Winston Van Chancellor.
HIGH SCHOOL: Louisville (Miss.).
COLLEGE: Mississippi State (1965).

HEAD COACHING RECORD

BACKGROUND: Head coach of the 2002 USA Basketball women's world championship team. ... WNBA Coach of the Year (1997, 1998, 1999). ... Led Comets to four consecutive championships (1997, 1998, 1999, 2000). ... Left Mississippi as the 16th all-time winningest women's college basketball coach. ... Led Mississippi to 14 NCAA Tournament appearances.

COLLEGIATE COACHING RECORD

Season Team	W	L	Pct.	Finish
78-79—Mississippi	31	9	.775	—
79-80—Mississippi	23	14	.622	—
80-81—Mississippi	14	12	.538	—
81-82—Mississippi	27	5	.844	—
82-83—Mississippi	26	6	.813	—
83-84—Mississippi	24	6	.800	—
84-85—Mississippi	29	3	.906	—
85-86—Mississippi	24	8	.750	—
86-87—Mississippi	25	5	.833	—
87-88—Mississippi	24	7	.774	—
88-89—Mississippi	23	8	.742	—
89-90—Mississippi	22	10	.688	—
90-91—Mississippi	20	9	.690	—
91-92—Mississippi	29	3	.906	—
92-93—Mississippi	19	10	.655	—
93-94—Mississippi	21	8	.724	—
94-95—Mississippi	21	8	.724	—
95-96—Mississippi	18	11	.621	—
96-97—Mississippi	16	11	.593	—
Totals (19 years)	436	153	.740	

WNBA COACHING RECORD

Season Team	W	L	Pct.	Finish	W	L	Pct.
1997—Houston	18	10	.643	1st/East	2	0	1.000
1998—Houston	27	3	.900	1st/West	4	1	.800
1999—Houston	26	6	.813	1st/West	4	2	.667
2000—Houston	27	5	.844	2nd/West	6	0	1.000
2001—Houston	19	13	.594	T3rd/West	0	2	.000
2002—Houston	24	8	.750	2nd/West	1	2	.333
2003—Houston	20	14	.588	2nd/West	0	1	.000
2004—Houston	13	21	.382	6th/West	—	—	—
2005—Houston	19	15	.559	3rd/West	2	3	.400
Totals (9 years)	193	95	.670		19	11	.633

NOTES:

1997—Defeated Charlotte in semifinals; defeated New York in the WNBA Championship Game.
1998—Defeated Charlotte, 2-0, in semifinals; defeated Phoenix, 2-1, in the WNBA Championship Series.
1999—Defeated Los Angeles, 2-1, in conference finals; defeated New York, 2-1, in Championship Series.
2000—Defeated Sacramento, 2-0, in first round; defeated Los Angeles, 2-0 in Western Conference Finals; defeated New York, 2-0 in WNBA Championship.
2001—Lost to Los Angeles, 2-0, in first round.
2002—Lost to Utah, 2-1, in first round.
2003—Lost to Sacramento, 2-0, in first round.
2005—Defeated Seattle, 2-1, in first round; lost to Sacramento, 2-0, in Western Conference Finals..

COWENS, DAVE   SKY

PERSONAL: Born October 25, 1948, in Newport, Ky. ... 6-9/230. (2,05/104,3). ... Full name: David William Cowens.
HIGH SCHOOL: Newport (Ky.) Central Catholic.
COLLEGE: Florida State.
TRANSACTIONS/CAREER NOTES: Selected by Boston Celtics in first round (fourth pick overall) of 1970 NBA Draft. ... Traded by Celtics to Milwaukee Bucks for G Quinn Buckner (September 9, 1982).
CAREER HONORS: Elected to Naismith Memorial Basketball Hall of Fame (1990).
MISCELLANEOUS: Member of NBA championship team (1974, 1976).

HEAD COACHING RECORD

BACKGROUND: Assistant coach, San Antonio Spurs (1994-95 and 1995-96). ... Assistant coach, Golden State Warriors (January 31-April 20, 2000).

NBA COACHING RECORD

Season Team	W	L	Pct.	Finish	W	L	Pct.
78-79—Boston	27	41	.397	5th/Atlantic Division	—	—	—
96-97—Charlotte	54	28	.659	6th/Central Division	0	3	.000
97-98—Charlotte	51	31	.622	3rd/Central Division	4	5	.444
98-99—Charlotte	4	11	.267		—	—	—
00-01—Golden State	17	65	.207	7th/Pacific Division	—	—	—
01-02—Golden State	9	15	.375		—	—	—
Totals (6 years)	162	191	.459	**Totals (2 years)**	4	8	.333

CBA COACHING RECORD

Season Team	W	L	Pct.	Finish	W	L	Pct.
84-85—Bay State	20	28	.417	6th/Atlantic Division	—	—	—

NOTES:
1978—Replaced Tom Sanders as Boston head coach (November), with record of 2-12.
1997—Lost to New York in Eastern Conference First Round.
1998—Defeated New Jersey, 3-1, in Eastern Conference First Round; lost to Chicago, 4-1, in Eastern Conference Semifinals.
1999—Resigned as Charlotte head coach (March 7); replaced by Paul Silas with club in seventh place

COLLEGIATE RECORD

NOTES: THE SPORTING NEWS All-America second team (1970).

Season Team	G	Min.	FGM	FGA	Pct.	FTM	FTA	Pct.	Reb.	Ast.	Pts.	RPG	APG	PPG
66-67—Florida State‡	18	...	105	208	.505	49	90	.544	357	...	259	19.8	...	14.4
67-68—Florida State	27	...	206	383	.538	96	131	.733	456	...	508	16.9	...	18.8
68-69—Florida State	25	...	202	384	.526	104	164	.634	437	...	508	17.5	...	20.3
69-70—Florida State	26	...	174	355	.490	115	169	.680	447	...	463	17.2	...	17.8
Varsity totals	78	...	582	1122	.519	315	464	.679	1340	...	1479	17.2	...	19.0

NBA REGULAR-SEASON RECORD

HONORS: NBA Most Valuable Player (1973). ... NBA Co-Rookie of the Year (1971). ... All-NBA second team (1973, 1975, 1976). ... NBA All-Defensive first team (1976). ... NBA All-Defensive second team (1975, 1980). ... NBA All-Rookie team (1971).

Season Team	G	Min.	FGM	FGA	Pct.	FTM	FTA	Pct.	Reb.	Ast.	PF	Dq.	Pts.	RPG	APG	PPG
70-71—Boston	81	3076	550	1302	.422	273	373	.732	1216	228	*350	15	1373	15.0	2.8	17.0
71-72—Boston	79	3186	657	1357	.484	175	243	.720	1203	245	*314	10	1489	15.2	3.1	18.8
72-73—Boston	82	3425	740	1637	.452	204	262	.779	1329	333	311	7	1684	16.2	4.1	20.5

									REBOUNDS							AVERAGES		
Season Team	G	Min.	FGM	FGA	Pct.	FTM	FTA	Pct.	Off.	Def.	Tot.	Ast.	St.	Blk.	TO	Pts.	RPG	APG	PPG
73-74—Boston	80	3352	645	1475	.437	228	274	.832	264	993	1257	354	95	101	...	1518	15.7	4.4	19.0
74-75—Boston	65	2632	569	1199	.475	191	244	.783	229	729	958	296	87	73	...	1329	14.7	4.6	20.4
75-76—Boston	78	3101	611	1305	.468	257	340	.756	335	911	1246	325	94	71	...	1479	16.0	4.2	19.0
76-77—Boston	50	1888	328	756	.434	162	198	.818	147	550	697	248	46	49	...	818	13.9	5.0	16.4
77-78—Boston	77	3215	598	1220	.490	239	284	.842	248	830	1078	351	102	67	217	1435	14.0	4.6	18.6
78-79—Boston	68	2517	488	1010	.483	151	187	.807	152	500	652	242	76	51	174	1127	9.6	3.6	16.6
79-80—Boston	66	2159	422	932	.453	95	122	.779	126	408	534	206	69	61	108	940	8.1	3.1	14.2
80-81—						Did not play—retired.													
81-82—						Did not play—retired.													
82-83—Milwaukee	40	1014	136	306	.444	52	63	.825	73	201	274	82	30	15	44	324	6.9	2.1	8.1
Totals	766	29565	5744	12499	.460	2027	2590	.783	...	...	10444	2910	599	488		54313516	13.6	3.8	17.6

Three-point field goals: 1979-80, 1-for-12 (.083). 1982-83, 0-for-2. Totals, 1-for-14 (.071).
Personal fouls/disqualifications: 1973-74, 294/7. 1974-75, 243/7. 1975-76, 314/10. 1976-77, 181/7. 1977-78, 297/5. 1978-79, 263/16. 1979-80, 216/2. 1982-83, 137/4. Totals, 2920/90.

NBA ALL-STAR GAME RECORD

NOTES: NBA All-Star Game Most Valuable Player (1973).

Season Team	Min.	FGM	FGA	Pct.	FTM	FTA	Pct.	Reb	Ast.	PF	Dq.	Pts.
1972—Boston	32	5	12	.417	4	5	.800	20	1	4	0	14
1973—Boston	30	7	15	.467	1	1	1.000	13	1	2	0	15

								REBOUNDS							
Season Team	Min.	FGM	FGA	Pct.	FTM	FTA	Pct.	Off.	Def.	Tot.	Ast.	PF	Dq.	St.	Blk.	TO	Pts.
1974—Boston	26	5	10	.500	1	3	.333	6	6	12	1	3	0	0	1	...	11
1975—Boston	15	3	7	.429	0	0	...	0	6	6	3	4	0	1	0	...	6

Season Team	Min.	FGM	FGA	Pct.	FTM	FTA	Pct.	REBOUNDS Off.	Def.	Tot.	Ast.	PF	Dq.	St.	Blk.	TO	Pts.
1976—Boston	23	6	13	.462	4	5	.800	8	8	16	1	3	0	1	0	...	16
1977—Boston								Selected, did not play—injured.									
1978—Boston	28	7	9	.778	0	0	...	6	8	14	5	5	0	2	0	2	14
Totals	154	33	66	.500	10	14	.714	...	...	81	12	21	0	4	1	2	76

COYLE, PAT — STORM

PERSONAL: Born September 5, 1960, in Philadelphia
HIGH SCHOOL: West Catholic (Philadelphia).
COLLEGE: Rutgers.

HEAD COACHING RECORD

BACKGROUND: Head coach at Loyola (Md.) College from 1992-1999, with an overall record of 100-77 (.565).

COLLEGIATE COACHING RECORD

Season Team	W	L	Pct.	Finish
92-93—Loyola College Maryland	14	15	.483	—
93-94—Loyola College Maryland	18	11	.621	—
94-95—Loyola College Maryland	20	9	.690	—
95-96—Loyola College Maryland	15	13	.536	—
96-97—Loyola College Maryland	9	19	.321	—
97-98—Loyola College Maryland	20	9	.690	—
98-99—Loyola College Maryland	4	1	.800	—
Totals (7 years)	100	77	.565	

WNBA COACHING RECORD

Season Team	W	L	Pct.	Finish	W	L	Pct.
2004—New York	11	7	.611	2nd/East	2	3	.400
2005—New York	18	16	.529	3rd/East	0	2	.529
Totals (2 years)	29	23	.558		2	5	.286

NOTES:

2004—Defeated Detroit, 2-1, in the first round; lost to Connecticut, 2-0, in the Eastern Conference finals.
2005—Lost to Indiana, 2-0, in the first round.

DONOVAN, ANNE — STORM

PERSONAL: Born November 1, 1961, in Ridgewood, N.J.
HIGH SCHOOL: Paramus Catholic (N.J.).
COLLEGE: Old Dominion (1983).
MISCELLANEOUS: Member of the gold medal-winning U.S. Olympic Teams in 1984 and 1988, as well the 1980 Olympic Team. ... One of only four male or female USA players to have been named to three Olympic squads. ... A member of 12 USA Basketball teams. ... Of a possible 11 medals, has won nine golds and two silvers. ... Inducted into the Naismith Memorial Basketball Hall of Fame in 1995. ... Inducted into the Women's Basketball Hall of Fame in 1999.

HEAD COACHING RECORD

BACKGROUND: Led Storm to WNBA Championship (2004). ... Named Storm head coach on December 18, 2002, becoming the first coach in WNBA history to take the helm of three different teams — Indiana (2000), Charlotte (2001-02) and Seattle (2003-). ... Led Charlotte to the WNBA Finals in 2001 after beginning the season with a 1-10 record. ... Head coach of Philadelphia Rage of ABL (1998). ... Served as head coach at East Carolina for three seasons (1995-1998). ... Led Lady Pirates to Colonial Athletic Association Tournament championship game in 1997. ... Served as assistant coach for 1997 USA Women's World Championship Qualifying Team that earned a silver medal. ... One of the most accomplished players in college history, led Old Dominion University to a 37-1 record and the AIAW national title as a freshman. ... Named the Naismith and Champion Player of the Year in 1983 as well as an All-American in 1981, 1982 and 1983. ... Finished collegiate career as Lady Monarchs' all-time leading scorer (2,179), rebounder (1,976) and shot blocker (801). ... Holds 25 ODU records. ... Played professionally in Shizuoka, Japan (1984-88) and Modena, Italy (1989).

COLLEGIATE COACHING RECORD

Season Team	W	L	Pct.	Finish
95-96—East Carolina	11	16	.407	—
96-97—East Carolina	13	16	.448	—
97-98—East Carolina	9	19	.321	—
Totals (3 years)	33	51	.393	

ABL COACHING RECORD

Season Team	W	L	Pct.	Finish
98-99—Philadelphia	9	5	.643	
Totals	9	5	.643	—

WNBA COACHING RECORD

Season Team	W	L	Pct.	Finish	W	L	Pct.
2000—Indiana	9	23	.281	7th/East	—	—	—

Season Team	W	L	Pct.	Finish	W	L	Pct.
2001—Charlotte	18	14	.563	4th/East	4	4	.500
2002—Charlotte	18	14	.563	T1st/East	0	2	.000
2003—Seattle	18	16	.529	T4th/West	—	—	—
2004—Seattle	20	14	.588	2nd/West	6	2	.750
2005—Seattle	20	14	.588	2nd/West	1	2	.750
Totals (6 years)	103	95	.520		11	10	.524

NOTES:

2001—Defeated Cleveland, 2-1, in first round; defeated New York, 2-1 in Eastern Conference Finals; lost to Los Angeles, 2-0 in WNBA Finals.

2002—Lost to Washington, 2-0, in first round.

2004—Defeated Minnesota, 2-0, in first round, defeated; Sacramento, 2-1, in Western Conference finals; defeated Connecticut, 2-1, in WNBA Championship.

2005—Lost to Houston, 2-1, in first round.

HUGHES, DAN — SILVER STARS

PERSONAL: Born April 14, 1955, in Lowell, Ohio ... Full Name: Daniel Dean Hughes.

HIGH SCHOOL: Fort Frye (Beverly, Ohio).

COLLEGE: Muskingum College (1977).

HEAD COACHING RECORD

BACKGROUND: Named WNBA Coach of the Year (2001). ... Led Rockers to an Eastern Conference-best 22-10 record in 2001 and their second consecutive trip to the WNBA Playoffs. ... In 1999, led the Charlotte Sting to the playoffs and their first ever playoff victory. ... Helped the University of Toledo women's basketball team to a 27-4 finish, Mid-American Conference regular season and tournament championships and an NCAA Tournament appearance as an assistant coach during the 1996-97 season. ... Named 1979 Sertoma Ohio Coach of the Year as the head coach of Madison Plains High School boys' basketball team.

WNBA COACHING RECORD

Season Team	W	L	Pct.	Finish	W	L	Pct.
1999—Charlotte	10	10	.500	T2nd/East	2	2	.500
2000—Cleveland	17	15	.531	2nd/East	3	3	.500
2001—Cleveland	22	10	.688	1st/East	1	2	.333
2002—Cleveland	10	22	.313	7th/East	—	—	—
2003—Cleveland	17	17	.500	4th/East	1	2	.333
2005—San Antonio	7	27	.206	7th/West	—	—	—
Totals (6 years)	83	101	.549		7	9	.438

NOTES:

1999—Defeated Detroit in the first round; lost to New York, 2-1, in the Eastern Conference Finals.

2000—Defeated Orlando, 2-1, in first round; lost to New York, 2-1, in Eastern Conference Finals.

2001—Lost to Charlotte, 2-1, in first round.

2003—Lost to Detroit, 2-1, in first round.

LAIMBEER, BILL — SHOCK

PERSONAL: Born May 19, 1957, in Boston ... Full Name: William Laimbeer Jr.. ... Name pronounced lam-BEER.

HIGH SCHOOL: Palos Verdes (Palos Verdes, Calif.).

JUNIOR COLLEGE: Owens Technical (Ohio).

COLLEGE: Notre Dame.

TRANSACTIONS/CAREER NOTES: Selected by Cleveland in third round (65th overall) of 1979 NBA Draft. ... Played in Italy (1979, 1980). ... Traded by Cleveland along with F Kenny Carr to Detroit for F Phil Hubbard, C Paul Mokeski and first- and second-round picks in the 1982 NBA Draft, February 16, 1982. ... Announced retirement, December 1, 1993. ... Special consultant, Detroit Shock, WNBA, April 18-June 19, 2002.

MISCELLANEOUS: Member of NBA Championship team (1989, 1990). ...Detroit's all-time leading rebounder (9,430).

HEAD COACHING RECORD

BACKGROUND: WNBA Coach of the Year (2003). ... Led Detroit to WNBA Championship (2003).

WNBA COACHING RECORD

Season Team	W	L	Pct.	Finish	W	L	Pct.
2002—Detroit	9	13	.409	8th/West	—	—	—
2003—Detroit	25	9	.735	1st/East	6	2	.750
2004—Detroit	17	17	.500	T3rd/East	1	2	.333
2005—Detroit	16	18	.471	T4th/East	0	2	.333
Totals (4 years)	67	57	.540		7	6	.538

NOTES:

2003—Defeated Houston, 2-1, in first round; defeated Connectict, 2-0, in Eastern Conference Finals; defeated Los Angeles, 2-1, in WNBA Championship.

2004—Lost to New York, 2-1, in first round.

2005—Lost to Connecticut, 2-0, in first round.

COLLEGIATE RECORD

Season Team	G	Min.	FGM	FGA	Pct.	FTM	FTA	Pct.	Reb.	Ast.	Pts.	RPG	APG	PPG
76-77—Owens Tech.								Did not play.						
75-76—Notre Dame	10	190	32	65	.492	18	23	.783	79	10	82	7.9	1.0	8.2

Season Team	G	Min.	FGM	FGA	Pct.	FTM	FTA	Pct.	Reb.	Ast.	Pts.	RPG	APG	PPG
												AVERAGES		
77-78—Notre Dame	29	654	97	175	.554	42	62	.677	190	31	236	6.6	1.1	8.1
78-79—Notre Dame	30	614	78	145	.538	35	50	.700	164	30	191	5.5	1.0	6.4
Totals	69	1458	207	385	.538	95	135	.704	433	71	509	6.3	1.0	7.4

ITALIAN LEAGUE RECORD

Season Team	G	Min.	FGM	FGA	Pct.	FTM	FTA	Pct.	Reb.	Ast.	Pts.	RPG	APG	PPG
												AVERAGES		
79-80—Brescia	29	...	258	465	.555	97	124	.782	363	...	613	12.5	...	21.1

NBA REGULAR-SEASON RECORD

Season Team	G	Min.	FGM	FGA	Pct.	FTM	FTA	Pct.	REBOUNDS Off.	Def.	Tot.	Ast.	St.	Blk.	TO	Pts.	AVERAGES RPG	APG	PPG
80-81—Cleveland	81	2460	337	670	.503	117	153	.765	266	427	693	216	56	78	132	791	8.6	2.7	9.8
81-82—Clev.-Det.	80	1829	265	536	.494	184	232	.793	234	383	617	100	39	64	121	718	7.7	1.3	9.0
82-83—Detroit	82	2871	436	877	.497	245	310	.790	282	711	993	263	51	118	176	1119	12.1	3.2	13.6
83-84—Detroit	82	2864	553	1044	.530	316	365	.866	329	674	*1003	149	49	84	151	1422	12.2	1.8	17.3
84-85—Detroit	82	2892	595	1177	.506	244	306	.797	295	718	1013	154	69	71	129	1438	12.4	1.9	17.5
85-86—Detroit	82	2891	545	1107	.492	266	319	.834	305	*770	*1075	146	59	65	133	1360	*13.1	1.8	16.6
86-87—Detroit	82	2854	506	1010	.501	245	274	.894	243	712	955	151	72	69	120	1263	11.6	1.8	15.4
87-88—Detroit	82	2897	455	923	.493	187	214	.874	165	667	832	199	66	78	136	1110	10.1	2.4	13.5
88-89—Detroit	81	2640	449	900	.499	178	212	.840	138	638	776	177	51	100	129	1106	9.6	2.2	13.7
89-90—Detroit	81	2675	380	785	.484	164	192	.854	166	614	780	171	57	84	98	981	9.6	2.1	12.1
90-91—Detroit	82	2668	372	778	.478	123	147	.837	173	564	737	157	38	56	98	904	9.0	1.9	11.0
91-92—Detroit	81	2234	342	727	.470	67	75	.893	104	347	451	160	51	54	102	783	5.6	2.0	9.7
92-93—Detroit	79	1933	292	574	.509	93	104	.894	110	309	419	127	46	40	59	687	5.3	1.6	8.7
93-94—Detroit	11	248	47	90	.522	11	13	.846	9	47	56	14	6	4	10	108	5.1	1.3	9.8
Totals	1068	33956	5574	11198	.498	2440	2916	.837	2819	7581	10400	2184	710	965	1594	13790	9.7	2.0	12.9

Three-point field goals: 1981-82, 4-for-13 (.308). 1982-83, 2-for-13 (.154). 1983-84, 0-for-11. 1984-85, 4-for-18 (.222). 1985-86, 4-for-14 (.286). 1986-87, 6-for-21 (.286). 1987-88, 13-for-39 (.333). 1988-89, 30-for-86 (.349). 1989-90, 57-for-158 (.361). 1990-91, 37-for-125 (.296). 1991-92, 32-for-85 (.376). 1992-93, 10-for-27 (.370). 1993-94, 3-for-9 (.333). Totals, 202-for-619 (.326).

Personal fouls/disqualifications: 1980-81, 332/14. 1981-82, 296/5. 1982-83, 320/9. 1983-84, 273/4. 1984-85, 308/4. 1985-86, 291/4. 1986-87, 283/4. 1987-88, 284/6. 1988-89, 259/2. 1989-90, 278/4. 1990-91, 242/3. 1991-92, 225/0. 1992-93, 212/4. 1993-94, 30/0. Totals, 3633/63.

NBA PLAYOFF RECORD

NOTES: Shares NBA Finals single-game record for most points in an overtime period—9 (June 7, 1990, vs. Portland).

Season Team	G	Min.	FGM	FGA	Pct.	FTM	FTA	Pct.	REBOUNDS Off.	Def.	Tot.	Ast.	St.	Blk.	TO	Pts.	AVERAGES RPG	APG	PPG
83-84—Detroit	5	165	29	51	.569	18	20	.900	14	48	62	12	4	3	12	76	12.4	2.4	15.2
84-85—Detroit	9	325	48	107	.449	36	51	.706	36	60	96	15	7	7	16	132	10.7	1.7	14.7
85-86—Detroit	4	168	34	68	.500	21	23	.913	20	36	56	1	2	3	8	90	14.0	0.3	22.5
86-87—Detroit	15	543	84	163	.515	15	24	.625	30	126	156	37	15	12	20	184	10.4	2.5	12.3
87-88—Detroit	23	779	114	250	.456	40	45	.889	43	178	221	44	18	19	30	273	9.6	1.9	11.9
88-89—Detroit	17	497	66	142	.465	25	31	.806	26	114	140	31	6	8	19	172	8.2	1.8	10.1
89-90—Detroit	20	667	91	199	.457	25	29	.862	41	170	211	28	23	18	16	222	10.6	1.4	11.1
90-91—Detroit	15	446	66	148	.446	27	31	.871	42	80	122	19	5	12	17	164	8.1	1.3	10.9
91-92—Detroit	5	145	17	46	.370	5	5	1.000	5	28	33	8	4	1	5	41	6.6	1.6	8.2
Totals	113	3735	549	1174	.468	212	259	.819	257	840	1097	195	84	83	143	1354	9.7	1.7	12.0

Three-point field goals: 1984-85, 0-for-2. 1985-86, 1-for-1. 1986-87, 1-for-5 (.200). 1987-88, 5-for-17 (.294). 1988-89, 15-for-42 (.357). 1989-90, 15-for-43 (.349). 1990-91, 5-for-17 (.294). 1991-92, 2-for-10 (.200). Totals, 44-for-137 (.321).

Personal fouls/disqualifications: 1983-84, 23/2. 1984-85, 32/1. 1985-86, 19/1. 1986-87, 53/2. 1987-88, 77/2. 1988-89, 55/1. 1989-90, 77/3. 1990-91, 54/0. 1991-92, 18/1. Totals, 408/13.

NBA ALL-STAR GAME RECORD

Season Team	Min.	FGM	FGA	Pct.	FTM	FTA	Pct.	REBOUNDS Off.	Def.	Tot.	Ast.	PF	Dq.	St.	Blk.	TO	Pts.
1983—Detroit	6	1	1	1.000	0	0	...	1	0	1	0	1	0	0	0	1	2
1984—Detroit	17	6	8	.750	1	1	1.000	1	4	5	0	3	0	1	2	0	13
1985—Detroit	11	2	4	.500	1	2	.500	1	2	3	1	1	0	0	0	0	5
1987—Detroit	11	4	7	.571	0	0	...	0	2	2	1	2	0	1	0	0	8
Totals	45	13	20	.650	2	3	.667	3	8	11	2	7	0	2	2	1	28

MCCONNELL SERIO, SUZIE — LYNX

PERSONAL: Born July 29, 1966, in Pittsburgh ... Full Name: Suzanne Theresa McConnell Serio.
HIGH SCHOOL: Seton LaSalle (Pittsburgh).
COLLEGE: Penn State.
TRANSACTIONS/CAREER NOTES: Selected by Cleveland in second round (16th overall) of WNBA Draft, April 29, 1998.

HEAD COACHING RECORD

BACKGROUND: WNBA Coach of the Year (2004).

WNBA COACHING RECORD

Season Team	W	L	Pct.	Finish	W	L	Pct.
2003—Minnesota	18	16	.529	T4th/West	1	2	.333
2004—Minnesota	18	16	.529	T3rd/West	0	2	.000

Season Team	W	L	Pct.	Finish		W	L	Pct.
2005—Minnesota	14	20	.412	6th/West		—	—	—
Totals (3 years)	50	52	.490			1	4	.200

NOTES:

2003—Lost to Los Angeles, 2-1, in first round.
2004—Lost to Seattle, 2-0, in first round.

COLLEGIATE RECORD

NOTES: Kodak All-America first team (1988). ... Naismith Award for small player of year (1988).

Season Team	G	Min.	FGM	FGA	Pct.	FTM	FTA	Pct.	Reb.	Ast.	Pts.	RPG	APG	PPG
												AVERAGES		
84-85—Penn State	33	...	157	343	.458	101	136	.743	0	321	415	2.8	9.7	12.6
85-86—Penn State	32	...	148	335	.442	86	109	.789	0	338	382	2.9	10.6	11.9
86-87—Penn State	30	...	169	337	.501	68	94	.723	0	355	418	4.7	11.8	13.9
87-88—Penn State	33	...	255	511	.499	116	143	.811	0	293	682	5.0	8.9	20.7
Totals	128	...	729	1526	.478	371	482	.770	0	1307	1897	3.9	10.2	14.8

Three-point field goals: 1986-87, 12-for-41 (.293). 1987-88, 56-for-140 (.400). Totals, 68-for-181 (.376).

OLYMPICS

NOTES: Member of gold medal-winning U.S. Olympic team (1988) and bronze medal-winning U.S. Olympic team (1992).

Season Team	G	Min.	FGM	FGA	Pct.	FTM	FTA	Pct.	Reb.	Ast.	Pts.	RPG	APG	PPG
												AVERAGES		
1988—United States	5	...	13	25	.520	11	12	.917	4	11	42	0.8	2.2	8.4
1988—United States	5	...	13	25	.520	11	12	.917	4	11	42	0.8	2.2	8.4
1992—United States	5	...	14	39	.359	1	2	.500	5	18	34	1.0	3.6	6.8
1992—United States	5	...	14	39	.359	1	2	.500	5	18	34	1.0	3.6	6.8
Totals	20	...	54	128	.422	24	28	.857	18	58	152	0.9	2.9	7.6

Three-point field goals: 1988-89, 5-for-7 (.714). 1988-89, 5-for-7 (.714). 1992-93, 5-for-19 (.263). 1992-93, 5-for-19 (.263). Totals, 20-for-52 (.385).

WNBA REGULAR-SEASON RECORD

HONORS: WNBA Newcomer of year (1998). ... WNBA Sportsmanship Award (1998, 2000). ... All-WNBA first team (1998).

Season Team	G	Min.	FGM	FGA	Pct.	FTM	FTA	Pct.	Off.	Def.	Tot.	Ast.	St.	Blk.	TO	Pts.	RPG	APG	PPG
									REBOUNDS								**AVERAGES**		
1998—Cleveland	28	882	80	176	.455	51	70	.729	8	54	62	178	49	5	104	240	2.2	6.4	8.6
1999—Cleveland	18	511	36	98	.367	16	19	.842	4	39	43	76	10	2	54	108	2.4	4.2	6.0
2000—Cleveland	32	705	58	140	.414	19	25	.760	9	41	50	119	15	1	69	173	1.6	3.7	5.4
Totals	78	2098	174	414	.420	86	114	.754	21	134	155	373	74	8	227	521	2.0	4.8	6.7

Three-point field goals: 1998, 29-for-71 (.408). 1999, 20-for-60 (.333). 2000, 38-for-97 (.392). Totals, 87-for-228 (.382).
Personal fouls/disqualifications: 1998, 48/0. 1999, 31/0. 2000, 30/0. Totals, 109/0.

WNBA PLAYOFF RECORD

Season Team	G	Min.	FGM	FGA	Pct.	FTM	FTA	Pct.	Off.	Def.	Tot.	Ast.	St.	Blk.	TO	Pts.	RPG	APG	PPG
									REBOUNDS								**AVERAGES**		
1998—Cleveland	3	99	7	14	.500	2	3	.667	3	4	7	15	8	1	9	19	2.3	5.0	6.3
2000—Cleveland	6	147	14	45	.311	2	2	1.000	3	11	14	25	5	1	16	39	2.3	4.2	6.5
Totals	9	246	21	59	.356	4	5	.800	6	15	21	40	13	2	25	58	2.3	4.4	6.4

Three-point field goals: 1998, 3-for-7 (.429). 2000, 9-for-36 (.250). Totals, 12-for-43 (.279).
Personal fouls/disqualifications: 1998, 9/0. 2000, 5/0. Totals, 14/0.

THIBAULT, MIKE — SUN

PERSONAL: Born September 28, 1950, in St. Paul, Minn. ... Full Name: Michael Francis Thibault.
HIGH SCHOOL: Bellarmine College Prep (San Jose, Calif.).
COLLEGE: St. Martin's College (Lacey, Wash.).

HEAD COACHING RECORD

BACKGROUND: Named head coach of Connecticut Sun on March 7, 2003. ... A 34-year coaching veteran. ... Joined the NBA as a scount for the Los Angeles Lakers in 1978. ... Has worked in various capacities for a number of NBA teams, including as an assistant coach/director of scouting for the Los Angeles Lakers (1978-82)-winning NBA Championships in '80 and '82-and the Chicago Bulls (1982-86), and as an assistant coach for the Milwaukee Bucks (1998-2002). ... Named World Basketball League Coach of the Year in 1988 during his one-year tenure as head coach of the Calgary 88's (record unavailable).

CBA COACHING RECORD

Season Team	W	L	Pct.	Finish
89-90—Omaha	29	27	.518	—
90-91—Omaha	39	17	.696	—
91-92—Omaha	37	19	.661	—
92-93—Omaha	28	28	.500	—
93-94—Omaha	30	26	.536	—
94-95—Omaha	26	30	.464	—
95-96—Omaha	28	28	.500	—
96-97—Omaha	22	34	.393	—
Totals (8 years)	239	209	.533	

NOTES:

1993—Defeated Grand Rapids, 4-2, in CBA Finals.
1994—Lost to Quad City, 4-1, in CBA Finals.

WNBA COACHING RECORD

Season	Team	W	L	Pct.	Finish	W	L	Pct.
2003—Connecticut		18	16	.529	T2nd/East	2	2	.500
2004—Connecticut		18	16	.529	T1st/East	5	3	.625
2005—Connecticut		26	8	.765	1st/East	5	3	.625
Totals (3 years)		62	40	.608		12	8	.600

NOTES:
2003—Defeated Charlotte, 2-0, in first round; lost to Detroit, 2-0, in Eastern Conference Finals.
2004—Defeated Washington, 2-1, in first round; defeated New York, 2-0, in Eastern Conference Finals; lost to Seattle, 2-1, in WNBA Championship.
2005—Defeated Detroit, 2-0, in first round; defeated Indiana, 2-0, in Eastern Conference Finals; lost to Sacramento, 3-1, in WNBA Championship.

WESTHEAD, PAUL — MERCURY

PERSONAL: Born February 21, 1939, in Malvern, Pa. ... Full Name: Paul W. Westhead.
HIGH SCHOOL: Malvern Prep (Malvern, Pa.).
COLLEGE: St. Joseph's.

COLLEGIATE RECORD

Season Team	G	Min.	FGM	FGA	Pct.	FTM	FTA	Pct.	Reb.	Ast.	Pts.	AVERAGES RPG	APG	PPG
58-59—St. Joseph's	2	—	0	1	.000	0	0	—	0	—	0	—	—	0.0
59-60—St. Joseph's	25	—	22	62	.355	6	12	.500	37	—	50	—	—	2.0
60-61—St. Joseph's	16	—	12	30	.400	7	13	.538	17	—	31	—	—	1.9
Totals	43	—	34	93	.366	13	25	.520	54	—	81	—	—	1.9

COLLEGIATE COACHING RECORD

NOTES: Assistant coach at Dayton (1963-63). ... Assistant coach at St. Joseph's (1968-69).

Season	Team	W	L	Pct.
70-71—LaSalle		20	7	.741
71-72—LaSalle		6	19	.240
72-73—LaSalle		15	10	.600
73-74—LaSalle		18	10	.643
74-75—LaSalle		22	7	.759
75-76—LaSalle		11	15	.423
76-77—LaSalle		17	12	.586
77-78—LaSalle		18	12	.600
78-79—LaSalle		15	13	.536
85-86—Loyola Marymount		19	11	.633
86-87—Loyola Marymount		12	16	.429
87-88—Loyola Marymount		28	4	.875
88-89—Loyola Marymount		20	11	.646
89-90—Loyola Marymount		26	6	.813
Totals (14 years)		247	153	.618

NBA COACHING RECORD

NOTES: Coach of NBA Championship team (1980).

Season	Team	W	L	Pct.	Finish	W	L	Pct.
79-80—Los Angeles		50	18	.735	1st/Pacific Division	12	4	.750
80-81—Los Angeles		54	28	.659	2nd/Pacific Division	1	2	.333
81-82—Los Angeles		7	4	.636		—	—	—
82-83—Chicago		28	54	.341	4th/Central Division	—	—	—
90-91—Denver		20	62	.244	7th/Midwest Division	—	—	—
91-92—Denver		24	58	.293		—	—	—
Totals (6 years)		183	224	.450	Totals (2 years)	13	6	.684

WHISENANT, JOHN — MONARCHS

PERSONAL: Born June 18, 1945, in Gore, Okla. ... Full Name: John H. Whisenant.
HIGH SCHOOL: Gore (Okla.).
COLLEGE: New Mexico State.

HEAD COACHING RECORD

BACKGROUND: Named WNBA Coach of the Year (2005). ... Led Monarchs to WNBA Championship (2005). ... Named head coach of Sacramento Monarchs, July 10, 2003. ... Has more than 30 years of baskeball experience, including as a head coach (51-35 record) and vice president of baskeball operations for the New Mexico Slam (IBL/CBA).

WNBA COACHING RECORD

Season	Team	W	L	Pct.	Finish	W	L	Pct.
2003—Sacramento		12	4	.750	3rd/West	3	3	.500
2004—Sacramento		18	16	.529	T3rd/West	3	3	.500
2005—Sacramento		25	9	.735	1st/West	7	1	.875
Totals (3 years)		55	29	.655		13	7	.650

HEAD COACHES

NOTES:
2003—Defeated Houston, 2-1, in first round; lost to Los Angeles, 2-1, in Western Conference Finals.
2004—Defeated Los Angeles, 2-1, in first round; lost to Seattle, 2-1, in Western Conference Finals.
2005—Defeated Los Angeles, 2-0, in first round; defeated Houstin, 2-0, in Western Conference Finals; defeated Connecticut, 3-1, in WNBA Championship.

WINTERS, BRIAN   FEVER

PERSONAL: Born March 1, 1952, in Rockaway, N.Y. ... Full Name: Brian Joseph Winters.
HIGH SCHOOL: Archbishop Molloy (Queens, N.Y.).
COLLEGE: South Carolina.
TRANSACTIONS/CAREER NOTES: Selected by Los Angeles in first round (12th overall) of 1974 NBA Draft. ... Traded by Los Angeles along with C Elmore Smith, F/C Dave Meyers and G/F Junior Bridgeman to Milwaukee for C Kareem Abdul-Jabbar and C Walt Wesley, June 16, 1975.

NBA COACHING RECORD

Season Team	W	L	Pct.	Finish	W	L	Pct.
				Regular Season			Playoffs
1995-96—Vancouver	15	67	.183	7th/Midwest Division	–	–	–
1997-98—Vancouver	8	35	.186				
2001-02—Golden State	13	46	.220	7th/Pacific Division	–	–	–
Totals (3 seasons)	36	148	.196				

WNBA COACHING RECORD

Season Team	W	L	Pct.	Finish	W	L	Pct.
2004—Indiana	15	19	.441	6th/East	–	–	–
2005—Indiana	21	13	.618	2nd/East	2	2	.500
Totals (2 years)	36	32	.529		2	2	.500

NOTES:
2005—Defeated New York, 2-0, in first round; lost to Connecticut, 2-0, in Eastern Conference Finals.

COLLEGIATE RECORD

Season Team	G	Min.	FGM	FGA	Pct.	FTM	FTA	Pct.	Reb.	Ast.	Pts.	RPG	APG	PPG
												AVERAGES		
70-71—S. Carolina	16	...	138	299	.462	92	108	.852	156	69	368	9.8	4.3	23.0
71-72—S. Carolina	29	692	90	175	.514	60	71	.845	82	55	240	2.8	1.9	8.3
72-73—S. Carolina	26	834	120	258	.465	59	81	.728	164	69	299	6.3	2.7	11.5
73-74—S. Carolina	27	1016	229	446	.513	82	100	.820	85	68	540	3.1	2.5	20.0
Totals	82	2542	439	879	.499	201	252	.798	331	192	1079	4.0	2.3	13.2

NBA REGULAR-SEASON RECORD

Season Team	G	Min.	FGM	FGA	Pct.	FTM	FTA	Pct.	Off.	Def.	Tot.	Ast.	St.	Blk.	TO	Pts.	RPG	APG	PPG
										REBOUNDS								AVERAGES	
74-75—Los Angeles	68	1516	359	810	.443	76	92	.826	39	99	138	195	74	18	...	794	2.0	2.9	11.7
75-76—Milwaukee	78	2795	618	1333	.464	180	217	.830	66	183	249	366	124	25	...	1416	3.2	4.7	18.2
76-77—Milwaukee	78	2717	652	1308	.498	205	242	.847	64	167	231	337	114	29	...	1509	3.0	4.3	19.3
77-78—Milwaukee	80	2751	674	1457	.463	246	293	.840	87	163	250	393	124	27	236	1594	3.1	4.9	19.9
78-79—Milwaukee	79	2575	662	1343	.493	237	277	.856	48	129	177	383	83	40	257	1561	2.2	4.8	19.8
79-80—Milwaukee	80	2623	535	1116	.479	184	214	.860	48	175	233	362	101	28	186	1292	2.8	4.5	16.2
80-81—Milwaukee	69	1771	331	697	.475	119	137	.869	32	108	140	185	70	10	136	799	2.0	2.7	11.6
81-82—Milwaukee	61	1829	404	806	.501	123	156	.788	51	119	170	253	57	9	118	967	2.8	4.1	15.9
82-83—Milwaukee	57	1361	255	587	.434	73	85	.859	35	75	110	156	45	4	81	605	1.9	2.7	10.6
Totals	650	19938	4490	9457	.475	1443	1713	.842	470	1218	1688	2630	792	190	1014	10537	2.6	4.0	16.2

Three-point field goals: 1979-80, 38-for-102 (.373). 1980-81, 18-for-51 (.353). 1981-82, 36-for-93 (.387). 1982-83, 22-for-68 (.324). Totals, 114-for-314 (.363).
Personal fouls/disqualifications: 1974-75, 168/1. 1975-76, 240/0. 1976-77, 228/1. 1977-78, 139/4. 1978-79, 243/1. 1979-80, 208/0. 1980-81, 185/2. 1981-82, 187/1. 1982-82, 132/2. Totals, 1830/12.

NBA PLAYOFF RECORD

Season Team	G	Min.	FGM	FGA	Pct.	FTM	FTA	Pct.	Off.	Def.	Tot.	Ast.	St.	Blk.	TO	Pts.	RPG	APG	PPG
										REBOUNDS								AVERAGES	
75-76—Milwaukee	3	126	39	62	.629	4	5	.800	3	4	7	15	5	2	...	82	2.3	5.0	27.3
76-77—Milwaukee	9	305	82	165	.497	20	27	.741	26	4	30	58	12	8	...	184	3.3	6.4	20.4
79-80—Milwaukee	7	268	46	100	.460	10	10	1.000	4	17	21	37	11	0	...	111	3.0	5.3	15.9
80-81—Milwaukee	7	181	28	61	.459	12	16	.750	4	19	23	22	10	1	...	70	3.3	3.1	10.0
81-82—Milwaukee	6	232	38	77	.494	20	24	.833	4	11	15	28	8	1	...	101	2.5	4.7	16.8
82-83—Milwaukee	9	240	36	84	.429	14	17	.824	7	15	22	32	6	4	...	89	2.4	3.6	9.9
Totals	41	1352	269	549	.490	80	99	.808	48	70	118	192	52	16	123	637	2.9	4.7	15.5

Three-point field goals: 1979-80. 9-for-21 (.429). 1980-81, 2-for-6 (.333). 1981-82, 5-for-10 (.500). 1982-83, 3-for-11 (.273). Totalks, 19-for-48 (.396).
Personal fouls/disqualifications: 1975-76, 11/1. 1977-78, 20/0. 1979-80, 25/1. 1980-81, 22/1. 1981-82, 23/0. 1982-83, 22/0. Totals, 123/3.

NBA ALL-STAR GAME RECORD

Season Team	Min.	FGM	FGA	Pct.	FTM	FTA	Pct.	Off.	Def.	Tot.	Ast.	PF	St.	Blk.	TO	Pts.
1977—Milwaukee	16	1	5	.200	0	0	...	0	2	2	1	2	1	0	...	2
1979—Milwaukee	14	4	7	.571	0	0	...	2	2	4	1	2	0	0	...	8
Totals	30	5	12	.417	0	0	...	2	4	6	2	4	1	0	...	10